*A*LMANAC OF
BUSINESS
AND
INDUSTRIAL
FINANCIAL
RATIOS

2008 EDITION

LEO TROY, Ph.D.

CCH
a Wolters Kluwer business

Editorial Staff

Production...Christopher Zwirek
Design ....Craig Arritola

This publication is designed to provide accurate and authoritative information in regard to the subject matter covered. It is sold with the understanding that the publisher is not engaged in rendering legal, accounting, or other professional service and that the author is not offering such advice in this publication. If legal advice or other professional assistance is required, the services of a competent professional person should be sought.

ISBN: 978-0-8080-1759-2

© 2007, CCH. All Rights Reserved.
4025 W. Peterson Avenue
Chicago, IL 60646-6085
1 800 248 3248
www.CCHGroup.com

Printed in the United States of America

Dedicated

To Alexander, Suzannah, Dale, Ariel Sarah Troy, Abigayle Hannah Troy, and Rachel Ilana Troy

Preface

Now in its 39th Edition, the *Almanac of Business and Industrial Financial Ratios* provides a precise benchmark for evaluating an individual company's financial performance. The performance data is derived from the latest available IRS figures on U.S. and international companies, and tracks 50 operating and financial factors in nearly 200 industries. The *Almanac* provides competitive norms in actual dollar amounts for revenue and capital factors, as well as important average operating costs in percent of net sales. It also provides other critical financial factors in percentage, including debt ratio, return on assets, return on equity, profit margin, and more. Beyond its reliable insights into corporate behavior, the *Almanac* can be used by other countries looking to model their economies on American performance.

Also included with the text, in a special pocket provided in the inside cover of the book, is a CD-ROM that contains all the materials found in the book including the explanatory discussion, the data tables, and the supporting index. Also included on the CD, but not in the book itself, is a special template that allows the reader to add individual company data of interest to compare and contrast with data from the book.

2008 Edition Highlights

The 2008 Edition of the *Almanac of Business and Industrial Financial Ratios* has been updated to include the following:

- **Broad scope:** *2008 Almanac* features the North American Industry Classification System (NAICS), so you can benchmark or analyze results consistently with corporations in the United States, Canada, and Mexico.

- **Most industry types:** *2008 Almanac* highlights most industry types, including industries with advanced technologies and newly emerging industries such as paging and wireless communications.

- **A truer picture** of corporate financial performance, since the data isn't based on a mixed bag of averages that might include partnerships or sole proprietors. *2008 Almanac* features a homogeneous universe of American corporate financial performance.

- **Many classifications:** *2008 Almanac* analyzes 197 industries with 50 financial performance items.

- **Benchmarks:** *2008 Almanac* provides 13 benchmarks, including such critical measures as Receipts to Cash Flow, Debt to Total Assets, and Return on Equity both before and after taxes.

- **Analytical tables:** *Table I, Corporations with and without Net Income (All Corporations), and Table II, Corporations with Net Income.*

- **Easier apples-to-apples comparisons:** Each table is divided into 13 asset sizes.

- **More comprehensive:** Total receipts of all corporations covered by *2008 Almanac* is $22.7 trillion, making the *Almanac* the Anatomy of American Corporate Capitalism.

Leo Troy, Ph. D.

October 2007

About the Author

Dr. Leo Troy is Professor of Economics at Rutgers University. He has been a faculty member of Rutgers for 50 years. In addition to authoring the widely praised *Almanac*, he has written many other books and articles published in leading journals. Professor Troy has been the recipient of numerous awards including two from the National Science Foundation, and two Fulbright grants. In addition, he has received numerous awards from private foundations. Dr. Troy received his Ph.D. from Columbia University and is a member of Phi Beta Kappa. He is a veteran of World War II with three battle stars and the combat infantry badge. He is the father of two children and is also a grandfather of three girls, including twins.

Acknowledgments

I wish to acknowledge the contributions of five people in particular for the development of the 39th Edition of the *Almanac:* Phil Wilson, Alan Kovar of Brighton Best, Lawrence R. Chodor, CPA, CVA, Wiss & Company, Marvin Sunshine, and Karen Kane.

Philip is responsible for the programming, which dealt with a very large amount of data, covering both the current and trend information. Alan, drawing upon his knowledge and experience as a CPA and Partner of Wiss and Company of Livingston, N.J., contributed significantly to the new content of the book. To Marvin Sunshine, Esq, my appreciation for actions and support that helped make the *Almanac* a continuing publication. Karen Kane is acknowledged for her contributions to the graphics of this issue.

Special acknowledgement is due my late friends and colleagues, Stan Katz, CPA, and Professor Emeritus of Accounting, Rutgers University, John Gilmour. I thank, too, Professor of Accounting, Rutgers University, David Zaumeyer, Ph.D., CPA, for recommending several ratios that continue to be included in the *Almanac*. I thank Mr. Ka-Neng Au, Business Librarian, Rutgers University, for significant contributions to the *Almanac*.

I wish to recognize, too, the cooperation of members of the Statistics of Income Division of the Internal Revenue Service—in particular, Ken Szeflinksi, Martha A. Harris, and Phyllis J. Whiles of the Corporation Returns Analysis Section. Without their data and its reliability, the Almanac would not be possible. Responsibility for the use of their facts and figures is, of course, solely my own. In this regard, I recall the valuable assistance I received from Barry Rosenstein, MBA, CPA, in checking procedures, in earlier editions, and which have continued into the current one. Finally, I wish to recognize the help of Suzannah B. Troy in bringing about the 39th annual edition of the *Almanac*. I anticipate continuation of her valuable assistance in subsequent editions.

INTRODUCTION

QUESTIONS, ANSWERS AND COMMENTS ON THE ALMANAC
Some users have requested further information on the use of the Almanac's ratios and statistics. This Q & A addition to the Almanac is in response to that demand.

1. What are the general purposes of the Almanac?

The goal of the Almanac is to provide users with a reliable and comprehensive source of standard financial ratios and financial statistics on all corporations, public and private, including those filing 1120S returns in the United States. Excluded are all individual proprietorships and partnerships. The Almanac makes available key business and financial statistics, which are consistent and neutral (unbiased by any commercial publisher or trade association).

2. What is the source and reliability of the Almanac's results?

The Almanac's results are computed from the Department of the Treasury, Internal Revenue Service's statistical sampling of the tax returns of all corporations. Dividends received from foreign corporations are included in total receipts of those corporations affected. The statistics apply to the company rather than the establishment.

3. Are international comparisons available?

Yes. Because of the adoption of a common system of industrial classification by the U.S., Canada and Mexico, known as the North American Industrial Classification System of industries (NAICS), under the North American Free Trade Agreement, users in Canada and Mexico can compare and contrast their results with those corporations in the United States.

4. What about comparisons within the U.S?

These are the most important applications of the Almanac. Results are available for each and every corporation within the U.S., whether public or private, and include small business corporations, those which file the 1120S tax return. Therefore, users can compare their corporate performance with that of their industry and asset size group of corporate enterprise in the United States.

5. How many corporations are covered in the Almanac?

The Almanac's results are derived from more than 5.5 million corporation tax returns. Furthermore, the user can easily determine the number of enterprises for the total of each industry and by each of the 12 asset size groups. This makes for a total of 13 asset size comparisons.

6. What about differences in the size of corporations?

In addition to the results for each industry, the Almanac displays 12 columns of performance by the size of assets. Again, this makes for a total of 13 asset size comparisons.

7. Does the Almanac distinguish between the profitability of corporations?

In a word, yes. Each industry is divided between two tables: Table I reports the results of all corporations in an industry, that is, those with and without net income. It is followed by a second table for the same industry, Table II, which reports only those corporations with net income.

8. How many items of information are there for each industry?

There are 50 indicators of corporate performance in each table and each industry and for all asset size groups, except where the IRS' data sample is too small, or it does not supply the necessary information.

9. Who are the users of the Almanac?

Accountants, corporate managers, business consultants, investors evaluating a corporate takeover, entrepreneurs considering new businesses, lawyers, and students of accounting, business, and management.

10. What accounting time period is covered?

The Internal Revenue Service provides the most recent statistics publicly available for the Almanac. For the 2008 Almanac, these statistics apply to the accounting period from July 2004 through June 2005.

WHAT'S NEW IN THIS EDITION

Beginning with the year 2002, the *Almanac of Business and Industrial Financial Ratios* began using the North American Industry Classification System (NAICS). NAICS replaces the Internal Revenue Service's own system, which it had used for many years, an adaptation of Standard Industrial Classification (SIC); all previous *Almanacs* had used that adaptation.

The new industrial classification system is the product of the North American Free Trade Agreement (NAFTA), and it replaces the existing classification systems not only of the United States but also of Canada and Mexico. Hence, the new system applies uniformly to the three countries, and users of the *Almanac 2008*, utilizing the new international industrial classification system, can now compare their results with corporations in all three nations.

In the United States, the new manual was created by the Office of Management and Budget (OMB). The NAICS system gives special attention to industries producing and furnishing advanced technologies, new and emerging industries, as well as service industries in general. NAICS divides the economy into 21 sectors, five in the predominantly goods-producing area, and 16 in the service producing area.

INDUSTRY SECTORS

Particularly noteworthy is NAICS's introduction of an Information sector. This sector assembles the industries from Newspaper Publishers (511110) to Internet Service Providers, Web Portals, and Data Processing Services (518115). Within this span, NAICS and therefore the *Almanac* include such important industries as software publishing, database and directory publishing, satellite telecommunications, paging and cellular, and other wireless communications. NAICS and the *Almanac* also provide a category of industries on Professional, Scientific, and Technical Services, industries in which human capital is the major input. The sector includes Legal Services (541115) and Scientific Research and Development Services (541700), as well as Management, Scientific, and Technical Services (541600) and Computer Systems Design and Related Services (541515).

Other important sectors are the Arts, Entertainment, and Recreation including Amusement, Gambling, and Recreation (713105), and the Health Care and Social Assistance including

Offices of Physicians (621115), Hospitals, Nursing, and Residential Care Facilities (622005). Within Manufacturing, the key goods sector industry, there is now a category embracing Computer and Electronic Product Manufacturing. It spans industries such as Computer and Peripheral Equipment (334110) to Navigational, Measuring, Electromedical, and Control Instruments (334500).

The source of the IRS's data are the tax returns of all *active* public and private corporations. Because the *Almanac's* data are derived only from corporate tax returns, there is a mixture of corporate with the financial performance of partnerships and individual proprietorships; the *Almanac's* information constitutes a **homogeneous universe**. The tax returns are classified by the IRS on the basis of the business activity which accounts for a corporation's largest percentage of total receipts. Large corporations with dissimilar business activities are included in only one industry, despite operations that are unrelated to the industry in which they are grouped.

The data developed by the IRS are derived from a stratified probability sample of corporation income tax returns. Where the sample data from the sample are small and should those numbers be used in a denominator, the result is reported as a hyphen (-) in the *Almanac*. Returns of the largest corporations are generally in the sample from year to year, but comparability can be affected by consolidations and mergers, changes in the law and the tax forms, and changes in the industrial classification system used over the years.

REPRESENTATIVE INDUSTRIES

The *Almanac* reports on nearly 200 industries. Minor industries are denoted by a six-digit code; major industries are designated by a three-digit industry code; industrial sectors by a two-digit code; and industrial divisions by a two-digit code. When the data are the same for minor, major, sector, and industrial division, the IRS reports only the industrial division, and similarly for other identities applicable to the major and sectoral industries; the *Almanac* follows this procedure.

Almanac 2008 continues the previous coverage of reporting information: for all industries, **Table I, Corporations with and without Net Income** (that is, the entire universe of active reporting corporations), and **Table II, Corporations with Net Income**, a subset of the universe. In the *Almanac 2008*, Table I covers over 5.5 million enterprises (corporations), and Table II covers 3.1 million corporations with net income. This implies that 2.4 million corporations reported deficits. The IRS defines net income (or deficit) as the companies' net profit or loss from taxable sources of income reduced by allowable deductions. Total receipts of the 5.5 million corporations reported in *Almanac 2008* was $22.7 trillion, up by $2 trillion.

The *Almanac* continues to report performance results not only by the total for each industry, but by 12 other asset size groups (a total of 13 asset size groups), providing 50 items of data and/or ratios on corporate performance:

Total

Zero
$1 to $500,000
$500,001 to $1,000,000
$1,000,001 to $5,000,000
$5,000,001 to $10,000,000
$10,000,001 to $25,000,000
$25,000,001 to $50,000,000
$50,000,001 to $100,000,000
$100,000,001 to $250,000,000
$250,000,001 to $500,000,000
$500,000,001 to $2,500,000,000
$2,500,000,001 or more

All data in Tables I and II cover an accounting period identified on all tables and are the most recent information available from the IRS. For the *Almanac 2008*, the accounting period is July 2004 through June 2005. The dating of the data is counterbalanced by the most extensive industrial coverage available in any report on financial performance, the number of items of corporate performance, and their availability in thirteen asset size groups. Moreover, the timing of the data are also counterbalanced by the stability of the *Almanac's* values as past trends have indicated. Therefore, the *Almanac's* financial results are reliable in assessing current corporate performance.

Beyond its reliable insights into corporate behavior on a micro basis, its comprehensive and detailed coverage make the *Almanac* the **Anatomy of American Corporate Capitalism**. In this macro sense, it constitutes **the** example to those countries desirous of modeling their economies on the American performance.

How to Use the Almanac

On the micro level, the *Almanac* multiplies manyfold the power of financial analysis to evaluate an individual company's financial performance: In contrast to many standard reports, the *Almanac* gives management, and analysts independent of any company, more of the fundamental analytical tools needed to compare their company with companies in the same industry and of the same asset size. The *Almanac* can enhance the value of any company's annual report because it affords the analyst and the stockholder detailed background of financial information for comparison.

All items and ratios are listed in Both Table I and Table II. No figures are reported in the *Almanac* when the IRS has either suppressed the underlying data, or the sample size, or other reasons affecting a calculated result, and where the ratio/item was not applicable to an industry. The 50 tax-based items that provide that financial analysis are as follows:

1. Number of Enterprises

These are the count of corporate tax returns filed by active corporations on one of the Form 1120-series returns.

> SPECIAL NOTE: Net Sales is used to compute the percentage of items 3 to 7 to Net Sales for all industries, except Finance, Insurance, and Real Estate (FIRE). For the FIRE industries, Total Receipts are used to compute the percentage of items 3 to 7.

Revenues ($ in thousands), Items 2 to 9

2. Operating Income (Net Sales)

This is the IRS item Business Receipts, the gross operating receipts reduced by the cost of returned goods and allowances.

3. Interest

Taxable interest includes interest on U.S. Government obligations, loans, notes, mortgages, arbitrage bonds, nonexempt private activity bonds, corporate bonds, bank deposits, and tax refunds; interest received from tax-exempt state or local municipal bonds and ESOP loans are not included in this item.

4. Rents

These are the gross amounts received from the use or occupancy of property by corporations whose principal activities did not involve operating rental properties.

5. Royalties

These are gross payments received for the use of property rights before taking deductions.

6. Other Portfolio Income

These consist of cash, notes, and accounts receivable, less allowance for bad debts and inventories.

7. Other Receipts

These receipts include such items as income from minor operations, cash discounts, claims, license rights, judgments, and joint ventures.

8. Total Receipts

Total receipts are the sum of ten items: 1. Business receipts; 2. Interest; 3. Interest on government obligations: state and local; 4. Rents; 5. Royalties; 6. Net capital gains (excluding long-term gains from regulated investment companies); 7. Net gain, noncapital assets; 8. Dividends received from domestic corporations; 9. Dividends received from foreign corporations; 10. Other receipts.

9. Average Total Receipts

Total receipts divided by the number of enterprises.

OPERATING COSTS/OPERATING INCOME, ITEMS 10 TO 22

10. Cost of Operations

This is the IRS's Costs of Goods Sold; it consists of the costs incurred in producing the goods or furnishing the services that generated the corporations' business receipts.

11. Salaries and Wages

These include the amount of salaries and wages paid as well as bonuses and director's fees, but no contributions to pension plans (see item 16) nor compensation of officers (see item 20).

12. Taxes Paid

Excludes Federal Income Taxes; they are the amounts paid for ordinary state and local taxes, social security, payroll taxes, unemployment insurance taxes, excise taxes, import and tariff duties, and business license and privilege taxes.

13. Interest Paid

These amounts consist of interest paid on all business indebtedness.

14. Depreciation

The charges allowed are governed principally by the IRS rules in effect in 1997, basically enacted in 1986, but also include other modifications. Hence, depreciation could represent amounts computed by different sets of rules.

15. Amortization and Depletion

Most amortization is calculated on a straight-line basis. Depletion is allowed for the exhaustion of natural deposits and timber.

16. Pensions, Profit-Sharing, Stock Bonus, and Annuity Plans

These are amounts deducted during the current year for qualified pension, profit-sharing, or other funded deferred compensation plans.

17. Employee Benefits

These are employer contributions to death benefit, insurance, health, accident, and sickness, and other welfare plans.

18. Advertising

Amounts include promotion and publicity expenses.

19. Other Expenses

These include expenses for repairs, bad debts, rent paid on business property, contributions and gifts, and expenses not allocable to specific deductible items.

20. Officers' Compensation

Salaries, wages, stock bonuses, bonds, and other forms of compensation are included in this item.

21. Operating Margin

This is the net income after all operating costs have been deducted.

22. Operating Margin Before Officers' Compensation

This measure takes into account the effect of Officers' Compensation on the operating margin.

SELECTED AVERAGE BALANCE SHEET ITEMS ($ IN THOUSANDS) ITEMS 23 TO 29

23. *Average Net Receivables*

The total of Notes and Accounts Receivable, less Allowance for Bad Debts, divided by the number of enterprises. Notes and Accounts Receivable are the gross amounts arising from business sales or services to customers on credit in the course of ordinary trade or business. This includes commercial paper, charge accounts, current intercompany receivables, property investment loans, and trade acceptances.

24. *Average Inventories*

Total inventories are divided by the number of enterprises. Inventories include finished goods, partially finished goods, new materials and supplies acquired for sale, merchandise on hand or in transit, and growing crops reported as assets by agricultural enterprises.

25. *Average Net Property, Plant and Equipment*

This includes depreciable assets less accumulated depreciation, depletable assets less accumulated depletion, and land; the sum is divided by the number of enterprises. Depreciable assets consist of end-of-year balance sheet tangible property, such as buildings and equipment used in trade or business, or held for the production of income, and that has a useful life of one year or more. The amount of accumulated depreciation represents the portion written off in the current year, as well as in prior years. Depletable assets represent the end-of-year value of mineral property, oil and gas wells, and other natural resources; standing timber; intangible development and drilling costs capitalized; and leases and leaseholds, subject to depletion. Accumulated depletion represents the cumulative adjustment of these assets.

26. *Average Total Assets*

Total Assets (and Total Liabilities) are amounts reported in the end-of-year balance sheet. Total Assets are net amounts after reduction from accumulated depreciation, accumulated amortization, accumulated depletion, and the reserve for bad debts. Total Liabilities include the claims of creditors and stockholders' equity, and were net after reduction by the cost of treasury stock. The average of total assets was obtained by dividing it by the number of enterprises.

27. *Average of Notes and Loans Payable, and Mortgages*

These liabilities were separated on the balance sheet according to the time to maturity of the obligations. Time to maturity was based on the date of the balance sheet, rather than the date of issue of the obligations. The total was divided by the number of enterprises.

28. *Average of All Other Liabilities*

These included accounts payable, and other liabilities including other current liabilities. The total was divided by the number of enterprises.

29. *Average Net Worth*

Net Worth represents the stockholders' equity in the corporation (total assets minus the claims of creditors). It consists of Capital Stock, Paid-In Capital Surplus, Retained Earnings Appropriated, Retained Earnings Unappropriated, less cost of treasury stock.

SELECTED FINANCIAL RATIOS, NUMBER OF TIMES TO ONE, RATIOS 30 TO 44

30. Current Ratio

The items that used Current Assets for this ratio are Cash; Notes and Accounts Receivable, Less: Allowance for Bad Debts; Inventories; Government Obligations; Tax-Exempt Securities; and Other Current Assets. For Current Liabilities, the following items were included: Accounts Payable; Mortgages and Notes Maturing in Less than 1 Year; and Other Current Liabilities.

This ratio, rated highest by CPAs as a measure of liquidity, gauges the ability of a company to meet its short-term financial obligations should it be compelled to liquidate its assets. However, it is not an absolute measure of the company's ability to meet its obligations. It is obtained by dividing current assets by current liabilities. The standard guideline has been a ratio of 2 to 1; however, some companies have found that in their experience, a ratio less than 2 to 1 is adequate, while others consider a larger one to be necessary. The ratio is affected by the method of valuation of inventory (LIFO or FIFO) and by inflation. The Almanac provides measures that can be treated as standards by size of asset.

31. Quick Ratio

This ratio is also known as the "Acid Test Ratio" because it is often used to estimate a company's general liquidity. There is some disagreement about the inclusion of inventory in the numerator because it may be slow moving, obsolete, or pledged to specific creditors, and, therefore, not be readily convertible into cash. The *Almanac* adopts a conservative approach and does not include the item in calculating the ratio. Excluding inventories and other current assets, the numerator is the same as that used in determining current assets. The denominator, current liabilities, is unchanged. The ratio of 1 to 1 has been considered a reasonable standard, but it is jeopardized because accounts and notes receivable may not be convertible into cash at face value and at short notice. The *Almanac* provides measures that can be treated as standards by size of asset.

32. Net Sales to Working Capital

This is an efficiency, or turnover, ratio that measures the rate at which current assets less current liabilities (Working Capital) is used in making sales. (In industries in Finance, Insurance, and Real Estate, total receipts rather than net sales is used.) A low ratio indicates a less efficient (profitable) use of working capital in making sales. The *Almanac* provides measures that can be treated as standards by size of asset. Working Capital is the difference between current assets and current liabilities.

33. Coverage Ratio

This ratio measures the number of times all interest paid by the company is covered by earnings before interest charges and taxes (EBIT). For that reason, the ratio is also known as the "times interest earned ratio." The ratio indicates the company's ability to service its debt based on its income.

34. Total Asset Turnover

The ratio is an efficiency ratio because it indicates the effectiveness of the company's use of its total assets in generating sales. It is measured by dividing net sales by total assets.

35. Inventory Turnover

Inventory turnover measures the liquidity of the inventory. It is computed by dividing the cost of goods sold by the average inventory. The result shows the number of times that the average inventory can be converted into receivables or cash. The ratio reflects both on the quality of the inventory and the efficiency of management. Typically, the higher the turnover rate, the more likely profits will be higher.

SPECIAL NOTE: Inventory turnover is not computed for industries in Finance, Insurance, and Real Estate.

36. Receivables Turnover

This ratio measures the liquidity of accounts receivable. It indicates the average collection period throughout the year. It is obtained by dividing sales average by net receivables. It is not computed in the Finance, Insurance, and Real Estate industries (although it is calculated for all other industries even though conventional analysis typically omits it) for many of the industries in the *Almanac*.

37. Total Liabilities to Net Worth

This ratio indicates the extent to which the company's funds are supplied by short- and long-term creditors compared to its owners. It is an indicator of the company's long-term debt paying ability. The ratio is one of the most important bearing on the company's capital structure. Net worth is defined in ratio 29.

38. Current Assets to Working Capital

The dependence of Working Capital in part on current assets is important to understanding this part of the source of Working Capital. Current Assets are defined in ratio 30 and Working Capital is defined in ratio 32.

39. Current Liabilities to Working Capital

The dependence of Working Capital in part on current liabilities is important to understanding this part of the source of Working Capital. Current Liabilities are defined in ratio 30 and Working Capital is defined in ratio 32.

40. Working Capital to Net Sales or Total Receipts

The purpose of this ratio is to determine the working capital needed in relation to projected sales or receipts. Working Capital is defined in ratio 32.

41. Inventory to Working Capital

This ratio, by showing the proportion of Working Capital invested in Inventory, indicates the part of Current Assets that are least liquid. Inventories which exceed working capital indicate that current liabilities exceed liquid current assets. Working Capital is defined in ratio 32.

42. Total Receipts to Cash Flow

Cash Flow is the difference between cash receipts and cash disbursements. The ratio of total receipts to cash flow could suggest steps which management might take to improve the company's cash position.

43. Cost of Goods to Cash Flow

This ratio can be the basis for projections of cash requirements needed to fund projected costs of production. Cash flow is defined in ratio 42.

44. Cash Flow to Total Debt

This ratio indicates the extent to which a company could service its total debt from cash flow. It is analogous to the coverage ratio; refer to ratio 33. Cash flow is defined in ratio 42.

SELECTED FINANCIAL FACTORS (IN PERCENTAGES), ITEMS 45 TO 50

45. Debt Ratio (Total Liabilities to Total Assets)

This ratio indicates the company's ability to pay all its debts. It measures the creditors' and owners' of the company's ability to withstand losses. It is an indicator of the long-run solvency of the firm.

46. Return on Total Assets

The ratio combines the turnover and profit ratios (Sales/Total Assets x [times] Profit/Sales) and yields the return on investment (Total Assets). The result is the end product of the DuPont System of financial analysis. The system takes into account both operating income and operating assets. In Table I of each industry, the Return on Investment (ROI) is net income less deficit before income taxes divided by total assets. In Table II of each industry, the ROI is net income before income taxes divided by Total Assets. Total Assets are used because management has discretion in the investment of the resources provided by both the creditors and owners.

47. Return on Equity Before Income Taxes

This ratio measures the profitability of the company's operations to owners, before income taxes. For Table I this is net income, less deficit before income taxes and before credits. For Table II this is net income minus income tax before credits.

48. Return on Equity After Income Taxes

This ratio measures the profitability of the company's operations to owners, after income taxes. For Table I this is net income, less deficit and minus income tax before credits. For Table II this is net income minus income tax and before credits.

49. Profit Margin (Before Income Tax)

This is net income before income tax divided by net sales (or total receipts) and indicates the contribution of sales to the profitability of the company. Competition, capital structure, and operating characteristics cause the margin to vary within and among industries. For Table I, net income less deficit and before income taxes is the numerator; for Table II it is net income before tax.

50. Profit Margin (After Income Tax)

This ratio is the same as ratio 49 except that income taxes are taken into account.

Table of Contents

Page references to tables for industries with net income are in italic

PRINCIPAL BUSINESS ACTIVITY (BASED ON NAICS)

ALMANAC
of Business and Industrial
FINANCIAL
RATIOS

39th ANNUAL EDITION
2008

Table I

Corporations with and without Net Income

AGRICULTURAL PRODUCTION

MONEY AMOUNTS AND SIZE OF ASSETS IN THOUSANDS OF DOLLARS

Item Description for Accounting Period 7/04 Through 6/05	Total	Zero Assets	Under 500	500 to 1,000	1,000 to 5,000	5,000 to 10,000	10,000 to 25,000	25,000 to 50,000	50,000 to 100,000	100,000 to 250,000	250,000 to 500,000	500,000 to 2,500,000	2,500,000 and over
Number of Enterprises 1	101205	9940	62326	13779	13471	969	451	130	70	50	11	7	0
Revenues ($ in Thousands)													
Net Sales 2	93163478	2088162	12554618	7534673	18869354	6297709	8274075	6583136	5628857	9123986	3368465	12840442	0
Interest 3	267949	10717	26684	24643	64872	12772	19236	17826	9473	21645	6441	53641	0
Rents 4	726172	4896	159563	181479	228598	43737	29621	14631	25894	20551	4826	12375	0
Royalties 5	243703	2915	5983	5844	19243	8591	7521	2001	3437	20976	2427	164765	0
Other Portfolio Income 6	1800126	192567	389207	153603	413792	154745	119285	43111	51819	117921	26063	138015	0
Other Receipts 7	7333044	278598	2467308	1039166	1955505	334881	466579	232564	68543	236015	62777	191108	0
Total Receipts 8	103534472	2577855	15603363	8939408	21551364	6852435	8916317	6893269	5788023	9541094	3470999	13400346	0
Average Total Receipts 9	1023	259	250	649	1600	7072	19770	53025	82686	190822	315545	1914335	•
Operating Costs/Operating Income (%)													
Cost of Operations 10	52.6	66.0	17.5	35.7	36.6	48.7	65.1	57.2	67.0	76.2	78.9	79.4	•
Salaries and Wages 11	8.2	7.7	11.9	8.9	11.9	9.3	6.6	6.0	5.6	4.7	3.0	5.4	•
Taxes Paid 12	2.2	3.3	3.2	3.5	3.2	2.4	1.6	1.3	1.5	1.8	1.7	0.7	•
Interest Paid 13	2.4	3.6	3.0	2.7	3.0	3.0	1.6	1.5	1.4	1.5	1.4	2.3	•
Depreciation 14	6.4	6.9	9.4	9.9	9.9	7.2	4.0	3.6	4.8	4.1	3.4	2.2	•
Amortization and Depletion 15	0.2	0.6	0.0	0.1	0.1	0.1	0.2	0.4	0.4	0.7	0.2	0.3	•
Pensions and Other Deferred Comp. 16	0.3	0.7	0.1	0.4	0.3	0.5	0.2	0.2	0.2	0.1	0.5	0.2	•
Employee Benefits 17	1.1	0.7	1.1	1.3	1.2	1.2	0.7	0.6	1.4	0.8	1.0	1.5	•
Advertising 18	0.5	0.3	0.3	0.3	0.4	0.3	0.3	0.2	0.1	0.3	0.1	1.3	•
Other Expenses 19	33.4	44.5	71.7	47.3	44.8	35.7	24.2	29.2	18.4	8.9	6.1	7.1	•
Officers' Compensation 20	2.0	0.4	3.8	4.2	2.8	2.5	1.2	1.0	0.7	0.7	0.7	0.4	•
Operating Margin 21	•	•	•	•	•	•	•	•	•	0.1	2.9	•	•
Operating Margin Before Officers' Comp. 22	•	•	•	•	•	•	•	•	•	0.9	3.6	•	•

Selected Average Balance Sheet ($ in Thousands)

Net Receivables 23	74	0	5	25	85	223	1829	5017	9762	17070	19090	320625	•
Inventories 24	89	0	11	36	162	687	2258	4704	12899	17012	47925	150157	•
Net Property, Plant and Equipment 25	432	0	91	418	1099	3962	6246	14618	29093	59616	122159	366386	•
Total Assets 26	944	0	170	702	1890	6717	15215	35930	69322	148948	312820	2287446	•
Notes and Loans Payable 27	478	0	155	334	1056	4280	7464	15947	29637	49150	69653	710933	•
All Other Liabilities 28	164	0	10	42	153	1028	2246	7049	14148	28096	77929	1018423	•
Net Worth 29	302	0	4	326	682	1410	5505	12934	25537	71702	165238	558090	•

Selected Financial Ratios (Times to 1)

Current Ratio 30	1.4	•	1.6	1.5	1.4	1.0	1.4	1.3	1.5	1.7	1.6	1.1	•
Quick Ratio 31	0.7	•	1.1	0.8	0.7	0.3	0.6	0.7	0.7	0.9	0.6	0.7	•
Net Sales to Working Capital 32	12.7	•	12.0	11.1	11.2	151.7	11.0	16.4	8.3	7.5	9.0	26.5	•
Coverage Ratio 33	1.8	•	1.8	2.6	1.0	0.3	2.3	3.3	1.8	4.1	5.1	2.8	•
Total Asset Turnover 34	1.0	•	1.2	0.8	0.7	1.0	1.2	1.4	1.2	1.2	1.0	0.8	•
Inventory Turnover 35	5.4	•	3.3	5.4	3.2	4.6	5.3	6.2	4.2	8.2	5.0	9.7	•
Receivables Turnover 36	12.9	•	49.1	20.7	17.3	24.4	10.7	10.4	8.0	11.1	15.5	6.1	•
Total Liabilities to Net Worth 37	2.1	•	37.2	1.2	1.8	3.8	1.8	1.8	1.7	1.1	0.9	3.1	•
Current Assets to Working Capital 38	3.8	•	2.7	3.1	3.6	42.1	3.7	4.8	3.0	2.4	2.7	9.0	•
Current Liabilities to Working Capital 39	2.8	•	1.7	2.1	2.6	41.1	2.7	3.8	2.0	1.4	1.7	8.0	•
Working Capital to Net Sales 40	0.1	•	0.1	0.1	0.1	0.0	0.1	0.1	0.1	0.1	0.1	0.0	•
Inventory to Working Capital 41	1.3	•	0.7	0.9	1.3	20.4	1.4	1.6	1.3	0.8	1.5	2.4	•
Total Receipts to Cash Flow 42	3.9	6.1	2.0	2.8	3.1	4.2	4.7	3.5	6.0	8.9	10.8	11.4	•
Cost of Goods to Cash Flow 43	2.0	4.0	0.3	1.0	1.1	2.1	3.1	2.0	4.0	6.8	8.5	9.1	•
Cash Flow to Total Debt 44	0.4	•	0.6	0.5	0.4	0.3	0.4	0.6	0.3	0.3	0.2	0.1	•

Selected Financial Factors (in Percentages)

Debt Ratio 45	68.0	•	97.4	53.5	63.9	79.0	63.8	64.0	63.2	51.9	47.2	75.6	•
Return on Total Assets 46	4.2	•	6.2	5.4	2.2	0.8	4.3	7.1	2.9	7.6	7.3	5.2	•
Return on Equity Before Income Taxes 47	6.0	•	103.4	7.2	•	•	6.7	13.6	3.6	12.0	11.1	13.8	•
Return on Equity After Income Taxes 48	3.9	•	88.6	6.5	•	•	5.4	11.9	1.9	8.6	6.6	10.2	•
Profit Margin (Before Income Tax) 49	2.0	•	2.3	4.3	•	•	2.0	3.5	1.1	4.7	6.0	4.2	•
Profit Margin (After Income Tax) 50	1.3	•	2.0	3.9	•	•	1.6	3.0	0.6	3.4	3.6	3.1	•

Table II

Corporations with Net Income

AGRICULTURAL PRODUCTION

MONEY AMOUNTS AND SIZE OF ASSETS IN THOUSANDS OF DOLLARS

Item Description for Accounting Period 7/04 Through 6/05	Total	Zero Assets	Under 100	101 to 250	251 to 500	501 to 1,000	1,001 to 5,000	5,001 to 10,000	10,001 to 25,000	25,001 to 50,000	50,001 to 100,000	100,001 to 250,000	250,001 and over
Number of Enterprises 1	51959	3541	30182	8859	8395	0	256	82	33	34	6	0	0
Revenues ($ in Thousands)													
Net Sales 2	65155630	336436	7855116	5224060	13540918	0	5973856	4642772	3645637	7518901	2583251	0	0
Interest 3	210073	4301	18859	20930	55544	0	16477	11117	4545	20045	1966	0	0
Rents 4	529730	2215	95111	134120	188580	0	24303	10657	8714	17852	3867	0	0
Royalties 5	226296	2301	5874	5511	17457	0	7117	1739	3410	15799	2427	0	0
Other Portfolio Income 6	1372823	146796	219878	111453	345072	0	92890	26809	31622	108172	21176	0	0
Other Receipts 7	5258843	154824	1547932	725667	1588074	0	295142	191989	54866	160391	53990	0	0
Total Receipts 8	72753395	646873	9742770	6221741	15735645	0	6409785	4885083	3748794	7841160	2666677	0	0
Average Total Receipts 9	1400	183	323	702	1874	•	25038	59574	113600	230622	444446	•	•
Operating Costs/Operating Income (%)													
Cost of Operations 10	53.6	41.2	18.7	39.8	32.5	•	68.8	58.0	61.1	78.1	77.8	•	•
Salaries and Wages 11	7.3	7.6	10.5	7.2	11.3	•	5.3	5.9	6.1	3.7	3.5	•	•
Taxes Paid 12	2.0	5.5	2.8	2.9	3.1	•	1.3	1.4	1.4	1.8	1.8	•	•
Interest Paid 13	1.8	5.0	2.3	1.8	2.7	•	1.2	1.1	0.9	1.0	0.5	•	•
Depreciation 14	5.4	5.5	7.0	7.9	9.1	•	3.0	3.4	3.1	3.3	3.3	•	•
Amortization and Depletion 15	0.2	0.7	0.0	0.0	0.1	•	0.3	0.1	0.3	0.3	0.1	•	•
Pensions and Other Deferred Comp. 16	0.2	0.6	0.1	0.5	0.4	•	0.2	0.2	0.3	0.1	0.5	•	•
Employee Benefits 17	1.0	1.2	1.0	1.3	1.2	•	0.6	0.5	0.6	0.9	1.0	•	•
Advertising 18	0.3	0.8	0.3	0.3	0.3	•	0.2	0.2	0.2	0.2	0.1	•	•
Other Expenses 19	29.1	45.2	62.5	42.9	44.3	•	18.5	25.7	22.3	6.6	4.8	•	•
Officers' Compensation 20	1.9	0.7	3.2	4.1	2.7	•	1.1	0.9	0.6	0.6	0.6	•	•
Operating Margin 21	•	•	•	•	•	•	•	2.5	3.1	3.2	5.9	•	•
Operating Margin Before Officers' Comp. 22	•	•	•	•	•	•	0.5	3.5	3.8	3.9	6.5	•	•

Selected Average Balance Sheet ($ in Thousands)

Net Receivables 23	75	0	6	24	72	•	2104	4974	8919	20722	19540	•
Inventories 24	123	0	10	44	199	•	2650	5351	15309	20038	78800	•
Net Property, Plant and Equipment 25	483	0	94	375	1064	•	5377	12845	26851	52810	152950	•
Total Assets 26	1078	0	192	697	1856	•	15415	36246	71459	146779	337022	•
Notes and Loans Payable 27	418	0	83	225	856	•	6708	14206	27255	40897	65238	•
All Other Liabilities 28	183	0	14	41	109	•	2329	6253	15878	28929	79007	•
Net Worth 29	476	0	95	431	891	•	6378	15787	28327	76953	192777	•

Selected Financial Ratios (Times to 1)

Current Ratio 30	1.6	•	1.7	2.2	1.4	•	1.4	1.4	1.7	1.9	2.7	•
Quick Ratio 31	0.8	•	1.3	1.2	0.7	•	0.7	0.7	0.7	1.0	0.9	•
Net Sales to Working Capital 32	10.4	•	11.6	6.2	11.9	•	11.1	10.9	8.9	6.9	5.7	•
Coverage Ratio 33	6.0	16.5	7.9	6.8	4.1	•	6.7	7.7	7.4	8.7	18.7	•
Total Asset Turnover 34	1.2	•	1.4	0.8	0.9	•	1.5	1.6	1.5	1.5	1.3	•
Inventory Turnover 35	5.5	•	4.9	5.4	2.6	•	6.1	6.1	4.4	8.6	4.3	•
Receivables Turnover 36	17.3	•	52.6	20.4	23.8	•	12.2	11.9	9.8	11.7		•
Total Liabilities to Net Worth 37	1.3	•	1.0	0.6	1.1	•	1.4	1.3	1.5	0.9	0.7	•
Current Assets to Working Capital 38	2.8	•	2.4	1.8	3.4	•	3.3	3.2	2.5	2.1	1.6	•
Current Liabilities to Working Capital 39	1.8	•	1.4	0.8	2.4	•	2.3	2.2	1.5	1.1	0.6	•
Working Capital to Net Sales 40	0.1	•	0.1	0.2	0.1	•	0.1	0.1	0.1	0.1	0.2	•
Inventory to Working Capital 41	1.1	•	0.4	0.5	1.4	•	1.4	1.1	1.1	0.7	1.0	•
Total Receipts to Cash Flow 42	3.4	1.1	1.7	2.7	2.5	•	4.8	3.4	3.9	8.5	9.1	•
Cost of Goods to Cash Flow 43	1.8	0.5	0.3	1.1	0.8	•	3.3	2.0	2.4	6.6	7.1	•
Cash Flow to Total Debt 44	0.6	•	1.5	0.8	0.7	•	0.5	0.8	0.7	0.4	0.3	•

Selected Financial Factors (in Percentages)

Debt Ratio 45	55.9	•	50.4	38.2	52.0	•	58.6	56.4	60.4	47.6	42.8	•
Return on Total Assets 46	12.3	•	24.3	10.3	9.6	•	11.8	13.9	10.6	12.8	12.4	•
Return on Equity Before Income Taxes 47	23.3	•	42.8	14.3	15.1	•	24.3	27.8	23.1	21.6	20.5	•
Return on Equity After Income Taxes 48	20.7	•	41.4	13.5	14.0	•	22.3	25.5	19.9	17.0	13.5	•
Profit Margin (Before Income Tax) 49	8.8	78.0	15.7	10.4	8.4	•	6.6	7.7	5.9	7.5	9.2	•
Profit Margin (After Income Tax) 50	7.8	68.8	15.1	9.8	7.7	•	6.1	7.1	5.1	5.9	6.1	•

Table I
Corporations with and without Net Income

FORESTRY AND LOGGING

MONEY AMOUNTS AND SIZE OF ASSETS IN THOUSANDS OF DOLLARS

Item Description for Accounting Period 7/04 Through 6/05	Total	Zero Assets	Under 500	500 to 1,000	1,000 to 5,000	5,000 to 10,000	10,000 to 25,000	25,000 to 50,000	50,000 to 100,000	100,000 to 250,000	250,000 to 500,000	500,000 to 2,500,000	2,500,000 and over
Number of Enterprises **1**	10683	742	7263	1438	1059	72	68	25	9	4	0	4	0
Revenues ($ in Thousands)													
Net Sales **2**	13351287	14211	2845424	1550647	4146039	221474	1025891	598419	275773	652664	0	2020746	0
Interest **3**	44466	17	2989	228	2756	2388	1510	2670	943	10112	0	20852	0
Rents **4**	53890	230	6119	494	5386	4975	3398	9446	289	19976	0	3576	0
Royalties **5**	2809	0	0	2305	14	220	139	0	0	0	0	131	0
Other Portfolio Income **6**	302929	2	11581	73469	81883	28676	12873	1761	15566	76527	0	593	0
Other Receipts **7**	137604	11795	6229	32243	4806	-17228	20365	11568	8680	24532	0	34613	0
Total Receipts **8**	13892985	26255	2872342	1659386	4240884	240505	1064176	623864	301251	783811	0	2080511	0
Average Total Receipts **9**	1300	35	395	1154	4005	3340	15650	24955	33472	195953	•	520128	•
Operating Costs/Operating Income (%)													
Cost of Operations **10**	65.2	3.8	56.2	34.0	67.1	90.0	74.6	81.7	88.1	87.7	•	75.8	•
Salaries and Wages **11**	7.1	1.7	7.3	12.2	9.6	1.8	5.9	4.4	3.8	3.8	•	1.2	•
Taxes Paid **12**	2.1	2.6	2.0	3.0	2.1	4.8	1.8	2.3	2.3	1.4	•	1.6	•
Interest Paid **13**	2.6	7.2	1.1	3.3	1.0	3.2	1.3	2.3	5.5	13.7	•	3.9	•
Depreciation **14**	6.8	5.7	8.0	17.3	6.2	1.4	4.3	4.9	2.0	6.8	•	1.7	•
Amortization and Depletion **15**	0.6	2.6	0.0	0.0	0.0	0.3	1.4	0.8	0.4	6.7	•	0.9	•
Pensions and Other Deferred Comp. **16**	0.3	•	0.0	0.0	0.5	0.2	0.4	0.2	0.1	0.2	•	0.2	•
Employee Benefits **17**	1.0	0.1	1.8	1.2	1.0	0.4	1.4	1.1	0.5	0.4	•	•	•
Advertising **18**	0.1	0.0	0.1	0.1	0.2	0.0	0.2	0.1	0.2	0.2	•	0.0	•
Other Expenses **19**	14.5	41.6	19.3	31.8	10.9	11.6	9.8	7.3	21.5	12.7	•	6.2	•
Officers' Compensation **20**	2.4	3.8	3.8	4.0	2.4	0.6	1.9	1.8	2.3	0.9	•	0.2	•
Operating Margin **21**	•	34.6	0.4	•	•	•	•	•	•	•	•	8.4	•
Operating Margin Before Officers' Comp. **22**	•	34.6	4.3	1.4	1.4	•	•	•	•	•	•	8.5	•

Selected Average Balance Sheet ($ in Thousands)

Net Receivables 23	69	0	7	33	138	488	1125	1868	1622	13996	66080
Inventories 24	128	0	4	11	153	32	1993	1183	6620	21118	211545
Net Property, Plant and Equipment 25	543	0	72	519	1130	1148	7308	15624	24624	224161	311665
Total Assets 26	1115	0	119	697	2054	8697	14888	35188	65039	295402	897503
Notes and Loans Payable 27	684	0	106	579	1189	6330	5043	12930	27122	283314	487512
All Other Liabilities 28	137	0	13	41	168	3185	1355	8594	6441	85213	49860
Net Worth 29	294	0	0	77	697	-818	8491	13664	31476	-73125	360131

Selected Financial Ratios (Times to 1)

Current Ratio 30	1.4	•	0.8	0.9	1.0	0.5	1.7	1.1	2.3	1.8	2.5
Quick Ratio 31	0.6	•	0.6	0.7	0.6	0.2	0.7	0.6	0.8	0.6	0.6
Net Sales to Working Capital 32	14.9	•	•	•	163.8	•	7.3	29.0	2.7	3.6	3.1
Coverage Ratio 33	1.5	17.6	2.2	1.0	2.3	•	1.5	•	•	•	3.9
Total Asset Turnover 34	1.1	•	3.3	1.5	1.9	0.4	1.0	0.7	0.5	0.6	0.6
Inventory Turnover 35	6.4	•	52.5	33.4	17.2	85.3	5.6	16.5	4.1	6.8	1.8
Receivables Turnover 36	19.9	•	54.5	43.8	34.8	10.4	14.3	13.2	21.5	7.5	9.0
Total Liabilities to Net Worth 37	2.8	•	255.3	8.1	1.9	•	0.8	1.6	1.1	•	1.5
Current Assets to Working Capital 38	3.7	•	•	•	22.1	•	2.4	11.0	1.8	2.2	1.7
Current Liabilities to Working Capital 39	2.7	•	•	•	21.1	•	1.4	10.0	0.8	1.2	0.7
Working Capital to Net Sales 40	0.1	•	•	•	0.0	•	0.1	0.0	0.4	0.3	0.3
Inventory to Working Capital 41	1.5	•	•	•	7.0	•	1.1	2.4	0.8	0.4	1.2
Total Receipts to Cash Flow 42	8.9	0.6	6.1	4.0	11.9	•	12.5	30.2	•	•	5.8
Cost of Goods to Cash Flow 43	5.8	0.0	3.4	1.4	8.0	•	9.3	24.7	•	•	4.4
Cash Flow to Total Debt 44	0.2	•	0.5	0.4	0.2	•	0.2	0.0	•	•	0.2

Selected Financial Factors (in Percentages)

Debt Ratio 45	73.6	•	99.6	89.0	66.1	109.4	43.0	61.2	51.6	124.8	59.9
Return on Total Assets 46	4.3	•	8.3	5.2	4.2	•	2.1	•	•	•	8.5
Return on Equity Before Income Taxes 47	5.6	•	1168.6	1.0	7.1	21.6	1.2	•	31.6	•	15.9
Return on Equity After Income Taxes 48	1.5	•	1126.1	•	6.2	32.7	0.2	•	31.6	•	9.1
Profit Margin (Before Income Tax) 49	1.3	119.3	1.4	0.1	1.3	•	0.7	•	•	•	11.3
Profit Margin (After Income Tax) 50	0.4	118.5	1.3	•	1.1	•	0.1	•	•	•	6.5

3

Table II

Corporations with Net Income

FORESTRY AND LOGGING

MONEY AMOUNTS AND SIZE OF ASSETS IN THOUSANDS OF DOLLARS

Item Description for Accounting Period 7/04 Through 6/05	Total	Zero Assets	Under 500	500 to 1,000	1,000 to 5,000	5,000 to 10,000	10,000 to 25,000	25,000 to 50,000	50,000 to 100,000	100,000 to 250,000	250,000 to 500,000	500,000 to 2,500,000	2,500,000 and over
Number of Enterprises 1	5756	460	3796	887	552	0	29	10	4	0	0	0	0
Revenues ($ in Thousands)													
Net Sales 2	9637554	13853	1789213	1179418	3434497	0	664413	438516	149545	0	0	0	0
Interest 3	29346	8	2721	204	1361	0	976	193	643	0	0	0	0
Rents 4	21014	189	9	494	3563	0	1339	7128	221	0	0	0	0
Royalties 5	2795	0	0	2305	0	0	139	0	0	0	0	0	0
Other Portfolio Income 6	147748	2	44	42914	49528	0	10102	934	15518	0	0	0	0
Other Receipts 7	107856	11796	5717	32014	-1228	0	15173	7826	1493	0	0	0	0
Total Receipts 8	9946313	25848	1797704	1257349	3487721	0	692142	454597	167420	0	0	0	0
Average Total Receipts 9	1728	56	474	1418	6318	•	23867	45460	41855	•	•	•	•
Operating Costs/Operating Income (%)													
Cost of Operations 10	64.3	3.9	54.5	26.2	71.0	•	76.1	85.0	85.7	•	•	•	•
Salaries and Wages 11	6.4	1.8	7.2	15.2	6.4	•	5.4	4.1	3.4	•	•	•	•
Taxes Paid 12	2.0	2.5	1.7	2.8	1.8	•	1.7	1.8	2.4	•	•	•	•
Interest Paid 13	1.7	7.4	1.1	2.5	0.9	•	1.1	0.9	0.4	•	•	•	•
Depreciation 14	5.3	5.9	7.2	13.1	4.6	•	3.8	2.1	2.1	•	•	•	•
Amortization and Depletion 15	0.2	2.5	0.0	0.0	0.0	•	0.4	0.1	0.7	•	•	•	•
Pensions and Other Deferred Comp. 16	0.3	•	0.0	0.0	0.0	•	0.5	0.1	•	•	•	•	•
Employee Benefits 17	0.7	0.1	0.4	0.4	1.1	•	1.4	0.7	0.6	•	•	•	•
Advertising 18	0.1	0.0	0.1	0.1	0.2	•	0.2	0.0	0.2	•	•	•	•
Other Expenses 19	12.4	34.2	17.4	37.0	8.3	•	5.8	4.8	4.0	•	•	•	•
Officers' Compensation 20	2.0	•	2.6	2.8	2.6	•	1.7	1.1	1.4	•	•	•	•
Operating Margin 21	4.7	41.7	7.9	•	2.5	•	1.8	•	•	•	•	•	•
Operating Margin Before Officers' Comp. 22	6.7	41.7	10.5	2.8	5.2	•	3.5	0.4	0.4	•	•	•	•

Selected Average Balance Sheet ($ in Thousands)

Net Receivables 23	95	0	13	51	201	•	1535	2638	2569
Inventories 24	208	0	7	11	282	•	2953	4041	5334
Net Property, Plant and Equipment 25	386	0	60	473	1048	•	6554	10364	15588
Total Assets 26	1088	0	132	730	2026	•	15277	36957	58551
Notes and Loans Payable 27	592	0	98	410	1134	•	5245	11189	15136
All Other Liabilities 28	97	0	10	61	209	•	2201	7491	3927
Net Worth 29	398	0	24	259	683	•	7832	18278	39488

Selected Financial Ratios (Times to 1)

Current Ratio 30	2.1	•	1.1	1.0	1.2	•	1.6	1.6	3.1
Quick Ratio 31	0.9	•	0.8	0.7	0.6	•	0.6	1.0	1.7
Net Sales to Working Capital 32	8.4	•	108.1	•	54.8	•	9.6	9.1	3.4
Coverage Ratio 33	5.6	18.3	8.4	3.6	5.4	•	6.5	4.3	28.2
Total Asset Turnover 34	1.5	•	3.6	1.8	3.1	•	1.5	1.2	0.6
Inventory Turnover 35	5.2	•	34.6	31.9	15.7	•	5.9	9.2	6.0
Receivables Turnover 36	24.2	•	38.0	41.6	43.4	•	15.9	•	•
Total Liabilities to Net Worth 37	1.7	•	4.5	1.8	2.0	•	1.0	1.0	0.5
Current Assets to Working Capital 38	1.9	•	12.9	•	6.6	•	2.7	2.6	1.5
Current Liabilities to Working Capital 39	0.9	•	11.9	•	5.6	•	1.7	1.6	0.5
Working Capital to Net Sales 40	0.1	•	0.0	•	0.0	•	0.1	0.1	0.3
Inventory to Working Capital 41	1.0	•	2.2	•	2.7	•	1.2	0.8	0.5
Total Receipts to Cash Flow 42	6.0	0.6	4.6	2.8	10.9	•	11.3	15.3	23.9
Cost of Goods to Cash Flow 43	3.8	0.0	2.5	0.7	7.8	•	8.6	13.0	20.5
Cash Flow to Total Debt 44	0.4	•	1.0	1.0	0.4	•	0.3	0.2	0.1

Selected Financial Factors (in Percentages)

Debt Ratio 45	63.4	•	81.8	64.5	66.3	•	48.7	50.5	32.6
Return on Total Assets 46	14.7	•	34.0	16.5	15.4	•	10.5	4.5	7.3
Return on Equity Before Income Taxes 47	33.1	•	164.1	33.6	37.3	•	17.3	7.0	10.4
Return on Equity After Income Taxes 48	27.5	•	162.6	30.5	35.6	•	14.7	6.2	9.4
Profit Margin (Before Income Tax) 49	7.9	128.2	8.4	6.5	4.1	•	5.9	2.9	11.0
Profit Margin (After Income Tax) 50	6.5	127.4	8.3	5.9	3.9	•	5.0	2.6	9.9

Table I

Corporations with and without Net Income

SUPPORT ACTIVITIES AND FISHING, HUNTING AND TRAPPING

MONEY AMOUNTS AND SIZE OF ASSETS IN THOUSANDS OF DOLLARS

Item Description for Accounting Period 7/04 Through 6/05	Total	Zero Assets	Under 500	500 to 1,000	1,000 to 5,000	5,000 to 10,000	10,000 to 25,000	25,000 to 50,000	50,000 to 100,000	100,000 to 250,000	250,000 to 500,000	500,000 to 2,500,000	2,500,000 and over
Number of Enterprises **1**	29665	3815	22457	1808	1198	245	104	29	9	0	0	0	0
Revenues ($ in Thousands)													
Net Sales **2**	18184362	388476	6341535	2038032	2947371	2221382	1886694	1029543	1331331	0	0	0	0
Interest **3**	22007	1534	4053	1659	5151	1860	2432	2936	2382	0	0	0	0
Rents **4**	25239	1	1189	6026	3985	9530	4170	263	74	0	0	0	0
Royalties **5**	595	0	0	0	0	107	86	0	402	0	0	0	0
Other Portfolio Income **6**	230196	26494	137386	13743	29184	7000	9500	5268	1621	0	0	0	0
Other Receipts **7**	815679	2383	304611	254620	69507	73413	52043	37147	21954	0	0	0	0
Total Receipts **8**	19278078	418888	6788774	2314080	3055198	2313292	1954925	1075157	1357764	0	0	0	0
Average Total Receipts **9**	650	110	302	1280	2550	9442	18797	37074	150863	•	•	•	•
Operating Costs/Operating Income (%)													
Cost of Operations **10**	54.6	40.3	42.9	56.8	45.1	64.3	72.4	79.9	71.6	•	•	•	•
Salaries and Wages **11**	10.3	1.2	10.4	10.8	14.0	13.1	6.8	4.9	7.4	•	•	•	•
Taxes Paid **12**	2.5	1.2	2.7	1.9	3.8	1.7	1.6	1.3	2.7	•	•	•	•
Interest Paid **13**	1.3	0.1	1.4	0.9	1.7	0.7	1.2	1.4	1.7	•	•	•	•
Depreciation **14**	4.4	2.2	3.9	5.0	5.5	4.8	3.3	4.4	4.3	•	•	•	•
Amortization and Depletion **15**	0.2	0.0	0.1	0.0	0.5	0.1	0.1	0.2	0.4	•	•	•	•
Pensions and Other Deferred Comp. **16**	0.3	•	0.1	0.8	0.1	0.8	0.2	0.2	0.1	•	•	•	•
Employee Benefits **17**	0.7	0.0	0.6	0.7	0.5	1.0	0.6	0.9	0.9	•	•	•	•
Advertising **18**	0.5	0.2	0.8	0.1	0.2	1.2	0.3	0.2	0.5	•	•	•	•
Other Expenses **19**	23.9	44.3	31.7	25.3	29.4	13.1	13.1	10.9	9.5	•	•	•	•
Officers' Compensation **20**	4.4	3.9	8.4	2.9	3.1	1.9	1.6	1.1	1.0	•	•	•	•
Operating Margin **21**	•	6.6	•	•	•	•	•	•	•	•	•	•	•
Operating Margin Before Officers' Comp. **22**	1.5	10.5	5.5	•	•	•	0.4	•	0.9	•	•	•	•

Selected Average Balance Sheet ($ in Thousands)

Net Receivables 23	47	0	6	33	220	1157	2989	6671	16388
Inventories 24	36	0	3	10	132	625	1883	5887	18451
Net Property, Plant and Equipment 25	154	0	39	297	1008	3072	5103	10357	39922
Total Assets 26	381	0	94	669	2036	7246	14533	33286	142670
Notes and Loans Payable 27	164	0	72	175	871	1709	5293	13221	57254
All Other Liabilities 28	66	0	9	67	304	993	3908	7996	42760
Net Worth 29	151	0	13	426	860	4544	5332	12069	42656

Selected Financial Ratios (Times to 1)

Current Ratio 30	1.5	•	1.9	2.0	1.2	2.2	1.3	1.4	1.3
Quick Ratio 31	1.0	•	1.5	1.4	0.9	1.6	0.8	0.8	0.5
Net Sales to Working Capital 32	11.5	•	17.4	8.7	26.1	5.1	11.0	7.6	10.6
Coverage Ratio 33	3.4	102.3	4.0	10.1	0.8	3.2	2.9	0.2	2.1
Total Asset Turnover 34	1.6	•	3.0	1.7	1.2	1.3	1.2	1.1	1.0
Inventory Turnover 35	9.2	•	35.9	64.3	8.4	9.3	7.0	4.8	5.7
Receivables Turnover 36	11.7	•	31.3	34.9	8.6	6.5	6.3	6.2	13.7
Total Liabilities to Net Worth 37	1.5	•	6.5	0.6	1.4	0.6	1.7	1.8	2.3
Current Assets to Working Capital 38	2.8	•	2.2	2.0	5.6	1.9	4.1	3.5	4.9
Current Liabilities to Working Capital 39	1.8	•	1.2	1.0	4.6	0.9	3.1	2.5	3.9
Working Capital to Net Sales 40	0.1	•	0.1	0.1	0.0	0.2	0.1	0.1	0.1
Inventory to Working Capital 41	0.6	•	0.2	0.1	0.9	0.3	1.2	1.2	2.4
Total Receipts to Cash Flow 42	4.7	2.1	3.8	3.7	4.1	8.1	8.0	12.0	11.1
Cost of Goods to Cash Flow 43	2.6	0.8	1.6	2.1	1.9	5.2	5.8	9.6	7.9
Cash Flow to Total Debt 44	0.6	•	0.9	1.3	0.5	0.4	0.2	0.1	0.1

Selected Financial Factors (in Percentages)

Debt Ratio 45	60.3	•	86.6	36.3	57.8	37.3	63.3	63.7	70.1
Return on Total Assets 46	7.1	•	16.7	15.5	1.7	2.6	4.5	0.3	3.7
Return on Equity Before Income Taxes 47	12.8	•	93.4	21.9	•	2.9	8.0	•	6.5
Return on Equity After Income Taxes 48	11.6	•	91.3	21.4	•	2.3	7.0	•	3.1
Profit Margin (Before Income Tax) 49	3.1	14.5	4.2	8.3	•	1.4	2.4	•	1.9
Profit Margin (After Income Tax) 50	2.9	12.7	4.1	8.1	•	1.2	2.1	•	0.9

Table II

Corporations with Net Income

SUPPORT ACTIVITIES AND FISHING, HUNTING AND TRAPPING

MONEY AMOUNTS AND SIZE OF ASSETS IN THOUSANDS OF DOLLARS

Item Description for Accounting Period 7/04 Through 6/05	Total	Zero Assets	Under 500	500 to 1,000	1,000 to 5,000	5,000 to 10,000	10,000 to 25,000	25,000 to 50,000	50,000 to 100,000	100,000 to 250,000	250,000 to 500,000	500,000 to 2,500,000	2,500,000 and over
Number of Enterprises 1	16346	2171	11893	1259	742	191	71	14	5	0	0	0	0
Revenues ($ in Thousands)													
Net Sales 2	13144404	327312	3793420	1998036	1661294	2194141	1489703	657360	1023139	0	0	0	0
Interest 3	15941	1534	3453	1536	4376	1302	1650	1159	930	0	0	0	0
Rents 4	11210	1	1089	2065	1508	2500	3890	83	74	0	0	0	0
Royalties 5	107	0	0	0	0	107	0	0	0	0	0	0	0
Other Portfolio Income 6	213641	26494	130648	13743	25284	6703	7404	1804	1560	0	0	0	0
Other Receipts 7	528891	2375	261328	86866	27134	71943	37520	19377	22348	0	0	0	0
Total Receipts 8	13914194	357716	4189938	2102246	1719596	2276696	1540167	679783	1048051	0	0	0	0
Average Total Receipts 9	851	165	352	1670	2318	11920	21692	48556	209610	•	•	•	•
Operating Costs/Operating Income (%)													
Cost of Operations 10	55.5	45.5	41.2	57.6	42.6	64.5	70.4	82.8	69.6	•	•	•	•
Salaries and Wages 11	10.2	0.3	12.1	7.2	16.1	12.5	6.6	3.0	7.7	•	•	•	•
Taxes Paid 12	2.2	0.6	2.7	1.2	3.5	1.5	1.5	1.0	3.3	•	•	•	•
Interest Paid 13	1.0	0.0	1.2	0.5	1.8	0.5	0.9	1.0	1.4	•	•	•	•
Depreciation 14	3.6	1.9	3.1	4.1	4.8	4.2	2.6	3.0	3.9	•	•	•	•
Amortization and Depletion 15	0.1	•	0.1	0.0	0.6	0.0	0.1	0.1	0.1	•	•	•	•
Pensions and Other Deferred Comp. 16	0.3	•	0.0	0.9	0.0	0.8	0.2	0.2	0.1	•	•	•	•
Employee Benefits 17	0.5	0.0	0.5	0.2	0.5	1.0	0.6	0.5	0.8	•	•	•	•
Advertising 18	0.4	0.1	0.4	0.1	0.3	1.2	0.3	0.1	0.3	•	•	•	•
Other Expenses 19	19.7	28.8	28.5	20.5	25.7	11.8	13.6	4.9	8.2	•	•	•	•
Officers' Compensation 20	3.2	3.9	6.5	2.0	2.1	1.9	1.5	1.4	1.0	•	•	•	•
Operating Margin 21	3.2	18.9	3.5	5.8	2.1	0.1	1.7	1.9	3.5	•	•	•	•
Operating Margin Before Officers' Comp. 22	6.4	22.8	10.0	7.7	4.2	2.0	3.2	3.4	4.5	•	•	•	•

Selected Average Balance Sheet ($ in Thousands)

Net Receivables 23	69	0	9	43	301	1370	3482	8092	22902
Inventories 24	49	0	3	13	118	722	1981	7951	54010
Net Property, Plant and Equipment 25	148	0	25	240	892	2300	4347	10703	51135
Total Assets 26	437	0	92	644	1998	7285	14150	34497	175192
Notes and Loans Payable 27	153	0	57	139	721	2041	4690	10997	47950
All Other Liabilities 28	85	0	9	65	317	1006	3999	12204	64057
Net Worth 29	199	0	26	440	959	4238	5461	11297	63185

Selected Financial Ratios (Times to 1)

Current Ratio 30	1.7	•	2.1	2.0	1.6	2.3	1.4	1.3	1.6
Quick Ratio 31	1.2	•	1.6	1.8	1.1	1.8	0.9	0.7	0.7
Net Sales to Working Capital 32	9.3	•	14.3	13.3	9.4	5.2	10.6	9.8	5.2
Coverage Ratio 33	10.0	669.8	12.3	23.0	4.1	8.2	6.4	6.3	5.3
Total Asset Turnover 34	1.8	•	3.5	2.5	1.1	1.6	1.5	1.4	1.2
Inventory Turnover 35	9.1	•	41.2	68.4	8.1	10.3	7.5	4.9	2.6
Receivables Turnover 36	12.4	•	34.0	38.8	8.5	8.3	6.3	•	•
Total Liabilities to Net Worth 37	1.2	•	2.5	0.5	1.1	0.7	1.6	2.1	1.8
Current Assets to Working Capital 38	2.4	•	1.9	2.0	2.8	1.8	3.8	4.0	2.6
Current Liabilities to Working Capital 39	1.4	•	0.9	1.0	1.8	0.8	2.8	3.0	1.6
Working Capital to Net Sales 40	0.1	•	0.1	0.1	0.1	0.2	0.1	0.1	0.2
Inventory to Working Capital 41	0.6	•	0.2	0.1	0.5	0.3	1.0	1.7	1.4
Total Receipts to Cash Flow 42	4.2	2.2	2.9	3.7	3.7	7.3	6.4	11.0	8.5
Cost of Goods to Cash Flow 43	2.3	1.0	1.2	2.1	1.6	4.7	4.5	9.1	5.9
Cash Flow to Total Debt 44	0.8	•	1.7	2.1	0.6	0.5	0.4	0.2	0.2

Selected Financial Factors (in Percentages)

Debt Ratio 45	54.5	•	71.7	31.6	52.0	41.8	61.4	67.3	63.9
Return on Total Assets 46	18.5	•	52.8	28.3	8.2	7.0	8.9	8.6	8.5
Return on Equity Before Income Taxes 47	36.7	•	171.5	39.6	13.0	10.5	19.4	22.2	19.2
Return on Equity After Income Taxes 48	35.1	•	169.6	38.9	12.0	9.8	18.0	21.6	15.0
Profit Margin (Before Income Tax) 49	9.1	28.2	14.0	11.0	5.6	3.9	5.1	5.3	5.9
Profit Margin (After Income Tax) 50	8.7	26.1	13.8	10.8	5.1	3.6	4.7	5.2	4.6

Table I

Corporations with and without Net Income

OIL AND GAS EXTRACTION

MONEY AMOUNTS AND SIZE OF ASSETS IN THOUSANDS OF DOLLARS

Item Description for Accounting Period 7/04 Through 6/05	Total	Zero Assets	Under 500	500 to 1,000	1,000 to 5,000	5,000 to 10,000	10,000 to 25,000	25,000 to 50,000	50,000 to 100,000	100,000 to 250,000	250,000 to 500,000	500,000 to 2,500,000	2,500,000 and over
Number of Enterprises 1	16807	881	11941	1070	1781	451	301	138	84	66	34	44	15
Revenues ($ in Thousands)													
Net Sales 2	104152751	473072	2495921	595705	5753764	1899293	2599861	2474385	2663116	3770816	4480934	21875891	55069993
Interest 3	1272602	4262	1294	610	9683	8034	11356	11673	18746	53903	18696	215621	918724
Rents 4	107206	29	0	1098	11269	1671	11292	13548	9932	5108	4219	10149	38892
Royalties 5	494043	1305	16514	12134	55536	20484	39191	42976	28027	32179	2298	94271	149128
Other Portfolio Income 6	2705020	575227	90302	33644	132291	71276	131682	147753	135443	290908	150288	398692	547518
Other Receipts 7	5761435	55778	171615	57720	337868	140854	228639	257314	409071	408952	124122	667293	2902204
Total Receipts 8	114493057	1109673	2775646	700911	6300411	2141612	3022021	2947649	3264335	4561866	4780557	23261917	59626459
Average Total Receipts 9	6812	1260	232	655	3538	4749	10040	21360	38861	69119	140605	528680	3975097
Operating Costs/Operating Income (%)													
Cost of Operations 10	48.9	21.2	7.2	12.1	57.9	30.5	45.0	36.3	29.5	29.5	22.5	47.7	56.7
Salaries and Wages 11	4.3	19.2	6.4	4.0	7.6	5.6	7.3	5.8	9.1	5.1	6.6	2.9	3.6
Taxes Paid 12	3.0	5.3	4.4	6.1	2.5	6.3	3.7	3.7	4.6	3.9	4.0	2.7	2.7
Interest Paid 13	4.3	8.0	1.1	0.9	1.1	1.6	1.9	2.3	2.1	5.3	4.6	3.2	5.5
Depreciation 14	5.8	18.5	4.2	8.7	3.2	5.5	7.1	7.4	7.7	9.0	10.0	5.6	5.3
Amortization and Depletion 15	5.0	7.3	1.3	4.5	2.3	4.1	4.3	6.0	5.9	8.3	7.4	7.7	3.9
Pensions and Other Deferred Comp. 16	0.6	8.3	1.2	0.6	0.5	0.5	0.4	0.2	1.0	0.3	0.3	0.3	0.6
Employee Benefits 17	0.6	0.7	0.9	0.5	0.5	3.4	0.7	0.7	0.6	0.9	0.7	0.7	0.5
Advertising 18	0.1	0.0	0.2	0.3	0.2	0.1	0.1	0.1	0.0	0.0	0.0	0.1	0.0
Other Expenses 19	21.6	57.5	61.9	47.2	18.6	29.7	29.4	28.7	30.6	31.1	29.8	25.1	15.4
Officers' Compensation 20	1.7	7.0	11.1	6.7	2.9	3.6	3.2	2.1	4.6	1.9	1.8	0.9	1.0
Operating Margin 21	4.2	•	0.0	8.6	2.6	9.2	•	6.6	4.2	4.8	12.4	3.2	4.8
Operating Margin Before Officers' Comp. 22	5.9	•	11.1	15.3	5.5	12.8	0.1	8.6	8.9	6.6	14.2	4.1	5.8

Selected Average Balance Sheet ($ in Thousands)

Net Receivables 23	1434	0	24	36	552	776	2072	4277	8275	15500	41820	86407	951773
Inventories 24	107	0	1	3	21	40	177	234	1076	1148	1236	9425	68086
Net Property, Plant and Equipment 25	6469	0	46	265	639	2172	5345	13319	29086	73863	189139	636741	4038289
Total Assets 26	14558	0	139	667	2443	7105	15550	35408	70497	161994	342978	1055061	10032570
Notes and Loans Payable 27	4266	0	89	80	773	1072	4228	8189	13869	40113	67953	269288	3221538
All Other Liabilities 28	3852	0	23	468	842	1364	3801	6922	17086	31048	104369	260873	2749169
Net Worth 29	6440	0	26	119	829	4669	7521	20296	39542	90834	170656	524900	4061863

Selected Financial Ratios (Times to 1)

Current Ratio 30	1.4	•	1.1	1.1	1.1	2.1	1.4	1.8	1.6	2.5	1.5	1.3	1.3
Quick Ratio 31	1.1	•	1.0	0.5	1.0	1.7	1.2	1.5	1.2	1.9	1.2	0.9	1.1
Net Sales to Working Capital 32	8.1	•	23.7	•	31.9	2.3	4.4	3.4	3.5	2.0	3.9	10.0	11.9
Coverage Ratio 33	4.3	11.1	11.1	31.8	11.6	14.4	7.7	12.0	13.8	5.9	5.3	4.0	3.4
Total Asset Turnover 34	0.4	•	1.5	0.8	1.3	0.6	0.6	0.5	0.4	0.4	0.4	0.5	0.4
Inventory Turnover 35	28.2	•	10.7	26.8	87.3	32.5	21.9	27.7	8.7	14.7	24.0	25.2	30.6
Receivables Turnover 36	4.5	•	9.9	4.7	7.4	6.6	4.6	4.4	4.7	3.5	3.7	6.1	3.9
Total Liabilities to Net Worth 37	1.3	•	4.2	4.6	1.9	0.5	1.1	0.7	0.8	0.8	1.0	1.0	1.5
Current Assets to Working Capital 38	3.6	•	7.9	•	10.6	1.9	3.3	2.3	2.8	1.7	2.8	4.0	4.5
Current Liabilities to Working Capital 39	2.6	•	6.9	•	9.6	0.9	2.3	1.3	1.8	0.7	1.8	3.0	3.5
Working Capital to Net Sales 40	0.1	•	0.0	•	0.0	0.4	0.2	0.3	0.3	0.5	0.3	0.1	0.1
Inventory to Working Capital 41	0.1	•	0.3	•	0.3	0.0	0.1	0.0	0.1	0.0	0.0	0.2	0.2
Total Receipts to Cash Flow 42	3.1	3.0	1.7	1.6	3.6	2.1	2.7	2.1	1.9	1.9	2.2	3.0	3.8
Cost of Goods to Cash Flow 43	1.5	0.6	0.1	0.2	2.1	0.7	1.2	0.8	0.6	0.6	0.5	1.5	2.2
Cash Flow to Total Debt 44	0.2	•	1.1	0.6	0.6	0.8	0.4	0.6	0.5	0.4	0.3	0.3	0.2

Selected Financial Factors (in Percentages)

Debt Ratio 45	55.8	•	80.9	82.2	66.1	34.3	51.6	42.7	43.9	43.9	50.2	50.2	59.5
Return on Total Assets 46	7.9	•	18.6	22.6	17.5	13.7	8.3	14.2	13.0	11.0	9.3	6.1	6.8
Return on Equity Before Income Taxes 47	13.7	•	88.8	122.6	47.1	19.4	15.0	22.7	21.4	16.2	15.3	9.2	11.9
Return on Equity After Income Taxes 48	10.4	•	86.3	113.0	44.6	17.8	13.5	19.8	18.4	12.0	11.9	6.9	8.4
Profit Margin (Before Income Tax) 49	14.2	80.9	11.2	26.2	12.1	21.6	13.1	25.7	26.7	25.8	19.8	9.7	13.1
Profit Margin (After Income Tax) 50	10.8	48.6	10.9	24.2	11.4	19.7	11.8	22.4	22.9	19.1	15.4	7.3	9.3

Table II

Corporations with Net Income

OIL AND GAS EXTRACTION

MONEY AMOUNTS AND SIZE OF ASSETS IN THOUSANDS OF DOLLARS

Item Description for Accounting Period 7/04 Through 6/05	Total	Zero Assets	Under 500	500 to 1,000	1,000 to 5,000	5,000 to 10,000	10,000 to 25,000	25,000 to 50,000	50,000 to 100,000	100,000 to 250,000	250,000 to 500,000	500,000 to 2,500,000	2,500,000 and over
Number of Enterprises **1**	9135	50	6009	944	1298	367	198	100	58	45	0	0	0
Revenues ($ in Thousands)													
Net Sales **2**	93452195	141926	1773830	591234	3886011	1734192	2244393	2156407	2152691	3167781	0	0	0
Interest **3**	1160790	3816	732	591	7466	4368	7885	8561	14359	46186	0	0	0
Rents **4**	88351	0	0	1095	11269	1372	10534	12698	9844	3937	0	0	0
Royalties **5**	437702	635	434	12126	55053	14614	39186	24875	25206	29647	0	0	0
Other Portfolio Income **6**	2440852	560892	87925	33634	120417	66863	121164	135904	106183	246738	0	0	0
Other Receipts **7**	5166032	71269	123983	57717	272025	129315	160388	240027	394666	351198	0	0	0
Total Receipts **8**	102745922	778538	1986904	696397	4352241	1950724	2583550	2578472	2702949	3845487	0	0	0
Average Total Receipts **9**	11248	15571	331	738	3353	5315	13048	25785	46603	85455	•	•	•
Operating Costs/Operating Income (%)													
Cost of Operations **10**	50.1	38.2	6.9	8.7	47.7	29.9	46.9	37.6	24.6	33.1	•	•	•
Salaries and Wages **11**	4.0	9.5	6.6	4.0	9.3	5.2	5.8	5.3	9.5	3.7	•	•	•
Taxes Paid **12**	2.9	3.5	4.6	6.1	3.1	4.9	3.4	3.6	4.9	3.7	•	•	•
Interest Paid **13**	4.0	5.6	0.7	0.9	1.1	1.3	1.2	1.7	1.8	2.5	•	•	•
Depreciation **14**	5.4	10.3	4.2	8.4	3.3	5.4	5.5	6.8	7.7	8.2	•	•	•
Amortization and Depletion **15**	4.4	5.7	1.8	3.9	2.1	4.0	3.7	6.2	5.4	6.2	•	•	•
Pensions and Other Deferred Comp. **16**	0.5	0.3	0.7	0.6	0.4	0.5	0.4	0.3	1.2	0.3	•	•	•
Employee Benefits **17**	0.6	0.4	0.7	0.5	0.7	3.5	0.6	0.8	0.7	0.8	•	•	•
Advertising **18**	0.0	0.0	0.2	0.3	0.2	0.0	0.1	0.1	0.0	0.0	•	•	•
Other Expenses **19**	18.8	33.1	50.1	45.6	20.2	23.6	19.7	21.8	28.1	22.3	•	•	•
Officers' Compensation **20**	1.4	2.2	5.9	6.8	2.9	2.7	2.6	1.8	3.2	1.5	•	•	•
Operating Margin **21**	7.9	•	17.7	14.4	9.0	18.9	10.1	14.2	12.8	17.7	•	•	•
Operating Margin Before Officers' Comp. **22**	9.2	•	23.6	21.2	21.6	11.9	12.7	15.9	16.0	19.3	•	•	•

Selected Average Balance Sheet ($ in Thousands)

Net Receivables 23	2378	0	46	38	618	723	2027	4752	9033	19536	•
Inventories 24	156	0	0	3	15	40	149	191	1482	1515	•
Net Property, Plant and Equipment 25	9831	0	58	264	679	1925	4735	13026	27143	62882	•
Total Assets 26	22725	0	159	678	2549	7188	15260	35062	70768	159897	•
Notes and Loans Payable 27	6398	0	57	87	697	803	3275	6612	14463	33510	•
All Other Liabilities 28	5998	0	15	488	824	1238	3061	6851	17462	35694	•
Net Worth 29	10329	0	87	103	1027	5146	8924	21599	38844	90693	•

Selected Financial Ratios (Times to 1)

Current Ratio 30	1.4	•	3.5	0.5	1.2	2.4	2.0	1.8	1.6	2.6	•
Quick Ratio 31	1.2	•	3.4	0.5	1.1	1.7	1.6	1.5	1.2	2.1	•
Net Sales to Working Capital 32	7.7	•	4.5	•	15.6	2.3	3.4	3.9	3.5	2.1	•
Coverage Ratio 33	5.5	79.0	41.5	38.6	19.9	23.9	21.4	20.9	22.7	16.5	•
Total Asset Turnover 34	0.5	•	1.9	0.9	1.2	0.7	0.7	0.6	0.5	0.4	•
Inventory Turnover 35	32.8	•	107.5	20.7	92.5	35.0	35.8	42.5	6.2	15.4	•
Receivables Turnover 36	4.6	•	7.3	9.6	6.0	8.8	6.3	4.9	4.7	3.8	•
Total Liabilities to Net Worth 37	1.2	•	0.8	5.6	1.5	0.4	0.7	0.6	0.8	0.8	•
Current Assets to Working Capital 38	3.2	•	1.4	•	6.2	1.7	2.0	2.3	2.7	1.6	•
Current Liabilities to Working Capital 39	2.2	•	0.4	•	5.2	0.7	1.0	1.3	1.7	0.6	•
Working Capital to Net Sales 40	0.1	•	0.2	•	0.1	0.4	0.3	0.3	0.3	0.5	•
Inventory to Working Capital 41	0.1	•	0.0	•	0.1	0.0	0.1	0.0	0.2	0.1	•
Total Receipts to Cash Flow 42	3.0	0.7	1.7	1.5	2.6	2.0	2.5	2.0	1.6	1.7	•
Cost of Goods to Cash Flow 43	1.5	0.3	0.1	0.1	1.3	0.6	1.2	0.8	0.4	0.6	•
Cash Flow to Total Debt 44	0.3	•	2.5	0.7	0.7	1.2	0.7	0.8	0.7	0.6	•

Selected Financial Factors (in Percentages)

Debt Ratio 45	54.5	•	45.3	84.8	59.7	28.4	41.5	38.4	45.1	43.3	•
Return on Total Assets 46	9.8	•	56.6	30.5	25.9	21.2	19.6	21.8	21.0	18.3	•
Return on Equity Before Income Taxes 47	17.7	•	100.9	196.0	61.0	28.4	31.9	33.7	36.6	30.3	•
Return on Equity After Income Taxes 48	14.0	•	99.3	183.3	58.2	27.4	30.1	29.9	32.1	24.2	•
Profit Margin (Before Income Tax) 49	17.9	437.6	29.7	32.2	20.9	30.9	25.1	33.7	38.3	39.0	•
Profit Margin (After Income Tax) 50	14.1	329.9	29.3	30.1	20.0	29.8	23.7	30.0	33.6	31.2	•

Table I

Corporations with and without Net Income

COAL MINING

MONEY AMOUNTS AND SIZE OF ASSETS IN THOUSANDS OF DOLLARS

Item Description for Accounting Period 7/04 Through 6/05	Total	Zero Assets	Under 500	500 to 1,000	1,000 to 5,000	5,000 to 10,000	10,000 to 25,000	25,000 to 50,000	50,000 to 100,000	100,000 to 250,000	250,000 to 500,000	500,000 to 2,500,000	2,500,000 and over
Number of Enterprises 1	1312	0	961	0	119	128	0	17	13	4	3	6	4
Revenues ($ in Thousands)													
Net Sales 2	16788227	0	581350	0	125007	1137441	0	663807	1506452	745498	160864	3449569	6666279
Interest 3	240570	0	0	0	0	935	0	118	556	3841	654	56483	140200
Rents 4	22113	0	0	0	0	592	0	2	553	1485	2678	2146	9303
Royalties 5	98158	0	80	0	26475	0	0	0	1772	60	13478	14944	34667
Other Portfolio Income 6	981778	0	20829	0	1223	10962	0	5121	21913	0	3871	503151	89899
Other Receipts 7	538600	0	1642	0	5027	18299	0	19742	11143	12797	39486	222299	148689
Total Receipts 8	18869446	0	603901	0	157732	1168229	0	688790	1542389	763681	221031	4248592	7089037
Average Total Receipts 9	14230	•	628	•	1325	9127	•	40517	118645	190920	73677	708099	1772259
Operating Costs/Operating Income (%)													
Cost of Operations 10	67.1	•	61.7	•	60.4	57.7	•	53.6	59.4	88.9	74.5	64.6	66.9
Salaries and Wages 11	4.0	•	0.3	•	1.8	6.4	•	6.2	5.6	1.1	2.4	7.2	1.9
Taxes Paid 12	7.0	•	8.4	•	6.1	4.8	•	4.5	3.5	1.9	6.7	8.0	8.6
Interest Paid 13	4.3	•	0.6	•	6.1	0.5	•	1.2	1.2	0.4	3.1	5.7	4.6
Depreciation 14	6.8	•	5.1	•	26.7	5.5	•	10.2	7.1	1.5	3.9	6.1	8.1
Amortization and Depletion 15	4.4	•	0.4	•	0.3	2.3	•	3.9	3.8	0.9	6.2	6.2	5.7
Pensions and Other Deferred Comp. 16	1.6	•	0.1	•	0.0	0.0	•	0.2	0.4	0.7	•	1.6	2.5
Employee Benefits 17	4.4	•	1.2	•	0.3	1.0	•	2.8	2.5	1.2	6.5	5.0	5.3
Advertising 18	0.0	•	0.0	•	0.0	0.0	•	0.0	0.0	0.0	0.0	0.1	0.1
Other Expenses 19	13.9	•	22.6	•	38.7	23.3	•	18.7	16.7	5.1	15.2	10.0	7.5
Officers' Compensation 20	0.8	•	6.3	•	0.1	0.5	•	1.8	0.4	0.1	0.2	1.2	0.2
Operating Margin 21	•	•	•	•	•	•	•	•	•	•	•	•	•
Operating Margin Before Officers' Comp. 22	•	•	•	•	•	•	•	•	•	•	•	•	•

Selected Average Balance Sheet ($ in Thousands)

Net Receivables 23	2795	18	31	434	•	4913	12421	12259	103644	185853	446324
Inventories 24	730	0	128	52	•	1025	2435	8877	8637	24501	167335
Net Property, Plant and Equipment 25	9881	38	997	1788	•	15273	30026	57870	121328	466440	2071256
Total Assets 26	24085	136	1359	8072	•	35188	71812	139059	430268	1209901	4746903
Notes and Loans Payable 27	7167	31	1099	2247	•	13206	23363	61232	205958	183494	1519931
All Other Liabilities 28	9356	67	141	1540	•	4790	22232	29948	184549	472899	1956319
Net Worth 29	7562	38	119	4285	•	17192	26216	47878	39762	553509	1270653

Selected Financial Ratios (Times to 1)

Current Ratio 30	1.8	0.8	0.1	4.1	•	1.7	1.0	0.9	2.3	1.8	2.0
Quick Ratio 31	1.2	0.4	0.1	3.7	•	1.4	0.8	0.5	2.1	1.3	1.3
Net Sales to Working Capital 32	4.7	•	•	2.9	•	8.3	•	•	0.6	3.8	3.0
Coverage Ratio 33	0.3	•	•	1.9	•	1.5	2.5	2.3	7.0	2.3	•
Total Asset Turnover 34	0.5	4.5	0.8	1.1	•	1.1	1.6	1.3	0.1	0.5	0.4
Inventory Turnover 35	11.8	•	4.9	98.5	•	20.4	28.3	18.7	4.6	15.1	6.7
Receivables Turnover 36	3.9	62.6	6.2	31.3	•	9.3	13.0	10.6	•	4.6	2.2
Total Liabilities to Net Worth 37	2.2	2.6	10.5	0.9	•	1.0	1.7	1.9	9.8	1.2	2.7
Current Assets to Working Capital 38	2.3	•	•	1.3	•	2.4	•	•	1.8	2.3	2.0
Current Liabilities to Working Capital 39	1.3	•	•	0.3	•	1.4	•	•	0.8	1.3	1.0
Working Capital to Net Sales 40	0.2	•	•	0.3	•	0.1	•	•	1.8	0.3	0.3
Inventory to Working Capital 41	0.3	•	•	0.0	•	0.2	•	•	0.1	0.2	0.3
Total Receipts to Cash Flow 42	24.9	6.1	4.6	7.7	•	7.0	7.7	22.7	3.6	17.3	•
Cost of Goods to Cash Flow 43	16.7	3.7	2.7	4.5	•	3.7	4.6	20.2	2.7	11.2	•
Cash Flow to Total Debt 44	0.0	1.0	0.2	0.3	•	0.3	0.1	0.1	0.0	0.1	•

Selected Financial Factors (in Percentages)

Debt Ratio 45	68.6	72.3	91.3	46.9	•	51.1	63.5	65.6	90.8	54.3	73.2
Return on Total Assets 46	0.7	•	•	1.2	•	2.1	5.0	1.4	2.7	6.3	•
Return on Equity Before Income Taxes 47	•	•	•	1.1	•	1.5	8.1	2.3	25.3	7.8	•
Return on Equity After Income Taxes 48	•	•	•	0.6	•	1.4	8.0	1.2	14.0	7.2	•
Profit Margin (Before Income Tax) 49	•	•	•	0.5	•	0.6	1.8	0.6	18.8	7.5	•
Profit Margin (After Income Tax) 50	•	•	•	0.3	•	0.6	1.8	0.3	10.4	7.0	•

Table II

Corporations with Net Income

COAL MINING

MONEY AMOUNTS AND SIZE OF ASSETS IN THOUSANDS OF DOLLARS

Item Description for Accounting Period 7/04 Through 6/05	Total	Zero Assets	Under 500	500 to 1,000	1,000 to 5,000	5,000 to 10,000	10,000 to 25,000	25,000 to 50,000	50,000 to 100,000	100,000 to 250,000	250,000 to 500,000	500,000 to 2,500,000	2,500,000 and over
Number of Enterprises **1**	294	0	152	11	11	73	22	10	7	4	0	3	0
Revenues ($ in Thousands)													
Net Sales **2**	5406450	0	335883	73653	12978	736995	645784	472146	857884	808990	0	1162136	0
Interest **3**	42388	0	0	9	0	316	1420	108	219	4057	0	36258	0
Rents **4**	6622	0	0	0	0	0	1740	2	537	4162	0	181	0
Royalties **5**	51238	0	0	0	26475	0	627	0	606	13538	0	9992	0
Other Portfolio Income **6**	498460	0	20222	2371	29	9561	15830	3406	21349	3871	0	421821	0
Other Receipts **7**	279893	0	1632	606	5002	8165	7290	7380	6237	51829	0	191755	0
Total Receipts **8**	6285051	0	357737	76639	44484	755037	672691	483042	886832	886447	0	2122143	0
Average Total Receipts **9**	21378	•	2354	6967	4044	10343	30577	48304	126690	221612	•	707381	•
Operating Costs/Operating Income (%)													
Cost of Operations **10**	63.5	•	73.9	55.6	49.5	57.0	69.0	53.6	60.5	86.9	•	54.4	•
Salaries and Wages **11**	7.1	•	0.6	•	0.4	9.3	4.5	5.4	3.6	1.1	•	14.8	•
Taxes Paid **12**	5.2	•	6.9	13.0	23.0	4.3	3.0	4.6	2.8	2.6	•	8.8	•
Interest Paid **13**	2.5	•	0.5	0.0	4.7	0.6	0.5	1.1	1.2	0.9	•	7.2	•
Depreciation **14**	5.5	•	1.5	1.2	2.2	5.3	4.4	9.6	7.1	1.6	•	7.2	•
Amortization and Depletion **15**	3.7	•	0.7	0.7	2.9	1.3	2.0	4.7	5.6	2.0	•	6.0	•
Pensions and Other Deferred Comp. **16**	0.6	•	•	0.0	0.4	0.0	0.3	0.3	0.5	0.6	•	1.4	•
Employee Benefits **17**	2.3	•	0.0	0.2	•	1.3	0.9	2.4	1.7	2.1	•	4.5	•
Advertising **18**	0.0	•	0.0	•	•	0.0	0.0	0.0	0.0	0.0	•	0.1	•
Other Expenses **19**	14.4	•	12.9	5.2	222.2	19.3	14.6	13.9	13.3	6.4	•	15.9	•
Officers' Compensation **20**	0.9	•	3.3	•	0.6	0.7	1.2	1.8	0.6	0.1	•	0.8	•
Operating Margin **21**	•	•	•	24.1	•	0.9	•	2.6	3.1	•	•	•	•
Operating Margin Before Officers' Comp. **22**	•	•	2.9	24.1	•	1.6	0.7	4.4	3.6	•	•	•	•

Selected Average Balance Sheet ($ in Thousands)

	Total									
Net Receivables 23	4399	116	38	132	407	1812	5869	13408	37507	300592
Inventories 24	486	0	0	268	49	531	839	2355	13152	23856
Net Property, Plant and Equipment 25	9041	109	149	955	2182	4449	12706	34113	115794	514364
Total Assets 26	25163	358	798	4035	8377	14245	34739	77969	286446	1442147
Notes and Loans Payable 27	5501	99	48	2275	3404	4154	14690	17521	107622	178921
All Other Liabilities 28	8354	163	556	827	950	4090	3576	20598	146239	497255
Net Worth 29	11309	96	194	933	4024	6001	16473	39850	32585	765970

Selected Financial Ratios (Times to 1)

	Total									
Current Ratio 30	1.8	0.8	1.1	0.7	6.5	1.5	2.1	1.1	1.4	1.8
Quick Ratio 31	1.3	0.6	1.0	0.6	6.0	1.0	1.7	0.9	1.0	1.2
Net Sales to Working Capital 32	4.6	•	80.7	•	2.2	14.1	7.0	82.7	7.8	2.4
Coverage Ratio 33	5.1	12.6	830.7	8.9	6.4	8.1	5.5	6.2	7.2	4.3
Total Asset Turnover 34	0.7	6.2	8.4	0.3	1.2	2.1	1.4	1.6	0.7	0.3
Inventory Turnover 35	24.0	•	•	2.2	117.5	38.2	30.2	31.5	13.4	11.1
Receivables Turnover 36	2.6	•	306.9	2.0	33.9	19.0	10.4	10.0	•	•
Total Liabilities to Net Worth 37	1.2	2.7	3.1	3.3	1.1	1.4	1.1	1.0	7.8	0.9
Current Assets to Working Capital 38	2.3	•	7.8	•	1.2	3.2	1.9	16.3	3.7	2.3
Current Liabilities to Working Capital 39	1.3	•	6.8	•	0.2	2.2	0.9	15.3	2.7	1.3
Working Capital to Net Sales 40	0.2	•	0.0	•	0.5	0.1	0.1	0.0	0.1	0.4
Inventory to Working Capital 41	0.2	•	•	•	0.0	0.3	0.2	1.8	0.5	0.1
Total Receipts to Cash Flow 42	6.4	6.9	3.3	0.4	7.4	7.1	7.2	6.8	10.8	5.1
Cost of Goods to Cash Flow 43	4.0	5.1	1.8	0.2	4.2	4.9	3.8	4.1	9.4	2.8
Cash Flow to Total Debt 44	0.2	1.2	3.4	0.9	0.3	0.5	0.4	0.5	0.1	0.1

Selected Financial Factors (in Percentages)

	Total									
Debt Ratio 45	55.1	73.1	75.7	76.9	52.0	57.9	52.6	48.9	88.6	46.9
Return on Total Assets 46	9.5	40.9	236.5	12.1	4.5	8.6	8.1	12.0	4.4	10.5
Return on Equity Before Income Taxes 47	17.0	140.0	973.8	46.5	7.9	17.9	14.1	19.7	33.1	15.3
Return on Equity After Income Taxes 48	15.8	136.7	947.9	46.5	7.0	16.5	13.9	19.5	21.1	14.5
Profit Margin (Before Income Tax) 49	10.4	6.1	28.2	36.8	3.2	3.7	4.9	6.4	5.3	24.0
Profit Margin (After Income Tax) 50	9.7	6.0	27.4	36.8	2.8	3.4	4.9	6.3	3.4	22.8

10

Table I

Corporations with and without Net Income

METAL ORE MINING

MONEY AMOUNTS AND SIZE OF ASSETS IN THOUSANDS OF DOLLARS

Item Description for Accounting Period 7/04 Through 6/05	Total	Zero Assets	Under 500	500 to 1,000	1,000 to 5,000	5,000 to 10,000	10,000 to 25,000	25,000 to 50,000	50,000 to 100,000	100,000 to 250,000	250,000 to 500,000	500,000 to 2,500,000	2,500,000 and over
Number of Enterprises **1**	1660	0	1384	0	15	27	0	21	5	5	7	7	7
Revenues ($ in Thousands)													
Net Sales **2**	21169204	0	52661	0	12	1866	0	179365	144410	422019	963462	2396363	16943175
Interest **3**	527627	0	218	0	108	360	0	3130	817	5042	12698	55985	447622
Rents **4**	24176	0	6630	0	8	0	0	71	0	0	116	522	16829
Royalties **5**	175182	0	0	0	0	0	0	91	0	23487	720	15304	135580
Other Portfolio Income **6**	637861	0	714	0	798	721	0	3198	0	92	4610	188300	437306
Other Receipts **7**	890947	0	27148	0	889	7622	0	51096	4685	10614	-2101	30659	653208
Total Receipts **8**	23424997	0	87371	0	1815	10569	0	236951	149912	461254	979505	2687133	18633720
Average Total Receipts **9**	14111	•	63	•	121	391	•	11283	29982	92251	139929	383876	2661960
Operating Costs/Operating Income (%)													
Cost of Operations **10**	53.5	•	0.2	•	•	304.3	•	66.2	63.8	84.7	51.6	70.0	50.3
Salaries and Wages **11**	3.1	•	0.1	•	34125.0	24.4	•	10.3	3.1	1.3	0.8	0.5	3.5
Taxes Paid **12**	2.2	•	9.1	•	8216.7	32.7	•	3.0	1.6	0.9	3.9	2.4	2.1
Interest Paid **13**	4.2	•	3.3	•	4833.3	40.2	•	1.4	3.1	3.5	3.3	6.6	3.9
Depreciation **14**	7.1	•	7.0	•	6025.0	85.5	•	9.3	7.8	10.8	6.8	6.8	7.0
Amortization and Depletion **15**	12.4	•	3.6	•	1673133.3	102.7	•	7.1	15.2	5.5	17.0	10.1	11.5
Pensions and Other Deferred Comp. **16**	1.4	•	8.3	•	•	0.3	•	0.2	0.2	0.1	0.3	1.1	1.5
Employee Benefits **17**	1.4	•	0.1	•	1866.7	2.1	•	1.6	0.1	0.1	2.4	2.4	1.3
Advertising **18**	0.1	•	•	•	1325.0	0.2	•	0.0	0.0	0.0	•	0.0	0.1
Other Expenses **19**	16.0	•	59.0	•	318275.0	3366.1	•	45.6	18.9	7.0	15.5	10.9	15.5
Officers' Compensation **20**	0.6	•	45.6	•	•	28.7	•	2.9	5.2	1.2	0.3	0.2	0.4
Operating Margin **21**	•	•	•	•	•	•	•	•	•	•	•	•	2.8
Operating Margin Before Officers' Comp. **22**	•	•	9.3	•	•	•	•	•	•	•	•	•	3.3

Selected Average Balance Sheet ($ in Thousands)

Item											
Net Receivables 23	7292	•	181	24	•	5764	•	110	21295	16393	48030	1626412
Inventories 24	1519	•	•	19	•	1712	2140	9204	29323	88599	226596	
Net Property, Plant and Equipment 25	11076	•	8	•	1547	5408	10873	20803	63440	165260	421354	1910481
Total Assets 26	46511	•	131	•	2526	7221	32408	78856	143821	339500	1035190	9289174
Notes and Loans Payable 27	5308	•	28	•	410	5339	7411	24323	15505	45294	225161	893592
All Other Liabilities 28	14674	•	53	•	797	2791	16933	16391	49548	137171	331676	2878596
Net Worth 29	26529	•	49	•	1319	-909	8063	38142	78768	157035	478353	5516986

Selected Financial Ratios (Times to 1)

Item										
Current Ratio 30	1.6	5.9	3.0	1.1	1.5	1.7	1.6	2.0	1.6	
Quick Ratio 31	1.3	5.9	2.9	1.0	1.1	1.5	0.9	1.1	1.3	
Net Sales to Working Capital 32	2.7	0.8	0.0	1.0	1.9	5.5	4.8	2.5	2.7	
Coverage Ratio 33	3.2	9.7	•	•	•	•	1.0	1.2	4.4	
Total Asset Turnover 34	0.3	0.3	0.0	0.0	0.3	0.6	0.4	0.3	0.3	
Inventory Turnover 35	4.5	•	11.3	3.3	8.6	7.8	2.4	2.7	5.4	
Receivables Turnover 36	2.4	1253.8	0.0	5.8	1.9	27.3	4.8	11.2	3.5	2.2
Total Liabilities to Net Worth 37	0.8	1.7	0.9	•	3.0	1.1	0.8	1.2	0.7	
Current Assets to Working Capital 38	2.6	1.2	1.5	14.9	2.9	2.4	2.6	2.0	2.7	
Current Liabilities to Working Capital 39	1.6	0.2	0.5	13.9	1.9	1.4	1.6	1.0	1.7	
Working Capital to Net Sales 40	0.4	1.3	569.1	1.0	0.5	0.2	0.2	0.4	0.4	
Inventory to Working Capital 41	0.3	•	0.0	0.5	0.4	0.3	1.0	0.6	0.3	
Total Receipts to Cash Flow 42	4.9	1.3	•	3.9	44.1	8.7	11.8	4.1		
Cost of Goods to Cash Flow 43	2.6	0.0	•	2.6	28.1	4.5	8.3	2.1		
Cash Flow to Total Debt 44	0.1	0.3	•	0.1	0.0	0.1	0.1	0.2		

Selected Financial Factors (in Percentages)

Item										
Debt Ratio 45	43.0	62.6	47.8	112.6	75.1	51.6	45.2	53.7	53.8	40.6
Return on Total Assets 46	3.6	9.2	•	•	•	1.4	2.6	4.5		
Return on Equity Before Income Taxes 47	4.3	22.0	260.1	•	•	0.0	0.8	5.8		
Return on Equity After Income Taxes 48	2.5	22.0	260.1	•	•	•	0.7	3.8		
Profit Margin (Before Income Tax) 49	9.0	28.3	•	•	•	0.0	1.1	13.2		
Profit Margin (After Income Tax) 50	5.3	28.3	•	•	•	•	1.0	8.7		

11

Table II

Corporations with Net Income

METAL ORE MINING

MONEY AMOUNTS AND SIZE OF ASSETS IN THOUSANDS OF DOLLARS

Item Description for Accounting Period 7/04 Through 6/05		Total	Zero Assets	Under 500	500 to 1,000	1,000 to 5,000	5,000 to 10,000	10,000 to 25,000	25,000 to 50,000	50,000 to 100,000	100,000 to 250,000	250,000 to 500,000	500,000 to 2,500,000	2,500,000 and over
Number of Enterprises	1	956	0	870	61	0	0	3	7	0	0	4	4	7
Revenues ($ in Thousands)														
Net Sales	2	19255191	0	47111	11866	0	0	0	358350	0	0	526158	1368531	16943175
Interest	3	501715	0	0	167	0	0	328	1825	0	0	5144	46630	447622
Rents	4	17490	0	0	0	0	0	0	23	0	0	116	522	16829
Royalties	5	174419	0	0	0	0	0	0	23524	0	0	11	15304	135580
Other Portfolio Income	6	630654	0	0	0	0	0	201	1688	0	0	4007	187451	437306
Other Receipts	7	866122	0	27148	1509	0	0	103276	56930	0	0	18847	5205	653208
Total Receipts	8	21445591	0	74259	13542	0	0	103805	442340	0	0	554283	1623643	18633720
Average Total Receipts	9	22433	•	85	222	•	•	34602	63191	•	•	138571	405911	2661960
Operating Costs/Operating Income (%)														
Cost of Operations	10	51.6	•	0.2	•	•	•	•	87.4	•	•	47.0	61.6	50.3
Salaries and Wages	11	3.1	•	•	•	•	•	•	0.3	•	•	0.2	0.2	3.5
Taxes Paid	12	2.1	•	4.7	0.4	•	•	•	0.5	•	•	0.5	2.7	2.1
Interest Paid	13	4.1	•	3.6	5.5	•	•	•	0.0	•	•	1.2	9.0	3.9
Depreciation	14	7.1	•	7.5	1.4	•	•	•	1.0	•	•	7.6	8.6	7.0
Amortization and Depletion	15	11.5	•	4.0	0.3	•	•	•	4.7	•	•	12.8	12.8	11.5
Pensions and Other Deferred Comp.	16	1.3	•	9.3	•	•	•	•	0.0	•	•	0.3	0.2	1.5
Employee Benefits	17	1.5	•	•	•	•	•	•	0.1	•	•	4.5	4.0	1.3
Advertising	18	0.1	•	•	•	•	•	•	0.0	•	•	•	0.0	0.1
Other Expenses	19	15.3	•	27.6	62.0	•	•	•	5.4	•	•	15.2	13.3	15.5
Officers' Compensation	20	0.5	•	37.6	•	•	•	•	0.9	•	•	0.5	0.1	0.4
Operating Margin	21	1.8	•	5.3	30.5	•	•	•	•	•	•	10.1	•	2.8
Operating Margin Before Officers' Comp.	22	2.3	•	43.0	30.5	•	•	•	0.5	•	•	10.7	•	3.3

Selected Average Balance Sheet ($ in Thousands)

Net Receivables 23	12329	0	0	5058	15562	9084	60408	1626412
Inventories 24	1395	0	4	0	3686	9732	78925	252781
Net Property, Plant and Equipment 25	16664	6	554	0	20083	168624	425839	1910481
Total Assets 26	75173	158	803	13692	61106	311615	1234886	9289174
Notes and Loans Payable 27	7824	45	207	2	10899	35236	238764	893592
All Other Liabilities 28	23446	9	115	2088	16273	78842	453389	2878596
Net Worth 29	43904	104	481	11602	33934	197537	542732	5516986

Selected Financial Ratios (Times to 1)

Current Ratio 30	1.6	3.6	0.3	5.8	3.0	1.1	1.5	1.6
Quick Ratio 31	1.3	3.6	0.2	4.6	2.6	0.8	0.8	1.3
Net Sales to Working Capital 32	2.8	1.5	•	2.6	•	40.9	3.8	2.7
Coverage Ratio 33	4.3	18.3	9.2	197.0	10293.9	13.9	1.7	4.4
Total Asset Turnover 34	0.3	0.3	0.2	•	0.8	0.4	0.3	0.3
Inventory Turnover 35	7.4	•	•	•	12.1	6.3	2.7	4.8
Receivables Turnover 36	2.6	•	•	•	•	18.1	•	•
Total Liabilities to Net Worth 37	0.7	0.5	0.7	0.2	0.8	0.6	1.3	0.7
Current Assets to Working Capital 38	2.7	1.4	•	1.2	1.5	19.2	2.9	2.7
Current Liabilities to Working Capital 39	1.7	0.4	•	0.2	0.5	18.2	1.9	1.7
Working Capital to Net Sales 40	0.4	0.7	•	•	0.4	0.0	0.3	0.4
Inventory to Working Capital 41	0.3	•	•	•	0.2	3.2	0.9	0.3
Total Receipts to Cash Flow 42	4.1	1.2	1.0	•	3.6	3.4	7.3	4.1
Cost of Goods to Cash Flow 43	2.1	0.0	•	0.0	3.1	1.6	4.5	2.1
Cash Flow to Total Debt 44	0.2	0.8	0.6	16.3	0.5	0.3	0.1	0.2

Selected Financial Factors (in Percentages)

Debt Ratio 45	41.6	34.3	40.1	15.3	44.5	36.6	56.1	40.6
Return on Total Assets 46	4.7	22.8	12.1	210.5	19.3	7.3	4.2	4.5
Return on Equity Before Income Taxes 47	6.2	32.8	18.1	247.2	34.7	10.6	4.0	5.8
Return on Equity After Income Taxes 48	4.3	32.8	18.0	241.3	32.9	8.0	3.8	3.8
Profit Margin (Before Income Tax) 49	13.5	62.9	44.7	23.0	44.7	16.0	6.3	13.2
Profit Margin (After Income Tax) 50	9.5	62.9	44.6	21.8	•	12.0	6.0	8.7

Table I

Corporations with and without Net Income

NONMETALLIC MINERAL MINING AND QUARRYING

MONEY AMOUNTS AND SIZE OF ASSETS IN THOUSANDS OF DOLLARS

Item Description for Accounting Period 7/04 Through 6/05	Total	Zero Assets	Under 500	500 to 1,000	1,000 to 5,000	5,000 to 10,000	10,000 to 25,000	25,000 to 50,000	50,000 to 100,000	100,000 to 250,000	250,000 to 500,000	500,000 to 2,500,000	2,500,000 and over
Number of Enterprises **1**	4649	6	3220	491	556	113	146	57	27	20	4	4	4
Revenues ($ in Thousands)													
Net Sales **2**	25037593	38705	529269	303660	1960453	988063	2096524	1378241	2035512	2575244	1505509	2863878	8762535
Interest **3**	157802	87	97	72	547	1118	4626	2766	4845	7171	660	11790	124023
Rents **4**	46734	243	0	48	924	1896	4143	7729	3104	7575	718	10051	10303
Royalties **5**	21348	0	0	0	2443	202	130	747	0	1894	95	11939	3898
Other Portfolio Income **6**	316872	287	274	0	61686	5790	19434	10628	17118	15823	10941	26989	147901
Other Receipts **7**	401126	1157	4129	244	15991	15239	25839	33274	17891	52839	22791	111726	100007
Total Receipts **8**	25981475	40479	533769	304024	2042044	1012308	2150696	1433385	2078470	2660546	1540714	3036373	9148667
Average Total Receipts **9**	5589	6746	166	619	3673	8958	14731	25147	76980	133027	385178	759093	2287167
Operating Costs/Operating Income (%)													
Cost of Operations **10**	62.8	72.8	45.9	47.1	55.9	44.6	63.8	63.8	72.6	63.0	67.9	66.2	63.2
Salaries and Wages **11**	4.5	6.0	13.0	5.6	3.0	9.2	4.4	3.6	4.3	5.0	3.3	3.2	4.4
Taxes Paid **12**	3.0	2.7	5.6	2.6	3.8	2.4	2.8	2.9	2.2	1.8	2.2	2.3	3.7
Interest Paid **13**	3.1	1.3	1.7	1.8	1.6	2.1	1.6	0.9	1.1	2.4	3.6	3.9	4.8
Depreciation **14**	7.9	5.4	6.2	3.3	7.6	11.0	9.2	9.4	7.6	8.6	5.3	8.6	7.3
Amortization and Depletion **15**	2.8	2.3	2.5	1.4	1.4	0.6	2.2	2.3	1.9	3.9	2.7	5.4	2.8
Pensions and Other Deferred Comp. **16**	1.2	0.8	•	0.1	0.6	0.1	0.6	0.5	0.5	0.8	1.0	1.5	1.9
Employee Benefits **17**	2.3	1.0	1.4	2.2	2.5	2.1	1.5	1.4	2.2	3.4	3.6	2.8	2.0
Advertising **18**	0.2	0.7	0.4	0.0	0.2	0.2	0.3	0.2	0.2	0.2	0.2	0.1	0.1
Other Expenses **19**	11.6	7.2	34.4	11.8	18.8	23.8	10.1	9.4	6.8	10.0	10.5	8.6	10.8
Officers' Compensation **20**	1.3	4.3	3.7	1.0	4.0	2.4	2.1	2.8	1.0	1.4	0.6	0.9	0.3
Operating Margin **21**	•	•	•	23.0	0.6	1.5	1.3	2.9	•	•	•	•	•
Operating Margin Before Officers' Comp. **22**	0.6	•	•	24.1	4.6	3.9	3.4	5.6	0.5	1.0	•	•	•

Selected Average Balance Sheet ($ in Thousands)

Net Receivables 23	1195	0	5	117	248	1418	2248	3555	10054	20101	54460	160752	779864
Inventories 24	470	0	3	28	164	341	1501	1967	6977	14590	36992	163515	208200
Net Property, Plant and Equipment 25	3079	0	20	326	1275	3240	6567	13496	34219	69534	228628	513106	1501628
Total Assets 26	9622	0	44	742	2338	6797	15323	32702	72166	160254	351658	1230538	6444480
Notes and Loans Payable 27	2718	0	69	239	1041	4066	4391	6374	26056	46826	278019	361177	1514487
All Other Liabilities 28	1866	0	8	208	379	892	2250	4398	18108	36524	44142	351577	1213859
Net Worth 29	5038	0	-33	295	918	1839	8682	21930	28001	76905	29498	517784	3916134

Selected Financial Ratios (Times to 1)

Current Ratio 30	1.6	·	0.4	1.2	2.0	1.2	2.4	2.5	1.5	2.1	1.4	1.4	1.6
Quick Ratio 31	1.0	·	0.3	1.0	1.5	1.0	1.6	1.7	0.8	1.1	0.7	0.8	1.0
Net Sales to Working Capital 32	5.5	·	·	12.2	6.8	24.8	3.9	3.3	9.1	4.7	11.5	7.4	4.2
Coverage Ratio 33	2.0	1.1	·	14.1	4.0	2.8	3.4	8.2	2.4	2.2	1.4	1.7	1.7
Total Asset Turnover 34	0.6	·	3.8	0.8	1.5	1.3	0.9	0.7	1.0	0.8	1.1	0.6	0.3
Inventory Turnover 35	7.2	·	24.6	10.2	12.0	11.4	6.1	7.8	7.8	5.6	6.9	2.9	6.7
Receivables Turnover 36	6.2	·	52.6	5.9	13.8	7.0	6.8	7.6	7.9	7.4	7.7	3.4	·
Total Liabilities to Net Worth 37	0.9	·	·	1.5	1.5	2.7	0.8	0.5	1.6	1.1	10.9	1.4	0.7
Current Assets to Working Capital 38	2.6	·	·	5.8	2.0	6.2	1.7	1.7	3.1	1.9	3.6	3.6	2.7
Current Liabilities to Working Capital 39	1.6	·	·	4.8	1.0	5.2	0.7	0.7	2.1	0.9	2.6	2.6	1.7
Working Capital to Net Sales 40	0.2	·	·	0.1	0.1	0.0	0.3	0.3	0.1	0.2	0.1	0.1	0.2
Inventory to Working Capital 41	0.5	·	·	0.7	0.5	0.9	0.4	0.3	0.9	0.6	1.2	0.9	0.4
Total Receipts to Cash Flow 42	10.4	23.7	13.9	3.3	6.8	6.4	10.2	7.7	18.2	9.2	16.4	13.1	11.9
Cost of Goods to Cash Flow 43	6.6	17.3	6.4	1.6	3.8	2.8	6.5	4.9	13.2	5.8	11.1	8.7	7.5
Cash Flow to Total Debt 44	0.1	·	0.2	0.4	0.4	0.3	0.2	0.3	0.1	0.2	0.1	0.1	0.1

Selected Financial Factors (in Percentages)

Debt Ratio 45	47.6	·	176.0	60.2	60.7	72.9	43.3	32.9	61.2	52.0	91.6	57.9	41.1
Return on Total Assets 46	3.5	·	·	20.8	9.5	7.8	5.1	5.7	2.8	4.2	5.3	3.8	2.6
Return on Equity Before Income Taxes 47	3.3	·	68.5	48.5	18.2	18.7	6.3	7.5	4.2	4.8	17.2	3.7	1.8
Return on Equity After Income Taxes 48	2.4	·	68.5	48.5	17.0	17.0	5.6	6.6	2.1	3.1	14.3	1.9	1.1
Profit Margin (Before Income Tax) 49	3.1	0.1	·	23.2	4.7	3.9	3.8	6.8	1.6	2.8	1.3	2.6	3.2
Profit Margin (After Income Tax) 50	2.2	·	·	23.1	4.4	3.6	3.4	6.0	0.8	1.9	1.1	1.4	2.0

Table II

Corporations with Net Income

NONMETALLIC MINERAL MINING AND QUARRYING

MONEY AMOUNTS AND SIZE OF ASSETS IN THOUSANDS OF DOLLARS

Item Description for Accounting Period 7/04 Through 6/05	Total	Zero Assets	Under 500	500 to 1,000	1,000 to 5,000	5,000 to 10,000	10,000 to 25,000	25,000 to 50,000	50,000 to 100,000	100,000 to 250,000	250,000 to 500,000	500,000 to 2,500,000	2,500,000 and over
Number of Enterprises 1	1863	3	675	404	525	71	105	40	16	14	0	0	0
Revenues ($ in Thousands)													
Net Sales 2	18647574	18487	87334	211137	1847282	587986	1565343	980168	1201428	1766570	0	0	0
Interest 3	64636	6	95	0	547	189	3184	2430	4278	6517	0	0	0
Rents 4	35355	8	0	48	924	1896	3236	2894	3097	3427	0	0	0
Royalties 5	18696	0	0	0	2443	202	130	283	0	80	0	0	0
Other Portfolio Income 6	296602	99	0	0	55362	5672	16306	7051	14524	15444	0	0	0
Other Receipts 7	323866	1103	31	-1082	15991	13784	21533	24542	9562	45429	0	0	0
Total Receipts 8	19386729	19703	87460	210103	1922549	609729	1609732	1017368	1232889	1837467	0	0	0
Average Total Receipts 9	10406	6568	130	520	3662	8588	15331	25434	77056	131248	•	•	•
Operating Costs/Operating Income (%)													
Cost of Operations 10	59.7	72.9	28.5	41.7	53.7	27.2	61.0	61.1	70.8	62.9	•	•	•
Salaries and Wages 11	4.5	3.4	4.0	5.5	3.2	12.3	4.4	3.4	4.2	5.1	•	•	•
Taxes Paid 12	2.8	3.1	5.6	1.8	3.8	2.7	2.7	2.9	2.4	1.7	•	•	•
Interest Paid 13	2.6	0.6	5.2	1.8	1.6	2.3	1.3	0.7	0.9	1.5	•	•	•
Depreciation 14	7.9	4.7	24.9	2.3	7.3	14.3	8.4	8.2	6.8	7.6	•	•	•
Amortization and Depletion 15	2.8	2.2	•	2.0	0.9	0.7	2.4	2.7	2.6	3.9	•	•	•
Pensions and Other Deferred Comp. 16	1.4	1.3	•	0.1	0.6	0.1	0.7	0.6	0.7	1.0	•	•	•
Employee Benefits 17	2.1	•	1.8	0.4	2.7	0.9	1.5	1.2	1.6	2.7	•	•	•
Advertising 18	0.2	0.3	0.8	0.0	0.3	0.2	0.3	0.2	0.2	0.2	•	•	•
Other Expenses 19	12.6	3.7	17.9	7.2	20.2	32.9	10.0	8.4	6.1	9.1	•	•	•
Officers' Compensation 20	1.3	4.1	•	1.5	4.2	2.2	2.3	2.9	1.0	1.4	•	•	•
Operating Margin 21	2.1	3.7	11.2	35.8	1.5	4.3	5.1	7.8	2.7	2.8	•	•	•
Operating Margin Before Officers' Comp. 22	3.4	7.9	11.2	37.2	5.8	6.5	7.4	10.6	3.8	4.3	•	•	•

Selected Average Balance Sheet ($ in Thousands)

Net Receivables 23	1192	0	0	34	242	1524	2381	3580	9633	18793
Inventories 24	820	0	15	25	161	103	1351	2154	6232	15181
Net Property, Plant and Equipment 25	5473	0	42	361	1312	3791	6161	12697	29134	66401
Total Assets 26	18414	0	97	724	2396	6881	14933	32013	68359	163853
Notes and Loans Payable 27	3432	0	49	243	1067	3744	3436	4922	11373	37742
All Other Liabilities 28	2385	0	0	164	345	735	1969	4443	12921	26648
Net Worth 29	12597	0	48	317	984	2401	9528	22648	44065	99463

Selected Financial Ratios (Times to 1)

Current Ratio 30	2.1	•	14.9	1.1	2.2	1.1	3.1	2.7	2.4	2.5
Quick Ratio 31	1.1	•	7.9	1.0	1.7	1.0	2.2	1.9	1.3	1.2
Net Sales to Working Capital 32	5.0	•	4.0	21.4	6.2	41.9	3.3	3.0	4.6	4.0
Coverage Ratio 33	3.3	19.3	3.2	20.9	4.5	4.5	7.2	18.6	6.6	5.6
Total Asset Turnover 34	0.5	•	1.3	0.7	1.5	1.2	1.0	0.8	1.1	0.8
Inventory Turnover 35	7.3	•	2.5	8.8	11.7	21.8	6.7	6.9	8.5	5.2
Receivables Turnover 36	9.9	•	48.6	•	14.9	7.6	6.8	7.8	9.1	7.4
Total Liabilities to Net Worth 37	0.5	•	1.0	1.3	1.4	1.9	0.6	0.4	0.6	0.6
Current Assets to Working Capital 38	1.9	•	1.1	8.8	1.8	10.7	1.5	1.6	1.7	1.7
Current Liabilities to Working Capital 39	0.9	•	0.1	7.8	0.8	9.7	0.5	0.6	0.7	0.7
Working Capital to Net Sales 40	0.2	•	0.3	0.0	0.2	0.0	0.3	0.3	0.2	0.2
Inventory to Working Capital 41	0.5	•	•	1.0	0.4	0.5	0.3	0.3	0.5	0.6
Total Receipts to Cash Flow 42	7.6	7.4	4.7	2.5	5.9	4.0	7.4	5.7	10.7	7.2
Cost of Goods to Cash Flow 43	4.5	5.4	1.3	1.0	3.2	1.1	4.5	3.5	7.6	4.5
Cash Flow to Total Debt 44	0.2	•	0.6	0.5	0.4	0.5	0.4	0.5	0.3	0.3

Selected Financial Factors (in Percentages)

Debt Ratio 45	31.6	•	50.1	56.2	58.9	65.1	36.2	29.3	35.5	39.3
Return on Total Assets 46	4.7	•	22.1	26.8	10.6	12.4	9.1	9.3	6.9	6.4
Return on Equity Before Income Taxes 47	4.8	•	30.4	58.1	20.1	27.7	12.3	12.5	9.1	8.6
Return on Equity After Income Taxes 48	3.9	•	30.4	58.1	18.9	25.6	11.4	11.2	6.8	6.8
Profit Margin (Before Income Tax) 49	6.1	10.3	11.4	35.3	5.6	8.0	7.9	11.6	5.3	6.8
Profit Margin (After Income Tax) 50	4.9	8.5	11.4	35.3	5.3	7.4	7.3	10.4	4.0	5.3

Table I

Corporations with and without Net Income

SUPPORT ACTIVITIES FOR MINING

MONEY AMOUNTS AND SIZE OF ASSETS IN THOUSANDS OF DOLLARS

Item Description for Accounting Period 7/04 Through 6/05	Total	Zero Assets	Under 500	500 to 1,000	1,000 to 5,000	5,000 to 10,000	10,000 to 25,000	25,000 to 50,000	50,000 to 100,000	100,000 to 250,000	250,000 to 500,000	500,000 to 2,500,000	2,500,000 and over
Number of Enterprises **1**	6481	899	3793	785	855	31	46	18	7	10	9	17	9
Revenues ($ in Thousands)													
Net Sales **2**	45546332	668271	2206032	1427899	2688692	301332	705211	871522	221668	1171239	1753438	8287669	25243359
Interest **3**	482899	503	1740	1140	3992	1516	1206	1895	2701	1826	19062	159010	288308
Rents **4**	202415	1897	2006	148	1736	1421	4085	13	526	327	38077	102436	49743
Royalties **5**	148303	0	26	5804	8479	44	1	54	0	60	7114	0	126719
Other Portfolio Income **6**	2008561	316910	20898	51094	44602	16390	13457	5170	2488	7841	17747	555190	956773
Other Receipts **7**	1594830	158	1976	6218	114820	3741	21403	4174	7094	44386	21942	805490	563433
Total Receipts **8**	49983340	987739	2232678	1492303	2862321	324444	745363	882828	234477	1225679	1857380	9909795	27228335
Average Total Receipts **9**	7712	1099	589	1901	3348	10466	16204	49046	33497	122568	206376	582929	3025371
Operating Costs/Operating Income (%)													
Cost of Operations **10**	56.0	55.0	8.8	31.4	31.4	54.3	52.6	48.3	50.9	45.4	60.4	44.5	68.5
Salaries and Wages **11**	11.4	6.9	21.4	21.5	20.0	6.8	14.5	12.3	10.8	15.7	4.3	10.3	9.7
Taxes Paid **12**	2.2	0.6	3.5	4.7	3.3	2.1	2.4	3.2	3.1	2.1	3.2	2.3	1.8
Interest Paid **13**	5.0	2.8	0.4	0.9	1.7	0.7	1.3	1.6	5.4	0.9	2.0	12.8	4.1
Depreciation **14**	9.2	5.8	4.2	4.9	10.3	6.1	6.0	10.9	7.4	9.6	11.9	17.1	7.2
Amortization and Depletion **15**	0.6	0.2	0.0	•	0.4	0.1	0.3	0.2	2.7	0.9	1.3	1.1	0.5
Pensions and Other Deferred Comp. **16**	1.6	2.4	0.1	0.2	0.3	0.4	0.2	0.2	0.2	0.3	0.2	0.2	2.7
Employee Benefits **17**	2.1	3.5	1.0	0.4	1.8	1.5	1.6	2.3	0.1	1.0	3.5	2.2	2.3
Advertising **18**	0.1	0.0	0.2	0.2	0.3	0.2	0.2	0.2	2.0	0.2	0.1	0.1	0.1
Other Expenses **19**	17.1	20.9	43.7	31.6	31.1	16.6	16.3	16.2	25.6	26.2	17.5	25.5	9.1
Officers' Compensation **20**	1.3	2.4	5.2	7.5	2.7	4.0	2.1	0.6	2.1	1.2	0.8	0.9	0.6
Operating Margin **21**	•	•	11.4	•	•	7.2	2.7	3.9	•	•	•	•	•
Operating Margin Before Officers' Comp. **22**	•	1.9	16.6	4.2	•	11.2	4.7	4.5	•	•	•	•	•

Selected Average Balance Sheet ($ in Thousands)

Net Receivables 23	1426	0	14	110	491	1652	4353	10276	15548	35559	72042	132826	542015
Inventories 24	296	0	1	15	76	89	683	995	2324	4404	8917	34114	118655
Net Property, Plant and Equipment 25	3657	0	46	215	953	1772	3442	14130	29187	40439	113009	589564	1158437
Total Assets 26	12418	0	123	712	2181	7583	15749	36069	78459	128328	322872	1152153	5739768
Notes and Loans Payable 27	3677	0	41	390	1369	1258	4581	12783	36919	61914	83585	396847	1482833
All Other Liabilities 28	2913	0	8	107	208	1517	3456	7064	29178	55531	58688	190669	1524852
Net Worth 29	5827	0	74	214	604	4808	7713	16222	12363	10882	180599	564637	2732083

Selected Financial Ratios (Times to 1)

Current Ratio 30	2.0	•	4.8	1.9	3.1	2.3	1.9	2.1	1.0	1.0	2.7	1.9	2.0
Quick Ratio 31	1.5	•	4.4	1.7	2.6	1.9	1.5	1.8	0.9	0.7	2.3	1.5	1.4
Net Sales to Working Capital 32	4.2	•	11.5	10.3	4.7	4.6	3.7	5.2	26.9	•	3.3	4.9	3.5
Coverage Ratio 33	1.7	18.1	30.3	2.3	2.9	22.2	7.5	4.2	0.2	2.5	1.5	1.3	1.5
Total Asset Turnover 34	0.6	•	4.7	2.6	1.4	1.3	1.0	1.3	0.4	0.9	0.6	0.4	0.5
Inventory Turnover 35	13.3	•	57.9	39.1	13.0	59.1	11.8	23.5	6.9	12.1	13.2	6.4	16.2
Receivables Turnover 36	5.2	•	36.2	17.2	7.7	5.7	3.6	5.2	1.7	4.3	2.9	3.5	5.6
Total Liabilities to Net Worth 37	1.1	•	0.7	2.3	2.6	0.6	1.0	1.2	5.3	10.8	0.8	1.0	1.1
Current Assets to Working Capital 38	2.0	•	1.3	2.1	1.5	1.8	2.1	1.9	22.9	•	1.6	2.1	2.0
Current Liabilities to Working Capital 39	1.0	•	0.3	1.1	0.5	0.8	1.1	0.9	21.9	•	0.6	1.1	1.0
Working Capital to Net Sales 40	0.2	•	0.1	0.1	0.2	0.2	0.3	0.2	0.0	•	0.3	0.2	0.3
Inventory to Working Capital 41	0.2	•	0.0	0.1	0.1	0.1	0.2	0.1	1.0	•	0.1	0.2	0.2
Total Receipts to Cash Flow 42	7.5	1.6	2.0	4.0	3.7	4.1	4.8	5.7	6.4	5.2	8.3	5.9	20.1
Cost of Goods to Cash Flow 43	4.2	0.9	0.2	1.2	1.2	2.2	2.5	2.7	3.3	2.3	5.0	2.6	13.8
Cash Flow to Total Debt 44	0.1	•	5.9	0.9	0.5	0.9	0.4	0.4	0.2	0.2	0.2	0.1	0.0

Selected Financial Factors (in Percentages)

Debt Ratio 45	53.1	•	40.0	69.9	72.3	36.6	51.0	55.0	84.2	91.5	44.1	51.0	52.4
Return on Total Assets 46	4.9	•	61.7	5.6	7.2	19.9	9.3	9.1	0.4	2.0	1.8	6.9	3.0
Return on Equity Before Income Taxes 47	4.5	•	99.4	10.6	17.2	30.0	16.5	15.4	•	14.0	1.0	3.0	2.1
Return on Equity After Income Taxes 48	3.3	•	94.9	8.0	13.3	25.3	13.4	14.8	•	•	0.5	2.6	1.0
Profit Margin (Before Income Tax) 49	3.7	47.3	12.6	1.3	3.3	14.9	8.3	5.2	•	1.3	0.9	3.5	2.1
Profit Margin (After Income Tax) 50	2.7	45.7	12.0	0.9	2.6	12.5	6.7	5.0	•	•	0.5	3.0	0.9

Table II

Corporations with Net Income

SUPPORT ACTIVITIES FOR MINING

MONEY AMOUNTS AND SIZE OF ASSETS IN THOUSANDS OF DOLLARS

Item Description for Accounting Period 7/04 Through 6/05	Total	Zero Assets	Under 500	500 to 1,000	1,000 to 5,000	5,000 to 10,000	10,000 to 25,000	25,000 to 50,000	50,000 to 100,000	100,000 to 250,000	250,000 to 500,000	500,000 to 2,500,000	2,500,000 and over
Number of Enterprises **1**	4264	451	2633	673	420	16	32	12	0	7	6	8	5
Revenues ($ in Thousands)													
Net Sales **2**	32382872	456754	1985196	1257891	1577930	261656	567396	649333	0	820229	916731	4748842	19140917
Interest **3**	403240	503	1572	765	1777	154	1055	2485	0	1430	18766	102767	271965
Rents **4**	140067	1897	920	0	44	5	3975	539	0	327	38064	81440	12855
Royalties **5**	136005	0	26	5804	8479	0	1	54	0	60	1	0	121579
Other Portfolio Income **6**	1779614	316910	20783	51094	42494	9826	12367	5037	0	5129	15181	424362	876430
Other Receipts **7**	1231801	68	1641	3411	109992	3811	18163	4963	0	41201	14451	719986	314114
Total Receipts **8**	36073599	776132	2010138	1318965	1740716	275452	602957	662411	0	866376	1003194	6077397	20737860
Average Total Receipts **9**	8460	1721	763	1960	4145	17216	18842	55201	•	124054	167199	759675	4147572
Operating Costs/Operating Income (%)													
Cost of Operations **10**	60.8	34.9	8.8	34.8	35.7	50.2	56.0	43.0	•	52.1	56.8	37.4	77.8
Salaries and Wages **11**	10.6	9.7	21.1	20.6	17.4	5.5	11.9	12.4	•	16.5	4.8	11.6	8.1
Taxes Paid **12**	2.2	0.9	3.4	4.0	2.9	2.0	2.1	3.6	•	2.2	2.1	3.0	1.6
Interest Paid **13**	4.4	4.0	0.4	0.8	0.6	0.2	1.0	0.9	•	0.9	1.6	15.7	3.2
Depreciation **14**	6.0	5.8	3.9	5.1	4.9	6.1	5.5	7.7	•	11.2	9.9	13.3	4.0
Amortization and Depletion **15**	0.4	0.3	0.0	•	0.5	0.0	0.2	0.0	•	1.1	0.4	1.3	0.3
Pensions and Other Deferred Comp. **16**	0.6	3.5	0.0	0.2	0.3	0.4	0.2	0.2	•	0.3	0.3	0.3	0.8
Employee Benefits **17**	1.9	5.1	1.0	0.2	1.1	1.6	1.6	2.0	•	0.5	2.3	2.2	2.1
Advertising **18**	0.1	0.0	0.1	0.2	0.2	0.2	0.1	0.1	•	0.2	0.1	0.1	0.1
Other Expenses **19**	14.7	28.6	43.3	25.3	28.1	13.5	13.3	19.8	•	9.4	26.2	29.1	5.6
Officers' Compensation **20**	1.3	3.5	3.7	8.4	2.7	3.0	1.7	0.6	•	1.5	1.4	1.0	0.5
Operating Margin **21**	•	3.6	14.2	0.1	5.6	17.2	6.4	9.7	•	4.1	•	•	•
Operating Margin Before Officers' Comp. **22**	•	7.1	17.9	8.5	8.2	20.2	8.1	10.2	•	5.7	•	•	•

Selected Average Balance Sheet ($ in Thousands)

Net Receivables 23	1427	0	8	113	822	2977	4416	13878	•	44398	84867	130445	684606
Inventories 24	267	0	1	16	117	140	808	771	•	7387	6945	65378	164812
Net Property, Plant and Equipment 25	2198	0	54	201	428	2305	3520	11033	•	40831	88242	421674	888865
Total Assets 26	12327	0	146	669	1953	8108	16099	42728	•	133965	318730	1056924	7688660
Notes and Loans Payable 27	2844	0	41	178	732	1002	3876	11470	•	41709	55062	337595	1597720
All Other Liabilities 28	3142	0	9	103	274	1602	3428	11125	•	43962	42386	204251	2144673
Net Worth 29	6341	0	96	388	947	5504	8796	20133	•	48293	221282	515078	3946268

Selected Financial Ratios (Times to 1)

Current Ratio 30	2.3	•	5.0	2.1	3.7	2.7	2.2	2.2	•	1.4	3.9	2.1	2.3
Quick Ratio 31	1.7	•	4.5	2.0	3.1	2.4	1.7	2.0	•	1.2	3.3	1.6	1.6
Net Sales to Working Capital 32	3.9	•	12.5	9.5	3.8	5.2	3.6	4.1	•	6.4	1.9	5.4	3.3
Coverage Ratio 33	3.1	19.2	38.8	6.9	26.1	91.4	13.8	14.5	•	12.4	3.5	1.9	2.7
Total Asset Turnover 34	0.6	•	5.2	2.8	1.9	2.0	1.1	1.3	•	0.9	0.5	0.6	0.5
Inventory Turnover 35	17.3	•	105.1	42.0	11.5	58.4	12.3	30.2	•	8.3	12.5	3.4	18.1
Receivables Turnover 36	6.0	•	84.5	•	5.4	9.0	4.5	4.5	•	•	2.1	•	•
Total Liabilities to Net Worth 37	0.9	•	0.5	0.7	1.1	0.5	0.8	1.1	•	1.8	0.4	1.1	0.9
Current Assets to Working Capital 38	1.7	•	1.3	1.9	1.4	1.6	1.8	1.8	•	3.3	1.3	1.9	1.7
Current Liabilities to Working Capital 39	0.7	•	0.3	0.9	0.4	0.6	0.8	0.8	•	2.3	0.3	0.9	0.7
Working Capital to Net Sales 40	0.3	•	0.1	0.1	0.3	0.2	0.3	0.2	•	0.2	0.5	0.2	0.3
Inventory to Working Capital 41	0.1	•	0.0	0.1	0.1	0.1	0.2	0.1	•	0.4	0.1	0.2	0.1
Total Receipts to Cash Flow 42	6.1	1.1	1.9	4.3	2.5	3.5	4.5	3.7	•	6.5	5.0	3.3	24.6
Cost of Goods to Cash Flow 43	3.7	0.4	0.2	1.5	0.9	1.8	2.5	1.6	•	3.4	2.8	1.2	19.1
Cash Flow to Total Debt 44	0.2	•	8.0	1.6	1.5	1.8	0.5	0.7	•	0.2	0.3	0.3	0.0

Selected Financial Factors (in Percentages)

Debt Ratio 45	48.6	•	34.6	41.9	51.5	32.1	45.4	52.9	•	64.0	30.6	51.3	48.7
Return on Total Assets 46	8.4	•	81.8	16.3	31.8	45.7	15.0	15.9	•	9.5	2.7	16.8	4.3
Return on Equity Before Income Taxes 47	11.1	•	121.9	24.0	63.0	66.6	25.5	31.4	•	24.3	2.7	16.4	5.3
Return on Equity After Income Taxes 48	9.5	•	116.9	22.3	57.9	58.6	21.5	29.6	•	17.2	2.1	15.4	3.8
Profit Margin (Before Income Tax) 49	9.2	73.5	15.4	5.0	15.9	22.4	12.6	11.7	•	10.0	3.9	14.2	5.4
Profit Margin (After Income Tax) 50	7.9	71.2	14.8	4.6	14.6	19.7	10.7	11.0	•	7.1	3.1	13.3	3.9

16

Table I

Corporations with and without Net Income

ELECTRIC POWER GENERATION, TRANSMISSION AND DISTRIBUTION

MONEY AMOUNTS AND SIZE OF ASSETS IN THOUSANDS OF DOLLARS

Item Description for Accounting Period 7/04 Through 6/05	Total	Zero Assets	Under 500	500 to 1,000	1,000 to 5,000	5,000 to 10,000	10,000 to 25,000	25,000 to 50,000	50,000 to 100,000	100,000 to 250,000	250,000 to 500,000	500,000 to 2,500,000	2,500,000 and over
Number of Enterprises 1	809	0	0	200	60	40	0	31	16	28	16	31	30
Revenues ($ in Thousands)													
Net Sales 2	250608164	0	0	94993	107094	1923159	0	965237	2371790	1604977	1603981	19212050	221864956
Interest 3	5326495	0	0	0	227	248730	0	14577	5456	24684	85312	549326	4371377
Rents 4	2063953	0	0	0	0	5468	0	1205	77	532	9492	46286	1999269
Royalties 5	31756	0	0	0	0	0	0	212	134	0	0	21245	10165
Other Portfolio Income 6	5026460	0	0	0	0	7597	0	34086	70751	128876	9511	489467	3034234
Other Receipts 7	6057129	0	0	4630	40204	110261	0	35929	25277	65206	114122	669886	4809365
Total Receipts 8	269113957	0	0	99623	147525	2295215	0	1051246	2473485	1824275	1822418	20988260	236089366
Average Total Receipts 9	332650	•	•	498	2459	57380	•	33911	154593	65153	113901	677041	7889646
Operating Costs/Operating Income (%)													
Cost of Operations 10	64.4	•	•	•	11.6	54.7	•	64.9	52.5	50.2	34.3	65.3	64.9
Salaries and Wages 11	4.0	•	•	2.4	26.1	8.0	•	9.1	1.7	3.3	3.9	4.5	3.9
Taxes Paid 12	3.5	•	•	5.8	3.8	8.8	•	1.7	0.7	2.5	2.8	3.3	3.6
Interest Paid 13	7.4	•	•	0.8	1.6	11.4	•	2.3	1.4	6.2	15.2	6.1	7.5
Depreciation 14	9.3	•	•	0.0	3.7	9.5	•	3.0	1.6	7.4	12.5	8.3	9.5
Amortization and Depletion 15	0.9	•	•	•	0.1	0.3	•	0.4	0.5	0.4	1.2	2.4	0.8
Pensions and Other Deferred Comp. 16	0.9	•	•	•	6.5	0.8	•	0.3	0.1	0.3	0.5	0.8	0.8
Employee Benefits 17	0.9	•	•	•	1.9	1.4	•	1.4	0.2	1.2	0.9	0.8	0.9
Advertising 18	0.1	•	•	0.0	0.1	0.0	•	0.0	0.2	0.1	0.0	0.2	0.1
Other Expenses 19	16.0	•	•	46.9	35.6	17.8	•	22.1	45.7	41.0	43.2	17.8	14.6
Officers' Compensation 20	0.3	•	•	16.4	2.8	1.3	•	1.2	0.3	1.1	0.9	0.3	0.3
Operating Margin 21	•	•	•	27.7	6.1	•	•	•	•	•	•	•	•
Operating Margin Before Officers' Comp. 22	•	•	•	44.1	9.0	•	•	•	•	•	•	•	•

Selected Average Balance Sheet ($ in Thousands)

Net Receivables 23	44039	•	0	32	370	•	10952	13725	13647	17949	91864	1047890
Inventories 24	10382	•	0	8	1159	•	520	1045	1359	3412	19362	254001
Net Property, Plant and Equipment 25	364969	•	2	199	4101	•	11585	24374	53047	152605	673769	8979057
Total Assets 26	717046	•	525	2649	7469	•	33696	68666	154355	348924	1192700	17763406
Notes and Loans Payable 27	306239	•	21	529	79089	•	16390	32472	77908	191778	663702	7246132
All Other Liabilities 28	229083	•	205	862	1113	•	13109	19820	41345	128255	276936	5751883
Net Worth 29	181724	•	299	1258	-72733	•	4198	16373	35102	28890	252063	4665391

Selected Financial Ratios (Times to 1)

Current Ratio 30	0.9	•	2.6	1.8	2.9	•	1.0	1.3	1.5	0.7	1.1	0.9
Quick Ratio 31	0.5	•	2.6	1.2	1.5	•	0.8	1.2	1.1	0.6	0.8	0.5
Net Sales to Working Capital 32	•	•	1.5	3.7	24.2	•	•	24.3	5.1	•	24.0	•
Coverage Ratio 33	1.0	•	43.7	28.1	1.5	•	2.1	0.7	1.0	0.9	0.9	0.9
Total Asset Turnover 34	0.4	•	0.9	0.7	6.4	•	0.9	2.2	0.4	0.3	0.5	0.4
Inventory Turnover 35	19.2	•	•	24.8	22.7	•	38.9	74.4	21.2	10.1	20.9	18.9
Receivables Turnover 36	6.5	•	•	36.3	159.9	•	3.7	13.6	4.6	4.7	6.8	6.4
Total Liabilities to Net Worth 37	2.9	•	0.8	1.1	•	•	7.0	3.2	3.4	11.1	3.7	2.8
Current Assets to Working Capital 38	•	•	1.6	2.2	1.5	•	•	4.1	3.0	•	7.9	•
Current Liabilities to Working Capital 39	•	•	0.6	1.2	0.5	•	•	3.1	2.0	•	6.9	•
Working Capital to Net Sales 40	0.7	•	0.7	0.3	0.0	•	•	0.0	0.2	•	0.0	•
Inventory to Working Capital 41	•	•	•	0.0	0.7	•	•	0.2	0.1	•	0.8	•
Total Receipts to Cash Flow 42	9.8	•	1.6	1.3	4.5	•	8.2	2.2	3.4	2.9	8.5	11.7
Cost of Goods to Cash Flow 43	6.3	•	•	0.2	2.5	•	5.3	1.2	1.7	1.0	5.5	7.6
Cash Flow to Total Debt 44	0.1	•	1.3	1.0	0.1	•	0.1	1.3	0.1	0.1	0.1	0.0

Selected Financial Factors (in Percentages)

Debt Ratio 45	74.7	•	43.1	52.5	1073.7	•	87.5	76.2	77.3	91.7	78.9	73.6
Return on Total Assets 46	3.1	•	30.2	30.7	107.9	•	4.4	2.2	2.2	3.8	2.9	3.0
Return on Equity Before Income Taxes 47	•	•	51.8	62.3	•	•	18.2	•	•	•	•	•
Return on Equity After Income Taxes 48	•	•	51.8	37.5	•	•	6.6	•	•	•	•	•
Profit Margin (Before Income Tax) 49	•	•	32.6	43.9	5.3	•	2.5	•	•	•	•	•
Profit Margin (After Income Tax) 50	•	•	32.6	26.4	3.6	•	0.9	•	•	•	•	•

Table II
Corporations with Net Income

ELECTRIC POWER GENERATION, TRANSMISSION AND DISTRIBUTION

MONEY AMOUNTS AND SIZE OF ASSETS IN THOUSANDS OF DOLLARS

Item Description for Accounting Period 7/04 Through 6/05		Total	Zero Assets	Under 500	500 to 1,000	1,000 to 5,000	5,000 to 10,000	10,000 to 25,000	25,000 to 50,000	50,000 to 100,000	100,000 to 250,000	250,000 to 500,000	500,000 to 2,500,000	2,500,000 and over
Number of Enterprises	1	407	23	0	0	56	27	20	19	7	16	9	13	17
Revenues ($ in Thousands)														
Net Sales	2	116135348	163528	0	0	99395	1881446	295749	568452	1723669	931242	947324	7354534	102065370
Interest	3	2122021	20787	0	0	209	248391	3756	2776	2990	8726	65241	161304	1607842
Rents	4	1474319	1026	0	0	0	3557	292	1021	2	339	7022	26277	1434783
Royalties	5	22642	0	0	0	0	0	0	212	46	0	0	21221	1163
Other Portfolio Income	6	3563289	1249968	0	0	0	7597	493	18116	70517	63827	4608	440815	1707348
Other Receipts	7	4792167	155172	0	0	39980	109585	21782	25535	8007	37124	85271	269123	4035956
Total Receipts	8	128109786	1590481	0	0	139584	2250576	322072	616112	1805231	1041258	1109466	8273274	110852462
Average Total Receipts	9	314766	69151	•	•	2493	83355	16104	32427	257890	65079	123274	636406	6520733
Operating Costs/Operating Income (%)														
Cost of Operations	10	56.4	42.4	•	•	5.7	54.6	63.9	56.3	42.0	39.8	34.3	51.9	57.5
Salaries and Wages	11	4.3	30.8	•	•	26.9	8.1	8.5	13.5	0.7	1.9	6.1	6.1	4.0
Taxes Paid	12	4.2	6.9	•	•	3.9	8.9	1.7	2.3	0.3	2.7	3.7	5.8	4.1
Interest Paid	13	7.3	12.8	•	•	0.7	11.6	3.4	1.8	0.6	5.0	14.8	5.3	7.5
Depreciation	14	10.3	13.1	•	•	3.7	9.4	1.8	3.8	0.7	8.3	11.8	7.0	10.8
Amortization and Depletion	15	1.0	2.2	•	•	0.0	0.3	1.1	0.3	0.5	0.4	1.8	5.0	0.8
Pensions and Other Deferred Comp.	16	1.1	0.1	•	•	7.0	0.8	1.2	0.5	0.0	0.3	0.7	0.2	1.1
Employee Benefits	17	1.2	0.0	•	•	1.9	1.3	0.3	1.9	0.1	1.3	1.6	1.6	1.2
Advertising	18	0.1	•	•	•	0.0	0.0	0.3	0.1	0.0	0.1	0.0	0.4	0.1
Other Expenses	19	19.4	561.6	•	•	29.1	17.3	14.7	15.2	56.8	45.7	34.1	18.3	17.6
Officers' Compensation	20	0.4	1.9	•	•	2.7	1.3	2.2	1.7	0.1	0.5	1.5	0.5	0.4
Operating Margin	21	•	•	•	•	18.1	•	0.8	2.6	•	•	•	•	•
Operating Margin Before Officers' Comp.	22	•	•	•	•	20.8	•	3.1	4.2	•	•	•	•	•

Selected Average Balance Sheet ($ in Thousands)

Net Receivables 23	45128	0	•	•	0	346	2394	5513	17893	8692	15958	75544	989116
Inventories 24	11793	0	•	•	8	1676	193	433	1185	1670	1385	19242	261434
Net Property, Plant and Equipment 25	383152	0	•	•	196	4047	4157	11754	22436	62782	127923	565268	8579664
Total Assets 26	763727	0	•	•	2711	8315	17356	32467	75156	154800	351428	1115193	16984046
Notes and Loans Payable 27	291145	0	•	•	432	5115	6289	13987	20435	82976	176019	521124	6359577
All Other Liabilities 28	244480	0	•	•	826	1170	5055	19235	27678	38870	104991	282788	5498922
Net Worth 29	228102	0	•	•	1453	2030	6012	-755	27043	32954	70418	311280	5125548

Selected Financial Ratios (Times to 1)

Current Ratio 30	0.9	•	•	•	2.1	3.5	1.6	0.8	1.2	1.2	1.1	1.2	0.9
Quick Ratio 31	0.5	•	•	•	1.3	1.6	1.2	0.5	1.0	0.8	0.9	0.9	0.5
Net Sales to Working Capital 32	•	•	•	•	3.3	24.7	6.6	•	48.1	12.9	31.2	20.5	•
Coverage Ratio 33	1.7	24.5	•	•	83.3	1.5	3.8	6.9	5.6	2.1	1.4	3.0	1.5
Total Asset Turnover 34	0.4	•	•	•	0.7	8.4	0.9	0.9	3.3	0.4	0.3	0.5	0.4
Inventory Turnover 35	13.7	•	•	•	12.2	22.7	49.0	38.9	87.2	13.9	26.0	15.3	13.2
Receivables Turnover 36	6.3	•	•	•	137.0	280.3	4.3	5.8	19.9	6.6	9.5	6.1	6.1
Total Liabilities to Net Worth 37	2.3	•	•	•	0.9	3.1	1.9	•	1.8	3.7	4.0	2.6	2.3
Current Assets to Working Capital 38	•	•	•	•	1.9	1.4	2.7	•	5.4	6.2	16.8	6.8	•
Current Liabilities to Working Capital 39	•	•	•	•	0.9	0.4	1.7	•	4.4	5.2	15.8	5.8	•
Working Capital to Net Sales 40	•	•	•	•	0.3	0.0	0.2	•	0.0	0.1	0.0	0.0	•
Inventory to Working Capital 41	•	•	•	•	•	0.7	0.1	•	0.2	0.4	0.5	0.8	•
Total Receipts to Cash Flow 42	5.4	0.1	•	•	1.2	4.5	4.3	5.5	1.7	2.3	2.8	4.2	6.5
Cost of Goods to Cash Flow 43	3.1	0.0	•	•	0.1	2.4	2.7	3.1	0.7	0.9	1.0	2.2	3.7
Cash Flow to Total Debt 44	0.1	•	•	•	1.2	2.5	0.3	0.2	3.0	0.2	0.1	0.2	0.1

Selected Financial Factors (in Percentages)

Debt Ratio 45	70.1	•	•	•	46.4	75.6	65.4	102.3	64.0	78.7	80.0	72.1	69.8
Return on Total Assets 46	4.6	•	•	•	38.8	147.2	11.1	11.8	11.4	4.0	6.4	7.9	4.1
Return on Equity Before Income Taxes 47	6.3	•	•	•	71.5	206.1	23.5	•	26.0	9.8	9.7	18.8	4.7
Return on Equity After Income Taxes 48	4.6	•	•	•	48.6	145.4	20.6	•	21.5	6.8	9.5	15.9	3.4
Profit Margin (Before Income Tax) 49	5.0	300.8	•	•	58.5	6.0	9.6	11.0	2.9	5.5	6.5	10.3	4.0
Profit Margin (After Income Tax) 50	3.7	196.8	•	•	39.8	4.2	8.4	8.3	2.4	3.9	6.3	8.7	2.9

Table I

Corporations with and without Net Income

NATURAL GAS DISTRIBUTION

MONEY AMOUNTS AND SIZE OF ASSETS IN THOUSANDS OF DOLLARS

Item Description for Accounting Period 7/04 Through 6/05	Total	Zero Assets	Under 500	500 to 1,000	1,000 to 5,000	5,000 to 10,000	10,000 to 25,000	25,000 to 50,000	50,000 to 100,000	100,000 to 250,000	250,000 to 500,000	500,000 to 2,500,000	2,500,000 and over
Number of Enterprises **1**	895	304	262	34	187	25	27	9	8	10	3	8	18
Revenues ($ in Thousands)													
Net Sales **2**	91199675	125821	26884	119437	481978	124186	2082215	301869	1059020	3451028	1431645	9366355	72629240
Interest **3**	1376980	667	0	31	50	680	762	526	1094	2102	2292	10994	1357781
Rents **4**	87934	985	0	0	0	745	95	704	2080	353	171	5560	77241
Royalties **5**	39896	0	0	0	0	0	0	0	26	373	0	0	39497
Other Portfolio Income **6**	2120973	72	0	0	567	1632	5781	1222	609	22500	1682	15457	2071450
Other Receipts **7**	4690853	422	0	765	3527	3931	7216	53242	7909	16409	13463	22067	4561900
Total Receipts **8**	99516311	127967	26884	120233	486122	131174	2096069	357563	1070738	3492765	1449253	9420433	80737109
Average Total Receipts **9**	111191	421	103	3536	2600	5247	77632	39729	133842	349276	483084	1177554	4485395
Operating Costs/Operating Income (%)													
Cost of Operations **10**	69.3	29.7	70.2	79.3	64.4	42.2	95.1	85.2	91.5	88.6	79.3	76.9	66.3
Salaries and Wages **11**	3.7	9.1	•	8.6	7.5	6.6	1.2	14.9	1.4	1.2	2.9	2.3	4.0
Taxes Paid **12**	2.2	5.3	0.8	0.3	1.5	4.3	0.3	2.9	0.7	0.8	2.1	2.4	2.3
Interest Paid **13**	5.1	6.9	•	0.4	2.0	0.5	0.3	2.3	0.6	1.1	1.3	2.7	5.9
Depreciation **14**	6.0	5.9	•	1.0	6.4	5.5	0.7	4.1	2.4	2.1	4.5	6.6	6.4
Amortization and Depletion **15**	0.4	0.4	•	•	0.2	0.2	0.1	0.9	0.1	0.2	0.4	0.3	0.5
Pensions and Other Deferred Comp. **16**	0.5	0.1	•	0.1	0.0	1.0	0.1	0.4	0.2	0.1	0.6	0.7	0.5
Employee Benefits **17**	1.0	1.3	•	1.8	1.1	1.4	0.1	0.5	0.5	0.2	0.5	0.7	1.1
Advertising **18**	0.0	0.0	•	0.0	0.7	0.3	0.2	0.1	0.0	0.1	0.1	0.1	0.0
Other Expenses **19**	19.4	37.0	25.6	5.2	14.3	18.6	1.6	6.0	2.6	3.5	6.6	8.0	22.7
Officers' Compensation **20**	0.3	0.2	•	0.9	1.6	3.6	0.3	0.6	0.5	0.2	0.3	0.2	0.3
Operating Margin **21**	•	4.1	3.4	2.2	0.4	15.7	0.0	•	•	1.7	1.5	•	•
Operating Margin Before Officers' Comp. **22**	•	4.2	3.4	3.1	1.9	19.3	0.3	•	0.1	1.9	1.9	•	•

Selected Average Balance Sheet ($ in Thousands)

Net Receivables 23	54377	0	0	50	174	210	4649	9395	18210	36337	48423	111026	2604192
Inventories 24	5054	0	0	85	79	75	639	1916	5386	6888	62878	93354	190429
Net Property, Plant and Equipment 25	84353	0	0	389	940	3411	5331	16549	25540	74515	173916	909839	3676584
Total Assets 26	249221	0	0	773	1803	7121	16687	37003	75551	171776	367658	1394995	11507918
Notes and Loans Payable 27	105656	0	0	201	760	451	4436	12171	9642	48845	135660	468546	4969512
All Other Liabilities 28	128324	0	0	424	130	1232	6951	12729	26092	68294	115674	482820	6076474
Net Worth 29	15242	0	0	148	912	5438	5300	12103	39816	54637	116324	443629	461932

Selected Financial Ratios (Times to 1)

Current Ratio 30	0.9	•	•	0.6	5.9	1.9	1.4	1.2	1.4	1.3	1.1	0.9	0.9
Quick Ratio 31	0.6	•	•	0.5	1.8	1.5	1.0	1.0	1.1	0.9	0.4	0.4	0.6
Net Sales to Working Capital 32	•	•	•	•	3.7	8.4	32.7	12.2	13.5	19.9	57.0	•	•
Coverage Ratio 33	1.3	1.8	•	7.4	1.6	43.9	3.4	1.2	2.3	3.7	3.1	0.9	1.3
Total Asset Turnover 34	0.4	•	•	4.5	1.4	0.7	4.6	0.9	1.8	2.0	1.3	0.8	0.4
Inventory Turnover 35	14.0	•	•	32.8	21.1	28.0	114.8	14.9	22.5	44.4	6.0	9.6	14.0
Receivables Turnover 36	1.6	•	88.3	•	15.4	15.0	•	•	6.9	12.4	10.0	9.3	1.3
Total Liabilities to Net Worth 37	15.4	•	•	4.2	1.0	0.3	2.1	2.1	0.9	2.1	2.2	2.1	23.9
Current Assets to Working Capital 38	•	•	•	•	1.2	2.2	3.8	6.0	3.4	4.5	17.0	•	•
Current Liabilities to Working Capital 39	•	•	•	•	0.2	1.2	2.8	5.0	2.4	3.5	16.0	•	•
Working Capital to Net Sales 40	•	•	•	•	0.3	0.1	0.0	0.1	0.1	0.1	0.0	•	•
Inventory to Working Capital 41	•	•	•	•	0.1	0.2	0.3	0.7	0.4	0.5	8.0	•	•
Total Receipts to Cash Flow 42	5.3	2.7	5.3	16.3	7.2	3.0	53.5	17.2	35.0	17.7	11.3	17.3	4.5
Cost of Goods to Cash Flow 43	3.7	0.8	3.7	12.9	4.6	1.3	50.9	14.6	32.0	15.7	8.9	13.3	3.0
Cash Flow to Total Debt 44	0.1	•	•	0.3	0.4	1.0	0.1	0.1	0.1	0.2	0.2	0.1	0.1

Selected Financial Factors (in Percentages)

Debt Ratio 45	93.9	•	•	80.9	49.4	23.6	68.2	67.3	47.3	68.2	68.4	68.2	96.0
Return on Total Assets 46	2.7	•	•	15.1	4.6	14.7	4.4	2.5	2.2	8.0	5.3	2.1	2.6
Return on Equity Before Income Taxes 47	9.6	•	•	68.5	3.5	18.8	9.8	1.0	2.3	18.3	11.3	•	13.6
Return on Equity After Income Taxes 48	3.9	•	•	68.5	1.7	15.2	7.5	•	1.9	13.8	11.2	•	5.3
Profit Margin (Before Income Tax) 49	1.4	5.8	3.4	2.9	1.2	20.6	0.7	0.4	0.7	2.9	2.8	•	1.6
Profit Margin (After Income Tax) 50	0.6	5.6	2.9	2.9	0.6	16.7	0.5	•	0.6	2.2	2.7	•	0.6

Table II

Corporations with Net Income

NATURAL GAS DISTRIBUTION

MONEY AMOUNTS AND SIZE OF ASSETS IN THOUSANDS OF DOLLARS

Item Description for Accounting Period 7/04 Through 6/05	Total	Zero Assets	Under 500	500 to 1,000	1,000 to 5,000	5,000 to 10,000	10,000 to 25,000	25,000 to 50,000	50,000 to 100,000	100,000 to 250,000	250,000 to 500,000	500,000 to 2,500,000	2,500,000 and over
Number of Enterprises 1	460	9	0	0	76	25	17	0	4	0	0	4	14
Revenues ($ in Thousands)													
Net Sales 2	66224954	97345	0	0	333194	124186	1833647	0	884818	0	0	6669854	51383432
Interest 3	641441	641	0	0	50	680	678	0	651	0	0	6820	627182
Rents 4	22753	478	0	0	0	745	95	0	0	0	0	1204	19035
Royalties 5	27112	0	0	0	0	0	0	0	0	0	0	0	26739
Other Portfolio Income 6	864603	52	0	0	567	1632	5660	0	0	0	0	4610	827139
Other Receipts 7	1513057	387	0	0	2787	3931	4242	0	7437	0	0	31907	1376333
Total Receipts 8	69293920	98903	0	0	336598	131174	1844322	0	892906	0	0	6714395	54259860
Average Total Receipts 9	150639	10989	.	.	4429	5247	108490	.	223226	.	.	1678599	3875704
Operating Costs/Operating Income (%)													
Cost of Operations 10	64.1	24.3	.	.	69.6	42.2	96.3	.	94.2	.	.	82.3	57.9
Salaries and Wages 11	3.7	10.8	.	.	4.3	6.6	1.0	.	0.7	.	.	0.8	4.3
Taxes Paid 12	2.2	6.1	.	.	1.3	4.3	0.2	.	0.5	.	.	2.0	2.5
Interest Paid 13	3.4	8.7	.	.	2.8	0.5	0.2	.	0.4	.	.	1.8	4.0
Depreciation 14	5.6	6.7	.	.	7.3	5.5	0.4	.	0.8	.	.	5.1	6.3
Amortization and Depletion 15	0.4	0.5	.	.	0.3	0.2	0.1	.	0.0	.	.	0.1	0.5
Pensions and Other Deferred Comp. 16	0.3	.	.	.	0.0	1.0	0.1	.	0.1	.	.	0.4	0.3
Employee Benefits 17	1.1	1.6	.	.	0.8	1.4	0.1	.	0.2	.	.	0.6	1.3
Advertising 18	0.0	0.1	.	.	0.3	0.3	0.0	.	0.0	.	.	0.0	0.0
Other Expenses 19	19.2	34.6	.	.	9.4	18.6	0.9	.	1.1	.	.	5.7	23.3
Officers' Compensation 20	0.3	.	.	.	1.2	3.6	0.2	.	0.3	.	.	0.1	0.3
Operating Margin 21	.	6.7	.	.	2.6	15.7	0.7	.	1.7	.	.	1.1	.
Operating Margin Before Officers' Comp. 22	0.0	6.7	.	.	3.8	19.3	0.9	.	2.0	.	.	1.2	.

Selected Average Balance Sheet ($ in Thousands)

Net Receivables 23	17975	0	•	•	284	210	4832	•	32289	•	•	160742	487263
Inventories 24	8192	0	•	•	112	75	588	•	6951	•	•	116946	202807
Net Property, Plant and Equipment 25	114520	0	•	•	2123	3411	3927	•	17506	•	•	978496	3388538
Total Assets 26	233551	0	•	•	2818	7121	16832	•	73150	•	•	1577474	6979012
Notes and Loans Payable 27	74345	0	•	•	1862	451	3962	•	11270	•	•	438705	2251509
All Other Liabilities 28	84386	0	•	•	261	1232	7266	•	37534	•	•	584527	2514220
Net Worth 29	74820	0	•	•	696	5438	5604	•	24346	•	•	554243	2213283

Selected Financial Ratios (Times to 1)

Current Ratio 30	0.9	•	•	•	2.1	1.9	1.5	•	1.3	•	•	1.1	0.9
Quick Ratio 31	0.5	•	•	•	1.7	1.5	1.1	•	1.1	•	•	0.5	0.4
Net Sales to Working Capital 32	•	•	•	•	12.8	8.4	31.5	•	18.1	•	•	42.9	•
Coverage Ratio 33	2.3	2.0	•	•	2.3	43.9	7.9	•	8.2	•	•	2.0	2.2
Total Asset Turnover 34	0.6	•	•	•	1.6	0.7	6.4	•	3.0	•	•	1.1	0.5
Inventory Turnover 35	11.3	•	•	•	27.2	28.0	176.7	•	30.0	•	•	11.7	10.5
Receivables Turnover 36	4.9	•	•	•	16.2	15.0	23.9	•	•	•	•	•	4.3
Total Liabilities to Net Worth 37	2.1	•	•	•	3.1	0.3	2.0	•	2.0	•	•	1.8	2.2
Current Assets to Working Capital 38	•	•	•	•	1.9	2.2	3.1	•	4.0	•	•	10.7	•
Current Liabilities to Working Capital 39	•	•	•	•	0.9	1.2	2.1	•	3.0	•	•	9.7	•
Working Capital to Net Sales 40	•	•	•	•	0.1	0.1	0.0	•	0.1	•	•	0.0	•
Inventory to Working Capital 41	•	•	•	•	0.2	0.2	0.2	•	0.6	•	•	3.0	•
Total Receipts to Cash Flow 42	4.6	2.5	•	•	8.8	3.0	59.6	•	27.5	•	•	19.3	3.8
Cost of Goods to Cash Flow 43	3.0	0.6	•	•	6.1	1.3	57.4	•	26.0	•	•	15.9	2.2
Cash Flow to Total Debt 44	0.2	•	•	•	0.2	1.0	0.2	•	0.2	•	•	0.1	0.2

Selected Financial Factors (in Percentages)

Debt Ratio 45	68.0	•	•	•	75.3	23.6	66.7	•	66.7	•	•	64.9	68.3
Return on Total Assets 46	4.8	•	•	•	10.1	14.7	9.2	•	9.2	•	•	3.8	4.7
Return on Equity Before Income Taxes 47	8.4	•	•	•	23.0	18.8	24.0	•	24.2	•	•	5.4	8.1
Return on Equity After Income Taxes 48	6.1	•	•	•	17.2	15.2	20.6	•	22.9	•	•	3.4	5.9
Profit Margin (Before Income Tax) 49	4.4	8.3	•	•	3.7	20.6	1.2	•	2.7	•	•	1.8	4.9
Profit Margin (After Income Tax) 50	3.2	8.1	•	•	2.7	16.7	1.1	•	2.5	•	•	1.1	3.5

Table I

Corporations with and without Net Income

WATER, SEWAGE AND OTHER SYSTEMS

MONEY AMOUNTS AND SIZE OF ASSETS IN THOUSANDS OF DOLLARS

Item Description for Accounting Period 7/04 Through 6/05	Total	Zero Assets	Under 500	500 to 1,000	1,000 to 5,000	5,000 to 10,000	10,000 to 25,000	25,000 to 50,000	50,000 to 100,000	100,000 to 250,000	250,000 to 500,000	500,000 to 2,500,000	2,500,000 and over
Number of Enterprises **1**	5356	0	0	541	500	69	40	0	6	9	4	8	0
Revenues ($ in Thousands)													
Net Sales **2**	6850470	0	0	216101	538622	196750	298640	0	63462	269364	429342	4047723	0
Interest **3**	152605	0	0	551	760	2075	259	0	2025	2191	1459	134385	0
Rents **4**	13305	0	0	0	0	717	462	0	308	1141	1570	8473	0
Royalties **5**	36	0	0	0	17	0	19	0	0	0	0	0	0
Other Portfolio Income **6**	112331	0	0	1055	15143	16795	1122	0	4925	2389	964	48363	0
Other Receipts **7**	111385	0	0	2584	16410	1875	3125	0	3351	6454	6458	66379	0
Total Receipts **8**	7240132	0	0	220291	570952	218212	303627	0	74071	281539	439793	4305323	0
Average Total Receipts **9**	1352	•	•	407	1142	3162	7591	•	12345	31282	109948	538165	•
Operating Costs/Operating Income (%)													
Cost of Operations **10**	28.2	•	•	30.5	41.2	38.2	37.4	•	33.7	27.9	35.6	27.3	•
Salaries and Wages **11**	7.6	•	•	11.9	5.3	12.2	19.8	•	6.4	9.1	11.9	5.5	•
Taxes Paid **12**	7.4	•	•	4.3	4.1	9.7	4.1	•	6.7	8.0	7.4	8.4	•
Interest Paid **13**	11.0	•	•	3.9	5.2	4.6	5.3	•	12.7	10.9	4.9	15.4	•
Depreciation **14**	17.8	•	•	8.2	11.9	11.1	9.8	•	20.6	26.1	15.6	21.0	•
Amortization and Depletion **15**	4.3	•	•	2.3	0.1	0.2	0.8	•	1.0	0.3	0.6	6.9	•
Pensions and Other Deferred Comp. **16**	1.0	•	•	0.5	0.5	0.1	0.2	•	1.2	1.7	0.7	1.1	•
Employee Benefits **17**	3.0	•	•	0.0	1.2	1.1	7.0	•	2.8	3.7	4.0	3.3	•
Advertising **18**	0.2	•	•	0.4	0.3	1.0	0.1	•	0.1	0.7	0.1	0.2	•
Other Expenses **19**	22.8	•	•	38.3	35.3	31.1	15.6	•	27.2	15.6	15.0	17.5	•
Officers' Compensation **20**	1.8	•	•	4.1	1.9	1.7	2.5	•	3.6	3.6	1.6	0.6	•
Operating Margin **21**	•	•	•	•	•	•	•	•	•	•	2.7	•	•
Operating Margin Before Officers' Comp. **22**	•	•	•	•	•	•	•	•	•	•	•	4.3	•

Selected Average Balance Sheet ($ in Thousands)

Net Receivables 23	173	•	54	76	437	838	•	889	3082	12227	79591	•
Inventories 24	37	•	50	9	38	65	•	388	13125	3737	3170	•
Net Property, Plant and Equipment 25	3743	•	388	1604	3450	11172	•	35818	111229	298092	1910856	•
Total Assets 26	6270	•	657	2294	6145	15869	•	59296	153629	371534	3347566	•
Notes and Loans Payable 27	2429	•	278	1382	3987	5859	•	29030	72162	98370	1281946	•
All Other Liabilities 28	1510	•	85	744	1348	5820	•	10235	43377	147768	736243	•
Net Worth 29	2331	•	293	168	809	4190	•	20031	38090	125396	1329376	•

Selected Financial Ratios (Times to 1)

Current Ratio 30	1.0	•	2.8	2.6	0.5	1.5	•	1.1	1.7	1.1	0.8	•
Quick Ratio 31	0.5	•	1.7	2.5	0.4	0.9	•	0.7	0.6	0.7	0.4	•
Net Sales to Working Capital 32	•	•	4.3	4.1	•	8.1	•	16.1	3.8	34.2	•	•
Coverage Ratio 33	1.0	•	0.4	0.8	1.0	0.8	•	1.1	0.7	2.0	0.9	•
Total Asset Turnover 34	0.2	•	0.6	0.5	0.5	0.5	•	0.2	0.2	0.3	0.2	•
Inventory Turnover 35	9.7	•	2.4	51.4	28.7	43.0	•	9.2	0.6	10.2	43.6	•
Receivables Turnover 36	8.5	•	8.3	10.3	7.9	9.7	•	9.0	11.2	9.2	8.0	•
Total Liabilities to Net Worth 37	1.7	•	1.2	12.6	6.6	2.8	•	2.0	3.0	2.0	1.5	•
Current Assets to Working Capital 38	•	•	1.6	1.6	•	3.2	•	8.4	2.5	11.2	•	•
Current Liabilities to Working Capital 39	•	•	0.6	0.6	•	2.2	•	7.4	1.5	10.2	•	•
Working Capital to Net Sales 40	•	•	0.2	0.2	•	0.1	•	0.1	0.3	0.0	•	•
Inventory to Working Capital 41	•	•	0.6	0.0	•	0.1	•	0.5	1.3	1.9	•	•
Total Receipts to Cash Flow 42	5.3	•	3.3	4.2	5.4	8.3	•	6.2	10.8	5.6	7.1	•
Cost of Goods to Cash Flow 43	1.5	•	1.0	1.7	2.0	3.1	•	2.1	3.0	2.0	1.9	•
Cash Flow to Total Debt 44	0.1	•	0.3	0.1	0.1	0.1	•	0.0	0.0	0.1	0.0	•

Selected Financial Factors (in Percentages)

Debt Ratio 45	62.8	•	55.4	92.7	86.8	73.6	•	66.2	75.2	66.2	60.3	•
Return on Total Assets 46	2.3	•	0.8	2.0	2.1	2.0	•	2.4	1.5	2.9	2.2	•
Return on Equity Before Income Taxes 47	0.2	•	•	•	0.0	•	•	0.4	•	4.4	•	•
Return on Equity After Income Taxes 48	•	•	•	•	•	•	•	•	•	2.5	•	•
Profit Margin (Before Income Tax) 49	0.5	•	•	•	0.0	•	•	0.8	•	5.1	•	•
Profit Margin (After Income Tax) 50	•	•	•	•	•	•	•	•	•	2.9	•	•

Table II

Corporations with Net Income

WATER, SEWAGE AND OTHER SYSTEMS

MONEY AMOUNTS AND SIZE OF ASSETS IN THOUSANDS OF DOLLARS

Item Description for Accounting Period 7/04 Through 6/05	Total	Zero Assets	Under 500	500 to 1,000	1,000 to 5,000	5,000 to 10,000	10,000 to 25,000	25,000 to 50,000	50,000 to 100,000	100,000 to 250,000	250,000 to 500,000	500,000 to 2,500,000	2,500,000 and over
Number of Enterprises 1	2340	0	2028	55	163	45	22	13	3	0	0	4	0
Revenues ($ in Thousands)													
Net Sales 2	2324213	0	324584	69639	219716	179072	120288	154169	31489	0	0	874625	0
Interest 3	12805	0	2468	216	631	1836	104	636	1896	0	0	2552	0
Rents 4	7084	0	0	0	0	717	12	570	295	0	0	3561	0
Royalties 5	36	0	0	0	17	0	19	0	0	0	0	0	0
Other Portfolio Income 6	106439	0	20151	0	15143	16795	689	333	4925	0	0	45929	0
Other Receipts 7	31463	0	1065	111	1452	1710	783	2938	3044	0	0	9623	0
Total Receipts 8	2482040	0	348268	69966	236959	200130	121895	158646	41649	0	0	936290	0
Average Total Receipts 9	1061	·	172	1272	1454	4447	5541	12204	13883	·	·	234072	·
Operating Costs/Operating Income (%)													
Cost of Operations 10	37.4	·	3.8	69.8	48.6	39.8	31.0	51.6	46.0	·	·	45.4	·
Salaries and Wages 11	6.2	·	8.5	5.8	6.5	12.1	10.9	4.0	5.2	·	·	4.3	·
Taxes Paid 12	6.3	·	2.3	1.3	3.3	8.6	5.4	7.6	7.0	·	·	6.5	·
Interest Paid 13	5.0	·	0.7	0.1	2.7	2.8	4.4	3.3	15.1	·	·	7.2	·
Depreciation 14	14.7	·	13.2	0.1	5.4	9.8	10.8	10.6	13.3	·	·	19.0	·
Amortization and Depletion 15	0.3	·	0.0	·	0.1	0.1	0.1	0.8	0.2	·	·	0.5	·
Pensions and Other Deferred Comp. 16	1.3	·	0.9	·	0.9	0.2	0.3	1.8	0.2	·	·	1.9	·
Employee Benefits 17	2.1	·	0.3	·	1.3	0.9	2.8	1.1	3.6	·	·	3.2	·
Advertising 18	0.1	·	0.1	0.2	0.1	1.1	0.1	0.1	0.0	·	·	0.0	·
Other Expenses 19	18.2	·	44.7	15.4	20.5	29.1	18.0	13.1	26.7	·	·	8.1	·
Officers' Compensation 20	1.9	·	4.0	3.7	1.9	1.8	3.3	1.2	4.9	·	·	0.6	·
Operating Margin 21	6.4	·	21.5	3.7	8.8	·	13.0	4.9	·	·	·	3.2	·
Operating Margin Before Officers' Comp. 22	8.3	·	25.5	7.4	10.7	·	16.4	6.0	·	·	·	3.8	·

Selected Average Balance Sheet ($ in Thousands)

Net Receivables 23	113	17	237	146	627	689	1425	1106	21956
Inventories 24	21	0	488	12	1	68	104	17	3872
Net Property, Plant and Equipment 25	2147	65	27	1347	3809	11015	23979	32681	632147
Total Assets 26	2971	127	777	2078	5952	14664	31226	54329	879102
Notes and Loans Payable 27	874	15	392	724	2255	4370	7682	20058	265632
All Other Liabilities 28	964	20	427	346	1634	5881	13392	8670	287005
Net Worth 29	1134	92	-43	1008	2063	4413	10152	25601	326466

Selected Financial Ratios (Times to 1)

Current Ratio 30	1.5	3.5	1.7	2.4	0.8	1.7	1.6	1.1	1.6
Quick Ratio 31	1.0	3.5	0.6	2.2	0.7	1.4	1.2	0.8	0.7
Net Sales to Working Capital 32	8.4	4.1	4.0	4.5	•	5.9	7.4	12.3	7.8
Coverage Ratio 33	3.7	41.1	30.8	7.1	2.9	4.2	3.3	1.7	2.4
Total Asset Turnover 34	0.3	1.3	1.6	0.6	0.7	0.4	0.4	0.2	0.2
Inventory Turnover 35	17.7	•	1.8	56.1	1533.5	24.8	58.7	278.6	25.6
Receivables Turnover 36	7.1	8.4	3.9	6.5	11.3	6.5	7.7	•	•
Total Liabilities to Net Worth 37	1.6	0.4	•	1.1	1.9	2.3	2.1	1.1	1.7
Current Assets to Working Capital 38	3.1	1.4	2.4	1.7	•	2.5	2.8	9.1	2.8
Current Liabilities to Working Capital 39	2.1	0.4	1.4	0.7	•	1.5	1.8	8.1	1.8
Working Capital to Net Sales 40	0.1	0.2	0.2	0.2	•	0.2	0.1	0.1	0.1
Inventory to Working Capital 41	0.2	•	1.6	0.1	•	0.1	0.1	0.0	0.1
Total Receipts to Cash Flow 42	4.2	1.7	6.4	4.3	4.6	3.5	5.4	6.8	7.4
Cost of Goods to Cash Flow 43	1.6	0.1	4.5	2.1	1.8	1.1	2.8	3.1	3.4
Cash Flow to Total Debt 44	0.1	2.6	0.2	0.3	0.2	0.2	0.1	0.1	0.1

Selected Financial Factors (in Percentages)

Debt Ratio 45	61.8	28.0	105.6	51.5	65.3	69.9	67.5	52.9	62.9
Return on Total Assets 46	6.1	37.1	7.0	12.6	5.5	7.0	4.2	4.8	4.4
Return on Equity Before Income Taxes 47	11.5	50.3	•	22.3	10.4	17.8	9.0	4.1	6.9
Return on Equity After Income Taxes 48	9.5	46.8	•	16.4	9.6	16.0	7.6	2.4	5.6
Profit Margin (Before Income Tax) 49	13.2	28.8	4.2	16.7	5.4	14.4	7.7	9.9	10.3
Profit Margin (After Income Tax) 50	10.9	26.7	4.0	12.3	5.0	12.9	6.5	5.9	8.3

Table I

Corporations with and without Net Income

COMBINATION GAS AND ELECTRIC

MONEY AMOUNTS AND SIZE OF ASSETS IN THOUSANDS OF DOLLARS

Item Description for Accounting Period 7/04 Through 6/05	Total	Zero Assets	Under 500	500 to 1,000	1,000 to 5,000	5,000 to 10,000	10,000 to 25,000	25,000 to 50,000	50,000 to 100,000	100,000 to 250,000	250,000 to 500,000	500,000 to 2,500,000	2,500,000 and over
Number of Enterprises **1**	37	0	0	0	0	0	0	0	0	0	0	3	30

Revenues ($ in Thousands)

Net Sales **2**	177501413	0	0	0	0	0	0	0	0	0	0	1791668	175349739
Interest **3**	3108905	0	0	0	0	0	0	0	0	0	0	3035	3103177
Rents **4**	1147122	0	0	0	0	0	0	0	0	0	0	8652	1138111
Royalties **5**	48563	0	0	0	0	0	0	0	0	0	0	0	47020
Other Portfolio Income **6**	5662279	0	0	0	0	0	0	0	0	0	0	1939	5659912
Other Receipts **7**	6120538	0	0	0	0	0	0	0	0	0	0	32814	6086610
Total Receipts **8**	193588820	0	0	0	0	0	0	0	0	0	0	1838108	191384569
Average Total Receipts **9**	5232130	•	•	•	•	•	•	•	•	•	•	612703	6379486

Operating Costs/Operating Income (%)

Cost of Operations **10**	49.8	•	•	•	•	•	•	•	•	•	•	56.5	49.7
Salaries and Wages **11**	6.2	•	•	•	•	•	•	•	•	•	•	4.8	6.2
Taxes Paid **12**	4.6	•	•	•	•	•	•	•	•	•	•	5.7	4.6
Interest Paid **13**	8.0	•	•	•	•	•	•	•	•	•	•	6.0	8.0
Depreciation **14**	10.8	•	•	•	•	•	•	•	•	•	•	10.9	10.8
Amortization and Depletion **15**	0.8	•	•	•	•	•	•	•	•	•	•	1.9	0.8
Pensions and Other Deferred Comp. **16**	1.8	•	•	•	•	•	•	•	•	•	•	2.4	1.8
Employee Benefits **17**	1.3	•	•	•	•	•	•	•	•	•	•	1.5	1.3
Advertising **18**	0.1	•	•	•	•	•	•	•	•	•	•	0.2	0.1
Other Expenses **19**	23.6	•	•	•	•	•	•	•	•	•	•	16.9	23.7
Officers' Compensation **20**	0.3	•	•	•	•	•	•	•	•	•	•	0.4	0.3
Operating Margin **21**	•	•	•	•	•	•	•	•	•	•	•	•	•
Operating Margin Before Officers' Comp. **22**	•	•	•	•	•	•	•	•	•	•	•	•	•

Selected Average Balance Sheet ($ in Thousands)

Net Receivables 23	1046970	89277	1280740
Inventories 24	257442	19812	315298
Net Property, Plant and Equipment 25	6305019	751488	7688756
Total Assets 26	15252898	1341580	18654449
Notes and Loans Payable 27	5197802	433573	6359212
All Other Liabilities 28	4899452	485520	5983888
Net Worth 29	5155644	422488	6311350

Selected Financial Ratios (Times to 1)

Current Ratio 30	1.0	0.9	1.0
Quick Ratio 31	0.6	0.5	0.6
Net Sales to Working Capital 32	•	•	•
Coverage Ratio 33	1.2	0.2	1.2
Total Asset Turnover 34	0.3	0.4	0.3
Inventory Turnover 35	9.3	17.0	9.2
Receivables Turnover 36	3.2	7.4	3.2
Total Liabilities to Net Worth 37	2.0	2.2	2.0
Current Assets to Working Capital 38	•	•	•
Current Liabilities to Working Capital 39	•	•	•
Working Capital to Net Sales 40	•	•	•
Inventory to Working Capital 41	•	•	•
Total Receipts to Cash Flow 42	5.3	12.6	5.2
Cost of Goods to Cash Flow 43	2.6	7.1	2.6
Cash Flow to Total Debt 44	0.1	0.1	0.1

Selected Financial Factors (in Percentages)

Debt Ratio 45	66.2	68.5	66.2
Return on Total Assets 46	3.1	0.6	3.1
Return on Equity Before Income Taxes 47	1.7	•	1.7
Return on Equity After Income Taxes 48	0.5	•	0.5
Profit Margin (Before Income Tax) 49	1.8	•	1.9
Profit Margin (After Income Tax) 50	0.5	•	0.5

Table II

Corporations with Net Income

COMBINATION GAS AND ELECTRIC

MONEY AMOUNTS AND SIZE OF ASSETS IN THOUSANDS OF DOLLARS

Item Description for Accounting Period 7/04 Through 6/05	Total	Zero Assets	Under 500	500 to 1,000	1,000 to 5,000	5,000 to 10,000	10,000 to 25,000	25,000 to 50,000	50,000 to 100,000	100,000 to 250,000	250,000 to 500,000	500,000 to 2,500,000	2,500,000 and over
Number of Enterprises 1	25	0	0	0	0	0	0	0	0	0	0	0	21

Revenues ($ in Thousands)

Item Description for Accounting Period 7/04 Through 6/05	Total	Zero Assets	Under 500	500 to 1,000	1,000 to 5,000	5,000 to 10,000	10,000 to 25,000	25,000 to 50,000	50,000 to 100,000	100,000 to 250,000	250,000 to 500,000	500,000 to 2,500,000	2,500,000 and over
Net Sales 2	126994399	0	0	0	0	0	0	0	0	0	0	0	126037132
Interest 3	1051231	0	0	0	0	0	0	0	0	0	0	0	1047282
Rents 4	940907	0	0	0	0	0	0	0	0	0	0	0	939142
Royalties 5	39984	0	0	0	0	0	0	0	0	0	0	0	38440
Other Portfolio Income 6	5369989	0	0	0	0	0	0	0	0	0	0	0	5368075
Other Receipts 7	5229649	0	0	0	0	0	0	0	0	0	0	0	5199536
Total Receipts 8	139626159	0	0	0	0	0	0	0	0	0	0	0	138629607
Average Total Receipts 9	5585046	•	•	•	•	•	•	•	•	•	•	•	6601410

Operating Costs/Operating Income (%)

Item Description for Accounting Period 7/04 Through 6/05	Total	Zero Assets	Under 500	500 to 1,000	1,000 to 5,000	5,000 to 10,000	10,000 to 25,000	25,000 to 50,000	50,000 to 100,000	100,000 to 250,000	250,000 to 500,000	500,000 to 2,500,000	2,500,000 and over
Cost of Operations 10	49.9	•	•	•	•	•	•	•	•	•	•	•	49.7
Salaries and Wages 11	6.5	•	•	•	•	•	•	•	•	•	•	•	6.5
Taxes Paid 12	4.5	•	•	•	•	•	•	•	•	•	•	•	4.5
Interest Paid 13	6.6	•	•	•	•	•	•	•	•	•	•	•	6.7
Depreciation 14	10.6	•	•	•	•	•	•	•	•	•	•	•	10.6
Amortization and Depletion 15	0.8	•	•	•	•	•	•	•	•	•	•	•	0.8
Pensions and Other Deferred Comp. 16	2.2	•	•	•	•	•	•	•	•	•	•	•	2.2
Employee Benefits 17	1.4	•	•	•	•	•	•	•	•	•	•	•	1.4
Advertising 18	0.1	•	•	•	•	•	•	•	•	•	•	•	0.1
Other Expenses 19	20.0	•	•	•	•	•	•	•	•	•	•	•	20.0
Officers' Compensation 20	0.3	•	•	•	•	•	•	•	•	•	•	•	0.3
Operating Margin 21	•	•	•	•	•	•	•	•	•	•	•	•	•
Operating Margin Before Officers' Comp. 22	•	•	•	•	•	•	•	•	•	•	•	•	•

Selected Average Balance Sheet ($ in Thousands)

Net Receivables 23	1129484
Inventories 24	196090
Net Property, Plant and Equipment 25	6231766
Total Assets 26	12668183
Notes and Loans Payable 27	4610342
All Other Liabilities 28	4885566
Net Worth 29	3172274

Selected Financial Ratios (Times to 1)

Current Ratio 30	1.0
Quick Ratio 31	0.6
Net Sales to Working Capital 32	
Coverage Ratio 33	2.1
Total Asset Turnover 34	0.4
Inventory Turnover 35	12.9
Receivables Turnover 36	5.3
Total Liabilities to Net Worth 37	3.0
Current Assets to Working Capital 38	
Current Liabilities to Working Capital 39	
Working Capital to Net Sales 40	
Inventory to Working Capital 41	
Total Receipts to Cash Flow 42	4.5
Cost of Goods to Cash Flow 43	2.2
Cash Flow to Total Debt 44	0.1

Selected Financial Factors (in Percentages)

Debt Ratio 45	75.0
Return on Total Assets 46	5.5
Return on Equity Before Income Taxes 47	11.5
Return on Equity After Income Taxes 48	8.6
Profit Margin (Before Income Tax) 49	7.2
Profit Margin (After Income Tax) 50	5.4

Selected Average Balance Sheet ($ in Thousands)

Net Receivables 23	1337407
Inventories 24	231634
Net Property, Plant and Equipment 25	7367326
Total Assets 26	14980092
Notes and Loans Payable 27	5454350
All Other Liabilities 28	5780541
Net Worth 29	3745201

Selected Financial Ratios (Times to 1)

Current Ratio 30	1.0
Quick Ratio 31	0.6
Net Sales to Working Capital 32	
Coverage Ratio 33	2.1
Total Asset Turnover 34	0.4
Inventory Turnover 35	12.9
Receivables Turnover 36	5.3
Total Liabilities to Net Worth 37	3.0
Current Assets to Working Capital 38	
Current Liabilities to Working Capital 39	
Working Capital to Net Sales 40	
Inventory to Working Capital 41	
Total Receipts to Cash Flow 42	4.4
Cost of Goods to Cash Flow 43	2.2
Cash Flow to Total Debt 44	0.1

Selected Financial Factors (in Percentages)

Debt Ratio 45	75.0
Return on Total Assets 46	5.6
Return on Equity Before Income Taxes 47	11.6
Return on Equity After Income Taxes 48	8.6
Profit Margin (Before Income Tax) 49	7.2
Profit Margin (After Income Tax) 50	5.4

24

Table I

Corporations with and without Net Income

CONSTRUCTION OF BUILDINGS

MONEY AMOUNTS AND SIZE OF ASSETS IN THOUSANDS OF DOLLARS

Item Description for Accounting Period 7/04 Through 6/05	Total	Zero Assets	Under 500	500 to 1,000	1,000 to 5,000	5,000 to 10,000	10,000 to 25,000	25,000 to 50,000	50,000 to 100,000	100,000 to 250,000	250,000 to 500,000	500,000 to 2,500,000	2,500,000 and over
Number of Enterprises 1	217787	30248	138554	18849	23898	3399	1945	504	217	90	35	35	12
Revenues ($ in Thousands)													
Net Sales 2	541781631	5756738	69935630	34132610	107919731	43711489	56874271	33445526	28179134	24149811	18543205	47791812	71341673
Interest 3	1174972	5763	16669	15414	59375	24032	30307	24435	20428	46976	32656	248076	650841
Rents 4	544101	6186	36198	31325	68355	43277	44987	28308	56988	32857	68234	95215	32172
Royalties 5	152893	2236	0	0	0	8	0	0	41	6102	286	107726	36492
Other Portfolio Income 6	1219719	184922	81969	84042	158380	36776	51762	35711	71689	62619	41273	258286	152288
Other Receipts 7	8456637	790997	687986	148033	735514	315800	504434	330423	332006	311331	425729	1227510	2646880
Total Receipts 8	553329953	6746842	70758452	34441424	108941355	44131382	57505761	33864403	28660286	24609696	19111383	49728625	74860346
Average Total Receipts 9	2541	223	511	1826	4559	12984	29566	67191	132075	273441	546040	1420818	6238362
Operating Costs/Operating Income (%)													
Cost of Operations 10	80.8	61.7	69.9	79.4	86.3	87.2	88.5	88.9	89.1	88.9	84.5	84.1	62.5
Salaries and Wages 11	3.8	8.0	6.2	3.4	2.9	2.4	2.5	2.6	2.8	2.7	3.8	4.2	5.3
Taxes Paid 12	1.1	1.5	1.8	1.5	1.0	0.9	0.7	0.7	0.6	0.6	0.8	1.0	1.4
Interest Paid 13	0.7	0.6	0.5	0.6	0.5	0.4	0.4	0.4	0.5	0.5	0.7	1.1	1.4
Depreciation 14	0.7	1.5	1.3	1.0	0.7	0.6	0.5	0.6	0.5	0.5	0.9	0.7	0.4
Amortization and Depletion 15	0.1	0.0	0.0	0.0	0.0	0.0	0.0	0.0	0.2	0.1	0.1	0.1	0.1
Pensions and Other Deferred Comp. 16	0.2	0.0	0.3	0.3	0.2	0.2	0.2	0.2	0.2	0.2	0.2	0.2	0.2
Employee Benefits 17	0.5	1.0	0.9	0.7	0.3	0.9	0.5	0.4	0.5	0.2	0.3	0.5	0.3
Advertising 18	0.3	0.5	0.3	0.4	0.2	0.2	0.2	0.2	0.2	0.3	0.5	0.3	0.7
Other Expenses 19	7.6	39.3	13.1	6.5	4.4	3.6	3.5	2.9	2.9	2.6	3.9	3.8	19.8
Officers' Compensation 20	2.0	1.8	4.7	3.5	2.4	1.8	1.5	1.2	1.0	0.7	0.9	0.9	0.6
Operating Margin 21	2.3	•	1.1	2.7	1.0	1.8	1.6	2.0	1.5	2.6	3.4	3.1	7.4
Operating Margin Before Officers' Comp. 22	4.3	•	5.8	6.2	3.4	3.6	3.0	3.1	2.5	3.3	4.3	4.0	8.0

Selected Average Balance Sheet ($ in Thousands)

Item													
Net Receivables 23	250	0	15	85	378	1618	4085	10337	21015	41167	81562	156628	536237
Inventories 24	335	0	16	199	510	1593	3029	6938	11429	41833	73746	255241	1862798
Net Property, Plant and Equipment 25	132	0	24	104	229	602	1382	3236	6628	15995	46678	147616	160195
Total Assets 26	1367	0	98	718	2157	6756	14859	34499	68059	152216	340022	942659	6373253
Notes and Loans Payable 27	529	0	62	382	969	2467	4931	10801	20269	41739	95108	239911	2746555
All Other Liabilities 28	480	0	26	202	800	2996	6653	15786	31764	66019	126697	357897	1434269
Net Worth 29	358	0	11	134	388	1293	3275	7913	16026	44458	118218	344850	2192429

Selected Financial Ratios (Times to 1)

Item													
Current Ratio 30	1.6	·	1.6	1.4	1.4	1.4	1.4	1.4	1.4	1.4	1.8	1.6	2.3
Quick Ratio 31	0.7	·	0.9	0.5	0.6	0.7	0.7	0.7	0.8	0.7	0.9	0.7	0.6
Net Sales to Working Capital 32	7.1	·	20.6	9.4	9.7	7.7	9.1	9.3	7.8	7.4	5.0	6.2	3.0
Coverage Ratio 33	7.7	3.3	5.8	6.8	4.6	7.2	7.9	9.5	7.9	9.4	10.9	7.6	9.8
Total Asset Turnover 34	1.8	·	5.2	2.5	2.1	1.9	2.0	1.9	1.9	1.8	1.6	1.4	0.9
Inventory Turnover 35	6.0	·	22.4	7.2	7.6	7.0	8.5	8.5	10.1	5.7	6.1	4.5	2.0
Receivables Turnover 36	10.5	·	34.6	21.9	12.2	8.7	7.6	7.1	6.5	7.6	6.2	8.2	12.4
Total Liabilities to Net Worth 37	2.8	·	8.2	4.4	4.6	4.2	3.5	3.4	3.2	2.4	1.9	1.7	1.9
Current Assets to Working Capital 38	2.7	·	2.6	2.8	3.6	3.3	3.7	3.8	3.3	3.3	2.2	2.6	1.8
Current Liabilities to Working Capital 39	1.7	·	1.6	1.8	2.6	2.3	2.7	2.8	2.3	2.3	1.2	1.6	0.8
Working Capital to Net Sales 40	0.1	·	0.0	0.1	0.1	0.1	0.1	0.1	0.1	0.1	0.2	0.2	0.3
Inventory to Working Capital 41	1.1	·	0.6	1.1	1.1	1.0	1.1	1.1	0.8	1.1	0.9	1.0	1.2
Total Receipts to Cash Flow 42	9.2	3.0	7.4	11.7	18.4	18.2	18.7	18.8	19.5	16.1	10.5	10.2	3.2
Cost of Goods to Cash Flow 43	7.4	1.9	5.2	9.3	15.9	15.9	16.6	16.7	17.3	14.3	8.8	8.6	2.0
Cash Flow to Total Debt 44	0.3	·	0.8	0.3	0.1	0.1	0.1	0.1	0.1	0.2	0.2	0.2	0.4

Selected Financial Factors (in Percentages)

Item													
Debt Ratio 45	73.8	·	89.1	81.3	82.0	80.9	78.0	77.1	76.5	70.8	65.2	63.4	65.6
Return on Total Assets 46	9.3	·	14.2	10.4	5.3	6.1	6.0	6.9	7.0	8.8	11.0	11.9	12.8
Return on Equity Before Income Taxes 47	31.0	·	107.5	47.3	23.0	27.4	23.8	26.8	26.0	27.0	28.8	28.2	33.4
Return on Equity After Income Taxes 48	25.1	·	105.1	45.8	21.6	25.9	22.6	24.7	25.1	24.6	26.5	21.3	21.9
Profit Margin (Before Income Tax) 49	4.5	1.3	2.3	3.5	2.0	2.8	2.7	3.2	3.2	4.5	6.4	7.1	12.3
Profit Margin (After Income Tax) 50	3.6	1.2	2.2	3.4	1.9	2.6	2.5	2.9	3.1	4.1	5.9	5.4	8.1

Table II

Corporations with Net Income

CONSTRUCTION OF BUILDINGS

MONEY AMOUNTS AND SIZE OF ASSETS IN THOUSANDS OF DOLLARS

Item Description for Accounting Period 7/04 Through 6/05	Total	Zero Assets	Under 500	500 to 1,000	1,000 to 5,000	5,000 to 10,000	10,000 to 25,000	25,000 to 50,000	50,000 to 100,000	100,000 to 250,000	250,000 to 500,000	500,000 to 2,500,000	2,500,000 and over
Number of Enterprises **1**	127243	15276	78845	13324	15192	2369	1523	390	170	79	31	32	12
Revenues ($ in Thousands)													
Net Sales **2**	435796536	4184210	4218358	27855534	75596776	33931319	48639637	28822436	23927028	22379233	16780446	38118886	71341673
Interest **3**	1100608	2862	9735	7950	38750	18021	23651	20198	14206	44170	32097	238125	650841
Rents **4**	416517	5918	17156	19087	25402	32045	29843	27018	34775	32684	68231	92185	32172
Royalties **5**	152892	2236	0	0	0	8	0	0	41	6102	286	107726	36492
Other Portfolio Income **6**	981130	182748	17947	43007	104355	23868	40467	30487	47442	58495	36256	243772	152288
Other Receipts **7**	7478479	852004	234952	134522	529997	234615	391963	304018	220045	348949	415322	1165215	2646880
Total Receipts **8**	445926162	5229978	4498148	28061100	76295280	34239876	49125561	29204157	24243537	22869633	17332638	39965909	74860346
Average Total Receipts **9**	3505	342	564	2106	5022	14453	32256	74882	142609	289489	559117	1248935	6238362
Operating Costs/Operating Income (%)													
Cost of Operations **10**	79.2	59.9	65.9	78.6	84.1	86.0	87.8	88.5	88.5	88.6	83.5	81.2	62.5
Salaries and Wages **11**	3.7	9.6	5.3	3.2	2.7	2.3	2.4	2.5	2.9	2.7	3.9	4.9	5.3
Taxes Paid **12**	1.1	1.7	1.6	1.4	1.0	0.8	0.7	0.6	0.6	0.6	0.8	1.2	1.4
Interest Paid **13**	0.7	0.4	0.4	0.6	0.5	0.4	0.3	0.3	0.4	0.5	0.7	1.3	1.4
Depreciation **14**	0.6	1.2	1.1	1.0	0.7	0.6	0.5	0.5	0.4	0.5	0.8	0.8	0.4
Amortization and Depletion **15**	0.1	0.0	0.0	0.0	0.0	0.0	0.0	0.0	0.3	0.0	0.1	0.2	0.1
Pensions and Other Deferred Comp. **16**	0.2	0.0	0.2	0.3	0.2	0.2	0.2	0.2	0.1	0.2	0.3	0.2	0.2
Employee Benefits **17**	0.4	1.1	0.5	0.5	0.3	0.9	0.5	0.4	0.5	0.2	0.3	0.4	0.3
Advertising **18**	0.3	0.5	0.3	0.3	0.2	0.2	0.2	0.2	0.2	0.3	0.5	0.4	0.7
Other Expenses **19**	7.5	34.4	13.0	5.9	4.1	3.3	2.8	2.8	2.2	2.4	4.1	4.2	19.8
Officers' Compensation **20**	1.8	1.7	4.8	3.4	2.4	1.8	1.5	1.1	1.0	0.8	1.0	1.1	0.6
Operating Margin **21**	4.4	•	6.8	4.8	3.7	3.5	3.2	2.9	2.9	3.1	4.0	4.2	7.4
Operating Margin Before Officers' Comp. **22**	6.2	•	11.5	8.2	6.1	5.3	4.7	4.0	3.9	3.9	5.0	5.2	8.0

Selected Average Balance Sheet ($ in Thousands)

Net Receivables 23	334	0	14	84	396	1669	4238	10817	21799	41458	83332	113117	536237
Inventories 24	504	0	17	191	586	1760	3211	7548	13180	43166	82352	274874	1862798
Net Property, Plant and Equipment 25	161	0	19	96	213	480	1208	2594	5832	15158	43597	156011	160195
Total Assets 26	1903		98	730	2161	6707	14881	34503	68777	152421	343842	906622	6373253
Notes and Loans Payable 27	699	0	44	373	896	2462	4492	9862	18764	40817	96324	248981	2746555
All Other Liabilities 28	630	0	20	197	729	2791	6598	15943	33113	66236	128872	312142	1434269
Net Worth 29	574	0	33	160	536	1454	3790	8698	16900	45369	118646	345498	2192429

Selected Financial Ratios (Times to 1)

Current Ratio 30	1.7	.	2.0	1.7	1.5	1.4	1.4	1.3	1.4	1.4	1.9	1.8	2.3
Quick Ratio 31	0.7	.	1.3	0.5	0.6	0.6	0.7	0.7	0.8	0.7	0.9	0.6	0.6
Net Sales to Working Capital 32	6.5	.	16.4	9.2	8.5	8.5	9.1	10.3	8.5	7.8	4.6	5.3	3.0
Coverage Ratio 33	11.0	39.6	20.0	11.0	10.1	11.7	13.6	13.4	12.9	11.4	12.2	7.7	9.8
Total Asset Turnover 34	1.8	.	5.7	2.9	2.3	2.1	2.1	2.1	2.0	1.9	1.6	1.3	0.9
Inventory Turnover 35	5.4	.	21.6	8.6	7.1	7.0	8.7	8.7	9.4	5.8	5.5	3.5	2.0
Receivables Turnover 36	10.8	.	41.0	25.2	13.9	9.3	8.1	7.5	6.9	8.3	6.5	8.4	12.4
Total Liabilities to Net Worth 37	2.3	.	1.9	3.6	3.0	3.6	2.9	3.0	3.1	2.4	1.9	1.6	1.9
Current Assets to Working Capital 38	2.5	.	2.0	2.5	3.0	3.4	3.5	3.9	3.3	3.3	2.1	2.3	1.8
Current Liabilities to Working Capital 39	1.5	.	1.0	1.5	2.0	2.4	2.5	2.9	2.3	2.3	1.1	1.3	0.8
Working Capital to Net Sales 40	0.2	.	0.1	0.1	0.1	0.1	0.1	0.1	0.1	0.1	0.2	0.2	0.3
Inventory to Working Capital 41	1.1	.	0.4	1.0	1.0	1.1	1.0	1.1	0.9	1.1	0.9	1.1	1.2
Total Receipts to Cash Flow 42	7.6	2.1	5.3	9.8	12.7	14.4	16.1	16.2	18.0	14.6	9.4	8.4	3.2
Cost of Goods to Cash Flow 43	6.0	1.3	3.5	7.7	10.7	12.4	14.2	14.3	15.9	12.9	7.9	6.8	2.0
Cash Flow to Total Debt 44	0.3	.	1.6	0.4	0.2	0.2	0.2	0.2	0.2	0.2	0.3	0.3	0.4

Selected Financial Factors (in Percentages)

Debt Ratio 45	69.8	.	65.9	78.1	75.2	78.3	74.5	74.8	75.4	70.2	65.5	61.9	65.6
Return on Total Assets 46	13.3	.	44.8	17.5	11.7	10.2	9.6	9.7	9.4	10.8	12.5	13.6	12.8
Return on Equity Before Income Taxes 47	40.1	.	124.7	72.5	42.6	43.2	35.1	35.5	35.5	33.1	33.3	31.0	33.4
Return on Equity After Income Taxes 48	33.9	.	123.4	70.7	41.0	41.3	33.8	33.0	34.4	30.4	30.6	23.5	21.9
Profit Margin (Before Income Tax) 49	6.7	14.4	7.4	5.5	4.6	4.4	4.2	4.2	4.3	5.3	7.3	9.0	12.3
Profit Margin (After Income Tax) 50	5.7	14.2	7.3	5.4	4.4	4.2	4.0	3.9	4.1	4.9	6.7	6.8	8.1

Table I

Corporations with and without Net Income

HEAVY AND CIVIL ENGINEERING CONSTRUCTION

MONEY AMOUNTS AND SIZE OF ASSETS IN THOUSANDS OF DOLLARS

Item Description for Accounting Period 7/04 Through 6/05	Total	Zero Assets	Under 500	500 to 1,000	1,000 to 5,000	5,000 to 10,000	10,000 to 25,000	25,000 to 50,000	50,000 to 100,000	100,000 to 250,000	250,000 to 500,000	500,000 to 2,500,000	2,500,000 and over
Number of Enterprises **1**	28340	1895	15057	4110	5070	1035	806	199	99	43	10	12	3
Revenues ($ in Thousands)													
Net Sales **2**	16756920	345688	11711636	8449912	31886311	14926580	24996212	12403622	11283302	9495922	5901552	16738146	15618036
Interest **3**	205510	312	6349	4393	17749	11178	19104	7961	13285	7740	14242	57189	46010
Rents **4**	145225	0	20474	9459	18034	2935	26018	14795	8739	2345	3928	19852	18645
Royalties **5**	82438	0	0	0	0	0	1139	1	167	8150	6488	7048	59444
Other Portfolio Income **6**	1366416	122824	132874	120654	164769	42893	116922	42851	42486	50062	11001	414850	104230
Other Receipts **7**	1890238	-4115	23158	8533	160572	112501	165810	111736	102832	163270	17680	419647	608615
Total Receipts **8**	16746747	1189491	11894491	8592951	32247435	15096087	25325205	12580966	11450811	9727489	5954891	17656732	16454980
Average Total Receipts **9**	5908	245	790	2091	6360	14586	31421	63221	115665	226221	595489	1471394	5484993
Operating Costs/Operating Income (%)													
Cost of Operations **10**	76.1	69.0	43.1	64.3	68.9	78.2	80.7	82.4	81.2	85.6	88.1	84.2	85.0
Salaries and Wages **11**	4.7	7.5	13.9	8.5	5.0	3.6	2.8	2.7	3.2	3.7	2.5	3.2	5.4
Taxes Paid **12**	1.9	3.1	3.4	3.0	2.3	1.9	1.6	1.5	1.6	1.0	0.9	1.8	0.9
Interest Paid **13**	0.7	0.5	0.7	0.9	0.6	0.5	0.5	0.5	0.6	1.1	1.0	0.9	0.8
Depreciation **14**	3.8	5.2	4.0	5.5	4.4	3.8	3.8	4.7	4.3	4.7	2.7	2.4	1.8
Amortization and Depletion **15**	0.2	0.1	0.0	0.0	0.0	0.0	0.0	0.1	0.2	0.3	0.3	0.7	0.5
Pensions and Other Deferred Comp. **16**	0.4	11.1	0.5	0.3	0.3	0.2	0.4	0.5	0.3	0.3	0.2	0.2	0.4
Employee Benefits **17**	1.2	1.2	1.4	1.1	1.0	2.1	1.3	1.1	1.2	1.1	0.9	0.9	1.2
Advertising **18**	0.1	0.1	0.4	0.3	0.1	0.1	0.1	0.1	0.1	0.1	0.1	0.1	0.1
Other Expenses **19**	8.9	20.9	22.3	10.8	13.8	7.0	6.4	5.0	6.1	5.6	3.8	5.7	6.4
Officers' Compensation **20**	2.3	1.7	9.2	3.6	3.3	1.8	1.7	1.4	1.0	1.0	0.6	0.7	0.7
Operating Margin **21**	•	•	1.0	1.7	0.4	0.7	0.8	0.1	0.2	•	•	•	•
Operating Margin Before Officers' Comp. **22**	2.0	•	10.3	5.3	3.6	2.6	2.5	1.5	1.3	•	•	•	•

Selected Average Balance Sheet ($ in Thousands)

Item													
Net Receivables 23	804	0	23	132	755	2452	5325	11597	19493	45239	90660	173763	687855
Inventories 24	106	0	4	15	105	455	419	899	2330	4751	10021	15278	217138
Net Property, Plant and Equipment 25	821	0	72	308	797	2081	4086	8811	19903	41892	82726	178404	979409
Total Assets 26	2971	0	174	673	2432	7216	15223	33574	67973	144694	313844	840893	4627766
Notes and Loans Payable 27	726	0	119	268	769	1805	3546	7602	15368	50058	73421	129109	525336
All Other Liabilities 28	1171	0	50	98	726	2443	5621	12929	21337	63860	109705	303525	3043650
Net Worth 29	1074	0	4	307	937	2969	6056	13044	31269	30776	130718	408258	1058780

Selected Financial Ratios (Times to 1)

Item													
Current Ratio 30	1.4	•	1.4	2.2	1.7	1.6	1.5	1.5	1.6	1.3	1.5	1.8	0.7
Quick Ratio 31	1.1	•	1.2	1.8	1.4	1.2	1.2	1.2	1.2	1.0	1.1	1.2	0.6
Net Sales to Working Capital 32	13.6	•	34.0	12.0	11.1	8.6	9.5	9.4	8.2	11.7	10.6	7.4	•
Coverage Ratio 33	3.9	26.9	5.1	4.6	3.5	4.5	5.1	4.0	3.9	•	0.8	6.4	3.9
Total Asset Turnover 34	1.9	•	4.5	3.1	2.6	2.0	2.0	1.9	1.7	1.5	1.9	1.7	1.1
Inventory Turnover 35	41.3	•	81.0	88.7	41.1	24.8	59.7	57.1	39.7	39.8	51.9	76.9	20.4
Receivables Turnover 36	6.8	•	35.1	16.8	8.2	5.4	6.1	5.6	5.8	5.5	5.6	6.3	5.4
Total Liabilities to Net Worth 37	1.8	•	41.2	1.2	1.6	1.4	1.5	1.6	1.2	3.7	1.4	1.1	3.4
Current Assets to Working Capital 38	3.8	•	3.3	1.8	2.4	2.7	3.0	3.1	2.7	4.2	3.1	2.2	•
Current Liabilities to Working Capital 39	2.8	•	2.3	0.8	1.4	1.7	2.0	2.1	1.7	3.2	2.1	1.2	•
Working Capital to Net Sales 40	0.1	•	0.0	0.1	0.1	0.1	0.1	0.1	0.1	0.1	0.1	0.1	•
Inventory to Working Capital 41	0.2	•	0.1	0.1	0.2	0.2	0.1	0.1	0.2	0.2	0.2	0.1	•
Total Receipts to Cash Flow 42	13.7	3.9	5.2	10.4	10.0	19.4	18.7	26.9	22.3	73.0	52.0	15.3	13.4
Cost of Goods to Cash Flow 43	10.4	2.7	2.2	6.7	6.9	15.2	15.1	22.1	18.1	62.5	45.8	12.9	11.4
Cash Flow to Total Debt 44	0.2	•	0.9	0.5	0.4	0.2	0.2	0.1	0.1	0.0	0.1	0.2	0.1

Selected Financial Factors (in Percentages)

Item													
Debt Ratio 45	63.9	•	97.6	54.4	61.5	58.9	60.2	61.1	54.0	78.7	58.3	51.4	77.1
Return on Total Assets 46	5.1	•	14.9	13.1	5.3	4.8	5.2	3.8	3.9	•	1.6	9.0	3.5
Return on Equity Before Income Taxes 47	10.6	•	504.2	22.5	10.0	9.0	10.5	7.4	6.2	•	•	15.7	11.5
Return on Equity After Income Taxes 48	9.0	•	488.6	21.2	9.0	7.6	9.3	6.7	5.5	•	•	12.0	10.3
Profit Margin (Before Income Tax) 49	2.0	14.0	2.7	3.4	1.5	1.9	2.0	1.6	1.7	•	•	4.6	2.3
Profit Margin (After Income Tax) 50	1.7	13.4	2.6	3.2	1.3	1.6	1.8	1.4	1.5	•	•	3.5	2.1

Table II

Corporations with Net Income

HEAVY AND CIVIL ENGINEERING CONSTRUCTION

MONEY AMOUNTS AND SIZE OF ASSETS IN THOUSANDS OF DOLLARS

Item Description for Accounting Period 7/04 Through 6/05	Total	Zero Assets	Under 500	500 to 1,000	1,000 to 5,000	5,000 to 10,000	10,000 to 25,000	25,000 to 50,000	50,000 to 100,000	100,000 to 250,000	250,000 to 500,000	500,000 to 2,500,000	2,500,000 and over
Number of Enterprises **1**	18387	1105	9550	3160	3029	717	575	135	70	29	0	0	0
Revenues ($ in Thousands)													
Net Sales **2**	118607092	208054	6908599	7102285	20853006	10910349	18880802	8780684	8130274	6094453	0	0	0
Interest **3**	149945	312	691	2958	10012	8808	14099	4610	11011	6081	0	0	0
Rents **4**	91459	0	3573	2529	12205	1910	12818	9945	7948	1360	0	0	0
Royalties **5**	69038	0	0	0	0	0	666	1	167	8150	0	0	0
Other Portfolio Income **6**	1084620	122085	103113	120576	119426	29740	81575	31216	27881	33190	0	0	0
Other Receipts **7**	1692021	1035	9886	8032	115591	104547	145287	89354	96172	137020	0	0	0
Total Receipts **8**	121694175	331486	7025862	7236380	21110240	11055354	19135247	8915810	8273453	6280254	0	0	0
Average Total Receipts **9**	6618	300	736	2290	6969	15419	33279	66043	118192	216560	·	·	·
Operating Costs/Operating Income (%)													
Cost of Operations **10**	74.9	45.6	34.0	63.4	65.2	76.8	79.2	80.7	80.8	81.0	·	·	·
Salaries and Wages **11**	4.5	9.9	16.4	8.7	4.6	3.5	2.8	2.6	3.4	3.7	·	·	·
Taxes Paid **12**	1.8	3.9	3.1	3.0	2.4	1.9	1.7	1.5	1.6	1.0	·	·	·
Interest Paid **13**	0.6	0.8	0.7	1.0	0.5	0.4	0.4	0.4	0.5	0.5	·	·	·
Depreciation **14**	3.5	6.7	3.0	5.3	3.9	3.3	3.6	4.7	3.9	4.8	·	·	·
Amortization and Depletion **15**	0.2	0.1	0.0	0.0	0.0	0.0	0.0	0.1	0.1	0.2	·	·	·
Pensions and Other Deferred Comp. **16**	0.4	18.4	0.3	0.3	0.4	0.2	0.4	0.6	0.3	0.3	·	·	·
Employee Benefits **17**	1.1	1.1	0.9	0.7	1.0	2.2	1.3	1.0	1.3	0.8	·	·	·
Advertising **18**	0.1	0.0	0.2	0.4	0.1	0.1	0.1	0.1	0.1	0.1	·	·	·
Other Expenses **19**	8.6	24.7	24.0	10.4	14.8	6.5	6.1	4.8	5.2	5.2	·	·	·
Officers' Compensation **20**	2.3	0.1	10.1	3.5	3.6	1.8	1.8	1.4	1.0	1.2	·	·	·
Operating Margin **21**	2.0	·	7.4	3.3	3.4	3.1	2.7	2.0	1.9	1.0	·	·	·
Operating Margin Before Officers' Comp. **22**	4.3	·	17.4	6.8	7.0	4.9	4.4	3.4	2.9	2.3	·	·	·

Selected Average Balance Sheet ($ in Thousands)

Net Receivables 23	865	0	24	143	739	2536	5710	11871	19666	42023
Inventories 24	83	0	0	17	105	244	388	774	2399	5694
Net Property, Plant and Equipment 25	868	0	46	317	781	1859	3897	8545	18563	42365
Total Assets 26	3209	0	142	683	2519	7265	15333	33380	69286	140644
Notes and Loans Payable 27	652	0	74	272	713	1453	3014	6334	13086	36456
All Other Liabilities 28	1230	0	60	93	807	2444	5619	12522	21484	37339
Net Worth 29	1328	0	8	317	999	3367	6699	14524	34716	66849

Selected Financial Ratios (Times to 1)

Current Ratio 30	1.5	•	1.7	2.4	1.8	1.7	1.6	1.5	1.7	1.8
Quick Ratio 31	1.2	•	1.5	2.0	1.4	1.4	1.3	1.3	1.3	1.4
Net Sales to Working Capital 32	11.5	•	23.2	12.0	10.7	7.6	8.6	8.9	7.4	6.2
Coverage Ratio 33	9.3	62.6	15.0	6.4	10.5	11.8	10.8	9.1	8.5	8.7
Total Asset Turnover 34	2.0	•	5.1	3.3	2.7	2.1	2.1	1.9	1.7	1.5
Inventory Turnover 35	58.1	•	240.9	82.7	42.8	47.9	67.1	67.8	39.1	29.9
Receivables Turnover 36	7.4	•	38.8	22.0	8.4	6.7	6.4	6.3	6.0	5.4
Total Liabilities to Net Worth 37	1.4	•	16.7	1.2	1.5	1.2	1.3	1.3	1.0	1.1
Current Assets to Working Capital 38	3.2	•	2.4	1.7	2.3	2.4	2.7	2.9	2.5	2.2
Current Liabilities to Working Capital 39	2.2	•	1.4	0.7	1.3	1.4	1.7	1.9	1.5	1.2
Working Capital to Net Sales 40	0.1	•	0.0	0.1	0.1	0.1	0.1	0.1	0.1	0.2
Inventory to Working Capital 41	0.2	•	0.0	0.2	0.2	0.2	0.1	0.1	0.1	0.1
Total Receipts to Cash Flow 42	10.4	1.6	3.6	9.1	7.4	13.5	14.0	18.4	17.2	14.4
Cost of Goods to Cash Flow 43	7.8	0.7	1.2	5.7	4.9	10.4	11.1	14.9	13.9	11.6
Cash Flow to Total Debt 44	0.3	•	1.5	0.7	0.6	0.3	0.3	0.2	0.2	0.2

Selected Financial Factors (in Percentages)

Debt Ratio 45	58.6	•	94.3	53.6	60.3	53.6	56.3	56.5	49.9	52.5
Return on Total Assets 46	10.4	•	50.3	20.4	13.9	10.0	9.5	7.7	7.0	6.9
Return on Equity Before Income Taxes 47	22.4	•	830.8	37.0	31.8	19.8	19.6	15.8	12.3	12.8
Return on Equity After Income Taxes 48	20.4	•	818.1	35.4	30.4	18.0	18.2	14.9	11.3	11.2
Profit Margin (Before Income Tax) 49	4.6	48.0	9.2	5.2	4.6	4.4	4.0	3.5	3.7	4.1
Profit Margin (After Income Tax) 50	4.2	46.9	9.1	5.0	4.4	4.0	3.7	3.3	3.4	3.6

28

Table I

Corporations with and without Net Income

LAND SUBDIVISION

MONEY AMOUNTS AND SIZE OF ASSETS IN THOUSANDS OF DOLLARS

Item Description for Accounting Period 7/04 Through 6/05	Total	Zero Assets	Under 500	500 to 1,000	1,000 to 5,000	5,000 to 10,000	10,000 to 25,000	25,000 to 50,000	50,000 to 100,000	100,000 to 250,000	250,000 to 500,000	500,000 to 2,500,000	2,500,000 and over
Number of Enterprises 1	45933	4214	27226	4008	8645	884	594	194	92	48	17	11	0
Revenues ($ in Thousands)													
Net Sales 2	41938324	408866	3702212	1592599	11591073	3960955	4820545	3959178	2203958	2595093	2097644	5006200	0
Interest 3	347493	1700	6578	282	51765	18715	18806	21978	32281	43527	41003	110857	0
Rents 4	580470	8240	17764	416	42452	20799	40841	43015	82984	49113	80790	194057	0
Royalties 5	4013	0	0	0	682	710	888	319	1414	0	0	0	0
Other Portfolio Income 6	846668	18673	11377	581	103928	78303	52288	27063	38925	54584	57226	403720	0
Other Receipts 7	2573695	18946	211865	4820	485446	194699	196787	158983	268306	242555	175765	615525	0
Total Receipts 8	46290663	456425	3949796	1598698	12275346	4274181	5130155	4210536	2627868	2984872	2452428	6330359	0
Average Total Receipts 9	1008	108	145	399	1420	4835	8637	21704	28564	62185	144260	575487	•
Operating Costs/Operating Income (%)													
Cost of Operations 10	71.8	79.8	66.0	54.1	76.8	74.1	75.4	73.0	62.7	67.6	62.8	73.5	•
Salaries and Wages 11	4.7	1.8	8.6	2.8	2.2	2.0	4.2	5.7	6.0	8.6	9.2	5.8	•
Taxes Paid 12	1.9	3.4	1.8	2.6	1.4	1.2	1.3	1.4	2.0	2.1	5.4	2.6	•
Interest Paid 13	3.4	3.7	1.6	2.7	2.4	3.6	2.4	3.8	5.2	4.3	6.5	5.5	•
Depreciation 14	1.6	3.5	1.0	0.9	0.9	0.9	1.6	2.1	4.7	2.9	2.1	1.9	•
Amortization and Depletion 15	0.1	0.6	0.0	0.0	0.0	0.1	0.1	0.2	0.2	0.2	0.5	0.2	•
Pensions and Other Deferred Comp. 16	0.4	•	0.6	0.2	0.7	0.1	0.2	0.2	0.3	0.5	0.4	0.0	•
Employee Benefits 17	0.5	0.3	1.0	0.3	0.3	0.2	0.4	0.3	0.4	0.8	1.4	0.9	•
Advertising 18	0.6	0.1	0.4	0.1	0.4	0.4	0.5	0.8	0.8	0.6	1.4	0.6	•
Other Expenses 19	10.8	33.2	11.8	9.8	9.1	10.9	8.5	7.6	17.2	15.8	15.6	10.1	•
Officers' Compensation 20	2.1	4.5	5.4	1.9	2.1	1.7	2.5	1.8	2.0	2.0	1.3	0.3	•
Operating Margin 21	2.0	•	1.8	24.6	3.8	4.9	2.9	3.2	•	2.0	•	•	•
Operating Margin Before Officers' Comp. 22	4.1	•	7.3	26.5	5.9	6.5	5.3	5.0	0.4	•	•	•	•

Selected Average Balance Sheet ($ in Thousands)

Item													
Net Receivables 23	146	0	7	54	223	390	1197	3106	4529	14289	17399	122254	•
Inventories 24	416	0	34	202	586	2719	3754	8969	13141	19300	62282	249969	•
Net Property, Plant and Equipment 25	398	0	32	137	498	1277	3697	8458	15896	40002	115173	204925	•
Total Assets 26	1740	0	142	721	2121	7186	15016	34561	68923	148708	348909	1220663	•
Notes and Loans Payable 27	992	0	136	405	1326	5104	9080	21378	32005	62660	220018	457657	•
All Other Liabilities 28	331	0	76	84	350	786	2405	5655	14208	29615	58470	257001	•
Net Worth 29	417	0	-70	232	445	1296	3530	7528	22709	56433	70421	506006	•

Selected Financial Ratios (Times to 1)

Item												
Current Ratio 30	1.9	•	1.2	3.1	1.8	2.2	2.0	1.9	2.6	1.9	1.8	1.8
Quick Ratio 31	0.6	•	0.4	0.6	0.5	0.6	0.6	0.6	0.8	0.8	0.6	0.7
Net Sales to Working Capital 32	2.2	•	11.0	1.4	2.5	1.9	1.9	2.3	1.2	1.9	2.3	2.0
Coverage Ratio 33	4.6	•	6.3	10.3	5.1	4.6	4.8	3.5	4.4	3.2	2.6	5.5
Total Asset Turnover 34	0.5	•	1.0	0.6	0.6	0.6	0.5	0.6	0.3	0.4	0.4	0.4
Inventory Turnover 35	1.6	•	2.6	1.1	1.8	1.2	1.6	1.7	1.1	1.9	1.2	1.3
Receivables Turnover 36	6.6	•	14.3	10.2	6.6	12.8	6.7	7.8	5.6	3.7	8.0	4.1
Total Liabilities to Net Worth 37	3.2	•	•	2.1	3.8	4.5	3.3	3.6	2.0	1.6	4.0	1.4
Current Assets to Working Capital 38	2.1	•	6.4	1.5	2.2	1.9	2.0	2.1	1.6	2.1	2.3	2.3
Current Liabilities to Working Capital 39	1.1	•	5.4	0.5	1.2	0.9	1.0	1.1	0.6	1.1	1.3	1.3
Working Capital to Net Sales 40	0.5	•	0.1	0.7	0.4	0.5	0.5	0.4	0.9	0.5	0.4	0.5
Inventory to Working Capital 41	1.1	•	2.9	0.8	1.1	1.0	1.0	1.1	0.7	0.7	1.5	1.3
Total Receipts to Cash Flow 42	5.0	•	5.6	3.0	5.9	4.8	6.6	6.4	3.2	4.6	4.6	3.6
Cost of Goods to Cash Flow 43	3.6	•	3.7	1.6	4.5	3.6	5.0	4.7	2.0	3.1	2.9	2.7
Cash Flow to Total Debt 44	0.1	•	0.1	0.3	0.1	0.2	0.1	0.1	0.2	0.1	0.1	0.2

Selected Financial Factors (in Percentages)

Item												
Debt Ratio 45	76.0	•	149.0	67.9	79.0	82.0	76.5	78.2	67.1	62.1	79.8	58.5
Return on Total Assets 46	8.3	•	9.7	15.3	7.7	10.2	6.3	7.9	7.9	5.0	5.9	11.4
Return on Equity Before Income Taxes 47	27.2	•	•	42.9	29.4	44.1	21.3	25.9	18.6	9.2	17.7	22.6
Return on Equity After Income Taxes 48	23.4	•	•	42.4	28.8	41.6	20.2	24.1	16.9	7.3	11.5	14.6
Profit Margin (Before Income Tax) 49	12.4	•	8.5	25.0	9.7	12.8	9.3	9.6	17.6	9.6	10.1	25.1
Profit Margin (After Income Tax) 50	10.7	•	8.4	24.7	9.5	12.0	8.8	8.9	16.0	7.7	6.6	16.2

Table II

Corporations with Net Income

LAND SUBDIVISION

MONEY AMOUNTS AND SIZE OF ASSETS IN THOUSANDS OF DOLLARS

Item Description for Accounting Period 7/04 Through 6/05	Total	Zero Assets	Under 500	500 to 1,000	1,000 to 5,000	5,000 to 10,000	10,000 to 25,000	25,000 to 50,000	50,000 to 100,000	100,000 to 250,000	250,000 to 500,000	500,000 to 2,500,000	2,500,000 and over
Number of Enterprises **1**	18408	852	9622	2116	4594	599	382	127	66	0	0	0	0
Revenues ($ in Thousands)													
Net Sales **2**	32894880	391857	2320801	1474988	7503237	3346831	3946695	3225543	1905796	0	0	0	0
Interest **3**	259603	701	4420	244	30751	15676	12618	12637	20425	0	0	0	0
Rents **4**	493225	8240	12203	416	34376	15876	34038	27914	65784	0	0	0	0
Royalties **5**	948	0	0	0	65	63	338	65	417	0	0	0	0
Other Portfolio Income **6**	796619	18493	7326	581	94416	74884	44178	17161	32100	0	0	0	0
Other Receipts **7**	2462356	119790	261454	3052	434373	189291	157733	133331	201421	0	0	0	0
Total Receipts **8**	36907631	539081	2606204	1479281	8097218	3642621	4195600	3417651	2225943	0	0	0	0
Average Total Receipts **9**	2005	633	271	699	1763	6081	10983	26911	33726	•	•	•	•
Operating Costs/Operating Income (%)													
Cost of Operations **10**	68.0	81.1	48.9	51.8	69.4	70.9	73.1	72.0	64.4	•	•	•	•
Salaries and Wages **11**	4.6	0.7	11.5	2.5	2.5	1.6	3.6	4.4	4.7	•	•	•	•
Taxes Paid **12**	1.9	2.6	1.6	2.2	1.6	1.3	1.2	1.3	1.7	•	•	•	•
Interest Paid **13**	2.9	1.0	1.8	1.9	2.0	3.5	1.9	1.7	3.3	•	•	•	•
Depreciation **14**	1.4	1.6	0.5	0.6	0.8	0.8	1.2	1.0	4.7	•	•	•	•
Amortization and Depletion **15**	0.1	0.4	0.0	0.0	0.0	0.1	0.1	0.1	0.2	•	•	•	•
Pensions and Other Deferred Comp. **16**	0.4	•	1.0	0.3	0.9	0.1	0.2	0.2	0.3	•	•	•	•
Employee Benefits **17**	0.5	0.2	1.1	0.3	0.3	0.1	0.3	0.2	0.2	•	•	•	•
Advertising **18**	0.5	0.1	0.6	0.0	0.5	0.4	0.5	0.7	0.6	•	•	•	•
Other Expenses **19**	8.9	12.1	10.9	9.3	7.9	11.0	6.6	5.2	10.4	•	•	•	•
Officers' Compensation **20**	2.0	0.7	6.4	1.7	2.5	1.8	2.4	1.8	1.8	•	•	•	•
Operating Margin **21**	8.7	•	15.8	29.3	11.6	8.4	8.9	11.3	7.5	•	•	•	•
Operating Margin Before Officers' Comp. **22**	10.8	0.2	22.2	31.1	14.1	10.2	11.3	13.1	9.3	•	•	•	•

Selected Average Balance Sheet ($ in Thousands)

Net Receivables 23	245	0	14	85	180	422	1161	3222	3117
Inventories 24	738	0	36	188	706	2520	4202	10662	14331
Net Property, Plant and Equipment 25	592	0	9	84	507	868	2942	7342	15758
Total Assets 26	2875	0	167	748	2146	7248	14963	34498	68890
Notes and Loans Payable 27	1444	0	74	450	1218	4574	8563	18634	32315
All Other Liabilities 28	445	0	9	95	275	686	2227	5229	11749
Net Worth 29	986	0	83	203	653	1988	4173	10635	24826

Selected Financial Ratios (Times to 1)

Current Ratio 30	2.1	·	3.3	3.2	2.0	2.2	2.1	1.9	2.7
Quick Ratio 31	0.7	·	1.2	0.7	0.6	0.5	0.5	0.6	0.7
Net Sales to Working Capital 32	2.2	·	3.3	2.1	2.6	2.2	2.1	2.6	1.2
Coverage Ratio 33	8.3	38.6	17.1	16.9	10.9	5.9	8.9	11.0	8.3
Total Asset Turnover 34	0.6	·	1.4	0.9	0.8	0.8	0.7	0.7	0.4
Inventory Turnover 35	1.6	·	3.3	1.9	1.6	1.6	1.8	1.7	1.3
Receivables Turnover 36	7.9	·	27.1	10.6	8.6	15.3	8.7	·	11.5
Total Liabilities to Net Worth 37	1.9	·	1.0	2.7	2.3	2.6	2.6	2.2	1.8
Current Assets to Working Capital 38	1.9	·	1.4	1.5	2.0	1.9	1.9	2.1	1.6
Current Liabilities to Working Capital 39	0.9	·	0.4	0.5	1.0	0.9	0.9	1.1	0.6
Working Capital to Net Sales 40	0.5	·	0.3	0.5	0.4	0.5	0.5	0.4	0.8
Inventory to Working Capital 41	1.0	·	0.6	0.9	1.1	1.1	1.0	1.1	0.8
Total Receipts to Cash Flow 42	3.8	2.3	2.8	2.7	3.9	4.0	5.1	4.7	3.2
Cost of Goods to Cash Flow 43	2.6	1.9	1.4	1.4	2.7	2.8	3.7	3.4	2.0
Cash Flow to Total Debt 44	0.3	·	1.0	0.5	0.3	0.3	0.2	0.2	0.2

Selected Financial Factors (in Percentages)

Debt Ratio 45	65.7	·	50.0	72.9	69.6	72.6	72.1	69.2	64.0
Return on Total Assets 46	14.8	·	43.3	29.4	16.4	16.0	11.9	13.9	11.6
Return on Equity Before Income Taxes 47	37.9	·	81.5	101.8	48.8	48.5	37.7	41.0	28.2
Return on Equity After Income Taxes 48	33.9	·	81.2	100.7	48.1	46.1	36.2	39.1	26.1
Profit Margin (Before Income Tax) 49	20.9	37.0	28.1	29.6	19.5	17.3	15.2	17.2	24.3
Profit Margin (After Income Tax) 50	18.7	33.6	28.0	29.3	19.2	16.4	14.6	16.4	22.4

Table I

Corporations with and without Net Income

ELECTRICAL CONTRACTORS

MONEY AMOUNTS AND SIZE OF ASSETS IN THOUSANDS OF DOLLARS

Item Description for Accounting Period 7/04 Through 6/05	Total	Zero Assets	Under 500	500 to 1,000	1,000 to 5,000	5,000 to 10,000	10,000 to 25,000	25,000 to 50,000	50,000 to 100,000	100,000 to 250,000	250,000 to 500,000	500,000 to 2,500,000	2,500,000 and over
Number of Enterprises 1	49872	5959	36840	2971	3205	601	226	47	14	6	3	0	0
Revenues ($ in Thousands)													
Net Sales 2	65023061	764242	15933901	5826075	16225113	9849898	7917624	3435424	2381747	1158111	1530924	0	0
Interest 3	53393	3	4712	1180	9829	3808	2352	460	324	6131	24593	0	0
Rents 4	17736	0	7384	1554	4823	1735	716	626	160	378	360	0	0
Royalties 5	1266	0	0	0	0	1266	0	0	0	0	0	0	0
Other Portfolio Income 6	80638	1476	40004	4498	12485	4151	5675	7524	1256	683	2885	0	0
Other Receipts 7	424226	42	47884	8904	46215	39249	22394	15027	17434	13339	213743	0	0
Total Receipts 8	65600320	765763	16033885	5842211	16298465	9900107	7948761	3459061	2400921	1178642	1772505	0	0
Average Total Receipts 9	1315	129	435	1966	5085	16473	35172	73597	171494	196440	590835	•	•
Operating Costs/Operating Income (%)													
Cost of Operations 10	67.0	59.1	45.7	62.5	73.5	75.4	77.8	79.2	79.7	81.8	71.1	•	•
Salaries and Wages 11	7.4	6.6	11.7	9.8	6.0	4.2	5.5	5.2	5.2	6.7	9.3	•	•
Taxes Paid 12	2.9	2.0	3.7	3.2	2.8	2.6	2.4	2.8	1.8	1.9	2.5	•	•
Interest Paid 13	0.6	0.2	0.5	0.4	0.4	0.5	0.3	0.5	0.1	1.8	5.5	•	•
Depreciation 14	1.7	2.2	2.3	1.6	1.4	1.4	1.0	1.1	1.1	1.7	5.0	•	•
Amortization and Depletion 15	0.1	•	0.1	0.0	0.0	0.0	0.0	0.1	0.0	0.2	1.5	•	•
Pensions and Other Deferred Comp. 16	0.5	0.0	0.4	0.8	0.4	0.7	0.6	0.4	0.7	0.1	0.2	•	•
Employee Benefits 17	2.8	0.6	1.7	2.1	2.6	5.2	3.8	2.4	2.4	2.1	1.7	•	•
Advertising 18	0.3	1.2	0.4	0.4	0.2	0.1	0.1	0.1	0.1	0.1	0.3	•	•
Other Expenses 19	9.8	16.5	19.3	10.1	6.5	4.8	4.7	5.1	4.3	4.3	23.3	•	•
Officers' Compensation 20	4.8	7.2	9.0	4.3	4.6	3.4	2.1	1.6	1.9	2.0	0.5	•	•
Operating Margin 21	2.2	4.4	5.1	4.8	1.5	1.7	1.6	1.4	2.8	•	•	•	•
Operating Margin Before Officers' Comp. 22	7.0	11.6	14.1	9.1	6.1	5.0	3.7	3.0	4.7	•	•	•	•

Selected Average Balance Sheet ($ in Thousands)

Net Receivables 23	224	0	21	298	972	3878	8283	16879	37505	47858	209470	•
Inventories 24	22	0	7	52	104	252	438	683	839	4548	21513	•
Net Property, Plant and Equipment 25	73	0	28	101	255	801	1284	3383	5058	18296	131050	•
Total Assets 26	495	0	90	663	1984	6985	14802	33674	66542	111119	766055	•
Notes and Loans Payable 27	128	0	40	192	332	1662	2537	6386	3991	38449	360905	•
All Other Liabilities 28	188	0	24	166	828	3095	6772	16189	34391	57347	126411	•
Net Worth 29	179	0	26	305	825	2227	5493	11099	28160	15323	278738	•

Selected Financial Ratios (Times to 1)

Current Ratio 30	1.6	•	1.6	2.3	1.7	1.5	1.6	1.5	1.7	1.3	1.5	•
Quick Ratio 31	1.3	•	1.3	1.9	1.3	1.2	1.3	1.2	1.4	0.9	1.1	•
Net Sales to Working Capital 32	9.3	•	22.0	6.8	8.2	9.1	7.3	8.0	7.1	13.7	3.5	•
Coverage Ratio 33	6.4	24.8	11.6	12.6	6.3	5.1	7.2	5.4	29.9	0.5	0.1	•
Total Asset Turnover 34	2.6	•	4.8	3.0	2.6	2.3	2.4	2.2	2.6	1.7	0.7	•
Inventory Turnover 35	39.8	•	29.2	23.4	35.6	49.1	62.3	84.8	161.8	34.7	16.9	•
Receivables Turnover 36	6.2	•	21.9	6.7	5.8	4.4	4.4	5.1	4.7	2.3	•	•
Total Liabilities to Net Worth 37	1.8	•	2.5	1.2	1.4	2.1	1.7	2.0	1.4	6.3	1.7	•
Current Assets to Working Capital 38	2.6	•	2.6	1.8	2.5	3.1	2.6	2.9	2.4	4.9	3.0	•
Current Liabilities to Working Capital 39	1.6	•	1.6	0.8	1.5	2.1	1.6	1.9	1.4	3.9	2.0	•
Working Capital to Net Sales 40	0.1	•	0.0	0.1	0.1	0.1	0.1	0.1	0.1	0.1	0.3	•
Inventory to Working Capital 41	0.1	•	0.3	0.2	0.1	0.1	0.1	0.1	0.0	0.1	0.1	•
Total Receipts to Cash Flow 42	9.1	5.1	4.5	7.9	14.4	18.0	19.3	19.7	16.2	61.6	6.6	•
Cost of Goods to Cash Flow 43	6.1	3.0	2.0	4.9	10.6	13.6	15.0	15.6	12.9	50.4	4.7	•
Cash Flow to Total Debt 44	0.5	•	1.5	0.7	0.3	0.2	0.2	0.2	0.3	0.0	0.2	•

Selected Financial Factors (in Percentages)

Debt Ratio 45	63.8	•	71.5	54.0	58.4	68.1	62.9	67.0	57.7	86.2	63.6	•
Return on Total Assets 46	9.7	•	30.3	16.3	6.1	6.3	5.5	5.6	9.4	1.6	0.3	•
Return on Equity Before Income Taxes 47	22.6	•	97.0	32.7	12.3	15.8	12.8	13.8	21.4	•	•	•
Return on Equity After Income Taxes 48	21.2	•	95.5	32.0	10.9	14.2	11.1	11.4	18.9	•	•	•
Profit Margin (Before Income Tax) 49	3.1	4.6	5.8	5.1	2.0	2.2	2.0	2.1	3.5	•	•	•
Profit Margin (After Income Tax) 50	2.9	4.5	5.7	5.0	1.8	1.9	1.7	1.7	3.1	•	•	•

Table II
Corporations with Net Income

ELECTRICAL CONTRACTORS

MONEY AMOUNTS AND SIZE OF ASSETS IN THOUSANDS OF DOLLARS

Item Description for Accounting Period 7/04 Through 6/05	Total	Zero Assets	Under 500	500 to 1,000	1,000 to 5,000	5,000 to 10,000	10,000 to 25,000	25,000 to 50,000	50,000 to 100,000	100,000 to 250,000	250,000 to 500,000	500,000 to 2,500,000	2,500,000 and over
Number of Enterprises **1**	30121	2772	22327	2068	2279	441	182	0	0	0	0	0	0
Revenues ($ in Thousands)													
Net Sales **2**	48643189	515863	11138842	424799	12771231	8094678	6576227	0	0	0	0	0	0
Interest **3**	15338	3	2131	1016	6696	2887	1959	0	0	0	0	0	0
Rents **4**	7221	0	517	1554	2549	1668	703	0	0	0	0	0	0
Royalties **5**	1266	0	0	0	0	1266	0	0	0	0	0	0	0
Other Portfolio Income **6**	63625	1476	38134	4168	9208	998	3424	0	0	0	0	0	0
Other Receipts **7**	166899	30	35898	8368	37948	32261	23581	0	0	0	0	0	0
Total Receipts **8**	48897538	517372	11215522	4239905	12827632	8133758	6605894	0	0	0	0	0	0
Average Total Receipts **9**	1623	187	502	2050	5629	18444	36296	·	·	·	·	·	·
Operating Costs/Operating Income (%)													
Cost of Operations **10**	65.9	48.1	41.5	59.2	73.1	75.6	76.8	·	·	·	·	·	·
Salaries and Wages **11**	7.2	7.6	11.9	9.1	6.2	4.2	5.4	·	·	·	·	·	·
Taxes Paid **12**	2.8	2.5	3.6	3.1	2.6	2.6	2.4	·	·	·	·	·	·
Interest Paid **13**	0.4	0.2	0.6	0.3	0.3	0.3	0.3	·	·	·	·	·	·
Depreciation **14**	1.5	2.6	2.3	1.7	1.3	1.2	0.9	·	·	·	·	·	·
Amortization and Depletion **15**	0.0	·	0.0	0.0	0.0	0.0	0.0	·	·	·	·	·	·
Pensions and Other Deferred Comp. **16**	0.5	0.0	0.3	1.0	0.4	0.7	0.6	·	·	·	·	·	·
Employee Benefits **17**	2.5	0.2	1.2	1.9	2.1	4.4	4.1	·	·	·	·	·	·
Advertising **18**	0.2	1.2	0.4	0.5	0.2	0.1	0.1	·	·	·	·	·	·
Other Expenses **19**	8.8	16.1	19.6	9.6	5.5	4.6	4.4	·	·	·	·	·	·
Officers' Compensation **20**	5.0	10.7	9.3	4.9	4.9	3.4	2.2	·	·	·	·	·	·
Operating Margin **21**	5.0	10.8	9.2	8.8	3.3	2.8	2.9	·	·	·	·	·	·
Operating Margin Before Officers' Comp. **22**	10.1	21.5	18.6	13.7	8.3	6.1	5.1	·	·	·	·	·	·

Selected Average Balance Sheet ($ in Thousands)

Net Receivables 23	258	0	20	264	1011	4050	8355
Inventories 24	19	0	5	54	66	221	382
Net Property, Plant and Equipment 25	77	0	34	107	236	746	1278
Total Assets 26	535	0	98	632	2024	6880	14770
Notes and Loans Payable 27	97	0	39	165	235	1227	1973
All Other Liabilities 28	216	0	23	127	908	3004	6704
Net Worth 29	222	0	36	340	882	2650	6094

Selected Financial Ratios (Times to 1)

Current Ratio 30	1.7	•	1.5	2.6	1.8	1.7	1.7
Quick Ratio 31	1.4	•	1.1	2.0	1.4	1.4	1.4
Net Sales to Working Capital 32	9.2	•	31.6	7.0	7.7	7.8	7.3
Coverage Ratio 33	16.4	72.0	17.9	29.8	15.8	10.3	13.0
Total Asset Turnover 34	3.0	•	5.1	3.2	2.8	2.7	2.4
Inventory Turnover 35	54.7	•	40.0	22.6	61.7	63.0	72.6
Receivables Turnover 36	7.0	•	23.8	10.6	6.7	4.8	4.6
Total Liabilities to Net Worth 37	1.4	•	1.7	0.9	1.3	1.6	1.4
Current Assets to Working Capital 38	2.4	•	3.1	1.6	2.3	2.5	2.5
Current Liabilities to Working Capital 39	1.4	•	2.1	0.6	1.3	1.5	1.5
Working Capital to Net Sales 40	0.1	•	0.0	0.1	0.1	0.1	0.1
Inventory to Working Capital 41	0.1	•	0.3	0.3	0.1	0.1	0.1
Total Receipts to Cash Flow 42	8.0	3.9	3.7	6.1	13.0	15.1	16.0
Cost of Goods to Cash Flow 43	5.3	1.9	1.5	3.6	9.5	11.4	12.3
Cash Flow to Total Debt 44	0.6	•	2.2	1.1	0.4	0.3	0.3

Selected Financial Factors (in Percentages)

Debt Ratio 45	58.5	•	63.2	46.2	56.4	61.5	58.7
Return on Total Assets 46	17.8	•	53.4	30.5	11.1	9.6	8.8
Return on Equity Before Income Taxes 47	40.3	•	137.1	54.8	23.8	22.4	19.8
Return on Equity After Income Taxes 48	38.5	•	135.4	54.0	22.0	20.6	17.9
Profit Margin (Before Income Tax) 49	5.5	11.1	9.9	9.1	3.7	3.2	3.3
Profit Margin (After Income Tax) 50	5.3	11.0	9.8	9.0	3.5	3.0	3.0

Table I

Corporations with and without Net Income

PLUMBING, HEATING, AND AIR-CONDITIONING CONTRACTORS

MONEY AMOUNTS AND SIZE OF ASSETS IN THOUSANDS OF DOLLARS

Item Description for Accounting Period 7/04 Through 6/05	Total	Zero Assets	Under 500	500 to 1,000	1,000 to 5,000	5,000 to 10,000	10,000 to 25,000	25,000 to 50,000	50,000 to 100,000	100,000 to 250,000	250,000 to 500,000	500,000 to 2,500,000	2,500,000 and over
Number of Enterprises **1**	65758	5632	51687	4122	3507	548	209	34	11	4	3	0	0
Revenues ($ in Thousands)													
Net Sales **2**	93398933	1104374	29729273	9110471	24626670	10630999	7359087	2989837	2260481	1363884	4813855	0	0
Interest **3**	31153	9	5363	5640	9894	3415	2785	1013	72	75	2887	0	0
Rents **4**	29881	67	2210	8077	12800	4150	992	1033	435	0	115	0	0
Royalties **5**	98	0	0	0	0	0	0	98	0	0	0	0	0
Other Portfolio Income **6**	174210	2807	65777	8272	32428	6520	4039	51369	1396	29	1572	0	0
Other Receipts **7**	176322	11328	35334	16271	74299	21472	29091	-34918	4200	5078	14171	0	0
Total Receipts **8**	94400597	1118585	29837957	9148731	24756091	10666556	7395994	3008432	2266584	1369066	4832600	0	0
Average Total Receipts **9**	1436	199	577	2219	7059	19465	35388	88483	206053	342266	1610867	·	·
Operating Costs/Operating Income (%)													
Cost of Operations **10**	66.8	48.4	49.8	61.8	74.4	77.1	80.4	84.0	77.8	79.0	83.9	·	·
Salaries and Wages **11**	8.3	9.1	13.0	7.2	6.5	5.0	4.9	5.3	8.0	8.2	4.5	·	·
Taxes Paid **12**	2.7	2.2	3.4	3.6	2.4	2.0	2.1	1.4	1.6	1.5	2.4	·	·
Interest Paid **13**	0.4	1.0	0.5	0.4	0.4	0.3	0.3	0.3	0.7	0.3	0.3	·	·
Depreciation **14**	1.5	2.7	2.1	2.0	1.2	1.1	0.8	0.7	0.6	0.9	0.5	·	·
Amortization and Depletion **15**	0.0	0.0	0.0	0.0	0.0	0.0	0.0	0.2	0.1	0.0	0.3	·	·
Pensions and Other Deferred Comp. **16**	0.5	0.2	0.5	0.5	0.5	0.8	0.4	0.6	0.1	0.1	0.2	·	·
Employee Benefits **17**	1.9	0.4	1.6	1.9	2.0	2.4	2.3	1.8	1.9	3.5	0.9	·	·
Advertising **18**	0.6	0.6	1.0	1.0	0.5	0.3	0.2	0.1	0.4	0.1	0.1	·	·
Other Expenses **19**	10.1	21.6	16.4	11.4	7.8	5.1	4.6	2.9	6.9	3.7	5.4	·	·
Officers' Compensation **20**	5.0	2.9	8.1	7.3	3.9	3.1	2.0	1.1	1.2	0.6	1.5	·	·
Operating Margin **21**	2.3	10.8	3.6	2.8	0.6	3.0	1.9	1.6	0.6	2.1	·	·	·
Operating Margin Before Officers' Comp. **22**	7.3	13.7	11.7	10.2	4.5	6.1	3.9	2.8	1.8	2.7	1.4	·	·

Selected Average Balance Sheet ($ in Thousands)

Net Receivables 23	198	0	22	256	1172	3969	8097	20901	43093	67899	454674	•
Inventories 24	22	0	8	44	126	306	531	2257	2339	5035	7080	•
Net Property, Plant and Equipment 25	61	0	29	145	268	835	1121	2934	5674	13647	26344	•
Total Assets 26	414	0	100	647	2130	7223	14379	35173	66847	144631	822873	•
Notes and Loans Payable 27	103	0	50	174	514	1113	2234	4654	19708	11697	57589	•
All Other Liabilities 28	200	0	29	210	1042	3935	9026	19171	40246	99541	543802	•
Net Worth 29	110	0	20	264	575	2175	3119	11347	6893	33392	221482	•

Selected Financial Ratios (Times to 1)

Current Ratio 30	1.5	•	1.7	2.1	1.4	1.5	1.5	1.4	1.6	1.1	1.1	•
Quick Ratio 31	1.2	•	1.4	1.8	1.2	1.2	1.2	1.1	1.1	1.1	0.9	•
Net Sales to Working Capital 32	13.3	•	23.2	8.7	13.6	9.0	8.5	8.8	14.0	7.5	24.6	•
Coverage Ratio 33	7.8	13.2	9.6	8.9	4.1	12.1	9.4	9.4	2.2	10.6	2.1	•
Total Asset Turnover 34	3.5	•	5.8	3.4	3.3	2.7	2.4	2.5	3.1	2.4	2.0	•
Inventory Turnover 35	43.1	•	35.4	30.8	41.5	48.9	53.3	32.7	68.4	53.5	190.1	•
Receivables Turnover 36	7.5	•	24.8	8.4	6.5	4.7	4.6	4.2	5.7	1.8	•	•
Total Liabilities to Net Worth 37	2.7	•	3.9	1.5	2.7	2.3	3.6	2.1	8.7	3.3	2.7	•
Current Assets to Working Capital 38	3.0	•	2.5	1.9	3.4	2.8	3.0	3.0	3.8	2.6	9.4	•
Current Liabilities to Working Capital 39	2.0	•	1.5	0.9	2.4	1.8	2.0	2.0	2.8	1.6	8.4	•
Working Capital to Net Sales 40	0.1	•	0.0	0.1	0.1	0.1	0.1	0.1	0.1	0.1	0.0	•
Inventory to Working Capital 41	0.2	•	0.3	0.1	0.3	0.2	0.2	0.2	0.2	0.1	0.1	•
Total Receipts to Cash Flow 42	9.4	3.3	5.6	8.1	14.8	14.5	18.0	45.2	15.4	21.9	26.4	•
Cost of Goods to Cash Flow 43	6.3	1.6	2.8	5.0	11.0	11.2	14.5	37.9	12.0	17.3	22.2	•
Cash Flow to Total Debt 44	0.5	•	1.3	0.7	0.3	0.3	0.2	0.1	0.2	0.1	0.1	•

Selected Financial Factors (in Percentages)

Debt Ratio 45	73.3	•	79.5	59.3	73.0	69.9	78.3	67.7	89.7	76.9	73.1	•
Return on Total Assets 46	10.8	•	25.7	12.5	5.0	9.7	6.7	6.2	4.9	6.4	1.4	•
Return on Equity Before Income Taxes 47	35.4	•	112.1	27.3	14.0	29.6	27.5	17.0	26.0	25.2	2.8	•
Return on Equity After Income Taxes 48	33.4	•	110.5	25.5	11.9	27.7	25.1	15.7	22.7	22.9	1.2	•
Profit Margin (Before Income Tax) 49	2.7	12.1	4.0	3.3	1.1	3.3	2.4	2.2	0.9	2.5	0.4	•
Profit Margin (After Income Tax) 50	2.6	12.1	3.9	3.0	1.0	3.1	2.2	2.0	0.8	2.2	0.2	•

Construction 238220

Table II

Corporations with Net Income

PLUMBING, HEATING, AND AIR-CONDITIONING CONTRACTORS

MONEY AMOUNTS AND SIZE OF ASSETS IN THOUSANDS OF DOLLARS

Item Description for Accounting Period 7/04 Through 6/05	Total	Zero Assets	Under 500	500 to 1,000	1,000 to 5,000	5,000 to 10,000	10,000 to 25,000	25,000 to 50,000	50,000 to 100,000	100,000 to 250,000	250,000 to 500,000	500,000 to 2,500,000	2,500,000 and over
Number of Enterprises 1	42392	3272	33027	2955	2423	508	167	0	0	0	0	0	0
Revenues ($ in Thousands)													
Net Sales 2	72735049	711663	21613589	6300069	18434989	10062708	6037607	0	0	0	0	0	0
Interest 3	22449	9	3760	3239	7322	3206	1580	0	0	0	0	0	0
Rents 4	19275	67	0	1629	12733	3399	971	0	0	0	0	0	0
Royalties 5	98	0	0	0	0	0	0	0	0	0	0	0	0
Other Portfolio Income 6	128372	240	42718	5212	18358	6291	3438	0	0	0	0	0	0
Other Receipts 7	117374	624	23126	11348	50423	19691	25908	0	0	0	0	0	0
Total Receipts 8	73022617	712603	21683193	6321497	18523825	10095295	6069504	0	0	0	0	0	0
Average Total Receipts 9	1723	218	657	2139	7645	19873	36344	•	•	•	•	•	•
Operating Costs/Operating Income (%)													
Cost of Operations 10	66.6	55.5	50.2	57.1	71.3	76.5	79.4	•	•	•	•	•	•
Salaries and Wages 11	7.7	3.6	11.3	7.9	7.3	5.0	4.9	•	•	•	•	•	•
Taxes Paid 12	2.6	1.7	3.2	3.9	2.4	2.0	2.1	•	•	•	•	•	•
Interest Paid 13	0.3	1.2	0.3	0.4	0.4	0.3	0.2	•	•	•	•	•	•
Depreciation 14	1.3	2.2	1.7	2.3	1.1	1.1	0.8	•	•	•	•	•	•
Amortization and Depletion 15	0.0	0.0	0.0	0.0	0.0	0.0	0.0	•	•	•	•	•	•
Pensions and Other Deferred Comp. 16	0.6	0.3	0.7	0.6	0.5	0.8	0.5	•	•	•	•	•	•
Employee Benefits 17	1.8	0.7	1.3	1.5	2.1	2.4	2.4	•	•	•	•	•	•
Advertising 18	0.5	0.1	0.7	1.0	0.5	0.3	0.2	•	•	•	•	•	•
Other Expenses 19	9.4	13.3	15.3	11.9	8.0	5.1	4.3	•	•	•	•	•	•
Officers' Compensation 20	4.9	1.8	8.2	7.9	4.0	3.0	2.1	•	•	•	•	•	•
Operating Margin 21	4.2	19.4	6.9	5.5	2.4	3.5	3.0	•	•	•	•	•	•
Operating Margin Before Officers' Comp. 22	9.2	21.2	15.1	13.4	6.4	6.5	5.2	•	•	•	•	•	•

Selected Average Balance Sheet ($ in Thousands)

Net Receivables 23	240	0	22	252	1236	4024	8172
Inventories 24	24	0	8	35	134	250	510
Net Property, Plant and Equipment 25	67	0	27	148	262	859	1115
Total Assets 26	493	0	102	639	2222	7296	14452
Notes and Loans Payable 27	102	0	39	180	542	1102	1817
All Other Liabilities 28	223	0	23	174	1019	3892	7508
Net Worth 29	168	0	40	285	661	2303	5126

Selected Financial Ratios (Times to 1)

Current Ratio 30	1.6	•	2.0	2.7	1.5	1.6	1.5
Quick Ratio 31	1.3	•	1.8	2.3	1.3	1.2	1.2
Net Sales to Working Capital 32	11.5	•	18.7	7.0	12.0	8.9	8.5
Coverage Ratio 33	14.9	17.3	25.2	14.0	8.6	14.3	15.7
Total Asset Turnover 34	3.5	•	6.4	3.3	3.4	2.7	2.5
Inventory Turnover 35	48.1	•	42.7	34.6	40.4	60.6	56.2
Receivables Turnover 36	7.8	•	27.9	8.3	6.9	5.6	4.5
Total Liabilities to Net Worth 37	1.9	•	1.6	1.2	2.4	2.2	1.8
Current Assets to Working Capital 38	2.6	•	2.0	1.6	2.9	2.8	2.9
Current Liabilities to Working Capital 39	1.6	•	1.0	0.6	1.9	1.8	1.9
Working Capital to Net Sales 40	0.1	•	0.1	0.1	0.1	0.1	0.1
Inventory to Working Capital 41	0.2	•	0.2	0.1	0.3	0.1	0.1
Total Receipts to Cash Flow 42	8.4	3.3	5.0	6.5	11.3	13.6	15.4
Cost of Goods to Cash Flow 43	5.6	1.9	2.5	3.7	8.0	10.4	12.3
Cash Flow to Total Debt 44	0.6	•	2.1	0.9	0.4	0.3	0.3

Selected Financial Factors (in Percentages)

Debt Ratio 45	65.9	•	60.9	55.3	70.2	68.4	64.5
Return on Total Assets 46	17.3	•	48.1	21.0	11.2	11.2	9.5
Return on Equity Before Income Taxes 47	47.3	•	118.1	43.6	33.1	32.9	25.0
Return on Equity After Income Taxes 48	45.3	•	116.8	41.3	30.4	30.9	23.2
Profit Margin (Before Income Tax) 49	4.6	19.6	7.2	5.8	2.9	3.8	3.5
Profit Margin (After Income Tax) 50	4.4	19.6	7.1	5.5	2.6	3.6	3.3

Table I

Corporations with and without Net Income

OTHER SPECIALTY TRADE CONTRACTORS

MONEY AMOUNTS AND SIZE OF ASSETS IN THOUSANDS OF DOLLARS

Item Description for Accounting Period 7/04 Through 6/05	Total	Zero Assets	Under 500	500 to 1,000	1,000 to 5,000	5,000 to 10,000	10,000 to 25,000	25,000 to 50,000	50,000 to 100,000	100,000 to 250,000	250,000 to 500,000	500,000 to 2,500,000	2,500,000 and over
Number of Enterprises **1**	314113	42015	239382	15204	14842	1564	831	176	65	27	7	0	0
Revenues ($ in Thousands)													
Net Sales **2**	334009620	5901741	118074690	40159526	86156003	24216522	27989021	12653874	9615268	7143403	2099570	0	0
Interest **3**	176231	6775	25060	17598	32610	9259	12785	14574	12986	10465	34119	0	0
Rents **4**	233918	12334	28971	6570	46195	5296	19676	15351	3440	28096	67989	0	0
Royalties **5**	10087	0	3489	0	0	740	3	2219	297	3319	19	0	0
Other Portfolio Income **6**	775422	77925	263324	68383	174513	24491	33526	29414	27354	56104	20383	0	0
Other Receipts **7**	1154631	11514	223746	197047	287349	93836	207453	62296	38306	21647	11445	0	0
Total Receipts **8**	336359909	6010289	118619280	40449124	86966670	24350144	28262464	12777728	9697651	7263034	2233525	0	0
Average Total Receipts **9**	1071	143	496	2660	5841	15569	34010	72601	149195	269001	319075	•	•
Operating Costs/Operating Income (%)													
Cost of Operations **10**	65.3	41.3	53.5	65.9	69.8	78.5	78.9	78.4	82.1	77.3	74.1	•	•
Salaries and Wages **11**	7.7	7.1	11.0	7.2	6.6	3.7	4.4	4.3	4.5	7.4	6.4	•	•
Taxes Paid **12**	2.3	2.1	2.8	2.5	2.4	1.8	1.8	1.6	1.4	1.5	1.1	•	•
Interest Paid **13**	0.5	0.9	0.5	0.4	0.5	0.4	0.5	0.6	0.7	1.9	3.8	•	•
Depreciation **14**	2.3	3.0	2.4	2.5	2.4	2.1	2.0	2.0	2.3	2.4	2.6	•	•
Amortization and Depletion **15**	0.1	0.2	0.0	0.3	0.0	0.0	0.0	0.1	0.2	0.6	1.5	•	•
Pensions and Other Deferred Comp. **16**	0.3	0.0	0.3	0.4	0.4	0.5	0.5	0.2	0.3	0.4	0.2	•	•
Employee Benefits **17**	1.3	1.1	1.0	1.0	1.8	1.4	1.6	1.4	1.3	0.8	1.1	•	•
Advertising **18**	0.4	0.5	0.6	0.4	0.5	0.1	0.2	0.2	0.2	0.1	0.2	•	•
Other Expenses **19**	12.9	32.8	18.0	13.3	10.3	6.3	6.8	8.5	5.4	6.3	14.7	•	•
Officers' Compensation **20**	4.5	7.6	6.8	4.8	3.5	2.8	1.7	1.3	1.2	1.2	0.8	•	•
Operating Margin **21**	2.1	3.5	3.1	1.3	1.9	2.4	1.5	1.4	0.5	0.1	•	•	•
Operating Margin Before Officers' Comp. **22**	6.6	11.0	9.9	6.1	5.4	5.3	3.2	2.7	1.7	1.2	1.2	•	•

Selected Average Balance Sheet ($ in Thousands)

	1	2	3	4	5	6	7	8	9	10	11	
Net Receivables 23	116	0	13	189	909	2994	6829	15169	30460	58717	72367	•
Inventories 24	15	0	4	39	107	355	597	1151	2288	3924	10369	•
Net Property, Plant and Equipment 25	73	0	29	198	437	1035	2353	5995	11900	29991	42488	•
Total Assets 26	318	0	77	693	2062	6765	14685	34007	68465	153437	433502	•
Notes and Loans Payable 27	108	0	49	227	595	1826	3177	8019	17942	37410	114040	•
All Other Liabilities 28	114	0	18	177	744	3194	6614	14816	30249	59627	158083	•
Net Worth 29	97	0	10	289	723	1745	4894	11172	20275	56400	161380	•

Selected Financial Ratios (Times to 1)

	1	2	3	4	5	6	7	8	9	10	11
Current Ratio 30	1.5	•	1.4	1.9	1.6	1.3	1.4	1.5	1.5	1.4	1.5
Quick Ratio 31	1.2	•	1.1	1.4	1.3	0.9	1.1	1.1	1.2	1.1	0.7
Net Sales to Working Capital 32	15.1	•	47.2	13.1	10.1	12.7	9.8	9.7	10.0	11.6	5.4
Coverage Ratio 33	6.2	7.2	8.4	5.6	5.8	8.5	6.4	5.3	2.8	1.9	1.0
Total Asset Turnover 34	3.3	•	6.4	3.8	2.8	2.3	2.3	2.1	2.2	1.7	0.7
Inventory Turnover 35	46.5	•	67.8	44.7	37.9	34.2	44.6	49.0	53.1	52.1	21.4
Receivables Turnover 36	9.6	•	37.3	12.1	6.9	5.7	5.3	5.3	5.1	4.7	3.8
Total Liabilities to Net Worth 37	2.3	•	6.4	1.4	1.9	2.9	2.0	2.0	2.4	1.7	1.7
Current Assets to Working Capital 38	3.0	•	3.5	2.1	2.6	4.2	3.2	3.2	3.1	3.7	3.2
Current Liabilities to Working Capital 39	2.0	•	2.5	1.1	1.6	3.2	2.2	2.2	2.1	2.7	2.2
Working Capital to Net Sales 40	0.1	•	0.0	0.1	0.1	0.1	0.1	0.1	0.1	0.1	0.2
Inventory to Working Capital 41	0.2	•	0.4	0.2	0.2	0.3	0.2	0.2	0.2	0.2	0.2
Total Receipts to Cash Flow 42	8.0	2.9	5.4	8.4	11.0	14.3	14.9	11.7	22.4	17.5	9.1
Cost of Goods to Cash Flow 43	5.2	1.2	2.9	5.6	7.7	11.2	11.7	9.2	18.3	13.5	6.7
Cash Flow to Total Debt 44	0.6	•	1.4	0.8	0.4	0.2	0.2	0.3	0.1	0.2	0.1

Selected Financial Factors (in Percentages)

	1	2	3	4	5	6	7	8	9	10	11
Debt Ratio 45	69.6	•	86.5	58.3	64.9	74.2	66.7	67.1	70.4	63.2	62.8
Return on Total Assets 46	11.3	•	26.2	9.4	8.5	7.8	6.7	6.2	4.3	6.2	2.6
Return on Equity Before Income Taxes 47	31.2	•	171.5	18.4	20.0	26.5	16.9	15.3	9.4	8.2	
Return on Equity After Income Taxes 48	29.4	•	168.1	17.5	18.6	24.1	15.2	13.4	6.9	6.3	
Profit Margin (Before Income Tax) 49	2.8	5.3	3.6	2.0	2.5	3.0	2.5	2.4	1.3	1.7	1.7
Profit Margin (After Income Tax) 50	2.7	5.1	3.5	1.9	2.3	2.7	2.2	2.1	0.9	1.3	1.3

Table II
Corporations with Net Income

OTHER SPECIALTY TRADE CONTRACTORS

MONEY AMOUNTS AND SIZE OF ASSETS IN THOUSANDS OF DOLLARS

Item Description for Accounting Period 7/04 Through 6/05	Total	Zero Assets	Under 500	500 to 1,000	1,000 to 5,000	5,000 to 10,000	10,000 to 25,000	25,000 to 50,000	50,000 to 100,000	100,000 to 250,000	250,000 to 500,000	500,000 to 2,500,000	2,500,000 and over
Number of Enterprises 1	203459	23352	155603	11856	10615	1191	645	127	45	0	0	0	0
Revenues ($ in Thousands)													
Net Sales 2	258459414	3812149	87177564	34825724	65146334	20792375	22862726	9749587	7154661	0	0	0	0
Interest 3	120998	6399	13872	13287	22853	5902	10295	11428	4556	0	0	0	0
Rents 4	163711	12334	14059	4622	23834	2108	18755	12497	1717	0	0	0	0
Royalties 5	6266	0	0	0	0	740	2	2219	7	0	0	0	0
Other Portfolio Income 6	548520	75448	163323	53269	140414	19264	22796	18083	18995	0	0	0	0
Other Receipts 7	904020	10890	141308	185320	182864	82484	182827	58135	31085	0	0	0	0
Total Receipts 8	260202929	3917220	87510126	35082222	65516299	20902873	23097401	9851949	7211021	0	0	0	0
Average Total Receipts 9	1279	168	562	2959	6172	17551	35810	77574	160245	·	·	·	·
Operating Costs/Operating Income (%)													
Cost of Operations 10	65.1	42.1	53.5	66.1	67.8	77.1	78.0	78.8	81.4	·	·	·	·
Salaries and Wages 11	7.2	6.8	9.9	7.2	6.7	3.8	4.5	4.1	4.1	·	·	·	·
Taxes Paid 12	2.2	1.7	2.6	2.4	2.4	1.7	1.8	1.6	1.5	·	·	·	·
Interest Paid 13	0.4	0.6	0.4	0.4	0.5	0.3	0.4	0.5	0.6	·	·	·	·
Depreciation 14	2.0	2.0	1.8	2.2	2.1	2.0	1.7	2.0	1.9	·	·	·	·
Amortization and Depletion 15	0.1	0.1	0.0	0.0	0.0	0.0	0.0	0.1	0.1	·	·	·	·
Pensions and Other Deferred Comp. 16	0.4	0.0	0.3	0.3	0.4	0.5	0.5	0.2	0.3	·	·	·	·
Employee Benefits 17	1.3	0.7	0.9	0.9	1.9	1.3	1.6	1.3	1.3	·	·	·	·
Advertising 18	0.4	0.3	0.6	0.3	0.4	0.1	0.2	0.2	0.2	·	·	·	·
Other Expenses 19	11.9	28.7	16.7	12.0	10.2	6.5	6.4	7.0	4.6	·	·	·	·
Officers' Compensation 20	4.3	6.5	6.4	4.2	3.7	2.8	1.8	1.3	1.3	·	·	·	·
Operating Margin 21	4.9	10.4	6.9	3.9	4.1	3.9	3.1	3.0	2.9	·	·	·	·
Operating Margin Before Officers' Comp. 22	9.1	17.0	13.3	8.1	7.8	6.7	4.9	4.3	4.1	·	·	·	·

Selected Average Balance Sheet ($ in Thousands)

Net Receivables 23	133	0	11	201	879	3348	7094	15642	31755
Inventories 24	16	0	30	113	331	577	1020		2817
Net Property, Plant and Equipment 25	74	0	25	187	409	1104	2162	5932	10969
Total Assets 26	350	0	76	701	2035	6619	14598	34317	68267
Notes and Loans Payable 27	99	0	35	190	552	1517	2714	7105	14482
All Other Liabilities 28	120	0	15	177	686	2895	6396	15231	30522
Net Worth 29	131	0	26	334	796	2207	5488	11981	23263

Selected Financial Ratios (Times to 1)

Current Ratio 30	1.7	•	1.8	2.0	1.8	1.5	1.5	1.5	1.6
Quick Ratio 31	1.3	•	1.5	1.6	1.4	1.2	1.2	1.2	1.3
Net Sales to Working Capital 32	13.3	•	32.5	13.2	9.2	10.6	9.0	9.4	9.0
Coverage Ratio 33	13.8	22.5	20.7	13.7	10.9	14.1	12.8	9.7	6.9
Total Asset Turnover 34	3.6	•	7.3	4.2	3.0	2.6	2.4	2.2	2.3
Inventory Turnover 35	50.6	•	72.4	65.1	37.0	40.7	47.9	59.3	45.9
Receivables Turnover 36	10.3	•	44.5	14.0	7.5	6.4	5.5	5.5	•
Total Liabilities to Net Worth 37	1.7	•	1.9	1.1	1.6	2.0	1.7	1.9	1.9
Current Assets to Working Capital 38	2.5	•	2.2	2.0	2.3	3.1	2.9	3.0	2.7
Current Liabilities to Working Capital 39	1.5	•	1.2	1.0	1.3	2.1	1.9	2.0	1.7
Working Capital to Net Sales 40	0.1	•	0.0	0.1	0.1	0.1	0.1	0.1	0.1
Inventory to Working Capital 41	0.2	•	0.2	0.2	0.2	0.2	0.2	0.1	0.2
Total Receipts to Cash Flow 42	7.0	2.6	4.8	7.5	9.1	11.7	12.1	11.4	16.0
Cost of Goods to Cash Flow 43	4.5	1.1	2.5	4.9	6.2	9.0	9.4	9.0	13.0
Cash Flow to Total Debt 44	0.8	•	2.3	1.1	0.5	0.3	0.3	0.3	0.2

Selected Financial Factors (in Percentages)

Debt Ratio 45	62.6	•	65.6	52.4	60.9	66.7	62.4	65.1	65.9
Return on Total Assets 46	21.7	•	56.0	21.1	15.4	12.6	10.9	10.2	9.8
Return on Equity Before Income Taxes 47	53.7	•	154.9	41.0	35.7	35.1	26.8	26.1	24.7
Return on Equity After Income Taxes 48	51.7	•	152.9	40.1	34.0	32.6	24.8	23.6	21.6
Profit Margin (Before Income Tax) 49	5.5	13.2	7.3	4.7	4.6	4.4	4.1	4.1	3.6
Profit Margin (After Income Tax) 50	5.3	12.9	7.2	4.6	4.4	4.1	3.8	3.7	3.2

Table I

Corporations with and without Net Income

ANIMAL FOOD AND GRAIN AND OILSEED MILLING

MONEY AMOUNTS AND SIZE OF ASSETS IN THOUSANDS OF DOLLARS

Item Description for Accounting Period 7/04 Through 6/05	Total	Zero Assets	Under 500	500 to 1,000	1,000 to 5,000	5,000 to 10,000	10,000 to 25,000	25,000 to 50,000	50,000 to 100,000	100,000 to 250,000	250,000 to 500,000	500,000 to 2,500,000	2,500,000 and over
Number of Enterprises **1**	1891	278	657	320	402	72	82	30	19	17	6	3	4
Revenues ($ in Thousands)													
Net Sales **2**	76110180	344371	237695	1016984	1614295	1548737	2975935	2605096	2551451	3828404	2863536	1824233	54699441
Interest **3**	421439	38	3	1578	1097	608	3560	2620	1620	3549	7073	18217	381474
Rents **4**	170935	0	570	2	84	43	2690	888	333	202	159	375	165589
Royalties **5**	332588	3	0	0	4075	0	456	0	25	220	459	36604	290745
Other Portfolio Income **6**	426338	10370	8418	12878	617	2642	4410	2815	1169	3692	181	65271	313868
Other Receipts **7**	1740779	-295	41322	3034	5759	8966	30753	27695	54299	22507	39946	6693	1500111
Total Receipts **8**	79202259	354487	288008	1034476	1625927	1560996	3017804	2639114	2608897	3855874	2911354	1951393	57351228
Average Total Receipts **9**	41884	1275	438	3233	4045	21680	36802	87970	137310	226975	485226	650464	14337807
Operating Costs/Operating Income (%)													
Cost of Operations **10**	76.9	78.0	73.0	73.7	77.9	79.4	78.8	81.3	82.6	74.0	71.6	82.6	76.6
Salaries and Wages **11**	3.3	6.0	19.0	3.7	6.1	7.5	5.3	3.8	3.9	4.6	3.9	1.3	2.8
Taxes Paid **12**	0.8	1.3	5.2	1.8	1.2	1.4	1.1	0.8	0.9	1.1	1.3	0.9	0.7
Interest Paid **13**	2.5	1.6	2.1	0.0	1.2	1.0	0.7	0.5	1.0	1.2	2.9	4.6	2.9
Depreciation **14**	2.4	2.1	1.4	0.5	2.3	2.5	3.1	2.3	2.5	3.4	4.5	2.6	2.3
Amortization and Depletion **15**	0.2	1.1	0.2	0.0	0.1	0.0	0.1	0.1	0.3	0.8	0.6	1.4	0.1
Pensions and Other Deferred Comp. **16**	0.6	2.6	•	0.6	0.1	0.2	0.2	0.5	0.2	0.4	1.3	0.7	0.6
Employee Benefits **17**	1.0	1.0	5.9	•	0.5	0.3	0.8	0.6	0.7	1.3	1.3	2.4	0.9
Advertising **18**	6.1	7.7	0.3	0.0	0.6	0.5	0.6	0.5	0.5	2.3	4.2	0.8	7.9
Other Expenses **19**	7.2	8.6	33.4	8.0	11.8	5.9	7.6	8.0	6.8	7.3	6.2	6.9	7.0
Officers' Compensation **20**	0.5	0.4	1.7	3.8	2.1	0.9	1.1	0.7	0.5	0.9	0.5	1.3	0.3
Operating Margin **21**	•	•	•	7.9	•	0.4	0.6	0.9	•	1.7	•	•	•
Operating Margin Before Officers' Comp. **22**	•	•	•	11.7	•	1.3	1.7	1.7	0.5	3.7	2.2	•	•

Selected Average Balance Sheet ($ in Thousands)

Net Receivables 23	2329	0	21	91	549	1767	2894	8420	14240	20739	64974	47055	592136
Inventories 24	3023	0	79	51	569	1300	2928	5955	12723	19057	36571	82258	968724
Net Property, Plant and Equipment 25	6700	0	74	11	801	3920	5914	10426	24618	57232	175705	203424	2027859
Total Assets 26	33023	0	165	647	2289	7814	15906	32863	73566	160244	375093	926085	12302012
Notes and Loans Payable 27	13483	0	165	4	1799	4124	4863	8703	23858	43795	106539	405198	5163271
All Other Liabilities 28	9437	0	65	68	628	1237	3456	10749	15351	51375	116802	176249	3609938
Net Worth 29	10103	0	-65	575	-138	2453	7587	13411	34357	65073	151751	344637	3528803

Selected Financial Ratios (Times to 1)

Current Ratio 30	1.1	•	1.1	8.2	1.3	2.3	1.7	1.7	1.5	1.6	1.1	1.1	1.0
Quick Ratio 31	0.5	•	0.5	6.3	0.6	1.4	1.0	1.0	0.7	0.9	0.7	0.5	0.4
Net Sales to Working Capital 32	61.9	•	88.1	6.5	15.1	10.5	10.7	12.2	12.2	9.8	35.8	39.4	•
Coverage Ratio 33	2.1	•	•	1534.8	•	2.2	4.1	5.5	3.3	4.0	2.2	1.6	2.1
Total Asset Turnover 34	1.2	•	2.2	4.9	1.8	2.8	2.3	2.6	1.8	1.4	1.3	0.7	1.1
Inventory Turnover 35	10.2	•	3.3	46.0	5.5	13.1	9.8	11.9	8.7	8.7	9.3	6.1	10.8
Receivables Turnover 36	17.1	•	6.4	43.9	8.4	10.8	12.3	11.9	9.5	11.7	6.8	6.6	23.9
Total Liabilities to Net Worth 37	2.3	•	•	0.1	•	2.2	1.1	1.5	1.1	1.5	1.5	1.7	2.5
Current Assets to Working Capital 38	11.3	•	16.9	1.1	4.5	1.8	2.4	2.5	3.1	2.6	9.8	9.2	•
Current Liabilities to Working Capital 39	10.3	•	15.9	0.1	3.5	0.8	1.4	1.5	2.1	1.6	8.8	8.2	•
Working Capital to Net Sales 40	0.0	•	0.0	0.2	0.1	0.1	0.1	0.1	0.1	0.1	0.0	0.0	•
Inventory to Working Capital 41	4.3	•	9.2	0.2	2.1	0.6	0.9	0.9	1.1	0.9	3.0	2.8	•
Total Receipts to Cash Flow 42	12.3	•	23.0	6.6	17.2	15.8	12.3	11.7	13.1	10.3	12.0	14.0	12.4
Cost of Goods to Cash Flow 43	9.5	•	16.8	4.9	13.4	12.6	9.7	9.5	10.8	7.6	8.6	11.5	9.5
Cash Flow to Total Debt 44	0.1	•	0.1	6.7	0.1	0.3	0.4	0.4	0.3	0.2	0.2	0.1	0.1

Selected Financial Factors (in Percentages)

Debt Ratio 45	69.4	•	139.3	11.1	106.0	68.6	52.3	59.2	53.3	59.4	59.5	62.8	71.3
Return on Total Assets 46	6.6	•	•	47.5	•	6.0	6.1	7.2	5.9	6.6	7.9	5.0	6.8
Return on Equity Before Income Taxes 47	11.5	•	118.3	53.4	89.8	10.6	9.7	14.5	8.7	12.2	10.5	5.3	12.3
Return on Equity After Income Taxes 48	7.7	•	118.3	53.2	90.8	7.5	8.4	13.1	6.5	10.3	7.8	2.3	8.1
Profit Margin (Before Income Tax) 49	2.9	•	•	9.7	•	1.2	2.0	2.2	2.2	3.5	3.3	3.0	3.2
Profit Margin (After Income Tax) 50	1.9	•	•	9.6	•	0.9	1.8	2.0	1.7	3.0	2.5	1.3	2.1

Table II
Corporations with Net Income

ANIMAL FOOD AND GRAIN AND OILSEED MILLING

MONEY AMOUNTS AND SIZE OF ASSETS IN THOUSANDS OF DOLLARS

Item Description for Accounting Period 7/04 Through 6/05	Total	Zero Assets	Under 500	500 to 1,000	1,000 to 5,000	5,000 to 10,000	10,000 to 25,000	25,000 to 50,000	50,000 to 100,000	100,000 to 250,000	250,000 to 500,000	500,000 to 2,500,000	2,500,000 and over
Number of Enterprises 1	833	0	400	0	174	27	64	19	14	12	0	0	4
Revenues ($ in Thousands)													
Net Sales 2	69038540	0	22280	0	576328	457375	2301517	1703378	1960806	3049492	0	0	54699441
Interest 3	417525	0	0	0	909	600	3164	682	949	2901	0	0	381474
Rents 4	167981	0	0	0	0	0	1143	301	321	92	0	0	165589
Royalties 5	327402	0	0	0	0	0	0	0	0	53	0	0	290745
Other Portfolio Income 6	412349	0	1163	0	396	1052	3947	1252	924	2900	0	0	313868
Other Receipts 7	1683893	0	16855	0	4215	8961	27235	12572	48308	19259	0	0	1500111
Total Receipts 8	72047690	0	40298	0	581848	467988	2337006	1718185	2011308	3074697	0	0	57351228
Average Total Receipts 9	86492	.	101	.	3344	17333	36516	90431	143665	256225	.	.	14337807
Operating Costs/Operating Income (%)													
Cost of Operations 10	76.5	.	48.3	.	78.3	73.2	77.0	78.1	81.0	73.0	.	.	76.6
Salaries and Wages 11	3.0	.	10.6	.	4.1	4.9	5.2	4.1	4.0	4.7	.	.	2.8
Taxes Paid 12	0.8	.	3.5	.	0.8	1.7	1.1	0.9	0.9	1.1	.	.	0.7
Interest Paid 13	2.5	.	2.2	.	0.2	0.8	0.6	0.3	1.0	0.8	.	.	2.9
Depreciation 14	2.4	.	5.4	.	1.7	1.9	2.8	2.6	1.9	3.0	.	.	2.3
Amortization and Depletion 15	0.2	.	0.1	.	0.0	0.0	0.1	0.1	0.2	0.7	.	.	0.1
Pensions and Other Deferred Comp. 16	0.6	.	.	.	0.0	0.5	0.3	0.6	0.2	0.4	.	.	0.6
Employee Benefits 17	1.0	.	0.4	.	0.3	0.5	0.9	0.8	0.7	1.4	.	.	0.9
Advertising 18	6.6	.	0.2	.	0.3	1.7	0.8	0.7	0.5	2.2	.	.	7.9
Other Expenses 19	7.0	.	97.8	.	9.7	10.5	7.8	7.1	7.9	7.5	.	.	7.0
Officers' Compensation 20	0.5	.	.	.	2.8	1.4	1.2	0.8	0.5	1.0	.	.	0.3
Operating Margin 21	.	.	.	.	1.8	3.0	2.2	3.9	1.3	4.3	.	.	.
Operating Margin Before Officers' Comp. 22	.	.	.	.	4.6	4.3	3.4	4.7	1.8	5.2	.	.	.

Selected Average Balance Sheet ($ in Thousands)

Net Receivables 23	4550	6	863	1200	3009	8095	13595	21999	592136
Inventories 24	6073	1	527	2902	2935	5945	13212	22446	968724
Net Property, Plant and Equipment 25	13583	69	1004	1315	5700	11026	21541	51798	2027859
Total Assets 26	70099	85	2843	6896	15894	32280	70285	156501	12302012
Notes and Loans Payable 27	27954	81	2153	2677	4335	7027	22825	35166	5163271
All Other Liabilities 28	20312	52	558	1273	3457	7207	14324	57192	3609938
Net Worth 29	21833	-48	132	2946	8102	18046	33137	64143	3528803

Selected Financial Ratios (Times to 1)

Current Ratio 30	1.1	0.2	2.8	3.4	1.9	2.0	1.7	1.8	1.0
Quick Ratio 31	0.5	0.2	1.8	1.8	1.1	1.2	0.8	1.0	0.4
Net Sales to Working Capital 32	57.9	•	3.6	4.7	9.2	10.3	9.7	8.8	•
Coverage Ratio 33	2.4	6.6	15.6	7.2	6.9	14.7	4.9	7.1	2.1
Total Asset Turnover 34	1.2	0.7	1.2	2.5	2.3	2.8	2.0	1.6	1.1
Inventory Turnover 35	10.4	41.9	4.9	4.3	9.4	11.8	8.6	8.3	10.8
Receivables Turnover 36	18.5	•	5.3	4.9	11.6	12.7	9.5	•	23.9
Total Liabilities to Net Worth 37	2.2	•	20.6	1.3	1.0	0.8	1.1	1.4	2.5
Current Assets to Working Capital 38	10.4	•	1.5	1.4	2.1	2.0	2.4	2.2	•
Current Liabilities to Working Capital 39	9.4	•	0.5	0.4	1.1	1.0	1.4	1.2	•
Working Capital to Net Sales 40	0.0	•	0.3	0.2	0.1	0.1	0.1	0.1	•
Inventory to Working Capital 41	4.0	•	0.6	0.6	0.8	0.8	0.9	0.8	•
Total Receipts to Cash Flow 42	11.5	1.0	9.4	7.5	9.9	9.6	9.7	8.6	12.4
Cost of Goods to Cash Flow 43	8.8	0.5	7.4	5.5	7.6	7.5	7.9	6.2	9.5
Cash Flow to Total Debt 44	0.1	0.4	0.1	0.6	0.5	0.7	0.4	0.3	0.1

Selected Financial Factors (in Percentages)

Debt Ratio 45	68.9	156.9	95.4	57.3	49.0	44.1	52.9	59.0	71.3
Return on Total Assets 46	7.3	9.5	3.5	14.8	9.9	14.1	9.6	9.5	6.8
Return on Equity Before Income Taxes 47	13.7	•	70.6	29.9	16.6	23.5	16.3	19.9	12.3
Return on Equity After Income Taxes 48	9.8	•	68.4	23.1	15.0	21.8	13.2	17.2	8.1
Profit Margin (Before Income Tax) 49	3.6	12.3	2.8	5.2	3.8	4.7	3.8	5.0	3.2
Profit Margin (After Income Tax) 50	2.6	12.3	2.7	4.0	3.4	4.4	3.1	4.3	2.1

38

Table I

Corporations with and without Net Income

SUGAR AND CONFECTIONERY PRODUCT

MONEY AMOUNTS AND SIZE OF ASSETS IN THOUSANDS OF DOLLARS

Item Description for Accounting Period 7/04 Through 6/05	Total	Zero Assets	Under 500	500 to 1,000	1,000 to 5,000	5,000 to 10,000	10,000 to 25,000	25,000 to 50,000	50,000 to 100,000	100,000 to 250,000	250,000 to 500,000	500,000 to 2,500,000	2,500,000 and over
Number of Enterprises 1	1180	17	832	119	105	28	33	11	15	7	4	4	4
Revenues ($ in Thousands)													
Net Sales 2	35589101	54912	770431	257395	380978	546962	1025374	472361	1704757	1704383	1159295	1951444	25560810
Interest 3	87087	174	0	0	645	438	356	337	294	50	12107	25392	47294
Rents 4	71144	4	0	0	0	385	875	2445	1572	30	100	38684	27048
Royalties 5	178486	0	0	0	0	0	106	598	4	1072	449	5871	170387
Other Portfolio Income 6	329986	101	0	0	3616	40	5177	289	518	0	202	33674	286370
Other Receipts 7	303420	0	290	1488	583	622	4756	2782	9770	-84	10910	53376	218925
Total Receipts 8	36559224	55191	770721	258883	385822	548447	1036644	478812	1716915	1705451	1183063	2108441	26310834
Average Total Receipts 9	30982	3247	926	2175	3674	19587	31413	43528	114461	243636	295766	527110	6577708
Operating Costs/Operating Income (%)													
Cost of Operations 10	52.1	78.9	60.5	70.3	52.0	69.7	75.9	74.6	67.8	76.8	63.6	69.9	45.3
Salaries and Wages 11	6.2	2.2	6.9	6.8	9.4	6.3	4.2	4.4	6.6	4.7	6.8	4.2	6.5
Taxes Paid 12	1.3	7.3	4.4	0.9	3.2	1.8	1.6	1.6	1.5	0.8	1.8	1.1	1.2
Interest Paid 13	2.7	10.4	0.0	0.4	1.6	1.1	0.7	1.9	1.0	1.9	7.8	1.8	2.9
Depreciation 14	3.3	2.1	3.5	0.7	4.2	1.5	3.6	3.4	2.7	3.5	4.5	3.6	3.3
Amortization and Depletion 15	0.8	•	0.0	0.1	1.0	0.0	0.5	0.2	0.2	0.3	2.6	0.1	0.9
Pensions and Other Deferred Comp. 16	2.5	0.9	•	3.5	1.1	0.8	0.2	0.2	0.7	0.3	0.9	1.3	3.1
Employee Benefits 17	1.7	0.3	•	1.3	1.1	0.4	1.1	1.3	1.8	1.7	2.0	1.2	1.9
Advertising 18	5.8	0.1	1.5	0.0	2.1	1.9	0.7	0.5	3.3	1.4	3.0	2.9	7.3
Other Expenses 19	21.6	80.7	15.4	10.7	13.7	10.4	8.6	10.6	10.6	8.5	10.9	16.3	25.4
Officers' Compensation 20	0.7	1.4	0.9	5.3	8.0	2.8	1.8	1.3	1.2	0.6	1.4	0.2	0.4
Operating Margin 21	1.3	•	6.8	0.1	2.6	3.3	1.1	•	2.5	•	•	•	2.0
Operating Margin Before Officers' Comp. 22	2.0	•	7.7	5.4	10.6	6.1	2.9	1.2	3.8	0.0	•	•	2.4

Selected Average Balance Sheet ($ in Thousands)

Net Receivables 23	5936	0	70	558	291	1642	2925	5576	11825	23477	49803	198300	1327816
Inventories 24	2964	0	28	170	426	1735	3330	10709	17950	38044	42776	124601	483236
Net Property, Plant and Equipment 25	6723	0	28	15	469	3181	5808	11284	21470	63047	100546	277372	1294730
Total Assets 26	38922	0	186	789	1860	7871	17049	31826	67453	166047	425341	869919	9249078
Notes and Loans Payable 27	16438	0	7	237	1029	3085	4182	14871	19657	74954	283708	164128	4064038
All Other Liabilities 28	12657	0	73	238	513	2078	3626	7763	14102	50060	-1212	303812	3189182
Net Worth 29	9827	0	106	314	318	2708	9241	9192	33695	41033	142845	401979	1995857

Selected Financial Ratios (Times to 1)

Current Ratio 30	0.7	•	2.2	2.3	1.5	1.9	1.6	2.1	1.8	2.0	0.9	1.5	0.6
Quick Ratio 31	0.4	•	1.8	1.7	0.6	1.0	0.8	0.8	0.8	0.8	0.4	0.8	0.4
Net Sales to Working Capital 32	•	•	10.9	5.2	10.1	9.9	10.8	4.6	7.4	7.0	•	3.7	•
Coverage Ratio 33	2.9	•	3787.1	2.8	3.4	4.3	4.2	1.6	4.3	0.7	0.6	4.0	3.1
Total Asset Turnover 34	0.8	•	5.0	2.7	2.0	2.5	1.8	1.3	1.7	1.5	0.7	0.6	0.7
Inventory Turnover 35	5.3	•	20.2	9.0	4.4	7.8	7.1	3.0	4.3	4.9	4.3	2.7	6.0
Receivables Turnover 36	6.1	•	•	3.9	11.9	•	10.9	7.6	10.1	10.7	5.5	2.7	6.1
Total Liabilities to Net Worth 37	3.0	•	0.8	1.5	4.9	1.9	0.8	2.5	1.0	3.0	2.0	1.2	3.6
Current Assets to Working Capital 38	•	•	1.9	1.8	3.1	2.1	2.8	1.9	2.3	2.0	•	3.1	•
Current Liabilities to Working Capital 39	•	•	0.9	0.8	2.1	1.1	1.8	0.9	1.3	1.0	•	2.1	•
Working Capital to Net Sales 40	0.1	•	0.1	0.2	0.1	0.1	0.1	0.2	0.1	0.1	•	0.3	•
Inventory to Working Capital 41	•	•	0.3	0.4	1.3	0.9	1.2	1.1	1.2	1.0	•	0.6	•
Total Receipts to Cash Flow 42	4.1	•	6.4	11.1	7.5	7.8	10.5	9.9	8.4	15.0	15.8	5.0	3.5
Cost of Goods to Cash Flow 43	2.2	•	3.9	7.8	3.9	5.5	7.9	7.4	5.7	11.5	10.1	3.5	1.6
Cash Flow to Total Debt 44	0.3	•	1.8	0.4	0.3	0.5	0.4	0.2	0.4	0.1	0.1	0.2	0.3

Selected Financial Factors (in Percentages)

Debt Ratio 45	74.8	•	43.1	60.1	82.9	65.6	45.8	71.1	50.0	75.3	66.4	53.8	78.4
Return on Total Assets 46	5.9	•	34.3	2.7	10.8	11.4	5.2	4.3	7.1	2.0	3.4	4.1	6.3
Return on Equity Before Income Taxes 47	15.3	•	60.4	4.4	44.4	25.5	7.4	5.8	10.9	•	•	6.6	19.8
Return on Equity After Income Taxes 48	9.9	•	60.4	3.9	33.6	21.4	6.2	5.1	9.2	•	•	3.9	12.9
Profit Margin (Before Income Tax) 49	5.0	•	6.9	0.6	3.9	3.5	2.2	1.2	3.2	•	•	5.4	6.2
Profit Margin (After Income Tax) 50	3.2	•	6.9	0.6	2.9	3.0	1.8	1.1	2.7	•	•	3.2	4.0

Table II

Corporations with Net Income

SUGAR AND CONFECTIONERY PRODUCT

MONEY AMOUNTS AND SIZE OF ASSETS IN THOUSANDS OF DOLLARS

Item Description for Accounting Period 7/04 Through 6/05	Total	Zero Assets	Under 500	500 to 1,000	1,000 to 5,000	5,000 to 10,000	10,000 to 25,000	25,000 to 50,000	50,000 to 100,000	100,000 to 250,000	250,000 to 500,000	500,000 to 2,500,000	2,500,000 and over
Number of Enterprises 1	1099	0	0	119	68	28	22	8	11	4	0	0	4
Revenues ($ in Thousands)													
Net Sales 2	3283992	0	0	257395	315644	546962	770266	321855	1370528	1334791	0	0	25560810
Interest 3	69101	0	0	0	576	438	200	337	161	5	0	0	47294
Rents 4	69643	0	0	0	0	385	278	1666	1572	5	0	0	27048
Royalties 5	171391	0	0	0	0	0	101	598	4	0	0	0	170387
Other Portfolio Income 6	301325	0	0	0	3616	40	5092	289	103	133	0	0	286370
Other Receipts 7	290065	0	0	1488	0	622	2811	2673	6508	4248	0	0	218925
Total Receipts 8	33585517	0	0	258883	319836	548447	777848	327418	1378876	1339182	0	0	26310834
Average Total Receipts 9	30560	•	•	2175	4703	19587	35398	40927	125352	334796	•	•	6577708
Operating Costs/Operating Income (%)													
Cost of Operations 10	50.2	•	•	70.3	52.1	69.7	75.7	71.7	66.4	70.9	•	•	45.3
Salaries and Wages 11	6.2	•	•	6.8	9.9	6.3	3.6	3.5	6.4	4.6	•	•	6.5
Taxes Paid 12	1.3	•	•	0.9	3.0	1.8	1.4	1.5	1.4	1.7	•	•	1.2
Interest Paid 13	2.5	•	•	0.4	1.9	1.1	0.4	2.1	0.6	1.7	•	•	2.9
Depreciation 14	3.2	•	•	0.7	4.7	1.5	2.9	3.2	2.5	3.8	•	•	3.3
Amortization and Depletion 15	0.7	•	•	0.1	1.2	0.0	0.1	0.2	0.1	0.3	•	•	0.9
Pensions and Other Deferred Comp. 16	2.6	•	•	3.5	0.5	0.8	0.3	0.2	0.7	0.5	•	•	3.1
Employee Benefits 17	1.7	•	•	1.3	1.3	0.4	1.0	1.5	1.9	1.9	•	•	1.9
Advertising 18	6.0	•	•	0.0	2.1	1.9	0.5	0.6	3.9	0.9	•	•	7.3
Other Expenses 19	22.5	•	•	10.7	13.0	10.4	8.5	12.4	11.0	9.1	•	•	25.4
Officers' Compensation 20	0.6	•	•	5.3	3.0	2.8	2.0	1.4	1.3	1.1	•	•	0.4
Operating Margin 21	2.3	•	•	0.1	7.4	3.3	3.6	1.6	3.9	3.5	•	•	2.0
Operating Margin Before Officers' Comp. 22	2.9	•	•	5.4	10.4	6.1	5.7	3.0	5.2	4.6	•	•	2.4

Selected Average Balance Sheet ($ in Thousands)

Net Receivables 23	5491	558	399	1642	3185	4708	13274	39782	1327816
Inventories 24	2662	135	529	1735	3209	10210	18317	48828	483236
Net Property, Plant and Equipment 25	6495	15	558	3181	5340	11580	23164	78503	1294730
Total Assets 26	38310	789	2242	7871	16450	31301	66141	201856	9249078
Notes and Loans Payable 27	16076	237	1354	3085	2822	13557	16466	110609	4064038
All Other Liabilities 28	12678	238	571	2078	3438	7103	13504	44153	3189182
Net Worth 29	9556	314	318	2708	10190	10641	36171	47094	1995857

Selected Financial Ratios (Times to 1)

Current Ratio 30	0.7	2.3	1.4	1.9	2.2	1.8	1.7	2.4	0.6
Quick Ratio 31	0.4	1.7	0.6	1.0	1.2	0.7	0.9	1.2	0.4
Net Sales to Working Capital 32	•	5.2	11.9	9.9	7.6	5.1	8.0	5.5	•
Coverage Ratio 33	3.4	2.8	5.5	4.3	13.4	2.6	8.0	3.3	3.1
Total Asset Turnover 34	0.8	2.7	2.1	2.5	2.1	1.3	1.9	1.7	0.7
Inventory Turnover 35	5.6	11.3	4.6	7.8	8.3	2.8	4.5	4.8	6.0
Receivables Turnover 36	6.5	5.8	10.9	•	11.5	7.0	9.9	•	6.1
Total Liabilities to Net Worth 37	3.0	1.5	6.0	1.9	0.6	1.9	0.8	3.3	3.6
Current Assets to Working Capital 38	•	1.8	3.4	2.1	1.9	2.2	2.4	1.7	•
Current Liabilities to Working Capital 39	•	0.8	2.4	1.1	0.9	1.2	1.4	0.7	•
Working Capital to Net Sales 40	•	0.2	0.1	0.1	0.1	0.2	0.1	0.2	•
Inventory to Working Capital 41	•	0.4	1.4	0.9	0.7	1.2	1.1	0.8	•
Total Receipts to Cash Flow 42	3.8	11.1	5.9	7.8	8.4	7.2	7.3	8.0	3.5
Cost of Goods to Cash Flow 43	1.9	7.8	3.1	5.5	6.3	5.2	4.8	5.7	1.6
Cash Flow to Total Debt 44	0.3	0.4	0.4	0.5	0.7	0.3	0.6	0.3	0.3

Selected Financial Factors (in Percentages)

Debt Ratio 45	75.1	60.1	85.8	65.6	38.1	66.0	45.3	76.7	78.4
Return on Total Assets 46	6.6	2.7	22.0	11.4	10.8	7.0	9.7	9.2	6.3
Return on Equity Before Income Taxes 47	18.7	4.4	127.1	25.5	16.1	12.6	15.5	27.3	19.8
Return on Equity After Income Taxes 48	12.8	3.9	110.4	21.4	14.5	11.7	13.4	23.0	12.9
Profit Margin (Before Income Tax) 49	6.0	0.6	8.7	3.5	4.7	3.3	4.5	3.9	6.2
Profit Margin (After Income Tax) 50	4.1	0.6	7.6	3.0	4.2	3.1	3.9	3.2	4.0

Table I
Corporations with and without Net Income

FRUIT AND VEGETABLE PRESERVING AND SPECIALTY FOOD

MONEY AMOUNTS AND SIZE OF ASSETS IN THOUSANDS OF DOLLARS

Item Description for Accounting Period 7/04 Through 6/05	Total	Zero Assets	Under 500	500 to 1,000	1,000 to 5,000	5,000 to 10,000	10,000 to 25,000	25,000 to 50,000	50,000 to 100,000	100,000 to 250,000	250,000 to 500,000	500,000 to 2,500,000	2,500,000 and over
Number of Enterprises 1	486	4	103	36	117	64	74	31	27	19	0	6	5
Revenues ($ in Thousands)													
Net Sales 2	39814984	670833	343	147907	652868	1412842	2180321	1696777	3154964	4602702	0	7613896	17681531
Interest 3	519833	3029	0	0	222	221	1636	1938	1821	3817	0	45966	461184
Rents 4	21635	0	0	0	201	82	1233	619	6379	3705	0	2561	6855
Royalties 5	449948	289	0	0	0	277	0	0	0	0	0	32418	416964
Other Portfolio Income 6	228555	1306	0	0	0	490	8583	20897	935	29582	0	12334	154428
Other Receipts 7	800730	843	0	1168	4327	9386	30767	28016	33467	59378	0	64311	569067
Total Receipts 8	41835685	676300	343	149075	657618	1423298	2222540	1748247	3197566	4699184	0	7771486	19290029
Average Total Receipts 9	86082	169075	3	4141	5621	22239	30034	56395	118428	247325	•	1295248	3858006
Operating Costs/Operating Income (%)													
Cost of Operations 10	68.4	77.3	67.3	83.6	76.1	65.5	73.7	76.9	76.5	72.6	•	59.4	67.8
Salaries and Wages 11	5.0	4.6	•	1.4	1.4	4.1	5.4	3.6	3.3	4.3	•	9.8	3.8
Taxes Paid 12	1.3	0.4	•	0.8	2.6	1.3	1.6	1.4	1.2	1.6	•	2.0	0.9
Interest Paid 13	3.1	4.7	•	0.6	0.4	0.5	1.5	1.5	1.4	1.1	•	3.0	4.6
Depreciation 14	2.8	3.7	•	4.4	1.5	1.1	2.7	3.0	3.2	4.1	•	3.6	2.1
Amortization and Depletion 15	1.0	6.0	•	0.5	0.0	1.7	0.2	0.2	0.3	0.2	•	1.6	1.2
Pensions and Other Deferred Comp. 16	0.6	0.0	•	•	1.1	0.1	0.2	0.2	0.3	0.2	•	0.5	0.8
Employee Benefits 17	1.4	0.6	•	0.5	3.3	1.9	1.1	1.1	2.4	1.2	•	2.2	0.9
Advertising 18	3.1	4.9	•	1.0	0.5	3.0	1.3	1.1	1.5	2.1	•	6.3	2.8
Other Expenses 19	14.6	9.6	62.4	5.5	6.4	20.7	11.1	11.3	8.6	10.0	•	12.3	18.6
Officers' Compensation 20	0.7	3.1	•	2.8	7.3	1.6	1.6	1.1	0.9	0.6	•	0.3	0.4
Operating Margin 21	•	•	•	•	•	•	•	•	0.3	2.0	•	•	•
Operating Margin Before Officers' Comp. 22	•	•	•	1.8	6.7	1.3	1.3	•	1.2	2.6	•	•	•

Selected Average Balance Sheet ($ in Thousands)

Line Item													
Net Receivables 23	19657	0	5	180	329	1493	2985	6083	10742	18178	•	76611	1581568
Inventories 24	10758	0	0	192	930	891	5054	10887	27353	56922	•	176844	292138
Net Property, Plant and Equipment 25	13886	0	0	361	384	1419	5294	11183	20977	65123	•	288476	465389
Total Assets 26	95575	0	5	938	1908	8993	16521	34779	72211	175073	•	1161457	6214120
Notes and Loans Payable 27	35337	0	1	229	289	3497	6197	14832	28281	45920	•	511022	2257428
All Other Liabilities 28	20608	0	0	467	387	1708	7236	8544	17958	45926	•	243387	1245204
Net Worth 29	39630	0	4	242	1232	3788	3088	11403	25973	83227	•	407048	2711488

Selected Financial Ratios (Times to 1)

Line Item													
Current Ratio 30	1.2	•	1.3	2.5	1.7	1.0	1.5	1.6	1.8		•	1.9	1.0
Quick Ratio 31	0.7	•	•	0.4	1.1	0.4	0.6	0.4	0.5		•	0.7	0.8
Net Sales to Working Capital 32	14.8	•	0.7	•	31.9	6.5	18.3	8.4	7.1	6.0	•	8.0	130.8
Coverage Ratio 33	2.5	•	0.5	1.3	•	2.1	2.2	2.1	4.7		•	1.3	2.9
Total Asset Turnover 34	0.9	•	0.7	4.4	2.9	2.5	1.8	1.6	1.6	1.4	•	1.1	0.6
Inventory Turnover 35	5.2	•	•	17.9	4.6	16.2	4.3	3.9	3.3	3.1	•	4.3	8.2
Receivables Turnover 36	4.4	•	•	45.7	10.7	•	10.0	9.2	10.9	13.1	•	17.8	2.4
Total Liabilities to Net Worth 37	1.4	0.3	2.9	0.5	1.4	4.3	2.0	1.8	1.1		•	1.9	1.3
Current Assets to Working Capital 38	6.3	1.0	4.5	1.7	2.5	68.2	2.9	2.6	2.3		•	2.1	77.5
Current Liabilities to Working Capital 39	5.3	•	3.5	0.7	1.5	67.2	1.9	1.6	1.3		•	1.1	76.5
Working Capital to Net Sales 40	0.1	1.4	0.0	0.2	0.1	0.0	0.1	0.1	0.2		•	0.1	0.0
Inventory to Working Capital 41	2.0	•	3.0	0.9	0.7	36.0	1.6	1.7	1.5		•	1.1	11.7
Total Receipts to Cash Flow 42	6.4	3.1	21.4	23.6	5.4	9.5	9.9	11.9	8.4		•	8.9	4.5
Cost of Goods to Cash Flow 43	4.4	2.1	17.9	18.0	3.5	7.0	7.6	9.1	6.1		•	5.3	3.1
Cash Flow to Total Debt 44	0.2	1.0	0.3	0.8	0.2	0.2	0.2	0.3			•	0.2	0.2

Selected Financial Factors (in Percentages)

Line Item													
Debt Ratio 45	58.5	•	22.7	74.2	35.5	57.9	81.3	67.2	64.0	52.5	•	65.0	56.4
Return on Total Assets 46	6.5	•	•	1.3	1.6	•	5.5	5.2	5.0	7.2	•	4.4	7.5
Return on Equity Before Income Taxes 47	9.4	•	•	0.6	•	15.3	8.5	7.3	11.9		•	3.2	11.3
Return on Equity After Income Taxes 48	6.0	•	•	•	•	13.0	6.3	5.6	7.9		•	1.2	7.5
Profit Margin (Before Income Tax) 49	4.5	•	•	0.1	•	1.6	1.8	1.6	4.1		•	1.0	8.6
Profit Margin (After Income Tax) 50	2.9	•	•	•	•	1.4	1.3	1.3	2.7		•	0.4	5.7

Table II

Corporations with Net Income

FRUIT AND VEGETABLE PRESERVING AND SPECIALTY FOOD

MONEY AMOUNTS AND SIZE OF ASSETS IN THOUSANDS OF DOLLARS

Item Description for Accounting Period 7/04 Through 6/05	Total	Zero Assets	Under 500	500 to 1,000	1,000 to 5,000	5,000 to 10,000	10,000 to 25,000	25,000 to 50,000	50,000 to 100,000	100,000 to 250,000	250,000 to 500,000	500,000 to 2,500,000	2,500,000 and over
Number of Enterprises 1	243	0	0	0	80	14	54	22	18	12	0	0	0
Revenues ($ in Thousands)													
Net Sales 2	30973466	0	0	0	566965	179116	1513395	1131173	2178768	3400235	0	0	0
Interest 3	508458	0	0	0	136	179	947	1679	692	3777	0	0	0
Rents 4	10923	0	0	0	201	70	873	584	666	3496	0	0	0
Royalties 5	443221	0	0	0	0	277	0	0	0	0	0	0	0
Other Portfolio Income 6	221611	0	0	0	0	487	5418	20605	833	28612	0	0	0
Other Receipts 7	690969	0	0	0	3732	3916	21612	20706	12073	56774	0	0	0
Total Receipts 8	32848648	0	0	0	571034	184045	1542245	1174747	2193032	3492894	0	0	0
Average Total Receipts 9	135180	·	·	·	7138	13146	28560	53398	121835	291074	·	·	·
Operating Costs/Operating Income (%)													
Cost of Operations 10	66.3	·	·	·	77.0	79.2	75.4	75.7	76.5	69.4	·	·	·
Salaries and Wages 11	5.2	·	·	·	1.6	2.4	4.1	3.8	2.8	4.7	·	·	·
Taxes Paid 12	1.3	·	·	·	2.2	1.3	1.7	1.3	1.1	1.8	·	·	·
Interest Paid 13	3.2	·	·	·	0.4	0.1	0.9	1.4	0.9	0.9	·	·	·
Depreciation 14	2.6	·	·	·	1.2	1.6	2.6	2.6	3.3	4.3	·	·	·
Amortization and Depletion 15	0.8	·	·	·	·	0.0	0.1	0.1	0.1	0.1	·	·	·
Pensions and Other Deferred Comp. 16	0.6	·	·	·	1.3	0.1	0.3	0.2	0.4	0.3	·	·	·
Employee Benefits 17	1.3	·	·	·	3.5	0.4	0.9	0.7	2.7	0.8	·	·	·
Advertising 18	3.4	·	·	·	0.5	0.7	0.9	0.7	0.7	2.2	·	·	·
Other Expenses 19	15.7	·	·	·	6.4	9.7	8.4	11.3	7.4	11.5	·	·	·
Officers' Compensation 20	0.6	·	·	·	5.5	1.8	1.6	1.3	1.0	0.5	·	·	·
Operating Margin 21	·	·	·	·	0.4	2.6	3.3	0.8	3.2	3.7	·	·	·
Operating Margin Before Officers' Comp. 22	·	·	·	·	5.9	4.4	4.9	2.1	4.2	4.1	·	·	·

Selected Average Balance Sheet ($ in Thousands)

Net Receivables 23	35821	355	871	2891	5752	12519	19772
Inventories 24	16485	1139	783	4873	10842	30831	60588
Net Property, Plant and Equipment 25	20799	299	2619	5208	10651	22290	73954
Total Assets 26	158683	2244	6873	16453	34368	73088	193728
Notes and Loans Payable 27	57127	390	134	5072	14099	24127	45847
All Other Liabilities 28	32330	514	522	6960	7365	17283	54541
Net Worth 29	69226	1339	6216	4421	12904	31678	93341

Selected Financial Ratios (Times to 1)

Current Ratio 30	1.1	2.4	7.6	1.1	1.5	1.8	1.6
Quick Ratio 31	0.7	0.9	5.8	0.4	0.6	0.5	0.5
Net Sales to Working Capital 32	17.7	6.7	4.1	35.1	7.9	6.1	7.4
Coverage Ratio 33	3.1	3.8	75.4	6.6	4.3	5.4	8.2
Total Asset Turnover 34	0.8	3.2	1.9	1.7	1.5	1.7	1.5
Inventory Turnover 35	5.1	4.8	12.9	4.3	3.6	3.0	3.2
Receivables Turnover 36	3.7	10.5	11.6	10.6	9.0	9.4	13.4
Total Liabilities to Net Worth 37	1.3	0.7	0.1	2.7	1.7	1.3	1.1
Current Assets to Working Capital 38	8.2	1.7	1.2	11.9	2.9	2.3	2.8
Current Liabilities to Working Capital 39	7.2	0.7	0.2	10.9	1.9	1.3	1.8
Working Capital to Net Sales 40	0.1	0.1	0.2	0.0	0.1	0.2	0.1
Inventory to Working Capital 41	2.3	1.1	0.2	6.6	1.6	1.5	1.7
Total Receipts to Cash Flow 42	5.4	19.8	7.4	8.2	8.2	10.3	6.4
Cost of Goods to Cash Flow 43	3.5	15.3	5.9	6.2	6.2	7.9	4.5
Cash Flow to Total Debt 44	0.3	0.4	2.6	0.3	0.3	0.3	0.4

Selected Financial Factors (in Percentages)

Debt Ratio 45	56.4	40.3	9.5	73.1	62.5	56.7	51.8
Return on Total Assets 46	8.1	4.7	10.1	10.4	9.1	7.8	10.6
Return on Equity Before Income Taxes 47	12.7	5.8	11.0	32.7	18.7	14.6	19.4
Return on Equity After Income Taxes 48	8.8	4.7	10.4	30.5	16.0	12.6	13.8
Profit Margin (Before Income Tax) 49	6.9	1.1	5.4	5.2	4.7	3.8	6.4
Profit Margin (After Income Tax) 50	4.8	0.9	5.0	4.8	4.0	3.3	4.5

Table I

Corporations with and without Net Income

DAIRY PRODUCT

MONEY AMOUNTS AND SIZE OF ASSETS IN THOUSANDS OF DOLLARS

Item Description for Accounting Period 7/04 Through 6/05	Total	Zero Assets	Under 500	500 to 1,000	1,000 to 5,000	5,000 to 10,000	10,000 to 25,000	25,000 to 50,000	50,000 to 100,000	100,000 to 250,000	250,000 to 500,000	500,000 to 2,500,000	2,500,000 and over
Number of Enterprises 1	850	138	385	0	141	60	61	29	18	8	4	6	0
Revenues ($ in Thousands)													
Net Sales 2	35025528	4452	186626	0	1493620	1747081	2684020	2782093	3187492	2862999	2956091	17121053	0
Interest 3	162693	637	180	0	632	976	1231	1665	2478	2367	4416	148109	0
Rents 4	10480	0	0	0	0	1413	2551	1313	993	495	0	3715	0
Royalties 5	5456	0	0	0	0	0	0	2693	0	8	0	2756	0
Other Portfolio Income 6	93192	88	2861	0	67477	92	3874	1425	1441	11467	2546	1919	0
Other Receipts 7	455325	261	0	0	39989	587	10797	9029	-18177	13482	5699	393661	0
Total Receipts 8	35752674	5438	189667	0	1601718	1750149	2702473	2798218	3174227	2890818	2968752	17671213	0
Average Total Receipts 9	42062	39	493	•	11360	29169	44303	96490	176346	361352	742188	2945202	•
Operating Costs/Operating Income (%)													
Cost of Operations 10	78.5	•	40.7	•	77.7	84.5	82.3	77.5	80.0	80.7	83.1	76.6	•
Salaries and Wages 11	4.6	•	24.3	•	8.0	3.3	4.4	7.2	4.1	3.7	2.1	4.6	•
Taxes Paid 12	1.0	3.7	3.5	•	1.9	1.0	1.0	1.2	0.9	0.9	0.8	0.9	•
Interest Paid 13	1.5	•	0.5	•	0.7	0.3	0.5	0.5	0.4	1.5	1.0	2.2	•
Depreciation 14	3.0	361.3	1.5	•	3.7	1.4	2.3	2.7	2.8	2.7	3.1	3.2	•
Amortization and Depletion 15	0.8	•	0.3	•	0.0	0.0	0.1	0.1	0.1	0.9	0.1	1.3	•
Pensions and Other Deferred Comp. 16	0.4	•	2.1	•	0.3	0.3	0.3	0.5	0.5	0.4	0.2	0.3	•
Employee Benefits 17	1.1	16.6	2.3	•	2.2	0.6	0.9	1.2	1.0	1.4	0.8	1.1	•
Advertising 18	1.7	•	2.9	•	0.2	1.0	0.7	0.5	1.4	1.9	3.0	2.1	•
Other Expenses 19	8.2	668.4	22.3	•	10.0	5.0	5.2	6.7	6.2	7.1	5.9	9.7	•
Officers' Compensation 20	0.6	•	8.6	•	1.4	2.2	1.0	0.7	0.5	0.3	0.2	0.4	•
Operating Margin 21	•	•	•	•	•	0.5	1.3	1.2	2.2	•	•	•	•
Operating Margin Before Officers' Comp. 22	•	•	•	•	2.7	2.7	2.2	1.9	2.7	•	•	•	•

Selected Average Balance Sheet ($ in Thousands)

Net Receivables 23	4410	0	19	•	796	2173	3621	7930	13264	23361	50790	402527	•
Inventories 24	2505	0	4	•	646	1105	2794	5143	13659	23728	45569	171911	•
Net Property, Plant and Equipment 25	7100	0	19	•	1225	2198	5400	14670	25402	54406	149670	579487	•
Total Assets 26	27961	0	187	•	3174	6322	15692	35620	70209	163530	315900	2840329	•
Notes and Loans Payable 27	8426	0	98	•	1074	919	4870	10152	13830	99316	144663	784038	•
All Other Liabilities 28	8202	0	22	•	863	2444	3735	10512	17168	44149	92098	855172	•
Net Worth 29	11333	0	67	•	1237	2959	7087	14956	39212	20066	79139	1201120	•

Selected Financial Ratios (Times to 1)

Current Ratio 30	1.1	•	1.9	•	1.5	1.7	1.7	1.4	1.9	1.4	1.4	0.9	•
Quick Ratio 31	0.7	•	1.7	•	0.9	1.1	0.9	0.8	1.0	0.9	0.7	0.6	•
Net Sales to Working Capital 32	40.9	•	8.6	•	15.9	18.5	12.5	20.7	10.8	16.6	21.0	•	•
Coverage Ratio 33	1.5	•	•	•	2.8	3.4	4.7	4.4	5.1	0.6	1.2	1.4	•
Total Asset Turnover 34	1.5	•	2.6	•	3.3	4.6	2.8	2.7	2.5	2.2	2.3	1.0	•
Inventory Turnover 35	12.9	•	44.7	•	12.7	22.3	13.0	14.5	10.4	12.2	13.5	12.7	•
Receivables Turnover 36	11.1	•	41.5	•	15.5	12.9	12.0	12.0	14.5	14.4	15.9	9.3	•
Total Liabilities to Net Worth 37	1.5	•	1.8	•	1.6	1.1	1.2	1.4	0.8	7.1	3.0	1.4	•
Current Assets to Working Capital 38	8.7	•	2.2	•	2.8	2.5	2.4	3.7	2.1	3.7	3.4	•	•
Current Liabilities to Working Capital 39	7.7	•	1.2	•	1.8	1.5	1.4	2.7	1.1	2.7	2.4	•	•
Working Capital to Net Sales 40	0.0	•	0.1	•	0.1	0.1	0.0	0.0	0.1	0.1	0.0	•	•
Inventory to Working Capital 41	2.6	•	0.1	•	1.1	0.7	0.9	1.1	0.9	1.1	1.4	•	•
Total Receipts to Cash Flow 42	13.6	•	12.5	•	13.1	21.0	17.1	14.7	14.2	20.9	19.5	11.1	•
Cost of Goods to Cash Flow 43	10.7	•	5.1	•	10.2	17.8	14.0	11.4	11.3	16.8	16.2	8.5	•
Cash Flow to Total Debt 44	0.2	•	0.3	•	0.4	0.4	0.3	0.3	0.4	0.1	0.2	0.2	•

Selected Financial Factors (in Percentages)

Debt Ratio 45	59.5	•	64.5	•	61.0	53.2	54.8	58.0	44.2	87.7	74.9	57.7	•
Return on Total Assets 46	3.3	•	•	•	6.4	4.3	6.9	6.2	5.5	1.9	2.9	3.1	•
Return on Equity Before Income Taxes 47	2.9	•	•	•	10.6	6.5	12.1	11.5	8.0	•	1.8	2.2	•
Return on Equity After Income Taxes 48	1.6	•	•	•	10.5	3.3	10.7	10.2	5.5	•	1.8	1.0	•
Profit Margin (Before Income Tax) 49	0.8	•	•	•	1.2	0.7	1.9	1.8	1.8	•	0.2	0.9	•
Profit Margin (After Income Tax) 50	0.4	•	•	•	1.2	0.3	1.7	1.6	1.2	•	0.2	0.4	•

43

Table II

Corporations with Net Income

DAIRY PRODUCT

MONEY AMOUNTS AND SIZE OF ASSETS IN THOUSANDS OF DOLLARS

Item Description for Accounting Period 7/04 Through 6/05	Total	Zero Assets	Under 500	500 to 1,000	1,000 to 5,000	5,000 to 10,000	10,000 to 25,000	25,000 to 50,000	50,000 to 100,000	100,000 to 250,000	250,000 to 500,000	500,000 to 2,500,000	2,500,000 and over
Number of Enterprises 1	285	0	0	0	66	46	41	22	13	8	0	0	0
Revenues ($ in Thousands)													
Net Sales 2	26913815	0	0	0	700015	1101834	1806651	2311406	2447453	3888610	0	0	0
Interest 3	155293	0	0	0	237	267	1162	1615	2284	2297	0	0	0
Rents 4	6995	0	0	0	0	0	2513	765	737	306	0	0	0
Royalties 5	4267	0	0	0	0	0	0	2693	0	0	0	0	0
Other Portfolio Income 6	74113	0	0	0	67292	53	2775	1096	698	314	0	0	0
Other Receipts 7	420321	0	0	0	38868	180	7530	7746	5826	12680	0	0	0
Total Receipts 8	27574804	0	0	0	806412	1102334	1820631	2325321	2456998	3904207	0	0	0
Average Total Receipts 9	96754	.	.	.	12218	23964	44406	105696	189000	488026	.	.	.
Operating Costs/Operating Income (%)													
Cost of Operations 10	78.6	.	.	.	71.5	76.9	81.7	80.3	80.9	79.8	.	.	.
Salaries and Wages 11	4.5	.	.	.	13.3	5.0	4.1	5.8	3.6	3.0	.	.	.
Taxes Paid 12	0.9	.	.	.	1.7	1.2	1.0	1.0	0.8	0.9	.	.	.
Interest Paid 13	1.4	.	.	.	0.5	0.2	0.4	0.5	0.4	0.9	.	.	.
Depreciation 14	2.9	.	.	.	5.0	1.6	2.0	2.4	2.7	3.6	.	.	.
Amortization and Depletion 15	0.6	.	.	.	0.0	0.0	0.1	0.1	0.0	0.2	.	.	.
Pensions and Other Deferred Comp. 16	0.4	.	.	.	0.6	0.4	0.2	0.5	0.3	0.4	.	.	.
Employee Benefits 17	0.9	.	.	.	3.7	0.7	0.7	1.0	0.6	1.2	.	.	.
Advertising 18	1.1	.	.	.	0.3	1.3	0.7	0.5	1.3	2.3	.	.	.
Other Expenses 19	7.8	.	.	.	13.7	7.2	5.2	5.6	5.8	5.9	.	.	.
Officers' Compensation 20	0.6	.	.	.	0.6	3.3	1.1	0.6	0.5	0.2	.	.	.
Operating Margin 21	0.3	.	.	.	.	2.2	2.9	1.7	3.1	1.7	.	.	.
Operating Margin Before Officers' Comp. 22	0.9	.	.	.	.	5.5	4.0	2.4	3.7	1.9	.	.	.

Selected Average Balance Sheet ($ in Thousands)

Net Receivables 23	11251	671	1817	3720	8875	15217	35322
Inventories 24	5507	566	1196	2626	5947	14987	28899
Net Property, Plant and Equipment 25	15862	731	2376	4810	14013	25980	90971
Total Assets 26	60885	2390	6148	15334	37840	69335	208781
Notes and Loans Payable 27	17065	424	730	3734	9608	14769	67203
All Other Liabilities 28	20087	939	2112	3491	11571	17628	55357
Net Worth 29	23733	1027	3306	8109	16660	36938	86221

Selected Financial Ratios (Times to 1)

Current Ratio 30	1.2	1.6	1.8	2.1	1.4	2.1	1.9
Quick Ratio 31	0.7	1.0	1.1	1.2	0.9	1.2	1.2
Net Sales to Working Capital 32	31.8	17.3	14.9	9.7	17.0	9.5	10.3
Coverage Ratio 33	2.9	9.5	11.5	10.9	5.8	10.0	3.3
Total Asset Turnover 34	1.6	4.4	3.9	2.9	2.8	2.7	2.3
Inventory Turnover 35	13.5	13.4	15.4	13.7	14.2	10.2	13.4
Receivables Turnover 36	10.4	15.1	12.0	11.1	12.3	14.0	•
Total Liabilities to Net Worth 37	1.6	1.3	0.9	0.9	1.3	0.9	1.4
Current Assets to Working Capital 38	7.2	2.6	2.3	1.9	3.3	1.9	2.1
Current Liabilities to Working Capital 39	6.2	1.6	1.3	0.9	2.3	0.9	1.1
Working Capital to Net Sales 40	0.0	0.1	0.1	0.1	0.1	0.1	0.1
Inventory to Working Capital 41	2.0	0.8	0.8	0.6	1.0	0.7	0.6
Total Receipts to Cash Flow 42	11.0	8.4	12.1	13.2	15.2	11.7	14.6
Cost of Goods to Cash Flow 43	8.7	6.0	9.3	10.8	12.2	9.5	11.6
Cash Flow to Total Debt 44	0.2	0.9	0.7	0.5	0.3	0.5	0.3

Selected Financial Factors (in Percentages)

Debt Ratio 45	61.0	57.1	46.2	47.1	56.0	46.7	58.7
Return on Total Assets 46	6.5	21.5	9.7	11.7	7.8	10.6	7.0
Return on Equity Before Income Taxes 47	11.0	44.7	16.4	20.0	14.7	17.9	11.8
Return on Equity After Income Taxes 48	9.1	44.4	12.7	18.2	13.2	14.3	11.1
Profit Margin (Before Income Tax) 49	2.8	4.3	2.3	3.7	2.3	3.5	2.1
Profit Margin (After Income Tax) 50	2.3	4.3	1.7	3.3	2.1	2.8	2.0

Table I

Corporations with and without Net Income

MEAT AND SEAFOOD PROCESSING

MONEY AMOUNTS AND SIZE OF ASSETS IN THOUSANDS OF DOLLARS

Item Description for Accounting Period 7/04 Through 6/05	Total	Zero Assets	Under 500	500 to 1,000	1,000 to 5,000	5,000 to 10,000	10,000 to 25,000	25,000 to 50,000	50,000 to 100,000	100,000 to 250,000	250,000 to 500,000	500,000 to 2,500,000	2,500,000 and over
Number of Enterprises **1**	2097	12	1222	198	287	130	118	46	39	28	5	8	3
Revenues ($ in Thousands)													
Net Sales **2**	132726904	97257	487397	306319	1821145	3147132	6170500	4278999	8519600	11972323	2399798	27204104	66322330
Interest **3**	217144	14	13	1075	464	3759	1969	1553	2227	8312	7839	55659	134261
Rents **4**	25148	398	3	33	1714	3307	1318	576	514	3345	17	9137	4787
Royalties **5**	31689	0	0	0	0	0	64	5	0	0	0	23546	8073
Other Portfolio Income **6**	447725	25263	0	2050	16967	7649	5155	7457	7522	11576	355	57274	306459
Other Receipts **7**	1119108	-4932	-3741	1027	17716	9888	20763	6957	44960	94929	6823	61480	863256
Total Receipts **8**	134567718	118000	483672	310504	1858006	3171715	6199769	4295547	8574823	12090485	2414832	27411200	67639166
Average Total Receipts **9**	64172	9833	396	1568	6474	24398	52540	93381	219867	431803	482966	3426400	22546389
Operating Costs/Operating Income (%)													
Cost of Operations **10**	82.5	77.8	59.1	67.8	81.4	81.4	83.3	83.3	83.8	82.7	73.7	79.9	84.0
Salaries and Wages **11**	4.0	3.1	9.4	5.9	4.4	4.6	3.9	3.6	3.0	2.8	2.4	5.1	4.0
Taxes Paid **12**	0.8	0.8	3.2	2.8	1.5	1.2	1.1	1.2	0.9	0.9	1.5	0.9	0.6
Interest Paid **13**	1.0	1.5	0.4	0.0	1.0	0.8	0.6	0.7	0.6	0.7	1.2	1.0	1.2
Depreciation **14**	1.9	1.9	0.8	1.1	2.6	1.4	1.7	2.8	2.3	2.0	2.9	1.9	1.8
Amortization and Depletion **15**	0.1	0.7	0.1		0.0	0.0	0.1	0.1	0.1	0.1	0.5	0.1	0.1
Pensions and Other Deferred Comp. **16**	0.3	0.5	•	0.1	0.1	0.1	0.2	0.4	0.2	0.1	0.4	0.4	0.3
Employee Benefits **17**	1.2	•	3.8	1.0	0.5	0.6	0.9	0.8	0.8	2.1	1.0	1.1	1.1
Advertising **18**	0.7	1.8	0.6	2.2	0.3	0.2	0.6	0.9	2.1	0.6	1.0	0.5	0.6
Other Expenses **19**	6.4	23.4	23.6	13.8	8.5	8.2	5.6	5.6	4.8	4.7	10.5	6.6	6.5
Officers' Compensation **20**	0.3	0.8	5.7	6.5	1.9	1.9	1.1	1.1	0.4	0.3	0.2	0.2	0.1
Operating Margin **21**	0.6	•	•	•	•	•	1.1	•	1.1	3.1	4.8	2.1	•
Operating Margin Before Officers' Comp. **22**	1.0	•	•	5.2	•	1.4	2.2	0.6	1.5	3.5	5.0	2.4	•

Selected Average Balance Sheet ($ in Thousands)

Net Receivables 23	5296	0	6	178	504	1891	3421	6216	14660	35024	29739	297694	1966691
Inventories 24	5190	0	3	59	179	736	3397	7224	13690	36486	64546	238260	2067706
Net Property, Plant and Equipment 25	7515	0	30	65	1780	1655	5686	12893	24120	53046	80072	419822	2511302
Total Assets 26	32075	0	53	656	2935	6990	15844	35044	69682	166746	308038	1592397	13389252
Notes and Loans Payable 27	9796	0	27	12	3623	3461	5712	14395	20032	51931	118491	295134	416426
All Other Liabilities 28	12265	0	13	27	689	1982	3524	8337	18764	42127	64437	662171	5637733
Net Worth 29	10013	0	13	617	-1377	1548	6608	12312	30885	72688	125109	635092	3587093

Selected Financial Ratios (Times to 1)

Current Ratio 30	1.4	•	0.8	8.1	1.7	1.0	1.7	1.2	1.5	1.8	1.7	1.4	1.3
Quick Ratio 31	0.5	•	0.6	6.5	1.2	0.6	0.9	0.6	0.8	0.9	0.7	0.7	0.3
Net Sales to Working Capital 32	13.9	•	•	5.7	16.1	•	14.8	30.6	18.1	10.4	10.0	15.4	12.7
Coverage Ratio 33	3.0	7.0	•	•	0.8	1.4	3.8	1.0	3.7	7.3	5.7	4.1	2.3
Total Asset Turnover 34	2.0	•	7.6	2.4	2.2	3.5	3.3	2.7	3.1	2.6	1.6	2.1	1.7
Inventory Turnover 35	10.1	•	81.0	17.8	28.9	26.8	12.8	10.7	13.4	9.7	5.5	11.4	9.0
Receivables Turnover 36	12.5	•	101.7	6.3	13.2	12.5	15.5	13.8	17.0	12.5	12.4	18.4	10.5
Total Liabilities to Net Worth 37	2.2	•	3.0	0.1	•	3.5	1.4	1.8	1.3	1.3	1.5	1.5	2.7
Current Assets to Working Capital 38	3.8	•	•	1.1	2.4	•	2.5	5.5	2.9	2.2	2.5	3.5	4.4
Current Liabilities to Working Capital 39	2.8	•	•	0.1	1.4	•	1.5	4.5	1.9	1.2	1.5	2.5	3.4
Working Capital to Net Sales 40	0.1	•	•	0.2	0.1	•	0.1	0.0	0.1	0.1	0.1	0.1	0.1
Inventory to Working Capital 41	1.1	•	•	0.2	0.6	1.0	1.0	2.3	1.2	1.0	1.3	1.3	1.1
Total Receipts to Cash Flow 42	14.2	5.5	17.0	9.7	19.7	16.3	16.7	23.8	17.4	12.8	6.7	12.7	14.8
Cost of Goods to Cash Flow 43	11.7	4.3	10.0	6.5	16.0	13.3	13.9	19.8	14.5	10.6	4.9	10.2	12.4
Cash Flow to Total Debt 44	0.2	•	0.6	4.1	0.1	0.3	0.3	0.2	0.3	0.4	0.4	0.3	0.2

Selected Financial Factors (in Percentages)

Debt Ratio 45	68.8	•	75.0	5.9	146.9	77.9	58.3	64.9	55.7	56.4	59.4	60.1	73.2
Return on Total Assets 46	6.1	•	•	•	1.7	3.9	7.0	1.8	7.4	12.2	10.2	8.8	4.7
Return on Equity Before Income Taxes 47	13.1	•	•	•	0.7	5.1	12.4	•	12.2	24.2	20.8	16.7	9.9
Return on Equity After Income Taxes 48	9.3	•	•	•	1.0	4.2	10.9	•	11.6	21.8	13.1	10.6	6.5
Profit Margin (Before Income Tax) 49	2.1	9.1	•	•	•	0.3	1.6	•	1.7	4.1	5.4	3.1	1.6
Profit Margin (After Income Tax) 50	1.5	7.7	•	•	0.3	•	1.4	•	1.6	3.7	3.4	2.0	1.0

Table II
Corporations with Net Income

MEAT AND SEAFOOD PROCESSING

MONEY AMOUNTS AND SIZE OF ASSETS IN THOUSANDS OF DOLLARS

Item Description for Accounting Period 7/04 Through 6/05	Total	Zero Assets	Under 500	500 to 1,000	1,000 to 5,000	5,000 to 10,000	10,000 to 25,000	25,000 to 50,000	50,000 to 100,000	100,000 to 250,000	250,000 to 500,000	500,000 to 2,500,000	2,500,000 and over
Number of Enterprises **1**	1240	0	760	133	107	60	86	29	25	0	0	0	3
Revenues ($ in Thousands)													
Net Sales **2**	111411408	0	479535	139445	1268882	1806467	4766741	2796190	5443316	0	0	0	66322330
Interest **3**	190974	0	13	879	151	3112	1253	1231	1846	0	0	0	134261
Rents **4**	22278	0	3	33	781	3104	1233	225	13	0	0	0	4787
Royalties **5**	31170	0	0	0	0	0	64	5	0	0	0	0	8073
Other Portfolio Income **6**	439455	0	0	1291	16007	6868	3616	3857	7491	0	0	0	306459
Other Receipts **7**	1151847	0	-1	422	11670	6525	17042	9574	46838	0	0	0	863256
Total Receipts **8**	113247132	0	479550	142070	1297491	1826076	4789949	2811082	5499504	0	0	0	67639166
Average Total Receipts **9**	91328	•	631	1068	12126	30435	55697	96934	219980	•	•	•	22546389
Operating Costs/Operating Income (%)													
Cost of Operations **10**	81.0	•	58.7	57.0	83.2	79.4	81.5	81.1	83.1	•	•	•	84.0
Salaries and Wages **11**	4.5	•	9.5	10.5	4.6	5.9	4.1	3.5	2.9	•	•	•	4.0
Taxes Paid **12**	0.9	•	3.2	3.9	1.2	1.2	1.1	1.3	0.9	•	•	•	0.6
Interest Paid **13**	1.0	•	0.3	0.0	0.5	0.7	0.4	0.6	0.4	•	•	•	1.2
Depreciation **14**	2.0	•	0.8	1.8	0.8	0.8	1.6	2.7	2.2	•	•	•	1.8
Amortization and Depletion **15**	0.1	•	•	•	0.0	0.0	0.1	0.1	0.0	•	•	•	0.1
Pensions and Other Deferred Comp. **16**	0.3	•	•	0.2	0.1	0.1	0.2	0.3	0.2	•	•	•	0.3
Employee Benefits **17**	1.3	•	3.9	0.0	0.0	0.6	0.9	0.8	0.9	•	•	•	1.1
Advertising **18**	0.7	•	0.6	0.1	0.2	0.1	0.7	0.7	2.3	•	•	•	0.6
Other Expenses **19**	6.7	•	16.4	17.4	7.7	8.1	5.8	4.6	3.9	•	•	•	6.5
Officers' Compensation **20**	0.3	•	5.8	10.2	2.0	1.7	1.1	1.2	0.2	•	•	•	0.1
Operating Margin **21**	1.2	•	0.7	•	•	1.4	2.4	3.2	2.8	•	•	•	•
Operating Margin Before Officers' Comp. **22**	1.6	•	6.5	9.2	1.7	3.0	3.5	4.4	3.1	•	•	•	•

Selected Average Balance Sheet ($ in Thousands)

Net Receivables 23	7024	9	169	807	2317	3628	6721	14306	1966691
Inventories 24	7851	3	5	403	980	3599	8182	15481	2067706
Net Property, Plant and Equipment 25	10833	47	46	773	1508	5484	12707	23477	2511302
Total Assets 26	47608	81	668	2416	7784	16011	33712	69981	13389252
Notes and Loans Payable 27	13566	12	1	1136	3551	5042	10905	12185	4164426
All Other Liabilities 28	17895	13	15	532	2646	3550	8570	19042	5637733
Net Worth 29	16148	56	652	748	1587	7418	14237	38754	3587093

Selected Financial Ratios (Times to 1)

Current Ratio 30	1.4	1.9	19.4	2.9	0.8	1.8	1.6	1.6	1.3
Quick Ratio 31	0.4	1.4	18.5	1.9	0.5	0.9	0.8	0.9	0.3
Net Sales to Working Capital 32	12.2	41.9	3.9	10.9	•	13.5	14.7	15.5	12.7
Coverage Ratio 33	4.0	3.1	15.3	4.7	4.5	7.7	7.4	10.9	2.3
Total Asset Turnover 34	1.9	7.8	1.6	4.9	3.9	3.5	2.9	3.1	1.7
Inventory Turnover 35	9.3	122.7	109.5	24.5	24.4	12.6	9.6	11.7	9.0
Receivables Turnover 36	12.6	100.3	5.5	12.8	•	15.6	12.0	15.4	10.5
Total Liabilities to Net Worth 37	1.9	0.4	0.0	2.2	3.9	1.2	1.4	0.8	2.7
Current Assets to Working Capital 38	3.5	2.1	1.1	1.5	•	2.3	2.8	2.5	4.4
Current Liabilities to Working Capital 39	2.5	1.1	0.1	0.5	•	1.3	1.8	1.5	3.4
Working Capital to Net Sales 40	0.1	0.0	0.3	0.1	0.1	0.1	0.1	0.1	0.1
Inventory to Working Capital 41	1.1	0.4	0.0	0.5	•	0.9	1.1	1.0	1.1
Total Receipts to Cash Flow 42	12.3	7.5	6.5	14.6	12.5	13.4	13.4	13.8	14.8
Cost of Goods to Cash Flow 43	10.0	4.4	3.7	12.1	9.9	10.9	10.9	11.5	12.4
Cash Flow to Total Debt 44	0.2	3.4	10.1	0.5	0.4	0.5	0.4	0.5	0.2

Selected Financial Factors (in Percentages)

Debt Ratio 45	66.1	30.7	2.4	69.0	79.6	53.7	57.8	44.6	73.2
Return on Total Assets 46	7.4	8.4	0.8	11.6	12.2	11.5	12.4	13.2	4.7
Return on Equity Before Income Taxes 47	16.4	8.1	0.8	29.5	46.6	21.5	25.5	21.7	9.9
Return on Equity After Income Taxes 48	12.4	7.2	0.7	28.0	44.8	19.7	23.7	21.0	6.5
Profit Margin (Before Income Tax) 49	2.9	0.7	0.5	1.9	2.5	2.9	3.8	3.9	1.6
Profit Margin (After Income Tax) 50	2.2	0.6	0.5	1.8	2.4	2.6	3.5	3.7	1.0

Table I

Corporations with and without Net Income

BAKERIES AND TORTILLA

MONEY AMOUNTS AND SIZE OF ASSETS IN THOUSANDS OF DOLLARS

Item Description for Accounting Period 7/04 Through 6/05	Total	Zero Assets	Under 500	500 to 1,000	1,000 to 5,000	5,000 to 10,000	10,000 to 25,000	25,000 to 50,000	50,000 to 100,000	100,000 to 250,000	250,000 to 500,000	500,000 to 2,500,000	2,500,000 and over
Number of Enterprises **1**	4224	763	2504	473	294	67	74	23	19	9	6	11	0
Revenues ($ in Thousands)													
Net Sales **2**	89131072	335337	985434	312884	1731497	1479186	2419686	2165731	2302535	1606066	3132112	72660604	0
Interest **3**	1712429	63	5	47	447	664	683	1369	526	6254	1796	1700576	0
Rents **4**	2068257	77	1176	1294	5740	0	187	3779	241	8	149	2055607	0
Royalties **5**	2466318	0	0	0	0	0	52	405	0	1768	64746	2399346	0
Other Portfolio Income **6**	2883001	21914	0	391	14	1102	1024	18301	1904	1706	391	2836257	0
Other Receipts **7**	2375398	454	11575	8316	19352	7630	4739	2628	20045	10224	56158	2234272	0
Total Receipts **8**	100636475	357845	998190	322932	1757050	1488582	2426371	2192213	2325251	1626026	3255352	83886662	0
Average Total Receipts **9**	23713	469	399	683	5976	22218	32789	95314	122382	180670	542559	7626060	•
Operating Costs/Operating Income (%)													
Cost of Operations **10**	53.2	51.5	45.3	61.3	71.1	65.3	65.8	68.5	59.6	72.1	62.7	50.7	•
Salaries and Wages **11**	7.1	12.6	19.4	8.3	7.9	7.2	7.6	8.9	13.6	6.2	14.0	6.3	•
Taxes Paid **12**	6.0	3.7	3.8	3.0	2.7	2.9	2.0	1.6	2.1	1.9	2.7	6.8	•
Interest Paid **13**	4.9	0.5	0.2	1.4	0.4	0.7	0.7	0.9	0.8	1.8	1.3	5.8	•
Depreciation **14**	3.8	2.0	1.6	2.6	5.8	4.2	3.7	4.3	4.9	5.4	4.1	3.7	•
Amortization and Depletion **15**	0.6	0.0	0.0	0.4	0.0	0.1	0.1	0.2	0.1	2.4	0.5	0.6	•
Pensions and Other Deferred Comp. **16**	1.7	0.9	•	•	0.0	0.5	0.3	0.8	1.9	0.8	0.5	1.9	•
Employee Benefits **17**	3.0	0.0	0.2	1.6	2.5	2.7	2.4	2.6	3.9	3.4	1.8	3.1	•
Advertising **18**	2.0	3.8	1.8	0.4	0.7	0.8	1.2	1.0	1.1	1.5	0.8	2.2	•
Other Expenses **19**	21.4	22.9	23.2	15.0	14.1	10.5	11.8	10.4	9.7	11.3	10.7	23.6	•
Officers' Compensation **20**	0.7	7.0	11.8	4.4	2.7	2.8	2.6	1.2	1.5	0.8	0.5	0.3	•
Operating Margin **21**	•	•	•	1.8	•	2.3	1.8	•	0.8	•	0.5	•	•
Operating Margin Before Officers' Comp. **22**	•	2.0	4.6	6.2	•	5.1	4.5	0.8	2.3	•	1.1	•	•

Selected Average Balance Sheet ($ in Thousands)

Net Receivables 23	2281	0	16	55	535	1628	3102	6481	10299	20918	47939	754343	•
Inventories 24	1111	0	15	27	363	1227	1568	4008	5845	13033	25404	353217	•
Net Property, Plant and Equipment 25	2615	0	28	195	1420	3515	6518	16901	32532	61362	100416	694402	•
Total Assets 26	32332	0	72	607	3287	8478	15388	36447	69500	151375	319608	11694227	•
Notes and Loans Payable 27	6208	0	57	310	1112	2475	4337	12707	15838	29905	68458	2179037	•
All Other Liabilities 28	11175	0	20	97	504	2045	3354	12729	16906	61222	82676	4103256	•
Net Worth 29	14949	0	-5	200	1670	3959	7697	11010	36757	60248	168474	5411935	•

Selected Financial Ratios (Times to 1)

Current Ratio 30	0.7	•	1.3	2.8	2.9	1.9	1.7	1.1	1.4	1.0	1.4	0.6
Quick Ratio 31	0.4	•	0.9	2.4	1.2	1.3	1.1	0.7	0.9	0.6	0.9	0.4
Net Sales to Working Capital 32	•	•	35.7	3.0	4.9	9.9	11.9	55.0	20.1	•	17.9	•
Coverage Ratio 33	3.5	4.8	•	4.7	•	5.5	4.0	1.9	3.3	•	4.4	3.6
Total Asset Turnover 34	0.6	•	5.5	1.1	1.8	2.6	2.1	2.6	1.7	1.2	1.6	0.6
Inventory Turnover 35	10.1	•	11.7	15.0	11.5	11.7	13.7	16.1	12.4	9.9	12.9	9.5
Receivables Turnover 36	10.1	•	13.3	11.4	12.9	10.2	11.4	13.8	11.2	9.5	12.8	9.8
Total Liabilities to Net Worth 37	1.2	•	•	2.0	1.0	1.1	1.0	2.3	0.9	1.5	0.9	1.2
Current Assets to Working Capital 38	•	•	4.0	1.6	1.5	2.1	2.5	8.1	3.7	•	3.6	•
Current Liabilities to Working Capital 39	•	•	3.0	0.6	0.5	1.1	1.5	7.1	2.7	•	2.6	•
Working Capital to Net Sales 40	•	•	0.0	0.3	0.2	0.1	0.1	0.0	0.0	•	0.1	•
Inventory to Working Capital 41	•	•	1.1	0.1	0.3	0.4	0.6	2.1	0.8	•	1.0	•
Total Receipts to Cash Flow 42	3.6	5.5	8.4	6.4	22.5	9.4	8.8	13.3	10.9	34.2	8.2	3.1
Cost of Goods to Cash Flow 43	1.9	2.8	3.8	3.9	16.0	6.2	5.8	9.1	6.5	24.7	5.1	1.6
Cash Flow to Total Debt 44	0.3	•	0.6	0.3	0.2	0.5	0.5	0.3	0.3	0.1	0.4	0.3

Selected Financial Factors (in Percentages)

Debt Ratio 45	53.8	•	106.6	67.0	49.2	53.3	50.0	69.8	47.1	60.2	47.3	53.7
Return on Total Assets 46	11.3	•	•	6.9	•	9.3	5.8	4.3	4.4	•	9.4	11.9
Return on Equity Before Income Taxes 47	17.6	•	483.8	16.5	•	16.3	8.8	6.7	5.8	•	13.8	18.7
Return on Equity After Income Taxes 48	11.7	•	486.4	16.5	•	12.1	7.5	4.1	5.3	•	10.4	12.6
Profit Margin (Before Income Tax) 49	12.5	1.8	•	5.0	•	2.9	2.1	0.8	1.7	•	4.5	15.3
Profit Margin (After Income Tax) 50	8.4	1.6	•	5.0	•	2.2	1.8	0.5	1.6	•	3.4	10.3

Table II

Corporations with Net Income

BAKERIES AND TORTILLA

MONEY AMOUNTS AND SIZE OF ASSETS IN THOUSANDS OF DOLLARS

Item Description for Accounting Period 7/04 Through 6/05	Total	Zero Assets	Under 500	500 to 1,000	1,000 to 5,000	5,000 to 10,000	10,000 to 25,000	25,000 to 50,000	50,000 to 100,000	100,000 to 250,000	250,000 to 500,000	500,000 to 2,500,000	2,500,000 and over
Number of Enterprises **1**	1268	304	466	209	150	52	43	14	16	0	6	8	0
Revenues ($ in Thousands)													
Net Sales **2**	76389077	312356	258648	101198	919141	1203713	1483978	1394140	1859598	0	3132112	65724195	0
Interest **3**	1650477	40	0	0	130	664	365	275	3076	0	1796	1644130	0
Rents **4**	2064311	77	0	0	5204	0	132	3659	196	0	149	2054894	0
Royalties **5**	2465643	0	0	0	0	0	0	405	1487	0	64746	2399005	0
Other Portfolio Income **6**	2760913	11415	0	0	14	1102	415	18067	2461	0	391	2727051	0
Other Receipts **7**	2322390	338	0	0	16323	1666	2530	852	10300	0	56158	2234220	0
Total Receipts **8**	87652811	324226	258648	101198	940812	1207145	1487420	1417398	1877118	0	3255352	76783495	0
Average Total Receipts **9**	69127	1067	555	484	6272	23214	34591	101243	117320	.	542559	9597937	.
Operating Costs/Operating Income (%)													
Cost of Operations **10**	52.1	49.8	64.1	50.0	60.5	62.9	64.5	73.0	58.2	.	62.7	50.4	.
Salaries and Wages **11**	6.1	12.4	6.3	.	8.8	7.5	7.0	6.8	14.0	.	14.0	5.4	.
Taxes Paid **12**	6.5	3.7	2.7	3.6	2.9	2.9	2.1	1.2	2.0	.	2.7	7.2	.
Interest Paid **13**	5.4	0.2	.	.	0.5	0.5	0.5	1.1	0.9	.	1.3	6.1	.
Depreciation **14**	3.8	1.1	0.7	0.2	1.9	3.3	3.3	2.8	4.7	.	4.1	3.8	.
Amortization and Depletion **15**	0.5	0.1	.	.	0.0	0.1	0.1	0.1	0.2	.	0.5	0.5	.
Pensions and Other Deferred Comp. **16**	1.6	0.9	.	.	0.2	0.5	0.2	0.6	1.9	.	0.5	1.7	.
Employee Benefits **17**	2.5	0.0	0.2	1.0	2.0	2.8	1.9	1.4	3.6	.	1.8	2.6	.
Advertising **18**	2.1	3.8	5.3	0.1	1.1	0.9	1.2	0.7	1.2	.	0.8	2.2	.
Other Expenses **19**	22.8	22.4	19.5	17.3	15.6	10.7	11.6	8.1	9.6	.	10.7	24.6	.
Officers' Compensation **20**	0.5	6.5	0.2	8.7	4.5	3.4	2.4	1.4	1.8	.	0.5	0.3	.
Operating Margin **21**	.	.	0.9	19.2	2.1	4.5	5.0	2.7	1.9	.	0.5	.	.
Operating Margin Before Officers' Comp. **22**	.	5.6	1.1	27.9	6.6	7.9	7.4	4.2	3.7	.	1.1	.	.

Selected Average Balance Sheet ($ in Thousands)

Net Receivables 23	6851	0	26	16	415	1676	2930	5971	9955	•	47939	983266	•
Inventories 24	3308	0	24	25	415	1175	1720	3856	4417	•	28702	465047	•
Net Property, Plant and Equipment 25	6272	0	86	6	955	2647	6628	17056	31972	•	100416	749164	•
Total Assets 26	102202	0	163	531	3223	8233	15701	36145	80034	•	319608	15514328	•
Notes and Loans Payable 27	18488	0	33	0	622	1705	3775	10212	19524	•	68458	2777101	•
All Other Liabilities 28	35386	0	26	14	433	2057	3438	11787	19009	•	82676	5446183	•
Net Worth 29	48328	0	104	517	2168	4471	8488	14146	41501	•	168474	7291044	•

Selected Financial Ratios (Times to 1)

Current Ratio 30	0.6	•	2.1	36.3	4.7	2.2	1.8	1.1	1.4	•	1.4	0.6	
Quick Ratio 31	0.4	•	1.5	33.7	1.4	1.6	1.2	0.7	1.0	•	0.9	0.3	
Net Sales to Working Capital 32	•	•	16.0	0.9	3.6	8.0	11.9	65.1	18.2	•	17.9	•	
Coverage Ratio 33	3.9	14.7	•	•	9.5	11.3	10.7	5.2	4.0	•	4.4	3.8	
Total Asset Turnover 34	0.6	•	3.4	0.9	1.9	2.8	2.2	2.8	1.5	•	1.6	0.5	
Inventory Turnover 35	9.5	•	14.8	9.8	8.9	12.4	13.0	18.8	15.3	•	11.4	8.9	
Receivables Turnover 36	9.8	•	5.6	10.7	10.8	11.3	11.6	17.2	12.6	•	•	9.4	
Total Liabilities to Net Worth 37	1.1	•	0.6	0.0	0.5	0.8	0.8	1.6	0.9	•	0.9	1.1	
Current Assets to Working Capital 38	•	•	1.9	1.0	1.3	1.8	2.3	8.3	3.5	•	3.6	•	
Current Liabilities to Working Capital 39	•	•	0.9	0.0	0.3	0.8	1.3	7.3	2.5	•	2.6	•	
Working Capital to Net Sales 40	•	•	0.1	1.1	0.3	0.1	0.1	0.0	0.1	•	0.1	•	
Inventory to Working Capital 41	•	•	0.4	0.1	0.1	0.3	0.6	2.5	0.7	•	1.0	•	
Total Receipts to Cash Flow 42	3.2	5.3	7.5	3.4	6.0	8.2	7.1	11.0	10.1	•	8.2	2.9	
Cost of Goods to Cash Flow 43	1.7	2.6	4.8	1.7	3.6	5.2	4.6	8.0	5.9	•	5.1	1.5	
Cash Flow to Total Debt 44	0.4	•	1.3	9.8	1.0	0.7	0.7	0.4	0.3	•	0.4	0.3	

Selected Financial Factors (in Percentages)

Debt Ratio 45	52.7	•	36.1	2.7	32.7	45.7	45.9	60.9	48.1	•	47.3	53.0	
Return on Total Assets 46	12.2	•	3.0	17.5	9.4	14.7	12.6	15.1	5.4	•	9.4	12.3	
Return on Equity Before Income Taxes 47	19.2	•	4.8	18.0	12.5	24.7	21.2	31.1	7.9	•	13.8	19.4	
Return on Equity After Income Taxes 48	13.1	•	4.1	18.0	12.2	19.9	19.2	27.6	7.4	•	10.4	13.1	
Profit Margin (Before Income Tax) 49	15.4	2.8	0.9	19.2	4.4	4.8	5.2	4.4	2.8	•	4.5	17.2	
Profit Margin (After Income Tax) 50	10.5	2.7	0.8	19.2	4.3	3.8	4.7	3.9	2.6	•	3.4	11.6	

Table I

Corporations with and without Net Income

OTHER FOOD

MONEY AMOUNTS AND SIZE OF ASSETS IN THOUSANDS OF DOLLARS

Item Description for Accounting Period 7/04 Through 6/05	Total	Zero Assets	Under 500	500 to 1,000	1,000 to 5,000	5,000 to 10,000	10,000 to 25,000	25,000 to 50,000	50,000 to 100,000	100,000 to 250,000	250,000 to 500,000	500,000 to 2,500,000	2,500,000 and over
Number of Enterprises **1**	3660	346	2078	393	364	191	137	73	32	26	9	10	0
Revenues ($ in Thousands)													
Net Sales **2**	69508655	425442	422450	563922	2014485	4317171	4583451	4676755	3908344	6227101	2567653	39801881	0
Interest **3**	2118187	1030	2	0	551	507	1789	3528	4219	10686	12709	2083166	0
Rents **4**	115187	200	0	0	475	140	1890	773	1451	809	9561	99889	0
Royalties **5**	551297	86	0	0	0	194	46	1670	21241	8898	2224	516938	0
Other Portfolio Income **6**	455412	35	85	112	3676	1100	11370	18546	6757	304686	6846	102198	0
Other Receipts **7**	847171	398	51164	12	5915	18052	8425	18406	18962	71627	22324	631885	0
Total Receipts **8**	73595909	427191	473701	564046	2025102	4337164	4606971	4719678	3960974	6623807	2621317	43235957	0
Average Total Receipts **9**	20108	1235	228	1435	5563	22708	33628	64653	123780	254762	291257	4323596	·
Operating Costs/Operating Income (%)													
Cost of Operations **10**	72.0	42.8	59.1	56.2	73.3	73.9	74.1	70.5	66.8	72.0	68.0	73.1	·
Salaries and Wages **11**	6.2	14.0	8.3	6.3	8.2	12.1	5.3	6.8	8.1	5.7	6.4	5.3	·
Taxes Paid **12**	1.3	3.2	2.7	3.3	1.8	1.2	1.3	1.4	1.6	1.3	1.5	1.2	·
Interest Paid **13**	5.4	4.5	1.0	1.7	0.7	0.2	0.8	1.2	1.3	3.2	1.9	8.2	·
Depreciation **14**	2.6	2.5	3.0	2.9	2.2	1.6	2.6	2.9	3.0	3.4	3.4	2.5	·
Amortization and Depletion **15**	0.5	0.2	0.1	0.0	0.4	0.0	0.2	0.6	0.7	0.5	1.2	0.4	·
Pensions and Other Deferred Comp. **16**	0.7	0.1	4.1	0.0	0.3	0.3	0.2	0.4	0.5	0.3	0.5	0.9	·
Employee Benefits **17**	1.0	1.0	0.1	0.0	0.9	0.7	0.9	1.5	2.0	1.1	1.2	0.8	·
Advertising **18**	2.9	0.5	1.0	1.5	1.3	0.6	1.4	1.8	2.0	3.5	2.2	3.6	·
Other Expenses **19**	9.6	15.9	53.8	16.7	11.0	6.0	9.1	9.7	12.0	9.4	11.2	9.0	·
Officers' Compensation **20**	1.0	2.9	13.2	7.9	4.5	1.7	2.0	1.4	1.1	0.8	1.1	0.3	·
Operating Margin **21**	·	12.3	·	3.3	·	1.8	2.1	1.7	0.9	·	1.4	·	·
Operating Margin Before Officers' Comp. **22**	·	15.2	·	11.2	·	3.4	4.1	3.1	1.9	·	2.5	·	·

Selected Average Balance Sheet ($ in Thousands)

Net Receivables 23	34540	0	22	45	454	1788	3452	6377	10916	20433	27727	12377792	•
Inventories 24	1472	0	5	36	469	1340	3689	7117	14885	24492	44330	239732	•
Net Property, Plant and Equipment 25	3008	0	49	243	490	2150	5267	10702	23241	43540	96632	597553	•
Total Assets 26	61605	0	105	843	1975	7185	16039	33900	73463	150757	354174	2070267	•
Notes and Loans Payable 27	6686	0	81	290	550	3557	5308	12714	19458	44101	100995	1897572	•
All Other Liabilities 28	39286	0	25	97	485	2016	4557	9297	21549	35474	60573	13967322	•
Net Worth 29	15633	0	-1	455	939	1611	6174	11889	32456	71182	192606	5005373	•

Selected Financial Ratios (Times to 1)

Current Ratio 30	1.0	•	0.9	4.3	1.8	1.9	1.4	1.4	1.5	2.1	2.8	1.0	•
Quick Ratio 31	0.9	•	0.6	3.9	0.9	1.1	0.7	0.7	0.7	1.0	1.1	0.9	•
Net Sales to Working Capital 32	116.1	•	•	4.8	10.0	11.1	12.4	13.5	10.7	6.0	2.7	•	•
Coverage Ratio 33	1.6	3.8	•	2.9	•	10.0	4.1	3.4	2.7	2.6	2.8	1.4	•
Total Asset Turnover 34	0.3	•	1.9	1.7	2.8	3.1	2.1	1.9	1.7	1.6	0.8	0.2	•
Inventory Turnover 35	9.3	•	22.5	22.7	8.6	12.5	6.7	6.3	5.5	7.0	4.4	12.1	•
Receivables Turnover 36	0.6	•	13.5	28.9	12.8	13.5	10.0	10.6	11.1	11.7	11.3	0.4	•
Total Liabilities to Net Worth 37	2.9	•	•	0.9	1.1	3.5	1.6	1.9	1.3	1.1	0.8	3.2	•
Current Assets to Working Capital 38	233.4	•	•	1.3	2.3	2.1	3.3	3.6	2.9	1.9	1.5	•	•
Current Liabilities to Working Capital 39	232.4	•	•	0.3	1.3	1.1	2.3	2.6	1.9	0.9	0.5	•	•
Working Capital to Net Sales 40	0.0	•	•	0.2	0.1	0.1	0.1	0.1	0.1	0.2	0.4	•	•
Inventory to Working Capital 41	9.3	•	•	0.1	0.9	0.6	1.4	1.5	1.3	0.6	0.6	•	•
Total Receipts to Cash Flow 42	9.9	4.0	20.2	7.0	28.8	14.5	10.3	9.6	8.3	11.6	7.8	9.5	•
Cost of Goods to Cash Flow 43	7.1	1.7	11.9	4.0	21.1	10.7	7.6	6.8	5.6	8.4	5.3	6.9	•
Cash Flow to Total Debt 44	0.0	•	0.1	0.5	0.2	0.3	0.3	0.3	0.4	0.3	0.2	0.0	•

Selected Financial Factors (in Percentages)

Debt Ratio 45	74.6	•	101.2	46.0	52.4	77.6	61.5	64.9	55.8	52.8	45.6	76.0	•
Return on Total Assets 46	2.6	•	•	8.6	•	7.8	7.2	7.8	5.9	13.2	4.4	2.3	•
Return on Equity Before Income Taxes 47	3.8	•	5358.8	10.4	•	31.5	14.1	15.7	8.3	17.1	5.1	2.9	•
Return on Equity After Income Taxes 48	2.6	•	5358.8	10.4	•	27.0	11.9	11.5	5.7	15.3	2.6	1.9	•
Profit Margin (Before Income Tax) 49	3.1	12.7	•	3.3	•	2.2	2.6	2.9	2.2	5.1	3.5	3.7	•
Profit Margin (After Income Tax) 50	2.1	11.6	•	3.3	•	1.9	2.2	2.1	1.5	4.6	1.8	2.4	•

Table II

Corporations with Net Income

OTHER FOOD

MONEY AMOUNTS AND SIZE OF ASSETS IN THOUSANDS OF DOLLARS

Item Description for Accounting Period 7/04 Through 6/05	Total	Zero Assets	Under 500	500 to 1,000	1,000 to 5,000	5,000 to 10,000	10,000 to 25,000	25,000 to 50,000	50,000 to 100,000	100,000 to 250,000	250,000 to 500,000	500,000 to 2,500,000	2,500,000 and over
Number of Enterprises 1	1573	342	373	393	108	156	98	47	21	19	0	0	0
Revenues ($ in Thousands)													
Net Sales 2	59962879	375002	219745	563922	679647	3995097	3410964	3167221	2797918	5152182	0	0	0
Interest 3	2113755	1030	0	0	257	364	1456	2036	3286	9819	0	0	0
Rents 4	111638	200	0	0	0	72	1661	22	709	607	0	0	0
Royalties 5	527696	86	0	0	0	194	45	1670	35	8451	0	0	0
Other Portfolio Income 6	445153	1	0	112	2272	264	10548	17362	1287	304263	0	0	0
Other Receipts 7	543171	404	0	12	1296	17030	14038	7677	11162	61378	0	0	0
Total Receipts 8	63704292	376723	219745	564046	683472	4013021	3438712	3195988	2814397	5536700	0	0	0
Average Total Receipts 9	40499	1102	589	1435	6328	25724	35089	68000	134019	291405	•	•	•
Operating Costs/Operating Income (%)													
Cost of Operations 10	71.7	39.2	56.7	56.2	73.6	73.3	72.6	67.9	67.1	71.7	•	•	•
Salaries and Wages 11	5.9	14.5	6.5	6.3	3.8	12.6	5.3	6.8	6.9	5.4	•	•	•
Taxes Paid 12	1.3	3.3	1.5	3.3	1.9	1.1	1.3	1.4	1.5	1.2	•	•	•
Interest Paid 13	5.9	4.9	1.3	1.7	0.6	0.1	0.6	0.9	1.0	3.4	•	•	•
Depreciation 14	2.5	1.9	2.0	2.9	1.9	1.4	2.3	2.6	3.0	2.8	•	•	•
Amortization and Depletion 15	0.4	0.2	•	0.0	0.2	0.0	0.1	0.7	0.4	0.5	•	•	•
Pensions and Other Deferred Comp. 16	0.7	0.0	•	0.0	0.2	0.2	0.2	0.4	0.6	0.3	•	•	•
Employee Benefits 17	0.9	0.0	•	0.0	1.4	0.6	1.0	1.4	1.9	1.2	•	•	•
Advertising 18	3.1	0.8	•	1.5	0.4	0.4	1.3	1.7	1.8	4.1	•	•	•
Other Expenses 19	8.8	17.1	24.7	16.7	9.2	5.6	8.6	9.6	10.8	9.0	•	•	•
Officers' Compensation 20	0.8	2.8	1.3	7.9	4.0	1.6	2.2	1.5	1.3	0.9	•	•	•
Operating Margin 21	•	14.7	6.0	3.3	2.9	3.0	4.4	5.0	3.7	•	•	•	•
Operating Margin Before Officers' Comp. 22	•	17.6	7.2	11.2	6.9	4.6	6.6	6.5	5.0	0.4	•	•	•

Selected Average Balance Sheet ($ in Thousands)

Net Receivables 23	79779	0	120	45	538	2015	3387	6668	11469	23183
Inventories 24	2791	0	11	22	858	1307	3575	7893	17782	28491
Net Property, Plant and Equipment 25	5616	0	24	243	590	2072	4722	9873	21437	39687
Total Assets 26	139098	0	256	843	2400	7171	15759	34346	71243	150903
Notes and Loans Payable 27	12836	0	195	290	438	3366	4394	11584	17388	28156
All Other Liabilities 28	90334	0	59	97	571	1968	4365	7985	21165	39198
Net Worth 29	35928	0	1	455	1391	1837	7000	14776	32690	83549

Selected Financial Ratios (Times to 1)

Current Ratio 30	1.0	•	1.0	4.3	2.3	2.0	1.6	1.7	1.7	2.3
Quick Ratio 31	0.9	•	0.6	3.9	1.3	1.3	0.8	0.8	0.7	1.2
Net Sales to Working Capital 32	•	•	1664.7	4.8	7.3	12.0	9.5	8.9	8.8	5.8
Coverage Ratio 33	1.8	4.1	5.6	2.9	6.9	24.5	9.5	8.1	5.4	3.0
Total Asset Turnover 34	0.3	•	2.3	1.7	2.6	3.6	2.2	2.0	1.9	1.8
Inventory Turnover 35	9.8	•	29.2	36.3	5.4	14.4	7.1	5.8	5.0	6.8
Receivables Turnover 36	0.5	•	7.1	62.9	6.9	15.5	11.1	10.1	11.3	11.1
Total Liabilities to Net Worth 37	2.9	•	181.3	0.9	0.7	2.9	1.3	1.3	1.2	0.8
Current Assets to Working Capital 38	•	•	578.3	1.3	1.8	2.0	2.6	2.4	2.5	1.8
Current Liabilities to Working Capital 39	•	•	577.3	0.3	0.8	1.0	1.6	1.4	1.5	0.8
Working Capital to Net Sales 40	•	•	0.0	0.2	0.1	0.1	0.1	0.1	0.1	0.2
Inventory to Working Capital 41	•	•	42.0	0.1	0.7	0.7	1.1	1.0	1.2	0.6
Total Receipts to Cash Flow 42	9.1	3.5	4.4	7.0	12.3	13.2	8.5	7.3	7.5	10.7
Cost of Goods to Cash Flow 43	6.5	1.4	2.5	4.0	9.0	9.6	6.1	5.0	5.0	7.7
Cash Flow to Total Debt 44	0.0	•	0.5	0.5	0.5	0.4	0.5	0.5	0.5	0.4

Selected Financial Factors (in Percentages)

Debt Ratio 45	74.2	•	99.5	46.0	42.0	74.4	55.6	57.0	54.1	44.6
Return on Total Assets 46	2.9	•	16.8	8.6	10.6	12.9	12.7	14.4	9.9	18.6
Return on Equity Before Income Taxes 47	5.0	•	2506.7	10.4	15.6	48.2	25.7	29.3	17.5	22.6
Return on Equity After Income Taxes 48	3.7	•	2506.7	10.4	12.8	43.4	23.0	24.0	13.6	20.6
Profit Margin (Before Income Tax) 49	4.7	15.2	6.0	3.3	3.4	3.5	5.2	6.4	4.3	7.0
Profit Margin (After Income Tax) 50	3.5	14.0	6.0	3.3	2.8	3.1	4.6	5.3	3.3	6.3

50

Table I

Corporations with and without Net Income

SOFT DRINK AND ICE

MONEY AMOUNTS AND SIZE OF ASSETS IN THOUSANDS OF DOLLARS

Item Description for Accounting Period 7/04 Through 6/05	Total	Zero Assets	Under 500	500 to 1,000	1,000 to 5,000	5,000 to 10,000	10,000 to 25,000	25,000 to 50,000	50,000 to 100,000	100,000 to 250,000	250,000 to 500,000	500,000 to 2,500,000	2,500,000 and over
Number of Enterprises 1	631	3	104	216	150	30	57	30	9	15	5	6	6
Revenues ($ in Thousands)													
Net Sales 2	49127185	134269	28801	246778	879210	469766	2013095	2355606	1140636	3665379	1667377	8151850	28374416
Interest 3	968559	25	0	303	85	248	602	1040	604	19018	4038	42023	900572
Rents 4	89787	0	0	0	3040	308	3713	1572	754	1096	400	5391	73513
Royalties 5	1165108	0	0	0	0	0	193	0	0	0	0	41191	1123725
Other Portfolio Income 6	881151	0	101	206	3257	21217	34465	4989	3301	10832	5525	3937	793320
Other Receipts 7	1834873	1758	0	63	134	29330	22722	25162	27835	49325	80695	66941	1530910
Total Receipts 8	54066663	136052	28902	247350	885726	520869	2074790	2388369	1173130	3745650	1758035	8311333	32796456
Average Total Receipts 9	85684	45351	278	1145	5905	17362	36400	79612	130348	249710	351607	1385222	5466076
Operating Costs/Operating Income (%)													
Cost of Operations 10	51.8	55.3	69.2	55.7	73.9	72.0	72.2	69.2	70.5	66.5	56.9	47.5	46.1
Salaries and Wages 11	12.8	17.3	1.4	5.7	10.4	7.5	8.4	10.4	9.7	10.3	13.6	10.9	14.4
Taxes Paid 12	2.0	3.3	2.2	2.8	2.1	1.6	1.6	1.5	2.2	1.6	3.0	1.6	2.1
Interest Paid 13	4.6	3.9	1.3	0.9	0.5	0.5	0.5	0.6	1.3	1.2	2.9	2.6	6.6
Depreciation 14	4.9	5.4	5.0	4.4	1.8	3.4	3.1	3.8	3.6	4.2	8.7	5.2	5.1
Amortization and Depletion 15	0.9	1.9	0.4	0.4	0.0	0.1	0.1	0.2	0.2	0.5	0.7	0.8	1.2
Pensions and Other Deferred Comp. 16	1.6	0.9	•	1.7	0.5	0.5	0.4	0.5	0.3	0.4	0.5	0.1	2.6
Employee Benefits 17	2.1	0.5	•	0.6	1.6	1.7	1.4	2.2	1.5	2.7	0.8	2.6	2.1
Advertising 18	3.1	16.4	3.9	1.3	1.0	1.0	3.2	2.3	2.1	1.7	1.7	0.7	4.1
Other Expenses 19	17.9	25.4	16.1	21.8	2.9	10.5	7.3	8.1	9.7	8.5	13.9	20.5	21.1
Officers' Compensation 20	0.5	0.9	0.0	5.7	5.4	0.9	0.9	0.9	0.7	0.6	0.6	0.3	0.3
Operating Margin 21	•	•	0.4	•	0.0	0.4	0.8	0.2	•	1.7	•	7.2	•
Operating Margin Before Officers' Comp. 22	•	•	0.4	4.6	5.4	1.3	1.7	1.1	•	2.3	•	7.5	•

Selected Average Balance Sheet ($ in Thousands)

Net Receivables 23	22784	0	32	142	861	1081	2599	6803	9970	21388	39875	157284	2045838
Inventories 24	3509	0	68	45	172	531	1678	3992	5068	10764	20452	54540	217026
Net Property, Plant and Equipment 25	20374	0	43	247	715	1995	5269	12668	25851	47842	141278	392989	1322703
Total Assets 26	131808	0	370	659	2011	6699	15202	36591	74360	154504	356313	1369077	11256751
Notes and Loans Payable 27	49891	0	198	235	694	2186	3883	13309	28816	29494	164171	603580	4245898
All Other Liabilities 28	34843	0	47	87	287	908	3511	10468	17148	34741	137472	283012	3052840
Net Worth 29	47074	0	126	337	1030	3605	7808	12814	28396	90269	54670	482486	3958013

Selected Financial Ratios (Times to 1)

Current Ratio 30	1.1	·	0.9	4.9	2.5	1.7	1.7	1.7	1.7	1.7	1.9	1.5	1.0
Quick Ratio 31	0.8	·	0.3	3.7	1.8	1.1	1.1	1.2	1.2	1.2	1.2	1.0	0.8
Net Sales to Working Capital 32	20.4	·	·	3.7	17.6	7.7	11.9	10.4	9.5	11.5	8.5	15.6	41.7
Coverage Ratio 33	3.2	·	1.6	0.0	2.5	21.7	8.1	3.4	1.6	4.1	1.7	4.5	3.0
Total Asset Turnover 34	0.6	·	0.7	1.7	2.9	2.3	2.1	1.7	1.6	1.6	0.9	1.0	0.4
Inventory Turnover 35	11.5	·	2.8	14.0	25.2	21.2	15.2	13.6	17.6	15.1	9.3	11.8	10.0
Receivables Turnover 36	4.5	·	·	12.0	7.0	19.6	14.2	12.4	13.5	11.8	6.6	8.2	3.2
Total Liabilities to Net Worth 37	1.8	·	1.9	1.0	1.0	0.9	0.9	1.9	1.6	0.7	5.5	1.8	1.8
Current Assets to Working Capital 38	9.0	·	·	1.3	1.7	2.4	2.4	2.3	2.4	2.4	2.1	3.1	25.4
Current Liabilities to Working Capital 39	8.0	·	·	0.3	0.7	1.4	1.4	1.3	1.4	1.4	1.1	2.1	24.4
Working Capital to Net Sales 40	0.0	·	·	0.3	0.1	0.1	0.1	0.1	0.1	0.1	0.1	0.1	0.0
Inventory to Working Capital 41	0.9	·	·	0.3	0.3	0.6	0.6	0.4	0.4	0.5	0.5	0.7	1.9
Total Receipts to Cash Flow 42	4.2	·	6.2	6.5	32.0	10.8	13.1	12.3	9.2	7.9	6.4	3.7	3.4
Cost of Goods to Cash Flow 43	2.2	·	4.3	3.6	23.7	7.8	9.1	8.6	6.1	4.6	4.5	1.8	1.6
Cash Flow to Total Debt 44	0.2	·	0.2	0.5	0.8	0.4	0.3	0.3	0.4	0.1	0.1	0.4	0.2

Selected Financial Factors (in Percentages)

Debt Ratio 45	64.3	·	66.1	48.8	48.8	46.2	48.6	65.0	61.8	41.6	84.7	64.8	64.8
Return on Total Assets 46	8.5	·	1.5	0.1	3.8	27.6	10.3	4.8	3.6	8.0	4.7	11.6	8.4
Return on Equity Before Income Taxes 47	16.4	·	1.6	•	4.5	48.9	17.5	9.6	3.7	10.4	12.9	25.7	16.0
Return on Equity After Income Taxes 48	10.5	·	1.5	•	4.0	45.3	15.0	7.9	2.4	8.6	5.4	17.6	9.9
Profit Margin (Before Income Tax) 49	9.9	·	0.7	•	0.8	11.3	3.9	1.6	0.8	3.8	2.1	9.1	13.4
Profit Margin (After Income Tax) 50	6.3	·	0.7	•	0.7	10.4	3.3	1.3	0.5	3.2	0.9	6.3	8.3

Table II
Corporations with Net Income

SOFT DRINK AND ICE

MONEY AMOUNTS AND SIZE OF ASSETS IN THOUSANDS OF DOLLARS

Item Description for Accounting Period 7/04 Through 6/05	Total	Zero Assets	Under 500	500 to 1000	251 to 500	501 to 1,000	1,001 to 5,000	5,001 to 10,000	10,001 to 25,000	25,001 to 50,000	50,001 to 100,000	100,001 to 250,000	250,001 and over
Number of Enterprises 1	489	0	0	131	0	19	37	19	5	12	0	6	0

Revenues ($ in Thousands)

Item	Total	Zero Assets	Under 500	500 to 1000	251 to 500	501 to 1,000	1,001 to 5,000	5,001 to 10,000	10,001 to 25,000	25,001 to 50,000	50,001 to 100,000	100,001 to 250,000	250,001 and over
Net Sales 2	33861916	0	0	189726	0	328509	1255272	1567728	603533	3336776	0	8151850	0
Interest 3	892252	0	0	8	0	248	550	565	600	18972	0	42023	0
Rents 4	48087	0	0	0	0	101	1480	861	754	1096	0	5391	0
Royalties 5	1165108	0	0	0	0	0	193	0	0	0	0	41191	0
Other Portfolio Income 6	873562	0	0	0	0	21217	34138	3193	378	10488	0	3937	0
Other Receipts 7	1770903	0	0	63	0	29285	16847	11449	6381	43824	0	66941	0
Total Receipts 8	38611828	0	0	189797	0	379360	1308480	1583796	611646	3411156	0	8311333	0
Average Total Receipts 9	78961	•	•	1449	•	19966	35364	83358	122329	284263	•	1385222	•

Operating Costs/Operating Income (%)

Item	Total	Zero Assets	Under 500	500 to 1000	251 to 500	501 to 1,000	1,001 to 5,000	5,001 to 10,000	10,001 to 25,000	25,001 to 50,000	50,001 to 100,000	100,001 to 250,000	250,001 and over
Cost of Operations 10	48.3	•	•	51.4	•	64.5	65.4	63.1	72.3	68.3	•	47.5	•
Salaries and Wages 11	11.0	•	•	6.0	•	10.0	9.8	11.9	6.1	9.5	•	10.9	•
Taxes Paid 12	1.9	•	•	3.1	•	1.8	1.7	1.6	2.4	1.7	•	1.6	•
Interest Paid 13	4.7	•	•	1.2	•	0.2	0.5	0.4	1.3	0.9	•	2.6	•
Depreciation 14	4.2	•	•	5.6	•	3.1	3.4	3.4	3.4	3.8	•	5.2	•
Amortization and Depletion 15	0.8	•	•	0.5	•	0.1	0.1	0.2	0.2	0.4	•	0.8	•
Pensions and Other Deferred Comp. 16	1.0	•	•	2.2	•	0.5	0.5	0.5	0.2	0.3	•	0.1	•
Employee Benefits 17	1.9	•	•	0.5	•	1.7	1.5	2.6	1.4	2.5	•	2.6	•
Advertising 18	3.9	•	•	1.7	•	1.2	4.8	3.1	1.8	1.8	•	0.7	•
Other Expenses 19	22.8	•	•	21.5	•	13.9	7.7	8.8	7.7	8.0	•	20.5	•
Officers' Compensation 20	0.5	•	•	5.1	•	1.0	0.9	1.1	1.2	0.5	•	0.3	•
Operating Margin 21	•	•	•	1.3	•	1.9	3.6	3.2	2.0	2.4	•	7.2	•
Operating Margin Before Officers' Comp. 22	•	•	•	6.4	•	2.9	4.5	4.3	3.2	2.9	•	7.5	•

Selected Average Balance Sheet ($ in Thousands)

Net Receivables 23	25259	151	1355	2303	6600	8929	23888	157284
Inventories 24	3626	66	361	1526	3504	4201	12929	60611
Net Property, Plant and Equipment 25	15303	308	1554	5017	10886	31116	46739	392989
Total Assets 26	112649	640	7599	15351	38056	71610	149955	1369077
Notes and Loans Payable 27	43213	388	1088	2885	8322	24161	14504	603580
All Other Liabilities 28	35437	77	1169	3469	9686	16788	36047	283012
Net Worth 29	33999	175	5342	8996	20048	30661	99404	482486

Selected Financial Ratios (Times to 1)

Current Ratio 30	1.1	3.5	4.0	2.0	2.2	1.4	1.9	1.5
Quick Ratio 31	0.8	2.1	3.2	1.4	1.5	0.7	1.3	1.0
Net Sales to Working Capital 32	21.1	7.0	5.9	9.6	7.6	18.2	9.9	15.6
Coverage Ratio 33	4.4	2.1	97.6	16.4	10.7	3.6	6.2	4.5
Total Asset Turnover 34	0.6	2.3	2.3	2.2	2.2	1.7	1.9	1.0
Inventory Turnover 35	9.2	11.2	30.9	14.5	14.9	20.8	14.7	10.6
Receivables Turnover 36	3.4	18.1	17.8	13.5	13.8			1.8
Total Liabilities to Net Worth 37	2.3	2.6	0.4	0.7	0.9	1.3	0.5	1.8
Current Assets to Working Capital 38	11.5	1.4	1.3	2.0	1.8	3.8	2.1	3.1
Current Liabilities to Working Capital 39	10.5	0.4	0.3	1.0	0.8	2.8	1.1	2.1
Working Capital to Net Sales 40	0.0	0.1	0.2	0.1	0.1	0.1	0.1	0.1
Inventory to Working Capital 41	1.0	0.5	0.2	0.4	0.3	0.6	0.5	0.7
Total Receipts to Cash Flow 42	3.0	5.8	4.5	7.4	8.9	11.0	9.1	3.7
Cost of Goods to Cash Flow 43	1.4	3.0	2.9	4.9	5.6	8.0	6.2	1.8
Cash Flow to Total Debt 44	0.3	0.5	1.7	0.7	0.5	0.3	0.6	0.4

Selected Financial Factors (in Percentages)

Debt Ratio 45	69.8	72.6	29.7	41.4	47.3	57.2	33.7	64.8
Return on Total Assets 46	12.7	5.6	39.9	18.3	10.1	7.7	10.1	11.6
Return on Equity Before Income Taxes 47	32.4	10.7	56.1	29.4	17.4	13.0	12.8	25.7
Return on Equity After Income Taxes 48	21.9	9.1	52.3	25.9	15.7	10.9	10.8	17.6
Profit Margin (Before Income Tax) 49	15.9	1.3	17.3	7.8	4.2	3.3	4.6	9.1
Profit Margin (After Income Tax) 50	10.8	1.1	16.2	6.9	3.8	2.8	3.9	6.3

Table I

Corporations with and without Net Income

BREWERIES

MONEY AMOUNTS AND SIZE OF ASSETS IN THOUSANDS OF DOLLARS

Item Description for Accounting Period 7/04 Through 6/05	Total	Zero Assets	Under 500	500 to 1,000	1,000 to 5,000	5,000 to 10,000	10,000 to 25,000	25,000 to 50,000	50,000 to 100,000	100,000 to 250,000	250,000 to 500,000	500,000 to 2,500,000	2,500,000 and over
Number of Enterprises 1	117	0	0	65	19	12	0	7	0	0	0	3	0
Revenues ($ in Thousands)													
Net Sales 2	24542152	0	0	16199	128583	112952	0	326092	0	0	0	23200074	0
Interest 3	35154	0	0	197	0	0	0	326	0	0	0	34155	0
Rents 4	25997	0	0	0	0	41	0	0	0	0	0	25956	0
Royalties 5	351671	0	0	0	0	0	0	172	0	0	0	351499	0
Other Portfolio Income 6	396233	0	0	0	0	14	0	0	0	0	0	395184	0
Other Receipts 7	292180	0	0	0	0	571	0	4507	0	0	0	281177	0
Total Receipts 8	25643387	0	0	16396	128583	113578	0	331097	0	0	0	24428045	0
Average Total Receipts 9	219174	.	.	252	6768	9465	.	47300	.	.	.	8096015	.
Operating Costs/Operating Income (%)													
Cost of Operations 10	41.7	.	.	76.3	91.2	64.6	.	64.7	.	.	.	40.4	.
Salaries and Wages 11	8.3	.	.	.	3.7	6.3	.	4.1	.	.	.	8.5	.
Taxes Paid 12	13.3	.	.	6.5	.	5.9	.	3.9	.	.	.	13.8	.
Interest Paid 13	2.4	.	.	.	0.1	0.9	.	1.2	.	.	.	2.5	.
Depreciation 14	5.7	.	.	.	.	4.2	.	6.8	.	.	.	5.9	.
Amortization and Depletion 15	0.3	.	.	.	.	0.3	.	0.1	.	.	.	0.4	.
Pensions and Other Deferred Comp. 16	1.7	.	.	.	.	0.4	.	0.7	.	.	.	1.8	.
Employee Benefits 17	1.6	.	.	.	.	1.8	.	0.8	.	.	.	1.7	.
Advertising 18	7.8	.	.	.	.	7.3	.	2.7	.	.	.	8.0	.
Other Expenses 19	8.2	.	.	18.0	4.8	9.8	.	10.8	.	.	.	8.0	.
Officers' Compensation 20	0.6	.	.	.	.	1.2	.	1.1	.	.	.	0.6	.
Operating Margin 21	8.3	.	.	.	0.3	.	.	3.2	.	.	.	8.4	.
Operating Margin Before Officers' Comp. 22	8.9	.	.	.	0.3	.	.	4.3	.	.	.	9.0	.

Selected Average Balance Sheet ($ in Thousands)

Net Receivables 23	9773	333	494	530	6730	339584
Inventories 24	8198	0	641	856	2603	293082
Net Property, Plant and Equipment 25	90370	0	0	2829	24321	3400536
Total Assets 26	194856	657	3144	5804	37789	7291427
Notes and Loans Payable 27	101268	0	2888	3524	19003	3842721
All Other Liabilities 28	59785	409	24	5112	3925	2298429
Net Worth 29	33803	248	231	-2832	14862	1150276

Selected Financial Ratios (Times to 1)

Current Ratio 30	0.9	1.6	69.2	0.3	2.3	0.9
Quick Ratio 31	0.5	1.5	42.1	0.1	1.6	0.5
Net Sales to Working Capital 32	·	1.0	4.1	·	8.2	·
Coverage Ratio 33	6.6	·	4.5	·	5.0	6.5
Total Asset Turnover 34	1.1	0.4	2.2	1.6	1.2	1.1
Inventory Turnover 35	10.7	·	9.6	7.1	11.6	10.7
Receivables Turnover 36	21.2	·	13.2	23.2	7.4	22.3
Total Liabilities to Net Worth 37	4.8	1.7	12.6	·	1.5	5.3
Current Assets to Working Capital 38	·	2.7	1.0	·	1.8	·
Current Liabilities to Working Capital 39	·	1.7	0.0	·	0.8	·
Working Capital to Net Sales 40	·	1.0	0.2	·	0.1	·
Inventory to Working Capital 41	·	·	0.4	·	0.5	·
Total Receipts to Cash Flow 42	5.3	238.2	20.0	20.5	7.2	5.2
Cost of Goods to Cash Flow 43	2.2	181.8	18.2	13.2	4.7	2.1
Cash Flow to Total Debt 44	0.2	0.0	0.1	0.1	0.3	0.2

Selected Financial Factors (in Percentages)

Debt Ratio 45	82.7	62.3	92.6	148.8	60.7	84.2
Return on Total Assets 46	16.8	0.2	0.8	·	7.3	17.0
Return on Equity Before Income Taxes 47	81.9	0.4	8.4	7.4	14.8	91.0
Return on Equity After Income Taxes 48	55.6	0.4	7.2	7.4	12.5	61.1
Profit Margin (Before Income Tax) 49	13.2	0.4	0.3	·	4.7	13.5
Profit Margin (After Income Tax) 50	9.0	0.4	0.2	·	4.0	9.1

53

Table II

Corporations with Net Income

BREWERIES

MONEY AMOUNTS AND SIZE OF ASSETS IN THOUSANDS OF DOLLARS

Item Description for Accounting Period 7/04 Through 6/05	Total	Zero Assets	Under 500	500 to 1,000	1,000 to 5,000	5,000 to 10,000	10,000 to 25,000	25,000 to 50,000	50,000 to 100,000	100,000 to 250,000	250,000 to 500,000	500,000 to 2,500,000	2,500,000 and over
Number of Enterprises 1	103	0	0	65	0	0	0	0	0	0	0	3	0
Revenues ($ in Thousands)													
Net Sales 2	24362663	0	0	16199	0	0	0	0	0	0	0	23200074	0
Interest 3	35088	0	0	197	0	0	0	0	0	0	0	34155	0
Rents 4	25956	0	0	0	0	0	0	0	0	0	0	25956	0
Royalties 5	351671	0	0	0	0	0	0	0	0	0	0	351499	0
Other Portfolio Income 6	396201	0	0	0	0	0	0	0	0	0	0	395184	0
Other Receipts 7	289785	0	0	0	0	0	0	0	0	0	0	281177	0
Total Receipts 8	25461364	0	0	16396	0	0	0	0	0	0	0	24288045	0
Average Total Receipts 9	247198	·	·	252	·	·	·	·	·	·	·	8096015	·
Operating Costs/Operating Income (%)													
Cost of Operations 10	41.5	·	·	76.3	·	·	·	·	·	·	·	40.4	·
Salaries and Wages 11	8.3	·	·	·	·	·	·	·	·	·	·	8.5	·
Taxes Paid 12	13.3	·	·	6.5	·	·	·	·	·	·	·	13.8	·
Interest Paid 13	2.4	·	·	·	·	·	·	·	·	·	·	2.5	·
Depreciation 14	5.8	·	·	·	·	·	·	·	·	·	·	5.9	·
Amortization and Depletion 15	0.3	·	·	·	·	·	·	·	·	·	·	0.4	·
Pensions and Other Deferred Comp. 16	1.7	·	·	·	·	·	·	·	·	·	·	1.8	·
Employee Benefits 17	1.6	·	·	·	·	·	·	·	·	·	·	1.7	·
Advertising 18	7.8	·	·	·	·	·	·	·	·	·	·	8.0	·
Other Expenses 19	8.2	·	·	18.0	·	·	·	·	·	·	·	8.0	·
Officers' Compensation 20	0.6	·	·	·	·	·	·	·	·	·	·	0.6	·
Operating Margin 21	8.4	·	·	·	·	·	·	·	·	·	·	8.4	·
Operating Margin Before Officers' Comp. 22	9.0	·	·	·	·	·	·	·	·	·	·	9.0	·

Selected Average Balance Sheet ($ in Thousands)

Net Receivables 23	11010	333	339584
Inventories 24	9081	0	287854
Net Property, Plant and Equipment 25	101347	0	3400536
Total Assets 26	219534	657	7291427
Notes and Loans Payable 27	114482	0	3842721
All Other Liabilities 28	67169	409	2298429
Net Worth 29	37883	248	1150276

Selected Financial Ratios (Times to 1)

Current Ratio 30	1.0	1.6	0.9
Quick Ratio 31	0.5	1.5	0.5
Net Sales to Working Capital 32		1.0	
Coverage Ratio 33	6.6		6.5
Total Asset Turnover 34	1.1	0.4	1.1
Inventory Turnover 35	10.8		10.9
Receivables Turnover 36	21.3		
Total Liabilities to Net Worth 37	4.8	1.7	5.3
Current Assets to Working Capital 38		2.7	
Current Liabilities to Working Capital 39		1.7	
Working Capital to Net Sales 40		1.0	
Inventory to Working Capital 41			
Total Receipts to Cash Flow 42	5.2	238.2	5.2
Cost of Goods to Cash Flow 43	2.2	181.8	2.1
Cash Flow to Total Debt 44	0.2	0.0	0.2

Selected Financial Factors (in Percentages)

Debt Ratio 45	82.7	62.3	84.2
Return on Total Assets 46	16.9	0.2	17.0
Return on Equity Before Income Taxes 47	83.3	0.4	91.0
Return on Equity After Income Taxes 48	56.6	0.4	61.1
Profit Margin (Before Income Tax) 49	13.3	0.4	13.5
Profit Margin (After Income Tax) 50	9.1	0.4	9.1

Table I

Corporations with and without Net Income

WINERIES AND DISTILLERIES

MONEY AMOUNTS AND SIZE OF ASSETS IN THOUSANDS OF DOLLARS

Item Description for Accounting Period 7/04 Through 6/05		Total	Zero Assets	Under 500	500 to 1,000	1,000 to 5,000	5,000 to 10,000	10,000 to 25,000	25,000 to 50,000	50,000 to 100,000	100,000 to 250,000	250,000 to 500,000	500,000 to 2,500,000	2,500,000 and over
Number of Enterprises	1	892	0	103	409	159	95	0	24	0	10	3	3	4
Revenues ($ in Thousands)														
Net Sales	2	20056873	0	32695	401075	243462	362154	0	599064	0	1144193	1021457	3149938	11545517
Interest	3	178658	0	0	132	1098	819	0	734	0	2389	3457	6926	160862
Rents	4	9925	0	0	0	0	0	0	170	0	1279	16	7247	810
Royalties	5	411628	0	0	0	0	0	0	1232	0	0	0	191	410200
Other Portfolio Income	6	150974	0	0	144	0	347	0	3134	0	21042	23	32312	68387
Other Receipts	7	318346	0	1488	35158	-1540	7106	0	15569	0	4881	4769	134382	88001
Total Receipts	8	21126404	0	34183	436509	243020	370426	0	619903	0	1173784	1029722	3330996	12273777
Average Total Receipts	9	23684	•	332	1067	1528	3899	•	25829	•	117378	343241	1110332	3068444
Operating Costs/Operating Income (%)														
Cost of Operations	10	52.1	•	36.6	56.6	31.3	44.8	•	58.7	•	67.9	49.0	60.6	47.9
Salaries and Wages	11	7.1	•	8.9	4.7	17.1	17.5	•	8.8	•	5.2	4.7	10.1	6.1
Taxes Paid	12	13.0	•	6.1	4.9	5.2	5.7	•	3.9	•	4.0	23.6	12.3	14.9
Interest Paid	13	4.2	•	0.6	4.5	2.6	2.9	•	1.5	•	3.6	1.2	0.9	5.8
Depreciation	14	3.4	•	4.7	2.6	6.9	8.3	•	7.3	•	4.2	2.4	5.3	2.2
Amortization and Depletion	15	1.7	•	•	0.3	0.2	0.1	•	0.4	•	1.3	1.3	0.3	2.6
Pensions and Other Deferred Comp.	16	0.4	•	•	0.1	1.7	0.2	•	0.3	•	0.6	0.4	0.7	0.4
Employee Benefits	17	1.0	•	4.6	0.8	1.7	1.6	•	1.5	•	1.1	0.9	1.1	0.9
Advertising	18	6.6	•	0.5	2.9	2.4	1.1	•	1.0	•	1.7	5.2	3.9	9.0
Other Expenses	19	10.1	•	27.8	15.5	22.8	12.1	•	12.0	•	7.6	2.7	12.6	9.5
Officers' Compensation	20	1.2	•	15.3	10.0	5.4	1.1	•	2.0	•	1.2	0.5	0.5	0.9
Operating Margin	21	•	•	•	•	2.5	4.7	•	2.5	•	1.6	8.1	•	•
Operating Margin Before Officers' Comp.	22	0.4	•	10.2	7.2	7.9	5.8	•	4.6	•	2.8	8.6	•	0.6

Selected Average Balance Sheet ($ in Thousands)

Net Receivables 23	6595	•	1	50	564	376	3428	•	19819	65221	132877	1164563
Inventories 24	7070	•	366	338	728	2625	10354	•	46103	141348	411214	669193
Net Property, Plant and Equipment 25	6737	•	32	160	572	3221	15047	•	45881	64266	384954	663436
Total Assets 26	38048	•	399	686	2096	6910	36324	•	155524	364340	1209416	5840167
Notes and Loans Payable 27	18885	•	492	1482	606	4526	7841	•	64283	69763	349381	3197224
All Other Liabilities 28	9116	•	30	39	214	353	5887	•	30288	77034	229766	1581150
Net Worth 29	10048	•	-123	-835	1276	2031	22596	•	60953	217543	630269	1061792

Selected Financial Ratios (Times to 1)

Current Ratio 30	1.9	•	1.7	5.3	4.8	5.5	2.3	•	2.2	2.8	2.4	1.6
Quick Ratio 31	0.8	•	0.0	1.2	2.3	1.0	0.8	•	0.6	0.8	0.5	0.9
Net Sales to Working Capital 32	3.0	•	2.2	2.8	1.4	1.3	2.5	•	2.6	2.4	2.7	3.4
Coverage Ratio 33	2.3	•	0.2	2.3	1.9	3.4	4.9	•	2.2	8.3	•	2.3
Total Asset Turnover 34	0.6	•	0.8	1.4	0.7	0.6	0.7	•	0.7	0.9	0.9	0.5
Inventory Turnover 35	1.7	•	0.3	1.6	0.7	0.6	1.4	•	1.7	1.2	1.5	2.1
Receivables Turnover 36	2.9	•	•	35.0	2.8	10.9	6.6	•	6.1	5.7	7.9	2.0
Total Liabilities to Net Worth 37	2.8	•	•	•	0.6	2.4	0.6	•	1.6	0.7	0.9	4.5
Current Assets to Working Capital 38	2.1	•	2.5	1.2	1.3	1.2	1.8	•	1.8	1.6	1.7	2.6
Current Liabilities to Working Capital 39	1.1	•	1.5	0.2	0.3	0.2	0.8	•	0.8	0.6	0.7	1.6
Working Capital to Net Sales 40	0.3	•	0.5	0.4	0.7	0.8	0.4	•	0.4	0.4	0.4	0.3
Inventory to Working Capital 41	1.0	•	2.5	1.0	0.7	0.9	1.1	•	1.2	1.1	1.1	0.9
Total Receipts to Cash Flow 42	7.9	•	6.4	5.6	6.1	6.8	6.3	•	9.1	9.2	12.5	7.2
Cost of Goods to Cash Flow 43	4.1	•	2.3	3.2	1.9	3.0	3.7	•	6.2	4.5	7.6	3.5
Cash Flow to Total Debt 44	0.1	•	0.1	0.1	0.3	0.1	0.3	•	0.1	0.3	0.1	0.1

Selected Financial Factors (in Percentages)

Debt Ratio 45	73.6	•	130.9	221.8	39.1	70.6	37.8	•	60.8	40.3	47.9	81.8
Return on Total Assets 46	5.6	•	0.1	15.0	3.6	5.5	5.2	•	5.8	9.5	•	6.5
Return on Equity Before Income Taxes 47	11.8	•	1.3	•	2.7	13.2	6.6	•	7.9	14.0	•	19.9
Return on Equity After Income Taxes 48	7.5	•	1.3	•	0.9	10.5	5.2	•	6.4	9.9	•	12.6
Profit Margin (Before Income Tax) 49	5.3	•	•	6.0	2.3	7.0	6.0	•	4.2	8.9	•	7.3
Profit Margin (After Income Tax) 50	3.3	•	•	5.9	0.7	5.6	4.7	•	3.4	6.3	•	4.6

Table II

Corporations with Net Income

WINERIES AND DISTILLERIES

MONEY AMOUNTS AND SIZE OF ASSETS IN THOUSANDS OF DOLLARS

Item Description for Accounting Period 7/04 Through 6/05	Total	Zero Assets	Under 500	500 to 1,000	1,000 to 5,000	5,000 to 10,000	10,000 to 25,000	25,000 to 50,000	50,000 to 100,000	100,000 to 250,000	250,000 to 500,000	500,000 to 2,500,000	2,500,000 and over
Number of Enterprises **1**	538	0	0	309	72	80	23	0	13	0	0	0	0
Revenues ($ in Thousands)													
Net Sales **2**	18213841	0	0	237403	218559	331162	323401	0	858475	0	0	0	0
Interest **3**	170793	0	0	92	1098	805	67	0	1162	0	0	0	0
Rents **4**	9250	0	0	0	0	0	66	0	211	0	0	0	0
Royalties **5**	411623	0	0	0	0	0	0	0	0	0	0	0	0
Other Portfolio Income **6**	137861	0	0	144	0	176	3513	0	15085	0	0	0	0
Other Receipts **7**	216663	0	0	34583	357	6362	9762	0	8662	0	0	0	0
Total Receipts **8**	19160031	0	0	272222	220014	338505	336809	0	883595	0	0	0	0
Average Total Receipts **9**	35613	•	•	881	3056	4231	14644	•	67969	•	•	•	•
Operating Costs/Operating Income (%)													
Cost of Operations **10**	50.5	•	•	45.8	27.9	44.1	46.6	•	60.5	•	•	•	•
Salaries and Wages **11**	6.7	•	•	6.0	17.1	15.8	8.4	•	5.1	•	•	•	•
Taxes Paid **12**	13.8	•	•	4.7	5.0	5.5	11.1	•	8.6	•	•	•	•
Interest Paid **13**	4.0	•	•	3.7	0.9	2.5	1.9	•	1.4	•	•	•	•
Depreciation **14**	2.9	•	•	3.4	6.7	6.9	5.2	•	3.6	•	•	•	•
Amortization and Depletion **15**	1.8	•	•	0.3	0.2	0.1	0.2	•	0.6	•	•	•	•
Pensions and Other Deferred Comp. **16**	0.5	•	•	0.1	1.9	0.2	0.3	•	0.5	•	•	•	•
Employee Benefits **17**	1.0	•	•	1.2	1.8	1.2	1.0	•	0.4	•	•	•	•
Advertising **18**	7.0	•	•	4.1	2.2	1.1	1.6	•	3.1	•	•	•	•
Other Expenses **19**	9.2	•	•	15.3	25.2	12.6	10.6	•	8.6	•	•	•	•
Officers' Compensation **20**	1.0	•	•	14.0	5.9	1.0	2.5	•	1.3	•	•	•	•
Operating Margin **21**	1.6	•	•	1.2	5.2	9.0	10.7	•	6.4	•	•	•	•
Operating Margin Before Officers' Comp. **22**	2.7	•	•	15.2	11.1	10.0	13.2	•	7.7	•	•	•	•

Selected Average Balance Sheet ($ in Thousands)

Net Receivables 23	6757	22	333	408	1796	7534
Inventories 24	9209	446	1072	2558	6458	20575
Net Property, Plant and Equipment 25	7877	98	714	2746	5884	15807
Total Assets 26	48368	674	2566	6430	17202	64970
Notes and Loans Payable 27	25641	433	640	4330	4659	18281
All Other Liabilities 28	12024	41	330	304	2341	12411
Net Worth 29	10704	200	1595	1796	10202	34278

Selected Financial Ratios (Times to 1)

Current Ratio 30	1.8	5.1	3.0	6.8	2.6	2.0
Quick Ratio 31	0.7	0.5	1.0	1.5	0.7	0.8
Net Sales to Working Capital 32	4.0	1.9	2.8	1.4	2.5	4.1
Coverage Ratio 33	2.9	5.3	7.4	5.5	8.7	7.9
Total Asset Turnover 34	0.7	1.1	1.2	0.6	0.8	1.0
Inventory Turnover 35	1.9	0.8	0.8	0.7	1.0	1.9
Receivables Turnover 36	3.9	51.9		10.8	7.4	8.9
Total Liabilities to Net Worth 37	3.5	2.4	0.6	2.6	0.7	0.9
Current Assets to Working Capital 38	2.3	1.2	1.5	1.2	1.6	2.0
Current Liabilities to Working Capital 39	1.3	0.2	0.5	0.2	0.6	1.0
Working Capital to Net Sales 40	0.2	0.5	0.4	0.7	0.4	0.2
Inventory to Working Capital 41	1.2	1.1	1.0	0.8	1.1	1.2
Total Receipts to Cash Flow 42	7.1	3.9	4.6	5.0	4.5	6.1
Cost of Goods to Cash Flow 43	3.6	1.8	1.3	2.2	2.1	3.7
Cash Flow to Total Debt 44	0.1	0.4	0.7	0.2	0.4	0.4

Selected Financial Factors (in Percentages)

Debt Ratio 45	77.9	70.3	37.8	72.1	40.7	47.2
Return on Total Assets 46	8.1	22.4	8.1	8.8	13.8	10.9
Return on Equity Before Income Taxes 47	24.1	60.9	11.2	25.8	20.5	18.0
Return on Equity After Income Taxes 48	17.3	60.4	7.9	22.2	19.1	14.1
Profit Margin (Before Income Tax) 49	7.6	15.9	5.9	11.2	14.9	9.4
Profit Margin (After Income Tax) 50	5.5	15.7	4.1	9.6	13.9	7.3

Table I

Corporations with and without Net Income

TOBACCO MANUFACTURING

MONEY AMOUNTS AND SIZE OF ASSETS IN THOUSANDS OF DOLLARS

Item Description for Accounting Period 7/04 Through 6/05	Total	Zero Assets	Under 500	500 to 1,000	1,000 to 5,000	5,000 to 10,000	10,000 to 25,000	25,000 to 50,000	50,000 to 100,000	100,000 to 250,000	250,000 to 500,000	500,000 to 2,500,000	2,500,000 and over
Number of Enterprises 1	20	0	0	0	0	0	0	0	0	0	6	0	3
Revenues ($ in Thousands)													
Net Sales 2	17746722	0	0	0	0	0	0	0	0	0	2203724	0	14622596
Interest 3	148593	0	0	0	0	0	0	0	0	0	82553	0	65663
Rents 4	17809	0	0	0	0	0	0	0	0	0	1687	0	16122
Royalties 5	99894	0	0	0	0	0	0	0	0	0	12135	0	87747
Other Portfolio Income 6	64711	0	0	0	0	0	0	0	0	0	4256	0	60443
Other Receipts 7	513503	0	0	0	0	0	0	0	0	0	16437	0	525371
Total Receipts 8	18591232	0	0	0	0	0	0	0	0	0	2320792	0	15377942
Average Total Receipts 9	929562	•	•	•	•	•	•	•	•	•	386799	•	5125981
Operating Costs/Operating Income (%)													
Cost of Operations 10	62.3	•	•	•	•	•	•	•	•	•	59.3	•	64.2
Salaries and Wages 11	5.7	•	•	•	•	•	•	•	•	•	5.4	•	5.8
Taxes Paid 12	2.1	•	•	•	•	•	•	•	•	•	3.6	•	0.6
Interest Paid 13	2.3	•	•	•	•	•	•	•	•	•	6.6	•	1.8
Depreciation 14	1.2	•	•	•	•	•	•	•	•	•	2.2	•	1.0
Amortization and Depletion 15	0.2	•	•	•	•	•	•	•	•	•	1.3	•	0.0
Pensions and Other Deferred Comp. 16	2.6	•	•	•	•	•	•	•	•	•	0.3	•	3.0
Employee Benefits 17	1.0	•	•	•	•	•	•	•	•	•	1.6	•	1.0
Advertising 18	5.3	•	•	•	•	•	•	•	•	•	1.3	•	6.1
Other Expenses 19	11.5	•	•	•	•	•	•	•	•	•	12.9	•	11.3
Officers' Compensation 20	0.8	•	•	•	•	•	•	•	•	•	1.7	•	0.6
Operating Margin 21	5.0	•	•	•	•	•	•	•	•	•	3.8	•	4.4
Operating Margin Before Officers' Comp. 22	5.7	•	•	•	•	•	•	•	•	•	5.4	•	4.9

Selected Average Balance Sheet ($ in Thousands)

Net Receivables 23	114875	47623	658586
Inventories 24	101288	41316	519787
Net Property, Plant and Equipment 25	99700	51705	522908
Total Assets 26	1248809	584566	6979804
Notes and Loans Payable 27	313670	157645	1729772
All Other Liabilities 28	513617	176234	3036284
Net Worth 29	421522	250686	2213748

Selected Financial Ratios (Times to 1)

Current Ratio 30	1.0	1.2	1.0
Quick Ratio 31	0.6	0.5	0.7
Net Sales to Working Capital 32	54.4	11.1	2559.1
Coverage Ratio 33	5.2	2.5	6.4
Total Asset Turnover 34	0.7	0.6	0.7
Inventory Turnover 35	5.5	5.3	6.0
Receivables Turnover 36	8.8	9.0	8.6
Total Liabilities to Net Worth 37	2.0	1.3	2.2
Current Assets to Working Capital 38	23.1	5.5	1079.5
Current Liabilities to Working Capital 39	22.1	4.5	1078.5
Working Capital to Net Sales 40	0.0	0.1	0.0
Inventory to Working Capital 41	6.7	1.8	305.4
Total Receipts to Cash Flow 42	5.0	4.9	5.0
Cost of Goods to Cash Flow 43	3.1	2.9	3.2
Cash Flow to Total Debt 44	0.2	0.2	0.2

Selected Financial Factors (in Percentages)

Debt Ratio 45	66.2	57.1	68.3
Return on Total Assets 46	8.7	10.2	8.0
Return on Equity Before Income Taxes 47	20.8	14.1	21.2
Return on Equity After Income Taxes 48	14.6	11.2	14.1
Profit Margin (Before Income Tax) 49	9.9	9.6	9.6
Profit Margin (After Income Tax) 50	6.9	7.7	6.4

57

Table II

Corporations with Net Income

TOBACCO MANUFACTURING

MONEY AMOUNTS AND SIZE OF ASSETS IN THOUSANDS OF DOLLARS

Item Description for Accounting Period 7/04 Through 6/05	Total	Zero Assets	Under 500	500 to 1,000	1,000 to 5,000	5,000 to 10,000	10,000 to 25,000	25,000 to 50,000	50,000 to 100,000	100,000 to 250,000	250,000 to 500,000	500,000 to 2,500,000	2,500,000 and over
Number of Enterprises **1**	16	0	0	0	0	0	0	0	0	0	0	0	3
Revenues ($ in Thousands)													
Net Sales **2**	16892326	0	0	0	0	0	0	0	0	0	0	0	14622596
Interest **3**	79691	0	0	0	0	0	0	0	0	0	0	0	65663
Rents **4**	17209	0	0	0	0	0	0	0	0	0	0	0	16122
Royalties **5**	92279	0	0	0	0	0	0	0	0	0	0	0	87747
Other Portfolio Income **6**	64600	0	0	0	0	0	0	0	0	0	0	0	60443
Other Receipts **7**	508751	0	0	0	0	0	0	0	0	0	0	0	525371
Total Receipts **8**	17654856	0	0	0	0	0	0	0	0	0	0	0	15377942
Average Total Receipts **9**	1103428	·	·	·	·	·	·	·	·	·	·	·	5125981
Operating Costs/Operating Income (%)													
Cost of Operations **10**	62.2	·	·	·	·	·	·	·	·	·	·	·	64.2
Salaries and Wages **11**	5.6	·	·	·	·	·	·	·	·	·	·	·	5.8
Taxes Paid **12**	1.8	·	·	·	·	·	·	·	·	·	·	·	0.6
Interest Paid **13**	1.8	·	·	·	·	·	·	·	·	·	·	·	1.8
Depreciation **14**	1.1	·	·	·	·	·	·	·	·	·	·	·	1.0
Amortization and Depletion **15**	0.2	·	·	·	·	·	·	·	·	·	·	·	0.0
Pensions and Other Deferred Comp. **16**	2.7	·	·	·	·	·	·	·	·	·	·	·	3.0
Employee Benefits **17**	1.0	·	·	·	·	·	·	·	·	·	·	·	1.0
Advertising **18**	5.4	·	·	·	·	·	·	·	·	·	·	·	6.1
Other Expenses **19**	11.4	·	·	·	·	·	·	·	·	·	·	·	11.3
Officers' Compensation **20**	0.7	·	·	·	·	·	·	·	·	·	·	·	0.6
Operating Margin **21**	6.1	·	·	·	·	·	·	·	·	·	·	·	4.4
Operating Margin Before Officers' Comp. **22**	6.8	·	·	·	·	·	·	·	·	·	·	·	4.9

Selected Average Balance Sheet ($ in Thousands)

Net Receivables 23	133889
Inventories 24	115277
Net Property, Plant and Equipment 25	116078
Total Assets 26	1496482
Notes and Loans Payable 27	361555
All Other Liabilities 28	617216
Net Worth 29	517711

Selected Financial Ratios (Times to 1)

Current Ratio 30	1.0
Quick Ratio 31	0.6
Net Sales to Working Capital 32	87.8
Coverage Ratio 33	6.9
Total Asset Turnover 34	0.7
Inventory Turnover 35	5.7
Receivables Turnover 36	9.3
Total Liabilities to Net Worth 37	1.9
Current Assets to Working Capital 38	37.1
Current Liabilities to Working Capital 39	36.1
Working Capital to Net Sales 40	0.0
Inventory to Working Capital 41	10.6
Total Receipts to Cash Flow 42	4.8
Cost of Goods to Cash Flow 43	3.0
Cash Flow to Total Debt 44	0.2

Selected Financial Factors (in Percentages)

Debt Ratio 45	65.4
Return on Total Assets 46	8.8
Return on Equity Before Income Taxes 47	21.8
Return on Equity After Income Taxes 48	15.5
Profit Margin (Before Income Tax) 49	10.7
Profit Margin (After Income Tax) 50	7.6

Also shown (right column values):

Net Receivables 23	658586
Inventories 24	519787
Net Property, Plant and Equipment 25	522908
Total Assets 26	6979804
Notes and Loans Payable 27	1729772
All Other Liabilities 28	3036284
Net Worth 29	2213748
Current Ratio 30	1.0
Quick Ratio 31	0.7
Net Sales to Working Capital 32	2559.1
Coverage Ratio 33	6.4
Total Asset Turnover 34	0.7
Inventory Turnover 35	6.0
Receivables Turnover 36	8.6
Total Liabilities to Net Worth 37	2.2
Current Assets to Working Capital 38	1079.5
Current Liabilities to Working Capital 39	1078.5
Working Capital to Net Sales 40	0.0
Inventory to Working Capital 41	305.4
Total Receipts to Cash Flow 42	5.0
Cost of Goods to Cash Flow 43	3.2
Cash Flow to Total Debt 44	0.2
Debt Ratio 45	68.3
Return on Total Assets 46	8.0
Return on Equity Before Income Taxes 47	21.2
Return on Equity After Income Taxes 48	14.1
Profit Margin (Before Income Tax) 49	9.6
Profit Margin (After Income Tax) 50	6.4

Table I

Corporations with and without Net Income

TEXTILE MILLS

MONEY AMOUNTS AND SIZE OF ASSETS IN THOUSANDS OF DOLLARS

Item Description for Accounting Period 7/04 Through 6/05	Total	Zero Assets	Under 500	500 to 1,000	1,000 to 5,000	5,000 to 10,000	10,000 to 25,000	25,000 to 50,000	50,000 to 100,000	100,000 to 250,000	250,000 to 500,000	500,000 to 2,500,000	2,500,000 and over
Number of Enterprises **1**	2182	457	1000	241	282	49	87	21	16	15	10	5	0
Revenues ($ in Thousands)													
Net Sales **2**	18592202	244424	903009	232016	936025	780897	2279624	1253366	1540516	2933774	3595688	3892361	0
Interest **3**	209835	468	0	46	3706	771	1166	2474	477	25892	4074	170759	0
Rents **4**	13748	0	0	0	4544	1719	1840	387	2	1186	2782	1289	0
Royalties **5**	78383	0	0	0	0	0	0	0	0	2166	21429	54788	0
Other Portfolio Income **6**	286395	623	0	60	84636	240	7221	9456	960	77430	8749	97022	0
Other Receipts **7**	200941	143	741	5049	2299	3507	10834	15371	27500	45613	41099	48788	0
Total Receipts **8**	19381504	245658	903750	237171	1031210	787134	2300685	1281054	1569455	3086061	3673821	4265507	0
Average Total Receipts **9**	8882	538	904	984	3657	16064	26445	61003	98091	205737	367382	853101	•
Operating Costs/Operating Income (%)													
Cost of Operations **10**	75.6	84.2	83.2	67.2	76.9	80.8	78.4	83.0	77.0	73.0	76.6	68.7	•
Salaries and Wages **11**	5.9	2.5	0.4	1.8	4.5	4.1	5.5	3.5	5.7	6.8	4.8	9.8	•
Taxes Paid **12**	1.8	1.4	0.9	3.6	2.1	0.9	2.1	2.1	1.9	1.6	1.8	1.7	•
Interest Paid **13**	2.5	0.5	1.3	1.1	0.8	1.1	1.0	1.2	1.4	3.0	2.3	4.9	•
Depreciation **14**	4.0	0.8	0.0	1.1	2.3	2.1	2.6	3.4	4.7	3.9	4.6	6.2	•
Amortization and Depletion **15**	0.4	0.7	0.0	0.0	0.1	0.2	0.1	0.2	0.4	1.1	0.5	0.5	•
Pensions and Other Deferred Comp. **16**	0.6	0.3	0.0	0.1	0.1	0.1	0.2	0.5	0.8	0.5	0.5	1.4	•
Employee Benefits **17**	1.3	1.5	0.0	0.1	1.5	0.5	1.5	2.0	1.2	1.5	0.8	1.7	•
Advertising **18**	0.6	0.0	0.0	0.0	0.1	0.2	0.2	0.2	0.7	0.4	0.3	1.7	•
Other Expenses **19**	9.5	10.3	6.2	18.5	15.6	9.7	7.1	10.8	6.4	10.9	9.4	9.5	•
Officers' Compensation **20**	1.4	1.0	2.0	8.5	4.6	1.1	2.2	0.9	1.0	0.9	1.1	0.5	•
Operating Margin **21**	•	•	5.9	•	•	•	•	•	•	•	•	•	•
Operating Margin Before Officers' Comp. **22**	•	•	7.8	6.5	•	0.3	1.4	•	•	•	•	•	•

Selected Average Balance Sheet ($ in Thousands)

	1	2	3	4	5	6	7	8	9	10	11	12	
Net Receivables 23	1206	0	88	72	625	2538	3237	7377	9612	25532	69549	111231	•
Inventories 24	1107	0	5	53	461	1464	4060	7464	15562	28702	53514	94169	•
Net Property, Plant and Equipment 25	1897	0	1	24	370	1347	4423	11485	26501	46224	109648	224326	•
Total Assets 26	8549	0	132	540	2235	7705	15397	37051	70285	165049	370232	1592474	•
Notes and Loans Payable 27	1845	0	53	23	548	2863	4790	24655	19884	32544	100471	185137	•
All Other Liabilities 28	2263	0	130	66	453	2372	3229	11837	14267	49623	77728	453591	•
Net Worth 29	4441	0	-51	452	1234	2470	7378	560	36134	82882	192033	953746	•

Selected Financial Ratios (Times to 1)

	1	2	3	4	5	6	7	8	9	10	11	12	
Current Ratio 30	2.1	•	0.9	5.8	2.4	1.8	1.9	1.0	2.6	2.0	1.6	3.7	•
Quick Ratio 31	1.2	•	0.8	1.0	1.5	0.9	0.9	0.6	1.2	1.0	0.8	2.6	•
Net Sales to Working Capital 32	4.5	•	2.4	3.7	6.3	5.8	5.8	•	4.6	5.2	6.6	2.1	•
Coverage Ratio 33	1.4	•	5.6	1.2	3.1	1.0	1.1	•	1.5	1.5	0.8	1.7	•
Total Asset Turnover 34	1.0	•	6.8	1.8	1.5	2.1	1.7	1.6	1.4	1.2	1.0	0.5	•
Inventory Turnover 35	5.8	•	159.6	12.2	5.5	8.8	5.1	6.6	4.8	5.0	5.1	5.7	•
Receivables Turnover 36	7.6	•	17.5	13.2	5.7	9.1	8.7	8.2	9.0	8.1	6.1	6.4	•
Total Liabilities to Net Worth 37	0.9	•	0.2	0.8	2.1	1.1	65.2	•	0.9	1.0	0.9	0.7	•
Current Assets to Working Capital 38	1.9	•	1.2	1.7	2.3	2.1	•	•	1.6	2.0	2.7	1.4	•
Current Liabilities to Working Capital 39	0.9	•	0.2	0.7	1.3	1.1	•	•	0.6	1.0	1.7	0.4	•
Working Capital to Net Sales 40	0.2	•	0.4	0.3	0.2	0.2	•	•	0.2	0.2	0.2	0.5	•
Inventory to Working Capital 41	0.6	•	0.1	0.5	0.9	0.9	•	•	0.7	0.9	1.1	0.2	•
Total Receipts to Cash Flow 42	13.8	17.1	8.8	6.5	14.9	16.3	17.8	•	18.6	13.0	13.5	10.0	•
Cost of Goods to Cash Flow 43	10.4	14.4	7.3	4.4	11.5	13.1	13.9	•	14.3	9.5	10.3	6.9	•
Cash Flow to Total Debt 44	0.2	0.6	1.7	0.2	0.2	0.2	•	•	0.2	0.2	0.2	0.1	•

Selected Financial Factors (in Percentages)

	1	2	3	4	5	6	7	8	9	10	11	12	
Debt Ratio 45	48.0	•	138.3	16.4	44.8	67.9	52.1	98.5	48.6	49.8	48.1	40.1	•
Return on Total Assets 46	3.3	49.3	2.3	3.5	2.2	1.9	•	2.9	5.5	1.7	•	4.1	•
Return on Equity Before Income Taxes 47	1.7	•	0.5	4.4	•	•	0.4	•	1.8	3.7	•	2.8	•
Return on Equity After Income Taxes 48	0.1	•	0.2	2.4	•	•	•	•	1.0	1.8	•	0.9	•
Profit Margin (Before Income Tax) 49	0.9	5.9	0.2	1.6	•	0.1	•	0.7	1.6	•	•	3.4	•
Profit Margin (After Income Tax) 50	0.1	5.9	0.1	0.9	•	•	•	0.4	0.8	•	•	1.1	•

Table II
Corporations with Net Income

TEXTILE MILLS

MONEY AMOUNTS AND SIZE OF ASSETS IN THOUSANDS OF DOLLARS

Item Description for Accounting Period 7/04 Through 6/05	Total	Zero Assets	Under 500	500 to 1,000	1,000 to 5,000	5,000 to 10,000	10,000 to 25,000	25,000 to 50,000	50,000 to 100,000	100,000 to 250,000	250,000 to 500,000	500,000 to 2,500,000	2,500,000 and over
Number of Enterprises 1	1788	451	0	60	153	38	53	9	11	9	0	0	0
Revenues ($ in Thousands)													
Net Sales 2	12105442	183673	0	207150	549444	681153	1513608	464926	1143458	1700028	0	0	0
Interest 3	53597	15	0	45	1297	112	657	660	353	12455	0	0	0
Rents 4	10016	0	0	0	3022	1606	338	150	2	834	0	0	0
Royalties 5	47377	0	0	0	0	0	0	0	0	1488	0	0	0
Other Portfolio Income 6	253404	412	0	59	82928	185	6130	7004	760	76504	0	0	0
Other Receipts 7	115883	0	0	792	1624	2493	7530	11957	5281	32778	0	0	0
Total Receipts 8	12585719	184100	0	208046	638315	685549	1528263	484697	1149854	1824087	0	0	0
Average Total Receipts 9	7039	408	•	3467	4172	18041	28835	53855	104532	202676	•	•	•
Operating Costs/Operating Income (%)													
Cost of Operations 10	72.9	83.9	•	74.0	77.2	79.2	76.1	79.2	76.3	70.2	•	•	•
Salaries and Wages 11	6.5	0.9	•	2.0	4.6	3.6	5.4	3.5	6.3	6.8	•	•	•
Taxes Paid 12	1.8	0.8	•	3.9	2.1	0.8	2.1	2.1	2.1	1.9	•	•	•
Interest Paid 13	1.0	0.6	•	0.2	0.5	1.0	0.8	1.3	0.4	1.6	•	•	•
Depreciation 14	3.4	0.3	•	0.8	2.2	1.5	1.7	3.3	2.9	4.6	•	•	•
Amortization and Depletion 15	0.3	1.0	•	•	0.0	0.2	0.0	0.1	0.0	1.3	•	•	•
Pensions and Other Deferred Comp. 16	0.6	0.0	•	0.1	0.1	0.0	0.2	0.3	0.4	0.6	•	•	•
Employee Benefits 17	1.1	0.9	•	0.1	1.8	0.5	1.1	1.3	1.2	1.8	•	•	•
Advertising 18	0.7	0.0	•	0.0	0.1	0.1	0.3	0.1	0.9	0.3	•	•	•
Other Expenses 19	8.4	2.3	•	9.3	18.2	8.2	6.9	5.0	4.7	9.5	•	•	•
Officers' Compensation 20	1.3	•	•	9.4	2.4	0.7	2.3	1.1	1.0	1.0	•	•	•
Operating Margin 21	1.9	9.4	•	0.4	•	4.1	2.9	2.7	3.8	0.4	•	•	•
Operating Margin Before Officers' Comp. 22	3.3	9.4	•	9.8	•	4.8	5.2	3.8	4.9	1.3	•	•	•

Selected Average Balance Sheet ($ in Thousands)

Net Receivables 23	936	0	•	281	704	2961	3249	6581	10434	24668
Inventories 24	760	0	•	125	430	1375	3919	7552	16307	27696
Net Property, Plant and Equipment 25	1229	0	•	68	308	1011	3346	9428	18122	50841
Total Assets 26	5915	0	•	610	2196	7734	14515	34745	67780	159978
Notes and Loans Payable 27	719	0	•	81	421	2699	3152	8028	6460	22328
All Other Liabilities 28	1176	0	•	256	507	2484	3557	7232	11939	43557
Net Worth 29	4020	0	•	273	1269	2551	7806	19484	49382	94082

Selected Financial Ratios (Times to 1)

Current Ratio 30	2.5	•	•	1.3	2.9	1.9	2.0	2.2	3.1	2.3
Quick Ratio 31	1.6	•	•	0.9	2.1	1.0	1.0	1.3	1.4	1.2
Net Sales to Working Capital 32	3.7	•	•	37.5	2.9	6.1	5.8	4.9	3.8	4.3
Coverage Ratio 33	7.1	15.9	•	5.1	14.0	5.7	5.6	6.1	12.4	5.7
Total Asset Turnover 34	1.1	•	•	5.7	1.6	2.3	2.0	1.5	1.5	1.2
Inventory Turnover 35	6.5	•	•	20.4	6.4	10.3	5.5	5.4	4.9	4.8
Receivables Turnover 36	8.8	•	•	•	6.2	9.6	10.0	6.7	10.3	8.0
Total Liabilities to Net Worth 37	0.5	•	•	1.2	0.7	2.0	0.9	0.8	0.4	0.7
Current Assets to Working Capital 38	1.7	•	•	4.6	1.5	2.1	2.0	1.9	1.5	1.7
Current Liabilities to Working Capital 39	0.7	•	•	3.6	0.5	1.1	1.0	0.9	0.5	0.7
Working Capital to Net Sales 40	0.3	•	•	0.0	0.3	0.2	0.2	0.2	0.3	0.2
Inventory to Working Capital 41	0.5	•	•	1.4	0.4	0.8	0.9	0.7	0.7	0.6
Total Receipts to Cash Flow 42	8.8	8.7	•	15.4	11.6	9.9	10.7	9.2	13.7	9.4
Cost of Goods to Cash Flow 43	6.4	7.3	•	11.4	9.0	7.9	8.2	7.3	10.5	6.6
Cash Flow to Total Debt 44	0.4	•	•	0.7	0.3	0.3	0.4	0.4	0.4	0.3

Selected Financial Factors (in Percentages)

Debt Ratio 45	32.0	•	•	55.2	42.2	67.0	46.2	43.9	27.1	41.2
Return on Total Assets 46	8.1	•	•	5.5	12.0	13.4	9.3	12.3	7.2	11.0
Return on Equity Before Income Taxes 47	10.2	•	•	9.9	19.3	33.5	14.1	18.4	9.1	15.4
Return on Equity After Income Taxes 48	8.1	•	•	8.4	15.9	30.3	13.0	16.1	8.3	12.6
Profit Margin (Before Income Tax) 49	6.1	9.6	•	0.8	6.8	4.8	3.9	6.9	4.3	7.6
Profit Margin (After Income Tax) 50	4.8	9.6	•	0.7	5.6	4.3	3.6	6.1	3.9	6.3

60

Table I

Corporations with and without Net Income

TEXTILE PRODUCT MILLS

MONEY AMOUNTS AND SIZE OF ASSETS IN THOUSANDS OF DOLLARS

Item Description for Accounting Period 7/04 Through 6/05	Total	Zero Assets	Under 500	500 to 1,000	1,000 to 5,000	5,000 to 10,000	10,000 to 25,000	25,000 to 50,000	50,000 to 100,000	100,000 to 250,000	250,000 to 500,000	500,000 to 2,500,000	2,500,000 and over
Number of Enterprises 1	2838	4	1855	364	409	30	90	44	17	14	4	6	0
Revenues ($ in Thousands)													
Net Sales 2	27654154	289286	450693	852584	1467779	441241	2633436	249049	1770567	2218283	1750600	13286635	0
Interest 3	185176	1113	0	2	298	75	1864	789	548	7792	6063	166632	0
Rents 4	9938	63	28	0	1402	7	763	1884	1243	1634	182	2732	0
Royalties 5	32449	0	0	0	0	0	0	2185	3	127	228	29905	0
Other Portfolio Income 6	185714	396	22036	104	1441	2159	4384	106443	6375	6167	997	35216	0
Other Receipts 7	203727	294	625	41	4597	1691	10947	40565	11907	17450	1868	113740	0
Total Receipts 8	28271158	291152	473382	852731	1475517	445173	2651394	2644915	1790643	2251453	1759938	13634860	0
Average Total Receipts 9	9962	72788	255	2343	3608	14839	29460	60112	105332	160818	439984	2272477	•
Operating Costs/Operating Income (%)													
Cost of Operations 10	70.6	89.4	59.3	69.8	60.8	68.1	75.9	72.0	77.0	76.0	72.1	68.4	•
Salaries and Wages 11	7.6	1.7	0.2	5.5	8.4	5.9	5.7	6.6	5.2	6.3	7.4	9.2	•
Taxes Paid 12	2.1	1.7	4.7	2.1	2.5	2.2	1.6	2.2	1.9	1.3	2.2	2.2	•
Interest Paid 13	2.6	0.7	0.6	0.4	0.6	2.9	0.9	1.2	1.4	1.6	3.5	3.8	•
Depreciation 14	2.4	1.2	0.4	0.6	3.4	2.6	2.2	3.0	3.1	2.5	4.5	2.0	•
Amortization and Depletion 15	0.4	0.0	0.0	•	0.0	0.1	0.2	0.3	0.3	0.2	1.3	0.4	•
Pensions and Other Deferred Comp. 16	0.4	0.0	0.1	0.1	0.7	0.6	0.3	0.4	0.4	0.2	0.8	0.5	•
Employee Benefits 17	2.0	1.9	0.0	1.3	1.6	3.1	1.4	1.7	2.4	1.5	1.9	2.4	•
Advertising 18	0.7	0.0	0.0	0.5	0.6	0.1	0.6	0.4	0.6	0.5	2.9	0.7	•
Other Expenses 19	11.5	23.5	27.4	12.8	17.3	8.9	8.2	12.6	8.0	13.1	6.6	11.5	•
Officers' Compensation 20	1.4	2.5	11.2	4.0	3.3	8.1	2.6	2.3	0.6	1.0	0.4	0.4	•
Operating Margin 21	•	•	•	3.0	0.7	•	0.5	•	•	•	•	•	•
Operating Margin Before Officers' Comp. 22	•	•	7.3	7.0	4.0	5.6	3.2	•	•	•	•	•	•

Selected Average Balance Sheet ($ in Thousands)

Net Receivables 23	951	0	20	300	382	1410	3640	7465	12718	29166	48834	146238	•
Inventories 24	2054	0	2	256	590	2349	4809	8331	16161	32243	78544	266689	•
Net Property, Plant and Equipment 25	1574	0	4	29	329	2165	3290	9293	19850	28666	138035	375565	•
Total Assets 26	7220	0	42	734	1812	6771	16215	34077	73401	155562	356469	1898552	•
Notes and Loans Payable 27	3268	0	105	355	687	3333	4383	11102	24038	50186	174455	979757	•
All Other Liabilities 28	1884	0	8	274	328	1518	4177	9052	19228	53865	125811	449252	•
Net Worth 29	2067	0	-71	105	797	1920	7654	13924	30134	51512	56202	469543	•

Selected Financial Ratios (Times to 1)

Current Ratio 30	1.3	•	1.6	2.0	1.8	1.8	1.8	1.8	1.6	1.6	1.7	1.0
Quick Ratio 31	0.5	•	1.6	1.0	0.6	0.7	0.8	0.9	0.8	0.7	0.6	0.2
Net Sales to Working Capital 32	13.5	•	17.3	7.1	5.8	6.8	6.3	6.6	7.5	5.1	7.2	•
Coverage Ratio 33	1.2	•	3.0	9.0	3.1	0.4	2.3	3.7	1.3	•	0.1	1.4
Total Asset Turnover 34	1.3	•	5.8	3.2	2.0	2.2	1.8	1.7	1.4	1.0	1.2	1.2
Inventory Turnover 35	3.3	•	59.2	6.4	3.7	4.3	4.6	4.9	5.0	3.7	4.0	5.7
Receivables Turnover 36	3.8	•	9.1	9.4	7.2	7.6	7.8	8.6	7.7	5.6	7.4	12.5
Total Liabilities to Net Worth 37	2.5	•	•	6.0	1.3	2.5	1.1	1.4	1.4	2.0	5.3	3.0
Current Assets to Working Capital 38	4.3	•	2.7	2.0	2.3	2.3	2.3	2.3	2.7	2.7	2.4	•
Current Liabilities to Working Capital 39	3.3	•	1.7	1.0	1.3	1.3	1.3	1.3	1.7	1.7	1.4	•
Working Capital to Net Sales 40	0.1	•	0.1	0.1	0.2	0.1	0.2	0.2	0.1	0.2	0.1	•
Inventory to Working Capital 41	2.1	•	0.0	1.0	0.8	1.1	1.1	1.0	1.1	1.1	1.2	•
Total Receipts to Cash Flow 42	11.3	•	4.3	8.3	6.6	20.1	13.1	11.8	16.1	11.4	60.7	10.4
Cost of Goods to Cash Flow 43	8.0	•	2.6	5.8	4.0	13.7	10.0	8.5	12.4	8.6	43.8	7.1
Cash Flow to Total Debt 44	0.2	•	0.5	0.4	0.5	0.2	0.3	0.2	0.1	0.1	0.0	0.1

Selected Financial Factors (in Percentages)

Debt Ratio 45	71.4	•	270.2	85.6	56.0	71.6	52.8	59.1	58.9	66.9	84.2	75.3
Return on Total Assets 46	4.3	•	9.7	10.8	3.6	2.6	3.9	7.5	2.5	•	0.4	6.0
Return on Equity Before Income Taxes 47	2.7	•	•	67.1	5.5	•	4.6	13.3	1.3	•	•	6.3
Return on Equity After Income Taxes 48	•	•	•	63.2	4.5	•	3.1	11.9	0.8	•	•	1.2
Profit Margin (Before Income Tax) 49	0.6	•	1.1	3.0	1.2	•	1.2	3.3	0.4	•	•	1.3
Profit Margin (After Income Tax) 50	•	•	1.0	2.8	1.0	•	0.8	2.9	0.2	•	•	0.3

Table II
Corporations with Net Income

TEXTILE PRODUCT MILLS

MONEY AMOUNTS AND SIZE OF ASSETS IN THOUSANDS OF DOLLARS

Item Description for Accounting Period 7/04 Through 6/05	Total	Zero Assets	Under 500	500 to 1,000	1,000 to 5,000	5,000 to 10,000	10,000 to 25,000	25,000 to 50,000	50,000 to 100,000	100,000 to 250,000	250,000 to 500,000	500,000 to 2,500,000	2,500,000 and over
Number of Enterprises 1	1847	0	0	364	218	14	54	31	10	7	0	0	0
Revenues ($ in Thousands)													
Net Sales 2	16019765	0	0	852584	1100970	230908	1755305	1876009	1085061	1748945	0	0	0
Interest 3	145955	0	0	2	230	0	561	549	192	3725	0	0	0
Rents 4	4808	0	0	0	1375	0	0	276	696	1634	0	0	0
Royalties 5	18209	0	0	0	0	0	0	0	3	73	0	0	0
Other Portfolio Income 6	69285	0	0	104	1352	57	1206	9105	5576	5357	0	0	0
Other Receipts 7	68520	0	0	41	2810	1460	8393	9681	8190	17692	0	0	0
Total Receipts 8	16326542	0	0	852731	1106737	232425	1765465	1895620	1099718	1777426	0	0	0
Average Total Receipts 9	8839	•	•	2343	5077	16602	32694	61149	109972	253918	•	•	•
Operating Costs/Operating Income (%)													
Cost of Operations 10	68.6	•	•	69.8	58.9	65.1	73.5	70.1	74.2	74.3	•	•	•
Salaries and Wages 11	7.4	•	•	5.5	8.9	4.5	5.8	6.4	5.7	6.1	•	•	•
Taxes Paid 12	1.9	•	•	2.1	2.3	1.2	1.4	2.2	2.2	1.3	•	•	•
Interest Paid 13	1.9	•	•	0.4	0.5	2.1	0.8	1.0	0.8	1.2	•	•	•
Depreciation 14	1.6	•	•	0.6	3.4	1.1	1.8	2.4	2.8	1.9	•	•	•
Amortization and Depletion 15	0.3	•	•	•	0.0	0.0	0.2	0.3	0.2	0.1	•	•	•
Pensions and Other Deferred Comp. 16	0.4	•	•	0.1	0.8	0.9	0.3	0.3	0.4	0.2	•	•	•
Employee Benefits 17	1.4	•	•	1.3	1.6	0.6	1.4	1.6	2.6	1.1	•	•	•
Advertising 18	0.8	•	•	0.5	0.5	0.2	0.6	0.4	0.6	0.5	•	•	•
Other Expenses 19	10.5	•	•	12.8	17.2	4.9	6.7	7.7	5.3	8.8	•	•	•
Officers' Compensation 20	1.7	•	•	4.0	3.3	15.0	3.1	2.0	0.8	1.1	•	•	•
Operating Margin 21	3.5	•	•	3.0	2.7	4.3	4.4	5.5	4.4	3.6	•	•	•
Operating Margin Before Officers' Comp. 22	5.2	•	•	7.0	6.0	19.3	7.5	7.5	5.2	4.7	•	•	•

Selected Average Balance Sheet ($ in Thousands)

Net Receivables 23	746	300	621	2055	3923	8076	12714	36799
Inventories 24	2180	315	685	2277	5412	8842	15374	52253
Net Property, Plant and Equipment 25	1057	29	349	613	2844	8143	17695	31467
Total Assets 26	5559	734	1851	6382	16206	33972	74658	163174
Notes and Loans Payable 27	1953	355	592	3323	3753	10472	14709	45700
All Other Liabilities 28	1083	274	442	1023	3877	9592	13458	54307
Net Worth 29	2522	105	817	2037	8576	13908	46491	63167

Selected Financial Ratios (Times to 1)

Current Ratio 30	1.6	2.0	1.8	3.7	2.3	1.8	2.3	1.5
Quick Ratio 31	0.6	1.0	1.0	1.4	1.1	0.9	1.1	0.6
Net Sales to Working Capital 32	9.7	7.1	7.9	4.0	5.1	6.1	5.2	7.2
Coverage Ratio 33	3.8	9.0	7.9	3.4	7.3	7.5	8.5	5.3
Total Asset Turnover 34	1.6	3.2	2.7	2.6	2.0	1.8	1.5	1.5
Inventory Turnover 35	2.7	5.2	4.3	4.7	4.4	4.8	5.2	3.6
Receivables Turnover 36	2.8	•	6.7	10.4	8.0	8.9	8.1	6.7
Total Liabilities to Net Worth 37	1.2	6.0	1.3	2.1	0.9	1.4	0.6	1.6
Current Assets to Working Capital 38	2.8	2.0	2.3	1.4	1.8	2.2	1.8	3.0
Current Liabilities to Working Capital 39	1.8	1.0	1.3	0.4	0.8	1.2	0.8	2.0
Working Capital to Net Sales 40	0.1	0.1	0.1	0.3	0.2	0.2	0.2	0.1
Inventory to Working Capital 41	1.6	1.0	1.0	0.8	0.8	1.0	0.7	1.6
Total Receipts to Cash Flow 42	7.2	8.3	5.9	12.3	9.7	7.9	10.7	8.2
Cost of Goods to Cash Flow 43	5.0	5.8	3.4	8.0	7.1	5.6	7.9	6.1
Cash Flow to Total Debt 44	0.4	0.4	0.8	0.3	0.4	0.4	0.4	0.3

Selected Financial Factors (in Percentages)

Debt Ratio 45	54.6	85.6	55.8	68.1	47.1	59.1	37.7	61.3
Return on Total Assets 46	11.6	10.8	10.1	18.2	11.5	13.5	9.7	9.9
Return on Equity Before Income Taxes 47	19.0	67.1	19.9	40.3	18.8	28.6	13.8	20.7
Return on Equity After Income Taxes 48	14.9	63.2	18.1	39.9	16.6	26.5	13.1	18.3
Profit Margin (Before Income Tax) 49	5.5	3.0	3.2	5.0	5.0	6.6	5.9	5.2
Profit Margin (After Income Tax) 50	4.3	2.8	2.9	4.9	4.4	6.1	5.6	4.6

Table I

Corporations with and without Net Income

APPAREL KNITTING MILLS

MONEY AMOUNTS AND SIZE OF ASSETS IN THOUSANDS OF DOLLARS

Item Description for Accounting Period 7/04 Through 6/05	Total	Zero Assets	Under 500	500 to 1,000	1,000 to 5,000	5,000 to 10,000	10,000 to 25,000	25,000 to 50,000	50,000 to 100,000	100,000 to 250,000	250,000 to 500,000	500,000 to 2,500,000	2,500,000 and over
Number of Enterprises 1	229	0	0	0	0	0	29	8	5	4	0	0	0
Revenues ($ in Thousands)													
Net Sales 2	3483894	0	0	0	0	0	819048	569675	567591	898017	0	0	0
Interest 3	2395	0	0	0	0	0	404	54	124	371	0	0	0
Rents 4	191	0	0	0	0	0	1	43	144	0	0	0	0
Royalties 5	21157	0	0	0	0	0	0	0	20697	460	0	0	0
Other Portfolio Income 6	46410	0	0	0	0	0	443	222	34761	3687	0	0	0
Other Receipts 7	24890	0	0	0	0	0	3697	1294	6880	2224	0	0	0
Total Receipts 8	3578937	0	0	0	0	0	823593	571288	630197	904759	0	0	0
Average Total Receipts 9	15629	·	·	·	·	·	28400	71411	126039	226190	·	·	·
Operating Costs/Operating Income (%)													
Cost of Operations 10	72.9	·	·	·	·	·	72.7	80.9	66.1	73.2	·	·	·
Salaries and Wages 11	5.6	·	·	·	·	·	5.6	4.6	9.8	4.5	·	·	·
Taxes Paid 12	2.3	·	·	·	·	·	2.1	2.3	1.1	2.0	·	·	·
Interest Paid 13	1.8	·	·	·	·	·	1.0	0.7	4.0	1.7	·	·	·
Depreciation 14	2.1	·	·	·	·	·	2.1	1.8	2.6	2.4	·	·	·
Amortization and Depletion 15	0.4	·	·	·	·	·	0.2	0.1	0.6	1.0	·	·	·
Pensions and Other Deferred Comp. 16	0.4	·	·	·	·	·	0.3	0.3	0.1	1.1	·	·	·
Employee Benefits 17	1.2	·	·	·	·	·	1.7	0.6	0.2	1.7	·	·	·
Advertising 18	2.0	·	·	·	·	·	1.8	0.4	2.3	3.7	·	·	·
Other Expenses 19	9.8	·	·	·	·	·	9.3	5.1	16.2	6.7	·	·	·
Officers' Compensation 20	1.9	·	·	·	·	·	2.7	1.0	1.7	0.6	·	·	·
Operating Margin 21	·	·	·	·	·	·	0.5	2.3	·	1.2	·	·	·
Operating Margin Before Officers' Comp. 22	1.5	·	·	·	·	·	3.2	3.3	·	1.8	·	·	·

Selected Average Balance Sheet ($ in Thousands)

Net Receivables 23	1936	3822	9399	15661	32976
Inventories 24	2850	5025	9988	16996	60453
Net Property, Plant and Equipment 25	1784	3582	4994	15406	32790
Total Assets 26	9133	15505	34352	73402	158532
Notes and Loans Payable 27	3214	5267	8630	51032	51397
All Other Liabilities 28	903	2846	7614	-42631	47124
Net Worth 29	5015	7392	18108	65001	60012

Selected Financial Ratios (Times to 1)

Current Ratio 30	2.1	2.1	2.3	1.7	1.8
Quick Ratio 31	0.9	1.0	1.1	0.7	0.6
Net Sales to Working Capital 32	4.9	5.4	4.8	6.1	5.2
Coverage Ratio 33	2.3	2.0	4.4	2.5	2.2
Total Asset Turnover 34	1.7	1.8	2.1	1.5	1.4
Inventory Turnover 35	3.9	4.1	5.8	4.4	2.7
Receivables Turnover 36	8.0	6.8	8.2	9.4	6.7
Total Liabilities to Net Worth 37	0.8	1.1	0.9	0.1	1.6
Current Assets to Working Capital 38	1.9	1.9	1.8	2.4	2.2
Current Liabilities to Working Capital 39	0.9	0.9	0.8	1.4	1.2
Working Capital to Net Sales 40	0.2	0.2	0.2	0.2	0.2
Inventory to Working Capital 41	0.9	0.9	0.8	1.2	1.4
Total Receipts to Cash Flow 42	11.0	11.8	16.8	6.6	14.7
Cost of Goods to Cash Flow 43	8.0	8.6	13.5	4.3	10.7
Cash Flow to Total Debt 44	0.3	0.3	0.3	2.1	0.2

Selected Financial Factors (in Percentages)

Debt Ratio 45	45.1	52.3	47.3	11.4	62.1
Return on Total Assets 46	7.1	3.7	6.8	15.8	5.3
Return on Equity Before Income Taxes 47	7.3	3.9	9.9	10.8	7.7
Return on Equity After Income Taxes 48	5.1	3.3	8.0	9.9	4.4
Profit Margin (Before Income Tax) 49	2.4	1.0	2.5	6.2	2.1
Profit Margin (After Income Tax) 50	1.7	0.9	2.0	5.7	1.2

Table II

Corporations with Net Income

APPAREL KNITTING MILLS

MONEY AMOUNTS AND SIZE OF ASSETS IN THOUSANDS OF DOLLARS

Item Description for Accounting Period 7/04 Through 6/05	Total	Zero Assets	Under 500	500 to 1,000	1,000 to 5,000	5,000 to 10,000	10,000 to 25,000	25,000 to 50,000	50,000 to 100,000	100,000 to 250,000	250,000 to 500,000	500,000 to 2,500,000	2,500,000 and over
Number of Enterprises **1**	114	0	0	0	69	0	19	0	5	0	0	0	0
Revenues ($ in Thousands)													
Net Sales **2**	2671328	0	0	0	273272	0	533081	0	567591	0	0	0	0
Interest **3**	1611	0	0	0	1041	0	324	0	124	0	0	0	0
Rents **4**	188	0	0	0	0	0	1	0	144	0	0	0	0
Royalties **5**	20697	0	0	0	0	0	0	0	20697	0	0	0	0
Other Portfolio Income **6**	46095	0	0	0	7215	0	245	0	34761	0	0	0	0
Other Receipts **7**	18746	0	0	0	8907	0	2781	0	6880	0	0	0	0
Total Receipts **8**	2758665	0	0	0	290435	0	536432	0	630197	0	0	0	0
Average Total Receipts **9**	24199	•	•	•	4209	•	28233	•	126039	•	•	•	•
Operating Costs/Operating Income (%)													
Cost of Operations **10**	73.0	•	•	•	66.1	•	72.9	•	66.1	•	•	•	•
Salaries and Wages **11**	5.7	•	•	•	3.6	•	5.4	•	9.8	•	•	•	•
Taxes Paid **12**	2.1	•	•	•	4.3	•	2.1	•	1.1	•	•	•	•
Interest Paid **13**	2.0	•	•	•	2.7	•	0.7	•	4.0	•	•	•	•
Depreciation **14**	1.9	•	•	•	1.1	•	2.0	•	2.6	•	•	•	•
Amortization and Depletion **15**	0.3	•	•	•	0.3	•	0.3	•	0.6	•	•	•	•
Pensions and Other Deferred Comp. **16**	0.4	•	•	•	•	•	0.3	•	0.1	•	•	•	•
Employee Benefits **17**	1.3	•	•	•	•	•	2.0	•	0.2	•	•	•	•
Advertising **18**	1.1	•	•	•	1.3	•	0.8	•	2.3	•	•	•	•
Other Expenses **19**	8.8	•	•	•	11.9	•	7.4	•	16.2	•	•	•	•
Officers' Compensation **20**	1.7	•	•	•	2.6	•	3.0	•	1.7	•	•	•	•
Operating Margin **21**	1.6	•	•	•	6.1	•	3.0	•	•	•	•	•	•
Operating Margin Before Officers' Comp. **22**	3.3	•	•	•	8.7	•	6.0	•	•	•	•	•	•

Selected Average Balance Sheet ($ in Thousands)

Net Receivables 23	2858	423	3499		15661
Inventories 24	4221	234	5503		16996
Net Property, Plant and Equipment 25	2534	437	3107		15406
Total Assets 26	13807	2866	14564		73402
Notes and Loans Payable 27	4931	366	3394		51032
All Other Liabilities 28	675	822	2491		-42631
Net Worth 29	8202	1678	8679		65001

Selected Financial Ratios (Times to 1)

Current Ratio 30	2.0	3.0	2.2		1.7
Quick Ratio 31	0.8	1.5	1.1		0.7
Net Sales to Working Capital 32	5.0	2.9	5.7		6.1
Coverage Ratio 33	3.5	5.5	5.9		2.5
Total Asset Turnover 34	1.7	1.4	1.9		1.5
Inventory Turnover 35	4.1	11.2	3.7		4.4
Receivables Turnover 36	8.9	14.0	6.5		9.4
Total Liabilities to Net Worth 37	0.7	0.7	0.7		0.1
Current Assets to Working Capital 38	2.0	1.5	1.8		2.4
Current Liabilities to Working Capital 39	1.0	0.5	0.8		1.4
Working Capital to Net Sales 40	0.2	0.3	0.2		0.2
Inventory to Working Capital 41	1.0	0.3	0.8		1.2
Total Receipts to Cash Flow 42	9.6	5.2	10.4		6.6
Cost of Goods to Cash Flow 43	7.0	3.4	7.6		4.3
Cash Flow to Total Debt 44	0.4	0.6	0.5		2.1

Selected Financial Factors (in Percentages)

Debt Ratio 45	40.6	41.4	40.4		11.4
Return on Total Assets 46	11.7	20.8	8.5		15.8
Return on Equity Before Income Taxes 47	14.1	29.1	11.8		10.8
Return on Equity After Income Taxes 48	11.3	19.7	11.0		9.9
Profit Margin (Before Income Tax) 49	4.9	12.3	3.7		6.2
Profit Margin (After Income Tax) 50	3.9	8.4	3.4		5.7

Table I

Corporations with and without Net Income

CUT AND SEW APPAREL CONTRACTORS AND MFRS.

MONEY AMOUNTS AND SIZE OF ASSETS IN THOUSANDS OF DOLLARS

Item Description for Accounting Period 7/04 Through 6/05	Total	Zero Assets	Under 500	500 to 1,000	1,000 to 5,000	5,000 to 10,000	10,000 to 25,000	25,000 to 50,000	50,000 to 100,000	100,000 to 250,000	250,000 to 500,000	500,000 to 2,500,000	2,500,000 and over
Number of Enterprises **1**	7260	1022	4743	637	528	134	102	41	23	15	6	4	4
Revenues ($ in Thousands)													
Net Sales **2**	42741040	254544	1820008	868904	3322435	2339693	4151568	2887435	2798594	2522061	2326707	4233865	15215225
Interest **3**	212311	58	132	17	189	117	1452	1068	942	9180	201	107790	91165
Rents **4**	31515	0	1456	0	22	29	261	1257	404	1206	0	6603	20277
Royalties **5**	923883	0	291	0	78	0	1727	9873	11158	2252	5453	279316	613734
Other Portfolio Income **6**	147112	6885	9962	6	85	578	3404	510	19578	10645	1108	20049	74302
Other Receipts **7**	756633	399	47334	0	12860	26716	54999	22888	23536	9809	57661	103997	396436
Total Receipts **8**	44812494	261886	1879183	868927	3335669	2367133	4213411	2923031	2854212	2555153	2391130	4751620	16411139
Average Total Receipts **9**	6173	256	396	1364	6318	17665	41308	71293	124096	170344	398522	1187905	4102785
Operating Costs/Operating Income (%)													
Cost of Operations **10**	64.6	71.1	37.5	63.9	68.5	65.1	72.1	70.3	71.6	66.7	62.0	66.9	61.8
Salaries and Wages **11**	10.1	2.5	19.3	11.4	8.5	13.8	9.1	7.6	8.1	11.8	7.8	9.6	10.2
Taxes Paid **12**	1.9	3.2	3.9	1.5	1.5	2.6	2.2	2.0	1.5	2.0	1.7	3.1	1.3
Interest Paid **13**	2.2	0.3	0.6	2.9	0.9	1.2	0.8	0.8	0.8	3.4	0.8	4.3	3.2
Depreciation **14**	1.1	1.3	1.8	1.5	0.5	0.7	0.7	0.7	1.1	2.0	1.3	2.1	1.0
Amortization and Depletion **15**	0.5	0.2	0.1	0.0	0.1	0.0	0.1	0.1	0.5	0.4	0.4	0.7	1.0
Pensions and Other Deferred Comp. **16**	0.5	0.1	0.2	•	0.2	0.1	0.2	0.2	0.3	0.4	0.8	0.5	0.7
Employee Benefits **17**	1.2	0.5	1.1	0.4	0.6	0.6	0.7	0.7	1.1	2.2	1.9	0.8	1.6
Advertising **18**	2.5	0.1	0.9	0.3	0.4	2.1	0.7	1.2	1.3	1.6	4.7	3.7	3.8
Other Expenses **19**	13.8	10.1	29.2	17.5	14.3	11.1	8.0	8.5	8.3	8.2	10.5	17.6	16.0
Officers' Compensation **20**	2.2	8.7	4.4	3.1	3.0	2.6	3.8	2.8	2.1	1.4	1.9	0.6	1.6
Operating Margin **21**	•	1.9	1.1	•	1.5	•	1.6	5.1	3.3	•	6.3	•	•
Operating Margin Before Officers' Comp. **22**	1.6	10.6	5.5	0.6	4.5	2.5	5.5	7.9	5.4	1.3	8.1	•	•

Selected Average Balance Sheet ($ in Thousands)

Net Receivables 23	824	0	236	3	584	1416	3622	7713	14763	29579	62417	190184	679443
Inventories 24	864	0	147	27	686	2154	6244	12133	19419	30479	76237	204583	521770
Net Property, Plant and Equipment 25	411	0	95	14	310	436	1539	2503	7923	17221	31180	119042	318727
Total Assets 26	4796	0	627	78	2090	6224	15488	31780	69327	162783	345971	1067268	4712838
Notes and Loans Payable 27	1278	0	279	49	908	1802	4238	7690	16763	65077	57158	228097	1195995
All Other Liabilities 28	1546	0	344	29	587	1545	5189	8359	11665	40783	83972	356950	1666348
Net Worth 29	1972	0	4	-0	595	2877	6061	15731	40899	56923	204841	482220	1850496

Selected Financial Ratios (Times to 1)

Current Ratio 30	1.5	•	0.9	1.2	2.1	2.7	1.7	2.4	2.7	1.9	3.8	1.6	1.1
Quick Ratio 31	0.8	•	0.5	0.5	1.0	1.1	0.7	1.0	1.2	0.9	2.3	0.8	0.6
Net Sales to Working Capital 32	7.6	•	•	64.6	7.2	5.3	8.3	4.7	4.1	4.3	2.2	5.9	27.5
Coverage Ratio 33	3.0	17.5	0.1	8.3	3.1	1.9	4.8	9.5	7.4	1.3	12.7	1.5	3.0
Total Asset Turnover 34	1.2	•	2.2	4.9	3.0	2.8	2.6	2.2	1.8	1.0	1.1	1.0	0.8
Inventory Turnover 35	4.4	•	5.9	5.3	6.3	5.3	4.7	4.1	4.5	3.7	3.2	3.5	4.5
Receivables Turnover 36	7.5	•	4.8	43.3	10.0	13.8	10.5	9.8	9.8	5.3	5.5	5.7	6.5
Total Liabilities to Net Worth 37	1.4	•	146.4	•	2.5	1.2	1.6	1.0	0.7	1.9	0.7	1.2	1.5
Current Assets to Working Capital 38	2.8	•	•	7.5	1.9	1.6	2.5	1.7	1.6	2.1	1.4	2.7	10.7
Current Liabilities to Working Capital 39	1.8	•	•	6.5	0.9	0.6	1.5	0.7	0.6	1.1	0.4	1.7	9.7
Working Capital to Net Sales 40	0.1	•	•	0.0	0.1	0.2	0.1	0.2	0.2	0.2	0.5	0.2	0.0
Inventory to Working Capital 41	1.1	•	•	3.9	0.8	0.8	1.1	0.9	0.8	0.7	0.4	1.2	3.7
Total Receipts to Cash Flow 42	6.7	7.8	9.2	3.8	7.5	10.1	10.7	7.6	8.4	19.6	5.5	6.5	5.4
Cost of Goods to Cash Flow 43	4.3	5.6	5.9	1.4	5.1	6.6	7.7	5.3	6.0	13.1	3.4	4.3	3.3
Cash Flow to Total Debt 44	0.3	•	0.2	1.3	0.6	0.5	0.4	0.6	0.5	0.1	0.5	0.3	0.2

Selected Financial Factors (in Percentages)

Debt Ratio 45	58.9	•	99.3	100.0	71.5	53.8	60.9	50.5	41.0	65.0	40.8	54.8	60.7
Return on Total Assets 46	8.3	•	0.9	24.6	8.4	6.4	10.4	15.8	10.8	4.7	11.0	6.5	7.8
Return on Equity Before Income Taxes 47	13.5	•	•	•	19.9	6.5	21.0	28.6	15.8	3.4	17.1	4.9	13.2
Return on Equity After Income Taxes 48	9.8	•	•	•	19.0	4.3	20.3	26.4	14.5	0.6	16.0	2.0	7.9
Profit Margin (Before Income Tax) 49	4.5	4.8	4.4	•	1.9	1.1	3.1	6.4	5.3	1.1	9.0	2.2	6.4
Profit Margin (After Income Tax) 50	3.3	4.8	4.3	•	1.8	0.7	3.0	5.9	4.9	0.2	8.5	0.9	3.8

Table II

Corporations with Net Income

CUT AND SEW APPAREL CONTRACTORS AND MFRS.

MONEY AMOUNTS AND SIZE OF ASSETS IN THOUSANDS OF DOLLARS

Item Description for Accounting Period 7/04 Through 6/05	Total	Zero Assets	Under 500	500 to 1,000	1,000 to 5,000	5,000 to 10,000	10,000 to 25,000	25,000 to 50,000	50,000 to 100,000	100,000 to 250,000	250,000 to 500,000	500,000 to 2,500,000	2,500,000 and over
Number of Enterprises **1**	3565	263	2095	527	448	83	74	33	19	0	0	0	0
Revenues ($ in Thousands)													
Net Sales **2**	34601201	128440	1367576	607593	2817120	1617440	3368639	2549102	2410465	0	0	0	0
Interest **3**	114501	0	132	17	129	87	585	1047	853	0	0	0	0
Rents **4**	23055	0	1456	0	0	29	109	1257	0	0	0	0	0
Royalties **5**	700211	0	291	0	78	0	0	29	0	0	0	0	0
Other Portfolio Income **6**	113092	6885	9962	6	48	492	302	507	17001	0	0	0	0
Other Receipts **7**	694155	138	44586	0	8752	10458	47573	20248	22603	0	0	0	0
Total Receipts **8**	36246215	135463	1424003	607616	2826127	1625806	3417208	2572190	2450922	0	0	0	0
Average Total Receipts **9**	10167	515	680	1153	6308	19588	46178	77945	128996	•	•	•	•
Operating Costs/Operating Income (%)													
Cost of Operations **10**	64.2	75.1	39.0	53.7	67.9	67.6	71.9	69.6	70.1	•	•	•	•
Salaries and Wages **11**	9.6	2.4	14.9	12.2	8.3	10.3	8.6	7.2	8.5	•	•	•	•
Taxes Paid **12**	2.0	1.2	3.7	1.6	1.6	2.9	2.3	1.7	1.6	•	•	•	•
Interest Paid **13**	1.4	0.2	0.5	3.3	0.9	1.2	0.8	0.6	0.7	•	•	•	•
Depreciation **14**	1.0	0.9	1.5	1.9	0.4	0.4	0.6	0.7	0.9	•	•	•	•
Amortization and Depletion **15**	0.5	•	•	0.0	0.1	0.0	0.0	0.1	0.3	•	•	•	•
Pensions and Other Deferred Comp. **16**	0.4	0.0	0.3	•	0.3	0.1	0.3	0.2	0.3	•	•	•	•
Employee Benefits **17**	1.1	0.4	1.2	0.6	0.6	0.3	0.7	0.6	0.9	•	•	•	•
Advertising **18**	2.3	0.0	1.1	0.5	0.4	2.6	0.7	1.1	1.3	•	•	•	•
Other Expenses **19**	12.9	3.2	28.1	15.9	13.0	8.6	6.4	8.1	8.2	•	•	•	•
Officers' Compensation **20**	2.3	2.7	4.4	4.4	2.8	2.6	4.1	3.0	2.2	•	•	•	•
Operating Margin **21**	2.3	13.7	5.3	5.8	3.7	3.4	3.5	7.2	4.9	•	•	•	•
Operating Margin Before Officers' Comp. **22**	4.6	16.4	9.7	10.2	6.6	5.9	7.6	10.2	7.1	•	•	•	•

Selected Average Balance Sheet ($ in Thousands)

Net Receivables 23	1422	0	5	276	587	1364	3865	7422	14760
Inventories 24	1370	0	33	128	685	2693	6665	13372	18181
Net Property, Plant and Equipment 25	644	0	12	110	348	226	1352	2504	7222
Total Assets 26	6733	0	89	631	2057	6414	15797	31541	69148
Notes and Loans Payable 27	1627	0	91	238	921	1593	3960	6133	16339
All Other Liabilities 28	1551	0	31	275	394	1805	5835	7256	13740
Net Worth 29	3555	0	-32	118	742	3017	6002	18153	39069

Selected Financial Ratios (Times to 1)

Current Ratio 30	2.3	•	1.2	1.0	2.7	2.5	1.7	2.5	3.1
Quick Ratio 31	1.2	•	0.6	0.7	1.4	1.0	0.7	1.0	1.4
Net Sales to Working Capital 32	4.9	•	46.3	•	6.2	5.5	9.1	4.9	3.9
Coverage Ratio 33	6.4	96.1	19.5	2.8	5.5	4.5	7.5	15.7	10.1
Total Asset Turnover 34	1.4	•	7.3	1.8	3.1	3.0	2.9	2.4	1.8
Inventory Turnover 35	4.5	•	7.7	4.8	6.2	4.9	4.9	4.0	4.9
Receivables Turnover 36	7.3	•	40.0	3.4	9.6	13.7	11.9	10.1	11.0
Total Liabilities to Net Worth 37	0.9	•	•	4.4	1.8	1.1	1.6	0.7	0.8
Current Assets to Working Capital 38	1.8	•	5.3	•	1.6	1.7	2.5	1.7	1.5
Current Liabilities to Working Capital 39	0.8	•	4.3	•	0.6	0.7	1.5	0.7	0.5
Working Capital to Net Sales 40	0.2	•	0.0	•	0.2	0.2	0.1	0.2	0.3
Inventory to Working Capital 41	0.7	•	2.7	•	0.7	0.9	1.2	0.8	0.7
Total Receipts to Cash Flow 42	5.8	4.6	3.1	5.8	7.0	9.0	10.5	6.8	7.5
Cost of Goods to Cash Flow 43	3.7	3.4	1.2	3.1	4.8	6.1	7.5	4.7	5.3
Cash Flow to Total Debt 44	0.5	•	1.8	0.4	0.7	0.6	0.4	0.9	0.6

Selected Financial Factors (in Percentages)

Debt Ratio 45	47.2	•	136.0	81.3	63.9	53.0	62.0	42.4	43.5
Return on Total Assets 46	12.5	•	72.6	16.6	15.1	15.8	16.4	21.2	13.6
Return on Equity Before Income Taxes 47	20.0	•	•	56.6	34.3	26.1	37.5	34.4	21.8
Return on Equity After Income Taxes 48	15.8	•	•	55.0	33.5	22.7	36.6	32.1	20.1
Profit Margin (Before Income Tax) 49	7.3	19.2	9.4	5.8	4.0	4.0	4.9	8.1	6.7
Profit Margin (After Income Tax) 50	5.8	19.2	9.3	5.6	3.5	4.0	4.8	7.5	6.2

Table I
Corporations with and without Net Income

APPAREL ACCESSORIES AND OTHER APPAREL

MONEY AMOUNTS AND SIZE OF ASSETS IN THOUSANDS OF DOLLARS

Item Description for Accounting Period 7/04 Through 6/05	Total	Zero Assets	Under 500	500 to 1,000	1,000 to 5,000	5,000 to 10,000	10,000 to 25,000	25,000 to 50,000	50,000 to 100,000	100,000 to 250,000	250,000 to 500,000	500,000 to 2,500,000	2,500,000 and over
Number of Enterprises **1**	3734	0	2692	453	0	0	40	22	12	4	0	0	0
Revenues ($ in Thousands)													
Net Sales **2**	11385234	0	1888879	826031	0	0	1147556	1563302	1379571	1053258	0	0	0
Interest **3**	11230	0	7	78	0	0	249	351	7345	633	0	0	0
Rents **4**	421	0	0	0	0	0	46	46	323	6	0	0	0
Royalties **5**	3329	0	0	0	0	0	0	5	68	3255	0	0	0
Other Portfolio Income **6**	49159	0	0	0	0	0	5993	336	28168	102	0	0	0
Other Receipts **7**	99171	0	9086	6025	0	0	33612	4389	-3971	8998	0	0	0
Total Receipts **8**	11548544	0	1897972	832134	0	0	1187456	1568429	1411504	1066252	0	0	0
Average Total Receipts **9**	3093	·	705	1837	·	·	29686	71292	117625	266563	·	·	·
Operating Costs/Operating Income (%)													
Cost of Operations **10**	64.5	·	58.2	60.1	·	·	68.2	71.1	65.5	64.0	·	·	·
Salaries and Wages **11**	9.8	·	12.5	7.5	·	·	8.6	6.2	7.2	9.5	·	·	·
Taxes Paid **12**	2.3	·	2.0	2.8	·	·	2.1	2.4	3.5	2.2	·	·	·
Interest Paid **13**	1.2	·	0.6	1.4	·	·	1.0	1.2	2.4	1.7	·	·	·
Depreciation **14**	1.3	·	1.1	1.2	·	·	1.1	1.2	1.3	1.5	·	·	·
Amortization and Depletion **15**	0.1	·	0.0	0.0	·	·	0.2	0.3	0.3	0.4	·	·	·
Pensions and Other Deferred Comp. **16**	0.3	·	0.4	0.9	·	·	0.2	0.1	0.4	0.1	·	·	·
Employee Benefits **17**	1.1	·	1.2	0.9	·	·	0.8	1.1	1.1	0.7	·	·	·
Advertising **18**	1.3	·	1.2	1.0	·	·	0.9	1.0	3.3	1.8	·	·	·
Other Expenses **19**	12.9	·	16.3	20.0	·	·	11.5	9.9	11.9	11.7	·	·	·
Officers' Compensation **20**	2.9	·	4.1	4.3	·	·	3.3	2.0	2.3	1.2	·	·	·
Operating Margin **21**	2.4	·	2.4	·	·	·	2.1	3.5	0.9	5.0	·	·	·
Operating Margin Before Officers' Comp. **22**	5.2	·	6.5	4.2	·	·	5.4	5.5	3.1	6.2	·	·	·

Selected Average Balance Sheet ($ in Thousands)

Net Receivables 23	320	64	143	•	4289	8130	19515	14533
Inventories 24	463	56	366	•	5088	10880	25512	39907
Net Property, Plant and Equipment 25	148	23	49	•	1667	3513	9362	12866
Total Assets 26	1308	180	745	•	15993	34076	69651	130695
Notes and Loans Payable 27	444	79	123	•	3965	12699	32937	54243
All Other Liabilities 28	422	50	414	•	3675	7107	18407	53496
Net Worth 29	442	51	209	•	8354	14269	18307	22956

Selected Financial Ratios (Times to 1)

Current Ratio 30	1.9	2.5	2.2	•	2.0	1.7	1.9	1.7
Quick Ratio 31	0.9	1.9	0.9	•	1.0	0.7	0.8	0.8
Net Sales to Working Capital 32	6.3	7.6	5.2	•	4.8	7.1	4.6	7.4
Coverage Ratio 33	4.4	5.9	1.5	•	6.8	4.3	2.6	4.6
Total Asset Turnover 34	2.3	3.9	2.4	•	1.8	2.1	1.7	2.0
Inventory Turnover 35	4.2	7.3	3.0	•	3.8	4.6	3.0	4.2
Receivables Turnover 36	9.9	9.5	15.3	•	6.2	8.9	6.8	23.4
Total Liabilities to Net Worth 37	2.0	2.5	2.6	•	0.9	1.4	2.8	4.7
Current Assets to Working Capital 38	2.1	1.7	1.9	•	2.0	2.3	2.1	2.5
Current Liabilities to Working Capital 39	1.1	0.7	0.9	•	1.0	1.3	1.1	1.5
Working Capital to Net Sales 40	0.2	0.1	0.2	•	0.2	0.1	0.2	0.1
Inventory to Working Capital 41	0.9	0.4	1.0	•	0.9	1.0	0.9	1.1
Total Receipts to Cash Flow 42	7.5	6.3	6.3	•	6.4	8.1	8.6	7.9
Cost of Goods to Cash Flow 43	4.8	3.7	3.8	•	4.3	5.8	5.6	5.1
Cash Flow to Total Debt 44	0.5	0.9	0.5	•	0.6	0.4	0.3	0.3

Selected Financial Factors (in Percentages)

Debt Ratio 45	66.2	71.6	72.0	•	47.8	58.1	73.7	82.4
Return on Total Assets 46	11.8	13.5	5.0	•	11.8	10.4	10.7	16.0
Return on Equity Before Income Taxes 47	26.9	39.5	5.7	•	19.3	19.1	25.2	71.3
Return on Equity After Income Taxes 48	24.4	39.3	4.2	•	17.9	14.5	19.7	65.5
Profit Margin (Before Income Tax) 49	3.9	2.9	0.6	•	5.6	3.8	4.0	6.2
Profit Margin (After Income Tax) 50	3.5	2.9	0.5	•	5.2	2.9	3.1	5.7

Table II
Corporations with Net Income

APPAREL ACCESSORIES AND OTHER APPAREL

MONEY AMOUNTS AND SIZE OF ASSETS IN THOUSANDS OF DOLLARS

Item Description for Accounting Period 7/04 Through 6/05	Total	Zero Assets	Under 500	500 to 1,000	1,000 to 5,000	5,000 to 10,000	10,000 to 25,000	25,000 to 50,000	50,000 to 100,000	100,000 to 250,000	250,000 to 500,000	500,000 to 2,500,000	2,500,000 and over
Number of Enterprises **1**	2384	0	1601	325	383	0	27	0	12	0	0	0	0
Revenues ($ in Thousands)													
Net Sales **2**	8808506	0	1346135	608202	2508367	0	867561	0	1863915	0	0	0	0
Interest **3**	9544	0	6	78	763	0	35	0	7711	0	0	0	0
Rents **4**	345	0	0	0	0	0	16	0	329	0	0	0	0
Royalties **5**	68	0	0	0	0	0	0	0	68	0	0	0	0
Other Portfolio Income **6**	37644	0	0	0	3245	0	5917	0	28270	0	0	0	0
Other Receipts **7**	91478	0	21	6025	37663	0	31934	0	11087	0	0	0	0
Total Receipts **8**	8947585	0	1346162	614305	2550038	0	905463	0	1911380	0	0	0	0
Average Total Receipts **9**	3753	•	841	1890	6658	•	33536	•	159282	•	•	•	•
Operating Costs/Operating Income (%)													
Cost of Operations **10**	63.4	•	58.1	60.9	65.0	•	67.9	•	60.5	•	•	•	•
Salaries and Wages **11**	9.2	•	10.6	6.5	11.9	•	7.8	•	8.5	•	•	•	•
Taxes Paid **12**	2.3	•	1.5	2.6	1.7	•	2.0	•	3.5	•	•	•	•
Interest Paid **13**	0.8	•	0.2	0.0	0.7	•	0.8	•	1.4	•	•	•	•
Depreciation **14**	0.8	•	0.5	0.4	0.6	•	1.0	•	1.2	•	•	•	•
Amortization and Depletion **15**	0.1	•	•	0.1	0.0	•	0.1	•	0.2	•	•	•	•
Pensions and Other Deferred Comp. **16**	0.3	•	0.5	1.2	0.1	•	0.2	•	0.2	•	•	•	•
Employee Benefits **17**	0.9	•	1.0	0.7	0.5	•	0.9	•	0.9	•	•	•	•
Advertising **18**	1.4	•	0.7	1.3	1.0	•	0.5	•	3.2	•	•	•	•
Other Expenses **19**	12.2	•	14.5	20.3	11.7	•	10.0	•	11.9	•	•	•	•
Officers' Compensation **20**	3.2	•	4.5	5.2	3.0	•	3.9	•	2.1	•	•	•	•
Operating Margin **21**	5.5	•	8.0	0.9	3.7	•	4.9	•	6.3	•	•	•	•
Operating Margin Before Officers' Comp. **22**	8.6	•	12.5	6.1	6.7	•	8.8	•	8.4	•	•	•	•

Selected Average Balance Sheet ($ in Thousands)

Net Receivables 23	368	71	89	501	5027	19071
Inventories 24	573	60	472	951	5380	28423
Net Property, Plant and Equipment 25	125	6	18	180	1456	8034
Total Assets 26	1475	161	822	2225	15320	82131
Notes and Loans Payable 27	366	41	52	446	4073	24407
All Other Liabilities 28	445	50	262	831	3641	21592
Net Worth 29	664	70	507	948	7606	36132

Selected Financial Ratios (Times to 1)

Current Ratio 30	2.2	3.0	2.5	2.2	2.1	2.2
Quick Ratio 31	1.0	2.9	0.9	0.7	1.1	1.0
Net Sales to Working Capital 32	5.6	8.6	4.2	6.3	4.8	4.3
Coverage Ratio 33	9.9	35.4	61.4	8.2	12.0	7.5
Total Asset Turnover 34	2.5	5.2	2.3	2.9	2.1	1.9
Inventory Turnover 35	4.1	8.1	2.4	4.5	4.1	3.3
Receivables Turnover 36	10.0	9.3	20.1	13.4	6.2	9.7
Total Liabilities to Net Worth 37	1.2	1.3	0.6	1.3	1.0	1.3
Current Assets to Working Capital 38	1.8	1.5	1.7	1.8	1.9	1.8
Current Liabilities to Working Capital 39	0.8	0.5	0.7	0.8	0.9	0.8
Working Capital to Net Sales 40	0.2	0.1	0.2	0.2	0.2	0.2
Inventory to Working Capital 41	0.8	0.0	1.1	1.1	0.8	0.7
Total Receipts to Cash Flow 42	6.2	5.0	5.9	7.7	5.6	6.0
Cost of Goods to Cash Flow 43	4.0	2.9	3.6	5.0	3.8	3.6
Cash Flow to Total Debt 44	0.7	1.8	1.0	0.7	0.7	0.6

Selected Financial Factors (in Percentages)

Debt Ratio 45	55.0	56.6	38.3	57.4	50.4	56.0
Return on Total Assets 46	20.0	42.9	4.5	18.0	21.2	20.7
Return on Equity Before Income Taxes 47	39.9	96.0	7.1	37.0	39.2	40.7
Return on Equity After Income Taxes 48	37.4	95.7	6.3	36.8	36.9	36.7
Profit Margin (Before Income Tax) 49	7.2	8.0	1.9	5.4	9.3	9.5
Profit Margin (After Income Tax) 50	6.7	7.9	1.7	5.3	8.7	8.5

Table I

Corporations with and without Net Income

LEATHER AND ALLIED PRODUCT MANUFACTURING

MONEY AMOUNTS AND SIZE OF ASSETS IN THOUSANDS OF DOLLARS

Item Description for Accounting Period 7/04 Through 6/05	Total	Zero Assets	Under 500	500 to 1,000	1,000 to 5,000	5,000 to 10,000	10,000 to 25,000	25,000 to 50,000	50,000 to 100,000	100,000 to 250,000	250,000 to 500,000	500,000 to 2,500,000	2,500,000 and over
Number of Enterprises 1	2191	1049	844	99	131	4	31	12	8	7	0	5	0
Revenues ($ in Thousands)													
Net Sales 2	9872426	52552	169507	34112	387335	102632	866031	1013707	1319379	1346297	0	4580876	0
Interest 3	15959	1	2	31	68	0	1418	704	650	4063	0	9021	0
Rents 4	5183	0	0	823	1358	0	399	827	0	1207	0	570	0
Royalties 5	79362	2	0	0	0	0	449	1770	266	38067	0	38808	0
Other Portfolio Income 6	27701	3582	2665	27	784	0	1058	3130	369	15004	0	1082	0
Other Receipts 7	79398	0	28	42	64	326	3941	5808	4581	35760	0	28847	0
Total Receipts 8	10080029	56137	172202	35035	389609	102958	873296	1025946	1325245	1440398	0	4659204	0
Average Total Receipts 9	4601	54	204	354	2974	25740	28171	85496	165656	205771	•	931841	•
Operating Costs/Operating Income (%)													
Cost of Operations 10	64.7	49.6	42.1	61.1	66.8	64.2	68.8	65.4	64.1	68.1	•	63.8	•
Salaries and Wages 11	9.1	4.5	8.7	25.8	8.2	11.1	8.3	9.3	8.9	9.4	•	9.2	•
Taxes Paid 12	1.8	3.9	1.4	4.6	3.3	1.1	1.9	2.1	2.5	1.6	•	1.3	•
Interest Paid 13	1.2	1.5	0.3	1.3	0.2	0.6	1.0	0.7	1.4	3.1	•	0.9	•
Depreciation 14	1.8	13.3	0.5	18.3	1.1	0.7	1.4	1.2	1.2	1.3	•	2.2	•
Amortization and Depletion 15	0.5	0.0	0.1	1.9	0.0	0.1	0.2	0.1	0.1	0.2	•	0.9	•
Pensions and Other Deferred Comp. 16	0.5	2.1	0.1	•	0.7	0.2	0.3	0.6	0.2	0.7	•	0.5	•
Employee Benefits 17	1.0	0.9	0.0	2.5	1.3	0.4	1.4	1.2	0.7	2.4	•	0.6	•
Advertising 18	2.1	0.1	1.3	1.6	0.7	1.1	1.1	3.1	1.7	2.9	•	2.1	•
Other Expenses 19	12.3	20.7	36.9	37.8	19.8	11.4	9.6	12.7	10.2	17.3	•	9.9	•
Officers' Compensation 20	2.3	13.1	7.1	9.2	4.0	2.4	2.5	1.4	5.5	2.1	•	1.2	•
Operating Margin 21	2.8	•	1.6	•	•	6.8	3.5	2.2	3.5	•	•	7.4	•
Operating Margin Before Officers' Comp. 22	5.1	3.3	8.8	•	•	9.2	6.0	3.6	9.0	•	•	8.6	•

Selected Average Balance Sheet ($ in Thousands)

	1	2	3	4	5	6	7	8	9	10	11	12
Net Receivables 23	748	0	19	11	127	2718	4163	13003	20307	57419	•	148664
Inventories 24	727	0	49	272	582	2609	4956	11191	29192	27587	•	111725
Net Property, Plant and Equipment 25	401	0	0	235	225	665	2189	4638	8251	19149	•	99658
Total Assets 26	3157	0	86	626	1492	8174	15881	38074	72169	200845	•	724446
Notes and Loans Payable 27	906	0	20	1568	289	3298	4477	8156	17444	69786	•	179352
All Other Liabilities 28	876	0	7	66	641	1490	3669	10280	21217	103414	•	137286
Net Worth 29	1375	0	59	-1008	562	3385	7735	19638	33507	27646	•	407808

Selected Financial Ratios (Times to 1)

	1	2	3	4	5	6	7	8	9	10	11	12
Current Ratio 30	2.1	•	11.6	18.1	1.6	4.2	2.0	2.3	2.2	1.6	•	2.2
Quick Ratio 31	1.1	•	5.6	6.7	0.4	2.6	0.9	1.2	1.0	0.8	•	1.4
Net Sales to Working Capital 32	4.2	•	2.7	1.2	6.7	4.9	4.9	5.2	5.3	4.1	•	3.7
Coverage Ratio 33	5.1	•	12.7	•	•	13.4	5.6	5.8	3.9	0.8	•	10.6
Total Asset Turnover 34	1.4	•	2.3	0.5	2.0	3.1	1.8	2.2	2.3	1.0	•	1.3
Inventory Turnover 35	4.0	•	1.7	0.8	3.4	6.3	3.9	4.9	3.6	4.8	•	5.2
Receivables Turnover 36	6.2	•	10.2	2.8	16.2	10.4	7.0	6.9	6.9	3.7	•	7.7
Total Liabilities to Net Worth 37	1.3	•	0.4	•	1.7	1.4	1.1	0.9	1.2	6.3	•	0.8
Current Assets to Working Capital 38	1.9	•	1.1	1.1	2.6	1.3	2.0	1.8	1.8	2.8	•	1.8
Current Liabilities to Working Capital 39	0.9	•	0.1	0.1	1.6	0.3	1.0	0.8	0.8	1.8	•	0.8
Working Capital to Net Sales 40	0.2	•	0.4	0.8	0.1	0.2	0.2	0.2	0.2	0.2	•	0.3
Inventory to Working Capital 41	0.7	•	0.6	0.7	1.1	0.5	0.9	0.7	0.9	0.7	•	0.6
Total Receipts to Cash Flow 42	7.2	29.0	3.1	•	9.8	6.0	7.9	7.6	7.9	8.5	•	6.6
Cost of Goods to Cash Flow 43	4.7	14.4	1.3	•	6.6	3.9	5.4	5.0	5.1	5.8	•	4.2
Cash Flow to Total Debt 44	0.3	•	2.5	•	0.3	0.9	0.4	0.6	0.5	0.1	•	0.4

Selected Financial Factors (in Percentages)

	1	2	3	4	5	6	7	8	9	10	11	12
Debt Ratio 45	56.4	•	31.0	260.9	62.3	58.6	51.3	48.4	53.6	86.2	•	43.7
Return on Total Assets 46	9.0	•	8.1	•	•	24.0	9.4	9.1	12.1	2.3	•	12.7
Return on Equity Before Income Taxes 47	16.6	•	10.8	21.0	•	53.7	15.9	14.6	19.3	•	•	20.4
Return on Equity After Income Taxes 48	13.4	•	10.5	21.0	•	53.7	14.8	12.1	18.4	•	•	17.0
Profit Margin (Before Income Tax) 49	5.1	•	3.2	•	•	7.1	4.4	3.4	3.9	•	•	9.1
Profit Margin (After Income Tax) 50	4.1	•	3.1	•	•	7.1	4.1	2.8	3.7	•	•	7.6

Table II
Corporations with Net Income

LEATHER AND ALLIED PRODUCT MANUFACTURING

MONEY AMOUNTS AND SIZE OF ASSETS IN THOUSANDS OF DOLLARS

Item Description for Accounting Period 7/04 Through 6/05	Total	Zero Assets	Under 500	500 to 1,000	1,000 to 5,000	5,000 to 10,000	10,000 to 25,000	25,000 to 50,000	50,000 to 100,000	100,000 to 250,000	250,000 to 500,000	500,000 to 2,500,000	2,500,000 and over
Number of Enterprises 1	730	0	613	49	17	0	24	9	0	3	0	5	0
Revenues ($ in Thousands)													
Net Sales 2	8084211	0	152701	29792	153031	0	673262	810014	0	629294	0	458876	0
Interest 3	11413	0	2	30	62	0	620	266	0	781	0	9021	0
Rents 4	2719	0	0	823	0	0	356	827	0	143	0	570	0
Royalties 5	40782	0	0	0	0	0	138	1106	0	462	0	38808	0
Other Portfolio Income 6	12412	0	2665	10	0	0	591	3128	0	1084	0	1082	0
Other Receipts 7	45353	0	1	29	38	0	3113	5802	0	1656	0	28847	0
Total Receipts 8	8196890	0	155369	30684	153131	0	678080	821143	0	633420	0	4665204	0
Average Total Receipts 9	11229	•	253	626	9008	•	28253	91238	•	211140	•	931841	•
Operating Costs/Operating Income (%)													
Cost of Operations 10	63.8	•	41.4	65.2	78.0	•	67.3	67.1	•	62.5	•	63.8	•
Salaries and Wages 11	9.0	•	9.6	8.5	7.8	•	8.4	8.4	•	10.0	•	9.2	•
Taxes Paid 12	1.7	•	1.5	3.4	1.5	•	2.0	1.9	•	1.9	•	1.3	•
Interest Paid 13	0.9	•	0.2	1.5	0.2	•	0.7	0.5	•	0.5	•	0.9	•
Depreciation 14	1.7	•	0.5	1.1	0.5	•	1.5	1.4	•	1.2	•	2.2	•
Amortization and Depletion 15	0.6	•	0.1	•	0.0	•	0.1	0.1	•	0.2	•	0.9	•
Pensions and Other Deferred Comp. 16	0.4	•	0.1	•	1.0	•	0.4	0.7	•	0.6	•	0.5	•
Employee Benefits 17	0.7	•	0.0	•	0.4	•	1.2	1.1	•	1.0	•	0.6	•
Advertising 18	2.0	•	1.3	0.4	0.5	•	1.3	2.0	•	3.0	•	2.1	•
Other Expenses 19	10.2	•	33.7	11.3	6.8	•	8.7	9.4	•	11.9	•	9.9	•
Officers' Compensation 20	2.3	•	7.9	9.8	2.8	•	2.9	1.4	•	0.7	•	1.2	•
Operating Margin 21	6.6	•	3.6	•	0.6	•	5.5	6.1	•	6.6	•	7.4	•
Operating Margin Before Officers' Comp. 22	8.9	•	11.6	8.6	3.4	•	8.4	7.5	•	7.3	•	8.6	•

Selected Average Balance Sheet ($ in Thousands)

Net Receivables 23	1955	27	20	195	4551	13535	100903	148664
Inventories 24	1688	11	155	1514	5009	10639	39276	146957
Net Property, Plant and Equipment 25	970	1	184	314	2017	5838	15208	99658
Total Assets 26	7606	68	606	2411	15764	37838	206069	724446
Notes and Loans Payable 27	1753	20	128	254	3620	8070	22276	179352
All Other Liabilities 28	1542	9	32	672	3677	9285	47511	137286
Net Worth 29	4311	39	447	1485	8467	20483	136281	407808

Selected Financial Ratios (Times to 1)

Current Ratio 30	2.5	6.5	11.7	2.0	2.2	2.2	5.3	2.2
Quick Ratio 31	1.5	5.4	6.7	0.8	1.1	1.1	3.8	1.4
Net Sales to Working Capital 32	3.7	4.8	1.8	10.2	4.4	6.0	1.7	3.7
Coverage Ratio 33	10.0	34.1	2.1	4.8	9.6	15.7	15.6	10.6
Total Asset Turnover 34	1.5	3.6	1.0	3.7	1.8	2.4	1.0	1.3
Inventory Turnover 35	4.2	9.6	2.6	4.6	3.8	5.7	3.3	4.0
Receivables Turnover 36	6.0	9.2		20.4	6.4	7.7		
Total Liabilities to Net Worth 37	0.8	0.7	0.4	0.6	0.9	0.8	0.5	0.8
Current Assets to Working Capital 38	1.7	1.2	1.1	2.0	1.8	1.8	1.2	1.8
Current Liabilities to Working Capital 39	0.7	0.2	0.1	1.0	0.8	0.8	0.2	0.8
Working Capital to Net Sales 40	0.3	0.2	0.6	0.1	0.2	0.2	0.6	0.3
Inventory to Working Capital 41	0.6	0.2	0.5	1.2	0.8	0.8	0.3	0.6
Total Receipts to Cash Flow 42	6.6	3.0	8.2	18.7	7.4	6.7	5.9	6.6
Cost of Goods to Cash Flow 43	4.2	1.2	5.3	14.6	5.0	4.5	3.7	4.2
Cash Flow to Total Debt 44	0.5	2.9	0.5	0.5	0.5	0.8	0.5	0.4

Selected Financial Factors (in Percentages)

Debt Ratio 45	43.3	42.5	26.3	38.4	46.3	45.9	33.9	43.7
Return on Total Assets 46	13.0	20.1	3.3	3.0	12.5	19.0	7.8	12.7
Return on Equity Before Income Taxes 47	20.6	34.0	2.4	3.8	20.8	32.8	11.1	20.4
Return on Equity After Income Taxes 48	17.6	33.3	2.4	3.2	19.6	29.6	7.2	17.0
Profit Margin (Before Income Tax) 49	8.0	5.4	1.8	0.6	6.3	7.5	7.2	9.1
Profit Margin (After Income Tax) 50	6.8	5.3	1.8	0.5	5.9	6.7	4.7	7.6

Table I

Corporations with and without Net Income

WOOD PRODUCT MANUFACTURING

MONEY AMOUNTS AND SIZE OF ASSETS IN THOUSANDS OF DOLLARS

Item Description for Accounting Period 7/04 Through 6/05	Total	Zero Assets	Under 500	500 to 1,000	1,000 to 5,000	5,000 to 10,000	10,000 to 25,000	25,000 to 50,000	50,000 to 100,000	100,000 to 250,000	250,000 to 500,000	500,000 to 2,500,000	2,500,000 and over
Number of Enterprises 1	13773	1510	7208	1563	2491	457	315	116	60	29	8	14	0
Revenues ($ in Thousands)													
Net Sales 2	100811980	942273	5597316	3731136	13136872	9414719	10411339	7845728	6679524	6801175	4267587	31981312	0
Interest 3	576794	1265	707	1262	6144	5967	4112	7573	14202	21781	1884	511896	0
Rents 4	41392	0	412	1992	6049	6020	5579	3933	5836	3451	306	7814	0
Royalties 5	45984	0	0	432	82	1	173	467	149	9676	0	35005	0
Other Portfolio Income 6	775490	6781	24968	3216	31054	10197	17867	21440	16186	13926	10395	619456	0
Other Receipts 7	546106	1919	1591	18132	135674	45193	58846	80390	58372	77123	47196	21672	0
Total Receipts 8	102797746	952238	5624994	3756170	13315875	9482097	10500916	7959531	6774269	6927132	4327368	33177155	0
Average Total Receipts 9	7464	631	780	2403	5346	20749	33336	68617	112904	238867	540921	2369797	•
Operating Costs/Operating Income (%)													
Cost of Operations 10	73.7	71.6	56.4	63.3	71.2	81.1	77.7	79.7	78.5	75.8	70.4	73.0	•
Salaries and Wages 11	5.4	4.5	12.9	6.5	7.0	4.0	4.1	3.7	4.3	4.4	6.5	5.0	•
Taxes Paid 12	1.6	1.4	2.6	2.3	2.1	1.5	1.6	1.6	1.5	1.7	1.4	1.2	•
Interest Paid 13	2.2	2.0	0.8	0.4	1.0	0.4	0.8	0.8	1.5	1.6	1.0	5.0	•
Depreciation 14	3.1	6.0	2.0	2.9	2.6	2.0	2.7	2.8	2.6	3.5	4.0	4.0	•
Amortization and Depletion 15	1.2	0.3	0.1	0.0	0.1	0.0	0.2	0.2	0.5	0.2	0.3	3.6	•
Pensions and Other Deferred Comp. 16	0.5	0.2	0.9	0.2	0.2	0.2	0.3	0.3	0.2	0.4	0.4	1.0	•
Employee Benefits 17	1.0	1.1	1.7	1.6	1.2	0.8	1.2	1.1	0.8	0.9	1.3	0.7	•
Advertising 18	0.6	0.6	0.3	0.2	0.2	0.2	0.3	0.5	0.5	1.0	1.4	0.9	•
Other Expenses 19	6.6	12.3	13.7	15.5	9.2	4.8	5.6	5.3	6.6	6.9	8.1	3.9	•
Officers' Compensation 20	1.6	2.8	8.0	3.8	2.9	1.6	1.3	1.1	0.7	0.7	0.5	0.5	•
Operating Margin 21	2.3	•	0.4	3.2	2.4	3.4	4.3	3.0	2.4	3.1	4.6	1.2	•
Operating Margin Before Officers' Comp. 22	4.0	•	8.5	7.0	5.2	5.0	5.5	4.0	3.1	3.8	5.2	1.7	•

Selected Average Balance Sheet ($ in Thousands)

Net Receivables 23	582	0	53	152	469	1773	2800	5539	11088	19004	37207	170014	•
Inventories 24	686	0	29	140	448	1865	4114	8465	14343	23568	42026	128827	•
Net Property, Plant and Equipment 25	1632	0	59	175	654	1696	4764	10717	21502	57293	118320	908897	•
Total Assets 26	7146	0	178	725	2158	7097	15064	34413	68829	152667	344358	4809454	•
Notes and Loans Payable 27	1735	0	107	240	1034	1843	5368	10382	24647	60699	59122	908819	•
All Other Liabilities 28	2505	0	28	120	474	1383	2839	6860	14244	25564	89552	2021015	•
Net Worth 29	2906	0	43	365	650	3870	6857	17172	29938	66403	195684	1879620	•

Selected Financial Ratios (Times to 1)

Current Ratio 30	1.2	•	2.6	2.8	1.6	2.3	2.0	1.8	1.6	2.4	1.7	0.9	•
Quick Ratio 31	0.3	•	1.8	1.8	0.8	1.2	0.9	0.7	0.8	1.2	0.9	0.1	•
Net Sales to Working Capital 32	18.5	•	11.3	7.4	11.0	7.2	7.4	8.2	8.2	5.6	9.6	•	•
Coverage Ratio 33	2.9	0.1	2.2	9.7	4.7	11.6	7.3	6.5	3.6	4.2	7.0	2.0	•
Total Asset Turnover 34	1.0	•	4.4	3.3	2.4	2.9	2.2	2.0	1.6	1.5	1.5	0.5	•
Inventory Turnover 35	7.9	•	15.2	10.8	8.4	9.0	6.2	6.4	6.1	7.5	8.9	12.9	•
Receivables Turnover 36	6.6	•	15.1	15.5	13.6	12.5	13.1	12.5	11.8	14.1	15.7	16.8	•
Total Liabilities to Net Worth 37	1.5	•	3.1	1.0	2.3	0.8	1.2	1.0	1.3	1.3	0.8	1.6	•
Current Assets to Working Capital 38	7.5	•	1.6	1.6	2.7	1.7	2.0	2.3	2.5	1.7	2.4	•	•
Current Liabilities to Working Capital 39	6.5	•	0.6	0.6	1.7	0.7	1.0	1.3	1.5	0.7	1.4	•	•
Working Capital to Net Sales 40	0.1	•	0.1	0.1	0.1	0.1	0.1	0.1	0.1	0.2	0.1	•	•
Inventory to Working Capital 41	1.8	•	0.4	0.5	1.1	0.7	1.0	1.1	1.2	0.7	0.9	•	•
Total Receipts to Cash Flow 42	11.3	11.2	9.8	6.9	10.0	13.2	10.8	11.9	11.0	9.5	7.8	14.3	•
Cost of Goods to Cash Flow 43	8.3	8.0	5.5	4.4	7.2	10.7	8.4	9.4	8.6	7.2	5.5	10.4	•
Cash Flow to Total Debt 44	0.2	•	0.6	1.0	0.3	0.5	0.4	0.3	0.3	0.3	0.5	0.1	•

Selected Financial Factors (in Percentages)

Debt Ratio 45	59.3	•	75.6	49.7	69.9	45.5	54.5	50.1	56.5	56.5	43.2	60.9	•
Return on Total Assets 46	6.7	•	7.3	14.3	11.5	13.1	12.9	10.3	8.6	9.9	11.0	4.7	•
Return on Equity Before Income Taxes 47	10.9	•	16.5	25.5	30.1	21.9	24.5	17.4	14.2	17.3	16.6	6.0	•
Return on Equity After Income Taxes 48	9.3	•	15.7	23.6	28.5	20.9	22.7	15.1	11.5	14.9	14.0	4.6	•
Profit Margin (Before Income Tax) 49	4.3	•	0.9	3.9	3.7	4.1	5.1	4.4	3.8	4.9	6.1	5.0	•
Profit Margin (After Income Tax) 50	3.7	•	0.9	3.6	3.5	3.9	4.7	3.8	3.1	4.2	5.1	3.8	•

Table II
Corporations with Net Income

WOOD PRODUCT MANUFACTURING

MONEY AMOUNTS AND SIZE OF ASSETS IN THOUSANDS OF DOLLARS

Item Description for Accounting Period 7/04 Through 6/05	Total	Zero Assets	Under 500	500 to 1,000	1,000 to 5,000	5,000 to 10,000	10,000 to 25,000	25,000 to 50,000	50,000 to 100,000	100,000 to 250,000	250,000 to 500,000	500,000 to 2,500,000	2,500,000 and over
Number of Enterprises **1**	7534	504	3233	1108	1868	399	251	89	43	23	5	11	0
Revenues ($ in Thousands)													
Net Sales **2**	84167569	524042	2902879	3112613	9906356	8511893	8848021	6262724	4606477	5662722	3471208	30358635	0
Interest **3**	540445	47	113	1098	4118	3701	3448	6301	10446	11852	1845	497477	0
Rents **4**	22897	0	0	1992	1642	2709	4855	2049	695	2246	306	6403	0
Royalties **5**	43972	0	0	0	82	1	167	467	46	9676	0	33533	0
Other Portfolio Income **6**	740544	1354	15997	2890	25566	9700	15245	17784	12137	11835	9376	618659	0
Other Receipts **7**	423764	1225	1352	13898	118815	31699	49571	54025	49770	69839	21838	11730	0
Total Receipts **8**	85939191	526668	2920341	3132491	10056579	8559703	8921307	6343350	4679571	5768170	3504573	31526437	0
Average Total Receipts **9**	11407	1045	903	2827	5384	21453	35543	71274	108827	250790	700915	2866040	•
Operating Costs/Operating Income (%)													
Cost of Operations **10**	73.7	71.3	55.9	63.1	69.4	81.1	77.2	79.7	76.5	75.6	71.2	73.1	•
Salaries and Wages **11**	5.0	3.7	12.0	6.9	7.5	3.8	3.9	3.3	4.3	4.3	4.1	4.8	•
Taxes Paid **12**	1.5	1.8	3.0	2.3	2.1	1.4	1.5	1.5	1.5	1.9	1.3	1.2	•
Interest Paid **13**	2.3	0.1	0.3	0.3	0.7	0.4	0.7	0.7	1.3	1.4	0.8	5.2	•
Depreciation **14**	3.1	2.6	0.9	2.9	2.6	2.0	2.5	2.7	2.9	3.2	3.5	4.1	•
Amortization and Depletion **15**	1.4	0.0	0.1	0.0	0.1	0.0	0.2	0.2	0.4	0.2	0.1	3.7	•
Pensions and Other Deferred Comp. **16**	0.6	0.3	0.2	0.3	0.2	0.2	0.2	0.4	0.3	0.4	0.3	1.0	•
Employee Benefits **17**	0.9	0.7	2.1	1.5	1.1	0.9	1.2	0.9	0.7	1.0	1.3	0.7	•
Advertising **18**	0.6	1.0	0.2	0.2	0.2	0.2	0.3	0.3	0.5	0.6	1.7	0.9	•
Other Expenses **19**	5.4	8.9	12.2	13.3	8.2	4.2	5.1	4.2	5.1	6.0	8.0	3.3	•
Officers' Compensation **20**	1.4	2.2	6.8	4.2	2.9	1.4	1.3	1.1	0.8	0.8	0.4	0.5	•
Operating Margin **21**	4.0	7.4	6.3	5.0	5.2	4.4	5.8	4.9	5.6	4.8	7.2	1.5	•
Operating Margin Before Officers' Comp. **22**	5.3	9.5	13.1	9.1	8.1	5.8	7.1	6.0	6.4	5.5	7.6	2.0	•

Selected Average Balance Sheet ($ in Thousands)

Net Receivables 23	889	0	75	176	500	1687	2880	5503	10360	18427	50530	210943	•
Inventories 24	969	0	41	108	455	1499	4023	7671	14019	22160	49406	231979	•
Net Property, Plant and Equipment 25	2383	0	31	172	549	1716	4590	9930	21867	60588	124937	996098	•
Total Assets 26	11661	0	215	759	2089	7025	15134	34058	67399	160666	323547	5870495	•
Notes and Loans Payable 27	2384	0	15	178	716	1783	4715	9482	22525	52177	78084	1006912	•
All Other Liabilities 28	4235	0	21	125	337	1271	2736	6663	12188	24832	80298	2526395	•
Net Worth 29	5042	0	179	456	1036	3971	7682	17913	32687	83657	165165	2337188	•

Selected Financial Ratios (Times to 1)

Current Ratio 30	1.1	•	7.1	3.0	2.3	2.5	2.2	1.9	2.0	2.5	2.2	0.9
Quick Ratio 31	0.3	•	5.1	2.2	1.3	1.2	1.0	0.7	0.9	1.3	1.1	0.1
Net Sales to Working Capital 32	17.7	•	6.2	7.6	7.0	7.2	6.7	8.0	6.3	5.5	7.7	•
Coverage Ratio 33	3.6	59.4	25.0	20.0	10.8	14.9	10.5	9.7	6.4	5.9	11.7	2.0
Total Asset Turnover 34	1.0	•	4.2	3.7	2.5	3.0	2.3	2.1	1.6	1.5	2.1	0.5
Inventory Turnover 35	8.5	•	12.3	16.4	8.1	11.5	6.8	7.3	5.8	8.4	10.0	8.7
Receivables Turnover 36	6.5	•	11.8	15.6	13.1	15.3	14.5	14.2	12.5	16.5	16.7	3.3
Total Liabilities to Net Worth 37	1.3	•	0.2	0.7	1.0	0.8	1.0	0.9	1.1	0.9	1.0	1.5
Current Assets to Working Capital 38	7.7	•	1.2	1.5	1.8	1.7	1.8	2.2	2.0	1.7	1.8	•
Current Liabilities to Working Capital 39	6.7	•	0.2	0.5	0.8	0.7	0.8	1.2	1.0	0.7	0.8	•
Working Capital to Net Sales 40	0.1	•	0.2	0.1	0.1	0.1	0.1	0.1	0.2	0.2	0.1	•
Inventory to Working Capital 41	1.7	•	0.3	0.3	0.7	0.7	0.9	1.0	0.9	0.7	0.7	•
Total Receipts to Cash Flow 42	10.4	6.4	6.7	7.1	8.2	12.3	9.5	10.8	8.9	8.7	6.6	14.7
Cost of Goods to Cash Flow 43	7.6	4.5	3.7	4.5	5.7	10.0	7.4	8.6	6.8	6.6	4.7	10.7
Cash Flow to Total Debt 44	0.2	•	3.7	1.3	0.6	0.6	0.5	0.4	0.3	0.4	0.7	0.1

Selected Financial Factors (in Percentages)

Debt Ratio 45	56.8	•	16.8	39.9	50.4	43.5	49.2	47.4	51.5	47.9	49.0	60.2
Return on Total Assets 46	8.0	•	30.2	21.8	18.6	16.2	17.0	14.3	13.6	12.2	19.2	5.0
Return on Equity Before Income Taxes 47	13.4	•	34.9	34.4	34.1	26.7	30.4	24.4	23.6	19.5	34.4	6.4
Return on Equity After Income Taxes 48	11.7	•	34.5	32.3	32.8	25.6	28.4	21.6	20.1	17.1	29.4	4.9
Profit Margin (Before Income Tax) 49	6.1	7.9	6.9	5.6	6.7	5.0	6.6	6.2	7.2	6.6	8.2	5.4
Profit Margin (After Income Tax) 50	5.3	7.3	6.9	5.2	6.4	4.8	6.2	5.5	6.1	5.8	7.0	4.2

Table I

Corporations with and without Net Income

PULP, PAPER, AND PAPERBOARD MILLS

MONEY AMOUNTS AND SIZE OF ASSETS IN THOUSANDS OF DOLLARS

Item Description for Accounting Period 7/04 Through 6/05	Total	Zero Assets	Under 500	500 to 1,000	1,000 to 5,000	5,000 to 10,000	10,000 to 25,000	25,000 to 50,000	50,000 to 100,000	100,000 to 250,000	250,000 to 500,000	500,000 to 2,500,000	2,500,000 and over
Number of Enterprises 1	252	0	0	0	0	0	21	20	9	12	7	21	7
Revenues ($ in Thousands)													
Net Sales 2	94395323	0	0	0	0	0	578938	1005935	1109177	2089715	2721096	20692047	64563003
Interest 3	542190	0	0	0	0	0	161	521	633	12202	1038	160990	366248
Rents 4	28207	0	0	0	0	0	474	115	9	498	2408	4414	20290
Royalties 5	189462	0	0	0	0	0	0	0	30	0	23	41994	147415
Other Portfolio Income 6	1600932	0	0	0	0	0	2519	1577	1583	51971	15065	511227	1004993
Other Receipts 7	2347392	0	0	0	0	0	711	8406	5473	35407	158674	289104	1831875
Total Receipts 8	99103506	0	0	0	0	0	582803	1016554	1116905	2189793	2898304	21699776	67933824
Average Total Receipts 9	393268	•	•	•	•	•	27753	50828	124101	182483	414043	1033323	9704832
Operating Costs/Operating Income (%)													
Cost of Operations 10	76.8	•	•	•	•	•	79.7	79.9	77.4	74.7	60.3	80.4	76.0
Salaries and Wages 11	4.3	•	•	•	•	•	4.5	4.0	4.2	4.5	4.4	4.0	4.4
Taxes Paid 12	1.4	•	•	•	•	•	1.7	1.7	1.1	1.3	1.1	1.3	1.4
Interest Paid 13	4.0	•	•	•	•	•	1.1	1.1	3.4	5.0	1.9	3.1	4.5
Depreciation 14	4.2	•	•	•	•	•	3.3	3.6	2.9	6.7	7.4	6.8	3.2
Amortization and Depletion 15	0.2	•	•	•	•	•	0.2	0.5	0.5	0.7	0.3	0.3	0.2
Pensions and Other Deferred Comp. 16	0.7	•	•	•	•	•	0.5	0.9	0.8	1.0	0.9	0.9	0.7
Employee Benefits 17	1.6	•	•	•	•	•	1.3	1.8	1.4	2.0	2.9	1.3	1.7
Advertising 18	0.3	•	•	•	•	•	0.1	0.3	0.5	0.1	0.2	0.3	0.3
Other Expenses 19	9.2	•	•	•	•	•	6.3	7.9	5.8	8.7	18.8	6.1	9.9
Officers' Compensation 20	0.3	•	•	•	•	•	1.1	1.1	0.9	1.2	0.2	0.5	0.1
Operating Margin 21	•	•	•	•	•	•	0.1	•	1.0	•	1.7	•	•
Operating Margin Before Officers' Comp. 22	•	•	•	•	•	•	1.2	•	2.0	•	1.8	•	•

Selected Average Balance Sheet ($ in Thousands)

Net Receivables 23	44919	•	3543	5449	11151	20724	34581	168330	994187
Inventories 24	35410	•	2289	6729	12265	19658	29713	88854	900355
Net Property, Plant and Equipment 25	214246	•	7160	15759	25414	88210	222937	573215	5489313
Total Assets 26	587929	•	15780	35501	64387	187121	338572	1138728	16782555
Notes and Loans Payable 27	224447	•	6364	19869	24235	140080	107558	346651	6533707
All Other Liabilities 28	150033	•	5205	11523	25687	36675	95151	362294	4064210
Net Worth 29	213449	•	4212	4109	14466	10365	135864	429782	6184638

Selected Financial Ratios (Times to 1)

Current Ratio 30	0.9	•	1.0	1.2	1.8	2.0	1.9	1.8	0.8
Quick Ratio 31	0.5	•	0.6	0.5	0.8	0.9	1.0	1.1	0.4
Net Sales to Working Capital 32	•	•	132.2	21.9	8.3	6.0	9.3	7.0	•
Coverage Ratio 33	1.5	•	1.7	•	1.5	0.7	5.4	1.0	1.7
Total Asset Turnover 34	0.6	•	1.7	1.4	1.9	0.9	1.1	0.9	0.5
Inventory Turnover 35	8.1	•	9.6	6.0	7.8	6.6	7.9	8.9	7.8
Receivables Turnover 36	8.2	•	8.2	7.6	12.9	9.3	15.6	6.4	8.6
Total Liabilities to Net Worth 37	1.8	•	2.7	7.6	3.5	17.1	1.5	1.6	1.7
Current Assets to Working Capital 38	•	•	34.8	6.6	2.3	2.0	2.1	2.2	•
Current Liabilities to Working Capital 39	•	•	33.8	5.6	1.3	1.0	1.1	1.2	•
Working Capital to Net Sales 40	•	•	0.0	0.0	0.1	0.2	0.1	0.1	•
Inventory to Working Capital 41	•	•	11.3	2.6	1.2	0.8	0.9	0.7	•
Total Receipts to Cash Flow 42	12.1	•	18.3	24.8	15.0	19.6	4.0	28.1	10.5
Cost of Goods to Cash Flow 43	9.3	•	14.6	19.8	11.6	14.7	2.4	22.6	8.0
Cash Flow to Total Debt 44	0.1	•	0.1	0.1	0.2	0.1	0.5	0.0	0.1

Selected Financial Factors (in Percentages)

Debt Ratio 45	63.7	•	73.3	88.4	77.5	94.5	59.9	62.3	63.1
Return on Total Assets 46	4.0	•	3.4	•	9.8	3.1	11.5	2.7	4.2
Return on Equity Before Income Taxes 47	3.9	•	5.3	•	14.7	•	23.5	•	4.6
Return on Equity After Income Taxes 48	2.5	•	3.7	•	13.2	•	17.7	•	3.4
Profit Margin (Before Income Tax) 49	2.2	•	0.8	•	1.7	•	8.2	•	3.1
Profit Margin (After Income Tax) 50	1.4	•	0.6	•	1.5	•	6.2	•	2.3

73

Table II

Corporations with Net Income

PULP, PAPER, AND PAPERBOARD MILLS

MONEY AMOUNTS AND SIZE OF ASSETS IN THOUSANDS OF DOLLARS

Item Description for Accounting Period 7/04 Through 6/05	Total	Zero Assets	Under 500	500 to 1,000	1,000 to 5,000	5,000 to 10,000	10,000 to 25,000	25,000 to 50,000	50,000 to 100,000	100,000 to 250,000	250,000 to 500,000	500,000 to 2,500,000	2,500,000 and over
Number of Enterprises 1	57	0	0	0	0	3	14	9	6	4	0	13	0
Revenues ($ in Thousands)													
Net Sales 2	67019316	0	0	0	0	30542	446892	492545	866177	847054	0	10281260	0
Interest 3	373666	0	0	0	0	263	142	108	310	3340	0	128794	0
Rents 4	25109	0	0	0	0	0	474	48	6	33	0	3966	0
Royalties 5	151388	0	0	0	0	0	0	0	30	0	0	4169	0
Other Portfolio Income 6	1464308	0	0	0	0	1408	2487	1523	135	84	0	485399	0
Other Receipts 7	1839932	0	0	0	0	2	623	3360	3454	13730	0	126975	0
Total Receipts 8	70873719	0	0	0	0	32215	450618	497584	870112	864241	0	11030563	0
Average Total Receipts 9	1243399	•	•	•	•	10738	32187	55287	145019	216060	•	848505	•
Operating Costs/Operating Income (%)													
Cost of Operations 10	75.0	•	•	•	•	85.4	78.5	78.6	77.1	68.8	•	75.9	•
Salaries and Wages 11	4.7	•	•	•	•	4.1	3.8	3.4	4.2	5.4	•	4.7	•
Taxes Paid 12	1.5	•	•	•	•	0.8	1.4	1.3	0.9	1.5	•	1.3	•
Interest Paid 13	4.0	•	•	•	•	0.3	0.9	1.0	3.2	2.0	•	3.2	•
Depreciation 14	3.3	•	•	•	•	2.0	3.0	2.6	2.2	5.4	•	6.2	•
Amortization and Depletion 15	0.2	•	•	•	•	0.5	0.2	0.0	0.4	0.1	•	0.2	•
Pensions and Other Deferred Comp. 16	0.6	•	•	•	•	0.5	0.6	0.7	0.4	2.3	•	0.9	•
Employee Benefits 17	1.5	•	•	•	•	1.2	1.0	1.2	1.2	1.9	•	1.2	•
Advertising 18	0.3	•	•	•	•	0.1	0.1	0.5	0.1	0.1	•	0.1	•
Other Expenses 19	9.3	•	•	•	•	2.2	6.0	7.0	6.7	9.2	•	6.8	•
Officers' Compensation 20	0.2	•	•	•	•	1.6	0.9	1.4	0.7	0.8	•	0.7	•
Operating Margin 21	•	•	•	•	•	1.2	3.6	2.3	2.9	2.6	•	•	•
Operating Margin Before Officers' Comp. 22	•	•	•	•	•	2.8	4.5	3.7	3.5	3.4	•	•	•

Selected Average Balance Sheet ($ in Thousands)

Net Receivables 23	109604	•	3605	3814	5943	11810	28163	•	96332
Inventories 24	75325	•	1448	2213	6014	23112	35088	•	64543
Net Property, Plant and Equipment 25	679268	•	1739	6881	13346	20484	86668	•	521978
Total Assets 26	1862163	•	8552	16341	32925	64048	191476	•	1000367
Notes and Loans Payable 27	725346	•	649	4253	11111	12861	79470	•	282666
All Other Liabilities 28	424349	•	13591	4976	7540	29103	40578	•	291521
Net Worth 29	712468	•	-5688	7112	14274	22084	71428	•	426179

Selected Financial Ratios (Times to 1)

Current Ratio 30	0.9	•	0.4	1.6	1.8	2.3	1.9	•	1.7
Quick Ratio 31	0.4	•	0.3	0.9	0.8	0.9	0.8	•	0.9
Net Sales to Working Capital 32	•	•	•	11.0	7.6	6.2	6.0	•	8.0
Coverage Ratio 33	2.4	•	24.5	5.6	4.2	2.0	3.3	•	3.0
Total Asset Turnover 34	0.6	•	1.2	2.0	1.7	2.3	1.1	•	0.8
Inventory Turnover 35	11.7	•	6.0	11.3	7.1	4.8	4.2	•	9.3
Receivables Turnover 36	13.1	•	•	9.8	8.2	•	•	•	11.1
Total Liabilities to Net Worth 37	1.6	•	•	1.3	1.3	1.9	1.7	•	1.3
Current Assets to Working Capital 38	•	•	•	2.7	2.3	1.8	2.1	•	2.4
Current Liabilities to Working Capital 39	•	•	•	1.7	1.3	0.8	1.1	•	1.4
Working Capital to Net Sales 40	•	•	•	0.1	0.1	0.2	0.2	•	0.1
Inventory to Working Capital 41	•	•	•	0.9	0.8	1.0	1.0	•	0.8
Total Receipts to Cash Flow 42	8.9	•	28.1	11.6	10.6	11.0	9.0	•	10.4
Cost of Goods to Cash Flow 43	6.7	•	24.0	9.1	8.3	8.5	6.2	•	7.9
Cash Flow to Total Debt 44	0.1	•	0.0	0.3	0.3	0.3	0.2	•	0.1

Selected Financial Factors (in Percentages)

Debt Ratio 45	61.7	•	166.5	56.5	56.6	65.5	62.7	•	57.4
Return on Total Assets 46	6.0	•	8.3	10.4	7.1	14.7	7.4	•	7.4
Return on Equity Before Income Taxes 47	9.1	•	•	19.7	12.5	21.6	13.7	•	11.5
Return on Equity After Income Taxes 48	7.3	•	•	18.3	11.3	20.2	10.1	•	9.1
Profit Margin (Before Income Tax) 49	5.5	•	6.7	4.4	3.3	3.3	4.6	•	6.2
Profit Margin (After Income Tax) 50	4.4	•	5.0	4.1	3.0	3.1	3.4	•	4.9

74

Table I

Corporations with and without Net Income

CONVERTED PAPER PRODUCT

MONEY AMOUNTS AND SIZE OF ASSETS IN THOUSANDS OF DOLLARS

Item Description for Accounting Period 7/04 Through 6/05	Total	Zero Assets	Under 500	500 to 1,000	1,000 to 5,000	5,000 to 10,000	10,000 to 25,000	25,000 to 50,000	50,000 to 100,000	100,000 to 250,000	250,000 to 500,000	500,000 to 2,500,000	2,500,000 and over
Number of Enterprises 1	3299	0	917	635	0	0	159	61	31	21	7	8	4
Revenues ($ in Thousands)													
Net Sales 2	80708754	0	1657681	1339946	0	0	4986900	3325472	2818222	4980016	2768613	8430889	39369602
Interest 3	1683757	0	0	0	0	0	4258	2166	3082	5125	10638	68457	1587459
Rents 4	96565	0	0	1	0	0	966	2040	2292	603	1607	5525	81766
Royalties 5	931716	0	0	0	0	0	160	3196	144	1546	454	64165	861359
Other Portfolio Income 6	1241731	0	46532	58	0	0	6954	7725	5280	5905	169107	110381	868088
Other Receipts 7	2501710	0	5740	524	0	0	14033	20852	59473	17650	28309	181454	2007945
Total Receipts 8	87164233	0	1709953	1340530	0	0	5013271	3361451	2888493	5010845	2978728	8860871	44776219
Average Total Receipts 9	26421	•	1865	2111	•	•	31530	55106	93177	238612	425533	1107609	11194055
Operating Costs/Operating Income (%)													
Cost of Operations 10	71.7	•	65.0	79.7	•	•	72.7	73.6	73.6	71.4	71.1	71.5	71.7
Salaries and Wages 11	8.0	•	5.5	7.3	•	•	6.4	6.5	6.9	6.2	7.1	6.8	9.3
Taxes Paid 12	1.4	•	1.9	1.3	•	•	2.0	1.8	1.7	1.6	1.8	1.7	0.9
Interest Paid 13	2.7	•	0.2	0.7	•	•	1.0	1.0	1.3	1.3	2.4	3.7	3.8
Depreciation 14	3.8	•	0.7	2.9	•	•	3.7	3.6	4.3	3.0	5.0	4.9	3.9
Amortization and Depletion 15	0.5	•	•	0.2	•	•	0.1	0.3	0.2	0.3	0.3	0.7	0.7
Pensions and Other Deferred Comp. 16	1.1	•	0.0	0.0	•	•	0.5	0.6	0.4	0.4	1.4	0.9	1.6
Employee Benefits 17	2.4	•	2.7	0.8	•	•	1.4	1.6	1.6	1.9	1.2	3.5	2.7
Advertising 18	0.7	•	0.1	0.2	•	•	0.2	0.2	0.4	0.8	1.0	0.1	1.1
Other Expenses 19	10.1	•	25.6	5.5	•	•	7.6	7.9	7.0	10.6	11.5	8.1	10.4
Officers' Compensation 20	1.0	•	6.1	2.5	•	•	2.2	1.6	1.3	0.6	0.7	0.3	0.3
Operating Margin 21	•	•	•	•	•	•	2.3	1.3	1.3	2.1	•	•	•
Operating Margin Before Officers' Comp. 22	•	•	1.5	•	•	•	4.5	2.9	2.7	2.7	•	•	•

Selected Average Balance Sheet ($ in Thousands)

Net Receivables 23	2642	•	27	275	•	•	3995	7851	11277	32185	47070	161028	922689
Inventories 24	1735	•	19	56	•	•	3004	6257	12805	24629	47997	94391	541592
Net Property, Plant and Equipment 25	6248	•	44	155	•	•	5640	11790	21346	49830	175456	441866	2661888
Total Assets 26	30294	•	150	673	•	•	15515	34399	65614	149566	388919	1071071	18446841
Notes and Loans Payable 27	8583	•	123	298	•	•	7276	11200	19838	42935	65820	486724	4598023
All Other Liabilities 28	12239	•	94	244	•	•	4542	7637	20156	45515	136692	238247	8322763
Net Worth 29	9472	•	-66	132	•	•	3696	15562	25620	61116	186507	346100	5526056

Selected Financial Ratios (Times to 1)

Current Ratio 30	0.6	•	1.0	1.8	•	1.3	1.9	1.5	1.7	1.0	1.6	0.4
Quick Ratio 31	0.4	•	0.8	1.5	•	0.7	1.1	0.7	1.0	0.4	0.9	0.3
Net Sales to Working Capital 32	•	•	415.3	10.1	•	16.5	6.7	8.8	8.0	•	8.3	•
Coverage Ratio 33	3.2	•	•	•	•	3.8	3.4	3.8	3.0	3.0	1.9	3.6
Total Asset Turnover 34	0.8	•	12.0	3.1	•	2.0	1.6	1.4	1.6	1.0	1.0	0.5
Inventory Turnover 35	10.1	•	63.1	30.1	•	7.6	6.4	5.2	6.9	5.9	8.0	13.0
Receivables Turnover 36	9.6	•	•	8.7	•	8.3	7.1	7.7	7.9	10.0	8.6	10.2
Total Liabilities to Net Worth 37	2.2	•	•	4.1	•	3.2	1.2	1.6	1.4	1.1	2.1	2.3
Current Assets to Working Capital 38	•	•	24.1	2.2	•	4.5	2.1	3.1	2.4	•	2.7	•
Current Liabilities to Working Capital 39	•	•	23.1	1.2	•	3.5	1.1	2.1	1.4	•	1.7	•
Working Capital to Net Sales 40	•	•	0.0	0.1	•	0.1	0.1	0.1	0.1	•	0.1	•
Inventory to Working Capital 41	•	•	4.3	0.3	•	1.6	0.8	1.4	0.8	•	0.8	•
Total Receipts to Cash Flow 42	8.0	•	10.9	51.9	•	12.6	12.1	11.2	9.0	7.1	10.4	6.2
Cost of Goods to Cash Flow 43	5.8	•	7.1	41.4	•	9.1	8.9	8.2	6.4	5.1	7.5	4.4
Cash Flow to Total Debt 44	0.1	•	0.8	0.1	•	0.2	0.2	0.2	0.3	0.3	0.1	0.1

Selected Financial Factors (in Percentages)

Debt Ratio 45	68.7	•	144.0	80.4	•	76.2	54.8	61.0	59.1	52.0	67.7	70.0
Return on Total Assets 46	6.9	•	•	•	•	7.6	5.5	7.1	6.1	7.3	6.7	7.3
Return on Equity Before Income Taxes 47	15.1	•	121.6	•	•	23.6	8.5	13.5	10.0	10.1	9.5	17.6
Return on Equity After Income Taxes 48	10.1	•	121.6	•	•	21.2	7.6	10.4	8.0	9.0	6.9	11.4
Profit Margin (Before Income Tax) 49	5.8	•	•	•	•	2.8	2.4	3.8	2.6	4.8	3.1	9.9
Profit Margin (After Income Tax) 50	3.9	•	•	•	•	2.5	2.2	2.9	2.1	4.3	2.3	6.4

Table II

Corporations with Net Income

CONVERTED PAPER PRODUCT

MONEY AMOUNTS AND SIZE OF ASSETS IN THOUSANDS OF DOLLARS

Item Description for Accounting Period 7/04 Through 6/05	Total	Zero Assets	Under 500	500 to 1,000	1,000 to 5,000	5,000 to 10,000	10,000 to 25,000	25,000 to 50,000	50,000 to 100,000	100,000 to 250,000	250,000 to 500,000	500,000 to 2,500,000	2,500,000 and over
Number of Enterprises **1**	2133	0	404	246	1069	187	115	45	21	16	0	5	0
Revenues ($ in Thousands)													
Net Sales **2**	53241980	0	599362	590674	6027488	2051751	3644510	2676940	1814756	3766253	0	5915967	0
Interest **3**	929542	0	0	0	1798	282	2211	1703	2118	4775	0	7023	0
Rents **4**	17649	0	0	0	1013	352	379	2040	2209	596	0	5426	0
Royalties **5**	865480	0	0	0	0	0	160	3196	139	1374	0	9371	0
Other Portfolio Income **6**	1058765	0	0	58	14397	2014	4860	7701	2971	5876	0	105483	0
Other Receipts **7**	1978148	0	0	464	123836	3184	12573	13990	46276	12978	0	56930	0
Total Receipts **8**	58091564	0	599366	591196	6168532	2057583	3664693	2705570	1868469	3791852	0	6100200	0
Average Total Receipts **9**	27235	.	1484	2403	5770	11003	31867	60124	88975	236991	.	1220040	.
Operating Costs/Operating Income (%)													
Cost of Operations **10**	64.1	.	76.8	70.1	67.8	64.5	70.7	72.7	72.4	71.0	.	71.7	.
Salaries and Wages **11**	10.1	.	2.2	9.5	8.6	7.9	6.6	6.6	5.9	6.3	.	6.2	.
Taxes Paid **12**	1.6	.	1.8	1.8	2.4	2.3	2.0	1.8	1.3	1.7	.	1.9	.
Interest Paid **13**	2.5	.	0.1	0.3	0.6	1.6	0.8	0.7	1.4	1.2	.	1.9	.
Depreciation **14**	4.3	.	0.1	3.2	3.0	4.6	3.4	3.2	3.8	3.1	.	5.2	.
Amortization and Depletion **15**	0.6	.	.	0.0	0.1	0.2	0.1	0.2	0.2	0.3	.	0.8	.
Pensions and Other Deferred Comp. **16**	1.4	.	0.0	.	0.3	0.3	0.5	0.7	0.5	0.4	.	1.1	.
Employee Benefits **17**	2.9	.	1.9	1.3	1.8	2.0	1.4	1.4	1.5	1.8	.	2.9	.
Advertising **18**	0.9	.	0.0	0.2	0.3	0.4	0.2	0.3	0.2	0.5	.	0.1	.
Other Expenses **19**	11.0	.	7.9	9.6	7.8	7.5	7.6	7.7	7.3	9.4	.	6.4	.
Officers' Compensation **20**	1.1	.	7.6	3.2	3.3	2.7	2.3	1.6	1.6	0.6	.	0.2	.
Operating Margin **21**	.	.	1.6	0.8	3.9	6.0	4.4	3.4	4.0	3.8	.	1.6	.
Operating Margin Before Officers' Comp. **22**	0.6	.	9.2	4.0	7.2	8.8	6.7	5.0	5.6	4.4	.	1.8	.

Selected Average Balance Sheet ($ in Thousands)

Item											
Net Receivables 23	3052	•	1	236	564	1173	4101	7909	11575	30508	116689
Inventories 24	1989	•	42	54	212	811	2820	6123	15603	22491	99064
Net Property, Plant and Equipment 25	6881	•	24	193	773	2917	5454	11760	18569	49631	482509
Total Assets 26	33369	•	37	730	2286	5941	15503	33478	65432	150768	1182483
Notes and Loans Payable 27	10713	•	16	118	611	3390	4642	8922	20176	41471	487125
All Other Liabilities 28	9428	•	2	223	584	357	3399	7199	21400	39114	249865
Net Worth 29	13227	•	18	389	1091	2193	7462	17357	23856	70183	445493

Selected Financial Ratios (Times to 1)

Item											
Current Ratio 30	1.0	•	6.2	2.6	1.6	1.0	2.1	2.0	1.5	2.2	1.2
Quick Ratio 31	0.6	•	1.3	2.1	1.0	0.7	1.2	1.1	0.7	1.3	0.5
Net Sales to Working Capital 32	184.2	•	141.4	6.9	12.4	88.8	7.0	6.8	8.2	6.2	27.6
Coverage Ratio 33	5.1	•	31.8	4.1	10.8	5.1	7.3	7.7	6.0	4.7	3.6
Total Asset Turnover 34	0.7	•	40.6	3.3	2.5	1.8	2.0	1.8	1.3	1.6	1.0
Inventory Turnover 35	8.0	•	27.5	31.0	18.0	8.7	7.9	7.1	4.0	7.4	8.6
Receivables Turnover 36	8.4	•	16.3	11.3	12.2		8.5	8.1	•	9.0	11.9
Total Liabilities to Net Worth 37	1.5	•	1.0	0.9	1.1	1.7	1.1	0.9	1.7	1.1	1.7
Current Assets to Working Capital 38	67.0	•	1.2	1.6	2.6	22.2	1.9	2.0	3.1	1.9	7.1
Current Liabilities to Working Capital 39	66.0	•	0.2	0.6	1.6	21.2	0.9	1.0	2.1	0.9	6.1
Working Capital to Net Sales 40	0.0	•	0.0	0.1	0.1	0.0	0.1	0.1	0.1	0.2	0.0
Inventory to Working Capital 41	15.4	•	0.9	0.3	0.6	6.6	0.7	0.7	1.5	0.6	2.6
Total Receipts to Cash Flow 42	5.7	•	17.4	14.1	9.2	8.7	9.7	9.9	7.9	8.3	10.0
Cost of Goods to Cash Flow 43	3.6	•	13.4	9.9	6.3	5.6	6.9	7.2	5.7	5.9	7.2
Cash Flow to Total Debt 44	0.2	•	4.6	0.5	0.5	0.3	0.4	0.4	0.3	0.4	0.2

Selected Financial Factors (in Percentages)

Item											
Debt Ratio 45	60.4	•	50.2	46.7	52.3	63.1	51.9	48.2	63.5	53.4	62.3
Return on Total Assets 46	9.7	•	68.3	3.9	17.0	14.6	11.8	9.2	11.0	8.7	6.8
Return on Equity Before Income Taxes 47	19.8	•	132.8	5.5	32.3	31.7	21.2	15.4	25.1	14.7	13.1
Return on Equity After Income Taxes 48	14.3	•	132.8	5.5	31.6	28.5	19.6	14.3	20.1	12.4	9.9
Profit Margin (Before Income Tax) 49	10.5	•	1.6	0.9	6.3	6.3	5.0	4.5	6.9	4.4	4.9
Profit Margin (After Income Tax) 50	7.6	•	1.6	0.9	6.1	5.7	4.6	4.2	5.6	3.7	3.7

Table I

Corporations with and without Net Income

PRINTING AND RELATED SUPPORT ACTIVITIES

MONEY AMOUNTS AND SIZE OF ASSETS IN THOUSANDS OF DOLLARS

Item Description for Accounting Period 7/04 Through 6/05	Total	Zero Assets	Under 500	500 to 1,000	1,000 to 5,000	5,000 to 10,000	10,000 to 25,000	25,000 to 50,000	50,000 to 100,000	100,000 to 250,000	250,000 to 500,000	500,000 to 2,500,000	2,500,000 and over
Number of Enterprises 1	33333	3300	22513	3384	3130	504	318	103	37	17	8	15	3
Revenues ($ in Thousands)													
Net Sales 2	87054278	648180	9608613	6452620	13831005	6799436	8540931	5784755	3353987	2880807	2558204	15108478	11487262
Interest 3	230480	23	1051	1290	8798	3494	5191	4169	2575	16515	23790	135355	28230
Rents 4	44419	0	132	6499	8198	1803	3453	397	62	2245	1125	19192	1314
Royalties 5	409268	0	0	0	0	2676	10768	3885	24	10376	30236	324783	26522
Other Portfolio Income 6	494548	5409	3729	77981	16773	26780	18109	5924	2315	2751	8407	326367	2
Other Receipts 7	1069922	25622	-3741	35083	129680	45380	77839	31407	26483	28438	119170	472500	82058
Total Receipts 8	89302915	679234	9609784	6573473	13994454	6879569	8656291	5830537	3385446	2941132	2740932	16386675	11625388
Average Total Receipts 9	2679	206	427	1943	4471	13650	27221	56607	91499	173008	342616	1092445	3875129
Operating Costs/Operating Income (%)													
Cost of Operations 10	60.3	29.6	47.9	51.5	58.7	66.4	66.2	66.3	65.6	58.3	64.6	55.8	72.2
Salaries and Wages 11	10.2	12.2	11.5	12.4	11.1	8.4	9.4	10.0	7.5	9.5	9.4	12.6	6.4
Taxes Paid 12	2.5	3.5	3.0	2.6	3.3	2.6	2.4	2.3	2.1	1.9	1.9	2.3	2.2
Interest Paid 13	1.9	1.1	1.0	1.0	1.4	1.4	1.2	1.1	1.9	3.6	3.9	2.5	3.0
Depreciation 14	4.7	3.5	3.3	3.9	5.4	4.6	5.0	5.0	4.9	5.6	3.6	5.1	4.5
Amortization and Depletion 15	0.4	0.1	0.2	0.0	0.2	0.2	0.2	0.2	0.5	1.2	1.0	0.6	0.6
Pensions and Other Deferred Comp. 16	0.5	0.2	0.3	0.6	0.3	0.4	0.5	0.6	0.5	0.8	1.3	0.8	0.5
Employee Benefits 17	2.0	1.2	1.2	0.9	1.4	0.9	1.7	2.3	1.9	2.3	3.9	3.8	2.2
Advertising 18	0.8	0.9	1.1	0.3	0.5	0.3	0.9	0.4	3.9	1.5	0.1	1.3	0.0
Other Expenses 19	13.2	37.0	22.2	18.1	10.5	10.2	8.8	8.0	8.9	17.3	18.5	15.7	8.2
Officers' Compensation 20	3.2	9.6	7.2	7.1	5.5	3.8	2.6	1.9	1.6	1.0	1.3	0.6	0.2
Operating Margin 21	0.3	1.1	1.0	1.6	1.8	0.8	1.1	1.8	0.8	•	•	•	0.1
Operating Margin Before Officers' Comp. 22	3.5	10.8	8.2	8.7	7.3	4.5	3.7	3.7	2.4	•	•	•	0.3

Selected Average Balance Sheet ($ in Thousands)

Net Receivables 23	369	0	25	199	528	1792	3965	8412	13525	20418	42343	226729	605120
Inventories 24	130	0	5	38	164	1072	1755	4118	8745	13756	23086	50456	183010
Net Property, Plant and Equipment 25	545	0	48	240	915	2511	5970	12112	22839	41575	72055	257266	1006032
Total Assets 26	1839	0	111	720	2125	7264	15282	33528	66516	146785	321058	1058021	4780971
Notes and Loans Payable 27	737	0	103	384	1009	2779	6129	11086	26393	69526	144782	358858	1526724
All Other Liabilities 28	547	0	40	179	490	1874	3707	8679	16833	32472	86795	339301	1737203
Net Worth 29	555	0	-33	157	626	2611	5446	13763	23291	44788	89481	359862	1517044

Selected Financial Ratios (Times to 1)

Current Ratio 30	1.4	•	1.1	1.8	1.4	1.5	1.4	1.6	1.5	1.4	1.3	1.3	1.1
Quick Ratio 31	1.0	•	0.9	1.6	1.1	0.9	1.0	1.1	0.9	0.8	0.7	1.0	0.7
Net Sales to Working Capital 32	14.3	•	98.8	10.5	15.7	10.7	11.4	9.0	8.9	14.0	15.5	10.9	34.0
Coverage Ratio 33	2.5	6.3	1.9	4.6	3.1	2.4	3.1	3.3	1.9	0.8	0.4	4.0	1.4
Total Asset Turnover 34	1.4	•	3.8	2.6	2.1	1.9	1.8	1.7	1.4	1.2	1.0	1.0	0.8
Inventory Turnover 35	12.2	•	43.9	25.5	15.8	8.4	10.1	9.0	6.8	7.2	8.9	11.1	15.1
Receivables Turnover 36	7.5	•	19.2	9.7	8.9	7.4	6.8	6.9	7.0	8.0	6.8	4.5	8.4
Total Liabilities to Net Worth 37	2.3	•	•	3.6	2.4	1.8	1.8	1.4	1.9	2.3	2.6	1.9	2.2
Current Assets to Working Capital 38	3.7	•	12.1	2.3	3.5	3.1	3.3	2.7	2.9	3.8	4.3	3.9	9.1
Current Liabilities to Working Capital 39	2.7	•	11.1	1.3	2.5	2.1	2.3	1.7	1.9	2.8	3.3	2.9	8.1
Working Capital to Net Sales 40	0.1	•	0.0	0.1	0.1	0.1	0.1	0.1	0.1	0.1	0.1	0.1	0.0
Inventory to Working Capital 41	0.7	•	1.2	0.2	0.6	0.9	0.8	0.7	0.8	1.2	1.2	0.6	1.7
Total Receipts to Cash Flow 42	8.3	2.7	6.5	6.0	10.1	11.9	11.6	12.4	11.9	8.3	10.1	5.3	14.5
Cost of Goods to Cash Flow 43	5.0	0.8	3.1	3.1	5.9	7.9	7.7	8.2	7.8	4.8	6.5	2.9	10.5
Cash Flow to Total Debt 44	0.2	•	0.5	0.6	0.3	0.2	0.2	0.2	0.2	0.2	0.1	0.3	0.1

Selected Financial Factors (in Percentages)

Debt Ratio 45	69.8	•	129.4	78.2	64.1	70.5	64.4	58.9	65.0	69.5	72.1	66.0	68.3
Return on Total Assets 46	6.7	•	7.8	11.9	6.2	9.0	6.5	6.3	4.9	3.4	1.6	9.3	3.5
Return on Equity Before Income Taxes 47	13.5	•	•	42.5	20.7	10.0	12.2	10.7	6.6	•	•	20.5	3.4
Return on Equity After Income Taxes 48	10.4	•	•	39.1	19.3	8.3	11.1	9.3	5.6	•	•	13.5	2.2
Profit Margin (Before Income Tax) 49	2.9	•	1.0	6.0	3.5	2.9	1.9	2.5	2.6	1.7	•	7.3	1.4
Profit Margin (After Income Tax) 50	2.2	•	0.9	5.4	3.2	2.7	1.6	2.3	2.3	1.5	•	4.8	0.9

Table II
Corporations with Net Income

PRINTING AND RELATED SUPPORT ACTIVITIES

MONEY AMOUNTS AND SIZE OF ASSETS IN THOUSANDS OF DOLLARS

Item Description for Accounting Period 7/04 Through 6/05	Total	Zero Assets	Under 500	500 to 1,000	1,000 to 5,000	5,000 to 10,000	10,000 to 25,000	25,000 to 50,000	50,000 to 100,000	100,000 to 250,000	250,000 to 500,000	500,000 to 2,500,000	2,500,000 and over
Number of Enterprises 1	17798	2149	10732	2160	2100	321	213	71	0	7	4	0	0
Revenues ($ in Thousands)													
Net Sales 2	62566128	345319	6279358	5000605	9464189	4410429	5961736	4329518	0	1361275	1299081	0	0
Interest 3	160926	23	557	658	5198	2823	2880	2986	0	58	5607	0	0
Rents 4	36893	0	79	6499	2674	1803	2576	197	0	1848	693	0	0
Royalties 5	381980	0	0	0	0	2090	10716	3700	0	37	17156	0	0
Other Portfolio Income 6	454142	4878	2944	67711	9949	20025	13753	4465	0	971	2129	0	0
Other Receipts 7	864916	8030	19012	32506	115315	35072	54918	24277	0	6039	21902	0	0
Total Receipts 8	64464985	358250	6301950	5107979	9597325	4472242	6046579	4365143	0	1370228	1346568	0	0
Average Total Receipts 9	3622	167	587	2365	4570	13932	28388	61481	•	195747	336642	•	•
Operating Costs/Operating Income (%)													
Cost of Operations 10	59.0	28.6	46.6	51.0	58.1	67.5	64.4	65.5	•	51.5	62.9	•	•
Salaries and Wages 11	10.0	4.3	10.3	12.5	10.3	8.5	9.4	10.3	•	7.5	11.2	•	•
Taxes Paid 12	2.4	3.7	2.6	2.2	3.2	2.6	2.4	2.1	•	1.0	1.7	•	•
Interest Paid 13	1.6	0.9	0.7	0.6	1.3	1.1	0.9	0.8	•	2.4	2.6	•	•
Depreciation 14	4.5	0.9	2.8	2.7	4.9	4.3	4.4	4.2	•	6.2	3.3	•	•
Amortization and Depletion 15	0.4	0.2	0.2	0.0	0.2	0.2	0.2	0.2	•	0.7	1.1	•	•
Pensions and Other Deferred Comp. 16	0.5	0.3	0.4	0.7	0.3	0.4	0.5	0.6	•	1.1	1.4	•	•
Employee Benefits 17	2.1	1.6	1.1	0.8	1.4	0.7	1.6	2.2	•	1.5	4.5	•	•
Advertising 18	0.9	1.2	0.7	0.3	0.4	0.3	1.1	0.5	•	2.7	0.2	•	•
Other Expenses 19	12.5	33.2	20.8	17.5	9.8	8.1	8.4	7.4	•	17.5	8.8	•	•
Officers' Compensation 20	3.0	11.4	7.5	7.3	5.0	3.1	2.7	1.9	•	1.1	1.7	•	•
Operating Margin 21	3.1	13.6	6.4	4.3	5.1	3.3	4.1	4.3	•	6.7	0.8	•	•
Operating Margin Before Officers' Comp. 22	6.1	25.1	13.9	11.6	10.1	6.4	6.7	6.2	•	7.8	2.5	•	•

Selected Average Balance Sheet ($ in Thousands)

Net Receivables 23	50112	18322	•	8880	3972	1666	510	242	31	0	499
Inventories 24	38372	20113	•	4089	1875	1013	159	16	5	0	163
Net Property, Plant and Equipment 25	69205	49268	•	11655	5701	2798	869	196	55	0	723
Total Assets 26	353531	137414	•	33886	15395	6985	2018	737	131	0	2513
Notes and Loans Payable 27	120087	68509	•	9197	4968	2387	795	215	85	0	832
All Other Liabilities 28	74742	29502	•	9102	3440	1878	463	185	50	0	747
Net Worth 29	158702	39403	•	15587	6987	2720	760	338	-4	0	935

Selected Financial Ratios (Times to 1)

Current Ratio 30	1.8	1.4	•	1.6	1.7	1.6	1.5	2.2	1.1	•	1.4
Quick Ratio 31	1.0	0.7	•	1.1	1.2	1.0	1.2	2.0	1.0	•	1.0
Net Sales to Working Capital 32	7.1	16.3	•	9.8	8.4	10.5	14.6	8.9	116.9	•	13.1
Coverage Ratio 33	2.7	4.1	•	7.3	6.9	5.1	6.1	11.3	10.4	20.1	4.8
Total Asset Turnover 34	0.9	1.4	•	1.8	1.8	2.0	2.2	3.1	4.5	•	1.4
Inventory Turnover 35	5.3	5.0	•	9.8	9.6	9.1	16.5	75.3	56.0	•	12.7
Receivables Turnover 36	•	7.5	•	7.4	7.2	•	9.3	11.3	23.4	•	7.9
Total Liabilities to Net Worth 37	1.2	2.5	•	1.2	1.2	1.6	1.7	1.2	•	•	1.7
Current Assets to Working Capital 38	2.2	3.8	•	2.8	2.4	2.7	3.2	1.8	12.8	•	3.4
Current Liabilities to Working Capital 39	1.2	2.8	•	1.8	1.4	1.7	2.2	0.8	11.8	•	2.4
Working Capital to Net Sales 40	0.1	0.1	•	0.1	0.1	0.1	0.1	0.1	0.0	•	0.1
Inventory to Working Capital 41	0.8	1.6	•	0.7	0.6	0.8	0.5	0.1	1.0	•	0.6
Total Receipts to Cash Flow 42	9.2	4.5	•	9.7	8.8	9.8	7.9	5.1	5.0	2.2	6.7
Cost of Goods to Cash Flow 43	5.8	2.3	•	6.4	5.6	6.6	4.6	2.6	2.3	0.6	4.0
Cash Flow to Total Debt 44	0.2	0.4	•	0.3	0.4	0.3	0.5	1.1	0.9	•	0.3

Selected Financial Factors (in Percentages)

Debt Ratio 45	55.1	71.3	•	54.0	54.6	61.1	62.3	54.2	103.0	•	62.8
Return on Total Assets 46	6.5	13.8	•	10.7	11.7	11.4	17.5	22.1	33.7	•	10.8
Return on Equity Before Income Taxes 47	9.2	36.5	•	20.2	22.0	23.6	38.8	44.1	•	•	23.1
Return on Equity After Income Taxes 48	6.0	33.4	•	18.4	20.7	21.0	37.1	41.6	•	•	19.5
Profit Margin (Before Income Tax) 49	4.5	7.4	•	5.2	5.5	4.7	6.5	6.4	6.8	17.6	6.1
Profit Margin (After Income Tax) 50	3.0	6.8	•	4.7	5.2	4.1	6.3	6.1	6.7	16.5	5.2

78

Table I

Corporations with and without Net Income

PETROLEUM REFINERIES (INCLUDING INTEGRATED)

MONEY AMOUNTS AND SIZE OF ASSETS IN THOUSANDS OF DOLLARS

Item Description for Accounting Period 7/04 Through 6/05	Total	Zero Assets	Under 500	500 to 1,000	1,000 to 5,000	5,000 to 10,000	10,000 to 25,000	25,000 to 50,000	50,000 to 100,000	100,000 to 250,000	250,000 to 500,000	500,000 to 2,500,000	2,500,000 and over
Number of Enterprises 1	715	5	657	0	3	0	5	4	8	4	4	7	18

Revenues ($ in Thousands)

Item	Total	Zero Assets	Under 500	500 to 1,000	1,000 to 5,000	5,000 to 10,000	10,000 to 25,000	25,000 to 50,000	50,000 to 100,000	100,000 to 250,000	250,000 to 500,000	500,000 to 2,500,000	2,500,000 and over
Net Sales 2	1169575312	9462458	855	0	12459	0	140941	674137	1004799	1395393	6832357	14069002	1135982910
Interest 3	12168110	5212	5	0	163	0	62	618	449	5558	1795	25729	12128517
Rents 4	1625262	2600	24	0	0	0	173	6	597	548	33637	11197	1576481
Royalties 5	887646	50509	0	0	110	0	0	0	0	11208	24	0	825795
Other Portfolio Income 6	18436405	57744	0	0	0	0	1467	1	8947	13352	65501	73391	18216005
Other Receipts 7	30756699	1138706	1297	0	45865	0	873	5156	10919	12737	11823	95420	29435901
Total Receipts 8	1233451434	10717229	2181	0	58597	0	143516	679918	1025711	1438796	6945137	14274739	1198165609
Average Total Receipts 9	1725107	2143446	3	•	19532	•	28703	169980	128214	359699	1736284	2039248	66564756

Operating Costs/Operating Income (%)

Item	Total	Zero Assets	Under 500	500 to 1,000	1,000 to 5,000	5,000 to 10,000	10,000 to 25,000	25,000 to 50,000	50,000 to 100,000	100,000 to 250,000	250,000 to 500,000	500,000 to 2,500,000	2,500,000 and over
Cost of Operations 10	86.3	87.7	30.2	•	36.6	•	77.0	94.6	89.8	91.3	92.0	86.3	86.3
Salaries and Wages 11	1.3	4.5	5.5	•	13.4	•	4.2	0.9	2.1	1.3	1.3	1.3	1.3
Taxes Paid 12	2.6	1.5	45.8	•	28.7	•	1.0	0.2	0.6	0.9	0.3	2.0	2.6
Interest Paid 13	1.3	2.8	143.0	•	1.8	•	0.9	0.3	0.8	0.1	0.6	1.0	1.3
Depreciation 14	1.5	1.1	0.5	•	2.1	•	1.8	0.9	1.6	1.2	1.3	1.6	1.5
Amortization and Depletion 15	0.4	0.3	49.9	•	•	•	1.4	0.1	0.3	0.2	0.0	1.3	0.4
Pensions and Other Deferred Comp. 16	0.3	0.3	•	•	0.6	•	0.2	0.1	0.0	0.0	0.5	0.2	0.3
Employee Benefits 17	0.2	1.0	•	•	•	•	0.2	0.2	0.3	0.3	0.3	0.1	0.2
Advertising 18	0.1	0.5	0.1	•	0.1	•	0.0	0.0	0.4	0.2	0.1	0.0	0.1
Other Expenses 19	4.3	3.3	98.8	•	16.3	•	15.0	1.7	3.5	3.2	3.6	4.2	4.3
Officers' Compensation 20	0.1	0.3	6.4	•	7.0	•	1.4	0.3	0.3	0.9	0.2	0.5	0.0
Operating Margin 21	1.6	•	•	•	•	•	•	0.7	0.4	0.4	0.0	•	1.7
Operating Margin Before Officers' Comp. 22	1.7	•	•	•	0.4	•	1.0	1.0	0.7	1.2	0.0	•	1.7

Selected Average Balance Sheet ($ in Thousands)

Net Receivables 23	830198	0	0	•	477	•	5335	11174	13500	28259	61864	109463	32904685
Inventories 24	31655	0	0	•	369	•	1612	4744	10137	10850	72676	89205	1198119
Net Property, Plant and Equipment 25	243738	0	0	•	1178	•	5483	10518	27806	29364	147539	241284	9552230
Total Assets 26	2375211	0	36	•	5723	•	17387	39442	64393	166736	364812	639882	9337197
Notes and Loans Payable 27	294790	0	63	•	303	•	11465	9775	13238	9385	123078	125775	11617794
All Other Liabilities 28	1221121	0	0	•	845	•	4729	15112	28136	58594	187890	253320	48335053
Net Worth 29	859299	0	-27	•	4575	•	1193	14556	23020	98756	53844	260786	33984350

Selected Financial Ratios (Times to 1)

Current Ratio 30	0.8	•	1.2	•	3.0	•	1.2	1.6	1.1	1.5	0.9	1.4	0.8
Quick Ratio 31	0.8	•	1.2	•	2.5	•	0.9	1.3	0.6	1.3	0.4	0.9	0.8
Net Sales to Working Capital 32	•	•	1.9	•	2.7	•	17.2	17.1	61.1	12.5	•	24.2	•
Coverage Ratio 33	7.5	4.6	0.1	•	206.1	•	•	7.2	4.0	24.7	3.6	1.8	7.7
Total Asset Turnover 34	0.7	•	0.0	•	0.7	•	1.6	4.3	2.0	2.1	4.7	3.1	0.7
Inventory Turnover 35	44.6	•	•	•	4.1	•	13.5	33.6	11.1	29.4	21.6	19.8	45.4
Receivables Turnover 36	3.5	•	155.5	•	•	•	5.1	13.9	11.2	10.8	28.0	20.7	3.4
Total Liabilities to Net Worth 37	1.8	•	•	•	0.3	•	13.6	1.7	1.8	0.7	5.8	1.5	1.8
Current Assets to Working Capital 38	•	•	5.4	•	1.5	•	5.4	2.6	14.5	2.9	•	3.6	•
Current Liabilities to Working Capital 39	•	•	4.4	•	0.5	•	4.4	1.6	13.5	1.9	•	2.6	•
Working Capital to Net Sales 40	•	•	0.5	•	0.4	•	0.1	0.1	0.0	0.1	•	0.0	•
Inventory to Working Capital 41	•	•	•	•	0.2	•	1.0	0.5	5.9	0.3	•	1.0	•
Total Receipts to Cash Flow 42	9.6	8.7	•	•	0.3	•	8.0	34.5	21.1	17.0	26.3	25.3	9.5
Cost of Goods to Cash Flow 43	8.3	7.7	•	•	0.1	•	6.1	32.6	18.9	15.6	24.2	22.2	8.2
Cash Flow to Total Debt 44	0.1	•	•	•	13.7	•	0.2	0.2	0.1	0.3	0.2	0.2	0.1

Selected Financial Factors (in Percentages)

Debt Ratio 45	63.8	•	173.2	•	20.1	•	93.1	63.1	64.3	40.8	85.2	59.2	63.8
Return on Total Assets 46	6.7	•	0.6	•	265.3	•	•	7.8	6.4	7.6	9.4	5.5	6.6
Return on Equity Before Income Taxes 47	16.0	•	6.1	•	330.3	•	•	18.3	13.4	12.3	46.0	5.9	15.8
Return on Equity After Income Taxes 48	10.3	•	6.3	•	221.7	•	•	11.9	9.7	8.8	38.2	2.1	10.2
Profit Margin (Before Income Tax) 49	8.4	10.1	•	•	363.8	•	1.6	2.5	2.5	3.5	1.4	0.8	8.5
Profit Margin (After Income Tax) 50	5.4	7.2	•	•	244.3	•	1.0	1.8	1.8	2.5	1.2	0.3	5.5

79

Table II

Corporations with Net Income

PETROLEUM REFINERIES (INCLUDING INTEGRATED)

MONEY AMOUNTS AND SIZE OF ASSETS IN THOUSANDS OF DOLLARS

Item Description for Accounting Period 7/04 Through 6/05	Total	Zero Assets	Under 500	500 to 1,000	1,000 to 5,000	5,000 to 10,000	10,000 to 25,000	25,000 to 50,000	50,000 to 100,000	100,000 to 250,000	250,000 to 500,000	500,000 to 2,500,000	2,500,000 and over
Number of Enterprises **1**	43	0	0	0	0	4	0	0	0	0	0	4	0
Revenues ($ in Thousands)													
Net Sales **2**	1144327900	0	0	0	0	40025	0	0	0	0	0	9109406	0
Interest **3**	11859063	0	0	0	0	124	0	0	0	0	0	15859	0
Rents **4**	1578321	0	0	0	0	138	0	0	0	0	0	9346	0
Royalties **5**	887640	0	0	0	0	0	0	0	0	0	0	0	0
Other Portfolio Income **6**	17709684	0	0	0	0	1440	0	0	0	0	0	72603	0
Other Receipts **7**	31668621	0	0	0	0	4909	0	0	0	0	0	39291	0
Total Receipts **8**	1208031229	0	0	0	0	46636	0	0	0	0	0	9246505	0
Average Total Receipts **9**	28093750	.	.	.	.	11659	.	.	.	.	.	2311626	.
Operating Costs/Operating Income (%)													
Cost of Operations **10**	86.5	.	.	.	.	32.9	.	.	.	.	.	88.8	.
Salaries and Wages **11**	1.3	.	.	.	.	13.7	.	.	.	.	.	1.6	.
Taxes Paid **12**	2.6	.	.	.	.	3.4	.	.	.	.	.	2.1	.
Interest Paid **13**	1.1	.	.	.	.	1.3	.	.	.	.	.	0.8	.
Depreciation **14**	1.4	.	.	.	.	2.7	.	.	.	.	.	1.1	.
Amortization and Depletion **15**	0.4	.	.	.	.	0.0	.	.	.	.	.	0.2	.
Pensions and Other Deferred Comp. **16**	0.3	.	.	.	.	1.0	.	.	.	.	.	0.2	.
Employee Benefits **17**	0.2	.	.	.	.	0.0	.	.	.	.	.	0.2	.
Advertising **18**	0.1	.	.	.	.	0.2	.	.	.	.	.	0.0	.
Other Expenses **19**	4.1	.	.	.	.	32.7	.	.	.	.	.	2.9	.
Officers' Compensation **20**	0.1	.	.	.	.	6.2	.	.	.	.	.	0.5	.
Operating Margin **21**	1.9	.	.	.	.	5.8	.	.	.	.	.	1.6	.
Operating Margin Before Officers' Comp. **22**	2.0	.	.	.	.	12.0	.	.	.	.	.	2.1	.

Selected Average Balance Sheet ($ in Thousands)

Net Receivables 23	13665362	2265	111756
Inventories 24	468284	682	90160
Net Property, Plant and Equipment 25	3664568	4332	214193
Total Assets 26	38482825	11610	658384
Notes and Loans Payable 27	4298850	4293	120760
All Other Liabilities 28	20086912	2807	269123
Net Worth 29	14097363	4510	268501

Selected Financial Ratios (Times to 1)

Current Ratio 30	0.8	1.1	1.4
Quick Ratio 31	0.8	0.8	0.9
Net Sales to Working Capital 32		32.1	23.9
Coverage Ratio 33	8.7	18.0	4.7
Total Asset Turnover 34	0.7	0.9	3.5
Inventory Turnover 35	49.2	4.8	22.4
Receivables Turnover 36	3.5		22.0
Total Liabilities to Net Worth 37	1.7	1.6	1.5
Current Assets to Working Capital 38	17.2	17.2	3.4
Current Liabilities to Working Capital 39		16.2	2.4
Working Capital to Net Sales 40		0.0	0.0
Inventory to Working Capital 41		2.2	1.1
Total Receipts to Cash Flow 42	9.4	1.9	19.1
Cost of Goods to Cash Flow 43	8.1	0.6	17.0
Cash Flow to Total Debt 44	0.1	0.7	0.3

Selected Financial Factors (in Percentages)

Debt Ratio 45	63.4	61.2	59.2
Return on Total Assets 46	6.9	20.4	13.6
Return on Equity Before Income Taxes 47	16.7	49.5	26.3
Return on Equity After Income Taxes 48	11.0	38.3	19.8
Profit Margin (Before Income Tax) 49	8.8	22.3	3.1
Profit Margin (After Income Tax) 50	5.8	17.3	2.3

Table I

Corporations with and without Net Income

ASPHALT PAVING, ROOFING, OTHER PETROLEUM AND COAL PRODUCTS

MONEY AMOUNTS AND SIZE OF ASSETS IN THOUSANDS OF DOLLARS

Item Description for Accounting Period 7/04 Through 6/05	Total	Zero Assets	Under 500	500 to 1,000	1,000 to 5,000	5,000 to 10,000	10,000 to 25,000	25,000 to 50,000	50,000 to 100,000	100,000 to 250,000	250,000 to 500,000	500,000 to 2,500,000	2,500,000 and over
Number of Enterprises 1	1316	41	690	234	201	53	56	17	11	6	4	3	0
Revenues ($ in Thousands)													
Net Sales 2	15745462	110276	232373	550212	2202340	580399	1805101	979866	1338069	1947741	1367851	4631235	0
Interest 3	20782	216	252	27	814	119	692	2352	126	3727	10096	2360	0
Rents 4	3426	718	0	0	243	0	2134	26	187	0	118	0	0
Royalties 5	21849	0	0	0	0	4	9	0	395	1711	2683	17047	0
Other Portfolio Income 6	251610	10139	0	0	905	588	3685	202091	930	4784	27809	680	0
Other Receipts 7	103695	1578	-100362	0	342	61956	4803	7360	24547	15138	35843	52490	0
Total Receipts 8	16146824	122927	132263	550239	2204644	643066	1816424	1191695	1364254	1973101	1444400	4703812	0
Average Total Receipts 9	12270	2998	192	2351	10968	12133	32436	70100	124023	328850	361100	1567937	•
Operating Costs/Operating Income (%)													
Cost of Operations 10	76.7	60.3	8.0	19.7	85.9	86.7	73.9	77.0	78.4	90.3	78.7	75.9	•
Salaries and Wages 11	4.7	11.1	0.1	27.7	4.3	4.6	5.7	4.2	5.0	2.2	1.5	3.9	•
Taxes Paid 12	1.1	1.7	0.2	4.6	0.7	1.2	1.6	1.2	0.9	0.6	1.8	0.6	•
Interest Paid 13	1.7	0.9	0.2	2.4	1.1	2.5	0.6	0.9	1.2	0.4	7.6	1.6	•
Depreciation 14	3.2	5.4	2.1	10.5	0.8	5.3	3.4	3.6	2.6	1.6	3.7	3.8	•
Amortization and Depletion 15	0.2	2.1	•	•	0.0	0.4	0.1	0.2	0.5	0.4	1.0	0.1	•
Pensions and Other Deferred Comp. 16	0.3	0.1	0.0	0.2	0.4	0.5	0.3	0.4	0.2	0.2	1.1	0.1	•
Employee Benefits 17	0.9	2.2	•	1.0	0.6	0.9	0.9	0.8	1.3	0.3	1.6	1.1	•
Advertising 18	0.5	0.3	0.0	0.1	1.1	0.1	0.5	0.5	0.4	0.1	0.0	0.6	•
Other Expenses 19	8.6	28.1	16.9	31.7	4.5	4.6	7.4	10.7	5.4	3.0	7.3	11.1	•
Officers' Compensation 20	1.0	4.9	0.1	2.3	1.8	1.9	1.8	1.7	0.8	0.3	0.6	0.4	•
Operating Margin 21	1.0	•	72.4	•	•	•	4.0	•	3.3	0.5	•	1.0	•
Operating Margin Before Officers' Comp. 22	2.1	•	72.5	2.1	0.5	•	5.7	0.6	4.2	0.9	•	1.4	•

Selected Average Balance Sheet ($ in Thousands)

Net Receivables 23	1379	0	0	203	892	1846	4327	7643	19240	28692	49966	178225
Inventories 24	694	0	0	0	54	600	2255	4579	10048	16821	74514	104699
Net Property, Plant and Equipment 25	2188	0	0	495	1168	3909	4969	11490	16119	40611	126893	306645
Total Assets 26	6234	0	61	791	2551	7557	15703	34480	74940	139654	406131	770486
Notes and Loans Payable 27	2941	0	42	431	3294	4438	3766	9364	25736	27938	256054	332543
All Other Liabilities 28	2030	0	385	336	1259	923	4140	12055	18944	37282	125166	218425
Net Worth 29	1264	0	-366	24	-2003	2196	7797	13060	30259	74434	24912	219519

Selected Financial Ratios (Times to 1)

Current Ratio 30	1.6	•	11.4	1.4	1.0	1.0	1.9	1.7	1.4	2.1	1.3	1.9
Quick Ratio 31	1.0	•	11.4	1.3	0.9	0.8	1.3	1.1	0.9	1.1	0.6	1.2
Net Sales to Working Capital 32	10.9	•	6.2	32.5	179.1	1612.2	7.1	7.2	9.3	9.9	11.7	8.6
Coverage Ratio 33	2.3	•	133.7	0.9	•	1.8	8.5	1.0	5.2	6.1	1.1	2.6
Total Asset Turnover 34	1.9	•	5.5	3.0	4.3	1.4	2.1	1.7	1.6	2.3	0.8	2.0
Inventory Turnover 35	13.2	•	•	•	175.6	15.8	10.6	9.7	9.5	17.4	3.6	11.2
Receivables Turnover 36	9.4	•	2979.1	13.7	15.9	6.6	7.4	8.2	6.3	11.9	3.4	•
Total Liabilities to Net Worth 37	3.9	•	•	32.0	•	2.4	1.0	1.6	1.5	0.9	15.3	2.5
Current Assets to Working Capital 38	2.7	•	1.1	3.6	21.0	463.0	2.1	2.5	3.2	1.9	4.5	2.2
Current Liabilities to Working Capital 39	1.7	•	0.1	2.6	20.0	462.0	1.1	1.5	2.2	0.9	3.5	1.2
Working Capital to Net Sales 40	0.1	•	0.2	0.0	0.0	0.0	0.1	0.1	0.1	0.1	0.1	0.1
Inventory to Working Capital 41	0.7	•	•	•	1.7	62.0	0.5	0.6	0.8	0.5	1.8	0.6
Total Receipts to Cash Flow 42	9.5	5.3	2.2	4.0	51.1	17.6	10.0	3.5	10.4	24.5	19.6	8.0
Cost of Goods to Cash Flow 43	7.3	3.2	0.2	0.8	43.9	15.3	7.4	2.7	8.2	22.1	15.5	6.1
Cash Flow to Total Debt 44	0.3	•	0.4	0.8	0.0	0.1	0.4	0.8	0.3	0.2	0.0	0.3

Selected Financial Factors (in Percentages)

Debt Ratio 45	79.7	•	701.2	97.0	178.5	70.9	50.3	62.1	59.6	46.7	93.9	71.5
Return on Total Assets 46	7.8	•	163.2	6.4	•	6.6	10.7	1.5	10.6	5.1	7.3	8.3
Return on Equity Before Income Taxes 47	22.2	•	•	•	6.3	10.4	19.0	•	21.2	8.1	14.1	17.9
Return on Equity After Income Taxes 48	18.2	•	•	•	6.4	10.4	17.7	•	20.7	4.8	9.8	15.1
Profit Margin (Before Income Tax) 49	2.3	•	29.3	•	•	2.1	4.6	•	5.3	1.9	1.0	2.5
Profit Margin (After Income Tax) 50	1.9	•	29.3	•	2.1	2.1	4.3	•	5.1	1.1	0.7	2.1

Table II

Corporations with Net Income

ASPHALT PAVING, ROOFING, OTHER PETROLEUM AND COAL PRODUCTS

MONEY AMOUNTS AND SIZE OF ASSETS IN THOUSANDS OF DOLLARS

Item Description for Accounting Period 7/04 Through 6/05	Total	Zero Assets	Under 500	500 to 1,000	1,000 to 5,000	5,000 to 10,000	10,000 to 25,000	25,000 to 50,000	50,000 to 100,000	100,000 to 250,000	250,000 to 500,000	500,000 to 2,500,000	2,500,000 and over
Number of Enterprises **1**	1031	0	0	0	0	40	42	0	0	6	0	3	0
Revenues ($ in Thousands)													
Net Sales **2**	12312424	0	0	0	0	437967	1293844	0	0	1850915	0	4631235	0
Interest **3**	19025	0	0	0	0	0	560	0	0	13446	0	2360	0
Rents **4**	1683	0	0	0	0	0	503	0	0	105	0	0	0
Royalties **5**	21450	0	0	0	0	0	8	0	0	4394	0	17047	0
Other Portfolio Income **6**	47473	0	0	0	0	1	3229	0	0	31631	0	680	0
Other Receipts **7**	85302	0	0	0	0	61394	2708	0	0	37723	0	52490	0
Total Receipts **8**	12487357	0	0	0	0	499362	1300852	0	0	1938214	0	4703812	0
Average Total Receipts **9**	12112	•	•	•	•	12484	30973	•	•	323036	•	1567937	•
Operating Costs/Operating Income (%)													
Cost of Operations **10**	78.4	•	•	•	•	94.1	71.5	•	•	87.5	•	75.9	•
Salaries and Wages **11**	3.6	•	•	•	•	1.0	5.9	•	•	2.4	•	3.9	•
Taxes Paid **12**	0.9	•	•	•	•	0.8	1.6	•	•	0.8	•	0.6	•
Interest Paid **13**	1.1	•	•	•	•	3.2	0.5	•	•	1.1	•	1.6	•
Depreciation **14**	2.8	•	•	•	•	6.0	3.1	•	•	1.9	•	3.8	•
Amortization and Depletion **15**	0.2	•	•	•	•	0.5	0.1	•	•	0.7	•	0.1	•
Pensions and Other Deferred Comp. **16**	0.2	•	•	•	•	0.2	0.3	•	•	0.3	•	0.1	•
Employee Benefits **17**	0.7	•	•	•	•	0.8	0.7	•	•	0.5	•	1.1	•
Advertising **18**	0.6	•	•	•	•	0.1	0.5	•	•	0.1	•	0.6	•
Other Expenses **19**	7.4	•	•	•	•	2.7	7.3	•	•	5.1	•	11.1	•
Officers' Compensation **20**	1.0	•	•	•	•	0.4	1.7	•	•	0.4	•	0.4	•
Operating Margin **21**	3.1	•	•	•	•	•	6.6	•	•	•	•	1.0	•
Operating Margin Before Officers' Comp. **22**	4.1	•	•	•	•	•	8.3	•	•	•	•	1.4	•

Selected Average Balance Sheet ($ in Thousands)

Net Receivables 23	1334	1950	4170	33610	178225
Inventories 24	678	415	1933	20867	104699
Net Property, Plant and Equipment 25	1894	4628	4554	60190	306645
Total Assets 26	5609	7968	14956	204809	770486
Notes and Loans Payable 27	1867	5694	3108	35447	332543
All Other Liabilities 28	1804	968	3530	67594	218425
Net Worth 29	1938	1305	8318	101768	219519

Selected Financial Ratios (Times to 1)

Current Ratio 30	1.6	0.7	2.1	1.0	1.9
Quick Ratio 31	1.1	0.6	1.5	0.5	1.2
Net Sales to Working Capital 32	11.3		6.4		8.6
Coverage Ratio 33	5.3	2.4	15.2	4.7	2.6
Total Asset Turnover 34	2.1	1.4	2.1	1.5	2.0
Inventory Turnover 35	13.8	24.8	11.4	12.9	11.2
Receivables Turnover 36	9.4	9.0			
Total Liabilities to Net Worth 37	1.9	5.1	0.8	1.0	2.5
Current Assets to Working Capital 38	2.7		1.9		2.2
Current Liabilities to Working Capital 39	1.7		0.9		1.2
Working Capital to Net Sales 40	0.1		0.2		0.1
Inventory to Working Capital 41	0.6		0.4		0.6
Total Receipts to Cash Flow 42	9.3	15.9	8.0	13.8	8.0
Cost of Goods to Cash Flow 43	7.3	15.0	5.7	12.1	6.1
Cash Flow to Total Debt 44	0.3	0.1	0.6	0.2	0.3

Selected Financial Factors (in Percentages)

Debt Ratio 45	65.4	83.6	44.4	50.3	71.5
Return on Total Assets 46	12.0	10.4	15.7	8.0	8.3
Return on Equity Before Income Taxes 47	28.2	37.1	26.3	12.7	17.9
Return on Equity After Income Taxes 48	24.9	37.1	24.7	9.7	15.1
Profit Margin (Before Income Tax) 49	4.6	4.4	7.1	4.2	2.5
Profit Margin (After Income Tax) 50	4.0	4.4	6.7	3.2	2.1

Table I

Corporations with and without Net Income

BASIC CHEMICAL

MONEY AMOUNTS AND SIZE OF ASSETS IN THOUSANDS OF DOLLARS

Item Description for Accounting Period 7/04 Through 6/05	Total	Zero Assets	Under 500	500 to 1,000	1,000 to 5,000	5,000 to 10,000	10,000 to 25,000	25,000 to 50,000	50,000 to 100,000	100,000 to 250,000	250,000 to 500,000	500,000 to 2,500,000	2,500,000 and over
Number of Enterprises 1	971	5	266	139	220	129	84	31	19	18	11	28	20
Revenues ($ in Thousands)													
Net Sales 2	122215921	801278	368996	290395	586335	915034	1882145	1578174	2028599	4077744	2997912	31571542	75060766
Interest 3	1711051	1048	0	0	2311	822	4125	799	1899	15398	20586	196723	1467340
Rents 4	299181	0	0	0	20	63	1934	1756	114	12334	3927	21594	257439
Royalties 5	2915103	2750	0	28429	462	0	414	1162	736	8039	1260	293048	2578805
Other Portfolio Income 6	2660562	33	0	7623	3041	393	2307	6408	20539	39740	15408	882367	1682701
Other Receipts 7	3452612	7158	1190	12360	4621	1189	27182	10906	9921	73759	102504	655537	2546286
Total Receipts 8	133197430	812267	370186	338807	596790	917501	1918107	1599205	2061808	4227014	3141597	33620811	83593337
Average Total Receipts 9	137176	162453	1392	2437	2713	7112	22835	51587	108516	234834	285600	1200743	4179667
Operating Costs/Operating Income (%)													
Cost of Operations 10	78.3	77.9	53.6	47.9	74.3	72.5	69.7	65.9	76.6	76.5	66.5	72.4	82.2
Salaries and Wages 11	5.8	2.8	10.3	14.3	7.9	5.7	7.6	7.5	4.3	6.3	6.4	6.7	5.4
Taxes Paid 12	1.4	0.7	1.0	6.3	2.2	3.3	1.6	1.7	2.6	0.9	1.3	1.1	1.4
Interest Paid 13	4.4	3.0	0.0	1.2	1.3	1.2	0.8	1.2	1.2	1.3	2.7	2.8	5.7
Depreciation 14	4.1	8.5	0.3	3.1	1.6	5.7	3.6	5.0	4.0	3.5	5.2	4.1	4.1
Amortization and Depletion 15	0.8	0.4	0.5	*	1.3	0.2	0.2	0.4	0.6	0.5	0.9	0.8	0.8
Pensions and Other Deferred Comp. 16	1.0	0.1	0.0	0.8	0.1	0.6	0.6	0.6	0.3	0.3	0.6	1.4	1.0
Employee Benefits 17	2.0	4.0	0.9	3.3	0.6	0.8	1.3	1.4	1.3	0.9	1.3	2.4	1.9
Advertising 18	0.6	0.0	0.2	0.0	0.5	0.2	0.3	0.4	0.1	0.2	0.2	1.8	0.2
Other Expenses 19	9.8	5.9	10.3	17.6	13.8	6.1	10.3	11.3	7.9	8.6	14.3	11.4	9.0
Officers' Compensation 20	0.5	0.3	2.7	13.1	4.3	2.1	2.0	1.4	1.2	0.7	0.7	0.6	0.3
Operating Margin 21	*	*	20.2	*	*	1.7	2.1	3.2	*	0.4	*	*	*
Operating Margin Before Officers' Comp. 22	*	*	22.9	5.5	*	3.8	4.1	4.6	1.0	1.1	0.6	*	*

Selected Average Balance Sheet ($ in Thousands)

Item													
Net Receivables 23	52321	0	166	376	726	1327	3873	9003	18879	27380	37108	166352	2192728
Inventories 24	13450	0	51	252	158	848	2492	5672	14627	17461	40429	145217	368960
Net Property, Plant and Equipment 25	47305	0	8	91	490	2552	5051	12612	20125	51590	110429	360757	1601955
Total Assets 26	257571	0	409	886	2257	6305	15913	36171	75329	163490	347426	1272739	10113475
Notes and Loans Payable 27	112813	0	0	813	708	6338	4228	13606	20415	62792	76056	392930	4716043
All Other Liabilities 28	74899	0	94	333	814	1107	3820	8446	24302	39602	78460	556770	2706186
Net Worth 29	69860	0	315	-260	736	-1140	7866	14118	30612	61096	192909	323039	2691246

Selected Financial Ratios (Times to 1)

Item													
Current Ratio 30	1.0	•	4.1	0.8	1.5	1.4	1.9	1.7	1.5	1.6	2.0	1.3	1.0
Quick Ratio 31	0.7	•	2.4	0.6	1.2	0.8	1.2	1.0	0.9	0.9	1.1	0.7	0.7
Net Sales to Working Capital 32	47.6	•	4.8	•	5.7	7.9	5.7	6.6	7.9	8.5	4.9	9.9	•
Coverage Ratio 33	1.3	0.3	558.7	8.4	•	2.7	6.1	4.7	2.2	4.3	2.9	1.5	1.1
Total Asset Turnover 34	0.5	•	3.4	2.4	1.2	1.1	1.4	1.4	1.4	1.4	0.8	0.9	0.4
Inventory Turnover 35	7.3	•	14.5	4.0	12.5	6.1	6.3	5.9	5.6	9.9	4.5	5.6	8.4
Receivables Turnover 36	2.2	•	12.2	4.4	4.5	6.2	6.6	6.2	6.1	9.6	6.0	8.1	1.5
Total Liabilities to Net Worth 37	2.7	•	0.3	•	2.1	•	1.0	1.6	1.5	1.7	0.8	2.9	2.8
Current Assets to Working Capital 38	31.1	•	1.3	•	3.1	3.3	2.1	2.4	3.0	2.6	2.0	3.9	•
Current Liabilities to Working Capital 39	30.1	•	0.3	•	2.1	2.3	1.1	1.4	2.0	1.6	1.0	2.9	•
Working Capital to Net Sales 40	0.0	•	0.2	•	0.2	0.1	0.2	0.2	0.1	0.1	0.2	0.1	•
Inventory to Working Capital 41	5.6	•	0.2	•	0.4	0.8	0.7	0.8	1.1	0.7	0.6	1.5	•
Total Receipts to Cash Flow 42	13.4	30.3	3.7	4.7	28.8	14.9	8.2	7.5	12.8	8.9	5.8	12.9	15.6
Cost of Goods to Cash Flow 43	10.5	23.6	2.0	2.3	21.4	10.8	5.7	4.9	9.8	6.8	3.8	9.3	12.8
Cash Flow to Total Debt 44	0.0	•	4.0	0.4	0.1	0.1	0.3	0.3	0.2	0.2	0.3	0.1	0.0

Selected Financial Factors (in Percentages)

Item													
Debt Ratio 45	72.9	•	23.0	129.4	67.4	118.1	50.6	61.0	59.4	62.6	44.5	74.6	73.4
Return on Total Assets 46	2.8	•	69.8	24.2	3.5	•	6.7	8.2	7.8	3.7	6.1	3.6	2.4
Return on Equity Before Income Taxes 47	2.3	•	90.6	•	•	•	11.4	16.5	15.9	4.9	7.2	4.4	1.1
Return on Equity After Income Taxes 48	0.9	•	90.6	•	•	•	8.4	15.3	11.4	3.1	4.1	1.8	0.1
Profit Margin (Before Income Tax) 49	1.3	•	20.6	9.0	2.0	•	4.6	4.0	1.4	4.3	5.1	1.3	0.8
Profit Margin (After Income Tax) 50	0.5	•	20.6	8.9	1.2	•	3.0	4.2	0.9	3.1	2.9	0.5	0.1

Table II

Corporations with Net Income

BASIC CHEMICAL

MONEY AMOUNTS AND SIZE OF ASSETS IN THOUSANDS OF DOLLARS

Item Description for Accounting Period 7/04 Through 6/05	Total	Zero Assets	Under 500	500 to 1,000	1,000 to 5,000	5,000 to 10,000	10,000 to 25,000	25,000 to 50,000	50,000 to 100,000	100,000 to 250,000	250,000 to 500,000	500,000 to 2,500,000	2,500,000 and over
Number of Enterprises 1	599	0	0	139	64	69	65	0	9	15	0	14	13
Revenues ($ in Thousands)													
Net Sales 2	60890891	0	0	290395	289250	612840	1615863	0	1209187	3219172	0	16995804	32543970
Interest 3	509990	0	0	0	693	797	3584	0	632	7679	0	118463	371017
Rents 4	163809	0	0	0	20	53	1932	0	39	2723	0	13542	143322
Royalties 5	1492244	0	0	28429	0	0	142	0	149	5420	0	241199	1211765
Other Portfolio Income 6	2025634	0	0	7623	1940	393	1205	0	13236	39740	0	636190	1304650
Other Receipts 7	1929065	0	0	12360	178	878	23430	0	7737	66282	0	324521	1380277
Total Receipts 8	67011633	0	0	338807	292081	614961	1646156	0	1230980	3341016	0	18329719	36955001
Average Total Receipts 9	111873	·	·	2437	4564	8912	25325	·	136776	222734	·	1309266	2842692
Operating Costs/Operating Income (%)													
Cost of Operations 10	69.1	·	·	47.9	72.9	71.6	69.0	·	76.5	74.8	·	69.9	68.6
Salaries and Wages 11	7.3	·	·	14.3	5.1	5.0	6.9	·	4.4	5.6	·	6.8	7.8
Taxes Paid 12	1.5	·	·	6.3	1.6	2.4	1.5	·	1.4	1.0	·	1.3	1.6
Interest Paid 13	3.8	·	·	1.2	0.4	0.5	0.7	·	0.9	1.4	·	2.5	5.4
Depreciation 14	4.9	·	·	3.1	0.8	2.5	2.9	·	2.5	3.3	·	3.2	6.4
Amortization and Depletion 15	0.8	·	·	·	0.0	0.2	0.2	·	0.3	0.5	·	1.0	0.9
Pensions and Other Deferred Comp. 16	1.2	·	·	0.8	0.1	0.5	0.6	·	0.3	0.3	·	1.1	1.5
Employee Benefits 17	2.2	·	·	3.3	0.4	1.2	1.3	·	1.2	1.0	·	1.5	2.8
Advertising 18	1.1	·	·	0.0	0.4	0.2	0.3	·	0.1	0.2	·	3.2	0.3
Other Expenses 19	11.2	·	·	17.6	10.0	6.1	9.2	·	5.8	9.0	·	10.2	12.1
Officers' Compensation 20	0.7	·	·	13.1	4.7	3.0	2.0	·	1.2	0.8	·	0.6	0.4
Operating Margin 21	·	·	·	·	3.6	6.7	5.4	·	5.4	2.1	·	·	·
Operating Margin Before Officers' Comp. 22	·	·	·	5.5	8.3	9.7	7.4	·	6.6	2.9	·	·	·

Selected Average Balance Sheet ($ in Thousands)

Net Receivables 23	22758	•	•	376	528	1108	4399	•	20137	26775	•	147748 775761
Inventories 24	12316	•	•	227	231	966	2498	•	12737	15929	•	192029 278252
Net Property, Plant and Equipment 25	38313	•	•	91	398	2728	4469	•	25519	50461	•	328244 1208194
Total Assets 26	187911	•	•	886	2636	6906	15695	•	74599	159115	•	1306529 6628091
Notes and Loans Payable 27	64556	•	•	813	277	1491	3647	•	24998	61432	•	350336 2425849
All Other Liabilities 28	59236	•	•	333	471	939	3989	•	24477	36101	•	553313 1987011
Net Worth 29	64118	•	•	-260	1888	4477	8058	•	25123	61582	•	402880 2215231

Selected Financial Ratios (Times to 1)

Current Ratio 30	1.2	•	0.8	2.8	2.6	2.1	•	1.6	1.8	•	1.2	1.1
Quick Ratio 31	0.7	•	0.6	2.5	1.2	1.3	•	0.9	1.0	•	0.5	0.7
Net Sales to Working Capital 32	12.8	•	•	3.4	3.9	5.0	•	9.0	7.3	•	13.5	19.5
Coverage Ratio 33	3.0	•	8.4	11.8	13.8	11.2	•	9.5	5.3	•	3.9	2.4
Total Asset Turnover 34	0.5	•	2.4	1.7	1.3	1.6	•	1.8	1.3	•	0.9	0.4
Inventory Turnover 35	5.7	•	4.4	14.3	6.6	6.9	•	8.1	10.1	•	4.4	6.2
Receivables Turnover 36	1.9	•	5.3	4.9	7.1	6.9	•	8.0	9.6	•	9.0	1.1
Total Liabilities to Net Worth 37	1.9	•	•	0.4	0.5	0.9	•	2.0	1.6	•	2.2	2.0
Current Assets to Working Capital 38	6.4	•	•	1.6	1.6	1.9	•	2.8	2.3	•	5.4	11.6
Current Liabilities to Working Capital 39	5.4	•	•	0.6	0.6	0.9	•	1.8	1.3	•	4.4	10.6
Working Capital to Net Sales 40	0.1	•	•	0.3	0.3	0.2	•	0.1	0.1	•	0.1	0.1
Inventory to Working Capital 41	1.5	•	•	0.2	0.4	0.6	•	1.1	0.6	•	2.4	1.8
Total Receipts to Cash Flow 42	6.9	•	4.7	8.0	8.1	6.8	•	8.4	7.5	•	8.5	6.4
Cost of Goods to Cash Flow 43	4.7	•	2.3	5.8	5.8	4.7	•	6.4	5.6	•	6.0	4.4
Cash Flow to Total Debt 44	0.1	•	0.4	0.8	0.4	0.5	•	0.3	0.3	•	0.2	0.1

Selected Financial Factors (in Percentages)

Debt Ratio 45	65.9	•	129.4	28.4	35.2	48.7	•	66.3	61.3	•	69.2	66.6
Return on Total Assets 46	6.1	•	24.2	8.6	9.7	12.6	•	14.5	10.2	•	9.0	4.8
Return on Equity Before Income Taxes 47	11.8	•	•	11.0	13.9	22.3	•	38.6	21.4	•	21.6	8.4
Return on Equity After Income Taxes 48	9.5	•	•	9.1	11.7	18.6	•	33.9	16.0	•	17.4	6.7
Profit Margin (Before Income Tax) 49	7.5	•	9.0	4.6	7.0	7.2	•	7.2	6.1	•	7.2	7.4
Profit Margin (After Income Tax) 50	6.0	•	8.9	3.8	5.9	6.0	•	6.3	4.6	•	5.8	5.9

Table I

Corporations with and without Net Income

RESIN, SYNTHETIC RUBBER AND FIBERS AND FILAMENTS

MONEY AMOUNTS AND SIZE OF ASSETS IN THOUSANDS OF DOLLARS

Item Description for Accounting Period 7/04 Through 6/05	Total	Zero Assets	Under 500	500 to 1,000	1,000 to 5,000	5,000 to 10,000	10,000 to 25,000	25,000 to 50,000	50,000 to 100,000	100,000 to 250,000	250,000 to 500,000	500,000 to 2,500,000	2,500,000 and over
Number of Enterprises **1**	826	0	0	0	0	52	23	15	10	6	5	5	3
Revenues ($ in Thousands)													
Net Sales **2**	35593895	0	0	0	0	443837	515847	876555	885682	654070	1843262	7374563	21948912
Interest **3**	1862541	0	0	0	0	90	348	808	9432	4093	9688	28462	1809585
Rents **4**	73425	0	0	0	0	85	73	1426	611	1065	729	4410	65017
Royalties **5**	727547	0	0	0	0	3461	0	50	132	0	1489	16523	705891
Other Portfolio Income **6**	455785	0	0	0	0	46	124	623	7279	971	52031	159591	235118
Other Receipts **7**	1075223	0	0	0	0	950	5983	2040	5329	3448	13557	139501	893885
Total Receipts **8**	39788416	0	0	0	0	448469	522375	881502	908465	663647	1920756	7723050	25665408
Average Total Receipts **9**	48170	•	•	•	•	8624	22712	58767	90846	110608	384151	1544610	8852803
Operating Costs/Operating Income (%)													
Cost of Operations **10**	70.2	•	•	•	•	62.0	74.4	68.9	81.1	78.1	78.9	83.3	64.6
Salaries and Wages **11**	2.6	•	•	•	•	5.0	6.1	6.0	3.7	4.6	4.8	3.2	1.8
Taxes Paid **12**	0.8	•	•	•	•	2.0	1.7	1.2	1.6	1.3	1.1	0.5	0.7
Interest Paid **13**	6.9	•	•	•	•	2.9	0.8	1.3	2.3	2.3	1.6	2.0	10.0
Depreciation **14**	3.5	•	•	•	•	1.6	2.8	4.3	3.9	4.3	2.9	2.3	3.9
Amortization and Depletion **15**	0.2	•	•	•	•	0.2	0.2	0.2	0.1	1.3	0.6	•	0.2
Pensions and Other Deferred Comp. **16**	0.5	•	•	•	•	1.9	0.5	0.8	0.1	0.1	0.3	0.9	0.3
Employee Benefits **17**	3.4	•	•	•	•	1.0	1.2	2.4	2.2	1.8	1.5	0.9	4.7
Advertising **18**	0.4	•	•	•	•	0.5	0.4	0.3	0.3	0.1	0.1	0.0	0.5
Other Expenses **19**	21.1	•	•	•	•	9.3	8.5	7.3	4.0	13.3	7.8	6.3	29.5
Officers' Compensation **20**	0.4	•	•	•	•	2.9	1.9	1.0	0.9	1.1	1.6	0.2	0.0
Operating Margin **21**	•	•	•	•	•	10.7	1.4	6.3	•	•	•	0.3	•
Operating Margin Before Officers' Comp. **22**	•	•	•	•	•	13.6	3.3	7.2	0.7	•	0.4	0.5	•

Selected Average Balance Sheet ($ in Thousands)

Net Receivables 23	9468	•	1213	3406	8568	11838	19936	38073	218738	1986354
Inventories 24	5107	•	862	3086	5419	12375	11677	41402	112282	1000101
Net Property, Plant and Equipment 25	15854	•	1160	5117	14486	23959	48773	125103	475071	3023680
Total Assets 26	126497	•	5951	15176	38604	71677	148232	365316	1482576	30687409
Notes and Loans Payable 27	19766	•	1020	4757	12668	16428	37597	76471	431658	4323870
All Other Liabilities 28	51263	•	674	4859	10337	19442	41117	59930	429197	13037146
Net Worth 29	55467	•	4257	5560	15598	35807	69518	228916	621720	13326394

Selected Financial Ratios (Times to 1)

Current Ratio 30	1.7	•	3.8	1.3	1.8	2.0	1.3	2.1	2.3	1.5
Quick Ratio 31	1.0	•	2.0	0.8	1.0	1.1	0.7	1.1	1.7	0.9
Net Sales to Working Capital 32	5.6	•	3.6	12.0	7.1	5.2	10.1	6.9	4.5	5.9
Coverage Ratio 33	1.5	•	5.0	4.1	6.3	2.1	•	3.6	3.5	1.3
Total Asset Turnover 34	0.3	•	1.4	1.5	1.5	1.2	0.7	1.0	1.0	0.2
Inventory Turnover 35	5.9	•	6.1	5.4	7.4	5.8	7.3	7.0	10.9	4.7
Receivables Turnover 36	5.0	•	9.0	6.8	7.0	7.7	6.2	10.0	7.7	4.0
Total Liabilities to Net Worth 37	1.3	•	0.4	1.7	1.5	1.0	1.1	0.6	1.4	1.3
Current Assets to Working Capital 38	2.5	•	1.4	4.5	2.3	2.0	4.2	1.9	1.8	2.9
Current Liabilities to Working Capital 39	1.5	•	0.4	3.5	1.3	1.0	3.2	0.9	0.8	1.9
Working Capital to Net Sales 40	0.2	•	0.3	0.1	0.1	0.2	0.1	0.1	0.2	0.2
Inventory to Working Capital 41	0.7	•	0.5	1.5	0.7	0.7	1.3	0.7	0.4	0.8
Total Receipts to Cash Flow 42	5.0	•	5.0	10.8	7.8	21.4	19.4	10.0	9.5	3.8
Cost of Goods to Cash Flow 43	3.5	•	3.1	8.0	5.4	17.4	15.1	7.9	7.9	2.5
Cash Flow to Total Debt 44	0.1	•	1.0	0.2	0.3	0.1	0.1	0.3	0.2	0.1

Selected Financial Factors (in Percentages)

Debt Ratio 45	56.2	•	28.5	63.4	59.6	50.0	53.1	37.3	58.1	56.6
Return on Total Assets 46	3.5	•	21.0	5.2	12.3	5.8	•	6.0	6.9	3.2
Return on Equity Before Income Taxes 47	2.7	•	23.5	10.7	25.6	6.0	•	6.9	11.7	1.8
Return on Equity After Income Taxes 48	2.0	•	22.6	8.2	24.8	3.8	•	4.4	7.4	1.4
Profit Margin (Before Income Tax) 49	3.5	•	11.7	2.6	6.8	2.4	•	4.3	4.9	3.3
Profit Margin (After Income Tax) 50	2.6	•	11.3	2.0	6.6	1.5	•	2.7	3.1	2.6

Table II
Corporations with Net Income

RESIN, SYNTHETIC RUBBER AND FIBERS AND FILAMENTS

MONEY AMOUNTS AND SIZE OF ASSETS IN THOUSANDS OF DOLLARS

Item Description for Accounting Period 7/04 Through 6/05	Total	Zero Assets	Under 500	500 to 1,000	1,000 to 5,000	5,000 to 10,000	10,000 to 25,000	25,000 to 50,000	50,000 to 100,000	100,000 to 250,000	250,000 to 500,000	500,000 to 2,500,000	2,500,000 and over
Number of Enterprises 1	218	0	0	0	124	49	15	0	7	0	0	0	3
Revenues ($ in Thousands)													
Net Sales 2	31623819	0	0	0	744872	374759	366706	0	745471	0	0	0	21948912
Interest 3	1843705	0	0	0	0	86	242	0	2793	0	0	0	1809585
Rents 4	70730	0	0	0	0	85	12	0	346	0	0	0	65017
Royalties 5	723234	0	0	0	0	3461	0	0	0	0	0	0	705891
Other Portfolio Income 6	422859	0	0	0	0	46	120	0	7500	0	0	0	235118
Other Receipts 7	948849	0	0	0	0	939	5844	0	5999	0	0	0	893885
Total Receipts 8	35633196	0	0	0	746217	379376	372924	0	762109	0	0	0	25658408
Average Total Receipts 9	163455	·	·	·	6018	7742	24862	·	108873	·	·	·	8552803
Operating Costs/Operating Income (%)													
Cost of Operations 10	68.8	·	·	·	67.3	56.5	70.7	·	77.4	·	·	·	64.6
Salaries and Wages 11	2.2	·	·	·	5.6	5.3	6.7	·	4.0	·	·	·	1.8
Taxes Paid 12	0.8	·	·	·	3.1	2.2	1.8	·	1.5	·	·	·	0.7
Interest Paid 13	7.3	·	·	·	0.3	2.8	0.7	·	1.0	·	·	·	10.0
Depreciation 14	3.4	·	·	·	4.4	1.9	2.3	·	3.0	·	·	·	3.9
Amortization and Depletion 15	0.2	·	·	·	·	0.2	0.1	·	0.1	·	·	·	0.2
Pensions and Other Deferred Comp. 16	0.3	·	·	·	0.7	2.2	0.6	·	0.1	·	·	·	0.3
Employee Benefits 17	3.7	·	·	·	4.4	1.0	1.4	·	2.0	·	·	·	4.7
Advertising 18	0.4	·	·	·	0.0	0.5	0.4	·	0.3	·	·	·	0.5
Other Expenses 19	22.4	·	·	·	10.3	10.0	8.6	·	6.2	·	·	·	29.5
Officers' Compensation 20	0.3	·	·	·	3.4	3.3	2.3	·	0.9	·	·	·	0.0
Operating Margin 21	·	·	·	·	0.5	14.1	4.3	·	3.4	·	·	·	·
Operating Margin Before Officers' Comp. 22	·	·	·	·	3.8	17.4	6.7	·	4.3	·	·	·	·

Selected Average Balance Sheet ($ in Thousands)

Net Receivables 23	33904	•	•	465	1149	3897	•	13497	•	1986354
Inventories 24	16058	•	•	607	1105	2593	•	12027	•	987855
Net Property, Plant and Equipment 25	54768	•	•	568	1220	3688	•	26410	•	3023680
Total Assets 26	461616	•	•	2066	5771	13348	•	77438	•	30687409
Notes and Loans Payable 27	68968	•	•	410	528	2872	•	9293	•	4323870
All Other Liabilities 28	187776	•	•	248	683	4141	•	20255	•	13037146
Net Worth 29	204873	•	•	1408	4560	6335	•	47890	•	13326394

Selected Financial Ratios (Times to 1)

Current Ratio 30	1.7	•	•	2.9	4.0	1.9	•	2.4	•	1.5
Quick Ratio 31	1.0	•	•	1.5	2.1	1.2	•	1.2	•	0.9
Net Sales to Working Capital 32	5.2	•	•	6.1	3.4	6.4	•	4.6	•	5.9
Coverage Ratio 33	1.7	•	•	3.3	6.4	9.6	•	7.0	•	1.3
Total Asset Turnover 34	0.3	•	•	2.9	1.3	1.8	•	1.4	•	0.2
Inventory Turnover 35	6.2	•	•	6.7	3.9	6.7	•	6.9	•	4.8
Receivables Turnover 36	4.9	•	•	•	•	7.3	•	9.3	•	•
Total Liabilities to Net Worth 37	1.3	•	•	0.5	0.3	1.1	•	0.6	•	1.3
Current Assets to Working Capital 38	2.5	•	•	1.5	1.3	2.2	•	1.7	•	2.9
Current Liabilities to Working Capital 39	1.5	•	•	0.5	0.3	1.2	•	0.7	•	1.9
Working Capital to Net Sales 40	0.2	•	•	0.2	0.3	0.2	•	0.2	•	0.2
Inventory to Working Capital 41	0.6	•	•	0.6	0.5	0.7	•	0.7	•	0.8
Total Receipts to Cash Flow 42	4.5	•	•	17.4	4.1	7.9	•	9.8	•	3.8
Cost of Goods to Cash Flow 43	3.1	•	•	11.7	2.3	5.6	•	7.6	•	2.5
Cash Flow to Total Debt 44	0.1	•	•	0.5	1.5	0.4	•	0.4	•	0.1

Selected Financial Factors (in Percentages)

Debt Ratio 45	55.6	•	•	31.9	21.0	52.5	•	38.2	•	56.6
Return on Total Assets 46	3.8	•	•	2.7	24.0	12.3	•	9.3	•	3.2
Return on Equity Before Income Taxes 47	3.4	•	•	2.8	25.6	23.3	•	12.9	•	1.8
Return on Equity After Income Taxes 48	2.6	•	•	2.6	24.7	20.0	•	10.6	•	1.4
Profit Margin (Before Income Tax) 49	4.8	•	•	0.7	15.3	6.0	•	5.8	•	3.3
Profit Margin (After Income Tax) 50	3.7	•	•	0.6	14.7	5.2	•	4.7	•	2.6

Table I

Corporations with and without Net Income

PHARMACEUTICAL AND MEDICINE

MONEY AMOUNTS AND SIZE OF ASSETS IN THOUSANDS OF DOLLARS

Item Description for Accounting Period 7/04 Through 6/05	Total	Zero Assets	Under 500	500 to 1,000	1,000 to 5,000	5,000 to 10,000	10,000 to 25,000	25,000 to 50,000	50,000 to 100,000	100,000 to 250,000	250,000 to 500,000	500,000 to 2,500,000	2,500,000 and over
Number of Enterprises 1	1131	30	386	90	159	129	100	58	57	48	15	30	28
Revenues ($ in Thousands)													
Net Sales 2	269911433	375769	61135	220932	426040	1439870	1569780	1789713	2825683	5823347	3246213	20917572	230415379
Interest 3	4161328	38452	757	131	557	2553	5530	13668	25092	53511	19682	204834	3796558
Rents 4	327757	277	34	0	376	255	439	76	711	2245	1584	13740	308019
Royalties 5	18400463	69409	2256	0	4927	0	10458	4861	18548	87197	13944	532002	17665861
Other Portfolio Income 6	7253403	15	33	3578	3404	1181	18653	3999	5199	93205	18200	321760	6784176
Other Receipts 7	15507144	723800	4935	358	14845	12524	52121	19476	80745	159416	270325	774913	13393691
Total Receipts 8	314761528	1207722	69150	224999	450149	1456383	1656981	1831793	2955978	6218921	3569948	22764821	272354684
Average Total Receipts 9	278304	40257	179	2500	2831	11290	16570	31583	51859	129561	237997	758827	9726953
Operating Costs/Operating Income (%)													
Cost of Operations 10	49.8	48.2	50.1	58.8	41.2	65.3	55.9	51.8	42.8	37.7	36.4	39.5	51.2
Salaries and Wages 11	15.1	31.7	27.0	10.6	17.7	5.8	13.5	13.8	17.0	11.2	17.0	14.2	15.3
Taxes Paid 12	1.6	9.6	3.1	3.1	3.2	2.3	2.7	2.8	2.5	2.0	2.0	1.9	1.4
Interest Paid 13	3.5	0.8	3.4	1.1	3.9	0.6	1.3	1.5	1.5	1.8	2.9	2.0	3.8
Depreciation 14	3.3	2.8	9.3	2.1	3.9	3.2	5.4	4.0	4.0	3.0	3.4	2.8	3.4
Amortization and Depletion 15	1.4	2.3	12.7	1.2	0.2	0.4	1.0	2.2	2.9	1.8	3.2	1.7	1.4
Pensions and Other Deferred Comp. 16	1.6	4.2	0.0	0.0	1.6	0.2	0.2	0.4	1.3	0.5	0.3	1.0	1.8
Employee Benefits 17	1.8	2.3	2.1	0.0	2.1	1.8	1.8	2.1	2.9	1.7	2.7	2.3	1.8
Advertising 18	4.2	3.8	0.1	0.1	3.0	0.7	1.1	4.2	3.7	1.8	2.7	4.0	4.3
Other Expenses 19	22.8	190.3	95.4	23.6	42.8	14.3	26.4	29.8	29.7	31.5	24.4	27.5	21.6
Officers' Compensation 20	0.6	16.1	9.2	2.3	7.1	5.5	4.4	3.5	3.3	1.7	2.8	1.1	0.3
Operating Margin 21	•	•	•	•	•	•	•	•	•	5.3	2.1	2.0	•
Operating Margin Before Officers' Comp. 22	•	•	•	•	5.3	•	•	•	•	7.0	4.9	3.1	•

Selected Average Balance Sheet ($ in Thousands)

Net Receivables 23	145549	0	13	194	439	1174	2333	4593	8607	18015	46360	171811	5595292
Inventories 24	29696	0	6	212	664	1106	2169	4814	6696	15923	31149	124997	980597
Net Property, Plant and Equipment 25	59044	0	53	218	491	2179	3724	7663	12432	25779	41723	147577	2091561
Total Assets 26	640800	0	118	824	1906	6504	16469	36736	70762	162530	375247	1197181	23797358
Notes and Loans Payable 27	227875	0	264	350	1334	1390	3998	8054	17208	37161	70312	284488	8713608
All Other Liabilities 28	203216	0	73	217	1040	1332	4581	7695	16811	33150	85773	279986	7725457
Net Worth 29	209708	0	-220	257	-468	3782	7890	20987	36743	92219	219162	632707	7358292

Selected Financial Ratios (Times to 1)

Current Ratio 30	1.1	•	0.6	2.1	1.1	2.2	1.8	2.7	1.9	2.1	2.8	2.1	1.0
Quick Ratio 31	0.8	•	0.5	1.0	0.7	1.4	1.2	1.6	1.2	1.1	1.7	1.2	0.7
Net Sales to Working Capital 32	14.8	•	•	8.4	26.6	5.8	3.6	2.2	2.7	3.3	1.6	2.3	83.6
Coverage Ratio 33	4.9	12.4	•	0.1	2.7	•	•	•	•	8.1	5.1	6.7	4.9
Total Asset Turnover 34	0.4	•	1.3	3.0	1.4	1.7	1.0	0.8	0.7	0.7	0.6	0.6	0.3
Inventory Turnover 35	4.0	•	12.5	6.8	1.7	6.6	4.0	3.3	3.2	2.9	2.5	2.2	4.3
Receivables Turnover 36	1.8	•	24.4	14.6	5.0	8.7	7.1	6.1	6.0	6.5	5.6	4.0	1.6
Total Liabilities to Net Worth 37	2.1	•	•	2.2	•	0.7	1.1	0.8	0.9	0.8	0.7	0.9	2.2
Current Assets to Working Capital 38	14.2	•	•	2.0	12.1	1.8	2.3	1.6	2.1	1.9	1.5	1.9	83.4
Current Liabilities to Working Capital 39	13.2	•	•	1.0	11.1	0.8	1.3	0.6	1.1	0.9	0.5	0.9	82.4
Working Capital to Net Sales 40	0.1	•	•	0.1	0.0	0.2	0.3	0.5	0.4	0.3	0.6	0.4	0.0
Inventory to Working Capital 41	1.9	•	•	0.9	4.3	0.6	0.5	0.3	0.4	0.4	0.3	0.4	10.4
Total Receipts to Cash Flow 42	3.3	0.5	•	6.7	6.3	8.4	7.8	7.5	5.1	2.4	2.9	2.9	3.4
Cost of Goods to Cash Flow 43	1.6	0.3	•	4.0	2.6	5.5	4.4	3.9	2.2	0.9	1.1	1.1	1.7
Cash Flow to Total Debt 44	0.2	•	•	0.6	0.2	0.5	0.2	0.3	0.3	0.7	0.5	0.4	0.1

Selected Financial Factors (in Percentages)

Debt Ratio 45	67.3	•	286.5	68.8	124.5	41.9	52.1	42.9	48.1	43.3	41.6	47.2	69.1
Return on Total Assets 46	6.5	•	•	0.3	•	2.6	•	•	•	10.8	8.7	7.9	6.5
Return on Equity Before Income Taxes 47	15.7	•	71.6	•	120.4	2.8	•	•	•	16.7	12.0	12.7	16.7
Return on Equity After Income Taxes 48	10.1	•	71.6	•	120.5	0.0	•	•	•	7.0	6.9	7.8	11.1
Profit Margin (Before Income Tax) 49	13.9	9.4	•	•	•	1.0	•	•	•	12.7	12.1	11.6	14.9
Profit Margin (After Income Tax) 50	8.9	•	•	•	•	0.0	•	•	•	5.4	7.0	7.1	9.9

87

Table II

Corporations with Net Income

PHARMACEUTICAL AND MEDICINE

MONEY AMOUNTS AND SIZE OF ASSETS IN THOUSANDS OF DOLLARS

Item Description for Accounting Period 7/04 Through 6/05	Total	Zero Assets	Under 500	500 to 1,000	1,000 to 5,000	5,000 to 10,000	10,000 to 25,000	25,000 to 50,000	50,000 to 100,000	100,000 to 250,000	250,000 to 500,000	500,000 to 2,500,000	2,500,000 and over
Number of Enterprises 1	460	23	0	87	73	104	45	25	21	29	8	17	0
Revenues ($ in Thousands)													
Net Sales 2	24879533	133598	0	218923	316431	1336146	1115421	1355919	1996403	4937240	2458272	16350640	0
Interest 3	3903370	36338	0	34	129	2148	1466	2761	7893	24935	5916	142594	0
Rents 4	280064	269	0	0	366	210	116	21	573	1522	96	7832	0
Royalties 5	17633060	69338	0	0	3980	0	8365	1849	8280	20513	3089	306194	0
Other Portfolio Income 6	7118793	15	0	0	3404	954	16039	3846	4594	63532	16288	260783	0
Other Receipts 7	13948149	721074	0	357	12805	10875	14882	6731	17501	114452	71361	490416	0
Total Receipts 8	291681969	960632	0	219314	337115	1350333	1156289	1371127	2035244	5162194	2555022	17558459	0
Average Total Receipts 9	634091	41767	•	2521	4618	12984	25695	54845	96916	178007	319378	1032851	•
Operating Costs/Operating Income (%)													
Cost of Operations 10	49.6	41.4	•	59.2	29.2	65.7	56.3	48.4	36.2	35.0	37.3	36.6	•
Salaries and Wages 11	14.8	16.2	•	9.7	14.7	5.0	7.4	10.6	12.5	7.3	14.4	12.1	•
Taxes Paid 12	1.5	18.5	•	3.1	3.1	2.0	1.9	1.9	2.0	1.5	2.0	1.8	•
Interest Paid 13	3.3	0.3	•	0.9	1.3	0.3	0.8	0.7	1.0	1.1	1.2	0.8	•
Depreciation 14	3.1	4.8	•	1.9	2.0	2.2	3.3	2.8	3.0	1.9	3.1	2.1	•
Amortization and Depletion 15	1.3	0.9	•	•	0.0	0.2	0.3	0.3	1.2	0.8	1.8	1.2	•
Pensions and Other Deferred Comp. 16	1.6	6.6	•	•	2.1	0.2	0.2	0.4	0.7	0.5	0.1	0.6	•
Employee Benefits 17	1.8	2.4	•	0.0	1.2	1.5	1.2	1.5	2.2	1.2	2.5	2.1	•
Advertising 18	4.2	2.2	•	0.1	3.4	0.7	1.0	5.2	3.9	1.9	2.3	4.5	•
Other Expenses 19	21.5	465.4	•	19.4	31.9	11.5	14.6	14.8	19.1	26.0	16.5	24.8	•
Officers' Compensation 20	0.5	1.2	•	1.9	6.2	5.2	2.7	2.3	2.7	1.2	2.4	0.9	•
Operating Margin 21	•	•	•	3.7	4.7	5.3	10.3	11.3	15.7	21.6	16.2	12.5	•
Operating Margin Before Officers' Comp. 22	•	•	•	5.6	10.9	10.5	13.0	13.6	18.4	22.8	18.6	13.3	•

Selected Average Balance Sheet ($ in Thousands)

Net Receivables 23	202765	53726	23802	14241	8767	3535	1311	690	201	•	0	347416
Inventories 24	178933	49007	20312	11279	7859	2956	1201	1042	219	•	0	64536
Net Property, Plant and Equipment 25	155826	53649	21616	17835	8474	3488	1925	576	220	•	0	127658
Total Assets 26	1249994	388576	163357	76372	36893	16174	6538	2153	826	•	0	1469588
Notes and Loans Payable 27	109991	35181	27885	10268	6372	3601	1009	954	310	•	0	512527
All Other Liabilities 28	334506	57078	39850	12984	9774	4270	1257	1055	216	•	0	467471
Net Worth 29	805498	296317	95621	53119	20747	8303	4272	144	300	•	0	489590

Selected Financial Ratios (Times to 1)

Current Ratio 30	2.2	4.0	1.6	2.1	2.6	2.1	2.4	1.2	2.5	•	1.1	
Quick Ratio 31	1.2	2.5	0.9	1.3	1.6	1.3	1.4	0.8	1.2	•	0.8	
Net Sales to Working Capital 32	3.0	1.9	6.9	4.4	3.7	4.6	5.9	18.1	7.1	•	16.6	
Coverage Ratio 33	25.6	17.9	25.7	19.1	18.9	17.7	21.1	9.4	5.2	615.9	6.1	
Total Asset Turnover 34	0.8	0.8	1.0	1.2	1.5	1.5	2.0	2.0	3.0	•	0.4	
Inventory Turnover 35	2.0	2.3	2.9	3.0	3.3	4.7	7.0	1.2	6.8	•	4.2	
Receivables Turnover 36	4.4	6.7	7.2	7.4	6.6	7.8	9.6	4.5	14.4	•	1.7	
Total Liabilities to Net Worth 37	0.6	0.3	0.7	0.4	0.8	0.9	0.5	13.9	1.8	•	2.0	
Current Assets to Working Capital 38	1.9	1.3	2.7	1.9	1.6	1.9	1.7	6.2	1.6	•	15.9	
Current Liabilities to Working Capital 39	0.9	0.3	1.7	0.9	0.6	0.9	0.7	5.2	0.6	•	14.9	
Working Capital to Net Sales 40	0.3	0.5	0.1	0.2	0.3	0.2	0.2	0.1	0.1	•	0.1	
Inventory to Working Capital 41	0.4	0.3	0.8	0.5	0.5	0.6	0.6	1.6	0.8	•	2.0	
Total Receipts to Cash Flow 42	2.4	2.8	2.0	2.9	3.9	4.0	6.7	2.7	6.2	0.2	3.1	
Cost of Goods to Cash Flow 43	0.9	1.1	0.7	1.0	1.9	2.3	4.4	0.8	3.7	0.1	1.6	
Cash Flow to Total Debt 44	0.9	1.2	1.3	1.4	0.9	0.8	0.8	0.8	0.8	•	0.2	

Selected Financial Factors (in Percentages)

Debt Ratio 45	35.6	23.7	41.5	30.4	43.8	48.7	34.7	93.3	63.7	•	66.7	
Return on Total Assets 46	16.5	16.9	29.2	23.2	19.2	22.8	13.1	25.2	14.8	•	7.4	
Return on Equity Before Income Taxes 47	24.7	21.0	47.9	31.6	32.4	41.9	19.1	336.8	32.9	•	18.7	
Return on Equity After Income Taxes 48	17.9	13.9	32.5	25.2	26.7	36.7	16.0	336.1	28.4	•	12.7	
Profit Margin (Before Income Tax) 49	20.6	20.2	26.9	17.7	12.4	14.1	6.3	11.2	3.9	159.7	16.9	
Profit Margin (After Income Tax) 50	15.0	13.4	18.2	14.1	10.2	12.3	5.3	11.2	3.4	104.5	11.5	

Table I

Corporations with and without Net Income

PAINT, COATING, AND ADHESIVE

MONEY AMOUNTS AND SIZE OF ASSETS IN THOUSANDS OF DOLLARS

Item Description for Accounting Period 7/04 Through 6/05	Total	Zero Assets	Under 500	500 to 1,000	1,000 to 5,000	5,000 to 10,000	10,000 to 25,000	25,000 to 50,000	50,000 to 100,000	100,000 to 250,000	250,000 to 500,000	500,000 to 2,500,000	2,500,000 and over
Number of Enterprises **1**	912	0	445	264	0	73	62	28	14	9	4	10	3
Revenues ($ in Thousands)													
Net Sales **2**	36093641	0	0	907550	0	1130888	2026434	1549216	1253104	1873344	1495797	7880352	16171750
Interest **3**	336863	0	0	593	0	975	1455	499	2175	8638	4366	194532	121986
Rents **4**	8143	0	0	0	0	146	507	141	212	34	1340	2066	3281
Royalties **5**	402226	0	0	0	0	630	426	1171	828	0	15715	104130	279327
Other Portfolio Income **6**	518592	0	0	1599	0	2	3853	10245	613	21507	1831	143658	306040
Other Receipts **7**	143305	0	0	5	0	2766	11835	3248	10337	5754	7925	16152	71480
Total Receipts **8**	37502770	0	0	909747	0	1135407	2044510	1564520	1267269	1909277	1526974	8340890	16953864
Average Total Receipts **9**	41121	•	•	3446	•	15554	32976	55876	90519	212142	381744	834089	5651288
Operating Costs/Operating Income (%)													
Cost of Operations **10**	59.6	•	•	63.2	•	58.5	68.3	59.8	70.3	61.2	64.3	64.7	53.5
Salaries and Wages **11**	11.3	•	•	8.6	•	7.4	10.2	9.5	7.0	11.7	10.7	9.1	14.0
Taxes Paid **12**	2.1	•	•	1.7	•	4.3	1.7	1.6	2.0	1.5	1.9	2.0	2.2
Interest Paid **13**	2.8	•	•	0.5	•	1.0	0.9	0.6	0.9	0.9	3.4	5.6	2.6
Depreciation **14**	2.4	•	•	0.2	•	3.2	1.9	2.2	2.7	1.9	1.9	2.7	2.6
Amortization and Depletion **15**	0.7	•	•	0.1	•	0.0	0.2	0.3	0.2	0.9	1.3	1.1	0.7
Pensions and Other Deferred Comp. **16**	1.4	•	•	2.0	•	0.5	0.5	0.5	1.1	2.0	0.4	1.2	2.0
Employee Benefits **17**	2.1	•	•	0.2	•	3.5	1.3	1.8	1.3	1.5	1.3	2.0	2.6
Advertising **18**	1.4	•	•	0.1	•	0.4	0.9	1.4	0.8	1.3	0.7	0.8	2.0
Other Expenses **19**	14.1	•	•	10.9	•	16.7	10.5	14.3	10.4	11.9	16.0	13.2	15.5
Officers' Compensation **20**	1.2	•	•	5.8	•	4.5	2.2	2.3	1.4	1.2	0.4	0.4	0.4
Operating Margin **21**	0.8	•	•	6.8	•	1.6	1.6	5.8	2.0	4.0	•	1.7	•
Operating Margin Before Officers' Comp. **22**	2.0	•	•	12.6	•	4.4	3.7	8.0	3.4	5.2	•	•	2.1

Selected Average Balance Sheet ($ in Thousands)

Net Receivables 23	6662	289	2141	4556	8704	13097	33278	62542	127490	1016156
Inventories 24	3763	265	1385	4374	6859	11428	17414	47320	67749	476228
Net Property, Plant and Equipment 25	6897	35	2469	3441	8020	18930	28258	38758	170640	1053118
Total Assets 26	38193	755	7001	16346	35186	71518	149901	298474	1105929	5594004
Notes and Loans Payable 27	9330	284	2679	5262	7188	17166	48875	131984	397884	750762
All Other Liabilities 28	15695	306	1679	4532	9120	16109	39338	83293	337068	3020578
Net Worth 29	13168	165	2644	6553	18878	38242	61687	83197	370977	1822664

Selected Financial Ratios (Times to 1)

Current Ratio 30	1.4	2.1	1.1	1.8	2.1	1.8	1.8	1.6	1.1	1.3
Quick Ratio 31	0.8	1.0	0.8	1.0	1.3	1.0	1.0	0.9	0.6	0.8
Net Sales to Working Capital 32	10.7	9.4	37.6	6.6	5.2	6.1	7.5	7.5	25.5	11.3
Coverage Ratio 33	2.8	15.2	1.3	3.8	12.4	4.5	7.9	0.8	1.5	3.8
Total Asset Turnover 34	1.0	4.6	2.2	2.0	1.6	1.3	1.4	1.3	0.7	1.0
Inventory Turnover 35	6.3	8.2	6.5	5.1	4.8	5.5	7.3	5.1	7.5	6.1
Receivables Turnover 36	6.4	13.6	4.9	7.7	6.3	6.8	8.0	6.1	6.2	6.2
Total Liabilities to Net Worth 37	1.9	3.6	1.6	1.5	0.9	0.9	1.4	2.6	2.0	2.1
Current Assets to Working Capital 38	3.7	1.9	8.5	2.2	1.9	2.2	2.3	2.6	10.1	4.0
Current Liabilities to Working Capital 39	2.7	0.9	7.5	1.2	0.9	1.2	1.3	1.6	9.1	3.0
Working Capital to Net Sales 40	0.1	0.1	0.0	0.2	0.2	0.2	0.1	0.1	0.0	0.1
Inventory to Working Capital 41	1.1	1.0	2.0	0.9	0.7	0.8	0.8	0.8	2.7	1.1
Total Receipts to Cash Flow 42	6.6	5.9	11.7	9.5	5.2	8.0	6.6	7.6	6.9	5.9
Cost of Goods to Cash Flow 43	3.9	3.7	6.9	6.5	3.1	5.6	4.0	4.9	4.5	3.2
Cash Flow to Total Debt 44	0.2	1.0	0.3	0.4	0.7	0.3	0.4	0.2	0.2	0.2

Selected Financial Factors (in Percentages)

Debt Ratio 45	65.5	78.1	62.2	59.9	46.3	46.5	58.8	72.1	66.5	67.4
Return on Total Assets 46	8.1	34.5	3.1	6.7	12.0	5.0	9.8	3.6	6.2	9.4
Return on Equity Before Income Taxes 47	15.1	147.6	2.0	12.3	20.6	7.3	20.8	•	6.5	21.4
Return on Equity After Income Taxes 48	10.0	147.6	0.1	9.6	17.1	5.2	17.1	•	3.3	13.9
Profit Margin (Before Income Tax) 49	5.0	7.1	0.3	2.5	7.0	3.1	6.2	•	3.0	7.2
Profit Margin (After Income Tax) 50	3.3	7.1	0.0	1.9	5.8	2.2	5.1	•	1.5	4.7

Table II

Corporations with Net Income

PAINT, COATING, AND ADHESIVE

MONEY AMOUNTS AND SIZE OF ASSETS IN THOUSANDS OF DOLLARS

Item Description for Accounting Period 7/04 Through 6/05	Total	Zero Assets	Under 500	500 to 1,000	1,000 to 5,000	5,000 to 10,000	10,000 to 25,000	25,000 to 50,000	50,000 to 100,000	100,000 to 250,000	250,000 to 500,000	500,000 to 2,500,000	2,500,000 and over
Number of Enterprises **1**	680	0	88	178	286	34	44	22	9	0	0	0	0
Revenues ($ in Thousands)													
Net Sales **2**	27595120	0	68433	816051	1297348	498298	1468745	1329841	739051	0	0	0	0
Interest **3**	135772	0	0	2	1460	723	1126	232	2138	0	0	0	0
Rents **4**	7076	0	0	0	0	146	444	141	212	0	0	0	0
Royalties **5**	360749	0	0	0	0	630	324	1171	7	0	0	0	0
Other Portfolio Income **6**	390711	0	0	0	4739	2	3378	10231	164	0	0	0	0
Other Receipts **7**	82101	0	0	6	10268	2015	6586	4202	6854	0	0	0	0
Total Receipts **8**	28571529	0	68433	816059	1313815	501814	1480603	1345818	748426	0	0	0	0
Average Total Receipts **9**	42017	·	778	4585	4594	14759	33650	61174	83158	·	·	·	·
Operating Costs/Operating Income (%)													
Cost of Operations **10**	58.2	·	59.1	63.0	62.1	61.5	67.3	57.1	62.3	·	·	·	·
Salaries and Wages **11**	11.6	·	10.2	8.7	6.7	10.5	9.8	9.6	7.7	·	·	·	·
Taxes Paid **12**	2.1	·	3.0	1.7	2.0	2.2	1.6	1.6	2.5	·	·	·	·
Interest Paid **13**	1.5	·	·	0.3	0.4	1.2	0.7	0.5	0.4	·	·	·	·
Depreciation **14**	2.3	·	0.7	0.0	0.8	1.5	1.9	2.2	2.9	·	·	·	·
Amortization and Depletion **15**	0.7	·	·	0.0	0.2	0.0	0.1	0.2	0.2	·	·	·	·
Pensions and Other Deferred Comp. **16**	1.5	·	·	2.2	0.5	1.1	0.5	0.5	0.8	·	·	·	·
Employee Benefits **17**	2.0	·	3.6	0.0	2.1	1.4	1.1	1.7	1.7	·	·	·	·
Advertising **18**	1.4	·	·	0.0	0.9	0.9	0.6	1.6	0.5	·	·	·	·
Other Expenses **19**	13.5	·	14.2	9.3	11.1	11.1	10.0	14.5	12.6	·	·	·	·
Officers' Compensation **20**	1.4	·	4.4	6.4	8.4	4.2	2.1	2.5	1.7	·	·	·	·
Operating Margin **21**	3.9	·	5.0	8.4	4.9	4.5	4.2	7.9	6.6	·	·	·	·
Operating Margin Before Officers' Comp. **22**	5.2	·	9.3	14.8	13.3	8.7	6.3	10.5	8.3	·	·	·	·

Selected Average Balance Sheet ($ in Thousands)

Net Receivables **23**	6418	133	357	769	1891	4528	8453	11593
Inventories **24**	4001	127	238	486	1396	4279	6850	11417
Net Property, Plant and Equipment **25**	6277	32	24	198	2868	3535	7886	20021
Total Assets **26**	35393	301	776	1987	8000	16205	35342	67724
Notes and Loans Payable **27**	8142	52	75	227	2130	4057	4879	8582
All Other Liabilities **28**	11949	115	424	619	2184	4418	8454	12937
Net Worth **29**	15302	134	277	1141	3686	7730	22009	46204

Selected Financial Ratios (Times to 1)

Current Ratio **30**	1.5	2.1	1.7	2.1	1.6	2.1	2.5	2.3
Quick Ratio **31**	0.9	1.0	0.9	1.4	1.0	1.1	1.5	1.2
Net Sales to Working Capital **32**	8.7	5.6	14.5	5.9	9.5	5.7	4.8	4.4
Coverage Ratio **33**	6.1	•	29.6	17.6	5.4	7.8	20.2	20.3
Total Asset Turnover **34**	1.1	2.6	5.9	2.3	1.8	2.1	1.7	1.2
Inventory Turnover **35**	5.9	3.6	12.1	5.8	6.5	5.3	5.0	4.5
Receivables Turnover **36**	6.3	6.5	15.8	•	•	7.9	7.1	•
Total Liabilities to Net Worth **37**	1.3	1.2	1.8	0.7	1.2	1.1	0.6	0.5
Current Assets to Working Capital **38**	2.9	1.9	2.3	1.9	2.6	1.9	1.7	1.8
Current Liabilities to Working Capital **39**	1.9	0.9	1.3	0.9	1.6	0.9	0.7	0.8
Working Capital to Net Sales **40**	0.1	0.2	0.1	0.2	0.1	0.2	0.2	0.2
Inventory to Working Capital **41**	0.9	1.0	1.1	0.6	0.9	0.8	0.6	0.6
Total Receipts to Cash Flow **42**	5.7	5.4	5.8	6.5	6.5	7.9	4.6	5.2
Cost of Goods to Cash Flow **43**	3.3	3.2	3.7	4.0	4.0	5.3	2.6	3.2
Cash Flow to Total Debt **44**	0.4	0.9	1.6	0.8	0.5	0.5	1.0	0.7

Selected Financial Factors (in Percentages)

Debt Ratio **45**	56.8	55.5	64.3	42.6	53.9	52.3	37.7	31.8
Return on Total Assets **46**	10.9	12.8	51.5	14.8	11.7	11.8	17.0	10.0
Return on Equity Before Income Taxes **47**	21.0	28.8	139.5	24.3	20.7	21.5	26.0	13.9
Return on Equity After Income Taxes **48**	15.1	28.8	139.5	24.0	17.7	18.3	22.1	11.3
Profit Margin (Before Income Tax) **49**	7.9	5.0	8.4	6.1	5.2	5.0	9.5	7.8
Profit Margin (After Income Tax) **50**	5.7	5.0	8.4	6.0	4.5	4.2	8.0	6.3

Table I

Corporations with and without Net Income

SOAP, CLEANING COMPOUND, AND TOILET PREPARATION

MONEY AMOUNTS AND SIZE OF ASSETS IN THOUSANDS OF DOLLARS

Item Description for Accounting Period 7/04 Through 6/05	Total	Zero Assets	Under 500	500 to 1,000	1,000 to 5,000	5,000 to 10,000	10,000 to 25,000	25,000 to 50,000	50,000 to 100,000	100,000 to 250,000	250,000 to 500,000	500,000 to 2,500,000	2,500,000 and over
Number of Enterprises 1	1517	6	910	280	162	41	49	22	12	10	8	8	9
Revenues ($ in Thousands)													
Net Sales 2	109960584	416348	688974	472072	1213010	524120	1507187	1406989	1044419	1597300	3207073	10088766	87494326
Interest 3	821889	44986	0	162	399	2089	1273	2644	967	3156	3174	106005	657034
Rents 4	101862	3118	0	0	2145	120	561	229	105	207	1670	52403	41304
Royalties 5	2565324	6432	0	0	4294	0	1263	263	91	1231	17332	347552	2186865
Other Portfolio Income 6	1616220	344980	1171	56	15246	229	1636	481	951	32560	33039	277965	907904
Other Receipts 7	1575882	37418	22674	501	2031	1439	4762	23421	-1079	39910	34914	180626	1229270
Total Receipts 8	116341761	853282	712819	472791	1237125	527997	1516682	1434027	1045454	1674364	3297202	11053317	92516703
Average Total Receipts 9	76692	142214	783	1689	7637	12878	30953	65183	87121	167436	412150	1381665	10279634
Operating Costs/Operating Income (%)													
Cost of Operations 10	61.3	57.2	55.8	53.1	62.4	60.3	62.1	65.8	57.3	55.0	59.2	42.2	63.8
Salaries and Wages 11	7.1	19.7	11.7	11.5	7.1	7.1	9.7	8.2	10.2	6.8	9.0	15.2	5.8
Taxes Paid 12	1.2	2.1	2.9	2.5	2.0	2.3	1.9	1.4	2.0	1.5	1.5	1.6	1.1
Interest Paid 13	2.7	62.3	3.2	0.6	0.2	1.0	1.1	0.9	1.6	1.7	1.7	3.5	2.5
Depreciation 14	2.3	3.2	1.1	2.3	0.7	1.7	2.1	2.0	2.2	2.5	3.3	1.9	2.3
Amortization and Depletion 15	1.2	0.5	•	0.0	0.0	0.1	0.3	0.2	1.0	0.6	0.8	0.8	1.4
Pensions and Other Deferred Comp. 16	1.1	0.9	•	0.3	0.8	0.2	0.5	0.4	0.7	0.5	0.6	1.1	1.1
Employee Benefits 17	1.4	3.0	0.0	2.4	0.9	0.9	1.7	1.3	1.1	1.4	1.1	3.2	1.2
Advertising 18	5.6	8.3	0.4	0.2	1.0	1.0	1.7	4.1	4.2	10.1	6.1	6.1	5.7
Other Expenses 19	14.4	44.4	28.6	16.1	20.8	19.1	13.7	11.0	13.7	12.9	14.0	25.8	12.8
Officers' Compensation 20	0.9	15.6	9.4	7.9	3.4	3.1	2.3	2.1	3.0	1.1	0.8	1.9	0.5
Operating Margin 21	0.9	•	•	3.0	1.2	3.2	3.0	2.6	3.0	5.8	1.9	•	1.8
Operating Margin Before Officers' Comp. 22	1.8	•	•	10.9	4.5	6.3	5.3	4.7	5.9	6.9	2.7	•	2.3

Selected Average Balance Sheet ($ in Thousands)

Net Receivables 23	14544	0	60	229	974	1152	3797	8623	14243	23231	56720	131044	2162070
Inventories 24	4467	0	126	123	720	1856	3722	9423	11682	20329	46504	172464	438900
Net Property, Plant and Equipment 25	10624	0	54	67	292	2095	3915	8899	9256	28547	76448	159575	1471422
Total Assets 26	99287	0	356	631	3295	6222	16478	36584	61317	145189	346420	1410542	14608161
Notes and Loans Payable 27	35263	0	200	503	408	1123	4847	8747	17701	41634	114927	450432	5275330
All Other Liabilities 28	23892	0	144	133	719	1243	5262	9037	15014	32148	85454	413516	3439894
Net Worth 29	40132	0	13	-5	2168	3855	6370	18800	28602	71408	146040	546594	5892936

Selected Financial Ratios (Times to 1)

Current Ratio 30	1.0	•	1.3	3.3	2.8	2.7	1.5	2.1	2.1	1.9	1.5	1.3	0.9
Quick Ratio 31	0.6	•	0.4	2.2	1.4	1.3	0.8	1.1	1.3	1.1	0.7	0.5	0.6
Net Sales to Working Capital 32	•	•	13.4	4.5	4.3	5.3	9.0	5.5	5.0	5.0	8.4	14.0	•
Coverage Ratio 33	4.1	0.8	•	5.9	13.7	4.9	4.4	6.1	2.9	7.4	3.9	4.1	4.6
Total Asset Turnover 34	0.7	•	2.1	2.7	2.3	2.1	1.9	1.7	1.4	1.1	1.2	0.9	0.7
Inventory Turnover 35	9.9	•	3.4	7.3	6.5	4.2	5.1	4.5	4.3	4.3	5.1	3.1	14.1
Receivables Turnover 36	4.9	•	10.3	7.8	4.5	10.9	7.7	6.4	6.2	8.0	7.6	8.6	4.5
Total Liabilities to Net Worth 37	1.5	•	26.7	•	0.5	0.6	1.6	0.9	1.1	1.0	1.4	1.6	1.5
Current Assets to Working Capital 38	•	•	3.9	1.4	1.6	1.6	2.8	1.9	1.9	2.1	2.9	4.7	•
Current Liabilities to Working Capital 39	•	•	2.9	0.4	0.6	0.6	1.8	0.9	0.9	1.1	1.9	3.7	•
Working Capital to Net Sales 40	•	•	0.1	0.2	0.2	0.2	0.1	0.2	0.2	0.2	0.1	0.1	•
Inventory to Working Capital 41	•	•	2.7	0.3	0.3	0.8	1.1	0.7	0.6	0.7	1.1	2.0	•
Total Receipts to Cash Flow 42	5.2	•	6.4	6.3	4.8	4.8	6.6	7.2	6.6	4.8	6.0	3.6	5.4
Cost of Goods to Cash Flow 43	3.2	•	3.6	3.4	3.0	2.9	4.1	4.7	3.8	2.7	3.5	1.5	3.4
Cash Flow to Total Debt 44	0.2	•	0.3	0.4	1.4	1.1	0.5	0.5	0.4	0.4	0.3	0.4	0.2

Selected Financial Factors (in Percentages)

Debt Ratio 45	59.6	•	96.4	100.8	34.2	38.0	61.3	48.6	53.4	50.8	57.8	61.2	59.7
Return on Total Assets 46	8.0	•	•	10.1	7.0	10.0	8.7	9.5	6.6	13.5	7.6	12.6	7.5
Return on Equity Before Income Taxes 47	15.1	•	•	•	9.9	12.9	17.5	15.5	9.2	23.8	13.4	24.5	14.5
Return on Equity After Income Taxes 48	9.8	•	•	•	8.6	10.3	15.7	12.5	7.9	19.1	8.2	14.9	9.4
Profit Margin (Before Income Tax) 49	8.4	•	•	3.1	2.9	3.9	3.6	4.6	3.0	10.6	4.9	10.6	8.8
Profit Margin (After Income Tax) 50	5.4	•	3.0	3.0	2.5	3.1	3.3	3.7	2.6	8.5	3.0	6.5	5.7

91

Table II

Corporations with Net Income

SOAP, CLEANING COMPOUND, AND TOILET PREPARATION

MONEY AMOUNTS AND SIZE OF ASSETS IN THOUSANDS OF DOLLARS

Item Description for Accounting Period 7/04 Through 6/05	Total	Zero Assets	Under 500	500 to 1,000	1,000 to 5,000	5,000 to 10,000	10,000 to 25,000	25,000 to 50,000	50,000 to 100,000	100,000 to 250,000	250,000 to 500,000	500,000 to 2,500,000	2,500,000 and over
Number of Enterprises **1**	527	3	0	280	145	19	29	17	6	0	5	0	0
Revenues ($ in Thousands)													
Net Sales **2**	102667770	299132	0	472072	1065447	290503	930407	1097945	542737	0	2736792	0	0
Interest **3**	685219	34476	0	162	395	12	453	1767	274	0	2351	0	0
Rents **4**	99845	3118	0	0	947	0	321	162	105	0	1606	0	0
Royalties **5**	2474942	6271	0	0	4294	0	612	168	91	0	17332	0	0
Other Portfolio Income **6**	1578978	344980	0	56	15246	7	117	442	677	0	33039	0	0
Other Receipts **7**	1526503	30734	0	501	1113	519	3905	20808	-1126	0	22502	0	0
Total Receipts **8**	109033257	718711	0	472791	1087442	291041	935815	1121292	542758	0	2813622	0	0
Average Total Receipts **9**	206894	239570	•	1689	7500	15318	32269	65958	90460	•	562724	•	•
Operating Costs/Operating Income (%)													
Cost of Operations **10**	61.6	52.0	•	53.1	60.0	53.1	57.7	67.4	46.8	•	58.6	•	•
Salaries and Wages **11**	6.8	18.1	•	11.5	7.1	9.0	9.8	6.6	12.0	•	9.0	•	•
Taxes Paid **12**	1.2	2.5	•	2.5	2.0	1.6	1.9	1.5	2.2	•	1.6	•	•
Interest Paid **13**	2.4	79.3	•	0.6	0.1	0.8	0.5	0.8	1.0	•	0.6	•	•
Depreciation **14**	2.3	3.3	•	2.3	0.7	2.0	1.5	1.7	2.4	•	3.4	•	•
Amortization and Depletion **15**	1.2	0.2	•	0.0	0.0	0.1	0.1	0.2	0.4	•	0.5	•	•
Pensions and Other Deferred Comp. **16**	1.1	1.2	•	0.3	0.8	0.2	0.4	0.3	1.1	•	0.7	•	•
Employee Benefits **17**	1.3	4.0	•	2.4	0.9	0.2	1.4	1.4	1.3	•	0.9	•	•
Advertising **18**	5.6	10.2	•	0.2	0.5	1.2	1.7	3.9	3.5	•	6.3	•	•
Other Expenses **19**	14.1	43.7	•	16.1	22.8	18.8	14.6	8.8	15.8	•	14.2	•	•
Officers' Compensation **20**	0.7	21.5	•	7.9	3.4	2.4	2.5	2.3	4.1	•	0.9	•	•
Operating Margin **21**	1.8	•	•	3.0	1.6	10.6	8.1	5.0	9.4	•	3.3	•	•
Operating Margin Before Officers' Comp. **22**	2.5	•	•	10.9	5.0	13.0	10.6	7.4	13.5	•	4.2	•	•

Selected Average Balance Sheet ($ in Thousands)

Net Receivables 23	39809	0	•	229	•	996	1344	4019	8992	13890	•	72475
Inventories 24	11547	0	•	97	626	3100	3730	10257	10258	•	•	67279
Net Property, Plant and Equipment 25	28405	0	•	67	278	1283	3389	8291	9974	•	•	96727
Total Assets 26	260242	0	•	631	3176	6259	15149	36814	57595	•	•	366465
Notes and Loans Payable 27	88397	0	•	503	203	1621	2755	7109	13107	•	•	52710
All Other Liabilities 28	63736	0	•	133	724	1633	4394	9359	14758	•	•	110243
Net Worth 29	108109	0	•	-5	2250	3006	7999	20345	29730	•	•	203512

Selected Financial Ratios (Times to 1)

Current Ratio 30	0.9	•	3.3	3.7	2.9	2.1	2.2	2.4	•	1.8
Quick Ratio 31	0.6	•	2.2	1.9	1.3	1.2	1.2	1.5	•	0.8
Net Sales to Working Capital 32	•	1.1	4.5	3.6	4.9	5.8	5.1	4.7	•	7.8
Coverage Ratio 33	4.9	•	5.9	37.0	13.8	18.8	10.2	10.4	•	11.1
Total Asset Turnover 34	0.7	•	2.7	2.3	2.4	2.1	1.8	1.6	•	1.5
Inventory Turnover 35	10.4	•	9.2	7.0	2.6	5.0	4.2	4.1	•	4.8
Receivables Turnover 36	4.9	•	8.9	4.3	8.8	7.9	5.7	•	•	•
Total Liabilities to Net Worth 37	1.4	•	•	0.4	1.1	0.9	0.8	0.9	•	0.8
Current Assets to Working Capital 38	•	•	1.4	1.4	1.5	1.9	1.9	1.7	•	2.3
Current Liabilities to Working Capital 39	•	•	0.4	0.4	0.5	0.9	0.9	0.7	•	1.3
Working Capital to Net Sales 40	•	•	0.2	0.3	0.2	0.2	0.2	0.2	•	0.1
Inventory to Working Capital 41	•	•	0.3	0.2	0.8	0.7	0.7	0.5	•	1.0
Total Receipts to Cash Flow 42	5.0	•	6.3	4.4	3.7	4.8	6.9	4.2	•	5.5
Cost of Goods to Cash Flow 43	3.1	•	3.4	2.6	1.9	2.7	4.7	2.0	•	3.2
Cash Flow to Total Debt 44	0.3	•	0.4	1.8	1.3	0.9	0.6	0.8	•	0.6

Selected Financial Factors (in Percentages)

Debt Ratio 45	58.5	•	100.8	29.2	52.0	47.2	44.7	48.4	•	44.5
Return on Total Assets 46	8.8	•	10.1	7.9	28.4	19.4	14.0	16.3	•	10.4
Return on Equity Before Income Taxes 47	16.9	•	10.9	54.9	34.8	22.8	28.6	•	•	17.1
Return on Equity After Income Taxes 48	11.2	•	•	9.5	49.0	32.5	19.2	26.1	•	11.1
Profit Margin (Before Income Tax) 49	9.4	4.2	3.1	3.3	10.8	8.7	7.2	9.4	•	6.4
Profit Margin (After Income Tax) 50	6.2	2.9	3.0	2.9	9.6	8.1	6.0	8.6	•	4.1

Table I

Corporations with and without Net Income

CHEMICAL PRODUCT AND PREPARATION

MONEY AMOUNTS AND SIZE OF ASSETS IN THOUSANDS OF DOLLARS

Item Description for Accounting Period 7/04 Through 6/05	Total	Zero Assets	Under 500	500 to 1,000	1,000 to 5,000	5,000 to 10,000	10,000 to 25,000	25,000 to 50,000	50,000 to 100,000	100,000 to 250,000	250,000 to 500,000	500,000 to 2,500,000	2,500,000 and over
Number of Enterprises **1**	3003	25	1933	285	374	104	121	56	37	26	20	19	3
Revenues ($ in Thousands)													
Net Sales **2**	53052918	1732810	893770	529952	1634831	1153719	3110641	2833515	2969862	4778200	6452707	15779795	11183116
Interest **3**	224292	7990	1	793	1750	2317	4625	3566	6949	21787	32191	99540	42785
Rents **4**	24709	385	0	1100	621	2783	1402	76	501	676	6523	8298	2344
Royalties **5**	466972	15	0	0	157	50	3818	11008	296	13079	90035	212922	135592
Other Portfolio Income **6**	617000	23515	1	0	11143	1919	2647	30837	9944	9896	149049	261076	116974
Other Receipts **7**	913097	139593	3881	1946	4528	46548	22700	30987	27049	70187	95951	462007	7717
Total Receipts **8**	55298988	1904308	897653	533791	1653030	1207336	3145833	2909989	3014601	4893825	6826456	16823638	11488528
Average Total Receipts **9**	18415	76172	464	1873	4420	11609	25999	51964	81476	188224	341323	885455	3829509
Operating Costs/Operating Income (%)													
Cost of Operations **10**	71.0	76.5	34.9	57.7	55.2	58.3	71.3	69.9	68.6	66.7	74.0	69.2	80.7
Salaries and Wages **11**	6.9	5.2	12.2	7.5	8.2	14.1	7.3	7.6	7.5	10.1	5.9	6.4	5.4
Taxes Paid **12**	1.4	1.5	3.5	2.7	2.3	2.5	1.6	1.5	1.6	1.9	1.3	1.5	0.8
Interest Paid **13**	2.4	6.4	1.6	0.9	1.0	1.5	0.9	0.8	1.7	1.9	2.1	3.7	1.7
Depreciation **14**	3.5	3.1	4.6	1.3	2.2	2.7	2.6	3.0	3.1	3.3	4.4	4.0	3.1
Amortization and Depletion **15**	1.0	1.8	0.0	0.0	0.1	0.3	0.2	0.3	0.7	0.8	1.1	1.4	0.9
Pensions and Other Deferred Comp. **16**	0.8	1.6	0.0	0.3	0.5	0.6	0.4	0.5	0.9	0.6	0.7	0.9	1.1
Employee Benefits **17**	1.5	0.9	0.8	0.1	1.7	1.6	1.1	1.4	1.6	1.9	1.6	2.1	0.8
Advertising **18**	1.1	0.2	1.4	0.5	0.4	0.8	0.5	0.5	0.6	0.3	0.5	2.2	0.8
Other Expenses **19**	12.2	10.9	24.1	12.9	21.5	12.7	11.1	11.4	10.6	12.2	10.4	14.2	9.0
Officers' Compensation **20**	1.3	1.0	8.7	8.9	5.3	4.4	2.2	2.2	1.4	0.7	1.1	0.5	0.4
Operating Margin **21**	•	•	8.1	7.3	1.6	0.4	0.6	0.8	1.8	•	•	•	•
Operating Margin Before Officers' Comp. **22**	•	•	16.8	16.2	6.8	4.9	2.8	3.0	3.2	0.4	•	•	•

Selected Average Balance Sheet ($ in Thousands)

Net Receivables 23	3131	0	42	199	343	1258	3864	7240	14626	28494	68526	165738	777232
Inventories 24	2012	0	21	215	395	1416	3139	6640	12317	25364	31122	104159	392476
Net Property, Plant and Equipment 25	3654	0	54	89	428	2357	4237	9086	15683	33955	91039	236105	548583
Total Assets 26	17702	0	129	674	1839	7454	15474	35939	70466	146743	360754	1222931	3498674
Notes and Loans Payable 27	5799	0	120	196	603	2343	4977	9195	25043	42284	117850	456657	826482
All Other Liabilities 28	5984	0	47	204	478	1427	4094	9380	19449	47848	114164	307665	2127139
Net Worth 29	5919	0	-38	274	759	3684	6403	17364	25974	56612	128741	458608	545053

Selected Financial Ratios (Times to 1)

Current Ratio 30	1.2	•	0.6	1.8	1.9	1.4	1.7	1.7	1.5	1.6	1.3	1.3	0.9
Quick Ratio 31	0.7	•	0.6	0.9	1.2	0.8	1.0	1.0	0.8	0.9	0.9	0.7	0.4
Net Sales to Working Capital 32	13.2	•	•	8.1	8.2	9.5	6.3	6.1	6.8	7.9	9.3	9.3	•
Coverage Ratio 33	1.6	1.1	6.4	10.0	3.8	4.4	2.8	5.7	3.0	2.2	2.5	1.3	0.1
Total Asset Turnover 34	1.0	•	3.6	2.8	2.4	1.5	1.7	1.4	1.1	1.3	0.9	0.7	1.1
Inventory Turnover 35	6.2	•	7.6	5.0	6.1	4.6	5.8	5.3	4.5	4.8	7.7	5.5	7.7
Receivables Turnover 36	6.2	•	7.5	10.9	9.1	6.2	6.5	7.3	6.0	6.5	6.1	5.5	5.7
Total Liabilities to Net Worth 37	2.0	•	•	1.5	1.4	1.0	1.4	1.1	1.7	1.6	1.8	1.7	5.4
Current Assets to Working Capital 38	5.3	•	•	2.3	2.1	3.4	2.4	2.4	3.0	2.8	4.0	4.3	•
Current Liabilities to Working Capital 39	4.3	•	•	1.3	1.1	2.4	1.4	1.4	2.0	1.8	3.0	3.3	•
Working Capital to Net Sales 40	0.1	•	•	0.1	0.1	0.1	0.2	0.2	0.1	0.1	0.1	0.1	•
Inventory to Working Capital 41	1.5	•	•	1.0	0.7	1.1	0.8	0.8	1.0	1.1	1.0	1.1	•
Total Receipts to Cash Flow 42	9.1	11.0	3.6	6.1	4.8	6.5	9.1	7.5	8.2	8.2	9.4	8.1	20.4
Cost of Goods to Cash Flow 43	6.4	8.4	1.3	3.5	2.7	3.8	6.5	5.2	5.6	5.5	6.9	5.6	16.5
Cash Flow to Total Debt 44	0.2	•	0.8	0.8	0.8	0.5	0.3	0.4	0.2	0.2	0.1	0.1	0.1

Selected Financial Factors (in Percentages)

Debt Ratio 45	66.6	•	129.2	59.3	58.7	50.6	58.6	51.7	63.1	61.4	64.3	62.5	84.4
Return on Total Assets 46	3.8	•	36.0	24.6	8.6	9.8	4.5	6.1	5.6	5.2	4.7	3.2	0.1
Return on Equity Before Income Taxes 47	4.4	•	•	54.3	15.3	15.3	7.0	10.4	10.2	7.5	8.0	1.8	•
Return on Equity After Income Taxes 48	2.3	•	•	50.4	11.5	8.8	4.0	7.3	7.0	5.3	5.7	0.4	•
Profit Margin (Before Income Tax) 49	1.5	1.0	8.5	8.0	2.7	5.1	1.7	3.6	3.3	2.3	3.2	1.0	•
Profit Margin (After Income Tax) 50	0.8	0.5	8.5	7.4	2.0	2.9	1.0	2.5	2.3	1.6	2.3	0.2	•

Table II

Corporations with Net Income

CHEMICAL PRODUCT AND PREPARATION

MONEY AMOUNTS AND SIZE OF ASSETS IN THOUSANDS OF DOLLARS

Item Description for Accounting Period 7/04 Through 6/05	Total	Zero Assets	Under 500	500 to 1,000	1,000 to 5,000	5,000 to 10,000	10,000 to 25,000	25,000 to 50,000	50,000 to 100,000	100,000 to 250,000	250,000 to 500,000	500,000 to 2,500,000	2,500,000 and over
Number of Enterprises 1	2342	10	1530	285	249	68	88	44	25	19	12	12	0
Revenues ($ in Thousands)													
Net Sales 2	36895524	1576169	806109	529952	1285902	877451	2400373	2339240	2133499	3955712	3092010	17899108	0
Interest 3	168019	7518	0	793	1195	2155	3359	2713	5866	13326	27842	103252	0
Rents 4	23108	385	0	1100	617	2783	1122	34	501	499	6259	9808	0
Royalties 5	426824	12	0	0	157	50	3818	11008	281	11150	74573	325775	0
Other Portfolio Income 6	432959	704	0	0	11122	725	2344	25328	6874	9873	142175	233815	0
Other Receipts 7	747007	139592	3880	1946	3787	45977	17808	23622	18567	22035	84117	385674	0
Total Receipts 8	38693441	1724380	809989	533791	1302780	929141	2428824	2401945	2165588	4012595	3426976	18957432	0
Average Total Receipts 9	16522	172438	529	1873	5232	13664	27600	54590	86624	211189	285581	1579786	•
Operating Costs/Operating Income (%)													
Cost of Operations 10	72.0	77.2	36.1	57.7	49.8	59.3	69.7	69.4	65.5	65.2	68.2	79.3	•
Salaries and Wages 11	6.3	4.6	8.4	7.5	7.8	12.7	7.0	7.5	8.0	9.8	6.8	4.6	•
Taxes Paid 12	1.5	1.6	3.2	2.7	2.6	2.5	1.5	1.5	1.8	1.9	1.4	1.1	•
Interest Paid 13	1.8	6.5	1.7	0.9	0.8	0.7	0.7	0.6	1.0	1.2	2.1	2.0	•
Depreciation 14	3.2	3.2	5.0	1.3	2.4	2.0	2.4	2.7	3.2	3.0	5.0	3.3	•
Amortization and Depletion 15	0.6	0.4	•	0.0	0.0	0.3	0.2	0.1	0.6	0.4	1.4	0.8	•
Pensions and Other Deferred Comp. 16	0.6	1.7	•	0.3	0.5	0.7	0.4	0.5	1.1	0.6	0.5	0.5	•
Employee Benefits 17	1.6	0.6	0.9	0.1	2.0	1.7	1.1	1.3	1.7	2.0	2.4	1.6	•
Advertising 18	0.6	0.0	1.5	0.5	0.3	0.6	0.5	0.5	0.6	0.3	0.7	0.8	•
Other Expenses 19	10.7	7.6	22.4	12.9	23.0	9.7	10.0	10.9	9.8	11.8	12.3	9.2	•
Officers' Compensation 20	1.4	0.9	9.6	8.9	5.5	4.3	2.1	2.3	1.4	0.7	1.8	0.3	•
Operating Margin 21	•	•	11.2	7.3	5.2	5.6	4.6	2.6	5.4	3.2	•	•	•
Operating Margin Before Officers' Comp. 22	1.1	•	20.8	16.2	10.8	9.9	6.8	4.9	6.8	3.9	•	•	•

Selected Average Balance Sheet ($ in Thousands)

Net Receivables 23	2670	0	50	199	357	1396	3732	7880	12717	27901	54180	313549
Inventories 24	1473	0	23	166	436	1567	3229	6297	11340	23655	26714	128202
Net Property, Plant and Equipment 25	2692	0	57	89	493	1369	4197	8407	16987	36593	64900	278100
Total Assets 26	13213	0	144	674	1931	7508	15242	35472	67680	143664	351302	1500171
Notes and Loans Payable 27	3303	0	140	196	583	1226	3608	7298	15403	37205	88832	370068
All Other Liabilities 28	4019	0	29	204	598	1020	4037	9556	15855	46678	103135	482985
Net Worth 29	5891	0	-25	274	750	5262	7598	18619	36422	59781	159335	647118

Selected Financial Ratios (Times to 1)

Current Ratio 30	1.4	•	0.8	1.8	1.5	2.7	2.0	1.9	2.3	1.5	1.9	1.2
Quick Ratio 31	0.8	•	0.7	0.9	1.0	1.6	1.1	1.1	1.3	0.8	1.2	0.7
Net Sales to Working Capital 32	9.5	•	•	8.1	15.2	4.4	5.8	5.3	4.2	9.5	4.2	17.2
Coverage Ratio 33	3.8	1.8	7.8	10.0	8.8	18.6	9.9	10.1	8.0	4.9	5.4	2.5
Total Asset Turnover 34	1.2	•	3.7	2.8	2.7	1.7	1.8	1.5	1.3	1.4	0.7	1.0
Inventory Turnover 35	7.7	•	8.3	6.5	5.9	4.9	5.9	5.9	4.9	5.7	6.6	9.2
Receivables Turnover 36	6.6	•	7.3	12.6	8.5	6.3	7.4	7.4	6.4	7.2	6.0	5.8
Total Liabilities to Net Worth 37	1.2	•	•	1.5	1.6	0.4	1.0	0.9	0.9	1.4	1.2	1.3
Current Assets to Working Capital 38	3.5	•	•	2.3	3.1	1.6	2.0	2.1	1.8	3.0	2.2	6.8
Current Liabilities to Working Capital 39	2.5	•	•	1.3	2.1	0.6	1.0	1.1	0.8	2.0	1.2	5.8
Working Capital to Net Sales 40	0.1	•	•	0.1	0.1	0.2	0.2	0.2	0.2	0.1	0.2	0.1
Inventory to Working Capital 41	1.0	•	•	1.0	0.9	0.5	0.7	0.7	0.6	1.2	0.5	1.8
Total Receipts to Cash Flow 42	7.4	9.0	3.4	6.1	3.8	5.3	7.0	6.7	6.7	6.9	5.7	9.7
Cost of Goods to Cash Flow 43	5.3	6.9	1.2	3.5	1.9	3.2	4.9	4.7	4.4	4.5	3.9	7.7
Cash Flow to Total Debt 44	0.3	•	0.9	0.8	1.2	1.1	0.5	0.5	0.4	0.4	0.2	0.2

Selected Financial Factors (in Percentages)

Debt Ratio 45	55.4	•	117.6	59.3	61.2	29.9	50.2	47.5	46.2	58.4	54.6	56.9
Return on Total Assets 46	8.0	•	49.2	24.6	19.7	20.8	11.6	9.0	9.9	8.7	8.1	5.0
Return on Equity Before Income Taxes 47	13.2	•	•	54.3	44.9	28.1	20.9	15.5	16.1	16.7	14.5	6.9
Return on Equity After Income Taxes 48	10.4	•	•	50.4	39.1	21.2	17.4	11.7	12.8	13.9	11.5	4.9
Profit Margin (Before Income Tax) 49	4.9	5.1	11.7	8.0	6.5	11.5	5.8	5.4	6.9	4.8	9.0	3.0
Profit Margin (After Income Tax) 50	3.9	4.6	11.7	7.4	5.7	8.6	4.9	4.1	5.4	4.0	7.1	2.1

Table I

Corporations with and without Net Income

PLASTICS PRODUCT

MONEY AMOUNTS AND SIZE OF ASSETS IN THOUSANDS OF DOLLARS

Item Description for Accounting Period 7/04 Through 6/05	Total	Zero Assets	Under 500	500 to 1,000	1,000 to 5,000	5,000 to 10,000	10,000 to 25,000	25,000 to 50,000	50,000 to 100,000	100,000 to 250,000	250,000 to 500,000	500,000 to 2,500,000	2,500,000 and over
Number of Enterprises 1	11151	682	5451	1403	2267	480	446	179	115	78	21	24	5
Revenues ($ in Thousands)													
Net Sales 2	106574089	1292368	2148997	2731992	10218808	5637778	12108690	9443823	10771048	15941960	6460494	19968055	9850074
Interest 3	312288	2361	999	2168	3995	1846	6631	9236	17440	29810	19100	158577	60126
Rents 4	41752	1413	0	495	1033	1856	1754	2003	6525	4637	7373	9217	5446
Royalties 5	211143	1789	25533	0	0	0	1081	5991	4124	31693	13840	56751	70341
Other Portfolio Income 6	636709	44136	19555	5335	7491	38225	22800	17218	29271	206945	125749	110355	9629
Other Receipts 7	1276366	3974	61793	7001	80603	32416	61647	78793	235072	152880	95836	194293	272059
Total Receipts 8	109052347	1346041	2256877	2746991	10311930	5712121	12202603	9557064	11063480	16367925	6722392	20497248	10267675
Average Total Receipts 9	9780	1974	414	1958	4549	11900	27360	53391	96204	209845	320114	854052	2053535
Operating Costs/Operating Income (%)													
Cost of Operations 10	71.1	63.4	69.4	60.8	64.0	65.4	72.9	71.2	73.4	75.4	71.6	75.1	66.2
Salaries and Wages 11	5.9	8.3	7.7	6.3	6.5	9.0	6.0	6.0	5.3	4.6	5.6	5.2	6.8
Taxes Paid 12	1.7	1.9	2.4	2.7	2.5	2.2	1.9	1.9	1.8	1.5	1.7	1.3	1.1
Interest Paid 13	2.4	4.6	1.2	0.6	1.0	1.0	1.0	1.4	1.6	1.6	2.8	4.4	5.6
Depreciation 14	4.0	3.5	1.2	2.0	3.4	4.0	4.2	4.3	4.9	3.8	4.7	4.5	3.4
Amortization and Depletion 15	0.5	2.3	0.0	0.2	0.1	0.3	0.2	0.3	0.7	0.5	0.6	0.9	0.5
Pensions and Other Deferred Comp. 16	0.5	0.3	0.0	0.6	0.4	0.2	0.4	0.4	0.4	0.5	0.3	0.5	0.9
Employee Benefits 17	1.6	1.1	0.5	1.4	1.7	1.2	1.6	1.5	1.7	1.8	1.7	1.7	1.9
Advertising 18	0.6	0.9	0.4	0.4	0.5	2.5	0.4	0.5	0.6	0.6	0.1	0.3	1.2
Other Expenses 19	9.7	14.4	19.6	12.8	10.7	10.3	7.5	8.3	9.1	9.0	9.9	8.4	13.5
Officers' Compensation 20	1.7	2.3	6.8	6.7	4.9	2.3	1.8	1.5	1.2	0.7	0.9	0.6	0.3
Operating Margin 21	0.2	•	•	5.4	4.4	1.6	2.3	2.8	•	•	0.1	•	•
Operating Margin Before Officers' Comp. 22	1.9	•	•	12.2	9.3	3.9	4.1	4.2	0.5	0.7	1.0	•	•

Selected Average Balance Sheet ($ in Thousands)

Net Receivables 23	1532	0	42	156	603	1306	3719	8047	13702	30665	60886	117497	695909
Inventories 24	966	0	24	142	460	988	3132	5819	11510	21253	35475	81362	162007
Net Property, Plant and Equipment 25	2117	0	11	209	543	2431	5194	11387	23128	42582	98492	259539	444919
Total Assets 26	8374	0	153	727	2086	6418	15457	35265	70611	145965	349044	1034706	3768555
Notes and Loans Payable 27	3667	0	110	203	715	2000	5770	13528	27511	47607	135011	562082	1846760
All Other Liabilities 28	2771	0	321	187	569	1340	4117	9414	16840	42196	76246	250903	2115982
Net Worth 29	1936	0	-277	337	802	3079	5570	12323	26259	56162	137787	221722	-194187

Selected Financial Ratios (Times to 1)

Current Ratio 30	1.4	•	1.3	2.3	1.7	1.7	1.5	1.4	1.4	1.8	1.7	1.6	0.7
Quick Ratio 31	0.7	•	0.9	1.5	1.0	1.0	0.8	0.8	0.7	0.9	1.0	0.7	0.5
Net Sales to Working Capital 32	10.3	•	16.2	7.5	8.2	8.7	9.2	9.4	10.8	7.0	5.7	6.3	•
Coverage Ratio 33	2.1	1.2	•	10.6	6.6	3.9	4.1	3.9	2.3	2.6	2.1	1.0	1.6
Total Asset Turnover 34	1.1	•	2.6	2.7	2.2	1.8	1.8	1.5	1.3	1.4	0.9	0.8	0.5
Inventory Turnover 35	7.0	•	11.6	8.4	6.3	7.8	6.3	6.5	6.0	7.3	6.2	7.7	8.1
Receivables Turnover 36	6.8	•	9.6	11.9	8.2	10.4	7.3	7.3	6.8	7.5	6.2	6.6	3.7
Total Liabilities to Net Worth 37	3.3	•	•	1.2	1.6	1.1	1.8	1.9	1.7	1.6	1.5	3.7	•
Current Assets to Working Capital 38	3.7	•	4.5	1.8	2.4	2.4	3.0	3.2	3.7	2.3	2.4	2.6	•
Current Liabilities to Working Capital 39	2.7	•	3.5	0.8	1.4	1.4	2.0	2.2	2.7	1.3	1.4	1.6	•
Working Capital to Net Sales 40	0.1	•	0.1	0.1	0.1	0.1	0.1	0.1	0.1	0.1	0.2	0.2	•
Inventory to Working Capital 41	1.2	•	1.2	0.5	0.8	0.9	1.1	1.1	1.4	0.8	0.7	0.7	•
Total Receipts to Cash Flow 42	10.0	8.5	9.8	7.0	7.7	9.5	11.6	9.5	11.0	10.3	8.3	17.2	6.6
Cost of Goods to Cash Flow 43	7.1	5.4	6.8	4.2	4.9	6.2	8.4	6.8	8.1	7.7	5.9	12.9	4.4
Cash Flow to Total Debt 44	0.1	•	0.1	0.7	0.5	0.4	0.2	0.2	0.2	0.2	0.2	0.1	0.1

Selected Financial Factors (in Percentages)

Debt Ratio 45	76.9	•	280.7	53.7	61.5	52.0	64.0	65.1	62.8	61.5	60.5	78.6	105.2
Return on Total Assets 46	5.7	•	•	17.7	13.6	7.3	7.0	8.0	5.0	6.0	5.3	3.6	4.6
Return on Equity Before Income Taxes 47	12.7	•	6.0	34.6	30.0	11.3	14.7	17.0	7.5	9.6	7.1	0.3	•
Return on Equity After Income Taxes 48	10.1	•	6.1	33.6	29.1	10.6	13.2	14.8	5.4	8.0	5.0	•	•
Profit Margin (Before Income Tax) 49	2.6	1.0	•	6.0	5.3	3.0	3.0	4.0	2.1	2.6	3.2	0.1	3.3
Profit Margin (After Income Tax) 50	2.0	0.5	•	5.8	5.2	2.8	2.7	3.5	1.5	2.2	2.2	•	1.7

95

Table II

Corporations with Net Income

PLASTICS PRODUCT

MONEY AMOUNTS AND SIZE OF ASSETS IN THOUSANDS OF DOLLARS

Item Description for Accounting Period 7/04 Through 6/05	Total	Zero Assets	Under 500	500 to 1,000	1,000 to 5,000	5,000 to 10,000	10,000 to 25,000	25,000 to 50,000	50,000 to 100,000	100,000 to 250,000	250,000 to 500,000	500,000 to 2,500,000	2,500,000 and over
Number of Enterprises **1**	5183	270	0	944	1773	288	312	125	68	0	13	14	0
Revenues ($ in Thousands)													
Net Sales **2**	73679725	571077	0	2146534	8440294	4074081	8820697	7008926	6410832	0	4522628	10636673	0
Interest **3**	267898	1014	0	999	2998	858	4875	6328	12682	0	12636	145678	0
Rents **4**	15815	50	0	0	1	1802	1245	1395	2335	0	4079	2200	0
Royalties **5**	179724	35	0	0	0	0	828	4753	1609	0	11634	51392	0
Other Portfolio Income **6**	473669	41808	0	4500	4635	33249	18373	14670	16403	0	47358	65335	0
Other Receipts **7**	938658	6272	0	4435	76233	28633	44046	42334	194269	0	31225	131031	0
Total Receipts **8**	75555489	620256	0	2156468	8524161	4138623	8890064	7078406	6638130	0	4629560	11032309	0
Average Total Receipts **9**	14578	2297	•	2284	4808	14370	28494	56627	97620	•	356120	788022	•
Operating Costs/Operating Income (%)													
Cost of Operations **10**	68.6	60.4	•	59.2	63.0	60.5	70.3	69.7	71.4	•	69.0	72.8	•
Salaries and Wages **11**	6.1	9.4	•	6.6	6.5	10.3	6.1	6.1	5.4	•	5.5	5.1	•
Taxes Paid **12**	1.8	2.7	•	2.5	2.4	2.0	1.9	2.0	1.9	•	1.9	1.5	•
Interest Paid **13**	2.0	2.1	•	0.5	0.8	0.5	0.7	1.0	1.4	•	1.9	4.1	•
Depreciation **14**	3.7	3.2	•	1.8	2.8	3.0	3.8	4.0	4.1	•	4.7	4.8	•
Amortization and Depletion **15**	0.4	0.9	•	0.0	0.1	0.2	0.2	0.2	0.3	•	0.5	1.0	•
Pensions and Other Deferred Comp. **16**	0.5	0.1	•	0.7	0.4	0.2	0.4	0.4	0.5	•	0.4	0.6	•
Employee Benefits **17**	1.5	1.5	•	1.2	1.6	1.2	1.5	1.5	1.6	•	1.6	1.2	•
Advertising **18**	0.7	0.7	•	0.4	0.5	3.4	0.4	0.4	0.7	•	0.1	0.2	•
Other Expenses **19**	9.5	10.7	•	11.5	10.1	10.9	7.3	7.2	8.4	•	9.1	9.4	•
Officers' Compensation **20**	1.6	2.3	•	7.5	5.1	2.0	2.0	1.5	1.1	•	0.5	0.2	•
Operating Margin **21**	3.5	6.2	•	7.9	6.6	5.8	5.4	6.1	3.5	•	4.7	•	•
Operating Margin Before Officers' Comp. **22**	5.2	8.4	•	15.5	11.7	7.8	7.4	7.6	4.6	•	5.2	•	•

Selected Average Balance Sheet ($ in Thousands)

Net Receivables 23	1899	0	•	153	562	1538	3858	8268	14117	•	63707	120448	•
Inventories 24	1364	0	•	121	423	1043	3153	5879	12829	•	36588	86612	•
Net Property, Plant and Equipment 25	2780	0	•	235	472	2081	4900	11056	21487	•	101477	200205	•
Total Assets 26	12272	0	•	763	1997	6201	15506	35330	69701	•	350861	1110084	•
Notes and Loans Payable 27	4961	0	•	153	583	1045	4445	10512	20651	•	109690	594384	•
All Other Liabilities 28	3831	0	•	154	504	1067	3507	8787	15969	•	61473	214513	•
Net Worth 29	3480	0	•	457	910	4089	7554	16031	33081	•	179697	301186	•

Selected Financial Ratios (Times to 1)

Current Ratio 30	1.5	•	•	3.2	1.9	2.4	1.9	1.6	1.7	•	2.4	1.5	•
Quick Ratio 31	0.8	•	•	2.0	1.2	1.5	1.1	1.0	0.9	•	1.5	0.5	•
Net Sales to Working Capital 32	8.4	•	•	6.5	7.6	6.4	6.6	7.5	6.8	•	4.4	5.9	•
Coverage Ratio 33	4.1	8.1	•	19.5	10.1	17.0	9.4	8.0	6.2	•	4.9	1.8	•
Total Asset Turnover 34	1.2	•	•	3.0	2.4	2.3	1.8	1.6	1.4	•	1.0	0.7	•
Inventory Turnover 35	7.2	•	•	11.1	7.1	8.2	6.3	6.6	5.2	•	6.6	6.4	•
Receivables Turnover 36	7.9	•	•	17.0	9.2	11.4	7.5	7.5	6.4	•	6.5	4.7	•
Total Liabilities to Net Worth 37	2.5	•	•	0.7	1.2	0.5	1.1	1.2	1.1	•	1.0	2.7	•
Current Assets to Working Capital 38	2.9	•	•	1.5	2.1	1.7	2.2	2.5	2.5	•	1.7	3.0	•
Current Liabilities to Working Capital 39	1.9	•	•	0.5	1.1	0.7	1.2	1.5	1.5	•	0.7	2.0	•
Working Capital to Net Sales 40	0.1	•	•	0.2	0.1	0.2	0.2	0.1	0.1	•	0.2	0.2	•
Inventory to Working Capital 41	0.9	•	•	0.5	0.7	0.6	0.8	0.9	0.9	•	0.5	0.7	•
Total Receipts to Cash Flow 42	7.4	4.6	•	6.1	6.7	6.5	8.6	7.9	7.4	•	7.1	10.3	•
Cost of Goods to Cash Flow 43	5.1	2.8	•	3.6	4.2	3.9	6.0	5.5	5.3	•	4.9	7.5	•
Cash Flow to Total Debt 44	0.2	•	•	1.2	0.6	1.0	0.4	0.4	0.3	•	0.3	0.1	•

Selected Financial Factors (in Percentages)

Debt Ratio 45	71.6	•	•	40.2	54.4	34.1	51.3	54.6	52.5	•	48.8	72.9	•
Return on Total Assets 46	9.6	•	•	26.4	20.1	18.0	12.5	12.8	11.4	•	9.1	5.2	•
Return on Equity Before Income Taxes 47	25.5	•	•	41.9	39.7	25.7	22.9	24.7	20.2	•	14.0	8.7	•
Return on Equity After Income Taxes 48	22.4	•	•	40.8	38.7	24.7	21.4	22.2	17.3	•	11.4	6.9	•
Profit Margin (Before Income Tax) 49	6.2	14.7	•	8.4	7.6	7.4	6.1	7.1	7.1	•	7.3	3.5	•
Profit Margin (After Income Tax) 50	5.5	13.4	•	8.2	7.4	7.1	5.7	6.4	6.1	•	5.9	2.7	•

Table I

Corporations with and without Net Income

RUBBER PRODUCT

MONEY AMOUNTS AND SIZE OF ASSETS IN THOUSANDS OF DOLLARS

Item Description for Accounting Period 7/04 Through 6/05	Total	Zero Assets	Under 500	500 to 1,000	1,000 to 5,000	5,000 to 10,000	10,000 to 25,000	25,000 to 50,000	50,000 to 100,000	100,000 to 250,000	250,000 to 500,000	500,000 to 2,500,000	2,500,000 and over
Number of Enterprises **1**	771	29	87	54	360	98	74	24	21	6	7	6	4
Revenues ($ in Thousands)													
Net Sales **2**	50867914	90990	137591	115353	3196065	1549305	2195747	1190421	2301502	777619	2819044	9305611	27188666
Interest **3**	293531	300	0	75	534	502	1512	2708	1108	3713	22042	129785	131252
Rents **4**	33053	94	0	0	0	0	686	1666	549	1769	1409	6907	19973
Royalties **5**	194610	0	0	0	0	0	1	409	488	3745	1406	38791	149770
Other Portfolio Income **6**	213929	7687	7659	0	547	5206	6245	669	7983	1537	27298	57007	92093
Other Receipts **7**	589203	4443	2648	325	8779	6047	17327	3978	12960	10129	57392	357150	108024
Total Receipts **8**	52192240	103514	147898	115753	3205925	1561060	2221518	1199851	2324590	798512	2928591	9895251	27689778
Average Total Receipts **9**	67694	3569	1700	2144	8905	15929	30021	49994	110695	133085	418370	1649208	6922444
Operating Costs/Operating Income (%)													
Cost of Operations **10**	74.2	81.1	49.9	79.8	69.8	68.3	73.4	72.7	75.3	66.5	71.6	77.3	74.6
Salaries and Wages **11**	5.6	8.8	21.2	4.9	8.0	10.1	6.8	5.8	4.4	8.2	5.8	8.2	4.0
Taxes Paid **12**	0.9	4.4	5.6	1.5	1.6	1.5	2.1	1.9	1.7	2.0	1.3	0.8	0.6
Interest Paid **13**	1.2	1.7	4.6	0.7	0.6	0.2	1.3	2.7	2.0	2.5	2.9	2.3	0.5
Depreciation **14**	2.4	3.3	0.9	1.7	1.1	3.1	3.0	3.1	3.4	2.6	1.7	3.7	2.0
Amortization and Depletion **15**	0.2	0.2	•	•	0.0	0.0	0.3	0.4	0.7	1.6	1.0	0.4	0.1
Pensions and Other Deferred Comp. **16**	0.7	0.5	0.0	•	0.5	0.3	0.5	0.4	0.5	0.9	2.1	0.4	0.7
Employee Benefits **17**	2.6	1.1	3.2	•	1.7	0.7	1.8	2.4	2.1	3.1	2.3	4.2	2.5
Advertising **18**	1.0	0.4	0.0	•	1.3	0.1	0.3	0.5	0.6	0.5	1.0	0.6	1.3
Other Expenses **19**	11.6	9.4	7.0	7.6	9.4	3.7	10.0	8.2	7.0	11.3	11.9	6.6	14.6
Officers' Compensation **20**	0.8	5.5	14.3	2.9	4.9	3.3	1.8	1.1	0.9	0.9	0.6	0.4	0.1
Operating Margin **21**	•	•	•	0.8	1.3	8.8	•	0.8	1.4	•	•	•	•
Operating Margin Before Officers' Comp. **22**	•	•	7.6	3.7	6.2	12.1	0.4	1.9	2.2	0.8	•	•	•

Selected Average Balance Sheet ($ in Thousands)

Net Receivables 23	10185	0	127	248	1045	1821	3842	7405	13349	15207	51840	228557	1173799
Inventories 24	8142	0	72	278	984	563	3584	6685	11029	20817	52967	196117	879227
Net Property, Plant and Equipment 25	13224	0	30	103	581	2064	5026	10143	19108	20271	69852	330330	1541781
Total Assets 26	55659	0	232	682	3034	6463	16666	32280	68701	139201	343546	1397739	6513229
Notes and Loans Payable 27	17366	0	1034	147	897	620	5406	19065	23067	53986	149272	254624	2167176
All Other Liabilities 28	24670	0	109	180	952	2033	5547	8509	21672	22213	102879	560907	3292744
Net Worth 29	13622	0	-911	355	1185	3810	5713	4706	23962	63001	91395	582207	1053308

Selected Financial Ratios (Times to 1)

Current Ratio 30	1.6	.	1.9	2.2	1.6	1.7	1.6	1.3	1.6	1.8	1.2	1.2	1.7
Quick Ratio 31	0.9	.	1.2	1.0	0.8	1.4	0.9	0.7	0.9	0.8	0.6	0.7	1.1
Net Sales to Working Capital 32	7.8	.	17.0	6.8	10.3	9.3	8.9	11.7	9.5	5.6	24.2	14.7	6.0
Coverage Ratio 33	2.3	.	1.2	2.6	3.8	52.1	0.8	1.6	2.2	2.0	1.7	1.9	2.8
Total Asset Turnover 34	1.2	.	6.8	3.1	2.9	2.4	1.8	1.5	1.6	0.9	1.2	1.1	1.0
Inventory Turnover 35	6.0	.	10.9	6.1	6.3	19.2	6.1	5.4	7.5	4.1	5.4	6.1	5.8
Receivables Turnover 36	6.8	.	12.7	8.6	7.7	12.5	7.7	6.6	7.9	11.3	8.5	7.0	6.2
Total Liabilities to Net Worth 37	3.1	.	.	0.9	1.6	0.7	1.9	5.9	1.9	1.2	2.8	1.4	5.2
Current Assets to Working Capital 38	2.8	.	2.2	1.8	2.6	2.4	2.8	4.2	2.7	2.2	7.5	5.2	2.4
Current Liabilities to Working Capital 39	1.8	.	1.2	0.8	1.6	1.4	1.8	3.2	1.7	1.2	6.5	4.2	1.4
Working Capital to Net Sales 40	0.1	.	0.1	0.1	0.1	0.1	0.1	0.1	0.1	0.2	0.0	0.1	0.2
Inventory to Working Capital 41	1.0	.	0.7	0.9	1.2	0.4	1.1	1.7	1.0	1.1	3.3	1.8	0.8
Total Receipts to Cash Flow 42	8.8	24.2	23.1	24.8	11.0	8.3	17.4	12.3	12.5	8.9	8.5	15.5	7.0
Cost of Goods to Cash Flow 43	6.5	19.6	11.5	19.8	7.7	5.7	12.8	9.0	9.4	5.9	6.1	12.0	5.2
Cash Flow to Total Debt 44	0.2	.	0.1	0.3	0.4	0.7	0.2	0.1	0.2	0.2	0.2	0.1	0.2

Selected Financial Factors (in Percentages)

Debt Ratio 45	75.5	.	492.7	47.9	61.0	41.1	65.7	85.4	65.1	54.7	73.4	58.3	83.8
Return on Total Assets 46	3.2	.	36.7	5.8	6.3	23.9	1.7	6.6	7.0	4.7	5.6	4.7	1.5
Return on Equity Before Income Taxes 47	7.4	.	.	6.9	11.9	39.7	.	16.8	10.9	5.3	8.4	5.2	5.9
Return on Equity After Income Taxes 48	6.0	.	.	5.9	10.1	37.7	.	9.9	8.2	3.7	7.0	3.2	5.8
Profit Margin (Before Income Tax) 49	1.5	.	0.8	1.1	1.6	9.6	.	1.6	2.4	2.6	1.9	2.0	0.9
Profit Margin (After Income Tax) 50	1.2	.	0.8	1.0	1.4	9.1	.	0.9	1.8	1.8	1.6	1.2	0.9

Table II

Corporations with Net Income

RUBBER PRODUCT

MONEY AMOUNTS AND SIZE OF ASSETS IN THOUSANDS OF DOLLARS

Item Description for Accounting Period 7/04 Through 6/05	Total	Zero Assets	Under 500	500 to 1,000	1,000 to 5,000	5,000 to 10,000	10,000 to 25,000	25,000 to 50,000	50,000 to 100,000	100,000 to 250,000	250,000 to 500,000	500,000 to 2,500,000	2,500,000 and over
Number of Enterprises **1**	545	26	0	54	271	98	46	17	16	0	3	0	0
Revenues ($ in Thousands)													
Net Sales **2**	34847053	52586	0	115353	2953552	1549305	1484838	895992	1926050	0	825487	0	0
Interest **3**	213302	300	0	75	444	502	561	2600	884	0	4006	0	0
Rents **4**	31201	61	0	0	0	0	285	1634	530	0	804	0	0
Royalties **5**	191090	0	0	0	0	0	1	7	474	0	904	0	0
Other Portfolio Income **6**	171634	5246	0	0	547	5206	3889	667	6312	0	20384	0	0
Other Receipts **7**	513596	3307	0	325	8624	6047	11710	2437	13862	0	27938	0	0
Total Receipts **8**	35967876	61500	0	115753	2963167	1561060	1501284	903337	1948112	0	879523	0	0
Average Total Receipts **9**	65996	2365	•	2144	10934	15929	32637	53137	121757	•	293174	•	•
Operating Costs/Operating Income (%)													
Cost of Operations **10**	70.9	80.7	•	79.8	70.0	68.3	69.6	68.9	75.6	•	65.8	•	•
Salaries and Wages **11**	6.8	8.6	•	4.9	7.3	10.1	7.3	6.4	3.9	•	6.4	•	•
Taxes Paid **12**	1.0	1.7	•	1.5	1.5	1.5	2.2	1.8	1.6	•	1.3	•	•
Interest Paid **13**	1.1	1.1	•	0.7	0.3	0.2	0.7	1.6	1.6	•	3.2	•	•
Depreciation **14**	2.8	2.0	•	1.7	0.6	3.1	2.7	2.5	3.5	•	1.1	•	•
Amortization and Depletion **15**	0.3	0.4	•	•	0.0	0.0	0.2	0.4	0.6	•	2.9	•	•
Pensions and Other Deferred Comp. **16**	0.7	0.6	•	•	0.5	0.3	0.5	0.4	0.4	•	0.5	•	•
Employee Benefits **17**	3.4	0.9	•	•	1.7	0.7	2.0	2.7	2.1	•	0.8	•	•
Advertising **18**	1.4	0.5	•	•	1.4	0.1	0.3	0.7	0.6	•	1.8	•	•
Other Expenses **19**	10.4	8.7	•	7.6	8.6	3.7	7.9	7.7	6.7	•	10.5	•	•
Officers' Compensation **20**	0.9	2.4	•	2.9	4.9	3.3	1.9	1.1	0.7	•	0.6	•	•
Operating Margin **21**	0.3	•	•	0.8	3.0	8.8	4.8	5.8	2.7	•	5.1	•	•
Operating Margin Before Officers' Comp. **22**	1.2	•	•	3.7	8.0	12.1	6.7	6.9	3.5	•	5.7	•	•

Selected Average Balance Sheet ($ in Thousands)

Net Receivables 23	10175	0	•	248	1311	1821	4158	7807	14491	•	30203
Inventories 24	6283	0	•	284	1117	510	3943	7260	10772	•	29739
Net Property, Plant and Equipment 25	11708	0	•	103	534	2064	4643	8798	20410	•	24266
Total Assets 26	49366	0	•	682	3389	6463	16311	31923	71956	•	309544
Notes and Loans Payable 27	12320	0	•	147	790	620	3755	13053	23147	•	143880
All Other Liabilities 28	20124	0	•	180	1054	2033	4421	8768	23045	•	49590
Net Worth 29	16922	0	•	355	1545	3810	8136	10102	25763	•	116073

Selected Financial Ratios (Times to 1)

Current Ratio 30	1.6	•	•	2.2	1.8	1.7	1.8	1.6	1.6	•	1.7
Quick Ratio 31	1.0	•	•	1.0	1.0	1.4	1.0	0.8	0.9	•	0.9
Net Sales to Working Capital 32	7.7	•	•	6.8	9.0	9.3	7.4	7.4	9.7	•	9.1
Coverage Ratio 33	4.4	9.6	•	2.6	10.9	52.1	9.4	5.1	3.5	•	4.8
Total Asset Turnover 34	1.3	•	•	3.1	3.2	2.4	2.0	1.7	1.7	•	0.9
Inventory Turnover 35	7.2	•	•	6.0	6.8	21.2	5.7	5.0	8.4	•	6.1
Receivables Turnover 36	7.5	•	•	•	8.5	13.1	7.6	6.8	9.0	•	•
Total Liabilities to Net Worth 37	1.9	•	•	0.9	1.2	0.7	1.0	2.2	1.8	•	1.7
Current Assets to Working Capital 38	2.6	•	•	1.8	2.3	2.4	2.3	2.7	2.7	•	2.4
Current Liabilities to Working Capital 39	1.6	•	•	0.8	1.3	1.4	1.3	1.7	1.7	•	1.4
Working Capital to Net Sales 40	0.1	•	•	0.1	0.1	0.1	0.1	0.1	0.1	•	0.1
Inventory to Working Capital 41	0.9	•	•	0.9	1.0	0.4	0.9	1.2	1.0	•	1.0
Total Receipts to Cash Flow 42	8.2	7.1	•	24.8	9.7	8.3	8.6	8.0	10.8	•	4.7
Cost of Goods to Cash Flow 43	5.8	5.7	•	19.8	6.8	5.7	6.0	5.5	8.1	•	3.1
Cash Flow to Total Debt 44	0.2	•	•	0.3	0.6	0.7	0.5	0.3	0.2	•	0.3

Selected Financial Factors (in Percentages)

Debt Ratio 45	65.7	•	•	47.9	54.4	41.1	50.1	68.4	64.2	•	62.5
Return on Total Assets 46	6.1	•	•	5.8	11.8	23.9	13.0	13.5	9.1	•	13.6
Return on Equity Before Income Taxes 47	13.9	•	•	6.9	23.6	39.7	23.3	34.4	18.1	•	28.7
Return on Equity After Income Taxes 48	12.4	•	•	5.9	21.8	37.7	21.1	29.8	14.9	•	26.1
Profit Margin (Before Income Tax) 49	3.7	9.4	•	1.1	3.3	9.6	5.9	6.6	3.9	•	12.1
Profit Margin (After Income Tax) 50	3.3	8.9	•	1.0	3.1	9.1	5.3	5.7	3.2	•	11.0

Table I

Corporations with and without Net Income

CLAY, REFRACTORY AND OTHER NONMETALLIC MINERAL PRODUCT

MONEY AMOUNTS AND SIZE OF ASSETS IN THOUSANDS OF DOLLARS

Item Description for Accounting Period 7/04 Through 6/05	Total	Zero Assets	Under 500	500 to 1,000	1,000 to 5,000	5,000 to 10,000	10,000 to 25,000	25,000 to 50,000	50,000 to 100,000	100,000 to 250,000	250,000 to 500,000	500,000 to 2,500,000	2,500,000 and over
Number of Enterprises 1	2829	430	1318	248	661	38	72	28	13	15	0	6	0
Revenues ($ in Thousands)													
Net Sales 2	19992097	528773	1031217	708305	3086365	458656	1503005	1339675	932140	2350767	0	8053195	0
Interest 3	211719	5091	1667	1376	644	91	1362	1725	1260	3672	0	194832	0
Rents 4	27316	3	0	4	0	0	883	19	2097	692	0	23618	0
Royalties 5	274193	0	0	0	4183	6817	1226	15	1122	1479	0	259352	0
Other Portfolio Income 6	123142	10460	16992	83	208	363	9290	1350	960	18968	0	64467	0
Other Receipts 7	403670	17002	-2681	376	42688	2297	25711	6420	49152	39986	0	222716	0
Total Receipts 8	21032137	561329	1047195	710144	3134088	468224	1541477	1349204	986731	2415564	0	8818180	0
Average Total Receipts 9	7434	1305	795	2863	4741	12322	21409	48186	75902	161038	·	1469697	·
Operating Costs/Operating Income (%)													
Cost of Operations 10	68.2	64.8	64.1	53.9	67.9	72.1	69.5	64.6	75.4	68.8	·	69.4	·
Salaries and Wages 11	7.2	4.1	6.3	6.5	7.0	6.9	6.8	7.0	6.8	7.5	·	7.8	·
Taxes Paid 12	1.9	2.7	1.9	3.5	2.5	2.2	2.3	2.1	2.0	2.0	·	1.3	·
Interest Paid 13	2.6	1.8	0.2	0.3	0.9	1.4	1.0	1.1	1.2	1.6	·	4.9	·
Depreciation 14	4.1	6.9	1.2	2.0	2.6	4.3	3.5	4.6	6.4	5.5	·	4.4	·
Amortization and Depletion 15	0.6	0.0	0.0	0.0	0.3	0.2	0.3	0.3	0.5	1.4	·	0.8	·
Pensions and Other Deferred Comp. 16	1.3	0.8	0.3	1.1	0.2	0.6	0.5	0.9	0.7	0.6	·	2.5	·
Employee Benefits 17	1.7	0.6	0.3	0.9	1.0	1.8	1.8	2.3	1.8	2.1	·	2.0	·
Advertising 18	0.7	0.7	0.1	0.6	0.6	0.5	0.4	0.6	0.8	0.5	·	0.9	·
Other Expenses 19	11.0	7.8	9.9	18.9	8.4	10.8	9.0	8.1	5.4	7.2	·	14.2	·
Officers' Compensation 20	2.5	1.6	16.2	12.6	2.7	5.7	2.5	2.1	1.3	0.9	·	0.4	·
Operating Margin 21	·	8.2	·	·	5.9	·	2.4	6.4	·	1.7	·	·	·
Operating Margin Before Officers' Comp. 22	0.8	9.8	15.6	12.4	8.6	·	4.9	8.5	·	2.6	·	·	·

Selected Average Balance Sheet ($ in Thousands)

Net Receivables 23	2951	0	20	247	394	2053	3012	6018	9938	37177	•	1141951
Inventories 24	728	0	12	45	456	3978	3264	7098	12418	24183	•	101208
Net Property, Plant and Equipment 25	1721	0	19	182	568	1768	4631	13283	29466	62816	•	387534
Total Assets 26	12599	0	157	669	1926	7448	15401	35668	65493	179314	•	4677734
Notes and Loans Payable 27	4456	0	109	184	633	2525	4275	9558	18466	55121	•	1710209
All Other Liabilities 28	4877	0	6	230	394	2021	3925	5755	11711	41294	•	2030138
Net Worth 29	3265	0	42	255	899	2902	7201	20355	35316	82899	•	937387

Selected Financial Ratios (Times to 1)

Current Ratio 30	1.4	•	27.8	1.8	2.2	1.7	1.8	2.5	1.8	2.0	•	1.2
Quick Ratio 31	0.8	•	23.0	1.5	1.2	0.8	0.9	1.2	0.9	1.1	•	0.7
Net Sales to Working Capital 32	4.5	•	6.5	15.8	7.7	6.4	5.7	4.2	5.8	3.7	•	3.3
Coverage Ratio 33	2.4	9.1	5.0	1.4	9.5	•	6.0	7.5	4.1	3.8	•	1.3
Total Asset Turnover 34	0.6	•	5.0	4.3	2.4	1.6	1.4	1.3	1.1	0.9	•	0.3
Inventory Turnover 35	6.6	•	42.0	34.6	7.0	2.2	4.4	4.4	4.4	4.5	•	9.2
Receivables Turnover 36	2.5	•	43.0	•	13.1	4.8	7.0	8.7	7.2	5.2	•	1.2
Total Liabilities to Net Worth 37	2.9	•	2.8	1.6	1.1	1.6	1.1	0.8	0.9	1.2	•	4.0
Current Assets to Working Capital 38	3.7	•	1.0	2.3	1.8	2.5	2.3	1.7	2.2	2.0	•	5.2
Current Liabilities to Working Capital 39	2.7	•	0.0	1.3	0.8	1.5	1.3	0.7	1.2	1.0	•	4.2
Working Capital to Net Sales 40	0.2	•	0.2	0.1	0.1	0.2	0.2	0.2	0.2	0.3	•	0.3
Inventory to Working Capital 41	0.5	•	0.1	0.2	0.8	1.3	0.9	0.7	0.9	0.7	•	0.3
Total Receipts to Cash Flow 42	8.8	5.2	12.0	7.2	8.6	50.7	8.3	7.3	14.2	10.3	•	8.4
Cost of Goods to Cash Flow 43	6.0	3.3	7.7	3.9	5.9	36.6	5.7	4.7	10.7	7.1	•	5.8
Cash Flow to Total Debt 44	0.1	•	0.6	1.0	0.5	0.1	0.3	0.4	0.2	0.2	•	0.0

Selected Financial Factors (in Percentages)

Debt Ratio 45	74.1	•	73.4	61.9	53.3	61.0	53.2	42.9	46.1	53.8	•	80.0
Return on Total Assets 46	3.5	•	5.7	1.5	20.2	•	8.4	10.9	5.5	5.4	•	1.8
Return on Equity Before Income Taxes 47	7.7	•	17.3	1.0	38.7	•	15.0	16.6	7.8	8.6	•	1.9
Return on Equity After Income Taxes 48	5.8	•	17.0	0.6	36.0	•	13.1	13.6	5.9	5.5	•	0.7
Profit Margin (Before Income Tax) 49	3.6	14.2	0.9	0.1	7.4	•	5.2	7.0	3.8	4.5	•	1.3
Profit Margin (After Income Tax) 50	2.7	9.7	0.9	0.1	6.9	•	4.5	5.8	2.9	2.9	•	0.5

99

Table II
Corporations with Net Income

CLAY, REFRACTORY AND OTHER NONMETALLIC MINERAL PRODUCT

MONEY AMOUNTS AND SIZE OF ASSETS IN THOUSANDS OF DOLLARS

Item Description for Accounting Period 7/04 Through 6/05	Total	Zero Assets	Under 500	500 to 1,000	1,000 to 5,000	5,000 to 10,000	10,000 to 25,000	25,000 to 50,000	50,000 to 100,000	100,000 to 250,000	250,000 to 500,000	500,000 to 2,500,000	2,500,000 and over
Number of Enterprises 1	1756	0	1051	85	457	0	51	24	0	0	0	0	0
Revenues ($ in Thousands)													
Net Sales 2	11425960	0	1030528	369135	2517947	0	1168220	1218075	0	0	0	0	0
Interest 3	68147	0	1667	1115	498	0	605	603	0	0	0	0	0
Rents 4	3338	0	0	4	0	0	484	19	0	0	0	0	0
Royalties 5	23164	0	0	0	4183	0	1223	15	0	0	0	0	0
Other Portfolio Income 6	111492	0	16992	0	123	0	7444	1261	0	0	0	0	0
Other Receipts 7	338569	0	1465	236	42360	0	22554	5347	0	0	0	0	0
Total Receipts 8	11970670	0	1050652	370490	2565111	0	1200530	1225320	0	0	0	0	0
Average Total Receipts 9	6817	·	1000	4359	5613	·	23540	51055	·	·	·	·	·
Operating Costs/Operating Income (%)													
Cost of Operations 10	65.5	·	64.1	44.9	65.7	·	67.4	64.1	·	·	·	·	·
Salaries and Wages 11	6.8	·	6.3	6.3	6.5	·	6.5	7.0	·	·	·	·	·
Taxes Paid 12	2.2	·	1.7	3.4	2.6	·	2.2	2.0	·	·	·	·	·
Interest Paid 13	1.7	·	0.2	0.0	0.9	·	0.8	0.9	·	·	·	·	·
Depreciation 14	3.8	·	1.2	0.9	2.7	·	3.1	4.1	·	·	·	·	·
Amortization and Depletion 15	0.6	·	0.0	0.0	0.1	·	0.3	0.3	·	·	·	·	·
Pensions and Other Deferred Comp. 16	0.6	·	0.3	2.1	0.2	·	0.5	1.0	·	·	·	·	·
Employee Benefits 17	1.4	·	0.3	0.8	0.6	·	1.8	2.1	·	·	·	·	·
Advertising 18	0.5	·	0.1	0.9	0.8	·	0.4	0.7	·	·	·	·	·
Other Expenses 19	9.5	·	9.8	21.4	8.9	·	8.0	7.6	·	·	·	·	·
Officers' Compensation 20	3.8	·	16.2	19.1	3.2	·	2.5	2.1	·	·	·	·	·
Operating Margin 21	3.5	·	·	0.1	7.9	·	6.5	8.1	·	·	·	·	·
Operating Margin Before Officers' Comp. 22	7.3	·	15.9	19.3	11.0	·	8.9	10.3	·	·	·	·	·

Selected Average Balance Sheet ($ in Thousands)

Net Receivables 23	1023	25	258	502	3081	6369
Inventories 24	654	3	60	402	2993	6598
Net Property, Plant and Equipment 25	1534	23	74	727	4403	12457
Total Assets 26	5434	185	779	2195	15725	36233
Notes and Loans Payable 27	1844	51	8	724	3699	9298
All Other Liabilities 28	1234	7	440	508	3355	5942
Net Worth 29	2356	128	331	963	8671	20994

Selected Financial Ratios (Times to 1)

Current Ratio 30	2.0	30.7	1.2	2.0	2.1	2.5
Quick Ratio 31	1.2	27.1	1.0	1.2	1.1	1.3
Net Sales to Working Capital 32	5.5	6.9	52.4	8.4	5.0	4.2
Coverage Ratio 33	5.9	8.1	46.4	12.3	13.2	11.1
Total Asset Turnover 34	1.2	5.3	5.6	2.5	1.5	1.4
Inventory Turnover 35	6.5	186.3	32.6	9.0	5.2	4.9
Receivables Turnover 36	8.5	55.6	15.1	13.6	8.4	9.5
Total Liabilities to Net Worth 37	1.3	0.4	1.4	1.3	0.8	0.7
Current Assets to Working Capital 38	2.0	1.0	6.3	2.0	1.9	1.7
Current Liabilities to Working Capital 39	1.0	0.0	5.3	1.0	0.9	0.7
Working Capital to Net Sales 40	0.2	0.1	0.0	0.1	0.2	0.2
Inventory to Working Capital 41	0.7	0.0	0.7	0.8	0.8	0.7
Total Receipts to Cash Flow 42	6.3	11.1	5.7	6.0	6.5	6.7
Cost of Goods to Cash Flow 43	4.1	7.1	2.6	3.9	4.4	4.3
Cash Flow to Total Debt 44	0.3	1.5	1.7	0.7	0.5	0.5

Selected Financial Factors (in Percentages)

Debt Ratio 45	56.6	31.0	57.5	56.1	44.9	42.1
Return on Total Assets 46	12.1	9.8	2.9	26.6	14.9	13.4
Return on Equity Before Income Taxes 47	23.1	12.5	6.8	55.6	25.0	21.0
Return on Equity After Income Taxes 48	18.9	12.4	5.8	52.0	22.8	17.7
Profit Margin (Before Income Tax) 49	8.4	1.6	0.5	9.7	9.4	8.7
Profit Margin (After Income Tax) 50	6.8	1.6	0.4	9.1	8.6	7.3

Table I
Corporations with and without Net Income

GLASS AND GLASS PRODUCT

MONEY AMOUNTS AND SIZE OF ASSETS IN THOUSANDS OF DOLLARS

Item Description for Accounting Period 7/04 Through 6/05	Total	Zero Assets	Under 500	500 to 1,000	1,000 to 5,000	5,000 to 10,000	10,000 to 25,000	25,000 to 50,000	50,000 to 100,000	100,000 to 250,000	250,000 to 500,000	500,000 to 2,500,000	2,500,000 and over
Number of Enterprises 1	1868	0	0	0	334	63	32	9	7	9	4	7	0
Revenues ($ in Thousands)													
Net Sales 2	23186249	0	0	0	1636178	791332	863626	507957	636038	1739885	1911012	13363447	0
Interest 3	96984	0	0	0	816	64	385	470	11	10814	5762	78663	0
Rents 4	14907	0	0	0	0	0	648	396	301	1692	417	11453	0
Royalties 5	96961	0	0	0	0	20	2	146	0	15520	1441	79832	0
Other Portfolio Income 6	146022	0	0	0	455	5004	12585	745	3921	2212	23527	94976	0
Other Receipts 7	209150	0	0	0	11279	1361	6571	1169	2411	59309	20894	106130	0
Total Receipts 8	23750273	0	0	0	1648728	797781	883817	510883	642682	1829432	1963053	14034501	0
Average Total Receipts 9	12714	•	•	•	4936	12663	27619	56765	91812	203270	490763	2004929	•
Operating Costs/Operating Income (%)													
Cost of Operations 10	67.0	•	•	•	62.0	77.8	69.8	68.5	68.4	80.8	65.8	68.1	•
Salaries and Wages 11	6.7	•	•	•	7.6	4.4	6.6	7.5	4.2	7.5	8.0	4.8	•
Taxes Paid 12	2.5	•	•	•	2.1	1.3	2.1	3.1	2.7	3.2	2.4	2.5	•
Interest Paid 13	3.3	•	•	•	0.5	0.9	1.2	1.6	1.1	2.1	1.3	4.6	•
Depreciation 14	4.6	•	•	•	1.7	1.6	4.0	3.3	3.6	4.8	3.9	5.4	•
Amortization and Depletion 15	0.3	•	•	•	0.0	0.0	0.2	0.1	0.2	0.4	0.3	0.4	•
Pensions and Other Deferred Comp. 16	1.3	•	•	•	0.1	0.1	0.4	0.3	0.7	1.1	0.3	2.0	•
Employee Benefits 17	3.3	•	•	•	1.4	0.5	2.1	1.6	4.0	2.6	4.6	4.0	•
Advertising 18	0.5	•	•	•	0.4	0.3	0.4	0.4	0.2	1.7	0.8	0.3	•
Other Expenses 19	11.8	•	•	•	10.0	9.3	11.6	9.4	7.0	10.3	12.6	11.3	•
Officers' Compensation 20	1.3	•	•	•	7.7	2.0	1.5	1.1	0.6	0.7	0.5	0.3	•
Operating Margin 21	•	•	•	•	6.3	1.7	0.1	2.9	7.2	•	•	•	•
Operating Margin Before Officers' Comp. 22	•	•	•	•	14.0	3.7	1.5	4.1	7.9	•	•	•	•

Selected Average Balance Sheet ($ in Thousands)

Net Receivables 23	1432	602	1903	3173	7117	13165	17703	79451	217691
Inventories 24	1607	426	1858	3260	6801	15631	21267	55097	272844
Net Property, Plant and Equipment 25	3616	689	1320	5062	9483	22368	44827	99705	719190
Total Assets 26	14962	1974	6336	15497	36212	64128	143029	388487	3163315
Notes and Loans Payable 27	6426	872	1642	6139	13835	24315	68596	103968	1326919
All Other Liabilities 28	3941	417	1522	3636	8590	16390	66633	122772	799560
Net Worth 29	4595	685	3172	5722	13787	23423	7800	161748	1036835

Selected Financial Ratios (Times to 1)

Current Ratio 30	1.2	3.1	2.7	1.3	1.5	1.5	0.8	2.4	1.1
Quick Ratio 31	0.6	2.0	1.5	0.8	0.9	0.7	0.4	1.1	0.5
Net Sales to Working Capital 32	16.2	5.9	4.9	13.0	9.0	8.8	•	4.3	24.8
Coverage Ratio 33	0.9	14.6	3.7	3.0	3.1	8.9	•	2.5	0.8
Total Asset Turnover 34	0.8	2.5	2.0	1.7	1.6	1.4	1.4	1.2	0.6
Inventory Turnover 35	5.2	7.1	5.3	5.8	5.7	4.0	7.3	5.7	4.9
Receivables Turnover 36	8.4	7.6	6.5	8.7	7.8	6.3	11.8	6.4	8.6
Total Liabilities to Net Worth 37	2.3	1.9	1.0	1.7	1.6	1.7	17.3	1.4	2.1
Current Assets to Working Capital 38	5.3	1.5	1.6	4.0	2.9	3.1	•	1.7	8.3
Current Liabilities to Working Capital 39	4.3	0.5	0.6	3.0	1.9	2.1	•	0.7	7.3
Working Capital to Net Sales 40	0.1	0.2	0.2	0.1	0.1	0.1	•	0.2	0.0
Inventory to Working Capital 41	2.0	0.5	0.6	1.6	1.1	1.5	•	0.6	3.2
Total Receipts to Cash Flow 42	13.7	7.0	9.2	8.9	9.4	7.4	•	11.0	16.2
Cost of Goods to Cash Flow 43	9.2	4.3	7.2	6.2	6.5	5.1	•	7.2	11.0
Cash Flow to Total Debt 44	0.1	0.5	0.4	0.3	0.3	0.3	•	0.2	0.1

Selected Financial Factors (in Percentages)

Debt Ratio 45	69.3	65.3	49.9	63.1	61.9	63.5	94.5	58.4	67.2
Return on Total Assets 46	2.5	18.9	6.7	6.4	8.0	13.3	•	4.1	2.3
Return on Equity Before Income Taxes 47	•	50.7	9.7	11.5	14.3	32.4	•	6.0	•
Return on Equity After Income Taxes 48	•	46.3	7.8	10.6	12.1	21.4	•	2.8	•
Profit Margin (Before Income Tax) 49	•	7.1	2.5	2.4	3.5	8.4	•	2.0	•
Profit Margin (After Income Tax) 50	•	6.5	2.0	2.2	3.0	5.5	•	1.0	•

Table II

Corporations with Net Income

GLASS AND GLASS PRODUCT

MONEY AMOUNTS AND SIZE OF ASSETS IN THOUSANDS OF DOLLARS

Item Description for Accounting Period 7/04 Through 6/05	Total	Zero Assets	Under 500	500 to 1000	251 to 500	501 to 1,000	1,001 to 5,000	5,001 to 10,000	10,001 to 25,000	25,001 to 50,000	50,001 to 100,000	100,001 to 250,000	250,001 and over
Number of Enterprises **1**	1329	0	700	228	305	0	17	6	0	0	0	3	0
Revenues ($ in Thousands)													
Net Sales **2**	13851967	0	554064	358075	1536559	0	476405	325253	0	0	0	7540301	0
Interest **3**	34046	0	0	0	719	0	225	469	0	0	0	28981	0
Rents **4**	2534	0	0	0	0	0	648	396	0	0	0	1075	0
Royalties **5**	12321	0	0	0	0	0	2	0	0	0	0	10858	0
Other Portfolio Income **6**	93423	0	1	2598	455	0	12390	717	0	0	0	61609	0
Other Receipts **7**	36374	0	0	0	9994	0	6320	840	0	0	0	6663	0
Total Receipts **8**	14030665	0	554065	360673	1547727	0	495990	327675	0	0	0	7649487	0
Average Total Receipts **9**	10557	•	792	1582	5075	•	29176	54612	•	•	•	2549829	•
Operating Costs/Operating Income (%)													
Cost of Operations **10**	63.2	•	32.8	46.6	61.7	•	69.6	68.0	•	•	•	64.0	•
Salaries and Wages **11**	6.5	•	20.7	4.4	7.6	•	5.6	6.2	•	•	•	5.7	•
Taxes Paid **12**	2.4	•	3.4	2.4	2.1	•	1.9	3.2	•	•	•	2.4	•
Interest Paid **13**	1.5	•	0.2	2.1	0.4	•	1.1	1.6	•	•	•	2.1	•
Depreciation **14**	4.9	•	0.3	8.4	1.7	•	3.7	2.9	•	•	•	6.5	•
Amortization and Depletion **15**	0.4	•	•	•	0.0	•	0.1	0.1	•	•	•	0.7	•
Pensions and Other Deferred Comp. **16**	1.5	•	•	•	0.1	•	0.5	0.3	•	•	•	2.5	•
Employee Benefits **17**	2.8	•	0.1	0.6	1.5	•	2.3	1.3	•	•	•	3.3	•
Advertising **18**	0.6	•	2.7	0.0	0.5	•	0.4	0.6	•	•	•	0.5	•
Other Expenses **19**	10.6	•	20.7	27.1	9.7	•	10.7	8.4	•	•	•	9.7	•
Officers' Compensation **20**	1.8	•	11.9	6.0	7.8	•	1.1	1.0	•	•	•	0.1	•
Operating Margin **21**	3.7	•	7.1	2.5	6.9	•	2.9	6.2	•	•	•	2.5	•
Operating Margin Before Officers' Comp. **22**	5.6	•	19.1	8.4	14.7	•	4.1	7.3	•	•	•	2.6	•

Selected Average Balance Sheet ($ in Thousands)

Net Receivables 23	1253	55	124	636	3016	6448	281062
Inventories 24	1363	42	365	457	3095	5518	380164
Net Property, Plant and Equipment 25	2743	8	271	681	4974	7208	887363
Total Assets 26	9054	220	851	2040	14998	38360	2828601
Notes and Loans Payable 27	2761	56	498	870	5190	11787	874164
All Other Liabilities 28	2385	52	162	416	3171	7605	745909
Net Worth 29	3907	112	192	754	6638	18968	1208527

Selected Financial Ratios (Times to 1)

Current Ratio 30	1.5	3.7	2.7	3.4	1.6	1.7	1.1
Quick Ratio 31	0.8	2.7	0.7	2.2	1.0	1.0	0.6
Net Sales to Working Capital 32	9.9	5.6	5.0	5.5	9.1	6.8	26.2
Coverage Ratio 33	4.4	31.9	2.5	19.1	7.2	5.3	2.9
Total Asset Turnover 34	1.2	3.6	1.8	2.5	1.9	1.4	0.9
Inventory Turnover 35	4.8	6.2	2.0	6.8	6.3	6.7	4.2
Receivables Turnover 36	8.1	10.7	•	8.3	8.5	12.0	8.0
Total Liabilities to Net Worth 37	1.3	1.0	3.4	1.7	1.3	1.0	1.3
Current Assets to Working Capital 38	3.0	1.4	1.6	1.4	2.7	2.4	7.9
Current Liabilities to Working Capital 39	2.0	0.4	0.6	0.4	1.7	1.4	6.9
Working Capital to Net Sales 40	0.1	0.2	0.2	0.2	0.1	0.1	0.0
Inventory to Working Capital 41	1.2	0.2	1.2	0.5	0.9	0.9	3.5
Total Receipts to Cash Flow 42	8.4	4.7	4.9	6.9	6.6	7.5	10.2
Cost of Goods to Cash Flow 43	5.3	1.5	2.3	4.2	4.6	5.1	6.6
Cash Flow to Total Debt 44	0.2	1.6	0.5	0.6	0.5	0.4	0.2

Selected Financial Factors (in Percentages)

Debt Ratio 45	56.8	49.0	77.4	63.0	55.7	50.6	57.3
Return on Total Assets 46	7.5	26.6	9.7	19.9	15.3	12.1	5.4
Return on Equity Before Income Taxes 47	13.5	50.5	26.0	51.0	29.7	19.8	8.3
Return on Equity After Income Taxes 48	11.0	50.5	24.5	46.6	28.3	17.5	6.3
Profit Margin (Before Income Tax) 49	5.1	7.1	3.2	7.6	7.0	6.9	4.0
Profit Margin (After Income Tax) 50	4.1	7.1	3.0	7.0	6.7	6.1	3.0

Table I

Corporations with and without Net Income

CEMENT, CONCRETE, LIME AND GYPSUM PRODUCT

MONEY AMOUNTS AND SIZE OF ASSETS IN THOUSANDS OF DOLLARS

Item Description for Accounting Period 7/04 Through 6/05	Total	Zero Assets	Under 500	500 to 1,000	1,000 to 5,000	5,000 to 10,000	10,000 to 25,000	25,000 to 50,000	50,000 to 100,000	100,000 to 250,000	250,000 to 500,000	500,000 to 2,500,000	2,500,000 and over
Number of Enterprises 1	4835	0	0	0	1461	249	167	53	22	21	9	14	8
Revenues ($ in Thousands)													
Net Sales 2	61520096	0	0	0	6518772	2723894	4436503	2744679	2299679	3815779	2643490	12193281	21366275
Interest 3	766845	0	0	0	5019	2300	3700	1818	2675	8844	21844	99704	618411
Rents 4	57807	0	0	0	9437	2390	2367	1176	1639	6497	3039	13620	14748
Royalties 5	43600	0	0	0	0	136	643	48	0	10875	9457	2971	18957
Other Portfolio Income 6	378646	0	0	0	39913	16534	18623	10780	10255	32455	34607	54502	124843
Other Receipts 7	968074	0	0	0	79485	4293	39264	16316	8182	109437	69221	165811	443354
Total Receipts 8	63735068	0	0	0	6652626	2749547	4501100	2774817	2322430	3983887	2781658	12529889	22586588
Average Total Receipts 9	13182	•	•	•	4553	11042	26953	52355	105565	189709	309073	894992	2823324
Operating Costs/Operating Income (%)													
Cost of Operations 10	65.3	•	•	•	64.2	68.1	70.1	68.5	72.4	68.5	67.2	65.8	63.8
Salaries and Wages 11	6.1	•	•	•	7.3	6.0	6.1	6.7	4.2	5.3	5.8	4.5	6.2
Taxes Paid 12	2.3	•	•	•	2.7	2.2	2.1	2.3	1.6	2.4	2.4	2.2	2.1
Interest Paid 13	3.4	•	•	•	1.0	1.2	0.8	0.9	0.8	1.2	3.6	3.7	6.1
Depreciation 14	6.0	•	•	•	4.7	5.3	4.9	5.6	5.6	5.6	6.5	7.1	5.8
Amortization and Depletion 15	1.0	•	•	•	0.1	0.0	0.2	0.4	0.4	0.8	1.9	1.4	1.5
Pensions and Other Deferred Comp. 16	0.8	•	•	•	0.4	0.4	0.4	0.8	0.4	0.7	0.7	0.7	1.3
Employee Benefits 17	2.3	•	•	•	1.8	1.5	1.3	2.3	1.8	2.0	2.1	2.5	3.0
Advertising 18	0.3	•	•	•	0.4	0.4	0.3	0.4	0.5	0.8	0.2	0.1	0.3
Other Expenses 19	9.6	•	•	•	14.2	10.1	9.1	7.5	5.9	8.2	9.3	7.7	9.2
Officers' Compensation 20	1.1	•	•	•	3.0	2.3	1.8	1.7	1.1	0.9	0.8	0.4	0.3
Operating Margin 21	1.8	•	•	•	0.2	2.4	2.8	2.8	5.3	3.6	•	4.0	0.5
Operating Margin Before Officers' Comp. 22	2.8	•	•	•	3.3	4.7	4.6	4.6	6.3	4.4	0.5	4.4	0.8

Selected Average Balance Sheet ($ in Thousands)

Item											
Net Receivables 23	2139	•	677	1496	4107	8187	17117	25392	45047	147212	545528
Inventories 24	912	•	220	839	1668	4367	6677	12111	24552	70736	211052
Net Property, Plant and Equipment 25	6338	•	864	3362	5639	15013	29247	61462	171030	698265	1639393
Total Assets 26	14908	•	2217	7443	15274	35459	71252	161727	383997	1293660	4400376
Notes and Loans Payable 27	4996	•	911	3879	4177	9804	14858	43824	125199	431114	1483689
All Other Liabilities 28	4381	•	459	1489	3457	7460	16933	34632	83264	331952	1567518
Net Worth 29	5532	•	846	2075	7640	18195	39460	83271	175535	530594	1349168

Selected Financial Ratios (Times to 1)

Item											
Current Ratio 30	1.2	•	1.7	1.5	1.9	2.0	1.8	2.3	1.8	1.2	0.9
Quick Ratio 31	0.8	•	1.3	0.8	1.3	1.2	1.2	1.5	1.1	0.7	0.6
Net Sales to Working Capital 32	16.6	•	8.4	9.3	6.7	5.9	7.2	5.4	6.7	14.6	•
Coverage Ratio 33	2.6	•	3.3	3.7	6.5	5.5	8.9	7.8	2.4	2.9	2.0
Total Asset Turnover 34	0.9	•	2.0	1.5	1.7	1.5	1.5	1.1	0.8	0.7	0.6
Inventory Turnover 35	9.1	•	13.0	8.9	11.2	8.1	11.3	10.3	8.0	8.1	8.1
Receivables Turnover 36	6.9	•	7.3	8.2	6.8	6.5	6.6	7.9	7.2	6.8	6.1
Total Liabilities to Net Worth 37	1.7	•	1.6	2.6	1.0	0.9	0.8	0.9	1.2	1.4	2.3
Current Assets to Working Capital 38	5.6	•	2.3	3.0	2.1	2.0	2.3	1.8	2.3	5.4	•
Current Liabilities to Working Capital 39	4.6	•	1.3	2.0	1.1	1.0	1.3	0.8	1.3	4.4	•
Working Capital to Net Sales 40	0.1	•	0.1	0.1	0.1	0.2	0.1	0.2	0.1	0.1	•
Inventory to Working Capital 41	1.3	•	0.5	0.9	0.4	0.5	0.5	0.4	0.5	1.2	•
Total Receipts to Cash Flow 42	8.3	•	8.7	9.9	9.6	11.6	9.7	7.4	8.6	8.4	7.7
Cost of Goods to Cash Flow 43	5.4	•	5.6	6.8	6.7	7.9	7.0	5.0	5.8	5.5	4.9
Cash Flow to Total Debt 44	0.2	•	0.4	0.2	0.4	0.3	0.3	0.3	0.2	0.1	0.1

Selected Financial Factors (in Percentages)

Item											
Debt Ratio 45	62.9	•	61.8	72.1	50.0	48.7	44.6	48.5	54.3	59.0	69.3
Return on Total Assets 46	7.6	•	6.6	6.7	8.4	7.0	10.4	10.3	6.6	7.0	7.5
Return on Equity Before Income Taxes 47	12.5	•	12.1	17.4	14.3	11.2	16.7	17.4	8.6	11.1	12.5
Return on Equity After Income Taxes 48	8.8	•	11.5	13.8	12.9	9.2	13.8	14.0	5.0	7.4	8.0
Profit Margin (Before Income Tax) 49	5.4	•	2.3	3.3	4.1	3.9	6.3	8.0	5.1	6.8	6.3
Profit Margin (After Income Tax) 50	3.8	•	2.2	2.6	3.7	3.2	5.2	6.4	3.0	4.5	4.0

Table II

Corporations with Net Income

CEMENT, CONCRETE, LIME AND GYPSUM PRODUCT

MONEY AMOUNTS AND SIZE OF ASSETS IN THOUSANDS OF DOLLARS

Item Description for Accounting Period 7/04 Through 6/05	Total	Zero Assets	Under 500	500 to 1,000	1,000 to 5,000	5,000 to 10,000	10,000 to 25,000	25,000 to 50,000	50,000 to 100,000	100,000 to 250,000	250,000 to 500,000	500,000 to 2,500,000	2,500,000 and over
Number of Enterprises 1	3122	18	1453	527	702	190	133	39	19	0	0	0	0
Revenues ($ in Thousands)													
Net Sales 2	5042987	218508	975950	679137	3941624	2357394	3548095	2121506	1988545	0	0	0	0
Interest 3	507965	93	815	1221	2810	2050	3345	1623	2207	0	0	0	0
Rents 4	45479	198	0	2195	808	1763	1871	679	1362	0	0	0	0
Royalties 5	43076	0	0	0	0	136	631	48	0	0	0	0	0
Other Portfolio Income 6	334961	3009	0	31961	23832	16382	9623	6746	7409	0	0	0	0
Other Receipts 7	808777	4451	830	15416	21781	3874	35026	11849	7087	0	0	0	0
Total Receipts 8	52165245	226259	977595	729930	3990855	2381599	3598591	2142451	2006610	0	0	0	0
Average Total Receipts 9	16709	12570	673	1385	5685	12535	27057	54935	105611	•	•	•	•
Operating Costs/Operating Income (%)													
Cost of Operations 10	64.7	57.2	42.9	55.3	61.3	65.5	69.8	66.6	70.6	•	•	•	•
Salaries and Wages 11	6.1	10.2	12.7	10.4	7.6	6.4	6.0	6.7	4.1	•	•	•	•
Taxes Paid 12	2.2	1.8	5.4	2.6	2.6	2.2	2.1	2.3	1.7	•	•	•	•
Interest Paid 13	3.0	1.4	1.3	1.1	0.6	1.2	0.6	0.8	0.8	•	•	•	•
Depreciation 14	5.5	6.5	4.4	5.8	4.1	5.2	4.5	5.0	5.6	•	•	•	•
Amortization and Depletion 15	1.0	0.3	0.1	0.2	0.0	0.0	0.1	0.3	0.4	•	•	•	•
Pensions and Other Deferred Comp. 16	0.9	0.3	•	1.5	0.4	0.5	0.5	0.8	0.5	•	•	•	•
Employee Benefits 17	2.4	1.7	0.2	1.9	2.0	1.5	1.4	2.3	1.9	•	•	•	•
Advertising 18	0.3	0.1	0.2	0.7	0.4	0.4	0.4	0.4	0.6	•	•	•	•
Other Expenses 19	8.9	18.7	21.2	16.7	12.7	10.5	8.3	7.6	6.2	•	•	•	•
Officers' Compensation 20	1.0	0.3	2.9	6.4	3.2	2.4	1.9	1.9	1.1	•	•	•	•
Operating Margin 21	4.0	1.4	8.7	•	5.2	4.1	4.5	5.3	6.6	•	•	•	•
Operating Margin Before Officers' Comp. 22	5.0	1.7	11.6	3.7	8.4	6.4	6.4	7.2	7.7	•	•	•	•

Selected Average Balance Sheet ($ in Thousands)

Net Receivables 23	2732	0	14	133	861	1796	3939	8593	16679
Inventories 24	1106	0	6	59	221	864	1611	4925	6853
Net Property, Plant and Equipment 25	8001	0	187	199	788	3261	5437	13907	28478
Total Assets 26	18608	0	249	670	2554	7184	15436	35776	71077
Notes and Loans Payable 27	6329	0	126	244	631	2758	3523	9001	15140
All Other Liabilities 28	4962	0	10	111	548	1602	3227	7823	15981
Net Worth 29	7317	0	114	315	1375	2824	8686	18952	39957

Selected Financial Ratios (Times to 1)

Current Ratio 30	1.4	•	1.8	3.3	2.4	1.6	2.2	2.1	1.8
Quick Ratio 31	0.9	•	1.3	2.5	1.9	1.1	1.5	1.3	1.2
Net Sales to Working Capital 32	9.8	•	41.5	4.9	6.0	10.0	5.7	5.4	7.4
Coverage Ratio 33	3.5	4.6	7.9	5.2	12.4	5.1	10.7	9.2	10.5
Total Asset Turnover 34	0.9	•	2.7	1.9	2.2	1.7	1.7	1.5	1.5
Inventory Turnover 35	9.4	•	44.9	12.1	15.6	9.4	11.6	7.4	10.8
Receivables Turnover 36	6.9	•	30.2	•	7.3	7.7	7.5	6.4	6.8
Total Liabilities to Net Worth 37	1.5	•	1.2	1.1	0.9	1.5	0.8	0.9	0.8
Current Assets to Working Capital 38	3.4	•	2.3	1.4	1.7	2.7	1.9	1.9	2.3
Current Liabilities to Working Capital 39	2.4	•	1.3	0.4	0.7	1.7	0.9	0.9	1.3
Working Capital to Net Sales 40	0.1	•	0.0	0.2	0.2	0.1	0.2	0.2	0.1
Inventory to Working Capital 41	0.7	•	0.6	0.2	0.3	0.8	0.4	0.5	0.5
Total Receipts to Cash Flow 42	7.5	5.0	4.5	7.3	7.3	8.3	8.5	9.2	8.5
Cost of Goods to Cash Flow 43	4.8	2.9	1.9	4.0	4.4	5.5	5.9	6.1	6.0
Cash Flow to Total Debt 44	0.2	•	1.1	0.5	0.7	0.3	0.5	0.4	0.4

Selected Financial Factors (in Percentages)

Debt Ratio 45	60.7	•	54.3	53.0	46.2	60.7	43.7	47.0	43.8
Return on Total Assets 46	9.1	•	27.4	11.3	15.4	10.9	11.2	10.7	12.3
Return on Equity Before Income Taxes 47	16.6	•	52.4	19.5	26.3	22.4	18.1	18.0	19.9
Return on Equity After Income Taxes 48	12.4	•	52.2	18.9	25.5	19.0	16.5	15.4	16.5
Profit Margin (Before Income Tax) 49	7.5	4.9	8.9	4.8	6.4	5.1	5.9	6.3	7.6
Profit Margin (After Income Tax) 50	5.6	4.5	8.9	4.6	6.2	4.3	5.4	5.4	6.3

Table I

Corporations with and without Net Income

IRON, STEEL MILLS AND STEEL PRODUCT

MONEY AMOUNTS AND SIZE OF ASSETS IN THOUSANDS OF DOLLARS

Item Description for Accounting Period 7/04 Through 6/05	Total	Zero Assets	Under 500	500 to 1,000	1,000 to 5,000	5,000 to 10,000	10,000 to 25,000	25,000 to 50,000	50,000 to 100,000	100,000 to 250,000	250,000 to 500,000	500,000 to 2,500,000	2,500,000 and over
Number of Enterprises 1	3309	12	1941	532	356	186	109	58	40	36	12	21	6
Revenues ($ in Thousands)													
Net Sales 2	109641688	514253	1162423	1104190	2195620	2399531	3535602	3506869	4542693	10337771	7037602	31572772	41732363
Interest 3	325884	115	0	192	89	1017	1974	1463	6756	35607	23500	100979	154193
Rents 4	56051	989	0	0	0	5	187	2101	1771	4094	1009	13702	32193
Royalties 5	305752	9	0	0	0	0	96	126	4399	3664	1827	240553	55079
Other Portfolio Income 6	535731	1	0	825	201	11857	6848	2408	67373	45567	22947	56335	321368
Other Receipts 7	1711260	99867	206	4503	27075	12826	56169	23135	63421	47936	145606	838295	392217
Total Receipts 8	112576366	615234	1162629	1109710	2222985	2425236	3600876	3536102	4686413	10474639	7232491	32822636	42687413
Average Total Receipts 9	34021	51270	599	2086	6244	13039	33036	60967	117160	290962	602708	1562983	7114569
Operating Costs/Operating Income (%)													
Cost of Operations 10	77.1	75.4	65.8	74.9	80.4	79.3	78.1	79.7	78.8	77.7	82.3	78.4	74.8
Salaries and Wages 11	3.0	13.2	10.9	6.7	4.7	3.8	3.7	4.2	3.4	3.3	1.9	3.5	2.0
Taxes Paid 12	1.3	0.4	2.2	2.8	1.5	1.5	1.4	1.3	1.4	1.2	1.2	1.1	1.5
Interest Paid 13	1.6	2.0	0.8	0.8	0.5	0.5	0.7	1.0	1.1	1.4	1.4	1.7	1.9
Depreciation 14	3.0	2.3	2.6	1.7	2.4	2.7	2.6	3.2	2.9	1.9	2.1	2.5	3.8
Amortization and Depletion 15	0.3	•	0.2	0.1	0.0	0.0	0.2	0.1	0.1	0.2	0.2	0.4	0.4
Pensions and Other Deferred Comp. 16	1.2	0.2	•	0.2	0.0	0.3	0.4	0.3	0.3	0.8	0.6	0.7	2.2
Employee Benefits 17	1.4	0.3	0.5	1.4	0.7	1.0	1.2	1.1	1.3	1.1	1.6	1.5	1.4
Advertising 18	0.1	0.0	0.1	0.1	0.1	0.1	0.2	0.1	0.1	0.2	0.0	0.1	0.0
Other Expenses 19	5.5	17.1	16.8	7.7	6.0	4.8	6.2	4.8	5.3	4.1	5.9	5.3	5.5
Officers' Compensation 20	0.7	0.5	4.3	2.9	3.1	1.8	2.0	1.8	0.9	0.4	0.3	0.3	0.5
Operating Margin 21	4.8	•	0.7	0.4	0.4	4.1	3.2	2.4	4.4	7.7	2.4	4.6	6.0
Operating Margin Before Officers' Comp. 22	5.5	•	0.1	3.6	3.6	5.8	5.2	4.2	5.3	8.1	2.7	4.9	6.5

Selected Average Balance Sheet ($ in Thousands)

Net Receivables 23	3921	0	54	195	777	1942	4145	8422	15324	31410	70501	187921	775101
Inventories 24	3965	0	26	62	946	1130	3962	7553	17725	41136	69516	204511	717005
Net Property, Plant and Equipment 25	7141	0	42	207	482	1827	3961	9399	18314	44615	77633	351695	1882224
Total Assets 26	22050	0	150	623	2717	6496	15562	33960	69247	160846	329858	1111240	5107680
Notes and Loans Payable 27	5786	0	106	313	1283	1203	6299	12279	19127	53492	91550	347651	933906
All Other Liabilities 28	9234	0	47	138	735	2212	4235	10088	93273	52230	117487	358131	2354708
Net Worth 29	7031	0	-3	172	699	3082	5028	11593	-43152	55124	120821	405458	1819066

Selected Financial Ratios (Times to 1)

Current Ratio 30	1.9	•	0.9	1.9	2.4	2.0	1.6	1.5	1.1	2.0	1.6	2.0	2.1
Quick Ratio 31	0.9	•	0.7	1.4	1.3	1.3	0.9	0.8	0.5	0.8	0.7	1.0	1.1
Net Sales to Working Capital 32	6.2	•	•	13.3	4.8	5.8	8.2	9.0	21.5	5.8	7.7	5.3	5.8
Coverage Ratio 33	5.7	5.3	•	2.6	4.1	10.3	8.1	4.3	7.9	7.6	4.5	5.9	5.4
Total Asset Turnover 34	1.5	•	4.0	3.3	2.3	2.0	2.1	1.8	1.6	1.8	1.8	1.4	1.4
Inventory Turnover 35	6.4	•	15.1	25.1	5.2	9.0	6.4	6.4	5.0	5.4	6.9	5.8	7.3
Receivables Turnover 36	9.4	•	8.1	18.1	6.6	7.3	7.9	8.8	8.1	10.2	10.7	8.2	10.8
Total Liabilities to Net Worth 37	2.1	•	•	2.6	2.9	1.1	2.1	1.9	•	1.9	1.7	1.7	1.8
Current Assets to Working Capital 38	2.1	•	•	2.1	1.7	2.1	2.6	3.0	8.1	2.0	2.7	2.0	1.9
Current Liabilities to Working Capital 39	1.1	•	•	1.1	0.7	1.1	1.6	2.0	7.1	1.0	1.7	1.0	0.9
Working Capital to Net Sales 40	0.2	•	•	0.1	0.2	0.2	0.1	0.1	0.0	0.2	0.1	0.2	0.2
Inventory to Working Capital 41	0.9	•	•	0.5	0.7	0.7	1.1	1.3	3.7	1.0	1.2	0.9	0.7
Total Receipts to Cash Flow 42	9.2	11.6	14.6	13.7	17.6	11.3	10.1	15.0	9.6	8.4	10.8	8.0	9.3
Cost of Goods to Cash Flow 43	7.1	8.8	9.6	10.3	14.1	9.0	7.9	11.9	7.6	6.5	8.9	6.3	6.9
Cash Flow to Total Debt 44	0.2	•	0.3	0.3	0.2	0.3	0.3	0.2	0.1	0.3	0.3	0.3	0.2

Selected Financial Factors (in Percentages)

Debt Ratio 45	68.1	•	101.9	72.4	74.3	52.6	67.7	65.9	162.3	65.7	63.4	63.5	64.4
Return on Total Assets 46	13.7	•	•	6.5	5.1	11.3	12.0	7.4	14.3	18.6	11.7	13.9	13.9
Return on Equity Before Income Taxes 47	35.5	•	899.9	14.5	14.9	21.5	32.5	16.8	•	47.1	24.9	31.6	31.8
Return on Equity After Income Taxes 48	27.9	•	899.9	14.1	12.4	19.5	29.9	13.8	•	39.1	18.7	23.7	25.1
Profit Margin (Before Income Tax) 49	7.5	8.5	•	1.2	1.7	5.1	5.0	3.2	7.6	9.0	5.1	8.5	8.3
Profit Margin (After Income Tax) 50	5.9	8.0	•	1.2	1.4	4.7	4.6	2.7	6.2	7.5	3.8	6.4	6.6

Table II

Corporations with Net Income

IRON, STEEL MILLS AND STEEL PRODUCT

MONEY AMOUNTS AND SIZE OF ASSETS IN THOUSANDS OF DOLLARS

Item Description for Accounting Period 7/04 Through 6/05	Total	Zero Assets	Under 500	500 to 1,000	1,000 to 5,000	5,000 to 10,000	10,000 to 25,000	25,000 to 50,000	50,000 to 100,000	100,000 to 250,000	250,000 to 500,000	500,000 to 2,500,000	2,500,000 and over
Number of Enterprises **1**	2315	0	1295	0	230	162	86	40	33	30	0	18	0
Revenues ($ in Thousands)													
Net Sales **2**	96711426	0	780908	0	1821856	2249955	2749721	2608204	4020543	9092443	0	27630845	0
Interest **3**	282492	0	0	0	78	726	759	448	5463	31588	0	95763	0
Rents **4**	41931	0	0	0	0	5	100	1004	946	1388	0	7188	0
Royalties **5**	298121	0	0	0	0	0	83	0	1760	3404	0	240553	0
Other Portfolio Income **6**	493961	0	0	0	197	8072	2722	2105	64717	32830	0	45765	0
Other Receipts **7**	1537494	0	0	0	27000	11387	14595	17658	56594	36771	0	812569	0
Total Receipts **8**	99365425	0	780908	0	1849131	2270145	2767980	2629419	4150023	9198424	0	28832683	0
Average Total Receipts **9**	42922	·	603	·	8040	14013	32186	65735	125758	306614	·	1601816	·
Operating Costs/Operating Income (%)													
Cost of Operations **10**	76.3	·	63.8	·	79.1	79.4	75.3	79.0	77.7	77.1	·	77.3	·
Salaries and Wages **11**	2.9	·	9.3	·	5.1	3.5	3.9	3.3	3.3	3.2	·	3.6	·
Taxes Paid **12**	1.3	·	1.7	·	1.3	1.5	1.5	1.3	1.4	1.1	·	1.2	·
Interest Paid **13**	1.5	·	0.5	·	0.3	0.3	0.7	0.7	1.1	1.1	·	1.6	·
Depreciation **14**	3.0	·	1.7	·	2.6	2.3	2.7	3.1	2.7	1.8	·	2.8	·
Amortization and Depletion **15**	0.3	·	0.3	·	0.0	0.0	0.1	0.1	0.1	0.1	·	0.3	·
Pensions and Other Deferred Comp. **16**	1.3	·	·	·	0.1	0.3	0.4	0.3	0.4	0.6	·	0.7	·
Employee Benefits **17**	1.2	·	0.1	·	0.7	0.9	1.3	0.9	1.2	0.9	·	1.4	·
Advertising **18**	0.1	·	0.1	·	0.1	0.1	0.1	0.1	0.1	0.2	·	0.1	·
Other Expenses **19**	5.1	·	16.0	·	4.5	4.2	4.7	3.4	5.0	3.9	·	5.0	·
Officers' Compensation **20**	0.7	·	4.4	·	3.2	1.7	2.3	2.1	1.0	0.4	·	0.3	·
Operating Margin **21**	6.4	·	2.2	·	3.1	5.7	6.8	5.7	6.0	9.4	·	5.7	·
Operating Margin Before Officers' Comp. **22**	7.1	·	6.6	·	6.3	7.4	9.2	7.7	7.0	9.8	·	6.0	·

Selected Average Balance Sheet ($ in Thousands)

Net Receivables 23	5054	27	1002	2084	4339	8418	16019	31811	196576
Inventories 24	3667	22	873	1206	3759	7537	16129	36118	161591
Net Property, Plant and Equipment 25	9325	41	687	1519	4017	8909	18041	43099	391120
Total Assets 26	27678	145	3168	6581	15391	33493	70767	159987	1159943
Notes and Loans Payable 27	6389	48	410	1063	5123	9460	18657	44826	342616
All Other Liabilities 28	9887	37	720	2155	3812	8390	22692	50980	302130
Net Worth 29	11402	60	2038	3362	6456	15643	29418	64181	515197

Selected Financial Ratios (Times to 1)

Current Ratio 30	2.1	1.3	2.9	2.2	1.7	1.8	1.9	2.1	2.1
Quick Ratio 31	1.0	0.7	2.0	1.4	0.9	0.9	0.9	0.9	1.0
Net Sales to Working Capital 32	5.6	37.0	4.9	5.1	7.3	7.1	5.9	5.7	5.0
Coverage Ratio 33	7.1	5.6	16.9	21.5	11.3	10.1	9.2	10.3	7.4
Total Asset Turnover 34	1.5	4.1	2.5	2.1	2.1	1.9	1.7	1.9	1.3
Inventory Turnover 35	8.7	17.2	7.2	9.1	6.4	6.8	5.9	6.5	7.3
Receivables Turnover 36	12.9	27.4	6.6	9.0	8.2	10.1	10.4	12.7	11.5
Total Liabilities to Net Worth 37	1.4	1.4	0.6	1.0	1.4	1.1	1.4	1.5	1.3
Current Assets to Working Capital 38	1.9	5.0	1.5	1.8	2.4	2.3	2.1	1.9	1.9
Current Liabilities to Working Capital 39	0.9	4.0	0.5	0.8	1.4	1.3	1.1	0.9	0.9
Working Capital to Net Sales 40	0.2	0.0	0.2	0.2	0.1	0.1	0.2	0.2	0.2
Inventory to Working Capital 41	0.8	1.9	0.4	0.6	1.0	1.0	1.0	1.0	0.9
Total Receipts to Cash Flow 42	8.2	7.6	14.2	10.2	9.1	11.2	8.6	7.5	7.2
Cost of Goods to Cash Flow 43	6.3	4.9	11.3	8.1	6.9	8.9	6.7	5.8	5.6
Cash Flow to Total Debt 44	0.3	0.9	0.5	0.4	0.4	0.3	0.3	0.4	0.3

Selected Financial Factors (in Percentages)

Debt Ratio 45	58.8	58.5	35.7	48.9	58.1	53.3	58.4	59.9	55.6
Return on Total Assets 46	16.1	10.9	12.2	14.6	17.1	14.0	17.9	22.3	15.4
Return on Equity Before Income Taxes 47	33.5	21.7	17.9	27.3	37.1	27.1	38.4	50.1	30.1
Return on Equity After Income Taxes 48	26.8	21.7	16.6	25.2	34.6	24.1	31.6	41.9	22.8
Profit Margin (Before Income Tax) 49	9.2	2.2	4.6	6.6	7.5	6.5	9.3	10.6	10.1
Profit Margin (After Income Tax) 50	7.3	2.2	4.3	6.1	7.0	5.8	7.6	8.9	7.6

Table I

Corporations with and without Net Income

NONFERROUS METAL PRODUCTION AND PROCESSING

MONEY AMOUNTS AND SIZE OF ASSETS IN THOUSANDS OF DOLLARS

Item Description for Accounting Period 7/04 Through 6/05	Total	Zero Assets	Under 500	500 to 1,000	1,000 to 5,000	5,000 to 10,000	10,000 to 25,000	25,000 to 50,000	50,000 to 100,000	100,000 to 250,000	250,000 to 500,000	500,000 to 2,500,000	2,500,000 and over
Number of Enterprises 1	1442	6	706	173	344	17	83	40	27	19	11	13	4
Revenues ($ in Thousands)													
Net Sales 2	63450168	266986	152603	403518	2440436	206990	2991678	2854553	2668526	4354955	5494254	14373021	27742647
Interest 3	1080943	40	1	1	594	101	839	2143	8447	6701	6173	131443	924460
Rents 4	92971	2	0	0	2188	0	610	475	222	47	719	52370	36339
Royalties 5	64766	335	0	0	0	0	128	8916	697	0	417	9232	45041
Other Portfolio Income 6	832082	2193	0	28	251	60	1209	1248	6907	4276	36735	108502	670676
Other Receipts 7	1273374	342	0	0	-31474	3745	10006	14347	253664	132121	118223	136624	635773
Total Receipts 8	66794304	269898	152604	403547	2411995	210896	3004470	2881682	2938463	4498100	5656521	14811192	29954936
Average Total Receipts 9	46321	44983	216	2333	7012	12406	36198	72042	108832	236742	514229	1139322	7388734
Operating Costs/Operating Income (%)													
Cost of Operations 10	82.0	127.0	64.6	73.6	85.2	74.7	81.3	83.7	80.5	85.2	83.8	80.2	81.6
Salaries and Wages 11	3.4	3.8	6.0	0.0	2.9	3.1	2.9	2.8	5.6	2.1	2.2	5.3	3.0
Taxes Paid 12	0.9	0.6	3.6	0.8	1.3	1.6	1.3	1.2	1.3	0.9	1.0	1.1	0.5
Interest Paid 13	3.1	6.4	0.0	0.4	0.8	2.2	0.6	0.7	1.4	1.2	1.5	2.5	5.0
Depreciation 14	2.8	2.1	0.5	0.4	1.3	2.8	2.3	2.7	3.4	2.9	2.5	3.1	2.9
Amortization and Depletion 15	0.8	0.4	•	0.4	0.0	0.2	0.0	0.1	0.2	0.1	0.4	0.5	1.4
Pensions and Other Deferred Comp. 16	0.4	0.5	•	•	0.4	1.3	0.4	0.3	0.5	0.3	0.3	0.5	0.3
Employee Benefits 17	1.1	4.9	1.6	0.7	0.9	0.8	1.4	1.4	1.9	1.4	1.7	1.4	0.6
Advertising 18	0.2	0.1	1.4	0.6	0.1	0.1	0.1	0.1	0.1	0.0	0.0	0.3	0.2
Other Expenses 19	7.1	7.0	20.4	2.1	5.0	13.3	4.7	4.6	12.0	3.1	6.5	8.1	7.5
Officers' Compensation 20	0.4	0.8	3.0	2.4	1.3	2.7	1.4	1.1	1.3	0.4	0.5	0.3	0.0
Operating Margin 21	•	•	•	18.5	0.7	•	3.5	1.3	•	2.3	•	•	•
Operating Margin Before Officers' Comp. 22	•	•	1.8	20.9	1.9	•	4.9	2.4	•	2.7	0.1	•	•

Selected Average Balance Sheet ($ in Thousands)

Net Receivables 23	20331	0	43	67	625	1419	4485	9651	14389	32896	67478	125249	6223639
Inventories 24	4005	0	12	78	596	3239	3258	9071	9366	25752	85454	154546	584606
Net Property, Plant and Equipment 25	10746	0	7	217	607	2533	4499	9933	19498	45033	90457	236221	2245618
Total Assets 26	77140	0	60	729	3033	6626	15652	35411	67114	147221	387965	1048818	21171112
Notes and Loans Payable 27	23948	0	75	202	1417	4670	4933	9926	18657	46229	176717	402375	6128721
All Other Liabilities 28	22250	0	15	62	991	2333	4490	10772	19705	60265	81793	559593	5256956
Net Worth 29	30942	0	-31	465	624	-377	6230	14714	28753	40727	129454	86850	9785436

Selected Financial Ratios (Times to 1)

Current Ratio 30	1.1	•	2.4	7.3	0.9	1.2	1.7	1.6	1.7	1.5	1.7	1.3	1.0
Quick Ratio 31	0.9	•	2.3	5.3	0.4	0.9	0.9	0.8	0.9	0.8	0.7	0.5	0.9
Net Sales to Working Capital 32	14.5	•	6.9	5.9	•	20.0	9.2	8.5	6.9	9.9	6.5	11.7	35.0
Coverage Ratio 33	2.3	•	•	44.0	0.4	0.6	7.4	4.3	2.3	5.6	2.7	0.9	2.5
Total Asset Turnover 34	0.6	•	3.6	3.2	2.3	1.8	2.3	2.0	1.5	1.6	1.3	1.1	0.3
Inventory Turnover 35	9.0	•	11.5	22.1	10.1	2.8	9.0	6.6	8.5	7.6	4.9	5.7	9.5
Receivables Turnover 36	2.5	•	6.2	39.3	13.0	1.6	8.8	7.8	8.8	7.7	7.0	1.3	•
Total Liabilities to Net Worth 37	1.5	•	•	0.6	3.9	•	1.5	1.4	1.3	2.6	2.0	11.1	1.2
Current Assets to Working Capital 38	9.5	•	1.7	1.2	•	5.9	2.5	2.7	2.4	3.1	2.3	4.3	37.8
Current Liabilities to Working Capital 39	8.5	•	0.7	0.2	•	4.9	1.5	1.7	1.4	2.1	1.3	3.3	36.8
Working Capital to Net Sales 40	0.1	•	0.1	0.2	•	0.0	0.1	0.1	0.1	0.1	0.2	0.1	0.0
Inventory to Working Capital 41	1.5	•	0.1	0.3	•	1.2	0.9	1.1	0.8	1.2	1.0	1.3	3.0
Total Receipts to Cash Flow 42	12.4	•	7.2	5.0	47.5	10.4	13.4	17.9	8.6	12.1	13.0	23.0	9.2
Cost of Goods to Cash Flow 43	10.2	•	4.6	3.6	40.5	7.8	10.9	15.0	7.0	10.3	10.9	18.5	7.5
Cash Flow to Total Debt 44	0.1	•	0.3	1.8	0.1	0.2	0.3	0.2	0.3	0.2	0.1	0.0	0.1

Selected Financial Factors (in Percentages)

Debt Ratio 45	59.9	•	151.0	36.2	79.4	105.7	60.2	58.4	57.2	72.3	66.6	91.7	53.8
Return on Total Assets 46	4.0	•	•	60.5	0.7	2.4	10.4	6.0	4.9	10.6	5.3	2.3	3.9
Return on Equity Before Income Taxes 47	5.6	•	8.6	92.7	•	28.1	22.6	11.0	6.6	31.5	9.9	•	5.1
Return on Equity After Income Taxes 48	3.8	•	8.7	92.7	•	30.6	21.3	7.9	4.7	22.6	8.1	•	3.6
Profit Margin (Before Income Tax) 49	3.9	•	•	18.5	•	•	3.9	2.3	1.9	5.6	2.6	•	7.3
Profit Margin (After Income Tax) 50	2.7	•	•	18.5	•	•	3.7	1.6	1.4	4.0	2.1	•	5.2

Table II

Corporations with Net Income

NONFERROUS METAL PRODUCTION AND PROCESSING

MONEY AMOUNTS AND SIZE OF ASSETS IN THOUSANDS OF DOLLARS

Item Description for Accounting Period 7/04 Through 6/05	Total	Zero Assets	Under 500	500 to 1,000	1,000 to 5,000	5,000 to 10,000	10,000 to 25,000	25,000 to 50,000	50,000 to 100,000	100,000 to 250,000	250,000 to 500,000	500,000 to 2,500,000	2,500,000 and over
Number of Enterprises 1	612	0	0	0	204	5	62	24	20	15	7	10	4
Revenues ($ in Thousands)													
Net Sales 2	52973397	0	0	0	1748169	99735	2222821	1826939	2179212	3296432	3894693	9712134	27242647
Interest 3	1050523	0	0	0	593	22	584	1569	2818	6598	4384	109457	924460
Rents 4	92062	0	0	0	2188	0	610	467	222	17	686	51531	36339
Royalties 5	54435	0	0	0	0	0	0	8916	0	0	2	140	45041
Other Portfolio Income 6	722265	0	0	0	251	60	597	656	6527	4269	25239	11798	670676
Other Receipts 7	1263630	0	0	0	1490	1398	6865	11650	251226	120785	95153	138946	635773
Total Receipts 8	56156312	0	0	0	1752691	101215	2231477	1850197	2440005	3428101	4020157	1002406	29954936
Average Total Receipts 9	91759	•	•	•	8592	20243	35992	77092	122000	228540	574308	1002401	7388734
Operating Costs/Operating Income (%)													
Cost of Operations 10	80.8	•	•	•	79.7	65.0	79.8	82.9	81.6	82.3	82.9	78.1	81.6
Salaries and Wages 11	3.4	•	•	•	3.9	5.6	2.8	2.8	6.0	2.2	2.6	5.3	3.0
Taxes Paid 12	0.8	•	•	•	1.5	1.4	1.2	1.0	1.2	1.0	0.9	1.2	0.5
Interest Paid 13	3.2	•	•	•	0.6	0.3	0.5	0.6	1.0	1.1	0.8	2.3	5.0
Depreciation 14	2.8	•	•	•	1.4	0.9	2.2	2.5	2.5	3.2	2.0	3.3	2.9
Amortization and Depletion 15	0.8	•	•	•	0.1	0.0	0.0	0.0	0.2	0.1	0.4	0.3	1.4
Pensions and Other Deferred Comp. 16	0.3	•	•	•	0.6	2.7	0.4	0.3	0.5	0.4	0.3	0.3	0.3
Employee Benefits 17	1.0	•	•	•	1.0	1.4	1.2	1.2	2.2	1.1	1.3	1.5	0.6
Advertising 18	0.2	•	•	•	0.1	0.2	0.1	0.1	0.1	0.1	0.0	0.3	0.2
Other Expenses 19	6.9	•	•	•	6.0	10.6	4.4	3.7	12.6	3.2	5.5	7.2	7.5
Officers' Compensation 20	0.4	•	•	•	1.3	2.6	1.5	1.1	0.9	0.5	0.6	0.3	0.0
Operating Margin 21	•	•	•	•	4.0	9.2	5.8	3.6	•	4.8	2.8	•	•
Operating Margin Before Officers' Comp. 22	•	•	•	•	5.2	11.9	7.3	4.7	•	5.3	3.4	•	•

Selected Average Balance Sheet ($ in Thousands)

Net Receivables 23	45964	688	2456	4378	10325	16107	34835	69080	121430	6223639
Inventories 24	6620	608	8073	3096	8466	11373	22558	59271	147333	584606
Net Property, Plant and Equipment 25	22514	729	727	4199	9952	16331	46818	101794	236048	2245618
Total Assets 26	168391	2480	7667	15072	37138	69330	150626	401272	939838	21171112
Notes and Loans Payable 27	49886	1070	473	4056	9139	16644	36578	135769	345671	6128721
All Other Liabilities 28	42263	582	1269	3931	11983	21451	57298	74201	236321	5256956
Net Worth 29	76242	827	5924	7085	16017	31234	56750	191303	357847	9785436

Selected Financial Ratios (Times to 1)

Current Ratio 30	1.1	1.8	5.1	1.9	1.6	2.0	1.5	1.8	2.0	1.0
Quick Ratio 31	0.9	1.0	3.7	1.1	0.9	1.1	0.9	0.8	0.8	0.9
Net Sales to Working Capital 32	11.3	11.7	3.8	7.6	8.6	5.8	8.8	7.1	5.3	35.0
Coverage Ratio 33	2.9	8.0	38.0	13.5	8.6	4.2	8.8	8.3	2.3	2.5
Total Asset Turnover 34	0.5	3.5	2.6	2.4	2.0	1.6	1.5	1.4	1.0	0.3
Inventory Turnover 35	10.6	11.2	1.6	9.2	7.5	7.8	8.0	7.8	5.2	9.5
Receivables Turnover 36	2.2	12.9	0.9	9.6	8.5	•	7.3	•	1.0	•
Total Liabilities to Net Worth 37	1.2	2.0	0.3	1.1	1.3	1.2	1.7	1.1	1.6	1.2
Current Assets to Working Capital 38	8.1	2.2	1.2	2.1	2.6	2.0	3.0	2.3	2.1	37.8
Current Liabilities to Working Capital 39	7.1	1.2	0.2	1.1	1.6	1.0	2.0	1.3	1.1	36.8
Working Capital to Net Sales 40	0.1	0.1	0.3	0.1	0.1	0.2	0.1	0.1	0.2	0.0
Inventory to Working Capital 41	1.1	0.9	0.3	0.8	1.1	0.6	1.1	0.8	0.6	3.0
Total Receipts to Cash Flow 42	9.7	13.2	5.1	10.5	13.9	7.5	8.6	10.1	12.0	9.2
Cost of Goods to Cash Flow 43	7.9	10.5	3.3	8.4	11.5	6.1	7.1	8.4	9.3	7.5
Cash Flow to Total Debt 44	0.1	0.4	2.3	0.4	0.3	0.4	0.3	0.3	0.1	0.1

Selected Financial Factors (in Percentages)

Debt Ratio 45	54.7	66.6	22.7	53.0	56.9	54.9	62.3	52.3	61.9	53.8
Return on Total Assets 46	4.8	16.8	28.6	16.0	11.2	6.7	14.6	9.5	5.4	3.9
Return on Equity Before Income Taxes 47	7.0	44.0	36.0	31.5	23.0	11.3	34.2	17.4	8.0	5.1
Return on Equity After Income Taxes 48	5.3	40.1	35.4	30.0	18.3	9.0	26.1	15.6	6.3	3.6
Profit Margin (Before Income Tax) 49	6.2	4.2	10.7	6.2	4.8	3.2	8.8	6.0	2.9	7.3
Profit Margin (After Income Tax) 50	4.7	3.9	10.5	5.9	3.8	2.6	6.7	5.3	2.3	5.2

Table I

Corporations with and without Net Income

FOUNDRIES

MONEY AMOUNTS AND SIZE OF ASSETS IN THOUSANDS OF DOLLARS

Item Description for Accounting Period 7/04 Through 6/05	Total	Zero Assets	Under 500	500 to 1,000	1,000 to 5,000	5,000 to 10,000	10,000 to 25,000	25,000 to 50,000	50,000 to 100,000	100,000 to 250,000	250,000 to 500,000	500,000 to 2,500,000	2,500,000 and over
Number of Enterprises **1**	1526	4	1180	0	166	63	67	20	13	0	6	6	0

Revenues ($ in Thousands)

Net Sales **2**	18654478	475600	708483	0	1209497	768697	1826726	1082731	1574738	0	3158633	7849373	0
Interest **3**	82518	4	0	0	916	140	1070	664	468	0	6901	72356	0
Rents **4**	2954	0	0	0	662	216	602	162	113	0	229	969	0
Royalties **5**	16782	0	0	0	0	0	0	177	0	0	15706	899	0
Other Portfolio Income **6**	16472	0	0	0	791	52	1800	932	2299	0	2247	8351	0
Other Receipts **7**	99367	3839	544	0	1186	12387	19048	4224	6559	0	2485	49096	0
Total Receipts **8**	18872571	479443	709027	0	1213052	781492	1849246	1088890	1584177	0	3186201	7981044	0
Average Total Receipts **9**	12367	119861	601	•	7308	12405	27601	54444	121860	•	531034	1330174	•

Operating Costs/Operating Income (%)

Cost of Operations **10**	74.2	80.2	55.6	•	71.1	80.9	77.6	76.5	72.9	•	79.5	72.4	•
Salaries and Wages **11**	6.4	2.0	8.2	•	4.4	5.4	4.7	3.8	4.6	•	5.6	8.3	•
Taxes Paid **12**	2.0	3.2	3.5	•	4.1	2.1	2.2	2.2	1.8	•	2.0	1.3	•
Interest Paid **13**	2.2	0.1	0.8	•	0.8	1.7	0.9	0.8	1.6	•	2.4	3.3	•
Depreciation **14**	3.6	3.7	2.6	•	3.5	3.2	2.9	4.5	5.5	•	4.0	3.3	•
Amortization and Depletion **15**	0.3	1.3	0.9	•	0.0	0.3	0.2	0.0	0.2	•	•	0.5	•
Pensions and Other Deferred Comp. **16**	0.8	0.1	•	•	1.3	1.0	0.4	0.6	1.0	•	0.4	1.0	•
Employee Benefits **17**	2.9	3.8	2.2	•	4.0	1.2	2.1	3.2	1.1	•	2.9	3.4	•
Advertising **18**	0.1	0.0	0.2	•	0.1	0.1	0.1	0.1	0.1	•	0.1	0.1	•
Other Expenses **19**	5.7	6.3	10.7	•	7.1	4.8	5.3	4.6	7.1	•	4.2	5.7	•
Officers' Compensation **20**	1.4	0.0	9.5	•	3.1	1.7	1.8	1.3	0.9	•	0.4	0.8	•
Operating Margin **21**	0.4	•	5.7	•	0.4	•	1.8	2.6	3.1	•	•	•	•
Operating Margin Before Officers' Comp. **22**	1.8	•	15.2	•	3.6	•	3.6	3.9	4.0	•	•	0.6	•

Selected Average Balance Sheet ($ in Thousands)

Net Receivables 23	1712	0	50	•	1041	1664	4367	7541	16664	•	82181	187139	•
Inventories 24	1245	0	35	•	679	1123	2525	4671	8408	•	50367	157078	•
Net Property, Plant and Equipment 25	2571	0	34	•	1145	2982	4841	13398	34157	•	111374	300154	•
Total Assets 26	11794	0	205	•	3512	7146	15130	33418	83359	•	380208	1945922	•
Notes and Loans Payable 27	3343	0	180	•	836	2460	4665	8124	25735	•	143268	487574	•
All Other Liabilities 28	3029	0	55	•	751	2062	4197	7850	21726	•	97825	499045	•
Net Worth 29	5422	0	-31	•	1925	2625	6269	17444	35898	•	139115	959304	•

Selected Financial Ratios (Times to 1)

Current Ratio 30	1.6	•	2.7	•	1.9	1.7	1.6	1.8	1.6	•	1.7	1.4	•
Quick Ratio 31	0.9	•	1.6	•	1.3	1.0	1.0	1.1	1.0	•	1.0	0.7	•
Net Sales to Working Capital 32	9.0	•	7.6	•	6.7	8.3	8.3	7.7	9.1	•	7.7	10.4	•
Coverage Ratio 33	1.8	3.5	8.1	•	1.9	0.5	4.5	4.9	3.3	•	0.9	1.5	•
Total Asset Turnover 34	1.0	•	2.9	•	2.1	1.7	1.8	1.6	1.5	•	1.4	0.7	•
Inventory Turnover 35	7.3	•	9.6	•	7.6	8.8	8.4	8.9	10.5	•	8.3	6.0	•
Receivables Turnover 36	7.5	•	13.5	•	7.2	7.4	7.0	7.7	9.0	•	6.5	7.6	•
Total Liabilities to Net Worth 37	1.2	•	•	•	0.8	1.7	1.4	0.9	1.3	•	1.7	1.0	•
Current Assets to Working Capital 38	2.8	•	1.6	•	2.1	2.4	2.7	2.3	2.8	•	2.5	3.4	•
Current Liabilities to Working Capital 39	1.8	•	0.6	•	1.1	1.4	1.7	1.3	1.8	•	1.5	2.4	•
Working Capital to Net Sales 40	0.1	•	0.1	•	0.1	0.1	0.1	0.1	0.1	•	0.1	0.1	•
Inventory to Working Capital 41	1.0	•	0.6	•	0.6	0.9	0.8	0.8	0.8	•	0.8	1.4	•
Total Receipts to Cash Flow 42	18.0	16.5	8.0	•	20.1	29.6	13.9	17.0	10.8	•	65.9	17.7	•
Cost of Goods to Cash Flow 43	13.4	13.3	4.5	•	14.3	23.9	10.8	13.0	7.9	•	52.4	12.8	•
Cash Flow to Total Debt 44	0.1	•	0.3	•	0.2	0.1	0.2	0.2	0.2	•	0.0	0.1	•

Selected Financial Factors (in Percentages)

Debt Ratio 45	54.0	•	115.0	•	45.2	63.3	58.6	47.8	56.9	•	63.4	50.7	•
Return on Total Assets 46	4.0	•	19.3	•	3.2	1.6	7.0	6.3	7.5	•	3.0	3.3	•
Return on Equity Before Income Taxes 47	3.8	•	•	•	2.7	•	13.2	9.7	12.1	•	•	2.3	•
Return on Equity After Income Taxes 48	2.4	•	•	•	1.7	•	11.1	8.4	8.2	•	•	1.3	•
Profit Margin (Before Income Tax) 49	1.7	0.2	5.8	•	0.7	•	3.0	3.1	3.6	•	•	1.7	•
Profit Margin (After Income Tax) 50	1.1	0.2	5.8	•	0.5	•	2.5	2.7	2.4	•	•	1.0	•

Table II

Corporations with Net Income

FOUNDRIES

MONEY AMOUNTS AND SIZE OF ASSETS IN THOUSANDS OF DOLLARS

Item Description for Accounting Period 7/04 Through 6/05	Total	Zero Assets	Under 500	500 to 1,000	1,000 to 5,000	5,000 to 10,000	10,000 to 25,000	25,000 to 50,000	50,000 to 100,000	100,000 to 250,000	250,000 to 500,000	500,000 to 2,500,000	2,500,000 and over
Number of Enterprises **1**	985	0	0	0	94	22	50	14	10	0	0	3	0
Revenues ($ in Thousands)													
Net Sales **2**	12632987	0	0	0	858362	282273	1505734	777136	1245572	0	0	5165948	0
Interest **3**	12536	0	0	0	354	90	1060	75	383	0	0	3793	0
Rents **4**	2256	0	0	0	655	39	554	162	12	0	0	719	0
Royalties **5**	16782	0	0	0	0	0	0	177	0	0	0	899	0
Other Portfolio Income **6**	6142	0	0	0	0	0	1485	222	2299	0	0	727	0
Other Receipts **7**	76232	0	0	0	272	4347	11946	2793	4896	0	0	31041	0
Total Receipts **8**	12746935	0	0	0	859643	286749	1520779	780565	1253162	0	0	5203127	0
Average Total Receipts **9**	12941	•	•	•	9145	13034	30416	55755	125316	•	•	1734376	•
Operating Costs/Operating Income (%)													
Cost of Operations **10**	71.3	•	•	•	70.9	77.7	75.9	75.5	71.2	•	•	66.1	•
Salaries and Wages **11**	7.6	•	•	•	4.2	3.3	4.4	3.7	4.7	•	•	11.1	•
Taxes Paid **12**	2.0	•	•	•	4.1	2.3	2.2	2.2	2.0	•	•	1.3	•
Interest Paid **13**	1.4	•	•	•	1.1	0.8	0.7	0.8	1.0	•	•	2.3	•
Depreciation **14**	3.3	•	•	•	2.9	4.5	2.9	3.8	4.1	•	•	3.1	•
Amortization and Depletion **15**	0.4	•	•	•	0.0	0.1	0.1	0.0	0.3	•	•	0.5	•
Pensions and Other Deferred Comp. **16**	0.8	•	•	•	0.5	0.4	0.4	0.3	1.1	•	•	1.4	•
Employee Benefits **17**	2.7	•	•	•	3.9	2.3	2.3	2.5	1.4	•	•	3.9	•
Advertising **18**	0.1	•	•	•	0.1	0.1	0.1	0.0	0.1	•	•	0.2	•
Other Expenses **19**	4.8	•	•	•	7.2	3.5	5.3	3.5	7.5	•	•	5.0	•
Officers' Compensation **20**	1.5	•	•	•	2.6	3.1	1.9	1.3	1.0	•	•	0.9	•
Operating Margin **21**	3.9	•	•	•	2.6	2.1	3.9	6.4	5.6	•	•	4.1	•
Operating Margin Before Officers' Comp. **22**	5.4	•	•	•	5.2	5.3	5.8	7.7	6.6	•	•	5.0	•

Selected Average Balance Sheet ($ in Thousands)

Net Receivables 23	1848	1413	1901	4610	8003	18152	276359
Inventories 24	1188	662	1870	2391	4138	11972	255238
Net Property, Plant and Equipment 25	2438	1539	3288	4889	14040	29311	361784
Total Assets 26	10396	3968	8481	15686	34517	83798	2085079
Notes and Loans Payable 27	2588	1288	1350	3865	7709	21260	564564
All Other Liabilities 28	3599	952	1783	4096	8305	20409	854850
Net Worth 29	4209	1728	5348	7725	18502	42128	665665

Selected Financial Ratios (Times to 1)

Current Ratio 30	1.6	1.4	2.4	1.8	1.7	2.1	1.4
Quick Ratio 31	1.0	0.9	1.4	1.1	1.0	1.4	0.7
Net Sales to Working Capital 32	8.2	12.9	5.3	7.2	8.6	5.9	11.0
Coverage Ratio 33	4.4	3.6	5.9	8.1	9.5	7.2	3.1
Total Asset Turnover 34	1.2	2.3	1.5	1.9	1.6	1.5	0.8
Inventory Turnover 35	7.7	9.8	5.3	9.6	10.1	7.4	4.5
Receivables Turnover 36	8.2	6.8	4.6	8.4	7.9		
Total Liabilities to Net Worth 37	1.5	1.3	0.6	1.0	0.9	1.0	2.1
Current Assets to Working Capital 38	2.6	3.4	1.7	2.3	2.5	1.9	3.8
Current Liabilities to Working Capital 39	1.6	2.4	0.7	1.3	1.5	0.9	2.8
Working Capital to Net Sales 40	0.1	0.1	0.2	0.1	0.1	0.2	0.1
Inventory to Working Capital 41	1.0	1.1	0.7	0.7	0.9	0.6	1.6
Total Receipts to Cash Flow 42	12.7	15.0	15.4	11.0	11.3	7.9	12.7
Cost of Goods to Cash Flow 43	9.1	10.7	12.0	8.4	8.6	5.7	8.4
Cash Flow to Total Debt 44	0.2	0.3	0.3	0.3	0.3	0.4	0.1

Selected Financial Factors (in Percentages)

Debt Ratio 45	59.5	56.4	36.9	50.8	46.4	49.7	68.1
Return on Total Assets 46	7.7	8.9	6.8	10.7	12.3	10.5	5.9
Return on Equity Before Income Taxes 47	14.8	14.8	8.9	19.0	20.5	18.0	12.4
Return on Equity After Income Taxes 48	12.0	12.8	8.3	16.7	18.7	13.6	9.7
Profit Margin (Before Income Tax) 49	4.8	2.8	3.7	4.9	6.8	6.1	4.8
Profit Margin (After Income Tax) 50	4.0	2.4	3.5	4.3	6.2	4.6	3.8

Table I

Corporations with and without Net Income

FORGING AND STAMPING

MONEY AMOUNTS AND SIZE OF ASSETS IN THOUSANDS OF DOLLARS

Item Description for Accounting Period 7/04 Through 6/05	Total	Zero Assets	Under 500	500 to 1,000	1,000 to 5,000	5,000 to 10,000	10,000 to 25,000	25,000 to 50,000	50,000 to 100,000	100,000 to 250,000	250,000 to 500,000	500,000 to 2,500,000	2,500,000 and over
Number of Enterprises 1	3073	0	0	0	647	155	139	48	30	17	0	0	0
Revenues ($ in Thousands)													
Net Sales 2	18932467	0	0	0	2496034	1694862	3699564	2754587	2792225	4065857	0	0	0
Interest 3	76711	0	0	0	1033	3764	2230	1062	2230	65863	0	0	0
Rents 4	3270	0	0	0	27	413	1201	850	752	27	0	0	0
Royalties 5	341	0	0	0	0	0	1	6	0	334	0	0	0
Other Portfolio Income 6	66890	0	0	0	7435	6156	17548	2395	6951	16737	0	0	0
Other Receipts 7	230372	0	0	0	56491	20297	34965	14439	16194	85165	0	0	0
Total Receipts 8	19310051	0	0	0	2561020	1725492	3755509	2773339	2818352	4233983	0	0	0
Average Total Receipts 9	6284	•	•	•	3958	11132	27018	57778	93945	249058	•	•	•
Operating Costs/Operating Income (%)													
Cost of Operations 10	72.7	•	•	•	67.4	73.1	76.0	78.6	73.4	72.7	•	•	•
Salaries and Wages 11	4.9	•	•	•	6.5	3.9	4.6	4.3	4.3	5.1	•	•	•
Taxes Paid 12	2.1	•	•	•	2.9	2.5	2.1	1.9	2.0	1.5	•	•	•
Interest Paid 13	1.4	•	•	•	0.7	0.8	0.8	0.9	1.1	3.3	•	•	•
Depreciation 14	3.8	•	•	•	2.3	2.4	3.6	3.3	5.2	4.8	•	•	•
Amortization and Depletion 15	0.3	•	•	•	0.0	0.1	0.1	0.2	0.4	1.0	•	•	•
Pensions and Other Deferred Comp. 16	0.6	•	•	•	0.5	0.4	0.7	0.5	0.7	0.9	•	•	•
Employee Benefits 17	2.2	•	•	•	3.6	0.9	2.1	1.5	2.1	2.8	•	•	•
Advertising 18	0.2	•	•	•	0.2	0.2	0.1	0.1	0.2	0.2	•	•	•
Other Expenses 19	8.0	•	•	•	13.2	12.6	5.5	4.9	5.7	6.5	•	•	•
Officers' Compensation 20	2.9	•	•	•	5.7	3.7	1.9	1.3	1.3	1.1	•	•	•
Operating Margin 21	0.8	•	•	•	•	•	2.4	2.4	3.6	0.0	•	•	•
Operating Margin Before Officers' Comp. 22	3.7	•	•	•	2.7	3.1	4.3	3.7	4.9	1.2	•	•	•

Selected Average Balance Sheet ($ in Thousands)

Net Receivables 23	954	587	1633	3958	9717	15126	40537
Inventories 24	711	481	1744	3059	5986	11595	26202
Net Property, Plant and Equipment 25	1178	407	1681	4972	12021	24140	58374
Total Assets 26	4092	2311	6978	15587	35506	69980	203527
Notes and Loans Payable 27	1218	576	2315	4632	11846	20966	62802
All Other Liabilities 28	1249	1373	1907	4041	9069	18653	57744
Net Worth 29	1626	362	2756	6914	14591	30361	82981

Selected Financial Ratios (Times to 1)

Current Ratio 30	1.7	1.6	1.5	1.8	1.6	1.5	1.7
Quick Ratio 31	1.0	1.1	0.8	1.0	1.0	0.8	0.9
Net Sales to Working Capital 32	6.8	5.8	8.5	6.7	8.1	7.6	6.7
Coverage Ratio 33	3.0	0.4	2.4	5.7	4.4	5.0	2.3
Total Asset Turnover 34	1.5	1.7	1.6	1.7	1.6	1.3	1.2
Inventory Turnover 35	6.3	5.4	4.6	6.6	7.5	5.9	6.6
Receivables Turnover 36	6.9	6.8	5.5	7.4	6.6	6.2	7.2
Total Liabilities to Net Worth 37	1.5	5.4	1.5	1.3	1.4	1.3	1.5
Current Assets to Working Capital 38	2.5	2.6	2.9	2.3	2.7	3.1	2.5
Current Liabilities to Working Capital 39	1.5	1.6	1.9	1.3	1.7	2.1	1.5
Working Capital to Net Sales 40	0.1	0.2	0.1	0.1	0.1	0.1	0.1
Inventory to Working Capital 41	0.8	0.7	1.2	0.8	0.9	1.0	0.9
Total Receipts to Cash Flow 42	12.2	12.2	14.2	13.0	15.5	11.2	10.5
Cost of Goods to Cash Flow 43	8.8	8.2	10.4	9.9	12.2	8.2	7.6
Cash Flow to Total Debt 44	0.2	0.2	0.2	0.2	0.2	0.2	0.2

Selected Financial Factors (in Percentages)

Debt Ratio 45	60.3	84.3	60.5	55.6	58.9	56.6	59.2
Return on Total Assets 46	6.3	0.4	3.1	8.1	6.5	7.5	8.9
Return on Equity Before Income Taxes 47	10.6		4.6	15.0	12.2	13.8	12.1
Return on Equity After Income Taxes 48	8.9		2.1	13.4	11.1	11.7	10.7
Profit Margin (Before Income Tax) 49	2.8		1.2	3.9	3.1	4.5	4.2
Profit Margin (After Income Tax) 50	2.4		0.5	3.5	2.8	3.8	3.7

Table II
Corporations with Net Income

FORGING AND STAMPING

MONEY AMOUNTS AND SIZE OF ASSETS IN THOUSANDS OF DOLLARS

Item Description for Accounting Period 7/04 Through 6/05	Total	Zero Assets	Under 500	500 to 1,000	1,000 to 5,000	5,000 to 10,000	10,000 to 25,000	25,000 to 50,000	50,000 to 100,000	100,000 to 250,000	250,000 to 500,000	500,000 to 2,500,000	2,500,000 and over
Number of Enterprises **1**	2020	0	1199	0	394	141	102	35	0	11	0	0	0
Revenues ($ in Thousands)													
Net Sales **2**	13942452	0	760062	0	1611563	1435917	2814584	2126252	0	2528868	0	0	0
Interest **3**	68804	0	472	0	647	364	1210	897	0	62982	0	0	0
Rents **4**	2602	0	0	0	0	83	899	850	0	23	0	0	0
Royalties **5**	341	0	0	0	0	0	1	6	0	334	0	0	0
Other Portfolio Income **6**	55697	0	0	0	5369	5095	16666	2391	0	16105	0	0	0
Other Receipts **7**	201762	0	38	0	51682	22362	25087	13058	0	73647	0	0	0
Total Receipts **8**	14271658	0	760572	0	1669261	1463821	2858447	2143454	0	2681959	0	0	0
Average Total Receipts **9**	7065	•	634	•	4237	10382	28024	61242	•	243814	•	•	•
Operating Costs/Operating Income (%)													
Cost of Operations **10**	70.4	•	55.1	•	64.3	71.9	74.2	76.9	•	67.2	•	•	•
Salaries and Wages **11**	5.1	•	5.4	•	6.2	4.3	4.7	4.4	•	6.2	•	•	•
Taxes Paid **12**	2.1	•	3.3	•	2.7	2.3	2.1	1.9	•	1.4	•	•	•
Interest Paid **13**	1.5	•	0.7	•	0.6	0.8	0.8	0.8	•	4.6	•	•	•
Depreciation **14**	3.3	•	4.3	•	2.5	2.3	3.2	3.2	•	3.9	•	•	•
Amortization and Depletion **15**	0.4	•	0.0	•	0.0	0.1	0.1	0.2	•	1.4	•	•	•
Pensions and Other Deferred Comp. **16**	0.7	•	0.1	•	0.7	0.5	0.7	0.5	•	1.1	•	•	•
Employee Benefits **17**	2.3	•	2.6	•	3.3	0.9	2.1	1.4	•	3.3	•	•	•
Advertising **18**	0.2	•	0.3	•	0.2	0.2	0.1	0.1	•	0.3	•	•	•
Other Expenses **19**	7.3	•	13.4	•	12.0	8.1	5.4	4.9	•	7.1	•	•	•
Officers' Compensation **20**	2.9	•	10.2	•	7.3	3.9	2.1	1.3	•	1.3	•	•	•
Operating Margin **21**	3.8	•	4.6	•	0.2	4.8	4.7	4.5	•	2.2	•	•	•
Operating Margin Before Officers' Comp. **22**	6.7	•	14.8	•	7.5	8.7	6.8	5.8	•	3.5	•	•	•

Selected Average Balance Sheet ($ in Thousands)

Net Receivables 23	1076	71	644	1524	4018	10495			37739
Inventories 24	755	16	469	1429	2938	5851			26808
Net Property, Plant and Equipment 25	1239	28	439	1683	4578	11713			53509
Total Assets 26	4432	185	1990	6827	15434	36471			199589
Notes and Loans Payable 27	1335	18	630	1917	4273	10521			69786
All Other Liabilities 28	1119	56	528	1492	3643	8950			55833
Net Worth 29	1978	112	832	3418	7519	17000			73971

Selected Financial Ratios (Times to 1)

Current Ratio 30	1.8	2.2	1.6	2.1	2.0	1.8			1.7
Quick Ratio 31	1.1	1.7	1.0	1.1	1.1	1.1			1.0
Net Sales to Working Capital 32	6.4	7.9	8.5	5.5	5.9	6.8			6.7
Coverage Ratio 33	5.0	7.7	6.9	9.5	9.1	7.7			2.8
Total Asset Turnover 34	1.6	3.4	2.1	1.5	1.8	1.7			1.2
Inventory Turnover 35	6.4	21.4	5.6	5.1	7.0	8.0			5.8
Receivables Turnover 36	6.8	16.0	6.3	5.6	8.1	7.0			6.2
Total Liabilities to Net Worth 37	1.2	0.7	1.4	1.0	1.1	1.1			1.7
Current Assets to Working Capital 38	2.3	1.9	2.6	1.9	2.0	2.3			2.5
Current Liabilities to Working Capital 39	1.3	0.9	1.6	0.9	1.0	1.3			1.5
Working Capital to Net Sales 40	0.2	0.1	0.1	0.2	0.2	0.1			0.1
Inventory to Working Capital 41	0.8	0.4	0.9	0.8	0.8	0.8			0.8
Total Receipts to Cash Flow 42	8.7	7.8	7.9	8.0	10.1	11.8			7.0
Cost of Goods to Cash Flow 43	6.2	4.3	5.1	5.8	7.5	9.1			4.7
Cash Flow to Total Debt 44	0.3	1.1	0.4	0.4	0.3	0.3			0.3

Selected Financial Factors (in Percentages)

Debt Ratio 45	55.4	39.5	58.2	49.9	51.3	53.4			62.9
Return on Total Assets 46	12.0	18.3	9.0	11.3	12.5	10.1			14.9
Return on Equity Before Income Taxes 47	21.5	26.3	18.4	20.1	22.9	18.8			25.9
Return on Equity After Income Taxes 48	19.4	24.5	16.8	17.9	20.9	17.5			23.3
Profit Margin (Before Income Tax) 49	6.2	4.7	3.7	6.8	6.2	5.3			8.3
Profit Margin (After Income Tax) 50	5.6	4.3	3.4	6.0	5.7	4.9			7.5

Table I

Corporations with and without Net Income

CUTLERY, HARDWARE, SPRING AND WIRE MACHINE SHOPS, NUT, BOLT

MONEY AMOUNTS AND SIZE OF ASSETS IN THOUSANDS OF DOLLARS

Item Description for Accounting Period 7/04 Through 6/05	Total	Zero Assets	Under 500	500 to 1,000	1,000 to 5,000	5,000 to 10,000	10,000 to 25,000	25,000 to 50,000	50,000 to 100,000	100,000 to 250,000	250,000 to 500,000	500,000 to 2,500,000	2,500,000 and over
Number of Enterprises **1**	20452	2010	13214	1698	2757	368	263	67	33	24	8	10	0
Revenues ($ in Thousands)													
Net Sales **2**	55412834	273885	4210517	2857500	10592949	4085149	6503365	3322807	3153902	4381501	3349458	12681800	0
Interest **3**	1124682	1074	2354	1479	7749	2521	3799	6373	3876	12430	11212	1071816	0
Rents **4**	19007	78	404	3943	3173	466	619	1164	159	4936	1272	2792	0
Royalties **5**	116727	320	24	0	0	81	34	1166	390	1513	2573	110626	0
Other Portfolio Income **6**	655289	31969	26114	3273	38219	9578	10723	13381	12267	25119	277929	206713	0
Other Receipts **7**	868298	490	22002	6997	75732	33804	31184	15718	60990	160718	-258	460925	0
Total Receipts **8**	58196837	307816	4261415	2873192	10711822	4131599	6549724	3360609	3231584	4586217	3642186	14453672	0
Average Total Receipts **9**	2846	153	322	1692	3887	11227	24904	50158	97927	191092	455273	1453467	•
Operating Costs/Operating Income (%)													
Cost of Operations **10**	63.4	47.3	47.5	62.2	64.0	67.2	70.0	74.1	73.0	66.9	69.2	56.4	•
Salaries and Wages **11**	7.7	12.9	11.2	6.4	6.5	4.2	6.2	4.8	6.0	10.3	5.9	10.2	•
Taxes Paid **12**	2.3	2.6	2.7	3.3	2.8	2.9	2.3	1.8	2.0	1.9	1.7	1.6	•
Interest Paid **13**	3.7	0.9	1.0	1.3	1.8	0.6	0.9	1.1	2.0	1.4	5.0	10.9	•
Depreciation **14**	3.8	17.0	4.6	5.8	4.2	5.6	3.8	4.2	3.7	3.1	3.3	2.3	•
Amortization and Depletion **15**	0.7	0.1	0.1	0.0	0.2	0.1	0.1	0.3	0.8	0.6	0.9	2.2	•
Pensions and Other Deferred Comp. **16**	0.8	0.7	0.2	0.7	0.5	0.7	0.5	0.5	0.5	0.8	1.4	1.3	•
Employee Benefits **17**	2.1	0.5	1.1	1.2	2.2	2.1	2.0	1.5	2.1	2.1	2.7	2.6	•
Advertising **18**	0.8	0.7	0.5	0.1	0.2	0.5	0.6	0.6	0.8	0.8	0.9	1.6	•
Other Expenses **19**	12.0	22.9	18.4	10.8	9.0	7.3	7.9	6.9	8.4	9.4	9.9	19.8	•
Officers' Compensation **20**	3.0	5.2	8.3	6.5	5.3	3.8	2.5	1.3	1.4	1.0	0.8	0.5	•
Operating Margin **21**	•	•	4.5	1.5	3.2	4.9	3.1	2.9	•	1.7	•	•	•
Operating Margin Before Officers' Comp. **22**	2.7	•	12.8	8.0	8.5	8.7	5.6	4.1	0.7	2.7	•	•	•

Selected Average Balance Sheet ($ in Thousands)

Net Receivables 23	437	0	22	167	495	1460	3542	7728	14458	29192	57888	337763	•
Inventories 24	309	0	18	108	380	1077	3625	6805	14826	27470	51883	149167	•
Net Property, Plant and Equipment 25	439	0	32	263	585	2181	4560	10078	21000	36073	77610	162859	•
Total Assets 26	2679	0	105	735	2148	6971	15208	33667	64339	158519	340787	2874940	•
Notes and Loans Payable 27	675	0	71	459	1011	1213	4664	10868	30077	48624	153604	351674	•
All Other Liabilities 28	1006	0	20	192	686	1484	3285	7359	18764	34484	122832	1376834	•
Net Worth 29	998	0	15	84	451	4274	7259	15440	15499	75412	64350	1146431	•

Selected Financial Ratios (Times to 1)

Current Ratio 30	1.7	•	2.4	1.5	1.3	2.3	1.9	2.1	2.3	1.9	1.5	1.5	•
Quick Ratio 31	1.0	•	1.6	1.1	0.8	1.5	1.0	1.1	0.9	1.0	0.8	1.0	•
Net Sales to Working Capital 32	6.7	•	8.6	11.8	13.0	4.6	5.6	5.2	3.6	5.3	8.9	6.5	•
Coverage Ratio 33	2.3	2.4	6.5	2.6	3.4	10.4	5.4	4.5	2.0	5.8	2.4	1.5	•
Total Asset Turnover 34	1.0	•	3.0	2.3	1.8	1.6	1.6	1.5	1.5	1.2	1.2	0.4	•
Inventory Turnover 35	5.6	•	8.6	9.7	6.5	6.9	4.8	5.4	4.7	4.4	5.6	4.8	•
Receivables Turnover 36	6.8	•	14.1	9.4	8.2	10.0	7.6	7.1	7.8	6.5	9.1	4.2	•
Total Liabilities to Net Worth 37	1.7	•	6.0	7.8	3.8	0.6	1.1	1.2	3.2	1.1	4.3	1.5	•
Current Assets to Working Capital 38	2.5	•	1.7	3.1	3.9	1.7	2.1	1.9	1.8	2.1	3.1	3.0	•
Current Liabilities to Working Capital 39	1.5	•	0.7	2.1	2.9	0.7	1.1	0.9	0.8	1.1	2.1	2.0	•
Working Capital to Net Sales 40	0.1	•	0.1	0.1	0.1	0.2	0.2	0.2	0.3	0.2	0.1	0.2	•
Inventory to Working Capital 41	0.8	•	0.5	0.6	1.4	0.5	0.9	0.8	0.7	0.8	1.3	0.8	•
Total Receipts to Cash Flow 42	7.3	5.6	5.5	10.2	9.3	9.8	10.2	10.5	12.9	7.0	12.1	4.4	•
Cost of Goods to Cash Flow 43	4.6	2.7	2.6	6.3	6.0	6.6	7.1	7.8	9.4	4.7	8.3	2.5	•
Cash Flow to Total Debt 44	0.2	•	0.6	0.3	0.2	0.4	0.3	0.3	0.2	0.3	0.1	0.2	•

Selected Financial Factors (in Percentages)

Debt Ratio 45	62.8	•	85.7	88.6	79.0	38.7	52.3	54.1	75.9	52.4	81.1	60.1	•
Return on Total Assets 46	8.7	•	20.2	7.7	11.2	10.7	7.7	7.6	6.1	9.1	14.7	7.4	•
Return on Equity Before Income Taxes 47	13.3	•	119.4	41.7	37.5	15.8	13.1	12.8	12.7	15.9	45.2	6.4	•
Return on Equity After Income Taxes 48	11.1	•	118.6	39.3	34.8	14.5	11.5	11.6	7.7	11.5	38.6	4.6	•
Profit Margin (Before Income Tax) 49	4.9	1.3	5.7	2.1	4.4	6.1	3.8	4.0	2.1	6.6	6.9	5.8	•
Profit Margin (After Income Tax) 50	4.1	•	5.6	2.0	4.1	5.6	3.4	3.6	1.3	4.8	5.9	4.2	•

113

Table II
Corporations with Net Income

CUTLERY, HARDWARE, SPRING AND WIRE MACHINE SHOPS, NUT, BOLT

MONEY AMOUNTS AND SIZE OF ASSETS IN THOUSANDS OF DOLLARS

Item Description for Accounting Period 7/04 Through 6/05	Total	Zero Assets	Under 500	500 to 1,000	1,000 to 5,000	5,000 to 10,000	10,000 to 25,000	25,000 to 50,000	50,000 to 100,000	100,000 to 250,000	250,000 to 500,000	500,000 to 2,500,000	2,500,000 and over
Number of Enterprises **1**	13297	847	8508	1160	2209	0	194	49	23	16	0	6	0
Revenues ($ in Thousands)													
Net Sales **2**	39798064	177851	2869788	1938256	8209641	0	5008437	2445427	2036049	2604212	0	8828640	0
Interest **3**	1102114	42	1133	1010	6949	0	3094	5703	1680	10806	0	1063710	0
Rents **4**	12011	0	404	77	3090	0	579	1164	159	4669	0	1448	0
Royalties **5**	110924	0	0	0	0	0	19	1165	0	1513	0	105831	0
Other Portfolio Income **6**	622861	30129	25899	1605	34621	0	8510	11263	12192	22327	0	191715	0
Other Receipts **7**	711263	-29	19251	6954	44961	0	20947	12014	20964	154350	0	405894	0
Total Receipts **8**	42357237	207993	2916475	1947902	8299262	0	5041586	2476736	2071044	2797877	0	10597238	0
Average Total Receipts **9**	3185	246	343	1679	3757	•	25988	50546	90045	174867	•	1766206	•
Operating Costs/Operating Income (%)													
Cost of Operations **10**	61.1	47.3	45.1	58.1	59.5	•	68.2	72.5	70.1	65.6	•	53.8	•
Salaries and Wages **11**	7.5	17.6	10.1	5.5	6.9	•	6.2	4.9	6.4	9.3	•	10.6	•
Taxes Paid **12**	2.3	2.8	2.5	3.6	2.8	•	2.2	1.8	2.3	2.1	•	1.6	•
Interest Paid **13**	4.4	0.3	1.1	0.6	1.8	•	0.8	1.1	1.7	1.2	•	15.2	•
Depreciation **14**	3.4	1.8	5.0	4.0	3.8	•	3.5	4.1	3.4	3.4	•	2.2	•
Amortization and Depletion **15**	0.8	•	0.1	0.0	0.2	•	0.1	0.2	0.4	0.7	•	2.7	•
Pensions and Other Deferred Comp. **16**	0.7	0.5	0.2	0.0	0.7	•	0.6	0.5	0.5	0.9	•	0.9	•
Employee Benefits **17**	2.2	0.6	0.7	1.7	2.3	•	1.8	1.5	2.4	2.3	•	2.6	•
Advertising **18**	0.7	0.2	0.4	0.2	0.2	•	0.6	0.7	0.8	0.9	•	1.2	•
Other Expenses **19**	11.6	17.5	14.5	10.0	9.8	•	7.6	6.1	7.4	7.7	•	20.9	•
Officers' Compensation **20**	3.3	4.9	8.8	7.9	6.0	•	2.6	1.4	1.7	1.1	•	0.5	•
Operating Margin **21**	2.0	6.5	11.5	7.4	5.9	•	5.8	5.3	3.0	4.8	•	•	•
Operating Margin Before Officers' Comp. **22**	5.3	11.4	20.3	15.3	11.9	•	8.5	6.7	4.7	5.8	•	•	•

Selected Average Balance Sheet ($ in Thousands)

Net Receivables 23	501	0	22	202	455	•	3678	8183	12306	28610	•	427043
Inventories 24	311	0	18	102	314	•	3473	6659	13108	31958	•	147374
Net Property, Plant and Equipment 25	435	0	34	146	485	•	4374	9847	16816	35337	•	162051
Total Assets 26	3276	0	120	696	2044	•	15351	33499	64331	160199	•	4091763
Notes and Loans Payable 27	632	0	64	275	790	•	4092	9674	22043	33366	•	451734
All Other Liabilities 28	1248	0	25	156	455	•	3032	7266	16007	35463	•	2027328
Net Worth 29	1396	0	30	266	800	•	8226	16559	26280	91371	•	1612700

Selected Financial Ratios (Times to 1)

Current Ratio 30	1.9	•	2.7	2.5	1.8	•	2.2	2.3	1.9	1.8	•	1.5
Quick Ratio 31	1.2	•	1.7	1.8	1.1	•	1.1	1.2	0.9	1.0	•	1.1
Net Sales to Working Capital 32	5.8	•	7.1	5.2	7.5	•	5.0	4.7	5.8	5.2	•	6.2
Coverage Ratio 33	3.0	72.2	12.9	13.8	4.8	•	9.5	7.1	4.1	11.8	•	1.6
Total Asset Turnover 34	0.9	•	2.8	2.4	1.8	•	1.7	1.5	1.4	1.0	•	0.4
Inventory Turnover 35	5.9	•	8.5	9.5	7.1	•	5.1	5.4	4.7	3.3	•	5.4
Receivables Turnover 36	7.1	•	15.2	9.2	9.8	•	8.1	7.2	7.9	5.0	•	4.1
Total Liabilities to Net Worth 37	1.3	•	2.9	1.6	1.6	•	0.9	1.0	1.4	0.8	•	1.5
Current Assets to Working Capital 38	2.1	•	1.6	1.7	2.2	•	1.8	1.8	2.2	2.3	•	2.9
Current Liabilities to Working Capital 39	1.1	•	0.6	0.7	1.2	•	0.8	0.8	1.2	1.3	•	1.9
Working Capital to Net Sales 40	0.2	•	0.1	0.2	0.1	•	0.2	0.2	0.2	0.2	•	0.2
Inventory to Working Capital 41	0.7	•	0.5	0.3	0.8	•	0.8	0.7	1.0	0.8	•	0.7
Total Receipts to Cash Flow 42	5.9	2.9	4.4	6.9	7.1	•	8.2	8.7	9.2	5.4	•	3.8
Cost of Goods to Cash Flow 43	3.6	1.4	2.0	4.0	4.3	•	5.6	6.3	6.4	3.5	•	2.1
Cash Flow to Total Debt 44	0.3	•	0.9	0.6	0.4	•	0.4	0.3	0.3	0.4	•	0.2

Selected Financial Factors (in Percentages)

Debt Ratio 45	57.4	•	74.7	61.8	60.9	•	46.4	50.6	59.1	43.0	•	60.6
Return on Total Assets 46	11.9	•	40.1	20.4	16.0	•	12.2	11.4	9.3	13.9	•	8.7
Return on Equity Before Income Taxes 47	18.6	•	145.9	49.5	32.4	•	20.3	19.8	17.3	22.3	•	8.2
Return on Equity After Income Taxes 48	16.2	•	145.3	48.4	30.5	•	18.4	18.3	13.1	16.9	•	6.1
Profit Margin (Before Income Tax) 49	8.7	23.5	13.1	7.9	7.0	•	6.5	6.6	5.1	12.5	•	9.0
Profit Margin (After Income Tax) 50	7.6	21.5	13.1	7.7	6.6	•	5.9	6.1	3.9	9.5	•	6.7

114

Table I

Corporations with and without Net Income

ARCHITECTURAL AND STRUCTURAL METALS

MONEY AMOUNTS AND SIZE OF ASSETS IN THOUSANDS OF DOLLARS

Item Description for Accounting Period 7/04 Through 6/05

	Total	Zero Assets	Under 500	500 to 1,000	1,000 to 5,000	5,000 to 10,000	10,000 to 25,000	25,000 to 50,000	50,000 to 100,000	100,000 to 250,000	250,000 to 500,000	500,000 to 2,500,000	2,500,000 and over
Number of Enterprises **1**	6339	5	3326	983	1548	204	178	41	21	20	5	7	0

Revenues ($ in Thousands)

	Total	Zero Assets	Under 500	500 to 1,000	1,000 to 5,000	5,000 to 10,000	10,000 to 25,000	25,000 to 50,000	50,000 to 100,000	100,000 to 250,000	250,000 to 500,000	500,000 to 2,500,000	2,500,000 and over
Net Sales **2**	36505700	467872	1597535	1869794	7733263	3395693	5069353	2281230	2283995	5638057	1449625	4719282	0
Interest **3**	158940	46	4302	1679	8074	1064	2975	2648	1271	20645	2223	114013	0
Rents **4**	20959	0	356	202	948	865	2156	1342	727	1447	10	12907	0
Royalties **5**	67408	0	0	0	0	0	30	128	378	150	204	66518	0
Other Portfolio Income **6**	125056	435	10443	13200	17470	7183	5182	1729	2319	10265	119	56713	0
Other Receipts **7**	409236	959	30667	7415	8413	22964	32040	163	17225	62742	12603	214042	0
Total Receipts **8**	37287299	469312	1643303	1892290	7768168	3427769	5111736	2287240	2305915	5733306	1464784	5183475	0
Average Total Receipts **9**	5882	93862	494	1925	5018	16803	28718	55786	109805	286665	292957	740496	•

Operating Costs/Operating Income (%)

	Total	Zero Assets	Under 500	500 to 1,000	1,000 to 5,000	5,000 to 10,000	10,000 to 25,000	25,000 to 50,000	50,000 to 100,000	100,000 to 250,000	250,000 to 500,000	500,000 to 2,500,000	2,500,000 and over
Cost of Operations **10**	71.2	80.0	67.5	70.2	68.8	76.0	74.4	74.8	72.8	74.5	67.1	63.9	•
Salaries and Wages **11**	7.0	3.6	6.4	6.7	6.4	5.2	6.2	6.2	6.4	7.9	9.6	9.9	•
Taxes Paid **12**	2.1	0.6	3.5	2.8	2.5	2.2	2.0	2.0	1.4	1.9	1.5	1.8	•
Interest Paid **13**	1.9	0.6	1.1	0.8	0.8	0.8	0.8	0.9	0.9	1.1	5.3	7.5	•
Depreciation **14**	2.6	0.3	1.9	1.1	1.9	2.4	2.3	2.4	1.8	2.4	3.5	5.4	•
Amortization and Depletion **15**	0.2	0.0	0.0	0.0	0.0	0.0	0.1	0.2	0.1	0.3	1.2	0.4	•
Pensions and Other Deferred Comp. **16**	0.5	0.1	0.0	0.3	0.4	0.4	0.4	0.3	0.3	0.6	0.3	1.4	•
Employee Benefits **17**	2.0	0.3	0.3	4.2	2.8	2.0	1.5	1.8	0.8	1.8	2.3	2.0	•
Advertising **18**	0.5	0.1	0.3	0.3	0.4	0.3	0.5	0.4	0.4	0.7	1.2	0.6	•
Other Expenses **19**	9.0	10.2	17.0	8.9	10.3	6.0	7.3	6.0	6.7	6.2	9.2	13.7	•
Officers' Compensation **20**	2.2	4.7	6.2	4.8	3.6	1.8	2.2	1.2	1.0	0.8	0.5	0.6	•
Operating Margin **21**	0.7	•	•	•	2.0	2.8	2.2	3.7	7.5	1.7	•	•	•
Operating Margin Before Officers' Comp. **22**	2.9	4.2	1.9	4.6	5.6	4.5	4.4	4.9	8.5	2.5	•	•	•

Selected Average Balance Sheet ($ in Thousands)

Net Receivables 23	1055	0	55	274	663	2181	5152	10293	19414	46760	70538	247477	•
Inventories 24	555	0	18	177	355	2230	2864	6069	12474	29180	40922	67511	•
Net Property, Plant and Equipment 25	853	0	26	74	477	1906	3390	8906	14842	43113	60304	239764	•
Total Assets 26	3748	0	133	714	2121	7484	15545	33972	68295	169120	333161	1023597	•
Notes and Loans Payable 27	1267	0	73	272	947	2693	4384	10245	19119	36412	168776	333052	•
All Other Liabilities 28	1212	0	41	167	653	2276	5083	9200	20559	56001	102442	365742	•
Net Worth 29	1269	0	19	274	521	2515	6078	14527	28617	76707	61944	324802	•

Selected Financial Ratios (Times to 1)

Current Ratio 30	1.8	•	1.7	3.5	1.7	1.7	1.6	1.8	1.8	1.8	1.5	1.8	•
Quick Ratio 31	1.1	•	1.2	2.4	1.1	0.9	0.9	1.2	0.9	1.0	0.9	1.3	•
Net Sales to Working Capital 32	6.4	•	11.3	4.3	8.4	8.2	7.3	5.6	6.2	6.6	6.6	3.8	•
Coverage Ratio 33	2.5	0.6	•	2.2	4.0	5.5	4.9	5.2	10.1	4.2	0.9	1.4	•
Total Asset Turnover 34	1.5	•	3.6	2.7	2.4	2.2	1.8	1.6	1.6	1.7	0.9	0.7	•
Inventory Turnover 35	7.4	•	17.7	7.6	9.7	5.7	7.4	6.9	6.4	7.2	4.8	6.4	•
Receivables Turnover 36	6.0	•	8.2	6.3	8.6	5.8	5.9	5.7	7.0	5.7	4.2	3.9	•
Total Liabilities to Net Worth 37	2.0	•	6.2	1.6	3.1	2.0	1.6	1.3	1.4	1.2	4.4	2.2	•
Current Assets to Working Capital 38	2.3	•	2.4	1.4	2.4	2.5	2.8	2.2	2.3	2.3	2.9	2.2	•
Current Liabilities to Working Capital 39	1.3	•	1.4	0.4	1.4	1.5	1.8	1.2	1.3	1.3	1.9	1.2	•
Working Capital to Net Sales 40	0.2	•	0.1	0.2	0.1	0.1	0.1	0.2	0.2	0.2	0.2	0.3	•
Inventory to Working Capital 41	0.7	•	0.4	0.4	0.7	1.0	0.9	0.6	0.9	0.7	1.1	0.5	•
Total Receipts to Cash Flow 42	11.1	10.8	11.8	14.4	10.8	13.7	11.9	11.9	7.3	13.0	14.6	8.6	•
Cost of Goods to Cash Flow 43	7.9	8.6	7.9	10.1	7.4	10.4	8.8	8.9	5.3	9.7	9.8	5.5	•
Cash Flow to Total Debt 44	0.2	•	0.4	0.3	0.2	0.2	0.3	0.2	0.4	0.2	0.1	0.1	•

Selected Financial Factors (in Percentages)

Debt Ratio 45	66.1	•	86.1	61.6	75.4	66.4	60.9	57.2	58.1	54.6	81.4	68.3	•
Return on Total Assets 46	7.5	•	•	4.8	7.8	10.1	7.0	8.0	14.9	7.4	4.0	7.0	•
Return on Equity Before Income Taxes 47	13.4	•	•	7.0	23.8	24.6	14.3	15.1	31.9	12.5	•	6.6	•
Return on Equity After Income Taxes 48	10.8	•	•	3.1	21.0	22.7	12.8	12.5	30.2	9.0	•	3.6	•
Profit Margin (Before Income Tax) 49	3.0	•	•	1.0	2.5	3.7	3.1	3.9	8.4	3.4	•	3.2	•
Profit Margin (After Income Tax) 50	2.4	•	•	0.5	2.2	3.4	2.7	3.3	7.9	2.5	•	1.8	•

Table II
Corporations with Net Income

ARCHITECTURAL AND STRUCTURAL METALS

MONEY AMOUNTS AND SIZE OF ASSETS IN THOUSANDS OF DOLLARS

Item Description for Accounting Period 7/04 Through 6/05	Total	Zero Assets	Under 500	500 to 1,000	1,000 to 5,000	5,000 to 10,000	10,000 to 25,000	25,000 to 50,000	50,000 to 100,000	100,000 to 250,000	250,000 to 500,000	500,000 to 2,500,000	2,500,000 and over
Number of Enterprises 1	4138	0	1845	730	1247	120	132	25	18	13	0	0	0
Revenues ($ in Thousands)													
Net Sales 2	26328953	0	1057782	1550931	5937073	2281379	3926048	1537952	1854688	4123928	0	0	0
Interest 3	138236	0	378	945	5390	888	2500	844	1232	18841	0	0	0
Rents 4	7304	0	356	202	928	0	1781	345	727	1215	0	0	0
Royalties 5	66404	0	0	0	0	0	30	0	378	141	0	0	0
Other Portfolio Income 6	111528	0	9395	12661	16690	7137	3366	536	2096	9669	0	0	0
Other Receipts 7	282782	0	22480	5731	3611	21804	28855	3311	16581	44502	0	0	0
Total Receipts 8	26935207	0	1090391	1570470	5963692	2311208	3962580	1542988	1875702	4198296	0	0	0
Average Total Receipts 9	6509	•	591	2151	4782	19260	30020	61720	104206	322946	•	•	•
Operating Costs/Operating Income (%)													
Cost of Operations 10	70.0	•	69.7	67.6	65.3	75.1	72.8	72.4	72.5	73.4	•	•	•
Salaries and Wages 11	6.7	•	5.0	7.1	6.3	5.7	6.1	5.7	6.0	7.9	•	•	•
Taxes Paid 12	2.0	•	2.7	3.1	2.5	1.6	1.9	2.0	1.4	2.0	•	•	•
Interest Paid 13	1.3	•	0.9	0.2	0.6	0.6	0.5	0.5	0.8	1.0	•	•	•
Depreciation 14	2.4	•	1.3	1.2	2.0	1.7	2.1	2.3	1.7	2.6	•	•	•
Amortization and Depletion 15	0.1	•	0.0	0.0	0.0	0.0	0.0	0.2	0.1	0.2	•	•	•
Pensions and Other Deferred Comp. 16	0.5	•	0.0	0.4	0.4	0.3	0.5	0.3	0.3	0.5	•	•	•
Employee Benefits 17	2.0	•	0.2	4.0	2.8	1.5	1.4	1.8	0.8	1.7	•	•	•
Advertising 18	0.5	•	0.1	0.4	0.3	0.2	0.5	0.5	0.4	0.8	•	•	•
Other Expenses 19	8.6	•	14.1	8.3	11.0	6.6	7.1	5.6	5.4	5.1	•	•	•
Officers' Compensation 20	2.2	•	5.0	5.6	3.6	1.6	2.2	1.3	1.2	0.8	•	•	•
Operating Margin 21	3.6	•	1.1	2.2	5.2	5.2	5.0	7.6	9.5	3.9	•	•	•
Operating Margin Before Officers' Comp. 22	5.8	•	6.0	7.8	8.7	6.8	7.2	8.9	10.7	4.7	•	•	•

Selected Average Balance Sheet ($ in Thousands)

Net Receivables 23	1035	73	276	685	2283	4921	9646	18970	45690
Inventories 24	559	23	147	232	2238	2954	6430	12148	33149
Net Property, Plant and Equipment 25	839	20	76	460	1378	3360	8552	14550	49296
Total Assets 26	3884	150	690	2058	7794	15569	34288	67116	178521
Notes and Loans Payable 27	1095	69	62	854	2067	3414	7068	16602	28807
All Other Liabilities 28	1197	50	175	657	2596	4784	7882	20655	65240
Net Worth 29	1563	30	453	548	3131	7371	19337	29860	84474

Selected Financial Ratios (Times to 1)

Current Ratio 30	1.8	1.6	3.7	1.9	1.7	1.9	2.1	1.9	1.8
Quick Ratio 31	1.1	1.1	2.6	1.3	0.9	1.1	1.3	1.0	1.0
Net Sales to Working Capital 32	6.4	12.5	4.9	7.1	7.9	5.8	5.2	5.4	7.2
Coverage Ratio 33	5.6	5.7	19.9	10.4	12.6	12.7	17.1	14.9	6.9
Total Asset Turnover 34	1.7	3.8	3.1	2.3	2.4	1.9	1.8	1.5	1.8
Inventory Turnover 35	8.0	17.4	9.7	13.4	6.4	7.3	6.9	6.1	7.0
Receivables Turnover 36	7.0	7.3	7.7	9.6	7.1	6.8	6.2	7.5	
Total Liabilities to Net Worth 37	1.5	4.0	0.5	2.8	1.5	1.1	0.8	1.2	1.1
Current Assets to Working Capital 38	2.2	2.6	1.4	2.1	2.4	2.1	1.9	2.1	2.3
Current Liabilities to Working Capital 39	1.2	1.6	0.4	1.1	1.4	1.1	0.9	1.1	1.3
Working Capital to Net Sales 40	0.2	0.1	0.2	0.1	0.1	0.2	0.2	0.2	0.1
Inventory to Working Capital 41	0.7	0.4	0.4	0.5	1.0	0.7	0.5	0.8	0.8
Total Receipts to Cash Flow 42	8.5	7.4	11.7	7.9	9.8	9.0	8.3	6.7	10.9
Cost of Goods to Cash Flow 43	6.0	5.2	7.9	5.1	7.3	6.5	6.0	4.8	8.0
Cash Flow to Total Debt 44	0.3	0.6	0.8	0.4	0.4	0.4	0.5	0.4	0.3

Selected Financial Factors (in Percentages)

Debt Ratio 45	59.5	79.9	34.3	73.4	59.8	52.7	43.6	55.5	52.7
Return on Total Assets 46	12.1	19.4	11.2	14.3	17.2	12.2	15.0	17.4	11.8
Return on Equity Before Income Taxes 47	24.5	79.3	16.2	48.6	39.4	23.8	25.0	36.5	21.4
Return on Equity After Income Taxes 48	21.3	76.1	13.1	45.4	36.8	22.1	21.9	34.5	16.9
Profit Margin (Before Income Tax) 49	6.0	4.2	3.5	5.6	6.5	5.9	7.9	10.6	5.7
Profit Margin (After Income Tax) 50	5.2	4.0	2.8	5.2	6.1	5.5	6.9	10.0	4.5

Table I

Corporations with and without Net Income

BOILER, TANK, AND SHIPPING CONTAINER

MONEY AMOUNTS AND SIZE OF ASSETS IN THOUSANDS OF DOLLARS

Item Description for Accounting Period 7/04 Through 6/05		Total	Zero Assets	Under 500	500 to 1,000	1,000 to 5,000	5,000 to 10,000	10,000 to 25,000	25,000 to 50,000	50,000 to 100,000	100,000 to 250,000	250,000 to 500,000	500,000 to 2,500,000	2,500,000 and over
Number of Enterprises	1	416	0	0	0	246	14	51	11	9	5	5	0	4
Revenues ($ in Thousands)														
Net Sales	2	18216043	0	0	0	811016	218671	1452878	544349	1005131	967502	3077547	0	10077179
Interest	3	126615	0	0	0	409	90	5076	850	157	4942	3466	0	111626
Rents	4	36867	0	0	0	4272	282	240	1030	722	0	5101	0	25220
Royalties	5	171724	0	0	0	7	0	276	0	236	0	4474	0	166731
Other Portfolio Income	6	77119	0	0	0	3248	152	9848	1876	2467	9	1866	0	57652
Other Receipts	7	339380	0	0	0	1073	272	6508	2304	8558	1057	23220	0	294613
Total Receipts	8	18967748	0	0	0	820025	219467	1474826	550409	1017271	973510	3115674	0	10733021
Average Total Receipts	9	45596	•	•	•	3333	15676	28918	50037	113030	194702	623135	•	2683255
Operating Costs/Operating Income (%)														
Cost of Operations	10	79.1	•	•	•	63.8	67.2	75.8	74.4	77.6	73.7	80.1	•	81.8
Salaries and Wages	11	4.5	•	•	•	13.3	6.7	5.7	4.2	7.2	6.0	2.6	•	3.8
Taxes Paid	12	1.4	•	•	•	3.5	1.9	2.1	1.8	1.1	2.0	1.5	•	0.9
Interest Paid	13	3.0	•	•	•	0.6	1.7	1.1	0.9	1.1	4.1	3.3	•	3.5
Depreciation	14	2.9	•	•	•	1.2	1.8	1.8	2.2	2.2	3.4	5.1	•	2.7
Amortization and Depletion	15	0.6	•	•	•	0.2	0.4	0.2	0.2	0.4	0.8	1.1	•	0.5
Pensions and Other Deferred Comp.	16	1.5	•	•	•	0.7	0.2	0.5	0.6	0.3	1.9	1.1	•	2.1
Employee Benefits	17	1.9	•	•	•	2.6	0.2	1.6	1.7	0.8	1.6	1.2	•	2.4
Advertising	18	0.2	•	•	•	0.5	0.4	0.5	0.3	0.3	0.5	0.2	•	0.0
Other Expenses	19	5.6	•	•	•	9.0	8.0	6.2	9.9	7.3	5.0	4.7	•	4.8
Officers' Compensation	20	1.0	•	•	•	4.2	2.1	1.9	1.5	1.1	0.3	0.2	•	0.8
Operating Margin	21	•	•	•	•	0.4	9.4	2.5	2.3	0.7	0.7	•	•	•
Operating Margin Before Officers' Comp.	22	•	•	•	•	4.6	11.5	4.5	3.8	1.7	1.1	•	•	•

Selected Average Balance Sheet ($ in Thousands)

Net Receivables 23	8618	672	1393	5158	10052	20465	39593	52778	594616
Inventories 24	3726	368	4747	2892	6407	10390	21922	68622	154321
Net Property, Plant and Equipment 25	8321	292	2439	3341	8271	13423	34180	170358	487631
Total Assets 26	54271	1877	6120	15877	35506	61719	166085	773278	3891767
Notes and Loans Payable 27	15242	601	4145	4287	9969	19667	82389	481919	681205
All Other Liabilities 28	24023	304	1280	5172	7035	24216	67153	206947	1984785
Net Worth 29	15006	972	694	6419	18502	17836	16542	84411	1225777

Selected Financial Ratios (Times to 1)

Current Ratio 30	1.1	3.3	1.4	1.8	2.6	1.4	1.4	2.3	0.8
Quick Ratio 31	0.6	2.0	0.8	1.1	1.5	0.9	0.8	0.5	0.6
Net Sales to Working Capital 32	26.1	3.2	15.3	5.7	3.8	10.9	7.1	3.3	•
Coverage Ratio 33	1.8	3.7	6.6	4.8	4.7	2.8	1.3	1.0	2.0
Total Asset Turnover 34	0.8	1.8	2.6	1.8	1.4	1.8	1.2	0.8	0.6
Inventory Turnover 35	9.3	5.7	2.2	7.5	5.7	8.3	6.5	7.2	13.3
Receivables Turnover 36	5.9	7.2	4.1	6.5	4.7	6.5	7.5	13.0	5.0
Total Liabilities to Net Worth 37	2.6	0.9	7.8	1.5	0.9	2.5	9.0	8.2	2.2
Current Assets to Working Capital 38	10.7	1.4	3.4	2.2	1.6	3.5	3.2	1.7	•
Current Liabilities to Working Capital 39	9.7	0.4	2.4	1.2	0.6	2.5	2.2	0.7	•
Working Capital to Net Sales 40	0.0	0.3	0.1	0.2	0.3	0.1	0.1	0.3	•
Inventory to Working Capital 41	2.5	0.6	0.9	0.7	0.5	1.1	0.7	0.4	•
Total Receipts to Cash Flow 42	15.5	14.4	6.0	11.7	9.7	13.1	19.8	29.2	14.7
Cost of Goods to Cash Flow 43	12.2	9.2	4.0	8.8	7.2	10.2	14.6	23.4	12.0
Cash Flow to Total Debt 44	0.1	0.3	0.5	0.3	0.3	0.2	0.1	0.0	0.1

Selected Financial Factors (in Percentages)

Debt Ratio 45	72.4	48.2	88.7	59.6	47.9	71.1	90.0	89.1	68.5
Return on Total Assets 46	4.5	3.6	29.2	9.2	6.0	5.3	6.3	2.8	4.5
Return on Equity Before Income Taxes 47	7.4	5.1	218.7	18.0	9.0	11.7	16.0	1.0	7.1
Return on Equity After Income Taxes 48	4.9	3.6	212.3	16.0	7.4	7.5	9.8	0.3	4.5
Profit Margin (Before Income Tax) 49	2.5	1.5	9.7	4.1	3.4	1.9	1.4	0.1	3.5
Profit Margin (After Income Tax) 50	1.7	1.1	9.4	3.6	2.8	1.2	0.8	0.0	2.2

Table II

Corporations with Net Income

BOILER, TANK, AND SHIPPING CONTAINER

MONEY AMOUNTS AND SIZE OF ASSETS IN THOUSANDS OF DOLLARS

Item Description for Accounting Period 7/04 Through 6/05	Total	Zero Assets	Under 500	500 to 1,000	1,000 to 5,000	5,000 to 10,000	10,000 to 25,000	25,000 to 50,000	50,000 to 100,000	100,000 to 250,000	250,000 to 500,000	500,000 to 2,500,000	2,500,000 and over
Number of Enterprises **1**	274	0	0	0	201	0	35	8	0	0	0	0	0
Revenues ($ in Thousands)													
Net Sales **2**	14141173	0	0	0	617062	0	1030680	494188	0	0	0	0	0
Interest **3**	113643	0	0	0	333	0	583	850	0	0	0	0	0
Rents **4**	34312	0	0	0	1717	0	240	1030	0	0	0	0	0
Royalties **5**	76270	0	0	0	7	0	276	0	0	0	0	0	0
Other Portfolio Income **6**	33801	0	0	0	3248	0	9827	1857	0	0	0	0	0
Other Receipts **7**	320079	0	0	0	285	0	5998	1356	0	0	0	0	0
Total Receipts **8**	14719278	0	0	0	622652	0	1047604	499281	0	0	0	0	0
Average Total Receipts **9**	53720	.	.	.	3098	.	29932	62410	.	.	.	.	.
Operating Costs/Operating Income (%)													
Cost of Operations **10**	79.1	.	.	.	59.8	.	73.4	73.6	.	.	.	.	.
Salaries and Wages **11**	4.4	.	.	.	13.5	.	5.4	4.1	.	.	.	.	.
Taxes Paid **12**	1.2	.	.	.	3.7	.	2.2	1.8	.	.	.	.	.
Interest Paid **13**	2.3	.	.	.	0.3	.	0.6	1.0	.	.	.	.	.
Depreciation **14**	3.1	.	.	.	0.8	.	1.7	2.2	.	.	.	.	.
Amortization and Depletion **15**	0.4	.	.	.	0.0	.	0.1	0.2	.	.	.	.	.
Pensions and Other Deferred Comp. **16**	0.7	.	.	.	0.8	.	0.5	0.6	.	.	.	.	.
Employee Benefits **17**	2.0	.	.	.	2.7	.	1.7	1.8	.	.	.	.	.
Advertising **18**	0.2	.	.	.	0.6	.	0.7	0.3	.	.	.	.	.
Other Expenses **19**	4.8	.	.	.	8.9	.	6.1	9.1	.	.	.	.	.
Officers' Compensation **20**	1.0	.	.	.	3.9	.	2.1	1.4	.	.	.	.	.
Operating Margin **21**	0.9	.	.	.	5.1	.	5.7	3.8	.	.	.	.	.
Operating Margin Before Officers' Comp. **22**	1.9	.	.	.	9.0	.	7.8	5.3	.	.	.	.	.

Selected Average Balance Sheet ($ in Thousands)

Net Receivables 23	9838	655	4429	9779
Inventories 24	3822	375	3065	6721
Net Property, Plant and Equipment 25	9531	218	3112	9194
Total Assets 26	65177	1774	15999	35009
Notes and Loans Payable 27	15503	468	3522	9971
All Other Liabilities 28	28281	291	5136	6897
Net Worth 29	21393	1015	7341	18141

Selected Financial Ratios (Times to 1)

Current Ratio 30	1.3	3.5	1.9	2.7
Quick Ratio 31	0.7	2.0	1.0	1.4
Net Sales to Working Capital 32	11.3	2.9	5.8	4.4
Coverage Ratio 33	3.2	18.7	13.5	5.9
Total Asset Turnover 34	0.8	1.7	1.8	1.8
Inventory Turnover 35	10.7	4.9	7.0	6.8
Receivables Turnover 36	6.0	7.7	8.1	6.4
Total Liabilities to Net Worth 37	2.0	0.7	1.2	0.9
Current Assets to Working Capital 38	4.7	1.4	2.2	1.6
Current Liabilities to Working Capital 39	3.7	0.4	1.2	0.6
Working Capital to Net Sales 40	0.1	0.3	0.2	0.2
Inventory to Working Capital 41	1.1	0.6	0.8	0.5
Total Receipts to Cash Flow 42	12.1	9.0	8.5	8.7
Cost of Goods to Cash Flow 43	9.5	5.4	6.2	6.4
Cash Flow to Total Debt 44	0.1	0.4	0.4	0.4

Selected Financial Factors (in Percentages)

Debt Ratio 45	67.2	42.8	54.1	48.2
Return on Total Assets 46	5.8	11.0	14.5	10.3
Return on Equity Before Income Taxes 47	12.1	18.1	29.2	16.5
Return on Equity After Income Taxes 48	9.4	16.3	26.7	14.2
Profit Margin (Before Income Tax) 49	5.0	6.0	7.3	4.8
Profit Margin (After Income Tax) 50	3.9	5.4	6.6	4.2

118

Table I

Corporations with and without Net Income

COATING, ENGRAVING, HEAT TREATING, AND ALLIED ACTIVITIES

MONEY AMOUNTS AND SIZE OF ASSETS IN THOUSANDS OF DOLLARS

Item Description for Accounting Period 7/04 Through 6/05	Total	Zero Assets	Under 500	500 to 1,000	1,000 to 5,000	5,000 to 10,000	10,000 to 25,000	25,000 to 50,000	50,000 to 100,000	100,000 to 250,000	250,000 to 500,000	500,000 to 2,500,000	2,500,000 and over
Number of Enterprises **1**	4572	3	3768	89	563	61	53	19	7	5	4	0	0
Revenues ($ in Thousands)													
Net Sales **2**	11485667	33354	2535497	142440	2741457	649250	1278817	829646	571093	976000	1728114	0	0
Interest **3**	15794	147	599	7	1864	858	1104	1072	3187	1526	5430	0	0
Rents **4**	15186	86	8202	0	3501	2663	380	71	33	10	240	0	0
Royalties **5**	5236	0	0	0	0	71	732	157	34	1003	3239	0	0
Other Portfolio Income **6**	43549	0	17859	18	11454	138	10512	994	565	712	1296	0	0
Other Receipts **7**	166386	4890	93056	4	25008	3204	7019	6775	1506	2489	22436	0	0
Total Receipts **8**	11731818	38477	2655213	142469	2783284	656184	1298564	838715	576418	981740	1760755	0	0
Average Total Receipts **9**	2566	12826	705	1601	4944	10757	24501	44143	82345	196348	440189	•	•
Operating Costs/Operating Income (%)													
Cost of Operations **10**	57.1	97.2	34.9	68.1	54.6	61.8	66.6	66.3	66.3	76.5	64.8	•	•
Salaries and Wages **11**	8.5	8.3	15.7	3.1	7.0	4.0	6.6	5.9	6.2	4.8	7.9	•	•
Taxes Paid **12**	3.1	0.9	3.9	4.0	4.2	3.4	2.7	2.8	2.3	2.1	1.6	•	•
Interest Paid **13**	1.6	3.4	0.5	0.1	1.2	1.0	1.7	1.3	2.8	2.3	3.5	•	•
Depreciation **14**	4.5	4.4	2.3	16.0	4.6	5.9	5.3	5.2	4.6	6.0	4.5	•	•
Amortization and Depletion **15**	0.5	0.8	0.0	•	0.0	0.0	0.4	0.2	0.9	1.7	1.8	•	•
Pensions and Other Deferred Comp. **16**	0.6	0.1	0.2	•	0.5	1.8	0.3	0.8	0.9	0.8	0.9	•	•
Employee Benefits **17**	2.3	2.2	2.0	2.9	2.8	3.2	3.0	2.1	1.8	2.3	1.5	•	•
Advertising **18**	0.3	•	0.2	0.3	0.3	0.2	0.2	0.2	0.3	0.1	0.7	•	•
Other Expenses **19**	14.4	3.5	25.7	12.2	18.5	8.9	9.7	7.4	6.8	5.1	8.4	•	•
Officers' Compensation **20**	5.7	•	14.8	4.1	5.3	4.4	2.4	1.9	1.3	1.0	2.0	•	•
Operating Margin **21**	1.3	•	•	•	0.9	5.4	1.1	6.0	5.9	•	2.4	•	•
Operating Margin Before Officers' Comp. **22**	6.9	•	14.6	•	6.2	9.8	3.5	7.8	7.2	•	4.4	•	•

Selected Average Balance Sheet ($ in Thousands)

	1	2	3	4	5	6	7	8	9	10	11
Net Receivables 23	339	0	46	230	659	1273	3931	7418	10040	28836	86199
Inventories 24	152	0	8	55	156	626	1876	3004	10268	12613	61026
Net Property, Plant and Equipment 25	542	0	63	368	911	3411	6382	13737	26191	55286	107410
Total Assets 26	1692	0	191	688	2337	7524	15732	32814	73075	153015	611624
Notes and Loans Payable 27	657	0	161	373	863	2486	6595	9450	31022	62849	165931
All Other Liabilities 28	493	0	69	172	556	1099	4075	7691	22481	49670	207930
Net Worth 29	542	0	-40	143	918	3939	5063	15672	19572	40495	237763

Selected Financial Ratios (Times to 1)

	1	2	3	4	5	6	7	8	9	10	11
Current Ratio 30	1.7	•	1.6	1.7	1.3	2.8	1.4	1.8	1.4	1.3	2.5
Quick Ratio 31	1.1	•	1.1	1.4	1.1	1.6	1.0	1.2	0.7	0.9	1.3
Net Sales to Working Capital 32	9.2	•	16.8	12.6	18.3	4.8	11.4	7.1	9.8	13.1	3.9
Coverage Ratio 33	3.1	•	10.7	•	3.0	7.8	2.6	6.6	3.4	0.1	2.2
Total Asset Turnover 34	1.5	•	3.5	2.3	2.1	1.4	1.5	1.3	1.1	1.3	0.7
Inventory Turnover 35	9.4	•	28.0	19.9	17.1	10.5	8.6	9.6	5.3	11.8	4.6
Receivables Turnover 36	7.8	•	15.7	•	7.6	9.4	6.5	8.0	7.8	8.8	4.5
Total Liabilities to Net Worth 37	2.1	•	•	3.8	1.5	0.9	2.1	1.1	2.7	2.8	1.6
Current Assets to Working Capital 38	2.5	•	2.8	2.4	4.0	1.5	3.5	2.3	3.2	4.1	1.7
Current Liabilities to Working Capital 39	1.5	•	1.8	1.4	3.0	0.5	2.5	1.3	2.2	3.1	0.7
Working Capital to Net Sales 40	0.1	•	0.1	0.1	0.1	0.2	0.1	0.1	0.1	0.1	0.3
Inventory to Working Capital 41	0.7	•	0.3	0.4	0.6	0.3	0.8	0.6	1.3	1.2	0.7
Total Receipts to Cash Flow 42	7.4	•	4.4	•	6.9	7.9	10.9	8.4	8.0	69.3	8.9
Cost of Goods to Cash Flow 43	4.2	•	1.5	•	3.8	4.9	7.3	5.5	5.3	53.0	5.8
Cash Flow to Total Debt 44	0.3	•	0.7	•	0.5	0.4	0.2	0.3	0.2	0.0	0.1

Selected Financial Factors (in Percentages)

	1	2	3	4	5	6	7	8	9	10	11
Debt Ratio 45	68.0	•	120.8	79.2	60.7	47.6	67.8	52.2	73.2	73.5	61.1
Return on Total Assets 46	7.4	•	17.6	•	7.7	10.5	6.7	11.0	10.7	0.2	5.4
Return on Equity Before Income Taxes 47	15.7	•	•	•	13.1	17.6	12.6	19.6	28.3	•	7.7
Return on Equity After Income Taxes 48	13.4	•	•	•	10.7	15.5	9.7	17.0	26.0	•	5.8
Profit Margin (Before Income Tax) 49	3.4	•	4.5	•	2.5	6.5	2.6	7.0	6.8	•	4.2
Profit Margin (After Income Tax) 50	2.9	•	4.5	•	2.0	5.7	2.0	6.1	6.2	•	3.2

Table II

Corporations with Net Income

COATING, ENGRAVING, HEAT TREATING, AND ALLIED ACTIVITIES

MONEY AMOUNTS AND SIZE OF ASSETS IN THOUSANDS OF DOLLARS

Item Description for Accounting Period 7/04 Through 6/05	Total	Zero Assets	Under 500	500 to 1,000	1,000 to 5,000	5,000 to 10,000	10,000 to 25,000	25,000 to 50,000	50,000 to 100,000	100,000 to 250,000	250,000 to 500,000	500,000 to 2,500,000	2,500,000 and over
Number of Enterprises **1**	2632	0	2123	60	333	0	39	16	7	0	0	0	0
Revenues ($ in Thousands)													
Net Sales **2**	8053120	0	1632887	138668	1805513	0	912559	723142	889390	0	0	0	0
Interest **3**	8829	0	264	7	1100	0	845	1072	1202	0	0	0	0
Rents **4**	13784	0	8202	0	2425	0	380	71	43	0	0	0	0
Royalties **5**	4006	0	0	0	0	0	610	157	0	0	0	0	0
Other Portfolio Income **6**	34497	0	17663	18	3792	0	10432	688	1125	0	0	0	0
Other Receipts **7**	141228	0	92783	5	4821	0	5773	6042	3364	0	0	0	0
Total Receipts **8**	8255464	0	1751799	138698	1817651	0	930599	731172	865124	0	0	0	0
Average Total Receipts **9**	3137	•	825	2312	5458	•	23862	45698	123589	•	•	•	•
Operating Costs/Operating Income (%)													
Cost of Operations **10**	57.1	•	33.6	68.0	54.8	•	67.2	65.3	65.1	•	•	•	•
Salaries and Wages **11**	8.3	•	16.6	2.1	7.0	•	5.8	5.7	6.9	•	•	•	•
Taxes Paid **12**	3.0	•	3.6	3.9	4.4	•	2.5	2.9	2.4	•	•	•	•
Interest Paid **13**	1.2	•	0.4	0.1	0.9	•	0.8	1.2	1.6	•	•	•	•
Depreciation **14**	3.9	•	2.0	6.8	4.4	•	4.0	5.4	4.0	•	•	•	•
Amortization and Depletion **15**	0.4	•	0.0	•	0.0	•	0.1	0.2	0.3	•	•	•	•
Pensions and Other Deferred Comp. **16**	0.8	•	0.3	•	0.7	•	0.3	0.7	1.2	•	•	•	•
Employee Benefits **17**	2.1	•	1.1	3.0	2.3	•	2.8	2.2	2.5	•	•	•	•
Advertising **18**	0.3	•	0.1	0.1	0.3	•	0.2	0.2	0.3	•	•	•	•
Other Expenses **19**	12.0	•	27.3	11.1	11.2	•	7.5	7.0	7.5	•	•	•	•
Officers' Compensation **20**	4.9	•	10.9	4.2	5.3	•	2.7	2.0	1.7	•	•	•	•
Operating Margin **21**	6.0	•	4.1	0.7	8.7	•	6.0	7.2	6.4	•	•	•	•
Operating Margin Before Officers' Comp. **22**	10.8	•	15.0	4.9	14.0	•	8.7	9.2	8.1	•	•	•	•

Selected Average Balance Sheet ($ in Thousands)

Net Receivables 23	402	42	322	702	4058	6894	16556
Inventories 24	176	10	42	96	1822	2345	16635
Net Property, Plant and Equipment 25	594	49	133	1015	5375	15293	34851
Total Assets 26	2001	172	582	2553	15008	33778	89756
Notes and Loans Payable 27	686	172	82	690	3965	10013	21523
All Other Liabilities 28	452	64	234	428	3875	7219	21145
Net Worth 29	863	-64	266	1435	7168	16546	47088

Selected Financial Ratios (Times to 1)

Current Ratio 30	2.1	1.5	1.7	2.1	1.6	1.9	2.1
Quick Ratio 31	1.3	1.2	1.4	1.9	1.2	1.3	1.3
Net Sales to Working Capital 32	7.0	23.1	12.5	9.6	7.8	7.0	5.6
Coverage Ratio 33	7.8	26.4	6.1	11.2	11.0	7.8	5.3
Total Asset Turnover 34	1.5	4.5	4.0	2.1	1.6	1.3	1.4
Inventory Turnover 35	9.9	24.9	37.6	31.0	8.6	12.6	4.8
Receivables Turnover 36	9.6	21.6	13.9	8.8	6.0	10.5	6.3
Total Liabilities to Net Worth 37	1.3		1.2	0.8	1.1	1.0	0.9
Current Assets to Working Capital 38	1.9	3.0	2.3	1.9	2.6	2.1	1.9
Current Liabilities to Working Capital 39	0.9	2.0	1.3	0.9	1.6	1.1	0.9
Working Capital to Net Sales 40	0.1	0.0	0.1	0.1	0.1	0.1	0.2
Inventory to Working Capital 41	0.6	0.5	0.4	0.1	0.6	0.6	0.7
Total Receipts to Cash Flow 42	6.0	3.3	13.7	6.1	8.0	7.9	7.4
Cost of Goods to Cash Flow 43	3.4	1.1	9.3	3.3	5.4	5.2	4.8
Cash Flow to Total Debt 44	0.4	1.0	0.5	0.8	0.4	0.3	0.4

Selected Financial Factors (in Percentages)

Debt Ratio 45	56.9	137.1	54.3	43.8	52.2	51.0	47.5
Return on Total Assets 46	14.8	52.8	3.6	21.8	13.6	12.7	11.9
Return on Equity Before Income Taxes 47	30.0		6.7	35.3	25.9	22.6	18.4
Return on Equity After Income Taxes 48	27.4		5.6	32.7	23.1	19.7	16.3
Profit Margin (Before Income Tax) 49	8.5	11.4	0.8	9.3	7.9	8.3	7.1
Profit Margin (After Income Tax) 50	7.7	11.4	0.7	8.6	7.1	7.2	6.2

Table I

Corporations with and without Net Income

OTHER FABRICATED METAL PRODUCT

MONEY AMOUNTS AND SIZE OF ASSETS IN THOUSANDS OF DOLLARS

Item Description for Accounting Period 7/04 Through 6/05		Total	Zero Assets	Under 500	500 to 1,000	1,000 to 5,000	5,000 to 10,000	10,000 to 25,000	25,000 to 50,000	50,000 to 100,000	100,000 to 250,000	250,000 to 500,000	500,000 to 2,500,000	2,500,000 and over
Number of Enterprises	1	18781	904	11054	1897	3661	598	366	139	71	42	21	15	12
Revenues ($ in Thousands)														
Net Sales	2	148577222	944458	5739576	3464185	19270288	8173392	10008006	7243658	7588814	7000185	8135951	10444439	60564271
Interest	3	2943291	3054	2080	687	6790	3876	7087	5693	6738	27528	15726	90871	2773160
Rents	4	549147	145	343	504	5816	599	4538	3807	1091	2032	7256	4392	518624
Royalties	5	1733589	2583	645	0	0	186	3697	682	1097	26200	32575	21508	1644417
Other Portfolio Income	6	1858889	50040	26854	9647	16219	30988	29753	25896	28109	80547	51258	49369	1460208
Other Receipts	7	1482498	82250	8977	36018	119010	33474	59105	60959	57681	96419	79312	71689	777604
Total Receipts	8	157144636	1082530	5778475	3511041	19418123	8242515	10112186	7340695	7683530	7232911	8322078	10682268	67738284
Average Total Receipts	9	8367	1197	523	1851	5304	13783	27629	52811	108219	172212	396289	712151	5644857
Operating Costs/Operating Income (%)														
Cost of Operations	10	66.7	65.2	53.4	62.8	67.0	72.0	70.9	70.4	71.2	67.4	69.2	70.0	64.8
Salaries and Wages	11	6.8	12.9	12.2	9.1	7.3	5.4	6.4	7.2	7.4	7.5	6.8	7.3	6.0
Taxes Paid	12	2.0	2.4	3.3	3.7	2.6	1.9	2.1	1.9	1.8	1.6	2.3	1.6	1.7
Interest Paid	13	3.2	3.4	1.1	0.8	0.9	0.7	1.0	1.2	1.3	2.4	1.8	3.5	5.8
Depreciation	14	3.2	1.7	3.1	2.6	2.8	3.6	2.9	3.2	3.5	3.2	3.2	2.8	3.4
Amortization and Depletion	15	0.7	1.1	0.0	0.3	0.0	0.0	0.2	0.2	0.3	0.4	0.3	0.6	1.4
Pensions and Other Deferred Comp.	16	0.9	0.4	0.2	0.4	0.7	0.3	0.6	0.7	0.9	1.0	0.8	0.8	1.3
Employee Benefits	17	2.2	1.7	1.6	1.1	1.6	1.5	1.8	1.7	2.1	2.0	2.7	2.3	2.8
Advertising	18	1.4	1.7	0.3	1.0	0.4	0.4	0.4	0.7	0.6	0.7	0.7	0.5	2.6
Other Expenses	19	10.6	25.0	16.4	12.8	10.0	6.1	7.7	7.5	6.9	9.7	9.8	8.2	12.4
Officers' Compensation	20	1.7	2.3	6.0	5.7	4.2	3.0	2.2	1.7	1.4	0.9	0.8	0.4	0.4
Operating Margin	21	0.5	•	2.3	•	2.3	5.1	3.8	3.6	2.6	3.1	1.7	2.0	•
Operating Margin Before Officers' Comp.	22	2.2	•	8.3	5.4	6.5	8.1	6.0	5.3	4.0	4.1	2.5	2.4	•

Selected Average Balance Sheet ($ in Thousands)

Net Receivables 23	1245	0	36	201	648	1941	4128	7727	16061	27667	65685	124841	911809
Inventories 24	855	0	19	131	496	1758	3839	8070	13327	28151	65025	121729	406648
Net Property, Plant and Equipment 25	1384	0	60	153	584	1929	3852	8890	19252	32173	75118	119523	1084842
Total Assets 26	12364	0	158	664	2300	6845	15709	34927	69461	154869	334380	927241	14476035
Notes and Loans Payable 27	4367	0	136	310	887	1938	4548	9781	20638	45256	105110	282664	5222716
All Other Liabilities 28	1999	0	32	145	602	1576	4151	7882	19884	36701	107873	258114	1838490
Net Worth 29	5998	0	-9	208	810	3331	7011	17265	28939	72913	121398	386463	7414829

Selected Financial Ratios (Times to 1)

Current Ratio 30	1.6	•	1.3	1.9	1.8	2.2	1.8	2.1	1.9	2.1	2.0	2.0	1.2
Quick Ratio 31	0.9	•	0.9	1.2	1.1	1.4	1.0	1.1	1.0	1.0	0.9	1.0	0.8
Net Sales to Working Capital 32	7.5	•	23.5	8.7	7.6	5.5	6.2	4.8	5.9	3.9	4.8	3.5	14.6
Coverage Ratio 33	3.1	0.1	3.7	2.2	4.3	10.0	6.0	5.2	4.0	3.7	3.3	2.3	2.9
Total Asset Turnover 34	0.6	•	3.3	2.7	2.3	2.0	1.7	1.5	1.5	1.1	1.2	0.8	0.3
Inventory Turnover 35	6.2	•	14.7	8.8	7.1	5.6	5.1	4.5	5.7	4.0	4.1	4.0	8.0
Receivables Turnover 36	6.5	•	17.1	9.3	8.3	6.4	6.9	6.9	8.5	5.4	6.2	4.5	5.9
Total Liabilities to Net Worth 37	1.1	•	•	2.2	1.8	1.1	1.2	1.0	1.4	1.1	1.8	1.4	1.0
Current Assets to Working Capital 38	2.7	•	3.9	2.1	2.3	1.8	2.3	1.9	2.1	1.9	2.0	2.0	5.1
Current Liabilities to Working Capital 39	1.7	•	2.9	1.1	1.3	0.8	1.3	0.9	1.1	0.9	1.0	1.0	4.1
Working Capital to Net Sales 40	0.1	•	0.0	0.1	0.1	0.2	0.2	0.2	0.2	0.3	0.2	0.3	0.1
Inventory to Working Capital 41	0.9	•	0.9	0.7	0.8	0.6	0.9	0.8	0.9	0.6	0.8	0.6	1.3
Total Receipts to Cash Flow 42	6.8	5.1	6.7	11.6	10.0	10.1	9.3	9.2	11.4	7.2	8.7	9.1	5.0
Cost of Goods to Cash Flow 43	4.5	3.4	3.6	7.3	6.7	7.3	6.6	6.5	8.1	4.9	6.0	6.3	3.2
Cash Flow to Total Debt 44	0.2	•	0.5	0.3	0.4	0.4	0.3	0.3	0.2	0.3	0.2	0.1	0.1

Selected Financial Factors (in Percentages)

Debt Ratio 45	51.5	•	106.0	68.6	64.8	51.3	55.4	50.6	58.3	52.9	63.7	58.3	48.8
Return on Total Assets 46	6.5	•	13.4	5.1	9.1	13.2	10.2	9.4	8.0	9.7	6.8	5.9	5.8
Return on Equity Before Income Taxes 47	9.1	•	•	8.7	19.9	24.4	19.0	15.4	14.4	14.9	12.9	7.9	7.4
Return on Equity After Income Taxes 48	6.5	•	•	7.7	18.5	22.9	17.3	13.3	12.1	11.5	9.4	5.5	4.8
Profit Margin (Before Income Tax) 49	6.9	•	3.0	1.0	3.1	6.0	4.9	5.1	3.9	6.5	4.0	4.4	10.8
Profit Margin (After Income Tax) 50	5.0	•	2.9	0.9	2.8	5.6	4.4	4.4	3.3	5.0	3.0	3.0	7.1

Table II

Corporations with Net Income

OTHER FABRICATED METAL PRODUCT

MONEY AMOUNTS AND SIZE OF ASSETS IN THOUSANDS OF DOLLARS

Item Description for Accounting Period 7/04 Through 6/05	Total	Zero Assets	Under 500	500 to 1,000	1,000 to 5,000	5,000 to 10,000	10,000 to 25,000	25,000 to 50,000	50,000 to 100,000	100,000 to 250,000	250,000 to 500,000	500,000 to 2,500,000	2,500,000 and over
Number of Enterprises **1**	10779	259	5853	1092	2554	495	283	111	58	33	16	0	0
Revenues ($ in Thousands)													
Net Sales **2**	129693551	341851	4187025	2216541	13956434	6894599	8053795	5773767	6167366	5749210	7142633	0	0
Interest **3**	2816299	58	1843	256	4913	2066	4961	2710	6686	24825	12539	0	0
Rents **4**	544566	144	4	504	5560	4	3196	2308	926	1814	7091	0	0
Royalties **5**	1604913	0	645	0	0	186	3378	631	1092	20145	32139	0	0
Other Portfolio Income **6**	1706229	46593	20910	4569	11468	30054	26885	15026	27799	67199	46240	0	0
Other Receipts **7**	1092820	12764	8273	30660	27920	23057	49794	38881	51303	72364	70147	0	0
Total Receipts **8**	137458378	401410	4218700	2252530	14006295	6949966	8142009	5833323	6255172	5935557	7310789	0	0
Average Total Receipts **9**	12752	1550	721	2063	5484	14040	28770	52552	107848	179865	456924	•	•
Operating Costs/Operating Income (%)													
Cost of Operations **10**	65.9	67.5	48.2	57.6	64.1	71.2	69.4	68.1	69.1	67.5	68.9	•	•
Salaries and Wages **11**	6.7	7.1	14.3	11.1	7.3	4.9	6.4	7.2	7.5	7.2	6.8	•	•
Taxes Paid **12**	1.9	2.9	3.1	3.8	2.6	1.8	2.1	1.9	1.8	1.5	2.3	•	•
Interest Paid **13**	3.3	1.1	0.9	0.6	0.7	0.7	0.8	0.9	1.2	1.7	1.6	•	•
Depreciation **14**	3.0	2.9	2.5	2.2	2.6	3.6	2.7	2.9	3.3	3.1	3.1	•	•
Amortization and Depletion **15**	0.8	0.4	0.0	0.3	0.0	0.0	0.2	0.1	0.3	0.2	0.4	•	•
Pensions and Other Deferred Comp. **16**	0.9	0.6	0.2	0.6	0.8	0.3	0.6	0.6	0.8	1.1	0.6	•	•
Employee Benefits **17**	2.3	0.9	1.9	1.1	1.4	1.3	1.8	1.8	2.2	2.0	2.5	•	•
Advertising **18**	1.5	0.5	0.3	1.2	0.4	0.3	0.4	0.7	0.7	0.6	0.5	•	•
Other Expenses **19**	10.1	6.4	15.1	12.0	9.4	5.6	7.2	7.4	7.3	7.8	9.3	•	•
Officers' Compensation **20**	1.6	1.1	7.1	6.1	4.6	3.0	2.2	1.8	1.4	1.0	0.7	•	•
Operating Margin **21**	2.1	8.6	6.4	3.4	6.0	7.2	6.1	6.6	4.5	6.4	3.2	•	•
Operating Margin Before Officers' Comp. **22**	3.7	9.7	13.5	9.4	10.6	10.2	8.3	8.4	5.9	7.4	3.9	•	•

Selected Average Balance Sheet ($ in Thousands)

Net Receivables 23	1911	0	36	195	655	1964	4231	7383	16061	29633	69536
Inventories 24	1185	0	25	161	447	1490	3751	7268	15870	27270	60971
Net Property, Plant and Equipment 25	2075	0	64	99	560	1943	3702	8267	19004	32055	77224
Total Assets 26	19958	0	194	658	2330	6902	15855	34840	69688	154741	339189
Notes and Loans Payable 27	6945	0	124	216	643	1934	4020	7543	16610	40457	108862
All Other Liabilities 28	3108	0	48	166	548	1434	3900	6724	17429	39227	107119
Net Worth 29	9905	0	22	277	1139	3534	7935	20573	35649	75057	123208

Selected Financial Ratios (Times to 1)

Current Ratio 30	1.6	•	1.5	2.1	2.3	2.5	2.0	2.6	2.2	2.2	1.9
Quick Ratio 31	0.9	•	0.9	1.3	1.4	1.6	1.1	1.3	1.2	1.1	0.9
Net Sales to Working Capital 32	8.1	•	18.2	8.7	6.1	5.0	5.4	4.1	4.9	3.7	5.8
Coverage Ratio 33	3.6	24.3	9.3	9.8	9.7	13.2	10.1	9.9	6.1	6.8	4.5
Total Asset Turnover 34	0.6	•	3.7	3.1	2.3	2.0	1.8	1.5	1.5	1.1	1.3
Inventory Turnover 35	6.7	•	14.0	7.3	7.8	6.7	5.3	4.9	4.6	4.3	5.0
Receivables Turnover 36	7.2	•	22.4	•	8.9	7.1	7.2	7.7	•	6.0	7.5
Total Liabilities to Net Worth 37	1.0	•	8.0	1.4	1.0	1.0	1.0	0.7	1.0	1.1	1.8
Current Assets to Working Capital 38	2.8	•	2.8	1.9	1.8	1.7	2.0	1.6	1.8	1.8	2.1
Current Liabilities to Working Capital 39	1.8	•	1.8	0.9	0.8	0.7	1.0	0.6	0.8	0.8	1.1
Working Capital to Net Sales 40	0.1	•	0.1	0.1	0.2	0.2	0.2	0.2	0.2	0.3	0.2
Inventory to Working Capital 41	0.9	•	0.8	0.7	0.6	0.5	0.8	0.7	0.7	0.6	1.0
Total Receipts to Cash Flow 42	6.2	3.2	5.5	8.5	7.7	8.6	7.9	7.4	9.0	6.5	7.9
Cost of Goods to Cash Flow 43	4.1	2.1	2.7	4.9	4.9	6.2	5.5	5.1	6.2	4.4	5.4
Cash Flow to Total Debt 44	0.2	•	0.7	0.6	0.6	0.5	0.5	0.5	0.3	0.3	0.3

Selected Financial Factors (in Percentages)

Debt Ratio 45	50.4	•	88.9	57.9	51.1	48.8	50.0	41.0	48.8	51.5	63.7
Return on Total Assets 46	7.3	•	29.7	17.2	16.7	17.5	14.3	12.8	10.8	12.8	9.5
Return on Equity Before Income Taxes 47	10.6	•	239.0	36.7	30.6	31.6	25.8	19.4	17.7	22.5	20.4
Return on Equity After Income Taxes 48	8.0	•	234.2	35.3	29.2	29.9	23.7	17.3	15.4	18.2	15.9
Profit Margin (Before Income Tax) 49	8.8	26.0	7.2	5.0	6.4	8.0	7.2	7.7	5.9	9.7	5.6
Profit Margin (After Income Tax) 50	6.6	25.2	7.1	4.8	6.1	7.6	6.6	6.8	5.2	7.8	4.4

Table I

Corporations with and without Net Income

AGRICULTURE, CONSTRUCTION, AND MINING MACHINERY

MONEY AMOUNTS AND SIZE OF ASSETS IN THOUSANDS OF DOLLARS

Item Description for Accounting Period 7/04 Through 6/05	Total	Zero Assets	Under 500	500 to 1,000	1,000 to 5,000	5,000 to 10,000	10,000 to 25,000	25,000 to 50,000	50,000 to 100,000	100,000 to 250,000	250,000 to 500,000	500,000 to 2,500,000	2,500,000 and over
Number of Enterprises 1	2850	5	1140	251	1124	118	99	40	17	27	10	10	8
Revenues ($ in Thousands)													
Net Sales 2	90087576	194896	318177	432195	5134035	1156841	2472462	1938160	1835888	4977447	3331441	12131710	56164326
Interest 3	2716473	249	42	66	2601	2180	2068	1314	5801	7297	32025	119981	2542849
Rents 4	900845	174	0	162	114	21	1811	3324	68	775	922	23773	869702
Royalties 5	544011	255	0	0	0	201	126	1189	327	481	30831	96338	414263
Other Portfolio Income 6	859645	166	3354	222	38668	6196	5474	4784	10053	6381	41072	172557	570717
Other Receipts 7	2875454	235	22871	4190	12998	9516	18956	24335	17715	84965	10940	139799	2528933
Total Receipts 8	97984004	195975	344444	436835	5188416	1174955	2500897	1973106	1869852	5077346	3447231	12684158	63090790
Average Total Receipts 9	34380	39195	302	1740	4616	9957	25262	49328	109991	188050	344723	1268416	7886349
Operating Costs/Operating Income (%)													
Cost of Operations 10	73.4	74.6	61.5	59.5	73.5	63.6	74.2	67.9	65.9	72.7	73.6	75.5	73.7
Salaries and Wages 11	6.0	8.3	9.4	15.8	6.4	7.4	6.4	8.3	8.3	8.2	6.7	6.8	5.3
Taxes Paid 12	0.9	0.7	2.9	2.2	2.0	2.7	1.8	1.7	1.5	1.4	1.4	1.0	0.6
Interest Paid 13	3.2	3.5	2.7	0.4	1.0	0.5	1.0	1.5	1.4	1.6	2.4	2.1	4.2
Depreciation 14	3.0	3.2	2.4	0.9	3.3	2.8	1.8	2.3	2.4	2.7	2.4	1.8	3.4
Amortization and Depletion 15	0.5	6.0	0.2	0.1	0.1	0.1	0.1	0.2	0.5	0.8	0.6	0.5	0.6
Pensions and Other Deferred Comp. 16	2.5	0.3	0.3	0.2	0.2	0.3	0.7	0.5	0.6	0.7	0.5	1.4	3.6
Employee Benefits 17	1.9	0.3	1.9	1.3	1.6	1.0	1.9	1.5	1.5	1.9	1.3	1.9	2.1
Advertising 18	0.4	0.2	0.8	1.5	0.6	2.7	0.9	0.9	1.0	1.0	0.4	0.6	0.3
Other Expenses 19	13.4	11.8	14.2	16.9	7.5	14.5	7.1	9.0	10.7	7.9	8.6	8.9	16.2
Officers' Compensation 20	0.7	2.6	10.9	4.0	3.0	3.6	1.7	1.7	0.9	1.0	0.4	0.7	0.2
Operating Margin 21	•	•	•	•	0.7	1.0	2.4	4.5	5.4	0.2	1.5	•	•
Operating Margin Before Officers' Comp. 22	•	•	3.8	1.2	3.7	4.5	4.1	6.2	6.3	1.1	2.0	•	•

Selected Average Balance Sheet ($ in Thousands)

Net Receivables 23	13332	0	67	109	382	993	3487	7630	16041	29074	65098	276240	4028025
Inventories 24	3895	0	27	561	572	2622	4940	8488	19374	34407	45311	162506	726587
Net Property, Plant and Equipment 25	4504	0	42	73	333	1048	2669	6856	12489	29480	51122	128868	1115493
Total Assets 26	44296	0	157	804	1999	5979	14732	35580	66210	149006	330957	1429496	12159412
Notes and Loans Payable 27	19210	0	129	314	668	828	3987	13033	18520	46552	91118	373768	5817190
All Other Liabilities 28	14303	0	60	111	381	1581	5327	8306	23253	42766	91581	457146	4019266
Net Worth 29	10783	0	-33	379	950	3569	5418	14240	24437	59688	148258	598582	2322957

Selected Financial Ratios (Times to 1)

Current Ratio 30	1.6	•	1.3	4.3	2.4	2.3	1.8	1.8	1.8	1.7	2.2	1.5	1.5
Quick Ratio 31	1.1	•	1.0	1.4	1.2	0.8	0.8	0.8	0.9	0.8	1.2	0.8	1.1
Net Sales to Working Capital 32	4.0	•	13.3	3.6	6.0	4.3	5.2	5.0	6.1	5.1	4.3	6.5	3.4
Coverage Ratio 33	2.0	•	1.4	•	2.7	6.2	4.4	5.3	6.3	2.4	3.3	3.0	1.7
Total Asset Turnover 34	0.7	•	1.8	2.1	2.3	1.6	1.7	1.4	1.6	1.2	1.0	0.8	0.6
Inventory Turnover 35	6.0	•	6.4	1.8	5.9	2.4	3.8	3.9	3.7	3.9	5.4	5.6	7.1
Receivables Turnover 36	2.5	•	5.7	6.4	15.0	10.3	7.3	7.7	5.9	6.9	6.3	4.9	1.8
Total Liabilities to Net Worth 37	3.1	•	•	1.1	1.1	0.7	1.7	1.5	1.7	1.5	1.2	1.4	4.2
Current Assets to Working Capital 38	2.8	•	4.8	1.3	1.7	1.8	2.3	2.2	2.3	2.4	1.8	3.0	2.9
Current Liabilities to Working Capital 39	1.8	•	3.8	0.3	0.7	0.8	1.3	1.2	1.3	1.4	0.8	2.0	1.9
Working Capital to Net Sales 40	0.2	•	0.1	0.3	0.2	0.2	0.2	0.2	0.2	0.2	0.2	0.2	0.3
Inventory to Working Capital 41	0.5	•	0.9	0.9	0.8	1.1	1.1	1.1	0.9	1.1	0.7	0.9	0.4
Total Receipts to Cash Flow 42	6.9	•	9.0	9.6	13.9	7.0	10.8	7.1	6.2	11.7	8.4	9.8	5.9
Cost of Goods to Cash Flow 43	5.1	•	5.6	5.7	10.2	4.5	8.0	4.8	4.1	8.5	6.2	7.4	4.3
Cash Flow to Total Debt 44	0.1	•	0.2	0.4	0.3	0.6	0.2	0.3	0.4	0.2	0.1	0.1	0.1

Selected Financial Factors (in Percentages)

Debt Ratio 45	75.7	•	121.0	52.9	52.5	40.3	63.2	60.0	63.1	59.9	55.2	58.1	80.9
Return on Total Assets 46	4.7	•	6.8	•	6.2	4.9	7.7	10.6	14.1	4.7	7.9	5.4	4.2
Return on Equity Before Income Taxes 47	9.8	•	•	•	8.3	6.9	16.2	21.4	32.1	6.8	12.4	8.6	9.5
Return on Equity After Income Taxes 48	7.1	•	•	•	7.3	4.4	13.3	18.2	26.2	4.5	9.0	6.0	6.9
Profit Margin (Before Income Tax) 49	3.3	•	1.2	1.7	1.7	2.5	3.5	6.3	7.3	2.2	5.5	4.3	3.1
Profit Margin (After Income Tax) 50	2.4	•	0.8	•	1.5	1.6	2.9	5.3	5.9	1.4	3.0	3.0	2.3

Table II

Corporations with Net Income

AGRICULTURE, CONSTRUCTION, AND MINING MACHINERY

MONEY AMOUNTS AND SIZE OF ASSETS IN THOUSANDS OF DOLLARS

Item Description for Accounting Period 7/04 Through 6/05	Total	Zero Assets	Under 500	500 to 1,000	1,000 to 5,000	5,000 to 10,000	10,000 to 25,000	25,000 to 50,000	50,000 to 100,000	100,000 to 250,000	250,000 to 500,000	500,000 to 2,500,000	2,500,000 and over
Number of Enterprises **1**	1264	0	279	182	591	36	79	36	0	18	0	0	0

Revenues ($ in Thousands)

	Total	Zero Assets	Under 500	500 to 1,000	1,000 to 5,000	5,000 to 10,000	10,000 to 25,000	25,000 to 50,000	50,000 to 100,000	100,000 to 250,000	250,000 to 500,000	500,000 to 2,500,000	2,500,000 and over
Net Sales **2**	80844804	0	191492	340237	2358110	391977	2082449	1809845	0	3117338	0	0	0
Interest **3**	2655122	0	42	34	1762	2175	1427	979	0	6338	0	0	0
Rents **4**	900420	0	0	162	114	0	1807	3324	0	724	0	0	0
Royalties **5**	530238	0	0	0	0	0	126	1189	0	350	0	0	0
Other Portfolio Income **6**	814859	0	3314	0	907	5564	4551	4354	0	5504	0	0	0
Other Receipts **7**	2776047	0	22870	3697	7553	6929	15223	23610	0	47960	0	0	0
Total Receipts **8**	88521490	0	217718	344130	2368446	406645	2105583	1843301	0	3178214	0	0	0
Average Total Receipts **9**	70033	•	780	1891	4008	11296	26653	51203	•	176567	•	•	•

Operating Costs/Operating Income (%)

	Total	Zero Assets	Under 500	500 to 1,000	1,000 to 5,000	5,000 to 10,000	10,000 to 25,000	25,000 to 50,000	50,000 to 100,000	100,000 to 250,000	250,000 to 500,000	500,000 to 2,500,000	2,500,000 and over
Cost of Operations **10**	73.2	•	66.2	55.8	72.4	66.0	73.5	67.2	•	70.1	•	•	•
Salaries and Wages **11**	5.7	•	6.1	18.0	4.8	4.8	6.1	8.2	•	8.8	•	•	•
Taxes Paid **12**	0.8	•	3.4	2.0	1.1	2.2	1.9	1.7	•	1.6	•	•	•
Interest Paid **13**	3.4	•	3.3	0.3	0.6	1.0	0.8	1.2	•	1.7	•	•	•
Depreciation **14**	2.9	•	1.0	0.9	0.8	2.6	1.7	2.2	•	2.4	•	•	•
Amortization and Depletion **15**	0.5	•	0.0	0.2	0.2	0.0	0.1	0.2	•	0.4	•	•	•
Pensions and Other Deferred Comp. **16**	2.7	•	0.1	0.2	0.4	0.8	0.7	0.5	•	0.7	•	•	•
Employee Benefits **17**	1.9	•	3.2	1.6	0.7	0.7	1.5	1.5	•	1.2	•	•	•
Advertising **18**	0.4	•	1.1	1.7	0.8	0.7	0.9	0.9	•	0.8	•	•	•
Other Expenses **19**	14.0	•	8.9	14.9	6.9	11.4	6.5	9.4	•	7.5	•	•	•
Officers' Compensation **20**	0.6	•	12.3	2.8	2.9	3.1	1.8	1.8	•	0.7	•	•	•
Operating Margin **21**	•	•	•	1.7	8.5	6.8	4.6	5.3	•	4.1	•	•	•
Operating Margin Before Officers' Comp. **22**	•	•	6.7	4.5	11.4	9.9	6.3	7.1	•	4.8	•	•	•

Selected Average Balance Sheet ($ in Thousands)

Net Receivables 23	28922	•	245	118	393	1230	3628	7647	•	28358
Inventories 24	6846	•	73	612	522	5858	4786	7600	•	32494
Net Property, Plant and Equipment 25	9307	•	85	73	260	1236	2698	6863	•	23449
Total Assets 26	93650	•	375	808	1842	6507	14981	35720	•	146598
Notes and Loans Payable 27	41260	•	331	361	483	1920	3507	12438	•	42915
All Other Liabilities 28	30378	•	165	74	296	2071	4369	7936	•	31618
Net Worth 29	22012	•	-120	374	1062	2516	7104	15346	•	72066

Selected Financial Ratios (Times to 1)

Current Ratio 30	1.6	•	1.4	8.6	3.1	2.1	2.0	1.9	•	2.2
Quick Ratio 31	1.1	•	1.4	2.8	1.9	0.7	0.9	0.9	•	1.1
Net Sales to Working Capital 32	3.8	•	8.9	3.4	4.6	4.4	4.7	4.8	•	3.7
Coverage Ratio 33	2.2	•	3.4	10.1	14.9	11.3	7.8	7.0	•	4.7
Total Asset Turnover 34	0.7	•	1.8	2.3	2.2	1.7	1.8	1.4	•	1.2
Inventory Turnover 35	6.8	•	6.3	1.7	5.5	1.2	4.0	4.4	•	3.7
Receivables Turnover 36	2.7	•	4.5	5.5	11.7	5.3	7.9	8.5	•	7.2
Total Liabilities to Net Worth 37	3.3	•	•	1.2	0.7	1.6	1.1	1.3	•	1.0
Current Assets to Working Capital 38	2.8	•	3.6	1.1	1.5	1.9	2.0	2.1	•	1.8
Current Liabilities to Working Capital 39	1.8	•	2.6	0.1	0.5	0.9	1.0	1.1	•	0.8
Working Capital to Net Sales 40	0.3	•	0.1	0.3	0.2	0.2	0.2	0.2	•	0.3
Inventory to Working Capital 41	0.5	•	0.1	0.8	0.5	1.2	1.0	1.0	•	0.9
Total Receipts to Cash Flow 42	6.3	•	6.3	7.0	7.2	5.2	9.1	6.5	•	8.1
Cost of Goods to Cash Flow 43	4.6	•	4.2	3.9	5.2	3.5	6.7	4.4	•	5.7
Cash Flow to Total Debt 44	0.1	•	0.2	0.6	0.7	0.5	0.4	0.4	•	0.3

Selected Financial Factors (in Percentages)

Debt Ratio 45	76.5	•	132.1	53.8	42.3	61.3	52.6	57.0	•	50.8
Return on Total Assets 46	5.1	•	20.8	7.2	20.8	19.2	11.5	11.7	•	9.2
Return on Equity Before Income Taxes 47	12.0	•	•	14.0	33.7	45.4	21.1	23.3	•	14.7
Return on Equity After Income Taxes 48	9.1	•	•	12.4	31.9	33.4	18.3	20.0	•	11.8
Profit Margin (Before Income Tax) 49	4.1	•	8.0	2.8	9.0	10.5	5.7	7.1	•	6.1
Profit Margin (After Income Tax) 50	3.1	•	7.4	2.5	8.5	7.7	4.9	6.1	•	4.9

124

Table I

Corporations with and without Net Income

INDUSTRIAL MACHINERY

MONEY AMOUNTS AND SIZE OF ASSETS IN THOUSANDS OF DOLLARS

Item Description for Accounting Period 7/04 Through 6/05	Total	Zero Assets	Under 500	500 to 1,000	1,000 to 5,000	5,000 to 10,000	10,000 to 25,000	25,000 to 50,000	50,000 to 100,000	100,000 to 250,000	250,000 to 500,000	500,000 to 2,500,000	2,500,000 and over
Number of Enterprises **1**	3567	35	1807	371	784	250	149	75	40	28	12	11	4
Revenues ($ in Thousands)													
Net Sales **2**	47278931	169104	433812	690636	3535020	3335178	3229950	3284352	2707494	4271419	3463389	5818691	16339886
Interest **3**	282751	161	42	1	2801	8197	9036	6911	18094	26066	17547	89761	104133
Rents **4**	55491	118	0	1898	1614	4537	2549	5799	1059	11508	597	206	25606
Royalties **5**	181687	0	0	0	93	1321	3070	9022	6409	25585	34143	29098	72945
Other Portfolio Income **6**	419958	119	5129	34623	4482	6840	11899	10676	22806	100214	104043	59738	59388
Other Receipts **7**	516403	3384	5331	10185	57371	82554	28606	42527	38918	37630	23267	113913	72719
Total Receipts **8**	48735221	172886	444314	737343	3601381	3438627	3285110	3359287	2794780	4472422	3642986	6111407	16674677
Average Total Receipts **9**	13663	4940	246	1987	4594	13755	22048	44790	69870	159729	303582	555582	4168669
Operating Costs/Operating Income (%)													
Cost of Operations **10**	65.7	69.0	64.8	62.5	64.0	70.5	69.6	68.4	68.0	66.2	67.8	61.3	64.5
Salaries and Wages **11**	10.3	8.0	5.1	6.5	11.3	8.2	8.9	8.9	10.0	11.8	9.6	12.6	10.2
Taxes Paid **12**	1.9	2.4	2.2	4.3	3.5	2.5	2.3	2.3	2.2	1.9	1.4	2.3	1.1
Interest Paid **13**	2.0	0.6	0.3	1.1	1.2	0.6	1.0	1.4	1.8	2.9	1.3	4.7	1.9
Depreciation **14**	2.9	1.5	2.5	2.5	2.0	1.4	2.3	2.8	2.7	2.8	1.5	4.4	3.5
Amortization and Depletion **15**	0.8	0.1	•	0.2	0.1	0.1	0.4	0.8	1.3	1.0	0.5	1.9	0.9
Pensions and Other Deferred Comp. **16**	0.6	0.4	•	•	0.6	0.4	0.8	0.6	0.9	1.0	0.8	1.1	0.3
Employee Benefits **17**	2.4	1.4	0.1	5.7	2.7	2.2	1.9	2.0	2.5	3.1	3.9	2.9	1.9
Advertising **18**	0.6	1.4	1.4	0.7	1.4	0.3	0.6	0.6	0.5	0.5	0.4	0.6	0.4
Other Expenses **19**	9.6	12.1	20.1	9.1	10.6	6.5	9.1	9.6	11.0	12.6	8.0	10.1	8.9
Officers' Compensation **20**	1.7	4.8	6.8	5.4	4.3	6.4	2.4	1.6	1.5	1.1	1.0	0.8	0.4
Operating Margin **21**	1.5	•	•	2.0	•	0.9	0.8	1.0	•	•	3.6	•	6.0
Operating Margin Before Officers' Comp. **22**	3.2	3.2	3.5	7.4	2.6	7.3	3.1	2.5	•	•	4.7	•	6.4

Selected Average Balance Sheet ($ in Thousands)

Net Receivables 23	2733	0	26	261	713	2790	4300	8627	14697	33909	57878	174351	727387
Inventories 24	1669	0	38	108	770	1207	4118	6668	10433	22787	26093	68979	425049
Net Property, Plant and Equipment 25	2124	0	12	233	448	995	2826	6713	12308	25727	37552	66360	887323
Total Assets 26	15289	0	107	844	2558	7514	15961	35415	68153	156258	337211	972096	5817592
Notes and Loans Payable 27	3776	0	6	321	1101	1766	4320	10435	15464	44338	83193	335119	1015870
All Other Liabilities 28	4431	0	11	278	1093	2004	5293	11300	19909	48337	106221	340958	1378398
Net Worth 29	7081	0	89	245	364	3743	6348	13680	32781	63583	147796	296018	3423324

Selected Financial Ratios (Times to 1)

Current Ratio 30	2.1	•	8.0	1.4	2.0	2.0	1.6	1.7	1.7	2.1	1.7	1.7	2.6
Quick Ratio 31	1.4	•	4.0	1.1	0.9	1.4	0.9	0.9	1.0	1.1	1.0	1.1	2.0
Net Sales to Working Capital 32	3.3	•	3.0	11.0	4.8	5.3	5.2	5.0	4.5	3.0	4.4	4.0	2.2
Coverage Ratio 33	3.3	2.2	•	9.3	1.2	7.8	3.4	3.2	1.5	1.1	7.2	1.5	5.3
Total Asset Turnover 34	0.9	•	2.3	2.2	1.8	1.8	1.4	1.2	1.0	1.0	0.9	0.5	0.7
Inventory Turnover 35	5.2	•	4.1	10.8	3.7	7.8	3.7	4.5	4.4	4.4	7.5	4.7	6.2
Receivables Turnover 36	5.5	•	8.8	7.7	7.0	5.8	5.3	5.7	4.5	4.9	6.1	3.1	7.0
Total Liabilities to Net Worth 37	1.2	•	0.2	2.4	6.0	1.0	1.5	1.6	1.1	1.5	1.3	2.3	0.7
Current Assets to Working Capital 38	1.9	•	1.1	3.5	2.0	2.0	2.6	2.4	2.5	1.9	2.4	2.4	1.6
Current Liabilities to Working Capital 39	0.9	•	0.1	2.5	1.0	1.0	1.6	1.4	1.5	0.9	1.4	1.4	0.6
Working Capital to Net Sales 40	0.3	•	0.3	0.1	0.2	0.2	0.2	0.2	0.2	0.3	0.2	0.2	0.4
Inventory to Working Capital 41	0.5	•	0.5	0.7	1.0	0.5	1.0	0.8	0.7	0.5	0.5	0.5	0.3
Total Receipts to Cash Flow 42	8.3	8.9	8.3	6.1	13.6	11.5	10.1	9.1	10.7	10.2	6.7	9.2	6.6
Cost of Goods to Cash Flow 43	5.4	6.1	5.4	3.8	8.7	8.1	7.0	6.2	7.3	6.7	4.5	5.7	4.3
Cash Flow to Total Debt 44	0.2	•	1.6	0.5	0.2	0.3	0.2	0.2	0.2	0.2	0.2	0.1	0.3

Selected Financial Factors (in Percentages)

Debt Ratio 45	53.7	•	16.7	71.0	85.8	50.2	60.2	61.4	51.9	59.3	56.2	69.5	41.2
Return on Total Assets 46	5.8	•	•	21.7	2.5	8.1	4.7	5.8	2.7	3.1	8.0	4.0	7.1
Return on Equity Before Income Taxes 47	8.7	•	•	66.8	2.4	14.2	8.4	10.4	1.7	0.5	15.8	4.6	9.9
Return on Equity After Income Taxes 48	6.4	•	•	66.8	•	13.0	6.5	7.8	•	•	12.1	2.6	7.5
Profit Margin (Before Income Tax) 49	4.6	0.7	•	8.8	0.2	4.0	2.5	3.2	0.8	0.2	8.1	2.6	8.3
Profit Margin (After Income Tax) 50	3.4	•	•	8.8	•	3.7	1.9	2.4	•	•	6.2	1.5	6.3

Table II

Corporations with Net Income

INDUSTRIAL MACHINERY

MONEY AMOUNTS AND SIZE OF ASSETS IN THOUSANDS OF DOLLARS

Item Description for Accounting Period 7/04 Through 6/05	Total	Zero Assets	Under 500	500 to 1,000	1,000 to 5,000	5,000 to 10,000	10,000 to 25,000	25,000 to 50,000	50,000 to 100,000	100,000 to 250,000	250,000 to 500,000	500,000 to 2,500,000	2,500,000 and over
Number of Enterprises **1**	1542	31	442	253	390	222	99	48	24	14	0	6	0

Revenues ($ in Thousands)

Item	Total	Zero Assets	Under 500	500 to 1,000	1,000 to 5,000	5,000 to 10,000	10,000 to 25,000	25,000 to 50,000	50,000 to 100,000	100,000 to 250,000	250,000 to 500,000	500,000 to 2,500,000	2,500,000 and over
Net Sales **2**	33613007	117840	138835	434771	1675477	2843683	2350631	2256363	1684562	2256382	0	2444940	0
Interest **3**	162416	62	0	1	2456	7329	3957	4741	10394	8191	0	6084	0
Rents **4**	42104	107	0	0	250	452	1194	3887	224	11454	0	0	0
Royalties **5**	89168	0	0	0	93	30	1454	3424	6122	14844	0	2295	0
Other Portfolio Income **6**	292805	67	5129	34579	678	6717	6790	9569	16459	5079	0	48763	0
Other Receipts **7**	367946	3396	5105	862	43929	80673	19968	28905	26031	24643	0	57330	0
Total Receipts **8**	34567446	121472	149069	470213	1722883	2938884	2383994	2306889	1743792	2320593	0	2559412	0
Average Total Receipts **9**	22417	3918	337	1859	4418	13238	24081	48060	72658	165757	•	426569	•

Operating Costs/Operating Income (%)

Item	Total	Zero Assets	Under 500	500 to 1,000	1,000 to 5,000	5,000 to 10,000	10,000 to 25,000	25,000 to 50,000	50,000 to 100,000	100,000 to 250,000	250,000 to 500,000	500,000 to 2,500,000	2,500,000 and over
Cost of Operations **10**	64.2	74.2	71.7	54.5	65.3	67.2	68.3	67.2	68.6	65.2	•	55.6	•
Salaries and Wages **11**	10.2	4.2	8.5	7.1	7.7	8.7	8.5	8.6	8.1	10.8	•	16.1	•
Taxes Paid **12**	1.8	2.4	2.4	4.3	3.0	2.6	2.3	2.2	2.1	2.1	•	2.4	•
Interest Paid **13**	1.5	0.5	1.0	1.4	1.2	0.6	0.9	1.2	1.2	2.1	•	1.7	•
Depreciation **14**	2.8	1.7	3.4	3.4	2.1	1.4	2.1	2.6	2.3	2.9	•	2.4	•
Amortization and Depletion **15**	0.7	0.1	•	0.3	0.1	0.1	0.2	0.6	0.5	1.0	•	1.9	•
Pensions and Other Deferred Comp. **16**	0.5	0.4	•	•	0.7	0.4	0.7	0.6	0.7	0.8	•	1.7	•
Employee Benefits **17**	2.2	0.9	0.3	6.4	1.5	2.2	1.9	1.9	2.4	2.2	•	2.6	•
Advertising **18**	0.4	1.5	0.4	0.3	0.9	0.3	0.6	0.6	0.5	0.6	•	0.7	•
Other Expenses **19**	8.4	8.6	14.7	7.4	9.7	6.6	7.7	8.6	7.8	8.4	•	8.4	•
Officers' Compensation **20**	1.7	1.1	•	4.8	5.1	7.0	2.4	1.7	1.6	1.4	•	1.3	•
Operating Margin **21**	5.5	4.6	•	10.1	2.7	2.8	4.5	4.2	4.3	2.6	•	5.2	•
Operating Margin Before Officers' Comp. **22**	7.2	5.7	•	14.9	7.8	9.8	6.9	5.9	5.9	4.0	•	6.5	•

Selected Average Balance Sheet ($ in Thousands)

Net Receivables 23	4200	0	35	208	668	2801	4677	9098	15228	25584	118780
Inventories 24	2155	0	69	121	627	1245	3727	6491	9428	19444	90010
Net Property, Plant and Equipment 25	3659	0	16	288	403	960	2901	6744	12130	29552	59462
Total Assets 26	25321	0	126	869	2385	7547	16074	36019	64861	145111	1044842
Notes and Loans Payable 27	5170	0	25	403	814	1623	3654	8909	13910	42565	238628
All Other Liabilities 28	6370	0	38	120	685	1831	5425	11802	15458	40721	238348
Net Worth 29	13781	0	63	346	885	4093	6996	15307	35493	61825	567866

Selected Financial Ratios (Times to 1)

Current Ratio 30	2.3	•	2.9	2.0	2.6	2.3	1.8	1.9	2.1	1.8	1.6
Quick Ratio 31	1.6	•	1.1	1.5	1.3	1.6	1.0	1.1	1.4	0.9	1.0
Net Sales to Working Capital 32	2.9	•	4.6	6.4	4.1	4.6	4.7	4.5	3.8	4.9	4.6
Coverage Ratio 33	6.5	17.2	6.0	13.8	5.7	10.4	7.9	6.4	7.8	3.7	7.2
Total Asset Turnover 34	0.9	•	2.5	2.0	1.8	1.7	1.5	1.3	1.1	1.1	0.4
Inventory Turnover 35	6.5	•	3.3	7.7	4.5	6.9	4.3	4.9	5.1	5.4	2.5
Receivables Turnover 36	6.8	•	6.5	8.5	6.4	5.4	5.8	5.9	4.9	7.8	2.5
Total Liabilities to Net Worth 37	0.8	•	1.0	1.5	1.7	0.8	1.3	1.4	0.8	1.3	0.8
Current Assets to Working Capital 38	1.7	•	1.5	2.0	1.6	1.8	2.2	2.1	1.9	2.2	2.8
Current Liabilities to Working Capital 39	0.7	•	0.5	1.0	0.6	0.8	1.2	1.1	0.9	1.2	1.8
Working Capital to Net Sales 40	0.3	•	0.2	0.2	0.2	0.2	0.2	0.2	0.3	0.2	0.2
Inventory to Working Capital 41	0.4	•	0.8	0.4	0.7	0.5	0.8	0.7	0.5	0.8	0.7
Total Receipts to Cash Flow 42	6.6	6.9	6.7	4.0	8.0	9.2	8.3	7.6	7.2	8.1	5.9
Cost of Goods to Cash Flow 43	4.3	5.1	4.8	2.2	5.2	6.2	5.7	5.1	5.0	5.3	3.3
Cash Flow to Total Debt 44	0.3	•	0.7	0.8	0.4	0.3	0.3	0.3	0.3	0.2	0.1

Selected Financial Factors (in Percentages)

Debt Ratio 45	45.6	•	50.1	60.2	62.9	45.8	56.5	57.5	45.3	57.4	45.7
Return on Total Assets 46	8.5	•	14.9	38.9	12.0	11.5	10.0	9.9	9.9	8.5	4.8
Return on Equity Before Income Taxes 47	13.3	•	24.9	90.7	26.7	19.2	20.1	19.8	15.7	14.5	7.7
Return on Equity After Income Taxes 48	10.5	•	24.8	90.7	20.3	18.0	17.5	16.1	12.0	11.7	5.8
Profit Margin (Before Income Tax) 49	8.4	7.7	5.0	18.3	5.5	6.1	5.9	6.4	8.0	5.6	10.7
Profit Margin (After Income Tax) 50	6.6	6.4	5.0	18.3	4.2	5.8	5.2	5.2	6.0	4.5	8.0

Table I

Corporations with and without Net Income

COMMERCIAL AND SERVICE INDUSTRY MACHINERY

MONEY AMOUNTS AND SIZE OF ASSETS IN THOUSANDS OF DOLLARS

Item Description for Accounting Period 7/04 Through 6/05	Total	Zero Assets	Under 500	500 to 1,000	1,000 to 5,000	5,000 to 10,000	10,000 to 25,000	25,000 to 50,000	50,000 to 100,000	100,000 to 250,000	250,000 to 500,000	500,000 to 2,500,000	2,500,000 and over
Number of Enterprises 1	1784	870	0	0	430	65	72	15	21	17	3	8	4
Revenues ($ in Thousands)													
Net Sales 2	42515816	172161	0	0	3219736	606499	1707671	630499	1703657	2934360	1435593	5790004	23984734
Interest 3	1189591	3	0	0	987	345	4612	1177	2421	7436	14114	61132	1097262
Rents 4	330284	0	0	0	3421	0	631	561	4501	7213	74	166606	144048
Royalties 5	798266	0	0	0	0	0	1069	0	385	1241	3812	27170	764589
Other Portfolio Income 6	362761	160	0	0	326	81	2236	212	3200	32888	72432	49078	202150
Other Receipts 7	1619973	-6251	0	0	10624	11643	11236	3890	16335	39821	7169	259012	1263156
Total Receipts 8	46816691	166073	0	0	3235094	618568	1727455	636339	1730499	3022959	1533194	6353002	27455939
Average Total Receipts 9	26243	191	.	.	7523	9516	23992	42423	82405	177821	511065	794125	6863985
Operating Costs/Operating Income (%)													
Cost of Operations 10	55.5	55.4	.	.	53.8	66.7	65.6	69.0	63.7	64.8	60.6	52.1	53.1
Salaries and Wages 11	16.8	27.2	.	.	21.4	7.0	10.2	9.4	10.3	9.6	14.9	17.7	18.3
Taxes Paid 12	2.2	4.9	.	.	2.1	2.3	2.5	2.4	2.0	1.7	0.9	2.9	2.1
Interest Paid 13	4.0	1.3	.	.	0.3	1.6	1.2	1.3	0.9	2.1	2.1	2.2	6.0
Depreciation 14	6.8	6.7	.	.	1.0	3.8	2.5	2.5	2.5	4.5	1.5	4.7	9.6
Amortization and Depletion 15	0.6	0.5	.	.	0.1	0.8	0.5	0.8	0.6	0.5	1.1	1.1	0.6
Pensions and Other Deferred Comp. 16	0.9	0.0	.	.	0.5	0.4	0.6	0.5	1.0	1.0	0.4	1.0	1.0
Employee Benefits 17	5.2	1.0	.	.	1.8	1.8	2.0	2.1	2.3	2.4	1.8	2.4	7.5
Advertising 18	1.6	0.5	.	.	1.1	0.7	0.9	0.5	1.2	1.0	2.4	0.6	2.0
Other Expenses 19	14.0	21.4	.	.	8.4	12.5	11.3	8.7	10.7	11.1	11.1	19.6	14.5
Officers' Compensation 20	1.2	7.9	.	.	3.9	3.9	2.4	1.7	1.5	1.6	0.5	0.9	0.6
Operating Margin 21	.	.	.	.	5.6	.	0.4	1.2	3.3	.	2.9	.	.
Operating Margin Before Officers' Comp. 22	.	.	.	.	9.5	2.4	2.8	2.9	4.8	1.5	3.3	.	.

Selected Average Balance Sheet ($ in Thousands)

Net Receivables 23	7779	0	•	856	1265	4010	5889	16728	32428	181183	229646	2432826
Inventories 24	2056	0	•	704	2260	3998	8758	12916	29242	55666	75758	324649
Net Property, Plant and Equipment 25	4886	0	•	402	2344	2894	7312	10624	26944	37333	145161	1521952
Total Assets 26	38937	0	•	3221	7161	15983	35426	68901	163893	416148	1119453	12839980
Notes and Loans Payable 27	16009	0	•	1123	2116	4561	9916	15887	64864	153039	328102	5724476
All Other Liabilities 28	12523	0	•	1041	2469	17391	9193	22129	42835	85976	330594	4047231
Net Worth 29	10406	0	•	1057	2576	-5969	16317	30886	56194	177133	460757	3068272

Selected Financial Ratios (Times to 1)

Current Ratio 30	1.4	•	•	2.2	1.5	0.6	1.9	1.6	1.4	2.0	1.7	1.3
Quick Ratio 31	0.9	•	•	1.4	0.7	0.3	1.0	0.9	0.7	1.5	1.1	1.0
Net Sales to Working Capital 32	5.9	•	•	5.6	6.5	•	4.3	5.3	7.5	3.6	4.3	5.3
Coverage Ratio 33	1.4	•	•	19.9	1.3	2.4	2.6	6.4	2.4	8.1	3.1	0.9
Total Asset Turnover 34	0.6	•	•	2.3	1.3	1.5	1.2	1.2	1.1	1.1	0.6	0.5
Inventory Turnover 35	6.4	•	•	5.7	2.8	3.9	3.3	4.0	3.8	5.2	5.0	9.8
Receivables Turnover 36	3.1	•	•	11.2	7.3	6.3	6.7	5.5	4.5	•	3.2	2.5
Total Liabilities to Net Worth 37	2.7	•	•	2.0	1.8	•	1.2	1.2	1.9	1.3	1.4	3.2
Current Assets to Working Capital 38	3.7	•	•	1.9	3.1	•	2.1	2.7	3.4	2.0	2.5	4.0
Current Liabilities to Working Capital 39	2.7	•	•	0.9	2.1	•	1.1	1.7	2.4	1.0	1.5	3.0
Working Capital to Net Sales 40	0.2	•	•	0.2	0.2	•	0.2	0.2	0.1	0.3	0.2	0.2
Inventory to Working Capital 41	0.5	•	•	0.6	1.3	•	0.9	0.9	1.3	0.4	0.5	0.2
Total Receipts to Cash Flow 42	8.8	•	•	8.0	9.4	8.7	10.7	7.1	8.6	5.2	5.4	10.9
Cost of Goods to Cash Flow 43	4.9	•	•	4.3	6.3	5.7	7.4	4.5	5.6	3.2	2.8	5.8
Cash Flow to Total Debt 44	0.1	•	•	0.4	0.2	0.1	0.2	0.3	0.2	0.4	0.2	0.1

Selected Financial Factors (in Percentages)

Debt Ratio 45	73.3	•	•	67.2	64.0	137.3	53.9	55.2	65.7	57.4	58.8	76.1
Return on Total Assets 46	3.5	•	•	14.9	2.6	4.1	4.1	7.0	5.2	19.6	4.4	2.6
Return on Equity Before Income Taxes 47	3.8	•	•	43.2	1.6	•	5.4	13.1	8.7	40.3	7.3	•
Return on Equity After Income Taxes 48	2.4	•	•	40.8	•	•	2.9	10.6	6.5	24.8	5.1	•
Profit Margin (Before Income Tax) 49	1.7	•	•	6.1	0.4	1.6	2.1	5.0	2.8	14.9	4.6	•
Profit Margin (After Income Tax) 50	1.0	•	•	5.8	•	1.0	1.1	4.0	2.1	9.2	3.2	•

Table II

Corporations with Net Income

COMMERCIAL AND SERVICE INDUSTRY MACHINERY

MONEY AMOUNTS AND SIZE OF ASSETS IN THOUSANDS OF DOLLARS

Item Description for Accounting Period 7/04 Through 6/05	Total	Zero Assets	Under 500	500 to 1,000	1,000 to 5,000	5,000 to 10,000	10,000 to 25,000	25,000 to 50,000	50,000 to 100,000	100,000 to 250,000	250,000 to 500,000	500,000 to 2,500,000	2,500,000 and over
Number of Enterprises **1**	1310	825	0	0	350	37	45	11	17	14	0	0	0
Revenues ($ in Thousands)													
Net Sales **2**	29921671	79833	0	0	2897235	476780	1019194	480125	1388539	3138800	0	0	0
Interest **3**	1158136	0	0	0	402	205	1777	1172	1928	14732	0	0	0
Rents **4**	180357	0	0	0	3421	0	604	561	2058	7107	0	0	0
Royalties **5**	530893	0	0	0	0	0	0	0	166	3969	0	0	0
Other Portfolio Income **6**	320396	0	0	0	326	73	1739	152	3132	77358	0	0	0
Other Receipts **7**	1486464	2712	0	0	9845	10928	7403	2192	17623	30977	0	0	0
Total Receipts **8**	33597917	82545	0	0	2911229	487986	1030717	484202	1413446	3272943	0	0	0
Average Total Receipts **9**	25647	100	•	•	8318	13189	22905	44018	83144	233782	•	•	•
Operating Costs/Operating Income (%)													
Cost of Operations **10**	52.2	34.5	•	•	48.9	66.4	61.8	66.2	60.8	62.6	•	•	•
Salaries and Wages **11**	20.7	28.1	•	•	22.4	4.6	9.6	8.0	10.6	9.8	•	•	•
Taxes Paid **12**	2.3	2.9	•	•	2.0	1.9	2.1	2.2	2.1	1.4	•	•	•
Interest Paid **13**	4.9	0.4	•	•	0.2	0.7	0.9	1.3	0.9	1.3	•	•	•
Depreciation **14**	7.4	11.1	•	•	0.8	3.3	2.0	2.1	2.4	2.2	•	•	•
Amortization and Depletion **15**	0.5	0.9	•	•	0.1	0.4	0.2	1.0	0.7	0.3	•	•	•
Pensions and Other Deferred Comp. **16**	1.2	0.0	•	•	0.6	0.5	0.6	0.5	1.0	1.0	•	•	•
Employee Benefits **17**	4.4	•	•	•	1.7	0.9	1.7	1.6	2.5	2.1	•	•	•
Advertising **18**	1.0	0.5	•	•	1.1	0.7	0.8	0.4	1.2	1.7	•	•	•
Other Expenses **19**	12.4	20.5	•	•	8.2	11.2	9.3	9.1	10.6	12.3	•	•	•
Officers' Compensation **20**	1.2	•	•	•	4.1	3.9	2.4	1.7	1.5	1.2	•	•	•
Operating Margin **21**	•	1.0	•	•	10.0	5.6	8.5	5.9	5.7	4.0	•	•	•
Operating Margin Before Officers' Comp. **22**	•	1.0	•	•	14.1	9.4	10.9	7.6	7.3	5.1	•	•	•

Selected Average Balance Sheet ($ in Thousands)

Net Receivables 23	9465	0	•	935	1590	4107	6552	16330	59610
Inventories 24	1935	0	•	617	2770	3955	9282	11815	28107
Net Property, Plant and Equipment 25	3565	0	•	288	1935	2419	6290	10740	25381
Total Assets 26	39652	0	•	3375	7284	15587	35727	68157	189061
Notes and Loans Payable 27	17389	0	•	899	1323	3062	8238	14790	70631
All Other Liabilities 28	10932	0	•	1023	2724	4931	9576	17907	43302
Net Worth 29	11331	0	•	1453	3237	7594	17913	35460	75128

Selected Financial Ratios (Times to 1)

Current Ratio 30	1.7	•	2.3	1.7	1.9	2.0	1.7	1.6
Quick Ratio 31	1.4	•	1.5	0.9	1.1	1.1	1.0	1.0
Net Sales to Working Capital 32	3.4	•	5.5	6.5	4.3	3.8	5.1	5.4
Coverage Ratio 33	1.9	11.9	47.8	12.6	11.6	6.0	10.0	8.9
Total Asset Turnover 34	0.6	•	2.5	1.8	1.5	1.2	1.2	1.2
Inventory Turnover 35	6.2	•	6.6	3.1	3.5	3.1	4.2	5.0
Receivables Turnover 36	2.6	•	12.7	7.1	6.0	•	6.1	4.4
Total Liabilities to Net Worth 37	2.5	•	1.3	1.3	1.1	1.0	0.9	1.5
Current Assets to Working Capital 38	2.4	•	1.8	2.4	2.1	2.0	2.5	2.5
Current Liabilities to Working Capital 39	1.4	•	0.8	1.4	1.1	1.0	1.5	1.5
Working Capital to Net Sales 40	0.3	•	0.2	0.2	0.2	0.3	0.2	0.2
Inventory to Working Capital 41	0.3	•	0.5	0.8	0.8	0.8	0.9	0.8
Total Receipts to Cash Flow 42	8.6	4.9	6.0	6.0	5.7	6.9	6.1	5.3
Cost of Goods to Cash Flow 43	4.5	1.7	3.0	4.0	3.5	4.6	3.7	3.3
Cash Flow to Total Debt 44	0.1	•	0.7	0.5	0.5	0.4	0.4	0.4

Selected Financial Factors (in Percentages)

Debt Ratio 45	71.4	•	56.9	55.6	51.3	49.9	48.0	60.3
Return on Total Assets 46	5.4	•	26.1	15.2	15.3	9.8	10.2	14.2
Return on Equity Before Income Taxes 47	9.1	•	59.4	31.5	28.6	16.3	17.6	31.7
Return on Equity After Income Taxes 48	7.3	•	57.3	26.0	25.6	13.2	14.9	21.9
Profit Margin (Before Income Tax) 49	4.5	4.4	10.4	7.9	9.6	6.7	7.6	10.6
Profit Margin (After Income Tax) 50	3.6	4.3	10.1	6.5	8.6	5.4	6.5	7.3

Table I

Corporations with and without Net Income

VENTILATION, HEATING, A.C. & COMMERCIAL REFRIGERATION EQUIP.

MONEY AMOUNTS AND SIZE OF ASSETS IN THOUSANDS OF DOLLARS

Item Description for Accounting Period 7/04 Through 6/05	Total	Zero Assets	Under 500	500 to 1,000	1,000 to 5,000	5,000 to 10,000	10,000 to 25,000	25,000 to 50,000	50,000 to 100,000	100,000 to 250,000	250,000 to 500,000	500,000 to 2,500,000	2,500,000 and over
Number of Enterprises 1	782	266	0	0	180	70	70	34	15	9	3	13	0
Revenues ($ in Thousands)													
Net Sales 2	32784548	450549	0	0	672981	932862	2200727	2175801	1626464	1475690	1649919	21447999	0
Interest 3	138609	566	0	0	744	763	3026	1204	3121	8119	18192	102779	0
Rents 4	7114	0	0	0	0	7	888	857	533	1314	10	3207	0
Royalties 5	198157	0	0	0	0	0	485	2461	2639	801	961	190809	0
Other Portfolio Income 6	325778	85129	0	0	45	29255	3505	3462	9120	6812	1475	186971	0
Other Receipts 7	271968	5557	0	0	-5414	15360	30679	5460	10105	17592	2748	186482	0
Total Receipts 8	33726174	541801	0	0	668356	978247	2239310	2189245	1651982	1510328	1673305	2211247	0
Average Total Receipts 9	43128	2037	•	•	3713	13975	31990	64390	110132	167814	557768	1701404	•
Operating Costs/Operating Income (%)													
Cost of Operations 10	73.2	66.7	•	•	69.2	61.2	71.5	69.1	66.6	71.6	78.7	74.8	•
Salaries and Wages 11	7.3	10.9	•	•	5.1	12.0	8.0	9.3	7.5	7.2	3.9	7.1	•
Taxes Paid 12	1.2	0.5	•	•	2.7	1.9	2.0	1.8	1.3	2.1	1.2	0.9	•
Interest Paid 13	1.9	8.9	•	•	0.6	1.0	0.6	0.5	0.6	2.6	1.2	2.3	•
Depreciation 14	1.6	1.8	•	•	1.6	2.7	2.2	2.2	3.0	1.9	0.7	1.4	•
Amortization and Depletion 15	0.7	0.3	•	•	0.2	0.0	0.1	0.2	0.6	0.5	0.9	0.9	•
Pensions and Other Deferred Comp. 16	0.7	0.2	•	•	0.2	0.5	0.6	0.6	0.6	0.8	0.6	0.7	•
Employee Benefits 17	2.2	0.1	•	•	2.1	3.9	1.7	2.5	2.3	2.3	1.5	2.2	•
Advertising 18	0.9	1.4	•	•	1.1	0.7	0.6	0.4	0.7	1.5	0.2	1.1	•
Other Expenses 19	9.1	22.2	•	•	7.8	12.2	8.3	6.3	9.1	8.1	5.0	9.5	•
Officers' Compensation 20	1.5	1.7	•	•	8.7	2.1	1.9	1.8	1.3	0.8	4.6	0.9	•
Operating Margin 21	•	•	•	•	0.8	1.7	2.5	5.3	6.4	0.6	1.5	•	•
Operating Margin Before Officers' Comp. 22	1.0	•	•	•	9.5	3.8	4.4	7.1	7.8	1.4	6.1	•	•

Selected Average Balance Sheet ($ in Thousands)

Item										
Net Receivables 23	6452	0	460	644	4842	9495	17432	20382	71312	275291
Inventories 24	4002	0	375	997	3469	7241	11996	31986	57090	148803
Net Property, Plant and Equipment 25	4763	0	204	1229	3793	8343	16992	19985	33407	192030
Total Assets 26	45764		1642	6489	16020	38099	76388	149040	374471	2226771
Notes and Loans Payable 27	10858	0	527	982	4224	6397	16188	49182	69414	531860
All Other Liabilities 28	21673	0	593	1316	4389	9484	18477	41129	101173	1164870
Net Worth 29	13233	0	522	4191	7407	22218	41722	58729	203884	530041

Selected Financial Ratios (Times to 1)

Item										
Current Ratio 30	1.0		1.8	4.3	1.8	2.2	2.0	1.5	1.7	0.8
Quick Ratio 31	0.6		1.1	3.2	1.1	1.4	0.6	1.0	0.5	
Net Sales to Working Capital 32	82.9	2.3	6.2	4.2	6.4	5.0	5.3	8.6	8.9	
Coverage Ratio 33	2.4		1.2	6.9	7.7	12.8	15.0	2.1	3.5	1.7
Total Asset Turnover 34	0.9		2.3	2.1	2.0	1.7	1.4	1.1	1.5	0.7
Inventory Turnover 35	7.7		6.9	8.2	6.5	6.1	6.0	3.7	7.6	8.3
Receivables Turnover 36	6.8		10.0	11.4	7.0	7.6	6.7	6.4	6.1	
Total Liabilities to Net Worth 37	2.5		2.1	0.5	1.2	0.7	0.8	1.5	0.8	3.2
Current Assets to Working Capital 38	28.7		2.2	1.3	2.2	1.8	2.0	3.0	2.4	
Current Liabilities to Working Capital 39	27.7		1.2	0.3	1.2	0.8	1.0	2.0	1.4	
Working Capital to Net Sales 40	0.0		0.2	0.2	0.2	0.2	0.2	0.1	0.1	
Inventory to Working Capital 41	8.6		0.7	0.3	0.8	0.6	0.6	1.4	0.9	
Total Receipts to Cash Flow 42	10.4	3.9	21.4	5.9	9.1	9.4	6.1	11.8	13.7	11.4
Cost of Goods to Cash Flow 43	7.6	2.6	14.8	3.6	6.5	6.5	4.1	8.4	10.8	8.5
Cash Flow to Total Debt 44	0.1		0.2	1.0	0.4	0.5	0.2	0.1	0.1	

Selected Financial Factors (in Percentages)

Item										
Debt Ratio 45	71.1		68.2	35.4	53.8	41.7	45.4	60.6	45.6	76.2
Return on Total Assets 46	4.3		1.6	14.6	9.6	10.8	12.6	6.0	6.0	2.9
Return on Equity Before Income Taxes 47	8.6		1.0	19.3	18.1	17.0	21.6	7.9	7.9	5.0
Return on Equity After Income Taxes 48	5.5		17.9	16.0	14.5	15.0	5.3	7.9	2.7	2.5
Profit Margin (Before Income Tax) 49	2.7	11.5	0.1	6.1	4.3	5.9	8.3	5.3	2.9	1.6
Profit Margin (After Income Tax) 50	1.7	4.6	5.6	3.8	5.0	5.8	1.9	1.0	0.8	

VENTILATION, HEATING, A.C. & COMMERCIAL REFRIGERATION EQUIP.

Table II

Corporations with Net Income

MONEY AMOUNTS AND SIZE OF ASSETS IN THOUSANDS OF DOLLARS

Item Description for Accounting Period 7/04 Through 6/05	Total	Zero Assets	Under 500	500 to 1,000	1,000 to 5,000	5,000 to 10,000	10,000 to 25,000	25,000 to 50,000	50,000 to 100,000	100,000 to 250,000	250,000 to 500,000	500,000 to 2,500,000	2,500,000 and over
Number of Enterprises 1	625	262	0	0	177	0	57	28	0	9	0	9	0
Revenues ($ in Thousands)													
Net Sales 2	27836542	426976	0	0	655243	0	1892231	1707523	0	2203143	0	18413862	0
Interest 3	65956	268	0	0	744	0	2818	1119	0	17413	0	39709	0
Rents 4	5622	0	0	0	0	0	857	833	0	1324	0	2068	0
Royalties 5	196752	0	0	0	0	0	485	2461	0	1723	0	189443	0
Other Portfolio Income 6	186461	83280	0	0	32	0	2827	3441	0	5676	0	52828	0
Other Receipts 7	241333	5496	0	0	-659	0	28320	3830	0	3270	0	179108	0
Total Receipts 8	28532666	516020	0	0	655360	0	1927538	1719207	0	2232549	0	1877018	0
Average Total Receipts 9	45652	1970	•	•	3703	•	33816	61400	•	248061	•	2097446	•
Operating Costs/Operating Income (%)													
Cost of Operations 10	72.6	65.6	•	•	69.0	•	70.6	67.6	•	70.6	•	75.0	•
Salaries and Wages 11	7.4	9.4	•	•	5.0	•	8.2	9.5	•	5.5	•	7.1	•
Taxes Paid 12	1.2	0.4	•	•	2.7	•	2.0	1.7	•	1.7	•	1.0	•
Interest Paid 13	1.5	9.4	•	•	0.5	•	0.6	0.4	•	1.2	•	1.7	•
Depreciation 14	1.7	1.9	•	•	1.6	•	2.0	2.1	•	1.6	•	1.5	•
Amortization and Depletion 15	0.4	0.3	•	•	0.2	•	0.1	0.3	•	0.8	•	0.4	•
Pensions and Other Deferred Comp. 16	0.8	0.2	•	•	0.2	•	0.6	0.7	•	1.0	•	0.9	•
Employee Benefits 17	2.2	0.1	•	•	1.6	•	1.6	2.1	•	2.1	•	2.3	•
Advertising 18	1.0	1.5	•	•	1.1	•	0.7	0.4	•	0.9	•	1.1	•
Other Expenses 19	8.2	10.4	•	•	7.7	•	8.1	6.3	•	5.7	•	8.4	•
Officers' Compensation 20	1.2	0.3	•	•	8.8	•	1.9	1.3	•	3.8	•	0.5	•
Operating Margin 21	1.8	0.5	•	•	1.6	•	3.7	7.6	•	5.3	•	0.2	•
Operating Margin Before Officers' Comp. 22	3.0	0.9	•	•	10.4	•	5.6	8.9	•	9.1	•	0.8	•

Selected Average Balance Sheet ($ in Thousands)

Net Receivables 23	6823	0	444	4964	8640	40656	332165
Inventories 24	3538	0	352	3384	7256	23999	140803
Net Property, Plant and Equipment 25	5016	0	175	3714	8401	23667	234317
Total Assets 26	41072	0	1600	16294	37849	213122	2210647
Notes and Loans Payable 27	8751	0	483	4487	5940	40603	478016
All Other Liabilities 28	19585	0	589	4228	8606	51503	1203349
Net Worth 29	12736	0	528	7579	23304	121016	529282

Selected Financial Ratios (Times to 1)

Current Ratio 30	1.1	1.9	2.4		1.7	0.9
Quick Ratio 31	0.6	1.2	1.1	1.5	1.1	0.5
Net Sales to Working Capital 32	43.2	6.0	6.3	4.6	8.1	
Coverage Ratio 33	4.0	4.2	10.0	21.0	6.8	2.8
Total Asset Turnover 34	1.1	2.3	2.0	1.6	1.1	0.9
Inventory Turnover 35	9.1	7.3	6.9	5.7	7.2	10.9
Receivables Turnover 36	7.5	10.9	8.0	7.9		7.0
Total Liabilities to Net Worth 37	2.2	2.0	1.1	0.6	0.8	3.2
Current Assets to Working Capital 38	14.5	2.1	2.1	1.7	2.4	
Current Liabilities to Working Capital 39	13.5	1.1	1.1	0.7	1.4	
Working Capital to Net Sales 40	0.0	0.2	0.2	0.2	0.1	
Inventory to Working Capital 41	4.1	0.7	0.8	0.6	0.8	
Total Receipts to Cash Flow 42	9.1	3.3	16.5	8.2	7.8	8.9	10.4
Cost of Goods to Cash Flow 43	6.6	2.2	11.4	5.8	5.2	6.3	7.8
Cash Flow to Total Debt 44	0.2	0.2	0.5	0.5	0.3	0.1

Selected Financial Factors (in Percentages)

Debt Ratio 45	69.0	67.0	53.5	38.4	43.2	76.1
Return on Total Assets 46	6.7	4.9	12.6	14.1	9.0	4.5
Return on Equity Before Income Taxes 47	16.3	11.3	24.4	21.7	13.5	12.0
Return on Equity After Income Taxes 48	12.2	10.2	21.9	18.8	9.3	8.4
Profit Margin (Before Income Tax) 49	4.6	27.7	1.6	5.6	8.3	6.7	3.1
Profit Margin (After Income Tax) 50	3.5	20.4	1.5	5.0	7.2	4.6	2.2

Table I
Corporations with and without Net Income

METALWORKING MACHINERY

Money Amounts and Size of Assets in Thousands of Dollars

Item Description for Accounting Period 7/04 Through 6/05	Total	Zero Assets	Under 500	500 to 1,000	1,000 to 5,000	5,000 to 10,000	10,000 to 25,000	25,000 to 50,000	50,000 to 100,000	100,000 to 250,000	250,000 to 500,000	500,000 to 2,500,000	2,500,000 and over
Number of Enterprises **1**	7179	507	4377	657	1304	141	113	47	17	11	0	4	0
Revenues ($ in Thousands)													
Net Sales **2**	23240277	55655	2395497	618627	5028698	1401395	2328414	1707938	1341526	1986462	0	6376066	0
Interest **3**	58879	1112	895	603	3464	1348	1911	4054	1122	18417	0	25953	0
Rents **4**	13142	0	0	2188	2752	2121	841	722	671	2359	0	1488	0
Royalties **5**	10232	0	0	0	0	41	0	561	0	3806	0	5824	0
Other Portfolio Income **6**	259049	0	17829	38626	9363	43967	2815	8313	27398	19857	0	90884	0
Other Receipts **7**	246030	1184	2184	5220	24975	4782	22561	11076	6862	77330	0	89852	0
Total Receipts **8**	23827609	57951	2416405	665264	5069252	1453654	2356542	1732664	1377579	2108231	0	6590067	0
Average Total Receipts **9**	3319	114	552	1013	3887	10310	20854	36865	81034	191657	.	1647517	.
Operating Costs/Operating Income (%)													
Cost of Operations **10**	65.7	69.6	37.5	63.5	67.2	66.9	69.2	68.5	69.5	71.7	.	70.5	.
Salaries and Wages **11**	7.9	13.6	9.3	7.8	4.5	4.7	6.8	7.4	9.7	10.3	.	10.3	.
Taxes Paid **12**	2.9	11.1	4.6	5.4	4.0	4.3	2.9	3.0	2.4	2.0	.	1.1	.
Interest Paid **13**	2.2	0.5	2.1	2.2	0.6	1.1	1.2	1.7	2.7	2.4	.	4.0	.
Depreciation **14**	3.7	0.7	5.9	3.5	3.5	5.9	4.3	6.5	4.0	2.3	.	2.1	.
Amortization and Depletion **15**	0.3	0.1	0.2	0.0	0.0	0.0	0.1	0.4	0.2	0.2	.	0.9	.
Pensions and Other Deferred Comp. **16**	0.6	.	0.3	0.7	0.5	2.1	0.4	0.7	1.1	0.8	.	0.4	.
Employee Benefits **17**	2.5	0.1	1.8	5.5	2.3	2.3	2.5	2.2	2.4	2.2	.	2.8	.
Advertising **18**	0.4	2.3	0.1	0.3	0.3	0.2	0.3	0.4	0.5	0.4	.	0.8	.
Other Expenses **19**	10.7	29.7	26.4	12.0	8.5	10.9	8.0	8.3	8.2	7.9	.	9.2	.
Officers' Compensation **20**	3.2	1.6	9.2	8.7	5.1	3.7	2.7	2.0	1.3	0.9	.	0.5	.
Operating Margin **21**	.	.	2.7	.	3.5	.	1.5	.	.	.	.	.	.
Operating Margin Before Officers' Comp. **22**	3.0	11.9	11.9	.	8.6	1.7	4.2	0.8	.	.	.	.	.

Selected Average Balance Sheet ($ in Thousands)

Net Receivables 23	715	0	42	170	641	1677	3919	9172	16045	38340	•	549929
Inventories 24	409	0	16	167	354	1459	2961	6464	9961	41882	•	204395
Net Property, Plant and Equipment 25	528	0	72	93	525	2066	4428	8948	15587	30818	•	229120
Total Assets 26	3416	0	176	739	2239	6349	14990	33926	67986	187855	•	3236464
Notes and Loans Payable 27	1430	0	163	573	588	1855	5062	10595	16315	57449	•	1543120
All Other Liabilities 28	921	0	46	300	420	2381	3809	8389	18557	50023	•	910498
Net Worth 29	1065	0	-33	-134	1232	2112	6118	14941	33114	80383	•	782846

Selected Financial Ratios (Times to 1)

Current Ratio 30	1.6	•	1.3	1.1	2.3	1.3	1.6	1.9	1.7	1.8	•	1.5
Quick Ratio 31	1.0	•	1.0	0.7	1.6	0.8	0.9	1.1	0.9	1.0	•	0.9
Net Sales to Working Capital 32	5.5	•	23.2	12.9	4.6	10.4	6.0	3.9	4.5	4.0	•	5.1
Coverage Ratio 33	2.1	•	2.7	0.0	8.7	2.4	3.3	1.1	1.3	3.5	•	1.3
Total Asset Turnover 34	0.9	•	3.1	1.3	1.7	1.6	1.4	1.1	1.2	1.0	•	0.5
Inventory Turnover 35	5.2	•	12.4	3.6	7.3	4.6	4.8	3.9	5.5	3.1	•	5.5
Receivables Turnover 36	4.8	•	13.7	4.8	7.0	5.6	5.4	4.1	5.6	4.6	•	3.1
Total Liabilities to Net Worth 37	2.2	•	•	•	0.8	2.0	1.4	1.3	1.1	1.3	•	3.1
Current Assets to Working Capital 38	2.6	•	4.0	8.6	1.8	4.1	2.6	2.2	2.3	2.3	•	3.2
Current Liabilities to Working Capital 39	1.6	•	3.0	7.6	0.8	3.1	1.6	1.2	1.3	1.3	•	2.2
Working Capital to Net Sales 40	0.2	•	0.0	0.1	0.2	0.1	0.2	0.3	0.2	0.3	•	0.2
Inventory to Working Capital 41	0.7	•	0.8	2.2	0.5	1.5	0.9	0.8	0.7	1.0	•	0.7
Total Receipts to Cash Flow 42	10.0	•	4.2	•	10.5	11.4	12.5	14.8	15.4	8.8	•	11.7
Cost of Goods to Cash Flow 43	6.6	•	1.6	•	7.1	7.6	8.7	10.2	10.7	6.3	•	8.2
Cash Flow to Total Debt 44	0.1	•	0.6	•	0.4	0.2	0.2	0.1	0.1	0.2	•	0.1

Selected Financial Factors (in Percentages)

Debt Ratio 45	68.8	•	118.8	118.2	45.0	66.7	59.2	56.0	51.3	57.2	•	75.8
Return on Total Assets 46	4.4	•	17.7	0.1	8.4	4.4	5.3	2.1	4.1	7.9	•	2.6
Return on Equity Before Income Taxes 47	7.5	•	•	15.2	13.5	7.8	9.0	0.5	2.0	13.1	•	2.7
Return on Equity After Income Taxes 48	6.6	•	•	15.3	12.9	7.2	8.2	•	1.1	10.9	•	2.1
Profit Margin (Before Income Tax) 49	2.5	•	3.6	•	4.3	1.7	2.7	0.2	0.8	5.8	•	1.3
Profit Margin (After Income Tax) 50	2.2	•	3.5	•	4.1	1.5	2.4	•	0.5	4.9	•	1.0

Table II

Corporations with Net Income

METALWORKING MACHINERY

MONEY AMOUNTS AND SIZE OF ASSETS IN THOUSANDS OF DOLLARS

Item Description for Accounting Period 7/04 Through 6/05	Total	Zero Assets	Under 500	500 to 1,000	1,000 to 5,000	5,000 to 10,000	10,000 to 25,000	25,000 to 50,000	50,000 to 100,000	100,000 to 250,000	250,000 to 500,000	500,000 to 2,500,000	2,500,000 and over
Number of Enterprises 1	3482	255	1840	379	778	105	77	27	9	0	0	0	0
Revenues ($ in Thousands)													
Net Sales 2	16868253	730	1241826	263629	3248105	1047492	1630040	954425	674241	0	0	0	0
Interest 3	47844	177	598	194	1257	596	1092	1182	509	0	0	0	0
Rents 4	6666	0	0	9	1391	647	675	568	668	0	0	0	0
Royalties 5	10034	0	0	0	0	0	0	404	0	0	0	0	0
Other Portfolio Income 6	177208	0	123	38529	8078	741	1741	7764	14695	0	0	0	0
Other Receipts 7	205385	479	908	964	12794	2540	12701	3528	5107	0	0	0	0
Total Receipts 8	17315390	1386	1243455	303325	3271625	1052016	1646249	967871	695220	0	0	0	0
Average Total Receipts 9	4973	5	676	800	4205	10019	21380	35847	77247	•	•	•	•
Operating Costs/Operating Income (%)													
Cost of Operations 10	65.5	•	38.6	59.0	63.3	65.8	66.2	65.9	66.5	•	•	•	•
Salaries and Wages 11	7.3	•	1.9	7.0	4.5	4.7	6.7	7.8	8.4	•	•	•	•
Taxes Paid 12	2.4	21.5	4.8	5.0	3.7	3.3	2.8	2.5	2.4	•	•	•	•
Interest Paid 13	2.2	•	2.2	1.5	0.5	1.2	1.0	1.5	0.8	•	•	•	•
Depreciation 14	3.3	•	5.0	3.4	3.8	5.9	4.2	4.4	4.1	•	•	•	•
Amortization and Depletion 15	0.4	•	0.4	•	0.0	0.0	0.1	0.6	0.1	•	•	•	•
Pensions and Other Deferred Comp. 16	0.5	•	0.1	1.3	0.6	0.6	0.5	0.8	1.4	•	•	•	•
Employee Benefits 17	2.5	•	2.7	5.7	1.9	1.5	2.5	1.7	2.7	•	•	•	•
Advertising 18	0.5	•	0.0	0.2	0.3	0.2	0.4	0.4	0.6	•	•	•	•
Other Expenses 19	9.8	•	27.7	10.0	6.9	6.9	7.3	8.0	8.6	•	•	•	•
Officers' Compensation 20	2.7	•	7.7	10.7	5.7	3.7	2.8	1.9	1.4	•	•	•	•
Operating Margin 21	2.8	79.6	9.0	•	8.9	6.2	5.6	4.6	3.0	•	•	•	•
Operating Margin Before Officers' Comp. 22	5.6	79.6	16.7	6.8	14.6	9.9	8.4	6.4	4.5	•	•	•	•

Selected Average Balance Sheet ($ in Thousands)

Net Receivables 23	1128	0	45	105	547	1781	3829	8766	14127
Inventories 24	580	0	15	207	356	1507	2569	6140	10268
Net Property, Plant and Equipment 25	771	0	96	67	561	1952	4246	7893	14572
Total Assets 26	5715	0	241	707	2346	6286	14830	32149	66929
Notes and Loans Payable 27	2323	0	214	172	397	1966	4240	8755	11577
All Other Liabilities 28	1496	0	76	304	308	1931	3565	6127	13400
Net Worth 29	1895	0	-49	231	1641	2389	7024	17267	41952

Selected Financial Ratios (Times to 1)

Current Ratio 30	1.7	•	1.1	1.8	3.2	1.6	1.9	2.0	1.9
Quick Ratio 31	1.1	•	0.8	0.9	2.4	0.9	1.1	1.2	1.0
Net Sales to Working Capital 32	4.8	•	68.5	2.5	4.1	6.9	4.8	3.7	4.2
Coverage Ratio 33	3.6	•	5.2	8.3	21.7	6.7	7.5	4.9	9.6
Total Asset Turnover 34	0.8	•	2.8	1.0	1.8	1.6	1.4	1.1	1.1
Inventory Turnover 35	5.5	•	17.0	2.0	7.4	4.4	5.5	3.8	4.9
Receivables Turnover 36	4.5	•	14.5	4.0	7.7	5.6	6.2	3.8	6.8
Total Liabilities to Net Worth 37	2.0	•	•	2.1	0.4	1.6	1.1	0.9	0.6
Current Assets to Working Capital 38	2.5	•	12.5	2.3	1.5	2.8	2.1	2.0	2.1
Current Liabilities to Working Capital 39	1.5	•	11.5	1.3	0.5	1.8	1.1	1.0	1.1
Working Capital to Net Sales 40	0.2	•	0.0	0.4	0.2	0.1	0.2	0.3	0.2
Inventory to Working Capital 41	0.7	•	2.6	0.7	0.3	1.1	0.7	0.7	0.7
Total Receipts to Cash Flow 42	7.9	0.6	3.2	32.7	7.0	9.2	8.9	8.3	8.4
Cost of Goods to Cash Flow 43	5.1	•	1.2	19.3	4.5	6.0	5.9	5.5	5.6
Cash Flow to Total Debt 44	0.2	•	0.7	0.0	0.8	0.3	0.3	0.3	0.4

Selected Financial Factors (in Percentages)

Debt Ratio 45	66.8	•	120.2	67.3	30.1	62.0	52.6	46.3	37.3
Return on Total Assets 46	6.7	•	31.7	12.5	17.9	12.4	10.7	8.2	8.4
Return on Equity Before Income Taxes 47	14.7	•	•	33.6	24.4	27.7	19.6	12.2	12.0
Return on Equity After Income Taxes 48	13.6	•	•	33.5	23.7	27.0	18.6	10.6	10.7
Profit Margin (Before Income Tax) 49	5.7	169.5	9.2	11.2	9.6	6.6	6.5	6.0	6.7
Profit Margin (After Income Tax) 50	5.3	153.8	9.0	11.1	9.3	6.5	6.2	5.2	6.0

Table I

Corporations with and without Net Income

ENGINE, TURBINE AND POWER TRANSMISSION EQUIPMENT

MONEY AMOUNTS AND SIZE OF ASSETS IN THOUSANDS OF DOLLARS

Item Description for Accounting Period 7/04 Through 6/05	Total	Zero Assets	Under 500	500 to 1,000	1,000 to 5,000	5,000 to 10,000	10,000 to 25,000	25,000 to 50,000	50,000 to 100,000	100,000 to 250,000	250,000 to 500,000	500,000 to 2,500,000	2,500,000 and over
Number of Enterprises 1	211	5	12	0	107	18	33	7	6	8	4	6	4
Revenues ($ in Thousands)													
Net Sales 2	4975299	253968	1241	0	407356	131632	911988	307720	407069	1908584	977366	5465763	30202611
Interest 3	488360	16	0	0	146	649	528	770	6623	10393	3827	53188	412219
Rents 4	406609	0	0	0	0	801	268	0	375	984	136	24965	379080
Royalties 5	452369	1283	0	0	0	0	175	0	3874	19807	724	17379	409127
Other Portfolio Income 6	127129	0	0	0	147	3695	1024	158	1435	16581	5	45476	58606
Other Receipts 7	395529	-2929	1	0	1796	6099	2758	-8	10954	19331	1068	110278	246184
Total Receipts 8	4245295	252338	1242	0	409445	142876	916741	308640	430330	1975680	983126	5717049	31707827
Average Total Receipts 9	203058	50468	104	·	3827	7938	27780	44091	71722	246960	245782	952842	7926957
Operating Costs/Operating Income (%)													
Cost of Operations 10	71.3	75.2	433.4	·	64.5	52.6	71.5	79.7	76.6	72.7	71.4	73.5	70.8
Salaries and Wages 11	13.6	7.2	43.4	·	7.2	8.1	6.4	5.2	8.3	6.5	6.8	7.8	15.9
Taxes Paid 12	1.4	1.2	37.0	·	2.4	3.5	1.9	1.1	2.5	1.8	1.8	1.3	1.3
Interest Paid 13	1.9	4.3	18.1	·	1.4	6.2	0.9	1.8	3.5	0.6	2.0	3.0	1.8
Depreciation 14	3.5	2.6	9.5	·	3.4	4.3	2.9	2.9	3.7	2.7	2.9	2.8	3.7
Amortization and Depletion 15	0.4	3.3	40.5	·	0.1	0.3	0.1	0.9	2.2	0.3	2.5	0.8	0.2
Pensions and Other Deferred Comp. 16	2.9	0.3	·	·	1.2	0.4	1.3	0.1	2.2	1.5	1.1	1.1	3.5
Employee Benefits 17	2.5	1.2	5.9	·	1.8	3.6	2.6	0.5	1.6	2.3	1.4	1.7	2.7
Advertising 18	0.7	0.3	6.4	·	0.5	0.4	0.5	0.1	0.4	0.7	0.2	0.9	0.8
Other Expenses 19	3.8	6.6	1258.1	·	6.6	13.9	7.5	7.4	13.2	8.7	9.4	6.9	2.3
Officers' Compensation 20	0.7	0.2	120.6	·	2.0	3.6	1.7	1.3	1.2	0.8	2.8	0.4	0.6
Operating Margin 21	·	·	·	·	9.0	3.0	2.7	·	·	1.4	·	·	·
Operating Margin Before Officers' Comp. 22	·	·	·	·	11.0	6.6	4.3	0.3	·	2.1	0.5	·	0.2

Selected Average Balance Sheet ($ in Thousands)

Net Receivables 23	34895	0	12	•	461	1479	3913	7406	12677	37250	43850	209092	1325422
Inventories 24	23017	0	12	•	307	1084	4395	8934	10507	34320	30217	161173	790757
Net Property, Plant and Equipment 25	31084	0	10	•	899	1426	4324	11122	12866	39132	60895	215682	1072078
Total Assets 26	201450	0	94	•	2773	6219	16672	34052	72029	182876	335679	1086710	7887342
Notes and Loans Payable 27	38286	0	360	•	1310	3482	4996	15753	18445	37311	118852	320953	1196442
All Other Liabilities 28	104792	0	492	•	697	1195	5580	9114	29312	63281	103894	470344	4460360
Net Worth 29	58371	0	-758	•	766	1542	6095	9185	24272	82283	112932	295413	2230540

Selected Financial Ratios (Times to 1)

Current Ratio 30	1.3	•	0.5	•	1.6	2.8	1.6	1.4	1.9	1.6	1.9	1.5	1.2
Quick Ratio 31	0.7	•	0.2	•	0.9	2.0	0.8	0.5	1.1	1.0	1.1	0.7	0.6
Net Sales to Working Capital 32	9.8	•	•	•	7.3	3.3	7.0	8.0	3.5	5.9	3.8	5.5	13.7
Coverage Ratio 33	2.0	0.3	•	•	8.0	2.9	4.5	0.6	•	9.5	0.1	2.5	1.8
Total Asset Turnover 34	1.0	•	1.1	•	1.4	1.2	1.7	1.3	0.9	1.3	0.7	0.8	1.0
Inventory Turnover 35	6.0	•	36.3	•	8.0	3.5	4.5	3.9	4.9	5.1	5.8	4.2	6.8
Receivables Turnover 36	6.2	•	•	•	13.5	5.8	7.4	4.2	7.2	6.3	6.1	4.7	6.4
Total Liabilities to Net Worth 37	2.5	•	•	•	2.6	3.0	1.7	2.7	2.0	1.2	2.0	2.7	2.5
Current Assets to Working Capital 38	4.5	•	•	•	2.8	1.6	2.7	3.6	2.1	2.6	2.1	3.0	6.0
Current Liabilities to Working Capital 39	3.5	•	•	•	1.8	0.6	1.7	2.6	1.1	1.6	1.1	2.0	5.0
Working Capital to Net Sales 40	0.1	•	•	•	0.1	0.3	0.1	0.1	0.3	0.2	0.3	0.2	0.1
Inventory to Working Capital 41	1.3	•	•	•	1.0	0.3	1.2	1.8	0.6	0.7	0.6	1.0	1.6
Total Receipts to Cash Flow 42	30.2	49.7	•	•	6.9	5.2	11.1	24.3	67.0	8.4	16.7	9.7	92.2
Cost of Goods to Cash Flow 43	21.5	37.4	•	•	4.4	2.7	8.0	19.4	51.4	6.1	11.9	7.1	65.3
Cash Flow to Total Debt 44	0.0	•	•	•	0.3	0.2	0.1	0.1	0.0	0.3	0.1	0.1	0.0

Selected Financial Factors (in Percentages)

Debt Ratio 45	71.0	•	905.5	•	72.4	75.2	63.4	73.0	66.3	55.0	66.4	72.8	71.7
Return on Total Assets 46	3.6	•	•	•	14.9	20.9	6.8	1.4	•	7.7	0.2	6.4	3.0
Return on Equity Before Income Taxes 47	6.2	•	255.6	•	47.2	54.8	14.5	•	•	15.3	•	14.3	4.6
Return on Equity After Income Taxes 48	3.8	•	255.6	•	33.2	39.9	12.8	•	•	9.7	•	9.2	3.1
Profit Margin (Before Income Tax) 49	1.9	•	•	•	9.5	11.6	3.2	•	•	5.3	•	4.6	1.4
Profit Margin (After Income Tax) 50	1.1	•	•	•	6.7	8.4	2.8	•	•	3.4	•	3.0	0.9

Table II

Corporations with Net Income

ENGINE, TURBINE AND POWER TRANSMISSION EQUIPMENT

MONEY AMOUNTS AND SIZE OF ASSETS IN THOUSANDS OF DOLLARS

Item Description for Accounting Period 7/04 Through 6/05	Total	Zero Assets	Under 500	500 to 1,000	1,000 to 5,000	5,000 to 10,000	10,000 to 25,000	25,000 to 50,000	50,000 to 100,000	100,000 to 250,000	250,000 to 500,000	500,000 to 2,500,000	2,500,000 and over
Number of Enterprises **1**	136	0	0	0	72	0	22	4	0	0	0	0	0
Revenues ($ in Thousands)													
Net Sales **2**	36581588	0	0	0	370419	0	629077	159839	0	0	0	0	0
Interest **3**	468599	0	0	0	67	0	369	132	0	0	0	0	0
Rents **4**	384702	0	0	0	0	0	268	0	0	0	0	0	0
Royalties **5**	439824	0	0	0	0	0	0	0	0	0	0	0	0
Other Portfolio Income **6**	121076	0	0	0	147	0	161	158	0	0	0	0	0
Other Receipts **7**	283108	0	0	0	416	0	2343	-9	0	0	0	0	0
Total Receipts **8**	38278897	0	0	0	371049	0	632218	160120	0	0	0	0	0
Average Total Receipts **9**	281462	•	•	•	5153	•	28737	40030	•	•	•	•	•
Operating Costs/Operating Income (%)													
Cost of Operations **10**	71.7	•	•	•	63.2	•	71.4	68.7	•	•	•	•	•
Salaries and Wages **11**	13.3	•	•	•	6.8	•	6.2	7.6	•	•	•	•	•
Taxes Paid **12**	1.3	•	•	•	2.3	•	1.6	1.5	•	•	•	•	•
Interest Paid **13**	1.9	•	•	•	1.1	•	0.8	1.0	•	•	•	•	•
Depreciation **14**	3.7	•	•	•	3.4	•	2.6	4.5	•	•	•	•	•
Amortization and Depletion **15**	0.3	•	•	•	0.1	•	0.0	1.0	•	•	•	•	•
Pensions and Other Deferred Comp. **16**	3.0	•	•	•	1.3	•	1.5	0.3	•	•	•	•	•
Employee Benefits **17**	2.3	•	•	•	1.7	•	2.4	0.9	•	•	•	•	•
Advertising **18**	0.8	•	•	•	0.5	•	0.6	0.1	•	•	•	•	•
Other Expenses **19**	2.8	•	•	•	6.1	•	6.2	8.6	•	•	•	•	•
Officers' Compensation **20**	0.7	•	•	•	1.6	•	1.7	2.0	•	•	•	•	•
Operating Margin **21**	•	•	•	•	11.8	•	5.0	3.7	•	•	•	•	•
Operating Margin Before Officers' Comp. **22**	•	•	•	•	13.5	•	6.7	5.7	•	•	•	•	•

Selected Average Balance Sheet ($ in Thousands)

Net Receivables 23	45990	507	3958	5836
Inventories 24	29346	707	3949	11255
Net Property, Plant and Equipment 25	43841	1041	4529	10990
Total Assets 26	268207	2809	16831	35524
Notes and Loans Payable 27	42260	1103	4816	9285
All Other Liabilities 28	139168	604	4411	8181
Net Worth 29	86780	1103	7604	18057

Selected Financial Ratios (Times to 1)

Current Ratio 30	1.5	1.9	2.0	2.2
Quick Ratio 31	0.8	1.0	1.0	0.7
Net Sales to Working Capital 32	7.3	6.2	5.3	3.5
Coverage Ratio 33	2.5	11.7	7.9	4.6
Total Asset Turnover 34	1.0	1.8	1.7	1.1
Inventory Turnover 35	6.6	4.6	5.2	2.4
Receivables Turnover 36	7.2		7.9	
Total Liabilities to Net Worth 37	2.1	1.5	1.2	1.0
Current Assets to Working Capital 38	3.1	2.1	2.0	1.8
Current Liabilities to Working Capital 39	2.1	1.1	1.0	0.8
Working Capital to Net Sales 40	0.1	0.2	0.2	0.3
Inventory to Working Capital 41	0.9	0.9	0.9	1.0
Total Receipts to Cash Flow 42	29.1	6.1	9.9	11.5
Cost of Goods to Cash Flow 43	20.9	3.8	7.1	7.9
Cash Flow to Total Debt 44	0.1	0.5	0.3	0.2

Selected Financial Factors (in Percentages)

Debt Ratio 45	67.6	60.8	54.8	49.2
Return on Total Assets 46	4.8	24.0	10.6	5.4
Return on Equity Before Income Taxes 47	8.9	55.9	20.5	8.3
Return on Equity After Income Taxes 48	6.5	41.5	18.6	6.8
Profit Margin (Before Income Tax) 49	2.9	12.0	5.5	3.8
Profit Margin (After Income Tax) 50	2.1	8.9	4.9	3.1

Table I
Corporations with and without Net Income

OTHER GENERAL PURPOSE MACHINERY

MONEY AMOUNTS AND SIZE OF ASSETS IN THOUSANDS OF DOLLARS

Item Description for Accounting Period 7/04 Through 6/05	Total	Zero Assets	Under 500	500 to 1,000	1,000 to 5,000	5,000 to 10,000	10,000 to 25,000	25,000 to 50,000	50,000 to 100,000	100,000 to 250,000	250,000 to 500,000	500,000 to 2,500,000	2,500,000 and over
Number of Enterprises 1	7459	287	5362	508	816	225	135	47	25	21	11	14	7
Revenues ($ in Thousands)													
Net Sales 2	55668288	188695	1457470	580439	3332278	2731982	3362206	2147389	2136200	3548960	4505198	8423562	23253907
Interest 3	1285503	896	602	168	991	8435	2774	2747	3621	14243	11583	100911	1138531
Rents 4	17347	23	0	298	1259	3000	3387	261	547	1964	2630	951	3027
Royalties 5	586512	0	0	0	4710	0	2146	406	49	3001	6413	114152	455635
Other Portfolio Income 6	1150275	310	0	743	3391	13736	3947	25703	2538	41347	85411	56893	916257
Other Receipts 7	514904	1397	18564	1181	12194	36076	22216	18283	37174	20239	93243	49490	204850
Total Receipts 8	59222829	191321	1476636	582829	3354823	2793229	3396676	2194789	2180129	3629754	4704478	8745959	25972207
Average Total Receipts 9	7940	667	275	1147	4111	12414	25161	46698	87205	172845	427680	624711	3710315
Operating Costs/Operating Income (%)													
Cost of Operations 10	66.7	71.3	41.7	55.9	64.2	64.9	69.8	70.5	69.9	68.0	67.5	65.4	68.0
Salaries and Wages 11	9.1	4.8	13.2	4.7	10.3	10.4	8.5	8.0	8.1	9.5	8.3	10.2	8.6
Taxes Paid 12	1.8	2.0	3.5	3.2	2.7	2.2	2.2	2.0	1.6	1.8	2.0	1.4	1.6
Interest Paid 13	4.4	3.6	0.6	1.8	1.0	1.1	0.8	1.3	1.0	1.4	1.2	2.5	8.5
Depreciation 14	2.5	2.2	2.3	1.7	2.1	2.3	2.5	2.8	2.8	3.2	2.8	2.1	2.5
Amortization and Depletion 15	0.8	2.1	0.1	0.0	0.3	0.3	0.2	0.7	0.4	0.7	0.6	1.1	1.1
Pensions and Other Deferred Comp. 16	1.0	0.4	0.4	0.4	0.3	1.0	0.5	1.0	0.5	0.8	0.5	1.7	1.2
Employee Benefits 17	2.4	1.9	1.2	3.9	2.2	2.0	1.8	1.8	1.6	2.0	2.7	3.5	2.4
Advertising 18	0.7	0.2	0.6	1.5	0.9	0.7	0.6	0.5	0.6	0.9	0.8	0.4	0.7
Other Expenses 19	11.6	18.1	19.5	16.3	11.4	8.8	8.5	9.1	9.9	12.5	7.2	12.5	12.6
Officers' Compensation 20	1.8	0.7	12.4	6.9	4.4	4.5	2.7	1.7	1.3	1.1	2.9	0.7	0.7
Operating Margin 21	•	•	4.6	3.7	0.3	1.7	2.0	0.6	2.3	•	3.5	•	•
Operating Margin Before Officers' Comp. 22	•	•	17.0	10.6	4.7	6.1	4.6	2.4	3.6	•	6.4	•	•

Selected Average Balance Sheet ($ in Thousands)

Net Receivables 23	1445	0	20	112	684	1890	4204	7009	15934	27978	93536	126837	706064
Inventories 24	926	0	15	233	621	1387	3596	7884	16448	24602	54335	72023	357353
Net Property, Plant and Equipment 25	983	0	13	124	310	1933	3251	6837	14363	29115	60074	71037	446859
Total Assets 26	14549	0	72	637	2039	7480	15488	35574	72739	166439	356586	878723	11308526
Notes and Loans Payable 27	4139	0	46	488	868	2138	4884	10476	19957	56032	57903	215668	3243239
All Other Liabilities 28	3551	0	29	102	1000	2061	4714	9463	21472	43620	124479	340581	2332931
Net Worth 29	6858	0	-3	48	170	3281	5891	15635	31310	66787	174204	322475	5732356

Selected Financial Ratios (Times to 1)

Current Ratio 30	1.4	•	1.5	4.7	1.6	1.7	1.6	1.8	1.6	1.4	1.8	1.4	1.2
Quick Ratio 31	0.8	•	0.9	1.9	1.0	0.9	0.9	0.9	0.8	0.7	1.1	0.9	0.7
Net Sales to Working Capital 32	8.1	•	16.2	3.2	7.2	6.5	6.1	5.4	5.4	7.9	4.6	6.7	13.8
Coverage Ratio 33	1.9	•	10.8	3.2	2.0	4.4	4.6	3.5	5.3	1.5	6.8	2.1	1.5
Total Asset Turnover 34	0.5	•	3.8	1.8	2.0	1.6	1.6	1.3	1.2	1.0	1.1	0.7	0.3
Inventory Turnover 35	5.4	•	7.6	2.7	4.2	5.7	4.8	4.1	3.6	4.7	5.1	5.5	6.3
Receivables Turnover 36	5.0	•	13.7	11.6	6.3	7.3	6.7	6.4	5.0	5.1	5.3	4.5	4.3
Total Liabilities to Net Worth 37	1.1	•	•	12.4	11.0	1.3	1.6	1.3	1.3	1.5	1.0	1.7	1.0
Current Assets to Working Capital 38	3.7	•	3.1	1.3	2.6	2.5	2.6	2.3	2.6	3.4	2.2	3.6	6.6
Current Liabilities to Working Capital 39	2.7	•	2.1	0.3	1.6	1.5	1.6	1.3	1.6	2.4	1.2	2.6	5.6
Working Capital to Net Sales 40	0.1	•	0.1	0.3	0.1	0.2	0.2	0.2	0.2	0.1	0.2	0.1	0.1
Inventory to Working Capital 41	1.0	•	0.8	0.7	0.9	0.9	1.0	0.9	1.0	1.2	0.7	0.8	1.5
Total Receipts to Cash Flow 42	8.4	28.5	5.3	5.4	10.2	9.5	10.3	10.2	8.0	12.3	7.1	7.4	8.5
Cost of Goods to Cash Flow 43	5.6	20.4	2.2	3.0	6.6	6.1	7.2	7.2	5.6	8.3	4.8	4.8	5.8
Cash Flow to Total Debt 44	0.1	•	0.7	0.4	0.2	0.3	0.3	0.2	0.3	0.1	0.3	0.1	0.1

Selected Financial Factors (in Percentages)

Debt Ratio 45	52.9	•	104.8	92.5	91.7	56.1	62.0	56.0	57.0	59.9	51.1	63.3	49.3
Return on Total Assets 46	4.2	•	24.4	10.6	3.9	8.0	6.1	5.7	6.4	2.1	9.3	3.4	3.9
Return on Equity Before Income Taxes 47	4.2	•	•	97.0	24.0	14.2	12.6	9.3	12.1	1.7	16.2	4.8	2.7
Return on Equity After Income Taxes 48	3.1	•	•	87.3	15.4	11.0	10.1	6.6	8.5	•	12.6	2.8	2.1
Profit Margin (Before Income Tax) 49	3.8	•	5.9	4.0	1.0	3.8	3.0	3.2	4.4	0.7	6.9	2.6	4.6
Profit Margin (After Income Tax) 50	2.9	•	5.8	3.6	0.6	3.0	2.4	2.3	3.1	•	5.4	1.5	3.7

135

Table II
Corporations with Net Income

OTHER GENERAL PURPOSE MACHINERY

MONEY AMOUNTS AND SIZE OF ASSETS IN THOUSANDS OF DOLLARS

Item Description for Accounting Period 7/04 Through 6/05	Total	Zero Assets	Under 500	500 to 1,000	1,000 to 5,000	5,000 to 10,000	10,000 to 25,000	25,000 to 50,000	50,000 to 100,000	100,000 to 250,000	250,000 to 500,000	500,000 to 2,500,000	2,500,000 and over
Number of Enterprises 1	4306	13	3009	0	533	158	102	34	18	18	0	10	7
Revenues ($ in Thousands)													
Net Sales 2	47625788	183101	1318281	0	2492147	1998211	2672592	1554957	1547280	2808318	0	5605622	23253907
Interest 3	1260610	195	257	0	854	3091	2128	1657	2271	13512	0	91435	1138531
Rents 4	14108	0	0	0	1120	2993	1642	132	533	1840	0	255	3027
Royalties 5	586221	0	0	0	4710	0	2146	406	0	3001	0	113910	455635
Other Portfolio Income 6	1101876	310	0	0	3328	6287	1346	14248	2102	41336	0	30901	916257
Other Receipts 7	448806	1022	8723	0	6654	21212	13359	13384	32231	19794	0	39452	204850
Total Receipts 8	51037409	184628	1327261	0	2508813	2031794	2693213	1584784	1584417	2887801	0	5881575	25972207
Average Total Receipts 9	11853	14202	441	•	4707	12859	26404	46611	88023	160433	•	588158	3710315
Operating Costs/Operating Income (%)													
Cost of Operations 10	65.9	71.7	39.9	•	63.4	63.7	67.8	69.5	66.1	63.9	•	64.3	68.0
Salaries and Wages 11	8.9	4.4	14.3	•	9.7	8.4	7.9	7.3	8.5	10.5	•	10.1	8.6
Taxes Paid 12	1.8	1.9	3.1	•	2.7	2.3	2.0	2.0	1.5	1.9	•	1.5	1.6
Interest Paid 13	4.9	3.6	0.4	•	0.8	0.6	0.7	1.1	0.9	1.6	•	3.1	8.5
Depreciation 14	2.5	2.1	2.2	•	1.8	2.6	2.3	2.6	3.2	2.7	•	2.6	2.5
Amortization and Depletion 15	0.8	2.1	0.0	•	0.0	0.2	0.2	0.3	0.3	0.9	•	1.3	1.1
Pensions and Other Deferred Comp. 16	1.1	0.4	0.4	•	0.3	0.8	0.5	1.1	0.6	1.0	•	2.0	1.2
Employee Benefits 17	2.2	1.9	1.1	•	2.4	1.5	1.8	2.0	1.4	2.1	•	1.7	2.4
Advertising 18	0.7	0.2	0.5	•	0.7	0.6	0.6	0.5	0.6	1.1	•	0.5	0.7
Other Expenses 19	11.3	6.9	17.3	•	10.5	8.0	8.1	7.5	11.0	10.0	•	11.9	12.6
Officers' Compensation 20	1.9	0.6	11.6	•	4.8	5.2	2.6	1.8	1.5	1.3	•	0.9	0.7
Operating Margin 21	•	4.2	9.2	•	2.8	6.3	5.3	4.1	4.3	3.0	•	0.3	•
Operating Margin Before Officers' Comp. 22	•	4.9	20.8	•	7.7	11.5	7.9	5.9	5.9	4.3	•	1.1	•

Selected Average Balance Sheet ($ in Thousands)

Net Receivables 23	2107	0	30	•	818	2093	4279	6649	17446	29007	•	96624	706064
Inventories 24	1129	0	10	•	567	1137	3496	6416	14249	23263	•	74436	371726
Net Property, Plant and Equipment 25	1474	0	20	•	300	2148	3004	6823	15415	24788	•	78388	446859
Total Assets 26	23552	0	93	•	2026	7360	15218	34779	71479	169281	•	935234	11308526
Notes and Loans Payable 27	6453	0	40	•	558	1169	3534	9712	13957	48328	•	196608	3243239
All Other Liabilities 28	5482	0	27	•	673	1378	4481	8000	21290	46771	•	380007	2332931
Net Worth 29	11617	0	26	•	796	4812	7203	17067	36232	74182	•	358619	5732356

Selected Financial Ratios (Times to 1)

Current Ratio 30	1.4	•	2.0	•	1.7	2.5	2.0	2.0	2.0	1.7	•	1.3	1.2
Quick Ratio 31	0.8	•	1.3	•	1.1	1.6	1.1	0.9	1.1	0.9	•	0.7	0.7
Net Sales to Working Capital 32	7.8	•	14.4	•	6.6	4.5	4.9	4.9	3.9	5.4	•	7.9	13.8
Coverage Ratio 33	2.1	2.4	27.9	•	5.7	14.7	9.6	6.8	8.6	5.1	•	2.8	1.5
Total Asset Turnover 34	0.5	•	4.7	•	2.3	1.7	1.7	1.3	1.2	0.9	•	0.6	0.3
Inventory Turnover 35	6.5	•	18.3	•	5.2	7.1	5.1	5.0	4.0	4.3	•	4.8	6.1
Receivables Turnover 36	6.3	•	15.5	•	6.3	7.0	7.5	7.9	5.3	5.0	•	•	•
Total Liabilities to Net Worth 37	1.0	•	2.6	•	1.5	0.5	1.1	1.0	1.0	1.3	•	1.6	1.0
Current Assets to Working Capital 38	3.5	•	2.0	•	2.4	1.6	2.0	2.0	2.0	2.5	•	4.3	6.6
Current Liabilities to Working Capital 39	2.5	•	1.0	•	1.4	0.6	1.0	1.0	1.0	1.5	•	3.3	5.6
Working Capital to Net Sales 40	0.1	•	0.1	•	0.2	0.2	0.2	0.2	0.3	0.2	•	0.1	0.1
Inventory to Working Capital 41	1.0	•	0.5	•	0.8	0.5	0.8	0.8	0.7	0.8	•	1.0	1.5
Total Receipts to Cash Flow 42	7.5	9.0	4.8	•	8.5	7.1	8.0	8.3	6.2	7.7	•	6.2	8.5
Cost of Goods to Cash Flow 43	5.0	6.4	1.9	•	5.4	4.5	5.4	5.7	4.1	4.9	•	4.0	5.8
Cash Flow to Total Debt 44	0.1	•	1.4	•	0.4	0.7	0.4	0.3	0.4	0.2	•	0.2	0.1

Selected Financial Factors (in Percentages)

Debt Ratio 45	50.7	•	72.0	•	60.7	34.6	52.7	50.9	49.3	56.2	•	61.7	49.3
Return on Total Assets 46	5.0	•	48.2	•	9.9	14.7	11.6	10.0	9.3	7.4	•	5.3	3.9
Return on Equity Before Income Taxes 47	5.4	•	165.7	•	20.7	20.9	21.9	17.4	16.1	13.5	•	8.8	2.7
Return on Equity After Income Taxes 48	4.3	•	164.7	•	17.9	17.9	19.1	14.1	11.8	9.5	•	6.3	2.1
Profit Margin (Before Income Tax) 49	5.6	5.2	9.8	•	3.5	8.0	6.0	6.5	6.8	6.4	•	5.6	4.6
Profit Margin (After Income Tax) 50	4.5	3.5	9.8	•	3.0	6.8	5.3	5.2	5.0	4.5	•	4.1	3.7

Table I

Corporations with and without Net Income

COMPUTER AND PERIPHERAL EQUIPMENT

MONEY AMOUNTS AND SIZE OF ASSETS IN THOUSANDS OF DOLLARS

Item Description for Accounting Period 7/04 Through 6/05	Total	Zero Assets	Under 500	500 to 1,000	1,000 to 5,000	5,000 to 10,000	10,000 to 25,000	25,000 to 50,000	50,000 to 100,000	100,000 to 250,000	250,000 to 500,000	500,000 to 2,500,000	2,500,000 and over
Number of Enterprises **1**	3342	32	2533	129	330	93	91	49	26	18	14	20	7
Revenues ($ in Thousands)													
Net Sales **2**	157724685	328786	833591	108406	1810693	1116298	2062167	2196963	2319726	3149955	4095512	18819333	120883255
Interest **3**	1429379	1597	43	4	2534	1743	5763	7122	7319	15645	43288	144266	1200054
Rents **4**	1100041	0	93	0	163	0	767	257	542	769	295	48962	1048192
Royalties **5**	24334171	0	0	0	79	1064	91	16288	14910	18133	190118	407129	23686359
Other Portfolio Income **6**	1870772	8	0	721	77	4975	7654	8289	2000	13554	31019	298756	1503716
Other Receipts **7**	1659251	2532	3946	468	8594	7694	25050	15025	96346	10028	24792	893536	571244
Total Receipts **8**	188118299	332923	837673	109599	1822140	1131774	2101492	2243944	2440843	3208084	4385024	20611982	148892820
Average Total Receipts **9**	56289	10404	331	850	5522	12170	23093	45795	93879	178227	313216	1030599	21270403
Operating Costs/Operating Income (%)													
Cost of Operations **10**	66.2	56.1	47.1	80.9	54.7	53.7	70.7	61.3	67.8	72.5	61.9	73.0	65.6
Salaries and Wages **11**	15.0	23.4	8.5	7.9	16.6	26.8	15.0	18.2	15.3	9.3	17.4	14.0	15.0
Taxes Paid **12**	1.9	2.3	3.0	1.5	2.7	2.1	1.7	2.0	1.1	1.2	1.8	1.3	2.0
Interest Paid **13**	0.9	1.0	3.9	1.0	0.9	1.1	0.8	0.5	1.3	1.9	1.2	0.7	0.8
Depreciation **14**	3.4	3.5	0.9	1.4	4.2	2.8	2.3	1.9	2.5	1.7	3.1	2.5	3.6
Amortization and Depletion **15**	0.4	1.9	0.1	0.1	1.1	0.9	1.0	1.5	0.9	0.9	1.9	1.0	0.2
Pensions and Other Deferred Comp. **16**	1.3	0.4	1.5	•	0.2	0.3	0.2	0.3	0.2	0.2	0.3	0.3	1.6
Employee Benefits **17**	2.0	3.0	2.4	0.0	1.3	1.6	1.5	1.7	1.6	1.5	1.4	1.6	2.1
Advertising **18**	1.8	0.2	0.2	3.6	1.3	0.7	0.9	2.1	0.4	1.3	2.0	1.4	1.9
Other Expenses **19**	21.3	22.4	18.1	35.9	14.5	23.9	12.5	15.5	15.5	11.3	14.6	11.6	23.7
Officers' Compensation **20**	0.6	1.1	14.7	5.3	6.8	2.1	3.0	2.4	1.3	1.0	1.8	0.7	0.3
Operating Margin **21**	•	•	•	•	•	•	•	•	•	•	•	•	•
Operating Margin Before Officers' Comp. **22**	•	•	14.3	•	2.5	•	•	•	•	•	•	•	•

Selected Average Balance Sheet ($ in Thousands)

Net Receivables 23	10831	0	27	16	756	1975	3737	8115	12600	34788	59694	157188	4288796
Inventories 24	3233	0	13	146	486	1349	2614	5064	8453	20118	39246	65402	1077449
Net Property, Plant and Equipment 25	5909	0	11	14	495	995	1858	2517	7933	11019	20427	94703	2369293
Total Assets 26	52226	0	78	681	2609	8109	15965	36720	66957	162431	371274	1110822	19615482
Notes and Loans Payable 27	14056	0	162	220	2821	2568	4041	6634	18132	32799	63470	156731	5655651
All Other Liabilities 28	21290	0	76	947	1047	2862	5461	15030	28152	55344	100204	317292	8501940
Net Worth 29	16881	0	-159	-485	-1259	2679	6463	15056	20673	74288	207600	636799	5457890

Selected Financial Ratios (Times to 1)

Current Ratio 30	1.2	•	0.6	0.5	1.6	2.2	1.7	2.2	1.7	1.6	2.4	2.1	1.1
Quick Ratio 31	0.7	•	0.5	0.2	1.0	1.3	1.1	1.5	1.0	1.0	1.5	1.3	0.6
Net Sales to Working Capital 32	10.4	•	•	•	7.4	3.5	4.9	3.2	5.2	5.5	2.4	2.9	27.3
Coverage Ratio 33	7.8	•	1.0	•	•	•	•	•	•	1.5	0.8	3.5	10.6
Total Asset Turnover 34	0.9	•	4.2	1.2	2.1	1.5	1.4	1.2	1.3	1.1	0.8	0.8	0.9
Inventory Turnover 35	9.7	•	11.6	4.6	6.2	4.8	6.1	5.4	7.2	6.3	4.6	10.5	10.5
Receivables Turnover 36	4.2	•	12.8	10.2	8.9	5.9	5.7	5.6	7.1	5.0	4.7	6.2	3.9
Total Liabilities to Net Worth 37	2.1	•	•	•	•	2.0	1.5	1.4	2.2	1.2	0.8	0.7	2.6
Current Assets to Working Capital 38	5.6	•	•	•	2.7	1.8	2.4	1.9	2.4	2.8	1.7	1.9	14.3
Current Liabilities to Working Capital 39	4.6	•	•	•	1.7	0.8	1.4	0.9	1.4	1.8	0.7	0.9	13.3
Working Capital to Net Sales 40	0.1	•	•	•	0.1	0.3	0.2	0.3	0.2	0.2	0.4	0.3	0.0
Inventory to Working Capital 41	0.7	•	•	•	0.9	0.3	0.5	0.4	0.6	0.5	0.3	0.2	1.5
Total Receipts to Cash Flow 42	4.2	•	7.7	•	12.1	17.2	57.5	12.3	9.2	11.4	8.4	9.6	3.6
Cost of Goods to Cash Flow 43	2.8	•	3.6	•	6.6	9.3	40.7	7.6	6.2	8.3	5.2	7.0	2.3
Cash Flow to Total Debt 44	0.3	•	0.2	•	0.1	0.1	0.0	0.2	0.2	0.2	0.2	0.2	0.3

Selected Financial Factors (in Percentages)

Debt Ratio 45	67.7	•	304.1	171.3	148.3	67.0	59.5	59.0	69.1	54.3	44.1	42.7	72.2
Return on Total Assets 46	6.2	•	17.1	•	•	•	•	•	•	3.2	0.8	2.2	7.8
Return on Equity Before Income Taxes 47	16.8	•	•	63.3	15.9	•	•	•	•	2.4	•	2.7	25.5
Return on Equity After Income Taxes 48	10.2	•	1.1	63.3	16.6	•	•	•	•	0.2	•	0.6	16.8
Profit Margin (Before Income Tax) 49	6.0	•	0.1	•	•	•	•	•	•	1.0	•	1.8	8.1
Profit Margin (After Income Tax) 50	3.6	•	•	•	•	•	•	•	•	0.1	•	0.4	5.3

Table II

Corporations with Net Income

COMPUTER AND PERIPHERAL EQUIPMENT

MONEY AMOUNTS AND SIZE OF ASSETS IN THOUSANDS OF DOLLARS

Item Description for Accounting Period 7/04 Through 6/05	Total	Zero Assets	Under 500	500 to 1,000	1,000 to 5,000	5,000 to 10,000	10,000 to 25,000	25,000 to 50,000	50,000 to 100,000	100,000 to 250,000	250,000 to 500,000	500,000 to 2,500,000	2,500,000 and over
Number of Enterprises 1	1220	10	0	0	257	36	43	16	13	12	7	12	0
Revenues ($ in Thousands)													
Net Sales 2	13292036	73164	0	0	1630884	570735	1263523	986981	1501520	2442954	1920246	12264984	0
Interest 3	1195720	4	0	0	1419	227	1976	1975	1283	7749	16641	88286	0
Rents 4	1057637	0	0	0	0	0	185	109	335	398	295	8028	0
Royalties 5	24039508	0	0	0	0	1064	0	0	709	13610	64045	383549	0
Other Portfolio Income 6	1780469	8	0	0	2	0	3076	5832	1956	1677	6344	261473	0
Other Receipts 7	1235668	2143	0	0	2006	576	11931	8716	87807	2103	1587	691435	0
Total Receipts 8	162201038	75319	0	0	1634311	572602	1280691	1003613	1593610	2448491	2009158	13697755	0
Average Total Receipts 9	132952	7532	•	•	6359	15906	29784	62726	122585	204041	287023	1141480	•
Operating Costs/Operating Income (%)													
Cost of Operations 10	65.8	69.2	•	•	54.3	50.2	70.5	66.8	69.1	74.4	60.1	74.2	•
Salaries and Wages 11	13.4	13.1	•	•	13.2	15.9	9.9	10.0	11.1	8.2	14.2	11.2	•
Taxes Paid 12	1.8	0.8	•	•	2.0	2.1	1.2	1.5	0.9	1.2	1.4	1.2	•
Interest Paid 13	0.8	2.1	•	•	0.3	0.3	0.4	0.6	1.8	0.7	0.9	0.3	•
Depreciation 14	3.4	0.4	•	•	3.8	1.4	1.3	1.2	1.5	1.6	2.6	2.4	•
Amortization and Depletion 15	0.2	0.1	•	•	0.0	0.2	0.2	0.3	0.7	0.2	0.5	0.4	•
Pensions and Other Deferred Comp. 16	1.4	0.3	•	•	0.2	0.6	0.2	0.4	0.2	0.2	0.3	0.4	•
Employee Benefits 17	1.9	2.0	•	•	1.1	1.1	0.9	1.2	1.8	0.6	1.2	1.2	•
Advertising 18	1.7	0.4	•	•	1.2	0.5	0.8	1.3	0.3	0.9	1.4	1.1	•
Other Expenses 19	23.5	6.1	•	•	10.3	13.0	7.6	8.9	12.0	9.4	13.4	9.5	•
Officers' Compensation 20	0.4	1.8	•	•	6.5	2.2	2.3	1.1	1.0	0.9	1.4	0.7	•
Operating Margin 21	•	3.8	•	•	7.1	12.6	4.6	6.8	•	1.7	2.7	•	•
Operating Margin Before Officers' Comp. 22	•	5.6	•	•	13.6	14.8	6.8	7.9	0.7	2.6	4.0	•	•

Selected Average Balance Sheet ($ in Thousands)

Net Receivables 23	26161	0	·	·	842	3260	4644	8476	12943	32272	52166	175625	·
Inventories 24	7465	0	·	·	506	1380	2842	7792	9414	21528	30007	79978	·
Net Property, Plant and Equipment 25	13514	0	·	·	506	600	1874	2504	8996	11680	20613	92290	·
Total Assets 26	118848	0	·	·	2550	7787	14755	34421	67023	167325	352617	1107386	·
Notes and Loans Payable 27	33973	0	·	·	635	1097	3665	3002	32979	15169	66884	83888	·
All Other Liabilities 28	47551	0	·	·	478	2628	6747	11077	32401	60522	82456	293654	·
Net Worth 29	37324	0	·	·	1436	4061	4342	20342	1643	91634	203277	729844	·

Selected Financial Ratios (Times to 1)

Current Ratio 30	1.2	·	·	·	2.8	2.8	1.5	2.3	1.7	1.6	4.0	2.4	·
Quick Ratio 31	0.7	·	·	·	1.7	2.1	1.0	1.5	0.9	1.0	2.6	1.4	·
Net Sales to Working Capital 32	13.8	·	·	·	4.6	3.5	7.6	4.4	7.5	5.7	1.5	2.8	·
Coverage Ratio 33	12.1	4.2	·	·	26.5	51.0	14.4	15.7	4.3	8.4	9.4	29.3	·
Total Asset Turnover 34	0.9	·	·	·	2.5	2.0	2.0	1.8	1.7	1.2	0.8	0.9	·
Inventory Turnover 35	9.6	·	·	·	6.8	5.8	7.3	5.3	8.5	7.0	5.5	9.5	·
Receivables Turnover 36	4.0	·	·	·	10.7	6.6	6.4	5.7	9.8	6.3	·	5.7	·
Total Liabilities to Net Worth 37	2.2	·	·	·	0.8	0.9	2.4	0.7	39.8	0.8	0.7	0.5	·
Current Assets to Working Capital 38	7.1	·	·	·	1.6	1.6	2.8	1.8	2.5	2.7	1.3	1.7	·
Current Liabilities to Working Capital 39	6.1	·	·	·	0.6	0.6	1.8	0.8	1.5	1.7	0.3	0.7	·
Working Capital to Net Sales 40	0.1	·	·	·	0.2	0.3	0.1	0.2	0.1	0.2	0.7	0.4	·
Inventory to Working Capital 41	0.9	·	·	·	0.6	0.3	0.7	0.5	0.7	0.5	0.2	0.2	·
Total Receipts to Cash Flow 42	3.4	9.1	·	·	6.4	4.1	8.6	6.4	6.1	9.1	5.1	6.0	·
Cost of Goods to Cash Flow 43	2.3	6.3	·	·	3.5	2.1	6.1	4.3	4.2	6.8	3.1	4.5	·
Cash Flow to Total Debt 44	0.4	·	·	·	0.9	1.0	0.3	0.7	0.3	0.3	0.4	0.4	·

Selected Financial Factors (in Percentages)

Debt Ratio 45	68.6	·	·	·	43.7	47.8	70.6	40.9	97.5	45.2	42.4	34.1	·
Return on Total Assets 46	9.1	·	·	·	18.9	26.9	12.6	16.5	13.2	7.2	6.2	8.9	·
Return on Equity Before Income Taxes 47	26.6	·	·	·	32.3	50.6	40.0	26.1	412.9	11.6	9.6	13.1	·
Return on Equity After Income Taxes 48	18.5	·	·	·	31.4	43.7	35.2	19.8	356.3	9.0	6.6	9.9	·
Profit Margin (Before Income Tax) 49	9.1	6.7	·	·	7.3	13.0	5.9	8.6	5.9	5.3	7.1	9.4	·
Profit Margin (After Income Tax) 50	6.3	5.8	·	·	7.1	11.2	5.2	6.5	5.1	4.1	4.9	7.1	·

138

Table I

Corporations with and without Net Income

COMMUNICATIONS EQUIPMENT

MONEY AMOUNTS AND SIZE OF ASSETS IN THOUSANDS OF DOLLARS

Item Description for Accounting Period 7/04 Through 6/05	Total	Zero Assets	Under 500	500 to 1,000	1,000 to 5,000	5,000 to 10,000	10,000 to 25,000	25,000 to 50,000	50,000 to 100,000	100,000 to 250,000	250,000 to 500,000	500,000 to 2,500,000	2,500,000 and over
Number of Enterprises 1	1396	99	517	97	401	62	90	32	26	25	18	17	12
Revenues ($ in Thousands)													
Net Sales 2	102426469	169077	175553	71852	1561520	588471	1499814	1085503	1815189	3742004	6682554	10630288	74404645
Interest 3	1591096	302	122	1246	1996	1624	5435	4655	15441	37308	32081	148177	1342709
Rents 4	379703	640	0	0	0	0	1921	1035	361	61	25791	18456	331438
Royalties 5	2958419	0	177	0	0	0	1695	481	4014	20539	19739	68796	2842979
Other Portfolio Income 6	1736999	7272	6686	0	5233	269	17442	16619	34225	40066	36227	534218	1038745
Other Receipts 7	1984551	25748	8452	5	109012	7668	18141	25838	10090	19373	18381	123103	1618734
Total Receipts 8	111077237	203039	190990	73103	1677761	598032	1544448	1134131	1879320	3885951	6814773	11523038	81579250
Average Total Receipts 9	79568	2051	369	754	4184	9646	17161	35442	72282	154374	378598	677826	6798271
Operating Costs/Operating Income (%)													
Cost of Operations 10	66.7	72.3	63.0	21.1	53.9	61.4	56.8	60.7	53.0	73.7	74.5	61.6	67.4
Salaries and Wages 11	17.2	28.7	9.7	39.8	27.7	29.6	23.5	20.0	19.7	14.9	9.5	14.4	17.8
Taxes Paid 12	1.5	2.6	4.4	5.4	3.3	3.5	2.9	2.8	1.9	1.8	1.0	2.0	1.3
Interest Paid 13	2.2	0.8	2.1	3.8	0.7	1.4	1.5	0.8	1.8	0.8	1.3	3.0	2.3
Depreciation 14	3.8	5.7	1.6	1.6	2.4	3.6	4.1	3.4	3.3	3.1	3.0	5.8	3.7
Amortization and Depletion 15	1.4	3.9	2.0	7.2	1.9	3.9	2.5	2.7	1.9	1.4	1.3	1.8	1.3
Pensions and Other Deferred Comp. 16	1.2	0.2	0.2	3.7	0.4	0.1	0.4	0.4	0.3	0.3	0.1	1.0	1.5
Employee Benefits 17	1.8	3.2	0.8	4.8	1.9	3.1	2.3	2.6	3.5	1.3	3.3	2.8	1.5
Advertising 18	1.1	0.5	0.2	1.9	0.6	1.2	0.7	0.8	0.5	0.5	0.4	1.5	1.2
Other Expenses 19	16.1	58.3	52.4	23.1	28.7	27.3	25.3	11.9	19.4	10.1	8.7	15.4	16.5
Officers' Compensation 20	0.7	3.5	10.9	16.3	6.3	5.9	3.5	2.8	2.1	1.5	0.5	0.8	0.4
Operating Margin 21	•	•	•	•	•	•	•	•	•	•	•	•	•
Operating Margin Before Officers' Comp. 22	•	•	•	•	•	•	•	•	•	•	•	•	•

Selected Average Balance Sheet ($ in Thousands)

Net Receivables 23	16174	0	11	52	542	1220	3103	7538	12199	26767	74720	152281	1402895
Inventories 24	5433	0	93	213	468	1271	2670	5498	8160	18081	20041	93243	351851
Net Property, Plant and Equipment 25	9380	0	8	22	154	720	2231	3599	8026	12785	26766	124670	794666
Total Assets 26	112962	0	231	750	2576	7331	15758	33519	66545	164751	352546	1287041	9954142
Notes and Loans Payable 27	18824	0	78	472	860	1767	6108	3661	12879	8584	56774	269759	1576092
All Other Liabilities 28	46296	0	228	518	1014	4315	5898	10750	17355	37535	125139	300398	4513570
Net Worth 29	47842	0	-75	-241	701	1249	3751	19107	36311	118632	170632	716885	3864480

Selected Financial Ratios (Times to 1)

Current Ratio 30	1.7	•	0.8	1.0	1.5	1.3	1.4	2.1	2.8	3.0	1.9	2.0	1.7
Quick Ratio 31	1.0	•	0.4	0.6	1.1	0.8	0.9	1.3	1.8	1.6	1.3	1.2	1.0
Net Sales to Working Capital 32	3.3	•	•	5.7	7.4	5.3	2.6	2.4	2.3	4.1	2.2	3.5	•
Coverage Ratio 33	•	•	•	•	•	•	•	•	•	•	•	0.4	•
Total Asset Turnover 34	0.6	•	1.5	1.0	1.5	1.3	1.1	1.0	1.0	0.9	1.1	0.5	0.6
Inventory Turnover 35	9.0	•	2.3	0.7	4.5	4.6	3.5	3.7	4.5	6.1	13.8	4.1	11.9
Receivables Turnover 36	4.6	•	20.6	3.0	7.2	9.8	5.9	5.0	5.9	4.8	5.8	3.1	4.7
Total Liabilities to Net Worth 37	1.4	•	•	•	2.7	4.9	3.2	0.8	0.8	0.4	1.1	0.8	1.6
Current Assets to Working Capital 38	2.3	•	•	•	2.9	4.0	3.4	1.9	1.6	1.5	2.2	2.0	2.5
Current Liabilities to Working Capital 39	1.3	•	•	•	1.9	3.0	2.4	0.9	0.6	0.5	1.2	1.0	1.5
Working Capital to Net Sales 40	0.3	•	•	•	0.2	0.1	0.2	0.4	0.4	0.4	0.2	0.4	0.3
Inventory to Working Capital 41	0.3	•	•	•	0.7	1.4	0.9	0.5	0.3	0.3	0.3	0.3	0.2
Total Receipts to Cash Flow 42	12.8	•	•	•	60.6	72.1	28.6	9.0	•	•	20.0	9.7	11.5
Cost of Goods to Cash Flow 43	8.6	•	•	•	32.7	41.0	17.4	4.8	•	•	14.9	6.0	7.8
Cash Flow to Total Debt 44	0.1	•	•	•	0.0	0.0	0.1	0.3	•	•	0.1	0.1	0.1

Selected Financial Factors (in Percentages)

Debt Ratio 45	57.6	•	132.4	132.1	72.8	83.0	76.2	43.0	45.4	28.0	51.6	44.3	61.2
Return on Total Assets 46	•	•	•	•	•	•	•	•	•	•	•	0.6	•
Return on Equity Before Income Taxes 47	•	•	174.0	82.3	•	•	•	•	•	•	•	•	•
Return on Equity After Income Taxes 48	•	•	174.0	82.8	•	•	•	•	•	•	•	•	•
Profit Margin (Before Income Tax) 49	•	•	•	•	•	•	•	•	•	•	•	•	•
Profit Margin (After Income Tax) 50	•	•	•	•	•	•	•	•	•	•	•	•	•

Table II

Corporations with Net Income

COMMUNICATIONS EQUIPMENT

MONEY AMOUNTS AND SIZE OF ASSETS IN THOUSANDS OF DOLLARS

Item Description for Accounting Period 7/04 Through 6/05	Total	Zero Assets	Under 500	500 to 1,000	1,000 to 5,000	5,000 to 10,000	10,000 to 25,000	25,000 to 50,000	50,000 to 100,000	100,000 to 250,000	250,000 to 500,000	500,000 to 2,500,000	2,500,000 and over
Number of Enterprises **1**	285	14	0	28	124	19	40	15	13	9	0	7	7
Revenues ($ in Thousands)													
Net Sales **2**	69975004	113245	0	23388	558815	360266	914901	754255	1250418	1776741	0	5027232	54670785
Interest **3**	1217851	1	0	1	301	8	1174	1792	2480	8572	0	55956	1138599
Rents **4**	322770	626	0	0	0	0	57	31	11	0	0	16732	279533
Royalties **5**	1597876	0	0	0	0	0	1695	384	3014	20470	0	41826	1530093
Other Portfolio Income **6**	788167	5138	0	0	0	0	1959	16350	21703	35790	0	519270	180176
Other Receipts **7**	1391555	2531	0	0	106591	288	9567	7246	6238	2814	0	91507	1154180
Total Receipts **8**	75293223	121541	0	23389	665707	360562	929353	780058	1283864	1844387	0	5752523	58953366
Average Total Receipts **9**	264187	8682	.	835	5369	18977	23234	52004	98759	204932	.	821789	8421909
Operating Costs/Operating Income (%)													
Cost of Operations **10**	67.1	71.3	.	36.3	59.4	56.3	56.3	59.7	53.5	71.6	.	52.7	67.7
Salaries and Wages **11**	16.6	6.7	.	37.5	26.0	12.4	13.9	11.0	15.0	12.2	.	12.4	18.2
Taxes Paid **12**	1.4	0.3	.	3.1	2.8	1.8	2.6	2.0	1.6	1.8	.	2.6	1.3
Interest Paid **13**	1.7	0.4	.	7.9	0.8	0.4	0.6	0.4	1.5	0.4	.	3.5	1.8
Depreciation **14**	4.1	1.3	.	.	1.1	1.4	2.0	2.0	2.2	2.7	.	8.0	4.1
Amortization and Depletion **15**	1.3	1.2	.	1.1	2.1	0.2	0.3	0.4	0.8	0.2	.	1.0	1.5
Pensions and Other Deferred Comp. **16**	1.4	0.0	.	0.4	0.2	0.1	0.6	0.3	0.3	0.5	.	2.1	1.6
Employee Benefits **17**	1.3	1.1	.	.	1.3	1.5	2.0	1.7	3.1	0.7	.	4.1	1.1
Advertising **18**	1.3	0.1	.	0.2	0.2	0.3	0.5	0.8	0.5	0.2	.	2.1	1.4
Other Expenses **19**	7.0	18.3	.	10.3	15.4	7.5	11.1	9.4	12.8	8.4	.	14.5	6.1
Officers' Compensation **20**	0.6	.	.	.	3.3	3.3	2.5	2.3	1.7	1.3	.	1.0	0.5
Operating Margin **21**	.	.	.	3.1	.	15.0	7.7	10.1	7.1	.	.	.	.
Operating Margin Before Officers' Comp. **22**	.	.	.	3.1	.	18.3	10.2	12.4	8.7	1.2	.	.	.

Selected Average Balance Sheet ($ in Thousands)

Net Receivables 23	38573	0	•	173	647	2190	3276	9506	17314	29428	•	230714	1146338
Inventories 24	14813	0	•	468	860	2165	3324	5357	6298	27960	•	150419	319222
Net Property, Plant and Equipment 25	26066	0	•	4	85	613	1720	3674	6563	12478	•	204863	782705
Total Assets 26	280876	0	•	840	2319	7621	15102	33352	66282	151296	•	1268486	9259955
Notes and Loans Payable 27	39489	0	•	788	1504	529	2307	2123	21041	9485	•	224908	1204675
All Other Liabilities 28	119022	0	•	12	707	6454	4236	12835	17735	41993	•	378305	4154892
Net Worth 29	122365	0	•	40	107	638	8559	18394	27506	99819	•	665273	3900388

Selected Financial Ratios (Times to 1)

Current Ratio 30	1.6	•	1.1	1.1	2.4	2.1	2.7	2.1	•	1.8	1.5	
Quick Ratio 31	1.0	•	0.3	0.6	0.5	1.2	1.2	1.8	1.2	•	1.1	0.9
Net Sales to Working Capital 32	5.3	•	16.6	36.5	25.3	3.7	3.7	3.4	•	2.9	5.9	
Coverage Ratio 33	3.3	16.8	1.4	9.4	37.2	16.0	31.3	7.9	9.5	•	4.0	2.8
Total Asset Turnover 34	0.9	•	1.0	1.9	2.5	1.5	1.5	1.5	1.3	•	0.6	0.8
Inventory Turnover 35	11.1	•	0.6	3.1	4.9	3.9	5.6	8.2	5.1	•	2.5	16.6
Receivables Turnover 36	7.4	•	1.8	7.3	12.7	7.3	6.4	7.9	4.6	•	2.1	9.5
Total Liabilities to Net Worth 37	1.3	•	20.2	20.6	10.9	0.8	0.8	1.4	0.5	•	0.9	1.4
Current Assets to Working Capital 38	2.7	•	15.6	15.2	9.5	1.7	1.9	1.6	1.9	•	2.2	3.0
Current Liabilities to Working Capital 39	1.7	•	14.6	14.2	8.5	0.7	0.9	0.6	0.9	•	1.2	2.0
Working Capital to Net Sales 40	0.2	•	0.1	0.0	0.0	0.3	0.3	0.3	0.3	•	0.3	0.2
Inventory to Working Capital 41	0.4	•	11.2	6.4	5.0	0.6	0.5	0.3	0.3	•	0.5	0.4
Total Receipts to Cash Flow 42	11.8	4.4	7.4	5.2	4.7	5.5	5.1	5.1	13.8	•	4.5	14.8
Cost of Goods to Cash Flow 43	7.9	3.1	2.7	3.1	2.7	3.1	3.1	2.7	9.9	•	2.4	10.1
Cash Flow to Total Debt 44	0.1	•	0.1	0.4	0.6	0.6	0.7	0.5	0.3	•	0.3	0.1

Selected Financial Factors (in Percentages)

Debt Ratio 45	56.4	•	95.3	95.4	91.6	43.3	44.8	58.5	34.0	•	47.6	57.9
Return on Total Assets 46	5.1	•	11.0	14.0	38.6	15.0	21.0	16.7	5.4	•	8.1	4.1
Return on Equity Before Income Taxes 47	8.2	•	66.2	270.3	448.2	24.9	36.9	35.3	7.3	•	11.6	6.3
Return on Equity After Income Taxes 48	6.0	•	56.3	234.6	444.9	21.6	30.6	28.3	6.2	•	8.4	4.5
Profit Margin (Before Income Tax) 49	4.1	6.6	3.1	6.4	15.1	9.3	13.5	10.1	3.7	•	10.7	3.1
Profit Margin (After Income Tax) 50	3.0	6.3	2.7	5.6	15.0	8.1	11.2	8.1	3.1	•	7.8	2.2

Table I
Corporations with and without Net Income

AUDIO AND VIDEO EQUIP., REPRODUCING MAGNETIC & OPTICAL MEDIA

MONEY AMOUNTS AND SIZE OF ASSETS IN THOUSANDS OF DOLLARS

Item Description for Accounting Period 7/04 Through 6/05	Total	Zero Assets	Under 500	500 to 1,000	1,000 to 5,000	5,000 to 10,000	10,000 to 25,000	25,000 to 50,000	50,000 to 100,000	100,000 to 250,000	250,000 to 500,000	500,000 to 2,500,000	2,500,000 and over
Number of Enterprises **1**	1644	397	597	98	372	60	44	29	19	16	6	7	0
Revenues ($ in Thousands)													
Net Sales **2**	21671500	27512	10237	43470	1576538	587373	946414	1246093	1751905	2561146	1300538	11620274	0
Interest **3**	156680	78	3	257	311	2359	2104	2748	5075	13296	12890	117559	0
Rents **4**	8856	0	0	917	65	979	156	1273	1349	150	916	3051	0
Royalties **5**	384790	0	0	0	0	682	13	1569	920	16176	20998	344431	0
Other Portfolio Income **6**	106148	0	0	421	6	29	602	15753	6117	9476	2850	70897	0
Other Receipts **7**	334255	3313	-1098	3173	69677	14072	7403	32623	8104	20408	98447	78132	0
Total Receipts **8**	22662229	30903	9142	48238	1646597	605494	956692	1300059	1773470	2620652	1436639	12234344	0
Average Total Receipts **9**	13785	78	15	492	4426	10092	21743	44830	93341	163791	239440	1747763	•
Operating Costs/Operating Income (%)													
Cost of Operations **10**	63.7	55.0	54.1	38.9	43.8	70.3	62.3	58.9	68.1	64.7	55.1	66.9	•
Salaries and Wages **11**	12.9	19.7	3.9	14.1	23.1	9.3	15.9	13.7	11.8	10.9	19.6	11.3	•
Taxes Paid **12**	1.6	2.4	11.3	3.4	3.8	2.3	2.0	1.7	1.3	1.6	2.2	1.2	•
Interest Paid **13**	1.6	0.6	8.0	7.1	1.0	0.4	1.6	0.8	1.1	1.5	2.4	1.8	•
Depreciation **14**	4.2	6.7	4.2	53.8	1.3	1.5	5.3	3.3	4.1	3.3	5.8	4.7	•
Amortization and Depletion **15**	0.9	1.0	0.2	11.3	0.3	0.6	0.7	2.0	0.5	0.7	2.7	0.8	•
Pensions and Other Deferred Comp. **16**	0.5	0.0	0.0	2.3	0.1	0.1	0.4	0.4	0.1	0.5	0.9	0.7	•
Employee Benefits **17**	2.7	2.2	0.6	1.8	2.9	2.1	1.6	3.6	1.5	1.7	2.9	3.0	•
Advertising **18**	1.8	2.1	•	1.0	2.8	0.7	1.3	1.7	1.6	1.6	0.8	1.9	•
Other Expenses **19**	16.7	62.7	510.1	58.0	20.0	17.3	16.9	15.6	15.3	12.3	12.2	17.4	•
Officers' Compensation **20**	1.5	1.9	3.7	18.9	5.3	6.7	2.8	1.9	1.4	2.1	1.8	0.4	•
Operating Margin **21**	•	•	•	•	•	•	•	•	•	•	•	•	•
Operating Margin Before Officers' Comp. **22**	•	•	•	0.8	•	•	•	•	•	•	1.3	•	•

Selected Average Balance Sheet ($ in Thousands)

Net Receivables 23	2408	0	3	37	471	1561	4007	8723	17365	24657	62461	307908	•
Inventories 24	1421	0	58	33	391	1192	2681	6823	10481	23385	31036	143775	•
Net Property, Plant and Equipment 25	1637	0	1	156	176	1666	3211	4671	7406	20662	43660	214426	•
Total Assets 26	13090	0	116	725	1890	7515	16162	33875	70499	159546	360983	1781971	•
Notes and Loans Payable 27	3409	0	22	642	615	1611	4356	6265	41978	33330	75027	435527	•
All Other Liabilities 28	5040	0	16	297	812	3120	5571	10779	29158	57399	95270	736585	•
Net Worth 29	4641	0	79	-214	464	2785	6235	16831	-637	68818	190686	609859	•

Selected Financial Ratios (Times to 1)

Current Ratio 30	1.4	•	8.7	0.9	1.6	1.3	1.7	1.8	1.7	2.4	1.2	•
Quick Ratio 31	0.8	•	3.3	0.7	1.2	0.9	1.1	1.1	1.0	1.8	0.5	•
Net Sales to Working Capital 32	6.5	•	0.2	•	6.8	9.9	5.1	4.3	4.9	4.2	1.9	13.1	•
Coverage Ratio 33	•	•	•	•	0.9	•	•	2.0	•	2.1	2.8	•
Total Asset Turnover 34	1.0	•	0.1	0.6	2.2	1.3	1.3	1.3	1.3	1.0	0.6	0.9	•
Inventory Turnover 35	5.9	•	0.2	5.3	4.7	5.8	5.0	3.7	6.0	4.4	3.8	7.7	•
Receivables Turnover 36	5.7	•	1.9	6.9	7.5	5.4	5.6	5.2	6.4	5.8	4.0	5.8	•
Total Liabilities to Net Worth 37	1.8	•	0.5	•	3.1	1.7	1.6	1.0	1.3	0.9	1.9	•
Current Assets to Working Capital 38	3.4	•	1.1	•	2.6	4.5	2.4	2.3	2.5	2.3	1.7	6.4	•
Current Liabilities to Working Capital 39	2.4	•	0.1	•	1.6	3.5	1.4	1.3	1.5	1.3	0.7	5.4	•
Working Capital to Net Sales 40	0.2	•	6.0	•	0.1	0.1	0.2	0.2	0.2	0.2	0.5	0.1	•
Inventory to Working Capital 41	0.7	•	0.7	•	0.6	1.0	0.6	0.8	0.6	0.6	0.3	1.1	•
Total Receipts to Cash Flow 42	9.4	7.1	•	•	6.1	16.2	24.8	7.5	15.6	8.2	7.0	9.6	•
Cost of Goods to Cash Flow 43	6.0	3.9	•	•	2.7	11.4	15.4	4.4	10.6	5.3	3.9	6.4	•
Cash Flow to Total Debt 44	0.2	•	•	•	0.5	0.1	0.1	0.3	0.1	0.2	0.2	0.1	•

Selected Financial Factors (in Percentages)

Debt Ratio 45	64.5	•	32.5	129.5	75.4	62.9	61.4	50.3	100.9	56.9	47.2	65.8	•
Return on Total Assets 46	•	•	•	•	1.9	•	•	1.9	•	3.1	3.9	•
Return on Equity Before Income Taxes 47	•	•	•	206.7	•	•	•	1.9	764.9	3.7	4.7	•
Return on Equity After Income Taxes 48	•	•	•	209.5	•	•	•	0.5	852.8	0.7	2.1	•
Profit Margin (Before Income Tax) 49	•	•	•	•	•	•	•	0.7	•	1.6	4.2	•
Profit Margin (After Income Tax) 50	•	•	•	•	•	•	•	0.2	•	0.3	1.8	•

Table II

Corporations with Net Income

AUDIO AND VIDEO EQUIP., REPRODUCING MAGNETIC & OPTICAL MEDIA

MONEY AMOUNTS AND SIZE OF ASSETS IN THOUSANDS OF DOLLARS

Item Description for Accounting Period 7/04 Through 6/05	Total	Zero Assets	Under 500	500 to 1,000	1,000 to 5,000	5,000 to 10,000	10,000 to 25,000	25,000 to 50,000	50,000 to 100,000	100,000 to 250,000	250,000 to 500,000	500,000 to 2,500,000	2,500,000 and over
Number of Enterprises 1	372	4	0	0	205	38	20	16	10	9	0	0	0
Revenues ($ in Thousands)													
Net Sales 2	8145848	5161	0	0	1002942	512078	514300	761889	854131	1906000	0	0	0
Interest 3	28752	64	0	0	24	2016	485	1532	2280	4594	0	0	0
Rents 4	4671	0	0	0	0	979	0	1273	1344	150	0	0	0
Royalties 5	44455	0	0	0	0	180	13	838	824	2906	0	0	0
Other Portfolio Income 6	20970	0	0	0	6	0	344	4753	1674	5634	0	0	0
Other Receipts 7	144601	3037	0	0	65484	12148	5259	29998	7332	4938	0	0	0
Total Receipts 8	8389297	8262	0	0	1068456	527401	520401	800283	867585	1924222	0	0	0
Average Total Receipts 9	22552	2066	•	•	5212	13879	26020	50018	86758	213802	•	•	•
Operating Costs/Operating Income (%)													
Cost of Operations 10	57.2	45.9	•	•	64.5	71.9	64.5	53.7	58.1	64.1	•	•	•
Salaries and Wages 11	11.5	29.4	•	•	7.2	6.2	10.9	10.8	9.6	9.6	•	•	•
Taxes Paid 12	1.6	2.6	•	•	2.9	2.2	1.5	1.7	1.5	1.5	•	•	•
Interest Paid 13	0.9	0.7	•	•	1.2	0.2	0.5	0.7	1.3	1.6	•	•	•
Depreciation 14	3.0	0.5	•	•	0.8	0.7	2.8	3.1	2.0	2.7	•	•	•
Amortization and Depletion 15	0.4	0.0	•	•	0.0	0.0	0.2	0.4	0.3	0.5	•	•	•
Pensions and Other Deferred Comp. 16	0.6	0.2	•	•	0.2	0.1	0.4	0.5	0.1	0.6	•	•	•
Employee Benefits 17	2.9	1.4	•	•	1.5	1.8	1.1	4.5	1.6	1.6	•	•	•
Advertising 18	2.9	3.0	•	•	1.9	0.3	1.4	1.7	2.2	1.6	•	•	•
Other Expenses 19	12.1	11.5	•	•	14.5	9.5	10.1	13.6	11.2	9.8	•	•	•
Officers' Compensation 20	2.2	5.1	•	•	4.0	6.5	2.3	2.0	1.6	1.1	•	•	•
Operating Margin 21	4.8	•	•	•	1.3	0.6	4.4	7.3	10.5	5.2	•	•	•
Operating Margin Before Officers' Comp. 22	7.0	4.8	•	•	5.4	7.1	6.7	9.3	12.1	6.4	•	•	•

Selected Average Balance Sheet ($ in Thousands)

Net Receivables 23	3070	0	•	518	2128	3911	9269	16865	26908
Inventories 24	3002	0	•	470	1161	3721	6418	7851	33833
Net Property, Plant and Equipment 25	2448	0	•	102	679	2287	4735	9668	23500
Total Assets 26	17501	0	•	1567	7405	14932	33918	70615	162113
Notes and Loans Payable 27	2610	0	•	341	1081	2921	4490	29889	32977
All Other Liabilities 28	4735	0	•	455	3334	4535	8613	16284	59472
Net Worth 29	10155	0	•	771	2990	7476	20815	24442	69664

Selected Financial Ratios (Times to 1)

Current Ratio 30	2.3	•	•	2.2	1.6	1.9	2.4	2.4	1.9
Quick Ratio 31	1.4	•	•	1.1	1.1	1.1	1.6	1.7	1.1
Net Sales to Working Capital 32	3.8	•	•	6.8	6.8	5.1	3.4	3.1	4.5
Coverage Ratio 33	10.3	91.8	•	7.6	23.8	12.5	18.8	10.4	4.9
Total Asset Turnover 34	1.3	•	•	3.1	1.8	1.7	1.4	1.2	1.3
Inventory Turnover 35	4.2	•	•	6.7	8.3	4.5	4.0	6.3	4.0
Receivables Turnover 36	5.7	•	•	9.3	6.9	5.8	6.4	8.0	6.4
Total Liabilities to Net Worth 37	0.7	•	•	1.0	1.5	1.0	0.6	1.9	1.3
Current Assets to Working Capital 38	1.8	•	•	1.8	2.7	2.1	1.7	1.7	2.1
Current Liabilities to Working Capital 39	0.8	•	•	0.8	1.7	1.1	0.7	0.7	1.1
Working Capital to Net Sales 40	0.3	•	•	0.1	0.1	0.2	0.3	0.3	0.2
Inventory to Working Capital 41	0.5	•	•	0.9	0.7	0.7	0.5	0.4	0.6
Total Receipts to Cash Flow 42	5.6	1.4	•	4.9	8.5	7.4	4.3	4.6	6.8
Cost of Goods to Cash Flow 43	3.2	0.7	•	3.1	6.1	4.8	2.3	2.7	4.3
Cash Flow to Total Debt 44	0.5	•	•	1.3	0.4	0.5	0.8	0.4	0.3

Selected Financial Factors (in Percentages)

Debt Ratio 45	42.0	•	•	50.8	59.6	49.9	38.6	65.4	57.0
Return on Total Assets 46	11.0	•	•	28.3	6.9	10.5	18.2	16.9	10.2
Return on Equity Before Income Taxes 47	17.2	•	•	50.0	16.3	19.3	28.1	44.0	19.0
Return on Equity After Income Taxes 48	13.8	•	•	47.3	12.7	16.4	26.0	39.6	13.8
Profit Margin (Before Income Tax) 49	8.0	59.8	•	7.9	3.6	5.6	12.3	12.6	6.3
Profit Margin (After Income Tax) 50	6.4	58.0	•	7.5	2.8	4.8	11.4	11.3	4.5

Table I

Corporations with and without Net Income

SEMICONDUCTOR AND OTHER ELECTRONIC COMPONENT

MONEY AMOUNTS AND SIZE OF ASSETS IN THOUSANDS OF DOLLARS

Item Description for Accounting Period 7/04 Through 6/05	Total	Zero Assets	Under 500	500 to 1,000	1,000 to 5,000	5,000 to 10,000	10,000 to 25,000	25,000 to 50,000	50,000 to 100,000	100,000 to 250,000	250,000 to 500,000	500,000 to 2,500,000	2,500,000 and over
Number of Enterprises **1**	6606	358	3138	867	1452	325	186	65	48	62	33	46	24
Revenues ($ in Thousands)													
Net Sales **2**	223434836	3526743	1541397	1577062	7257113	3548839	3235361	2636576	4318442	10014452	9149637	31112370	145516844
Interest **3**	2821248	19207	1626	703	11399	4247	11887	8771	12763	51494	86789	382022	2230340
Rents **4**	106588	1833	1364	1123	1510	588	2494	4494	4883	4045	9036	16429	58788
Royalties **5**	3570539	111281	29	0	2713	390	950	2437	5502	125622	197201	509769	2614646
Other Portfolio Income **6**	2014745	15582	605	24805	6769	12905	35569	5964	13449	68285	120609	833337	876867
Other Receipts **7**	3026166	40575	4469	7709	-19141	26388	33657	36875	27723	63019	77388	437411	2290091
Total Receipts **8**	234974122	3715221	1549490	1611402	7260363	3593357	3319918	2695117	4382762	10326917	9640660	33291338	153587576
Average Total Receipts **9**	35570	10378	494	1859	5000	11056	17849	41463	91308	166563	292141	723725	6399482
Operating Costs/Operating Income (%)													
Cost of Operations **10**	68.1	68.0	52.4	52.9	56.8	63.4	64.0	66.9	72.7	66.3	70.4	66.7	69.4
Salaries and Wages **11**	10.1	8.8	14.9	11.3	15.5	14.9	14.4	11.3	10.6	12.3	13.5	14.9	8.1
Taxes Paid **12**	1.1	1.7	4.1	2.1	3.4	2.8	2.6	1.8	1.4	1.9	2.0	1.5	0.6
Interest Paid **13**	2.0	1.3	0.6	1.4	1.1	0.7	1.1	1.0	0.8	0.8	2.2	1.8	2.3
Depreciation **14**	4.9	7.0	1.7	0.7	2.7	3.2	3.8	3.5	3.7	3.6	3.8	5.6	5.2
Amortization and Depletion **15**	1.1	3.8	0.4	0.1	0.3	0.5	0.6	0.8	0.5	1.0	0.9	1.6	1.1
Pensions and Other Deferred Comp. **16**	0.6	0.4	0.3	0.7	0.5	0.4	0.4	0.5	0.4	0.4	0.3	0.4	0.7
Employee Benefits **17**	1.6	0.8	3.6	1.0	2.0	2.5	2.0	1.9	1.4	2.4	1.7	2.0	1.4
Advertising **18**	1.3	0.4	0.0	3.1	0.5	0.9	0.6	0.8	0.6	0.6	0.3	0.4	1.7
Other Expenses **19**	10.3	21.6	24.5	16.6	13.8	13.9	14.4	12.6	12.4	12.8	10.1	9.7	9.3
Officers' Compensation **20**	0.9	1.0	3.7	6.6	5.1	3.2	4.1	2.4	1.2	1.6	0.9	0.9	0.3
Operating Margin **21**	•	•	•	3.6	•	•	•	•	•	•	•	•	•
Operating Margin Before Officers' Comp. **22**	•	•	•	10.2	3.3	•	•	•	•	•	•	•	0.2

Selected Average Balance Sheet ($ in Thousands)

Net Receivables 23	6143	0	10	166	664	1431	2616	7108	13228	33377	46633	184398	1054103
Inventories 24	2919	0	20	77	587	1919	2828	5222	10927	20626	31677	64331	458564
Net Property, Plant and Equipment 25	6417	0	12	69	543	1139	2666	5715	12111	25542	40834	169086	1207426
Total Assets 26	41894	0	98	780	2402	7862	15256	33529	72084	171667	341711	1094163	7874968
Notes and Loans Payable 27	6175	0	107	228	1031	1761	3557	8065	14411	18301	47618	205447	1006458
All Other Liabilities 28	12617	0	15	567	682	2641	3647	8267	23428	45619	73981	283100	2513749
Net Worth 29	23102	0	-24	-15	688	3460	8053	17197	34245	107747	220112	605616	4354762

Selected Financial Ratios (Times to 1)

Current Ratio 30	1.8	·	2.1	1.9	1.8	2.1	2.4	2.3	1.9	2.6	2.2	2.1	1.6
Quick Ratio 31	1.1	·	1.6	1.0	1.1	1.2	1.5	1.4	1.2	1.7	1.3	1.5	0.9
Net Sales to Working Capital 32	4.2	·	19.9	5.6	6.9	3.4	2.9	3.3	4.2	2.6	2.7	2.2	5.4
Coverage Ratio 33	2.9	·	·	5.3	·	·	·	·	·	0.5	0.9	2.3	3.6
Total Asset Turnover 34	0.8	·	5.0	2.3	2.1	1.4	1.1	1.2	1.2	0.9	0.8	0.6	0.8
Inventory Turnover 35	7.9	·	13.0	12.6	4.8	3.6	3.9	5.2	6.0	5.2	6.2	7.0	9.2
Receivables Turnover 36	5.8	·	16.1	16.7	7.9	6.8	6.1	6.9	6.1	5.6	5.4	3.5	6.3
Total Liabilities to Net Worth 37	0.8	·	·	·	2.5	1.3	0.9	0.9	1.1	0.6	0.6	0.8	0.8
Current Assets to Working Capital 38	2.3	·	1.9	2.1	2.3	1.9	1.7	1.8	2.2	1.6	1.8	1.9	2.8
Current Liabilities to Working Capital 39	1.3	·	0.9	1.1	1.3	0.9	0.7	0.8	1.2	0.6	0.8	0.9	1.8
Working Capital to Net Sales 40	0.2	·	0.1	0.2	0.1	0.3	0.3	0.3	0.2	0.4	0.4	0.5	0.2
Inventory to Working Capital 41	0.4	·	0.4	0.4	0.8	0.6	0.5	0.5	0.6	0.3	0.3	0.2	0.5
Total Receipts to Cash Flow 42	8.6	9.0	10.8	6.1	12.9	23.0	19.3	11.7	16.9	10.7	14.4	11.6	7.5
Cost of Goods to Cash Flow 43	5.9	6.1	5.7	3.2	7.3	14.6	12.3	7.9	12.3	7.1	10.2	7.8	5.2
Cash Flow to Total Debt 44	0.2	·	0.4	0.4	0.2	0.1	0.1	0.2	0.1	0.2	0.2	0.1	0.2

Selected Financial Factors (in Percentages)

Debt Ratio 45	44.9	·	124.6	101.9	71.3	56.0	47.2	48.7	52.5	37.2	35.6	44.7	44.7
Return on Total Assets 46	4.7	·	·	16.6	·	·	·	·	0.4	·	1.6	2.5	6.4
Return on Equity Before Income Taxes 47	5.5	·	119.1	·	·	·	·	·	·	·	·	2.6	8.4
Return on Equity After Income Taxes 48	2.6	·	123.2	·	·	·	·	·	·	·	·	1.1	4.8
Profit Margin (Before Income Tax) 49	3.8	·	·	5.8	·	·	·	·	·	·	·	2.3	6.0
Profit Margin (After Income Tax) 50	1.8	·	·	5.7	·	·	·	·	·	·	·	1.0	3.5

Table II
Corporations with Net Income

SEMICONDUCTOR AND OTHER ELECTRONIC COMPONENT

MONEY AMOUNTS AND SIZE OF ASSETS IN THOUSANDS OF DOLLARS

Item Description for Accounting Period 7/04 Through 6/05	Total	Zero Assets	Under 500	500 to 1,000	1,000 to 5,000	5,000 to 10,000	10,000 to 25,000	25,000 to 50,000	50,000 to 100,000	100,000 to 250,000	250,000 to 500,000	500,000 to 2,500,000	2,500,000 and over
Number of Enterprises **1**	4049	315	1793	555	957	186	98	32	21	38	15	24	13
Revenues ($ in Thousands)													
Net Sales **2**	158183366	147725	978499	1566693	5249228	2520589	2298085	1592115	2814077	6988475	4184413	16475039	113366428
Interest **3**	1466344	427	734	387	1957	1236	2996	2679	3932	34929	33998	136791	1246277
Rents **4**	54696	23	0	1123	1510	0	1600	3213	391	1976	1778	6955	36126
Royalties **5**	1184949	0	0	0	0	7	42	2396	5464	61553	39637	153556	922293
Other Portfolio Income **6**	1455432	8461	0	24805	3504	11559	31662	2075	1989	49877	47909	642437	631151
Other Receipts **7**	2270723	3953	225	5343	17571	14817	20519	20559	18377	95438	25317	323351	1725258
Total Receipts **8**	164615510	160589	979458	1598351	5273770	2548208	2354904	1623037	2844230	7232248	4333052	17738129	117929533
Average Total Receipts **9**	40656	510	546	2880	5511	13700	24030	50720	135440	190322	288870	739089	9071503
Operating Costs/Operating Income (%)													
Cost of Operations **10**	65.1	70.1	48.6	53.2	53.7	62.3	61.4	63.9	71.9	62.1	64.0	60.8	66.7
Salaries and Wages **11**	9.2	5.0	18.8	10.7	13.4	10.9	10.0	7.8	7.2	11.2	13.8	16.9	7.5
Taxes Paid **12**	1.0	1.2	4.4	2.0	3.5	2.7	2.3	1.4	1.1	1.7	2.3	1.6	0.6
Interest Paid **13**	1.2	0.5	0.0	1.3	0.5	0.3	0.7	0.8	0.3	0.5	0.8	0.7	1.4
Depreciation **14**	5.1	1.9	1.1	0.2	2.3	2.1	2.9	3.0	2.3	3.3	3.1	5.7	5.6
Amortization and Depletion **15**	0.7	0.1	•	0.0	0.1	0.1	0.1	0.3	0.6	0.6	0.4	0.6	0.8
Pensions and Other Deferred Comp. **16**	0.7	0.1	•	0.7	0.7	0.5	0.4	0.7	0.5	0.5	0.4	0.4	0.8
Employee Benefits **17**	1.5	0.8	5.2	0.9	1.7	2.2	1.6	1.1	1.1	2.2	1.4	2.3	1.2
Advertising **18**	1.6	0.6	0.0	3.1	0.5	1.0	0.6	0.7	0.7	0.4	0.4	0.4	2.0
Other Expenses **19**	7.8	7.9	11.8	13.2	11.8	9.1	8.4	10.5	9.0	11.8	6.0	6.2	7.5
Officers' Compensation **20**	0.8	13.3	1.5	6.3	4.9	2.6	3.9	2.2	0.7	1.4	1.0	1.2	0.2
Operating Margin **21**	5.5	•	8.5	8.3	6.9	6.2	7.8	7.6	4.8	4.4	6.4	3.4	5.6
Operating Margin Before Officers' Comp. **22**	6.2	11.8	10.0	14.7	11.8	8.7	11.6	9.8	5.4	5.8	7.4	4.5	5.8

Selected Average Balance Sheet ($ in Thousands)

Net Receivables 23	6304	0	8	257	677	1717	3364	8477	14903	34433	39477	171881	1343133
Inventories 24	2319	0	33	119	505	1893	3576	5564	12634	19676	24485	46253	416036
Net Property, Plant and Equipment 25	7914	0	7	42	476	1240	2887	6428	9739	26789	38048	180559	1900547
Total Assets 26	40088	0	85	737	2150	8427	14832	32636	71830	178878	355282	1009165	9056206
Notes and Loans Payable 27	4448	0	38	42	529	1427	2575	6851	11221	11668	38076	89102	1022013
All Other Liabilities 28	10425	0	14	308	501	1124	3536	8777	18417	34552	67066	217763	2520509
Net Worth 29	25215	0	33	387	1120	5876	8720	17009	42192	132658	253140	702300	5513683

Selected Financial Ratios (Times to 1)

Current Ratio 30	2.2	•	4.5	2.0	2.1	4.4	2.5	2.5	2.4	3.4	2.7	3.2	1.9
Quick Ratio 31	1.4	•	3.2	1.4	1.4	2.4	1.5	1.5	1.5	2.2	1.8	2.4	1.1
Net Sales to Working Capital 32	3.7	•	11.3	8.8	6.7	2.6	3.9	3.7	4.7	2.3	2.2	1.7	4.7
Coverage Ratio 33	9.6	15.1	295.7	8.8	15.7	26.8	14.8	13.4	19.6	18.3	14.1	18.9	8.3
Total Asset Turnover 34	1.0	•	6.4	3.8	2.6	1.6	1.6	1.5	1.9	1.0	0.8	0.7	1.0
Inventory Turnover 35	11.0	•	8.0	12.6	5.8	4.5	4.0	5.7	7.6	5.8	7.3	9.0	14.0
Receivables Turnover 36	8.2	•	11.2	16.7	8.2	8.8	6.5	7.7	8.3	6.7	7.4	4.3	9.5
Total Liabilities to Net Worth 37	0.6	•	1.6	0.9	0.9	0.4	0.7	0.9	0.7	0.3	0.4	0.4	0.6
Current Assets to Working Capital 38	1.9	•	1.3	2.0	1.9	1.3	1.7	1.7	1.7	1.4	1.6	1.4	2.1
Current Liabilities to Working Capital 39	0.9	•	0.3	1.0	0.9	0.3	0.7	0.7	0.7	0.4	0.6	0.4	1.1
Working Capital to Net Sales 40	0.3	•	0.1	0.1	0.1	0.4	0.3	0.3	0.2	0.4	0.5	0.6	0.2
Inventory to Working Capital 41	0.3	•	0.3	0.6	0.6	0.5	0.6	0.6	0.5	0.3	0.2	0.1	0.4
Total Receipts to Cash Flow 42	6.3	8.9	7.1	5.5	6.6	8.1	6.5	5.4	7.5	5.9	7.2	6.6	6.2
Cost of Goods to Cash Flow 43	4.1	6.3	3.4	3.0	3.5	5.1	4.0	3.5	5.4	3.6	4.6	4.0	4.2
Cash Flow to Total Debt 44	0.4	•	1.5	1.5	0.8	0.7	0.6	0.6	0.6	0.7	0.4	0.3	0.4

Selected Financial Factors (in Percentages)

Debt Ratio 45	37.1	•	60.8	47.5	47.9	30.3	41.2	47.9	41.3	25.8	29.3	30.4	39.1
Return on Total Assets 46	11.0	•	55.2	44.7	20.1	12.1	17.3	15.9	11.5	8.8	8.6	8.6	11.3
Return on Equity Before Income Taxes 47	15.7	•	140.3	75.4	36.1	16.7	27.4	28.2	18.5	11.2	11.3	11.7	16.3
Return on Equity After Income Taxes 48	11.4	•	135.1	74.9	33.9	15.5	23.8	25.6	16.0	9.2	9.5	9.2	11.2
Profit Margin (Before Income Tax) 49	10.1	7.2	8.6	10.4	7.4	7.2	10.2	9.6	5.8	8.1	10.2	12.0	10.3
Profit Margin (After Income Tax) 50	7.4	6.7	8.2	10.3	6.9	6.7	8.9	8.7	5.1	6.7	8.7	9.4	7.1

Table I

Corporations with and without Net Income

NAVIGATIONAL, MEASURING, ELECTROMEDICAL, AND CONTROL

MONEY AMOUNTS AND SIZE OF ASSETS IN THOUSANDS OF DOLLARS

Item Description for Accounting Period 7/04 Through 6/05	Total	Zero Assets	Under 500	500 to 1,000	1,000 to 5,000	5,000 to 10,000	10,000 to 25,000	25,000 to 50,000	50,000 to 100,000	100,000 to 250,000	250,000 to 500,000	500,000 to 2,500,000	2,500,000 and over
Number of Enterprises **1**	3098	43	1128	860	609	246	76	40	30	27	10	20	8
Revenues ($ in Thousands)													
Net Sales **2**	52541063	106251	309073	1348280	3316077	2595854	1611360	1614916	2657298	3573422	2439432	13848187	19120910
Interest **3**	734808	170	311	38	3897	1125	1603	3105	12508	18691	20376	81255	591727
Rents **4**	86654	0	1895	9	192	4793	326	1099	9449	1002	426	18094	49370
Royalties **5**	646259	0	57822	0	0	1059	635	2224	0	15648	4467	245289	319114
Other Portfolio Income **6**	285717	544	0	1650	2632	11388	2413	12377	16011	60260	7357	136439	34647
Other Receipts **7**	1142903	6108	21	3364	12252	32876	13055	27638	21945	44209	18354	206739	756346
Total Receipts **8**	55437404	113073	369122	1353341	3335050	2647095	1629392	1661359	2717211	3713232	2490412	14536003	20872114
Average Total Receipts **9**	17895	2630	327	1574	5476	10761	21439	41534	90574	137527	249041	726800	2609014
Operating Costs/Operating Income (%)													
Cost of Operations **10**	58.3	66.4	61.0	45.6	61.0	47.6	57.3	55.1	55.0	53.5	51.6	56.6	63.8
Salaries and Wages **11**	15.9	27.9	10.0	10.8	12.6	15.4	14.2	14.7	14.5	16.2	17.9	16.5	16.6
Taxes Paid **12**	2.0	4.0	3.8	2.9	2.9	2.8	2.6	2.5	2.6	2.5	1.8	1.4	1.7
Interest Paid **13**	2.6	1.1	1.1	0.5	1.1	1.0	0.9	1.3	1.4	1.0	1.7	1.8	4.7
Depreciation **14**	3.0	1.2	1.7	0.8	1.5	2.1	2.6	2.6	2.1	2.9	3.5	2.8	3.8
Amortization and Depletion **15**	1.3	3.7	0.9	0.1	0.2	0.1	0.3	1.0	0.7	0.7	2.2	1.4	1.9
Pensions and Other Deferred Comp. **16**	1.8	0.8	0.0	0.4	0.4	0.8	0.5	0.8	0.8	0.9	0.2	1.6	3.0
Employee Benefits **17**	2.8	2.6	3.3	1.6	2.9	2.9	2.0	3.0	1.6	3.0	2.3	2.9	3.1
Advertising **18**	0.9	0.7	0.5	2.1	1.0	1.9	1.2	1.6	2.3	0.6	1.0	0.5	0.7
Other Expenses **19**	13.0	9.6	36.1	17.0	12.9	13.4	12.0	16.2	15.9	13.3	17.9	13.7	10.5
Officers' Compensation **20**	2.1	2.1	14.1	9.4	4.5	6.8	3.2	2.2	2.3	2.0	1.5	2.0	0.5
Operating Margin **21**	•	•	•	8.6	•	5.0	3.4	•	0.7	3.5	•	•	•
Operating Margin Before Officers' Comp. **22**	•	•	•	18.0	3.3	11.8	6.6	1.2	3.0	5.5	•	0.9	•

Selected Average Balance Sheet ($ in Thousands)

Net Receivables 23	3334	0	20	147	955	1860	3660	7200	14172	29952	64966	161964	431625
Inventories 24	2199	0	6	185	630	1944	3147	6149	11521	22201	40362	86305	278204
Net Property, Plant and Equipment 25	2497	0	4	51	316	1258	2689	5694	7959	23437	56241	114613	378493
Total Assets 26	26035	0	111	713	2614	7548	15306	36538	73300	172288	395041	1022612	5323888
Notes and Loans Payable 27	6431	0	40	338	939	2518	3017	6218	11438	12347	84260	261025	1397103
All Other Liabilities 28	6163	0	44	122	765	2047	3637	9518	17478	36272	77105	214834	1342453
Net Worth 29	13441	0	26	253	909	2983	8653	20802	44385	123669	233676	546753	2584332

Selected Financial Ratios (Times to 1)

Current Ratio 30	1.5	·	1.2	3.7	2.3	1.9	2.4	2.1	2.1	3.4	2.9	1.5	1.1
Quick Ratio 31	0.8	·	1.1	2.0	1.4	1.1	1.4	1.2	1.3	2.2	2.1	0.9	0.5
Net Sales to Working Capital 32	5.3	·	25.3	3.9	4.8	4.2	3.6	3.6	3.6	1.9	1.9	5.2	26.4
Coverage Ratio 33	2.1	·	·	18.1	0.4	8.0	6.2	2.6	3.3	8.6	1.3	3.9	1.0
Total Asset Turnover 34	0.7	·	2.5	2.2	2.1	1.4	1.4	1.1	1.2	0.8	0.6	0.7	0.4
Inventory Turnover 35	4.5	·	25.8	3.9	5.3	2.6	3.9	3.6	4.2	3.2	3.1	4.5	5.5
Receivables Turnover 36	4.8	·	11.5	13.0	5.8	5.6	5.8	5.8	6.0	4.6	2.6	4.4	5.0
Total Liabilities to Net Worth 37	0.9	·	3.2	1.8	1.9	1.5	0.8	0.8	0.7	0.4	0.7	0.9	1.1
Current Assets to Working Capital 38	3.2	·	5.0	1.4	1.8	2.1	1.7	1.9	1.9	1.4	1.5	2.9	18.2
Current Liabilities to Working Capital 39	2.2	·	4.0	0.4	0.8	1.1	0.7	0.9	0.9	0.4	0.5	1.9	17.2
Working Capital to Net Sales 40	0.2	·	0.0	0.3	0.2	0.2	0.3	0.3	0.3	0.5	0.5	0.2	0.0
Inventory to Working Capital 41	0.7	·	0.4	0.6	0.6	0.7	0.5	0.6	0.5	0.3	0.3	0.7	3.2
Total Receipts to Cash Flow 42	8.3	·	7.0	4.9	10.1	5.5	6.8	6.4	6.0	5.7	6.5	6.5	17.0
Cost of Goods to Cash Flow 43	4.8	·	4.3	2.2	6.2	2.6	3.9	3.5	3.3	3.0	3.3	3.7	10.9
Cash Flow to Total Debt 44	0.2	·	0.5	0.7	0.3	0.4	0.5	0.4	0.5	0.5	0.2	0.2	0.1

Selected Financial Factors (in Percentages)

Debt Ratio 45	48.4	·	76.1	64.5	65.2	60.5	43.5	43.1	39.4	28.2	40.8	46.5	51.5
Return on Total Assets 46	3.5	·	·	20.9	0.9	11.1	7.4	3.6	5.6	6.6	1.4	4.6	2.2
Return on Equity Before Income Taxes 47	3.4	·	·	55.6	·	24.7	10.9	3.9	6.4	8.2	0.6	6.4	0.2
Return on Equity After Income Taxes 48	2.2	·	·	54.9	·	21.6	8.7	0.9	3.5	6.3	·	4.1	·
Profit Margin (Before Income Tax) 49	2.7	·	·	9.0	·	7.0	4.5	2.0	3.2	7.6	0.5	5.0	0.2
Profit Margin (After Income Tax) 50	1.7	·	·	8.9	·	6.1	3.6	0.5	1.7	5.9	·	3.2	·

145

NAVIGATIONAL, MEASURING, ELECTROMEDICAL, AND CONTROL

Table II

Corporations with Net Income

MONEY AMOUNTS AND SIZE OF ASSETS IN THOUSANDS OF DOLLARS

Item Description for Accounting Period 7/04 Through 6/05	Total	Zero Assets	Under 500	500 to 1,000	1,000 to 5,000	5,000 to 10,000	10,000 to 25,000	25,000 to 50,000	50,000 to 100,000	100,000 to 250,000	250,000 to 500,000	500,000 to 2,500,000	2,500,000 and over
Number of Enterprises **1**	1930	20	398	0	393	219	59	26	22	22	6	15	0

Revenues ($ in Thousands)

Net Sales **2**	37641741	69034	248537	0	1938901	2479448	1326403	1270034	2047544	2938218	1609946	12061926	0
Interest **3**	639977	135	31	0	3607	406	1079	1525	9672	16145	8987	70644	0
Rents **4**	31605	0	1895	0	192	1063	186	1010	9126	931	163	10453	0
Royalties **5**	415527	0	0	0	0	1059	2	1346	0	14829	2714	243668	0
Other Portfolio Income **6**	260770	13	0	0	920	10028	2045	6195	14950	59847	1615	132111	0
Other Receipts **7**	724680	5642	21	0	8847	11445	6608	24437	19461	43458	17188	108638	0
Total Receipts **8**	39714300	74824	250484	0	1952467	2503449	1336323	1304547	2100753	3073428	1640613	12627440	0
Average Total Receipts **9**	20577	3741	629	•	4968	11431	22650	50175	95489	139701	273436	841829	•

Operating Costs/Operating Income (%)

Cost of Operations **10**	54.5	59.0	60.1	•	50.3	46.8	56.1	54.7	56.1	52.7	48.8	55.3	•
Salaries and Wages **11**	14.8	17.8	1.3	•	15.1	14.4	12.3	13.0	11.1	15.9	18.4	15.5	•
Taxes Paid **12**	1.8	2.0	2.9	•	3.0	2.7	2.4	2.2	2.2	2.4	1.5	1.4	•
Interest Paid **13**	2.7	1.2	0.4	•	0.9	0.9	0.6	1.4	1.4	1.1	1.7	1.8	•
Depreciation **14**	2.4	1.2	1.3	•	1.6	1.9	2.2	2.3	1.9	2.7	2.8	2.8	•
Amortization and Depletion **15**	1.7	5.6	1.1	•	0.2	0.0	0.2	0.8	0.7	0.6	2.5	1.5	•
Pensions and Other Deferred Comp. **16**	1.5	0.9	•	•	0.7	0.9	0.5	0.9	0.8	1.0	0.3	1.5	•
Employee Benefits **17**	2.7	2.9	3.4	•	2.9	2.7	2.0	3.0	1.5	3.1	2.5	2.7	•
Advertising **18**	0.9	0.7	0.2	•	1.2	2.0	1.2	1.3	2.6	0.6	1.2	0.5	•
Other Expenses **19**	14.9	3.4	14.4	•	13.9	12.5	10.3	12.7	14.4	12.1	16.5	14.8	•
Officers' Compensation **20**	2.1	1.6	9.0	•	4.7	6.8	3.1	1.8	1.5	2.1	1.6	1.2	•
Operating Margin **21**	0.0	3.7	5.9	•	5.6	8.4	9.0	5.7	5.8	5.6	2.3	1.0	•
Operating Margin Before Officers' Comp. **22**	2.1	5.3	15.0	•	10.3	15.2	12.1	7.5	7.3	7.7	3.9	2.2	•

Selected Average Balance Sheet ($ in Thousands)

Net Receivables 23	3519	0	50	•	791	1962	3814	7773	14189	30372	70342	177973	•
Inventories 24	2336	0	4	•	708	1888	2998	6886	11726	20027	20127	91680	•
Net Property, Plant and Equipment 25	2824	0	6	•	271	1306	2774	6218	8472	22888	59649	133286	•
Total Assets 26	30315	0	144	•	2744	7731	14878	35492	70073	177449	404572	1075928	•
Notes and Loans Payable 27	6978	0	10	•	703	2602	2926	7017	10029	11756	96652	265772	•
All Other Liabilities 28	6756	0	47	•	843	2112	3186	10991	17448	36165	76703	244527	•
Net Worth 29	16581	0	86	•	1197	3017	8766	17484	42596	129528	231218	565629	•

Selected Financial Ratios (Times to 1)

Current Ratio 30	1.8	•	1.6	•	2.3	1.9	2.6	2.0	2.2	3.6	2.5	1.8	•
Quick Ratio 31	0.9	•	1.5	•	1.2	1.0	1.6	1.1	1.4	2.3	1.9	1.1	•
Net Sales to Working Capital 32	3.8	•	20.6	•	4.2	4.5	3.6	4.6	3.7	1.8	2.7	4.4	•
Coverage Ratio 33	3.3	11.1	17.1	•	7.9	11.9	18.3	7.3	6.9	10.9	3.6	4.7	•
Total Asset Turnover 34	0.6	•	4.3	•	1.8	1.5	1.5	1.4	1.3	0.8	0.7	0.7	•
Inventory Turnover 35	4.6	•	90.7	•	3.5	2.8	4.2	3.9	4.4	3.5	6.5	4.9	•
Receivables Turnover 36	5.9	•	•	•	6.6	6.1	6.3	6.3	6.4	5.3	•	5.4	•
Total Liabilities to Net Worth 37	0.8	•	0.7	•	1.3	1.6	0.7	1.0	0.6	0.4	0.7	0.9	•
Current Assets to Working Capital 38	2.3	•	2.6	•	1.8	2.1	1.6	2.0	1.8	1.4	1.7	2.3	•
Current Liabilities to Working Capital 39	1.3	•	1.6	•	0.8	1.1	0.6	1.0	0.8	0.4	0.7	1.3	•
Working Capital to Net Sales 40	0.3	•	0.0	•	0.2	0.2	0.3	0.2	0.3	0.6	0.4	0.2	•
Inventory to Working Capital 41	0.5	•	0.1	•	0.7	0.8	0.5	0.7	0.5	0.3	0.2	0.6	•
Total Receipts to Cash Flow 42	5.6	7.4	5.9	•	5.6	5.0	5.4	5.1	4.8	5.1	5.7	5.4	•
Cost of Goods to Cash Flow 43	3.0	4.4	3.5	•	2.8	2.3	3.0	2.8	2.7	2.7	2.8	3.0	•
Cash Flow to Total Debt 44	0.3	•	1.8	•	0.6	0.5	0.7	0.5	0.7	0.5	0.3	0.3	•

Selected Financial Factors (in Percentages)

Debt Ratio 45	45.3	•	40.0	•	56.4	61.0	41.1	50.7	39.2	27.0	42.8	47.4	•
Return on Total Assets 46	5.7	•	30.9	•	12.9	15.0	15.5	13.6	13.0	8.7	4.1	6.5	•
Return on Equity Before Income Taxes 47	7.3	•	48.6	•	25.9	35.2	24.9	23.7	18.3	10.8	5.2	9.7	•
Return on Equity After Income Taxes 48	5.7	•	47.5	•	21.3	31.8	22.0	18.4	14.1	8.7	3.7	6.8	•
Profit Margin (Before Income Tax) 49	6.2	12.1	6.7	•	6.3	9.4	9.7	8.5	8.4	10.5	4.5	6.8	•
Profit Margin (After Income Tax) 50	4.9	11.4	6.6	•	5.2	8.5	8.6	6.6	6.5	8.4	3.2	4.8	•

Table I

Corporations with and without Net Income

ELECTRICAL LIGHTING EQUIPMENT AND HOUSEHOLD APPLIANCE

MONEY AMOUNTS AND SIZE OF ASSETS IN THOUSANDS OF DOLLARS

Item Description for Accounting Period 7/04 Through 6/05	Total	Zero Assets	Under 500	500 to 1,000	1,000 to 5,000	5,000 to 10,000	10,000 to 25,000	25,000 to 50,000	50,000 to 100,000	100,000 to 250,000	250,000 to 500,000	500,000 to 2,500,000	2,500,000 and over
Number of Enterprises 1	1202	0	0	0	159	0	59	15	9	17	6	4	5
Revenues ($ in Thousands)													
Net Sales 2	131043973	0	0	0	917523	0	1691618	1004182	1027781	3937881	2377227	6128687	109719082
Interest 3	28168709	0	0	0	16	0	758	227	1354	5697	537	8771	28126659
Rents 4	28008	0	0	0	0	0	964	109	397	2102	832	16700	2798
Royalties 5	1714470	0	0	0	6064	0	0	259	125	9218	263	37130	1657843
Other Portfolio Income 6	8126754	0	0	0	196	0	5066	833	6276	4734	3218	16145	8061289
Other Receipts 7	15054096	0	0	0	3850	0	7282	5378	-3515	37156	33287	16629	14840386
Total Receipts 8	184136010	0	0	0	927649	0	1705688	1010988	1032418	3996788	2415364	6224062	162408057
Average Total Receipts 9	153191	•	•	•	5834	•	28910	67399	114713	235105	402561	1556016	32481611
Operating Costs/Operating Income (%)													
Cost of Operations 10	58.5	•	•	•	64.4	•	64.8	67.2	59.8	64.0	67.7	66.6	57.2
Salaries and Wages 11	12.5	•	•	•	9.8	•	8.5	5.0	10.8	7.9	5.1	11.9	13.2
Taxes Paid 12	1.1	•	•	•	3.4	•	1.8	1.8	1.6	1.6	1.6	1.7	0.9
Interest Paid 13	21.1	•	•	•	2.7	•	0.7	1.0	1.0	1.0	1.4	1.5	24.8
Depreciation 14	9.8	•	•	•	1.5	•	1.9	2.2	2.5	2.3	3.5	2.1	11.3
Amortization and Depletion 15	1.6	•	•	•	1.2	•	0.2	0.4	0.5	0.4	2.1	0.3	1.8
Pensions and Other Deferred Comp. 16	0.9	•	•	•	0.0	•	0.5	0.3	0.9	0.5	0.2	1.0	0.8
Employee Benefits 17	1.6	•	•	•	2.1	•	1.6	0.7	2.0	1.7	2.3	2.1	1.6
Advertising 18	1.0	•	•	•	0.3	•	1.1	5.5	1.7	3.7	4.6	1.1	0.7
Other Expenses 19	28.9	•	•	•	14.7	•	14.4	13.0	14.8	10.3	10.1	12.0	32.3
Officers' Compensation 20	0.5	•	•	•	1.2	•	2.4	1.5	7.1	1.9	1.0	0.3	0.3
Operating Margin 21	•	•	•	•	•	•	2.2	1.4	•	4.8	0.5	•	•
Operating Margin Before Officers' Comp. 22	•	•	•	•	•	•	4.6	2.8	4.4	6.7	1.4	•	•

Selected Average Balance Sheet ($ in Thousands)

Net Receivables 23	202208	•	613	•	4018	11570	18571	45658	42934	218591	48076354
Inventories 24	7067	•	1263	•	4060	10326	18706	36656	32919	239394	1160066
Net Property, Plant and Equipment 25	46217	•	814	•	2739	5704	13478	27000	57819	139617	10729205
Total Assets 26	822675	•	3594	•	15274	34705	73934	151655	315098	1560621	195007186
Notes and Loans Payable 27	325566	•	1950	•	4453	8437	19277	36742	75671	325469	77595465
All Other Liabilities 28	252663	•	1513	•	4741	10856	20288	46858	119613	345909	59958309
Net Worth 29	244446	•	131	•	6080	15412	34369	68056	119813	889242	57453411

Selected Financial Ratios (Times to 1)

Current Ratio 30	0.8	•	0.9	•	1.8	2.4	2.0	2.2	2.1	1.8	0.8
Quick Ratio 31	0.7	•	0.3	•	0.9	1.2	1.2	1.2	1.0	0.9	0.7
Net Sales to Working Capital 32	•	•	•	•	6.3	4.5	4.7	4.4	5.4	6.4	•
Coverage Ratio 33	1.4	•	0.9	•	5.2	3.0	•	7.5	2.4	1.7	1.4
Total Asset Turnover 34	0.1	•	1.6	•	1.9	1.9	1.5	1.5	1.3	1.0	0.1
Inventory Turnover 35	9.0	•	2.9	•	4.6	4.4	3.7	4.0	8.1	4.3	10.8
Receivables Turnover 36	0.7	•	8.3	•	8.1	5.6	5.8	5.3	12.3	5.6	0.6
Total Liabilities to Net Worth 37	2.4	•	26.4	•	1.5	1.3	1.2	1.2	1.6	0.8	2.4
Current Assets to Working Capital 38	•	•	•	•	2.3	1.7	2.0	1.9	1.9	2.2	•
Current Liabilities to Working Capital 39	•	•	•	•	1.3	0.7	1.0	0.9	0.9	1.2	•
Working Capital to Net Sales 40	•	•	•	•	0.2	0.2	0.2	0.2	0.2	0.2	•
Inventory to Working Capital 41	•	•	•	•	1.0	0.7	0.7	0.7	0.6	0.8	•
Total Receipts to Cash Flow 42	3.9	•	7.5	•	7.7	7.2	10.0	6.6	9.1	9.0	3.5
Cost of Goods to Cash Flow 43	2.3	•	4.8	•	5.0	4.9	6.0	4.2	6.1	6.0	2.0
Cash Flow to Total Debt 44	0.0	•	0.2	•	0.4	0.5	0.3	0.4	0.2	0.3	0.0

Selected Financial Factors (in Percentages)

Debt Ratio 45	70.3	•	96.4	•	60.2	55.6	53.5	55.1	62.0	43.0	70.5
Return on Total Assets 46	3.9	•	4.1	•	7.1	5.8	•	11.1	4.2	2.5	3.8
Return on Equity Before Income Taxes 47	3.6	•	•	•	14.4	8.8	•	21.5	6.4	1.7	3.5
Return on Equity After Income Taxes 48	2.4	•	•	•	12.1	6.5	•	18.7	5.6	0.5	2.3
Profit Margin (Before Income Tax) 49	8.0	•	3.1	•	3.1	2.0	•	6.3	1.9	1.0	9.0
Profit Margin (After Income Tax) 50	5.3	•	2.6	•	2.6	1.5	•	5.5	1.7	0.3	6.0

147

Table II

Corporations with Net Income

ELECTRICAL LIGHTING EQUIPMENT AND HOUSEHOLD APPLIANCE

MONEY AMOUNTS AND SIZE OF ASSETS IN THOUSANDS OF DOLLARS

Item Description for Accounting Period 7/04 Through 6/05	Total	Zero Assets	Under 500	500 to 1,000	1,000 to 5,000	5,000 to 10,000	10,000 to 25,000	25,000 to 50,000	50,000 to 100,000	100,000 to 250,000	250,000 to 500,000	500,000 to 2,500,000	2,500,000 and over
Number of Enterprises **1**	742	0	489	0	147	26	42	9	0	13	0	0	0
Revenues ($ in Thousands)													
Net Sales **2**	120896417	0	63397	0	904611	369259	1346442	570167	0	3232540	0	0	0
Interest **3**	28151518	0	9	0	3	1	418	170	0	5441	0	0	0
Rents **4**	22035	0	0	0	0	0	180	0	0	0	0	0	0
Royalties **5**	1657269	0	0	0	6064	80	0	1	0	506	0	0	0
Other Portfolio Income **6**	8116851	0	0	0	196	0	2110	227	0	3681	0	0	0
Other Receipts **7**	14976938	0	3174	0	3851	612	6006	2411	0	36018	0	0	0
Total Receipts **8**	173821028	0	66580	0	914725	369952	1355156	572976	0	3278186	0	0	0
Average Total Receipts **9**	234260	•	136	•	6223	14229	32266	63664	•	252168	•	•	•
Operating Costs/Operating Income (%)													
Cost of Operations **10**	57.3	•	48.9	•	64.2	61.1	63.4	66.1	•	61.3	•	•	•
Salaries and Wages **11**	13.1	•	4.8	•	9.3	9.5	8.3	5.8	•	8.6	•	•	•
Taxes Paid **12**	1.0	•	1.7	•	3.4	2.9	1.8	1.8	•	1.6	•	•	•
Interest Paid **13**	22.8	•	2.7	•	2.4	0.9	0.7	1.0	•	0.9	•	•	•
Depreciation **14**	10.4	•	0.2	•	1.5	0.9	1.5	2.7	•	2.3	•	•	•
Amortization and Depletion **15**	1.7	•	0.5	•	0.0	0.1	0.1	0.2	•	0.3	•	•	•
Pensions and Other Deferred Comp. **16**	0.8	•	•	•	0.0	0.3	0.5	0.4	•	0.6	•	•	•
Employee Benefits **17**	1.6	•	0.0	•	2.1	1.8	1.4	1.0	•	1.8	•	•	•
Advertising **18**	0.8	•	2.8	•	0.3	1.4	1.2	1.8	•	3.6	•	•	•
Other Expenses **19**	30.3	•	31.3	•	14.2	15.4	13.0	9.6	•	10.6	•	•	•
Officers' Compensation **20**	0.4	•	4.9	•	1.1	2.2	2.4	2.1	•	1.9	•	•	•
Operating Margin **21**	•	•	2.1	•	1.6	3.7	5.9	7.5	•	6.6	•	•	•
Operating Margin Before Officers' Comp. **22**	•	•	6.9	•	2.7	5.8	8.3	9.7	•	8.5	•	•	•

Selected Average Balance Sheet ($ in Thousands)

Net Receivables 23	325849	7	648	1697	4386	8803	52541
Inventories 24	9524	9	973	3024	3895	11063	36052
Net Property, Plant and Equipment 25	72846	2	871	544	2469	6581	28363
Total Assets 26	1320526	59	3635	7358	14749	32702	154464
Notes and Loans Payable 27	524669	9	1806	2469	3358	8960	33823
All Other Liabilities 28	404192	14	1487	2461	4817	6344	47456
Net Worth 29	391664	36	342	2427	6573	17398	73184

Selected Financial Ratios (Times to 1)

Current Ratio 30	0.8	0.8	0.9	1.6	2.0	3.2	2.5
Quick Ratio 31	0.7	0.4	0.3	0.5	1.1	1.5	1.5
Net Sales to Working Capital 32			5.8	6.1	6.1	3.9	4.0
Coverage Ratio 33	1.4	3.6	2.2	5.4	11.1	9.3	10.0
Total Asset Turnover 34	0.1	2.2	1.7	1.9	2.2	1.9	1.6
Inventory Turnover 35	9.8	7.2	4.1	2.9	5.2	3.8	4.2
Receivables Turnover 36	0.6	34.6	13.8	7.0	8.6	5.2	1.1
Total Liabilities to Net Worth 37	2.4	0.6	9.6	2.0	1.2	0.9	1.7
Current Assets to Working Capital 38				2.7	2.0	1.5	
Current Liabilities to Working Capital 39				1.7	1.0	0.5	0.7
Working Capital to Net Sales 40			1.7	0.2	0.2	0.3	0.2
Inventory to Working Capital 41				1.8	0.8	0.7	0.6
Total Receipts to Cash Flow 42	3.7	3.1	6.3	5.5	6.8	6.1	5.8
Cost of Goods to Cash Flow 43	2.1	1.5	4.1	3.3	4.3	4.0	3.6
Cash Flow to Total Debt 44	0.0	1.8	0.3	0.5	0.6	0.7	0.5

Selected Financial Factors (in Percentages)

Debt Ratio 45	70.3	38.7	90.6	67.0	55.4	46.8	52.6
Return on Total Assets 46	3.9	21.7	8.6	9.1	15.8	17.4	14.4
Return on Equity Before Income Taxes 47	3.7	25.6	49.5	22.5	32.2	29.3	27.3
Return on Equity After Income Taxes 48	2.5	25.6	47.7	22.4	29.1	25.8	23.9
Profit Margin (Before Income Tax) 49	9.0	7.1	2.8	3.8	6.6	8.0	8.0
Profit Margin (After Income Tax) 50	6.0	7.1	2.7	3.8	6.0	7.1	7.0

Table I

Corporations with and without Net Income

ELECTRICAL EQUIPMENT

MONEY AMOUNTS AND SIZE OF ASSETS IN THOUSANDS OF DOLLARS

Item Description for Accounting Period 7/04 Through 6/05	Total	Zero Assets	Under 500	500 to 1,000	1,000 to 5,000	5,000 to 10,000	10,000 to 25,000	25,000 to 50,000	50,000 to 100,000	100,000 to 250,000	250,000 to 500,000	500,000 to 2,500,000	2,500,000 and over
Number of Enterprises **1**	1757	0	0	288	330	0	55	22	13	10	6	8	3
Revenues ($ in Thousands)													
Net Sales **2**	36211709	0	0	405787	1666880	0	1908564	1076449	1182390	1804306	2180206	5498717	18466566
Interest **3**	349176	0	0	88	1698	0	1244	1488	9503	5670	2881	27305	298776
Rents **4**	70540	0	0	0	405	0	1931	436	72	1010	0	615	66071
Royalties **5**	245256	0	0	61	0	0	2023	37	1020	1011	5265	15335	220290
Other Portfolio Income **6**	422866	0	0	0	492	0	11563	2906	6309	2084	13490	212199	171520
Other Receipts **7**	446924	0	0	161	5275	0	5794	1304	14044	19606	6662	180803	206375
Total Receipts **8**	37746471	0	0	406097	1674750	0	1931119	1082620	1213338	1833687	2208504	5934974	19429598
Average Total Receipts **9**	21483	·	·	1410	5075	·	35111	49210	93334	183369	368084	741872	6476533
Operating Costs/Operating Income (%)													
Cost of Operations **10**	69.4	·	·	60.2	64.5	·	76.6	73.4	68.8	58.2	62.8	72.4	69.6
Salaries and Wages **11**	6.5	·	·	6.9	8.4	·	6.8	7.7	9.4	13.3	6.1	7.6	5.3
Taxes Paid **12**	1.8	·	·	2.6	2.5	·	1.6	1.7	1.6	2.2	2.4	1.1	1.9
Interest Paid **13**	2.4	·	·	1.2	0.8	·	0.7	1.4	1.6	0.3	0.6	1.0	4.0
Depreciation **14**	2.3	·	·	2.2	1.8	·	2.0	3.0	3.0	3.4	3.3	2.3	2.3
Amortization and Depletion **15**	0.7	·	·	0.1	0.1	·	0.2	0.3	1.0	0.7	0.6	1.6	0.7
Pensions and Other Deferred Comp. **16**	1.3	·	·	0.1	0.9	·	0.5	0.6	0.7	1.1	1.5	0.3	1.9
Employee Benefits **17**	2.4	·	·	1.1	1.0	·	1.8	1.6	2.6	1.9	2.2	2.3	2.8
Advertising **18**	0.5	·	·	0.6	0.5	·	0.2	0.6	0.6	1.0	0.3	1.0	0.4
Other Expenses **19**	9.8	·	·	16.9	9.0	·	7.7	6.8	10.0	12.9	11.1	9.8	9.9
Officers' Compensation **20**	1.2	·	·	11.0	3.5	·	1.7	1.5	1.2	0.9	0.9	0.7	0.6
Operating Margin **21**	1.6	·	·	·	6.9	·	0.3	1.4	·	4.0	8.4	·	0.6
Operating Margin Before Officers' Comp. **22**	2.7	·	·	8.1	10.4	·	1.9	3.0	0.7	4.9	9.3	0.6	1.2

Selected Average Balance Sheet ($ in Thousands)

Net Receivables 23	6329	241	479	4731	8564	12633	31216	39807	303494	2362680
Inventories 24	2074	129	1059	3746	8141	10698	25875	37549	107520	412096
Net Property, Plant and Equipment 25	2940	67	397	2959	7851	13722	34090	82366	98195	931397
Total Assets 26	36696	576	2397	16517	34411	69429	166673	350788	1165067	15708079
Notes and Loans Payable 27	4014	223	907	4029	10828	21606	10787	41276	119736	1515493
All Other Liabilities 28	10266	204	513	4825	9594	16847	45997	111758	364239	4264316
Net Worth 29	22416	149	976	7663	13988	30976	109889	197754	681091	9928270

Selected Financial Ratios (Times to 1)

Current Ratio 30	1.1	1.9	3.0	2.0	2.1	1.7	2.4	1.9	1.6	0.8
Quick Ratio 31	0.8	1.0	1.0	1.1	1.1	0.8	1.4	0.9	1.2	0.7
Net Sales to Working Capital 32	15.7	6.3	4.0	6.4	4.8	6.7	3.0	6.0	3.6	•
Coverage Ratio 33	3.9	•	10.0	3.2	2.4	2.6	19.6	18.1	10.6	2.9
Total Asset Turnover 34	0.6	2.4	2.1	2.1	1.4	1.3	1.1	1.0	0.6	0.4
Inventory Turnover 35	6.9	6.6	3.1	7.1	4.4	5.9	4.1	6.1	4.6	10.4
Receivables Turnover 36	3.1	9.7	8.4	7.4	5.6	7.6	5.8	8.0	2.8	2.3
Total Liabilities to Net Worth 37	0.6	2.9	1.5	1.2	1.5	1.2	0.5	0.8	0.7	0.6
Current Assets to Working Capital 38	7.8	2.2	1.5	2.0	1.9	2.4	1.7	2.2	2.7	•
Current Liabilities to Working Capital 39	6.8	1.2	0.5	1.0	0.9	1.4	0.7	1.2	1.7	•
Working Capital to Net Sales 40	0.1	0.2	0.2	0.2	0.2	0.1	0.3	0.2	0.3	•
Inventory to Working Capital 41	1.7	0.8	1.0	0.7	0.7	1.0	0.4	0.8	0.6	•
Total Receipts to Cash Flow 42	7.6	9.0	7.3	14.0	12.9	9.4	5.9	5.2	8.0	7.4
Cost of Goods to Cash Flow 43	5.3	5.4	4.7	10.7	9.5	6.5	3.4	3.2	5.8	5.1
Cash Flow to Total Debt 44	0.2	0.4	0.5	0.3	0.2	0.3	0.5	0.5	0.2	0.1

Selected Financial Factors (in Percentages)

Debt Ratio 45	38.9	74.2	59.3	53.6	59.3	55.4	34.1	43.6	41.5	36.8
Return on Total Assets 46	5.3	•	17.2	4.4	4.8	5.4	6.4	11.1	6.4	4.5
Return on Equity Before Income Taxes 47	6.4	•	37.9	6.6	6.9	7.4	9.2	18.5	9.9	4.7
Return on Equity After Income Taxes 48	4.4	•	35.5	5.0	5.2	5.2	7.3	11.4	6.4	3.2
Profit Margin (Before Income Tax) 49	7.0	•	7.3	1.5	2.0	2.5	5.6	10.1	9.8	7.5
Profit Margin (After Income Tax) 50	4.8	•	6.9	1.1	1.5	1.8	4.4	6.2	6.3	5.1

149

Table II

Corporations with Net Income

ELECTRICAL EQUIPMENT

MONEY AMOUNTS AND SIZE OF ASSETS IN THOUSANDS OF DOLLARS

Item Description for Accounting Period 7/04 Through 6/05	Total	Zero Assets	Under 500	500 to 1,000	1,000 to 5,000	5,000 to 10,000	10,000 to 25,000	25,000 to 50,000	50,000 to 100,000	100,000 to 250,000	250,000 to 500,000	500,000 to 2,500,000	2,500,000 and over
Number of Enterprises **1**	1164	0	691	65	245	77	39	13	8	7	0	0	0
Revenues ($ in Thousands)													
Net Sales **2**	31760075	0	417382	83044	1468171	1032434	1424225	652762	620434	1566197	0	0	0
Interest **3**	335932	0	0	75	1632	191	935	529	9004	1774	0	0	0
Rents **4**	69547	0	0	0	405	0	1389	0	72	1010	0	0	0
Royalties **5**	231396	0	0	0	0	0	1988	0	996	631	0	0	0
Other Portfolio Income **6**	417019	0	0	0	442	884	11181	1122	4696	2059	0	0	0
Other Receipts **7**	440259	0	0	0	5091	1545	5056	3751	11823	19256	0	0	0
Total Receipts **8**	33254228	0	417382	83119	1475741	1035054	1444774	658164	647025	1590927	0	0	0
Average Total Receipts **9**	28569	•	604	1279	6023	13442	37045	50628	80878	227275	•	•	•
Operating Costs/Operating Income (%)													
Cost of Operations **10**	68.6	•	85.9	26.8	63.5	65.7	74.6	70.6	63.9	61.2	•	•	•
Salaries and Wages **11**	6.7	•	0.0	9.9	8.3	6.6	6.9	8.6	10.3	11.9	•	•	•
Taxes Paid **12**	1.9	•	0.3	2.4	2.4	1.4	1.6	1.6	1.8	1.9	•	•	•
Interest Paid **13**	2.6	•	0.0	0.5	0.8	0.2	0.5	0.7	1.2	0.3	•	•	•
Depreciation **14**	2.2	•	0.2	2.6	1.8	0.8	1.9	2.8	2.1	2.2	•	•	•
Amortization and Depletion **15**	0.8	•	•	0.1	0.1	0.0	0.1	0.3	0.7	0.7	•	•	•
Pensions and Other Deferred Comp. **16**	1.4	•	•	•	0.6	0.6	0.5	0.7	0.5	1.2	•	•	•
Employee Benefits **17**	2.3	•	0.5	0.1	1.0	0.8	1.3	1.1	1.4	1.3	•	•	•
Advertising **18**	0.5	•	•	1.3	0.4	0.2	0.3	0.8	1.1	1.0	•	•	•
Other Expenses **19**	9.3	•	9.3	13.2	8.8	5.7	7.6	6.2	12.3	9.9	•	•	•
Officers' Compensation **20**	1.1	•	2.1	32.5	3.2	5.0	1.8	1.5	0.9	0.7	•	•	•
Operating Margin **21**	2.7	•	1.8	10.6	9.2	12.9	3.0	5.2	3.8	7.6	•	•	•
Operating Margin Before Officers' Comp. **22**	3.7	•	3.9	43.1	12.4	17.9	4.7	6.7	4.7	8.3	•	•	•

Selected Average Balance Sheet ($ in Thousands)

Net Receivables 23	8925	0	403	515	2126	4655	8181	11821	40519
Inventories 24	2613	0	197	868	993	3545	6865	13485	31072
Net Property, Plant and Equipment 25	3869	2	10	441	568	2946	7391	10039	28778
Total Assets 26	51847	25	602	2596	5998	16862	33211	68530	163750
Notes and Loans Payable 27	5316	0	72	1052	692	3626	6666	15734	14119
All Other Liabilities 28	14203	1	200	430	1525	4591	7134	15971	59864
Net Worth 29	32328	23	330	1115	3781	8645	19411	36825	89767

Selected Financial Ratios (Times to 1)

Current Ratio 30	1.1	8.2	3.0	4.0	2.7	2.2	2.3	1.9	1.8
Quick Ratio 31	0.8	8.2	2.0	1.3	1.9	1.2	1.3	0.8	1.0
Net Sales to Working Capital 32	18.5	59.1	3.2	4.0	4.1	6.0	4.9	4.8	4.8
Coverage Ratio 33	4.4	458.4	20.7	13.9	73.9	10.4	9.9	8.3	30.2
Total Asset Turnover 34	0.5	24.5	2.1	2.3	2.2	2.2	1.5	1.1	1.4
Inventory Turnover 35	7.2		1.7	4.4	8.9	7.7	5.2	3.7	4.4
Receivables Turnover 36	2.9			9.5	10.1	8.1	6.7		
Total Liabilities to Net Worth 37	0.6	0.1	0.8	1.3	0.6	1.0	0.7	0.9	0.8
Current Assets to Working Capital 38	9.4	1.1	1.5	1.3	1.6	1.9	1.8	2.2	2.2
Current Liabilities to Working Capital 39	8.4	0.1	0.5	0.3	0.6	0.9	0.8	1.2	1.2
Working Capital to Net Sales 40	0.1	0.0	0.3	0.2	0.2	0.2	0.2	0.2	0.2
Inventory to Working Capital 41	2.0		0.5	0.9	0.5	0.7	0.7	0.8	0.7
Total Receipts to Cash Flow 42	7.1	12.8	4.8	6.3	5.7	9.9	8.8	5.5	5.6
Cost of Goods to Cash Flow 43	4.9	11.0	1.3	4.0	3.8	7.4	6.2	3.5	3.4
Cash Flow to Total Debt 44	0.2	33.2	1.0	0.6	1.1	0.4	0.4	0.4	0.5

Selected Financial Factors (in Percentages)

Debt Ratio 45	37.6	5.8	45.2	57.1	37.0	48.7	41.6	46.3	45.2
Return on Total Assets 46	6.0	43.0	23.9	24.2	29.8	10.6	10.0	11.0	12.9
Return on Equity Before Income Taxes 47	7.4	45.5	41.5	52.3	46.6	18.7	15.4	17.9	22.7
Return on Equity After Income Taxes 48	5.3	45.5	30.4	49.5	44.5	16.6	13.4	14.9	19.3
Profit Margin (Before Income Tax) 49	8.7	1.8	10.7	9.7	13.1	4.4	6.0	8.5	9.1
Profit Margin (After Income Tax) 50	6.3	1.8	7.8	9.2	12.6	3.9	5.2	7.1	7.8

Table I

Corporations with and without Net Income

OTHER ELECTRICAL EQUIPMENT AND COMPONENT

MONEY AMOUNTS AND SIZE OF ASSETS IN THOUSANDS OF DOLLARS

Item Description for Accounting Period 7/04 Through 6/05	Total	Zero Assets	Under 500	500 to 1,000	1,000 to 5,000	5,000 to 10,000	10,000 to 25,000	25,000 to 50,000	50,000 to 100,000	100,000 to 250,000	250,000 to 500,000	500,000 to 2,500,000	2,500,000 and over
Number of Enterprises **1**	4227	339	1702	419	906	434	215	93	51	29	17	17	3
Revenues ($ in Thousands)													
Net Sales **2**	53610605	1098119	797915	909691	5131301	4848937	5140514	4790453	4134348	3702140	4905150	11114713	7037323
Interest **3**	363846	11903	21	266	979	1974	5922	5894	12862	20338	34240	174802	94646
Rents **4**	29713	23	0	157	1392	184	1525	750	1806	1386	1514	5232	15742
Royalties **5**	286528	0	0	0	72	179	1227	73435	8147	20759	30762	58326	93621
Other Portfolio Income **6**	294876	31553	0	35	444	7041	9522	17373	63913	33134	12201	79729	39929
Other Receipts **7**	633870	22736	3015	8193	105451	62326	52703	33652	47605	138921	54447	123278	-18453
Total Receipts **8**	55219438	1164334	800951	918342	5239639	4920641	5211413	4921557	4268681	3916678	5038314	11556080	7262808
Average Total Receipts **9**	13064	3435	471	2192	5783	11338	24239	52920	83700	135058	296371	679769	2420936
Operating Costs/Operating Income (%)													
Cost of Operations **10**	66.4	74.6	51.2	58.2	63.3	71.8	68.2	67.2	68.4	66.2	68.9	63.8	65.8
Salaries and Wages **11**	10.2	8.9	11.7	11.8	11.1	9.4	9.4	10.2	11.4	13.8	7.7	8.5	12.6
Taxes Paid **12**	2.0	1.1	2.5	2.1	3.1	2.9	2.2	1.9	2.1	1.4	1.6	1.8	1.6
Interest Paid **13**	2.1	3.3	0.6	0.4	1.8	1.5	0.9	0.8	1.9	1.8	2.4	3.9	1.9
Depreciation **14**	2.7	2.4	0.9	2.9	2.8	1.5	2.3	2.6	3.5	3.3	3.1	2.9	2.7
Amortization and Depletion **15**	0.7	3.8	0.0	0.0	0.2	0.4	0.4	0.3	0.7	0.5	1.6	1.2	0.4
Pensions and Other Deferred Comp. **16**	0.6	1.3	0.2	0.4	0.2	0.6	0.4	0.7	0.4	0.5	0.5	0.8	1.2
Employee Benefits **17**	2.0	1.5	0.1	1.9	1.1	1.3	1.9	2.1	1.9	2.4	2.7	2.5	2.4
Advertising **18**	1.1	0.9	0.4	1.1	0.6	0.5	0.6	0.7	0.7	0.7	0.9	1.4	3.0
Other Expenses **19**	11.2	20.4	33.8	13.3	11.0	8.3	10.4	9.7	8.7	15.0	12.7	13.8	5.2
Officers' Compensation **20**	1.8	1.4	4.2	5.2	4.3	2.5	2.8	1.7	2.0	1.2	0.7	0.8	0.7
Operating Margin **21**	•	•	•	2.6	0.4	•	0.6	2.1	•	•	•	•	2.5
Operating Margin Before Officers' Comp. **22**	0.8	•	•	7.9	4.7	1.8	3.4	3.8	0.3	•	•	•	3.2

Selected Average Balance Sheet ($ in Thousands)

Net Receivables 23	2166	0	21	239	624	1668	3878	7945	16448	26980	93234	124319	280128
Inventories 24	1568	0	13	218	609	2008	3631	8062	13812	18270	41642	80814	162873
Net Property, Plant and Equipment 25	1785	0	20	77	903	1174	2754	5895	14026	27997	49337	107818	269838
Total Assets 26	14264	0	116	689	2740	6338	15210	33233	70505	154118	384110	978640	5661623
Notes and Loans Payable 27	3797	0	97	194	1805	2485	3653	4987	17696	30953	123072	369355	556459
All Other Liabilities 28	3686	0	89	194	877	1483	3964	11336	19963	36144	110192	190717	1607630
Net Worth 29	6782	0	-70	302	58	2370	7592	16910	32846	87021	150847	418567	3497534

Selected Financial Ratios (Times to 1)

Current Ratio 30	1.7	•	0.7	2.2	1.3	1.9	2.0	2.0	1.9	2.2	1.9	1.4	1.3
Quick Ratio 31	0.9	•	0.6	1.4	0.7	1.0	1.1	1.1	1.0	1.3	1.2	0.9	0.6
Net Sales to Working Capital 32	5.5	•	•	6.4	15.4	5.0	4.6	4.5	4.1	3.0	3.2	7.1	9.6
Coverage Ratio 33	2.0	•	•	9.4	2.4	1.5	3.2	7.0	1.8	0.6	1.1	1.7	4.4
Total Asset Turnover 34	0.9	•	4.1	3.1	2.1	1.8	1.6	1.5	1.1	0.8	0.8	0.7	0.4
Inventory Turnover 35	5.4	•	18.6	5.8	5.9	4.0	4.5	4.3	4.0	4.6	4.8	5.2	9.5
Receivables Turnover 36	6.3	•	30.2	7.4	8.7	8.0	6.4	6.0	5.2	4.5	3.4	5.4	•
Total Liabilities to Net Worth 37	1.1	•	•	1.3	1.7	2.1	1.0	1.0	1.1	0.8	1.5	1.3	0.6
Current Assets to Working Capital 38	2.5	•	•	1.8	4.3	2.1	2.0	2.0	2.1	1.9	2.2	3.5	4.1
Current Liabilities to Working Capital 39	1.5	•	•	0.8	3.3	1.1	1.0	1.0	1.1	0.9	1.2	2.5	3.1
Working Capital to Net Sales 40	0.2	•	•	0.2	0.1	0.2	0.2	0.2	0.2	0.3	0.3	0.1	0.1
Inventory to Working Capital 41	0.7	•	•	0.6	1.8	0.9	0.7	0.7	0.7	0.4	0.5	0.8	0.7
Total Receipts to Cash Flow 42	9.2	27.9	5.4	7.2	9.2	14.0	9.9	7.9	13.2	8.3	9.0	7.1	11.7
Cost of Goods to Cash Flow 43	6.1	20.8	2.8	4.2	5.8	10.1	6.7	5.3	9.0	5.5	6.2	4.5	7.7
Cash Flow to Total Debt 44	0.2	•	0.5	0.8	0.2	0.2	0.3	0.4	0.2	0.2	0.1	0.2	0.1

Selected Financial Factors (in Percentages)

Debt Ratio 45	52.5	•	160.4	56.2	97.9	62.6	50.1	49.1	53.4	43.5	60.7	57.2	38.2
Return on Total Assets 46	3.8	•	•	12.6	8.8	3.9	4.6	8.7	4.0	0.9	1.9	4.5	3.4
Return on Equity Before Income Taxes 47	4.0	•	35.7	25.7	246.1	3.7	6.3	14.6	3.9	•	0.3	4.3	4.3
Return on Equity After Income Taxes 48	2.1	•	35.9	24.7	194.6	1.4	4.0	11.7	1.8	•	•	3.1	2.6
Profit Margin (Before Income Tax) 49	2.1	•	•	3.6	2.5	0.8	2.0	4.8	1.6	•	0.1	2.8	6.3
Profit Margin (After Income Tax) 50	1.1	•	•	3.4	2.0	0.3	1.3	3.8	0.7	•	•	2.0	3.9

Table II

Corporations with Net Income

OTHER ELECTRICAL EQUIPMENT AND COMPONENT

MONEY AMOUNTS AND SIZE OF ASSETS IN THOUSANDS OF DOLLARS

Item Description for Accounting Period 7/04 Through 6/05

	Total	Zero Assets	Under 100	100 to 250	251 to 500	501 to 1,000	1,001 to 5,000	5,001 to 10,000	10,001 to 25,000	25,001 to 50,000	50,001 to 100,000	100,001 to 250,000	250,001 and over
Number of Enterprises 1	2815	318	966	353	627	257	156	62	0	17	12	0	0
Revenues ($ in Thousands)													
Net Sales 2	37558409	188478	589729	860943	3791473	2761146	3996804	3303873	0	2662399	3203032	0	0
Interest 3	182697	213	0	263	644	1312	3172	3966	0	9320	22634	0	0
Rents 4	21842	23	0	157	1392	126	1373	547	0	1083	1111	0	0
Royalties 5	232658	0	0	0	0	179	1224	73435	0	20181	5709	0	0
Other Portfolio Income 6	196744	121	0	0	405	665	7095	15219	0	29018	9048	0	0
Other Receipts 7	496289	11310	0	5152	10341	53624	43872	23281	0	117095	41368	0	0
Total Receipts 8	38718639	200145	589729	866515	3804255	2817052	4053540	3420321	0	2839096	3282902	0	0
Average Total Receipts 9	13754	629	610	2455	6067	10961	25984	55166	•	167006	273575	•	•
Operating Costs/Operating Income (%)													
Cost of Operations 10	64.3	63.0	48.4	58.5	60.6	70.2	66.8	65.3	•	63.2	62.1	•	•
Salaries and Wages 11	8.5	4.5	11.0	12.4	9.3	7.4	8.7	9.6	•	10.7	7.5	•	•
Taxes Paid 12	2.1	2.4	2.1	2.2	2.9	2.6	2.1	1.8	•	1.3	1.9	•	•
Interest Paid 13	1.5	2.4	0.1	0.4	1.3	1.0	0.7	0.8	•	1.0	3.2	•	•
Depreciation 14	2.4	1.5	0.2	3.1	2.8	1.2	2.0	2.3	•	2.3	3.1	•	•
Amortization and Depletion 15	0.4	2.3	0.0	0.0	0.1	0.2	0.2	0.2	•	0.5	1.6	•	•
Pensions and Other Deferred Comp. 16	0.7	0.4	0.3	0.4	0.2	0.8	0.5	0.7	•	0.5	0.7	•	•
Employee Benefits 17	2.1	2.7	0.0	2.0	1.1	1.3	1.8	2.1	•	2.3	3.0	•	•
Advertising 18	1.1	1.1	0.0	1.2	0.5	0.7	0.5	0.6	•	0.7	0.6	•	•
Other Expenses 19	10.2	11.9	29.8	10.6	9.4	4.4	8.3	8.0	•	15.0	13.6	•	•
Officers' Compensation 20	1.8	0.9	4.9	5.5	4.2	3.1	2.7	1.6	•	1.0	0.8	•	•
Operating Margin 21	4.9	6.7	3.3	3.8	7.6	7.1	5.6	6.8	•	1.5	1.9	•	•
Operating Margin Before Officers' Comp. 22	6.7	7.6	8.2	9.3	11.8	10.2	8.4	8.5	•	2.5	2.7	•	•

Selected Average Balance Sheet ($ in Thousands)

Net Receivables 23	2138	0	26	239	692	1568	4041	7877	•	31957	77057
Inventories 24	1481	0	6	185	581	2134	3670	8381	•	18998	40680
Net Property, Plant and Equipment 25	1675	0	1	91	680	1252	2574	5111	•	24636	52811
Total Assets 26	13299	0	126	723	2545	6234	14995	32637	•	155114	376988
Notes and Loans Payable 27	2962	0	14	186	1113	2255	3320	4717	•	17979	138991
All Other Liabilities 28	3755	0	79	166	703	1016	3994	11203	•	39271	93220
Net Worth 29	6582	0	34	371	729	2962	7681	16717	•	97863	144777

Selected Financial Ratios (Times to 1)

Current Ratio 30	1.9	•	0.9	2.7	1.4	2.5	2.1	2.2	•	2.2	2.0
Quick Ratio 31	1.1	•	0.8	1.8	0.8	1.4	1.2	1.2	•	1.4	1.2
Net Sales to Working Capital 32	5.0	•	•	6.1	12.0	4.1	4.5	4.2	•	3.5	2.7
Coverage Ratio 33	6.2	6.8	36.4	11.8	7.3	10.6	11.8	14.6	•	9.2	2.4
Total Asset Turnover 34	1.0	•	4.8	3.4	2.4	1.7	1.7	1.6	•	1.0	0.7
Inventory Turnover 35	5.8	•	50.1	7.7	6.3	3.5	4.7	4.2	•	5.2	4.1
Receivables Turnover 36	7.3	•	36.0	•	8.6	6.9	6.9	5.9	•	5.6	•
Total Liabilities to Net Worth 37	1.0	•	2.7	1.0	2.5	1.1	1.0	1.0	•	0.6	1.6
Current Assets to Working Capital 38	2.1	•	•	1.6	3.4	1.7	1.9	1.8	•	1.8	2.0
Current Liabilities to Working Capital 39	1.1	•	•	0.6	2.4	0.7	0.9	0.8	•	0.8	1.0
Working Capital to Net Sales 40	0.2	•	•	0.2	0.1	0.2	0.2	0.2	•	0.3	0.4
Inventory to Working Capital 41	0.6	•	•	0.5	1.3	0.7	0.7	0.7	•	0.4	0.4
Total Receipts to Cash Flow 42	6.3	•	4.6	8.2	6.7	8.5	7.4	6.0	•	4.7	6.0
Cost of Goods to Cash Flow 43	4.0	2.7	2.2	4.8	4.0	6.0	4.9	3.9	•	3.0	3.7
Cash Flow to Total Debt 44	0.3	•	1.5	0.8	0.5	0.4	0.5	0.6	•	0.6	0.2

Selected Financial Factors (in Percentages)

Debt Ratio 45	50.5	•	73.0	48.8	71.3	52.5	48.8	48.8	•	36.9	61.6
Return on Total Assets 46	9.6	•	16.2	16.3	21.8	17.4	13.3	18.2	•	9.5	5.5
Return on Equity Before Income Taxes 47	16.3	•	58.4	29.1	65.8	33.1	23.7	33.0	•	13.5	8.4
Return on Equity After Income Taxes 48	13.3	•	57.7	28.1	59.8	30.1	20.6	28.5	•	9.5	6.1
Profit Margin (Before Income Tax) 49	8.0	14.0	3.3	4.4	7.9	9.1	7.1	10.4	•	8.4	4.6
Profit Margin (After Income Tax) 50	6.6	11.2	3.2	4.3	7.2	8.3	6.2	8.9	•	5.9	3.3

Table I

Corporations with and without Net Income

MOTOR VEHICLES AND PARTS

MONEY AMOUNTS AND SIZE OF ASSETS IN THOUSANDS OF DOLLARS

Item Description for Accounting Period 7/04 Through 6/05	Total	Zero Assets	Under 500	500 to 1,000	1,000 to 5,000	5,000 to 10,000	10,000 to 25,000	25,000 to 50,000	50,000 to 100,000	100,000 to 250,000	250,000 to 500,000	500,000 to 2,500,000	2,500,000 and over
Number of Enterprises **1**	4742	397	2050	515	953	179	225	135	102	79	39	46	21
Revenues ($ in Thousands)													
Net Sales **2**	662951129	786919	3285990	662570	4859842	3148726	6984323	7781993	12724699	22236365	19795579	56145518	524538606
Interest **3**	36986579	3761	127	1334	2068	2841	4224	5754	9683	30572	84224	322945	36519046
Rents **4**	19183558	1207	2	0	165	51	1404	1816	7042	9589	13611	14536	19134135
Royalties **5**	6007650	14051	0	64	1112	46	739	4448	4477	23068	18304	156453	5784888
Other Portfolio Income **6**	12849064	7244	66052	0	8531	20507	21356	8759	19433	47084	139752	183292	12327054
Other Receipts **7**	19272423	7515	26843	18210	20365	30620	49924	43918	121030	308098	161500	400164	18084234
Total Receipts **8**	757250403	820697	3379014	682178	4892083	3202791	7061970	7846688	12886364	22654776	20212970	57222908	616387963
Average Total Receipts **9**	159690	2067	1648	1325	5133	17893	31387	58124	126337	286769	518281	1243976	29351808
Operating Costs/Operating Income (%)													
Cost of Operations **10**	81.4	75.6	87.9	65.8	70.5	82.0	78.0	78.7	80.5	83.0	81.0	78.9	81.8
Salaries and Wages **11**	3.3	6.4	3.0	5.5	7.1	3.7	5.3	4.6	3.2	3.9	3.7	4.3	3.1
Taxes Paid **12**	0.9	1.7	2.6	2.0	2.6	1.7	1.9	1.7	1.5	1.4	1.4	1.4	0.7
Interest Paid **13**	4.6	3.4	0.7	2.5	1.6	0.8	1.0	0.8	1.0	0.9	2.5	2.3	5.4
Depreciation **14**	7.8	4.5	0.7	5.3	2.7	2.3	2.8	4.6	4.2	3.2	4.1	4.0	8.8
Amortization and Depletion **15**	0.4	0.2	0.0	0.4	0.1	0.0	0.2	0.2	0.3	0.3	0.5	0.6	0.3
Pensions and Other Deferred Comp. **16**	2.3	0.5	0.1	•	0.7	0.1	0.3	0.3	0.4	0.3	0.4	0.8	2.8
Employee Benefits **17**	1.6	1.9	1.2	1.2	1.1	1.1	1.5	1.9	2.1	1.7	1.8	2.3	1.5
Advertising **18**	1.5	0.1	0.5	0.2	0.6	0.4	0.6	0.4	0.3	0.3	0.2	0.3	1.9
Other Expenses **19**	10.5	12.1	8.1	13.3	10.7	7.0	7.5	6.1	6.0	4.8	6.2	7.2	11.5
Officers' Compensation **20**	0.2	1.1	1.7	3.7	3.4	1.4	1.6	0.8	0.6	0.4	0.5	0.3	0.1
Operating Margin **21**	•	•	•	0.1	•	•	•	•	•	•	•	•	•
Operating Margin Before Officers' Comp. **22**	•	•	•	3.8	2.3	0.9	1.0	0.7	0.5	0.1	•	•	•

Selected Average Balance Sheet ($ in Thousands)

Item													
Net Receivables 23	109943	0	15	164	526	1557	3910	7704	16543	35454	64737	183961	23955192
Inventories 24	7713	0	97	234	647	1742	3917	6505	12550	26741	44365	102723	1129397
Net Property, Plant and Equipment 25	35458	0	38	234	580	1591	4339	12693	26456	44983	93098	237476	6838459
Total Assets 26	283675	0	134	844	2254	6467	15511	35815	74396	153544	351995	1045623	59585749
Notes and Loans Payable 27	107926	0	311	563	1124	2372	5852	13054	24762	48178	145241	407621	22644626
All Other Liabilities 28	120483	0	63	100	877	2078	4937	10010	23907	53305	100577	378859	25689567
Net Worth 29	55266	0	-240	182	253	2017	4721	12751	25727	52061	106177	259143	11251555

Selected Financial Ratios (Times to 1)

Item													
Current Ratio 30	1.3	•	1.5	1.7	1.3	1.5	1.5	1.5	1.2	1.3	1.5	1.3	1.3
Quick Ratio 31	1.1	•	0.2	0.7	0.6	0.7	0.7	0.8	0.7	0.7	0.9	0.7	1.1
Net Sales to Working Capital 32	4.2	38.0	6.2	13.8	12.3	9.5	12.5	15.9	21.0	15.9	9.8	12.5	3.6
Coverage Ratio 33	1.0	0.1	2.2	0.7	2.6	1.6	1.9	2.2	2.7	1.8	1.4	0.9	1.0
Total Asset Turnover 34	0.5	•	11.9	1.5	2.3	2.7	2.0	1.6	1.7	1.8	1.4	1.2	0.4
Inventory Turnover 35	14.8	14.5	3.6	8.3	5.6	6.2	7.0	8.0	8.7	9.3	9.4		18.1
Receivables Turnover 36	1.4	48.4	7.1	8.9	13.0	8.0	7.9	7.8	8.8	7.3	7.9		1.2
Total Liabilities to Net Worth 37	4.1	•	3.6	7.9	2.2	2.3	1.8	1.9	2.3	3.0	4.4		4.3
Current Assets to Working Capital 38	4.4	3.1	2.5	4.1	3.1	3.0	4.1	6.0	4.6	2.9	4.4		4.4
Current Liabilities to Working Capital 39	3.4	2.1	1.5	3.1	2.1	2.0	3.1	5.0	3.6	1.9	3.4		3.4
Working Capital to Net Sales 40	0.2	0.0	0.2	0.1	0.1	0.1	0.1	0.0	0.1	0.1	0.1		0.3
Inventory to Working Capital 41	0.2	2.6	1.0	1.9	1.5	1.2	1.5	2.1	1.6	1.0	1.2		0.2
Total Receipts to Cash Flow 42	10.7	30.9	8.7	13.6	16.6	16.8	18.6	17.8	18.7	23.1	20.4		9.6
Cost of Goods to Cash Flow 43	8.7	27.1	5.7	9.6	13.6	13.1	14.6	14.3	15.5	18.7	16.1		7.9
Cash Flow to Total Debt 44	0.1	•	0.2	0.1	0.2	0.1	0.1	0.1	0.1	0.1	0.1		0.1

Selected Financial Factors (in Percentages)

Item													
Debt Ratio 45	80.5	278.4	78.5	88.8	68.8	69.6	64.4	65.4	66.1	69.8	75.2		81.1
Return on Total Assets 46	2.4	•	8.4	2.5	5.3	3.2	2.5	3.7	4.7	3.8	2.4		2.3
Return on Equity Before Income Taxes 47	0.5	•	23.9	21.4	10.3	3.9	3.4	5.8	8.8	•	•		0.4
Return on Equity After Income Taxes 48	•	•	23.9	20.4	7.6	1.0	0.5	3.4	5.6	•	•		•
Profit Margin (Before Income Tax) 49	0.2	•	3.0	1.2	1.2	0.6	0.8	1.2	1.6	0.1	•		0.2
Profit Margin (After Income Tax) 50	•	•	2.9	0.9	0.2	0.7	0.1	0.1	1.0	•	•		•

Table II
Corporations with Net Income

MOTOR VEHICLES AND PARTS

MANUFACTURING 336105

MONEY AMOUNTS AND SIZE OF ASSETS IN THOUSANDS OF DOLLARS

Item Description for Accounting Period 7/04 Through 6/05	Total	Zero Assets	Under 500	500 to 1,000	1,000 to 5,000	5,000 to 10,000	10,000 to 25,000	25,000 to 50,000	50,000 to 100,000	100,000 to 250,000	250,000 to 500,000	500,000 to 2,500,000	2,500,000 and over
Number of Enterprises **1**	2450	15	1009	343	568	126	141	78	61	53	21	22	13
Revenues ($ in Thousands)													
Net Sales **2**	480484899	363252	600951	461548	2929364	2716008	4858953	5110717	8712622	15998708	13115312	30903032	39714431
Interest **3**	24123274	155	121	83	1553	2613	2216	3601	6723	18569	25086	48219	24014335
Rents **4**	12261231	1207	0	0	29	36	792	1123	5602	7626	7352	5673	12231791
Royalties **5**	2802534	2121	0	64	1106	46	714	3385	4090	21689	5119	91181	2673019
Other Portfolio Income **6**	9398399	4559	0	0	7069	18800	17993	3821	15211	40715	10663	108624	9170946
Other Receipts **7**	15397286	3495	2991	18032	21394	28088	29438	30443	61204	253936	74032	233165	14641068
Total Receipts **8**	544467623	374789	604063	479727	2960515	2765591	4910106	5153090	8805452	16341243	13237564	31389894	457445590
Average Total Receipts **9**	222232	24986	599	1399	5212	21949	34823	66065	144352	308325	630360	1426813	35188122
Operating Costs/Operating Income (%)													
Cost of Operations **10**	79.8	69.8	67.9	60.9	69.2	82.2	76.0	76.2	79.4	81.0	80.0	78.4	80.1
Salaries and Wages **11**	3.2	5.8	3.7	4.3	7.0	3.8	5.2	4.5	3.4	4.1	3.6	4.1	3.0
Taxes Paid **12**	0.9	1.6	3.2	2.5	2.8	1.5	1.7	1.8	1.4	1.5	1.3	1.3	0.8
Interest Paid **13**	4.0	0.8	0.5	2.7	0.7	0.4	0.7	0.7	0.8	0.8	1.1	0.7	4.7
Depreciation **14**	7.4	5.2	1.8	7.2	1.9	1.7	2.3	2.9	3.2	2.5	3.5	3.1	8.3
Amortization and Depletion **15**	0.4	0.1	0.1	0.2	0.1	0.0	0.1	0.1	0.2	0.3	0.4	0.4	0.4
Pensions and Other Deferred Comp. **16**	3.1	0.4	0.5	•	1.2	0.1	0.3	0.4	0.4	0.4	0.5	0.8	3.6
Employee Benefits **17**	1.6	1.7	2.1	1.7	1.2	0.9	1.4	2.0	2.1	1.7	1.6	2.1	1.6
Advertising **18**	1.7	0.0	1.4	0.3	0.3	0.4	0.5	0.5	0.4	0.3	0.3	0.2	2.0
Other Expenses **19**	9.4	10.3	13.4	15.2	9.1	6.5	6.2	5.5	4.7	4.9	4.0	5.9	10.2
Officers' Compensation **20**	0.2	0.2	3.8	3.4	2.5	1.3	1.8	0.9	0.6	0.4	0.5	0.3	0.1
Operating Margin **21**	•	4.1	1.7	1.6	4.2	1.2	3.8	4.5	3.4	2.2	3.3	2.7	•
Operating Margin Before Officers' Comp. **22**	•	4.4	5.5	5.1	6.7	2.5	5.6	5.4	3.9	2.6	3.8	3.0	•

Selected Average Balance Sheet ($ in Thousands)

Net Receivables 23	147783	0	25	191	510	1647	4133	8816	17972	37985	75956	219329	26975393
Inventories 24	10353	0	109	185	655	1657	4155	7167	14821	28602	56380	105337	1349526
Net Property, Plant and Equipment 25	51193	0	34	304	493	1237	3629	9446	23006	42573	105162	224181	8676972
Total Assets 26	368372	0	159	863	2189	6435	15201	35123	75451	155949	359045	956898	65566057
Notes and Loans Payable 27	133758	0	61	605	619	1841	4456	9892	18939	43228	108900	214939	24230184
All Other Liabilities 28	164103	0	40	93	609	1990	4681	9617	24633	51292	97597	354989	29684096
Net Worth 29	70511	0	58	165	962	2604	6064	15614	31879	61429	152548	386970	11751777

Selected Financial Ratios (Times to 1)

Current Ratio 30	1.4	•	2.7	1.3	2.2	1.4	1.7	1.6	1.4	1.5	1.7	1.6	1.4
Quick Ratio 31	1.2	•	0.8	0.6	1.2	0.6	1.0	0.9	0.8	0.8	1.0	1.0	1.2
Net Sales to Working Capital 32	3.9	•	7.5	12.0	6.6	14.9	7.7	8.2	11.7	10.8	8.4	8.1	3.4
Coverage Ratio 33	1.5	10.5	5.1	3.0	8.7	7.9	7.9	9.2	6.7	6.7	4.9	7.1	1.4
Total Asset Turnover 34	0.5	•	3.8	1.6	2.4	3.3	2.3	1.9	1.9	1.9	1.7	1.5	0.5
Inventory Turnover 35	15.1	•	3.7	4.4	5.4	10.7	6.3	7.0	7.7	8.5	8.9	10.5	18.0
Receivables Turnover 36	1.6	•	10.9	12.2	8.9	19.0	8.5	7.8	7.8	8.0	8.7	8.2	1.3
Total Liabilities to Net Worth 37	4.2	•	1.8	4.2	1.3	1.5	1.5	1.2	1.4	1.5	1.4	1.5	4.6
Current Assets to Working Capital 38	3.8	•	1.6	4.5	1.9	3.2	2.3	2.6	3.3	3.1	2.4	2.8	3.8
Current Liabilities to Working Capital 39	2.8	•	0.6	3.5	0.9	2.2	1.3	1.6	2.3	2.1	1.4	1.8	2.8
Working Capital to Net Sales 40	0.3	•	0.1	0.1	0.2	0.1	0.1	0.1	0.1	0.1	0.1	0.1	0.3
Inventory to Working Capital 41	0.2	•	1.1	2.0	0.8	1.6	0.9	1.0	1.2	1.1	0.8	0.7	0.2
Total Receipts to Cash Flow 42	9.7	6.2	7.8	6.7	8.7	13.3	10.6	10.6	12.2	12.2	13.6	11.0	9.4
Cost of Goods to Cash Flow 43	7.8	4.3	5.3	4.1	6.0	10.9	8.1	8.1	9.7	9.9	10.9	8.6	7.5
Cash Flow to Total Debt 44	0.1	•	0.8	0.3	0.5	0.4	0.4	0.3	0.3	0.3	0.2	0.2	0.1

Selected Financial Factors (in Percentages)

Debt Ratio 45	80.9	•	63.7	80.9	56.1	59.5	60.1	55.5	57.7	60.6	57.5	59.6	82.1
Return on Total Assets 46	3.3	•	10.5	12.9	14.0	11.4	12.9	11.3	10.0	10.1	9.3	7.5	2.9
Return on Equity Before Income Taxes 47	6.1	•	23.3	45.4	28.2	24.6	28.3	22.7	20.1	21.7	17.4	16.0	4.3
Return on Equity After Income Taxes 48	4.6	•	22.7	43.7	24.3	21.6	24.8	18.5	16.8	17.6	12.9	11.5	3.3
Profit Margin (Before Income Tax) 49	2.2	7.3	2.3	5.5	5.3	3.0	5.0	5.4	4.5	4.4	4.3	4.4	1.7
Profit Margin (After Income Tax) 50	1.7	6.8	2.2	5.3	4.5	2.6	4.4	4.4	3.8	3.6	3.2	3.2	1.3

154

Table I

Corporations with and without Net Income

AEROSPACE PRODUCT AND PARTS

MONEY AMOUNTS AND SIZE OF ASSETS IN THOUSANDS OF DOLLARS

Item Description for Accounting Period 7/04 Through 6/05	Total	Zero Assets	Under 500	500 to 1,000	1,000 to 5,000	5,000 to 10,000	10,000 to 25,000	25,000 to 50,000	50,000 to 100,000	100,000 to 250,000	250,000 to 500,000	500,000 to 2,500,000	2,500,000 and over
Number of Enterprises 1	1576	25	1007	120	127	115	84	39	16	12	8	13	9
Revenues ($ in Thousands)													
Net Sales 2	189121203	426333	271611	92342	665035	841725	1543605	1315794	1374836	1951340	2146434	8332166	170015982
Interest 3	1718633	2426	240	0	447	1184	554	1977	4326	5129	21536	24999	1655816
Rents 4	1427905	780	0	0	0	0	712	329	1478	5835	5019	43196	1370557
Royalties 5	1926490	1320	0	0	0	0	1	0	1404	0	3761	25857	1894148
Other Portfolio Income 6	1876870	723	1436	0	488	272	3065	13701	3139	9647	5332	54722	1784347
Other Receipts 7	1567053	70	141	910	-2580	1756	25206	-7985	12407	18122	55747	58062	1405190
Total Receipts 8	197638154	431652	273428	93252	663390	844937	1573143	1323816	1397590	1990073	2237829	8539002	178270040
Average Total Receipts 9	125405	17266	272	777	5224	7347	18728	33944	87349	165839	279729	656846	19807782
Operating Costs/Operating Income (%)													
Cost of Operations 10	75.5	70.8	62.7	55.2	62.5	61.3	68.5	68.2	64.2	72.0	64.6	71.4	76.3
Salaries and Wages 11	3.9	9.7	6.2	10.5	10.1	10.1	6.2	7.8	7.8	5.1	7.9	7.0	3.5
Taxes Paid 12	1.3	1.4	1.5	1.7	1.6	1.5	2.5	2.3	2.1	2.4	2.5	2.3	1.2
Interest Paid 13	2.3	1.9	1.2	0.8	1.3	0.7	1.4	2.5	1.5	2.0	8.3	5.0	2.1
Depreciation 14	3.1	2.3	1.3	4.6	2.4	2.3	3.7	2.9	4.3	3.1	3.3	2.9	3.1
Amortization and Depletion 15	0.5	1.5	0.1	0.0	0.3	0.0	0.2	1.0	*	1.2	2.4	0.9	0.4
Pensions and Other Deferred Comp. 16	1.9	1.0	*	2.3	0.1	0.3	0.5	0.5	0.6	0.9	0.7	1.5	2.0
Employee Benefits 17	4.1	3.1	0.8	0.1	1.0	1.4	2.3	2.2	2.2	2.7	2.5	3.1	4.3
Advertising 18	0.2	0.2	2.5	2.6	0.2	0.7	0.5	0.2	0.5	0.2	0.3	0.2	0.2
Other Expenses 19	10.1	24.3	34.7	26.5	5.9	17.3	10.5	12.1	13.6	7.7	14.4	6.8	10.1
Officers' Compensation 20	0.5	4.4	2.3	11.5	3.0	2.0	2.9	1.8	1.4	2.1	2.6	0.9	0.3
Operating Margin 21	*	*	*	*	11.6	2.3	1.0	*	6.3	0.5	*	*	*
Operating Margin Before Officers' Comp. 22	*	*	*	*	14.6	4.3	3.8	0.1	7.7	2.6	*	*	*

Selected Average Balance Sheet ($ in Thousands)

Net Receivables 23	22382	0	17	55	718	941	2804	5659	11142	22114	40765	227944	3429096
Inventories 24	12617	0	30	652	685	1593	4788	8940	16767	36929	52139	131524	1770679
Net Property, Plant and Equipment 25	20852	0	29	22	881	819	2982	4701	14856	36680	44025	155349	3237986
Total Assets 26	151298	0	106	775	2833	7411	15701	34307	74607	150876	341254	1322677	23494202
Notes and Loans Payable 27	40033	0	121	321	996	3945	5399	7973	20104	48130	176130	461640	5919731
All Other Liabilities 28	69130	0	6	365	533	867	3832	7944	19953	39833	97526	536878	11060432
Net Worth 29	42134	0	-21	90	1304	2599	6470	18390	34549	62914	67597	324160	6514038

Selected Financial Ratios (Times to 1)

Current Ratio 30	1.2	•	3.3	1.8	3.1	1.0	2.1	2.8	2.5	2.6	1.7	1.2	1.1
Quick Ratio 31	0.7	•	2.7	0.1	2.1	0.4	0.9	1.3	1.2	1.1	0.8	0.8	0.7
Net Sales to Working Capital 32	19.4	•	5.3	2.3	3.8	•	3.5	2.5	3.4	2.9	5.0	9.8	27.6
Coverage Ratio 33	1.8	•	•	•	9.9	4.7	3.0	0.5	6.4	2.1	0.4	1.1	1.9
Total Asset Turnover 34	0.8	•	2.5	1.0	1.8	1.0	1.2	1.0	1.2	1.1	0.8	0.5	0.8
Inventory Turnover 35	7.2	•	5.6	0.7	4.8	2.8	2.6	2.6	3.3	3.2	3.3	3.5	8.1
Receivables Turnover 36	5.8	•	17.9	•	7.3	9.3	7.0	6.4	8.2	7.7	5.9	3.6	5.8
Total Liabilities to Net Worth 37	2.6	•	•	7.6	1.2	1.9	1.4	0.9	1.2	1.4	4.0	3.1	2.6
Current Assets to Working Capital 38	7.4	•	1.4	2.3	1.5	•	1.9	1.6	1.7	1.6	2.4	6.8	9.9
Current Liabilities to Working Capital 39	6.4	•	0.4	1.3	0.5	•	0.9	0.6	0.7	0.6	1.4	5.8	8.9
Working Capital to Net Sales 40	0.1	•	0.2	0.4	0.3	•	0.3	0.4	0.3	0.3	0.2	0.1	0.0
Inventory to Working Capital 41	2.0	•	0.3	2.0	0.5	•	1.0	0.6	0.8	0.7	1.0	2.1	2.6
Total Receipts to Cash Flow 42	10.6	62.2	7.7	13.4	6.3	5.8	9.2	11.8	5.1	12.3	14.6	18.5	10.5
Cost of Goods to Cash Flow 43	8.0	44.0	4.8	7.4	4.0	3.6	6.3	8.0	3.3	8.9	9.5	13.2	8.0
Cash Flow to Total Debt 44	0.1	•	0.3	0.1	0.5	0.3	0.2	0.2	0.4	0.1	0.1	0.0	0.1

Selected Financial Factors (in Percentages)

Debt Ratio 45	72.2	•	•	88.4	54.0	64.9	58.8	46.4	53.7	58.3	80.2	75.5	72.3
Return on Total Assets 46	3.2	•	120.3	•	23.3	3.4	5.0	1.3	10.7	4.4	2.3	2.8	3.2
Return on Equity Before Income Taxes 47	5.0	•	160.6	•	45.5	7.6	8.1	•	19.4	5.5	•	1.3	5.5
Return on Equity After Income Taxes 48	3.0	•	160.6	•	44.7	7.2	6.8	•	17.6	4.7	•	•	3.4
Profit Margin (Before Income Tax) 49	1.8	•	•	•	11.3	2.7	2.9	•	7.8	2.1	•	0.7	1.9
Profit Margin (After Income Tax) 50	1.0	•	•	•	11.1	2.6	2.4	•	7.1	1.8	•	•	1.2

Table II
Corporations with Net Income

AEROSPACE PRODUCT AND PARTS

MONEY AMOUNTS AND SIZE OF ASSETS IN THOUSANDS OF DOLLARS

Item Description for Accounting Period 7/04 Through 6/05		Total	Zero Assets	Under 500	500 to 1,000	1,000 to 5,000	5,000 to 10,000	10,000 to 25,000	25,000 to 50,000	50,000 to 100,000	100,000 to 250,000	250,000 to 500,000	500,000 to 2,500,000	2,500,000 and over
Number of Enterprises	1	418	3	95	59	92	49	56	25	13	7	3	10	5
Revenues ($ in Thousands)														
Net Sales	2	119715666	276643	93601	55869	390426	626004	1096125	999434	1269139	1140370	831805	5943271	106992979
Interest	3	394814	3	31	0	331	41	440	1143	1308	3496	3962	11649	372410
Rents	4	187780	59	0	0	0	0	417	322	1463	4530	5	37160	143824
Royalties	5	1445700	1172	0	0	0	1	0	0	1404	0	0	16719	1426405
Other Portfolio Income	6	969087	723	1436	0	488	134	2011	12327	3055	9287	2946	47403	889279
Other Receipts	7	1319129	35	0	74	-2640	4796	27350	10636	9331	12520	23251	21277	1211495
Total Receipts	8	124032176	278635	95068	55943	388605	630975	1126344	1023862	1285700	1170203	861969	6077479	111037392
Average Total Receipts	9	296728	92878	1001	948	4224	12877	20113	40954	98900	167172	287323	607748	22207478
Operating Costs/Operating Income (%)														
Cost of Operations	10	74.5	68.8	57.5	59.6	48.8	57.4	65.0	64.6	64.0	67.6	63.5	68.1	75.6
Salaries and Wages	11	5.2	6.0	•	•	9.8	10.1	5.4	6.7	6.3	6.4	11.3	7.2	4.9
Taxes Paid	12	1.7	1.0	2.5	1.2	1.8	0.9	2.3	1.9	2.0	2.1	2.8	2.6	1.6
Interest Paid	13	1.8	2.7	1.9	1.0	1.4	0.1	1.0	1.7	0.8	1.4	1.8	4.1	1.7
Depreciation	14	2.0	2.8	0.6	3.3	3.9	1.5	3.5	2.4	3.8	3.0	4.0	3.2	1.8
Amortization and Depletion	15	0.6	2.3	0.4	•	0.5	0.0	0.1	0.4	0.2	0.8	1.3	1.0	0.5
Pensions and Other Deferred Comp.	16	2.8	0.4	•	3.8	0.2	0.4	0.4	0.5	0.6	0.6	0.5	0.6	3.0
Employee Benefits	17	3.5	3.6	2.3	•	1.1	0.5	2.0	1.9	1.9	2.5	2.4	3.5	3.6
Advertising	18	0.3	0.1	0.3	0.6	0.2	0.8	0.3	0.2	0.4	0.1	0.4	0.3	0.3
Other Expenses	19	7.3	10.0	24.5	14.5	5.7	11.4	8.2	9.8	8.3	8.7	10.3	6.3	7.2
Officers' Compensation	20	0.6	0.2	6.6	15.3	4.0	2.2	3.2	2.0	1.2	3.0	1.9	0.9	0.5
Operating Margin	21	•	2.1	3.4	0.7	22.6	14.7	8.6	7.9	10.4	3.7	•	2.2	•
Operating Margin Before Officers' Comp.	22	0.5	2.3	10.0	15.9	26.6	16.9	11.8	9.9	11.6	6.7	1.5	3.1	•

Selected Average Balance Sheet ($ in Thousands)

Net Receivables 23	47836	0	29	36	568	1277	2976	6446	10026	25840	54641	263369	3287827
Inventories 24	22734	0	228	542	466	1757	4244	9587	16387	33672	70451	94640	1455088
Net Property, Plant and Equipment 25	40130	0	19	4	1120	959	3140	4461	14355	36370	44806	137396	2877103
Total Assets 26	360360	0	284	601	3069	5865	15456	34920	74793	162469	351440	1248662	26521884
Notes and Loans Payable 27	90870	0	213	363	747	141	3738	6072	15719	22851	66174	461860	6464766
All Other Liabilities 28	154947	0	52	0	494	978	3344	8435	15191	45143	84332	346971	12007013
Net Worth 29	114544	0	19	238	1828	4746	8374	20412	43883	94475	200933	439831	8050105

Selected Financial Ratios (Times to 1)

Current Ratio 30	1.2	•	1.0	4.8	3.9	4.7	2.4	3.3	2.6	3.4	2.2	1.3	1.2
Quick Ratio 31	0.7	•	0.4	0.3	2.9	1.7	1.1	1.5	1.2	1.6	0.9	0.9	0.7
Net Sales to Working Capital 32	15.6	•	177.9	2.0	3.0	3.5	3.3	2.4	3.6	2.1	3.0	6.3	23.8
Coverage Ratio 33	3.4	2.1	3.6	1.8	17.1	246.6	12.1	7.2	15.1	5.0	2.8	2.1	3.3
Total Asset Turnover 34	0.8	•	3.5	1.6	1.4	2.2	1.3	1.1	1.3	1.0	0.8	0.5	0.8
Inventory Turnover 35	9.4	•	2.5	1.0	4.4	4.2	3.0	2.7	3.8	3.3	2.5	4.3	11.1
Receivables Turnover 36	6.5	•	18.6	•	6.6	12.7	7.7	7.3	9.3	7.3	•	3.5	6.8
Total Liabilities to Net Worth 37	2.1	•	13.9	1.5	0.7	0.2	0.8	0.7	0.7	0.7	0.7	1.8	2.3
Current Assets to Working Capital 38	5.3	•	41.2	1.3	1.3	1.3	1.7	1.4	1.6	1.4	1.8	4.6	7.3
Current Liabilities to Working Capital 39	4.3	•	40.2	0.3	0.3	0.3	0.7	0.4	0.6	0.4	0.8	3.6	6.3
Working Capital to Net Sales 40	0.1	•	0.0	0.5	0.3	0.3	0.3	0.4	0.3	0.5	0.3	0.2	0.0
Inventory to Working Capital 41	1.5	•	26.7	1.1	0.3	0.8	0.8	0.6	0.8	0.5	0.8	1.2	1.9
Total Receipts to Cash Flow 42	12.0	8.6	5.6	7.3	3.8	4.2	5.8	5.6	5.5	7.7	8.9	11.3	12.9
Cost of Goods to Cash Flow 43	9.0	5.9	3.2	4.3	1.8	2.4	3.8	3.6	3.5	5.2	5.7	7.7	9.8
Cash Flow to Total Debt 44	0.1	•	0.7	0.4	0.9	2.7	0.5	0.5	0.6	0.3	0.2	0.1	0.1

Selected Financial Factors (in Percentages)

Debt Ratio 45	68.2	•	93.3	60.4	40.4	19.1	45.8	41.5	41.3	41.9	42.8	64.8	69.6
Return on Total Assets 46	4.9	•	23.9	2.8	32.5	33.9	15.7	13.7	16.1	7.1	4.0	4.1	4.7
Return on Equity Before Income Taxes 47	11.0	•	256.5	3.2	51.3	41.7	26.6	20.2	25.7	9.8	4.5	6.3	10.7
Return on Equity After Income Taxes 48	8.2	•	256.5	2.7	50.6	41.2	25.0	18.4	23.9	8.9	3.7	4.7	7.7
Profit Margin (Before Income Tax) 49	4.4	2.9	5.0	0.8	22.1	15.5	11.4	10.3	11.5	5.7	3.3	4.6	4.0
Profit Margin (After Income Tax) 50	3.3	2.8	5.0	0.7	21.8	15.3	10.7	9.4	10.7	5.2	2.7	3.5	2.9

Table I

Corporations with and without Net Income

SHIP AND BOAT BUILDING

MONEY AMOUNTS AND SIZE OF ASSETS IN THOUSANDS OF DOLLARS

Item Description for Accounting Period 7/04 Through 6/05	Total	Zero Assets	Under 500	500 to 1,000	1,000 to 5,000	5,000 to 10,000	10,000 to 25,000	25,000 to 50,000	50,000 to 100,000	100,000 to 250,000	250,000 to 500,000	500,000 to 2,500,000	2,500,000 and over
Number of Enterprises **1**	3534	386	2519	192	310	29	51	29	8	7	3	0	0
Revenues ($ in Thousands)													
Net Sales **2**	29751243	135615	1405613	152319	2723929	307403	1435346	2026399	1294169	2100148	18170301	0	0
Interest **3**	17840	55	159	6	1589	1252	977	359	324	4884	8236	0	0
Rents **4**	32731	0	0	0	4732	75	150	5	0	842	26928	0	0
Royalties **5**	5888	0	0	0	0	0	105	1426	0	25	4332	0	0
Other Portfolio Income **6**	54073	5420	90	0	1119	8288	2247	7262	226	776	28646	0	0
Other Receipts **7**	417462	375	1	-17	29501	42068	12802	14366	22765	21645	273955	0	0
Total Receipts **8**	30279237	141465	1405863	152308	2760870	359086	1451627	2049817	1317484	2128320	18512398	0	0
Average Total Receipts **9**	8568	366	558	793	8906	12382	28463	70683	164686	304046	6170799	•	•
Operating Costs/Operating Income (%)													
Cost of Operations **10**	76.2	73.3	71.6	33.4	72.5	74.4	78.9	76.6	75.7	70.6	77.9	•	•
Salaries and Wages **11**	3.5	7.3	2.9	18.9	6.5	4.3	3.5	3.7	3.2	6.8	2.5	•	•
Taxes Paid **12**	2.0	1.8	1.5	2.1	2.0	2.5	1.4	1.7	2.0	1.9	2.2	•	•
Interest Paid **13**	0.9	0.6	0.3	0.1	0.6	1.3	1.2	0.7	0.2	2.3	0.9	•	•
Depreciation **14**	1.7	1.8	0.5	0.8	1.8	3.5	2.4	2.4	2.1	2.3	1.6	•	•
Amortization and Depletion **15**	0.9	0.0	0.2	0.0	0.0	0.0	0.1	0.2	0.1	0.1	1.4	•	•
Pensions and Other Deferred Comp. **16**	0.5	0.2	•	•	0.1	1.0	0.3	0.4	0.8	0.3	0.6	•	•
Employee Benefits **17**	2.0	1.8	0.0	2.4	1.3	1.2	1.2	1.0	3.3	1.9	2.4	•	•
Advertising **18**	0.5	1.2	0.6	0.1	1.0	0.4	1.0	1.2	1.0	1.5	0.1	•	•
Other Expenses **19**	7.3	6.9	20.8	8.3	10.7	23.7	7.2	7.1	6.4	12.2	5.1	•	•
Officers' Compensation **20**	1.4	0.4	4.0	4.3	4.2	2.7	1.7	1.4	1.0	1.0	0.8	•	•
Operating Margin **21**	3.0	4.6	•	29.6	•	•	1.1	3.7	4.3	•	4.5	•	•
Operating Margin Before Officers' Comp. **22**	4.4	5.1	1.5	33.9	3.4	•	2.9	5.1	5.2	0.0	5.3	•	•

Selected Average Balance Sheet ($ in Thousands)

Net Receivables 23	709	0	24	162	334	525	2054	5757	6241	20216	611235
Inventories 24	1082	0	8	5	769	4421	3722	7419	20490	29557	711094
Net Property, Plant and Equipment 25	1012	0	27	117	676	1127	4228	11651	22473	54657	709187
Total Assets 26	6165	0	87	528	2973	7285	15979	34963	71032	149008	5630910
Notes and Loans Payable 27	1513	0	94	33	803	4656	7385	9222	13002	22907	1270082
All Other Liabilities 28	1957	0	54	49	1119	1237	6202	12268	18286	29541	1787820
Net Worth 29	2695	0	-61	446	1051	1393	2392	13472	39744	96559	2573008

Selected Financial Ratios (Times to 1)

Current Ratio 30	1.4	•	0.5	5.9	1.5	2.7	1.2	1.5	1.9	2.0	1.3
Quick Ratio 31	0.5	•	0.5	5.9	0.4	0.9	0.5	0.8	0.7	0.9	0.4
Net Sales to Working Capital 32	12.6	•	•	2.6	11.9	3.3	21.6	10.4	8.0	7.6	13.4
Coverage Ratio 33	6.6	15.7	•	318.6	2.0	2.4	2.9	7.9	26.0	1.1	8.8
Total Asset Turnover 34	1.4	•	6.4	1.5	3.0	1.5	1.8	2.0	2.3	1.1	1.1
Inventory Turnover 35	5.9	•	52.2	50.8	8.3	1.8	6.0	7.2	6.0	7.2	6.6
Receivables Turnover 36	11.3	•	22.6	•	30.3	8.4	11.3	13.3	28.6	12.6	•
Total Liabilities to Net Worth 37	1.3	•	•	0.2	1.8	4.2	5.7	1.6	0.8	0.5	1.2
Current Assets to Working Capital 38	3.7	•	•	1.2	2.9	1.6	7.0	2.9	2.1	2.0	4.3
Current Liabilities to Working Capital 39	2.7	•	•	0.2	1.9	0.6	6.0	1.9	1.1	1.0	3.3
Working Capital to Net Sales 40	0.1	•	•	0.4	0.1	0.3	0.0	0.1	0.1	0.1	0.1
Inventory to Working Capital 41	1.4	•	•	0.0	1.4	0.9	3.1	1.0	1.1	0.6	1.6
Total Receipts to Cash Flow 42	9.6	7.0	6.8	3.0	11.8	4.4	13.0	9.6	8.5	9.0	10.0
Cost of Goods to Cash Flow 43	7.3	5.1	4.9	1.0	8.6	3.3	10.3	7.4	6.4	6.4	7.8
Cash Flow to Total Debt 44	0.3	•	0.6	3.2	0.4	0.4	0.2	0.3	0.6	0.6	0.2

Selected Financial Factors (in Percentages)

Debt Ratio 45	56.3	•	170.0	15.5	64.7	80.9	85.0	61.5	44.0	35.2	54.3
Return on Total Assets 46	8.2	•	•	44.6	3.5	4.5	6.2	11.1	14.4	5.3	8.4
Return on Equity Before Income Taxes 47	16.0	•	22.7	52.6	4.9	13.7	27.1	25.3	24.7	1.0	16.4
Return on Equity After Income Taxes 48	11.0	•	22.8	52.6	4.2	13.7	19.5	23.3	22.7	•	10.8
Profit Margin (Before Income Tax) 49	5.1	8.9	•	29.6	0.6	1.8	2.3	4.9	6.1	0.3	6.9
Profit Margin (After Income Tax) 50	3.5	8.7	•	29.6	0.5	1.7	1.8	4.5	5.6	•	4.6

Table II

Corporations with Net Income

SHIP AND BOAT BUILDING

MONEY AMOUNTS AND SIZE OF ASSETS IN THOUSANDS OF DOLLARS

Item Description for Accounting Period 7/04 Through 6/05	Total	Zero Assets	Under 500	500 to 1,000	1,000 to 5,000	5,000 to 10,000	10,000 to 25,000	25,000 to 50,000	50,000 to 100,000	100,000 to 250,000	250,000 to 500,000	500,000 to 2,500,000	2,500,000 and over
Number of Enterprises **1**	1692	0	0	192	200	5	32	22	0	0	0	0	0
Revenues ($ in Thousands)													
Net Sales **2**	26059558	0	0	152319	1848164	180683	1081071	1767304	0	0	0	0	0
Interest **3**	12188	0	0	6	1122	3	872	206	0	0	0	0	0
Rents **4**	31838	0	0	0	4732	0	121	5	0	0	0	0	0
Royalties **5**	5863	0	0	0	0	0	105	1426	0	0	0	0	0
Other Portfolio Income **6**	44833	0	0	0	1094	37	1634	7061	0	0	0	0	0
Other Receipts **7**	338732	0	0	-17	12449	1337	11185	10521	0	0	0	0	0
Total Receipts **8**	26493012	0	0	152308	1867561	182060	1094988	1786523	0	0	0	0	0
Average Total Receipts **9**	15658	•	•	793	9338	36412	34218	81206	•	•	•	•	•
Operating Costs/Operating Income (%)													
Cost of Operations **10**	77.1	•	•	33.4	79.3	74.0	76.5	75.9	•	•	•	•	•
Salaries and Wages **11**	2.9	•	•	18.9	2.5	2.1	3.4	3.1	•	•	•	•	•
Taxes Paid **12**	2.0	•	•	2.1	1.5	1.7	1.3	1.6	•	•	•	•	•
Interest Paid **13**	0.8	•	•	0.1	0.7	0.4	0.9	0.5	•	•	•	•	•
Depreciation **14**	1.7	•	•	0.8	1.7	1.0	2.0	2.1	•	•	•	•	•
Amortization and Depletion **15**	1.0	•	•	0.0	0.0	0.0	0.1	0.0	•	•	•	•	•
Pensions and Other Deferred Comp. **16**	0.5	•	•	•	0.1	1.7	0.3	0.3	•	•	•	•	•
Employee Benefits **17**	2.1	•	•	2.4	1.0	1.5	1.1	0.8	•	•	•	•	•
Advertising **18**	0.4	•	•	0.1	1.5	0.6	1.1	1.2	•	•	•	•	•
Other Expenses **19**	5.8	•	•	8.3	6.6	4.0	6.5	7.4	•	•	•	•	•
Officers' Compensation **20**	1.2	•	•	4.3	4.5	0.9	1.8	1.3	•	•	•	•	•
Operating Margin **21**	4.6	•	•	29.6	0.5	12.2	5.2	5.6	•	•	•	•	•
Operating Margin Before Officers' Comp. **22**	5.9	•	•	33.9	5.1	13.1	6.9	6.9	•	•	•	•	•

Selected Average Balance Sheet ($ in Thousands)

Net Receivables 23	1339	162	198	1658	1864	6149
Inventories 24	2035	5	808	12577	3609	6885
Net Property, Plant and Equipment 25	1817	117	723	1835	4330	12025
Total Assets 26	11915	528	2950	7449	14923	35881
Notes and Loans Payable 27	2674	33	900	2705	4777	7794
All Other Liabilities 28	3772	49	963	1705	4594	12548
Net Worth 29	5470	446	1088	3038	5552	15540

Selected Financial Ratios (Times to 1)

Current Ratio 30	1.4	5.9	1.5	2.4	1.6	1.6
Quick Ratio 31	0.5	5.9	0.2	1.4	0.7	0.8
Net Sales to Working Capital 32	12.2	2.6	12.9	12.1	10.7	10.2
Coverage Ratio 33	9.6	318.6	3.2	34.4	8.2	15.7
Total Asset Turnover 34	1.3	1.5	3.1	4.9	2.3	2.2
Inventory Turnover 35	5.8	50.8	9.1	2.1	7.2	8.9
Receivables Turnover 36	10.8		34.2	5.5	13.6	15.1
Total Liabilities to Net Worth 37	1.2	0.2	1.7	1.5	1.7	1.3
Current Assets to Working Capital 38	3.6	1.2	3.0	1.7	2.8	2.7
Current Liabilities to Working Capital 39	2.6	0.2	2.0	0.7	1.8	1.7
Working Capital to Net Sales 40	0.1	0.4	0.1	0.1	0.1	0.1
Inventory to Working Capital 41	1.3	0.0	1.4	0.6	1.2	1.0
Total Receipts to Cash Flow 42	9.5	3.0	16.7	6.3	8.9	8.0
Cost of Goods to Cash Flow 43	7.4	1.0	13.2	4.7	6.8	6.1
Cash Flow to Total Debt 44	0.3	3.2	0.3	1.3	0.4	0.5

Selected Financial Factors (in Percentages)

Debt Ratio 45	54.1	15.5	63.1	59.2	62.8	56.7
Return on Total Assets 46	9.6	44.6	7.1	64.8	16.7	16.0
Return on Equity Before Income Taxes 47	18.8	52.6	13.4	154.1	39.5	34.6
Return on Equity After Income Taxes 48	13.7	52.6	12.3	154.1	34.2	32.4
Profit Margin (Before Income Tax) 49	6.7	29.6	1.6	13.0	6.5	6.7
Profit Margin (After Income Tax) 50	4.9	29.6	1.5	13.0	5.6	6.3

Table I

Corporations with and without Net Income

OTHER TRANSPORTATION EQUIPMENT AND RAILROAD ROLLING STOCK

MONEY AMOUNTS AND SIZE OF ASSETS IN THOUSANDS OF DOLLARS

Item Description for Accounting Period 7/04 Through 6/05	Total	Zero Assets	Under 500	500 to 1,000	1,000 to 5,000	5,000 to 10,000	10,000 to 25,000	25,000 to 50,000	50,000 to 100,000	100,000 to 250,000	250,000 to 500,000	500,000 to 2,500,000	2,500,000 and over
Number of Enterprises 1	1509	423	497	191	229	79	42	16	9	9	7	7	0
Revenues ($ in Thousands)													
Net Sales 2	28445533	153488	39351	187156	1380662	912526	1439688	1239172	672439	1842993	4465725	16112332	0
Interest 3	840463	731	3	5	514	154	223	387	606	4662	13900	819277	0
Rents 4	180646	502	0	0	0	3223	43	115	57	94	2565	174047	0
Royalties 5	55791	0	0	0	0	318	0	218	4762	0	100	50393	0
Other Portfolio Income 6	257891	14307	1141	1844	661	29	2676	1223	418	23329	50936	161323	0
Other Receipts 7	593995	1284	19115	111	17575	1141	7656	5299	1672	40447	45142	454560	0
Total Receipts 8	30374319	170312	59610	189116	1399412	917391	1450286	1246414	679954	1911525	4578368	17771932	0
Average Total Receipts 9	20129	403	120	990	6111	11613	34531	77901	75550	212392	654053	2538847	•
Operating Costs/Operating Income (%)													
Cost of Operations 10	72.8	85.2	86.8	86.1	74.2	69.8	76.2	79.7	78.9	78.5	82.8	68.0	•
Salaries and Wages 11	6.2	6.5	6.8	7.6	7.6	9.1	5.4	5.4	6.3	5.1	3.5	6.9	•
Taxes Paid 12	1.5	0.7	1.8	3.8	3.2	1.7	1.6	1.9	1.5	1.2	0.7	1.5	•
Interest Paid 13	2.6	1.5	4.3	1.1	0.5	0.5	0.6	0.8	1.5	1.9	1.5	3.6	•
Depreciation 14	3.5	0.6	2.7	6.2	3.3	2.8	2.1	1.7	1.5	2.2	2.5	4.3	•
Amortization and Depletion 15	0.5	0.5	0.2	•	0.1	0.3	0.1	0.1	0.7	0.8	0.6	0.6	•
Pensions and Other Deferred Comp. 16	0.4	0.0	1.3	0.0	0.3	0.1	0.2	0.5	0.3	0.3	0.2	0.6	•
Employee Benefits 17	2.0	0.1	3.2	0.3	3.4	1.9	1.5	1.4	1.1	1.8	1.3	2.3	•
Advertising 18	0.9	0.1	5.7	1.4	0.3	0.2	0.6	0.4	0.9	0.4	1.2	0.9	•
Other Expenses 19	10.5	5.0	102.6	40.1	9.3	8.1	6.9	4.6	3.0	7.6	6.6	12.8	•
Officers' Compensation 20	0.7	1.5	9.8	11.6	2.1	1.1	1.4	1.9	1.1	1.0	0.2	0.3	•
Operating Margin 21	•	•	•	•	•	4.4	3.4	1.4	3.2	1.3	•	•	•
Operating Margin Before Officers' Comp. 22	•	0.0	•	•	•	5.5	4.8	3.4	4.2	0.1	•	•	•

Selected Average Balance Sheet ($ in Thousands)

Net Receivables **23**	4766	0	0	109	577	1125	4468	8618	12194	37176	57337	825485
Inventories **24**	2146	0	5	17	547	2137	4900	9433	19881	28124	68166	233410
Net Property, Plant and Equipment **25**	3310	0	41	174	621	1424	3518	8368	6282	22643	95954	496116
Total Assets **26**	16979	0	63	713	2750	5668	16428	38805	71952	154878	382393	2620912
Notes and Loans Payable **27**	3707	0	83	477	1390	1066	4231	11203	22018	30856	98201	505631
All Other Liabilities **28**	8326	0	25	39	5873	2237	5354	12322	31644	70284	148757	1234582
Net Worth **29**	4945	0	-44	197	-4513	2364	6843	15281	18289	53737	135436	880699

Selected Financial Ratios (Times to 1)

Current Ratio **30**	1.8	•	0.9	3.5	0.9	1.7	1.8	1.4	1.4	1.6	1.3	1.9
Quick Ratio **31**	1.0	•	0.4	1.6	0.5	0.5	0.9	0.6	0.6	0.8	0.6	1.2
Net Sales to Working Capital **32**	4.3	•	•	2.8	•	7.1	7.0	12.1	6.0	5.7	15.6	2.9
Coverage Ratio **33**	3.0	7.3	•	•	•	10.0	8.5	3.5	3.9	2.5	1.9	3.3
Total Asset Turnover **34**	1.1	•	1.2	1.4	2.2	2.0	2.1	2.0	1.0	1.3	1.7	0.9
Inventory Turnover **35**	6.4	•	13.7	49.4	8.2	3.8	5.3	6.5	3.0	5.7	7.8	6.7
Receivables Turnover **36**	5.2	•	133.4	•	11.1	10.0	8.9	9.4	5.0	7.1	11.4	3.9
Total Liabilities to Net Worth **37**	2.4	•	•	2.6	•	1.4	1.4	1.5	2.9	1.9	1.8	2.0
Current Assets to Working Capital **38**	2.3	•	•	1.4	•	2.5	2.3	3.4	3.5	2.6	4.1	2.1
Current Liabilities to Working Capital **39**	1.3	•	•	0.4	•	1.5	1.3	2.4	2.5	1.6	3.1	1.1
Working Capital to Net Sales **40**	0.2	•	•	0.4	•	0.1	0.1	0.1	0.2	0.2	0.1	0.3
Inventory to Working Capital **41**	0.6	•	•	0.0	•	1.6	1.0	1.7	1.5	0.8	2.1	0.4
Total Receipts to Cash Flow **42**	7.5	22.5	7.6	•	27.7	9.4	10.3	18.5	16.6	12.8	15.5	5.4
Cost of Goods to Cash Flow **43**	5.4	19.1	6.6	•	20.6	6.5	7.9	14.7	13.1	10.0	12.9	3.7
Cash Flow to Total Debt **44**	0.2	•	0.1	•	0.0	0.4	0.3	0.2	0.1	0.2	0.2	0.2

Selected Financial Factors (in Percentages)

Debt Ratio **45**	70.9	•	169.4	72.3	264.1	58.3	60.6	74.6	65.3	64.6		66.4
Return on Total Assets **46**	8.6	•	•	•	•	11.2	9.9	5.7	5.9	6.3	4.6	10.6
Return on Equity Before Income Taxes **47**	19.6	•	132.7	•	4.0	24.1	20.9	10.3	17.3	10.8	6.1	22.0
Return on Equity After Income Taxes **48**	12.4	•	132.7	•	4.1	24.0	20.3	7.6	9.7	7.4	4.3	14.2
Profit Margin (Before Income Tax) **49**	5.1	9.5	•	•	•	4.9	4.2	2.0	4.2	2.8	1.3	8.4
Profit Margin (After Income Tax) **50**	3.3	8.5	•	•	•	4.9	4.0	1.5	2.4	1.9	0.9	5.4

159

Table II
Corporations with Net Income

OTHER TRANSPORTATION EQUIPMENT AND RAILROAD ROLLING STOCK

MONEY AMOUNTS AND SIZE OF ASSETS IN THOUSANDS OF DOLLARS

Item Description for Accounting Period 7/04 Through 6/05	Total	Zero Assets	Under 500	500 to 1,000	1,000 to 5,000	5,000 to 10,000	10,000 to 25,000	25,000 to 50,000	50,000 to 100,000	100,000 to 250,000	250,000 to 500,000	500,000 to 2,500,000	2,500,000 and over
Number of Enterprises **1**	227	0	0	0	104	56	33	11	0	0	0	4	0

Revenues ($ in Thousands)

Item Description for Accounting Period 7/04 Through 6/05	Total	Zero Assets	Under 500	500 to 1,000	1,000 to 5,000	5,000 to 10,000	10,000 to 25,000	25,000 to 50,000	50,000 to 100,000	100,000 to 250,000	250,000 to 500,000	500,000 to 2,500,000	2,500,000 and over
Net Sales **2**	21367504	0	0	0	1155150	655369	1350068	881311	0	0	0	1273238	0
Interest **3**	802415	0	0	0	160	115	191	336	0	0	0	787188	0
Rents **4**	179841	0	0	0	0	3101	43	114	0	0	0	173365	0
Royalties **5**	54713	0	0	0	0	318	0	218	0	0	0	49415	0
Other Portfolio Income **6**	231778	0	0	0	661	29	2655	1218	0	0	0	159630	0
Other Receipts **7**	533465	0	0	0	10268	709	7449	1954	0	0	0	452534	0
Total Receipts **8**	23169716	0	0	0	1166239	659641	1360406	885151	0	0	0	14360370	0
Average Total Receipts **9**	102069	•	•	•	11214	11779	41224	80468	•	•	•	3590092	•

Operating Costs/Operating Income (%)

Item Description for Accounting Period 7/04 Through 6/05	Total	Zero Assets	Under 500	500 to 1,000	1,000 to 5,000	5,000 to 10,000	10,000 to 25,000	25,000 to 50,000	50,000 to 100,000	100,000 to 250,000	250,000 to 500,000	500,000 to 2,500,000	2,500,000 and over
Cost of Operations **10**	70.3	•	•	•	69.4	63.7	75.8	80.7	•	•	•	66.8	•
Salaries and Wages **11**	6.3	•	•	•	9.1	11.7	5.3	5.1	•	•	•	6.5	•
Taxes Paid **12**	1.6	•	•	•	3.2	1.8	1.6	1.8	•	•	•	1.5	•
Interest Paid **13**	2.8	•	•	•	0.3	0.5	0.5	0.5	•	•	•	3.9	•
Depreciation **14**	3.4	•	•	•	1.2	3.3	1.9	1.8	•	•	•	4.0	•
Amortization and Depletion **15**	0.5	•	•	•	0.0	0.0	0.1	0.1	•	•	•	0.5	•
Pensions and Other Deferred Comp. **16**	0.5	•	•	•	0.3	0.1	0.2	0.6	•	•	•	0.6	•
Employee Benefits **17**	2.2	•	•	•	3.8	2.2	1.5	1.5	•	•	•	2.4	•
Advertising **18**	0.9	•	•	•	0.3	0.3	0.6	0.3	•	•	•	1.2	•
Other Expenses **19**	10.7	•	•	•	9.0	7.9	6.6	2.7	•	•	•	13.9	•
Officers' Compensation **20**	0.6	•	•	•	2.5	1.2	1.4	1.8	•	•	•	0.3	•
Operating Margin **21**	0.3	•	•	•	0.9	7.4	4.5	3.1	•	•	•	•	•
Operating Margin Before Officers' Comp. **22**	0.9	•	•	•	3.4	8.6	5.9	5.0	•	•	•	•	•

Selected Average Balance Sheet ($ in Thousands)

Net Receivables 23	26031	864	913	4264	9302	1235370
Inventories 24	9975	637	2503	5150	9575	477634
Net Property, Plant and Equipment 25	15672	449	1435	3951	9349	625880
Total Assets 26	85067	3247	5699	16780	39068	3647387
Notes and Loans Payable 27	14691	457	477	3848	8161	554815
All Other Liabilities 28	38456	1103	2207	5230	12790	1774895
Net Worth 29	31921	1686	3015	7701	18118	1317677

Selected Financial Ratios (Times to 1)

Current Ratio 30	2.1	2.1	1.7	1.9	1.6	2.2
Quick Ratio 31	1.2	0.8	0.5	0.9	0.8	1.3
Net Sales to Working Capital 32	3.2	8.5	6.5	7.5	9.6	2.3
Coverage Ratio 33	4.1	6.6	17.2	11.1	8.5	3.9
Total Asset Turnover 34	1.1	3.4	2.1	2.4	2.1	0.9
Inventory Turnover 35	6.6	12.1	3.0	6.0	6.8	4.5
Receivables Turnover 36	5.0	16.8	9.7	10.7	9.4	
Total Liabilities to Net Worth 37	1.7	0.9	0.9	1.2	1.2	1.8
Current Assets to Working Capital 38	1.9	1.9	2.4	2.1	2.7	1.8
Current Liabilities to Working Capital 39	0.9	0.9	1.4	1.1	1.7	0.8
Working Capital to Net Sales 40	0.3	0.1	0.2	0.1	0.1	0.4
Inventory to Working Capital 41	0.5	0.6	1.7	1.1	1.3	0.4
Total Receipts to Cash Flow 42	5.9	12.5	7.4	9.5	18.0	4.5
Cost of Goods to Cash Flow 43	4.1	8.7	4.7	7.2	14.6	3.0
Cash Flow to Total Debt 44	0.3	0.6	0.6	0.5	0.2	0.3

Selected Financial Factors (in Percentages)

Debt Ratio 45	62.5	48.1	47.1	54.1	53.6	63.9
Return on Total Assets 46	12.8	7.5	17.6	14.2	8.3	13.2
Return on Equity Before Income Taxes 47	25.7	12.3	31.4	28.1	15.7	27.1
Return on Equity After Income Taxes 48	18.3	11.6	31.3	27.4	12.4	18.0
Profit Margin (Before Income Tax) 49	8.7	1.9	8.1	5.3	3.6	11.2
Profit Margin (After Income Tax) 50	6.2	1.8	8.1	5.2	2.8	7.5

Table I

Corporations with and without Net Income

FURNITURE AND RELATED PRODUCT MANUFACTURING

MONEY AMOUNTS AND SIZE OF ASSETS IN THOUSANDS OF DOLLARS

Item Description for Accounting Period 7/04 Through 6/05	Total	Zero Assets	Under 500	500 to 1,000	1,000 to 5,000	5,000 to 10,000	10,000 to 25,000	25,000 to 50,000	50,000 to 100,000	100,000 to 250,000	250,000 to 500,000	500,000 to 2,500,000	2,500,000 and over
Number of Enterprises **1**	12376	675	8529	1537	1089	255	174	53	25	20	6	12	0

Revenues ($ in Thousands)

	Total	Zero Assets	Under 500	500 to 1,000	1,000 to 5,000	5,000 to 10,000	10,000 to 25,000	25,000 to 50,000	50,000 to 100,000	100,000 to 250,000	250,000 to 500,000	500,000 to 2,500,000	2,500,000 and over
Net Sales **2**	59896754	149671	4394057	2904015	7293462	4885799	5835679	3272458	3500236	4916617	2741634	20003125	0
Interest **3**	98258	21	304	277	2972	3432	2086	2050	2894	16018	26895	41311	0
Rents **4**	46176	24	287	0	545	745	2911	2114	669	2993	7140	28749	0
Royalties **5**	60912	0	0	0	0	4664	555	93	667	4296	4103	46535	0
Other Portfolio Income **6**	220322	2905	3976	0	21704	39446	32395	22037	2659	7095	45732	42374	0
Other Receipts **7**	890505	1021	47107	1374	53310	28217	44777	53193	13212	25886	23487	598916	0
Total Receipts **8**	61212927	153642	4445731	2905666	7371993	4962303	5918403	3351945	3520337	4972905	2848991	20761010	0
Average Total Receipts **9**	4946	228	521	1890	6770	19460	34014	63244	140813	248645	474832	1730084	•

Operating Costs/Operating Income (%)

	Total	Zero Assets	Under 500	500 to 1,000	1,000 to 5,000	5,000 to 10,000	10,000 to 25,000	25,000 to 50,000	50,000 to 100,000	100,000 to 250,000	250,000 to 500,000	500,000 to 2,500,000	2,500,000 and over
Cost of Operations **10**	67.3	59.4	51.4	63.8	67.3	67.1	72.0	73.1	73.8	68.7	67.6	67.7	•
Salaries and Wages **11**	8.0	15.2	11.0	6.5	8.5	10.5	7.2	6.1	4.9	6.3	6.2	8.6	•
Taxes Paid **12**	2.4	2.7	3.9	2.7	2.5	2.3	2.2	2.0	1.9	1.7	1.9	2.4	•
Interest Paid **13**	1.1	4.4	0.8	1.2	0.8	0.9	0.8	0.6	1.1	1.6	2.6	1.3	•
Depreciation **14**	2.3	1.0	2.1	1.7	2.8	1.7	1.9	2.0	2.2	2.0	3.0	2.5	•
Amortization and Depletion **15**	0.3	5.6	0.1	0.1	0.0	0.1	0.1	0.1	0.4	0.3	0.3	0.5	•
Pensions and Other Deferred Comp. **16**	0.5	0.3	0.2	0.2	0.4	0.5	0.3	0.5	0.4	0.5	0.5	0.6	•
Employee Benefits **17**	1.7	1.0	0.9	1.6	0.9	0.8	1.8	2.2	1.6	1.7	3.1	2.0	•
Advertising **18**	1.6	0.7	0.4	0.2	1.2	1.0	1.2	1.1	1.4	2.9	2.6	2.3	•
Other Expenses **19**	11.6	22.1	20.1	13.8	12.5	9.2	9.3	9.0	8.9	11.4	13.0	10.9	•
Officers' Compensation **20**	2.3	1.3	8.6	4.2	3.5	3.5	2.0	1.6	1.1	1.1	1.0	0.9	•
Operating Margin **21**	0.9	•	0.6	4.1	•	2.5	1.2	1.5	2.4	1.8	•	0.4	•
Operating Margin Before Officers' Comp. **22**	3.2	•	9.2	8.3	3.1	6.0	3.2	3.1	3.5	3.0	1.3	1.3	•

Selected Average Balance Sheet ($ in Thousands)

Net Receivables 23	534	0	36	281	687	2090	3992	7677	17466	27111	51747	18248
Inventories 24	499	0	23	132	736	2239	4001	7974	19158	31814	56911	152142
Net Property, Plant and Equipment 25	600	0	43	133	570	1570	4057	8629	18409	33604	99230	244608
Total Assets 26	2822	0	121	660	2404	7624	15428	34763	73140	150784	345180	1406650
Notes and Loans Payable 27	884	0	69	353	993	2197	4777	8160	22245	40331	131596	396586
All Other Liabilities 28	747	0	38	167	747	2265	4125	8537	16276	35885	34031	397593
Net Worth 29	1191	0	14	140	665	3162	6526	18066	34620	74569	179553	612471

Selected Financial Ratios (Times to 1)

Current Ratio 30	1.7	•	1.5	1.8	1.7	2.0	1.8	2.2	2.3	2.7	1.3	1.4
Quick Ratio 31	0.8	•	1.0	1.3	0.9	1.0	1.0	1.1	1.1	1.4	0.7	0.6
Net Sales to Working Capital 32	8.3	•	21.1	8.4	9.4	7.0	7.3	5.3	6.0	4.8	16.0	10.2
Coverage Ratio 33	3.7	•	3.3	4.4	1.8	5.7	4.4	7.1	3.7	2.8	1.9	4.4
Total Asset Turnover 34	1.7	•	4.3	2.9	2.8	2.5	2.2	1.8	1.9	1.6	1.3	1.2
Inventory Turnover 35	6.5	•	11.6	9.1	6.1	5.7	6.0	5.7	5.4	5.3	5.4	7.4
Receivables Turnover 36	9.1	•	12.6	9.3	9.7	9.4	8.6	8.8	7.8	9.4	7.2	9.0
Total Liabilities to Net Worth 37	1.4	•	7.6	3.7	2.6	1.4	1.4	0.9	1.1	1.0	0.9	1.3
Current Assets to Working Capital 38	2.5	•	2.9	2.3	2.4	2.0	2.2	1.8	1.8	1.6	4.2	3.4
Current Liabilities to Working Capital 39	1.5	•	1.9	1.3	1.4	1.0	1.2	0.8	0.8	0.6	3.2	2.4
Working Capital to Net Sales 40	0.1	•	0.0	0.1	0.1	0.1	0.1	0.2	0.2	0.2	0.1	0.1
Inventory to Working Capital 41	0.9	•	0.9	0.6	1.0	0.9	0.9	0.8	0.8	0.7	1.6	0.9
Total Receipts to Cash Flow 42	8.4	21.3	5.8	8.4	11.0	10.4	9.2	9.5	8.1	7.9	7.5	•
Cost of Goods to Cash Flow 43	5.6	12.6	3.0	5.3	7.4	6.7	7.5	6.7	7.0	5.6	5.3	5.1
Cash Flow to Total Debt 44	0.4	•	0.4	0.4	0.4	0.4	0.4	0.4	0.4	0.4	0.4	0.3

Selected Financial Factors (in Percentages)

Debt Ratio 45	57.8	•	88.4	78.8	72.4	58.5	57.7	48.0	52.7	50.5	48.0	56.5
Return on Total Assets 46	7.3	•	11.0	15.3	3.9	12.4	7.4	8.1	7.7	7.5	6.7	6.6
Return on Equity Before Income Taxes 47	12.8	•	66.0	55.6	6.4	24.6	13.4	13.4	11.8	9.8	6.3	11.6
Return on Equity After Income Taxes 48	9.9	•	64.6	55.4	4.8	23.3	11.8	11.5	9.8	6.7	2.0	8.2
Profit Margin (Before Income Tax) 49	3.1	•	1.8	4.1	0.6	4.1	2.6	3.9	2.9	3.0	2.5	4.3
Profit Margin (After Income Tax) 50	2.4	•	1.8	4.1	0.5	3.8	2.3	3.4	2.4	2.0	0.8	3.0

Table II

Corporations with Net Income

FURNITURE AND RELATED PRODUCT MANUFACTURING

MONEY AMOUNTS AND SIZE OF ASSETS IN THOUSANDS OF DOLLARS

Item Description for Accounting Period 7/04 Through 6/05	Total	Zero Assets	Under 500	500 to 1,000	1,000 to 5,000	5,000 to 10,000	10,000 to 25,000	25,000 to 50,000	50,000 to 100,000	100,000 to 250,000	250,000 to 500,000	500,000 to 2,500,000	2,500,000 and over
Number of Enterprises 1	8509	401	6011	1063	579	0	126	46	16	14	0	9	0
Revenues ($ in Thousands)													
Net Sales 2	46825063	40290	3349105	1859715	4921384	0	4400362	2826285	2483832	3818952	0	16465800	0
Interest 3	64063	0	247	31	2800	0	1557	2026	2118	2901	0	29443	0
Rents 4	19880	0	287	0	545	0	2428	2114	666	418	0	5859	0
Royalties 5	23954	0	0	0	0	0	438	93	240	60	0	19020	0
Other Portfolio Income 6	173581	0	1174	0	21269	0	30212	20242	631	3868	0	37800	0
Other Receipts 7	517172	0	46824	1098	35592	0	29641	49544	10148	9183	0	309628	0
Total Receipts 8	47623713	40290	3397637	1860844	4981590	0	4464638	2900304	2497635	3835382	0	16867550	0
Average Total Receipts 9	5597	100	565	1751	8604	•	35434	63050	156102	273956	•	1874172	•
Operating Costs/Operating Income (%)													
Cost of Operations 10	66.0	49.1	50.4	60.3	65.3	•	70.3	72.5	72.4	66.7	•	66.9	•
Salaries and Wages 11	7.6	•	8.5	5.8	7.6	•	7.1	6.1	4.4	6.1	•	8.0	•
Taxes Paid 12	2.3	0.1	3.7	2.9	2.4	•	2.1	2.1	1.9	1.7	•	2.3	•
Interest Paid 13	0.8	•	0.8	1.2	0.4	•	0.7	0.6	0.9	0.6	•	1.0	•
Depreciation 14	2.1	•	2.2	1.5	2.5	•	1.8	2.1	2.0	2.0	•	2.2	•
Amortization and Depletion 15	0.3	•	0.1	0.1	0.0	•	0.1	0.1	0.1	0.2	•	0.6	•
Pensions and Other Deferred Comp. 16	0.4	•	0.2	0.2	0.6	•	0.4	0.5	0.4	0.4	•	0.5	•
Employee Benefits 17	1.6	•	0.7	1.8	1.2	•	1.6	2.0	1.5	2.0	•	1.8	•
Advertising 18	1.5	0.1	0.4	0.2	1.0	•	1.3	1.1	1.3	3.1	•	1.7	•
Other Expenses 19	11.3	33.7	21.8	14.4	11.7	•	8.9	9.0	8.5	9.9	•	11.1	•
Officers' Compensation 20	2.4	4.0	9.0	4.6	4.4	•	2.0	1.6	1.3	1.3	•	0.8	•
Operating Margin 21	3.6	13.0	2.2	7.3	2.8	•	3.6	2.5	5.2	6.1	•	3.1	•
Operating Margin Before Officers' Comp. 22	6.0	17.0	11.3	11.8	7.2	•	5.6	4.0	6.6	7.3	•	3.9	•

Selected Average Balance Sheet ($ in Thousands)

Net Receivables 23	568	0	39	197	852	•	4176	7731	17420	30569	•	175948
Inventories 24	533	0	15	159	747	•	3961	7556	20281	34742	•	181951
Net Property, Plant and Equipment 25	638	0	41	140	556	•	4110	8825	21157	36184	•	240082
Total Assets 26	2999	0	129	639	2618	•	15245	35021	75179	159037	•	1389433
Notes and Loans Payable 27	766	0	67	295	801	•	4464	7549	19414	24928	•	349218
All Other Liabilities 28	754	0	39	116	897	•	3817	8202	14882	30575	•	360119
Net Worth 29	1480	0	23	229	921	•	6964	19270	40883	103535	•	680096

Selected Financial Ratios (Times to 1)

Current Ratio 30	1.9	•	1.5	2.1	2.0	•	1.9	2.3	2.4	3.2	•	1.5
Quick Ratio 31	1.0	•	1.1	1.3	1.2	•	1.1	1.1	1.1	1.7	•	0.8
Net Sales to Working Capital 32	8.0	•	20.8	7.2	9.2	•	7.1	5.1	6.5	4.2	•	10.4
Coverage Ratio 33	7.9	•	5.8	7.3	11.7	•	8.3	9.8	7.7	11.2	•	6.8
Total Asset Turnover 34	1.8	•	4.3	2.7	3.2	•	2.3	1.8	2.1	1.7	•	1.3
Inventory Turnover 35	6.8	•	18.5	6.6	7.4	•	6.2	5.9	5.5	5.2	•	6.7
Receivables Turnover 36	9.7	•	15.4	11.0	10.9	•	8.5	9.2	7.9	9.3	•	9.3
Total Liabilities to Net Worth 37	1.0	•	4.6	1.8	1.8	•	1.2	0.8	0.8	0.5	•	1.0
Current Assets to Working Capital 38	2.2	•	2.8	2.0	2.0	•	2.1	1.8	1.7	1.4	•	2.9
Current Liabilities to Working Capital 39	1.2	•	1.8	1.0	1.0	•	1.1	0.8	0.7	0.4	•	1.9
Working Capital to Net Sales 40	0.1	•	0.0	0.1	0.1	•	0.1	0.2	0.2	0.2	•	0.1
Inventory to Working Capital 41	0.8	•	0.7	0.7	0.7	•	0.8	0.8	0.8	0.6	•	1.0
Total Receipts to Cash Flow 42	7.2	3.0	4.8	6.5	8.8	•	8.6	8.3	7.7	6.9	•	6.8
Cost of Goods to Cash Flow 43	4.8	1.5	2.4	3.9	5.8	•	6.1	6.1	5.6	4.6	•	4.5
Cash Flow to Total Debt 44	0.5	•	1.1	0.7	0.6	•	0.5	0.5	0.6	0.7	•	0.4

Selected Financial Factors (in Percentages)

Debt Ratio 45	50.7	•	82.0	64.2	64.8	•	54.3	45.0	45.6	34.9	•	51.1
Return on Total Assets 46	11.2	•	19.3	23.2	14.4	•	13.1	10.0	13.7	12.2	•	8.6
Return on Equity Before Income Taxes 47	19.9	•	88.6	56.0	37.5	•	25.3	16.3	21.9	17.1	•	15.0
Return on Equity After Income Taxes 48	16.5	•	87.4	55.8	35.2	•	23.2	14.2	19.3	13.8	•	10.9
Profit Margin (Before Income Tax) 49	5.3	13.0	3.7	7.3	4.1	•	5.0	5.1	5.8	6.5	•	5.6
Profit Margin (After Income Tax) 50	4.4	13.0	3.6	7.3	3.8	•	4.6	4.5	5.1	5.2	•	4.1

Table I

Corporations with and without Net Income

MEDICAL EQUIPMENT AND SUPPLIES

MONEY AMOUNTS AND SIZE OF ASSETS IN THOUSANDS OF DOLLARS

Item Description for Accounting Period 7/04 Through 6/05	Total	Zero Assets	Under 500	500 to 1,000	1,000 to 5,000	5,000 to 10,000	10,000 to 25,000	25,000 to 50,000	50,000 to 100,000	100,000 to 250,000	250,000 to 500,000	500,000 to 2,500,000	2,500,000 and over
Number of Enterprises **1**	8983	1062	5742	377	1213	139	191	84	62	46	20	35	11
Revenues ($ in Thousands)													
Net Sales **2**	91337731	1619746	1910301	607796	4990543	1656592	3600492	3701072	3708441	6693117	5183141	22975915	34690575
Interest **3**	1308894	51995	6437	354	3693	4679	11289	12846	18082	26291	39970	196919	936340
Rents **4**	55215	247	0	1	185	101	110	746	7032	12729	10001	18580	5482
Royalties **5**	1823962	0	0	0	423	4520	4447	12222	5769	11647	27243	125105	1632586
Other Portfolio Income **6**	785380	14727	13656	2696	57907	12025	21003	14453	14852	41332	20841	375320	196569
Other Receipts **7**	2964951	15993	34402	181	35598	25671	46786	27371	310721	90775	54815	390198	1932439
Total Receipts **8**	98276133	1702708	1964796	611028	5088349	1703588	3684127	3768710	4064897	6875891	5336011	24082037	39393991
Average Total Receipts **9**	10940	1603	342	1621	4195	12256	19289	44866	65563	149476	266801	688058	3581272
Operating Costs/Operating Income (%)													
Cost of Operations **10**	49.4	51.3	31.3	61.0	61.5	50.5	50.3	54.4	45.7	46.0	46.9	43.8	52.7
Salaries and Wages **11**	16.2	15.5	15.7	12.5	11.8	20.8	18.2	14.7	20.6	15.9	14.0	15.2	17.3
Taxes Paid **12**	1.9	1.6	4.0	2.9	3.8	2.4	2.5	2.0	2.5	1.8	1.8	1.9	1.4
Interest Paid **13**	3.1	7.6	1.2	2.1	1.0	1.2	1.2	1.1	1.1	2.4	2.3	2.3	4.7
Depreciation **14**	3.4	3.7	2.9	2.0	1.7	1.8	3.6	2.7	4.1	2.8	4.1	3.6	3.6
Amortization and Depletion **15**	1.5	3.9	0.1	0.2	0.5	0.9	0.8	0.9	0.9	1.1	2.1	1.3	1.9
Pensions and Other Deferred Comp. **16**	0.8	0.4	0.4	0.0	0.3	0.3	0.6	0.4	0.8	0.4	0.9	0.7	1.1
Employee Benefits **17**	2.8	4.0	1.3	1.3	1.2	1.5	2.5	2.3	2.6	2.4	2.0	2.3	3.7
Advertising **18**	1.2	1.2	0.6	0.9	1.4	1.6	1.2	2.2	2.6	2.2	1.0	1.0	0.9
Other Expenses **19**	19.7	20.9	22.8	20.8	17.0	23.2	20.9	17.5	24.6	18.0	18.8	22.4	18.0
Officers' Compensation **20**	2.2	1.3	15.7	7.3	5.2	2.9	4.1	2.6	3.4	1.7	1.2	2.1	0.8
Operating Margin **21**	•	4.2	•	•	•	•	•	•	•	5.5	4.8	3.3	•
Operating Margin Before Officers' Comp. **22**	0.1	19.9	•	•	•	•	1.7	•	•	7.2	6.0	5.5	•

Selected Average Balance Sheet ($ in Thousands)

Net Receivables 23	2513	0	15	185	570	1768	3080	7027	11891	35409	55417	146698	1063392
Inventories 24	1249	0	8	214	392	1880	2967	6053	6741	17351	42076	75584	416013
Net Property, Plant and Equipment 25	1667	0	27	122	263	840	2627	4867	10875	21235	43947	123794	596712
Total Assets 26	13932	0	71	646	1889	7253	16098	33946	71958	173669	378150	923704	5721618
Notes and Loans Payable 27	3758	0	31	326	582	1614	3604	7148	7195	43840	56433	270677	1652147
All Other Liabilities 28	3920	0	23	260	498	1828	3942	10122	14764	34564	74492	193969	1976130
Net Worth 29	6255	0	17	59	809	3811	8552	16675	49999	95265	247226	459058	2093341

Selected Financial Ratios (Times to 1)

Current Ratio 30	1.6	•	1.0	1.3	2.2	2.6	2.3	2.3	2.9	1.9	2.4	1.4	1.5
Quick Ratio 31	1.0	•	0.7	0.7	1.4	1.4	1.5	1.3	1.6	1.2	1.4	0.9	0.9
Net Sales to Working Capital 32	4.7	•	4824.0	15.9	5.4	3.6	3.1	3.8	2.1	3.6	3.1	6.7	5.0
Coverage Ratio 33	3.2	0.2	7.1	•	•	•	1.9	1.9	1.9	4.6	4.5	4.7	3.0
Total Asset Turnover 34	0.7	•	4.7	2.5	2.2	1.6	1.2	1.3	0.8	0.8	0.7	0.7	0.6
Inventory Turnover 35	4.0	•	13.6	4.6	6.5	3.2	3.2	4.0	4.1	3.9	2.9	3.8	4.0
Receivables Turnover 36	4.1	•	34.3	6.4	7.0	6.0	6.1	6.2	5.4	4.5	3.6	5.2	2.9
Total Liabilities to Net Worth 37	1.2	•	3.2	9.9	1.3	0.9	0.9	1.0	0.4	0.8	0.5	1.0	1.7
Current Assets to Working Capital 38	2.5	•	444.7	4.5	1.9	1.6	1.8	1.8	1.5	2.1	1.7	3.3	3.1
Current Liabilities to Working Capital 39	1.5	•	443.7	3.5	0.9	0.6	0.8	0.8	0.5	1.1	0.7	2.3	2.1
Working Capital to Net Sales 40	0.2	•	0.0	0.1	0.2	0.3	0.3	0.3	0.5	0.3	0.3	0.1	0.2
Inventory to Working Capital 41	0.6	•	120.4	2.0	0.6	0.4	0.5	0.5	0.2	0.4	0.4	0.8	0.7
Total Receipts to Cash Flow 42	4.4	9.0	4.2	18.7	12.0	6.2	7.1	6.2	4.5	4.1	4.1	3.6	4.2
Cost of Goods to Cash Flow 43	2.2	4.6	1.3	11.4	7.4	3.1	3.6	3.4	2.0	1.9	1.9	1.6	2.2
Cash Flow to Total Debt 44	0.3	•	1.5	0.1	0.3	0.6	0.4	0.4	0.6	0.5	0.5	0.4	0.2

Selected Financial Factors (in Percentages)

Debt Ratio 45	55.1	•	76.2	90.8	57.2	47.5	46.9	50.9	30.5	45.1	34.6	50.3	63.4
Return on Total Assets 46	7.1	•	38.9	•	•	•	•	2.7	1.8	9.1	6.9	7.9	7.9
Return on Equity Before Income Taxes 47	10.7	•	140.2	•	•	•	•	2.6	1.3	13.0	8.3	12.5	14.5
Return on Equity After Income Taxes 48	7.0	•	136.2	•	•	•	•	•	•	8.4	5.6	8.5	10.4
Profit Margin (Before Income Tax) 49	6.6	•	7.1	•	•	•	•	1.0	1.1	8.5	7.9	8.7	9.6
Profit Margin (After Income Tax) 50	4.3	•	6.9	•	•	•	•	1.0	1.1	5.5	5.4	5.9	6.9

Table II
Corporations with Net Income

MEDICAL EQUIPMENT AND SUPPLIES

MONEY AMOUNTS AND SIZE OF ASSETS IN THOUSANDS OF DOLLARS

Item Description for Accounting Period 7/04 Through 6/05	Total	Zero Assets	Under 500	500 to 1,000	1,000 to 5,000	5,000 to 10,000	10,000 to 25,000	25,000 to 50,000	50,000 to 100,000	100,000 to 250,000	250,000 to 500,000	500,000 to 2,500,000	2,500,000 and over
Number of Enterprises **1**	5336	378	3531	0	775	103	96	44	34	34	16	29	0
Revenues ($ in Thousands)													
Net Sales **2**	68878396	1216242	1396957	0	3669192	1524933	2518384	2443038	2464546	5539692	4218145	19179648	0
Interest **3**	1068478	46939	4920	0	823	1827	2028	7608	6974	23180	31101	178478	0
Rents **4**	45191	247	0	0	0	77	18	405	86	12723	9909	18192	0
Royalties **5**	1506364	0	0	0	0	4520	3651	5034	3090	9915	27131	68129	0
Other Portfolio Income **6**	721497	14434	1202	0	57614	11505	15387	12700	7516	21662	20620	369216	0
Other Receipts **7**	2545726	17011	34193	0	5761	17786	29728	17345	201078	79577	48894	322177	0
Total Receipts **8**	74765652	1294873	1437272	0	3733390	1560648	2569196	2486130	2683290	5686749	4355800	20135840	0
Average Total Receipts **9**	14012	3426	407	·	4817	15152	26762	56503	78920	167257	272238	694339	·
Operating Costs/Operating Income (%)													
Cost of Operations **10**	46.8	47.2	31.7	·	56.8	50.0	50.4	52.7	49.5	44.2	44.6	45.4	·
Salaries and Wages **11**	15.0	10.9	14.5	·	9.3	16.9	13.7	11.9	13.3	15.2	14.1	13.6	·
Taxes Paid **12**	2.0	1.3	4.2	·	3.7	2.0	2.2	1.8	2.1	1.9	1.8	1.9	·
Interest Paid **13**	3.0	7.6	0.7	·	0.5	0.8	0.6	0.8	1.0	1.6	1.9	2.1	·
Depreciation **14**	3.3	3.5	2.4	·	1.2	1.4	2.7	2.4	2.9	2.6	4.6	3.6	·
Amortization and Depletion **15**	1.3	3.4	0.0	·	0.0	0.3	0.3	0.5	0.8	1.0	1.3	1.2	·
Pensions and Other Deferred Comp. **16**	0.9	0.2	0.6	·	0.2	0.3	0.7	0.5	1.0	0.4	1.0	0.7	·
Employee Benefits **17**	2.5	4.5	0.4	·	0.9	1.0	2.0	1.9	1.9	2.4	2.0	2.3	·
Advertising **18**	1.2	1.2	0.6	·	1.7	1.5	1.2	2.7	2.6	2.6	0.8	1.0	·
Other Expenses **19**	19.5	18.4	21.4	·	14.2	16.9	14.0	14.4	17.4	16.8	19.5	21.3	·
Officers' Compensation **20**	1.8	0.3	10.3	·	4.8	2.1	3.5	2.5	1.9	1.6	1.3	1.3	·
Operating Margin **21**	2.8	1.6	13.3	·	6.8	6.9	8.6	8.0	5.7	9.7	7.2	5.6	·
Operating Margin Before Officers' Comp. **22**	4.6	1.9	23.6	·	11.6	9.0	12.1	10.4	7.6	11.4	8.5	6.9	·

Selected Average Balance Sheet ($ in Thousands)

Net Receivables 23	2584	0	24	•	621	2105	4077	8433	12294	38889	54865	150252
Inventories 24	1423	0	6	•	405	1464	3781	5954	7841	17229	41997	78768
Net Property, Plant and Equipment 25	1997	0	28	•	212	811	2922	5373	10044	23783	47537	122954
Total Assets 26	17256	0	85	•	1705	7175	16294	34251	72070	178805	374668	907709
Notes and Loans Payable 27	3997	0	25	•	308	1580	2887	5734	7359	30039	43642	263880
All Other Liabilities 28	4972	0	34	•	448	1360	4055	10400	13102	36821	78975	196963
Net Worth 29	8287	0	26	•	950	4235	9352	18117	51609	111945	252051	446865

Selected Financial Ratios (Times to 1)

Current Ratio 30	1.6	•	1.0	•	2.6	2.5	2.4	2.3	3.4	2.3	2.5	1.4
Quick Ratio 31	0.9	•	0.7	•	1.6	1.2	1.4	1.4	2.0	1.5	1.5	0.9
Net Sales to Working Capital 32	5.6	•	•	•	5.8	4.7	4.2	4.4	2.4	3.1	2.9	6.4
Coverage Ratio 33	5.2	2.1	23.6	•	19.4	13.3	22.1	13.3	17.1	9.1	6.6	6.4
Total Asset Turnover 34	0.7	•	4.6	•	2.8	2.1	1.6	1.6	1.0	0.9	0.7	0.7
Inventory Turnover 35	4.2	•	21.2	•	6.6	5.1	3.5	4.9	4.6	4.2	2.8	3.8
Receivables Turnover 36	5.3	•	28.3	•	7.0	7.1	6.4	7.0	6.2	4.8	3.7	5.2
Total Liabilities to Net Worth 37	1.1	•	2.3	•	0.8	0.7	0.7	0.9	0.4	0.6	0.5	1.0
Current Assets to Working Capital 38	2.7	•	•	•	1.6	1.7	1.7	1.8	1.4	1.8	1.7	3.3
Current Liabilities to Working Capital 39	1.7	•	•	•	0.6	0.7	0.7	0.8	0.4	0.8	0.7	2.3
Working Capital to Net Sales 40	0.2	•	•	•	0.2	0.2	0.2	0.2	0.4	0.3	0.3	0.2
Inventory to Working Capital 41	0.7	•	•	•	0.5	0.5	0.6	0.5	0.3	0.4	0.4	0.8
Total Receipts to Cash Flow 42	3.5	4.2	3.2	•	5.9	4.2	4.5	4.6	3.3	3.6	3.6	3.5
Cost of Goods to Cash Flow 43	1.7	2.0	1.0	•	3.3	2.1	2.3	2.4	1.6	1.6	1.6	1.6
Cash Flow to Total Debt 44	0.4	•	2.1	•	1.1	1.2	0.8	0.8	1.1	0.7	0.6	0.4

Selected Financial Factors (in Percentages)

Debt Ratio 45	52.0	•	69.3	•	44.3	41.0	42.6	47.1	28.4	37.4	32.7	50.8
Return on Total Assets 46	11.7	•	78.3	•	24.9	20.6	20.6	17.2	16.4	13.1	8.8	9.7
Return on Equity Before Income Taxes 47	19.7	•	244.0	•	42.4	32.3	34.3	30.1	21.6	18.6	11.1	16.6
Return on Equity After Income Taxes 48	14.9	•	239.8	•	41.7	28.7	29.5	25.5	17.3	13.2	7.8	11.6
Profit Margin (Before Income Tax) 49	12.7	8.1	16.2	•	8.5	9.3	12.2	9.8	15.4	12.8	10.6	11.2
Profit Margin (After Income Tax) 50	9.6	6.3	15.9	•	8.4	8.2	10.5	8.3	12.3	9.1	7.5	7.9

164

Table I

Corporations with and without Net Income

OTHER MISCELLANEOUS MANUFACTURING

MONEY AMOUNTS AND SIZE OF ASSETS IN THOUSANDS OF DOLLARS

Item Description for Accounting Period 7/04 Through 6/05	Total	Zero Assets	Under 500	500 to 1,000	1,000 to 5,000	5,000 to 10,000	10,000 to 25,000	25,000 to 50,000	50,000 to 100,000	100,000 to 250,000	250,000 to 500,000	500,000 to 2,500,000	2,500,000 and over
Number of Enterprises 1	24707	927	18683	1494	2376	422	438	173	75	65	25	23	4
Revenues ($ in Thousands)													
Net Sales 2	100527886	890582	6811362	3195542	14331822	5248693	11367341	8966181	6147578	10801906	7783914	14805351	10177615
Interest 3	769267	923	3296	767	6926	10039	7256	13214	7858	21449	66303	132744	498492
Rents 4	49515	1	0	0	2277	89	4834	2766	3622	6280	18669	6248	4728
Royalties 5	571950	4536	0	0	0	360	2432	11204	15326	4941	29439	436531	67180
Other Portfolio Income 6	793183	2777	19525	3533	34901	26987	27187	22449	29299	111958	249964	113066	151539
Other Receipts 7	1714013	47664	19238	32666	114549	118453	75344	73974	154187	43466	57160	200361	776949
Total Receipts 8	104425814	946483	6853421	3232508	14490475	5404621	11484394	9089788	6357870	10990000	8205449	15694301	11676503
Average Total Receipts 9	4227	1021	367	2164	6099	12807	26220	52542	84772	169077	328218	682361	2919126
Operating Costs/Operating Income (%)													
Cost of Operations 10	64.8	68.9	54.9	56.8	69.3	59.0	69.1	66.4	66.2	62.9	62.5	68.8	61.3
Salaries and Wages 11	8.7	10.1	9.6	12.6	6.7	10.5	8.3	8.9	8.2	9.1	9.6	8.2	9.1
Taxes Paid 12	1.9	1.5	2.9	2.7	2.1	1.9	1.9	1.9	1.5	1.6	1.8	1.6	2.0
Interest Paid 13	2.5	2.2	1.1	0.8	0.7	1.2	1.1	1.2	2.2	1.8	3.2	2.8	9.9
Depreciation 14	2.7	2.6	1.8	1.9	1.9	2.4	2.4	2.5	2.9	3.2	4.0	2.2	4.3
Amortization and Depletion 15	0.6	0.8	0.1	0.1	0.1	0.2	0.3	0.4	0.8	0.7	1.6	1.3	0.9
Pensions and Other Deferred Comp. 16	0.6	0.4	0.5	0.2	0.5	0.5	0.4	0.4	0.7	0.5	0.6	0.5	1.2
Employee Benefits 17	1.6	1.5	1.9	0.8	1.0	2.1	1.5	1.6	1.9	1.6	2.2	2.1	0.9
Advertising 18	1.7	2.5	1.6	0.6	0.7	1.6	1.1	1.6	1.8	1.7	2.0	3.7	1.2
Other Expenses 19	12.9	17.1	17.3	18.2	10.8	12.0	10.0	9.9	15.1	11.4	11.1	12.6	18.8
Officers' Compensation 20	2.7	1.9	9.4	5.4	4.8	4.7	2.4	2.7	1.7	1.5	0.8	0.7	0.4
Operating Margin 21	•	•	•	0.1	1.3	3.9	1.5	2.4	•	4.0	0.6	•	•
Operating Margin Before Officers' Comp. 22	2.0	•	8.3	5.4	6.1	8.5	3.9	5.1	•	5.5	1.4	•	•

Selected Average Balance Sheet ($ in Thousands)

Net Receivables 23	638	0	31	165	569	1766	3984	9075	15065	30793	46688	133925	537277
Inventories 24	547	0	32	187	664	2176	4003	8200	13501	22444	47832	75529	391412
Net Property, Plant and Equipment 25	531	0	17	137	469	1119	3095	6995	12029	27266	63088	76931	605798
Total Assets 26	3422	0	111	652	2282	7709	15680	34260	69817	147819	360872	888314	3933495
Notes and Loans Payable 27	1194	0	75	235	847	2170	5396	11437	25319	44850	118433	295347	1480340
All Other Liabilities 28	922	0	51	166	594	1485	4535	9627	20152	34810	87671	235593	1121843
Net Worth 29	1307	0	-15	250	841	4054	5750	13196	24347	68159	154768	357373	1331311

Selected Financial Ratios (Times to 1)

Current Ratio 30	1.7	•	1.3	2.8	2.0	2.2	1.7	1.7	1.7	1.9	1.5	1.5	1.9
Quick Ratio 31	0.9	•	0.7	1.7	1.0	1.1	0.9	0.9	0.9	1.0	0.7	0.8	1.1
Net Sales to Working Capital 32	5.7	•	18.3	7.2	7.7	4.2	5.9	5.7	5.2	4.6	6.3	5.6	3.8
Coverage Ratio 33	2.3	•	0.6	2.6	4.2	6.8	3.4	4.0	1.3	4.2	2.9	1.8	1.6
Total Asset Turnover 34	1.2	•	3.3	3.3	2.6	1.6	1.7	1.5	1.2	1.1	0.9	0.7	0.6
Inventory Turnover 35	4.8	•	6.2	6.5	6.3	3.4	4.5	4.2	4.0	4.7	4.1	5.9	4.0
Receivables Turnover 36	6.6	•	10.4	12.3	11.2	6.9	6.8	5.9	5.5	6.2	6.3	5.5	4.4
Total Liabilities to Net Worth 37	1.6	•	•	1.6	1.7	0.9	1.7	1.6	1.9	1.2	1.3	1.5	2.0
Current Assets to Working Capital 38	2.4	•	4.4	1.6	2.0	1.8	2.4	2.4	2.4	2.1	2.8	2.8	2.2
Current Liabilities to Working Capital 39	1.4	•	3.4	0.6	1.0	0.8	1.4	1.4	1.4	1.1	1.8	1.8	1.2
Working Capital to Net Sales 40	0.2	•	0.1	0.1	0.1	0.2	0.2	0.2	0.2	0.2	0.2	0.2	0.3
Inventory to Working Capital 41	0.8	•	1.8	0.5	0.9	0.8	1.0	0.9	0.9	0.7	1.0	0.8	0.6
Total Receipts to Cash Flow 42	7.6	10.8	8.7	6.8	9.6	6.2	9.7	8.6	7.5	6.7	8.1	8.0	5.0
Cost of Goods to Cash Flow 43	5.0	7.5	4.8	3.8	6.7	3.7	6.7	5.7	5.0	4.2	5.0	5.5	3.1
Cash Flow to Total Debt 44	0.3	•	0.3	0.8	0.4	0.5	0.3	0.3	0.2	0.3	0.2	0.2	0.2

Selected Financial Factors (in Percentages)

Debt Ratio 45	61.8	•	113.1	61.6	63.1	47.4	63.3	61.5	65.1	53.9	57.1	59.8	66.2
Return on Total Assets 46	6.9	•	2.2	6.5	8.3	12.9	6.0	7.6	3.3	8.5	7.9	3.6	10.0
Return on Equity Before Income Taxes 47	10.3	•	10.5	10.3	17.2	21.0	11.5	14.9	1.9	14.1	12.1	4.0	10.5
Return on Equity After Income Taxes 48	7.6	•	13.3	9.5	15.4	19.1	9.1	12.5	•	11.6	9.3	1.9	6.1
Profit Margin (Before Income Tax) 49	3.3	•	•	1.2	2.4	6.8	2.5	3.8	0.6	5.8	6.0	2.2	5.5
Profit Margin (After Income Tax) 50	2.5	•	•	1.1	2.1	6.2	2.0	3.2	•	4.7	4.6	1.1	3.2

165

Table II

Corporations with Net Income

OTHER MISCELLANEOUS MANUFACTURING

Money Amounts and Size of Assets in Thousands of Dollars

Item Description for Accounting Period 7/04 Through 6/05	Total	Zero Assets	Under 500	500 to 1,000	1,000 to 5,000	5,000 to 10,000	10,000 to 25,000	25,000 to 50,000	50,000 to 100,000	100,000 to 250,000	250,000 to 500,000	500,000 to 2,500,000	2,500,000 and over
Number of Enterprises 1	12798	344	9041	0	1613	329	307	125	46	47	17	13	0
Revenues ($ in Thousands)													
Net Sales 2	7701206	620698	3907490	0	11267160	4599158	8565926	6899201	4368628	8793401	5884966	10310287	0
Interest 3	698333	572	142	0	3884	8744	3869	7329	2582	11368	63213	98365	0
Rents 4	41630	0	0	0	2206	73	3440	1977	2330	5725	16465	4686	0
Royalties 5	515370	2611	0	0	0	360	760	6128	2719	4301	28012	404828	0
Other Portfolio Income 6	712991	1607	5208	0	34549	26784	24307	18300	12412	108138	228645	103986	0
Other Receipts 7	1431619	48516	4746	0	49274	115600	51664	45076	50216	50177	28413	182051	0
Total Receipts 8	80101149	674004	3917586	0	11357073	4750719	8649966	6978011	4438887	8973110	6249714	11104203	0
Average Total Receipts 9	6259	1959	433	•	7041	14440	28176	55824	96498	190917	367630	854169	•
Operating Costs/Operating Income (%)													
Cost of Operations 10	64.2	68.5	52.1	•	69.6	57.6	67.1	66.0	65.7	61.4	59.2	70.8	•
Salaries and Wages 11	8.3	6.6	7.5	•	6.0	10.2	8.0	8.4	7.5	9.1	10.4	7.3	•
Taxes Paid 12	1.8	1.3	2.3	•	2.0	1.8	1.9	1.9	1.4	1.5	1.6	1.4	•
Interest Paid 13	2.2	1.5	0.6	•	0.5	1.1	0.8	1.0	1.6	1.3	2.6	2.5	•
Depreciation 14	2.5	2.4	1.7	•	1.3	2.4	2.2	2.0	2.5	3.2	4.4	1.8	•
Amortization and Depletion 15	0.5	0.5	0.1	•	0.0	0.2	0.2	0.3	0.4	0.6	1.0	1.3	•
Pensions and Other Deferred Comp. 16	0.6	0.4	0.4	•	0.5	0.5	0.5	0.5	0.4	0.5	0.6	0.5	•
Employee Benefits 17	1.5	1.2	2.1	•	1.0	2.2	1.4	1.4	1.7	1.5	1.8	1.8	•
Advertising 18	1.8	2.4	1.5	•	0.7	1.6	1.2	1.6	1.4	1.8	2.4	4.1	•
Other Expenses 19	11.5	13.6	15.3	•	8.7	11.3	8.8	9.1	10.5	10.9	11.2	10.7	•
Officers' Compensation 20	2.5	1.2	8.1	•	4.9	4.8	2.4	2.0	1.4	1.5	0.9	0.4	•
Operating Margin 21	2.6	0.4	8.3	•	4.7	6.4	5.6	5.8	5.4	6.8	3.9	•	•
Operating Margin Before Officers' Comp. 22	5.1	1.7	16.4	•	9.7	11.2	8.0	7.8	6.8	8.3	4.8	•	•

Selected Average Balance Sheet ($ in Thousands)

Net Receivables 23	917	0	42	•	554	1927	4189	9536	16723	33121	51901	153243	•
Inventories 24	727	0	35	•	691	2270	3977	7991	15939	22484	51574	84069	•
Net Property, Plant and Equipment 25	740	0	20	•	372	1219	2964	6157	11688	28954	76203	82434	•
Total Assets 26	4731	0	127	•	2206	8145	15384	33431	69448	149531	379447	1061275	•
Notes and Loans Payable 27	1398	0	52	•	639	2106	4199	9779	20970	38695	90718	339254	•
All Other Liabilities 28	1276	0	40	•	591	1514	3980	9210	17914	33921	97215	317826	•
Net Worth 29	2057	0	34	•	975	4524	7206	14442	30564	76915	191514	404195	•

Selected Financial Ratios (Times to 1)

Current Ratio 30	1.9	•	1.9	•	2.1	2.3	2.0	1.8	2.0	2.2	2.0	1.3	•
Quick Ratio 31	1.0	•	1.0	•	1.1	1.2	1.1	1.0	1.1	1.2	0.9	0.7	•
Net Sales to Working Capital 32	5.4	•	9.2	•	8.3	4.3	5.0	5.4	4.6	4.5	4.2	8.3	•
Coverage Ratio 33	4.3	7.2	15.2	•	12.3	9.9	9.3	8.0	5.5	8.1	4.8	3.3	•
Total Asset Turnover 34	1.3	•	3.4	•	3.2	1.7	1.8	1.7	1.4	1.3	0.9	0.7	•
Inventory Turnover 35	5.3	•	6.4	•	7.0	3.5	4.7	4.6	3.9	5.1	4.0	6.7	•
Receivables Turnover 36	7.2	•	10.5	•	12.5	7.3	7.1	6.4	5.5	6.7	6.4	5.6	•
Total Liabilities to Net Worth 37	1.3	•	2.7	•	1.3	0.8	1.1	1.3	1.3	0.9	1.0	1.6	•
Current Assets to Working Capital 38	2.1	•	2.2	•	1.9	1.7	2.0	2.2	2.0	1.8	2.0	3.9	•
Current Liabilities to Working Capital 39	1.1	•	1.2	•	0.9	0.7	1.0	1.2	1.0	0.8	1.0	2.9	•
Working Capital to Net Sales 40	0.2	•	0.1	•	0.1	0.2	0.2	0.2	0.2	0.2	0.2	0.1	•
Inventory to Working Capital 41	0.7	•	0.8	•	0.8	0.7	0.8	0.8	0.7	0.6	0.7	1.0	•
Total Receipts to Cash Flow 42	6.3	5.1	5.1	•	8.6	5.5	7.5	7.0	6.4	5.6	6.3	7.0	•
Cost of Goods to Cash Flow 43	4.0	3.5	2.7	•	6.0	3.2	5.0	4.6	4.2	3.5	3.7	4.9	•
Cash Flow to Total Debt 44	0.4	•	0.9	•	0.7	0.7	0.5	0.4	0.4	0.5	0.3	0.2	•

Selected Financial Factors (in Percentages)

Debt Ratio 45	56.5	•	72.9	•	55.8	44.5	53.2	56.8	56.0	48.6	49.5	61.9	•
Return on Total Assets 46	12.1	•	31.4	•	19.0	18.5	13.4	13.1	11.8	12.8	11.7	6.3	•
Return on Equity Before Income Taxes 47	21.3	•	108.2	•	39.6	29.9	25.5	26.6	21.8	21.8	18.3	11.5	•
Return on Equity After Income Taxes 48	18.0	•	105.7	•	37.2	27.7	22.9	23.5	18.6	18.7	14.9	8.2	•
Profit Margin (Before Income Tax) 49	7.3	9.0	8.6	•	5.5	9.7	6.6	7.0	7.0	8.9	10.1	5.8	•
Profit Margin (After Income Tax) 50	6.2	8.7	8.4	•	5.2	9.0	5.9	6.2	6.0	7.7	8.2	4.2	•

Table I
Corporations with and without Net Income

MOTOR VEHICLE AND MOTOR VEHICLE PARTS AND SUPPLIES

MONEY AMOUNTS AND SIZE OF ASSETS IN THOUSANDS OF DOLLARS

Item Description for Accounting Period 7/04 Through 6/05	Total	Zero Assets	Under 500	500 to 1,000	1,000 to 5,000	5,000 to 10,000	10,000 to 25,000	25,000 to 50,000	50,000 to 100,000	100,000 to 250,000	250,000 to 500,000	500,000 to 2,500,000	2,500,000 and over
Number of Enterprises 1	15427	956	9276	1972	2299	410	293	104	50	31	15	16	6
Revenues ($ in Thousands)													
Net Sales 2	231046334	1938952	12663640	3639102	12249652	8541031	10537997	8354117	7044214	8311833	13951635	35239665	108574495
Interest 3	1990259	2822	1117	1823	12449	5634	7191	5406	8406	26056	44583	100095	1774677
Rents 4	541130	2409	1468	306	4623	1168	4999	13365	8393	4620	14650	71845	413284
Royalties 5	24941	0	0	0	0	0	82	6	409	2279	1030	1736	19399
Other Portfolio Income 6	1045865	21095	16194	1201	6570	15398	18704	16848	6857	56696	18494	162593	705216
Other Receipts 7	2707187	11177	13165	105176	87631	33746	90032	49380	41853	50159	56444	249007	1919417
Total Receipts 8	237355716	1976455	12695584	3747608	12360925	8596977	10659005	8439122	7110132	8451643	14086836	35824941	113406488
Average Total Receipts 9	15386	2067	1369	1900	5377	20968	36379	81145	142203	272634	939122	2239059	18901081
Operating Costs/Operating Income (%)													
Cost of Operations 10	81.3	82.9	86.1	72.6	72.1	84.5	77.1	77.4	76.5	78.7	87.6	83.7	81.4
Salaries and Wages 11	4.2	5.4	3.5	8.8	8.0	5.1	8.0	7.9	7.4	6.3	3.4	3.5	2.9
Taxes Paid 12	0.8	1.1	0.9	1.6	1.6	0.8	1.2	1.3	1.5	1.0	0.5	0.7	0.6
Interest Paid 13	0.7	0.5	0.2	0.6	0.6	0.7	0.6	0.6	0.6	1.0	0.4	0.4	0.9
Depreciation 14	4.3	0.6	0.5	1.0	0.8	0.5	1.1	1.6	1.3	1.5	1.3	1.9	7.7
Amortization and Depletion 15	0.1	0.3	0.1	0.0	0.1	0.1	0.1	0.1	0.1	0.2	0.1	0.1	0.1
Pensions and Other Deferred Comp. 16	0.2	0.0	0.1	0.2	0.2	0.1	0.2	0.2	0.2	0.1	0.1	0.2	0.2
Employee Benefits 17	0.5	0.6	0.2	0.9	0.8	0.3	0.7	0.9	0.7	1.1	0.6	0.5	0.3
Advertising 18	2.8	0.4	0.3	0.4	1.1	0.3	0.6	0.5	0.6	0.6	0.9	2.9	4.6
Other Expenses 19	5.4	6.2	6.7	10.6	10.5	5.5	7.5	7.0	7.6	7.3	3.5	5.8	4.0
Officers' Compensation 20	0.7	1.1	2.0	4.1	3.1	1.3	1.5	1.4	0.8	0.6	0.3	0.3	0.1
Operating Margin 21	•	0.9	•	•	1.3	0.8	1.5	1.0	2.6	1.4	1.2	•	•
Operating Margin Before Officers' Comp. 22	•	2.1	1.6	3.3	4.5	2.2	3.0	2.4	3.4	2.0	1.5	0.2	0.2

Selected Average Balance Sheet ($ in Thousands)

Net Receivables 23	2424	0	43	146	445	2162	4325	9387	16900	28732	69023	174654	4497042
Inventories 24	1714	0	78	357	881	3150	5975	12799	23561	54162	74562	336434	1544019
Net Property, Plant and Equipment 25	1976	0	15	41	223	341	1622	5741	8804	20514	48974	151322	4050582
Total Assets 26	8750	0	195	659	1995	6849	15219	33877	67785	159566	318317	1072837	14370294
Notes and Loans Payable 27	3051	0	83	180	575	2299	4993	12824	21182	49929	77441	258507	5496755
All Other Liabilities 28	3318	0	87	214	600	2543	5396	10399	22483	47775	102785	473197	5526181
Net Worth 29	2381	0	25	266	820	2007	4831	10653	24120	61862	138091	341132	3347358

Selected Financial Ratios (Times to 1)

Current Ratio 30	1.5	•	1.6	2.1	2.2	1.5	1.5	1.5	1.6	1.5	1.6	1.3	1.5
Quick Ratio 31	0.8	•	0.8	0.9	0.8	0.6	0.7	0.7	0.7	0.6	0.7	0.5	0.9
Net Sales to Working Capital 32	8.4	•	22.0	6.0	6.1	10.3	8.4	9.6	7.8	7.6	13.1	14.3	6.9
Coverage Ratio 33	3.6	6.8	0.0	4.7	5.0	3.3	5.7	4.2	6.4	4.1	5.9	4.8	2.9
Total Asset Turnover 34	1.7	•	7.0	2.8	2.7	3.0	2.4	2.4	2.1	1.7	2.9	2.1	1.3
Inventory Turnover 35	7.1	•	15.1	3.7	4.4	5.6	4.6	4.9	4.6	3.9	10.9	5.5	9.5
Receivables Turnover 36	6.4	•	31.4	12.1	12.2	11.0	9.0	9.0	9.2	9.6	13.7	11.4	4.2
Total Liabilities to Net Worth 37	2.7	•	6.7	1.5	1.4	2.4	2.2	2.2	1.8	1.6	1.3	2.1	3.3
Current Assets to Working Capital 38	3.1	•	2.7	1.9	1.9	3.1	2.9	3.1	2.8	3.0	2.8	4.4	3.2
Current Liabilities to Working Capital 39	2.1	•	1.7	0.9	0.9	2.1	1.9	2.1	1.8	2.0	1.8	3.4	2.2
Working Capital to Net Sales 40	0.1	•	0.0	0.2	0.2	0.1	0.1	0.1	0.1	0.1	0.1	0.1	0.1
Inventory to Working Capital 41	1.0	•	1.2	1.1	1.1	1.7	1.5	1.6	1.4	1.7	1.2	2.4	0.6
Total Receipts to Cash Flow 42	16.3	15.3	22.6	10.2	10.2	18.9	12.0	14.5	10.9	11.3	20.9	15.3	19.3
Cost of Goods to Cash Flow 43	13.3	12.7	19.4	7.4	7.3	16.0	9.2	11.2	8.3	8.9	18.3	12.8	15.7
Cash Flow to Total Debt 44	0.1	•	0.4	0.5	0.4	0.2	0.3	0.2	0.3	0.2	0.2	0.2	0.1

Selected Financial Factors (in Percentages)

Debt Ratio 45	72.8	•	87.1	59.7	58.9	70.7	68.3	68.6	64.4	61.2	56.6	68.2	76.7
Return on Total Assets 46	4.3	•	0.0	7.6	7.4	6.6	7.7	6.4	8.6	7.0	7.5	4.2	3.3
Return on Equity Before Income Taxes 47	11.4	•	•	14.8	14.4	15.6	20.0	15.5	20.5	13.6	14.4	10.5	9.2
Return on Equity After Income Taxes 48	7.2	•	•	13.2	12.7	12.3	17.5	13.6	16.2	10.2	11.8	6.9	4.0
Profit Margin (Before Income Tax) 49	1.8	2.8	•	2.1	2.2	1.5	2.7	2.1	3.5	3.1	2.1	1.6	1.7
Profit Margin (After Income Tax) 50	1.1	1.7	•	1.9	2.0	1.2	2.3	1.8	2.8	2.4	1.8	1.1	0.7

167

Table II

Corporations with Net Income

MOTOR VEHICLE AND MOTOR VEHICLE PARTS AND SUPPLIES

MONEY AMOUNTS AND SIZE OF ASSETS IN THOUSANDS OF DOLLARS

Item Description for Accounting Period 7/04 Through 6/05	Total	Zero Assets	Under 500	500 to 1,000	1,000 to 5,000	5,000 to 10,000	10,000 to 25,000	25,000 to 50,000	50,000 to 100,000	100,000 to 250,000	250,000 to 500,000	500,000 to 2,500,000	2,500,000 and over
Number of Enterprises **1**	9533	14	5665	1262	1822	348	245	84	43	0	0	16	0
Revenues ($ in Thousands)													
Net Sales **2**	163927562	1566999	9616093	2730340	8940750	7792389	9163294	6832487	6272338	0	0	92269217	0
Interest **3**	498318	833	890	1759	11917	4555	6730	4499	8093	0	0	393993	0
Rents **4**	223225	2239	1468	306	4375	1161	4964	8652	7612	0	0	176999	0
Royalties **5**	22279	0	0	0	0	0	82	6	398	0	0	18484	0
Other Portfolio Income **6**	305388	17039	15126	37	3959	13400	16198	7744	6657	0	0	156597	0
Other Receipts **7**	918609	7573	8473	102633	84706	27253	80577	40085	34069	0	0	433244	0
Total Receipts **8**	165895381	1594683	9642050	2835075	9045707	7838758	9271845	6893473	6329167	0	0	93848534	0
Average Total Receipts **9**	17402	113906	1702	2246	4965	22525	37844	82065	147190	•	•	5865533	•
Operating Costs/Operating Income (%)													
Cost of Operations **10**	80.8	85.6	86.0	74.5	69.0	85.1	77.5	77.6	76.2	•	•	81.7	•
Salaries and Wages **11**	4.3	3.7	3.5	8.1	7.6	4.8	7.6	7.5	7.1	•	•	3.0	•
Taxes Paid **12**	0.9	0.9	0.8	1.3	1.7	0.8	1.2	1.3	1.5	•	•	0.7	•
Interest Paid **13**	0.4	0.3	0.2	0.4	0.6	0.6	0.5	0.5	0.5	•	•	0.2	•
Depreciation **14**	1.8	0.4	0.3	0.7	0.9	0.5	1.0	1.3	1.3	•	•	2.4	•
Amortization and Depletion **15**	0.1	0.0	0.1	0.0	0.0	0.0	0.0	0.1	0.1	•	•	0.1	•
Pensions and Other Deferred Comp. **16**	0.2	0.0	0.0	0.3	0.3	0.1	0.2	0.2	0.2	•	•	0.2	•
Employee Benefits **17**	0.4	0.4	0.2	1.1	0.9	0.2	0.6	0.9	0.7	•	•	0.3	•
Advertising **18**	2.8	0.3	0.2	0.4	1.1	0.3	0.5	0.4	0.6	•	•	4.5	•
Other Expenses **19**	5.2	4.1	5.5	8.1	11.6	4.8	7.0	6.5	7.5	•	•	4.1	•
Officers' Compensation **20**	0.7	0.2	1.9	3.5	3.7	1.4	1.5	1.4	0.7	•	•	0.2	•
Operating Margin **21**	2.4	3.9	1.4	1.5	2.6	1.4	2.5	2.3	3.5	•	•	2.6	•
Operating Margin Before Officers' Comp. **22**	3.2	4.1	3.3	5.0	6.3	2.8	4.0	3.8	4.2	•	•	2.8	•

Selected Average Balance Sheet ($ in Thousands)

Net Receivables 23	1340	0	51	177	415	2294	4472	9740	16976	417357
Inventories 24	1922	0	88	388	883	2849	5888	12587	23121	371006
Net Property, Plant and Equipment 25	1016	0	16	26	174	349	1539	5225	9598	426622
Total Assets 26	6934	0	213	651	1973	6890	15277	33602	69104	2554831
Notes and Loans Payable 27	1553	0	82	122	563	2070	4629	10439	19914	484349
All Other Liabilities 28	2402	0	75	214	557	2578	5313	10855	22785	924310
Net Worth 29	2979	0	56	316	853	2242	5335	12308	26404	1146172

Selected Financial Ratios (Times to 1)

Current Ratio 30	1.4	•	2.2	2.4	2.3	1.5	1.6	1.6	1.5	1.6
Quick Ratio 31	0.6	•	1.2	1.1	0.8	0.7	0.7	0.7	0.7	0.7
Net Sales to Working Capital 32	13.0	•	17.3	6.1	5.2	10.1	7.9	9.1	8.0	21.7
Coverage Ratio 33	11.4	17.7	11.1	14.7	4.6	8.5	7.8	9.3	16.6	
Total Asset Turnover 34	2.5	•	8.0	3.3	2.5	3.2	2.4	2.4	2.1	2.3
Inventory Turnover 35	7.2	•	16.6	4.2	3.8	6.7	4.9	5.0	4.8	12.7
Receivables Turnover 36	10.7	•	32.1	12.0	12.3	11.5	9.4	8.9	9.7	19.9
Total Liabilities to Net Worth 37	1.3	•	2.8	1.1	1.3	2.1	1.9	1.7	1.6	1.2
Current Assets to Working Capital 38	3.5	•	1.9	1.7	1.8	2.8	2.7	2.9	2.8	5.9
Current Liabilities to Working Capital 39	2.5	•	0.9	0.7	0.8	1.8	1.7	1.9	1.8	4.9
Working Capital to Net Sales 40	0.1	•	0.1	0.2	0.2	0.1	0.1	0.1	0.1	0.0
Inventory to Working Capital 41	1.5	•	0.8	0.9	1.0	1.5	1.4	1.5	1.4	2.2
Total Receipts to Cash Flow 42	12.9	12.7	17.7	8.6	8.1	18.8	11.1	13.0	10.0	13.5
Cost of Goods to Cash Flow 43	10.4	10.9	15.2	6.4	5.6	16.0	8.6	10.1	7.6	11.0
Cash Flow to Total Debt 44	0.3	•	0.6	0.7	0.5	0.3	0.3	0.3	0.3	0.3

Selected Financial Factors (in Percentages)

Debt Ratio 45	57.0	•	73.9	51.5	56.8	67.5	65.1	63.4	61.8	55.1
Return on Total Assets 46	9.9	•	14.7	19.0	11.0	8.4	10.3	9.0	10.4	9.4
Return on Equity Before Income Taxes 47	21.0	•	51.3	36.6	22.0	20.2	25.9	21.4	24.3	19.7
Return on Equity After Income Taxes 48	15.6	•	49.3	34.5	19.9	16.8	23.3	19.4	19.7	13.0
Profit Margin (Before Income Tax) 49	3.6	5.7	1.7	5.3	3.8	2.0	3.7	3.2	4.4	3.9
Profit Margin (After Income Tax) 50	2.7	4.2	1.6	5.0	3.5	1.7	3.3	2.9	3.6	2.6

168

Table I

Corporations with and without Net Income

LUMBER AND OTHER CONSTRUCTION MATERIALS

MONEY AMOUNTS AND SIZE OF ASSETS IN THOUSANDS OF DOLLARS

Item Description for Accounting Period 7/04 Through 6/05	Total	Zero Assets	Under 500	500 to 1,000	1,000 to 5,000	5,000 to 10,000	10,000 to 25,000	25,000 to 50,000	50,000 to 100,000	100,000 to 250,000	250,000 to 500,000	500,000 to 2,500,000	2,500,000 and over
Number of Enterprises 1	13599	1966	5469	1463	3006	1073	407	126	63	16	4	6	0
Revenues ($ in Thousands)													
Net Sales 2	120172916	880295	3784057	4308144	20365053	23257702	18850179	13702410	12002573	6536796	1900687	14585020	0
Interest 3	118473	540	2322	2086	16754	7414	8049	8128	9204	5060	9286	49631	0
Rents 4	162883	5954	0	9848	6311	8192	6935	3677	1153	2028	1298	117487	0
Royalties 5	45262	0	12596	0	4	40	99	0	639	0	0	31885	0
Other Portfolio Income 6	246194	3842	24647	19377	20797	8950	17486	4456	27964	53150	2117	63410	0
Other Receipts 7	670352	-781	6806	10457	152306	93258	93771	57365	76236	40222	5450	135257	0
Total Receipts 8	121416080	889850	3830428	4349912	20561225	23375556	18976519	13776036	12117769	6637256	1918838	14982690	0
Average Total Receipts 9	8928	453	700	2973	6840	21785	46625	109334	192346	414828	479710	2497115	•
Operating Costs/Operating Income (%)													
Cost of Operations 10	80.6	74.3	68.4	76.7	77.3	82.5	80.4	83.6	80.8	79.3	82.8	84.5	•
Salaries and Wages 11	6.0	13.8	5.3	7.3	6.6	4.6	6.7	5.5	6.3	7.6	4.5	5.1	•
Taxes Paid 12	1.1	1.7	1.6	1.5	1.3	1.1	1.0	0.8	1.0	1.0	1.1	0.9	•
Interest Paid 13	0.6	0.6	0.3	0.3	0.5	0.6	0.5	0.5	0.6	0.8	1.5	1.0	•
Depreciation 14	1.1	0.3	0.7	1.1	1.0	0.9	1.1	0.8	1.2	1.6	2.2	1.8	•
Amortization and Depletion 15	0.1	0.1	0.0	0.0	0.0	0.0	0.0	0.0	0.1	0.2	0.5	0.2	•
Pensions and Other Deferred Comp. 16	0.3	0.2	1.2	0.2	0.4	0.3	0.3	0.2	0.2	0.4	0.4	0.3	•
Employee Benefits 17	0.6	0.4	0.7	0.4	0.7	0.5	0.6	0.5	0.7	0.6	1.1	0.7	•
Advertising 18	0.3	0.1	0.7	0.4	0.3	0.2	0.3	0.2	0.2	0.3	0.1	0.1	•
Other Expenses 19	5.7	9.3	11.9	7.5	7.0	4.9	5.1	4.2	5.6	5.7	5.5	4.9	•
Officers' Compensation 20	1.6	2.1	6.2	3.8	2.6	1.5	1.5	0.9	0.8	0.9	0.1	0.8	•
Operating Margin 21	2.0	•	3.1	0.8	2.3	2.9	2.5	2.7	2.4	1.6	0.1	•	•
Operating Margin Before Officers' Comp. 22	3.7	•	9.3	4.6	4.9	4.4	4.0	3.6	3.2	2.5	0.3	0.5	•

Selected Average Balance Sheet ($ in Thousands)

Net Receivables 23	1005	0	26	207	855	2357	5360	12250	21072	64502	104303	271206
Inventories 24	827	0	45	210	789	2275	4854	10230	18595	36989	42995	114337
Net Property, Plant and Equipment 25	559	0	22	69	269	1050	2103	4550	11558	32612	54594	425974
Total Assets 26	3146	0	146	687	2363	6763	15140	33873	68201	167834	294548	1337882
Notes and Loans Payable 27	1103	0	63	187	759	2309	4687	11458	25320	65117	129991	518500
All Other Liabilities 28	876	0	45	129	725	1609	4147	9143	18156	53936	102828	384636
Net Worth 29	1168	0	38	371	880	2845	6306	13272	24725	48780	61728	434746

Selected Financial Ratios (Times to 1)

Current Ratio 30	1.8	•	2.0	2.7	1.9	2.1	1.8	1.7	1.8	1.2	1.5	1.6
Quick Ratio 31	1.0	•	1.1	1.4	1.1	1.0	0.9	0.9	0.8	0.8	0.9	1.0
Net Sales to Working Capital 32	8.9	•	12.5	7.8	7.2	7.7	8.8	9.9	8.8	17.5	10.9	12.4
Coverage Ratio 33	6.5	•	15.2	6.3	8.2	7.1	7.6	7.9	6.6	1.7	5.1	4.5
Total Asset Turnover 34	2.8	•	4.7	4.3	2.9	3.2	3.1	3.2	2.8	1.6	2.4	1.8
Inventory Turnover 35	8.6	•	10.5	10.8	6.6	7.9	7.7	8.9	8.3	9.1	8.8	18.0
Receivables Turnover 36	9.4	•	20.1	14.3	7.9	9.6	9.3	9.4	10.7	5.2	7.0	10.3
Total Liabilities to Net Worth 37	1.7	•	2.8	0.9	1.7	1.4	1.4	1.6	1.8	3.8	2.4	2.1
Current Assets to Working Capital 38	2.2	•	2.0	1.6	2.1	1.9	2.3	2.4	2.3	5.8	3.1	2.7
Current Liabilities to Working Capital 39	1.2	•	1.0	0.6	1.1	0.9	1.3	1.4	1.3	4.8	2.1	1.7
Working Capital to Net Sales 40	0.1	•	0.1	0.1	0.1	0.1	0.1	0.1	0.1	0.1	0.1	0.1
Inventory to Working Capital 41	0.9	•	0.9	0.7	0.9	0.9	1.0	1.0	1.1	1.5	1.1	0.8
Total Receipts to Cash Flow 42	14.0	20.7	8.4	14.9	12.0	13.8	14.9	16.1	13.9	14.7	18.4	16.4
Cost of Goods to Cash Flow 43	11.3	15.4	5.8	11.4	9.3	11.4	12.0	13.5	11.3	11.6	15.2	13.8
Cash Flow to Total Debt 44	0.3	•	0.8	0.6	0.4	0.4	0.4	0.3	0.3	0.2	0.2	0.2

Selected Financial Factors (in Percentages)

Debt Ratio 45	62.9	•	73.9	46.0	62.8	57.9	58.3	60.8	63.7	70.9	79.0	67.5
Return on Total Assets 46	10.7	•	21.8	8.9	10.6	12.7	11.1	11.8	11.0	9.5	4.1	8.3
Return on Equity Before Income Taxes 47	24.3	•	77.8	13.9	25.1	26.0	23.1	26.3	25.7	26.3	8.2	19.9
Return on Equity After Income Taxes 48	21.3	•	74.5	12.2	24.0	24.4	20.9	23.9	22.7	20.5	5.3	13.1
Profit Margin (Before Income Tax) 49	3.2	•	4.3	1.8	3.3	3.4	3.1	3.2	3.3	3.1	1.1	3.6
Profit Margin (After Income Tax) 50	2.8	•	4.1	1.5	3.1	3.2	2.8	2.9	2.9	2.4	0.7	2.3

169

Table II
Corporations with Net Income

LUMBER AND OTHER CONSTRUCTION MATERIALS

MONEY AMOUNTS AND SIZE OF ASSETS IN THOUSANDS OF DOLLARS

Item Description for Accounting Period 7/04 Through 6/05	Total	Zero Assets	Under 500	500 to 1,000	1,000 to 5,000	5,000 to 10,000	10,000 to 25,000	25,000 to 50,000	50,000 to 100,000	100,000 to 250,000	250,000 to 500,000	500,000 to 2,500,000	2,500,000 and over
Number of Enterprises **1**	9851	1261	3460	1219	2398	949	369	116	56	0	0	0	0

Revenues ($ in Thousands)

Net Sales **2**	106839980	504352	3211134	3250356	17523123	21459530	17787814	12718897	11309874	0	0	0	0
Interest **3**	72077	281	488	1883	13350	6163	7618	6543	8287	0	0	0	0
Rents **4**	41232	100	0	9847	6208	8192	6282	3334	898	0	0	0	0
Royalties **5**	45255	0	12596	0	0	40	99	0	635	0	0	0	0
Other Portfolio Income **6**	194115	2855	15823	18305	19939	8163	15645	3860	26577	0	0	0	0
Other Receipts **7**	471347	955	890	10224	128691	86542	89524	50836	62120	0	0	0	0
Total Receipts **8**	107664006	508543	3240931	3290615	17691311	21568630	17906982	12783470	11408391	0	0	0	0
Average Total Receipts **9**	10929	403	937	2699	7378	22728	48528	110202	203721	•	•	•	•

Operating Costs/Operating Income (%)

Cost of Operations **10**	80.2	64.5	67.8	74.6	76.3	82.9	80.5	83.3	81.0	•	•	•	•
Salaries and Wages **11**	6.0	17.9	5.3	7.7	6.9	4.3	6.6	5.6	6.3	•	•	•	•
Taxes Paid **12**	1.1	2.0	1.2	1.6	1.3	1.0	1.0	0.9	1.0	•	•	•	•
Interest Paid **13**	0.5	0.6	0.2	0.4	0.4	0.5	0.4	0.4	0.6	•	•	•	•
Depreciation **14**	1.0	0.3	0.7	0.9	1.0	0.7	1.0	0.8	1.0	•	•	•	•
Amortization and Depletion **15**	0.1	0.1	0.0	0.0	0.0	0.0	0.0	0.0	0.1	•	•	•	•
Pensions and Other Deferred Comp. **16**	0.3	0.3	1.0	0.2	0.4	0.3	0.3	0.3	0.2	•	•	•	•
Employee Benefits **17**	0.6	0.3	0.6	0.4	0.7	0.4	0.6	0.5	0.7	•	•	•	•
Advertising **18**	0.3	0.2	0.6	0.4	0.4	0.2	0.3	0.2	0.2	•	•	•	•
Other Expenses **19**	5.3	9.5	11.0	7.7	6.2	4.8	4.9	4.2	5.3	•	•	•	•
Officers' Compensation **20**	1.6	1.7	5.4	4.2	2.6	1.6	1.5	0.9	0.8	•	•	•	•
Operating Margin **21**	3.1	2.6	6.1	1.9	3.7	3.3	2.9	3.0	2.8	•	•	•	•
Operating Margin Before Officers' Comp. **22**	4.7	4.3	11.5	6.1	6.3	4.9	4.4	3.9	3.6	•	•	•	•

Selected Average Balance Sheet ($ in Thousands)

Net Receivables 23	1259	0	24	209	841	2490	5557	12459	22356
Inventories 24	983	0	29	208	762	2338	4723	10002	18355
Net Property, Plant and Equipment 25	574	0	17	59	273	965	1994	4499	10756
Total Assets 26	3581	0	137	687	2383	6812	15163	33618	68188
Notes and Loans Payable 27	1172	0	47	162	607	2282	4554	11057	24900
All Other Liabilities 28	1009	0	33	115	711	1510	4122	8941	18563
Net Worth 29	1400	0	57	410	1064	3020	6487	13620	24725

Selected Financial Ratios (Times to 1)

Current Ratio 30	1.8	•	2.7	2.9	2.1	2.2	1.8	1.8	1.8
Quick Ratio 31	1.0	•	1.7	1.5	1.2	1.1	1.0	0.9	0.9
Net Sales to Working Capital 32	8.7	•	14.2	6.7	7.2	7.5	8.8	9.6	9.1
Coverage Ratio 33	8.8	7.0	44.4	9.9	12.3	8.3	9.0	9.0	7.6
Total Asset Turnover 34	3.0	•	6.8	3.9	3.1	3.3	3.2	3.3	3.0
Inventory Turnover 35	8.9	•	21.6	9.6	7.3	8.0	8.2	9.1	8.9
Receivables Turnover 36	9.6	•	30.0	12.7	8.6	9.5	9.6	9.8	11.1
Total Liabilities to Net Worth 37	1.6	•	1.4	0.7	1.2	1.3	1.3	1.5	1.8
Current Assets to Working Capital 38	2.2	•	1.6	1.5	2.0	1.9	2.2	2.3	2.3
Current Liabilities to Working Capital 39	1.2	•	0.6	0.5	1.0	0.9	1.2	1.3	1.3
Working Capital to Net Sales 40	0.1	•	0.1	0.1	0.1	0.1	0.1	0.1	0.1
Inventory to Working Capital 41	0.9	•	0.5	0.7	0.8	0.9	1.0	1.0	1.1
Total Receipts to Cash Flow 42	13.3	9.9	7.1	12.3	11.3	13.2	14.4	15.4	13.8
Cost of Goods to Cash Flow 43	10.7	6.4	4.8	9.2	8.6	10.9	11.6	12.8	11.2
Cash Flow to Total Debt 44	0.4	•	1.7	0.8	0.5	0.5	0.4	0.4	0.3

Selected Financial Factors (in Percentages)

Debt Ratio 45	60.9	•	58.1	40.3	55.3	55.7	57.2	59.5	63.7
Return on Total Assets 46	13.6	•	48.8	13.5	15.4	14.4	12.7	13.0	12.5
Return on Equity Before Income Taxes 47	30.9	•	113.7	20.4	31.8	28.6	26.4	28.5	30.0
Return on Equity After Income Taxes 48	27.5	•	110.2	18.6	30.6	26.9	24.1	26.0	26.7
Profit Margin (Before Income Tax) 49	4.0	3.4	7.0	3.1	4.6	3.8	3.6	3.5	3.7
Profit Margin (After Income Tax) 50	3.5	3.2	6.8	2.9	4.5	3.6	3.2	3.2	3.3

PROFESSIONAL AND COMMERCIAL EQUIPMENT AND SUPPLIES

Table I

Corporations with and without Net Income

MONEY AMOUNTS AND SIZE OF ASSETS IN THOUSANDS OF DOLLARS

Item Description for Accounting Period 7/04 Through 6/05	Total	Zero Assets	Under 500	500 to 1,000	1,000 to 5,000	5,000 to 10,000	10,000 to 25,000	25,000 to 50,000	50,000 to 100,000	100,000 to 250,000	250,000 to 500,000	500,000 to 2,500,000	2,500,000 and over
Number of Enterprises **1**	35112	5249	23069	2352	3457	471	287	96	60	30	19	15	7
Revenues ($ in Thousands)													
Net Sales **2**	188066736	4395229	11397771	4334629	33195921	13961556	11284677	7401035	11238370	8446822	11681660	28350305	42378761
Interest **3**	457323	2255	1166	1744	9263	3799	8523	11412	10294	21203	33839	98272	255552
Rents **4**	173450	0	0	2119	4304	593	2191	792	4091	2320	1751	33512	121778
Royalties **5**	181105	0	0	0	206	0	384	0	41933	5969	18820	34826	78967
Other Portfolio Income **6**	176314	24	5691	1763	29150	931	15085	2718	6209	7562	43711	26388	37082
Other Receipts **7**	1165339	12468	54911	61994	154517	19726	106762	22766	59458	110115	135728	149388	277506
Total Receipts **8**	190220267	4409976	11459539	4402249	33393361	13986605	11417622	7438723	11360355	8593991	11915509	28692691	43149646
Average Total Receipts **9**	5418	840	497	1872	9660	29696	39783	77487	189339	286466	627132	1912846	6164235
Operating Costs/Operating Income (%)													
Cost of Operations **10**	77.3	92.2	55.3	58.8	81.8	82.2	76.8	74.2	81.3	73.0	79.1	80.3	76.5
Salaries and Wages **11**	7.5	4.2	9.2	12.3	7.4	7.4	8.9	9.0	7.1	8.8	9.4	6.8	6.3
Taxes Paid **12**	0.9	0.4	1.8	1.8	0.9	0.9	1.1	1.1	0.8	1.0	1.0	0.7	0.8
Interest Paid **13**	0.7	0.5	0.5	0.7	0.3	0.5	0.5	0.5	0.5	0.7	0.5	0.9	1.2
Depreciation **14**	1.4	0.2	1.0	0.8	0.5	0.6	0.9	1.2	0.9	1.4	1.5	1.1	2.9
Amortization and Depletion **15**	0.2	0.2	0.0	0.1	0.0	0.1	0.2	0.3	0.4	0.3	0.4	0.3	0.2
Pensions and Other Deferred Comp. **16**	0.2	0.0	0.3	0.3	0.2	0.1	0.2	0.2	0.1	0.2	0.2	0.2	0.2
Employee Benefits **17**	0.7	0.1	0.6	0.7	0.6	0.7	0.7	0.7	0.8	1.1	0.9	0.8	0.8
Advertising **18**	0.8	0.2	0.9	2.2	0.3	0.3	0.8	0.7	0.5	1.3	1.3	1.3	0.9
Other Expenses **19**	7.7	4.4	19.8	15.1	5.8	5.5	8.4	8.6	6.1	9.9	6.3	5.7	7.7
Officers' Compensation **20**	1.4	0.6	7.7	5.4	2.0	1.0	1.5	1.2	0.6	0.8	0.7	0.2	0.2
Operating Margin **21**	1.2	•	2.9	2.0	0.3	0.9	0.1	2.2	0.9	1.6	•	1.7	2.3
Operating Margin Before Officers' Comp. **22**	2.5	•	10.7	7.4	2.3	1.9	1.6	3.4	1.5	2.4	•	1.9	2.5

Selected Average Balance Sheet ($ in Thousands)

Net Receivables 23	648	0	22	214	812	2630	5775	10970	26015	50789	105552	305381	758434
Inventories 24	385	0	22	200	423	2471	4059	8665	16783	31181	61742	135657	395603
Net Property, Plant and Equipment 25	186	0	16	63	266	618	1296	3500	7341	12162	26087	88306	208853
Total Assets 26	2500	0	93	716	2114	7092	15244	35864	72861	160614	359397	1086344	4737137
Notes and Loans Payable 27	683	0	71	219	570	2807	3714	6992	18126	38794	93921	230429	1328920
All Other Liabilities 28	924	0	40	238	961	3030	6870	15837	30300	60467	150799	433580	1389046
Net Worth 29	893	0	-18	259	583	1255	4659	13035	24436	61353	114677	422335	2019171

Selected Financial Ratios (Times to 1)

Current Ratio 30	1.4	•	1.4	1.8	1.5	1.4	1.5	1.5	1.4	1.6	1.1	1.7	1.3
Quick Ratio 31	0.8	•	0.8	1.0	1.0	0.8	0.9	0.9	0.8	0.9	0.7	1.0	0.6
Net Sales to Working Capital 32	12.5	•	22.6	7.3	16.9	15.9	10.1	8.1	12.4	7.2	22.9	7.8	14.7
Coverage Ratio 33	4.5	•	7.4	6.2	4.2	3.2	3.6	6.3	5.5	6.4	3.5	4.3	4.6
Total Asset Turnover 34	2.1	•	5.3	2.6	4.5	4.2	2.6	2.1	2.6	1.8	1.7	1.7	1.3
Inventory Turnover 35	10.7	•	12.2	5.4	18.6	9.9	7.4	6.6	9.1	6.6	7.9	11.2	11.7
Receivables Turnover 36	8.3	•	26.1	7.6	12.2	11.6	7.1	7.3	8.1	6.3	4.9	6.0	8.0
Total Liabilities to Net Worth 37	1.8	•	•	1.8	2.6	4.7	2.3	1.8	2.0	1.6	2.1	1.6	1.3
Current Assets to Working Capital 38	3.4	•	3.4	2.3	2.9	3.3	3.2	2.9	3.5	2.8	7.7	2.5	4.6
Current Liabilities to Working Capital 39	2.4	•	2.4	1.3	1.9	2.3	2.2	1.9	2.5	1.8	6.7	1.5	3.6
Working Capital to Net Sales 40	0.1	•	0.0	0.1	0.1	0.1	0.1	0.1	0.1	0.1	0.0	0.1	0.1
Inventory to Working Capital 41	0.9	•	1.0	0.9	0.8	1.3	1.0	1.0	1.2	0.8	2.0	0.6	1.1
Total Receipts to Cash Flow 42	11.5	169.1	5.1	6.4	18.8	17.6	12.1	9.7	14.0	8.6	16.9	13.0	9.3
Cost of Goods to Cash Flow 43	8.9	155.9	2.8	3.7	15.4	14.4	9.3	7.2	11.4	6.3	13.3	10.5	7.1
Cash Flow to Total Debt 44	0.3	•	0.9	0.6	0.3	0.3	0.3	0.3	0.3	0.3	0.1	0.2	0.2

Selected Financial Factors (in Percentages)

Debt Ratio 45	64.3	•	119.5	63.9	72.4	82.3	69.4	63.7	66.5	61.8	68.1	61.1	57.4
Return on Total Assets 46	6.6	•	21.4	10.8	5.2	6.6	4.4	6.9	6.5	7.7	2.9	6.5	6.9
Return on Equity Before Income Taxes 47	14.4	•	•	25.1	14.3	25.5	10.5	15.9	15.9	17.0	6.4	12.8	12.7
Return on Equity After Income Taxes 48	10.9	•	•	23.4	12.6	22.5	7.2	12.5	11.7	12.7	5.1	8.0	9.5
Profit Margin (Before Income Tax) 49	2.4	•	3.5	3.5	0.9	1.1	1.2	2.7	2.1	3.7	1.2	2.9	4.2
Profit Margin (After Income Tax) 50	1.8	•	3.4	3.3	0.8	1.0	0.8	2.1	1.5	2.8	0.9	1.8	3.2

Table II

Corporations with Net Income

PROFESSIONAL AND COMMERCIAL EQUIPMENT AND SUPPLIES

MONEY AMOUNTS AND SIZE OF ASSETS IN THOUSANDS OF DOLLARS

Item Description for Accounting Period 7/04 Through 6/05	Total	Zero Assets	Under 500	500 to 1,000	1,000 to 5,000	5,000 to 10,000	10,000 to 25,000	25,000 to 50,000	50,000 to 100,000	100,000 to 250,000	250,000 to 500,000	500,000 to 2,500,000	2,500,000 and over
Number of Enterprises 1	23411	2221	16017	1982	2453	352	215	76	43	20	12	0	0
Revenues ($ in Thousands)													
Net Sales 2	157460191	4094751	9734768	3770838	28108668	9983996	9412641	6107207	8660177	6555362	7650542	0	0
Interest 3	314331	1072	216	1518	6847	2691	5740	9539	4662	5087	27858	0	0
Rents 4	139592	0	0	38	4285	593	1112	457	4091	2300	1751	0	0
Royalties 5	140382	0	0	0	88	0	283	0	3107	5969	18793	0	0
Other Portfolio Income 6	143738	4	5691	1193	25518	913	12509	2296	3424	7244	41925	0	0
Other Receipts 7	939043	11868	19529	39881	151243	15854	92870	16562	54210	95608	47244	0	0
Total Receipts 8	159137277	4107695	9760204	3813468	28296649	10004047	9525155	6136061	8729671	6671570	7788113	0	0
Average Total Receipts 9	6798	1849	609	1924	11536	28421	44303	80738	203016	333578	649009	.	.
Operating Costs/Operating Income (%)													
Cost of Operations 10	77.3	93.7	54.5	57.4	82.9	81.6	76.7	74.4	80.3	72.5	79.0	.	.
Salaries and Wages 11	7.0	2.0	8.1	11.9	7.0	6.6	8.5	8.2	6.9	8.6	8.5	.	.
Taxes Paid 12	0.9	0.2	1.6	1.7	0.8	0.8	1.1	1.1	0.8	1.1	1.0	.	.
Interest Paid 13	0.5	0.3	0.5	0.6	0.2	0.2	0.4	0.5	0.4	0.4	0.5	.	.
Depreciation 14	1.3	0.1	0.9	0.7	0.4	0.6	0.8	1.2	0.8	0.8	1.6	.	.
Amortization and Depletion 15	0.1	0.1	0.0	0.1	0.0	0.0	0.1	0.2	0.2	0.2	0.3	.	.
Pensions and Other Deferred Comp. 16	0.2	0.0	0.3	0.3	0.2	0.1	0.2	0.3	0.1	0.2	0.2	.	.
Employee Benefits 17	0.6	0.0	0.5	0.7	0.5	0.7	0.7	0.7	0.8	1.1	0.8	.	.
Advertising 18	0.8	0.1	0.7	2.4	0.2	0.3	0.7	0.7	0.6	1.5	1.6	.	.
Other Expenses 19	7.2	2.6	18.6	14.2	4.5	5.5	7.2	7.7	6.0	9.8	5.3	.	.
Officers' Compensation 20	1.3	0.3	7.9	5.5	1.8	1.2	1.5	1.2	0.6	0.6	0.5	.	.
Operating Margin 21	2.7	0.8	6.3	4.7	1.5	2.3	2.1	4.0	2.4	3.2	0.6	.	.
Operating Margin Before Officers' Comp. 22	4.0	1.0	14.2	10.2	3.4	3.4	3.6	5.1	3.0	3.8	1.1	.	.

Selected Average Balance Sheet ($ in Thousands)

Net Receivables 23	758	0	21	205	899	2188	6222	11092	25687	48813	105125
Inventories 24	433	0	18	181	405	2642	3878	8625	16204	38566	69003
Net Property, Plant and Equipment 25	186	0	16	44	301	425	1348	3701	7447	14582	30874
Total Assets 26	2737	0	98	699	2162	6730	15523	35320	71215	162727	352813
Notes and Loans Payable 27	701	0	58	205	491	1844	3202	7066	18694	27041	107328
All Other Liabilities 28	1009	0	32	228	908	2966	6837	15478	30319	64671	153492
Net Worth 29	1027	0	8	265	764	1920	5484	12776	22201	71015	91993

Selected Financial Ratios (Times to 1)

Current Ratio 30	1.5	·	2.0	1.8	1.7	1.4	1.5	1.6	1.4	1.6	1.0
Quick Ratio 31	0.8	·	1.2	1.0	1.2	0.7	0.9	0.9	0.8	0.9	0.6
Net Sales to Working Capital 32	12.4	·	16.2	7.4	15.5	15.5	10.2	8.3	14.5	7.1	·
Coverage Ratio 33	8.0	4.9	13.9	10.5	11.1	10.9	8.9	10.3	8.8	13.6	6.9
Total Asset Turnover 34	2.5	·	6.2	2.7	5.3	4.2	2.8	2.3	2.8	2.0	1.8
Inventory Turnover 35	12.0	·	18.3	6.0	23.5	8.8	8.7	6.9	10.0	6.2	7.3
Receivables Turnover 36	9.5	·	32.5	8.3	14.1	12.6	7.7	8.1	9.1	6.8	5.3
Total Liabilities to Net Worth 37	1.7	·	11.6	1.6	1.8	2.5	1.8	1.8	2.2	1.3	2.8
Current Assets to Working Capital 38	3.2	·	2.0	2.2	2.4	3.3	2.9	2.8	3.8	2.6	·
Current Liabilities to Working Capital 39	2.2	·	1.0	1.2	1.4	2.3	1.9	1.8	2.8	1.6	·
Working Capital to Net Sales 40	0.1	·	0.1	0.1	0.1	0.1	0.1	0.1	0.1	0.1	·
Inventory to Working Capital 41	0.9	·	0.6	0.9	0.6	1.5	1.0	1.0	1.4	0.8	·
Total Receipts to Cash Flow 42	10.3	37.3	4.6	5.8	17.7	14.3	10.9	8.9	12.0	7.4	15.2
Cost of Goods to Cash Flow 43	7.9	35.0	2.5	3.3	14.7	11.6	8.4	6.6	9.7	5.4	12.0
Cash Flow to Total Debt 44	0.4	·	1.5	0.8	0.5	0.4	0.4	0.4	0.3	0.5	0.2

Selected Financial Factors (in Percentages)

Debt Ratio 45	62.5	·	92.1	62.0	64.7	71.5	64.7	63.8	68.8	56.4	73.9
Return on Total Assets 46	10.7	·	43.8	17.6	12.7	11.5	10.4	11.2	10.5	11.7	6.3
Return on Equity Before Income Taxes 47	25.0	·	511.6	42.0	32.8	36.5	26.2	27.9	29.8	24.8	20.6
Return on Equity After Income Taxes 48	20.4	·	502.8	40.0	31.0	33.9	22.5	23.5	23.3	19.2	18.1
Profit Margin (Before Income Tax) 49	3.8	1.1	6.5	5.9	2.2	2.5	3.3	4.4	3.3	5.4	3.0
Profit Margin (After Income Tax) 50	3.1	0.9	6.4	5.6	2.1	2.3	2.8	3.7	2.6	4.2	2.6

Table I

Corporations with and without Net Income

METAL AND MINERAL (EXCEPT PETROLEUM)

MONEY AMOUNTS AND SIZE OF ASSETS IN THOUSANDS OF DOLLARS

Item Description for Accounting Period 7/04 Through 6/05	Total	Zero Assets	Under 500	500 to 1,000	1,000 to 5,000	5,000 to 10,000	10,000 to 25,000	25,000 to 50,000	50,000 to 100,000	100,000 to 250,000	250,000 to 500,000	500,000 to 2,500,000	2,500,000 and over
Number of Enterprises **1**	4906	516	2098	627	907	330	215	94	55	31	17	12	3
Revenues ($ in Thousands)													
Net Sales **2**	113740539	1157808	1297978	1258923	6701256	6361544	10031278	8776088	9449385	11254479	11185251	33663463	12603085
Interest **3**	424159	7060	566	288	1606	3195	2613	5221	6022	22567	17718	164958	192345
Rents **4**	59196	394	0	0	3113	299	1760	1187	1532	3291	12746	16365	18508
Royalties **5**	203451	0	0	0	320	0	434	2	32	155	0	202164	343
Other Portfolio Income **6**	162953	66	3855	3578	1422	9465	6906	9618	9154	5900	30653	17316	65018
Other Receipts **7**	805528	41930	1841	3431	30592	27676	23057	59326	55543	47674	286988	47795	179680
Total Receipts **8**	115395826	1207258	1304240	1266220	6738309	6402179	10066048	8851442	9521668	11334066	11553356	34112061	13058979
Average Total Receipts **9**	23521	2340	622	2019	7429	19401	46819	94164	173121	365615	678433	2842672	4352993
Operating Costs/Operating Income (%)													
Cost of Operations **10**	86.8	91.6	73.9	64.7	77.6	81.0	84.4	86.1	84.7	88.2	83.1	90.2	94.6
Salaries and Wages **11**	3.2	3.0	3.9	3.5	5.5	4.2	3.6	3.1	3.1	2.1	4.6	2.9	1.7
Taxes Paid **12**	0.6	0.5	1.3	1.7	1.1	0.8	0.7	0.6	0.6	0.7	0.9	0.5	0.2
Interest Paid **13**	1.0	7.5	0.8	1.1	0.4	0.6	0.4	0.5	0.6	0.6	0.6	0.9	2.7
Depreciation **14**	0.8	0.2	1.7	1.0	1.1	0.8	0.6	0.6	0.7	0.6	1.2	0.7	0.8
Amortization and Depletion **15**	0.1	0.2	0.0	0.0	0.0	0.0	0.1	0.1	0.0	0.1	0.2	0.1	0.5
Pensions and Other Deferred Comp. **16**	0.2	0.1	0.6	0.3	0.4	0.2	0.2	0.2	0.3	0.3	0.3	0.3	0.0
Employee Benefits **17**	0.5	0.3	1.2	0.7	0.5	0.3	0.4	0.3	0.4	0.5	1.2	0.5	0.4
Advertising **18**	0.1	0.0	0.1	0.2	0.1	0.2	0.1	0.1	0.0	0.0	0.1	0.0	0.0
Other Expenses **19**	3.9	4.5	9.2	11.2	6.5	4.8	3.6	3.2	4.0	2.8	4.7	2.3	5.4
Officers' Compensation **20**	1.0	0.4	6.9	7.2	2.8	2.1	1.8	1.4	1.0	0.6	0.3	0.2	0.2
Operating Margin **21**	1.9	•	0.4	8.3	3.9	5.0	4.0	3.8	4.5	3.7	2.7	1.4	•
Operating Margin Before Officers' Comp. **22**	2.8	•	7.2	15.5	6.7	7.2	5.8	5.2	5.6	4.3	3.1	1.5	•

Selected Average Balance Sheet ($ in Thousands)

Net Receivables 23	2962	0	32	113	757	2106	5476	11167	22017	54615	81966	299259	964689
Inventories 24	2499	0	31	146	688	2481	5704	11511	25083	40890	100032	288776	359750
Net Property, Plant and Equipment 25	1458	0	25	82	263	675	1425	3482	6808	15326	54485	177139	684797
Total Assets 26	10434	0	145	677	2743	6904	15606	34109	69939	154356	367033	1119543	3607938
Notes and Loans Payable 27	3430	0	83	101	683	2252	4731	12759	22860	38626	86136	404404	1413342
All Other Liabilities 28	4062	0	21	106	981	1956	5816	12027	21952	61789	122945	448952	1766495
Net Worth 29	2942	0	41	470	1079	2696	5059	9323	25128	53941	157953	266187	428101

Selected Financial Ratios (Times to 1)

Current Ratio 30	1.5	•	2.0	3.1	1.9	1.7	1.6	1.5	1.8	1.6	1.8	1.3	1.1
Quick Ratio 31	0.7	•	1.4	2.1	1.0	0.8	0.8	0.7	0.8	0.8	0.8	0.6	0.7
Net Sales to Working Capital 32	10.0	•	12.4	5.8	7.4	8.2	9.1	9.6	6.8	7.4	6.4	15.3	26.1
Coverage Ratio 33	4.4	0.5	2.0	9.1	11.1	10.6	11.7	10.4	10.4	8.7	10.7	3.9	•
Total Asset Turnover 34	2.2	•	4.3	3.0	2.7	2.8	3.0	2.7	2.5	2.4	1.8	2.5	1.2
Inventory Turnover 35	8.1	•	14.8	8.9	8.3	6.3	6.9	7.0	5.8	7.8	5.5	8.8	11.0
Receivables Turnover 36	8.3	•	14.1	12.0	11.2	9.2	9.5	10.1	8.7	8.8	8.1	6.6	•
Total Liabilities to Net Worth 37	2.5	•	2.5	0.4	1.5	1.6	2.1	2.7	1.8	1.9	1.3	3.2	7.4
Current Assets to Working Capital 38	3.0	•	2.0	1.5	2.1	2.4	2.6	2.9	2.3	2.6	2.3	4.0	10.0
Current Liabilities to Working Capital 39	2.0	•	1.0	0.5	1.1	1.4	1.6	1.9	1.3	1.6	1.3	3.0	9.0
Working Capital to Net Sales 40	0.1	•	0.1	0.2	0.1	0.1	0.1	0.1	0.1	0.1	0.2	0.1	0.0
Inventory to Working Capital 41	1.3	•	0.4	0.5	0.9	1.1	1.2	1.4	1.2	1.0	1.1	1.8	2.2
Total Receipts to Cash Flow 42	16.1	•	14.3	5.8	10.8	10.8	14.0	14.2	11.7	15.1	10.9	23.3	68.4
Cost of Goods to Cash Flow 43	14.0	•	10.5	3.8	8.4	8.8	11.9	12.2	9.9	13.3	9.1	21.1	64.6
Cash Flow to Total Debt 44	0.2	•	0.4	1.7	0.4	0.4	0.3	0.3	0.3	0.2	0.3	0.1	0.0

Selected Financial Factors (in Percentages)

Debt Ratio 45	71.8	•	71.7	30.5	60.7	61.0	67.6	72.7	64.1	65.1	57.0	76.2	88.1
Return on Total Assets 46	9.5	•	7.2	28.8	13.1	17.5	14.3	14.1	14.4	11.6	11.5	9.1	•
Return on Equity Before Income Taxes 47	26.0	•	12.8	36.9	30.2	40.5	40.5	46.5	36.4	29.4	24.3	28.4	•
Return on Equity After Income Taxes 48	20.4	•	9.3	36.7	28.3	36.9	35.5	40.4	30.7	22.6	19.8	18.7	•
Profit Margin (Before Income Tax) 49	3.3	•	0.9	8.6	4.4	5.7	4.4	4.6	5.3	4.4	5.8	2.7	•
Profit Margin (After Income Tax) 50	2.6	•	0.6	8.6	4.1	5.2	3.9	4.0	4.5	3.4	4.8	1.8	•

Table II
Corporations with Net Income

METAL AND MINERAL (EXCEPT PETROLEUM)

MONEY AMOUNTS AND SIZE OF ASSETS IN THOUSANDS OF DOLLARS

Item Description for Accounting Period 7/04 Through 6/05	Total	Zero Assets	Under 500	500 to 1,000	1,000 to 5,000	5,000 to 10,000	10,000 to 25,000	25,000 to 50,000	50,000 to 100,000	100,000 to 250,000	250,000 to 500,000	500,000 to 2,500,000	2,500,000 and over
Number of Enterprises **1**	3681	96	1562	557	755	326	196	81	51	0	17	0	0
Revenues ($ in Thousands)													
Net Sales **2**	91235770	1059273	1122567	1187945	5526737	6298459	9195852	7642107	8825858	0	11185251	0	0
Interest **3**	247986	7046	288	283	1132	2962	2210	3848	5945	0	17718	0	0
Rents **4**	53748	345	0	0	3049	191	1723	1183	1532	0	12746	0	0
Royalties **5**	202352	0	0	0	0	0	434	0	32	0	0	0	0
Other Portfolio Income **6**	149507	66	332	3577	235	9306	6565	8656	8000	0	30653	0	0
Other Receipts **7**	794573	41755	945	3417	30647	27599	21747	53002	53638	0	286988	0	0
Total Receipts **8**	9263936	1108485	1124132	1195222	5561800	6338517	9228531	7708796	8895005	0	11533356	0	0
Average Total Receipts **9**	25179	11547	720	2146	7367	19443	47084	95170	174412	•	678433	•	•
Operating Costs/Operating Income (%)													
Cost of Operations **10**	84.8	92.8	75.2	67.4	75.5	80.8	83.7	85.1	84.4	•	83.1	•	•
Salaries and Wages **11**	3.6	1.9	3.3	3.4	6.1	4.2	3.7	3.2	3.0	•	4.6	•	•
Taxes Paid **12**	0.7	0.4	1.1	1.6	1.2	0.8	0.8	0.6	0.7	•	0.9	•	•
Interest Paid **13**	0.7	0.5	0.5	0.9	0.4	0.6	0.4	0.4	0.5	•	0.6	•	•
Depreciation **14**	0.8	0.2	1.5	1.0	1.2	0.8	0.6	0.6	0.7	•	1.2	•	•
Amortization and Depletion **15**	0.1	0.2	0.0	0.0	0.0	0.0	0.0	0.0	0.0	•	0.2	•	•
Pensions and Other Deferred Comp. **16**	0.3	0.1	0.7	0.4	0.5	0.2	0.2	0.2	0.3	•	0.3	•	•
Employee Benefits **17**	0.6	0.2	0.8	0.7	0.6	0.3	0.4	0.3	0.4	•	1.2	•	•
Advertising **18**	0.1	0.0	0.0	0.1	0.1	0.2	0.1	0.1	0.1	•	0.1	•	•
Other Expenses **19**	4.0	4.4	8.0	8.2	6.6	4.8	3.6	3.2	3.8	•	4.7	•	•
Officers' Compensation **20**	1.1	0.4	6.0	7.1	2.9	2.1	1.8	1.4	1.0	•	0.3	•	•
Operating Margin **21**	3.4	•	2.9	9.1	5.0	5.2	4.6	5.0	5.1	•	2.7	•	•
Operating Margin Before Officers' Comp. **22**	4.4	•	8.9	16.2	7.9	7.3	6.4	6.4	6.1	•	3.1	•	•

Selected Average Balance Sheet ($ in Thousands)

Net Receivables 23	3452	0	42	113	724	2101	5476	11329	22438	81966
Inventories 24	2627	0	21	134	647	2432	5466	11109	23158	85905
Net Property, Plant and Equipment 25	1154	0	24	78	254	673	1395	2946	6499	54485
Total Assets 26	11274	0	138	682	2797	6900	15578	34196	70374	367033
Notes and Loans Payable 27	3284	0	39	84	408	2256	4491	10684	21761	86136
All Other Liabilities 28	4144	0	21	116	895	1933	5695	11773	22136	122945
Net Worth 29	3846	0	77	482	1494	2710	5392	11739	26477	157953

Selected Financial Ratios (Times to 1)

Current Ratio 30	1.6	•	1.9	3.1	2.1	1.7	1.7	1.6	1.8	1.8
Quick Ratio 31	0.8	•	1.5	2.2	1.1	0.9	0.8	0.8	0.8	0.8
Net Sales to Working Capital 32	7.7	•	17.3	6.2	6.7	8.2	8.7	8.5	6.5	6.4
Coverage Ratio 33	7.9	7.8	7.2	11.5	15.0	10.8	13.5	14.2	12.4	10.7
Total Asset Turnover 34	2.2	•	5.2	3.1	2.6	2.8	3.0	2.8	2.5	1.8
Inventory Turnover 35	8.0	•	25.8	10.7	8.5	6.4	7.2	7.2	6.3	6.4
Receivables Turnover 36	9.8	•	15.3	12.6	12.4	10.1	10.0	10.6	9.6	10.4
Total Liabilities to Net Worth 37	1.9	•	0.8	0.4	0.9	1.5	1.9	1.9	1.7	1.3
Current Assets to Working Capital 38	2.6	•	2.1	1.5	1.9	2.4	2.5	2.6	2.2	2.3
Current Liabilities to Working Capital 39	1.6	•	1.1	0.5	0.9	1.4	1.5	1.6	1.2	1.3
Working Capital to Net Sales 40	0.1	•	0.1	0.2	0.1	0.1	0.1	0.1	0.2	0.2
Inventory to Working Capital 41	1.1	•	0.3	0.4	0.8	1.1	1.2	1.3	1.2	1.1
Total Receipts to Cash Flow 42	12.7	14.0	12.3	6.4	9.7	10.7	13.1	12.3	11.1	10.9
Cost of Goods to Cash Flow 43	10.8	13.0	9.3	4.3	7.3	8.7	10.9	10.4	9.3	9.1
Cash Flow to Total Debt 44	0.3	•	1.0	1.7	0.6	0.4	0.4	0.3	0.4	0.3

Selected Financial Factors (in Percentages)

Debt Ratio 45	65.9	•	44.0	29.4	46.6	60.7	65.4	65.7	62.4	57.0
Return on Total Assets 46	12.4	•	18.5	32.5	15.8	17.9	16.2	17.4	15.7	11.5
Return on Equity Before Income Taxes 47	31.8	•	28.4	42.0	27.5	41.4	43.4	47.0	38.3	24.3
Return on Equity After Income Taxes 48	26.1	•	25.9	41.7	25.9	37.7	38.4	41.5	32.5	19.8
Profit Margin (Before Income Tax) 49	4.9	3.6	3.1	9.5	5.6	5.8	5.0	5.8	5.9	5.8
Profit Margin (After Income Tax) 50	4.0	3.0	2.8	9.4	5.3	5.3	4.4	5.2	5.0	4.8

174

Table I

Corporations with and without Net Income

ELECTRICAL GOODS

MONEY AMOUNTS AND SIZE OF ASSETS IN THOUSANDS OF DOLLARS

Item Description for Accounting Period 7/04 Through 6/05	Total	Zero Assets	Under 500	500 to 1,000	1,000 to 5,000	5,000 to 10,000	10,000 to 25,000	25,000 to 50,000	50,000 to 100,000	100,000 to 250,000	250,000 to 500,000	500,000 to 2,500,000	2,500,000 and over
Number of Enterprises **1**	23820	4400	12201	2098	3597	769	397	168	82	48	26	29	5
Revenues ($ in Thousands)													
Net Sales **2**	245720428	2946906	7231463	3425530	25255105	13598603	15552625	14338564	12745387	17858139	15862561	66854594	50050950
Interest **3**	498018	2087	7672	4331	7898	3417	9658	11537	19265	17438	23165	230509	161041
Rents **4**	184511	5491	0	0	959	4020	2108	1639	18715	1073	2900	32105	115502
Royalties **5**	573088	0	0	0	0	0	3138	14751	747	3056	11715	42152	497529
Other Portfolio Income **6**	513027	2490	689	34	7914	30383	13002	25170	8941	11942	96528	212719	103217
Other Receipts **7**	2397423	38049	174667	53195	85144	86793	97639	171138	74637	167656	95016	884242	469244
Total Receipts **8**	249886495	2995023	7414491	3483090	25357020	13723216	15678170	14562799	12867692	18059304	16091885	68256321	51397483
Average Total Receipts **9**	10491	681	608	1660	7049	17846	39492	86683	156923	376236	618919	2353666	10279497
Operating Costs/Operating Income (%)													
Cost of Operations **10**	81.5	82.6	65.1	76.9	73.4	77.3	79.2	81.5	80.6	87.2	87.2	87.4	78.5
Salaries and Wages **11**	6.3	6.5	10.4	6.8	10.3	8.4	7.5	6.8	7.3	4.4	4.8	4.7	5.3
Taxes Paid **12**	0.8	0.7	1.7	1.3	1.1	1.1	1.0	0.9	0.9	0.7	0.7	0.4	0.7
Interest Paid **13**	0.6	0.3	0.6	0.4	0.4	0.7	0.4	0.4	0.5	0.4	0.4	0.9	0.7
Depreciation **14**	0.7	0.5	0.7	0.7	0.5	0.6	0.7	0.8	0.8	0.4	0.8	0.7	1.0
Amortization and Depletion **15**	1.3	0.5	1.0	0.2	0.0	0.1	0.1	0.1	0.1	0.1	0.6	0.2	5.6
Pensions and Other Deferred Comp. **16**	0.3	0.1	0.5	0.2	0.2	0.4	0.3	0.2	0.3	0.2	0.1	0.2	0.4
Employee Benefits **17**	0.6	0.7	0.7	0.5	0.6	0.6	0.6	0.5	0.7	0.4	0.3	0.6	0.6
Advertising **18**	0.8	0.6	0.6	0.3	0.4	0.5	0.5	0.6	0.6	0.7	0.7	0.8	1.4
Other Expenses **19**	6.4	7.2	14.9	9.3	8.7	7.8	6.2	6.9	5.9	5.2	4.3	4.2	7.5
Officers' Compensation **20**	0.9	1.0	5.3	5.8	2.8	1.8	1.4	1.0	0.7	0.4	0.4	0.1	0.1
Operating Margin **21**	•	•	•	•	1.5	0.8	2.0	0.2	1.5	0.0	•	•	•
Operating Margin Before Officers' Comp. **22**	0.8	0.3	3.7	3.4	4.4	2.6	3.5	1.2	2.2	0.4	0.2	•	•

Selected Average Balance Sheet ($ in Thousands)

Net Receivables 23	1381	0	48	158	824	2424	5917	13033	26496	55940	100128	266139	1489569
Inventories 24	1035	0	40	223	691	2324	4717	9961	19012	40114	60262	202447	990288
Net Property, Plant and Equipment 25	375	0	12	64	192	593	1199	2969	6368	8163	20422	84597	527195
Total Assets 26	4940	0	146	684	2199	7153	15314	34427	71076	147495	329584	1013292	7666452
Notes and Loans Payable 27	1112	0	85	167	683	2519	3670	6710	15065	43926	46053	173742	1709612
All Other Liabilities 28	2195	0	67	296	894	2963	6644	15860	28364	60435	155010	407944	3790404
Net Worth 29	1634	0	-7	221	623	1670	5000	11856	27647	43134	128521	431606	2166436

Selected Financial Ratios (Times to 1)

Current Ratio 30	1.4	•	1.6	2.0	1.7	1.5	1.6	1.5	1.7	1.5	1.3	1.5	1.2
Quick Ratio 31	0.7	•	1.0	1.0	1.0	0.8	0.9	0.9	1.0	0.9	0.8	0.8	0.5
Net Sales to Working Capital 32	10.1	•	12.8	5.9	9.3	8.0	8.0	8.6	6.7	9.6	13.9	11.4	11.2
Coverage Ratio 33	3.6	3.8	2.6	•	5.6	3.5	7.3	5.4	5.6	3.8	5.0	3.1	2.6
Total Asset Turnover 34	2.1	•	4.1	2.4	3.2	2.5	2.6	2.5	2.2	2.5	1.9	2.3	1.3
Inventory Turnover 35	8.1	•	9.6	5.6	7.5	5.9	6.6	7.0	6.6	8.1	8.8	10.0	7.9
Receivables Turnover 36	7.6	•	13.3	9.3	8.7	8.1	6.9	7.0	6.1	6.6	6.4	8.8	6.6
Total Liabilities to Net Worth 37	2.0	•	•	2.1	2.5	3.3	2.1	1.9	1.6	2.4	1.6	1.3	2.5
Current Assets to Working Capital 38	3.3	•	2.7	2.0	2.5	2.9	2.7	2.8	2.5	3.1	4.9	2.9	5.3
Current Liabilities to Working Capital 39	2.3	•	1.7	1.0	1.5	1.9	1.7	1.8	1.5	2.1	3.9	1.9	4.3
Working Capital to Net Sales 40	0.1	•	0.1	0.2	0.1	0.1	0.1	0.1	0.1	0.1	0.1	0.1	0.1
Inventory to Working Capital 41	1.1	•	0.8	0.8	0.9	1.1	1.0	1.1	0.9	1.0	1.5	1.1	1.3
Total Receipts to Cash Flow 42	14.8	14.9	8.2	15.5	10.9	12.6	12.9	13.9	13.7	17.6	20.9	20.1	13.6
Cost of Goods to Cash Flow 43	12.0	12.3	5.4	11.9	8.0	9.7	10.2	11.4	11.0	15.4	18.3	17.6	10.7
Cash Flow to Total Debt 44	0.2	•	0.5	0.2	0.4	0.3	0.3	0.3	0.3	0.2	0.1	0.2	0.1

Selected Financial Factors (in Percentages)

Debt Ratio 45	66.9	•	104.6	67.7	71.7	76.7	67.4	65.6	61.1	70.8	61.0	57.4	71.7
Return on Total Assets 46	4.8	6.1	•	•	7.5	6.0	8.4	5.4	6.5	4.0	3.4	6.1	2.5
Return on Equity Before Income Taxes 47	10.4	•	•	•	21.9	18.5	22.3	12.8	13.8	10.0	7.0	9.7	5.4
Return on Equity After Income Taxes 48	8.1	•	•	•	19.1	16.4	19.4	10.3	10.9	6.6	5.7	7.1	3.7
Profit Margin (Before Income Tax) 49	1.6	1.0	0.9	•	1.9	1.7	2.8	1.8	2.4	1.2	1.5	1.8	1.2
Profit Margin (After Income Tax) 50	1.3	0.7	0.7	•	1.7	1.6	2.5	1.4	1.9	0.8	1.2	1.3	0.8

Table II

Corporations with Net Income

ELECTRICAL GOODS

MONEY AMOUNTS AND SIZE OF ASSETS IN THOUSANDS OF DOLLARS

Item Description for Accounting Period 7/04 Through 6/05	Total	Zero Assets	Under 500	500 to 1,000	1,000 to 5,000	5,000 to 10,000	10,000 to 25,000	25,000 to 50,000	50,000 to 100,000	100,000 to 250,000	250,000 to 500,000	500,000 to 2,500,000	2,500,000 and over
Number of Enterprises **1**	14775	2350	7192	1214	2851	571	325	126	66	0	17	23	0

Revenues ($ in Thousands)

Item	Total	Zero Assets	Under 500	500 to 1,000	1,000 to 5,000	5,000 to 10,000	10,000 to 25,000	25,000 to 50,000	50,000 to 100,000	100,000 to 250,000	250,000 to 500,000	500,000 to 2,500,000	2,500,000 and over
Net Sales **2**	211794472	2673371	4496169	2240134	21735054	11590757	13476488	11770852	10946975	0	13862742	59537303	0
Interest **3**	418728	380	7474	1000	6513	1878	8160	8140	8429	0	13828	199554	0
Rents **4**	172538	12	0	0	819	3884	1929	1191	18080	0	2747	28656	0
Royalties **5**	537076	0	0	0	0	0	2971	236	96	0	7823	28186	0
Other Portfolio Income **6**	445332	1729	677	13	4103	22653	8132	18949	2134	0	78506	210512	0
Other Receipts **7**	1965043	31609	166382	22628	69198	73974	73889	110327	53724	0	58451	700412	0
Total Receipts **8**	215333189	2707101	4670702	2263775	21815687	11693146	13571569	11909695	11029438	0	14024097	60704623	0
Average Total Receipts **9**	14574	1152	649	1865	7652	20478	41759	94521	167113	•	824947	2639331	•

Operating Costs/Operating Income (%)

Item	Total	Zero Assets	Under 500	500 to 1,000	1,000 to 5,000	5,000 to 10,000	10,000 to 25,000	25,000 to 50,000	50,000 to 100,000	100,000 to 250,000	250,000 to 500,000	500,000 to 2,500,000	2,500,000 and over
Cost of Operations **10**	81.2	82.7	59.8	78.2	73.0	77.3	78.5	80.9	80.1	•	87.3	87.5	•
Salaries and Wages **11**	6.1	5.7	13.1	6.1	10.2	7.7	7.6	6.5	7.2	•	4.5	4.5	•
Taxes Paid **12**	0.7	0.5	1.8	1.1	1.1	1.0	1.0	0.8	0.9	•	0.7	0.4	•
Interest Paid **13**	0.5	0.3	0.1	0.5	0.4	0.5	0.4	0.3	0.4	•	0.3	0.8	•
Depreciation **14**	0.7	0.4	0.8	0.6	0.5	0.5	0.6	0.6	0.7	•	0.7	0.6	•
Amortization and Depletion **15**	1.4	0.5	0.0	0.1	0.0	0.0	0.1	0.1	0.1	•	0.5	0.2	•
Pensions and Other Deferred Comp. **16**	0.2	0.1	0.7	0.1	0.3	0.3	0.3	0.2	0.3	•	0.1	0.2	•
Employee Benefits **17**	0.6	0.6	0.7	0.3	0.6	0.4	0.6	0.5	0.6	•	0.2	0.7	•
Advertising **18**	0.8	0.6	0.6	0.2	0.4	0.4	0.5	0.4	0.6	•	0.6	0.7	•
Other Expenses **19**	6.1	5.4	15.1	6.6	7.9	7.0	5.8	5.9	5.7	•	3.7	4.0	•
Officers' Compensation **20**	0.8	0.5	5.0	3.5	2.7	1.7	1.4	1.0	0.7	•	0.3	0.1	•
Operating Margin **21**	0.9	2.9	2.2	2.8	2.8	3.0	3.2	2.7	2.6	•	1.0	0.4	•
Operating Margin Before Officers' Comp. **22**	1.7	3.5	7.1	6.3	5.6	4.7	4.6	3.8	3.4	•	1.3	0.5	•

Selected Average Balance Sheet ($ in Thousands)

Net Receivables 23	1849	0	37	200	884	2734	5976	13744	27257	•	116725	283444	•
Inventories 24	1283	0	29	226	711	2071	4613	9913	18512	•	84719	195220	•
Net Property, Plant and Equipment 25	505	0	13	60	177	604	1184	2702	5995	•	25358	86748	•
Total Assets 26	6535	0	146	686	2238	7161	15295	34415	70910	•	336265	1091587	•
Notes and Loans Payable 27	1332	0	37	161	649	2380	3425	6931	12787	•	49853	166130	•
All Other Liabilities 28	2900	0	56	234	872	2511	5684	14411	29270	•	146624	429520	•
Net Worth 29	2303	0	53	292	718	2270	6186	13073	28854	•	139788	495938	•

Selected Financial Ratios (Times to 1)

Current Ratio 30	1.5	•	2.1	2.1	1.7	1.7	1.8	1.7	1.7	•	1.5	1.6	•
Quick Ratio 31	0.7	•	1.4	1.2	0.9	1.0	1.0	1.0	1.0	•	0.9	0.8	•
Net Sales to Working Capital 32	10.1	•	10.1	5.8	9.3	7.8	7.3	8.2	7.1	•	10.3	11.4	•
Coverage Ratio 33	6.0	17.6	42.2	9.4	9.7	8.2	10.9	13.0	10.1	•	9.7	4.0	•
Total Asset Turnover 34	2.2	•	4.3	2.7	3.4	2.8	2.7	2.7	2.3	•	2.4	2.4	•
Inventory Turnover 35	9.1	•	13.0	6.4	7.8	7.6	7.1	7.6	7.2	•	8.4	11.6	•
Receivables Turnover 36	8.5	•	17.7	9.9	9.0	8.5	7.6	7.3	6.7	•	•	10.6	•
Total Liabilities to Net Worth 37	1.8	•	1.7	1.4	2.1	2.2	1.5	1.6	1.5	•	1.4	1.2	•
Current Assets to Working Capital 38	3.2	•	1.9	1.9	2.4	2.5	2.3	2.5	2.5	•	3.0	2.8	•
Current Liabilities to Working Capital 39	2.2	•	0.9	0.9	1.4	1.5	1.3	1.5	1.5	•	2.0	1.8	•
Working Capital to Net Sales 40	0.1	•	0.1	0.2	0.1	0.1	0.1	0.1	0.1	•	0.1	0.1	•
Inventory to Working Capital 41	1.0	•	0.5	0.7	0.9	0.8	0.9	0.9	0.9	•	1.1	1.0	•
Total Receipts to Cash Flow 42	13.3	11.6	5.6	11.6	10.2	10.6	11.9	11.8	12.4	•	19.2	18.8	•
Cost of Goods to Cash Flow 43	10.8	9.6	3.3	9.1	7.4	8.2	9.4	9.6	10.0	•	16.7	16.5	•
Cash Flow to Total Debt 44	0.3	•	1.2	0.4	0.5	0.4	0.4	0.4	0.3	•	0.2	0.2	•

Selected Financial Factors (in Percentages)

Debt Ratio 45	64.8	•	63.6	57.5	67.9	68.3	59.6	62.0	59.3	•	58.4	54.6	•
Return on Total Assets 46	7.0	•	26.6	11.6	12.1	12.5	11.6	11.5	8.8	•	6.4	7.4	•
Return on Equity Before Income Taxes 47	16.6	•	71.4	24.3	33.8	34.6	26.1	28.0	19.5	•	13.9	12.2	•
Return on Equity After Income Taxes 48	13.9	•	67.9	22.2	30.8	32.5	23.2	24.9	16.0	•	12.0	9.4	•
Profit Margin (Before Income Tax) 49	2.7	4.2	6.1	3.8	3.2	3.9	3.9	3.9	3.4	•	2.4	2.3	•
Profit Margin (After Income Tax) 50	2.2	3.9	5.8	3.5	2.9	3.6	3.5	3.5	2.8	•	2.1	1.8	•

Table I

Corporations with and without Net Income

HARDWARE, PLUMBING, HEATING EQUIPMENT, AND SUPPLIES

MONEY AMOUNTS AND SIZE OF ASSETS IN THOUSANDS OF DOLLARS

Item Description for Accounting Period 7/04 Through 6/05	Total	Zero Assets	Under 500	500 to 1,000	1,000 to 5,000	5,000 to 10,000	10,000 to 25,000	25,000 to 50,000	50,000 to 100,000	100,000 to 250,000	250,000 to 500,000	500,000 to 2,500,000	2,500,000 and over
Number of Enterprises **1**	14099	344	8431	2030	2259	586	293	87	40	15	4	9	0
Revenues ($ in Thousands)													
Net Sales **2**	90415145	171169	4885830	4642027	12914150	10648534	11118433	7454174	6467225	5719144	2901841	23492619	0
Interest **3**	135887	78	114	2686	13120	5103	8595	4363	8754	2526	454	90093	0
Rents **4**	21797	28	335	1368	2330	1299	2297	2359	3481	40	2060	6200	0
Royalties **5**	61738	0	0	0	0	1	947	2669	0	7911	0	50211	0
Other Portfolio Income **6**	84531	17465	17700	3292	11619	3172	7282	5528	4165	8547	687	5072	0
Other Receipts **7**	1670826	2806	62187	248356	164125	292924	83280	77149	66718	109405	52759	511118	0
Total Receipts **8**	92389924	191546	4966166	4897729	13105344	10951033	11220834	7546242	6550343	5847573	2957801	24155313	0
Average Total Receipts **9**	6553	557	589	2413	5801	18688	38296	86738	163759	389838	739450	2683924	•
Operating Costs/Operating Income (%)													
Cost of Operations **10**	74.7	73.1	66.7	68.6	72.0	71.1	74.8	76.6	79.1	80.6	72.3	77.6	•
Salaries and Wages **11**	9.2	8.6	9.9	11.1	9.1	10.9	9.6	8.7	7.7	7.2	10.6	8.8	•
Taxes Paid **12**	1.4	2.4	2.0	1.9	1.6	1.5	1.3	1.4	1.1	1.1	1.2	1.2	•
Interest Paid **13**	0.8	0.7	0.2	0.6	0.5	0.4	0.5	0.6	0.7	0.6	0.5	1.5	•
Depreciation **14**	0.8	0.7	0.5	0.6	0.8	1.3	0.7	0.7	0.8	0.8	1.2	0.8	•
Amortization and Depletion **15**	0.1	0.0	0.0	0.1	0.1	0.0	0.1	0.1	0.2	0.0	0.3	0.2	•
Pensions and Other Deferred Comp. **16**	0.4	2.1	0.4	0.7	0.5	0.5	0.3	0.5	0.3	0.3	0.4	0.3	•
Employee Benefits **17**	0.9	1.3	0.7	1.2	0.9	1.0	0.7	0.8	0.9	0.7	1.6	0.9	•
Advertising **18**	0.5	0.3	1.1	0.4	0.4	0.8	0.5	0.5	0.4	0.4	0.9	0.2	•
Other Expenses **19**	8.4	28.5	14.5	10.6	8.3	8.5	7.1	7.0	6.1	6.7	8.2	8.6	•
Officers' Compensation **20**	2.2	8.0	5.3	8.0	4.9	2.9	2.0	1.2	0.8	0.4	0.2	0.2	•
Operating Margin **21**	0.6	•	•	•	0.9	1.1	2.3	2.0	1.9	1.3	2.8	•	•
Operating Margin Before Officers' Comp. **22**	2.8	•	4.1	4.2	5.8	4.0	4.3	3.2	2.7	1.7	3.0	•	•

Selected Average Balance Sheet ($ in Thousands)

Net Receivables 23	780	0	28	246	721	2146	5019	11808	20853	48851	83648	331120
Inventories 24	840	0	24	211	895	2853	5986	11235	21496	48391	98326	312371
Net Property, Plant and Equipment 25	263	0	10	67	178	663	1280	3384	7869	17693	63925	132288
Total Assets 26	2611	0	86	734	2242	6805	15273	34541	65607	147098	400035	1292933
Notes and Loans Payable 27	819	0	70	213	471	1621	4269	10283	17205	39335	74116	532545
All Other Liabilities 28	863	0	48	290	733	2044	4446	10624	21669	55584	157194	418468
Net Worth 29	928	0	-33	230	1038	3140	6558	13633	26733	52179	168726	341920

Selected Financial Ratios (Times to 1)

Current Ratio 30	1.9	•	1.4	1.7	2.2	2.0	1.8	1.8	1.9	1.6	1.8	1.9
Quick Ratio 31	1.0	•	0.9	1.0	1.1	0.9	0.8	0.9	1.0	0.8	1.0	1.0
Net Sales to Working Capital 32	7.1	•	31.7	9.5	5.9	6.3	6.6	6.9	6.8	8.3	5.8	7.2
Coverage Ratio 33	4.7	•	3.7	3.9	5.9	9.7	6.9	6.5	5.6	7.4	11.4	2.6
Total Asset Turnover 34	2.5	•	6.8	3.1	2.5	2.7	2.5	2.5	2.5	2.6	1.8	2.0
Inventory Turnover 35	5.7	•	16.3	7.4	4.6	4.5	4.7	5.8	5.9	6.3	5.3	6.5
Receivables Turnover 36	8.4	•	20.5	10.5	7.0	9.2	7.6	8.1	7.9	9.9	9.0	8.1
Total Liabilities to Net Worth 37	1.8	•	•	2.2	1.2	1.2	1.3	1.5	1.5	1.8	1.4	2.8
Current Assets to Working Capital 38	2.1	•	3.8	2.4	1.9	2.0	2.2	2.3	2.1	2.6	2.3	2.1
Current Liabilities to Working Capital 39	1.1	•	2.8	1.4	0.9	1.0	1.2	1.3	1.1	1.6	1.3	1.1
Working Capital to Net Sales 40	0.1	•	0.0	0.1	0.2	0.2	0.2	0.1	0.1	0.1	0.2	0.1
Inventory to Working Capital 41	1.0	•	1.1	1.0	0.8	1.0	1.1	1.0	0.9	1.3	0.8	0.9
Total Receipts to Cash Flow 42	10.9	29.6	8.3	10.7	11.4	9.6	12.0	11.9	13.0	11.8	9.0	10.7
Cost of Goods to Cash Flow 43	8.1	21.6	5.5	7.3	8.2	6.8	9.0	9.1	10.3	9.5	6.5	8.3
Cash Flow to Total Debt 44	0.4	•	0.6	0.4	0.4	0.5	0.4	0.3	0.3	0.3	0.3	0.3

Selected Financial Factors (in Percentages)

Debt Ratio 45	64.4	•	138.3	68.6	53.7	53.9	57.1	60.5	59.3	64.5	57.8	73.6
Return on Total Assets 46	8.7	•	4.0	7.4	7.3	11.7	9.2	9.5	9.4	10.6	9.4	7.9
Return on Equity Before Income Taxes 47	19.2	•	•	17.4	13.2	22.7	18.3	20.4	19.0	25.8	20.3	18.6
Return on Equity After Income Taxes 48	15.5	•	•	14.5	11.2	21.7	15.8	17.3	14.6	20.3	19.4	11.6
Profit Margin (Before Income Tax) 49	2.8	•	0.4	1.8	2.4	3.9	3.2	3.3	3.1	3.5	4.7	2.4
Profit Margin (After Income Tax) 50	2.2	•	0.4	1.5	2.0	3.7	2.7	2.8	2.4	2.8	4.5	1.5

Table II

Corporations with Net Income

HARDWARE, PLUMBING, HEATING EQUIPMENT, AND SUPPLIES

MONEY AMOUNTS AND SIZE OF ASSETS IN THOUSANDS OF DOLLARS

Item Description for Accounting Period 7/04 Through 6/05	Total	Zero Assets	Under 500	500 to 1,000	1,000 to 5,000	5,000 to 10,000	10,000 to 25,000	25,000 to 50,000	50,000 to 100,000	100,000 to 250,000	250,000 to 500,000	500,000 to 2,500,000	2,500,000 and over
Number of Enterprises **1**	9237	66	4666	1752	1833	516	268	78	36	0	0	6	0
Revenues ($ in Thousands)													
Net Sales **2**	78290401	87910	3082878	4248006	11231640	9103071	10366291	6687132	5933775	0	0	20044730	0
Interest **3**	128191	64	61	1689	9390	4403	7892	4308	8274	0	0	89164	0
Rents **4**	18263	28	335	1368	2146	1066	1816	1677	3481	0	0	4246	0
Royalties **5**	57261	0	0	0	0	1	947	2669	0	0	0	45734	0
Other Portfolio Income **6**	72999	17464	14852	2529	11157	2560	7139	5286	4150	0	0	4947	0
Other Receipts **7**	1603973	2786	55131	243241	154387	282623	79326	72272	47323	0	0	508980	0
Total Receipts **8**	80171088	108252	3153257	4496833	11408720	9393724	10463411	6773344	5997003	0	0	21097801	0
Average Total Receipts **9**	8679	1640	676	2567	6224	18205	39043	86838	166583	•	•	3516300	•
Operating Costs/Operating Income (%)													
Cost of Operations **10**	74.8	60.3	63.3	67.7	71.7	69.4	74.7	76.4	79.0	•	•	80.0	•
Salaries and Wages **11**	9.3	10.0	7.6	11.2	8.7	11.6	9.5	8.6	7.6	•	•	8.9	•
Taxes Paid **12**	1.4	4.5	1.7	1.9	1.6	1.6	1.3	1.4	1.1	•	•	1.3	•
Interest Paid **13**	0.7	0.9	0.2	0.5	0.4	0.4	0.5	0.5	0.5	•	•	1.3	•
Depreciation **14**	0.8	0.9	0.5	0.6	0.8	1.4	0.7	0.7	0.8	•	•	0.7	•
Amortization and Depletion **15**	0.1	0.0	0.0	0.1	0.0	0.0	0.0	0.1	0.1	•	•	0.2	•
Pensions and Other Deferred Comp. **16**	0.4	4.0	0.3	0.7	0.6	0.5	0.3	0.5	0.4	•	•	0.3	•
Employee Benefits **17**	0.9	0.5	0.1	1.2	0.8	1.1	0.7	0.9	1.0	•	•	0.9	•
Advertising **18**	0.4	0.5	1.4	0.3	0.4	0.9	0.5	0.5	0.4	•	•	0.2	•
Other Expenses **19**	7.5	5.8	14.4	10.6	7.8	8.7	6.7	6.8	5.6	•	•	6.4	•
Officers' Compensation **20**	2.2	15.6	4.5	8.4	5.1	2.8	2.1	1.2	0.9	•	•	0.1	•
Operating Margin **21**	1.5	•	6.0	•	1.9	1.6	2.9	2.5	2.7	•	•	•	•
Operating Margin Before Officers' Comp. **22**	3.7	12.6	10.5	5.1	7.0	4.5	5.0	3.6	3.5	•	•	•	•

Selected Average Balance Sheet ($ in Thousands)

Net Receivables 23	1036	0	26	243	746	2048	5106	11957	21222	•	437062
Inventories 24	1077	0	16	198	856	2828	5985	11058	20685	•	383302
Net Property, Plant and Equipment 25	334	0	9	62	190	642	1246	3294	8562	•	158263
Total Assets 26	3361	0	84	739	2209	6613	15326	34724	65357	•	1626905
Notes and Loans Payable 27	987	0	17	178	459	1496	3989	10054	16327	•	650845
All Other Liabilities 28	1039	0	31	306	694	1993	4375	9680	22565	•	504137
Net Worth 29	1335	0	35	255	1056	3124	6962	14990	26465	•	471923

Selected Financial Ratios (Times to 1)

Current Ratio 30	2.0	•	2.0	1.6	2.3	2.0	1.9	1.9	1.8	•	2.1
Quick Ratio 31	1.0	•	1.6	0.9	1.2	0.9	0.9	1.0	0.9	•	1.1
Net Sales to Working Capital 32	6.8	•	19.0	10.4	5.8	6.0	6.4	6.3	7.4	•	6.9
Coverage Ratio 33	6.7	22.8	55.7	5.7	9.8	12.1	8.6	7.9	8.0	•	3.2
Total Asset Turnover 34	2.5	•	7.9	3.3	2.8	2.7	2.5	2.5	2.5	•	2.1
Inventory Turnover 35	5.9	•	26.3	8.3	5.1	4.3	4.8	5.9	6.3	•	7.1
Receivables Turnover 36	8.6	•	26.0	11.5	8.0	9.1	7.7	8.2	8.5	•	8.0
Total Liabilities to Net Worth 37	1.5	•	1.4	1.9	1.1	1.1	1.2	1.3	1.5	•	2.4
Current Assets to Working Capital 38	2.0	•	2.0	2.6	1.7	2.0	2.1	2.1	2.3	•	1.9
Current Liabilities to Working Capital 39	1.0	•	1.0	1.6	0.7	1.0	1.1	1.1	1.3	•	0.9
Working Capital to Net Sales 40	0.1	•	0.1	0.1	0.2	0.2	0.2	0.2	0.1	•	0.1
Inventory to Working Capital 41	0.9	•	0.4	1.0	0.8	1.0	1.1	0.9	1.0	•	0.8
Total Receipts to Cash Flow 42	10.5	18.0	4.9	9.9	10.6	8.8	11.7	11.4	12.8	•	12.8
Cost of Goods to Cash Flow 43	7.9	10.9	3.1	6.7	7.6	6.1	8.7	8.7	10.1	•	10.3
Cash Flow to Total Debt 44	0.4	•	2.7	0.5	0.5	0.6	0.4	0.4	0.3	•	0.2

Selected Financial Factors (in Percentages)

Debt Ratio 45	60.3	•	58.0	65.5	52.2	52.8	54.6	56.8	59.5	•	71.0
Return on Total Assets 46	11.5	•	66.8	10.2	10.8	14.0	10.9	10.6	10.7	•	9.1
Return on Equity Before Income Taxes 47	24.7	•	156.3	24.4	20.2	27.2	21.2	21.4	23.2	•	21.8
Return on Equity After Income Taxes 48	20.9	•	154.2	21.3	17.8	26.1	18.6	18.3	19.7	•	14.2
Profit Margin (Before Income Tax) 49	3.9	20.1	8.3	2.6	3.5	4.8	3.8	3.7	3.7	•	3.0
Profit Margin (After Income Tax) 50	3.3	13.5	8.2	2.2	3.1	4.6	3.3	3.2	3.2	•	2.0

Table I

Corporations with and without Net Income

MACHINERY, EQUIPMENT, AND SUPPLIES

MONEY AMOUNTS AND SIZE OF ASSETS IN THOUSANDS OF DOLLARS

Item Description for Accounting Period 7/04 Through 6/05	Total	Zero Assets	Under 500	500 to 1,000	1,000 to 5,000	5,000 to 10,000	10,000 to 25,000	25,000 to 50,000	50,000 to 100,000	100,000 to 250,000	250,000 to 500,000	500,000 to 2,500,000	2,500,000 and over
Number of Enterprises **1**	51984	5637	31225	4472	8069	1391	775	211	97	64	25	18	0
Revenues ($ in Thousands)													
Net Sales **2**	198985949	3378461	15928518	9139414	42401687	24458781	24212422	13269904	10852753	14405018	11851837	29087154	0
Interest **3**	422847	3305	6404	5265	30596	13614	23723	15790	26389	48346	19623	229792	0
Rents **4**	187481	1191	0	7308	35863	14864	13160	11021	11392	10194	24342	58145	0
Royalties **5**	27632	0	0	0	6	2150	989	1022	35	8371	4493	10566	0
Other Portfolio Income **6**	1309436	46588	23904	13492	81407	66082	129349	72968	145196	220365	185403	324681	0
Other Receipts **7**	2205999	23747	190257	50599	570993	227719	215593	155048	104929	258991	243631	164491	0
Total Receipts **8**	203139344	3453292	16149083	9216078	43120552	24783210	24595236	13525753	11140694	14951285	12329329	29874829	0
Average Total Receipts **9**	3908	613	517	2061	5344	17817	31736	64103	114853	233614	493173	1659713	.
Operating Costs/Operating Income (%)													
Cost of Operations **10**	74.8	91.3	63.2	69.8	73.4	77.4	76.9	77.4	76.0	75.3	77.0	75.9	.
Salaries and Wages **11**	7.7	2.7	7.0	8.0	8.1	8.3	7.9	7.9	8.1	6.9	7.3	7.7	.
Taxes Paid **12**	1.3	0.4	1.7	1.8	1.5	1.2	1.1	1.2	1.2	1.0	1.0	1.3	.
Interest Paid **13**	0.8	0.6	0.6	1.0	0.6	0.6	0.7	0.8	1.2	1.0	1.5	0.9	.
Depreciation **14**	2.2	0.8	1.2	1.9	1.4	1.2	2.2	2.1	3.7	4.5	5.3	1.9	.
Amortization and Depletion **15**	0.1	0.0	0.1	0.1	0.1	0.1	0.1	0.2	0.2	0.2	0.2	0.2	.
Pensions and Other Deferred Comp. **16**	0.4	0.0	0.6	0.2	0.4	0.4	0.3	0.3	0.3	0.3	0.4	0.6	.
Employee Benefits **17**	0.9	0.3	0.9	0.8	0.8	0.7	0.9	0.7	0.9	1.6	1.4	1.0	.
Advertising **18**	0.5	0.2	0.5	0.6	0.5	0.4	0.4	0.5	0.6	0.4	0.2	0.7	.
Other Expenses **19**	8.2	4.7	14.4	10.9	8.9	7.0	7.0	7.3	7.3	8.5	7.4	6.3	.
Officers' Compensation **20**	2.2	1.0	7.4	5.0	3.2	2.2	1.5	1.2	0.8	0.8	0.5	0.4	.
Operating Margin **21**	0.9	.	2.4	.	1.1	0.7	0.9	0.5	.	.	.	3.0	.
Operating Margin Before Officers' Comp. **22**	3.1	.	9.8	5.0	4.3	2.8	2.4	1.6	0.6	0.5	.	3.5	.

Selected Average Balance Sheet ($ in Thousands)

Net Receivables 23	507	0	36	198	605	2204	3930	8766	17690	39233	75700	298455	•
Inventories 24	607	0	34	216	872	2701	5750	12559	18997	52036	102061	216551	•
Net Property, Plant and Equipment 25	276	0	19	107	274	764	2088	4647	14132	23654	71297	150390	•
Total Assets 26	1902	0	129	734	2173	6895	15286	33971	68090	160365	348555	1102974	•
Notes and Loans Payable 27	603	0	67	316	722	1888	5080	11020	25701	46932	125096	249958	•
All Other Liabilities 28	651	0	36	224	768	2739	5278	12099	20174	55808	126880	349108	•
Net Worth 29	648	0	26	194	683	2268	4929	10852	22215	56625	96579	503909	•

Selected Financial Ratios (Times to 1)

Current Ratio 30	1.6	•	2.1	1.9	1.6	1.5	1.5	1.5	1.4	1.5	1.4	1.9	•
Quick Ratio 31	0.8	•	1.2	1.0	0.7	0.7	0.6	0.6	0.6	0.7	0.6	1.0	•
Net Sales to Working Capital 32	7.2	•	9.9	7.7	7.7	9.6	7.7	7.7	8.3	5.7	7.3	4.6	•
Coverage Ratio 33	4.7	1.3	6.9	1.8	5.5	4.3	4.4	4.1	3.1	4.7	2.2	7.4	•
Total Asset Turnover 34	2.0	•	4.0	2.8	2.4	2.6	2.0	1.9	1.6	1.4	1.4	1.5	•
Inventory Turnover 35	4.7	•	9.6	6.6	4.4	5.0	4.2	3.9	4.5	3.3	3.6	5.7	•
Receivables Turnover 36	7.9	•	14.1	11.7	8.3	8.8	8.5	7.8	7.1	5.8	6.7	5.6	•
Total Liabilities to Net Worth 37	1.9	•	4.0	2.8	2.2	2.0	2.1	2.1	2.1	1.8	2.6	1.2	•
Current Assets to Working Capital 38	2.6	•	1.9	2.1	2.6	3.1	2.9	3.2	3.4	2.9	3.3	2.1	•
Current Liabilities to Working Capital 39	1.6	•	0.9	1.1	1.6	2.1	1.9	2.2	2.4	1.9	2.3	1.1	•
Working Capital to Net Sales 40	0.1	•	0.1	0.1	0.1	0.1	0.1	0.1	0.1	0.2	0.1	0.2	•
Inventory to Working Capital 41	1.2	•	0.7	0.8	1.2	1.5	1.5	1.6	1.7	1.3	1.8	0.7	•
Total Receipts to Cash Flow 42	11.0	31.6	7.0	11.4	10.3	13.0	12.6	12.3	12.6	10.6	13.8	10.0	•
Cost of Goods to Cash Flow 43	8.2	28.8	4.4	7.9	7.5	10.1	9.7	9.5	9.6	8.0	10.7	7.6	•
Cash Flow to Total Debt 44	0.3	•	0.7	0.3	0.3	0.3	0.2	0.2	0.2	0.2	0.1	0.3	•

Selected Financial Factors (in Percentages)

Debt Ratio 45	65.9	•	80.0	73.5	68.6	67.1	67.8	68.1	67.4	64.7	72.3	54.3	•
Return on Total Assets 46	7.6	•	17.6	5.0	8.3	6.6	6.4	5.8	6.0	6.3	4.4	9.7	•
Return on Equity Before Income Taxes 47	17.6	•	75.1	8.1	21.7	15.5	15.5	13.8	12.4	14.0	8.8	18.4	•
Return on Equity After Income Taxes 48	13.9	•	73.2	6.6	19.9	13.3	13.0	10.8	9.7	11.5	5.1	11.5	•
Profit Margin (Before Income Tax) 49	3.0	0.2	3.8	0.8	2.8	2.0	2.4	2.4	2.5	3.5	1.8	5.7	•
Profit Margin (After Income Tax) 50	2.4	0.0	3.7	0.6	2.6	1.7	2.1	1.9	1.9	2.9	1.0	3.6	•

Table II

Corporations with Net Income

MACHINERY, EQUIPMENT, AND SUPPLIES

MONEY AMOUNTS AND SIZE OF ASSETS IN THOUSANDS OF DOLLARS

Item Description for Accounting Period 7/04 Through 6/05	Total	Zero Assets	Under 500	500 to 1,000	1,000 to 5,000	5,000 to 10,000	10,000 to 25,000	25,000 to 50,000	50,000 to 100,000	100,000 to 250,000	250,000 to 500,000	500,000 to 2,500,000	2,500,000 and over
Number of Enterprises **1**	34483	1884	21267	3294	5964	1144	613	159	74	52	17	15	0
Revenues ($ in Thousands)													
Net Sales **2**	161034501	2695730	13135999	7638545	34490656	20321100	19920658	10719931	8145892	12643120	8699451	22623420	0
Interest **3**	313176	1482	1987	4542	25409	11436	19977	13448	20539	32106	9114	173136	0
Rents **4**	144226	0	0	7168	25888	14657	10596	9031	5197	9962	14435	47292	0
Royalties **5**	18829	0	0	0	6	27	983	951	35	8371	351	8105	0
Other Portfolio Income **6**	866928	1667	12759	11105	60413	39381	88691	44040	89852	159776	51535	307704	0
Other Receipts **7**	1914252	10383	120110	46073	553616	222484	187386	113402	67823	215871	230826	146282	0
Total Receipts **8**	164291912	2709262	13270855	7707433	35155988	20609085	20228291	10900803	8329338	13069206	9005712	23305939	0
Average Total Receipts **9**	4764	1438	624	2340	5895	18015	32999	68559	112559	251331	529748	1553729	.
Operating Costs/Operating Income (%)													
Cost of Operations **10**	74.0	93.3	64.4	68.7	72.7	77.6	76.9	77.2	76.2	75.6	78.1	70.6	.
Salaries and Wages **11**	7.6	0.8	5.4	7.6	8.0	8.0	7.6	7.5	7.6	6.2	7.2	9.3	.
Taxes Paid **12**	1.3	0.1	1.7	1.7	1.4	1.2	1.1	1.2	1.2	1.0	1.0	1.6	.
Interest Paid **13**	0.7	0.1	0.5	0.9	0.6	0.6	0.6	0.7	0.9	0.8	1.0	0.9	.
Depreciation **14**	1.8	0.2	0.9	2.0	1.3	0.8	1.8	1.6	2.9	4.4	3.2	2.0	.
Amortization and Depletion **15**	0.1	0.0	0.1	0.1	0.1	0.0	0.1	0.1	0.1	0.2	0.2	0.3	.
Pensions and Other Deferred Comp. **16**	0.4	0.0	0.6	0.1	0.5	0.4	0.3	0.3	0.3	0.3	0.4	0.7	.
Employee Benefits **17**	0.9	0.1	0.9	0.7	0.8	0.8	0.8	0.7	0.8	1.5	1.5	1.2	.
Advertising **18**	0.5	0.1	0.4	0.6	0.5	0.4	0.4	0.5	0.7	0.4	0.1	0.8	.
Other Expenses **19**	7.6	2.9	12.5	9.7	8.6	6.2	6.5	7.0	6.7	7.6	6.4	6.6	.
Officers' Compensation **20**	2.2	0.3	7.0	5.3	3.1	2.3	1.5	1.1	0.8	0.7	0.5	0.5	.
Operating Margin **21**	2.8	2.0	5.6	2.6	2.5	1.8	2.2	2.2	1.9	1.4	0.4	5.3	.
Operating Margin Before Officers' Comp. **22**	5.0	2.3	12.6	7.8	5.6	4.0	3.8	3.3	2.7	2.1	0.9	5.9	.

Selected Average Balance Sheet ($ in Thousands)

Net Receivables 23	612	0	42	223	611	2266	3922	8800	18404	40419	81366	306510
Inventories 24	702	0	34	178	886	2687	5620	12863	18144	48005	102428	232339
Net Property, Plant and Equipment 25	296	0	18	124	256	597	1804	4159	12546	24113	59922	149464
Total Assets 26	2236	0	135	737	2194	6806	15186	34193	67323	163907	344632	1120783
Notes and Loans Payable 27	659	0	49	293	658	1784	4699	10465	22290	46441	116231	277743
All Other Liabilities 28	702	0	36	223	683	2521	5185	11995	20239	55631	130052	271291
Net Worth 29	875	0	51	220	853	2501	5303	11733	24793	61834	98349	571749

Selected Financial Ratios (Times to 1)

Current Ratio 30	1.7	·	2.2	1.7	1.9	1.6	1.6	1.5	1.4	1.5	1.5	2.0
Quick Ratio 31	0.8	·	1.3	1.0	0.9	0.8	0.7	0.6	0.7	0.7	0.6	1.1
Net Sales to Working Capital 32	6.8	·	10.4	10.0	7.0	8.1	7.2	7.2	7.8	5.8	7.1	4.1
Coverage Ratio 33	7.9	37.9	13.3	4.7	8.8	6.7	6.9	6.9	5.5	7.2	4.8	10.0
Total Asset Turnover 34	2.1	·	4.6	3.1	2.6	2.6	2.1	2.0	1.6	1.5	1.5	1.3
Inventory Turnover 35	4.9	·	11.8	9.0	4.7	5.1	4.4	4.0	4.6	3.8	3.9	4.6
Receivables Turnover 36	8.6	·	17.2	12.8	9.3	8.7	9.4	8.5	7.1	7.2	7.5	5.7
Total Liabilities to Net Worth 37	1.6	·	1.7	2.3	1.6	1.7	1.9	1.9	1.7	1.7	2.5	1.0
Current Assets to Working Capital 38	2.4	·	1.8	2.4	2.2	2.6	2.8	2.9	3.3	2.8	3.0	2.0
Current Liabilities to Working Capital 39	1.4	·	0.8	1.4	1.2	1.6	1.8	1.9	2.3	1.8	2.0	1.0
Working Capital to Net Sales 40	0.1	·	0.1	0.1	0.1	0.1	0.1	0.1	0.1	0.2	0.1	0.2
Inventory to Working Capital 41	1.1	·	0.6	0.9	1.1	1.3	1.5	1.5	1.6	1.4	1.6	0.7
Total Receipts to Cash Flow 42	9.5	19.3	6.5	9.3	9.0	12.3	11.3	10.7	10.8	9.9	11.2	8.0
Cost of Goods to Cash Flow 43	7.1	18.0	4.2	6.4	6.5	9.5	8.7	8.3	8.3	7.5	8.8	5.6
Cash Flow to Total Debt 44	0.4	·	1.1	0.5	0.5	0.3	0.3	0.3	0.2	0.2	0.2	0.3

Selected Financial Factors (in Percentages)

Debt Ratio 45	60.9	·	62.3	70.1	61.1	63.2	65.1	65.7	63.2	62.3	71.5	49.0
Return on Total Assets 46	11.5	·	32.9	14.0	13.1	9.7	9.4	8.9	8.3	8.2	7.3	12.5
Return on Equity Before Income Taxes 47	25.6	·	80.8	36.8	29.8	22.5	23.1	22.3	18.4	18.7	20.3	22.1
Return on Equity After Income Taxes 48	21.5	·	79.4	34.9	27.9	20.2	20.2	18.6	15.3	15.9	14.9	14.7
Profit Margin (Before Income Tax) 49	4.8	2.5	6.7	3.5	4.4	3.2	3.8	3.9	4.2	4.8	3.9	8.4
Profit Margin (After Income Tax) 50	4.0	2.4	6.6	3.3	2.8	2.8	3.3	3.2	3.4	4.0	2.9	5.6

Table I

Corporations with and without Net Income

FURNITURE, SPORTS, TOYS, JEWELRY, OTHER DURABLE GOODS

Money Amounts and Size of Assets in Thousands of Dollars

Item Description for Accounting Period 7/04 Through 6/05	Total	Zero Assets	Under 500	500 to 1,000	1,000 to 5,000	5,000 to 10,000	10,000 to 25,000	25,000 to 50,000	50,000 to 100,000	100,000 to 250,000	250,000 to 500,000	500,000 to 2,500,000	2,500,000 and over
Number of Enterprises 1	70914	8131	48334	4955	6806	1395	832	240	115	61	25	15	3
Revenues ($ in Thousands)													
Net Sales 2	223151978	1641255	21540669	9217771	39792301	21456356	29507683	19613966	17065539	14584018	9815903	25084538	13831980
Interest 3	298666	4438	4991	8299	15274	8719	18055	9789	32385	53305	26953	71357	45099
Rents 4	103171	1553	2264	4016	8826	3861	6460	4667	5997	1575	12176	34530	17247
Royalties 5	342037	246	0	5208	1942	1222	7434	2755	41629	58399	33686	83503	106012
Other Portfolio Income 6	365967	36930	29668	7917	36267	27369	27906	6195	22534	61972	58165	32266	18785
Other Receipts 7	2050446	28623	187558	34217	335649	82335	169863	97469	124950	284502	353653	288362	63259
Total Receipts 8	226312265	1713045	21765150	9277428	40190259	21579862	29737401	19734841	17293034	15043771	10300536	25594556	14082382
Average Total Receipts 9	3191	211	450	1872	5905	15469	35742	82229	150374	246619	412021	1706304	4694127
Operating Costs/Operating Income (%)													
Cost of Operations 10	76.7	65.6	64.7	70.4	74.4	76.5	78.3	77.2	80.5	74.7	76.2	83.8	88.6
Salaries and Wages 11	6.0	8.9	6.3	6.8	6.5	6.8	6.2	6.3	5.0	6.6	7.4	4.0	4.3
Taxes Paid 12	1.1	1.9	1.3	1.6	1.3	1.2	1.1	1.0	1.0	1.2	1.1	0.7	0.5
Interest Paid 13	0.7	1.9	0.5	0.6	0.5	0.6	0.6	0.6	0.8	1.4	1.4	0.7	0.8
Depreciation 14	0.9	0.9	1.0	0.9	0.8	1.1	0.8	0.9	1.0	1.2	1.7	0.8	0.6
Amortization and Depletion 15	0.2	0.3	0.1	0.1	0.0	0.1	0.1	0.1	0.2	0.5	0.5	0.2	0.9
Pensions and Other Deferred Comp. 16	0.2	0.1	0.4	0.1	0.3	0.1	0.2	0.2	0.2	0.2	0.1	0.2	0.1
Employee Benefits 17	0.5	0.9	0.5	0.5	0.4	0.5	0.5	0.5	0.5	1.0	1.0	0.5	0.2
Advertising 18	1.3	0.5	0.8	0.7	0.7	0.9	1.1	1.5	1.4	2.2	2.4	2.1	2.3
Other Expenses 19	9.1	18.1	17.2	13.7	10.3	8.0	7.3	7.7	7.5	9.6	10.3	5.9	2.7
Officers' Compensation 20	2.0	3.9	5.6	3.9	3.1	2.5	1.6	1.2	0.9	1.0	0.5	0.3	0.4
Operating Margin 21	1.2	•	1.7	0.8	1.7	1.8	2.2	2.7	1.0	0.3	•	0.9	•
Operating Margin Before Officers' Comp. 22	3.2	0.8	7.3	4.7	4.8	4.3	3.8	3.9	2.0	1.4	•	1.2	•

Selected Average Balance Sheet ($ in Thousands)

Net Receivables 23	393	0	19	175	620	2182	5472	12192	19865	43928	92081	171669	509747
Inventories 24	402	0	36	289	857	2508	5175	11712	18895	35684	67155	158349	292239
Net Property, Plant and Equipment 25	143	0	16	73	219	757	1263	3414	7670	13475	31677	63514	385979
Total Assets 26	1460	0	110	706	2238	6769	15329	34791	69981	158178	338598	797602	3609135
Notes and Loans Payable 27	431	0	72	265	577	2177	4493	11654	21702	49787	103186	115895	809459
All Other Liabilities 28	560	0	34	237	966	2587	6253	12559	26365	49354	123313	305398	1605391
Net Worth 29	469	0	4	204	695	2006	4583	10578	21914	59037	112100	376308	1194284

Selected Financial Ratios (Times to 1)

Current Ratio 30	1.6	•	2.2	2.0	1.6	1.5	1.6	1.6	1.7	1.4	1.5	1.2	
Quick Ratio 31	0.8	•	1.1	1.0	0.8	0.7	0.8	0.8	1.0	0.8	0.7	0.6	
Net Sales to Working Capital 32	8.4	•	9.7	6.6	8.4	8.0	7.7	8.1	8.1	5.5	7.5	10.6	16.1
Coverage Ratio 33	4.7	1.7	6.9	3.7	6.1	4.7	5.7	6.4	4.0	3.6	3.0	5.5	1.9
Total Asset Turnover 34	2.2	•	4.1	2.6	2.3	2.3	2.3	2.1	2.1	1.5	1.2	2.1	1.3
Inventory Turnover 35	6.0	•	7.9	4.5	4.7	5.4	5.4	5.4	6.3	5.0	4.5	8.9	14.0
Receivables Turnover 36	8.5	•	22.8	9.0	9.5	7.6	7.0	7.1	8.4	5.5	4.3	9.3	•
Total Liabilities to Net Worth 37	2.1	•	25.7	2.5	2.2	2.4	2.3	2.3	2.2	2.0	1.1	2.0	
Current Assets to Working Capital 38	2.8	•	1.9	2.0	2.7	3.0	2.8	2.8	2.8	3.7	3.0	5.1	
Current Liabilities to Working Capital 39	1.8	•	0.9	1.0	1.7	2.0	1.8	1.8	1.8	2.7	2.0	4.1	
Working Capital to Net Sales 40	0.1	•	0.1	0.2	0.1	0.1	0.1	0.1	0.1	0.1	0.1	0.1	
Inventory to Working Capital 41	1.1	•	0.9	0.9	1.3	1.4	1.2	1.2	0.9	1.3	1.0	1.0	
Total Receipts to Cash Flow 42	10.6	6.8	6.7	8.6	9.7	12.9	11.5	10.6	11.8	9.1	9.6	12.5	47.3
Cost of Goods to Cash Flow 43	8.1	4.4	4.4	6.1	7.2	9.9	9.0	8.2	9.5	6.8	7.3	10.5	41.9
Cash Flow to Total Debt 44	0.3	•	0.6	0.4	0.4	0.2	0.3	0.3	0.3	0.3	0.2	0.3	0.0

Selected Financial Factors (in Percentages)

Debt Ratio 45	67.9	•	96.3	71.1	68.9	70.4	70.1	69.6	68.7	62.7	66.9	52.8	66.9
Return on Total Assets 46	7.4	•	13.1	5.3	8.5	6.8	8.4	9.3	7.0	7.6	4.9	8.1	2.0
Return on Equity Before Income Taxes 47	18.1	•	299.6	13.5	22.9	18.1	23.3	25.9	16.6	14.5	9.8	14.1	2.9
Return on Equity After Income Taxes 48	15.3	•	290.5	11.8	21.4	15.8	21.1	23.4	13.2	10.7	7.1	9.2	2.8
Profit Margin (Before Income Tax) 49	2.7	1.3	2.8	1.5	2.7	2.4	3.0	3.4	2.5	3.6	2.8	3.2	0.7
Profit Margin (After Income Tax) 50	2.3	0.5	2.7	1.3	2.5	2.1	2.7	3.0	2.0	2.6	2.0	2.1	0.7

Table II

Corporations with Net Income

FURNITURE, SPORTS, TOYS, JEWELRY, OTHER DURABLE GOODS

MONEY AMOUNTS AND SIZE OF ASSETS IN THOUSANDS OF DOLLARS

Item Description for Accounting Period 7/04 Through 6/05	Total	Zero Assets	Under 500	500 to 1,000	1,000 to 5,000	5,000 to 10,000	10,000 to 25,000	25,000 to 50,000	50,000 to 100,000	100,000 to 250,000	250,000 to 500,000	500,000 to 2,500,000	2,500,000 and over
Number of Enterprises **1**	41677	2800	27449	3767	5539	1092	665	195	87	0	20	0	0
Revenues ($ in Thousands)													
Net Sales **2**	183414749	16028017	1172462	7850833	34544417	17940235	24969439	17010289	14547667	0	8087403	0	0
Interest **3**	199973	3901	1796	6750	12220	7179	14474	7712	13190	0	10002	0	0
Rents **4**	68492	1413	2	0	5122	1702	3958	4531	3310	0	10176	0	0
Royalties **5**	229106	1	0	149	1848	1222	6294	1746	28988	0	29446	0	0
Other Portfolio Income **6**	277606	36906	11088	1419	32502	19427	15104	5714	20477	0	56205	0	0
Other Receipts **7**	1730471	26659	174085	18321	298613	55653	145182	87026	90184	0	346661	0	0
Total Receipts **8**	185920397	16214988	1241342	7877472	34894722	18025418	25154451	17117018	14703816	0	8539893	0	0
Average Total Receipts **9**	4461	591	443	2091	6300	16507	37826	87780	169009	•	426995	•	•
Operating Costs/Operating Income (%)													
Cost of Operations **10**	76.7	64.7	63.8	71.2	73.6	76.5	78.3	77.8	82.0	•	73.9	•	•
Salaries and Wages **11**	5.8	7.1	6.1	6.5	6.6	6.5	6.1	5.9	4.2	•	8.1	•	•
Taxes Paid **12**	1.1	1.9	1.2	1.5	1.3	1.2	1.1	0.9	0.9	•	1.2	•	•
Interest Paid **13**	0.6	1.2	0.3	0.3	0.5	0.6	0.5	0.5	0.5	•	1.4	•	•
Depreciation **14**	0.9	0.5	0.9	0.7	0.8	1.1	0.7	0.9	0.9	•	1.9	•	•
Amortization and Depletion **15**	0.2	0.2	0.1	0.0	0.0	0.0	0.1	0.1	0.2	•	0.5	•	•
Pensions and Other Deferred Comp. **16**	0.2	0.1	0.5	0.1	0.3	0.1	0.2	0.2	0.1	•	0.2	•	•
Employee Benefits **17**	0.4	0.5	0.3	0.4	0.3	0.4	0.4	0.4	0.4	•	1.1	•	•
Advertising **18**	1.3	0.2	0.7	0.4	0.6	0.7	1.0	1.3	1.2	•	2.7	•	•
Other Expenses **19**	8.0	14.6	15.1	12.3	9.8	7.1	6.5	6.8	6.2	•	10.3	•	•
Officers' Compensation **20**	2.0	4.2	5.7	3.6	3.0	2.4	1.6	1.2	0.8	•	0.6	•	•
Operating Margin **21**	2.9	4.8	5.3	2.8	3.1	3.4	3.7	4.1	2.6	•	•	•	•
Operating Margin Before Officers' Comp. **22**	4.9	9.0	10.9	6.4	6.1	5.8	5.2	5.2	3.4	•	•	•	•

Selected Average Balance Sheet ($ in Thousands)

Net Receivables 23	553	0	27	203	655	2377	5697	13015	20973	•	97785
Inventories 24	515	0	34	268	852	2354	5188	11361	19010	•	64148
Net Property, Plant and Equipment 25	168	0	17	60	215	749	1216	3199	6931	•	31003
Total Assets 26	1939	0	128	711	2291	6679	15408	35070	69831	•	325499
Notes and Loans Payable 27	495	0	58	249	561	1848	4100	9821	18516	•	92753
All Other Liabilities 28	714	0	41	243	908	2468	6147	12635	24943	•	127308
Net Worth 29	730	0	29	219	822	2363	5161	12614	26372	•	105438

Selected Financial Ratios (Times to 1)

Current Ratio 30	1.7	•	2.2	2.0	1.7	1.6	1.6	1.6	1.7	•	1.3
Quick Ratio 31	0.9	•	1.3	1.1	0.8	0.8	0.9	0.9	0.8	•	0.7
Net Sales to Working Capital 32	7.8	•	10.5	6.7	7.7	7.2	7.8	7.8	7.9	•	8.2
Coverage Ratio 33	8.2	10.0	19.9	10.8	10.1	9.6	11.0	7.6		•	4.0
Total Asset Turnover 34	2.3	•	4.5	2.9	2.7	2.5	2.4	2.5	2.4	•	1.2
Inventory Turnover 35	6.6	•	10.8	5.5	5.4	5.3	5.7	6.0	7.2	•	4.7
Receivables Turnover 36	8.7	•	23.8	9.2	10.1	7.8	7.2	7.6	9.3	•	4.4
Total Liabilities to Net Worth 37	1.7	•	3.4	2.3	1.8	1.8	2.0	1.8	1.6	•	2.1
Current Assets to Working Capital 38	2.5	•	1.8	2.0	2.4	2.7	2.6	2.6	2.5	•	4.0
Current Liabilities to Working Capital 39	1.5	•	0.8	1.0	1.4	1.7	1.6	1.6	1.5	•	3.0
Working Capital to Net Sales 40	0.1	•	0.1	0.1	0.1	0.1	0.1	0.1	0.1	•	0.1
Inventory to Working Capital 41	1.0	•	0.7	0.8	1.2	1.1	1.1	1.1	1.1	•	1.3
Total Receipts to Cash Flow 42	9.8	4.7	5.7	8.2	9.0	11.4	10.7	9.9	11.5	•	8.4
Cost of Goods to Cash Flow 43	7.5	3.1	3.6	5.8	6.6	8.7	8.4	7.7	9.4	•	6.2
Cash Flow to Total Debt 44	0.4	•	1.0	0.5	0.5	0.3	0.3	0.4	0.3	•	0.2

Selected Financial Factors (in Percentages)

Debt Ratio 45	62.3	•	77.2	69.3	64.1	64.6	66.5	64.0	62.2	•	67.6
Return on Total Assets 46	11.2	•	30.8	10.0	12.4	10.9	12.0	12.8	10.0	•	7.1
Return on Equity Before Income Taxes 47	26.2	•	128.4	29.6	31.2	26.9	32.1	32.4	23.0	•	16.5
Return on Equity After Income Taxes 48	23.2	•	126.2	27.6	29.7	24.4	29.7	29.8	19.2	•	12.8
Profit Margin (Before Income Tax) 49	4.3	10.7	6.4	3.1	4.1	3.9	4.4	4.7	3.6	•	4.3
Profit Margin (After Income Tax) 50	3.8	9.7	6.3	2.9	3.9	3.5	4.1	4.3	3.0	•	3.3

Table I

Corporations with and without Net Income

PAPER AND PAPER PRODUCT

MONEY AMOUNTS AND SIZE OF ASSETS IN THOUSANDS OF DOLLARS

Item Description for Accounting Period 7/04 Through 6/05	Total	Zero Assets	Under 500	500 to 1,000	1,000 to 5,000	5,000 to 10,000	10,000 to 25,000	25,000 to 50,000	50,000 to 100,000	100,000 to 250,000	250,000 to 500,000	500,000 to 2,500,000	2,500,000 and over
Number of Enterprises 1	9694	550	7219	835	830	74	107	41	20	13	0	4	0
Revenues ($ in Thousands)													
Net Sales 2	46317270	440781	2738680	1743306	6300700	1416473	5818558	4650353	4732277	8559876	0	9916268	0
Interest 3	27423	1297	298	577	1434	1175	1962	1379	1331	2013	0	15955	0
Rents 4	11321	113	0	0	4329	130	417	784	758	275	0	4514	0
Royalties 5	12520	137	0	0	0	0	0	1	1556	3508	0	7318	0
Other Portfolio Income 6	55249	47	3634	1321	15239	3350	17154	527	1785	11447	0	741	0
Other Receipts 7	278530	11693	24735	4426	98402	6941	35397	19125	22984	35353	0	19478	0
Total Receipts 8	46702313	454068	2767347	1749630	6420104	1428069	5873488	4672169	4760691	8612472	0	9964274	0
Average Total Receipts 9	4818	826	383	2095	7735	19298	54892	113955	238035	662498	·	2491068	·
Operating Costs/Operating Income (%)													
Cost of Operations 10	82.6	68.5	57.1	73.6	78.8	83.5	84.7	84.1	83.7	90.0	·	85.4	·
Salaries and Wages 11	5.6	11.3	5.8	6.6	7.9	6.5	5.7	6.5	5.0	4.0	·	5.0	·
Taxes Paid 12	0.8	1.5	1.3	1.6	1.2	1.3	0.8	0.8	0.7	0.5	·	0.6	·
Interest Paid 13	0.8	7.0	0.9	0.3	0.6	0.6	0.4	0.4	0.5	0.6	·	1.3	·
Depreciation 14	0.6	1.1	0.8	0.7	0.6	0.9	0.5	0.6	0.5	0.3	·	0.9	·
Amortization and Depletion 15	0.2	3.1	0.1	0.0	0.0	0.0	0.0	0.1	0.1	0.1	·	0.5	·
Pensions and Other Deferred Comp. 16	0.2	0.5	0.3	0.1	0.3	0.2	0.2	0.2	0.2	0.1	·	0.2	·
Employee Benefits 17	0.5	0.7	0.6	0.1	0.7	0.5	0.4	0.5	0.4	0.3	·	0.5	·
Advertising 18	0.3	1.2	0.9	0.2	0.1	0.3	0.2	0.3	0.2	0.0	·	0.4	·
Other Expenses 19	6.5	16.6	22.5	12.5	6.6	4.4	4.9	4.8	7.7	3.3	·	4.8	·
Officers' Compensation 20	1.5	2.0	6.8	4.7	3.4	1.7	1.2	0.8	0.9	0.3	·	0.1	·
Operating Margin 21	0.4	·	2.9	·	·	·	0.9	0.8	0.1	0.6	·	0.4	·
Operating Margin Before Officers' Comp. 22	1.9	·	9.7	4.4	3.3	1.7	2.2	1.7	0.9	0.9	·	0.5	·

Selected Average Balance Sheet ($ in Thousands)

Net Receivables 23	589	0	30	183	801	1978	6933	15335	33597	89103	333082
Inventories 24	343	0	8	221	649	1984	4151	9935	17372	32913	191784
Net Property, Plant and Equipment 25	158	0	12	34	169	1011	1568	2878	7608	11678	152119
Total Assets 26	1520	0	85	636	1934	6857	15630	34722	78660	185016	1099766
Notes and Loans Payable 27	573	0	71	114	779	1984	4734	12158	23951	58888	476671
All Other Liabilities 28	598	0	36	200	759	2323	6237	12800	29199	82046	431265
Net Worth 29	349	0	-21	322	396	2550	4660	9764	25511	44082	191830

Selected Financial Ratios (Times to 1)

Current Ratio 30	1.5	•	1.0	2.5	1.8	1.7	1.5	1.6	1.6	1.6	1.1
Quick Ratio 31	0.9	•	0.8	1.5	1.1	0.8	0.9	0.9	0.9	1.2	0.7
Net Sales to Working Capital 32	13.7	•	197.1	6.1	10.4	9.1	13.4	10.2	10.1	13.1	32.5
Coverage Ratio 33	2.6	•	5.4	1.2	4.2	2.2	5.7	4.0	2.3	3.2	1.6
Total Asset Turnover 34	3.1	•	4.4	3.3	3.9	2.8	3.5	3.3	3.0	3.6	2.3
Inventory Turnover 35	11.5	•	26.5	6.9	9.2	8.1	11.1	9.6	11.4	18.0	11.0
Receivables Turnover 36	8.2	•	12.2	9.6	8.6	8.0	7.5	8.2	7.2	7.9	8.0
Total Liabilities to Net Worth 37	3.4	•	•	1.0	3.9	1.7	2.4	2.6	2.1	3.2	4.7
Current Assets to Working Capital 38	3.1	•	23.8	1.7	2.2	2.5	3.2	2.6	2.8	2.7	7.8
Current Liabilities to Working Capital 39	2.1	•	22.8	0.7	1.2	1.5	2.2	1.6	1.8	1.7	6.8
Working Capital to Net Sales 40	0.1	•	0.0	0.2	0.1	0.1	0.1	0.1	0.1	0.1	0.0
Inventory to Working Capital 41	1.0	•	4.6	0.6	0.9	1.1	0.9	0.9	0.8	0.6	2.8
Total Receipts to Cash Flow 42	16.4	29.3	4.4	10.0	16.3	26.1	19.4	22.3	14.0	30.5	22.3
Cost of Goods to Cash Flow 43	13.6	20.1	2.5	7.3	12.8	21.8	16.4	18.7	11.7	27.5	19.0
Cash Flow to Total Debt 44	0.2	•	0.8	0.7	0.3	0.2	0.3	0.2	0.3	0.2	0.1

Selected Financial Factors (in Percentages)

Debt Ratio 45	77.1	•	125.1	49.3	79.5	62.8	70.2	71.9	67.6	76.2	82.6
Return on Total Assets 46	6.3	•	21.3	1.3	9.2	3.8	7.9	5.6	3.5	6.3	4.9
Return on Equity Before Income Taxes 47	16.9	•	•	0.4	34.1	5.7	21.9	14.9	6.1	18.2	10.8
Return on Equity After Income Taxes 48	13.9	•	•	0.1	33.5	4.3	19.9	13.2	5.2	14.8	3.6
Profit Margin (Before Income Tax) 49	1.2	•	3.9	0.1	1.8	0.8	1.9	1.3	0.7	1.2	0.8
Profit Margin (After Income Tax) 50	1.0	•	3.8	0.0	1.7	0.6	1.7	1.1	0.6	1.0	0.3

Table II

Corporations with Net Income

PAPER AND PAPER PRODUCT

MONEY AMOUNTS AND SIZE OF ASSETS IN THOUSANDS OF DOLLARS

Item Description for Accounting Period 7/04 Through 6/05	Total	Zero Assets	Under 500	500 to 1,000	1,000 to 5,000	5,000 to 10,000	10,000 to 25,000	25,000 to 50,000	50,000 to 100,000	100,000 to 250,000	250,000 to 500,000	500,000 to 2,500,000	2,500,000 and over
Number of Enterprises **1**	6093	270	4481	0	593	54	94	36	14	0	3	0	0

Revenues ($ in Thousands)

Item Description for Accounting Period 7/04 Through 6/05	Total	Zero Assets	Under 500	500 to 1,000	1,000 to 5,000	5,000 to 10,000	10,000 to 25,000	25,000 to 50,000	50,000 to 100,000	100,000 to 250,000	250,000 to 500,000	500,000 to 2,500,000	2,500,000 and over
Net Sales **2**	35609235	71302	1793960	0	5552754	1243803	5280012	4123063	3613705	0	6116262	0	0
Interest **3**	18062	21	298	0	1051	309	1824	1379	1186	0	9638	0	0
Rents **4**	6542	109	0	0	4329	41	245	784	758	0	0	0	0
Royalties **5**	1	0	0	0	0	0	0	1	0	0	0	0	0
Other Portfolio Income **6**	44089	0	3476	0	15115	18	17150	511	1635	0	56	0	0
Other Receipts **7**	237367	139	24735	0	96288	2055	34073	16864	21386	0	4133	0	0
Total Receipts **8**	35915296	71571	1822469	0	5669537	1246226	5333304	4142602	3638670	0	6130089	0	0
Average Total Receipts **9**	5895	265	407	•	9561	23078	56737	115072	259905	•	2043363	•	•

Operating Costs/Operating Income (%)

Item Description for Accounting Period 7/04 Through 6/05	Total	Zero Assets	Under 500	500 to 1,000	1,000 to 5,000	5,000 to 10,000	10,000 to 25,000	25,000 to 50,000	50,000 to 100,000	100,000 to 250,000	250,000 to 500,000	500,000 to 2,500,000	2,500,000 and over
Cost of Operations **10**	83.7	85.4	62.8	•	80.1	85.0	84.7	84.2	84.4	•	87.0	•	•
Salaries and Wages **11**	5.4	1.2	5.9	•	7.7	6.2	5.7	6.2	4.5	•	4.0	•	•
Taxes Paid **12**	0.8	0.4	1.1	•	1.1	1.3	0.8	0.8	0.6	•	0.7	•	•
Interest Paid **13**	0.5	0.1	1.0	•	0.3	0.4	0.4	0.4	0.4	•	1.0	•	•
Depreciation **14**	0.5	0.6	0.4	•	0.5	0.6	0.4	0.6	0.4	•	0.7	•	•
Amortization and Depletion **15**	0.1	0.1	0.2	•	0.0	0.0	0.0	0.1	0.0	•	0.2	•	•
Pensions and Other Deferred Comp. **16**	0.2	0.0	0.5	•	0.3	0.3	0.2	0.2	0.1	•	0.3	•	•
Employee Benefits **17**	0.4	0.3	0.7	•	0.7	0.6	0.4	0.5	0.2	•	0.4	•	•
Advertising **18**	0.2	0.0	1.0	•	0.1	0.2	0.2	0.3	0.2	•	0.1	•	•
Other Expenses **19**	5.3	9.6	14.9	•	5.6	2.5	4.6	4.8	7.2	•	2.8	•	•
Officers' Compensation **20**	1.4	2.4	3.6	•	3.3	1.8	1.3	0.8	0.9	•	0.2	•	•
Operating Margin **21**	1.6	•	7.9	•	0.4	1.3	1.3	1.2	0.9	•	2.7	•	•
Operating Margin Before Officers' Comp. **22**	2.9	2.3	11.5	•	3.7	3.1	2.6	2.0	1.8	•	2.8	•	•

Selected Average Balance Sheet ($ in Thousands)

Net Receivables 23	708	0	30	•	960	2419	7074	15095	38164	•	241976
Inventories 24	355	0	8	•	593	2465	3873	8607	16098	•	102319
Net Property, Plant and Equipment 25	165	0	12	•	131	831	1518	2837	6454	•	114827
Total Assets 26	1756	0	85	•	1885	6840	15743	34523	78111	•	956099
Notes and Loans Payable 27	533	0	30	•	573	1998	4327	11472	22840	•	336950
All Other Liabilities 28	718	0	35	•	759	2398	6222	12756	30571	•	391911
Net Worth 29	505	0	21	•	553	2444	5193	10296	24700	•	227238

Selected Financial Ratios (Times to 1)

Current Ratio 30	1.5	•	1.1	•	1.8	1.6	1.5	1.6	1.5	•	1.0
Quick Ratio 31	0.9	•	0.9	•	1.2	0.9	1.0	0.9	1.0	•	0.6
Net Sales to Working Capital 32	14.6	•	65.1	•	13.4	10.7	12.6	10.4	10.8	•	•
Coverage Ratio 33	5.6	3.4	10.8	•	8.2	4.5	7.3	5.3	5.0	•	4.0
Total Asset Turnover 34	3.3	•	4.7	•	5.0	3.4	3.6	3.3	3.3	•	2.1
Inventory Turnover 35	13.8	•	33.1	•	12.6	7.9	12.3	11.2	13.5	•	17.3
Receivables Turnover 36	9.0	•	13.3	•	10.2	8.1	8.1	9.2	7.0	•	10.4
Total Liabilities to Net Worth 37	2.5	•	3.0	•	2.4	1.8	2.0	2.4	2.2	•	3.2
Current Assets to Working Capital 38	3.2	•	7.9	•	2.3	2.6	2.9	2.6	2.8	•	•
Current Liabilities to Working Capital 39	2.2	•	6.9	•	1.3	1.6	1.9	1.6	1.8	•	•
Working Capital to Net Sales 40	0.1	•	0.0	•	0.1	0.1	0.1	0.1	0.1	•	•
Inventory to Working Capital 41	0.9	•	1.5	•	0.7	1.1	0.9	0.9	0.8	•	•
Total Receipts to Cash Flow 42	16.1	12.7	4.7	•	16.5	34.4	18.9	20.6	12.8	•	21.0
Cost of Goods to Cash Flow 43	13.5	10.8	3.0	•	13.2	29.2	16.0	17.4	10.8	•	18.3
Cash Flow to Total Debt 44	0.3	•	1.3	•	0.4	0.2	0.3	0.2	0.4	•	0.1

Selected Financial Factors (in Percentages)

Debt Ratio 45	71.3	•	75.0	•	70.6	64.3	67.0	70.2	68.4	•	76.2
Return on Total Assets 46	9.8	•	48.8	•	14.0	6.3	9.4	6.7	6.7	•	8.2
Return on Equity Before Income Taxes 47	28.1	•	177.4	•	41.9	13.8	24.7	18.3	16.9	•	25.9
Return on Equity After Income Taxes 48	24.7	•	175.2	•	41.3	11.9	22.6	16.5	15.5	•	17.8
Profit Margin (Before Income Tax) 49	2.4	0.3	9.5	•	2.5	1.5	2.3	1.6	1.6	•	2.9
Profit Margin (After Income Tax) 50	2.1	0.3	9.3	•	2.4	1.3	2.1	1.5	1.5	•	2.0

Table I

Corporations with and without Net Income

DRUGS AND DRUGGISTS' SUNDRIES

MONEY AMOUNTS AND SIZE OF ASSETS IN THOUSANDS OF DOLLARS

Item Description for Accounting Period 7/04 Through 6/05	Total	Zero Assets	Under 500	500 to 1,000	1,000 to 5,000	5,000 to 10,000	10,000 to 25,000	25,000 to 50,000	50,000 to 100,000	100,000 to 250,000	250,000 to 500,000	500,000 to 2,500,000	2,500,000 and over
Number of Enterprises **1**	5849	108	4008	445	840	199	103	41	32	24	16	21	11
Revenues ($ in Thousands)													
Net Sales **2**	334093993	281776	1518486	883662	6687163	3223332	4017010	3131859	5764144	5743153	13540201	26767107	262536099
Interest **3**	716132	131	25	977	3241	3255	2363	6366	7126	11745	25139	93175	562587
Rents **4**	492571	0	0	0	123	116	565	1685	765	148	1893	3147	484130
Royalties **5**	1917673	0	0	1867	360	278	172	9748	11566	28626	221061	492381	1151615
Other Portfolio Income **6**	703150	0	3	5912	15565	7877	8233	617	1823	17390	4487	85340	555905
Other Receipts **7**	4158995	-2543	5153	40994	57219	38938	30988	74114	107519	47199	210375	560308	2988730
Total Receipts **8**	342082514	279364	1523667	933412	6763671	3273796	4059331	3224389	5892943	5848261	14003156	28001458	268279066
Average Total Receipts **9**	58486	2587	380	2098	8052	16451	39411	78644	184154	243678	875197	1333403	24389006
Operating Costs/Operating Income (%)													
Cost of Operations **10**	87.0	74.2	66.7	64.4	81.3	76.6	75.5	73.2	77.6	74.3	81.0	53.7	92.1
Salaries and Wages **11**	3.3	9.0	3.9	8.0	5.0	6.4	8.3	7.7	6.1	7.4	6.1	8.1	2.2
Taxes Paid **12**	0.4	0.8	1.0	2.8	0.8	0.9	1.0	1.0	0.8	0.7	0.6	0.9	0.3
Interest Paid **13**	0.5	0.1	0.6	0.6	0.5	1.1	0.7	0.9	0.3	1.2	0.6	1.7	0.3
Depreciation **14**	0.5	1.6	0.4	1.0	0.4	0.5	0.8	0.8	0.5	1.0	0.6	1.1	0.4
Amortization and Depletion **15**	0.3	0.1	0.1	0.6	0.1	0.1	0.2	0.3	0.4	1.4	0.5	0.7	0.2
Pensions and Other Deferred Comp. **16**	0.1	0.5	0.8	0.5	0.1	0.3	0.2	0.3	0.1	0.1	0.2	0.6	0.1
Employee Benefits **17**	0.4	0.1	0.2	0.8	0.4	0.6	0.7	0.9	0.4	0.9	0.4	0.8	0.3
Advertising **18**	0.9	6.6	1.0	0.6	1.0	1.0	1.4	3.0	2.0	2.4	0.7	2.8	0.6
Other Expenses **19**	5.4	15.8	18.6	12.4	9.0	7.7	8.9	10.6	11.1	11.7	9.5	23.5	2.7
Officers' Compensation **20**	0.4	0.2	6.9	5.0	1.9	2.2	1.9	1.1	0.8	0.5	0.4	0.9	0.1
Operating Margin **21**	0.8	•	•	•	•	2.6	0.5	0.2	•	•	•	5.2	0.6
Operating Margin Before Officers' Comp. **22**	1.2	•	6.7	8.4	1.6	4.8	2.4	1.3	0.8	•	•	6.1	0.7

Selected Average Balance Sheet ($ in Thousands)

Net Receivables 23	4139	0	55	180	635	1882	4335	10011	20215	26329	93451	171039	1434673
Inventories 24	5081	0	20	311	500	3449	4290	8893	16857	29568	64062	157223	2000823
Net Property, Plant and Equipment 25	1626	0	4	38	200	319	1303	3433	5790	9491	31355	88555	563154
Total Assets 26	26278	0	130	653	2281	7846	15229	33922	80008	151917	358614	977369	10361967
Notes and Loans Payable 27	4128	0	91	154	778	3318	5169	9588	13012	51275	87077	298414	1105845
All Other Liabilities 28	11091	0	60	353	1153	2882	5876	15425	32975	49267	147954	301906	4613501
Net Worth 29	11059	0	-21	146	350	1646	4185	8909	34022	51375	123583	377049	4642620

Selected Financial Ratios (Times to 1)

Current Ratio 30	1.4	•	1.8	1.1	1.4	1.5	1.3	1.3	1.7	1.3	1.6	1.7	1.3
Quick Ratio 31	0.7	•	1.3	0.7	0.7	0.6	0.7	0.7	1.0	0.7	0.8	0.9	0.6
Net Sales to Working Capital 32	14.4	•	7.1	44.0	13.6	6.9	14.2	15.7	7.7	13.3	8.2	5.6	19.0
Coverage Ratio 33	7.6	•	1.2	15.7	2.6	4.7	3.3	4.4	7.7	1.3	5.4	6.8	9.3
Total Asset Turnover 34	2.2	•	2.9	3.0	3.5	2.1	2.6	2.3	2.3	1.6	2.4	1.3	2.3
Inventory Turnover 35	9.8	•	12.5	4.1	12.9	3.6	6.9	6.3	8.3	6.0	10.7	4.4	11.0
Receivables Turnover 36	12.4	•	10.8	4.1	17.4	6.5	9.4	7.6	8.8	8.1	13.4	7.3	13.9
Total Liabilities to Net Worth 37	1.4	•	•	3.5	5.5	3.8	2.6	2.8	1.4	2.0	1.9	1.6	1.2
Current Assets to Working Capital 38	3.7	•	2.2	10.7	3.3	2.9	4.2	4.9	2.5	4.4	2.6	2.4	4.3
Current Liabilities to Working Capital 39	2.7	•	1.2	9.7	2.3	1.9	3.2	3.9	1.5	3.4	1.6	1.4	3.3
Working Capital to Net Sales 40	0.1	•	0.1	0.0	0.1	0.1	0.1	0.1	0.1	0.1	0.1	0.2	0.1
Inventory to Working Capital 41	1.3	•	0.5	3.4	1.2	1.5	1.7	1.8	0.7	1.5	0.8	0.7	1.6
Total Receipts to Cash Flow 42	12.4	20.6	6.4	5.3	12.1	9.7	11.3	8.0	8.1	9.0	8.6	3.1	19.8
Cost of Goods to Cash Flow 43	10.8	15.3	4.3	3.4	9.9	7.4	8.6	5.9	6.3	6.7	7.0	1.7	18.2
Cash Flow to Total Debt 44	0.3	•	0.4	0.7	0.3	0.3	0.3	0.4	0.5	0.3	0.4	0.7	0.2

Selected Financial Factors (in Percentages)

Debt Ratio 45	57.9	•	116.1	77.7	84.6	79.0	72.5	73.7	57.5	66.2	65.5	61.4	55.2
Return on Total Assets 46	8.2	•	2.2	29.1	4.8	10.8	5.6	9.2	5.7	2.4	8.1	15.0	7.3
Return on Equity Before Income Taxes 47	16.9	•	•	122.0	18.9	40.6	14.4	27.1	11.6	1.6	19.1	33.3	14.5
Return on Equity After Income Taxes 48	11.7	•	•	115.4	12.0	33.9	11.6	21.8	7.9	•	12.7	21.7	10.2
Profit Margin (Before Income Tax) 49	3.3	•	0.1	9.0	0.8	4.1	1.5	3.2	2.2	0.3	2.8	9.9	2.8
Profit Margin (After Income Tax) 50	2.3	•	0.0	8.5	0.5	3.4	1.2	2.5	1.5	•	1.8	6.4	2.0

185

Table II

Corporations with Net Income

DRUGS AND DRUGGISTS' SUNDRIES

MONEY AMOUNTS AND SIZE OF ASSETS IN THOUSANDS OF DOLLARS

Item Description for Accounting Period 7/04 Through 6/05	Total	Zero Assets	Under 500	500 to 1,000	1,000 to 5,000	5,000 to 10,000	10,000 to 25,000	25,000 to 50,000	50,000 to 100,000	100,000 to 250,000	250,000 to 500,000	500,000 to 2,500,000	2,500,000 and over
Number of Enterprises 1	3255	0	1992	0	538	156	70	30	22	17	11	17	0
Revenues ($ in Thousands)													
Net Sales 2	320986661	0	1260534	0	4720805	2817294	3243870	2475680	4980417	4134095	11385966	22628601	0
Interest 3	677178	0	25	0	2833	3138	1257	3420	5597	4257	13770	79314	0
Rents 4	490780	0	0	0	123	100	488	142	660	148	1842	3147	0
Royalties 5	1845939	0	0	0	0	199	30	9748	3472	27440	219681	431887	0
Other Portfolio Income 6	693810	0	3	0	15563	6455	6827	539	263	17385	4486	80475	0
Other Receipts 7	3901694	0	3955	0	32015	9423	10945	29772	21020	39954	212294	512588	0
Total Receipts 8	328596062	0	1264517	0	4771339	2836609	3263417	2519301	5011429	4223279	11833039	23736012	0
Average Total Receipts 9	100951	.	635	.	8869	18183	46620	83977	227792	248428	1076185	1396236	.
Operating Costs/Operating Income (%)													
Cost of Operations 10	87.5	.	66.2	.	79.7	76.4	78.2	77.4	81.6	76.7	80.9	48.1	.
Salaries and Wages 11	3.1	.	3.4	.	4.5	5.7	6.2	5.7	3.4	5.3	6.0	8.9	.
Taxes Paid 12	0.4	.	0.9	.	0.7	0.8	0.9	0.7	0.5	0.5	0.6	1.0	.
Interest Paid 13	0.5	.	0.4	.	0.6	1.1	0.3	0.5	0.2	1.1	0.5	1.8	.
Depreciation 14	0.5	.	0.4	.	0.3	0.4	0.6	0.6	0.2	1.0	0.6	1.2	.
Amortization and Depletion 15	0.3	.	0.0	.	0.0	0.0	0.1	0.3	0.2	0.9	0.3	0.8	.
Pensions and Other Deferred Comp. 16	0.1	.	0.9	.	0.1	0.4	0.2	0.2	0.1	0.1	0.2	0.4	.
Employee Benefits 17	0.4	.	.	.	0.3	0.3	0.5	0.6	0.2	0.9	0.4	0.9	.
Advertising 18	0.8	.	0.1	.	1.1	0.7	1.0	1.6	1.0	0.9	0.5	3.1	.
Other Expenses 19	4.9	.	16.0	.	8.0	6.6	6.7	6.7	7.9	9.8	9.6	24.8	.
Officers' Compensation 20	0.3	.	6.5	.	2.0	2.4	1.9	1.1	0.7	0.5	0.2	1.0	.
Operating Margin 21	1.3	.	5.1	.	2.7	5.1	3.3	4.5	3.9	2.3	0.2	7.8	.
Operating Margin Before Officers' Comp. 22	1.6	.	11.6	.	4.7	7.5	5.2	5.6	4.6	2.8	0.4	8.8	.

Selected Average Balance Sheet ($ in Thousands)

Net Receivables 23	6882	38	685	2133	4866	10248	23343	24115	108719	176634
Inventories 24	8599	30	439	2495	4935	9790	20241	33948	73064	159107
Net Property, Plant and Equipment 25	2731	8	124	341	1233	3087	3832	11038	32690	102548
Total Assets 26	44569	180	2453	8078	14950	32889	78563	142043	357792	1046016
Notes and Loans Payable 27	6460	46	798	1772	3844	7846	14445	42064	62608	340594
All Other Liabilities 28	18897	87	1041	3074	5551	12521	34207	43747	153845	339462
Net Worth 29	19112	48	615	3232	5554	12522	29912	56232	141338	365960

Selected Financial Ratios (Times to 1)

Current Ratio 30	1.4	1.6	1.6	1.6	1.7	1.5	1.7	1.3	1.8	1.6
Quick Ratio 31	0.7	0.9	0.8	0.6	0.8	0.9	1.0	0.6	1.0	0.8
Net Sales to Working Capital 32	15.2	11.7	10.6	6.3	9.4	10.1	8.8	15.8	8.8	6.3
Coverage Ratio 33	8.9	15.2	7.4	6.0	12.1	12.9	22.7	5.2	9.0	8.0
Total Asset Turnover 34	2.2	3.5	3.6	2.2	3.1	2.5	2.9	1.7	2.9	1.3
Inventory Turnover 35	10.0	13.9	15.9	5.5	7.3	6.5	9.1	5.5	11.5	4.0
Receivables Turnover 36	12.7	26.7	18.0	8.6	9.8	7.8	9.3	7.3	13.8	7.2
Total Liabilities to Net Worth 37	1.3	2.8	3.0	1.5	1.7	1.6	1.6	1.5	1.5	1.9
Current Assets to Working Capital 38	3.7	2.7	2.5	2.6	2.5	2.9	2.4	4.8	2.3	2.7
Current Liabilities to Working Capital 39	2.7	1.7	1.5	1.6	1.5	1.9	1.4	3.8	1.3	1.7
Working Capital to Net Sales 40	0.1	0.1	0.1	0.2	0.1	0.1	0.1	0.1	0.1	0.2
Inventory to Working Capital 41	1.4	0.9	0.8	1.4	1.0	1.1	0.8	1.7	0.8	0.7
Total Receipts to Cash Flow 42	12.4	5.6	9.7	9.0	10.8	8.4	8.4	7.4	7.6	2.8
Cost of Goods to Cash Flow 43	10.8	3.7	7.8	6.9	8.5	6.5	6.8	5.7	6.2	1.3
Cash Flow to Total Debt 44	0.3	0.9	0.5	0.4	0.5	0.5	0.6	0.4	0.6	0.7

Selected Financial Factors (in Percentages)

Debt Ratio 45	57.1	73.5	74.9	60.0	62.8	61.9	61.9	60.4	60.5	65.0
Return on Total Assets 46	9.3	20.3	15.7	15.5	13.0	16.9	13.6	9.4	13.6	18.6
Return on Equity Before Income Taxes 47	19.2	71.5	54.1	32.2	32.1	41.1	34.2	19.3	30.5	46.6
Return on Equity After Income Taxes 48	13.8	69.4	48.0	27.9	29.0	35.9	28.1	16.7	22.3	31.8
Profit Margin (Before Income Tax) 49	3.7	5.4	3.8	5.8	3.8	6.2	4.5	4.5	4.2	12.8
Profit Margin (After Income Tax) 50	2.7	5.2	3.4	5.0	3.5	5.5	3.7	3.9	3.0	8.7

Table I

Corporations with and without Net Income

APPAREL, PIECE GOODS, AND NOTIONS

MONEY AMOUNTS AND SIZE OF ASSETS IN THOUSANDS OF DOLLARS

Item Description for Accounting Period 7/04 Through 6/05	Total	Zero Assets	Under 500	500 to 1,000	1,000 to 5,000	5,000 to 10,000	10,000 to 25,000	25,000 to 50,000	50,000 to 100,000	100,000 to 250,000	250,000 to 500,000	500,000 to 2,500,000	2,500,000 and over
Number of Enterprises **1**	26567	3181	18006	2853	1646	428	273	92	44	22	8	12	0
Revenues ($ in Thousands)													
Net Sales **2**	85359421	1168160	8116327	6350582	10599473	8825689	10068990	7842515	4991768	5078207	2218039	20099672	0
Interest **3**	119807	752	2136	3112	4014	1375	3914	11225	4386	8819	6923	73150	0
Rents **4**	35356	141	0	462	3211	423	1867	1807	754	14758	4542	7391	0
Royalties **5**	872122	1236	0	0	3672	1018	5592	11995	9504	20822	21436	796846	0
Other Portfolio Income **6**	335350	0	14971	14027	5195	6360	9662	5445	3468	35892	26892	213439	0
Other Receipts **7**	1012043	76444	43626	11129	-5011	77085	86701	105454	39060	22917	23372	531267	0
Total Receipts **8**	87734099	1246733	8177060	6379312	10610554	8911950	10176726	7978441	5048940	5181415	2301204	21721765	0
Average Total Receipts **9**	3302	392	454	2236	6446	20822	37277	86722	114749	235519	287650	1810147	•
Operating Costs/Operating Income (%)													
Cost of Operations **10**	68.4	67.1	66.3	75.4	75.0	72.3	72.4	72.3	67.2	61.0	60.6	61.4	•
Salaries and Wages **11**	8.5	8.5	6.4	5.5	6.0	8.3	7.8	7.6	9.1	9.6	10.0	11.9	•
Taxes Paid **12**	2.3	1.8	1.9	1.7	2.3	2.2	2.4	3.1	1.6	3.6	3.1	2.0	•
Interest Paid **13**	0.9	1.0	0.4	0.4	0.6	0.8	0.8	0.8	1.2	1.0	0.7	1.3	•
Depreciation **14**	1.0	0.8	0.7	0.3	0.4	0.3	0.5	0.6	1.5	1.5	1.6	1.9	•
Amortization and Depletion **15**	0.2	0.0	0.1	0.1	0.1	0.0	0.1	0.2	0.3	0.1	0.2	0.5	•
Pensions and Other Deferred Comp. **16**	0.3	0.1	0.3	0.7	0.3	0.2	0.2	0.4	0.3	0.3	0.2	0.3	•
Employee Benefits **17**	0.5	0.3	0.3	0.2	0.4	0.7	0.4	0.4	0.9	1.0	0.9	0.6	•
Advertising **18**	1.8	1.7	0.7	1.3	0.7	0.7	0.9	1.1	2.0	2.4	3.3	3.8	•
Other Expenses **19**	12.8	23.5	18.5	11.3	10.9	10.2	9.6	9.0	11.0	13.3	15.1	15.7	•
Officers' Compensation **20**	2.5	5.3	5.4	3.7	2.4	2.6	2.6	2.1	1.3	1.8	1.5	1.3	•
Operating Margin **21**	0.9	•	•	•	1.0	1.6	2.3	2.5	3.6	4.4	3.0	•	•
Operating Margin Before Officers' Comp. **22**	3.4	•	4.5	3.1	3.4	4.3	4.9	4.7	4.8	6.2	4.5	0.6	•

Selected Average Balance Sheet ($ in Thousands)

Net Receivables 23	383	0	18	187	731	1782	4849	10030	16766	36306	46353	265922
Inventories 24	390	0	35	186	613	2368	5401	10837	19700	44003	59783	199904
Net Property, Plant and Equipment 25	179	0	8	40	113	772	987	2260	7794	19248	37160	202283
Total Assets 26	1884	0	106	665	2287	7107	15407	34120	70079	150283	298163	1943664
Notes and Loans Payable 27	541	0	102	237	627	1700	5206	11800	21736	38236	74147	433863
All Other Liabilities 28	588	0	43	338	1062	2927	5291	11018	19171	35240	54342	530627
Net Worth 29	755	0	-39	90	597	2480	4910	11301	29172	76807	169675	979175

Selected Financial Ratios (Times to 1)

Current Ratio 30	1.7	•	2.2	1.4	1.6	1.5	1.7	1.6	1.7	2.1	2.7	1.6
Quick Ratio 31	0.8	•	1.2	0.8	0.8	0.6	0.8	0.7	0.8	1.1	1.3	0.7
Net Sales to Working Capital 32	6.5	•	9.4	12.9	8.6	10.0	7.1	8.5	5.6	3.9	2.5	4.8
Coverage Ratio 33	5.8	•	0.6	0.6	2.9	4.3	5.0	6.4	5.0	7.2	11.5	8.1
Total Asset Turnover 34	1.7	•	4.3	3.3	2.8	2.9	2.4	2.5	1.6	1.5	0.9	0.9
Inventory Turnover 35	5.6	•	8.5	9.0	7.9	6.3	4.9	5.7	3.9	3.2	2.8	5.1
Receivables Turnover 36	8.1	•	22.2	12.8	8.5	9.0	8.0	8.9	6.8	6.0	4.5	6.2
Total Liabilities to Net Worth 37	1.5	•	•	6.4	2.8	1.9	2.1	2.0	1.4	1.0	0.8	1.0
Current Assets to Working Capital 38	2.5	•	1.8	3.4	2.6	2.9	2.5	2.8	2.4	1.9	1.6	2.8
Current Liabilities to Working Capital 39	1.5	•	0.8	2.4	1.6	1.9	1.5	1.8	1.4	0.9	0.6	1.8
Working Capital to Net Sales 40	0.2	•	0.1	0.1	0.1	0.1	0.1	0.1	0.2	0.3	0.4	0.2
Inventory to Working Capital 41	0.8	•	0.7	1.4	0.8	1.3	1.0	1.2	0.9	0.8	0.5	0.7
Total Receipts to Cash Flow 42	7.3	6.4	7.7	12.0	10.0	9.0	9.1	8.5	7.7	6.3	5.9	4.9
Cost of Goods to Cash Flow 43	5.0	4.3	5.1	9.0	7.5	6.5	6.6	6.2	5.2	3.8	3.6	3.0
Cash Flow to Total Debt 44	0.4	•	0.4	0.3	0.4	0.5	0.4	0.4	0.4	0.5	0.4	0.4

Selected Financial Factors (in Percentages)

Debt Ratio 45	59.9	•	136.4	86.4	73.9	65.1	68.1	66.9	58.4	48.9	43.1	49.6
Return on Total Assets 46	8.5	•	0.9	0.8	4.6	10.1	10.2	12.6	9.8	11.3	7.0	9.1
Return on Equity Before Income Taxes 47	17.6	•	1.9	•	11.6	22.1	25.6	31.9	18.9	19.0	11.2	15.9
Return on Equity After Income Taxes 48	12.9	•	3.2	•	9.8	20.7	22.8	29.7	15.9	15.2	7.4	10.3
Profit Margin (Before Income Tax) 49	4.1	•	•	•	1.1	2.7	3.4	4.2	4.9	6.3	6.9	9.3
Profit Margin (After Income Tax) 50	3.0	•	•	•	0.9	2.5	3.0	3.9	4.1	5.1	4.5	6.0

Table II

Corporations with Net Income

APPAREL, PIECE GOODS, AND NOTIONS

MONEY AMOUNTS AND SIZE OF ASSETS IN THOUSANDS OF DOLLARS

Item Description for Accounting Period 7/04 Through 6/05	Total	Zero Assets	Under 500	500 to 1,000	1,000 to 5,000	5,000 to 10,000	10,000 to 25,000	25,000 to 50,000	50,000 to 100,000	100,000 to 250,000	250,000 to 500,000	500,000 to 2,500,000	2,500,000 and over
Number of Enterprises 1	16078	1339	10858	1951	1218	360	210	78	27	0	0	0	0
Revenues ($ in Thousands)													
Net Sales 2	72560672	806026	6359311	4554763	8596113	7936378	8053678	6898979	3387623	0	0	0	0
Interest 3	98624	314	1006	3103	1428	520	2674	8144	1831	0	0	0	0
Rents 4	21630	54	0	462	939	423	1392	912	735	0	0	0	0
Royalties 5	731405	0	0	0	37	1018	4441	11995	7804	0	0	0	0
Other Portfolio Income 6	318898	0	14340	13988	1933	53	8946	5117	501	0	0	0	0
Other Receipts 7	720172	64013	17544	1607	11888	64521	61556	77426	30973	0	0	0	0
Total Receipts 8	74451401	870407	6392201	4573923	8612338	8002913	8132687	7002573	3429467	0	0	0	0
Average Total Receipts 9	4631	650	589	2344	7071	22230	38727	89777	127017	·	·	·	·
Operating Costs/Operating Income (%)													
Cost of Operations 10	68.3	71.6	71.3	75.6	74.6	71.9	72.6	72.1	63.3	·	·	·	·
Salaries and Wages 11	8.3	4.5	3.9	4.7	6.1	8.3	7.1	7.4	9.4	·	·	·	·
Taxes Paid 12	2.1	1.2	1.6	0.8	2.4	2.0	2.5	2.9	1.7	·	·	·	·
Interest Paid 13	0.7	0.4	0.1	0.3	0.5	0.8	0.7	0.7	1.0	·	·	·	·
Depreciation 14	0.9	0.5	0.5	0.2	0.3	0.3	0.4	0.5	1.4	·	·	·	·
Amortization and Depletion 15	0.2	·	0.0	0.0	0.1	0.0	0.0	0.2	0.3	·	·	·	·
Pensions and Other Deferred Comp. 16	0.3	0.2	0.3	0.6	0.3	0.1	0.2	0.2	0.3	·	·	·	·
Employee Benefits 17	0.5	0.3	0.1	0.3	0.4	0.7	0.3	0.3	1.0	·	·	·	·
Advertising 18	1.8	1.2	0.6	1.5	0.4	0.7	0.8	1.0	2.1	·	·	·	·
Other Expenses 19	11.4	8.3	13.5	10.4	9.8	9.8	8.2	8.0	10.9	·	·	·	·
Officers' Compensation 20	2.1	2.6	3.9	3.6	2.1	2.4	2.7	2.3	1.4	·	·	·	·
Operating Margin 21	3.4	9.3	4.2	2.1	3.1	3.1	4.6	4.4	7.3	·	·	·	·
Operating Margin Before Officers' Comp. 22	5.5	11.9	8.1	5.6	5.2	5.5	7.3	6.7	8.7	·	·	·	·

Selected Average Balance Sheet ($ in Thousands)

Net Receivables 23	538	0	16	146	798	1882	4990	10324	16639
Inventories 24	533	0	43	179	583	2400	5736	10105	22774
Net Property, Plant and Equipment 25	249	0	9	37	120	793	857	1963	7386
Total Assets 26	2602	0	120	650	2358	6971	15317	33581	72207
Notes and Loans Payable 27	650	0	36	141	560	1606	4150	10666	20827
All Other Liabilities 28	699	0	40	327	1070	3036	5237	10112	18697
Net Worth 29	1252	0	44	182	729	2329	5931	12803	32683

Selected Financial Ratios (Times to 1)

Current Ratio 30	1.9	•	2.5	1.7	1.8	1.5	1.8	1.8	1.9
Quick Ratio 31	0.9	•	1.4	1.0	0.9	0.6	0.8	0.8	0.9
Net Sales to Working Capital 32	5.9	•	9.5	9.8	7.9	10.7	6.6	7.2	5.4
Coverage Ratio 33	10.0	45.0	34.2	10.6	7.3	6.2	9.2	9.2	10.0
Total Asset Turnover 34	1.7	•	4.9	3.6	3.0	3.2	2.5	2.6	1.7
Inventory Turnover 35	5.8	•	9.7	9.8	9.0	6.6	4.9	6.3	3.5
Receivables Turnover 36	8.2	•	29.1	15.0	8.4	10.2	7.9	9.7	6.6
Total Liabilities to Net Worth 37	1.1	•	1.8	2.6	2.2	2.0	1.6	1.6	1.2
Current Assets to Working Capital 38	2.2	•	1.7	2.4	2.3	2.9	2.3	2.3	2.1
Current Liabilities to Working Capital 39	1.2	•	0.7	1.4	1.3	1.9	1.3	1.3	1.1
Working Capital to Net Sales 40	0.2	•	0.1	0.1	0.1	0.1	0.2	0.1	0.2
Inventory to Working Capital 41	0.7	•	0.6	1.0	0.6	1.3	0.9	1.0	0.9
Total Receipts to Cash Flow 42	6.7	4.1	7.1	9.8	8.9	8.3	8.2	8.0	6.0
Cost of Goods to Cash Flow 43	4.6	2.9	5.1	7.4	6.6	5.9	5.9	5.7	3.8
Cash Flow to Total Debt 44	0.5	•	1.1	0.5	0.5	0.6	0.5	0.5	0.5

Selected Financial Factors (in Percentages)

Debt Ratio 45	51.9	•	63.8	72.0	69.1	66.6	61.3	61.9	54.7
Return on Total Assets 46	12.5	•	23.7	9.9	11.5	14.8	15.7	17.5	16.9
Return on Equity Before Income Taxes 47	23.4	•	63.6	32.1	32.0	37.3	36.1	40.9	33.5
Return on Equity After Income Taxes 48	18.8	•	61.6	30.7	30.0	35.5	33.0	38.5	29.1
Profit Margin (Before Income Tax) 49	6.5	17.3	4.7	2.5	3.3	3.9	5.6	5.9	8.7
Profit Margin (After Income Tax) 50	5.2	14.3	4.6	2.4	3.1	3.7	5.1	5.6	7.6

Table I

Corporations with and without Net Income

GROCERY AND RELATED PRODUCT

MONEY AMOUNTS AND SIZE OF ASSETS IN THOUSANDS OF DOLLARS

Item Description for Accounting Period 7/04 Through 6/05	Total	Zero Assets	Under 500	500 to 1,000	1,000 to 5,000	5,000 to 10,000	10,000 to 25,000	25,000 to 50,000	50,000 to 100,000	100,000 to 250,000	250,000 to 500,000	500,000 to 2,500,000	2,500,000 and over
Number of Enterprises **1**	32671	3987	19150	2780	4980	934	527	166	71	37	14	20	3
Revenues ($ in Thousands)													
Net Sales **2**	423100200	4257935	15826937	9449391	54549903	33156770	34644063	24110729	20352557	21283953	23460927	72368556	109538479
Interest **3**	4313228	5914	11955	1249	11753	10186	15100	8803	8852	20514	7596	160891	4050414
Rents **4**	1060410	150	1110	1263	45317	8710	7729	2231	2952	44748	9367	110224	826610
Royalties **5**	972144	1062	0	0	0	0	4479	0	341	20177	10	6096	883979
Other Portfolio Income **6**	2995596	20926	7081	1709	13852	6473	35047	9704	3284	19851	21851	37109	2818707
Other Receipts **7**	6451860	62824	131072	14851	312160	107046	215715	190895	182885	180010	255629	955952	3842824
Total Receipts **8**	438893438	4348811	15978155	9468463	54932985	33289185	34922133	24322362	20550871	21569253	23755380	73694828	122061013
Average Total Receipts **9**	13434	1091	834	3406	11031	35642	66266	146520	289449	582953	1696813	3684741	40687004
Operating Costs/Operating Income (%)													
Cost of Operations **10**	84.1	90.1	76.7	81.3	86.0	88.2	85.6	85.4	88.2	84.9	88.5	86.7	78.7
Salaries and Wages **11**	5.3	3.3	5.3	4.7	3.9	3.3	4.8	5.2	3.7	4.7	4.2	4.8	7.9
Taxes Paid **12**	0.9	0.6	1.2	1.1	0.8	0.6	0.7	1.0	0.6	1.5	0.6	0.6	1.3
Interest Paid **13**	0.7	0.2	0.4	0.3	0.3	0.3	0.3	0.4	0.4	0.4	0.4	0.6	1.4
Depreciation **14**	1.0	0.3	1.2	0.8	0.7	0.6	0.7	0.7	0.7	0.9	0.9	0.8	1.7
Amortization and Depletion **15**	0.1	0.1	0.1	0.0	0.1	0.0	0.1	0.0	0.1	0.1	0.1	0.2	0.2
Pensions and Other Deferred Comp. **16**	0.3	0.1	0.1	0.1	0.2	0.2	0.1	0.2	0.1	0.2	0.2	0.2	0.6
Employee Benefits **17**	0.6	0.7	0.5	0.3	0.4	0.3	0.5	0.5	0.4	0.5	0.6	0.6	0.9
Advertising **18**	0.5	0.1	0.2	0.3	0.2	0.3	0.4	0.4	0.9	0.8	0.2	0.4	0.7
Other Expenses **19**	6.1	10.7	9.1	7.4	5.6	4.9	5.0	4.9	3.6	5.8	4.4	6.8	7.0
Officers' Compensation **20**	0.8	0.5	3.4	4.2	1.8	1.1	1.0	0.7	0.9	0.4	0.2	0.1	0.2
Operating Margin **21**	•	•	1.8	•	0.1	0.3	0.7	0.6	0.3	•	•	•	•
Operating Margin Before Officers' Comp. **22**	0.5	•	5.3	3.6	1.9	1.4	1.6	1.3	1.2	0.2	•	•	•

Selected Average Balance Sheet ($ in Thousands)

Line Item													
Net Receivables 23	1020	0	24	201	759	2764	5201	10699	20670	36293	94729	122003	4943011
Inventories 24	617	0	20	139	467	1624	3956	9408	20386	44058	90381	224521	2029875
Net Property, Plant and Equipment 25	724	0	33	118	326	889	2513	5828	10292	28981	85228	196404	3667778
Total Assets 26	11704	0	140	695	2132	6982	15359	34493	69879	151307	349622	961443	10404433
Notes and Loans Payable 27	1531	0	71	279	658	2125	4462	10878	22402	44743	78231	412753	8621530
All Other Liabilities 28	3003	0	35	255	776	2681	5489	11573	24121	56770	183468	188114	25134039
Net Worth 29	7171	0	35	161	698	2176	5408	12041	23357	49794	87923	360576	70288863

Selected Financial Ratios (Times to 1)

Line Item													
Current Ratio 30	1.4	•	1.7	1.7	1.7	1.4	1.5	1.5	1.6	1.5	1.4	1.3	1.3
Quick Ratio 31	0.8	•	1.2	1.1	1.1	0.9	0.9	0.8	0.8	0.7	0.7	0.4	0.8
Net Sales to Working Capital 32	12.4	•	27.2	15.8	16.3	21.1	16.9	17.6	15.0	17.6	26.9	38.2	5.7
Coverage Ratio 33	6.2	•	8.7	•	3.8	3.8	5.3	5.2	4.5	3.7	3.4	1.3	8.5
Total Asset Turnover 34	1.1	•	5.9	4.9	5.1	5.1	4.3	4.2	4.1	3.8	4.8	3.8	0.4
Inventory Turnover 35	17.7	•	31.2	19.8	20.2	19.3	14.2	13.2	12.4	11.1	16.4	14.0	14.2
Receivables Turnover 36	15.1	•	32.1	18.4	13.9	14.1	13.0	14.1	14.4	16.5	17.1	15.2	•
Total Liabilities to Net Worth 37	0.6	•	3.1	3.3	2.1	2.2	1.8	1.9	2.0	2.0	3.0	1.7	0.5
Current Assets to Working Capital 38	3.6	•	2.3	2.4	2.4	3.4	2.9	3.0	2.7	3.0	3.5	4.8	4.0
Current Liabilities to Working Capital 39	2.6	•	1.3	1.4	1.4	2.4	1.9	2.0	1.7	2.0	2.5	3.8	3.0
Working Capital to Net Sales 40	0.1	•	0.0	0.1	0.1	0.0	0.1	0.1	0.1	0.1	0.0	0.0	0.2
Inventory to Working Capital 41	0.7	•	0.6	0.8	0.7	1.2	1.1	1.2	1.2	1.3	1.5	1.8	0.3
Total Receipts to Cash Flow 42	12.8	19.9	10.1	18.9	20.0	24.6	19.0	19.1	24.9	17.3	24.1	17.6	6.7
Cost of Goods to Cash Flow 43	10.8	17.9	7.7	15.4	17.2	21.7	16.2	16.3	22.0	14.7	21.3	15.3	5.3
Cash Flow to Total Debt 44	0.2	•	0.8	0.3	0.4	0.3	0.3	0.3	0.2	0.3	0.3	0.3	0.2

Selected Financial Factors (in Percentages)

Line Item													
Debt Ratio 45	38.7	•	75.3	76.8	67.3	68.8	64.8	65.1	66.6	67.1	74.9	62.5	32.4
Return on Total Assets 46	4.4	•	18.6	•	5.4	4.9	7.8	7.8	6.5	6.3	6.3	2.7	4.2
Return on Equity Before Income Taxes 47	6.1	•	66.7	•	12.2	11.5	18.0	17.9	15.1	13.9	17.6	1.6	5.5
Return on Equity After Income Taxes 48	4.2	•	66.2	•	11.0	10.1	16.2	15.8	12.5	10.5	13.5	0.2	3.7
Profit Margin (Before Income Tax) 49	3.4	•	2.8	•	0.8	0.7	1.5	1.5	1.2	1.2	0.9	0.2	10.6
Profit Margin (After Income Tax) 50	2.3	•	2.8	•	0.7	0.6	1.3	1.3	1.0	0.9	0.7	0.0	7.1

Table II

Corporations with Net Income

GROCERY AND RELATED PRODUCT

MONEY AMOUNTS AND SIZE OF ASSETS IN THOUSANDS OF DOLLARS

Item Description for Accounting Period 7/04 Through 6/05		Total	Zero Assets	Under 500	500 to 1,000	1,000 to 5,000	5,000 to 10,000	10,000 to 25,000	25,000 to 50,000	50,000 to 100,000	100,000 to 250,000	250,000 to 500,000	500,000 to 2,500,000	2,500,000 and over
Number of Enterprises	1	22349	2197	13446	1383	3929	710	427	139	64	25	0	14	0
Revenues ($ in Thousands)														
Net Sales	2	358315319	1066458	12952578	4151694	47561050	26940569	29157534	20842253	18351536	14045604	0	51932886	0
Interest	3	4157309	2550	10750	960	10357	8703	6868	7653	5002	9695	0	38688	0
Rents	4	1006585	150	631	694	45026	8294	6508	2019	2927	19122	0	85960	0
Royalties	5	947483	1062	0	0	0	0	1907	0	341	4323	0	55861	0
Other Portfolio Income	6	2937813	11217	3382	1050	11350	4298	13975	8760	2674	13979	0	27464	0
Other Receipts	7	6003186	37809	52792	4501	292136	86635	181139	112447	178384	112356	0	880114	0
Total Receipts	8	373367695	1119246	13020133	4158899	47919919	27048499	29367931	20973132	18540864	14205079	0	53020953	0
Average Total Receipts	9	16706	509	968	3007	12196	38096	68777	150886	289701	568203	•	3787211	•
Operating Costs/Operating Income (%)														
Cost of Operations	10	83.8	83.3	77.2	81.7	86.2	88.0	85.6	84.9	88.3	81.9	•	87.1	•
Salaries and Wages	11	5.5	3.1	4.4	3.8	3.7	3.1	4.6	5.3	3.5	5.4	•	5.4	•
Taxes Paid	12	1.0	0.8	1.0	1.1	0.8	0.7	0.7	1.0	0.6	2.0	•	0.7	•
Interest Paid	13	0.7	0.2	0.4	0.2	0.3	0.2	0.3	0.3	0.3	0.4	•	0.6	•
Depreciation	14	1.0	0.2	1.1	0.5	0.6	0.6	0.6	0.7	0.7	1.0	•	0.9	•
Amortization and Depletion	15	0.1	0.1	0.1	0.0	0.0	0.0	0.0	0.0	0.1	0.1	•	0.2	•
Pensions and Other Deferred Comp.	16	0.3	0.1	0.1	0.2	0.2	0.1	0.2	0.2	0.1	0.2	•	0.3	•
Employee Benefits	17	0.6	0.2	0.4	0.3	0.3	0.3	0.5	0.5	0.4	0.6	•	0.6	•
Advertising	18	0.5	0.3	0.2	0.1	0.1	0.2	0.3	0.4	1.0	0.9	•	0.5	•
Other Expenses	19	5.6	5.7	8.0	6.4	5.3	4.6	4.7	4.5	3.5	5.8	•	5.1	•
Officers' Compensation	20	0.8	1.3	3.1	3.3	1.8	1.2	1.0	0.7	1.0	0.5	•	0.1	•
Operating Margin	21	0.2	4.6	4.0	2.3	0.7	1.0	1.5	1.3	0.4	1.1	•	•	•
Operating Margin Before Officers' Comp.	22	1.0	5.9	7.1	5.6	2.5	2.2	2.5	2.1	1.5	1.7	•	•	•

Selected Average Balance Sheet ($ in Thousands)

Net Receivables 23	1325	0	28	185	798	2897	5353	10628	20322	38708	•	123763
Inventories 24	756	0	19	173	458	1643	4067	9503	19666	51016	•	259914
Net Property, Plant and Equipment 25	918	0	31	50	345	800	2239	5720	9832	26489	•	220436
Total Assets 26	16353	0	152	709	2189	6776	15169	34318	69806	154071	•	941960
Notes and Loans Payable 27	1854	0	52	130	668	2173	4031	10047	21257	40914	•	280962
All Other Liabilities 28	4224	0	37	175	746	2675	5398	11261	24408	57416	•	324359
Net Worth 29	10275	0	63	404	775	1928	5740	13010	24141	55741	•	336639

Selected Financial Ratios (Times to 1)

Current Ratio 30	1.4	•	2.0	3.1	1.8	1.4	1.6	1.6	1.6	1.6	•	1.1
Quick Ratio 31	0.8	•	1.4	2.0	1.2	0.8	0.9	0.8	0.8	0.8	•	0.4
Net Sales to Working Capital 32	11.6	•	25.3	7.4	16.2	25.4	15.4	16.5	14.5	14.4	•	115.9
Coverage Ratio 33	7.4	41.2	12.3	12.6	6.5	6.7	9.0	7.0	5.5	6.6	•	2.3
Total Asset Turnover 34	1.0	•	6.3	4.2	5.5	5.6	4.5	4.4	4.1	3.6	•	3.9
Inventory Turnover 35	17.8	•	39.6	14.2	22.8	20.3	14.4	13.4	12.9	9.0	•	12.4
Receivables Turnover 36	15.3	•	35.9	14.5	15.0	14.9	13.1	14.7	15.3	14.3	•	15.6
Total Liabilities to Net Worth 37	0.6	•	1.4	0.8	1.8	2.5	1.6	1.6	1.9	1.8	•	1.8
Current Assets to Working Capital 38	3.6	•	2.0	1.5	2.2	3.7	2.6	2.8	2.6	2.8	•	12.7
Current Liabilities to Working Capital 39	2.6	•	1.0	0.5	1.2	2.7	1.6	1.8	1.6	1.8	•	11.7
Working Capital to Net Sales 40	0.1	•	0.0	0.1	0.0	0.0	0.1	0.1	0.1	0.1	•	0.0
Inventory to Working Capital 41	0.6	•	0.5	0.4	0.6	1.3	1.0	1.1	1.2	1.2	•	6.2
Total Receipts to Cash Flow 42	12.0	7.0	9.2	13.0	18.5	23.2	17.0	18.7	23.6	14.2	•	22.3
Cost of Goods to Cash Flow 43	10.1	5.8	7.1	10.6	15.9	20.4	14.5	15.9	20.9	11.6	•	19.4
Cash Flow to Total Debt 44	0.2	•	1.2	0.8	0.5	0.3	0.4	0.4	0.3	0.4	•	0.3

Selected Financial Factors (in Percentages)

Debt Ratio 45	37.2	•	58.7	43.0	64.6	71.5	62.2	62.1	65.4	63.8	•	64.3
Return on Total Assets 46	5.0	•	31.1	11.3	9.3	9.2	11.4	10.0	7.4	10.1	•	5.1
Return on Equity Before Income Taxes 47	6.9	•	69.2	18.2	22.3	27.4	26.7	22.6	17.4	23.8	•	8.0
Return on Equity After Income Taxes 48	5.0	•	68.8	18.0	21.0	25.3	24.6	20.3	14.6	19.3	•	5.9
Profit Margin (Before Income Tax) 49	4.4	9.6	4.5	2.5	1.4	1.4	2.2	2.0	1.5	2.4	•	0.7
Profit Margin (After Income Tax) 50	3.2	8.4	4.5	2.4	1.3	1.3	2.1	1.8	1.2	1.9	•	0.5

Table I

Corporations with and without Net Income

FARM PRODUCT RAW MATERIAL

MONEY AMOUNTS AND SIZE OF ASSETS IN THOUSANDS OF DOLLARS

Item Description for Accounting Period 7/04 Through 6/05	Total	Zero Assets	Under 500	500 to 1,000	1,000 to 5,000	5,000 to 10,000	10,000 to 25,000	25,000 to 50,000	50,000 to 100,000	100,000 to 250,000	250,000 to 500,000	500,000 to 2,500,000	2,500,000 and over
Number of Enterprises **1**	5313	34	2925	765	1083	327	109	23	26	11	3	4	3
Revenues ($ in Thousands)													
Net Sales **2**	103186681	465509	2887888	2536263	9761208	8389807	5428822	2234434	4358755	8438136	4845750	5184471	48655639
Interest **3**	1168420	546	287	4340	5204	4248	4046	2982	14423	8552	8256	17015	1098521
Rents **4**	155516	118	941	458	9108	4692	2168	3894	3859	1398	289	54794	73797
Royalties **5**	82459	7494	0	0	0	120	6870	0	0	0	0	17192	50783
Other Portfolio Income **6**	742601	13556	7	19349	6080	4646	14106	1494	11161	6262	756	10482	654702
Other Receipts **7**	1842277	12105	49281	112425	135262	81867	67483	28871	51385	19637	8539	75650	1199771
Total Receipts **8**	107177954	499328	2938404	2672835	9916862	8485380	5523495	2271675	4439583	8473985	4863590	5359604	51733213
Average Total Receipts **9**	20173	14686	1005	3494	9157	25949	50674	98768	170753	770362	1621197	1339901	17244404
Operating Costs/Operating Income (%)													
Cost of Operations **10**	91.6	79.4	82.4	85.7	87.1	92.8	88.8	89.4	92.3	96.3	96.2	87.5	92.8
Salaries and Wages **11**	2.6	6.5	3.7	3.8	3.7	1.9	3.4	3.6	1.6	1.0	1.0	5.9	2.3
Taxes Paid **12**	0.6	1.3	0.7	0.8	0.8	0.4	0.7	0.5	0.4	0.1	0.1	0.7	0.6
Interest Paid **13**	1.6	0.5	0.6	0.2	0.7	0.4	0.5	0.4	0.8	0.3	0.4	1.4	2.8
Depreciation **14**	1.0	1.1	0.9	0.9	1.1	0.6	1.0	1.3	0.8	0.3	0.2	1.1	1.2
Amortization and Depletion **15**	0.1	0.2	0.0	0.0	0.0	0.0	0.0	0.0	0.0	0.0	0.0	0.2	0.1
Pensions and Other Deferred Comp. **16**	0.4	0.3	0.2	0.0	0.1	0.2	0.1	0.1	0.1	0.1	0.0	0.3	0.7
Employee Benefits **17**	0.5	0.8	0.1	0.4	0.5	0.1	0.3	0.2	0.3	0.1	0.2	0.9	0.6
Advertising **18**	0.1	0.2	0.2	0.2	0.1	0.1	0.2	0.1	0.1	0.0	0.0	0.1	0.1
Other Expenses **19**	3.5	6.1	8.3	6.3	5.3	2.7	4.5	4.7	3.8	1.4	1.4	3.8	3.1
Officers' Compensation **20**	0.7	0.3	2.0	2.6	1.5	1.0	0.6	0.6	0.5	0.2	0.1	0.4	0.6
Operating Margin **21**	•	3.3	0.9	•	•	•	•	•	•	0.2	0.3	•	•
Operating Margin Before Officers' Comp. **22**	•	3.6	2.9	1.7	0.6	0.6	0.4	•	•	0.4	0.4	•	•

Selected Average Balance Sheet ($ in Thousands)

Net Receivables 23	4149	0	39	165	575	2912	4369	10193	16318	51024	119820	158152	5846094
Inventories 24	1816	0	3	51	419	1142	3741	9896	15174	61108	105697	335318	1804297
Net Property, Plant and Equipment 25	1230	0	43	164	606	1184	3112	7177	10271	19892	39675	105591	1235637
Total Assets 26	13030	0	167	740	2347	6902	15239	34807	69643	176766	305436	747834	17749929
Notes and Loans Payable 27	4308	0	99	165	1021	1691	4862	9013	23335	60687	140915	238253	5809116
All Other Liabilities 28	5329	0	96	189	722	3652	5716	14655	22115	64341	110041	378144	7276697
Net Worth 29	3392	0	-28	386	604	1558	4661	11139	24193	51737	54480	131438	4664116

Selected Financial Ratios (Times to 1)

Current Ratio 30	1.3	0.8	•	3.2	2.2	1.2	1.4	1.3	1.4	1.6	1.5	1.4	1.2
Quick Ratio 31	0.7	0.8	•	2.6	1.0	0.9	0.7	0.8	0.6	0.7	0.7	0.4	0.7
Net Sales to Working Capital 32	12.1	•	•	10.7	10.3	29.9	16.2	16.4	11.9	14.5	19.2	8.5	10.0
Coverage Ratio 33	2.3	21.9	5.6	30.0	1.9	2.8	4.3	2.5	2.6	2.8	2.5	1.8	2.2
Total Asset Turnover 34	1.5	•	5.9	4.5	3.8	3.7	3.3	2.8	2.4	4.3	5.3	1.7	0.9
Inventory Turnover 35	9.8	•	236.0	55.8	18.7	20.9	11.8	8.8	10.2	12.1	14.7	3.4	8.3
Receivables Turnover 36	3.8	•	26.5	16.8	13.8	10.7	11.5	8.8	12.5	14.0	10.6	9.2	2.1
Total Liabilities to Net Worth 37	2.8	•	•	0.9	2.9	3.4	2.3	2.1	1.9	2.4	4.6	4.7	2.8
Current Assets to Working Capital 38	4.8	•	•	1.4	1.8	6.3	3.6	4.1	3.2	2.7	3.1	3.6	6.0
Current Liabilities to Working Capital 39	3.8	•	•	0.4	0.8	5.3	2.6	3.1	2.2	1.7	2.1	2.6	5.0
Working Capital to Net Sales 40	0.1	•	•	0.1	0.1	0.0	0.1	0.1	0.1	0.1	0.1	0.1	0.1
Inventory to Working Capital 41	1.1	•	•	0.2	0.5	1.3	1.3	1.2	1.4	0.9	1.1	2.1	1.1
Total Receipts to Cash Flow 42	27.6	7.4	11.2	11.0	21.5	33.0	20.8	22.5	22.5	57.0	65.2	35.7	31.2
Cost of Goods to Cash Flow 43	25.3	5.8	9.2	9.4	18.7	30.7	18.5	20.1	20.8	54.9	62.7	31.2	28.9
Cash Flow to Total Debt 44	0.1	•	0.5	0.9	0.2	0.1	0.2	0.2	0.2	0.1	0.1	0.1	0.0

Selected Financial Factors (in Percentages)

Debt Ratio 45	74.0	116.7	•	47.8	74.3	77.4	69.4	68.0	65.3	70.7	82.2	82.4	73.7
Return on Total Assets 46	5.6	18.9	•	21.1	5.0	4.4	6.6	2.9	4.7	3.9	5.9	4.4	5.5
Return on Equity Before Income Taxes 47	12.4	•	•	39.0	9.3	12.4	16.5	5.4	8.4	8.6	19.8	11.3	11.2
Return on Equity After Income Taxes 48	8.6	•	•	34.8	8.1	11.3	14.0	4.2	5.4	5.5	13.6	8.3	7.2
Profit Margin (Before Income Tax) 49	2.2	10.6	2.6	4.5	0.6	0.8	1.5	0.6	0.6	0.6	0.7	1.1	3.2
Profit Margin (After Income Tax) 50	1.5	8.3	2.6	4.1	0.5	0.7	1.3	0.5	0.4	0.4	0.5	0.8	2.1

Table II

Corporations with Net Income

FARM PRODUCT RAW MATERIAL

MONEY AMOUNTS AND SIZE OF ASSETS IN THOUSANDS OF DOLLARS

Item Description for Accounting Period 7/04 Through 6/05	Total	Zero Assets	Under 500	500 to 1,000	1,000 to 5,000	5,000 to 10,000	10,000 to 25,000	25,000 to 50,000	50,000 to 100,000	100,000 to 250,000	250,000 to 500,000	500,000 to 2,500,000	2,500,000 and over
Number of Enterprises 1	3288	31	1497	554	832	232	0	20	19	0	3	0	0
Revenues ($ in Thousands)													
Net Sales 2	83333712	247610	2117558	1127393	8527719	5388592	0	1794117	3094629	0	4845750	0	0
Interest 3	880209	546	32	3400	4454	2374	0	2865	13308	0	8256	0	0
Rents 4	148277	118	5	330	8861	4566	0	2428	563	0	289	0	0
Royalties 5	82339	7494	0	0	0	0	0	0	0	0	0	0	0
Other Portfolio Income 6	718827	13550	0	15826	4010	2515	0	1321	3211	0	756	0	0
Other Receipts 7	1499236	11784	9215	27448	117927	37688	0	26276	47316	0	8539	0	0
Total Receipts 8	86657600	281102	2126810	1174397	8662971	5435735	0	1827007	3159027	0	4863590	0	0
Average Total Receipts 9	26356	9068	1421	2120	10412	23430	•	91350	166265	•	1621197	•	•
Operating Costs/Operating Income (%)													
Cost of Operations 10	91.4	64.7	80.3	73.7	87.5	92.4	•	88.9	93.3	•	96.2	•	•
Salaries and Wages 11	2.6	11.2	2.9	5.6	3.4	1.6	•	3.4	1.2	•	1.0	•	•
Taxes Paid 12	0.6	2.3	0.6	1.2	0.8	0.4	•	0.5	0.4	•	0.1	•	•
Interest Paid 13	1.5	0.3	0.4	0.1	0.6	0.3	•	0.4	0.8	•	0.4	•	•
Depreciation 14	1.0	1.8	0.5	1.6	0.9	0.4	•	1.2	0.6	•	0.2	•	•
Amortization and Depletion 15	0.1	0.4	0.0	•	0.0	0.1	•	0.0	0.0	•	0.0	•	•
Pensions and Other Deferred Comp. 16	0.4	0.6	0.3	0.0	0.1	0.2	•	0.1	0.1	•	0.0	•	•
Employee Benefits 17	0.4	1.3	0.0	0.2	0.4	0.1	•	0.2	0.3	•	0.2	•	•
Advertising 18	0.1	0.3	0.2	0.5	0.1	0.1	•	0.1	0.1	•	0.0	•	•
Other Expenses 19	3.3	10.2	7.1	8.7	5.0	2.2	•	5.2	2.8	•	1.4	•	•
Officers' Compensation 20	0.8	0.5	2.4	1.6	1.5	1.4	•	0.7	0.4	•	0.1	•	•
Operating Margin 21	•	6.5	5.3	6.8	•	0.9	•	0.0	0.0	•	0.3	•	•
Operating Margin Before Officers' Comp. 22	•	7.0	7.7	8.4	1.3	2.3	•	0.5	0.5	•	0.4	•	•

Selected Average Balance Sheet ($ in Thousands)

Net Receivables 23	6075	0	75	145	616	2771	•	9766	17143	119820
Inventories 24	2341	0	4	43	454	1213	•	9140	15985	105697
Net Property, Plant and Equipment 25	1555	0	48	114	462	941	•	6104	6168	39675
Total Assets 26	16926	0	258	715	2356	6813	•	33271	69482	305436
Notes and Loans Payable 27	4422	0	57	26	943	879	•	8757	22277	140915
All Other Liabilities 28	7695	0	179	124	821	4152	•	14662	20879	110041
Net Worth 29	4809	0	22	565	592	1782	•	9851	26326	54480

Selected Financial Ratios (Times to 1)

Current Ratio 30	1.2	•	0.8	3.4	2.3	1.2	•	1.3	1.5	1.5
Quick Ratio 31	0.8	•	0.8	2.6	1.0	0.9	•	0.8	0.6	0.7
Net Sales to Working Capital 32	12.7	•	•	6.5	9.9	27.6	•	16.4	11.0	19.2
Coverage Ratio 33	3.0	59.8	14.7	204.3	3.3	8.1	•	3.5	3.7	2.5
Total Asset Turnover 34	1.5	•	5.5	2.8	4.4	3.4	•	2.7	2.3	5.3
Inventory Turnover 35	9.9	•	319.2	34.9	19.7	17.7	•	8.7	9.5	14.7
Receivables Turnover 36	3.8	•	31.1	12.5	15.5	11.8	•	8.4	11.3	10.6
Total Liabilities to Net Worth 37	2.5	•	10.9	0.3	3.0	2.8	•	2.4	1.6	4.6
Current Assets to Working Capital 38	5.1	•	•	1.4	1.7	6.5	•	4.3	3.1	3.1
Current Liabilities to Working Capital 39	4.1	•	•	0.4	0.7	5.5	•	3.3	2.1	2.1
Working Capital to Net Sales 40	0.1	•	•	0.2	0.1	0.0	•	0.1	0.1	0.1
Inventory to Working Capital 41	1.2	•	•	0.2	0.4	1.1	•	1.3	1.4	1.1
Total Receipts to Cash Flow 42	24.9	4.1	9.1	5.5	19.4	26.5	•	18.0	22.6	65.2
Cost of Goods to Cash Flow 43	22.8	2.6	7.3	4.0	17.0	24.5	•	16.0	21.1	62.7
Cash Flow to Total Debt 44	0.1	•	0.7	2.5	0.3	0.2	•	0.2	0.2	0.1

Selected Financial Factors (in Percentages)

Debt Ratio 45	71.6	•	91.6	20.9	74.9	73.8	•	70.4	62.1	82.2
Return on Total Assets 46	6.7	•	33.7	31.4	8.5	7.0	•	4.2	6.8	5.9
Return on Equity Before Income Taxes 47	15.9	•	374.2	39.5	23.7	23.5	•	10.2	13.1	19.8
Return on Equity After Income Taxes 48	11.5	•	373.1	35.6	22.0	22.1	•	8.7	9.6	13.6
Profit Margin (Before Income Tax) 49	3.0	20.0	5.7	11.0	1.4	1.8	•	1.1	2.1	0.7
Profit Margin (After Income Tax) 50	2.2	15.7	5.7	9.9	1.3	1.7	•	1.0	1.5	0.5

Table I
Corporations with and without Net Income

CHEMICAL AND ALLIED PRODUCTS

MONEY AMOUNTS AND SIZE OF ASSETS IN THOUSANDS OF DOLLARS

Item Description for Accounting Period 7/04 Through 6/05	Total	Zero Assets	Under 500	500 to 1,000	1,000 to 5,000	5,000 to 10,000	10,000 to 25,000	25,000 to 50,000	50,000 to 100,000	100,000 to 250,000	250,000 to 500,000	500,000 to 2,500,000	2,500,000 and over
Number of Enterprises 1	9073	908	5483	708	1433	232	178	63	32	17	4	14	0
Revenues ($ in Thousands)													
Net Sales 2	59799941	986724	1834974	1918472	9909674	4628710	7153704	5419709	4850485	4255010	2168951	16673529	0
Interest 3	107142	396	262	109	5101	4353	3328	3773	7551	13540	665	68063	0
Rents 4	19853	0	0	0	1927	715	1363	606	2310	7117	772	5043	0
Royalties 5	86500	12	0	0	0	0	82	848	0	633	0	84924	0
Other Portfolio Income 6	249848	43654	312	217	13157	12301	2195	9840	4156	14253	3170	146593	0
Other Receipts 7	923058	17953	17603	31632	36144	31567	63478	63286	210778	44977	48011	357629	0
Total Receipts 8	61186342	1048739	1853151	1950430	9966003	4677646	7224150	5498062	5075280	4335530	2221569	17335781	0
Average Total Receipts 9	6744	1155	338	2755	6955	20162	40585	87271	158602	255031	555392	1238270	•
Operating Costs/Operating Income (%)													
Cost of Operations 10	78.3	72.5	64.3	52.6	75.5	76.6	82.1	83.4	83.5	90.0	84.4	76.8	•
Salaries and Wages 11	6.1	2.9	9.7	17.3	6.0	6.1	5.3	5.1	4.3	2.4	3.6	7.0	•
Taxes Paid 12	1.0	0.7	2.2	2.3	1.2	1.0	0.8	0.8	0.9	0.6	0.5	1.1	•
Interest Paid 13	1.2	4.4	0.6	0.6	0.5	0.4	0.5	0.6	0.5	1.2	0.4	2.4	•
Depreciation 14	1.7	1.7	0.8	1.2	0.9	1.1	1.1	1.3	1.2	0.7	1.8	3.3	•
Amortization and Depletion 15	0.3	0.2	0.0	0.0	0.1	0.0	0.1	0.1	0.2	0.5	0.0	0.6	•
Pensions and Other Deferred Comp. 16	0.4	0.0	0.1	0.9	0.3	0.4	0.3	0.2	0.4	0.1	0.2	0.5	•
Employee Benefits 17	0.8	0.0	1.4	1.3	0.6	0.5	0.4	0.5	0.8	0.3	0.1	1.4	•
Advertising 18	0.3	0.2	0.2	0.4	0.6	0.2	0.2	0.1	0.2	0.3	0.7	0.1	•
Other Expenses 19	8.4	14.3	13.6	15.8	8.3	9.0	7.0	5.4	9.9	3.1	7.8	9.3	•
Officers' Compensation 20	1.7	5.6	6.6	8.4	3.0	2.0	1.5	1.1	0.6	0.6	0.2	0.6	•
Operating Margin 21	•	•	0.6	•	2.9	2.7	0.7	1.5	•	0.3	0.3	•	•
Operating Margin Before Officers' Comp. 22	1.6	3.1	7.2	7.7	5.9	4.8	2.2	2.5	•	0.8	0.5	•	•

Selected Average Balance Sheet ($ in Thousands)

Net Receivables 23	805	0	24	290	738	2541	5439	12679	23006	41706	83068	126435
Inventories 24	596	0	16	139	386	2430	3878	7914	16375	27092	57311	121584
Net Property, Plant and Equipment 25	715	0	24	120	240	795	2186	4082	12504	15838	69524	296417
Total Assets 26	3700	0	105	677	2267	7292	14981	35238	70053	156439	279438	1190403
Notes and Loans Payable 27	1157	0	70	316	612	1142	4276	9699	18601	53571	86934	394488
All Other Liabilities 28	1379	0	35	383	739	3997	6111	11336	29102	60725	83423	426082
Net Worth 29	1163	0	-0	-22	916	2154	4594	14204	22350	42143	109081	369832

Selected Financial Ratios (Times to 1)

Current Ratio 30	1.4	•	1.1	1.2	1.9	1.5	1.4	1.6	1.4	1.1	1.2	1.3
Quick Ratio 31	0.8	•	0.8	0.8	1.3	0.9	0.8	1.0	0.8	0.6	0.7	0.6
Net Sales to Working Capital 32	12.2	•	46.1	32.9	8.1	10.1	11.9	9.0	11.4	29.0	22.5	13.4
Coverage Ratio 33	3.0	1.9	3.6	2.5	8.3	10.8	4.2	6.2	5.4	3.0	7.6	1.5
Total Asset Turnover 34	1.8	•	3.2	4.0	3.0	2.7	2.7	2.4	2.2	1.6	1.9	1.0
Inventory Turnover 35	8.7	•	13.6	10.3	13.5	6.3	8.5	9.1	7.7	8.3	8.0	7.5
Receivables Turnover 36	8.4	•	16.4	10.1	8.8	7.2	7.8	7.8	6.4	7.2	5.7	9.5
Total Liabilities to Net Worth 37	2.2	•	•	•	1.5	2.4	2.3	1.5	2.1	2.7	1.6	2.2
Current Assets to Working Capital 38	3.5	•	8.7	6.3	2.1	3.0	3.4	2.6	3.7	10.0	6.5	4.2
Current Liabilities to Working Capital 39	2.5	•	7.7	5.3	1.1	2.0	2.4	1.6	2.7	9.0	5.5	3.2
Working Capital to Net Sales 40	0.1	•	0.0	0.0	0.1	0.1	0.1	0.1	0.1	0.0	0.0	0.1
Inventory to Working Capital 41	1.2	•	2.2	1.8	0.5	1.1	1.2	0.9	1.4	3.8	2.4	1.4
Total Receipts to Cash Flow 42	11.6	8.2	9.0	7.1	9.8	9.9	13.7	14.0	9.0	21.7	11.0	13.5
Cost of Goods to Cash Flow 43	9.1	5.9	5.8	3.7	7.4	7.6	11.2	11.7	7.5	19.5	9.3	10.4
Cash Flow to Total Debt 44	0.2	•	0.4	0.5	0.5	0.4	0.3	0.3	0.4	0.1	0.3	0.1

Selected Financial Factors (in Percentages)

Debt Ratio 45	68.6	•	100.2	103.2	59.6	70.5	69.3	59.7	68.1	73.1	61.0	68.9
Return on Total Assets 46	6.1	•	7.1	6.5	12.1	11.4	5.9	8.5	6.1	5.6	6.0	3.6
Return on Equity Before Income Taxes 47	12.8	•	•	•	26.4	34.9	14.7	17.6	15.5	13.9	13.4	3.8
Return on Equity After Income Taxes 48	10.3	•	•	•	25.0	31.1	12.4	15.6	11.4	8.8	10.1	2.1
Profit Margin (Before Income Tax) 49	2.3	3.8	1.6	1.0	3.5	3.8	1.7	2.9	2.3	2.3	2.7	1.2
Profit Margin (After Income Tax) 50	1.8	3.6	1.5	0.4	3.3	3.4	1.4	2.6	1.7	1.5	2.0	0.6

Table II

Corporations with Net Income

CHEMICAL AND ALLIED PRODUCTS

MONEY AMOUNTS AND SIZE OF ASSETS IN THOUSANDS OF DOLLARS

Item Description for Accounting Period 7/04 Through 6/05	Total	Zero Assets	Under 500	500 to 1,000	1,000 to 5,000	5,000 to 10,000	10,000 to 25,000	25,000 to 50,000	50,000 to 100,000	100,000 to 250,000	250,000 to 500,000	500,000 to 2,500,000	2,500,000 and over
Number of Enterprises **1**	4868	452	2304	462	1178	221	143	56	24	12	4	11	0
Revenues ($ in Thousands)													
Net Sales **2**	50738517	638110	1232086	1292557	9275907	4528013	6184235	4974777	3874204	3133077	2168951	13436602	0
Interest **3**	86726	110	106	68	4523	4302	2068	3639	5912	4568	665	60766	0
Rents **4**	18360	0	0	0	1860	715	578	601	1837	7116	772	4881	0
Royalties **5**	85854	0	0	0	0	0	82	848	0	0	0	84924	0
Other Portfolio Income **6**	208061	40560	312	217	13026	12301	1394	2384	1565	11032	3170	122099	0
Other Receipts **7**	648163	8325	17464	31553	31736	31430	47994	57438	28864	32960	48011	312384	0
Total Receipts **8**	51785681	687105	1249968	1324395	9327052	4576761	6236351	5039687	3912382	3188753	2221569	14021656	0
Average Total Receipts **9**	10638	1520	543	2867	7918	20709	43611	89994	163016	265729	555392	1274696	•
Operating Costs/Operating Income (%)													
Cost of Operations **10**	79.9	73.8	64.2	58.9	75.2	76.3	82.7	83.7	84.6	89.8	84.4	81.2	•
Salaries and Wages **11**	5.1	0.5	7.4	13.6	5.9	6.1	4.8	4.9	4.2	2.2	3.6	4.7	•
Taxes Paid **12**	1.0	0.3	1.7	2.1	1.2	1.1	0.8	0.8	0.9	0.6	0.5	1.0	•
Interest Paid **13**	0.8	0.2	0.5	0.8	0.5	0.4	0.4	0.4	0.4	0.7	0.4	1.8	•
Depreciation **14**	1.2	0.3	0.4	0.8	0.9	1.1	0.8	0.7	1.1	0.8	1.8	1.8	•
Amortization and Depletion **15**	0.2	0.1	0.0	0.0	0.1	0.0	0.0	0.1	0.1	0.5	0.0	0.5	•
Pensions and Other Deferred Comp. **16**	0.4	0.0	0.1	1.3	0.3	0.4	0.3	0.2	0.4	0.1	0.2	0.6	•
Employee Benefits **17**	0.7	0.1	0.8	0.3	0.6	0.5	0.4	0.5	0.7	0.2	0.1	1.3	•
Advertising **18**	0.3	0.2	0.2	0.3	0.6	0.2	0.2	0.1	0.2	0.3	0.7	0.1	•
Other Expenses **19**	7.4	13.2	12.2	14.8	8.2	9.0	6.1	4.6	4.4	2.7	7.8	8.3	•
Officers' Compensation **20**	1.6	6.9	5.8	6.3	2.9	2.0	1.5	1.1	0.6	0.5	0.2	0.6	•
Operating Margin **21**	1.5	4.3	6.7	0.8	3.6	3.0	2.1	2.8	2.6	1.5	0.3	•	•
Operating Margin Before Officers' Comp. **22**	3.1	11.1	12.5	7.2	6.5	5.0	3.5	3.9	3.2	2.0	0.5	•	•

Selected Average Balance Sheet ($ in Thousands)

Net Receivables 23	1330	0	38	324	826	2575	5872	13475	22497	46906	83068	151394	•
Inventories 24	873	0	16	104	398	2335	3940	8224	17858	29577	56894	116444	•
Net Property, Plant and Equipment 25	898	0	43	68	261	826	1672	3279	10979	17553	69524	234075	•
Total Assets 26	5420	0	163	685	2363	7377	14953	34626	70450	155998	279438	1138448	•
Notes and Loans Payable 27	1393	0	44	357	627	1094	3839	8574	14285	43029	86934	299897	•
All Other Liabilities 28	2077	0	38	422	792	3979	6122	11705	32459	65403	83423	417232	•
Net Worth 29	1950	0	82	-94	943	2304	4992	14346	23705	47566	109081	421320	•

Selected Financial Ratios (Times to 1)

Current Ratio 30	1.4	•	1.4	1.2	1.8	1.5	1.5	1.6	1.3	1.0	1.2	1.3	•
Quick Ratio 31	0.8	•	1.0	0.9	1.3	0.9	0.9	0.9	0.7	0.5	0.7	0.6	•
Net Sales to Working Capital 32	12.1	•	21.5	27.9	9.2	9.9	10.4	9.3	13.8	•	22.5	12.1	•
Coverage Ratio 33	5.5	55.7	15.9	5.3	9.8	12.1	8.1	11.2	10.5	5.7	7.6	2.6	•
Total Asset Turnover 34	1.9	•	3.3	4.1	3.3	2.8	2.9	2.6	2.3	1.7	1.9	1.1	•
Inventory Turnover 35	9.5	•	21.5	15.8	14.9	6.7	9.1	9.0	7.6	7.9	8.0	8.5	•
Receivables Turnover 36	8.4	•	24.8	11.3	9.3	7.6	8.1	8.1	6.8	6.6	•	1.7	•
Total Liabilities to Net Worth 37	1.8	•	1.0	•	1.5	2.2	2.0	1.4	2.0	2.3	1.6	1.7	•
Current Assets to Working Capital 38	3.5	•	3.5	5.7	2.2	2.8	2.9	2.7	4.2	•	6.5	4.1	•
Current Liabilities to Working Capital 39	2.5	•	2.5	4.7	1.2	1.8	1.9	1.7	3.2	•	5.5	3.1	•
Working Capital to Net Sales 40	0.1	•	0.0	0.0	0.1	0.1	0.1	0.1	0.1	0.0	0.0	0.1	•
Inventory to Working Capital 41	1.1	•	0.8	1.4	0.5	1.0	1.1	1.0	1.8	•	2.4	1.1	•
Total Receipts to Cash Flow 42	11.0	6.0	6.2	6.7	9.3	9.7	12.6	13.1	14.0	18.5	11.0	11.7	•
Cost of Goods to Cash Flow 43	8.8	4.4	4.0	3.9	7.0	7.4	10.4	11.0	11.9	16.6	9.3	9.5	•
Cash Flow to Total Debt 44	0.3	•	1.1	0.5	0.6	0.4	0.3	0.3	0.2	0.1	0.3	0.1	•

Selected Financial Factors (in Percentages)

Debt Ratio 45	64.0	•	50.0	113.8	60.1	68.8	66.6	58.6	66.4	69.5	61.0	63.0	•
Return on Total Assets 46	8.7	•	28.6	16.7	15.3	12.3	9.6	11.6	9.0	7.1	6.0	5.1	•
Return on Equity Before Income Taxes 47	19.7	•	53.5	•	34.4	36.1	25.3	25.4	24.2	19.3	13.4	8.5	•
Return on Equity After Income Taxes 48	16.9	•	52.5	•	32.6	32.3	22.7	23.1	19.1	12.9	10.1	6.5	•
Profit Margin (Before Income Tax) 49	3.7	11.9	8.2	3.3	4.1	4.1	2.9	4.1	3.6	3.5	2.7	2.9	•
Profit Margin (After Income Tax) 50	3.2	11.6	8.0	2.4	3.9	3.6	2.6	3.7	2.8	2.3	2.0	2.2	•

Table I

Corporations with and without Net Income

PETROLEUM AND PETROLEUM PRODUCTS

MONEY AMOUNTS AND SIZE OF ASSETS IN THOUSANDS OF DOLLARS

Item Description for Accounting Period 7/04 Through 6/05	Total	Zero Assets	Under 500	500 to 1,000	1,000 to 5,000	5,000 to 10,000	10,000 to 25,000	25,000 to 50,000	50,000 to 100,000	100,000 to 250,000	250,000 to 500,000	500,000 to 2,500,000	2,500,000 and over
Number of Enterprises **1**	8835	431	4357	740	2258	508	339	119	35	25	8	11	5
Revenues ($ in Thousands)													
Net Sales **2**	294783026	38661056	2698565	3718206	34786819	25776950	31251475	22660589	20536915	20881987	24996603	39004073	29809790
Interest **3**	316121	9474	425	2313	14934	7486	11730	6839	2904	8663	1349	75469	174536
Rents **4**	243648	0	2	1384	27883	31257	40866	23684	4906	8413	7926	88578	8749
Royalties **5**	69185	0	0	0	115	488	27	1956	0	37	0	131	66433
Other Portfolio Income **6**	3828781	9397	176	7026	60222	23767	46111	25171	12983	57108	5924	60312	3520582
Other Receipts **7**	1295608	60390	7704	4863	204355	79168	156630	115451	55049	121476	6239	68661	415619
Total Receipts **8**	300536369	38740317	2706872	3733792	35094328	25919116	31506839	22833690	20612757	21077684	25018041	39297224	33995709
Average Total Receipts **9**	34017	89885	621	5046	15542	51022	92941	191880	588936	843107	3127255	3572475	6799142
Operating Costs/Operating Income (%)													
Cost of Operations **10**	91.8	99.0	77.3	89.5	90.1	89.5	92.5	93.1	95.7	95.0	98.3	97.0	69.4
Salaries and Wages **11**	1.7	0.3	10.3	2.0	3.1	2.4	2.3	2.1	1.2	1.3	0.6	0.4	2.5
Taxes Paid **12**	0.9	0.0	1.7	2.3	0.7	3.8	0.7	0.5	0.6	0.3	0.1	0.2	2.5
Interest Paid **13**	0.6	0.2	0.3	0.1	0.3	0.2	0.3	0.3	0.1	0.3	0.1	0.5	3.5
Depreciation **14**	0.9	0.0	0.6	0.9	0.8	0.6	0.8	0.9	0.5	0.6	0.2	0.5	4.3
Amortization and Depletion **15**	0.2	0.0	0.1	0.0	0.0	0.0	0.0	0.0	0.0	0.1	0.0	0.1	1.9
Pensions and Other Deferred Comp. **16**	0.2	0.0	0.3	0.0	0.0	0.0	0.1	0.0	0.0	0.1	0.0	0.0	1.1
Employee Benefits **17**	0.2	0.0	0.2	0.2	0.2	0.2	0.2	0.2	0.1	0.2	0.0	0.1	0.4
Advertising **18**	0.0	0.0	0.1	0.2	0.1	0.1	0.1	0.1	0.0	0.0	0.0	0.0	0.0
Other Expenses **19**	3.3	0.4	6.7	3.3	4.3	2.4	3.0	2.7	1.4	1.6	0.7	1.2	14.4
Officers' Compensation **20**	0.4	0.0	2.3	1.5	1.0	0.4	0.4	0.3	0.3	0.2	0.2	0.1	0.5
Operating Margin **21**	•	0.1	0.2	0.1	•	0.3	•	•	0.0	0.3	•	•	•
Operating Margin Before Officers' Comp. **22**	0.2	0.1	2.4	1.6	0.3	0.7	0.0	0.0	0.3	0.5	•	•	•

Selected Average Balance Sheet ($ in Thousands)

Net Receivables 23	2035	0	30	254	840	2303	4999	10634	27969	57354	113090	312386	976929
Inventories 24	685	0	18	80	307	651	1667	3777	8700	21805	127768	136015	100512
Net Property, Plant and Equipment 25	4696	0	17	145	650	2186	4348	11585	16172	35791	55426	200621	6354288
Total Assets 26	13600	0	116	740	2359	7142	15156	34199	66829	160356	347318	924864	16326999
Notes and Loans Payable 27	3050	0	39	141	775	2209	4560	11613	19209	38568	101680	256123	3121287
All Other Liabilities 28	3697	0	16	219	800	2247	5963	12627	30444	73325	224721	414331	3341660
Net Worth 29	6852	0	62	380	784	2686	4633	9960	17176	48463	20917	254410	9864052

Selected Financial Ratios (Times to 1)

Current Ratio 30	1.3	•	5.7	2.2	1.4	1.6	1.2	1.2	1.3	1.3	1.0	1.4	1.2
Quick Ratio 31	0.8	•	4.6	1.6	1.0	1.2	0.9	0.8	0.9	0.9	0.5	0.9	0.7
Net Sales to Working Capital 32	35.1	•	8.9	18.8	36.6	29.6	54.3	63.4	59.8	31.8	•	20.2	13.4
Coverage Ratio 33	4.2	2.7	2.7	4.6	1.6	4.7	2.5	2.9	3.6	5.7	•	2.1	5.3
Total Asset Turnover 34	2.5	•	5.3	6.8	6.5	7.1	6.1	5.6	8.8	5.2	9.0	3.8	0.4
Inventory Turnover 35	44.7	•	26.0	56.1	45.2	69.7	51.1	46.9	64.6	36.4	24.0	25.3	41.2
Receivables Turnover 36	15.8	•	17.7	23.0	19.2	22.9	20.0	19.6	24.3	16.0	22.6	12.9	4.7
Total Liabilities to Net Worth 37	1.0	•	0.9	0.9	2.0	1.7	2.3	2.4	2.9	2.3	15.6	2.6	0.7
Current Assets to Working Capital 38	4.4	•	1.2	1.9	3.4	2.6	5.2	6.1	4.6	4.0	•	3.4	5.7
Current Liabilities to Working Capital 39	3.4	•	0.2	0.9	2.4	1.6	4.2	5.1	3.6	3.0	•	2.4	4.7
Working Capital to Net Sales 40	0.0	•	0.1	0.1	0.0	0.0	0.0	0.0	0.0	0.0	•	0.0	0.1
Inventory to Working Capital 41	0.8	•	0.2	0.3	0.8	0.4	1.0	1.3	1.1	1.0	•	1.1	0.2
Total Receipts to Cash Flow 42	23.3	201.0	16.7	34.2	32.3	39.5	41.2	41.6	76.4	42.2	397.9	80.8	3.8
Cost of Goods to Cash Flow 43	21.4	198.9	12.9	30.6	29.1	35.4	38.1	38.7	73.2	40.1	391.2	78.4	2.6
Cash Flow to Total Debt 44	0.2	•	0.7	0.4	0.3	0.3	0.2	0.2	0.2	0.2	0.0	0.1	0.2

Selected Financial Factors (in Percentages)

Debt Ratio 45	49.6	•	47.0	48.7	66.8	62.4	69.4	70.9	74.3	69.8	94.0	72.5	39.6
Return on Total Assets 46	6.1	•	4.0	4.6	2.8	7.9	3.9	4.6	4.6	7.6	•	4.0	6.7
Return on Equity Before Income Taxes 47	9.3	•	4.8	7.0	3.1	16.6	7.7	10.3	12.8	20.6	•	7.4	9.0
Return on Equity After Income Taxes 48	6.3	•	2.0	6.4	2.1	15.6	6.4	7.9	10.4	16.3	•	5.8	6.0
Profit Margin (Before Income Tax) 49	1.9	0.3	0.5	0.5	0.2	0.9	0.4	0.5	0.4	1.2	•	0.5	14.9
Profit Margin (After Income Tax) 50	1.3	0.1	0.2	0.5	0.1	0.8	0.3	0.4	0.3	0.9	•	0.4	9.9

Table II

Corporations with Net Income

PETROLEUM AND PETROLEUM PRODUCTS

MONEY AMOUNTS AND SIZE OF ASSETS IN THOUSANDS OF DOLLARS

Item Description for Accounting Period 7/04 Through 6/05	Total	Zero Assets	Under 500	500 to 1,000	1,000 to 5,000	5,000 to 10,000	10,000 to 25,000	25,000 to 50,000	50,000 to 100,000	100,000 to 250,000	250,000 to 500,000	500,000 to 2,500,000	2,500,000 and over
Number of Enterprises **1**	4585	0	1801	576	1359	447	242	81	24	0	4	8	0
Revenues ($ in Thousands)													
Net Sales **2**	216935039	0	1150029	3397207	20796778	22613323	23167591	17106490	13104120	0	12451789	31605553	0
Interest **3**	297038	0	215	1546	10743	6642	9768	5524	2904	0	324	72664	0
Rents **4**	201960	0	0	1384	19502	20148	31578	19081	4906	0	0	88199	0
Royalties **5**	69059	0	0	0	115	488	7	1951	0	0	0	28	0
Other Portfolio Income **6**	3778982	0	13	557	50923	16858	29828	20066	11133	0	3902	60299	0
Other Receipts **7**	979905	0	4818	4863	74203	66987	104235	77657	47552	0	790	63090	0
Total Receipts **8**	222261983	0	1155075	3405557	20952264	22724446	23343007	17230769	13170615	0	12456805	31889833	0
Average Total Receipts **9**	48476	•	641	5912	15417	50838	96459	212726	548776	•	3114201	3986229	•
Operating Costs/Operating Income (%)													
Cost of Operations **10**	90.7	•	75.5	89.8	90.3	89.0	92.7	93.6	95.7	•	97.9	96.9	•
Salaries and Wages **11**	1.6	•	5.5	2.0	2.6	2.4	2.1	1.9	1.3	•	0.4	0.4	•
Taxes Paid **12**	1.1	•	1.7	1.9	0.7	4.2	0.7	0.5	0.2	•	0.1	0.2	•
Interest Paid **13**	0.7	•	0.5	0.1	0.3	0.2	0.2	0.2	0.1	•	0.1	0.5	•
Depreciation **14**	1.1	•	0.9	0.7	0.8	0.6	0.7	0.7	0.5	•	0.1	0.6	•
Amortization and Depletion **15**	0.3	•	0.2	0.0	0.0	0.0	0.0	0.0	0.0	•	0.0	0.1	•
Pensions and Other Deferred Comp. **16**	0.2	•	0.6	0.0	0.1	0.0	0.0	0.0	0.0	•	0.0	0.1	•
Employee Benefits **17**	0.2	•	0.3	0.2	0.2	0.1	0.1	0.2	0.1	•	0.0	0.1	•
Advertising **18**	0.0	•	0.0	0.2	0.1	0.1	0.1	0.0	0.0	•	0.0	0.0	•
Other Expenses **19**	3.6	•	6.8	3.1	3.6	2.3	2.7	2.3	1.5	•	0.4	1.3	•
Officers' Compensation **20**	0.4	•	4.7	1.5	1.1	0.4	0.5	0.3	0.1	•	0.2	0.0	•
Operating Margin **21**	0.2	•	3.3	0.4	0.2	0.6	0.1	0.2	0.2	•	0.8	•	•
Operating Margin Before Officers' Comp. **22**	0.6	•	8.0	1.9	1.3	0.9	0.5	0.5	0.3	•	1.0	•	•

Selected Average Balance Sheet ($ in Thousands)

Net Receivables 23	3226	•	35	271	951	2391	5522	11608	29297	•	139804	305521
Inventories 24	962	•	26	79	333	651	1749	3705	7834	•	180837	124767
Net Property, Plant and Equipment 25	8484	•	11	152	616	2118	3759	10327	16020	•	38425	260924
Total Assets 26	23931	•	153	755	2377	7228	15134	34559	66439	•	354258	969962
Notes and Loans Payable 27	5060	•	53	148	716	2147	4081	9492	18155	•	67289	263652
All Other Liabilities 28	6233	•	22	223	854	2233	6101	13537	29383	•	228762	468478
Net Worth 29	12638	•	78	383	807	2848	4952	11530	18901	•	58208	237831

Selected Financial Ratios (Times to 1)

Current Ratio 30	1.3	•	5.1	2.2	1.4	1.7	1.3	1.3	1.4	•	1.2	1.3
Quick Ratio 31	0.8	•	3.9	1.6	1.0	1.3	1.0	0.9	1.0	•	0.6	0.8
Net Sales to Working Capital 32	30.5	•	6.4	20.1	36.5	25.9	42.5	53.3	45.9	•	72.6	28.0
Coverage Ratio 33	5.1	•	7.9	5.9	4.2	5.8	4.7	5.2	5.8	•	9.4	2.5
Total Asset Turnover 34	2.0	•	4.2	7.8	6.4	7.0	6.3	6.1	8.2	•	8.8	4.1
Inventory Turnover 35	44.6	•	18.6	67.3	41.6	69.1	50.8	53.4	66.7	•	16.9	30.7
Receivables Turnover 36	13.8	•	13.5	30.1	15.3	22.8	18.7	19.5	19.5	•	18.2	15.1
Total Liabilities to Net Worth 37	0.9	•	1.0	1.0	1.9	1.5	2.1	2.0	2.5	•	5.1	3.1
Current Assets to Working Capital 38	4.3	•	1.2	1.9	3.6	2.4	4.2	4.9	3.8	•	7.2	4.2
Current Liabilities to Working Capital 39	3.3	•	0.2	0.9	2.6	1.4	3.2	3.9	2.8	•	6.2	3.2
Working Capital to Net Sales 40	0.0	•	0.2	0.0	0.0	0.0	0.0	0.0	0.0	•	0.0	0.0
Inventory to Working Capital 41	0.7	•	0.3	0.3	0.7	0.4	0.8	1.0	0.7	•	3.2	1.4
Total Receipts to Cash Flow 42	18.1	•	10.5	33.5	29.2	37.7	37.3	40.4	56.0	•	92.6	66.2
Cost of Goods to Cash Flow 43	16.4	•	7.9	30.1	26.4	33.6	34.6	37.8	53.7	•	90.7	64.1
Cash Flow to Total Debt 44	0.2	•	0.8	0.5	0.3	0.3	0.3	0.2	0.2	•	0.1	0.1

Selected Financial Factors (in Percentages)

Debt Ratio 45	47.2	•	49.3	49.2	66.1	60.6	67.3	66.6	71.6	•	83.6	75.5
Return on Total Assets 46	7.0	•	18.0	6.5	8.2	9.0	6.5	7.0	7.0	•	7.9	5.5
Return on Equity Before Income Taxes 47	10.7	•	31.0	10.7	18.4	18.8	15.6	17.0	20.5	•	42.9	13.5
Return on Equity After Income Taxes 48	7.6	•	25.7	9.9	16.7	17.7	13.8	13.9	17.3	•	28.8	11.1
Profit Margin (Before Income Tax) 49	2.9	•	3.8	0.7	1.0	1.1	0.8	0.9	0.7	•	0.8	0.8
Profit Margin (After Income Tax) 50	2.0	•	3.1	0.6	0.9	1.0	0.7	0.8	0.6	•	0.5	0.7

Table I

Corporations with and without Net Income

BEER, WINE, AND DISTILLED ALCOHOLIC BEVERAGE

MONEY AMOUNTS AND SIZE OF ASSETS IN THOUSANDS OF DOLLARS

Item Description for Accounting Period 7/04 Through 6/05	Total	Zero Assets	Under 500	500 to 1,000	1,000 to 5,000	5,000 to 10,000	10,000 to 25,000	25,000 to 50,000	50,000 to 100,000	100,000 to 250,000	250,000 to 500,000	500,000 to 2,500,000	2,500,000 and over
Number of Enterprises **1**	2992	60	1189	165	827	362	219	93	36	26	7	7	0
Revenues ($ in Thousands)													
Net Sales **2**	70752675	118865	418524	472220	9882559	8236792	10589459	8585576	5834610	8026987	4752529	13834553	0
Interest **3**	39296	3647	2033	460	3500	2468	1428	1101	1579	7717	2167	13198	0
Rents **4**	85879	0	0	0	5906	358	1136	541	5572	1740	12221	58405	0
Royalties **5**	82269	0	0	0	0	0	5140	0	0	111	2048	74970	0
Other Portfolio Income **6**	177955	2145	3	82	23438	8615	7935	7138	8116	48481	4002	68001	0
Other Receipts **7**	912404	57379	7206	3050	47514	74102	90921	179710	113719	94014	41965	202823	0
Total Receipts **8**	72050478	182036	427766	475812	9962917	8322335	10696019	8774066	5963596	8179050	4814932	14251950	0
Average Total Receipts **9**	24081	3034	360	2884	12047	22990	48840	94345	165655	314579	687847	2035993	•
Operating Costs/Operating Income (%)													
Cost of Operations **10**	75.0	80.2	50.3	74.8	75.4	74.6	74.3	75.8	76.2	73.3	76.3	75.7	•
Salaries and Wages **11**	8.4	11.9	3.7	6.5	9.4	8.4	8.4	8.3	8.2	7.8	9.2	8.1	•
Taxes Paid **12**	2.8	4.5	1.8	3.8	1.6	2.2	3.5	3.4	2.5	3.3	2.5	3.3	•
Interest Paid **13**	0.7	19.7	0.4	0.5	0.5	0.5	0.5	0.5	0.5	0.7	1.0	1.2	•
Depreciation **14**	0.8	0.9	0.9	1.3	0.7	1.0	0.9	0.9	1.2	0.7	0.4	0.8	•
Amortization and Depletion **15**	0.4	4.5	0.1	0.0	0.2	0.1	0.4	0.5	0.3	0.3	0.4	0.8	•
Pensions and Other Deferred Comp. **16**	0.4	0.3	2.2	0.0	0.4	0.8	0.4	0.3	0.3	0.2	0.3	0.3	•
Employee Benefits **17**	0.8	1.5	0.1	0.2	1.1	0.7	0.9	0.8	0.7	0.7	0.8	0.7	•
Advertising **18**	1.2	1.3	1.0	0.6	0.7	0.7	1.1	1.2	1.6	1.6	2.0	1.5	•
Other Expenses **19**	6.1	13.8	13.8	12.4	6.7	6.0	5.5	6.1	5.6	5.9	6.2	6.1	•
Officers' Compensation **20**	1.4	1.0	12.1	1.8	1.9	2.4	1.5	1.2	0.9	1.2	2.8	0.2	•
Operating Margin **21**	1.8	•	13.6	•	1.5	2.8	2.6	1.0	1.8	4.2	•	1.4	•
Operating Margin Before Officers' Comp. **22**	3.2	•	25.6	3.4	•	5.2	4.1	2.1	2.7	5.4	•	1.6	•

Selected Average Balance Sheet ($ in Thousands)

Net Receivables 23	1696	0	28	89	597	909	2468	6337	10220	31721	59335	209586
Inventories 24	2031	0	37	102	835	1575	2874	5849	15119	31134	68711	249384
Net Property, Plant and Equipment 25	1209	0	14	129	393	1204	2654	5421	11124	15049	17251	117349
Total Assets 26	9464	0	124	642	2595	6971	15341	34325	69698	152359	338584	1142860
Notes and Loans Payable 27	2735	0	55	274	890	2034	4443	10126	22349	52711	93227	265400
All Other Liabilities 28	3274	0	45	274	924	1818	3344	8713	15280	34780	129992	623885
Net Worth 29	3455	0	24	94	780	3119	7555	15486	32068	64868	115365	253575

Selected Financial Ratios (Times to 1)

Current Ratio 30	1.6	•	1.0	1.1	1.5	2.0	1.8	1.6	1.8	1.6	1.5	1.5
Quick Ratio 31	0.8	•	0.8	0.5	0.8	1.1	1.0	0.9	0.9	0.8	0.7	0.6
Net Sales to Working Capital 32	12.3	•	•	49.5	21.1	11.4	13.8	13.5	9.8	10.0	10.8	10.6
Coverage Ratio 33	6.1	1.7	38.1	•	5.8	9.0	8.7	6.9	9.6	9.4	0.4	4.7
Total Asset Turnover 34	2.5	•	2.8	4.5	4.6	3.3	3.2	2.7	2.3	2.0	2.0	1.7
Inventory Turnover 35	8.7	•	4.7	21.0	10.8	10.8	12.5	12.0	8.2	7.3	7.5	6.0
Receivables Turnover 36	14.6	•	14.5	48.7	21.5	27.3	18.6	16.1	15.4	10.0	12.2	10.1
Total Liabilities to Net Worth 37	1.7	•	4.2	5.9	2.3	1.2	1.0	1.2	1.2	1.3	1.9	3.5
Current Assets to Working Capital 38	2.6	•	•	7.9	3.1	2.0	2.2	2.6	2.3	2.5	2.9	2.9
Current Liabilities to Working Capital 39	1.6	•	•	6.9	2.1	1.0	1.2	1.6	1.3	1.5	1.9	1.9
Working Capital to Net Sales 40	0.1	•	•	0.0	0.0	0.1	0.1	0.1	0.1	0.1	0.1	0.1
Inventory to Working Capital 41	1.1	•	•	2.0	1.4	0.9	0.8	0.9	1.0	1.0	1.1	1.4
Total Receipts to Cash Flow 42	12.0	5.5	3.7	11.4	13.8	12.1	13.4	12.6	12.1	9.4	21.4	10.8
Cost of Goods to Cash Flow 43	9.0	4.4	1.9	8.6	10.4	9.1	9.9	9.6	9.2	6.9	16.4	8.2
Cash Flow to Total Debt 44	0.3	•	1.0	0.5	0.5	0.5	0.5	0.4	0.4	0.4	0.1	0.2

Selected Financial Factors (in Percentages)

Debt Ratio 45	63.5	•	80.7	85.4	69.9	55.3	50.8	54.9	54.0	57.4	65.9	77.8
Return on Total Assets 46	11.0	•	45.9	•	12.8	14.0	12.7	10.0	10.3	13.9	0.8	10.0
Return on Equity Before Income Taxes 47	25.1	•	232.1	•	35.1	27.9	22.8	19.0	20.0	29.1	•	35.6
Return on Equity After Income Taxes 48	21.8	•	231.5	•	32.9	26.9	22.0	17.9	18.5	26.3	•	26.3
Profit Margin (Before Income Tax) 49	3.7	13.2	15.8	•	2.3	3.8	3.6	3.2	3.9	6.1	•	4.6
Profit Margin (After Income Tax) 50	3.2	3.4	15.7	•	2.2	3.7	3.4	3.0	3.7	5.5	•	3.4

Table II

Corporations with Net Income

BEER, WINE, AND DISTILLED ALCOHOLIC BEVERAGE

MONEY AMOUNTS AND SIZE OF ASSETS IN THOUSANDS OF DOLLARS

Item Description for Accounting Period 7/04 Through 6/05	Total	Zero Assets	Under 500	500 to 1,000	1,000 to 5,000	5,000 to 10,000	10,000 to 25,000	25,000 to 50,000	50,000 to 100,000	100,000 to 250,000	250,000 to 500,000	500,000 to 2,500,000	2,500,000 and over
Number of Enterprises 1	2145	5	723	109	622	351	188	77	32	0	0	7	0
Revenues ($ in Thousands)													
Net Sales 2	65196303	112052	362885	222219	8183638	7943654	9652442	7205829	5558350	0	0	13834553	0
Interest 3	37191	3625	1841	141	2873	2468	1105	784	1297	0	0	13198	0
Rents 4	84992	0	0	0	5906	358	813	541	5572	0	0	58405	0
Royalties 5	82269	0	0	0	0	0	5140	0	0	0	0	74970	0
Other Portfolio Income 6	169550	2145	0	0	22630	8580	6362	4865	4508	0	0	68001	0
Other Receipts 7	862384	57280	706	184	47021	59688	91725	172101	100503	0	0	202823	0
Total Receipts 8	66432689	175102	365432	222544	8262068	8014748	9757587	7384120	5670230	0	0	14251950	0
Average Total Receipts 9	30971	35020	505	2042	13283	22834	51902	95898	177195	•	•	2035993	•
Operating Costs/Operating Income (%)													
Cost of Operations 10	74.9	73.2	50.9	72.6	73.7	74.5	74.2	75.5	76.8	•	•	75.7	•
Salaries and Wages 11	8.2	12.3	2.1	8.3	10.1	8.2	8.4	8.1	8.0	•	•	8.1	•
Taxes Paid 12	2.9	4.4	1.5	1.5	1.7	2.2	3.5	3.5	2.6	•	•	3.3	•
Interest Paid 13	0.7	20.3	0.4	0.3	0.5	0.5	0.4	0.5	0.4	•	•	1.2	•
Depreciation 14	0.8	0.9	0.9	2.3	0.8	1.0	0.9	0.9	1.1	•	•	0.8	•
Amortization and Depletion 15	0.4	4.7	0.1	0.0	0.2	0.1	0.4	0.4	0.3	•	•	0.8	•
Pensions and Other Deferred Comp. 16	0.4	0.3	•	0.0	0.5	0.8	0.4	0.3	0.4	•	•	0.3	•
Employee Benefits 17	0.8	1.6	•	1.3	1.3	0.6	0.9	0.9	0.7	•	•	0.7	•
Advertising 18	1.2	1.3	0.5	1.3	0.5	0.7	0.9	1.3	1.6	•	•	1.5	•
Other Expenses 19	5.9	5.5	8.2	10.4	6.5	5.9	5.3	5.8	5.0	•	•	6.1	•
Officers' Compensation 20	1.2	0.9	8.2	2.4	2.0	2.4	1.4	1.1	0.9	•	•	0.2	•
Operating Margin 21	2.6	•	27.2	0.9	2.3	3.3	3.2	1.8	2.3	•	•	1.4	•
Operating Margin Before Officers' Comp. 22	3.9	•	35.4	3.3	4.4	5.7	4.6	2.9	3.2	•	•	1.6	•

Selected Average Balance Sheet ($ in Thousands)

Net Receivables 23	2118	0	2	16	485	823	2517	6308	10584	•	209586
Inventories 24	2552	0	25	103	783	1458	2966	5938	15158	•	249384
Net Property, Plant and Equipment 25	1568	0	22	165	478	1229	2701	5497	11133	•	117349
Total Assets 26	12081	0	99	566	2654	6972	15488	34494	70798	•	1142860
Notes and Loans Payable 27	3379	0	37	241	829	2066	4297	9014	22338	•	265400
All Other Liabilities 28	4199	0	4	44	802	1680	3279	8835	16261	•	623885
Net Worth 29	4503	0	58	282	1023	3226	7912	16646	32199	•	253575

Selected Financial Ratios (Times to 1)

Current Ratio 30	1.7	•	4.8	3.1	1.6	2.1	2.0	1.7	1.8	•	1.5
Quick Ratio 31	0.8	•	1.6	2.0	0.7	1.1	1.1	0.9	0.9	•	0.6
Net Sales to Working Capital 32	12.1	•	18.6	10.0	20.4	10.9	13.1	13.2	9.6	•	10.6
Coverage Ratio 33	7.2	2.5	64.6	4.8	8.1	9.5	10.9	9.9	10.9	•	4.7
Total Asset Turnover 34	2.5	•	5.1	3.6	5.0	3.2	3.3	2.7	2.5	•	1.7
Inventory Turnover 35	8.9	•	10.1	14.4	12.4	11.6	12.8	11.9	8.8	•	6.0
Receivables Turnover 36	15.1	•	33.4	68.7	31.5	29.6	19.4	15.9	16.3	•	10.1
Total Liabilities to Net Worth 37	1.7	•	0.7	1.0	1.6	1.2	1.0	1.1	1.2	•	3.5
Current Assets to Working Capital 38	2.5	•	1.3	1.5	2.6	1.9	2.0	2.5	2.2	•	2.9
Current Liabilities to Working Capital 39	1.5	•	0.3	0.5	1.6	0.9	1.0	1.5	1.2	•	1.9
Working Capital to Net Sales 40	0.1	•	0.1	0.1	0.0	0.1	0.1	0.1	0.1	•	0.1
Inventory to Working Capital 41	1.1	•	0.8	0.5	1.2	0.8	0.8	0.9	1.0	•	1.4
Total Receipts to Cash Flow 42	11.2	2.9	2.9	11.1	12.8	11.8	12.5	11.4	12.3	•	10.8
Cost of Goods to Cash Flow 43	8.4	2.1	1.5	8.1	9.5	8.8	9.3	8.6	9.4	•	8.2
Cash Flow to Total Debt 44	0.4	•	4.2	0.6	0.6	0.5	0.5	0.5	0.4	•	0.2

Selected Financial Factors (in Percentages)

Debt Ratio 45	62.7	•	41.6	50.3	61.5	53.7	48.9	51.7	54.5	•	77.8
Return on Total Assets 46	13.3	•	143.2	4.6	18.6	15.1	15.7	12.8	11.4	•	10.0
Return on Equity Before Income Taxes 47	30.7	•	241.5	7.4	42.2	29.2	27.8	23.9	22.7	•	35.6
Return on Equity After Income Taxes 48	27.3	•	241.1	6.5	40.0	28.2	27.0	22.7	21.1	•	26.3
Profit Margin (Before Income Tax) 49	4.6	30.6	27.9	1.0	3.3	4.2	4.3	4.3	4.2	•	4.6
Profit Margin (After Income Tax) 50	4.0	20.1	27.8	0.9	3.1	4.0	4.2	4.0	3.9	•	3.4

Table I
Corporations with and without Net Income

MISCELLANEOUS NONDURABLE GOODS

MONEY AMOUNTS AND SIZE OF ASSETS IN THOUSANDS OF DOLLARS

Item Description for Accounting Period 7/04 Through 6/05		Total	Zero Assets	Under 500	500 to 1,000	1,000 to 5,000	5,000 to 10,000	10,000 to 25,000	25,000 to 50,000	50,000 to 100,000	100,000 to 250,000	250,000 to 500,000	500,000 to 2,500,000	2,500,000 and over
Number of Enterprises	1	34778	4498	22514	3853	2754	568	366	106	53	35	11	15	4
Revenues ($ in Thousands)														
Net Sales	2	140407077	1810419	13366158	9321161	20529208	15324503	16162276	9711709	6937152	12511658	6591053	20802128	7339651
Interest	3	248735	4422	4671	5645	22962	9466	8933	7640	11572	26829	30115	63658	52821
Rents	4	40755	85	1758	569	5003	2847	4509	3076	959	4261	161	16821	705
Royalties	5	89226	0	0	0	1664	1826	2157	369	3843	6438	1447	32201	39282
Other Portfolio Income	6	775165	4185	20793	5006	58977	7966	14504	6737	51762	25120	21770	77525	480821
Other Receipts	7	1804621	41704	23466	48318	163702	29948	163833	83456	67640	152120	188166	143528	698743
Total Receipts	8	143365579	1860815	13416846	9380699	20781516	15376556	16356212	9812987	7072928	12726426	6832712	21135861	8612023
Average Total Receipts	9	4122	414	596	2435	7546	27071	44689	92575	133451	363612	621156	1409057	2153006
Operating Costs/Operating Income (%)														
Cost of Operations	10	78.3	76.4	72.6	69.3	82.2	84.4	80.1	81.6	80.7	77.1	89.6	74.1	69.8
Salaries and Wages	11	6.7	6.9	5.6	10.7	4.8	4.9	6.5	5.7	5.8	7.3	3.5	8.3	13.3
Taxes Paid	12	1.3	0.9	1.1	2.5	1.3	0.9	1.4	1.3	1.1	1.0	0.5	1.3	1.8
Interest Paid	13	0.7	1.2	0.4	0.5	0.3	0.5	0.5	0.7	0.9	1.0	1.0	0.9	1.6
Depreciation	14	1.1	1.1	0.7	1.1	0.5	0.5	0.7	0.8	1.1	1.0	0.6	1.7	4.1
Amortization and Depletion	15	0.2	0.7	0.1	0.0	0.1	0.1	0.1	0.1	0.3	0.3	0.3	0.3	1.1
Pensions and Other Deferred Comp.	16	0.3	0.2	0.4	0.2	0.2	0.2	0.2	0.2	0.2	0.2	0.2	0.3	0.6
Employee Benefits	17	0.6	0.6	0.6	0.5	0.3	0.3	0.5	0.5	0.7	0.7	0.4	0.8	1.4
Advertising	18	0.7	0.4	0.6	0.7	0.6	0.3	0.6	0.9	1.0	1.7	0.2	0.7	0.2
Other Expenses	19	8.3	17.3	13.5	10.5	7.2	5.7	6.9	6.3	6.6	8.3	4.6	8.2	14.1
Officers' Compensation	20	1.6	1.4	4.1	3.1	2.4	1.0	1.3	1.0	1.0	0.5	1.0	0.5	1.1
Operating Margin	21	0.3	•	0.2	1.0	0.2	1.2	1.1	0.9	0.6	0.8	•	3.0	•
Operating Margin Before Officers' Comp.	22	1.9	•	4.3	4.1	2.6	2.2	2.4	1.9	1.6	1.3	•	3.4	•

Selected Average Balance Sheet ($ in Thousands)

Net Receivables 23	452	0	18	267	761	2115	4771	11179	15445	41657	111261	117524	695788
Inventories 24	384	0	36	190	582	2365	4292	9683	18497	29663	50389	203546	319335
Net Property, Plant and Equipment 25	270	0	17	134	241	601	1814	4158	9375	20085	15725	165658	630002
Total Assets 26	1929	0	112	754	2165	7064	15165	34633	69100	158877	373922	900275	3903892
Notes and Loans Payable 27	524	0	51	281	575	2744	4141	11690	19818	50866	103853	166003	906112
All Other Liabilities 28	666	0	44	240	970	2486	5514	11781	22769	60321	159096	300056	1086422
Net Worth 29	739	0	18	234	620	1835	5511	11162	26512	47690	110973	434216	1911358

Selected Financial Ratios (Times to 1)

Current Ratio 30	1.5	•	1.7	1.6	1.6	1.3	1.6	1.6	1.6	1.6	1.0	1.6	1.2
Quick Ratio 31	0.8	•	0.9	1.0	1.1	0.7	0.9	0.9	0.8	0.9	0.7	0.7	0.8
Net Sales to Working Capital 32	11.4	•	18.7	10.9	11.4	21.1	10.4	9.0	7.4	9.0	509.0	8.7	8.3
Coverage Ratio 33	5.1	•	2.7	4.2	5.2	4.0	5.7	3.9	3.7	3.5	2.7	6.5	10.7
Total Asset Turnover 34	2.1	•	5.3	3.2	3.4	3.8	2.9	2.6	1.9	2.3	1.6	1.5	0.5
Inventory Turnover 35	8.2	•	11.9	8.8	10.5	9.6	8.2	7.7	5.7	9.3	10.7	5.0	4.0
Receivables Turnover 36	9.6	•	25.9	10.3	9.6	12.2	9.6	8.9	8.1	9.3	5.7	8.8	•
Total Liabilities to Net Worth 37	1.6	•	5.3	2.2	2.5	2.9	1.8	2.1	1.6	2.3	2.4	1.1	1.0
Current Assets to Working Capital 38	3.2	•	2.5	2.5	2.6	4.2	2.7	2.6	2.6	2.6	162.6	2.7	6.5
Current Liabilities to Working Capital 39	2.2	•	1.5	1.5	1.6	3.2	1.7	1.6	1.6	1.6	161.6	1.7	5.5
Working Capital to Net Sales 40	0.1	•	0.1	0.1	0.1	0.0	0.1	0.1	0.1	0.1	0.0	0.1	0.1
Inventory to Working Capital 41	1.1	•	1.0	0.9	0.8	1.9	1.1	1.0	1.0	0.9	38.9	1.2	1.5
Total Receipts to Cash Flow 42	11.3	13.0	10.8	14.2	14.2	16.4	13.0	14.2	13.1	10.7	19.9	9.7	4.9
Cost of Goods to Cash Flow 43	8.8	10.0	7.5	11.7	11.7	13.9	10.4	11.6	10.6	8.3	17.8	7.2	3.4
Cash Flow to Total Debt 44	0.3	•	0.4	0.3	0.3	0.3	0.4	0.3	0.2	0.3	0.1	0.3	0.2

Selected Financial Factors (in Percentages)

Debt Ratio 45	61.7	•	84.1	69.0	71.4	74.0	63.7	67.8	61.6	70.0	70.3	51.8	51.0
Return on Total Assets 46	7.3	•	5.0	6.8	6.1	7.9	8.0	7.0	6.4	7.8	4.4	8.6	7.9
Return on Equity Before Income Taxes 47	15.3	•	19.5	16.7	17.2	22.8	18.1	16.2	12.2	18.6	9.4	15.0	14.7
Return on Equity After Income Taxes 48	11.7	•	15.8	15.8	15.3	21.1	15.9	13.3	10.0	13.4	7.5	11.8	9.3
Profit Margin (Before Income Tax) 49	2.8	•	0.6	1.6	1.4	1.5	2.3	2.0	2.5	2.5	1.7	4.7	15.3
Profit Margin (After Income Tax) 50	2.1	•	0.5	1.5	1.3	1.4	2.0	1.6	2.0	1.8	1.4	3.7	9.7

Table II

Corporations with Net Income

MISCELLANEOUS NONDURABLE GOODS

MONEY AMOUNTS AND SIZE OF ASSETS IN THOUSANDS OF DOLLARS

Item Description for Accounting Period 7/04 Through 6/05	Total	Zero Assets	Under 500	500 to 1,000	1,000 to 5,000	5,000 to 10,000	10,000 to 25,000	25,000 to 50,000	50,000 to 100,000	100,000 to 250,000	250,000 to 500,000	500,000 to 2,500,000	2,500,000 and over
Number of Enterprises 1	19239	2176	11303	0	2024	498	290	84	34	29	8	12	0
Revenues ($ in Thousands)													
Net Sales 2	114186895	621954	9788052	0	14006187	14083453	13426970	7672580	5755000	10466083	5135470	19278086	0
Interest 3	170448	4295	2604	0	11424	6840	7508	6862	8237	17365	22924	37486	0
Rents 4	31149	85	1478	0	3701	1438	4261	2328	940	1232	0	14440	0
Royalties 5	81157	0	0	0	0	1819	1557	292	2295	2644	1251	32189	0
Other Portfolio Income 6	740312	647	16927	0	58805	7692	8333	5929	49503	18621	21389	68035	0
Other Receipts 7	1532037	36429	16765	0	71245	27122	135018	75921	63726	130511	138703	125901	0
Total Receipts 8	116741998	663410	9825826	0	14151362	14128364	13583647	7763912	5879701	10636456	5319737	19556137	0
Average Total Receipts 9	6068	305	869	•	6992	28370	46840	92428	172932	366774	664967	1629678	•
Operating Costs/Operating Income (%)													
Cost of Operations 10	77.4	81.0	72.0	•	80.4	84.2	79.5	80.6	82.3	73.8	89.9	73.5	•
Salaries and Wages 11	6.8	4.0	5.5	•	4.5	4.9	6.4	6.2	4.9	7.5	2.7	8.4	•
Taxes Paid 12	1.3	0.9	1.0	•	1.5	0.8	1.4	1.0	1.0	1.1	0.5	1.3	•
Interest Paid 13	0.5	2.0	0.2	•	0.3	0.5	0.4	0.7	0.6	0.9	0.7	0.5	•
Depreciation 14	1.1	0.6	0.6	•	0.5	0.5	0.7	0.8	0.9	1.1	0.5	1.7	•
Amortization and Depletion 15	0.2	0.6	0.1	•	0.0	0.1	0.1	0.1	0.2	0.4	0.3	0.3	•
Pensions and Other Deferred Comp. 16	0.3	0.1	0.6	•	0.3	0.2	0.2	0.2	0.2	0.2	0.2	0.3	•
Employee Benefits 17	0.6	0.6	0.6	•	0.3	0.3	0.5	0.5	0.6	0.7	0.3	0.7	•
Advertising 18	0.6	0.5	0.4	•	0.3	0.3	0.6	0.5	0.9	2.0	0.1	0.8	•
Other Expenses 19	7.8	4.7	11.7	•	7.0	5.6	6.5	6.5	5.2	8.6	4.1	8.2	•
Officers' Compensation 20	1.5	1.5	4.2	•	2.5	1.0	1.4	1.1	0.9	0.5	1.0	0.5	•
Operating Margin 21	1.9	3.5	3.2	•	2.3	1.7	2.3	1.8	2.1	3.2	•	3.8	•
Operating Margin Before Officers' Comp. 22	3.4	5.0	7.4	•	4.8	2.7	3.7	2.9	3.0	3.8	0.5	4.3	•

Selected Average Balance Sheet ($ in Thousands)

	1	2	3	4	5	6	7	8	9	10	11	
Net Receivables 23	650	0	27	742	2094	4843	11319	16136	44168	124475	103874	•
Inventories 24	560	0	31	563	2209	4322	10287	21664	29112	43120	224587	•
Net Property, Plant and Equipment 25	361	0	17	191	551	1790	3472	8441	20873	18141	193082	•
Total Assets 26	2666	0	128	2085	7135	15277	34509	68839	159064	387566	943020	•
Notes and Loans Payable 27	547	0	30	448	2729	3848	11378	14123	49765	83363	110906	•
All Other Liabilities 28	927	0	52	868	2399	5331	11654	22607	54767	181810	329754	•
Net Worth 29	1192	0	46	768	2007	6098	11477	32109	54532	122392	502359	•

Selected Financial Ratios (Times to 1)

	1	2	3	4	5	6	7	8	9	10	11	
Current Ratio 30	1.6		1.7	1.7	1.4	1.7	1.6	1.7	1.7	1.0	1.8	•
Quick Ratio 31	0.9		1.0	1.2	0.7	0.9	0.9	0.8	0.9	0.8	0.8	•
Net Sales to Working Capital 32	9.1		22.2	9.8	19.0	9.5	8.5	8.3	8.1	290.1	7.7	•
Coverage Ratio 33	9.7	6.2	20.9	11.8	5.2	10.0	5.6	7.5	6.3	5.2	10.6	•
Total Asset Turnover 34	2.2		6.8	3.3	4.0	3.0	2.6	2.5	2.3	1.7	1.7	•
Inventory Turnover 35	8.2		19.9	9.9	10.8	8.5	7.2	6.4	9.1	13.4	5.3	•
Receivables Turnover 36	9.9		27.8	8.7	13.4	10.1	8.9	10.4	9.3			•
Total Liabilities to Net Worth 37	1.2		1.8	1.7	2.6	1.5	2.0	1.1	1.9	2.2	0.9	•
Current Assets to Working Capital 38	2.6		2.5	2.4	3.6	2.4	2.6	2.4	2.5	94.4	2.2	•
Current Liabilities to Working Capital 39	1.6		1.5	1.4	2.6	1.4	1.6	1.4	1.5	93.4	1.2	•
Working Capital to Net Sales 40	0.1		0.0	0.1	0.1	0.1	0.1	0.1	0.1	0.0	0.1	•
Inventory to Working Capital 41	0.9		0.8	0.7	1.6	1.0	1.0	1.0	0.8	19.5	1.1	•
Total Receipts to Cash Flow 42	9.8	7.2	7.7	11.7	15.4	11.5	12.3	12.6	8.3	17.4	9.2	•
Cost of Goods to Cash Flow 43	7.6	5.8	5.5	13.0	9.2	9.9	9.9	10.3	6.2	15.6	6.8	•
Cash Flow to Total Debt 44	0.4	1.4	0.4	0.4	0.4	0.3	0.4	0.4	0.4	0.1	0.4	•

Selected Financial Factors (in Percentages)

	1	2	3	4	5	6	7	8	9	10	11	
Debt Ratio 45	55.3		63.8	63.2	71.9	60.1	66.7	53.4	65.7	68.4	46.7	•
Return on Total Assets 46	11.4		25.4	12.0	9.9	11.7	9.8	11.9	13.1	6.3	9.9	•
Return on Equity Before Income Taxes 47	22.9		66.8	29.9	28.5	26.3	24.2	22.1	32.2	16.0	16.9	•
Return on Equity After Income Taxes 48	18.9		64.0	27.8	26.7	23.8	20.7	19.3	26.7	13.6	13.5	•
Profit Margin (Before Income Tax) 49	4.6	10.2	3.6	3.3	2.0	3.5	3.0	4.2	4.9	3.1	5.3	•
Profit Margin (After Income Tax) 50	3.8	8.1	3.4	3.1	1.9	3.1	2.6	3.7	4.0	2.6	4.2	•

Table I

Corporations with and without Net Income

WHOLESALE ELECTRONIC MARKETS AND AGENTS AND BROKERS

MONEY AMOUNTS AND SIZE OF ASSETS IN THOUSANDS OF DOLLARS

Item Description for Accounting Period 7/04 Through 6/05	Total	Zero Assets	Under 500	500 to 1,000	1,000 to 5,000	5,000 to 10,000	10,000 to 25,000	25,000 to 50,000	50,000 to 100,000	100,000 to 250,000	250,000 to 500,000	500,000 to 2,500,000	2,500,000 and over
Number of Enterprises **1**	10436	1712	8528	107	77	0	8	0	0	4	0	0	0

Revenues ($ in Thousands)

Item	Total	Zero Assets	Under 500	500 to 1,000	1,000 to 5,000	5,000 to 10,000	10,000 to 25,000	25,000 to 50,000	50,000 to 100,000	100,000 to 250,000	250,000 to 500,000	500,000 to 2,500,000	2,500,000 and over
Net Sales **2**	4318042	126181	2588193	42262	316681	0	37781	0	0	1206943	0	0	0
Interest **3**	3294	6	515	158	301	0	1	0	0	2313	0	0	0
Rents **4**	2463	0	0	0	0	0	0	0	0	2463	0	0	0
Royalties **5**	217	0	0	0	0	0	0	0	0	217	0	0	0
Other Portfolio Income **6**	5527	0	798	0	7	0	2	0	0	4719	0	0	0
Other Receipts **7**	46845	457	28239	0	197	0	255	0	0	17699	0	0	0
Total Receipts **8**	4376388	126644	2617745	42420	317186	0	38039	0	0	1234354	0	0	0
Average Total Receipts **9**	419	74	307	396	4119	•	4755	•	•	308588	•	•	•

Operating Costs/Operating Income (%)

Item	Total	Zero Assets	Under 500	500 to 1,000	1,000 to 5,000	5,000 to 10,000	10,000 to 25,000	25,000 to 50,000	50,000 to 100,000	100,000 to 250,000	250,000 to 500,000	500,000 to 2,500,000	2,500,000 and over
Cost of Operations **10**	0.3	•	•	•	2.8	•	6.1	•	•	•	•	•	•
Salaries and Wages **11**	24.3	1.0	12.3	4.6	34.9	•	28.7	•	•	50.2	•	•	•
Taxes Paid **12**	3.0	3.5	2.2	3.9	2.7	•	2.8	•	•	4.8	•	•	•
Interest Paid **13**	1.2	0.1	1.0	1.5	0.1	•	3.9	•	•	2.1	•	•	•
Depreciation **14**	2.2	1.2	1.5	3.2	0.2	•	2.2	•	•	4.4	•	•	•
Amortization and Depletion **15**	0.6	0.0	0.0	•	0.0	•	1.2	•	•	2.1	•	•	•
Pensions and Other Deferred Comp. **16**	2.0	0.0	2.1	•	2.3	•	1.4	•	•	2.0	•	•	•
Employee Benefits **17**	3.3	0.1	3.1	3.1	2.4	•	0.7	•	•	4.7	•	•	•
Advertising **18**	0.8	0.2	0.8	1.4	0.3	•	5.4	•	•	0.8	•	•	•
Other Expenses **19**	39.7	48.8	46.5	24.8	31.9	•	30.3	•	•	26.8	•	•	•
Officers' Compensation **20**	16.9	36.8	23.5	34.9	15.0	•	4.7	•	•	0.8	•	•	•
Operating Margin **21**	5.7	8.3	7.0	22.6	7.4	•	12.6	•	•	1.3	•	•	•
Operating Margin Before Officers' Comp. **22**	22.6	45.1	30.5	57.5	22.4	•	17.3	•	•	2.2	•	•	•

Selected Average Balance Sheet ($ in Thousands)

Net Receivables 23	62	0	0	320	947	8444	119283
Inventories 24	1	0	0	0	2	791	1410
Net Property, Plant and Equipment 25	68	0	18	39	26	2330	133349
Total Assets 26	326	0	61	631	1505	16626	641184
Notes and Loans Payable 27	121	0	39	0	84	5166	219642
All Other Liabilities 28	78	0	12	368	1126	9829	128223
Net Worth 29	126	0	10	264	295	1632	293319

Selected Financial Ratios (Times to 1)

Current Ratio 30	1.2		0.9	1.2	1.3	1.1	1.5
Quick Ratio 31	1.0		0.6	1.2	1.3	1.0	1.2
Net Sales to Working Capital 32	16.3			6.3	14.4	3.9	4.5
Coverage Ratio 33	6.9	134.5	9.4	16.3	109.2	4.4	2.9
Total Asset Turnover 34	1.3		5.0	0.6	2.7	0.3	0.5
Inventory Turnover 35	1.2				49.2	0.4	
Receivables Turnover 36	10.5		161762.1		4.3	0.5	
Total Liabilities to Net Worth 37	1.6		5.3	1.4	4.1	9.2	1.2
Current Assets to Working Capital 38	5.1			6.9	4.4	10.4	3.1
Current Liabilities to Working Capital 39	4.1			5.9	3.4	9.4	2.1
Working Capital to Net Sales 40	0.1			0.2	0.1	0.3	0.2
Inventory to Working Capital 41	0.0				0.0		0.0
Total Receipts to Cash Flow 42	2.4	1.9	2.0	2.2	2.6	2.7	4.0
Cost of Goods to Cash Flow 43	0.0				0.1		0.2
Cash Flow to Total Debt 44	0.9		3.0	0.5	1.3	0.1	0.2

Selected Financial Factors (in Percentages)

Debt Ratio 45	61.2		84.1	58.2	80.4	90.2	54.3
Return on Total Assets 46	10.7		45.9	15.3	20.7	4.9	2.9
Return on Equity Before Income Taxes 47	23.5		258.3	34.4	104.7	38.4	4.1
Return on Equity After Income Taxes 48	21.6		255.1	30.3	89.3	38.2	2.7
Profit Margin (Before Income Tax) 49	7.2	8.7	8.2	23.0	7.5	13.3	4.0
Profit Margin (After Income Tax) 50	6.6	8.6	8.1	20.3	6.4	13.2	2.6

Table II

Corporations with Net Income

WHOLESALE ELECTRONIC MARKETS AND AGENTS AND BROKERS

MONEY AMOUNTS AND SIZE OF ASSETS IN THOUSANDS OF DOLLARS

Item Description for Accounting Period 7/04 Through 6/05	Total	Zero Assets	Under 500	500 to 1000	251 to 500	501 to 1,000	1,001 to 5,000	5,001 to 10,000	10,001 to 25,000	25,001 to 50,000	50,001 to 100,000	100,001 to 250,000	250,001 and over
Number of Enterprises **1**	7442	1354	5910	107	61	0	0	0	0	0	0	0	0
Revenues ($ in Thousands)													
Net Sales **2**	4030779	108597	2335327	42262	314445	0	0	0	0	0	0	0	0
Interest **3**	2802	0	29	158	301	0	0	0	0	0	0	0	0
Rents **4**	2463	0	0	0	0	0	0	0	0	0	0	0	0
Royalties **5**	217	0	0	0	0	0	0	0	0	0	0	0	0
Other Portfolio Income **6**	5124	0	397	0	7	0	0	0	0	0	0	0	0
Other Receipts **7**	46305	0	28217	0	197	0	0	0	0	0	0	0	0
Total Receipts **8**	4087690	108597	2363970	42420	314950	0	0	0	0	0	0	0	0
Average Total Receipts **9**	549	80	400	396	5163	·	·	·	·	·	·	·	·
Operating Costs/Operating Income (%)													
Cost of Operations **10**	0.3	·	·	·	2.8	·	·	·	·	·	·	·	·
Salaries and Wages **11**	23.3	0.9	9.4	4.6	34.7	·	·	·	·	·	·	·	·
Taxes Paid **12**	2.9	3.5	2.0	3.9	2.7	·	·	·	·	·	·	·	·
Interest Paid **13**	1.2	·	1.0	1.5	0.1	·	·	·	·	·	·	·	·
Depreciation **14**	1.9	1.3	0.9	3.2	0.2	·	·	·	·	·	·	·	·
Amortization and Depletion **15**	0.6	·	0.0	·	0.0	·	·	·	·	·	·	·	·
Pensions and Other Deferred Comp. **16**	2.1	·	2.3	·	2.3	·	·	·	·	·	·	·	·
Employee Benefits **17**	2.9	·	2.3	3.1	2.4	·	·	·	·	·	·	·	·
Advertising **18**	0.8	·	0.9	1.4	0.2	·	·	·	·	·	·	·	·
Other Expenses **19**	39.6	30.8	47.9	24.8	32.1	·	·	·	·	·	·	·	·
Officers' Compensation **20**	17.0	40.3	24.4	34.9	15.0	·	·	·	·	·	·	·	·
Operating Margin **21**	7.2	23.1	9.0	22.6	7.4	·	·	·	·	·	·	·	·
Operating Margin Before Officers' Comp. **22**	24.2	63.4	33.4	57.5	22.4	·	·	·	·	·	·	·	·

Selected Average Balance Sheet ($ in Thousands)

Net Receivables 23	82	0	0	320	695
Inventories 24	1	0	0	0	3
Net Property, Plant and Equipment 25	88	0	19	39	31
Total Assets 26	396	0	41	631	1365
Notes and Loans Payable 27	156	0	42	0	104
All Other Liabilities 28	102	0	15	368	872
Net Worth 29	138	0	-15	264	388

Selected Financial Ratios (Times to 1)

Current Ratio 30	1.1	•	0.3	1.2	1.6
Quick Ratio 31	0.9	•	0.3	1.2	1.5
Net Sales to Working Capital 32	35.9	•	•	6.3	13.7
Coverage Ratio 33	8.2	•	11.6	16.3	109.3
Total Asset Turnover 34	1.4	•	9.5	0.6	3.8
Inventory Turnover 35	1.5	•	•	•	49.2
Receivables Turnover 36	11.8	•	467065.4	•	9.4
Total Liabilities to Net Worth 37	1.9	•	•	1.4	2.5
Current Assets to Working Capital 38	9.9	•	•	6.9	2.8
Current Liabilities to Working Capital 39	8.9	•	•	5.9	1.8
Working Capital to Net Sales 40	0.0	•	•	0.2	0.1
Inventory to Working Capital 41	0.1	•	•	•	0.0
Total Receipts to Cash Flow 42	2.3	2.1	1.8	2.2	2.6
Cost of Goods to Cash Flow 43	0.0	•	•	•	0.1
Cash Flow to Total Debt 44	0.9	•	3.8	0.5	2.0

Selected Financial Factors (in Percentages)

Debt Ratio 45	65.1	•	136.4	58.2	71.5
Return on Total Assets 46	13.5	•	106.5	15.3	28.9
Return on Equity Before Income Taxes 47	34.1	•	•	34.4	100.5
Return on Equity After Income Taxes 48	31.7	•	•	30.3	85.7
Profit Margin (Before Income Tax) 49	8.7	23.1	10.2	23.0	7.6
Profit Margin (After Income Tax) 50	8.1	23.0	10.1	20.3	6.5

Table I

Corporations with and without Net Income

NEW AND USED CAR DEALERS

MONEY AMOUNTS AND SIZE OF ASSETS IN THOUSANDS OF DOLLARS

Item Description for Accounting Period 7/04 Through 6/05	Total	Zero Assets	Under 500	500 to 1,000	1,000 to 5,000	5,000 to 10,000	10,000 to 25,000	25,000 to 50,000	50,000 to 100,000	100,000 to 250,000	250,000 to 500,000	500,000 to 2,500,000	2,500,000 and over
Number of Enterprises 1	49789	5912	21726	3140	8910	5296	3850	731	160	42	10	8	3
Revenues ($ in Thousands)													
Net Sales 2	693219596	4166998	15924716	9590557	92573981	147769613	224855487	86313404	33981036	17274884	8620255	20276671	31871994
Interest 3	1382766	2753	14062	27386	133585	159565	199686	92619	38421	59745	28630	336736	289578
Rents 4	250553	142	149	0	23074	22503	33072	26337	39850	51238	13623	29161	11404
Royalties 5	136944	0	0	0	0	0	28	50	0	4630	0	364	131872
Other Portfolio Income 6	817190	43117	43592	14245	37710	71548	122396	81263	159114	53534	38823	131270	20577
Other Receipts 7	11623922	128929	8972	69758	1590723	2425032	3824246	1549026	635925	427081	150611	680054	133567
Total Receipts 8	707430971	4341939	15991491	9701946	94359073	150448261	229034915	88062699	34854346	17871112	8851942	21454256	32458992
Average Total Receipts 9	14209	734	736	3090	10590	28408	59490	120469	217840	425503	885194	2681782	10819664
Operating Costs/Operating Income (%)													
Cost of Operations 10	88.3	90.3	84.4	87.3	87.5	89.1	89.2	88.8	88.3	87.2	84.5	83.5	85.2
Salaries and Wages 11	4.8	3.9	2.5	2.9	4.6	4.7	4.7	4.9	5.1	5.7	4.6	6.7	6.3
Taxes Paid 12	0.8	1.6	1.6	0.9	0.8	0.8	0.7	0.7	0.7	0.8	0.8	1.0	1.4
Interest Paid 13	0.5	0.5	0.5	0.5	0.5	0.5	0.4	0.5	0.5	0.6	0.8	1.3	1.2
Depreciation 14	0.6	0.1	0.2	0.4	0.3	0.3	0.4	0.6	1.3	0.9	3.4	5.5	0.5
Amortization and Depletion 15	0.1	0.0	0.0	0.0	0.0	0.0	0.0	0.0	0.1	0.1	0.1	0.3	0.5
Pensions and Other Deferred Comp. 16	0.1	0.1	0.1	0.1	0.1	0.1	0.1	0.1	0.1	0.0	0.1	0.0	0.0
Employee Benefits 17	0.4	0.4	0.2	0.2	0.5	0.5	0.4	0.4	0.4	0.5	0.5	0.6	0.5
Advertising 18	1.2	1.3	0.8	0.5	1.3	1.3	1.1	1.1	1.1	1.3	0.8	1.1	1.0
Other Expenses 19	3.8	8.3	7.3	5.3	4.6	3.5	3.4	3.3	3.4	4.7	3.2	4.5	3.7
Officers' Compensation 20	0.7	1.7	2.0	1.7	1.1	0.8	0.6	0.6	0.5	0.5	0.5	0.2	0.0
Operating Margin 21	•	•	0.3	0.1	•	•	•	•	•	•	0.7	•	•
Operating Margin Before Officers' Comp. 22	•	•	2.4	1.9	•	•	•	•	•	•	1.2	•	•

Selected Average Balance Sheet ($ in Thousands)

Net Receivables 23	437	0	16	166	368	685	1645	3986	8418	16736	41894	116430	442309
Inventories 24	2132	0	80	436	1678	4775	8951	18010	30455	59683	92313	587950	1448438
Net Property, Plant and Equipment 25	433	0	14	52	163	497	1346	3905	11207	23127	103707	372992	723269
Total Assets 26	3904	0	137	703	2558	7039	15031	33507	66734	139175	320660	1341591	5438329
Notes and Loans Payable 27	2599	0	104	394	1661	5244	10992	23849	45633	87886	213444	577145	1943133
All Other Liabilities 28	480	0	27	117	336	701	1654	3332	7704	18269	37441	343915	768984
Net Worth 29	826	0	6	191	560	1094	2385	6327	13398	33020	69774	420531	2726211

Selected Financial Ratios (Times to 1)

Current Ratio 30	1.2	•	2.5	2.7	1.4	1.2	1.2	1.2	1.2	1.2	1.3	1.2	1.1
Quick Ratio 31	0.3	•	0.8	1.0	0.3	0.3	0.3	0.3	0.4	0.4	0.4	0.4	0.3
Net Sales to Working Capital 32	23.8	•	10.2	7.8	15.7	24.9	30.0	24.5	26.0	29.8	18.1	27.7	87.1
Coverage Ratio 33	2.5	•	2.4	3.4	2.3	1.8	2.7	3.3	3.1	3.3	5.4	1.8	2.4
Total Asset Turnover 34	3.6	•	5.4	4.3	4.1	4.0	3.9	3.5	3.2	3.0	2.7	1.9	2.0
Inventory Turnover 35	5.8	•	7.7	6.1	5.4	5.2	5.8	5.8	6.2	6.0	7.9	3.6	6.2
Receivables Turnover 36	31.0	•	40.6	16.9	29.5	40.9	36.8	30.2	27.6	18.1	31.3	8.0	•
Total Liabilities to Net Worth 37	3.7	•	20.4	2.7	3.6	5.4	5.3	4.3	4.0	3.2	3.6	2.2	1.0
Current Assets to Working Capital 38	5.2	•	1.7	1.6	3.5	5.6	6.5	5.7	5.9	7.3	3.9	5.9	16.3
Current Liabilities to Working Capital 39	4.2	•	0.7	0.6	2.5	4.6	5.5	4.7	4.9	6.3	2.9	4.9	15.3
Working Capital to Net Sales 40	0.0	•	0.1	0.1	0.1	0.0	0.0	0.0	0.0	0.0	0.1	0.0	0.0
Inventory to Working Capital 41	3.7	•	1.1	1.0	2.5	4.3	4.8	3.9	3.9	4.5	2.2	3.7	11.9
Total Receipts to Cash Flow 42	29.2	88.3	18.1	19.3	24.3	36.7	32.1	29.4	28.8	25.6	17.4	24.4	23.7
Cost of Goods to Cash Flow 43	25.8	79.7	15.3	16.9	21.3	32.7	28.6	26.1	25.4	22.3	14.7	20.4	20.2
Cash Flow to Total Debt 44	0.2	•	0.3	0.3	0.2	0.1	0.1	0.1	0.1	0.2	0.2	0.1	0.2

Selected Financial Factors (in Percentages)

Debt Ratio 45	78.9	•	95.3	72.8	78.1	84.5	84.1	81.1	79.9	76.3	78.2	68.7	49.9
Return on Total Assets 46	4.6	•	6.9	8.0	4.6	3.2	4.4	5.2	5.2	5.5	11.2	4.2	5.5
Return on Equity Before Income Taxes 47	12.9	•	87.3	20.6	11.8	8.9	17.5	19.0	17.6	16.3	42.2	5.9	6.3
Return on Equity After Income Taxes 48	11.3	•	82.0	20.3	11.2	8.1	16.6	18.0	15.7	14.1	37.1	2.2	4.1
Profit Margin (Before Income Tax) 49	0.8	•	0.8	1.3	0.6	0.3	0.7	1.0	1.1	1.3	3.4	1.0	1.6
Profit Margin (After Income Tax) 50	0.7	•	0.7	1.3	0.6	0.3	0.7	1.0	1.0	1.1	3.0	0.4	1.1

Table II

Corporations with Net Income

NEW AND USED CAR DEALERS

MONEY AMOUNTS AND SIZE OF ASSETS IN THOUSANDS OF DOLLARS

Item Description for Accounting Period 7/04 Through 6/05	Total	Zero Assets	Under 500	500 to 1,000	1,000 to 5,000	5,000 to 10,000	10,000 to 25,000	25,000 to 50,000	50,000 to 100,000	100,000 to 250,000	250,000 to 500,000	500,000 to 2,500,000	2,500,000 and over
Number of Enterprises 1	28682	2211	11562	2168	5855	3500	2647	560	124	36	0	0	3
Revenues ($ in Thousands)													
Net Sales 2	518837860	793045	10999092	7962905	67102499	102457953	162582004	68251003	26855834	15173335	0	0	31871994
Interest 3	1179549	1527	10502	25093	98464	107358	144197	69453	29779	57666	0	0	289578
Rents 4	171432	102	131	0	19059	16628	20607	14993	24154	40516	0	0	11404
Royalties 5	136578	0	0	0	0	0	28	48	0	4630	0	0	131872
Other Portfolio Income 6	526866	23865	33738	14049	33829	60178	82667	56042	80996	36078	0	0	20577
Other Receipts 7	8892060	108911	16558	39773	1162300	1700956	2878353	1248514	544838	375008	0	0	133567
Total Receipts 8	529744345	927450	11060021	8041820	68416151	104343073	165707856	69640053	27535601	15687233	0	0	32458992
Average Total Receipts 9	18470	419	957	3709	11685	29812	62602	124357	222061	435756	•	•	10819664
Operating Costs/Operating Income (%)													
Cost of Operations 10	88.1	79.3	82.9	86.7	87.9	88.8	88.9	88.6	88.2	87.3	•	•	85.2
Salaries and Wages 11	4.8	2.7	2.6	2.7	4.5	4.6	4.7	4.9	5.3	5.5	•	•	6.3
Taxes Paid 12	0.8	2.9	1.8	0.7	0.8	0.8	0.7	0.7	0.7	0.8	•	•	1.4
Interest Paid 13	0.5	0.2	0.5	0.5	0.4	0.4	0.4	0.4	0.5	0.5	•	•	1.2
Depreciation 14	0.4	0.2	0.1	0.3	0.3	0.3	0.4	0.5	0.8	0.8	•	•	0.5
Amortization and Depletion 15	0.1	0.0	0.0	0.1	0.0	0.0	0.0	0.0	0.0	0.1	•	•	0.5
Pensions and Other Deferred Comp. 16	0.1	0.0	0.0	0.1	0.1	0.1	0.1	0.1	0.1	0.1	•	•	0.0
Employee Benefits 17	0.4	0.2	0.2	0.1	0.4	0.5	0.4	0.4	0.4	0.5	•	•	0.5
Advertising 18	1.1	2.7	0.9	0.5	1.3	1.2	1.1	1.1	1.1	1.2	•	•	1.0
Other Expenses 19	3.6	15.0	6.6	5.3	3.9	3.3	3.2	3.3	3.2	4.7	•	•	3.7
Officers' Compensation 20	0.7	5.4	1.5	1.8	1.0	0.8	0.7	0.6	0.6	0.5	•	•	0.0
Operating Margin 21	•	•	2.8	1.3	•	•	•	•	•	•	•	•	•
Operating Margin Before Officers' Comp. 22	0.1	•	4.3	3.1	0.5	0.0	0.1	0.1	•	•	•	•	•

Selected Average Balance Sheet ($ in Thousands)

Net Receivables 23	553	0	22	160	438	664	1685	4130	8193	14906	•	442309
Inventories 24	2712	0	91	450	1790	4798	9378	17893	32377	61723	•	148438
Net Property, Plant and Equipment 25	519	0	12	55	159	515	1303	3763	9897	24391	•	723269
Total Assets 26	4935	0	151	702	2705	6934	15129	33418	67247	139981	•	5438329
Notes and Loans Payable 27	3068	0	77	324	1604	4877	10791	22947	43864	86009	•	1943133
All Other Liabilities 28	598	0	25	130	353	752	1412	3419	8118	18396	•	768984
Net Worth 29	1269	0	49	249	748	1305	2926	7052	15264	35577	•	2726211

Selected Financial Ratios (Times to 1)

Current Ratio 30	1.3	•	3.3	2.8	1.5	1.3	1.2	1.3	1.2	1.2	•	1.1
Quick Ratio 31	0.3	•	1.2	1.0	0.4	0.3	0.3	0.4	0.4	0.4	•	0.3
Net Sales to Working Capital 32	21.7	•	10.2	9.1	14.3	23.2	25.3	21.8	22.2	28.1	•	87.1
Coverage Ratio 33	4.1	35.4	7.7	5.7	4.7	3.7	4.7	4.7	4.4	3.9	•	2.4
Total Asset Turnover 34	3.7	•	6.3	5.2	4.2	4.2	4.1	3.6	3.2	3.0	•	2.0
Inventory Turnover 35	5.9	•	8.7	7.1	5.6	5.4	5.8	6.0	5.9	6.0	•	6.2
Receivables Turnover 36	30.5	•	44.8	20.2	28.4	42.2	36.2	30.5	28.3	•	•	•
Total Liabilities to Net Worth 37	2.9	•	2.1	1.8	2.6	4.3	4.2	3.7	3.4	2.9	•	1.0
Current Assets to Working Capital 38	4.6	•	1.4	1.6	3.0	4.9	5.3	4.9	5.1	6.7	•	16.3
Current Liabilities to Working Capital 39	3.6	•	0.4	0.6	2.0	3.9	4.3	3.9	4.1	5.7	•	15.3
Working Capital to Net Sales 40	0.0	•	0.1	0.1	0.0	0.0	0.0	0.0	0.0	0.0	•	0.0
Inventory to Working Capital 41	3.2	•	0.9	0.9	2.1	3.7	3.9	3.3	3.4	4.1	•	11.9
Total Receipts to Cash Flow 42	25.4	7.0	13.0	16.4	23.7	30.3	27.7	26.1	25.8	24.7	•	23.7
Cost of Goods to Cash Flow 43	22.3	5.6	10.8	14.2	20.8	26.9	24.7	23.2	22.8	21.6	•	20.2
Cash Flow to Total Debt 44	0.2	•	0.7	0.5	0.2	0.2	0.2	0.2	0.2	0.2	•	0.2

Selected Financial Factors (in Percentages)

Debt Ratio 45	74.3	•	67.6	64.5	72.3	81.2	80.7	78.9	77.3	74.6	•	49.9
Return on Total Assets 46	7.2	•	24.1	14.6	7.6	6.1	6.9	7.0	7.0	6.2	•	5.5
Return on Equity Before Income Taxes 47	21.1	•	64.7	33.9	21.8	23.9	27.9	26.1	23.6	18.2	•	6.3
Return on Equity After Income Taxes 48	19.4	•	63.4	33.5	21.1	22.9	26.8	24.9	21.6	15.9	•	4.1
Profit Margin (Before Income Tax) 49	1.5	8.3	3.3	2.3	1.4	1.1	1.3	1.5	1.7	1.5	•	1.6
Profit Margin (After Income Tax) 50	1.4	7.8	3.3	2.3	1.4	1.0	1.3	1.4	1.5	1.3	•	1.1

204

Table I

Corporations with and without Net Income

OTHER MOTOR VEHICLE AND PARTS DEALERS

MONEY AMOUNTS AND SIZE OF ASSETS IN THOUSANDS OF DOLLARS

Item Description for Accounting Period 7/04 Through 6/05	Total	Zero Assets	Under 500	500 to 1,000	1,000 to 5,000	5,000 to 10,000	10,000 to 25,000	25,000 to 50,000	50,000 to 100,000	100,000 to 250,000	250,000 to 500,000	500,000 to 2,500,000	2,500,000 and over
Number of Enterprises **1**	43311	4745	25065	4762	7340	833	398	89	46	18	7	8	0
Revenues ($ in Thousands)													
Net Sales **2**	133305903	1192317	14512714	8228164	39760692	12388359	14802616	7495922	7204182	5047841	3247617	19425481	0
Interest **3**	131441	169	7840	6594	24923	13921	16920	16566	6535	11391	17560	9022	0
Rents **4**	93934	68	6916	5012	17079	2219	12910	6528	17314	167	11719	14001	0
Royalties **5**	41019	0	0	0	466	577	2	82	0	21417	35	18439	0
Other Portfolio Income **6**	236330	18376	12704	11056	44609	10570	39846	22624	28540	33482	2686	11838	0
Other Receipts **7**	1517789	-3352	67117	99776	366676	191655	169344	58999	107383	49487	36351	374352	0
Total Receipts **8**	135326416	1207578	14607291	8350602	40214445	12607301	15041638	7600721	7363954	5163785	3315968	19853133	0
Average Total Receipts **9**	3125	254	583	1754	5479	15135	37793	85401	160086	286877	473710	2481642	•
Operating Costs/Operating Income (%)													
Cost of Operations **10**	72.5	73.6	67.2	69.2	76.2	77.6	80.7	80.1	77.6	74.9	67.7	56.0	•
Salaries and Wages **11**	9.3	8.5	8.8	9.4	7.6	6.9	7.4	7.1	8.1	8.8	13.8	16.5	•
Taxes Paid **12**	1.8	2.0	2.5	2.4	1.5	1.4	1.2	1.3	1.3	1.5	1.7	2.9	•
Interest Paid **13**	1.0	1.1	0.9	0.8	1.0	1.1	0.8	0.8	1.1	1.3	0.9	1.1	•
Depreciation **14**	1.6	1.2	1.1	1.0	0.8	2.4	1.3	2.0	2.7	2.8	3.5	2.2	•
Amortization and Depletion **15**	0.1	0.1	0.0	0.1	0.0	0.1	0.0	0.0	0.1	0.4	1.2	0.1	•
Pensions and Other Deferred Comp. **16**	0.2	0.2	0.1	0.1	0.2	0.2	0.2	0.2	0.2	0.6	0.3	0.1	•
Employee Benefits **17**	0.7	0.2	0.3	0.6	0.5	0.5	0.7	0.9	0.7	1.0	1.4	1.5	•
Advertising **18**	1.2	0.7	1.3	0.9	1.2	1.1	0.9	0.9	0.9	1.0	1.2	1.8	•
Other Expenses **19**	9.1	13.8	13.3	12.9	7.7	6.9	5.8	6.1	7.1	7.6	8.7	13.3	•
Officers' Compensation **20**	1.8	1.8	4.6	3.3	2.1	1.6	1.1	0.8	0.7	0.4	0.5	0.3	•
Operating Margin **21**	0.8	•	•	•	1.2	0.3	•	•	•	•	•	4.1	•
Operating Margin Before Officers' Comp. **22**	2.6	•	4.4	2.6	3.3	1.8	1.1	0.7	0.4	0.2	•	4.4	•

Selected Average Balance Sheet ($ in Thousands)

Net Receivables 23	128	0	16	68	178	541	1802	5647	8748	22110	29471	104805	•
Inventories 24	660	0	63	386	1355	3986	7876	15262	29371	51850	60124	585660	•
Net Property, Plant and Equipment 25	242	0	28	113	266	1203	2193	6156	13782	34302	58972	400071	•
Total Assets 26	1376	0	141	688	2137	7084	14731	33896	70146	154940	312505	1768356	•
Notes and Loans Payable 27	579	0	80	325	795	3830	7817	18230	35607	68074	89088	534734	•
All Other Liabilities 28	409	0	39	113	785	1520	3719	8713	18947	36045	74881	606479	•
Net Worth 29	389	0	21	250	557	1735	3196	6953	15592	50820	148536	627143	•

Selected Financial Ratios (Times to 1)

Current Ratio 30	1.4	•	2.1	2.9	1.6	1.4	1.4	1.2	1.2	1.3	1.1	1.1	•
Quick Ratio 31	0.3	•	0.7	0.7	0.3	0.3	0.3	0.4	0.3	0.4	0.3	0.2	•
Net Sales to Working Capital 32	11.1	•	11.2	5.0	8.2	9.7	12.1	17.6	19.4	17.2	43.3	37.3	•
Coverage Ratio 33	3.4	•	1.5	2.0	3.4	2.9	2.9	2.7	2.8	2.6	2.2	6.6	•
Total Asset Turnover 34	2.2	•	4.1	2.5	2.5	2.1	2.5	2.5	2.2	1.8	1.5	1.4	•
Inventory Turnover 35	3.4	•	6.1	3.1	3.0	2.9	3.8	4.4	4.1	4.1	5.2	2.3	•
Receivables Turnover 36	24.2	•	34.0	26.4	30.2	25.2	21.8	16.4	19.2	10.3	13.1	27.0	•
Total Liabilities to Net Worth 37	2.5	•	5.7	1.8	2.8	3.1	3.6	3.9	3.5	2.0	1.1	1.8	•
Current Assets to Working Capital 38	3.4	•	1.9	1.5	2.7	3.5	3.8	5.3	6.0	5.0	11.3	13.7	•
Current Liabilities to Working Capital 39	2.4	•	0.9	0.5	1.7	2.5	2.8	4.3	5.0	4.0	10.3	12.7	•
Working Capital to Net Sales 40	0.1	•	0.1	0.2	0.1	0.1	0.1	0.1	0.1	0.1	0.0	0.0	•
Inventory to Working Capital 41	2.5	•	1.2	1.1	2.1	2.7	2.7	3.4	4.2	2.9	6.9	9.7	•
Total Receipts to Cash Flow 42	11.7	11.4	10.8	10.1	12.8	14.6	18.2	18.4	14.7	12.7	15.5	6.9	•
Cost of Goods to Cash Flow 43	8.5	8.4	7.2	7.0	9.8	11.4	14.7	14.7	11.4	9.5	10.5	3.8	•
Cash Flow to Total Debt 44	0.3	•	0.4	0.4	0.3	0.2	0.2	0.2	0.2	0.2	0.2	0.3	•

Selected Financial Factors (in Percentages)

Debt Ratio 45	71.8	•	85.0	63.7	73.9	75.5	78.3	79.5	77.8	67.2	52.5	64.5	•
Return on Total Assets 46	7.4	•	5.9	3.8	8.4	6.5	6.2	5.3	6.7	6.0	3.1	10.2	•
Return on Equity Before Income Taxes 47	18.6	•	13.9	5.3	22.7	17.6	18.7	16.0	19.5	11.4	3.5	24.4	•
Return on Equity After Income Taxes 48	15.1	•	12.1	4.7	21.7	15.2	16.2	14.0	18.2	9.6	1.3	16.2	•
Profit Margin (Before Income Tax) 49	2.4	•	0.5	0.8	2.3	2.1	1.6	1.3	1.9	2.1	1.1	6.3	•
Profit Margin (After Income Tax) 50	1.9	•	0.4	0.7	2.2	1.8	1.4	1.2	1.8	1.7	0.4	4.2	•

205

Table II

Corporations with Net Income

OTHER MOTOR VEHICLE AND PARTS DEALERS

MONEY AMOUNTS AND SIZE OF ASSETS IN THOUSANDS OF DOLLARS

Item Description for Accounting Period 7/04 Through 6/05	Total	Zero Assets	Under 500	500 to 1,000	1,000 to 5,000	5,000 to 10,000	10,000 to 25,000	25,000 to 50,000	50,000 to 100,000	100,000 to 250,000	250,000 to 500,000	500,000 to 2,500,000	2,500,000 and over
Number of Enterprises **1**	25786	1833	13956	3250	5621	688	313	68	35	12	0	0	0
Revenues ($ in Thousands)													
Net Sales **2**	108589454	912335	10685286	5723716	33290037	11158711	12254810	6105636	5950377	3242829	0	0	0
Interest **3**	104328	30	3175	6114	16620	9755	14869	13993	3488	11235	0	0	0
Rents **4**	77087	68	5931	894	9125	1536	12589	5983	16969	145	0	0	0
Royalties **5**	19133	0	0	0	0	577	0	77	0	5	0	0	0
Other Portfolio Income **6**	166682	17101	2250	9506	40864	10116	30300	18289	19318	17318	0	0	0
Other Receipts **7**	1316167	2106	36770	88668	304485	177652	140479	43808	92941	25361	0	0	0
Total Receipts **8**	110272851	931640	10733412	5828898	33661131	11358347	12453047	6187786	6083093	3296893	0	0	0
Average Total Receipts **9**	4276	508	769	1794	5988	16509	39786	90997	173803	274741	.	.	.
Operating Costs/Operating Income (%)													
Cost of Operations **10**	72.3	76.9	67.5	67.8	75.5	77.8	80.5	81.0	78.7	69.9	.	.	.
Salaries and Wages **11**	9.2	7.2	7.9	9.7	7.7	7.1	7.3	6.7	8.0	10.5	.	.	.
Taxes Paid **12**	1.7	1.9	2.2	2.5	1.5	1.4	1.2	1.2	1.2	1.8	.	.	.
Interest Paid **13**	0.9	1.2	0.9	0.8	0.8	1.1	0.8	0.6	0.9	1.0	.	.	.
Depreciation **14**	1.2	1.1	1.0	1.2	0.7	0.9	1.1	1.5	1.5	2.6	.	.	.
Amortization and Depletion **15**	0.1	0.0	0.0	0.2	0.0	0.1	0.0	0.0	0.1	0.3	.	.	.
Pensions and Other Deferred Comp. **16**	0.2	0.0	0.1	0.2	0.2	0.2	0.2	0.2	0.2	0.7	.	.	.
Employee Benefits **17**	0.7	0.1	0.3	0.7	0.5	0.5	0.7	0.8	0.6	1.4	.	.	.
Advertising **18**	1.2	0.6	1.2	0.9	1.2	1.2	0.9	0.9	1.0	1.3	.	.	.
Other Expenses **19**	8.6	8.1	11.9	11.3	7.5	6.8	5.5	5.3	6.5	8.6	.	.	.
Officers' Compensation **20**	1.7	1.2	4.2	3.9	2.2	1.4	1.1	0.7	0.7	0.4	.	.	.
Operating Margin **21**	2.1	1.5	2.7	0.8	2.2	1.6	0.7	0.9	0.6	1.7	.	.	.
Operating Margin Before Officers' Comp. **22**	3.8	2.7	6.9	4.7	4.4	3.0	1.8	1.7	1.3	2.1	.	.	.

Selected Average Balance Sheet ($ in Thousands)

Net Receivables 23	177	0	22	82	200	562	1806	5694	9458	28024
Inventories 24	876	0	64	405	1370	4333	7939	16259	31638	38672
Net Property, Plant and Equipment 25	282	0	32	144	268	998	1944	5102	11184	32357
Total Assets 26	1796	0	165	718	2149	7299	14701	33235	68982	144904
Notes and Loans Payable 27	720	0	79	319	758	3954	7429	17124	33716	50755
All Other Liabilities 28	532	0	46	122	757	1653	3711	8160	20420	35964
Net Worth 29	543	0	40	277	634	1693	3561	7950	14846	58185

Selected Financial Ratios (Times to 1)

Current Ratio 30	1.4	•	2.0	2.8	1.6	1.4	1.4	1.3	1.3	1.5
Quick Ratio 31	0.4	•	0.8	0.9	0.3	0.3	0.3	0.4	0.3	0.7
Net Sales to Working Capital 32	11.4	•	13.4	5.3	8.4	9.2	12.3	14.5	14.6	10.0
Coverage Ratio 33	5.1	3.9	4.6	4.5	5.1	4.1	4.0	4.5	4.2	4.3
Total Asset Turnover 34	2.3	•	4.6	2.5	2.8	2.2	2.7	2.7	2.5	1.9
Inventory Turnover 35	3.5	•	8.0	3.0	3.3	2.9	4.0	4.5	4.2	4.9
Receivables Turnover 36	24.6	•	41.3	22.9	30.5	26.4	23.5	18.4	19.5	•
Total Liabilities to Net Worth 37	2.3	•	3.1	1.6	2.4	3.3	3.1	3.2	3.6	1.5
Current Assets to Working Capital 38	3.4	•	2.0	1.5	2.5	3.3	3.7	4.3	4.4	2.9
Current Liabilities to Working Capital 39	2.4	•	1.0	0.5	1.5	2.3	2.7	3.3	3.4	1.9
Working Capital to Net Sales 40	0.1	•	0.1	0.2	0.1	0.1	0.1	0.1	0.1	0.1
Inventory to Working Capital 41	2.5	•	1.2	1.1	2.0	2.6	2.7	2.9	3.2	1.4
Total Receipts to Cash Flow 42	10.5	10.8	9.1	9.7	11.5	12.5	16.6	17.0	13.5	10.0
Cost of Goods to Cash Flow 43	7.6	8.3	6.1	6.6	8.7	9.7	13.4	13.8	10.6	7.0
Cash Flow to Total Debt 44	0.3	•	0.7	0.4	0.3	0.2	0.2	0.2	0.2	0.3

Selected Financial Factors (in Percentages)

Debt Ratio 45	69.8	•	75.9	61.4	70.5	76.8	75.8	76.1	78.5	59.8
Return on Total Assets 46	10.7	•	18.7	8.5	11.4	9.8	8.3	7.8	9.1	8.1
Return on Equity Before Income Taxes 47	28.5	•	60.7	17.1	31.1	32.0	25.5	25.5	32.2	15.5
Return on Equity After Income Taxes 48	24.3	•	58.9	16.3	29.9	29.1	22.7	23.1	30.5	13.5
Profit Margin (Before Income Tax) 49	3.7	3.6	3.2	2.7	3.3	3.3	2.3	2.3	2.8	3.3
Profit Margin (After Income Tax) 50	3.1	3.6	3.1	2.6	3.2	3.0	2.1	2.0	2.7	2.9

Table I
Corporations with and without Net Income

FURNITURE AND HOME FURNISHINGS STORES

MONEY AMOUNTS AND SIZE OF ASSETS IN THOUSANDS OF DOLLARS

Item Description for Accounting Period 7/04 Through 6/05	Total	Zero Assets	Under 500	500 to 1,000	1,000 to 5,000	5,000 to 10,000	10,000 to 25,000	25,000 to 50,000	50,000 to 100,000	100,000 to 250,000	250,000 to 500,000	500,000 to 2,500,000	2,500,000 and over
Number of Enterprises 1	42801	3120	31107	4304	3725	275	175	39	19	22	6	9	0
Revenues ($ in Thousands)													
Net Sales 2	88718778	785579	18676156	7915230	18337211	4497357	7657001	3205489	2552871	6802615	3474153	14815116	0
Interest 3	307754	12	2012	19135	52537	5663	6421	10674	28937	44564	48294	89505	0
Rents 4	42971	11	1932	1319	4375	7326	2730	1888	1745	3703	3365	14576	0
Royalties 5	25034	0	0	0	15	181	0	111	2878	14791	4923	2135	0
Other Portfolio Income 6	120596	1654	22318	3302	5436	9017	5575	2141	702	4587	27824	38042	0
Other Receipts 7	770963	3464	40712	35510	73633	46605	118669	76034	24805	155635	44619	151275	0
Total Receipts 8	89986096	790720	18743130	7974496	18473207	4566149	7790396	3296337	2611938	7025895	3603178	15110649	0
Average Total Receipts 9	2102	253	603	1853	4959	16604	44517	84521	137470	319359	600530	1678961	•
Operating Costs/Operating Income (%)													
Cost of Operations 10	59.6	67.8	62.5	61.1	61.6	61.4	61.8	60.7	56.6	57.6	59.5	51.4	•
Salaries and Wages 11	12.0	10.2	8.5	11.2	11.8	12.1	13.0	15.0	14.4	13.8	13.5	14.3	•
Taxes Paid 12	2.3	1.7	2.0	3.0	1.9	1.9	1.8	2.2	2.0	2.2	2.6	2.9	•
Interest Paid 13	0.6	0.6	0.5	0.8	0.6	0.4	0.5	0.5	0.6	0.8	0.7	0.8	•
Depreciation 14	1.5	1.1	1.1	0.8	1.0	1.1	1.0	2.0	2.1	1.5	2.2	3.1	•
Amortization and Depletion 15	0.2	0.0	0.1	0.0	0.0	0.1	0.2	0.2	0.2	0.4	0.1	0.3	•
Pensions and Other Deferred Comp. 16	0.2	0.1	0.1	0.2	0.2	0.1	0.2	0.2	0.2	0.3	0.2	0.2	•
Employee Benefits 17	0.9	0.6	0.4	1.2	0.6	0.7	0.8	1.1	0.9	0.7	1.9	1.6	•
Advertising 18	4.1	2.9	3.2	4.2	3.5	3.9	4.5	4.1	4.5	5.6	6.7	4.4	•
Other Expenses 19	15.2	17.8	16.1	13.2	14.9	16.6	13.8	13.5	17.2	17.5	15.6	14.5	•
Officers' Compensation 20	2.6	1.8	4.8	4.9	3.0	2.5	1.5	1.1	0.9	0.5	0.6	0.6	•
Operating Margin 21	1.0	•	0.7	•	0.8	•	0.9	•	0.4	•	•	5.8	•
Operating Margin Before Officers' Comp. 22	3.5	•	5.5	4.2	3.8	1.6	2.4	0.5	1.4	•	•	6.3	•

Selected Average Balance Sheet ($ in Thousands)

Net Receivables 23	119	0	22	93	308	825	3074	6902	9676	22796	40757	97788
Inventories 24	314	0	51	276	789	2914	5684	11990	22770	43641	97324	386395
Net Property, Plant and Equipment 25	224	0	26	139	345	1099	3023	6872	20510	36769	101786	443127
Total Assets 26	953	0	138	658	1909	6471	15299	34083	72441	146416	356240	1556186
Notes and Loans Payable 27	260	0	63	295	573	1814	3625	8651	16497	49667	55694	283783
All Other Liabilities 28	384	0	43	210	674	2171	6583	14750	26093	54548	151744	747703
Net Worth 29	309	0	32	153	662	2486	5091	10682	29851	42201	148802	524700

Selected Financial Ratios (Times to 1)

Current Ratio 30	1.6	•	1.9	1.9	1.9	1.7	1.5	1.3	1.8	1.2	2.1	1.4
Quick Ratio 31	0.5	•	0.8	0.6	0.6	0.5	0.6	0.5	0.7	0.5	0.5	0.4
Net Sales to Working Capital 32	9.3	•	13.4	8.2	7.4	7.6	12.0	15.2	7.3	21.5	5.7	7.7
Coverage Ratio 33	4.7	•	3.1	1.0	3.4	2.7	6.3	5.7	5.4	3.8	1.3	10.1
Total Asset Turnover 34	2.2	•	4.3	2.8	2.6	2.5	2.9	2.4	1.9	2.1	1.6	1.1
Inventory Turnover 35	3.9	•	7.3	4.1	3.8	3.4	4.8	4.2	3.3	4.1	3.5	2.2
Receivables Turnover 36	17.9	•	30.5	17.2	16.9	20.4	15.0	13.6	12.5	15.3	14.6	15.8
Total Liabilities to Net Worth 37	2.1	•	3.3	3.3	1.9	1.6	2.0	2.2	1.4	2.5	1.4	2.0
Current Assets to Working Capital 38	2.6	•	2.1	2.1	2.2	2.4	3.1	4.3	2.3	5.8	1.9	3.3
Current Liabilities to Working Capital 39	1.6	•	1.1	1.1	1.2	1.4	2.1	3.3	1.3	4.8	0.9	2.3
Working Capital to Net Sales 40	0.1	•	0.1	0.1	0.1	0.1	0.1	0.1	0.1	0.0	0.2	0.1
Inventory to Working Capital 41	1.5	•	1.2	1.4	1.3	1.6	1.7	2.1	1.3	2.8	1.3	1.9
Total Receipts to Cash Flow 42	9.0	14.0	9.6	11.6	10.5	9.6	8.8	9.3	7.8	7.1	10.1	6.9
Cost of Goods to Cash Flow 43	5.3	9.5	6.0	7.1	6.5	5.9	5.4	5.6	4.4	4.1	6.0	3.5
Cash Flow to Total Debt 44	0.4	•	0.6	0.3	0.4	0.4	0.5	0.4	0.4	0.4	0.3	0.2

Selected Financial Factors (in Percentages)

Debt Ratio 45	67.6	•	76.8	76.7	65.3	61.6	66.7	68.7	58.8	71.2	58.2	66.3
Return on Total Assets 46	6.6	•	6.8	2.2	5.6	2.6	9.0	6.7	6.2	6.5	1.5	9.0
Return on Equity Before Income Taxes 47	16.0	•	19.7	•	11.3	4.2	22.7	17.6	12.2	16.7	0.9	24.0
Return on Equity After Income Taxes 48	12.0	•	18.8	•	10.3	2.8	21.5	14.8	10.4	12.9	•	16.1
Profit Margin (Before Income Tax) 49	2.4	•	1.1	1.5	1.5	0.6	2.6	2.3	2.7	2.3	0.2	7.7
Profit Margin (After Income Tax) 50	1.8	•	1.0	1.4	1.4	0.4	2.5	1.9	2.3	1.8	•	5.1

Table II
Corporations with Net Income

FURNITURE AND HOME FURNISHINGS STORES

MONEY AMOUNTS AND SIZE OF ASSETS IN THOUSANDS OF DOLLARS

Item Description for Accounting Period 7/04 Through 6/05	Total	Zero Assets	Under 500	500 to 1,000	1,000 to 5,000	5,000 to 10,000	10,000 to 25,000	25,000 to 50,000	50,000 to 100,000	100,000 to 250,000	250,000 to 500,000	500,000 to 2,500,000	2,500,000 and over
Number of Enterprises **1**	24875	1803	18242	2139	2300	178	144	28	13	16	0	0	0
Revenues ($ in Thousands)													
Net Sales **2**	67901074	421107	13155977	3975089	13543307	3964664	6354534	2318619	2041600	4992188	0	0	0
Interest **3**	272511	0	1096	10950	42873	745	5336	10485	22075	42841	0	0	0
Rents **4**	35519	11	1932	0	1697	6288	2178	1648	1697	3703	0	0	0
Royalties **5**	18229	0	0	0	0	181	0	0	0	14791	0	0	0
Other Portfolio Income **6**	117696	1654	21271	2974	5396	8933	4597	2131	693	4183	0	0	0
Other Receipts **7**	538829	2728	20308	14326	38888	31885	96688	67059	21264	93052	0	0	0
Total Receipts **8**	68883858	425500	13200584	4003339	13632161	4012696	6463333	2399942	2087329	5150758	0	0	0
Average Total Receipts **9**	2769	236	724	1872	5927	22543	44884	85712	160564	321922	·	·	·
Operating Costs/Operating Income (%)													
Cost of Operations **10**	58.9	67.0	62.7	60.2	60.9	61.3	62.5	60.9	58.2	56.9	·	·	·
Salaries and Wages **11**	11.8	8.7	7.6	9.5	11.4	11.8	12.8	14.3	14.4	14.2	·	·	·
Taxes Paid **12**	2.2	2.0	1.8	2.8	1.8	1.9	1.8	2.2	1.9	2.0	·	·	·
Interest Paid **13**	0.5	0.4	0.4	0.6	0.5	0.3	0.4	0.4	0.4	0.7	·	·	·
Depreciation **14**	1.5	0.5	1.1	0.9	1.0	0.7	0.9	1.5	1.7	1.3	·	·	·
Amortization and Depletion **15**	0.2	0.0	0.2	0.1	0.0	0.0	0.0	0.0	0.0	0.5	·	·	·
Pensions and Other Deferred Comp. **16**	0.2	0.1	0.1	0.2	0.2	0.1	0.2	0.2	0.2	0.3	·	·	·
Employee Benefits **17**	0.9	0.3	0.4	0.9	0.6	0.7	0.7	1.1	0.9	0.9	·	·	·
Advertising **18**	4.0	0.6	3.2	5.2	3.2	3.9	4.2	4.1	4.0	4.5	·	·	·
Other Expenses **19**	14.1	14.1	13.7	12.3	14.5	15.5	12.8	13.6	15.3	16.1	·	·	·
Officers' Compensation **20**	2.4	1.3	5.1	4.4	3.2	2.4	1.5	1.1	0.7	0.7	·	·	·
Operating Margin **21**	3.3	5.0	3.8	3.0	2.7	1.3	2.1	0.5	2.1	1.9	·	·	·
Operating Margin Before Officers' Comp. **22**	5.7	6.3	8.8	7.4	6.0	3.8	3.6	1.6	2.8	2.5	·	·	·

Selected Average Balance Sheet ($ in Thousands)

Net Receivables 23	157	0	26	81	344	889	3342	7440	8734	23662
Inventories 24	400	0	48	290	850	3104	5267	13344	28484	32739
Net Property, Plant and Equipment 25	315	0	26	147	404	1094	2904	6651	20959	35818
Total Assets 26	1224	0	143	644	2069	6587	15393	34485	73351	142248
Notes and Loans Payable 27	281	0	54	138	485	1712	3267	7738	15975	37114
All Other Liabilities 28	435	0	38	176	718	2728	6271	14372	27060	49342
Net Worth 29	508	0	50	329	866	2146	5855	12374	30316	55792

Selected Financial Ratios (Times to 1)

Current Ratio 30	1.7	•	2.2	2.1	2.0	1.4	1.5	1.5	1.9	1.6
Quick Ratio 31	0.6	•	1.1	0.7	0.7	0.4	0.6	0.6	0.5	0.7
Net Sales to Working Capital 32	8.9	•	13.3	7.8	7.5	15.0	10.9	10.6	7.4	9.8
Coverage Ratio 33	9.6	15.7	10.9	7.4	7.6	9.4	10.2	11.1	10.9	8.0
Total Asset Turnover 34	2.2	•	5.0	2.9	2.8	3.4	2.9	2.4	2.1	2.2
Inventory Turnover 35	4.0	•	9.5	3.9	4.2	4.4	5.2	3.8	3.2	5.4
Receivables Turnover 36	17.8	•	35.4	13.7	18.4	24.6	15.3	12.4	14.5	14.5
Total Liabilities to Net Worth 37	1.4	•	1.8	1.0	1.4	2.1	1.6	1.8	1.4	1.5
Current Assets to Working Capital 38	2.5	•	1.8	1.9	2.0	3.6	2.9	3.2	2.1	2.6
Current Liabilities to Working Capital 39	1.5	•	0.8	0.9	1.0	2.6	1.9	2.2	1.1	1.6
Working Capital to Net Sales 40	0.1	•	0.1	0.1	0.1	0.1	0.1	0.1	0.1	0.1
Inventory to Working Capital 41	1.4	•	0.9	1.3	1.2	2.3	1.5	1.6	1.4	1.2
Total Receipts to Cash Flow 42	7.8	6.6	8.1	8.8	9.2	8.6	8.3	7.8	7.7	6.0
Cost of Goods to Cash Flow 43	4.6	4.4	5.1	5.3	5.6	5.3	5.2	4.7	4.5	3.4
Cash Flow to Total Debt 44	0.5	•	1.0	0.7	0.5	0.6	0.6	0.5	0.5	0.6

Selected Financial Factors (in Percentages)

Debt Ratio 45	58.5	•	64.8	48.8	58.1	67.4	62.0	64.1	58.7	60.8
Return on Total Assets 46	11.7	•	22.7	12.3	11.1	9.6	12.1	10.5	10.2	12.5
Return on Equity Before Income Taxes 47	25.2	•	58.7	20.8	23.1	26.3	28.8	26.7	22.4	27.9
Return on Equity After Income Taxes 48	21.1	•	57.7	20.0	21.8	23.8	27.5	23.3	19.6	24.0
Profit Margin (Before Income Tax) 49	4.7	6.1	4.1	3.7	3.4	2.5	3.8	4.0	4.3	5.0
Profit Margin (After Income Tax) 50	3.9	6.1	4.0	3.5	3.2	2.3	3.7	3.5	3.8	4.3

Table I

Corporations with and without Net Income

ELECTRONICS AND APPLIANCE STORES

MONEY AMOUNTS AND SIZE OF ASSETS IN THOUSANDS OF DOLLARS

Item Description for Accounting Period 7/04 Through 6/05	Total	Zero Assets	Under 500	500 to 1,000	1,000 to 5,000	5,000 to 10,000	10,000 to 25,000	25,000 to 50,000	50,000 to 100,000	100,000 to 250,000	250,000 to 500,000	500,000 to 2,500,000	2,500,000 and over
Number of Enterprises 1	33576	3860	24646	2192	2441	205	132	37	22	17	13	8	3
Revenues ($ in Thousands)													
Net Sales 2	114491420	843901	11706519	6275973	13300458	4229105	5157857	4206695	3712937	5097835	7694158	8850353	43415629
Interest 3	250378	308	7213	4157	3138	1016	3154	9590	3264	3397	44827	53648	116665
Rents 4	62534	0	6357	287	2172	588	3306	6	180	4	6122	3380	40131
Royalties 5	58149	0	0	0	0	0	1585	3186	130	27626	11771	7251	6600
Other Portfolio Income 6	278089	1605	17785	20263	65534	12812	15790	31263	1911	830	27660	9012	73623
Other Receipts 7	2153748	-5767	135577	9539	132630	21151	63508	20973	32897	416953	48130	691487	586673
Total Receipts 8	117294318	840047	11873451	631019	13503932	4264672	5245200	4271713	3751319	5546645	7832668	9615131	44239321
Average Total Receipts 9	3493	218	482	2879	5532	20803	39736	115452	170514	326273	602513	1201891	14746440
Operating Costs/Operating Income (%)													
Cost of Operations 10	70.3	66.8	55.6	68.5	69.9	68.5	69.7	78.0	67.0	75.3	69.9	71.6	73.8
Salaries and Wages 11	11.0	13.8	14.9	11.0	10.7	11.9	12.0	10.1	14.3	13.4	12.0	13.9	8.5
Taxes Paid 12	1.7	1.1	2.6	1.6	1.9	1.3	1.5	1.0	1.6	1.3	1.3	1.5	1.9
Interest Paid 13	0.4	0.4	0.7	0.5	0.7	0.4	0.5	0.2	0.6	0.3	0.9	0.4	0.2
Depreciation 14	1.4	0.6	1.1	0.7	1.1	2.6	1.3	0.6	2.0	2.6	1.6	1.9	1.4
Amortization and Depletion 15	0.2	0.5	0.1	0.2	0.1	0.2	0.4	0.1	0.4	0.2	0.8	0.3	0.0
Pensions and Other Deferred Comp. 16	0.1	0.1	0.3	0.2	0.2	0.4	0.2	0.2	0.1	0.1	0.1	0.0	0.1
Employee Benefits 17	0.6	0.4	0.5	1.0	0.7	1.2	0.8	0.5	1.1	1.1	0.9	0.9	0.3
Advertising 18	2.1	1.5	2.2	1.1	2.3	3.4	1.6	1.0	0.8	2.3	2.3	1.2	2.5
Other Expenses 19	9.8	17.4	15.6	9.5	9.6	7.5	10.4	7.2	10.2	9.9	9.3	11.9	8.1
Officers' Compensation 20	1.8	3.3	7.6	3.8	3.4	1.9	1.5	1.0	1.1	0.6	1.1	0.6	0.2
Operating Margin 21	0.4	•	•	2.0	•	0.7	0.0	•	0.8	•	•	•	2.9
Operating Margin Before Officers' Comp. 22	2.2	•	6.5	5.9	2.8	2.6	1.5	0.9	1.9	•	1.0	•	3.0

Selected Average Balance Sheet ($ in Thousands)

Net Receivables 23	198	0	17	227	457	986	4451	13390	17712	32657	88207	55485	257058
Inventories 24	322	0	40	184	592	1199	3027	4200	10218	25680	59591	408180	1648804
Net Property, Plant and Equipment 25	223	0	17	58	360	1143	1649	2440	10002	27469	41190	99118	1165891
Total Assets 26	1394	0	120	736	2044	7203	15773	33724	68008	164025	332150	870678	5626414
Notes and Loans Payable 27	274	0	67	280	598	1749	6377	3474	19201	22953	44002	172712	455926
All Other Liabilities 28	655	0	65	264	786	4143	8642	20901	29953	83906	183684	347252	2629905
Net Worth 29	465	0	-13	192	659	1310	754	9349	18854	57166	104465	350715	2540583

Selected Financial Ratios (Times to 1)

Current Ratio 30	1.4	•	1.3	1.8	1.7	1.3	1.2	1.3	1.1	1.7	1.2	1.1	1.6
Quick Ratio 31	0.6	•	0.7	1.1	0.9	0.8	0.8	0.9	0.7	0.9	0.8	0.4	0.3
Net Sales to Working Capital 32	13.2	•	23.6	11.8	9.0	15.0	20.3	17.7	44.7	7.4	17.6	50.3	10.9
Coverage Ratio 33	7.3	•	1.4	6.2	2.2	4.9	4.4	7.1	4.2	6.9	3.6	10.8	20.4
Total Asset Turnover 34	2.4	•	4.0	3.9	2.7	2.9	2.5	3.4	2.5	1.8	1.8	1.3	2.6
Inventory Turnover 35	7.5	•	6.7	10.6	6.4	11.8	9.0	21.1	11.1	8.8	6.9	1.9	6.5
Receivables Turnover 36	16.6	•	27.5	15.6	11.3	20.8	8.7	9.5	10.7	6.3	8.5	7.4	•
Total Liabilities to Net Worth 37	2.0	•	•	2.8	2.1	4.5	19.9	2.6	2.6	1.9	2.2	1.5	1.2
Current Assets to Working Capital 38	3.4	•	4.4	2.2	2.5	3.9	6.0	4.3	11.1	2.5	6.2	14.6	2.7
Current Liabilities to Working Capital 39	2.4	•	3.4	1.2	1.5	2.9	5.0	3.3	10.1	1.5	5.2	13.6	1.7
Working Capital to Net Sales 40	0.1	•	0.0	0.1	0.1	0.1	0.0	0.1	0.0	0.1	0.1	0.0	0.1
Inventory to Working Capital 41	1.3	•	2.0	0.8	1.0	0.8	1.7	0.8	2.7	0.8	1.7	5.5	1.2
Total Receipts to Cash Flow 42	10.7	19.1	8.7	11.1	12.5	14.0	11.8	15.4	11.0	11.6	13.8	8.4	10.2
Cost of Goods to Cash Flow 43	7.5	12.8	4.8	7.6	8.8	9.6	8.2	12.0	7.4	8.7	9.7	6.0	7.5
Cash Flow to Total Debt 44	0.3	•	0.4	0.5	0.3	0.3	0.2	0.3	0.3	0.2	0.2	0.3	0.5

Selected Financial Factors (in Percentages)

Debt Ratio 45	66.7	•	110.5	74.0	67.7	81.8	95.2	72.3	72.3	65.1	68.5	59.7	54.8
Return on Total Assets 46	7.9	•	3.9	11.9	4.2	5.4	5.5	5.7	6.2	3.6	5.4	6.1	12.5
Return on Equity Before Income Taxes 47	20.4	•	•	38.4	7.2	23.8	88.3	17.7	17.1	8.8	12.3	13.7	26.4
Return on Equity After Income Taxes 48	14.4	•	•	34.8	6.0	21.3	74.3	13.3	14.7	8.4	10.1	9.6	17.2
Profit Margin (Before Income Tax) 49	2.8	•	0.3	2.6	0.9	1.5	1.7	1.5	1.9	1.7	2.2	4.4	4.6
Profit Margin (After Income Tax) 50	2.0	•	0.2	2.3	0.7	1.4	1.4	1.1	1.6	1.6	1.8	3.1	3.0

Table II
Corporations with Net Income

ELECTRONICS AND APPLIANCE STORES

MONEY AMOUNTS AND SIZE OF ASSETS IN THOUSANDS OF DOLLARS

Item Description for Accounting Period 7/04 Through 6/05	Total	Zero Assets	Under 500	500 to 1,000	1,000 to 5,000	5,000 to 10,000	10,000 to 25,000	25,000 to 50,000	50,000 to 100,000	100,000 to 250,000	250,000 to 500,000	500,000 to 2,500,000	2,500,000 and over
Number of Enterprises 1	18473	1988	13284	1386	1529	119	93	27	0	13	8	0	3
Revenues ($ in Thousands)													
Net Sales 2	96196829	194654	7240676	3922602	9396893	3373544	4315082	3539672	0	3875849	5866636	0	43415629
Interest 3	229095	39	6991	3725	1737	782	1611	3656	0	1426	36968	0	116665
Rents 4	51824	0	3394	287	2149	444	1662	1	0	0	1555	0	40131
Royalties 5	24124	0	0	0	0	0	0	3186	0	2902	4185	0	6600
Other Portfolio Income 6	217865	971	960	19548	60948	12675	10362	117	0	830	27659	0	73623
Other Receipts 7	2055176	2	132863	7211	126039	24519	28258	16390	0	365896	49770	0	586673
Total Receipts 8	98774913	195666	7384884	3953373	9587766	3411964	4356975	3563022	0	4246903	5986773	0	44239321
Average Total Receipts 9	5347	98	556	2852	6271	28672	46849	131964	•	326685	748347	•	14746440
Operating Costs/Operating Income (%)													
Cost of Operations 10	71.8	39.5	52.4	66.3	70.5	79.1	71.3	81.4	•	75.3	74.5	•	73.8
Salaries and Wages 11	9.8	8.0	13.5	11.2	10.1	5.6	10.5	8.1	•	12.9	8.8	•	8.5
Taxes Paid 12	1.6	0.6	2.6	1.2	1.6	0.8	1.3	0.7	•	1.1	1.2	•	1.9
Interest Paid 13	0.3	0.1	0.5	0.5	0.5	0.1	0.3	0.1	•	0.2	0.7	•	0.2
Depreciation 14	1.3	0.8	1.0	0.6	0.8	0.7	1.1	0.4	•	2.6	1.2	•	1.4
Amortization and Depletion 15	0.1	0.0	0.0	0.3	0.0	0.1	0.1	0.1	•	0.2	0.2	•	0.0
Pensions and Other Deferred Comp. 16	0.1	•	0.5	0.1	0.2	0.2	0.3	0.2	•	0.1	0.1	•	0.1
Employee Benefits 17	0.5	•	0.3	0.8	0.6	0.7	0.7	0.3	•	1.2	0.4	•	0.3
Advertising 18	2.1	0.9	1.5	1.0	2.5	4.2	1.7	1.1	•	2.4	2.1	•	2.5
Other Expenses 19	8.6	32.1	14.3	9.0	8.4	5.8	7.7	4.6	•	6.4	7.3	•	8.1
Officers' Compensation 20	1.5	3.4	9.0	2.9	3.3	0.6	1.4	1.0	•	0.8	0.9	•	0.2
Operating Margin 21	2.1	14.6	4.5	6.1	1.4	2.2	3.5	1.9	•	•	2.4	•	2.9
Operating Margin Before Officers' Comp. 22	3.6	18.0	13.4	9.0	4.8	2.8	4.9	2.9	•	•	3.4	•	3.0

Selected Average Balance Sheet ($ in Thousands)

Net Receivables 23	260	0	16	220	431	1071	4724	15081	•	22453	103560	•	257058
Inventories 24	492	0	35	157	737	1963	3718	4905	•	25788	67490	•	1648804
Net Property, Plant and Equipment 25	338	0	17	63	323	877	1636	2611	•	28810	41876	•	1165891
Total Assets 26	2020	0	124	731	2095	6982	15784	34988	•	154757	327960	•	5626414
Notes and Loans Payable 27	294	0	53	216	479	188	2481	2511	•	25082	25076	•	455926
All Other Liabilities 28	906	0	32	262	820	3824	8906	21232	•	67599	172907	•	2629905
Net Worth 29	820	0	39	254	795	2970	4396	11245	•	62076	129978	•	2540583

Selected Financial Ratios (Times to 1)

Current Ratio 30	1.6	•	2.3	1.9	1.8	1.4	1.4	1.4	•	1.4	1.4	•	1.6
Quick Ratio 31	0.6	•	1.3	1.3	1.0	1.0	0.9	1.0	•	0.7	0.8	•	0.3
Net Sales to Working Capital 32	11.4	•	10.5	11.2	12.6	7.9	12.8	17.5	•	12.2	12.9	•	10.9
Coverage Ratio 33	14.6	211.7	14.3	15.1	7.5	26.8	14.8	18.2	•	31.3	7.3	•	20.4
Total Asset Turnover 34	2.6	•	4.4	3.9	2.9	4.1	2.9	3.7	•	1.9	2.2	•	2.6
Inventory Turnover 35	7.6	•	8.3	12.0	5.9	11.4	8.9	21.8	•	8.7	8.1	•	6.5
Receivables Turnover 36	19.9	•	39.8	15.2	12.0	23.9	9.8	9.8	•	11.3	•	•	•
Total Liabilities to Net Worth 37	1.5	•	2.2	1.9	1.6	1.4	2.6	2.1	•	1.5	1.5	•	1.2
Current Assets to Working Capital 38	2.8	•	1.7	2.1	2.3	2.1	3.4	3.8	•	3.8	3.8	•	2.7
Current Liabilities to Working Capital 39	1.8	•	0.7	1.1	1.3	1.1	2.4	2.8	•	2.8	2.8	•	1.7
Working Capital to Net Sales 40	0.1	•	0.1	0.1	0.1	0.1	0.1	0.1	•	0.1	0.1	•	0.1
Inventory to Working Capital 41	1.1	•	0.7	0.7	0.8	0.9	1.1	0.7	•	1.3	1.2	•	1.2
Total Receipts to Cash Flow 42	9.6	2.9	6.1	7.8	10.5	12.6	10.0	15.9	•	10.0	11.2	•	10.2
Cost of Goods to Cash Flow 43	6.9	1.1	3.2	5.2	7.4	10.0	7.1	12.9	•	7.5	8.3	•	7.5
Cash Flow to Total Debt 44	0.5	•	1.1	0.8	0.5	0.6	0.4	0.3	•	0.3	0.3	•	0.5

Selected Financial Factors (in Percentages)

Debt Ratio 45	59.4	•	68.8	65.3	62.0	57.5	72.1	67.9	•	59.9	60.4	•	54.8
Return on Total Assets 46	13.0	•	30.5	28.7	11.7	14.0	14.2	9.9	•	12.7	11.6	•	12.5
Return on Equity Before Income Taxes 47	29.9	•	90.9	77.1	26.7	31.6	47.7	29.2	•	30.8	25.3	•	26.4
Return on Equity After Income Taxes 48	23.7	•	89.3	72.8	25.0	29.7	44.3	24.3	•	30.3	22.4	•	17.2
Profit Margin (Before Income Tax) 49	4.7	14.9	6.5	6.9	3.5	3.3	4.5	2.5	•	6.4	4.5	•	4.6
Profit Margin (After Income Tax) 50	3.7	14.7	6.3	6.5	3.2	3.1	4.2	2.1	•	6.3	4.0	•	3.0

Table I

Corporations with and without Net Income

HOMES CENTERS; PAINT AND WALLPAPER STORES

MONEY AMOUNTS AND SIZE OF ASSETS IN THOUSANDS OF DOLLARS

Item Description for Accounting Period 7/04 Through 6/05	Total	Zero Assets	Under 500	500 to 1,000	1,000 to 5,000	5,000 to 10,000	10,000 to 25,000	25,000 to 50,000	50,000 to 100,000	100,000 to 250,000	250,000 to 500,000	500,000 to 2,500,000	2,500,000 and over
Number of Enterprises 1	3369	255	2164	334	514	41	40	7	7	4	0	0	3
Revenues ($ in Thousands)													
Net Sales 2	124727814	12128	1931504	391661	3044839	667751	1498588	528463	892460	2620130	0	0	113140291
Interest 3	192532	3	153	681	3061	2038	2465	303	868	23985	0	0	158974
Rents 4	15780	0	0	274	1643	674	212	36	0	3703	0	0	9238
Royalties 5	117956	0	0	0	0	0	1393	0	0	0	0	0	116563
Other Portfolio Income 6	63517	0	138	1350	1103	1455	474	721	268	1695	0	0	56313
Other Receipts 7	1441223	-248	1863	11438	41301	489	10851	4393	8634	39385	0	0	1323116
Total Receipts 8	126558822	11883	1933658	405404	3091947	672407	1513983	533916	902230	2688898	0	0	11804495
Average Total Receipts 9	37566	47	894	1214	6015	16400	37850	76274	128890	672224	•	•	38268165
Operating Costs/Operating Income (%)													
Cost of Operations 10	67.6	1.1	63.1	66.9	70.5	70.7	73.5	72.3	73.4	71.3	•	•	67.4
Salaries and Wages 11	11.5	35.8	12.3	6.9	10.5	11.5	10.4	12.4	10.6	12.3	•	•	11.5
Taxes Paid 12	2.1	1.4	5.6	1.4	2.5	1.9	1.4	1.7	1.4	1.2	•	•	2.1
Interest Paid 13	0.4	1.6	0.2	2.6	0.5	0.7	0.6	0.3	0.5	0.9	•	•	0.4
Depreciation 14	2.5	•	0.8	1.0	0.9	1.5	1.3	1.6	2.1	1.4	•	•	2.6
Amortization and Depletion 15	0.0	•	0.0	0.0	0.1	0.0	0.0	0.0	0.0	0.2	•	•	0.0
Pensions and Other Deferred Comp. 16	0.2	•	0.1	0.2	0.3	0.4	0.2	0.3	0.0	0.1	•	•	0.2
Employee Benefits 17	0.3	•	0.5	0.2	0.9	1.2	0.8	1.0	0.9	1.6	•	•	0.3
Advertising 18	1.6	1.3	1.2	1.2	0.7	1.0	1.0	1.2	0.7	0.4	•	•	1.7
Other Expenses 19	6.6	69.9	13.1	18.9	8.1	6.4	7.4	7.8	7.6	7.0	•	•	6.4
Officers' Compensation 20	0.2	0.1	2.8	5.2	3.1	2.8	1.2	0.9	0.7	0.4	•	•	0.0
Operating Margin 21	6.8	•	0.2	•	2.0	2.0	2.0	0.4	1.7	3.2	•	•	7.4
Operating Margin Before Officers' Comp. 22	7.1	•	3.0	0.6	5.1	4.7	3.3	1.3	2.4	3.6	•	•	7.4

Selected Average Balance Sheet ($ in Thousands)

Net Receivables 23	10530	0	38	90	590	907	3618	5224	13826	94208	•	11455343
Inventories 24	4965	0	100	339	680	2778	4697	15068	33926	61295	•	5093716
Net Property, Plant and Equipment 25	9141	0	10	73	242	1209	2472	8821	13288	73209	•	10010142
Total Assets 26	41922	0	174	700	2185	6712	14016	32053	65617	426712	•	45424643
Notes and Loans Payable 27	4367	0	67	522	624	1903	4377	5445	30681	83594	•	4410468
All Other Liabilities 28	15879	0	84	152	428	1544	3189	7158	8319	168894	•	17356666
Net Worth 29	21676	0	23	27	1134	3265	6451	19450	26617	174225	•	23657508

Selected Financial Ratios (Times to 1)

Current Ratio 30	1.1	•	1.7	1.2	3.1	2.2	2.4	2.4	5.0	1.9	•	1.1
Quick Ratio 31	0.8	•	0.7	0.4	1.6	0.7	1.1	0.8	2.5	1.4	•	0.7
Net Sales to Working Capital 32	20.4	•	13.3	22.1	5.0	7.0	6.4	6.3	3.5	5.1	•	27.2
Coverage Ratio 33	21.2	•	2.9	0.6	8.8	4.6	5.8	5.4	6.4	7.5	•	23.7
Total Asset Turnover 34	0.9	•	5.1	1.7	2.7	2.4	2.7	2.4	1.9	1.5	•	0.8
Inventory Turnover 35	5.0	•	5.7	2.3	6.1	4.1	5.9	3.6	2.8	7.6	•	5.0
Receivables Turnover 36	6.4	•	19.3	7.5	10.7	•	13.3	9.6	3.6	•	•	6.2
Total Liabilities to Net Worth 37	0.9	•	6.4	25.1	0.9	1.1	1.2	0.6	1.5	1.4	•	0.9
Current Assets to Working Capital 38	9.5	•	2.4	6.3	1.5	1.9	1.7	1.7	1.3	2.1	•	13.1
Current Liabilities to Working Capital 39	8.5	•	1.4	5.3	0.5	0.9	0.7	0.7	0.3	1.1	•	12.1
Working Capital to Net Sales 40	0.0	•	0.1	0.0	0.2	0.1	0.2	0.2	0.3	0.2	•	0.0
Inventory to Working Capital 41	2.9	•	1.3	4.1	0.6	1.2	0.9	1.1	0.6	0.5	•	3.9
Total Receipts to Cash Flow 42	7.8	1.8	11.7	6.7	10.5	15.3	12.2	14.3	12.2	8.7	•	7.6
Cost of Goods to Cash Flow 43	5.3	0.0	7.4	4.5	7.4	10.8	9.0	10.3	8.9	6.2	•	5.1
Cash Flow to Total Debt 44	0.2	•	0.5	0.3	0.5	0.3	0.4	0.4	0.3	0.3	•	0.2

Selected Financial Factors (in Percentages)

Debt Ratio 45	48.3	•	86.5	96.2	48.1	51.4	54.0	39.3	59.4	59.2	•	47.9
Return on Total Assets 46	8.0	•	2.8	2.5	10.9	8.1	9.9	4.2	6.4	10.3	•	7.9
Return on Equity Before Income Taxes 47	14.7	•	13.8	•	18.6	13.0	17.8	5.6	13.2	21.8	•	14.6
Return on Equity After Income Taxes 48	9.9	•	6.4	•	18.0	8.1	17.1	4.4	11.6	15.3	•	9.8
Profit Margin (Before Income Tax) 49	8.6	•	0.4	•	3.6	2.6	3.1	1.5	2.8	5.8	•	9.2
Profit Margin (After Income Tax) 50	5.8	•	0.2	•	3.5	1.6	2.9	1.1	2.4	4.1	•	6.1

Table II

Corporations with Net Income

HOMES CENTERS; PAINT AND WALLPAPER STORES

MONEY AMOUNTS AND SIZE OF ASSETS IN THOUSANDS OF DOLLARS

Item Description for Accounting Period 7/04 Through 6/05	Total	Zero Assets	Under 500	500 to 1,000	1,000 to 5,000	5,000 to 10,000	10,000 to 25,000	25,000 to 50,000	50,000 to 100,000	100,000 to 250,000	250,000 to 500,000	500,000 to 2,500,000	2,500,000 and over
Number of Enterprises 1	1786	0	977	279	441	0	34	4	0	4	0	0	3
Revenues ($ in Thousands)													
Net Sales 2	123828469	0	1669572	300705	2882135	0	1382627	315641	0	2620130	0	0	113140291
Interest 3	189752	0	153	620	2069	0	1743	276	0	23985	0	0	158974
Rents 4	15530	0	0	274	1572	0	203	2	0	3703	0	0	9238
Royalties 5	117956	0	0	0	0	0	1393	0	0	0	0	0	116563
Other Portfolio Income 6	60693	0	138	153	482	0	365	673	0	1695	0	0	56313
Other Receipts 7	1436473	0	1769	10280	40702	0	10898	2136	0	39385	0	0	1323116
Total Receipts 8	125644873	0	1671632	312032	2926960	0	1397229	318728	0	2688898	0	0	114804495
Average Total Receipts 9	70352	•	1711	1118	6637	•	41095	79682	•	672224	•	•	38268165
Operating Costs/Operating Income (%)													
Cost of Operations 10	67.6	•	64.8	67.0	70.4	•	73.5	69.5	•	71.3	•	•	67.4
Salaries and Wages 11	11.5	•	10.7	4.5	10.4	•	10.2	13.8	•	12.3	•	•	11.5
Taxes Paid 12	2.1	•	6.1	1.1	2.5	•	1.4	1.7	•	1.2	•	•	2.1
Interest Paid 13	0.4	•	0.0	1.3	0.4	•	0.6	0.4	•	0.9	•	•	0.4
Depreciation 14	2.5	•	0.5	1.1	0.9	•	1.3	1.2	•	1.4	•	•	2.6
Amortization and Depletion 15	0.0	•	0.0	0.0	0.1	•	0.0	0.1	•	0.2	•	•	0.0
Pensions and Other Deferred Comp. 16	0.2	•	0.1	0.2	0.3	•	0.2	0.3	•	0.1	•	•	0.2
Employee Benefits 17	0.3	•	0.5	0.0	0.9	•	0.8	1.1	•	1.6	•	•	0.3
Advertising 18	1.6	•	1.1	1.1	0.7	•	0.9	1.0	•	0.4	•	•	1.7
Other Expenses 19	6.6	•	11.4	17.5	7.9	•	7.2	7.3	•	7.0	•	•	6.4
Officers' Compensation 20	0.2	•	2.4	5.7	3.1	•	1.2	0.9	•	0.4	•	•	0.0
Operating Margin 21	6.9	•	2.3	0.4	2.4	•	2.6	2.8	•	3.2	•	•	7.4
Operating Margin Before Officers' Comp. 22	7.2	•	4.7	6.1	5.5	•	3.8	3.7	•	3.6	•	•	7.4

Selected Average Balance Sheet ($ in Thousands)

Net Receivables 23	19836	80	89	642	3878	8402	94208	11455343
Inventories 24	9238	173	186	744	4550	10220	61295	5093716
Net Property, Plant and Equipment 25	17206	7	85	266	2372	9348	73209	10010142
Total Assets 26	78779	284	723	2274	13778	34091	426712	45424643
Notes and Loans Payable 27	8028	20	479	598	4197	6468	83594	4410468
All Other Liabilities 28	29887	160	139	423	3162	7392	168894	17356666
Net Worth 29	40864	103	105	1253	6419	20230	174225	23657508

Selected Financial Ratios (Times to 1)

Current Ratio 30	1.1	1.6	1.0	3.2	2.6	2.6	1.9	1.1
Quick Ratio 31	0.8	0.8	0.4	1.8	1.2	1.3	1.4	0.7
Net Sales to Working Capital 32	20.9	17.3	957.7	5.0	6.5	5.9	5.1	27.2
Coverage Ratio 33	22.0	57.9	4.2	11.4	7.1	11.7	7.5	23.7
Total Asset Turnover 34	0.9	6.0	1.5	2.9	3.0	2.3	1.5	0.8
Inventory Turnover 35	5.1	6.4	3.9	6.2	6.6	5.4	7.6	5.0
Receivables Turnover 36	6.4	18.6	9.0	10.9	13.5	•	•	6.2
Total Liabilities to Net Worth 37	0.9	1.7	5.9	0.8	1.1	0.7	1.4	0.9
Current Assets to Working Capital 38	9.7	2.6	255.5	1.4	1.6	1.6	2.1	13.1
Current Liabilities to Working Capital 39	8.7	1.6	254.5	0.4	0.6	0.6	1.1	12.1
Working Capital to Net Sales 40	0.0	0.1	0.0	0.2	0.2	0.2	0.2	0.0
Inventory to Working Capital 41	3.0	1.2	153.1	0.6	0.8	0.8	0.5	3.9
Total Receipts to Cash Flow 42	7.8	11.1	5.3	10.2	11.5	11.1	8.7	7.6
Cost of Goods to Cash Flow 43	5.2	7.2	3.5	7.2	8.5	7.7	6.2	5.1
Cash Flow to Total Debt 44	0.2	0.9	0.3	0.6	0.5	0.5	0.3	0.2

Selected Financial Factors (in Percentages)

Debt Ratio 45	48.1	63.6	85.5	44.9	53.4	40.7	59.2	47.9
Return on Total Assets 46	8.0	15.0	8.2	12.6	12.5	9.6	10.3	7.9
Return on Equity Before Income Taxes 47	14.8	40.5	43.0	20.9	23.1	14.8	21.8	14.6
Return on Equity After Income Taxes 48	10.0	36.9	41.7	20.2	22.3	12.7	15.3	9.8
Profit Margin (Before Income Tax) 49	8.7	2.5	4.2	4.0	3.6	3.8	5.8	9.2
Profit Margin (After Income Tax) 50	5.9	2.2	4.0	3.9	3.5	3.3	4.1	6.1

Table I

Corporations with and without Net Income

HARDWARE STORES

MONEY AMOUNTS AND SIZE OF ASSETS IN THOUSANDS OF DOLLARS

Item Description for Accounting Period 7/04 Through 6/05	Total	Zero Assets	Under 500	500 to 1,000	1,000 to 5,000	5,000 to 10,000	10,000 to 25,000	25,000 to 50,000	50,000 to 100,000	100,000 to 250,000	250,000 to 500,000	500,000 to 2,500,000	2,500,000 and over
Number of Enterprises 1	7904	948	3073	2009	1674	142	47	11	0	0	0	0	0
Revenues ($ in Thousands)													
Net Sales 2	17283904	140647	2232622	3128363	6725192	1992314	1878325	1186440	0	0	0	0	0
Interest 3	19878	3	2385	4078	10101	972	1294	1045	0	0	0	0	0
Rents 4	12028	0	5248	613	2835	28	1657	1646	0	0	0	0	0
Royalties 5	7	0	0	0	7	0	0	0	0	0	0	0	0
Other Portfolio Income 6	53777	0	27091	3097	16914	2035	4221	420	0	0	0	0	0
Other Receipts 7	160847	0	19473	30834	63640	17371	25971	3558	0	0	0	0	0
Total Receipts 8	17530441	140650	2286819	3166985	6818689	2012720	1911468	1193109	0	0	0	0	0
Average Total Receipts 9	2218	148	744	1576	4073	14174	40670	108464	•	•	•	•	•
Operating Costs/Operating Income (%)													
Cost of Operations 10	64.0	65.6	61.1	63.3	64.6	61.1	70.1	62.7	•	•	•	•	•
Salaries and Wages 11	13.3	3.4	13.0	11.6	14.0	16.5	12.0	12.7	•	•	•	•	•
Taxes Paid 12	2.4	2.4	2.6	2.6	2.4	2.3	1.7	2.0	•	•	•	•	•
Interest Paid 13	0.6	3.8	0.5	0.6	0.9	0.2	0.4	0.4	•	•	•	•	•
Depreciation 14	1.5	0.7	1.0	1.5	1.8	1.5	1.2	1.5	•	•	•	•	•
Amortization and Depletion 15	0.1	0.0	0.0	0.1	0.1	0.0	0.0	0.1	•	•	•	•	•
Pensions and Other Deferred Comp. 16	0.3	•	0.0	0.3	0.3	0.3	0.5	0.4	•	•	•	•	•
Employee Benefits 17	1.1	0.1	1.8	1.0	0.9	1.1	1.3	1.4	•	•	•	•	•
Advertising 18	1.6	0.6	1.3	2.0	1.3	1.4	1.5	3.6	•	•	•	•	•
Other Expenses 19	11.1	34.7	12.9	11.6	10.9	9.4	8.2	11.9	•	•	•	•	•
Officers' Compensation 20	3.4	•	8.3	4.7	2.5	2.8	1.0	0.6	•	•	•	•	•
Operating Margin 21	0.7	•	•	0.8	0.4	3.5	2.2	2.6	•	•	•	•	•
Operating Margin Before Officers' Comp. 22	4.0	•	5.8	5.5	2.8	6.2	3.2	3.2	•	•	•	•	•

Selected Average Balance Sheet ($ in Thousands)

Net Receivables 23	129	0	60	71	239	877	2866	2869
Inventories 24	402	0	159	307	781	1755	5733	22061
Net Property, Plant and Equipment 25	190	0	22	89	373	2316	3829	11111
Total Assets 26	949	0	289	670	1819	7269	15438	42251
Notes and Loans Payable 27	304	0	89	195	806	633	3991	9854
All Other Liabilities 28	190	0	63	124	374	1017	3665	10332
Net Worth 29	456	0	136	352	639	5619	7782	22065

Selected Financial Ratios (Times to 1)

Current Ratio 30	2.8	•	2.5	3.9	2.7	3.5	2.0	2.1
Quick Ratio 31	0.9	•	1.0	1.3	0.9	1.2	0.7	0.3
Net Sales to Working Capital 32	5.2	•	5.5	4.1	5.1	4.5	8.0	7.7
Coverage Ratio 33	4.3	•	0.9	4.5	3.0	19.6	10.1	8.2
Total Asset Turnover 34	2.3	•	2.5	2.3	2.2	1.9	2.6	2.6
Inventory Turnover 35	3.5	•	2.8	3.2	3.3	4.9	4.9	3.1
Receivables Turnover 36	17.8	•	13.7	19.0	17.5	18.4	15.0	43.1
Total Liabilities to Net Worth 37	1.1	•	1.1	0.9	1.8	0.3	1.0	0.9
Current Assets to Working Capital 38	1.6	•	1.7	1.3	1.6	1.4	2.0	1.9
Current Liabilities to Working Capital 39	0.6	•	0.7	0.3	0.6	0.4	1.0	0.9
Working Capital to Net Sales 40	0.2	•	0.2	0.2	0.2	0.2	0.1	0.1
Inventory to Working Capital 41	1.0	•	1.0	0.9	1.0	0.6	1.3	1.5
Total Receipts to Cash Flow 42	11.4	9.6	12.8	11.8	12.4	8.9	11.0	9.1
Cost of Goods to Cash Flow 43	7.3	6.3	7.8	7.5	8.0	5.4	7.7	5.7
Cash Flow to Total Debt 44	0.4	•	0.4	0.4	0.3	1.0	0.5	0.6

Selected Financial Factors (in Percentages)

Debt Ratio 45	52.0	•	52.8	47.6	64.8	22.7	49.6	47.8
Return on Total Assets 46	6.4	•	1.1	6.1	5.8	9.0	11.4	9.2
Return on Equity Before Income Taxes 47	10.1	•	•	9.1	10.9	11.1	20.4	15.5
Return on Equity After Income Taxes 48	9.1	•	•	8.8	9.2	10.7	18.8	13.8
Profit Margin (Before Income Tax) 49	2.1	•	•	2.0	1.7	4.4	4.0	3.2
Profit Margin (After Income Tax) 50	1.9	•	•	2.0	1.5	4.3	3.7	2.8

213

RETAIL TRADE 444130

Table II
Corporations with Net Income

HARDWARE STORES

MONEY AMOUNTS AND SIZE OF ASSETS IN THOUSANDS OF DOLLARS

Item Description for Accounting Period 7/04 Through 6/05	Total	Zero Assets	Under 500	500 to 1,000	1,000 to 5,000	5,000 to 10,000	10,000 to 25,000	25,000 to 50,000	50,000 to 100,000	100,000 to 250,000	250,000 to 500,000	500,000 to 2,500,000	2,500,000 and over
Number of Enterprises **1**	5071	0	1548	1480	1205	0	43	0	0	0	0	0	0
Revenues ($ in Thousands)													
Net Sales **2**	13253887	0	957645	2384259	5026164	0	1771040	0	0	0	0	0	0
Interest **3**	15118	0	1037	3096	7750	0	1218	0	0	0	0	0	0
Rents **4**	6540	0	1	587	2663	0	1615	0	0	0	0	0	0
Royalties **5**	7	0	0	0	7	0	0	0	0	0	0	0	0
Other Portfolio Income **6**	51545	0	27080	3096	15770	0	3143	0	0	0	0	0	0
Other Receipts **7**	119655	0	15888	17734	45144	0	19963	0	0	0	0	0	0
Total Receipts **8**	13446652	0	1001651	2408772	5097498	0	1796979	0	0	0	0	0	0
Average Total Receipts **9**	2652	.	647	1628	4230	.	41790	.	.	.	.	.	.
Operating Costs/Operating Income (%)													
Cost of Operations **10**	64.3	.	60.9	64.0	64.7	.	70.5	.	.	.	.	.	.
Salaries and Wages **11**	12.6	.	11.4	10.4	12.8	.	11.6	.	.	.	.	.	.
Taxes Paid **12**	2.2	.	2.2	2.2	2.3	.	1.6	.	.	.	.	.	.
Interest Paid **13**	0.5	.	0.3	0.6	0.7	.	0.4	.	.	.	.	.	.
Depreciation **14**	1.6	.	1.5	1.6	1.7	.	1.2	.	.	.	.	.	.
Amortization and Depletion **15**	0.1	.	0.0	0.0	0.1	.	0.0	.	.	.	.	.	.
Pensions and Other Deferred Comp. **16**	0.3	.	0.1	0.3	0.4	.	0.4	.	.	.	.	.	.
Employee Benefits **17**	1.0	.	1.3	1.0	0.9	.	1.2	.	.	.	.	.	.
Advertising **18**	1.6	.	1.2	2.0	1.2	.	1.5	.	.	.	.	.	.
Other Expenses **19**	10.2	.	13.7	11.5	9.9	.	7.3	.	.	.	.	.	.
Officers' Compensation **20**	2.9	.	6.8	4.1	2.8	.	1.0	.	.	.	.	.	.
Operating Margin **21**	2.6	.	0.6	2.2	2.4	.	3.2	.	.	.	.	.	.
Operating Margin Before Officers' Comp. **22**	5.5	.	7.4	6.3	5.2	.	4.2	.	.	.	.	.	.

Selected Average Balance Sheet ($ in Thousands)

Net Receivables 23	151	36	69	272	2922
Inventories 24	474	148	304	845	5554
Net Property, Plant and Equipment 25	241	13	96	365	4078
Total Assets 26	1131	245	671	1849	15712
Notes and Loans Payable 27	243	33	166	508	3481
All Other Liabilities 28	200	36	144	284	3465
Net Worth 29	687	177	361	1057	8766

Selected Financial Ratios (Times to 1)

Current Ratio 30	3.1	4.7	3.3	3.3	2.1
Quick Ratio 31	1.1	1.9	1.2	1.4	0.7
Net Sales to Working Capital 32	5.0	4.4	4.5	4.6	7.9
Coverage Ratio 33	8.6	15.9	6.4	6.3	13.2
Total Asset Turnover 34	2.3	2.5	2.4	2.3	2.6
Inventory Turnover 35	3.6	2.5	3.4	3.2	5.2
Receivables Turnover 36	17.7	15.9	21.0	15.4	15.7
Total Liabilities to Net Worth 37	0.6	0.4	0.9	0.7	0.8
Current Assets to Working Capital 38	1.5	1.3	1.4	1.4	1.9
Current Liabilities to Working Capital 39	0.5	0.3	0.4	0.4	0.9
Working Capital to Net Sales 40	0.2	0.2	0.2	0.2	0.1
Inventory to Working Capital 41	0.9	0.8	0.9	0.8	1.2
Total Receipts to Cash Flow 42	9.6	8.1	10.5	9.9	10.7
Cost of Goods to Cash Flow 43	6.2	4.9	6.7	6.4	7.5
Cash Flow to Total Debt 44	0.6	1.1	0.5	0.5	0.6

Selected Financial Factors (in Percentages)

Debt Ratio 45	39.2	28.0	46.2	42.8	44.2
Return on Total Assets 46	10.6	13.9	9.1	10.2	13.3
Return on Equity Before Income Taxes 47	15.4	18.1	14.3	15.1	22.0
Return on Equity After Income Taxes 48	14.4	16.9	13.9	13.7	20.4
Profit Margin (Before Income Tax) 49	4.1	5.2	3.2	3.8	4.7
Profit Margin (After Income Tax) 50	3.8	4.8	3.1	3.5	4.3

214

Table I

Corporations with and without Net Income

OTHER BUILDING MATERIAL DEALERS

MONEY AMOUNTS AND SIZE OF ASSETS IN THOUSANDS OF DOLLARS

Item Description for Accounting Period 7/04 Through 6/05	Total	Zero Assets	Under 500	500 to 1,000	1,000 to 5,000	5,000 to 10,000	10,000 to 25,000	25,000 to 50,000	50,000 to 100,000	100,000 to 250,000	250,000 to 500,000	500,000 to 2,500,000	2,500,000 and over
Number of Enterprises **1**	17067	6	11163	2064	3103	457	193	52	14	7	3	4	0
Revenues ($ in Thousands)													
Net Sales **2**	68181134	175385	6043779	5519944	18192498	9416592	8117077	4690820	3350473	2692501	1908852	8073214	0
Interest **3**	95551	156	2103	4421	21050	3155	6255	5476	838	2695	10618	38785	0
Rents **4**	23055	0	0	1766	5624	60	10436	4433	119	184	208	226	0
Royalties **5**	234	0	0	0	0	0	34	200	0	0	0	0	0
Other Portfolio Income **6**	86489	1325	17535	13119	16656	2533	21451	3334	1183	351	6355	2646	0
Other Receipts **7**	359871	7154	6810	50550	100144	16614	68002	30550	35502	11234	23840	9468	0
Total Receipts **8**	68746334	184020	6070227	5589800	18335972	9438954	8223255	4734813	3388115	2706965	1949873	8124339	0
Average Total Receipts **9**	4028	30670	544	2708	5909	20654	42608	91054	242008	386709	649958	2031085	•
Operating Costs/Operating Income (%)													
Cost of Operations **10**	73.8	70.9	64.6	70.0	73.0	77.2	75.6	73.8	81.1	77.0	77.1	74.7	•
Salaries and Wages **11**	8.7	9.9	7.7	8.6	8.6	8.4	9.4	9.4	7.3	9.1	9.9	9.2	•
Taxes Paid **12**	1.6	1.5	2.1	2.6	1.6	1.4	1.4	1.6	0.9	1.3	1.7	1.0	•
Interest Paid **13**	0.5	0.4	0.6	0.4	0.5	0.4	0.5	0.5	0.3	0.4	1.0	1.0	•
Depreciation **14**	1.2	0.8	2.0	0.9	0.9	1.0	1.4	1.4	0.8	1.4	1.4	1.5	•
Amortization and Depletion **15**	0.1	0.0	0.2	0.0	0.0	0.0	0.2	0.0	0.0	•	0.4	0.3	•
Pensions and Other Deferred Comp. **16**	0.3	0.2	0.1	0.6	0.4	0.2	0.3	0.4	0.3	0.2	0.2	0.2	•
Employee Benefits **17**	0.8	0.8	0.4	0.9	0.8	0.7	0.9	1.0	0.6	0.8	0.9	1.4	•
Advertising **18**	0.6	1.2	1.6	0.6	0.8	0.3	0.5	0.8	0.3	0.3	0.3	0.3	•
Other Expenses **19**	7.6	6.8	15.7	9.4	7.4	6.5	6.4	6.3	5.5	5.5	4.8	6.0	•
Officers' Compensation **20**	2.1	0.6	4.3	4.1	3.1	1.5	1.4	1.1	0.7	0.7	0.8	0.5	•
Operating Margin **21**	2.6	6.8	0.8	2.2	2.8	2.5	1.9	3.7	2.0	3.3	1.6	3.9	•
Operating Margin Before Officers' Comp. **22**	4.7	7.4	5.1	6.3	5.9	4.0	3.4	4.8	2.7	3.9	2.4	4.4	•

Selected Average Balance Sheet ($ in Thousands)

Net Receivables 23	415	0	23	206	605	2447	5250	10671	23656	48057	88172	227917
Inventories 24	405	0	49	274	707	2064	3970	8769	14927	35878	92192	174628
Net Property, Plant and Equipment 25	236	0	33	68	274	759	2971	7285	15816	36994	71910	169384
Total Assets 26	1390	0	138	712	2056	7018	15198	34134	67349	141570	364758	845040
Notes and Loans Payable 27	383	0	74	146	496	1852	4307	8620	17100	32202	132507	217976
All Other Liabilities 28	395	0	42	190	571	1733	3792	8358	21760	36868	71706	344452
Net Worth 29	612	0	22	376	990	3433	7098	17157	28489	72500	160545	282612

Selected Financial Ratios (Times to 1)

Current Ratio 30	2.1	·	1.7	3.0	2.5	2.2	1.9	2.0	1.8	2.0	2.8	1.4
Quick Ratio 31	1.1	·	0.7	1.7	1.3	1.3	1.1	1.1	1.1	1.2	1.3	0.8
Net Sales to Working Capital 32	7.5	·	13.8	6.7	6.0	6.2	8.0	7.6	11.4	8.3	4.9	13.6
Coverage Ratio 33	7.3	30.4	3.2	10.9	8.4	8.3	7.2	10.7	11.3	9.6	4.9	5.4
Total Asset Turnover 34	2.9	·	3.9	3.8	2.9	2.9	2.8	2.6	3.6	2.7	1.7	2.4
Inventory Turnover 35	7.3	·	7.1	6.8	6.1	7.7	8.0	7.6	13.0	8.3	5.3	8.6
Receivables Turnover 36	10.2	·	22.5	12.2	10.3	9.2	8.9	8.4	11.2	8.9	5.6	10.3
Total Liabilities to Net Worth 37	1.3	·	5.3	0.9	1.1	1.0	1.1	1.0	1.4	1.0	1.3	2.0
Current Assets to Working Capital 38	1.9	·	2.4	1.5	1.7	1.8	2.1	2.0	2.2	2.0	1.6	3.3
Current Liabilities to Working Capital 39	0.9	·	1.4	0.5	0.7	0.8	1.1	1.0	1.2	1.0	0.6	2.3
Working Capital to Net Sales 40	0.1	·	0.1	0.2	0.2	0.2	0.1	0.1	0.1	0.1	0.2	0.1
Inventory to Working Capital 41	0.8	·	1.4	0.6	0.7	0.7	0.8	0.8	0.8	0.7	0.8	1.4
Total Receipts to Cash Flow 42	11.5	6.2	7.7	10.3	11.6	14.0	13.0	10.8	14.0	12.6	13.9	11.4
Cost of Goods to Cash Flow 43	8.5	4.4	5.0	7.2	8.5	10.8	9.8	8.0	11.3	9.7	10.7	8.5
Cash Flow to Total Debt 44	0.4	·	0.6	0.8	0.5	0.4	0.4	0.5	0.4	0.4	0.2	0.3

Selected Financial Factors (in Percentages)

Debt Ratio 45	56.0	·	84.1	47.3	51.9	51.1	53.3	49.7	57.7	48.8	56.0	66.6
Return on Total Assets 46	11.3	·	7.0	14.4	11.5	9.2	10.3	13.5	12.3	11.6	8.2	13.3
Return on Equity Before Income Taxes 47	22.2	·	30.1	24.9	21.0	16.5	19.0	24.3	26.5	20.3	14.8	32.5
Return on Equity After Income Taxes 48	19.8	·	28.6	23.8	19.4	15.0	17.4	21.3	24.7	16.4	9.8	26.7
Profit Margin (Before Income Tax) 49	3.4	11.6	1.2	3.5	3.5	2.7	3.2	4.6	3.2	3.8	3.7	4.5
Profit Margin (After Income Tax) 50	3.0	11.2	1.2	3.3	3.3	2.5	2.9	4.1	2.9	3.1	2.5	3.7

Table II

Corporations with Net Income

OTHER BUILDING MATERIAL DEALERS

MONEY AMOUNTS AND SIZE OF ASSETS IN THOUSANDS OF DOLLARS

Item Description for Accounting Period 7/04 Through 6/05	Total	Zero Assets	Under 500	500 to 1,000	1,000 to 5,000	5,000 to 10,000	10,000 to 25,000	25,000 to 50,000	50,000 to 100,000	100,000 to 250,000	250,000 to 500,000	500,000 to 2,500,000	2,500,000 and over
Number of Enterprises 1	11146	0	5823	1981	2723	365	173	0	0	7	3	4	0
Revenues ($ in Thousands)													
Net Sales 2	60777830	0	4128895	5431258	16631551	7707198	7176450	0	0	2692501	1908852	8073214	0
Interest 3	88987	0	1645	4230	16982	2607	5438	0	0	2695	10618	38785	0
Rents 4	15502	0	0	1766	4527	24	4015	0	0	184	208	226	0
Royalties 5	233	0	0	0	0	0	33	0	0	0	0	0	0
Other Portfolio Income 6	51418	0	5316	12937	9640	2058	6274	0	0	351	6355	2646	0
Other Receipts 7	316241	0	3608	50371	91830	11608	65141	0	0	11234	23840	9468	0
Total Receipts 8	61250211	0	4139464	5500562	16754530	7723495	7257351	0	0	2706965	1949873	8124339	0
Average Total Receipts 9	5495	•	711	2777	6153	21160	41950	•	•	386709	649958	2031085	•
Operating Costs/Operating Income (%)													
Cost of Operations 10	73.5	•	66.5	69.9	72.7	76.2	74.8	•	•	77.0	77.1	74.7	
Salaries and Wages 11	8.6	•	5.1	8.5	8.5	8.4	9.5	•	•	9.1	9.9	9.2	
Taxes Paid 12	1.6	•	2.1	2.6	1.6	1.5	1.4	•	•	1.3	1.7	1.0	
Interest Paid 13	0.5	•	0.3	0.4	0.4	0.4	0.4	•	•	0.4	1.0	1.0	
Depreciation 14	1.2	•	1.8	0.9	0.9	1.0	1.4	•	•	1.4	1.4	1.5	
Amortization and Depletion 15	0.1	•	0.0	0.0	0.0	0.0	0.0	•	•	•	0.4	0.3	
Pensions and Other Deferred Comp. 16	0.3	•	0.1	0.6	0.4	0.2	0.3	•	•	0.2	0.2	0.2	
Employee Benefits 17	0.9	•	0.2	0.9	0.8	0.7	0.8	•	•	0.8	0.9	1.4	
Advertising 18	0.6	•	0.9	0.6	0.8	0.3	0.5	•	•	0.3	0.3	0.3	
Other Expenses 19	7.3	•	14.8	9.3	7.4	6.6	6.1	•	•	5.5	4.8	6.0	
Officers' Compensation 20	2.0	•	3.7	4.1	3.1	1.4	1.5	•	•	0.7	0.8	0.5	
Operating Margin 21	3.4	•	4.5	2.4	3.3	3.3	3.2	•	•	3.3	1.6	3.9	
Operating Margin Before Officers' Comp. 22	5.4	•	8.1	6.4	6.4	4.7	4.6	•	•	3.9	2.4	4.4	

Selected Average Balance Sheet ($ in Thousands)

Net Receivables 23	576	25	209	635	2491	5219	48057	88172	227917
Inventories 24	544	59	251	696	2250	4022	34086	92192	174628
Net Property, Plant and Equipment 25	318	40	69	258	783	2785	36994	71910	169384
Total Assets 26	1889	144	714	2077	6942	15143	141570	364758	845040
Notes and Loans Payable 27	491	73	152	462	1885	3856	32202	132507	217976
All Other Liabilities 28	534	34	197	586	1778	3663	36868	71706	344452
Net Worth 29	863	36	365	1029	3279	7623	72500	160545	282612

Selected Financial Ratios (Times to 1)

Current Ratio 30	2.2	2.3	2.9	2.5	2.2	2.0	2.0	2.8	1.4
Quick Ratio 31	1.2	1.0	1.6	1.4	1.2	1.2	1.2	1.3	0.8
Net Sales to Working Capital 32	7.4	12.5	7.0	5.9	6.5	7.3	8.3	4.9	13.6
Coverage Ratio 33	9.2	16.9	11.2	10.2	10.1	10.8	9.6	4.9	5.4
Total Asset Turnover 34	2.9	4.9	3.8	2.9	3.0	2.7	2.7	1.7	2.4
Inventory Turnover 35	7.4	8.1	7.6	6.4	7.2	7.7	8.7	5.3	8.6
Receivables Turnover 36	10.3	23.0	13.2	10.8	8.8	9.0		5.6	10.3
Total Liabilities to Net Worth 37	1.2	3.0	1.0	1.0	1.1	1.0	1.0	1.3	2.0
Current Assets to Working Capital 38	1.9	1.8	1.5	1.6	1.8	2.0	2.0	1.6	3.3
Current Liabilities to Working Capital 39	0.9	0.8	0.5	0.6	0.8	1.0	1.0	0.6	2.3
Working Capital to Net Sales 40	0.1	0.1	0.1	0.2	0.2	0.1	0.1	0.2	0.1
Inventory to Working Capital 41	0.8	1.0	0.6	0.7	0.8	0.8	0.7	0.8	1.4
Total Receipts to Cash Flow 42	10.7	6.1	10.2	11.0	12.5	11.5	12.6	13.9	11.4
Cost of Goods to Cash Flow 43	7.9	4.0	7.2	8.0	9.5	8.6	9.7	10.7	8.5
Cash Flow to Total Debt 44	0.5	1.1	0.8	0.5	0.5	0.5	0.4	0.2	0.3

Selected Financial Factors (in Percentages)

Debt Ratio 45	54.3	74.8	48.9	50.5	52.8	49.7	48.8	56.0	66.6
Return on Total Assets 46	13.5	24.9	15.3	13.2	11.9	12.9	11.6	8.2	13.3
Return on Equity Before Income Taxes 47	26.4	92.6	27.3	24.1	22.8	23.2	20.3	14.8	32.5
Return on Equity After Income Taxes 48	23.8	90.9	26.1	22.3	20.8	21.6	16.4	9.8	26.7
Profit Margin (Before Income Tax) 49	4.2	4.7	3.6	4.1	3.5	4.3	3.8	3.7	4.5
Profit Margin (After Income Tax) 50	3.8	4.7	3.5	3.8	3.2	4.0	3.1	2.5	3.7

Table I

Corporations with and without Net Income

LAWN AND GARDEN EQUIPMENT AND SUPPLIES STORES

MONEY AMOUNTS AND SIZE OF ASSETS IN THOUSANDS OF DOLLARS

Item Description for Accounting Period 7/04 Through 6/05	Total	Zero Assets	Under 500	500 to 1,000	1,000 to 5,000	5,000 to 10,000	10,000 to 25,000	25,000 to 50,000	50,000 to 100,000	100,000 to 250,000	250,000 to 500,000	500,000 to 2,500,000	2,500,000 and over
Number of Enterprises **1**	11360	769	8050	1508	812	180	33	5	3	0	0	0	0
Revenues ($ in Thousands)													
Net Sales **2**	14594048	1067	3234908	3137748	3810699	2487271	1179106	504338	238911	0	0	0	0
Interest **3**	11031	0	1247	890	5919	1713	996	222	44	0	0	0	0
Rents **4**	10311	0	0	609	7611	0	1226	864	0	0	0	0	0
Royalties **5**	43	0	0	0	0	0	43	0	0	0	0	0	0
Other Portfolio Income **6**	22221	4641	0	1486	8553	3458	1034	3047	3	0	0	0	0
Other Receipts **7**	60221	0	1498	3240	18658	20409	11237	854	4325	0	0	0	0
Total Receipts **8**	14697875	5708	3237653	3143973	3851440	2512851	1193642	509325	243283	0	0	0	0
Average Total Receipts **9**	1294	7	402	2085	4743	13960	36171	101865	81094	•	•	•	•
Operating Costs/Operating Income (%)													
Cost of Operations **10**	71.0	458.1	69.2	62.4	73.9	79.5	73.9	64.5	71.5	•	•	•	•
Salaries and Wages **11**	10.3	•	10.3	14.8	8.5	7.6	8.8	13.8	9.6	•	•	•	•
Taxes Paid **12**	2.2	189.6	3.4	2.5	1.9	1.2	1.4	3.1	0.7	•	•	•	•
Interest Paid **13**	0.8	46.0	0.8	0.7	0.5	1.0	0.8	2.2	1.2	•	•	•	•
Depreciation **14**	1.3	296.5	1.3	1.6	1.2	0.6	1.5	3.0	1.4	•	•	•	•
Amortization and Depletion **15**	0.1	•	0.0	0.0	0.1	0.0	0.0	0.8	0.0	•	•	•	•
Pensions and Other Deferred Comp. **16**	0.3	•	0.0	0.3	0.2	0.8	0.2	0.1	0.1	•	•	•	•
Employee Benefits **17**	0.6	•	0.1	0.6	0.6	0.8	0.6	1.5	1.8	•	•	•	•
Advertising **18**	1.1	2.4	1.1	1.1	1.2	0.6	1.1	3.6	0.1	•	•	•	•
Other Expenses **19**	9.6	702.5	12.8	9.5	7.8	6.2	10.0	17.4	11.6	•	•	•	•
Officers' Compensation **20**	3.0	2168.3	3.7	4.3	2.6	1.8	1.1	0.8	0.7	•	•	•	•
Operating Margin **21**	•	•	•	2.3	1.4	•	0.5	•	1.1	•	•	•	•
Operating Margin Before Officers' Comp. **22**	2.7	•	1.0	6.5	4.1	1.8	1.6	•	1.8	•	•	•	•

Selected Average Balance Sheet ($ in Thousands)

Net Receivables 23	65	0	14	111	187	768	2722	1397	24075
Inventories 24	235	0	52	251	1328	3733	5944	9427	26315
Net Property, Plant and Equipment 25	96	0	31	178	356	448	3424	15855	4114
Total Assets 26	507	0	111	717	2110	6307	15298	32278	90596
Notes and Loans Payable 27	231	0	88	257	623	2232	5972	18035	111991
All Other Liabilities 28	165	0	32	174	672	2081	5361	18635	54871
Net Worth 29	111	0	-9	287	816	1994	3965	-4392	-76266

Selected Financial Ratios (Times to 1)

Current Ratio 30	1.5	•	1.6	2.5	1.6	1.5	1.3	0.4	0.4
Quick Ratio 31	0.4	•	0.5	1.1	0.3	0.3	0.4	0.1	0.3
Net Sales to Working Capital 32	11.3	•	14.9	6.8	7.7	8.1	14.4	•	•
Coverage Ratio 33	1.5	•	•	4.6	5.6	2.0	3.1	•	3.4
Total Asset Turnover 34	2.5	•	3.6	2.9	2.2	2.2	2.3	3.1	0.9
Inventory Turnover 35	3.9	•	5.3	5.2	2.6	2.9	4.4	6.9	2.2
Receivables Turnover 36	19.9	•	25.8	19.7	22.3	•	11.4	64.0	3.8
Total Liabilities to Net Worth 37	3.6	•	•	1.5	1.6	2.2	2.9	•	•
Current Assets to Working Capital 38	3.2	•	2.7	1.7	2.6	2.9	4.3	•	•
Current Liabilities to Working Capital 39	2.2	•	1.7	0.7	1.6	1.9	3.3	•	•
Working Capital to Net Sales 40	0.1	•	0.1	0.1	0.1	0.1	0.1	•	•
Inventory to Working Capital 41	2.1	•	1.7	0.9	2.0	2.2	2.7	•	•
Total Receipts to Cash Flow 42	14.5	•	16.9	12.1	12.0	19.1	10.2	•	8.9
Cost of Goods to Cash Flow 43	10.3	•	11.7	7.5	8.8	15.2	7.5	•	6.4
Cash Flow to Total Debt 44	0.2	•	0.2	0.4	0.3	0.2	0.3	•	0.1

Selected Financial Factors (in Percentages)

Debt Ratio 45	78.1	•	108.1	60.0	61.4	68.4	74.1	113.6	184.2
Return on Total Assets 46	3.0	•	•	9.3	6.8	4.3	5.9	•	3.7
Return on Equity Before Income Taxes 47	4.5	•	114.2	18.1	14.4	6.9	15.4	229.8	•
Return on Equity After Income Taxes 48	3.3	•	115.8	16.8	13.6	6.8	14.0	229.8	•
Profit Margin (Before Income Tax) 49	0.4	•	•	2.5	2.5	1.0	1.7	•	3.0
Profit Margin (After Income Tax) 50	0.3	•	•	2.3	2.4	1.0	1.6	•	3.0

Table II

Corporations with Net Income

LAWN AND GARDEN EQUIPMENT AND SUPPLIES STORES

MONEY AMOUNTS AND SIZE OF ASSETS IN THOUSANDS OF DOLLARS

Item Description for Accounting Period 7/04 Through 6/05	Total	Zero Assets	Under 500	500 to 1,000	1,000 to 5,000	5,000 to 10,000	10,000 to 25,000	25,000 to 50,000	50,000 to 100,000	100,000 to 250,000	250,000 to 500,000	500,000 to 2,500,000	2,500,000 and over
Number of Enterprises 1	5142	0	3244	1015	740	0	29	0	0	0	0	0	0
Revenues ($ in Thousands)													
Net Sales 2	11087324	0	1710298	2488777	3513579	0	1008194	0	0	0	0	0	0
Interest 3	10462	0	945	887	5803	0	908	0	0	0	0	0	0
Rents 4	7213	0	0	609	5532	0	989	0	0	0	0	0	0
Royalties 5	0	0	0	0	0	0	0	0	0	0	0	0	0
Other Portfolio Income 6	16893	0	0	798	8553	0	1034	0	0	0	0	0	0
Other Receipts 7	49519	0	342	3237	18538	0	8518	0	0	0	0	0	0
Total Receipts 8	11171411	0	1711585	2494308	3552005	0	1019643	0	0	0	0	0	0
Average Total Receipts 9	2173	•	528	2457	4800	•	35160	•	•	•	•	•	•
Operating Costs/Operating Income (%)													
Cost of Operations 10	71.4	•	68.5	61.9	73.8	•	75.1	•	•	•	•	•	•
Salaries and Wages 11	9.8	•	10.4	14.1	8.6	•	8.7	•	•	•	•	•	•
Taxes Paid 12	2.0	•	3.4	2.5	2.0	•	1.4	•	•	•	•	•	•
Interest Paid 13	0.5	•	0.4	0.3	0.6	•	0.8	•	•	•	•	•	•
Depreciation 14	1.2	•	0.9	1.6	1.3	•	1.5	•	•	•	•	•	•
Amortization and Depletion 15	0.1	•	0.0	0.0	0.1	•	0.0	•	•	•	•	•	•
Pensions and Other Deferred Comp. 16	0.2	•	0.0	0.4	0.2	•	0.2	•	•	•	•	•	•
Employee Benefits 17	0.6	•	0.2	0.5	0.6	•	0.5	•	•	•	•	•	•
Advertising 18	1.0	•	1.0	1.0	1.2	•	1.2	•	•	•	•	•	•
Other Expenses 19	8.5	•	11.6	9.8	7.5	•	8.2	•	•	•	•	•	•
Officers' Compensation 20	2.5	•	1.7	3.9	2.6	•	1.1	•	•	•	•	•	•
Operating Margin 21	2.1	•	1.8	4.1	1.7	•	1.1	•	•	•	•	•	•
Operating Margin Before Officers' Comp. 22	4.6	•	3.5	8.0	4.3	•	2.2	•	•	•	•	•	•

Selected Average Balance Sheet ($ in Thousands)

Net Receivables 23	106	12	125	170	2868
Inventories 24	391	75	309	1109	5897
Net Property, Plant and Equipment 25	131	18	156	381	3372
Total Assets 26	795	108	762	2116	15522
Notes and Loans Payable 27	240	38	141	614	5914
All Other Liabilities 28	234	25	159	643	5270
Net Worth 29	322	44	462	859	4339

Selected Financial Ratios (Times to 1)

Current Ratio 30	1.8	2.8	2.9	1.6	1.4
Quick Ratio 31	0.5	0.8	1.3	0.3	0.5
Net Sales to Working Capital 32	8.2	10.3	6.5	8.0	12.1
Coverage Ratio 33	6.2	5.8	16.1	6.0	3.7
Total Asset Turnover 34	2.7	4.9	3.2	2.2	2.2
Inventory Turnover 35	3.9	4.8	4.9	3.2	4.4
Receivables Turnover 36	20.0	29.3	18.3	26.5	11.0
Total Liabilities to Net Worth 37	1.5	1.4	0.6	1.5	2.6
Current Assets to Working Capital 38	2.3	1.6	1.5	2.7	3.8
Current Liabilities to Working Capital 39	1.3	0.6	0.5	1.7	2.8
Working Capital to Net Sales 40	0.1	0.1	0.2	0.1	0.1
Inventory to Working Capital 41	1.5	1.0	0.7	2.0	2.3
Total Receipts to Cash Flow 42	11.5	10.1	9.8	11.7	11.6
Cost of Goods to Cash Flow 43	8.2	6.9	6.1	8.7	8.7
Cash Flow to Total Debt 44	0.4	0.8	0.8	0.3	0.3

Selected Financial Factors (in Percentages)

Debt Ratio 45	59.6	58.7	39.4	59.4	72.0
Return on Total Assets 46	9.1	11.0	14.9	7.5	6.9
Return on Equity Before Income Taxes 47	19.0	22.0	23.1	15.4	17.9
Return on Equity After Income Taxes 48	18.1	21.2	21.8	14.5	16.5
Profit Margin (Before Income Tax) 49	2.8	1.9	4.3	2.8	2.2
Profit Margin (After Income Tax) 50	2.7	1.8	4.1	2.6	2.1

Table I

Corporations with and without Net Income

FOOD AND BEVERAGE STORES

MONEY AMOUNTS AND SIZE OF ASSETS IN THOUSANDS OF DOLLARS

Item Description for Accounting Period 7/04 Through 6/05	Total	Zero Assets	Under 500	500 to 1,000	1,000 to 5,000	5,000 to 10,000	10,000 to 25,000	25,000 to 50,000	50,000 to 100,000	100,000 to 250,000	250,000 to 500,000	500,000 to 2,500,000	2,500,000 and over
Number of Enterprises 1	80565	7919	62648	4999	4108	502	196	74	47	29	12	22	8
Revenues ($ in Thousands)													
Net Sales 2	468847507	1331413	38523421	13981563	39007466	16747563	13740682	10558468	12443540	14065356	9532356	81772349	217143330
Interest 3	574927	300	9783	5459	11939	4487	6848	5672	4670	10196	1827	85456	428289
Rents 4	854218	63	3307	3716	36337	14528	18980	18875	11569	15521	19477	148974	562871
Royalties 5	1222656	0	0	0	0	0	18	0	72	23990	155217	1023993	
Other Portfolio Income 6	734208	31194	79040	20132	21989	7757	24045	71420	12144	7584	28653	218572	211673
Other Receipts 7	5646972	71428	506939	178401	265483	215372	166568	83343	154461	137722	213276	854021	2799964
Total Receipts 8	477880488	1434398	39122490	14189271	39343214	16989707	13957141	10737778	12626456	14260369	9814955	83234589	222170120
Average Total Receipts 9	5932	181	624	2838	9577	33844	71210	145105	268648	491737	817913	3783390	27771265
Operating Costs/Operating Income (%)													
Cost of Operations 10	73.9	74.1	73.2	73.3	75.5	77.6	76.1	75.1	73.3	74.5	72.5	73.8	73.5
Salaries and Wages 11	10.0	7.2	7.5	9.3	8.4	8.7	10.0	9.3	10.7	10.8	12.3	10.9	10.4
Taxes Paid 12	1.7	2.0	2.2	1.6	1.6	1.6	1.5	1.6	2.3	1.7	1.5	1.8	1.6
Interest Paid 13	0.9	0.2	0.4	0.7	0.4	0.5	0.4	0.5	0.4	0.6	0.6	0.8	1.2
Depreciation 14	2.0	0.9	1.2	1.5	1.4	1.3	1.4	1.7	2.0	1.7	2.2	2.0	2.3
Amortization and Depletion 15	0.1	0.1	0.2	0.1	0.1	0.1	0.1	0.1	0.1	0.1	0.2	0.1	0.1
Pensions and Other Deferred Comp. 16	0.4	0.1	0.1	0.1	0.1	0.1	0.2	0.2	0.3	0.4	0.4	0.3	0.7
Employee Benefits 17	1.4	0.4	0.3	0.5	1.0	0.7	1.1	1.4	1.2	1.5	1.4	1.6	1.8
Advertising 18	0.8	1.0	0.7	1.0	1.0	1.1	0.8	0.8	1.0	0.9	0.8	0.8	0.6
Other Expenses 19	8.9	18.1	13.0	10.4	8.5	8.0	8.3	9.6	8.5	7.4	8.6	8.5	8.5
Officers' Compensation 20	0.6	2.6	2.9	2.3	1.3	0.6	0.7	0.6	0.5	0.4	0.2	0.1	0.1
Operating Margin 21	•	•	•	•	0.8	•	•	•	•	0.0	•	•	•
Operating Margin Before Officers' Comp. 22	•	1.3	•	1.4	2.1	0.2	0.2	•	0.2	0.4	•	•	•

Selected Average Balance Sheet ($ in Thousands)

Net Receivables 23	129	0	5	38	138	826	1171	2447	4193	7180	17659	59965	823284
Inventories 24	333	0	33	122	400	1278	3446	6640	11479	22072	52225	196160	1816270
Net Property, Plant and Equipment 25	900	0	34	237	769	3128	5812	14551	31959	65043	137908	630381	5423432
Total Assets 26	2208	0	113	676	2108	7543	15931	35944	71112	150820	370481	1250016	13695764
Notes and Loans Payable 27	710	0	86	339	842	3463	5663	12480	22487	41160	79271	405170	3848302
All Other Liabilities 28	1018	0	14	193	436	2115	4829	12497	21183	41321	156175	444864	7694648
Net Worth 29	481	0	13	144	831	1965	5439	10968	27442	68340	135035	399982	2152814

Selected Financial Ratios (Times to 1)

Current Ratio 30	1.1	•	2.6	1.4	1.9	1.4	1.4	1.2	1.1	1.2	1.1	1.4	0.9
Quick Ratio 31	0.4	•	0.9	0.7	0.8	0.6	0.6	0.5	0.5	0.5	0.4	0.5	0.3
Net Sales to Working Capital 32	133.5	•	17.6	40.6	19.4	34.8	34.7	63.2	205.2	56.1	67.9	33.7	•
Coverage Ratio 33	2.4	6.1	1.0	1.9	5.1	3.1	3.9	2.7	3.7	3.5	4.4	2.3	2.1
Total Asset Turnover 34	2.6	•	5.5	4.1	4.5	4.4	4.4	4.0	3.7	3.2	2.1	3.0	2.0
Inventory Turnover 35	12.9	•	13.6	16.8	17.9	20.3	15.5	16.1	16.9	16.4	11.0	14.0	11.0
Receivables Turnover 36	47.5	•	148.5	81.7	71.1	59.5	62.1	60.4	69.2	72.2	39.7	67.7	34.0
Total Liabilities to Net Worth 37	3.6	•	7.8	3.7	1.5	2.8	1.9	2.3	1.6	1.2	1.7	2.1	5.4
Current Assets to Working Capital 38	16.5	•	1.6	3.5	2.1	3.6	3.8	6.8	18.3	5.4	7.9	3.8	•
Current Liabilities to Working Capital 39	15.5	•	0.6	2.5	1.1	2.6	2.8	5.8	17.3	4.4	6.9	2.8	•
Working Capital to Net Sales 40	0.0	•	0.1	0.0	0.1	0.0	0.0	0.0	0.0	0.0	0.0	0.0	•
Inventory to Working Capital 41	7.7	•	1.0	1.6	0.9	1.4	1.7	3.1	8.0	2.6	4.3	2.0	•
Total Receipts to Cash Flow 42	14.1	8.0	13.0	12.9	13.3	14.9	15.4	14.8	16.0	17.6	14.0	15.4	13.7
Cost of Goods to Cash Flow 43	10.4	5.9	9.5	9.5	10.1	11.6	11.8	11.1	11.7	13.1	10.1	11.3	10.1
Cash Flow to Total Debt 44	0.2	•	0.5	0.4	0.6	0.4	0.4	0.4	0.4	0.3	0.2	0.3	0.2

Selected Financial Factors (in Percentages)

Debt Ratio 45	78.2	•	88.7	78.7	60.6	73.9	65.9	69.5	61.4	54.7	63.6	68.0	84.3
Return on Total Assets 46	5.4	•	2.2	5.4	9.4	7.0	6.3	5.3	6.0	6.3	6.0	5.5	5.1
Return on Equity Before Income Taxes 47	14.3	•	0.4	11.9	19.3	18.1	13.7	10.9	11.4	10.0	12.8	9.9	17.2
Return on Equity After Income Taxes 48	10.1	•	•	10.4	18.3	15.5	12.0	9.2	9.8	8.0	11.2	5.9	10.9
Profit Margin (Before Income Tax) 49	1.2	0.9	0.0	0.6	1.7	1.1	1.1	0.8	1.2	1.4	2.2	1.1	1.4
Profit Margin (After Income Tax) 50	0.8	0.9	•	0.5	1.6	0.9	0.9	0.7	1.0	1.1	1.9	0.6	0.9

Table II

Corporations with Net Income

FOOD AND BEVERAGE STORES

MONEY AMOUNTS AND SIZE OF ASSETS IN THOUSANDS OF DOLLARS

Item Description for Accounting Period 7/04 Through 6/05	Total	Zero Assets	Under 500	500 to 1,000	1,000 to 5,000	5,000 to 10,000	10,000 to 25,000	25,000 to 50,000	50,000 to 100,000	100,000 to 250,000	250,000 to 500,000	500,000 to 2,500,000	2,500,000 and over
Number of Enterprises 1	40299	3060	30911	3048	2626	371	144	0	30	23	8	19	0
Revenues ($ in Thousands)													
Net Sales 2	337432769	933797	22804056	9737443	28609111	10578367	10993254	0	8663465	11162425	6793421	53781884	0
Interest 3	438077	280	7605	4056	9761	3809	5457	0	2394	9150	730	82616	0
Rents 4	542089	63	1904	277	32931	9485	15644	0	8614	12959	8269	100847	0
Royalties 5	1174612	0	0	0	0	0	18	0	50	0	19366	154717	0
Other Portfolio Income 6	433635	19892	68278	18700	17323	3313	23348	0	8658	7339	28456	23398	0
Other Receipts 7	4041890	49308	323592	126171	189346	55107	131742	0	93499	103160	195956	624571	0
Total Receipts 8	344063072	1003340	23205435	9886647	28858472	10665081	11169463	0	8776680	11295033	7046198	54768033	0
Average Total Receipts 9	8538	328	751	3244	10990	28706	77566	•	292556	491088	880775	2882528	•
Operating Costs/Operating Income (%)													
Cost of Operations 10	73.0	76.9	73.1	72.3	75.8	72.6	76.8	•	73.1	74.2	73.5	71.9	•
Salaries and Wages 11	10.1	7.9	7.2	9.1	8.2	10.0	9.5	•	10.4	10.6	12.4	11.2	•
Taxes Paid 12	1.8	1.7	2.3	1.5	1.3	2.0	1.4	•	1.9	1.6	1.3	2.2	•
Interest Paid 13	0.8	0.1	0.4	0.5	0.3	0.5	0.3	•	0.4	0.3	0.5	0.9	•
Depreciation 14	2.1	0.6	0.9	1.5	1.0	1.1	1.2	•	1.8	1.7	2.3	2.3	•
Amortization and Depletion 15	0.1	0.0	0.2	0.1	0.1	0.1	0.0	•	0.1	0.1	0.0	0.2	•
Pensions and Other Deferred Comp. 16	0.5	0.2	0.1	0.1	0.1	0.1	0.2	•	0.3	0.5	0.4	0.5	•
Employee Benefits 17	1.5	0.6	0.3	0.4	0.7	0.7	1.0	•	1.2	1.5	0.9	1.9	•
Advertising 18	0.8	1.1	0.7	1.0	1.1	1.5	0.7	•	1.0	0.9	0.8	0.8	•
Other Expenses 19	8.5	10.4	11.3	10.5	8.1	8.3	7.7	•	8.4	7.2	7.9	7.3	•
Officers' Compensation 20	0.5	1.8	2.4	2.0	1.0	1.0	0.7	•	0.6	0.4	0.2	0.2	•
Operating Margin 21	0.4	•	1.1	0.9	2.1	2.2	0.5	•	0.8	1.0	•	0.8	•
Operating Margin Before Officers' Comp. 22	0.8	0.5	3.5	2.9	3.2	3.1	1.2	•	1.4	1.4	•	0.9	•

Selected Average Balance Sheet ($ in Thousands)

Net Receivables 23	181	0	6	34	106	978	1193	3402	6517	23828	50629
Inventories 24	507	0	41	142	416	1416	3514	13177	20409	62017	172256
Net Property, Plant and Equipment 25	1442	0	34	219	597	2588	5383	32678	66788	145352	604180
Total Assets 26	3248	0	131	670	2074	7326	16085	73545	151397	377819	1162829
Notes and Loans Payable 27	1085	0	74	278	532	2399	3936	20096	27571	73993	376097
All Other Liabilities 28	1193	0	16	125	476	2030	4642	22142	39823	155401	349110
Net Worth 29	970	0	41	268	1066	2897	7506	31307	84003	148425	437621

Selected Financial Ratios (Times to 1)

Current Ratio 30	0.9	•	2.9	2.0	2.0	1.5	1.5	1.2	1.3	1.3	1.3
Quick Ratio 31	0.4	•	1.0	0.9	0.9	0.8	0.7	0.5	0.6	0.5	0.5
Net Sales to Working Capital 32	•	53.2	15.6	20.6	19.0	23.7	26.6	82.2	46.4	37.2	37.5
Coverage Ratio 33	3.9	•	8.7	6.0	10.2	7.2	8.3	6.3	7.8	8.2	3.9
Total Asset Turnover 34	2.6	•	5.6	4.8	5.3	3.9	4.7	3.9	3.2	2.2	2.4
Inventory Turnover 35	12.1	•	13.2	16.2	19.9	14.6	16.7	16.0	17.6	10.1	11.8
Receivables Turnover 36	48.4	•	140.3	116.7	82.3	41.7	69.2	77.4	81.5	31.1	•
Total Liabilities to Net Worth 37	2.3	•	2.2	1.5	0.9	1.5	1.1	1.3	0.8	1.5	1.7
Current Assets to Working Capital 38	•	•	1.5	2.0	2.0	3.1	2.8	7.1	4.4	4.7	4.8
Current Liabilities to Working Capital 39	•	•	0.5	1.0	1.0	2.1	1.8	6.1	3.4	3.7	3.8
Working Capital to Net Sales 40	•	•	0.1	0.0	0.1	0.0	0.0	0.0	0.0	0.0	0.0
Inventory to Working Capital 41	•	•	0.9	0.9	0.8	1.0	1.3	3.1	2.0	2.4	2.3
Total Receipts to Cash Flow 42	12.4	8.7	10.2	10.7	11.7	11.0	14.0	13.9	15.1	12.7	13.4
Cost of Goods to Cash Flow 43	9.1	6.7	7.5	7.7	8.9	8.0	10.7	10.1	11.2	9.3	9.6
Cash Flow to Total Debt 44	0.3	•	0.8	0.7	0.9	0.6	0.6	0.5	0.5	0.3	0.3

Selected Financial Factors (in Percentages)

Debt Ratio 45	70.1	•	68.9	60.0	48.6	60.5	53.3	57.4	44.5	60.7	62.4
Return on Total Assets 46	7.9	•	18.1	14.1	17.6	12.9	11.4	9.9	8.0	8.9	8.5
Return on Equity Before Income Taxes 47	19.7	•	51.7	29.3	30.8	28.0	21.5	19.6	12.6	20.0	16.7
Return on Equity After Income Taxes 48	15.6	•	50.4	28.0	29.7	26.1	19.8	17.4	10.6	17.8	12.5
Profit Margin (Before Income Tax) 49	2.3	6.2	2.8	2.5	3.0	2.9	2.1	2.1	2.2	3.5	2.6
Profit Margin (After Income Tax) 50	1.8	6.1	2.8	2.3	2.9	2.7	1.9	1.9	1.8	3.1	1.9

Table I

Corporations with and without Net Income

BEER, WINE, AND LIQUOR STORES

MONEY AMOUNTS AND SIZE OF ASSETS IN THOUSANDS OF DOLLARS

Item Description for Accounting Period 7/04 Through 6/05		Total	Zero Assets	Under 500	500 to 1,000	1,000 to 5,000	5,000 to 10,000	10,000 to 25,000	25,000 to 50,000	50,000 to 100,000	100,000 to 250,000	250,000 to 500,000	500,000 to 2,500,000	2,500,000 and over
Number of Enterprises	1	15173	622	12613	1310	521	83	17	4	3	0	0	0	0
Revenues ($ in Thousands)														
Net Sales	2	17514679	53016	9659672	1745299	2483815	1669756	675240	441139	786743	0	0	0	0
Interest	3	4744	0	545	2388	1223	1	123	182	282	0	0	0	0
Rents	4	3487	0	0	74	2223	0	682	0	508	0	0	0	0
Royalties	5	0	0	0	0	0	0	0	0	0	0	0	0	0
Other Portfolio Income	6	31045	0	2070	9364	14431	693	3423	45	1016	0	0	0	0
Other Receipts	7	255989	113	141629	45482	56893	3860	2558	1424	4032	0	0	0	0
Total Receipts	8	17809944	53129	9803916	1802607	2558585	1674310	682026	442790	792581	0	0	0	0
Average Total Receipts	9	1174	85	777	1376	4911	20172	40119	110698	264194	•	•	•	•
Operating Costs/Operating Income (%)														
Cost of Operations	10	79.3	90.9	78.7	80.8	80.2	81.8	78.7	76.0	77.2	•	•	•	•
Salaries and Wages	11	5.6	•	5.3	4.5	5.7	6.2	7.9	8.9	7.0	•	•	•	•
Taxes Paid	12	2.0	5.7	2.2	2.2	2.5	0.6	1.3	1.5	1.2	•	•	•	•
Interest Paid	13	0.6	0.5	0.6	1.6	0.4	0.2	0.6	0.7	0.2	•	•	•	•
Depreciation	14	0.9	2.2	0.8	1.2	0.3	0.9	0.9	1.5	1.5	•	•	•	•
Amortization and Depletion	15	0.3	•	0.2	0.7	0.2	0.0	0.4	0.1	0.1	•	•	•	•
Pensions and Other Deferred Comp.	16	0.1	•	0.0	0.0	0.2	0.5	0.1	0.1	0.1	•	•	•	•
Employee Benefits	17	0.4	•	0.4	0.1	0.4	0.7	0.6	0.5	1.1	•	•	•	•
Advertising	18	0.6	•	0.4	0.3	0.9	0.2	1.9	1.7	1.0	•	•	•	•
Other Expenses	19	7.8	17.9	8.3	8.1	8.5	3.5	6.6	7.2	9.2	•	•	•	•
Officers' Compensation	20	2.7	•	3.4	4.0	1.8	1.1	1.5	1.4	0.4	•	•	•	•
Operating Margin	21	•	•	•	•	•	4.0	•	0.3	1.0	•	•	•	•
Operating Margin Before Officers' Comp.	22	2.4	•	3.0	0.6	0.7	5.1	1.2	1.7	1.4	•	•	•	•

Selected Average Balance Sheet ($ in Thousands)

Net Receivables 23	21	0	1	0	114	2718	513	1546	3581
Inventories 24	152	0	90	237	822	1853	6939	27884	32198
Net Property, Plant and Equipment 25	60	0	33	128	154	1036	2638	7496	31346
Total Assets 26	355	0	193	641	1634	6708	15521	35950	97612
Notes and Loans Payable 27	172	0	104	453	649	2281	3446	14242	21444
All Other Liabilities 28	78	0	33	66	549	1957	6001	11086	26817
Net Worth 29	105	0	56	122	436	2470	6075	10622	49351

Selected Financial Ratios (Times to 1)

Current Ratio 30	2.2	•	2.7	2.3	1.9	1.8	1.7	1.9	1.6
Quick Ratio 31	0.7	•	0.8	0.7	0.5	1.1	0.4	0.4	0.2
Net Sales to Working Capital 32	9.3	•	9.5	8.3	8.2	8.8	9.6	9.8	17.8
Coverage Ratio 33	3.1	•	2.8	0.9	5.2	23.9	2.2	2.0	11.6
Total Asset Turnover 34	3.3	•	4.0	2.1	2.9	3.0	2.6	3.1	2.7
Inventory Turnover 35	6.0	•	6.7	4.5	4.6	8.9	4.5	3.0	6.3
Receivables Turnover 36	64.4	•	274.2	324.8	59.6	10.2	79.8	37.6	•
Total Liabilities to Net Worth 37	2.4	•	2.4	4.2	2.7	1.7	1.6	2.4	1.0
Current Assets to Working Capital 38	1.8	•	1.6	1.8	2.1	2.2	2.5	2.1	2.7
Current Liabilities to Working Capital 39	0.8	•	0.6	0.8	1.1	1.2	1.5	1.1	1.7
Working Capital to Net Sales 40	0.1	•	0.1	0.1	0.1	0.1	0.1	0.1	0.1
Inventory to Working Capital 41	1.2	•	1.1	1.1	1.4	0.9	1.7	1.7	2.2
Total Receipts to Cash Flow 42	16.8	319.4	16.5	25.4	14.3	14.2	25.9	23.2	15.8
Cost of Goods to Cash Flow 43	13.3	290.4	13.0	20.5	11.4	11.6	20.3	17.7	12.2
Cash Flow to Total Debt 44	0.3	•	0.3	0.1	0.3	0.3	0.2	0.2	0.3

Selected Financial Factors (in Percentages)

Debt Ratio 45	70.4	•	70.9	80.9	73.3	63.2	60.9	70.5	49.4
Return on Total Assets 46	6.4	•	6.8	3.2	6.8	13.5	3.3	4.3	5.1
Return on Equity Before Income Taxes 47	14.7	•	15.0	•	20.5	35.1	4.6	7.4	9.2
Return on Equity After Income Taxes 48	12.9	•	14.5	•	14.9	34.7	3.8	6.0	5.8
Profit Margin (Before Income Tax) 49	1.3	•	1.1	•	1.9	4.3	0.7	0.7	1.7
Profit Margin (After Income Tax) 50	1.2	•	1.1	•	1.4	4.3	0.6	0.6	1.1

Table II
Corporations with Net Income

BEER, WINE, AND LIQUOR STORES

MONEY AMOUNTS AND SIZE OF ASSETS IN THOUSANDS OF DOLLARS

Item Description for Accounting Period 7/04 Through 6/05	Total	Zero Assets	Under 500	500 to 1,000	1,000 to 5,000	5,000 to 10,000	10,000 to 25,000	25,000 to 50,000	50,000 to 100,000	100,000 to 250,000	250,000 to 500,000	500,000 to 2,500,000	2,500,000 and over
Number of Enterprises **1**	11011	378	9513	696	324	0	11	0	0	0	0	0	0
Revenues ($ in Thousands)													
Net Sales **2**	13671252	30989	7633313	1115359	1768671	0	478527	0	0	0	0	0	0
Interest **3**	2628	0	541	345	1223	0	55	0	0	0	0	0	0
Rents **4**	3408	0	0	0	2217	0	682	0	0	0	0	0	0
Royalties **5**	0	0	0	0	0	0	0	0	0	0	0	0	0
Other Portfolio Income **6**	31008	0	2070	9364	14410	0	3408	0	0	0	0	0	0
Other Receipts **7**	210806	113	123944	19925	55928	0	1803	0	0	0	0	0	0
Total Receipts **8**	13919102	31102	7759868	1144993	1842449	0	484475	0	0	0	0	0	0
Average Total Receipts **9**	1264	82	816	1645	5687	•	44043	•	•	•	•	•	•
Operating Costs/Operating Income (%)													
Cost of Operations **10**	78.9	78.6	78.4	79.6	79.4	•	78.3	•	•	•	•	•	•
Salaries and Wages **11**	5.6	•	5.3	3.6	6.5	•	7.0	•	•	•	•	•	•
Taxes Paid **12**	1.4	0.6	1.6	1.8	1.4	•	1.3	•	•	•	•	•	•
Interest Paid **13**	0.4	0.8	0.4	0.8	0.4	•	0.4	•	•	•	•	•	•
Depreciation **14**	0.7	3.5	0.5	0.8	0.4	•	0.9	•	•	•	•	•	•
Amortization and Depletion **15**	0.2	•	0.2	0.5	0.2	•	0.2	•	•	•	•	•	•
Pensions and Other Deferred Comp. **16**	0.1	•	0.0	0.0	0.2	•	0.1	•	•	•	•	•	•
Employee Benefits **17**	0.4	•	0.4	0.0	0.5	•	0.5	•	•	•	•	•	•
Advertising **18**	0.5	•	0.4	0.2	0.9	•	1.2	•	•	•	•	•	•
Other Expenses **19**	7.4	12.2	7.7	8.4	8.9	•	6.4	•	•	•	•	•	•
Officers' Compensation **20**	3.0	•	3.9	4.2	2.3	•	1.6	•	•	•	•	•	•
Operating Margin **21**	1.2	4.3	1.2	0.0	•	•	2.2	•	•	•	•	•	•
Operating Margin Before Officers' Comp. **22**	4.2	4.3	5.1	4.2	1.2	•	3.8	•	•	•	•	•	•

Selected Average Balance Sheet ($ in Thousands)

Net Receivables 23	27	0	1	0	142	362
Inventories 24	150	0	78	338	977	7913
Net Property, Plant and Equipment 25	52	0	25	37	219	2603
Total Assets 26	363	0	201	640	1769	14873
Notes and Loans Payable 27	139	0	81	367	637	2119
All Other Liabilities 28	80	0	35	65	537	5728
Net Worth 29	144	0	85	209	594	7027

Selected Financial Ratios (Times to 1)

Current Ratio 30	2.5	•	3.2	3.6	2.2	1.8
Quick Ratio 31	0.9	•	1.1	1.0	0.7	0.3
Net Sales to Working Capital 32	8.6	•	8.6	6.3	7.2	10.1
Coverage Ratio 33	9.0	6.9	8.8	4.4	8.7	9.6
Total Asset Turnover 34	3.4	•	4.0	2.5	3.1	2.9
Inventory Turnover 35	6.5	•	8.1	3.8	4.4	4.3
Receivables Turnover 36	60.9	•	1690.1	208.1	51.0	100.7
Total Liabilities to Net Worth 37	1.5	•	1.4	2.1	2.0	1.1
Current Assets to Working Capital 38	1.7	•	1.5	1.4	1.8	2.3
Current Liabilities to Working Capital 39	0.7	•	0.5	0.4	0.8	1.3
Working Capital to Net Sales 40	0.1	•	0.1	0.2	0.1	0.1
Inventory to Working Capital 41	1.0	•	0.9	0.8	1.0	1.6
Total Receipts to Cash Flow 42	13.7	5.9	13.3	15.9	12.6	15.9
Cost of Goods to Cash Flow 43	10.8	4.7	10.4	12.7	10.0	12.5
Cash Flow to Total Debt 44	0.4	•	0.5	0.2	0.4	0.3

Selected Financial Factors (in Percentages)

Debt Ratio 45	60.3	•	57.8	67.4	66.4	52.8
Return on Total Assets 46	11.7	•	13.1	8.6	10.7	11.1
Return on Equity Before Income Taxes 47	26.1	•	27.4	20.5	28.3	21.1
Return on Equity After Income Taxes 48	24.3	•	27.0	16.5	21.7	20.0
Profit Margin (Before Income Tax) 49	3.0	4.7	2.9	2.7	3.1	3.4
Profit Margin (After Income Tax) 50	2.8	4.7	2.9	2.1	2.4	3.2

Table I

Corporations with and without Net Income

HEALTH AND PERSONAL CARE STORES

MONEY AMOUNTS AND SIZE OF ASSETS IN THOUSANDS OF DOLLARS

Item Description for Accounting Period 7/04 Through 6/05	Total	Zero Assets	Under 500	500 to 1,000	1,000 to 5,000	5,000 to 10,000	10,000 to 25,000	25,000 to 50,000	50,000 to 100,000	100,000 to 250,000	250,000 to 500,000	500,000 to 2,500,000	2,500,000 and over
Number of Enterprises 1	37337	3169	27337	4760	1844	102	61	21	14	12	7	3	7
Revenues ($ in Thousands)													
Net Sales 2	224693443	1526178	22984580	17882415	11495630	2315816	2468617	1568173	2589609	5423408	2913390	6824133	146701495
Interest 3	281399	5795	1350	3943	9694	227	1722	1585	764	3658	1676	42875	208108
Rents 4	115631	11782	2206	4332	4331	3149	440	2	1140	571	1372	3435	82870
Royalties 5	164437	49640	0	0	0	6807	0	0	0	0	2830	97651	7509
Other Portfolio Income 6	119716	5790	29676	6802	2641	929	5989	572	449	2514	1028	1178	62148
Other Receipts 7	1601074	89484	39452	45277	44288	22775	36392	16017	19933	109054	4279	80619	1093507
Total Receipts 8	226975700	1688669	23057264	17942769	11556584	2349703	2513160	1586349	2611895	5539205	2924575	7049891	148155637
Average Total Receipts 9	6079	533	843	3769	6267	23036	41199	75540	186564	461600	417796	2349964	21165091
Operating Costs/Operating Income (%)													
Cost of Operations 10	75.8	45.1	69.3	76.2	72.1	65.0	69.8	57.2	65.0	69.5	62.1	62.4	79.1
Salaries and Wages 11	9.1	20.7	7.5	6.9	10.9	10.7	11.2	15.1	13.8	12.8	9.1	16.3	8.7
Taxes Paid 12	1.2	4.1	1.7	1.4	1.4	1.5	1.5	1.9	1.5	1.8	1.8	2.3	0.9
Interest Paid 13	0.6	1.6	0.3	0.2	0.4	0.6	0.5	0.9	1.0	1.3	1.9	1.0	0.6
Depreciation 14	1.0	1.3	0.7	0.5	0.8	1.2	0.8	1.9	1.2	1.2	2.6	1.9	1.1
Amortization and Depletion 15	0.2	0.7	0.1	0.1	0.1	0.2	0.2	0.2	0.3	0.4	0.5	0.7	0.3
Pensions and Other Deferred Comp. 16	0.2	0.1	0.2	0.5	0.3	0.3	0.2	0.1	0.2	0.2	0.1	0.3	0.2
Employee Benefits 17	0.6	0.1	0.4	0.3	0.5	0.5	0.8	0.8	1.0	1.3	0.8	1.3	0.6
Advertising 18	1.0	6.4	1.2	0.4	1.1	3.8	2.2	7.1	1.2	1.3	1.4	1.1	0.8
Other Expenses 19	7.5	30.4	10.4	5.9	8.4	9.1	10.3	13.5	9.1	11.8	17.4	14.1	6.1
Officers' Compensation 20	1.3	2.2	5.3	5.4	3.0	1.2	1.6	1.1	1.0	0.3	1.3	0.4	0.1
Operating Margin 21	1.5	•	2.9	2.3	1.1	5.8	0.9	0.2	4.6	•	1.0	•	1.6
Operating Margin Before Officers' Comp. 22	2.8	•	8.2	7.7	4.1	7.0	2.5	1.3	5.7	•	2.3	•	1.6

Selected Average Balance Sheet ($ in Thousands)

Net Receivables 23	281	0	16	90	306	1685	3693	6604	13036	23284	36255	172990	1042062
Inventories 24	511	0	58	212	435	1863	3637	9418	19300	55528	49094	316141	1835884
Net Property, Plant and Equipment 25	434	0	22	104	175	1200	1838	7128	14595	26177	64787	418537	1736230
Total Assets 26	2222	0	153	713	1741	6646	15204	35418	73048	149754	338171	1326189	8667429
Notes and Loans Payable 27	523	0	71	206	411	2559	4284	13670	28217	82633	100289	318200	1713582
All Other Liabilities 28	645	0	42	177	475	2192	10085	11674	24771	41829	123372	304732	2500575
Net Worth 29	1054	0	40	329	855	1896	836	10075	20060	25293	114510	703257	4453272

Selected Financial Ratios (Times to 1)

Current Ratio 30	1.5	.	2.4	2.6	2.5	2.0	0.9	1.3	1.9	1.7	1.0	1.9	1.4
Quick Ratio 31	0.6	.	1.1	1.3	1.3	1.4	0.5	0.6	0.7	0.6	0.4	0.7	0.5
Net Sales to Working Capital 32	15.9	.	12.9	12.5	8.1	9.7	.	17.4	8.7	12.4	78.6	7.0	19.6
Coverage Ratio 33	5.3	.	11.1	14.1	5.1	13.8	6.6	2.5	6.7	1.2	1.7	2.3	5.3
Total Asset Turnover 34	2.7	.	5.5	5.3	3.6	3.4	2.7	2.1	2.5	3.0	1.2	1.7	2.4
Inventory Turnover 35	8.9	.	10.1	13.5	10.3	7.9	7.8	4.5	6.2	5.7	5.3	4.5	9.0
Receivables Turnover 36	24.7	.	49.9	49.3	21.0	9.6	11.5	9.0	14.3	17.1	21.9	16.7	24.2
Total Liabilities to Net Worth 37	1.1	.	2.8	1.2	1.0	2.5	17.2	2.5	2.6	4.9	2.0	0.9	0.9
Current Assets to Working Capital 38	2.9	.	1.7	1.6	1.7	2.0	.	4.7	2.2	2.3	22.9	2.1	3.6
Current Liabilities to Working Capital 39	1.9	.	0.7	0.6	0.7	1.0	.	3.7	1.2	1.3	21.9	1.1	2.6
Working Capital to Net Sales 40	0.1	.	0.1	0.1	0.1	0.1	0.1	0.1	0.1	0.1	0.0	0.1	0.1
Inventory to Working Capital 41	1.5	.	0.9	0.8	0.6	0.5	.	2.0	0.8	1.3	13.4	0.7	2.0
Total Receipts to Cash Flow 42	14.3	6.0	10.0	15.5	13.6	7.0	9.5	9.2	8.6	12.6	8.6	9.4	16.9
Cost of Goods to Cash Flow 43	10.8	2.7	6.9	11.8	9.8	4.6	6.6	5.3	5.6	8.7	5.3	5.8	13.4
Cash Flow to Total Debt 44	0.4	.	0.7	0.6	0.5	0.7	0.3	0.3	0.4	0.3	0.2	0.4	0.3

Selected Financial Factors (in Percentages)

Debt Ratio 45	52.6	.	73.8	53.9	50.9	71.5	94.5	71.6	72.5	83.1	66.1	47.0	48.6
Return on Total Assets 46	8.4	.	19.2	15.1	7.3	26.7	8.6	4.8	16.2	4.8	4.0	4.0	7.7
Return on Equity Before Income Taxes 47	14.4	.	66.7	30.5	12.0	86.8	132.5	10.1	50.3	4.3	4.8	4.2	12.1
Return on Equity After Income Taxes 48	10.9	.	64.8	29.7	10.7	85.1	118.0	8.5	45.6	.	4.0	3.6	8.0
Profit Margin (Before Income Tax) 49	2.5	.	3.2	2.7	1.6	7.3	2.7	1.4	5.5	0.2	1.3	1.3	2.6
Profit Margin (After Income Tax) 50	1.9	.	3.1	2.6	1.5	7.1	2.4	1.1	4.9	.	1.1	1.1	1.7

Table II

Corporations with Net Income

HEALTH AND PERSONAL CARE STORES

MONEY AMOUNTS AND SIZE OF ASSETS IN THOUSANDS OF DOLLARS

Item Description for Accounting Period 7/04 Through 6/05	Total	Zero Assets	Under 500	500 to 1,000	1,000 to 5,000	5,000 to 10,000	10,000 to 25,000	25,000 to 50,000	50,000 to 100,000	100,000 to 250,000	250,000 to 500,000	500,000 to 2,500,000	2,500,000 and over
Number of Enterprises **1**	24490	632	18682	3559	1428	0	41	12	0	0	0	3	0
Revenues ($ in Thousands)													
Net Sales **2**	204426670	399474	18310377	15541134	10191288	0	1894273	1079939	0	0	0	6824133	0
Interest **3**	273357	4338	942	2750	7756	0	974	691	0	0	0	42875	0
Rents **4**	93457	0	407	4230	4106	0	23	0	0	0	0	3435	0
Royalties **5**	134125	20934	0	0	0	0	0	0	0	0	0	97651	0
Other Portfolio Income **6**	104902	5616	20596	3250	2636	0	4172	388	0	0	0	1178	0
Other Receipts **7**	1369310	588	33476	31904	39073	0	26761	12099	0	0	0	80619	0
Total Receipts **8**	206401821	430950	18365798	15583268	10244859	0	1926203	1093117	0	0	0	7049891	0
Average Total Receipts **9**	8428	682	983	4379	7174	•	46981	91093	•	•	•	2349964	•
Operating Costs/Operating Income (%)													
Cost of Operations **10**	76.5	61.3	70.7	77.1	73.2	•	71.1	59.7	•	•	•	62.4	•
Salaries and Wages **11**	8.7	8.6	6.4	6.3	10.1	•	10.4	12.1	•	•	•	16.3	•
Taxes Paid **12**	1.1	1.0	1.5	1.4	1.3	•	1.4	1.7	•	•	•	2.3	•
Interest Paid **13**	0.5	0.1	0.2	0.2	0.3	•	0.4	0.3	•	•	•	1.0	•
Depreciation **14**	1.0	0.5	0.7	0.4	0.7	•	0.7	1.4	•	•	•	1.9	•
Amortization and Depletion **15**	0.2	0.1	0.0	0.0	0.0	•	0.2	0.1	•	•	•	0.7	•
Pensions and Other Deferred Comp. **16**	0.3	0.0	0.3	0.5	0.3	•	0.2	0.1	•	•	•	0.3	•
Employee Benefits **17**	0.5	0.2	0.4	0.2	0.5	•	0.8	0.7	•	•	•	1.3	•
Advertising **18**	0.9	0.6	1.1	0.3	1.1	•	0.6	8.2	•	•	•	1.1	•
Other Expenses **19**	6.9	19.8	8.7	5.0	6.8	•	9.1	8.9	•	•	•	14.1	•
Officers' Compensation **20**	1.1	1.5	5.1	5.0	3.0	•	1.5	1.0	•	•	•	0.4	•
Operating Margin **21**	2.2	6.3	4.9	3.5	2.6	•	3.5	5.8	•	•	•	•	•
Operating Margin Before Officers' Comp. **22**	3.3	7.8	10.0	8.6	5.7	•	5.0	6.9	•	•	•	•	•

Selected Average Balance Sheet ($ in Thousands)

Net Receivables 23	389	0	20	87	348	4261	7946	172990
Inventories 24	695	0	62	247	465	3525	10618	228275
Net Property, Plant and Equipment 25	583	0	21	92	175	1543	7338	418537
Total Assets 26	3023	0	168	727	1763	15289	36457	1326189
Notes and Loans Payable 27	625	0	43	131	373	2485	6902	318200
All Other Liabilities 28	871	0	43	200	488	6375	9078	304732
Net Worth 29	1527	0	81	396	901	6429	20478	703257

Selected Financial Ratios (Times to 1)

Current Ratio 30	1.5	•	2.7	2.5	2.5	1.6	1.8	1.9
Quick Ratio 31	0.6	•	1.3	1.2	1.4	1.0	1.0	0.7
Net Sales to Working Capital 32	16.6	•	12.2	13.7	8.8	12.3	8.9	7.0
Coverage Ratio 33	7.2	119.1	23.1	23.8	10.7	14.2	25.4	2.3
Total Asset Turnover 34	2.8	•	5.8	6.0	4.0	3.0	2.5	1.7
Inventory Turnover 35	9.2	•	11.2	13.6	11.2	9.3	5.1	6.2
Receivables Turnover 36	24.5	•	48.6	53.3	22.2	11.7	8.5	•
Total Liabilities to Net Worth 37	1.0	•	1.1	0.8	1.0	1.4	0.8	0.9
Current Assets to Working Capital 38	2.9	•	1.6	1.7	1.7	2.6	2.2	2.1
Current Liabilities to Working Capital 39	1.9	•	0.6	0.7	0.7	1.6	1.2	1.1
Working Capital to Net Sales 40	0.1	•	0.1	0.1	0.1	0.1	0.1	0.1
Inventory to Working Capital 41	1.5	•	0.8	0.8	0.6	0.8	0.8	0.7
Total Receipts to Cash Flow 42	13.7	3.7	9.3	14.2	12.8	8.2	7.7	9.4
Cost of Goods to Cash Flow 43	10.5	2.3	6.6	11.0	9.3	5.8	4.6	5.8
Cash Flow to Total Debt 44	0.4	•	1.2	0.9	0.6	0.6	0.7	0.4

Selected Financial Factors (in Percentages)

Debt Ratio 45	49.5	•	51.4	45.5	48.9	57.9	•	43.8
Return on Total Assets 46	10.2	•	31.7	23.9	14.1	16.9	•	18.1
Return on Equity Before Income Taxes 47	17.3	•	62.4	42.1	25.0	37.4	•	31.0
Return on Equity After Income Taxes 48	13.6	•	61.0	41.2	23.4	34.6	•	29.6
Profit Margin (Before Income Tax) 49	3.2	14.2	5.2	3.8	3.2	5.2	7.1	3.6
Profit Margin (After Income Tax) 50	2.5	13.9	5.1	3.7	3.0	4.8	6.7	1.3

Table I

Corporations with and without Net Income

GASOLINE STATIONS

RETAIL TRADE
447100

MONEY AMOUNTS AND SIZE OF ASSETS IN THOUSANDS OF DOLLARS

Item Description for Accounting Period 7/04 Through 6/05	Total	Zero Assets	Under 500	500 to 1,000	1,000 to 5,000	5,000 to 10,000	10,000 to 25,000	25,000 to 50,000	50,000 to 100,000	100,000 to 250,000	250,000 to 500,000	500,000 to 2,500,000	2,500,000 and over
Number of Enterprises 1	37195	3072	24724	4966	3759	377	177	64	25	14	8	9	0
Revenues ($ in Thousands)													
Net Sales 2	194151748	910484	50096352	15577764	23398734	14853555	15138092	12347286	6459532	9259078	11939780	34171091	0
Interest 3	65784	582	4126	3164	12749	7907	2791	4801	743	3168	7567	18186	0
Rents 4	135322	47	10186	8138	33572	7593	13513	9129	5117	6486	17501	24040	0
Royalties 5	25804	0	0	0	0	0	209	2	0	693	0	24900	0
Other Portfolio Income 6	271289	7346	8685	9747	54276	9286	29097	13325	17612	13094	60114	48704	0
Other Receipts 7	1432024	76419	419552	80165	189802	58436	116001	56265	60185	111351	77429	186420	0
Total Receipts 8	196081971	994878	50538901	15678978	23689133	14936777	15299703	12430808	6543189	9393870	12102391	34473341	0
Average Total Receipts 9	5272	324	2044	3157	6302	39620	86439	194231	261728	670991	1512799	3830371	•
Operating Costs/Operating Income (%)													
Cost of Operations 10	87.6	89.0	87.4	87.3	87.8	85.5	88.9	89.0	88.6	89.5	86.9	87.2	•
Salaries and Wages 11	3.8	1.5	3.3	3.9	3.8	4.5	3.9	3.2	3.9	3.7	4.6	4.2	•
Taxes Paid 12	1.2	1.5	1.4	1.1	1.1	1.9	1.1	1.4	0.7	1.6	0.7	0.7	•
Interest Paid 13	0.5	0.1	0.2	0.6	0.9	0.4	0.4	0.4	0.6	0.4	0.3	0.6	•
Depreciation 14	1.3	0.2	0.6	1.4	1.3	1.3	1.2	1.2	1.6	1.3	1.8	2.0	•
Amortization and Depletion 15	0.1	0.1	0.1	0.2	0.1	0.1	0.1	0.1	0.0	0.0	0.1	0.1	•
Pensions and Other Deferred Comp. 16	0.0	0.0	0.0	0.0	0.0	0.0	0.0	0.0	0.1	0.1	0.2	0.1	•
Employee Benefits 17	0.2	0.3	0.0	0.1	0.1	0.3	0.2	0.2	0.3	0.2	0.5	0.3	•
Advertising 18	0.1	0.0	0.1	0.1	0.1	0.1	0.1	0.1	0.2	0.2	0.3	0.2	•
Other Expenses 19	5.1	14.1	6.4	5.1	4.8	5.4	4.6	4.2	4.5	3.5	4.5	4.4	•
Officers' Compensation 20	0.6	2.4	1.1	0.6	1.0	0.4	0.3	0.3	0.3	0.2	0.2	0.1	•
Operating Margin 21	•	•	•	•	•	0.1	•	•	•	•	•	0.2	•
Operating Margin Before Officers' Comp. 22	0.1	0.3	0.3	0.3	•	0.5	0.1	0.1	•	•	0.0	0.2	•

Selected Average Balance Sheet ($ in Thousands)

	1	2	3	4	5	6	7	8	9	10	11	12
Net Receivables 23	89	0	17	17	121	778	1622	3656	8117	11168	42100	94407
Inventories 24	112	0	50	68	123	650	1505	3145	5328	14904	35188	87916
Net Property, Plant and Equipment 25	515	0	79	420	1084	2888	8201	18404	32981	60284	173718	473761
Total Assets 26	1043	0	216	698	1771	6493	15238	35062	71149	152341	382571	998184
Notes and Loans Payable 27	492	0	137	490	1133	2814	6900	13127	26463	45402	153972	285810
All Other Liabilities 28	272	0	37	86	348	1415	4740	10687	21759	47495	116232	364205
Net Worth 29	279	0	42	122	290	2265	3598	11247	22927	59444	112367	348170

Selected Financial Ratios (Times to 1)

	1	2	3	4	5	6	7	8	9	10	11	12
Current Ratio 30	1.3	•	2.5	1.7	1.3	1.5	1.1	1.1	1.1	1.0	0.8	1.1
Quick Ratio 31	0.7	•	1.1	0.8	0.8	0.7	0.7	0.6	0.5	0.4	•	0.7
Net Sales to Working Capital 32	65.6	•	33.0	47.1	53.4	41.9	132.6	261.8	162.5	•	•	101.4
Coverage Ratio 33	2.0	0.6	1.4	1.5	1.2	2.7	1.3	2.5	1.9	3.3	4.7	2.8
Total Asset Turnover 34	5.0	•	9.4	4.5	3.5	6.1	5.6	5.5	3.6	4.3	3.9	3.8
Inventory Turnover 35	40.9	•	35.7	40.3	44.3	51.8	50.5	54.6	43.0	39.7	36.9	37.7
Receivables Turnover 36	60.0	•	121.8	96.7	43.6	55.8	56.6	60.5	34.5	69.3	38.8	44.9
Total Liabilities to Net Worth 37	2.7	•	4.2	4.7	5.1	1.9	3.2	2.1	2.1	1.6	2.4	1.9
Current Assets to Working Capital 38	4.3	•	1.7	2.5	4.0	2.9	8.1	16.5	15.6	•	•	8.7
Current Liabilities to Working Capital 39	3.3	•	0.7	1.5	3.0	1.9	7.1	15.5	14.6	•	•	7.7
Working Capital to Net Sales 40	0.0	•	0.0	0.0	0.0	0.0	0.0	0.0	0.0	•	•	0.0
Inventory to Working Capital 41	1.5	•	0.8	1.1	1.3	0.8	2.4	4.7	3.5	•	•	2.4
Total Receipts to Cash Flow 42	26.8	10.4	26.5	27.7	28.0	23.7	31.1	28.7	27.9	29.9	27.0	25.3
Cost of Goods to Cash Flow 43	23.5	9.3	23.2	24.1	24.6	20.3	27.6	25.5	24.7	26.7	23.5	22.1
Cash Flow to Total Debt 44	0.3	•	0.4	0.2	0.2	0.4	0.2	0.3	0.2	0.2	0.2	0.2

Selected Financial Factors (in Percentages)

	1	2	3	4	5	6	7	8	9	10	11	12
Debt Ratio 45	73.3	•	80.7	82.6	83.6	65.1	76.4	67.9	67.8	61.0	70.6	65.1
Return on Total Assets 46	4.7	•	2.9	4.2	3.8	6.2	3.3	4.9	4.1	5.6	5.7	6.2
Return on Equity Before Income Taxes 47	8.9	•	4.4	7.9	3.0	11.4	3.4	9.2	6.1	10.0	15.2	11.5
Return on Equity After Income Taxes 48	7.5	•	3.8	7.6	1.6	10.8	2.3	8.4	5.6	9.0	12.6	9.3
Profit Margin (Before Income Tax) 49	0.5	•	0.1	0.3	0.1	0.7	0.1	0.5	0.5	0.9	1.1	1.1
Profit Margin (After Income Tax) 50	0.4	•	0.1	0.3	0.1	0.6	0.1	0.5	0.5	0.8	1.0	0.9

Table II

Corporations with Net Income

GASOLINE STATIONS

MONEY AMOUNTS AND SIZE OF ASSETS IN THOUSANDS OF DOLLARS

Item Description for Accounting Period 7/04 Through 6/05	Total	Zero Assets	Under 500	500 to 1,000	1,000 to 5,000	5,000 to 10,000	10,000 to 25,000	25,000 to 50,000	50,000 to 100,000	100,000 to 250,000	250,000 to 500,000	500,000 to 2,500,000	2,500,000 and over
Number of Enterprises 1	19064	1239	12739	2758	1869	280	94	47	14	9	0	0	0
Revenues ($ in Thousands)													
Net Sales 2	140738192	707486	34467277	10254672	13718613	11436075	8408665	9193488	3832461	4159019	0	0	0
Interest 3	54928	26	2799	1767	8258	7211	2053	3577	315	3168	0	0	0
Rents 4	100997	47	2549	3005	28077	4338	7339	6067	1548	6486	0	0	0
Royalties 5	25802	0	0	0	0	0	209	0	0	693	0	0	0
Other Portfolio Income 6	230632	5834	8622	6192	50130	7242	16148	10758	7330	9710	0	0	0
Other Receipts 7	1085116	41198	338396	30855	136864	55008	65121	39770	29094	102023	0	0	0
Total Receipts 8	142235667	754591	34819643	10296491	13941942	11509874	8499535	9253660	3870748	4281099	0	0	0
Average Total Receipts 9	7461	609	2733	3733	7460	41107	90421	196886	276482	475678	•	•	•
Operating Costs/Operating Income (%)													
Cost of Operations 10	87.3	89.9	86.8	87.8	87.9	86.0	89.4	89.3	89.2	83.0	•	•	•
Salaries and Wages 11	3.8	1.6	3.2	3.4	3.3	4.3	3.5	3.3	3.5	5.8	•	•	•
Taxes Paid 12	1.2	1.5	1.5	1.0	0.9	2.2	0.8	1.3	0.7	3.1	•	•	•
Interest Paid 13	0.4	0.2	0.2	0.5	0.8	0.3	0.4	0.3	0.6	0.6	•	•	•
Depreciation 14	1.2	0.2	0.6	1.0	1.1	1.0	1.1	1.0	1.5	1.5	•	•	•
Amortization and Depletion 15	0.1	0.0	0.1	0.1	0.1	0.1	0.0	0.0	0.0	0.0	•	•	•
Pensions and Other Deferred Comp. 16	0.1	0.1	0.0	0.0	0.0	0.0	0.0	0.0	0.0	0.2	•	•	•
Employee Benefits 17	0.2	0.5	0.1	0.1	0.2	0.3	0.1	0.2	0.3	0.3	•	•	•
Advertising 18	0.1	0.0	0.1	0.0	0.1	0.1	0.1	0.1	0.1	0.3	•	•	•
Other Expenses 19	4.9	8.1	6.1	4.8	4.6	4.7	4.4	3.7	3.3	5.3	•	•	•
Officers' Compensation 20	0.5	2.7	1.1	0.5	1.1	0.4	0.3	0.3	0.3	0.3	•	•	•
Operating Margin 21	0.2	•	0.3	0.8	•	0.6	•	0.3	0.6	•	•	•	•
Operating Margin Before Officers' Comp. 22	0.7	•	1.4	1.3	1.0	1.0	0.1	0.6	0.8	•	•	•	•

Selected Average Balance Sheet ($ in Thousands)

Net Receivables 23	119	0	21	16	123	767	1765	3704	8713	10402
Inventories 24	155	0	66	75	130	704	1664	3208	6244	11798
Net Property, Plant and Equipment 25	656	0	65	402	1006	2778	7483	17702	32906	52166
Total Assets 26	1409	0	237	664	1762	6598	14694	34784	75022	151480
Notes and Loans Payable 27	568	0	103	460	1022	2525	5644	12955	31257	35990
All Other Liabilities 28	373	0	36	108	284	1443	3971	10165	20321	48892
Net Worth 29	468	0	98	96	456	2631	5080	11664	23444	66599

Selected Financial Ratios (Times to 1)

Current Ratio 30	1.4	•	3.5	1.5	1.4	1.7	1.2	1.2	1.2	0.9
Quick Ratio 31	0.7	•	1.5	0.7	0.9	0.8	0.8	0.7	0.6	0.4
Net Sales to Working Capital 32	59.3	•	29.2	66.6	52.3	33.6	89.8	111.6	65.5	•
Coverage Ratio 33	3.9	13.0	8.3	3.3	3.0	4.5	3.3	3.9	3.4	5.2
Total Asset Turnover 34	5.2	•	11.4	5.6	4.2	6.2	6.1	5.6	3.6	3.1
Inventory Turnover 35	41.7	•	35.5	43.4	49.6	49.9	48.1	54.5	39.1	32.5
Receivables Turnover 36	60.6	•	139.7	224.0	36.2	55.6	50.1	55.7	30.8	56.0
Total Liabilities to Net Worth 37	2.0	•	1.4	5.9	2.9	1.5	1.9	2.0	2.2	1.3
Current Assets to Working Capital 38	3.9	•	1.4	3.2	3.3	2.4	5.5	7.4	6.7	•
Current Liabilities to Working Capital 39	2.9	•	0.4	2.2	2.3	1.4	4.5	6.4	5.7	•
Working Capital to Net Sales 40	0.0	•	0.0	0.0	0.0	0.0	0.0	0.0	0.0	•
Inventory to Working Capital 41	1.3	•	0.7	1.4	1.1	0.6	1.5	1.8	1.5	•
Total Receipts to Cash Flow 42	23.3	13.9	20.8	24.1	21.7	22.7	27.1	28.5	26.4	16.7
Cost of Goods to Cash Flow 43	20.3	12.5	18.1	21.1	19.0	19.5	24.2	25.5	23.5	13.9
Cash Flow to Total Debt 44	0.3	•	0.9	0.3	0.3	0.5	0.3	0.3	0.2	0.3

Selected Financial Factors (in Percentages)

Debt Ratio 45	66.8	•	58.5	85.5	74.1	60.1	65.4	66.5	68.8	56.0
Return on Total Assets 46	8.8	•	16.9	9.5	9.7	9.6	7.2	7.4	7.9	9.2
Return on Equity Before Income Taxes 47	19.7	•	35.8	45.9	24.9	18.7	14.6	16.4	17.8	16.9
Return on Equity After Income Taxes 48	18.1	•	35.4	45.2	23.1	18.0	13.1	15.3	17.1	15.8
Profit Margin (Before Income Tax) 49	1.2	2.1	1.3	1.2	1.5	1.2	0.8	1.0	1.5	2.4
Profit Margin (After Income Tax) 50	1.1	2.0	1.3	1.2	1.4	1.2	0.7	0.9	1.5	2.3

Table I

Corporations with and without Net Income

CLOTHING AND CLOTHING ACCESSORIES STORES

MONEY AMOUNTS AND SIZE OF ASSETS IN THOUSANDS OF DOLLARS

Item Description for Accounting Period 7/04 Through 6/05	Total	Zero Assets	Under 500	500 to 1,000	1,000 to 5,000	5,000 to 10,000	10,000 to 25,000	25,000 to 50,000	50,000 to 100,000	100,000 to 250,000	250,000 to 500,000	500,000 to 2,500,000	2,500,000 and over
Number of Enterprises **1**	56949	5801	43065	4884	2624	264	139	60	32	26	24	23	6
Revenues ($ in Thousands)													
Net Sales **2**	159733553	893407	16107412	6242992	8526256	3123712	4468540	3952744	4678531	8485505	15070474	38164743	50019238
Interest **3**	810221	3934	2867	2183	8688	4396	7346	4177	1243	23520	44627	209678	497561
Rents **4**	150063	0	1293	493	5266	340	5597	1491	727	714	44971	31148	58024
Royalties **5**	835727	0	43	0	0	0	133	20	6343	14807	77154	340065	397161
Other Portfolio Income **6**	706711	3761	18429	873	4721	5159	2118	2598	1582	3878	23223	275102	365266
Other Receipts **7**	1649169	8458	26893	45562	54222	17093	83037	85226	78610	90809	211303	728865	219092
Total Receipts **8**	163885444	909560	16156937	6292103	8599153	3150700	4566771	4046256	4767036	8619233	15471752	39749601	51556342
Average Total Receipts **9**	2878	157	375	1288	3277	11934	32854	67438	148970	331509	644656	1728244	8592724
Operating Costs/Operating Income (%)													
Cost of Operations **10**	54.4	63.2	51.6	56.9	59.1	55.3	57.3	57.1	53.2	55.1	53.0	54.1	54.1
Salaries and Wages **11**	13.9	10.1	11.1	13.3	12.7	15.3	13.8	15.2	14.8	14.8	15.3	13.8	14.4
Taxes Paid **12**	2.3	1.9	2.4	2.2	2.1	2.9	2.2	2.5	2.4	2.6	2.5	2.2	2.1
Interest Paid **13**	0.9	0.6	0.6	0.9	0.9	0.5	0.9	0.8	0.7	0.5	0.7	0.7	1.4
Depreciation **14**	2.6	1.1	0.8	0.8	0.9	1.1	1.4	2.0	1.9	2.7	2.9	3.5	3.2
Amortization and Depletion **15**	0.3	0.3	0.1	0.1	0.1	0.3	0.2	0.1	0.1	0.3	0.1	0.3	0.4
Pensions and Other Deferred Comp. **16**	0.3	0.0	0.1	0.1	0.6	0.1	0.2	0.2	0.1	0.1	0.2	0.2	0.4
Employee Benefits **17**	1.0	0.5	0.5	0.7	0.7	0.3	0.8	0.8	1.1	0.9	1.1	1.1	1.2
Advertising **18**	2.5	2.0	2.4	2.9	3.4	3.8	3.3	2.9	2.9	2.0	2.4	2.7	2.1
Other Expenses **19**	18.0	28.1	22.4	16.8	13.9	17.4	17.4	18.9	20.3	20.6	19.8	18.8	15.5
Officers' Compensation **20**	1.9	0.8	7.7	4.7	5.3	1.5	2.2	1.8	1.0	0.8	0.7	0.9	0.4
Operating Margin **21**	2.0	•	0.3	0.8	0.5	1.2	0.3	•	1.6	•	1.4	1.6	4.7
Operating Margin Before Officers' Comp. **22**	3.9	•	8.0	5.4	5.8	2.8	2.5	•	2.5	0.6	2.1	2.5	5.2

Selected Average Balance Sheet ($ in Thousands)

Net Receivables 23	118	0	4	29	94	1185	1870	3462	4006	10205	17608	46964	580512
Inventories 24	517	0	74	420	986	3514	7417	13429	32553	58100	99415	322441	1087472
Net Property, Plant and Equipment 25	370	0	11	92	220	824	2560	7017	16399	51919	99862	258666	1392791
Total Assets 26	1604	0	134	676	1789	6774	15565	35171	70650	163144	361837	1092120	5199104
Notes and Loans Payable 27	341	0	50	274	556	1952	4426	11840	13594	30652	65835	114313	1195908
All Other Liabilities 28	669	0	50	174	572	2938	5792	16100	34578	57869	134002	352236	2851111
Net Worth 29	594	0	34	228	660	1884	5347	7230	22478	74623	162000	625571	1152085

Selected Financial Ratios (Times to 1)

Current Ratio 30	1.8	•	2.1	2.8	2.3	1.4	1.6	1.3	1.5	1.4	1.7	1.9	1.7
Quick Ratio 31	0.6	•	0.6	0.6	0.5	0.4	0.5	0.4	0.4	0.4	0.5	0.6	0.7
Net Sales to Working Capital 32	6.7	•	6.7	3.6	4.0	8.4	7.1	11.3	8.4	12.7	8.0	6.3	7.2
Coverage Ratio 33	6.3	•	2.1	2.6	2.6	4.9	3.8	1.2	6.3	3.6	6.6	9.0	7.1
Total Asset Turnover 34	1.7	•	2.8	1.9	1.8	1.7	2.1	1.9	2.1	2.0	1.7	1.5	1.6
Inventory Turnover 35	2.9	•	2.6	1.7	1.9	1.9	2.5	2.8	2.4	3.1	3.3	2.8	4.1
Receivables Turnover 36	25.9	•	80.1	41.4	37.1	10.1	17.5	20.8	38.2	33.7	31.0	32.2	17.9
Total Liabilities to Net Worth 37	1.7	•	2.9	2.0	1.7	2.6	1.9	3.9	2.1	1.2	1.2	0.7	3.5
Current Assets to Working Capital 38	2.3	•	1.9	1.6	1.8	3.8	2.6	4.2	2.9	3.3	2.5	2.1	2.5
Current Liabilities to Working Capital 39	1.3	•	0.9	0.6	0.8	2.8	1.6	3.2	1.9	2.3	1.5	1.1	1.5
Working Capital to Net Sales 40	0.1	•	0.1	0.3	0.2	0.1	0.1	0.1	0.1	0.1	0.1	0.2	0.1
Inventory to Working Capital 41	1.3	•	1.4	1.2	1.3	2.4	1.6	2.5	1.9	2.1	1.3	1.2	1.1
Total Receipts to Cash Flow 42	7.3	10.3	7.5	8.8	10.2	8.7	8.0	10.4	6.5	10.3	7.2	6.9	6.6
Cost of Goods to Cash Flow 43	4.0	6.5	3.9	5.0	6.0	4.8	4.6	5.9	3.4	5.7	3.8	3.7	3.6
Cash Flow to Total Debt 44	0.4	•	0.5	0.3	0.3	0.3	0.4	0.2	0.5	0.4	0.4	0.5	0.3

Selected Financial Factors (in Percentages)

Debt Ratio 45	62.9	•	74.5	66.3	63.1	72.2	65.6	79.4	68.2	54.3	55.2	42.7	77.8
Return on Total Assets 46	10.1	•	3.2	4.7	4.0	4.6	6.9	1.7	8.7	3.6	8.1	10.0	15.7
Return on Equity Before Income Taxes 47	22.9	•	6.5	8.6	6.5	13.1	14.7	1.1	22.9	5.7	15.3	15.5	61.0
Return on Equity After Income Taxes 48	15.1	•	6.1	7.5	5.2	11.9	12.7	•	16.5	1.4	9.0	10.5	39.7
Profit Margin (Before Income Tax) 49	4.8	•	0.6	1.5	1.3	2.1	2.5	0.1	3.5	1.3	3.9	5.8	8.4
Profit Margin (After Income Tax) 50	3.2	•	0.6	1.3	1.1	1.9	2.1	•	2.5	0.3	2.3	4.0	5.5

Table II

Corporations with Net Income

CLOTHING AND CLOTHING ACCESSORIES STORES

MONEY AMOUNTS AND SIZE OF ASSETS IN THOUSANDS OF DOLLARS

Item Description for Accounting Period 7/04 Through 6/05	Total	Zero Assets	Under 500	500 to 1,000	1,000 to 5,000	5,000 to 10,000	10,000 to 25,000	25,000 to 50,000	50,000 to 100,000	100,000 to 250,000	250,000 to 500,000	500,000 to 2,500,000	2,500,000 and over
Number of Enterprises 1	30874	2271	22204	3980	1967	221	105	40	27	0	17	0	6

Revenues ($ in Thousands)

Net Sales 2	138354674	507762	9188646	5186099	6866663	2711369	3468449	2874225	4340163	0	12169939	0	50019238
Interest 3	760201	515	1320	1520	6518	1654	5967	1398	1094	0	40980	0	497561
Rents 4	129685	0	224	1	3352	0	2189	1454	720	0	31861	0	58024
Royalties 5	816403	0	43	0	0	0	0	0	6343	0	66155	0	397161
Other Portfolio Income 6	692376	320	16132	871	3437	5158	1938	1723	1524	0	19987	0	365266
Other Receipts 7	1268920	1621	17649	25625	41923	11803	38159	56023	89852	0	126429	0	219092
Total Receipts 8	142022259	510218	9224014	5214116	6921893	2729984	3516702	2934823	4439696	0	12455351	0	51556342
Average Total Receipts 9	4600	225	415	1310	3519	12353	33492	73371	164433	•	732668	•	8592724

Operating Costs/Operating Income (%)

Cost of Operations 10	54.2	55.9	53.1	57.1	59.3	54.6	57.2	56.7	52.7	•	53.9	•	54.1
Salaries and Wages 11	13.8	9.4	9.1	12.8	11.9	15.2	12.9	14.3	15.0	•	14.4	•	14.4
Taxes Paid 12	2.2	1.7	2.2	2.1	1.9	3.0	2.0	2.4	2.5	•	2.5	•	2.1
Interest Paid 13	0.9	0.7	0.5	0.8	0.6	0.4	0.6	0.6	0.5	•	0.4	•	1.4
Depreciation 14	2.6	0.9	0.6	0.6	0.6	1.0	1.3	1.8	1.9	•	2.9	•	3.2
Amortization and Depletion 15	0.3	0.0	0.1	0.1	0.0	0.4	0.1	0.1	0.1	•	0.0	•	0.4
Pensions and Other Deferred Comp. 16	0.3	0.1	0.1	0.1	0.6	0.1	0.2	0.2	0.1	•	0.2	•	0.4
Employee Benefits 17	1.0	0.3	0.4	0.8	0.6	0.3	0.6	0.7	1.1	•	1.0	•	1.2
Advertising 18	2.5	1.0	2.3	2.1	3.7	4.0	3.0	2.6	2.9	•	2.6	•	2.1
Other Expenses 19	16.9	20.8	18.1	15.4	12.5	17.1	15.5	16.1	20.2	•	17.2	•	15.5
Officers' Compensation 20	1.6	1.1	7.0	4.6	5.4	1.2	2.4	1.9	0.9	•	0.8	•	0.4
Operating Margin 21	3.9	8.3	6.5	3.3	3.0	2.6	4.2	2.6	2.0	•	4.0	•	4.7
Operating Margin Before Officers' Comp. 22	5.4	9.4	13.5	7.8	8.3	3.8	6.6	4.6	2.9	•	4.7	•	5.2

Selected Average Balance Sheet ($ in Thousands)

Net Receivables 23	198	0	4	32	91	1163	1926	3678	4398	•	18736	•	580512
Inventories 24	772	0	82	399	1027	3149	7402	12895	28309	•	103325	•	1087472
Net Property, Plant and Equipment 25	602	0	9	85	151	674	2310	6596	17864	•	111643	•	1392791
Total Assets 26	2543	0	147	689	1823	6497	15535	35303	71491	•	386723	•	5199104
Notes and Loans Payable 27	484	0	43	269	460	1550	3433	9378	12285	•	39712	•	1195908
All Other Liabilities 28	1062	0	44	141	513	2764	5733	12500	35550	•	127250	•	2851111
Net Worth 29	997	0	61	278	851	2183	6369	13425	23655	•	219762	•	1152085

Selected Financial Ratios (Times to 1)

Current Ratio 30	1.9	•	2.3	3.4	2.5	1.4	1.7	1.8	1.8	•	1.6	•	1.7
Quick Ratio 31	0.6	•	0.6	0.8	0.5	0.5	0.5	0.5	0.5	•	0.4	•	0.7
Net Sales to Working Capital 32	6.4	•	6.1	3.3	3.8	8.6	6.3	6.6	8.2	•	7.6	•	7.2
Coverage Ratio 33	8.7	14.3	16.3	5.5	7.0	8.4	10.7	8.3	9.2	•	14.9	•	7.1
Total Asset Turnover 34	1.8	•	2.8	1.9	1.9	1.9	2.1	2.0	2.2	•	1.9	•	1.6
Inventory Turnover 35	3.1	•	2.7	1.9	2.0	2.1	2.6	3.2	3.0	•	3.7	•	4.1
Receivables Turnover 36	26.1	•	66.2	42.0	44.0	10.5	17.3	21.3	54.8	•	28.9	•	17.9
Total Liabilities to Net Worth 37	1.6	•	1.4	1.5	1.1	2.0	1.4	1.6	2.0	•	0.8	•	3.5
Current Assets to Working Capital 38	2.2	•	1.8	1.4	1.7	3.7	2.3	2.3	2.8	•	2.3	•	2.5
Current Liabilities to Working Capital 39	1.2	•	0.8	0.4	0.7	2.7	1.3	1.3	1.8	•	1.3	•	1.5
Working Capital to Net Sales 40	0.2	•	0.2	0.3	0.3	0.1	0.2	0.2	0.1	•	0.1	•	0.1
Inventory to Working Capital 41	1.2	•	1.2	1.1	1.3	2.3	1.5	1.4	1.8	•	1.1	•	1.1
Total Receipts to Cash Flow 42	6.7	5.5	6.1	8.0	8.4	8.0	6.9	8.0	6.3	•	7.1	•	6.6
Cost of Goods to Cash Flow 43	3.7	3.1	3.3	4.5	5.0	4.4	3.9	4.5	3.3	•	3.8	•	3.6
Cash Flow to Total Debt 44	0.4	•	0.8	0.4	0.4	0.5	0.4	0.4	0.5	•	0.6	•	0.3

Selected Financial Factors (in Percentages)

Debt Ratio 45	60.8	•	58.6	59.6	53.4	66.4	59.0	62.0	66.9	•	43.2	•	77.8
Return on Total Assets 46	13.4	•	20.6	8.8	8.4	7.0	13.0	10.8	10.9	•	12.3	•	15.7
Return on Equity Before Income Taxes 47	30.3	•	46.9	17.7	15.4	18.4	28.8	25.0	29.4	•	20.2	•	61.0
Return on Equity After Income Taxes 48	21.7	•	46.4	16.7	14.1	17.2	26.5	23.6	22.2	•	13.7	•	39.7
Profit Margin (Before Income Tax) 49	6.7	8.7	6.9	3.8	3.3	3.3	5.5	4.7	4.3	•	6.2	•	8.4
Profit Margin (After Income Tax) 50	4.8	7.7	6.8	3.4	3.1	3.1	5.1	4.4	3.3	•	4.2	•	5.5

228

Table I

Corporations with and without Net Income

SPORTING GOODS, HOBBY, BOOK, AND MUSIC STORES

MONEY AMOUNTS AND SIZE OF ASSETS IN THOUSANDS OF DOLLARS

Item Description for Accounting Period 7/04 Through 6/05	Total	Zero Assets	Under 500	500 to 1,000	1,000 to 5,000	5,000 to 10,000	10,000 to 25,000	25,000 to 50,000	50,000 to 100,000	100,000 to 250,000	250,000 to 500,000	500,000 to 2,500,000	2,500,000 and over
Number of Enterprises 1	33037	4699	22620	3336	1949	285	71	21	13	13	13	16	0
Revenues ($ in Thousands)													
Net Sales 2	77674318	635950	8332390	4746917	7978516	3989842	2279564	1588825	1457379	3164291	7455861	36044784	0
Interest 3	86032	1208	1494	979	5378	2608	2254	909	1628	3040	7091	59443	0
Rents 4	42833	0	2270	482	2569	606	213	1879	894	0	1366	32554	0
Royalties 5	241982	0	0	0	278	2314	139	0	0	1586	35409	202256	0
Other Portfolio Income 6	781778	11	2242	18430	10132	4471	2335	8853	8859	393	14890	711162	0
Other Receipts 7	995597	841	146702	11401	44689	76262	36007	18153	9089	36474	195873	420104	0
Total Receipts 8	79822540	638010	848098	4778209	8041562	4076103	2320512	1618619	1477849	3205784	7710490	37470303	0
Average Total Receipts 9	2416	136	375	1432	4126	14302	32683	77077	113681	246599	593115	2341894	•
Operating Costs/Operating Income (%)													
Cost of Operations 10	62.3	64.5	59.8	64.2	61.5	70.6	61.1	58.9	58.7	63.1	62.8	62.0	•
Salaries and Wages 11	11.8	7.3	8.6	9.7	12.2	10.3	13.4	12.1	15.7	12.4	12.2	12.5	•
Taxes Paid 12	2.2	2.1	2.3	1.9	2.1	1.4	2.1	1.7	2.2	2.1	2.0	2.4	•
Interest Paid 13	0.9	0.4	1.0	0.7	0.8	0.8	0.9	0.7	0.7	1.0	0.8	0.9	•
Depreciation 14	2.2	0.6	1.3	1.1	1.7	1.4	1.4	1.6	2.6	2.8	2.4	2.8	•
Amortization and Depletion 15	0.3	0.2	0.3	0.0	0.1	0.1	0.2	0.3	0.2	0.4	0.5	0.4	•
Pensions and Other Deferred Comp. 16	0.2	0.0	0.1	0.2	0.3	0.1	0.2	0.1	0.2	0.1	0.1	0.2	•
Employee Benefits 17	0.7	0.2	0.8	0.5	0.5	0.6	0.6	0.6	0.9	0.8	0.7	0.7	•
Advertising 18	2.2	1.1	1.8	2.6	2.0	1.8	3.9	3.3	4.5	3.7	3.2	1.8	•
Other Expenses 19	15.8	21.8	20.0	13.7	14.7	10.2	14.9	15.6	15.2	12.2	16.6	16.1	•
Officers' Compensation 20	1.8	3.9	6.1	4.3	2.9	1.5	1.7	1.4	1.5	0.9	0.5	0.6	•
Operating Margin 21	•	•	•	1.1	1.2	1.1	•	3.4	•	0.5	•	•	•
Operating Margin Before Officers' Comp. 22	1.5	1.9	3.9	5.4	4.1	2.6	1.4	4.9	•	1.4	•	0.2	•

Selected Average Balance Sheet ($ in Thousands)

Net Receivables 23	76	0	3	34	201	559	2039	4696	6389	16506	23146	58435
Inventories 24	556	0	78	343	960	3164	6742	12542	27229	63435	173440	532288
Net Property, Plant and Equipment 25	304	0	20	117	320	747	2673	5282	12238	31681	84014	399346
Total Assets 26	1392	0	133	698	1893	6784	15383	35224	66750	135987	327331	1644467
Notes and Loans Payable 27	368	0	79	161	795	2397	5957	7432	17342	49742	78098	321876
All Other Liabilities 28	523	0	55	226	663	2026	5994	12592	18361	48402	147439	620689
Net Worth 29	501	0	-0	311	436	2361	3432	15201	31047	37843	101794	701903

Selected Financial Ratios (Times to 1)

Current Ratio 30	1.6	•	1.5	2.4	1.8	1.5	1.2	1.9	1.7	1.7	1.4	1.6
Quick Ratio 31	0.4	•	0.3	0.6	0.6	0.3	0.4	0.7	0.5	0.5	0.2	0.4
Net Sales to Working Capital 32	7.1	•	10.9	4.9	6.6	8.8	17.3	6.0	6.1	6.4	8.6	6.4
Coverage Ratio 33	3.7	•	0.6	3.6	3.4	5.3	2.7	8.4	•	2.8	2.8	4.8
Total Asset Turnover 34	1.7	•	2.8	2.0	2.2	2.1	2.1	2.1	1.7	1.8	1.8	1.4
Inventory Turnover 35	2.6	•	2.8	2.7	2.6	3.1	2.9	3.6	2.4	2.4	2.1	2.6
Receivables Turnover 36	30.8	•	89.4	47.4	16.7	30.2	16.4	13.5	13.8	16.9	21.3	44.1
Total Liabilities to Net Worth 37	1.8	•	•	1.2	3.3	1.9	3.5	1.3	1.1	2.6	2.2	1.3
Current Assets to Working Capital 38	2.6	•	2.9	1.7	2.2	3.2	6.0	2.1	2.4	2.5	3.4	2.6
Current Liabilities to Working Capital 39	1.6	•	1.9	0.7	1.2	2.2	5.0	1.1	1.4	1.5	2.4	1.6
Working Capital to Net Sales 40	0.1	•	0.1	0.2	0.2	0.1	0.1	0.2	0.2	0.2	0.1	0.2
Inventory to Working Capital 41	1.7	•	2.3	1.3	1.4	2.4	3.8	1.2	1.4	1.5	2.7	1.6
Total Receipts to Cash Flow 42	9.1	8.3	9.1	9.6	9.1	12.9	9.8	6.4	14.7	12.3	9.3	8.5
Cost of Goods to Cash Flow 43	5.7	5.3	5.4	6.1	5.6	9.1	6.0	3.8	8.6	7.8	5.8	5.3
Cash Flow to Total Debt 44	0.3	•	0.3	0.4	0.3	0.2	0.3	0.6	0.2	0.2	0.3	0.3

Selected Financial Factors (in Percentages)

Debt Ratio 45	64.0	•	100.3	55.5	77.0	65.2	77.7	56.8	53.5	72.2	68.9	57.3
Return on Total Assets 46	5.6	•	1.7	5.1	6.1	8.3	5.0	12.9	•	5.0	4.0	6.3
Return on Equity Before Income Taxes 47	11.5	•	376.0	8.2	18.8	19.2	14.2	26.4	•	11.6	8.4	11.6
Return on Equity After Income Taxes 48	8.6	•	434.8	7.8	17.0	17.7	11.2	23.9	•	7.7	4.4	8.6
Profit Margin (Before Income Tax) 49	2.5	•	•	1.8	2.0	3.2	1.5	5.3	•	1.8	1.5	3.6
Profit Margin (After Income Tax) 50	1.8	•	•	1.7	1.8	3.0	1.2	4.8	•	1.2	0.8	2.7

229

Table II

Corporations with Net Income

SPORTING GOODS, HOBBY, BOOK, AND MUSIC STORES

MONEY AMOUNTS AND SIZE OF ASSETS IN THOUSANDS OF DOLLARS

Item Description for Accounting Period 7/04 Through 6/05	Total	Zero Assets	Under 500	500 to 1,000	1,000 to 5,000	5,000 to 10,000	10,000 to 25,000	25,000 to 50,000	50,000 to 100,000	100,000 to 250,000	250,000 to 500,000	500,000 to 2,500,000	2,500,000 and over
Number of Enterprises 1	19338	2632	13064	1935	1378	217	57	18	7	9	8	13	0
Revenues ($ in Thousands)													
Net Sales 2	60771424	510336	4398508	3202788	6128473	3451727	1695987	1490431	1010841	2401070	4888374	31592889	0
Interest 3	64434	0	440	948	3473	2434	1425	767	1258	982	6671	46037	0
Rents 4	27521	0	255	482	2201	206	205	1493	778	0	668	21232	0
Royalties 5	204067	0	0	0	68	2314	139	0	0	1586	17938	182022	0
Other Portfolio Income 6	742930	0	2204	1294	9822	4471	2167	8841	8697	238	759	704434	0
Other Receipts 7	726129	84	121757	5352	27478	53827	34560	13671	3720	19586	51142	394955	0
Total Receipts 8	62536505	510420	4523164	3210864	6171515	3514979	1734483	1515203	1025294	2423462	4965552	32941569	0
Average Total Receipts 9	3234	194	346	1659	4479	16198	30430	84178	146471	269274	620694	2533967	•
Operating Costs/Operating Income (%)													
Cost of Operations 10	62.3	64.7	57.1	64.9	62.7	70.3	60.6	59.3	59.5	61.2	63.3	61.9	•
Salaries and Wages 11	11.7	6.6	8.0	8.4	10.8	10.0	13.0	11.6	14.7	13.4	11.8	12.7	•
Taxes Paid 12	2.1	1.5	2.5	1.9	2.0	1.4	1.9	1.6	2.0	2.1	1.6	2.4	•
Interest Paid 13	0.8	0.3	0.6	0.4	0.8	0.6	0.7	0.8	0.6	0.7	0.7	0.9	•
Depreciation 14	2.3	0.5	1.1	1.0	1.2	1.3	1.2	1.5	1.4	2.6	2.7	2.9	•
Amortization and Depletion 15	0.3	0.3	0.1	0.0	0.1	0.1	0.3	0.3	0.1	0.1	0.7	0.4	•
Pensions and Other Deferred Comp. 16	0.2	•	0.1	0.3	0.3	0.1	0.2	0.1	0.3	0.1	0.1	0.2	•
Employee Benefits 17	0.5	0.1	0.3	0.3	0.3	0.5	0.7	0.5	0.4	0.6	0.7	0.6	•
Advertising 18	2.1	0.7	1.0	2.2	1.7	1.9	4.3	3.4	5.2	4.4	3.3	1.6	•
Other Expenses 19	14.4	11.6	19.3	11.1	13.8	9.2	13.0	15.2	12.2	11.4	12.2	15.5	•
Officers' Compensation 20	1.6	4.5	6.2	4.6	2.8	1.2	1.9	1.5	1.1	1.1	0.4	0.6	•
Operating Margin 21	1.8	9.3	3.6	4.8	3.4	3.3	2.1	4.3	2.5	2.4	2.6	0.3	•
Operating Margin Before Officers' Comp. 22	3.4	13.8	9.8	9.4	6.3	4.5	4.0	5.8	3.6	3.5	2.9	1.0	•

Selected Average Balance Sheet ($ in Thousands)

Net Receivables 23	85	0	5	32	234	502	1939	5185	5629	20532	32840	30368	•
Inventories 24	681	0	58	412	1001	3499	6436	12570	32829	54285	166389	597300	•
Net Property, Plant and Equipment 25	423	0	22	99	212	695	2236	4796	11802	30143	79707	465876	•
Total Assets 26	1891	0	131	721	1891	7027	15104	36073	68606	132222	335286	1805584	•
Notes and Loans Payable 27	416	0	51	132	614	2090	3647	8599	18884	41323	72068	336569	•
All Other Liabilities 28	644	0	46	233	372	2174	4858	13967	23137	39942	126060	642137	•
Net Worth 29	832	0	33	357	905	2763	6599	13507	26585	50957	137158	826878	•

Selected Financial Ratios (Times to 1)

Current Ratio 30	1.8	•	2.0	2.3	2.5	1.3	1.7	1.8	1.6	2.1	1.6	1.7	•
Quick Ratio 31	0.4	•	0.6	0.5	0.8	0.3	0.5	0.6	0.4	0.8	0.4	0.4	•
Net Sales to Working Capital 32	6.3	•	7.0	5.0	4.9	12.7	6.6	6.9	8.9	5.3	6.7	6.2	•
Coverage Ratio 33	7.2	28.5	11.7	12.5	6.4	9.7	6.8	8.9	7.4	5.9	6.9	6.4	•
Total Asset Turnover 34	1.7	•	2.6	2.3	2.4	2.3	2.0	2.3	2.1	2.0	1.8	1.3	•
Inventory Turnover 35	2.9	•	3.3	2.6	2.8	3.2	2.8	3.9	2.6	3.0	2.3	2.5	•
Receivables Turnover 36	35.7	•	76.1	47.5	17.9	33.4	15.6	20.0	20.1	•	15.7	•	•
Total Liabilities to Net Worth 37	1.3	•	2.9	1.0	1.1	1.5	1.3	1.7	1.6	1.6	1.4	1.2	•
Current Assets to Working Capital 38	2.3	•	2.0	1.8	1.7	4.1	2.4	2.3	2.8	1.9	2.5	2.4	•
Current Liabilities to Working Capital 39	1.3	•	1.0	0.8	0.7	3.1	1.4	1.3	1.8	0.9	1.5	1.4	•
Working Capital to Net Sales 40	0.2	•	0.1	0.2	0.2	0.1	0.2	0.1	0.1	0.2	0.2	0.2	•
Inventory to Working Capital 41	1.5	•	1.4	1.4	1.1	3.2	1.5	1.4	1.8	1.1	1.9	1.5	•
Total Receipts to Cash Flow 42	8.1	6.1	6.0	8.4	7.7	11.0	7.8	6.3	10.5	10.7	9.6	8.1	•
Cost of Goods to Cash Flow 43	5.1	3.9	3.4	5.5	4.8	7.7	4.7	3.7	6.3	6.6	6.1	5.0	•
Cash Flow to Total Debt 44	0.4	•	0.6	0.5	0.6	0.3	0.4	0.6	0.3	0.3	0.3	0.3	•

Selected Financial Factors (in Percentages)

Debt Ratio 45	56.0	•	74.7	50.5	52.1	60.7	56.3	62.6	61.2	61.5	59.1	54.2	•
Return on Total Assets 46	9.1	•	18.1	12.5	11.5	13.1	10.1	15.3	9.5	8.1	8.8	7.4	•
Return on Equity Before Income Taxes 47	17.9	•	65.3	23.3	20.2	29.8	19.7	36.4	21.3	17.6	18.5	13.6	•
Return on Equity After Income Taxes 48	14.9	•	64.1	22.7	19.0	28.1	17.7	33.0	15.4	13.4	13.7	10.5	•
Profit Margin (Before Income Tax) 49	4.7	9.4	6.4	5.0	4.1	5.2	4.4	5.9	3.9	3.4	4.2	4.6	•
Profit Margin (After Income Tax) 50	4.0	9.3	6.3	4.9	3.9	4.9	3.9	5.4	2.8	2.6	3.1	3.6	•

Table I
Corporations with and without Net Income

GENERAL MERCHANDISE STORES

MONEY AMOUNTS AND SIZE OF ASSETS IN THOUSANDS OF DOLLARS

Item Description for Accounting Period 7/04 Through 6/05	Total	Zero Assets	Under 500	500 to 1,000	1,000 to 5,000	5,000 to 10,000	10,000 to 25,000	25,000 to 50,000	50,000 to 100,000	100,000 to 250,000	250,000 to 500,000	500,000 to 2,500,000	2,500,000 and over
Number of Enterprises **1**	12333	1565	9806	404	429	32	32	15	10	9	8	7	16
Revenues ($ in Thousands)													
Net Sales **2**	545859277	24986480	3143137	515085	2469400	54740	1023510	1212008	1087161	2238656	5035032	22049888	481557179
Interest **3**	3473775	104275	520	1664	1459	1369	1043	354	20315	2867	23341	57616	3258951
Rents **4**	873288	0	792	0	2377	142	925	152	8642	6115	2944	26504	824695
Royalties **5**	2905003	0	0	0	154	0	11827	0	0	0	1122	45030	2846870
Other Portfolio Income **6**	5360337	931495	16264	290	2653	1552	407	550	1893	106	403	12022	4392701
Other Receipts **7**	12063626	479027	7407	23096	11695	475	13942	29464	15714	55584	33959	503048	10890218
Total Receipts **8**	570535306	26501277	3168120	540135	2487738	545278	1051654	1242528	1133725	2303328	5096801	22694108	503770614
Average Total Receipts **9**	46261	16934	323	1337	5799	17040	32864	82835	113372	255925	637100	3242015	31485663
Operating Costs/Operating Income (%)													
Cost of Operations **10**	71.9	66.6	60.3	73.4	63.0	71.0	66.6	68.3	59.4	63.8	63.8	72.6	72.4
Salaries and Wages **11**	11.2	10.0	11.0	9.9	12.7	10.7	13.4	14.4	13.9	14.4	13.7	9.9	11.3
Taxes Paid **12**	1.8	1.6	3.1	1.3	3.3	1.8	1.9	2.1	2.5	1.8	1.7	1.6	1.8
Interest Paid **13**	1.0	1.2	0.8	0.8	0.8	0.2	0.5	0.6	0.8	0.5	0.9	0.7	1.0
Depreciation **14**	2.2	3.2	1.2	0.9	0.8	2.1	1.1	1.5	2.5	1.6	2.9	2.0	2.2
Amortization and Depletion **15**	0.1	0.0	0.0	0.5	0.0	0.0	0.2	0.0	0.0	0.1	0.2	0.0	0.1
Pensions and Other Deferred Comp. **16**	0.5	1.4	0.0	1.0	0.8	0.2	0.2	0.2	0.3	0.2	0.2	0.3	0.5
Employee Benefits **17**	0.8	0.6	0.0	0.5	0.6	1.2	1.0	0.8	1.1	1.1	1.7	1.7	0.8
Advertising **18**	1.4	0.0	0.3	0.4	1.5	1.9	1.4	1.6	3.8	1.9	1.9	1.5	1.5
Other Expenses **19**	8.6	11.2	20.4	12.5	13.0	14.9	12.1	11.6	21.6	13.9	11.1	9.9	8.2
Officers' Compensation **20**	0.1	0.0	4.3	3.8	2.5	1.0	1.1	0.3	0.8	1.6	0.5	0.4	0.1
Operating Margin **21**	0.3	4.1	•	•	1.0	•	0.6	•	•	•	1.4	•	0.2
Operating Margin Before Officers' Comp. **22**	0.4	2.9	•	•	3.5	•	1.7	•	•	0.7	2.0	•	0.3

Selected Average Balance Sheet ($ in Thousands)

Net Receivables 23	1462	0	3	6	111	102	1195	4747	4865	19435	29387	74926	1053424
Inventories 24	5451	0	61	193	1516	5253	7075	15572	23142	47265	125479	494301	3760067
Net Property, Plant and Equipment 25	6805	0	27	50	251	1531	3159	7280	19401	26880	86384	420068	4950363
Total Assets 26	21896	0	129	655	2056	7773	16319	35868	78814	129441	338558	1285266	15791574
Notes and Loans Payable 27	5580	0	62	250	499	724	3199	9996	14234	20047	61971	267877	4057366
All Other Liabilities 28	7452	0	26	58	540	3298	19711	9736	121276	94728	83888	485747	5273416
Net Worth 29	8864	0	40	348	1016	3752	-6591	16135	-56697	14666	192700	531642	6460792

Selected Financial Ratios (Times to 1)

Current Ratio 30	1.2	•	2.9	3.2	2.5	2.0	2.7	2.5	0.4	2.2	1.9	1.3	1.2
Quick Ratio 31	0.4	•	0.5	1.0	0.6	1.1	0.9	0.7	0.2	0.8	0.5	0.3	0.4
Net Sales to Working Capital 32	28.9	•	5.6	5.5	6.6	5.8	4.4	5.7	•	5.6	7.2	21.1	30.2
Coverage Ratio 33	6.2	9.1	0.3	0.8	3.3	•	7.8	2.6	•	5.0	3.8	4.5	6.1
Total Asset Turnover 34	2.0	•	2.5	1.9	2.8	2.2	2.0	2.3	1.4	1.9	1.9	2.5	1.9
Inventory Turnover 35	5.8	•	3.2	4.8	2.4	2.3	3.0	3.5	2.8	3.4	3.2	4.6	5.8
Receivables Turnover 36	23.0	•	69.7	209.9	29.4	12.4	24.7	18.9	16.0	16.0	20.6	32.8	21.6
Total Liabilities to Net Worth 37	1.5	•	2.2	0.9	1.0	1.1	•	1.2	•	7.8	0.8	1.4	1.4
Current Assets to Working Capital 38	5.9	•	1.5	1.5	1.6	2.0	1.6	1.7	•	1.9	2.1	4.1	6.4
Current Liabilities to Working Capital 39	4.9	•	0.5	0.5	0.6	1.0	0.6	0.7	•	0.9	1.1	3.1	5.4
Working Capital to Net Sales 40	0.0	•	0.2	0.2	0.2	0.2	0.2	0.2	•	0.2	0.1	0.0	0.0
Inventory to Working Capital 41	3.5	•	1.1	0.7	1.2	0.8	1.0	1.0	•	1.1	1.4	3.0	3.7
Total Receipts to Cash Flow 42	10.2	8.1	12.6	15.8	10.9	28.2	9.0	15.7	8.5	8.7	11.2	11.7	10.2
Cost of Goods to Cash Flow 43	7.3	5.4	7.6	11.6	6.8	20.0	6.0	10.7	5.0	5.5	7.2	8.5	7.4
Cash Flow to Total Debt 44	0.3	•	0.3	0.3	0.5	0.1	0.2	0.3	0.1	0.3	0.4	0.4	0.3

Selected Financial Factors (in Percentages)

Debt Ratio 45	59.5	•	69.0	46.9	50.5	51.7	140.4	55.0	171.9	88.7	43.1	58.6	59.1
Return on Total Assets 46	11.9	•	0.5	1.2	7.0	•	7.4	3.5	•	4.7	6.7	7.4	11.2
Return on Equity Before Income Taxes 47	24.5	•	•	•	9.8	•	•	4.9	4.9	33.4	8.7	13.9	22.8
Return on Equity After Income Taxes 48	16.9	•	•	•	9.0	•	•	3.0	5.9	31.0	6.6	9.1	14.9
Profit Margin (Before Income Tax) 49	4.9	10.1	•	•	1.7	•	3.3	1.0	•	2.0	2.7	2.3	4.9
Profit Margin (After Income Tax) 50	3.4	10.1	•	•	1.6	•	2.7	0.6	•	1.8	2.0	1.5	3.2

231

Table II

Corporations with Net Income

GENERAL MERCHANDISE STORES

MONEY AMOUNTS AND SIZE OF ASSETS IN THOUSANDS OF DOLLARS

Item Description for Accounting Period 7/04 Through 6/05	Total	Zero Assets	Under 500	500 to 1,000	1,000 to 5,000	5,000 to 10,000	10,000 to 25,000	25,000 to 50,000	50,000 to 100,000	100,000 to 250,000	250,000 to 500,000	500,000 to 2,500,000	2,500,000 and over
Number of Enterprises 1	6550	270	5623	234	336	9	24	10	6	0	8	7	0
Revenues ($ in Thousands)													
Net Sales 2	509021507	24936239	2208348	189980	2002059	100439	904060	927410	858104	0	5035032	22049888	0
Interest 3	3112722	104270	179	487	948	285	315	133	13257	0	23341	57616	0
Rents 4	784745	0	0	0	121	0	925	152	8547	0	2944	26504	0
Royalties 5	1986784	0	0	0	152	0	11827	0	0	0	1122	45030	0
Other Portfolio Income 6	5321238	931495	12156	0	419	0	141	501	54	0	403	12022	0
Other Receipts 7	11900593	469899	5377	20941	3312	108	6045	13061	13791	0	33959	503048	0
Total Receipts 8	532127589	26441903	2226060	211408	2007011	100832	923313	941257	893753	·	5096801	22694108	0
Average Total Receipts 9	81241	97933	396	903	5973	11204	38471	94126	148959	·	637100	3242015	·
Operating Costs/Operating Income (%)													
Cost of Operations 10	72.9	66.6	57.0	59.5	62.1	47.3	66.8	71.4	60.5	·	63.8	72.6	·
Salaries and Wages 11	11.0	10.0	11.0	11.5	12.2	12.7	12.9	12.5	12.9	·	13.7	9.9	·
Taxes Paid 12	1.8	1.6	2.7	2.0	3.4	3.8	1.8	1.9	2.2	·	1.7	1.6	·
Interest Paid 13	0.9	1.2	0.7	2.1	0.9	0.4	0.5	0.6	0.8	·	0.9	0.7	·
Depreciation 14	2.2	3.2	0.6	2.4	0.8	2.2	1.0	1.3	1.9	·	2.9	2.0	·
Amortization and Depletion 15	0.1	·	0.0	1.3	0.0	0.0	0.3	0.0	0.0	·	0.2	0.0	·
Pensions and Other Deferred Comp. 16	0.5	1.4	·	2.6	1.0	0.3	0.2	0.2	0.3	·	0.2	0.3	·
Employee Benefits 17	0.8	0.6	·	0.2	0.6	0.1	0.9	0.6	1.2	·	1.7	1.7	·
Advertising 18	1.3	·	0.1	0.0	1.4	2.1	1.4	0.7	3.1	·	1.9	1.5	·
Other Expenses 19	7.7	11.1	20.1	16.6	12.1	21.1	10.6	8.7	17.3	·	11.1	9.9	·
Officers' Compensation 20	0.1	0.0	3.7	5.6	2.4	2.5	1.1	0.3	0.8	·	0.5	0.4	·
Operating Margin 21	0.7	4.2	4.1	·	3.1	7.5	2.6	1.8	·	·	1.4	·	·
Operating Margin Before Officers' Comp. 22	0.8	4.2	7.8	1.8	5.5	10.0	3.7	2.1	·	·	2.0	·	·

Selected Average Balance Sheet ($ in Thousands)

Net Receivables 23	2619	0		1	127	353	1135	6407	7270	29387	74926
Inventories 24	9056	0		69	1568	638	8078	14148	26279	123380	494301
Net Property, Plant and Equipment 25	11870	0		26	267	2184	3090	8234	18169	86384	420068
Total Assets 26	38032	0		122	1913	5527	16957	36501	76841	338558	1285266
Notes and Loans Payable 27	9278	0		59	542	727	3059	7363	16521	61971	267877
All Other Liabilities 28	12660	0		35	392	1394	4067	8992	19660	83888	485747
Net Worth 29	16094	0	28	199	978	3407	9830	20146	40659	192700	531642

Selected Financial Ratios (Times to 1)

Current Ratio 30	1.2	•	2.1	1.1	3.4	2.1	2.5	2.6	2.8	1.9	1.3
Quick Ratio 31	0.4	•	0.4	0.3	0.8	1.6	0.7	1.0	1.0	0.5	0.3
Net Sales to Working Capital 32	33.5	•	8.9	107.3	6.4	9.5	5.0	6.0	5.0	7.2	21.1
Coverage Ratio 33	6.8	9.2	7.6	4.6	4.8	19.3	11.4	6.6	4.7	3.8	4.5
Total Asset Turnover 34	2.0	•	3.2	1.4	3.1	2.0	2.2	2.5	1.9	1.9	2.5
Inventory Turnover 35	6.3	•	3.3	6.0	2.4	8.3	3.1	4.7	3.3	3.3	4.6
Receivables Turnover 36	23.1	•	•	2968.4	25.8	22.4	32.1	•	13.9	•	32.8
Total Liabilities to Net Worth 37	1.4	•	3.3	2.0	1.0	0.6	0.7	0.8	0.9	0.8	1.4
Current Assets to Working Capital 38	6.6	•	1.9	18.3	1.4	1.9	1.7	1.6	1.6	2.1	4.1
Current Liabilities to Working Capital 39	5.6	•	0.9	17.3	0.4	0.9	0.7	0.6	0.6	1.1	3.1
Working Capital to Net Sales 40	0.0	•	0.1	0.0	0.2	0.1	0.2	0.2	0.2	0.1	0.0
Inventory to Working Capital 41	4.0	•	1.6	10.8	1.1	0.4	1.1	0.9	0.8	1.4	3.0
Total Receipts to Cash Flow 42	10.8	8.0	8.2	7.7	9.7	5.2	8.8	14.7	7.0	11.2	11.7
Cost of Goods to Cash Flow 43	7.9	5.3	4.7	4.6	6.0	2.4	5.9	10.5	4.2	7.2	8.5
Cash Flow to Total Debt 44	0.3	•	0.5	0.3	0.7	1.0	0.6	0.4	0.6	0.4	0.4

Selected Financial Factors (in Percentages)

Debt Ratio 45	57.7	•	76.8	66.2	48.9	38.4	42.0	44.8	47.1	43.1	58.6
Return on Total Assets 46	12.8	•	18.1	13.2	13.2	16.9	11.4	9.9	7.2	6.7	7.4
Return on Equity Before Income Taxes 47	25.8	•	67.6	30.6	20.4	25.9	17.9	15.3	10.8	8.7	13.9
Return on Equity After Income Taxes 48	17.8	•	67.5	24.4	19.2	17.1	15.5	13.0	8.3	6.6	9.1
Profit Margin (Before Income Tax) 49	5.3	10.3	4.9	7.5	3.3	7.9	4.7	3.3	3.1	2.7	2.3
Profit Margin (After Income Tax) 50	3.7	10.3	4.9	6.0	3.2	5.2	4.0	2.8	2.4	2.0	1.5

Table I
Corporations with and without Net Income

MISCELLANEOUS STORE RETAILERS

MONEY AMOUNTS AND SIZE OF ASSETS IN THOUSANDS OF DOLLARS

Item Description for Accounting Period 7/04 Through 6/05		Total	Zero Assets	Under 500	500 to 1,000	1,000 to 5,000	5,000 to 10,000	10,000 to 25,000	25,000 to 50,000	50,000 to 100,000	100,000 to 250,000	250,000 to 500,000	500,000 to 2,500,000	2,500,000 and over
Number of Enterprises	1	91005	12755	68283	4924	4493	245	186	57	23	19	5	11	4
Revenues ($ in Thousands)														
Net Sales	2	135294812	1465115	29288542	9265857	19485059	3032384	5026194	3869577	2710453	5073735	2048898	17103621	36925377
Interest	3	320535	2484	5383	5306	26322	6731	4285	9423	4520	4623	9926	75346	166186
Rents	4	159154	0	5929	1663	15195	160	4543	1172	6451	1545	6326	90329	25841
Royalties	5	186830	0	0	115	1845	61956	3101	1105	0	21709	0	6585	90413
Other Portfolio Income	6	1137794	84140	32865	4260	40905	4869	12736	12081	14147	4645	47152	57421	822570
Other Receipts	7	2131067	132422	204664	29406	200719	64560	117323	65422	27896	5663	87100	341749	854147
Total Receipts	8	139230192	1684161	29537383	9306607	19770045	3170660	5168182	3958780	2763467	5111920	2199402	17675051	38884534
Average Total Receipts	9	1530	132	433	1890	4400	12941	27786	69452	120151	269048	439880	1606823	9721134
Operating Costs/Operating Income (%)														
Cost of Operations	10	63.7	51.7	56.0	62.0	69.2	63.4	67.7	62.2	62.7	58.9	49.4	55.4	73.0
Salaries and Wages	11	11.5	13.9	11.0	11.5	9.8	13.8	12.0	13.1	12.5	11.8	15.9	14.7	10.4
Taxes Paid	12	2.0	5.2	2.5	2.5	1.8	1.9	1.8	1.9	1.5	2.0	1.9	2.3	1.3
Interest Paid	13	1.0	0.7	0.8	0.7	0.8	1.2	0.8	1.0	1.3	0.9	2.5	0.7	1.3
Depreciation	14	1.7	0.7	1.1	1.2	1.0	1.5	1.9	2.2	1.4	2.5	3.1	3.6	1.6
Amortization and Depletion	15	0.2	0.1	0.2	0.2	0.1	0.1	0.1	0.2	0.4	0.1	0.3	0.3	0.3
Pensions and Other Deferred Comp.	16	0.1	0.2	0.1	0.1	0.3	0.4	0.3	0.3	0.1	0.1	0.0	0.2	0.0
Employee Benefits	17	1.0	2.2	0.6	0.4	0.8	0.6	0.9	0.9	0.8	1.0	2.8	1.8	1.0
Advertising	18	2.0	1.3	1.5	1.4	1.0	1.4	1.4	1.5	3.7	2.6	3.4	2.9	2.7
Other Expenses	19	14.5	32.2	20.0	16.2	12.0	14.2	11.5	14.2	17.9	14.8	19.8	14.3	10.1
Officers' Compensation	20	2.3	2.6	5.7	3.5	3.6	2.8	1.6	1.7	0.7	0.9	0.8	0.6	0.1
Operating Margin	21	•	•	0.6	0.2	•	•	0.2	0.8	•	4.3	0.0	3.2	•
Operating Margin Before Officers' Comp.	22	2.3	•	6.2	3.8	3.4	1.6	1.8	2.5	•	5.2	0.8	3.8	•

Selected Average Balance Sheet ($ in Thousands)

Net Receivables 23	135	0	12	111	350	1524	2425	6106	13505	15085	44647	117136	1520217
Inventories 24	201	0	44	303	819	2860	5229	13252	24765	49691	68975	217341	845823
Net Property, Plant and Equipment 25	133	0	18	142	346	898	3026	6416	10789	26423	91134	298813	746722
Total Assets 26	786	0	108	687	2004	6774	14378	36461	69239	148494	354047	1098445	6766528
Notes and Loans Payable 27	226	0	57	320	738	2281	4546	10882	21655	56215	159436	163214	1395176
All Other Liabilities 28	308	0	23	172	573	2321	5220	10827	30141	43711	99313	408022	3582356
Net Worth 29	252	0	27	195	693	2172	4611	14752	17443	48568	95299	527209	1788996

Selected Financial Ratios (Times to 1)

Current Ratio 30	1.7	•	2.4	2.1	1.9	1.4	1.5	1.8	1.5	1.6	1.6	1.6	1.5
Quick Ratio 31	0.7	•	1.0	0.9	0.7	0.6	0.6	0.7	0.6	0.4	0.8	0.5	0.7
Net Sales to Working Capital 32	7.5	•	9.8	7.4	6.3	7.5	8.1	6.1	7.1	7.9	7.7	7.2	6.8
Coverage Ratio 33	4.0	6.8	2.8	2.0	2.6	3.8	4.9	4.2	0.3	6.7	4.4	10.3	3.6
Total Asset Turnover 34	1.9	•	4.0	2.7	2.2	1.8	1.9	1.9	1.7	1.8	1.2	1.4	1.4
Inventory Turnover 35	4.7	•	5.4	3.9	3.7	2.7	3.5	3.2	3.0	3.2	2.9	4.0	8.0
Receivables Turnover 36	9.4	•	30.0	17.4	12.5	8.1	10.5	11.7	9.8	19.8	13.3	14.5	4.5
Total Liabilities to Net Worth 37	2.1	•	3.0	2.5	1.9	2.1	2.1	1.5	3.0	2.1	2.7	1.1	2.8
Current Assets to Working Capital 38	2.5	•	1.7	1.9	2.1	3.2	2.9	2.3	2.9	2.7	2.6	2.6	3.0
Current Liabilities to Working Capital 39	1.5	•	0.7	0.9	1.1	2.2	1.9	1.3	1.9	1.7	1.6	1.6	2.0
Working Capital to Net Sales 40	0.1	•	0.1	0.1	0.2	0.1	0.1	0.2	0.1	0.1	0.1	0.1	0.1
Inventory to Working Capital 41	1.0	•	0.9	1.1	1.2	1.5	1.5	1.2	1.6	1.5	1.0	1.1	0.6
Total Receipts to Cash Flow 42	8.5	4.6	7.5	9.4	10.0	7.4	9.7	7.9	8.0	7.9	5.0	6.9	10.4
Cost of Goods to Cash Flow 43	5.4	2.4	4.2	5.9	6.9	4.7	6.6	4.9	5.0	4.6	2.5	3.8	7.6
Cash Flow to Total Debt 44	0.3	•	0.7	0.4	0.3	0.4	0.3	0.4	0.3	0.3	0.3	0.4	0.2

Selected Financial Factors (in Percentages)

Debt Ratio 45	67.9	•	74.7	71.6	65.4	67.9	67.9	59.5	74.8	67.3	73.1	52.0	73.6
Return on Total Assets 46	7.4	•	8.8	3.7	4.5	8.2	7.0	7.5	0.7	10.6	12.4	10.3	6.5
Return on Equity Before Income Taxes 47	17.2	•	22.4	6.6	8.0	19.0	17.5	14.1	•	27.7	35.5	19.4	17.7
Return on Equity After Income Taxes 48	12.8	•	21.3	6.2	6.3	15.5	15.7	12.8	•	25.6	23.9	13.5	11.3
Profit Margin (Before Income Tax) 49	2.9	4.1	1.4	0.7	1.3	3.3	3.0	3.1	•	5.0	8.3	6.6	3.4
Profit Margin (After Income Tax) 50	2.2	3.8	1.4	0.6	1.0	2.7	2.7	2.8	•	4.6	5.6	4.6	2.2

Table II
Corporations with Net Income

MISCELLANEOUS STORE RETAILERS

MONEY AMOUNTS AND SIZE OF ASSETS IN THOUSANDS OF DOLLARS

Item Description for Accounting Period 7/04 Through 6/05	Total	Zero Assets	Under 500	500 to 1,000	1,000 to 5,000	5,000 to 10,000	10,000 to 25,000	25,000 to 50,000	50,000 to 100,000	100,000 to 250,000	250,000 to 500,000	500,000 to 2,500,000	2,500,000 and over
Number of Enterprises 1	48017	5693	35387	3456	3063	192	135	40	15	16	5	11	4
Revenues ($ in Thousands)													
Net Sales 2	113052425	864429	17855899	7146119	14846440	2763847	4167830	2594819	1840280	4894866	2048898	17103621	36925377
Interest 3	299719	1831	2888	4506	16209	6637	2981	7116	1578	4516	9926	75346	166186
Rents 4	149024	0	4834	0	15139	160	2134	763	2290	1207	6326	90329	25841
Royalties 5	184502	0	0	115	0	61956	2852	872	0	21709	0	6585	90413
Other Portfolio Income 6	1097383	26859	68854	1469	30173	4789	10960	8456	14147	4530	47152	57421	822570
Other Receipts 7	1915030	135550	128564	18960	132880	61029	88732	54238	16235	-4151	87100	341749	854147
Total Receipts 8	116698083	1063678	18026030	7171169	15040841	2898418	4275489	2666264	1874530	4922677	2199402	17675051	38884534
Average Total Receipts 9	2430	187	509	2075	4910	15096	31670	66657	124969	307667	439880	1606823	9721134
Operating Costs/Operating Income (%)													
Cost of Operations 10	64.1	41.4	54.6	62.0	68.6	64.8	68.4	62.4	63.0	58.2	49.4	55.4	73.0
Salaries and Wages 11	11.2	14.9	10.1	10.8	9.0	13.1	11.4	12.2	11.7	12.0	15.9	14.7	10.4
Taxes Paid 12	1.9	6.2	2.3	2.5	1.7	1.9	1.7	1.8	1.6	2.1	1.9	2.3	1.3
Interest Paid 13	0.9	0.3	0.5	0.6	0.7	0.8	0.7	0.8	0.7	0.9	2.5	0.7	1.3
Depreciation 14	1.7	0.5	0.8	1.2	0.9	1.5	1.7	1.8	1.2	2.4	3.1	3.6	1.6
Amortization and Depletion 15	0.2	0.0	0.1	0.1	0.0	0.1	0.1	0.2	0.1	0.1	0.3	0.3	0.3
Pensions and Other Deferred Comp. 16	0.2	0.0	0.2	0.1	0.3	0.4	0.3	0.4	0.0	0.1	0.0	0.2	0.0
Employee Benefits 17	1.0	2.6	0.6	0.4	0.7	0.5	0.8	0.7	0.7	1.0	2.8	1.8	1.0
Advertising 18	2.0	1.3	1.1	1.3	1.0	1.2	1.1	1.1	1.6	2.6	3.4	2.9	2.7
Other Expenses 19	13.3	25.5	19.0	15.5	10.7	13.1	10.3	13.1	15.8	14.7	19.8	14.3	10.1
Officers' Compensation 20	1.9	0.6	5.4	3.2	3.3	2.9	1.6	2.3	1.0	0.9	0.8	0.6	0.1
Operating Margin 21	1.7	6.5	5.3	2.3	3.2	•	2.0	3.2	2.7	4.8	0.0	3.2	•
Operating Margin Before Officers' Comp. 22	3.6	7.1	10.7	5.5	6.5	2.6	3.6	5.5	3.7	5.7	0.8	3.8	•

Selected Average Balance Sheet ($ in Thousands)

Net Receivables 23	228	0	13	111	393	1675	2473	6927	9588	14565	44647	117136	1520217
Inventories 24	290	0	46	289	897	2500	5059	12147	27622	55048	54801	245245	867320
Net Property, Plant and Equipment 25	209	0	15	142	302	815	2824	5044	12021	27932	91134	298813	746722
Total Assets 26	1290	0	115	683	2091	6421	14516	35548	73079	154563	354047	1098445	6766528
Notes and Loans Payable 27	319	0	44	271	680	1651	4294	9850	19980	61804	159436	163214	1395176
All Other Liabilities 28	526	0	21	187	623	2604	4787	9588	24106	47343	99313	408022	3582356
Net Worth 29	444	0	49	225	789	2166	5435	16110	28993	45415	95299	527209	1788996

Selected Financial Ratios (Times to 1)

Current Ratio 30	1.7	•	2.9	2.0	2.1	1.4	1.6	1.9	1.7	1.5	1.6	1.6	1.5
Quick Ratio 31	0.7	•	1.3	0.9	0.8	0.7	0.6	0.8	0.5	0.4	0.8	0.5	0.7
Net Sales to Working Capital 32	7.2	•	8.7	8.7	5.6	9.1	8.1	5.7	6.0	8.7	7.7	7.2	6.8
Coverage Ratio 33	6.4	92.0	12.8	5.3	7.4	6.6	7.5	8.0	7.8	7.2	4.4	10.3	3.6
Total Asset Turnover 34	1.8	•	4.4	3.0	2.3	2.2	2.1	1.8	1.7	2.0	1.2	1.4	1.4
Inventory Turnover 35	5.2	•	6.1	4.4	3.7	3.7	4.2	3.3	2.8	3.2	3.7	3.5	7.8
Receivables Turnover 36	8.8	•	27.5	17.8	13.2	9.3	11.8	10.5	12.4	24.6	•	•	7.8
Total Liabilities to Net Worth 37	1.9	•	1.3	2.0	1.7	2.0	1.7	1.2	1.5	2.4	2.7	1.1	2.8
Current Assets to Working Capital 38	2.5	•	1.5	2.0	1.9	3.3	2.7	2.2	2.4	2.8	2.6	2.6	3.0
Current Liabilities to Working Capital 39	1.5	•	0.5	1.0	0.9	2.3	1.7	1.2	1.4	1.8	1.6	1.6	2.0
Working Capital to Net Sales 40	0.1	•	0.1	0.1	0.2	0.1	0.1	0.2	0.2	0.1	0.1	0.1	0.1
Inventory to Working Capital 41	0.9	•	0.8	1.0	1.1	1.6	1.4	1.0	1.5	1.7	1.0	1.1	0.6
Total Receipts to Cash Flow 42	7.6	2.2	5.7	7.9	8.2	7.1	9.1	6.3	6.3	7.8	5.0	6.9	10.4
Cost of Goods to Cash Flow 43	4.9	0.9	3.1	4.9	5.6	4.6	6.2	3.9	4.0	4.6	2.5	3.8	7.6
Cash Flow to Total Debt 44	0.4	•	1.4	0.6	0.5	0.5	0.4	0.5	0.4	0.4	0.3	0.4	0.2

Selected Financial Factors (in Percentages)

Debt Ratio 45	65.6	•	57.2	67.1	62.3	66.3	62.6	54.7	60.3	70.6	73.1	52.0	73.6
Return on Total Assets 46	10.7	•	29.7	9.7	12.1	12.1	11.2	12.4	8.7	12.4	12.4	10.3	6.5
Return on Equity Before Income Taxes 47	26.3	•	64.0	24.0	27.7	30.5	26.0	23.9	19.1	36.4	35.5	19.4	17.7
Return on Equity After Income Taxes 48	21.6	•	62.9	23.5	25.6	26.0	23.9	22.2	16.0	33.7	23.9	13.5	11.3
Profit Margin (Before Income Tax) 49	5.0	29.5	6.3	2.6	4.5	4.6	4.6	5.9	4.5	5.4	8.3	6.6	3.4
Profit Margin (After Income Tax) 50	4.1	29.0	6.1	2.6	4.2	3.9	4.2	5.5	3.8	5.0	5.6	4.6	2.2

Table I

Corporations with and without Net Income

NONSTORE RETAILERS

MONEY AMOUNTS AND SIZE OF ASSETS IN THOUSANDS OF DOLLARS

Item Description for Accounting Period 7/04 Through 6/05	Total	Zero Assets	Under 500	500 to 1,000	1,000 to 5,000	5,000 to 10,000	10,000 to 25,000	25,000 to 50,000	50,000 to 100,000	100,000 to 250,000	250,000 to 500,000	500,000 to 2,500,000	2,500,000 and over
Number of Enterprises **1**	48341	6714	35462	3046	2502	291	155	82	29	28	13	17	3
Revenues ($ in Thousands)													
Net Sales **2**	114529953	2513606	16408558	9033096	18183178	7998977	7520584	7410455	3609768	7572209	8268897	13096193	12914430
Interest **3**	421157	49	3634	5150	10759	6002	3869	8831	13625	18679	137471	122551	90537
Rents **4**	110499	274	3511	8468	7398	2738	1209	5009	2886	5148	26488	44343	3025
Royalties **5**	215058	0	0	0	10587	0	2041	844	41906	0	2016	84401	73263
Other Portfolio Income **6**	286407	21368	65244	4621	21478	12956	31998	17101	2366	896	1399	76394	30585
Other Receipts **7**	2365505	13835	42657	33453	105034	38833	75538	96404	51278	229333	94832	514906	1069406
Total Receipts **8**	117928579	2549132	16523604	9084788	18338434	8059506	7635239	7538644	3721829	7826265	8531103	13938788	14181246
Average Total Receipts **9**	2440	380	466	2983	7330	27696	49260	91935	128339	279509	656239	819929	4727082
Operating Costs/Operating Income (%)													
Cost of Operations **10**	66.7	77.8	65.5	64.6	70.7	67.6	70.1	64.5	57.5	65.6	65.1	60.2	71.9
Salaries and Wages **11**	9.0	1.7	6.7	12.4	7.2	7.4	8.1	8.5	8.5	9.5	5.6	11.5	14.9
Taxes Paid **12**	1.5	4.8	2.2	2.7	1.3	1.1	1.1	1.2	1.4	1.3	1.0	1.3	0.8
Interest Paid **13**	0.8	0.7	0.5	0.7	0.6	0.4	0.5	0.5	1.0	0.8	1.0	2.1	1.1
Depreciation **14**	1.7	1.2	1.6	2.1	2.0	1.2	1.4	1.6	1.7	1.3	1.5	1.9	1.7
Amortization and Depletion **15**	0.3	0.4	0.2	0.2	0.3	0.1	0.1	0.3	0.4	0.6	0.4	0.7	0.1
Pensions and Other Deferred Comp. **16**	0.2	0.1	0.2	0.3	0.3	0.2	0.3	0.2	0.2	0.2	0.1	0.3	0.0
Employee Benefits **17**	0.8	0.1	0.4	0.6	0.7	0.7	0.6	0.9	0.9	0.8	0.6	1.8	0.9
Advertising **18**	3.2	0.7	1.7	0.6	1.9	3.9	3.4	7.5	5.5	4.0	6.0	3.1	3.7
Other Expenses **19**	14.8	18.5	14.4	13.1	11.2	14.7	13.1	13.8	23.2	13.4	18.6	18.2	15.2
Officers' Compensation **20**	2.2	1.3	5.5	4.1	2.8	2.0	1.3	0.9	1.0	0.9	0.7	1.5	0.2
Operating Margin **21**	•	•	1.2	•	0.9	0.7	•	0.2	•	1.5	•	•	•
Operating Margin Before Officers' Comp. **22**	0.9	•	6.7	2.8	3.7	2.7	1.2	1.1	2.4	2.4	0.0	•	•

Selected Average Balance Sheet ($ in Thousands)

Net Receivables 23	167	0	17	177	495	1714	3468	7077	12346	29082	60723	47019	436288
Inventories 24	145	0	15	132	420	1286	3074	5223	11471	27780	52055	74580	237631
Net Property, Plant and Equipment 25	146	0	16	202	463	1130	2802	4976	10029	17763	30588	85274	298337
Total Assets 26	1205	0	82	751	2190	6882	15547	34274	69821	155397	337983	894391	4804492
Notes and Loans Payable 27	351	0	44	311	821	1892	4801	6591	19245	38816	61733	196042	1609070
All Other Liabilities 28	344	0	28	249	666	2989	6410	13708	23984	43970	112262	224052	1002879
Net Worth 29	510	0	10	191	703	2001	4336	13974	26592	72611	163989	474297	2192543

Selected Financial Ratios (Times to 1)

Current Ratio 30	1.6	•	1.4	1.5	1.5	1.5	1.5	1.6	1.7	1.7	2.1	1.7	1.5
Quick Ratio 31	1.0	•	1.0	0.9	0.9	0.9	0.9	0.9	0.9	0.9	1.3	0.8	1.0
Net Sales to Working Capital 32	10.7	•	28.4	20.2	16.2	16.5	14.5	11.7	6.4	7.4	6.2	6.9	6.2
Coverage Ratio 33	3.0	•	4.7	•	4.0	4.6	4.0	5.0	2.8	6.8	3.4	3.1	0.4
Total Asset Turnover 34	2.0	•	5.7	4.0	3.3	4.0	3.1	2.6	1.8	1.7	1.9	0.9	0.9
Inventory Turnover 35	10.9	•	20.5	14.5	12.3	14.5	11.1	11.2	6.2	6.4	8.0	6.2	13.0
Receivables Turnover 36	14.4	•	30.4	19.6	14.1	16.7	13.9	16.0	7.5	10.0	9.8	16.0	10.2
Total Liabilities to Net Worth 37	1.4	•	7.6	2.9	2.1	2.4	2.6	1.5	1.6	1.1	1.1	0.9	1.2
Current Assets to Working Capital 38	2.7	•	3.3	3.1	3.0	3.1	3.1	2.8	2.3	2.5	1.9	2.3	2.9
Current Liabilities to Working Capital 39	1.7	•	2.3	2.1	2.0	2.1	2.1	1.8	1.3	1.5	0.9	1.3	1.9
Working Capital to Net Sales 40	0.1	•	0.0	0.0	0.1	0.1	0.1	0.1	0.2	0.1	0.2	0.1	0.2
Inventory to Working Capital 41	0.6	•	0.9	1.0	0.7	0.9	0.9	0.8	0.7	0.8	0.5	0.6	0.3
Total Receipts to Cash Flow 42	7.0	32.5	7.3	9.8	9.7	6.9	7.9	7.1	4.3	6.1	5.1	5.1	7.6
Cost of Goods to Cash Flow 43	4.7	25.3	4.8	6.3	6.8	4.7	5.5	4.6	2.5	4.0	3.3	3.0	5.5
Cash Flow to Total Debt 44	0.5	•	0.9	0.5	0.5	0.8	0.5	0.6	0.7	0.5	0.7	0.4	0.2

Selected Financial Factors (in Percentages)

Debt Ratio 45	57.7	•	88.3	74.5	67.9	70.9	72.1	59.2	61.9	53.3	51.5	47.0	54.4
Return on Total Assets 46	5.0	•	14.0	•	7.7	7.3	6.3	6.4	4.8	9.9	6.7	5.6	0.4
Return on Equity Before Income Taxes 47	7.8	•	94.3	•	18.1	19.8	16.9	12.5	8.2	18.0	9.7	7.1	•
Return on Equity After Income Taxes 48	6.1	•	91.3	•	16.2	17.6	15.2	9.6	5.1	17.0	7.5	4.5	•
Profit Margin (Before Income Tax) 49	1.7	•	1.9	•	1.7	1.4	1.5	1.9	1.7	4.8	2.5	4.4	•
Profit Margin (After Income Tax) 50	1.3	•	1.9	•	1.6	1.3	1.4	1.5	1.1	4.6	1.9	2.8	•

Table II

Corporations with Net Income

NONSTORE RETAILERS

MONEY AMOUNTS AND SIZE OF ASSETS IN THOUSANDS OF DOLLARS

Item Description for Accounting Period 7/04 Through 6/05	Total	Zero Assets	Under 500	500 to 1,000	1,000 to 5,000	5,000 to 10,000	10,000 to 25,000	25,000 to 50,000	50,000 to 100,000	100,000 to 250,000	250,000 to 500,000	500,000 to 2,500,000	2,500,000 and over
Number of Enterprises 1	25095	2886	18591	1514	1698	190	105	58	16	18	7	12	0
Revenues ($ in Thousands)													
Net Sales 2	82507873	2082941	11138648	4565217	13172176	5859621	5678930	5908535	2466694	5400699	5781175	20453235	0
Interest 3	300194	38	1363	3413	8219	4446	1569	6682	12735	14142	128193	119394	0
Rents 4	34002	274	0	8347	3121	2557	860	3781	2519	5148	1252	6143	0
Royalties 5	121468	0	0	0	10578	0	1909	844	40764	0	2016	65358	0
Other Portfolio Income 6	188200	21368	55197	1652	17407	11657	24338	11165	900	594	1258	42662	0
Other Receipts 7	1875288	202	17731	12668	68425	24828	60063	51551	18726	203541	25677	1391880	0
Total Receipts 8	85027025	2104823	11212939	4591297	13279926	5903109	5767669	5982558	2542338	5624124	5939571	22078672	0
Average Total Receipts 9	3388	729	603	3033	7821	31069	54930	103148	158896	312451	848510	1839889	•
Operating Costs/Operating Income (%)													
Cost of Operations 10	67.6	77.5	63.0	62.7	67.2	69.6	70.7	64.4	58.7	65.5	60.8	73.6	•
Salaries and Wages 11	7.5	1.0	6.5	12.0	7.2	6.8	7.1	7.5	7.4	10.0	5.4	8.2	•
Taxes Paid 12	1.4	5.7	2.1	3.0	1.3	1.1	1.0	1.0	1.3	1.4	0.8	0.9	•
Interest Paid 13	0.6	0.3	0.3	0.3	0.5	0.2	0.3	0.4	0.4	0.5	0.7	1.2	•
Depreciation 14	1.2	0.8	1.3	1.3	1.5	1.0	1.0	1.3	1.1	1.1	1.0	1.1	•
Amortization and Depletion 15	0.2	0.0	0.0	0.1	0.2	0.1	0.1	0.2	0.1	0.2	0.4	0.3	•
Pensions and Other Deferred Comp. 16	0.2	0.1	0.2	0.5	0.3	0.2	0.1	0.2	0.2	0.3	0.1	0.2	•
Employee Benefits 17	0.6	0.1	0.3	0.4	0.7	0.7	0.6	0.9	0.6	0.8	0.4	0.8	•
Advertising 18	3.1	0.8	1.8	0.9	2.5	4.2	3.4	7.5	4.6	3.6	8.0	1.5	•
Other Expenses 19	13.3	12.9	12.9	11.0	12.1	11.8	12.3	12.4	22.3	11.8	17.2	14.2	•
Officers' Compensation 20	2.3	1.4	6.3	3.9	3.2	1.9	1.1	0.9	1.0	0.8	0.7	1.0	•
Operating Margin 21	2.0	2.3	5.4	3.7	3.4	2.5	2.4	3.2	2.4	4.2	4.3	•	•
Operating Margin Before Officers' Comp. 22	4.2	3.7	11.6	7.6	6.6	4.4	3.4	4.1	3.4	4.9	5.0	•	•

Selected Average Balance Sheet ($ in Thousands)

Item	No.												
Net Receivables	23	198	0	18	234	563	2046	3868	8109	13328	30417	77748	62725
Inventories	24	204	0	22	125	508	1043	3315	5601	13878	33559	71703	122275
Net Property, Plant and Equipment	25	151	0	18	163	347	1159	2345	4678	5932	14914	35110	106833
Total Assets	26	1232	0	107	710	2299	6924	15336	34230	72527	150801	314533	1079719
Notes and Loans Payable	27	306	0	43	209	671	1161	3815	6011	13981	25863	52033	282848
All Other Liabilities	28	403	0	21	244	693	2623	5637	12369	23069	43278	89005	384080
Net Worth	29	523	0	43	258	935	3140	5883	15850	35477	81660	173494	412791

Selected Financial Ratios (Times to 1)

Item	No.												
Current Ratio	30	1.8	•	2.1	1.7	1.7	1.8	1.5	1.7	2.1	2.0	2.3	1.8
Quick Ratio	31	1.0	•	1.5	1.3	1.1	1.1	0.9	1.0	1.0	1.0	1.3	0.8
Net Sales to Working Capital	32	10.0	•	14.8	14.5	12.3	13.5	14.5	11.2	5.5	6.6	6.8	7.7
Coverage Ratio	33	9.6	13.6	22.7	13.3	10.0	16.2	13.2	11.9	14.0	19.3	10.5	5.3
Total Asset Turnover	34	2.7	•	5.6	4.2	3.4	4.5	3.5	3.0	2.1	2.0	2.6	1.6
Inventory Turnover	35	10.9	•	17.2	15.1	10.3	20.6	11.5	11.7	6.5	5.9	7.0	10.3
Receivables Turnover	36	16.0	•	34.8	13.8	12.6	15.5	14.5	16.4	7.6	9.5	10.0	24.3
Total Liabilities to Net Worth	37	1.4	•	1.5	1.8	1.2	1.6	1.6	1.2	1.0	0.8	0.8	1.6
Current Assets to Working Capital	38	2.2	•	1.9	2.4	2.5	2.3	2.9	2.5	1.9	2.0	1.7	2.3
Current Liabilities to Working Capital	39	1.2	•	0.9	1.4	1.5	1.3	1.9	1.5	0.9	1.0	0.7	1.3
Working Capital to Net Sales	40	0.1	•	0.1	0.1	0.1	0.1	0.1	0.1	0.2	0.2	0.1	0.1
Inventory to Working Capital	41	0.6	•	0.6	0.4	0.6	0.5	0.9	0.7	0.6	0.7	0.6	0.5
Total Receipts to Cash Flow	42	6.1	8.9	6.1	7.5	7.5	7.5	7.0	6.4	3.7	5.4	4.4	5.6
Cost of Goods to Cash Flow	43	4.1	6.9	3.9	4.7	5.0	5.2	4.9	4.1	2.2	3.5	2.7	4.1
Cash Flow to Total Debt	44	0.8	•	1.5	0.9	0.8	1.1	0.8	0.9	1.1	0.8	1.3	0.5

Selected Financial Factors (in Percentages)

Item	No.												
Debt Ratio	45	57.6	•	60.0	63.7	59.3	54.6	61.6	53.7	51.1	45.8	44.8	61.8
Return on Total Assets	46	15.1	•	35.4	19.5	15.7	15.2	14.9	14.7	12.6	17.5	20.4	9.7
Return on Equity Before Income Taxes	47	31.9	•	84.5	49.6	34.8	31.5	36.0	29.1	23.9	30.6	33.4	20.6
Return on Equity After Income Taxes	48	28.7	•	83.3	48.1	32.7	29.5	34.1	25.5	19.7	29.2	29.5	16.2
Profit Margin (Before Income Tax)	49	5.1	3.3	6.0	4.2	4.2	3.2	3.9	4.5	5.5	8.3	7.0	5.0
Profit Margin (After Income Tax)	50	4.6	3.2	5.9	4.1	3.9	3.0	3.7	4.0	4.5	8.0	6.2	3.9

Table I

Corporations with and without Net Income

AIR TRANSPORTATION

MONEY AMOUNTS AND SIZE OF ASSETS IN THOUSANDS OF DOLLARS

Item Description for Accounting Period 7/04 Through 6/05	Total	Zero Assets	Under 500	500 to 1,000	1,000 to 5,000	5,000 to 10,000	10,000 to 25,000	25,000 to 50,000	50,000 to 100,000	100,000 to 250,000	250,000 to 500,000	500,000 to 2,500,000	2,500,000 and over
Number of Enterprises **1**	10188	1630	6572	641	996	140	111	49	11	11	5	13	9
Revenues ($ in Thousands)													
Net Sales **2**	122120260	546574	1989294	505306	2111577	1297194	1746161	1926970	777988	2932665	3136694	15355057	89794780
Interest **3**	435663	113	172	123	7329	690	2127	3424	654	840	3449	60292	356451
Rents **4**	295776	0	5	0	930	2999	356	52	364	1711	630	8723	280005
Royalties **5**	27033	0	0	0	0	9	0	0	0	409	0	23818	2798
Other Portfolio Income **6**	1240151	121527	106760	66	100722	15363	9323	33879	2496	5675	8468	117500	718373
Other Receipts **7**	4548307	17583	29636	607	14588	10422	57927	33472	14961	-23988	2926	169432	4220739
Total Receipts **8**	128667190	685797	2125867	506102	2235146	1326677	1815894	1997797	796463	2917312	3152167	15734822	95373146
Average Total Receipts **9**	12629	421	323	790	2244	9476	16359	40771	72406	265210	630433	1210371	10597016
Operating Costs/Operating Income (%)													
Cost of Operations **10**	20.8	62.8	29.4	78.6	48.2	58.0	49.4	50.1	29.7	30.3	41.4	15.3	17.5
Salaries and Wages **11**	22.5	5.3	5.7	4.2	9.4	6.5	11.8	7.7	12.4	12.6	22.5	20.1	25.0
Taxes Paid **12**	3.0	1.0	1.9	0.5	1.8	3.0	2.3	1.7	1.8	2.0	2.2	3.4	3.1
Interest Paid **13**	3.2	1.6	1.5	3.9	2.0	2.2	2.2	1.3	1.5	1.4	1.0	3.0	3.5
Depreciation **14**	10.5	12.2	5.1	8.1	17.7	13.3	10.8	8.7	4.5	6.2	7.0	9.7	10.9
Amortization and Depletion **15**	0.4	0.2	0.0	0.0	0.0	0.0	0.2	•	0.5	0.3	0.5	1.0	0.4
Pensions and Other Deferred Comp. **16**	1.8	0.1	0.4	0.0	0.1	0.1	0.2	0.1	0.4	0.5	1.8	0.9	2.2
Employee Benefits **17**	3.1	0.4	1.0	0.0	0.8	0.9	1.8	1.3	1.2	1.8	2.2	2.1	3.6
Advertising **18**	0.8	0.0	0.5	0.0	0.1	0.2	0.5	0.4	0.1	0.1	0.4	0.8	0.9
Other Expenses **19**	46.7	40.2	48.0	17.0	35.5	22.1	35.3	37.0	42.8	40.1	22.8	51.7	48.1
Officers' Compensation **20**	0.4	3.7	2.8	•	1.6	1.7	1.3	1.0	2.0	0.6	0.5	0.7	0.2
Operating Margin **21**	•	•	3.7	•	•	•	•	•	2.9	4.1	•	•	•
Operating Margin Before Officers' Comp. **22**	•	•	6.5	•	•	•	•	•	4.9	4.8	•	•	•

Selected Average Balance Sheet ($ in Thousands)

Line Item													
Net Receivables 23	661	0	10	389	204	1858	1976	4405	8174	26746	34425	68692	452539
Inventories 24	218	0	0	0	0	13	530	791	2686	8925	14890	21266	179594
Net Property, Plant and Equipment 25	9142	0	49	134	1164	2421	9330	17575	21650	54499	175315	549880	8941160
Total Assets 26	14854	0	91	823	2037	6758	15654	35039	63500	148508	369200	1040570	14008823
Notes and Loans Payable 27	6274	0	162	1194	1666	6287	9942	17005	24977	58913	92241	488173	5542597
All Other Liabilities 28	8811	0	29	320	580	3900	3937	9081	41625	55567	216733	381727	8916887
Net Worth 29	-231	0	-100	-691	-209	-3429	1775	8954	-3102	34028	60226	170669	-450661

Selected Financial Ratios (Times to 1)

Line Item													
Current Ratio 30	0.9	•	1.5	1.6	1.2	1.8	0.9	1.4	1.6	1.1	1.0	1.1	0.8
Quick Ratio 31	0.6	•	1.5	1.6	1.1	1.4	0.7	1.1	1.0	0.6	0.7	0.8	0.5
Net Sales to Working Capital 32	•	•	25.5	4.0	15.2	5.8	•	10.3	6.9	35.7	130.1	26.0	•
Coverage Ratio 33	•	•	8.2	•	•	•	•	•	4.5	3.6	•	•	•
Total Asset Turnover 34	0.8	•	3.3	1.0	1.4	1.0	1.0	1.1	1.1	1.8	1.7	1.1	0.7
Inventory Turnover 35	11.4	•	•	4092.9	78.7	60.5	14.7	24.9	7.8	9.0	17.4	8.5	9.7
Receivables Turnover 36	18.8	•	26.5	2.3	11.5	4.9	7.8	11.0	9.2	10.1	22.1	17.7	22.7
Total Liabilities to Net Worth 37	•	•	•	•	•	•	7.8	•	2.9	3.4	5.1	5.1	•
Current Assets to Working Capital 38	•	•	3.0	2.6	5.2	2.2	•	3.6	2.7	9.7	34.3	8.0	•
Current Liabilities to Working Capital 39	•	•	2.0	1.6	4.2	1.2	•	2.6	1.7	8.7	33.3	7.0	•
Working Capital to Net Sales 40	•	•	0.0	0.2	0.1	0.2	•	0.1	0.1	0.0	0.0	0.0	•
Inventory to Working Capital 41	•	•	•	0.0	0.0	0.0	•	0.2	0.3	1.3	3.4	0.4	•
Total Receipts to Cash Flow 42	4.3	3.1	1.9	160.4	16.8	10.3	8.3	6.6	3.7	4.1	13.4	4.6	4.1
Cost of Goods to Cash Flow 43	0.9	1.9	0.6	126.0	8.1	6.0	4.1	3.3	1.1	1.2	5.6	0.7	0.7
Cash Flow to Total Debt 44	0.2	0.8	0.0	0.1	0.1	0.1	0.1	0.2	0.3	0.6	0.2	0.3	0.2

Selected Financial Factors (in Percentages)

Line Item													
Debt Ratio 45	101.6	•	210.6	184.0	110.3	150.7	88.7	74.4	104.9	77.1	83.7	83.6	103.2
Return on Total Assets 46	•	40.3	•	•	•	•	•	•	7.6	9.0	•	•	•
Return on Equity Before Income Taxes 47	409.1	•	•	13.9	115.7	15.0	•	•	28.3	•	•	•	203.8
Return on Equity After Income Taxes 48	412.7	•	•	13.9	122.3	15.1	•	•	21.2	•	•	•	203.8
Profit Margin (Before Income Tax) 49	10.6	•	•	•	•	•	•	5.3	•	•	•	3.6	•
Profit Margin (After Income Tax) 50	10.6	•	•	•	•	•	•	5.1	•	•	•	2.7	•

237

Table II
Corporations with Net Income

AIR TRANSPORTATION

MONEY AMOUNTS AND SIZE OF ASSETS IN THOUSANDS OF DOLLARS

Item Description for Accounting Period 7/04 Through 6/05	Total	Zero Assets	Under 500	500 to 1,000	1,000 to 5,000	5,000 to 10,000	10,000 to 25,000	25,000 to 50,000	50,000 to 100,000	100,000 to 250,000	250,000 to 500,000	500,000 to 2,500,000	2,500,000 and over
Number of Enterprises **1**	3965	349	2898	277	331	53	24	17	4	8	0	4	0

Revenues ($ in Thousands)

	Total	Zero Assets	Under 500	500 to 1,000	1,000 to 5,000	5,000 to 10,000	10,000 to 25,000	25,000 to 50,000	50,000 to 100,000	100,000 to 250,000	250,000 to 500,000	500,000 to 2,500,000	2,500,000 and over
Net Sales **2**	14958317	50968	1733283	447977	1540679	826944	609694	871442	428598	3123172	0	5325559	0
Interest **3**	37961	106	0	123	1067	49	540	1607	482	995	0	32992	0
Rents **4**	4134	0	5	0	0	0	36	52	321	1913	0	1807	0
Royalties **5**	23625	0	0	0	0	0	0	0	0	0	0	23625	0
Other Portfolio Income **6**	405231	121467	106760	66	97968	7841	2242	30181	82	4355	0	34269	0
Other Receipts **7**	226460	13038	28676	607	13862	1076	12371	21507	2333	5660	0	127332	0
Total Receipts **8**	15655728	185579	1868724	448773	1653576	835910	624883	924789	431816	3136095	0	5545584	0
Average Total Receipts **9**	3948	532	645	1620	4996	15772	26037	54399	107954	392012	•	1386396	•

Operating Costs/Operating Income (%)

	Total	Zero Assets	Under 500	500 to 1,000	1,000 to 5,000	5,000 to 10,000	10,000 to 25,000	25,000 to 50,000	50,000 to 100,000	100,000 to 250,000	250,000 to 500,000	500,000 to 2,500,000	2,500,000 and over
Cost of Operations **10**	31.8	41.2	21.7	87.9	58.2	61.5	59.3	58.8	18.3	44.3	•	4.2	•
Salaries and Wages **11**	13.1	7.1	5.6	4.7	5.9	5.3	9.4	7.6	11.7	9.9	•	22.9	•
Taxes Paid **12**	2.8	5.7	1.5	0.5	0.8	3.0	1.8	1.9	1.7	2.0	•	4.8	•
Interest Paid **13**	1.2	15.9	1.0	0.0	0.1	1.3	0.9	1.0	0.7	0.9	•	1.9	•
Depreciation **14**	4.5	5.9	1.4	0.1	3.9	10.7	3.6	3.7	3.6	2.1	•	6.7	•
Amortization and Depletion **15**	0.8	2.2	0.0	•	0.0	0.0	0.0	•	0.5	0.0	•	2.5	•
Pensions and Other Deferred Comp. **16**	0.9	0.2	0.4	0.0	0.0	0.1	0.3	0.1	0.7	0.6	•	1.9	•
Employee Benefits **17**	1.3	0.9	1.1	0.0	0.6	0.8	1.6	1.4	0.9	1.1	•	1.8	•
Advertising **18**	0.4	0.2	0.3	0.0	0.1	0.2	0.3	0.6	0.0	0.4	•	0.6	•
Other Expenses **19**	38.5	39.9	50.7	6.8	25.2	12.5	18.7	26.7	43.6	31.7	•	52.9	•
Officers' Compensation **20**	1.4	1.0	2.6	•	1.8	2.3	1.6	1.3	2.6	0.6	•	1.3	•
Operating Margin **21**	3.3	•	13.6	•	3.4	2.5	2.5	•	15.6	6.3	•	•	•
Operating Margin Before Officers' Comp. **22**	4.7	•	16.2	•	5.2	4.8	4.1	•	18.3	6.9	•	•	•

Selected Average Balance Sheet ($ in Thousands)

Line	Item											
23	Net Receivables	305	0	18	109	556	1126	3583	3702	5809	36165	105648
24	Inventories	123	0	0	0	12	11	1020	1257	3318	12448	34940
25	Net Property, Plant and Equipment	875	0	6	106	537	3483	6549	15303	16626	45531	552676
26	Total Assets	2223	0	79	744	2542	6804	15529	34430	55620	191363	1116536
27	Notes and Loans Payable	692	0	29	179	1153	6196	5235	14607	9697	33798	304063
28	All Other Liabilities	858	0	31	200	613	1033	3907	14328	20262	116898	411106
29	Net Worth	674	0	20	365	776	-425	6387	5495	25661	40667	401367

Selected Financial Ratios (Times to 1)

Line	Item											
30	Current Ratio	1.4	•	1.9	1.7	2.8	1.7	1.6	1.4	1.4	1.1	1.3
31	Quick Ratio	1.2	•	1.9	1.7	2.7	1.3	1.1	1.0	1.2	0.7	1.1
32	Net Sales to Working Capital	12.4	•	18.0	11.3	4.0	11.9	8.5	9.9	11.9	29.2	17.4
33	Coverage Ratio	7.4	16.3	21.5	106.0	91.8	3.8	6.4	5.6	24.6	8.2	2.4
34	Total Asset Turnover	1.7	•	7.5	2.2	1.8	2.3	1.6	1.5	1.9	2.0	1.2
35	Inventory Turnover	9.7	•	•	•	218.8	900.2	14.8	24.0	5.9	13.9	1.6
36	Receivables Turnover	8.9	•	31.7	•	10.1	5.6	6.5	15.1	11.9	10.1	15.1
37	Total Liabilities to Net Worth	2.3	•	3.0	1.0	2.3	•	1.4	5.3	1.2	3.7	1.8
38	Current Assets to Working Capital	3.3	•	2.1	2.4	1.5	2.5	2.7	3.6	3.3	8.9	4.5
39	Current Liabilities to Working Capital	2.3	•	1.1	1.4	0.5	1.5	1.7	2.6	2.3	7.9	3.5
40	Working Capital to Net Sales	0.1	•	0.1	0.1	0.3	0.1	0.1	0.1	0.1	0.0	0.1
41	Inventory to Working Capital	0.2	•	•	•	0.0	0.0	0.3	0.4	0.1	0.9	0.2
42	Total Receipts to Cash Flow	3.1	0.4	1.5	17.5	5.7	8.5	5.8	5.5	2.4	5.3	2.5
43	Cost of Goods to Cash Flow	1.0	0.2	0.3	15.4	3.3	5.2	3.4	3.2	0.4	2.4	0.1
44	Cash Flow to Total Debt	0.8	•	6.5	0.2	0.5	0.3	0.5	0.3	1.5	0.5	0.7

Selected Financial Factors (in Percentages)

Line	Item											
45	Debt Ratio	69.7	•	75.3	50.9	69.5	106.2	58.9	84.0	53.9	78.7	64.1
46	Return on Total Assets	15.5	•	169.1	0.4	19.9	11.0	9.6	8.4	32.9	15.5	5.4
47	Return on Equity Before Income Taxes	44.2	•	652.7	0.7	64.5	•	19.7	43.4	68.5	63.8	8.7
48	Return on Equity After Income Taxes	41.0	•	652.4	0.7	59.2	•	16.3	42.1	67.0	50.1	7.7
49	Profit Margin (Before Income Tax)	7.9	243.9	21.4	0.2	10.8	3.6	5.0	4.6	16.4	6.6	2.6
50	Profit Margin (After Income Tax)	7.3	243.7	21.4	0.2	9.9	3.5	4.1	4.5	16.0	5.2	2.3

238

Table I

Corporations with and without Net Income

RAIL TRANSPORTATION

MONEY AMOUNTS AND SIZE OF ASSETS IN THOUSANDS OF DOLLARS

Item Description for Accounting Period 7/04 Through 6/05	Total	Zero Assets	Under 500	500 to 1,000	1,000 to 5,000	5,000 to 10,000	10,000 to 25,000	25,000 to 50,000	50,000 to 100,000	100,000 to 250,000	250,000 to 500,000	500,000 to 2,500,000	2,500,000 and over
Number of Enterprises **1**	426	10	185	56	88	24	23	12	8	6	3	5	7
Revenues ($ in Thousands)													
Net Sales **2**	48481080	0	53697	46200	367092	27564	209676	225954	245092	395731	589702	2201386	44118986
Interest **3**	1134496	29	354	1	583	891	1328	508	2425	1024	703	18287	1108363
Rents **4**	583335	0	3347	0	337	86	1969	2178	3065	5223	5054	26475	535602
Royalties **5**	25026	0	0	0	15	0	1	0	259	1807	0	583	22361
Other Portfolio Income **6**	594257	9312	0	0	4223	11	1662	12527	3352	5879	2872	84934	469486
Other Receipts **7**	2482896	-1722	-1	10	9828	82	9848	4195	8153	391	47930	64376	2339802
Total Receipts **8**	53301090	7619	57397	46211	382078	28634	224484	245362	262346	410055	646261	2396041	48594600
Average Total Receipts **9**	125120	762	310	825	4342	1193	9760	20447	32793	68342	215420	479208	6942086
Operating Costs/Operating Income (%)													
Cost of Operations **10**	33.2	•	•	0.4	10.8	19.3	18.5	19.6	14.1	41.6	26.6	8.0	35.0
Salaries and Wages **11**	19.6	•	13.0	1.0	19.3	14.4	14.7	17.7	22.4	7.9	17.2	23.5	19.6
Taxes Paid **12**	6.8	•	9.2	0.1	2.1	2.6	6.5	4.2	6.2	4.1	2.7	7.5	6.9
Interest Paid **13**	7.0	•	17.6	2.0	0.7	1.6	2.1	1.9	1.0	1.6	3.2	5.9	7.3
Depreciation **14**	11.0	•	3.6	0.2	6.9	10.7	13.1	15.4	13.4	8.5	12.7	16.6	10.8
Amortization and Depletion **15**	0.2	•	•	0.2	0.0	0.1	0.1	0.0	0.0	1.1	1.1	0.2	0.2
Pensions and Other Deferred Comp. **16**	0.5	•	•	•	0.0	5.0	0.5	1.7	2.2	0.1	1.4	0.3	0.5
Employee Benefits **17**	4.0	•	2.0	•	0.9	4.4	2.3	3.1	4.3	1.4	3.3	4.4	4.0
Advertising **18**	0.1	•	0.1	0.2	0.2	0.0	0.4	0.1	0.1	0.1	0.0	0.0	0.1
Other Expenses **19**	24.1	•	60.6	96.9	57.8	50.8	37.2	24.8	31.3	31.8	32.7	43.6	22.4
Officers' Compensation **20**	0.4	•	•	0.2	2.7	0.8	4.1	2.1	1.5	0.7	1.7	0.4	0.3
Operating Margin **21**	•	•	•	•	•	•	0.5	9.5	3.3	1.3	•	•	•
Operating Margin Before Officers' Comp. **22**	•	•	•	•	1.3	•	4.6	11.5	4.8	1.9	•	•	•

Selected Average Balance Sheet ($ in Thousands)

Net Receivables 23	11452	0	60	1	476	280	2095	4582	3365	13865	38580	86676	579461
Inventories 24	2312	0	0	8	17	27	225	361	1953	2238	5919	7003	127293
Net Property, Plant and Equipment 25	283690	0	140	6	972	2982	8743	24590	50220	81911	289179	922789	16256848
Total Assets 26	398902	0	263	525	2169	6088	14920	34135	76635	122739	407654	1303270	22810782
Notes and Loans Payable 27	83927	0	11	152	667	238	3650	8295	15178	19803	151092	343059	4726523
All Other Liabilities 28	164214	0	38	75	593	1565	6177	9540	27442	41748	109581	489814	9478525
Net Worth 29	150761	0	213	298	910	4285	5093	16299	34014	61188	146981	470398	8605734

Selected Financial Ratios (Times to 1)

Current Ratio 30	0.7	•	3.2	7.7	1.2	7.8	1.0	1.3	0.8	1.0	0.8	1.0	0.7
Quick Ratio 31	0.4	•	3.0	0.0	1.0	7.4	0.8	1.0	0.6	0.7	0.5	0.8	0.4
Net Sales to Working Capital 32	•	•	•	1.8	32.7	0.4	255.4	10.9	•	•	•	329.7	•
Coverage Ratio 33	1.4	•	1.0	0.4	4.8	•	4.5	10.6	11.1	4.1	3.2	0.8	1.4
Total Asset Turnover 34	0.3	•	1.1	1.6	1.9	0.2	0.6	0.6	0.4	0.5	0.5	0.3	0.3
Inventory Turnover 35	16.4	•	•	0.4	27.0	8.2	7.5	10.2	2.2	12.2	8.8	5.0	17.3
Receivables Turnover 36	9.1	•	3.6	•	9.4	2.1	4.8	4.4	5.2	4.5	5.1	6.5	9.6
Total Liabilities to Net Worth 37	1.6	•	0.2	0.8	1.4	0.4	1.9	1.1	1.3	1.0	1.8	1.8	1.7
Current Assets to Working Capital 38	•	•	1.5	1.1	5.4	1.1	142.7	4.9	•	•	•	149.4	•
Current Liabilities to Working Capital 39	•	•	0.5	0.1	4.4	0.1	141.7	3.9	•	•	•	148.4	•
Working Capital to Net Sales 40	•	•	0.3	0.6	0.0	2.3	0.0	0.1	•	•	•	0.0	•
Inventory to Working Capital 41	•	•	•	0.0	•	0.0	6.5	0.2	•	•	•	10.1	•
Total Receipts to Cash Flow 42	6.6	•	2.2	1.1	2.7	2.6	3.0	2.9	2.9	3.8	4.0	4.2	7.2
Cost of Goods to Cash Flow 43	2.2	•	•	0.0	0.3	0.5	0.5	0.6	0.4	1.6	1.1	0.3	2.5
Cash Flow to Total Debt 44	0.1	•	2.7	3.5	1.2	0.2	0.3	0.4	0.2	0.3	0.2	0.1	0.1

Selected Financial Factors (in Percentages)

Debt Ratio 45	62.2	•	18.9	43.2	58.1	29.6	65.9	52.2	55.6	50.1	63.9	63.9	62.3
Return on Total Assets 46	2.8	•	20.3	1.3	6.5	•	5.9	11.4	4.6	3.5	4.9	1.5	2.8
Return on Equity Before Income Taxes 47	2.2	•	1.1	•	12.2	•	13.5	21.5	9.3	5.3	9.3	•	2.2
Return on Equity After Income Taxes 48	1.5	•	0.8	•	11.1	•	10.7	17.2	5.4	2.5	8.5	•	1.4
Profit Margin (Before Income Tax) 49	2.9	•	0.8	•	2.7	•	7.6	18.6	10.4	4.9	7.0	•	3.0
Profit Margin (After Income Tax) 50	2.0	•	0.6	•	2.4	•	6.0	14.9	6.0	2.3	6.3	•	2.0

Table II

Corporations with Net Income

RAIL TRANSPORTATION

MONEY AMOUNTS AND SIZE OF ASSETS IN THOUSANDS OF DOLLARS

Item Description for Accounting Period 7/04 Through 6/05	Total	Zero Assets	Under 500	500 to 1,000	1,000 to 5,000	5,000 to 10,000	10,000 to 25,000	25,000 to 50,000	50,000 to 100,000	100,000 to 250,000	250,000 to 500,000	500,000 to 2,500,000	2,500,000 and over
Number of Enterprises 1	252	0	92	0	61	3	14	8	5	0	0	0	0
Revenues ($ in Thousands)													
Net Sales 2	43973396	0	53650	0	145525	27217	161656	177215	165586	0	0	0	0
Interest 3	981809	0	0	0	0	0	451	232	2250	0	0	0	0
Rents 4	518488	0	3347	0	335	86	1604	2066	2609	0	0	0	0
Royalties 5	22621	0	0	0	0	0	0	0	259	0	0	0	0
Other Portfolio Income 6	512081	0	0	0	3847	11	549	12479	1337	0	0	0	0
Other Receipts 7	932366	0	0	0	7668	82	8630	279	7933	0	0	0	0
Total Receipts 8	46940761	0	56997	0	157375	27396	172891	192271	179974	0	0	0	0
Average Total Receipts 9	186273	•	620	•	2580	9132	12349	24034	35995	•	•	•	•
Operating Costs/Operating Income (%)													
Cost of Operations 10	35.0	•	•	•	27.1	19.6	18.7	11.5	15.2	•	•	•	•
Salaries and Wages 11	18.0	•	13.0	•	8.0	12.1	13.2	18.8	19.4	•	•	•	•
Taxes Paid 12	6.6	•	9.1	•	5.3	2.6	6.2	4.3	7.1	•	•	•	•
Interest Paid 13	6.8	•	17.6	•	1.2	1.6	1.5	1.6	1.0	•	•	•	•
Depreciation 14	10.3	•	3.7	•	13.7	7.5	8.4	15.0	10.6	•	•	•	•
Amortization and Depletion 15	0.2	•	•	•	•	0.1	0.1	0.1	0.0	•	•	•	•
Pensions and Other Deferred Comp. 16	0.5	•	•	•	•	1.2	0.6	2.1	1.4	•	•	•	•
Employee Benefits 17	3.5	•	2.0	•	2.3	4.1	2.4	3.1	2.8	•	•	•	•
Advertising 18	0.0	•	0.1	•	0.4	0.0	0.2	0.1	0.1	•	•	•	•
Other Expenses 19	21.6	•	59.9	•	36.1	30.1	29.1	26.0	29.1	•	•	•	•
Officers' Compensation 20	0.4	•	•	•	6.8	0.8	4.2	1.9	1.5	•	•	•	•
Operating Margin 21	•	•	•	•	•	20.3	15.4	15.6	11.9	•	•	•	•
Operating Margin Before Officers' Comp. 22	•	•	•	•	5.9	21.0	19.7	17.5	13.4	•	•	•	•

Selected Average Balance Sheet ($ in Thousands)

Net Receivables 23	15780	39	366	2240	2029	5282	2970
Inventories 24	2861	0	30	190	239	470	1253
Net Property, Plant and Equipment 25	428235	180	665	5203	8640	26133	49793
Total Assets 26	595719	236	1578	8917	15110	37063	75968
Notes and Loans Payable 27	119280	23	607	1907	3905	8097	12437
All Other Liabilities 28	255696	77	218	1881	4015	9399	23336
Net Worth 29	220743	136	752	5128	7190	19567	40195

Selected Financial Ratios (Times to 1)

Current Ratio 30	0.6	0.7	2.1	2.2	1.4	1.4	1.7
Quick Ratio 31	0.4	0.5	1.6	1.5	1.1	1.2	1.4
Net Sales to Working Capital 32			8.6	4.5	8.3	7.7	4.7
Coverage Ratio 33	1.6	1.1	7.0	14.2	16.4	16.7	20.8
Total Asset Turnover 34	0.3	2.5	1.5	1.0	0.8	0.6	0.4
Inventory Turnover 35	21.4		21.6	9.3	9.0	5.4	4.0
Receivables Turnover 36	12.5	4.9	5.4		5.1	4.5	10.5
Total Liabilities to Net Worth 37	1.7	0.7	1.1	0.7	1.1	0.9	0.9
Current Assets to Working Capital 38			1.9	1.8	3.5	3.5	2.4
Current Liabilities to Working Capital 39			0.9	0.8	2.5	2.5	1.4
Working Capital to Net Sales 40			0.1	0.2	0.1	0.1	0.2
Inventory to Working Capital 41				0.1	0.1	0.2	0.1
Total Receipts to Cash Flow 42	7.1	2.2	2.9	2.2	2.4	2.3	2.3
Cost of Goods to Cash Flow 43	2.5		0.8	0.4	0.5	0.3	0.4
Cash Flow to Total Debt 44	0.1	2.6	1.0	1.1	0.6	0.6	0.4

Selected Financial Factors (in Percentages)

Debt Ratio 45	62.9	42.4	52.3	42.5	52.4	47.2	47.1
Return on Total Assets 46	3.1	46.0	12.7	22.9	18.2	15.8	9.4
Return on Equity Before Income Taxes 47	3.0	4.2	22.8	36.9	36.0	28.1	16.9
Return on Equity After Income Taxes 48	2.1	3.2	20.9	30.9	32.7	22.7	11.7
Profit Margin (Before Income Tax) 49	3.8	1.0	7.2	20.9	22.4	24.8	20.6
Profit Margin (After Income Tax) 50	2.7	0.7	6.6	17.5	20.3	20.0	14.2

Table I

Corporations with and without Net Income

WATER TRANSPORTATION

MONEY AMOUNTS AND SIZE OF ASSETS IN THOUSANDS OF DOLLARS

Item Description for Accounting Period 7/04 Through 6/05	Total	Zero Assets	Under 500	500 to 1,000	1,000 to 5,000	5,000 to 10,000	10,000 to 25,000	25,000 to 50,000	50,000 to 100,000	100,000 to 250,000	250,000 to 500,000	500,000 to 2,500,000	2,500,000 and over
Number of Enterprises **1**	3142	307	1485	438	753	13	67	24	16	21	5	13	0
Revenues ($ in Thousands)													
Net Sales **2**	20669037	190000	2763491	260022	808979	87765	1424828	807719	902415	1795376	737085	10891356	0
Interest **3**	86615	294	486	407	852	119	2755	207	1783	1946	13105	64660	0
Rents **4**	100943	0	0	6685	0	0	2869	533	2250	1208	0	87398	0
Royalties **5**	2	0	0	0	0	0	0	0	0	2	0	0	0
Other Portfolio Income **6**	429747	307	20967	0	4277	13255	8596	2937	6214	221272	13582	138342	0
Other Receipts **7**	374136	-69882	78934	1766	6756	925	29694	9110	2293	18004	4026	292510	0
Total Receipts **8**	21660480	120719	2863878	268880	820864	102064	1468742	820506	914955	2037808	767798	11474266	0
Average Total Receipts **9**	6894	393	1929	614	1090	7851	21922	34188	57185	97038	153560	882636	•
Operating Costs/Operating Income (%)													
Cost of Operations **10**	48.8	26.1	95.7	4.2	23.6	56.0	53.2	41.8	42.4	41.1	33.1	43.0	•
Salaries and Wages **11**	9.3	8.1	1.3	25.4	14.3	2.3	10.4	14.1	11.5	8.3	5.8	10.4	•
Taxes Paid **12**	1.7	1.1	0.3	5.0	2.5	1.1	2.3	2.5	2.4	1.9	1.1	1.8	•
Interest Paid **13**	2.3	1.4	0.0	1.8	2.1	3.1	1.5	2.2	2.3	3.0	10.2	2.3	•
Depreciation **14**	8.5	12.0	0.1	10.3	19.6	6.4	5.2	7.6	7.0	14.2	21.6	8.5	•
Amortization and Depletion **15**	0.3	0.2	0.0	•	0.0	0.1	0.1	0.1	0.1	0.2	0.3	0.4	•
Pensions and Other Deferred Comp. **16**	0.7	•	0.4	0.3	0.1	0.2	0.3	0.3	1.2	0.4	0.8	0.9	•
Employee Benefits **17**	2.1	0.3	0.1	1.1	1.2	0.4	1.5	5.6	2.0	2.3	1.4	2.6	•
Advertising **18**	0.2	0.2	•	0.2	0.0	0.2	0.4	0.2	0.1	0.1	0.0	0.3	•
Other Expenses **19**	26.8	27.6	2.8	38.4	39.4	10.9	21.8	23.4	31.0	27.8	35.1	31.6	•
Officers' Compensation **20**	1.3	1.4	2.1	6.6	2.8	5.7	1.6	1.6	1.5	0.9	0.9	0.9	•
Operating Margin **21**	•	21.6	•	6.8	•	13.8	1.7	0.6	•	0.9	•	•	•
Operating Margin Before Officers' Comp. **22**	•	23.0	•	13.4	•	19.5	3.2	2.2	0.0	0.7	•	•	•

Selected Average Balance Sheet ($ in Thousands)

Net Receivables 23	843	0	0	117	44	6392	2662	4478	9586	13508	45914	117631	•
Inventories 24	74	0	0	0	0	14	236	164	1202	1147	2451	12089	•
Net Property, Plant and Equipment 25	4223	0	0	369	1508	586	8648	21323	35402	84856	155729	595771	•
Total Assets 26	7978	89	614	2314	7949	16205	34526	70057	138984	333998	1169098		•
Notes and Loans Payable 27	3356	1	443	1366	515	6553	16987	23532	62928	196295	445243		•
All Other Liabilities 28	1889	35	120	639	6743	3914	5760	21832	27775	54354	281249		•
Net Worth 29	2733	53	51	691	11779	5738	24692	48281	83349	442606			•

Selected Financial Ratios (Times to 1)

Current Ratio 30	1.1	•	1.5	1.2	0.7	1.1	1.2	1.4	1.0	1.0	1.8	1.0	•
Quick Ratio 31	0.7	•	1.5	0.7	0.2	1.0	0.9	1.2	0.6	0.8	1.4	0.7	•
Net Sales to Working Capital 32	67.5	•	98.5	16.7	•	19.8	27.3	12.1	108.5	•	4.8	114.1	•
Coverage Ratio 33	3.3	•	25.2	6.6	•	10.7	4.2	2.0	1.0	5.4	0.6	4.1	•
Total Asset Turnover 34	0.8	•	21.0	1.0	0.5	0.8	1.3	1.0	0.8	0.6	0.4	0.7	•
Inventory Turnover 35	43.3	•	•	•	1538.7	•	264.9	48.0	85.9	19.9	30.7	19.9	29.8
Receivables Turnover 36	8.1	•	223.8	6.2	13.6	1.8	9.5	6.7	5.1	8.1	3.5	7.2	•
Total Liabilities to Net Worth 37	1.9	•	0.7	11.1	6.5	10.5	1.8	1.9	1.8	1.9	3.0	1.6	•
Current Assets to Working Capital 38	18.6	•	2.8	6.4	•	20.8	7.2	3.3	47.0	•	2.3	32.3	•
Current Liabilities to Working Capital 39	17.6	•	1.8	5.4	•	19.8	6.2	2.3	46.0	•	1.3	31.3	•
Working Capital to Net Sales 40	0.0	•	0.0	0.1	•	0.1	0.0	0.1	0.0	•	0.2	0.0	•
Inventory to Working Capital 41	0.8	•	•	•	•	0.3	0.1	0.1	3.5	•	0.1	1.8	•
Total Receipts to Cash Flow 42	4.4	•	28.6	2.5	3.6	2.8	5.3	5.9	4.1	4.1	3.8	3.6	•
Cost of Goods to Cash Flow 43	2.1	•	27.4	0.1	0.9	1.6	2.8	2.4	1.7	1.7	1.2	1.5	•
Cash Flow to Total Debt 44	0.3	•	1.8	0.4	0.1	0.3	0.4	0.3	0.3	0.2	0.2	0.3	•

Selected Financial Factors (in Percentages)

Debt Ratio 45	65.7	•	40.6	91.7	86.7	91.3	64.6	65.9	64.8	65.3	75.0	62.1	•
Return on Total Assets 46	6.3	•	18.1	11.6	•	28.2	8.2	4.2	1.9	10.0	2.8	6.9	•
Return on Equity Before Income Taxes 47	12.9	•	29.3	119.5	•	294.1	17.5	6.2	0.1	23.4	•	13.9	•
Return on Equity After Income Taxes 48	8.4	•	28.9	109.6	•	278.9	13.8	5.6	•	15.4	•	9.3	•
Profit Margin (Before Income Tax) 49	5.4	•	0.8	10.2	•	30.1	4.7	2.2	0.0	13.2	•	7.3	•
Profit Margin (After Income Tax) 50	3.5	•	0.8	9.4	•	28.5	3.7	2.0	•	8.7	•	4.9	•

Table II

Corporations with Net Income

WATER TRANSPORTATION

MONEY AMOUNTS AND SIZE OF ASSETS IN THOUSANDS OF DOLLARS

Item Description for Accounting Period 7/04 Through 6/05	Total	Zero Assets	Under 500	500 to 1,000	1,000 to 5,000	5,000 to 10,000	10,000 to 25,000	25,000 to 50,000	50,000 to 100,000	100,000 to 250,000	250,000 to 500,000	500,000 to 2,500,000	2,500,000 and over
Number of Enterprises **1**	1315	0	533	0	232	13	42	12	8	0	0	10	0
Revenues ($ in Thousands)													
Net Sales **2**	17708898	0	2736125	0	761636	87765	1188180	445108	583437	0	0	10020302	0
Interest **3**	62803	0	32	0	129	119	2514	184	1139	0	0	55687	0
Rents **4**	98283	0	0	0	0	0	725	18	2250	0	0	87398	0
Royalties **5**	0	0	0	0	0	0	0	0	0	0	0	0	0
Other Portfolio Income **6**	354262	0	20967	0	3575	13255	8275	2087	3373	0	0	73115	0
Other Receipts **7**	340320	0	2518	0	4926	925	27761	7181	1059	0	0	285955	0
Total Receipts **8**	18564566	0	2759642	0	770266	102064	1227455	454578	591258	0	0	10522457	0
Average Total Receipts **9**	14118	•	5178	•	3320	7851	29225	37882	73907	•	•	1052246	•
Operating Costs/Operating Income (%)													
Cost of Operations **10**	50.1	•	96.6	•	25.1	56.0	54.1	21.4	47.7	•	•	43.8	•
Salaries and Wages **11**	9.2	•	1.2	•	13.8	2.3	10.2	19.2	9.6	•	•	10.2	•
Taxes Paid **12**	1.6	•	0.1	•	1.9	1.1	2.2	2.7	2.2	•	•	1.8	•
Interest Paid **13**	1.8	•	0.0	•	1.5	3.1	1.3	2.2	1.8	•	•	2.2	•
Depreciation **14**	5.4	•	0.1	•	9.0	6.4	4.2	5.8	4.4	•	•	5.8	•
Amortization and Depletion **15**	0.1	•	•	•	0.0	0.1	0.1	0.2	0.2	•	•	0.2	•
Pensions and Other Deferred Comp. **16**	0.6	•	•	•	0.1	0.2	0.3	0.2	1.3	•	•	0.9	•
Employee Benefits **17**	2.2	•	0.0	•	1.3	0.4	1.3	8.9	1.5	•	•	2.8	•
Advertising **18**	0.2	•	•	•	0.0	0.2	0.4	0.1	0.0	•	•	0.2	•
Other Expenses **19**	26.4	•	1.6	•	35.6	10.9	20.8	33.7	24.5	•	•	31.6	•
Officers' Compensation **20**	1.0	•	0.2	•	1.1	5.7	1.6	1.6	1.7	•	•	0.9	•
Operating Margin **21**	1.3	•	•	•	10.6	13.8	3.4	3.9	5.0	•	•	5.0	•
Operating Margin Before Officers' Comp. **22**	2.3	•	0.2	•	11.7	19.5	5.1	5.5	6.7	•	•	0.4	•

Selected Average Balance Sheet ($ in Thousands)

Net Receivables 23	1684	0	116	6392	3525	4451	13840	135304
Inventories 24	130	0	0	0	174	63	1758	11832
Net Property, Plant and Equipment 25	6217	1	1756	586	7664	17866	36899	552877
Total Assets 26	12178	180	2364	7949	16450	34225	76314	1095837
Notes and Loans Payable 27	4542	0	1016	515	6005	17402	20977	405127
All Other Liabilities 28	3726	97	732	6743	4742	6393	27009	343232
Net Worth 29	3909	84	615	691	5703	10430	28328	347478

Selected Financial Ratios (Times to 1)

Current Ratio 30	1.1	1.1	0.6	1.1	1.3	1.5	1.3	1.1
Quick Ratio 31	0.8	1.1	0.2	1.0	1.0	1.3	0.8	0.7
Net Sales to Working Capital 32	38.7		355.4	19.8	17.2	9.7	11.1	63.6
Coverage Ratio 33	5.9	25.6	8.9	10.7	6.3	3.7	4.5	5.3
Total Asset Turnover 34	1.1	28.5	1.4	0.8	1.7	1.1	1.0	0.9
Inventory Turnover 35	51.8				88.2	127.0	19.8	37.1
Receivables Turnover 36	8.8	221.6	29.2	1.8	9.8	6.0	5.2	8.0
Total Liabilities to Net Worth 37	2.1	1.2	2.8	10.5	1.9	2.3	1.7	2.2
Current Assets to Working Capital 38	9.6		7.7	20.8	4.4	3.0	4.7	16.6
Current Liabilities to Working Capital 39	8.6		6.7	19.8	3.4	2.0	3.7	15.6
Working Capital to Net Sales 40	0.0		0.0	0.1	0.1	0.1	0.1	0.0
Inventory to Working Capital 41	0.4				0.1	0.0	0.5	0.8
Total Receipts to Cash Flow 42	3.8	40.9	2.4	2.8	4.8	3.7	3.5	3.3
Cost of Goods to Cash Flow 43	1.9	39.5	0.6	1.6	2.6	0.8	1.7	1.5
Cash Flow to Total Debt 44	0.4	1.3	0.8	0.3	0.6	0.4	0.4	0.4

Selected Financial Factors (in Percentages)

Debt Ratio 45	67.9	53.5	74.0	91.3	65.3	69.5	62.9	68.3
Return on Total Assets 46	11.8	25.2	18.4	28.2	13.8	8.9	7.8	10.7
Return on Equity Before Income Taxes 47	30.6	52.1	62.7	294.1	33.4	21.1	16.3	27.3
Return on Equity After Income Taxes 48	23.1	51.4	61.1	278.9	27.4	19.8	12.7	19.7
Profit Margin (Before Income Tax) 49	8.9	0.9	11.8	30.1	6.7	5.9	6.4	9.5
Profit Margin (After Income Tax) 50	6.7	0.8	11.5	28.5	5.5	5.6	4.9	6.8

Table I

Corporations with and without Net Income

TRUCK TRANSPORTATION

MONEY AMOUNTS AND SIZE OF ASSETS IN THOUSANDS OF DOLLARS

Item Description for Accounting Period 7/04 Through 6/05	Total	Zero Assets	Under 500	500 to 1,000	1,000 to 5,000	5,000 to 10,000	10,000 to 25,000	25,000 to 50,000	50,000 to 100,000	100,000 to 250,000	250,000 to 500,000	500,000 to 2,500,000	2,500,000 and over
Number of Enterprises 1	96839	15834	69336	5098	5357	589	371	110	65	39	17	23	0
Revenues ($ in Thousands)													
Net Sales 2	187163013	2933263	33801904	10658466	32821627	9254849	14887265	8101057	8458182	9623299	8089931	48533169	0
Interest 3	315004	2479	8072	7902	11832	7922	10203	10861	6279	11280	10571	227602	0
Rents 4	354065	3210	6095	4931	21152	8245	20115	19022	22518	12355	48297	188124	0
Royalties 5	149946	0	0	0	514	8810	31	5	1	223	21090	119270	0
Other Portfolio Income 6	1530964	141023	125958	133316	365962	79949	113443	72697	59928	88110	73822	276756	0
Other Receipts 7	3020582	164209	123682	27709	183568	134265	93316	92541	42881	307177	54448	1796791	0
Total Receipts 8	192533574	3244184	34065711	10832324	33404655	9494040	15124373	8296183	8589789	10042444	8298159	51141712	0
Average Total Receipts 9	1988	205	491	2125	6236	16119	40767	75420	132151	257499	488127	2223553	•
Operating Costs/Operating Income (%)													
Cost of Operations 10	32.3	33.0	30.5	23.8	42.7	26.2	40.2	37.4	33.2	23.7	21.7	29.7	•
Salaries and Wages 11	18.5	9.7	14.1	19.3	12.9	22.7	15.2	17.1	19.7	20.5	23.6	24.6	•
Taxes Paid 12	3.9	2.5	3.5	4.4	3.4	3.9	4.0	3.6	4.4	4.3	4.5	4.4	•
Interest Paid 13	1.0	1.9	0.8	1.2	1.0	1.0	0.9	1.1	1.1	1.2	1.4	1.0	•
Depreciation 14	5.7	5.2	4.4	7.8	5.5	5.3	5.3	6.7	6.7	6.8	9.1	5.4	•
Amortization and Depletion 15	0.1	0.3	0.0	0.0	0.1	0.1	0.1	0.1	0.1	0.2	0.2	0.2	•
Pensions and Other Deferred Comp. 16	0.7	2.4	0.2	0.7	0.3	0.2	0.3	0.4	0.2	0.6	0.9	1.5	•
Employee Benefits 17	2.7	4.9	1.2	1.5	1.9	1.7	2.0	2.1	3.2	3.0	3.4	4.6	•
Advertising 18	0.2	0.2	0.2	0.1	0.3	0.2	0.2	0.3	0.2	0.2	0.3	0.1	•
Other Expenses 19	33.7	46.0	40.4	38.1	28.7	36.7	31.3	32.0	30.5	41.3	33.9	30.2	•
Officers' Compensation 20	1.7	4.3	3.4	3.0	2.4	1.9	1.2	0.9	0.8	0.5	0.5	0.5	•
Operating Margin 21	•	•	1.3	0.1	0.9	0.2	•	•	•	•	0.7	•	•
Operating Margin Before Officers' Comp. 22	1.1	4.7	•	3.1	3.2	2.1	0.5	•	0.6	•	1.2	•	•

Selected Average Balance Sheet ($ in Thousands)

	1	2	3	4	5	6	7	8	9	10	11	12
Net Receivables 23	191	0	13	127	557	1994	4441	9027	14434	34286	59629	299308
Inventories 24	8	0	2	8	16	89	181	321	1325	1191	2360	9542
Net Property, Plant and Equipment 25	359	0	42	353	842	2510	6777	17337	34867	76278	182046	493392
Total Assets 26	837	0	80	707	2039	7214	15216	33209	67431	147808	328904	1378762
Notes and Loans Payable 27	342	0	67	432	1044	3507	6614	15285	27786	52624	111585	380939
All Other Liabilities 28	231	0	16	89	392	1501	3827	8103	17934	40237	91528	484465
Net Worth 29	265	0	-3	186	603	2206	4774	9820	21712	54946	125791	513358

Selected Financial Ratios (Times to 1)

	1	2	3	4	5	6	7	8	9	10	11	12
Current Ratio 30	1.3	•	1.1	2.0	1.3	1.3	1.3	1.1	1.0	1.3	1.4	1.4
Quick Ratio 31	1.0	•	0.9	1.4	1.1	1.0	1.0	0.8	1.0	1.0	1.0	1.1
Net Sales to Working Capital 32	25.7	•	293.1	15.2	26.8	18.3	27.4	49.5	169.5	22.3	19.2	15.6
Coverage Ratio 33	3.3	1.2	3.8	2.4	3.7	3.7	2.0	1.7	2.3	2.8	3.4	4.1
Total Asset Turnover 34	2.3	•	6.1	3.0	2.2	2.2	2.6	2.2	1.9	1.7	1.4	1.5
Inventory Turnover 35	77.4	•	94.4	61.2	167.4	46.1	88.9	85.9	32.6	49.1	43.7	65.6
Receivables Turnover 36	10.7	•	36.3	17.6	8.9	10.4	9.3	8.9	9.5	7.8	8.4	7.8
Total Liabilities to Net Worth 37	2.2	•	•	2.8	2.4	2.3	2.2	2.4	2.1	1.7	1.6	1.7
Current Assets to Working Capital 38	4.3	•	17.1	2.0	4.1	4.0	4.8	8.9	29.9	4.7	3.7	3.8
Current Liabilities to Working Capital 39	3.3	•	16.1	1.0	3.1	3.0	3.8	7.9	28.9	3.7	2.7	2.8
Working Capital to Net Sales 40	0.0	•	0.0	0.1	0.0	0.0	0.0	0.0	0.0	0.0	0.1	0.1
Inventory to Working Capital 41	0.1	•	0.9	0.1	0.1	0.1	0.1	0.2	1.9	0.1	0.1	0.1
Total Receipts to Cash Flow 42	3.7	3.0	3.3	3.1	4.2	3.6	4.4	4.6	4.2	4.0	3.1	3.7
Cost of Goods to Cash Flow 43	1.2	1.0	1.0	0.7	1.8	1.0	1.8	1.7	1.4	0.9	0.7	1.1
Cash Flow to Total Debt 44	0.9	•	1.8	1.3	1.0	0.9	0.7	0.7	0.7	0.7	0.8	0.7

Selected Financial Factors (in Percentages)

	1	2	3	4	5	6	7	8	9	10	11	12
Debt Ratio 45	68.4	•	103.5	73.7	70.4	69.4	68.6	70.4	67.8	62.8	61.8	62.8
Return on Total Assets 46	7.6	•	17.4	8.7	10.8	8.4	4.6	4.0	4.8	5.6	6.7	6.1
Return on Equity Before Income Taxes 47	16.6	•	•	19.3	26.7	20.1	7.2	5.5	8.3	9.7	12.3	12.4
Return on Equity After Income Taxes 48	13.6	•	•	17.7	25.2	16.7	5.6	3.4	6.8	7.4	10.2	8.3
Profit Margin (Before Income Tax) 49	2.3	0.3	2.1	1.7	2.6	2.8	0.9	0.7	1.4	2.2	3.3	3.0
Profit Margin (After Income Tax) 50	1.9	0.1	2.0	1.6	2.5	2.3	0.7	0.5	1.1	1.6	2.7	2.0

Table II

Corporations with Net Income

TRUCK TRANSPORTATION

MONEY AMOUNTS AND SIZE OF ASSETS IN THOUSANDS OF DOLLARS

Item Description for Accounting Period 7/04 Through 6/05	Total	Zero Assets	Under 500	500 to 1,000	1,000 to 5,000	5,000 to 10,000	10,000 to 25,000	25,000 to 50,000	50,000 to 100,000	100,000 to 250,000	250,000 to 500,000	500,000 to 2,500,000	2,500,000 and over
Number of Enterprises **1**	57070	7257	41587	3278	4073	482	228	59	45	27	13	20	0
Revenues ($ in Thousands)													
Net Sales **2**	142895087	1773503	21628383	7885934	25511799	7286355	9958473	4862456	6392458	6344404	6084738	45166584	0
Interest **3**	284717	59	2303	5301	9699	6459	7053	3813	5410	9182	8986	226453	0
Rents **4**	301818	0	0	4910	17247	6882	7876	7225	19687	3936	47504	186551	0
Royalties **5**	149629	0	0	0	199	8810	31	5	0	223	21090	119270	0
Other Portfolio Income **6**	1175777	32685	65458	117368	329523	63903	75988	44438	40658	73494	62927	269334	0
Other Receipts **7**	2818567	156004	96429	24023	136322	108501	68538	52864	26048	300938	53320	1795579	0
Total Receipts **8**	147625595	1962251	21792573	8037536	26004789	7480910	10117959	4970801	6484261	6732177	6278565	47763771	0
Average Total Receipts **9**	2587	270	524	2452	6385	15521	44377	84251	144095	249340	482967	2388189	•
Operating Costs/Operating Income (%)													
Cost of Operations **10**	32.1	35.8	30.3	20.6	38.2	17.6	44.1	39.7	33.2	28.3	27.5	31.4	•
Salaries and Wages **11**	18.7	10.0	14.1	20.5	14.2	26.4	13.7	16.9	18.4	17.4	18.0	23.9	•
Taxes Paid **12**	4.0	2.3	3.7	4.6	3.6	3.8	4.1	3.4	4.3	3.9	3.9	4.4	•
Interest Paid **13**	0.9	0.8	0.8	1.1	0.9	1.0	0.7	0.8	1.0	1.0	1.2	1.0	•
Depreciation **14**	5.2	3.5	3.9	7.1	5.0	4.7	3.8	4.6	6.0	6.8	9.7	5.3	•
Amortization and Depletion **15**	0.1	0.1	0.0	0.0	0.1	0.0	0.0	0.1	0.1	0.1	0.1	0.1	•
Pensions and Other Deferred Comp. **16**	0.6	0.0	0.2	1.0	0.3	0.2	0.3	0.4	0.2	0.1	0.4	1.4	•
Employee Benefits **17**	2.7	0.6	1.2	1.6	2.1	1.7	1.8	1.9	2.8	1.4	1.8	4.9	•
Advertising **18**	0.2	0.2	0.2	0.1	0.2	0.2	0.2	0.3	0.2	0.3	0.3	0.1	•
Other Expenses **19**	32.8	34.5	37.6	38.6	30.6	40.5	28.6	29.8	31.7	41.7	34.5	29.4	•
Officers' Compensation **20**	1.7	5.2	3.6	3.0	2.6	2.1	1.2	0.8	0.8	0.6	0.5	0.5	•
Operating Margin **21**	0.8	7.0	4.5	1.9	2.1	1.8	1.6	1.5	1.3	•	2.1	•	•
Operating Margin Before Officers' Comp. **22**	2.5	12.2	8.1	4.8	3.9	3.9	2.8	2.3	2.0	2.6	•	•	•

Selected Average Balance Sheet ($ in Thousands)

Item													
Net Receivables 23	261	0	13	156	563	1910	4863	10120	15059	34159	62461	324206	•
Inventories 24	9	0	1	6	15	57	227	437	1736	710	2421	8956	•
Net Property, Plant and Equipment 25	455	0	43	395	812	2252	5957	15099	34468	64740	189357	524882	•
Total Assets 26	1089	0	85	755	2036	7189	15077	33843	68698	142585	329028	1387106	•
Notes and Loans Payable 27	377	0	56	430	979	3343	5407	12223	27090	39693	105246	330086	•
All Other Liabilities 28	314	0	19	104	362	1456	3813	9566	16487	39004	88310	511380	•
Net Worth 29	398	0	10	222	695	2391	5857	12055	25121	63887	135472	545641	•

Selected Financial Ratios (Times to 1)

Item												
Current Ratio 30	1.4	•	1.2	2.4	1.5	1.4	1.5	1.3	1.2	1.5	1.3	1.4
Quick Ratio 31	1.1	•	1.0	1.7	1.3	1.2	1.2	1.1	0.9	1.2	1.1	1.0
Net Sales to Working Capital 32	20.0	•	119.4	12.9	19.7	16.2	17.9	25.2	38.7	13.5	21.5	15.4
Coverage Ratio 33	5.4	23.0	7.9	4.6	5.5	5.5	5.8	5.9	3.6	5.5	5.5	4.3
Total Asset Turnover 34	2.3	•	6.1	3.2	3.1	2.1	2.9	2.4	2.1	1.6	1.4	1.6
Inventory Turnover 35	86.0	•	158.8	88.9	158.8	46.4	84.9	74.8	27.2	93.7	53.2	79.2
Receivables Turnover 36	10.9	•	35.6	18.9	11.3	9.1	9.3	9.9	10.0	7.6	8.0	8.7
Total Liabilities to Net Worth 37	1.7	•	7.3	2.4	1.9	2.0	1.6	1.8	1.7	1.2	1.4	1.5
Current Assets to Working Capital 38	3.6	•	7.2	1.7	3.1	3.6	3.1	4.7	6.7	3.1	4.2	3.8
Current Liabilities to Working Capital 39	2.6	•	6.2	0.7	2.1	2.6	2.1	3.7	5.7	2.1	3.2	2.8
Working Capital to Net Sales 40	0.0	•	0.0	0.1	0.1	0.1	0.1	0.0	0.0	0.1	0.0	0.1
Inventory to Working Capital 41	0.1	•	0.4	0.0	0.1	0.0	0.1	0.1	0.5	0.0	0.1	0.1
Total Receipts to Cash Flow 42	3.5	2.3	3.0	2.7	3.8	3.0	4.2	4.3	3.9	4.1	2.9	3.7
Cost of Goods to Cash Flow 43	1.1	0.8	0.9	0.5	1.5	0.5	1.8	1.7	1.3	1.2	0.8	1.2
Cash Flow to Total Debt 44	1.0	•	2.3	1.7	1.2	1.0	1.1	0.9	0.8	0.7	0.8	0.7

Selected Financial Factors (in Percentages)

Item												
Debt Ratio 45	63.5	•	87.9	70.7	65.9	66.7	61.2	64.4	63.4	55.2	58.8	60.7
Return on Total Assets 46	11.6	•	36.7	15.5	15.4	11.6	11.2	10.9	7.7	9.2	9.2	7.1
Return on Equity Before Income Taxes 47	25.9	•	265.2	41.1	36.8	28.5	23.8	25.5	15.3	16.8	18.2	13.8
Return on Equity After Income Taxes 48	22.5	•	260.4	39.0	35.1	24.6	21.7	22.3	13.5	13.9	15.6	9.4
Profit Margin (Before Income Tax) 49	4.1	17.7	5.2	3.8	4.1	4.5	3.2	3.7	2.7	4.6	5.3	3.3
Profit Margin (After Income Tax) 50	3.6	17.4	5.1	3.6	3.9	3.9	2.9	3.3	2.4	3.8	4.5	2.3

Table I

Corporations with and without Net Income

TRANSIT AND GROUND PASSENGER TRANSPORTATION

MONEY AMOUNTS AND SIZE OF ASSETS IN THOUSANDS OF DOLLARS

Item Description for Accounting Period 7/04 Through 6/05	Total	Zero Assets	Under 500	500 to 1,000	1,000 to 5,000	5,000 to 10,000	10,000 to 25,000	25,000 to 50,000	50,000 to 100,000	100,000 to 250,000	250,000 to 500,000	500,000 to 2,500,000	2,500,000 and over
Number of Enterprises 1	25969	2449	20734	1166	1403	131	59	15	6	5	0	3	0
Revenues ($ in Thousands)													
Net Sales 2	23632995	284238	3483158	536812	7082655	1494504	1520009	522514	604021	1428792	0	6676290	0
Interest 3	158857	1	535	223	3436	1652	1863	3605	1410	32102	0	114030	0
Rents 4	38178	0	12	0	18539	2715	506	2032	697	8385	0	5292	0
Royalties 5	2	0	0	0	0	0	0	0	0	2	0	0	0
Other Portfolio Income 6	236920	126	5318	16713	97750	28868	5480	3593	1578	69463	0	8230	0
Other Receipts 7	156569	0	38236	9877	49090	2483	7133	10025	18551	5626	0	15552	0
Total Receipts 8	24223521	284365	3527259	563625	7251470	1530022	1534991	541769	626257	1544370	0	6819394	0
Average Total Receipts 9	933	116	170	483	5169	11680	26017	36118	104376	308874	·	2273131	·
Operating Costs/Operating Income (%)													
Cost of Operations 10	32.5	41.8	15.2	22.2	45.5	57.4	44.8	26.7	21.4	34.4	·	20.8	·
Salaries and Wages 11	21.0	14.6	23.9	26.6	12.7	4.9	16.6	27.7	36.8	22.5	·	30.4	·
Taxes Paid 12	4.3	2.0	3.8	4.5	3.8	4.4	4.3	4.7	4.9	5.8	·	4.9	·
Interest Paid 13	2.5	1.0	2.1	4.3	1.3	1.3	1.1	1.8	1.6	5.3	·	4.0	·
Depreciation 14	7.3	7.6	6.0	9.2	5.7	15.8	6.9	12.0	5.6	5.3	·	7.9	·
Amortization and Depletion 15	0.8	0.2	0.8	1.5	0.1	0.0	0.1	0.3	0.3	2.1	·	1.6	·
Pensions and Other Deferred Comp. 16	0.6	·	·	·	0.5	0.3	1.3	0.2	0.3	1.0	·	1.1	·
Employee Benefits 17	1.8	0.9	0.6	1.4	0.7	0.9	4.3	3.1	5.0	6.2	·	1.9	·
Advertising 18	0.6	1.8	0.9	0.7	0.6	0.4	0.4	0.7	0.4	0.4	·	0.4	·
Other Expenses 19	28.6	24.4	43.1	29.3	24.8	16.6	18.1	21.3	28.5	28.3	·	30.9	·
Officers' Compensation 20	2.4	3.5	4.9	5.0	4.0	1.7	1.7	1.2	1.3	0.1	·	0.0	·
Operating Margin 21	·	2.1	·	·	0.3	·	0.4	0.3	·	·	·	·	·
Operating Margin Before Officers' Comp. 22	0.0	5.6	3.6	0.2	4.3	2.1	2.1	1.5	·	·	·	·	·

Selected Average Balance Sheet ($ in Thousands)

Net Receivables 23	80	0	8	7	490	944	2298	4444	12543	30938	•	224158
Inventories 24	6	0	0	3	9	158	146	932	1888	1041	•	20908
Net Property, Plant and Equipment 25	222	0	25	115	851	4420	6814	14073	25998	103622	•	687666
Total Assets 26	595	0	85	630	1900	7289	14858	34800	74260	271804	•	2045899
Notes and Loans Payable 27	293	0	68	473	1197	5006	6356	17205	25741	141533	•	606939
All Other Liabilities 28	121	0	12	16	356	1045	2850	4457	21774	66540	•	516632
Net Worth 29	180	0	5	140	348	1238	5652	13138	26746	63732	•	922328

Selected Financial Ratios (Times to 1)

Current Ratio 30	1.2	•	1.4	0.5	1.2	0.7	1.4	1.4	1.1	0.9	•	1.3
Quick Ratio 31	0.8	•	1.1	0.3	0.9	0.6	0.9	0.9	0.8	0.6	•	0.7
Net Sales to Working Capital 32	35.6	•	31.6	•	42.1	•	16.2	11.5	34.8	•	•	15.9
Coverage Ratio 33	1.1	3.1	1.0	1.1	3.1	•	2.2	3.2	•	0.4	•	0.6
Total Asset Turnover 34	1.5	•	2.0	0.7	2.7	1.6	1.7	1.0	1.4	1.1	•	1.1
Inventory Turnover 35	52.2	•	441.8	29.8	257.4	41.4	79.1	10.0	11.4	94.5	•	22.1
Receivables Turnover 36	11.8	•	23.0	•	11.3	11.8	12.5	7.2	9.1	13.5	•	10.5
Total Liabilities to Net Worth 37	2.3	•	17.3	3.5	4.5	4.9	1.6	1.6	1.8	3.3	•	1.2
Current Assets to Working Capital 38	7.4	•	3.6	•	6.8	•	3.7	3.7	8.1	•	•	4.8
Current Liabilities to Working Capital 39	6.4	•	2.6	•	5.8	•	2.7	2.7	7.1	•	•	3.8
Working Capital to Net Sales 40	0.0	•	0.0	•	0.0	•	0.1	0.1	0.0	•	•	0.1
Inventory to Working Capital 41	0.2	•	0.0	•	0.1	•	0.1	0.3	0.7	•	•	0.2
Total Receipts to Cash Flow 42	4.6	4.4	2.8	6.0	5.8	8.2	7.2	5.8	5.5	6.4	•	4.0
Cost of Goods to Cash Flow 43	1.5	1.8	0.4	1.3	2.7	4.7	3.2	1.5	1.2	2.2	•	0.8
Cash Flow to Total Debt 44	0.5	0.8	0.8	0.2	0.6	0.2	0.4	0.3	0.4	0.2	•	0.5

Selected Financial Factors (in Percentages)

Debt Ratio 45	69.7	•	94.5	77.7	81.7	83.0	62.0	62.2	64.0	76.6	•	54.9
Return on Total Assets 46	4.1	•	4.2	3.3	10.4	•	4.4	5.8	•	2.0	•	2.5
Return on Equity Before Income Taxes 47	0.9	•	•	0.7	38.5	•	6.4	10.5	•	•	•	•
Return on Equity After Income Taxes 48	0.1	•	•	•	35.6	•	5.6	9.5	•	•	•	•
Profit Margin (Before Income Tax) 49	0.2	2.2	•	0.2	2.7	•	1.4	3.9	•	•	•	•
Profit Margin (After Income Tax) 50	0.0	2.2	•	•	2.5	•	1.2	3.6	•	•	•	•

Table II

Corporations with Net Income

TRANSIT AND GROUND PASSENGER TRANSPORTATION

MONEY AMOUNTS AND SIZE OF ASSETS IN THOUSANDS OF DOLLARS

Item Description for Accounting Period 7/04 Through 6/05	Total	Zero Assets	Under 500	500 to 1,000	1,000 to 5,000	5,000 to 10,000	10,000 to 25,000	25,000 to 50,000	50,000 to 100,000	100,000 to 250,000	250,000 to 500,000	500,000 to 2,500,000	2,500,000 and over
Number of Enterprises 1	13337	0	9888	0	976	56	37	10	0	0	0	0	0
Revenues ($ in Thousands)													
Net Sales 2	10502549	0	2253005	0	4773652	786863	1062017	390214	0	0	0	0	0
Interest 3	15270	0	268	0	1580	933	1630	3603	0	0	0	0	0
Rents 4	10746	0	0	0	483	1193	433	2032	0	0	0	0	0
Royalties 5	0	0	0	0	0	0	0	0	0	0	0	0	0
Other Portfolio Income 6	165613	0	648	0	77349	185	2489	1553	0	0	0	0	0
Other Receipts 7	74906	0	20771	0	27494	1683	4922	9751	0	0	0	0	0
Total Receipts 8	10769084	0	2274692	0	4880558	790857	1071491	407153	0	0	0	0	0
Average Total Receipts 9	807	·	230	·	5001	14122	28959	40715	·	·	·	·	·
Operating Costs/Operating Income (%)													
Cost of Operations 10	34.1	·	12.1	·	44.0	65.5	51.2	18.7	·	·	·	·	·
Salaries and Wages 11	18.3	·	28.7	·	10.5	4.7	12.9	32.8	·	·	·	·	·
Taxes Paid 12	4.3	·	3.9	·	4.0	3.9	4.2	5.0	·	·	·	·	·
Interest Paid 13	1.3	·	1.4	·	1.1	1.0	0.8	1.3	·	·	·	·	·
Depreciation 14	5.2	·	4.4	·	4.8	5.6	5.1	9.1	·	·	·	·	·
Amortization and Depletion 15	0.1	·	0.0	·	0.0	0.0	0.1	0.4	·	·	·	·	·
Pensions and Other Deferred Comp. 16	0.5	·	·	·	0.5	0.3	1.3	0.2	·	·	·	·	·
Employee Benefits 17	1.6	·	0.4	·	0.8	1.2	4.1	3.7	·	·	·	·	·
Advertising 18	0.5	·	0.5	·	0.5	0.4	0.4	0.8	·	·	·	·	·
Other Expenses 19	27.0	·	35.6	·	26.0	13.7	15.1	24.6	·	·	·	·	·
Officers' Compensation 20	4.4	·	6.5	·	5.1	2.3	1.8	1.5	·	·	·	·	·
Operating Margin 21	2.9	·	6.5	·	2.7	1.3	2.9	2.0	·	·	·	·	·
Operating Margin Before Officers' Comp. 22	7.3	·	13.0	·	7.8	3.6	4.7	3.4	·	·	·	·	·

Selected Average Balance Sheet ($ in Thousands)

Net Receivables 23	76	10	560	1894	2687	4379
Inventories 24	4	0	7	134	111	712
Net Property, Plant and Equipment 25	129	20	772	2874	5672	13061
Total Assets 26	360	64	1896	7403	14723	36004
Notes and Loans Payable 27	193	47	1065	4092	5573	15540
All Other Liabilities 28	67	8	348	1289	2887	5478
Net Worth 29	100	9	484	2022	6263	14985

Selected Financial Ratios (Times to 1)

Current Ratio 30	1.3	1.6	1.3	1.3	1.5	1.4
Quick Ratio 31	1.0	1.4	1.1	1.1	1.0	1.0
Net Sales to Working Capital 32	23.6	30.9	23.4	14.7	12.0	11.0
Coverage Ratio 33	5.3	6.3	5.5	2.8	5.6	5.9
Total Asset Turnover 34	2.2	3.6	2.6	1.9	1.9	1.1
Inventory Turnover 35	65.8	333.6	292.9	68.8	132.9	10.3
Receivables Turnover 36	9.5	21.9	9.9	7.6	12.6	9.3
Total Liabilities to Net Worth 37	2.6	5.8	2.9	2.7	1.4	1.4
Current Assets to Working Capital 38	4.3	2.6	4.4	4.0	2.8	3.3
Current Liabilities to Working Capital 39	3.3	1.6	3.4	3.0	1.8	2.3
Working Capital to Net Sales 40	0.0	0.0	0.0	0.1	0.1	0.1
Inventory to Working Capital 41	0.1	0.0	0.0	0.1	0.0	0.1
Total Receipts to Cash Flow 42	4.3	2.7	5.5	7.4	7.3	4.7
Cost of Goods to Cash Flow 43	1.5	0.3	2.4	4.8	3.8	0.9
Cash Flow to Total Debt 44	0.7	1.6	0.6	0.4	0.5	0.4

Selected Financial Factors (in Percentages)

Debt Ratio 45	72.4	85.3	74.5	72.7	57.5	58.4
Return on Total Assets 46	14.8	31.7	15.7	5.3	8.9	8.2
Return on Equity Before Income Taxes 47	43.4	181.5	50.4	12.5	17.2	16.4
Return on Equity After Income Taxes 48	40.5	179.8	47.4	8.8	16.1	15.2
Profit Margin (Before Income Tax) 49	5.5	7.5	5.0	1.8	3.7	6.3
Profit Margin (After Income Tax) 50	5.1	7.4	4.7	1.3	3.5	5.8

Table I

Corporations with and without Net Income

PIPELINE TRANSPORTATION

MONEY AMOUNTS AND SIZE OF ASSETS IN THOUSANDS OF DOLLARS

Item Description for Accounting Period 7/04 Through 6/05	Total	Zero Assets	Under 500	500 to 1,000	1,000 to 5,000	5,000 to 10,000	10,000 to 25,000	25,000 to 50,000	50,000 to 100,000	100,000 to 250,000	250,000 to 500,000	500,000 to 2,500,000	2,500,000 and over
Number of Enterprises **1**	430	52	0	162	159	13	12	10	4	8	3	6	0
Revenues ($ in Thousands)													
Net Sales **2**	5005881	174417	0	521533	50401	124071	274547	638111	252687	224773	452561	2292781	0
Interest **3**	22195	26	0	0	338	244	257	806	181	5031	1229	14082	0
Rents **4**	6553	0	0	0	0	691	14	78	4	4812	0	953	0
Royalties **5**	0	0	0	0	0	0	0	0	0	0	0	0	0
Other Portfolio Income **6**	146268	116384	0	0	0	43	21	175	0	4169	102	25375	0
Other Receipts **7**	188078	7797	0	0	10727	256	11512	5020	-124	19334	19256	114299	0
Total Receipts **8**	5368975	298624	0	521533	61466	125305	286351	644190	252748	258119	473148	2447490	0
Average Total Receipts **9**	12486	5743	•	3219	387	9639	23863	64419	63187	32265	157716	407915	•
Operating Costs/Operating Income (%)													
Cost of Operations **10**	44.0	91.3	•	45.3	•	41.1	71.7	55.3	13.3	3.6	28.9	45.1	•
Salaries and Wages **11**	7.7	0.8	•	19.6	•	1.2	1.8	2.7	27.7	6.9	3.1	6.9	•
Taxes Paid **12**	4.0	1.6	•	1.9	1.6	4.6	1.5	3.5	6.7	4.9	4.8	4.5	•
Interest Paid **13**	7.6	1.9	•	0.5	0.1	0.2	0.7	0.8	0.7	16.5	6.9	12.9	•
Depreciation **14**	11.5	2.5	•	0.4	42.6	4.0	4.1	3.2	5.0	22.9	17.9	16.0	•
Amortization and Depletion **15**	0.5	0.1	•	0.4	•	0.1	0.1	0.1	0.1	1.3	0.1	0.7	•
Pensions and Other Deferred Comp. **16**	0.7	•	•	•	•	•	0.1	0.3	0.9	1.0	0.5	1.1	•
Employee Benefits **17**	1.0	0.1	•	•	•	0.2	0.5	0.5	6.4	0.8	0.5	1.1	•
Advertising **18**	0.1	0.0	•	0.7	0.0	0.0	0.0	0.0	0.0	0.0	•	0.0	•
Other Expenses **19**	15.1	7.8	•	15.1	25.7	17.3	10.8	20.5	25.2	53.9	13.7	9.7	•
Officers' Compensation **20**	0.5	0.5	•	2.5	•	0.0	0.9	0.4	•	•	0.2	0.3	•
Operating Margin **21**	7.3	•	•	13.6	30.0	31.2	8.0	12.8	14.1	•	23.3	1.5	•
Operating Margin Before Officers' Comp. **22**	7.9	•	•	16.1	30.0	31.2	8.9	13.1	14.1	•	23.5	1.8	•

Selected Average Balance Sheet ($ in Thousands)

Net Receivables 23	2212	0	•	307	556	719	3237	6539	6859	32858	15197	60555	•
Inventories 24	236	0	•	185	0	178	578	2454	187	418	6249	2067	•
Net Property, Plant and Equipment 25	17511	0	•	29	1302	6410	7328	19452	38132	79119	264871	895336	•
Total Assets 26	29470	0	•	940	3775	8793	15768	36836	64196	164634	330809	1446921	•
Notes and Loans Payable 27	12652	0	•	176	1234	645	3944	8240	9710	57285	232085	647325	•
All Other Liabilities 28	8439	0	•	107	1331	1942	3358	10775	31050	55312	61556	412507	•
Net Worth 29	8379	0	•	656	1210	6206	8466	17822	23436	52037	37168	387089	•

Selected Financial Ratios (Times to 1)

Current Ratio 30	0.9	•	•	7.3	11.3	1.3	1.7	1.3	1.8	1.2	0.4	0.6	•
Quick Ratio 31	0.7	•	•	5.5	11.3	1.0	1.3	0.9	1.1	1.0	0.3	0.5	•
Net Sales to Working Capital 32	•	•	•	4.8	0.4	15.0	8.8	23.5	5.3	4.0	•	•	•
Coverage Ratio 33	2.9	34.4	•	28.5	689.9	190.2	19.7	17.9	21.4	1.2	5.0	1.6	•
Total Asset Turnover 34	0.4	•	•	3.4	0.1	1.1	1.5	1.7	1.0	0.2	0.5	0.3	•
Inventory Turnover 35	21.7	•	•	7.9	•	22.0	28.4	14.4	45.0	2.4	7.0	83.4	•
Receivables Turnover 36	5.4	•	•	•	0.6	6.5	6.6	11.1	8.0	0.9	10.2	6.5	•
Total Liabilities to Net Worth 37	2.5	•	•	0.4	2.1	0.4	0.9	1.1	1.7	2.2	7.9	2.7	•
Current Assets to Working Capital 38	•	•	•	1.2	1.1	3.9	2.5	4.7	2.2	6.1	•	•	•
Current Liabilities to Working Capital 39	•	•	•	0.2	0.1	2.9	1.5	3.7	1.2	5.1	•	•	•
Working Capital to Net Sales 40	•	•	•	0.2	2.6	0.1	0.1	0.0	0.2	0.3	•	•	•
Inventory to Working Capital 41	•	•	•	0.3	•	0.3	0.3	0.9	0.0	0.0	•	•	•
Total Receipts to Cash Flow 42	4.0	3.6	•	3.8	1.5	2.2	4.8	3.1	3.6	2.1	2.5	6.5	•
Cost of Goods to Cash Flow 43	1.8	3.3	•	1.7	•	0.9	3.4	1.7	0.5	0.1	0.7	2.9	•
Cash Flow to Total Debt 44	0.1	•	•	3.0	0.1	1.7	0.7	1.1	0.4	0.1	0.2	0.1	•

Selected Financial Factors (in Percentages)

Debt Ratio 45	71.6	•	•	30.2	68.0	29.4	46.3	51.6	63.5	68.4	88.8	73.2	•
Return on Total Assets 46	8.6	•	•	48.4	4.4	35.1	18.8	25.1	14.6	3.3	15.8	5.3	•
Return on Equity Before Income Taxes 47	19.6	•	•	66.9	13.6	49.5	33.2	49.1	38.1	1.6	113.0	7.2	•
Return on Equity After Income Taxes 48	12.6	•	•	66.9	13.6	34.8	18.1	32.4	26.1	•	67.6	3.0	•
Profit Margin (Before Income Tax) 49	14.1	64.7	•	13.6	51.9	32.2	12.3	13.7	14.1	3.1	27.8	7.3	•
Profit Margin (After Income Tax) 50	9.0	49.0	•	13.6	51.9	22.6	6.7	9.1	9.7	•	16.7	3.0	•

Table II

Corporations with Net Income

PIPELINE TRANSPORTATION

MONEY AMOUNTS AND SIZE OF ASSETS IN THOUSANDS OF DOLLARS

Item Description for Accounting Period 7/04 Through 6/05	Total	Zero Assets	Under 500	500 to 1,000	1,000 to 5,000	5,000 to 10,000	10,000 to 25,000	25,000 to 50,000	50,000 to 100,000	100,000 to 250,000	250,000 to 500,000	500,000 to 2,500,000	2,500,000 and over
Number of Enterprises **1**	415	0	0	0	159	13	6	10	0	0	0	3	0
Revenues ($ in Thousands)													
Net Sales **2**	3561474	0	0	0	50401	124071	84436	638111	0	0	0	1254231	0
Interest **3**	17463	0	0	0	338	244	166	806	0	0	0	9561	0
Rents **4**	5594	0	0	0	0	691	7	78	0	0	0	1	0
Royalties **5**	0	0	0	0	0	0	0	0	0	0	0	0	0
Other Portfolio Income **6**	140564	0	0	0	0	43	0	175	0	0	0	24990	0
Other Receipts **7**	203493	0	0	0	10727	256	10484	5020	0	0	0	136002	0
Total Receipts **8**	3928588	0	0	0	61466	125305	95093	644190	0	0	0	1424785	0
Average Total Receipts **9**	9466	·	·	·	387	9639	15849	64419	·	·	·	474928	·
Operating Costs/Operating Income (%)													
Cost of Operations **10**	34.6	·	·	·	·	41.1	26.5	55.3	·	·	·	19.0	·
Salaries and Wages **11**	10.4	·	·	·	·	1.2	4.1	2.7	·	·	·	12.6	·
Taxes Paid **12**	4.7	·	·	·	1.6	4.6	4.2	3.5	·	·	·	6.7	·
Interest Paid **13**	7.4	·	·	·	0.1	0.2	0.7	0.8	·	·	·	16.7	·
Depreciation **14**	11.1	·	·	·	42.6	4.0	5.6	3.2	·	·	·	21.0	·
Amortization and Depletion **15**	0.1	·	·	·	·	0.1	0.0	0.1	·	·	·	0.0	·
Pensions and Other Deferred Comp. **16**	0.7	·	·	·	·	·	·	0.3	·	·	·	1.3	·
Employee Benefits **17**	1.3	·	·	·	·	0.2	0.7	0.5	·	·	·	1.8	·
Advertising **18**	0.1	·	·	·	0.0	0.0	·	0.0	·	·	·	0.0	·
Other Expenses **19**	14.0	·	·	·	25.7	17.3	17.7	20.5	·	·	·	9.8	·
Officers' Compensation **20**	0.6	·	·	·	·	0.0	·	0.4	·	·	·	0.3	·
Operating Margin **21**	15.0	·	·	·	30.0	31.2	40.5	12.8	·	·	·	10.6	·
Operating Margin Before Officers' Comp. **22**	15.6	·	·	·	30.0	31.2	40.5	13.1	·	·	·	10.9	·

Selected Average Balance Sheet ($ in Thousands)

Net Receivables 23	1271	556	719	1798	6539	73825
Inventories 24	214	0	178	956	2454	1703
Net Property, Plant and Equipment 25	13789	1302	6410	9812	19452	1396504
Total Assets 26	21180	3775	8793	16619	36836	1961088
Notes and Loans Payable 27	8624	1234	645	1135	8240	828453
All Other Liabilities 28	5969	1331	1942	3562	10775	550806
Net Worth 29	6587	1210	6206	11922	17822	581829

Selected Financial Ratios (Times to 1)

Current Ratio 30	1.6	11.3	1.3	2.5	1.3	0.8
Quick Ratio 31	1.2	11.3	1.0	1.7	0.9	0.7
Net Sales to Working Capital 32	9.6	0.4	15.0	3.8	23.5	
Coverage Ratio 33	4.3	689.9	190.2	80.5	17.9	2.3
Total Asset Turnover 34	0.4	0.1	1.1	0.8	1.7	0.2
Inventory Turnover 35	13.9		22.0	3.9	14.4	46.7
Receivables Turnover 36	7.2	0.6	7.9	5.7	11.1	
Total Liabilities to Net Worth 37	2.2	2.1	0.4	0.4	1.1	2.4
Current Assets to Working Capital 38	2.8	1.1	3.9	1.7	4.7	
Current Liabilities to Working Capital 39	1.8	0.1	2.9	0.7	3.7	
Working Capital to Net Sales 40	0.1	2.6	0.1	0.3	0.0	
Inventory to Working Capital 41	0.2		0.3	0.3	0.9	
Total Receipts to Cash Flow 42	3.0	1.5	2.2	1.5	3.1	3.3
Cost of Goods to Cash Flow 43	1.0		0.9	0.4	1.7	0.6
Cash Flow to Total Debt 44	0.2	0.1	1.7	2.1	1.1	0.1

Selected Financial Factors (in Percentages)

Debt Ratio 45	68.9	68.0	29.4	28.3	51.6	70.3
Return on Total Assets 46	13.0	4.4	35.1	45.5	25.1	8.3
Return on Equity Before Income Taxes 47	32.1	13.6	49.5	62.7	49.1	16.0
Return on Equity After Income Taxes 48	22.9	13.6	34.8	41.2	32.4	10.4
Profit Margin (Before Income Tax) 49	24.7	51.9	32.2	53.1	13.7	22.3
Profit Margin (After Income Tax) 50	17.5	51.9	22.6	34.9	9.1	14.5

Table I

Corporations with and without Net Income

OTHER TRANSPORTATION AND SUPPORT ACTIVITIES

MONEY AMOUNTS AND SIZE OF ASSETS IN THOUSANDS OF DOLLARS

Item Description for Accounting Period 7/04 Through 6/05	Total	Zero Assets	Under 500	500 to 1,000	1,000 to 5,000	5,000 to 10,000	10,000 to 25,000	25,000 to 50,000	50,000 to 100,000	100,000 to 250,000	250,000 to 500,000	500,000 to 2,500,000	2,500,000 and over
Number of Enterprises 1	38330	5191	27454	2663	2423	246	204	64	33	30	9	9	3
Revenues ($ in Thousands)													
Net Sales 2	173855798	7682401	21018404	9291483	12553914	5414802	7057602	4892964	3455593	7861551	3245495	9664333	81717255
Interest 3	1043970	1934	3500	3210	10083	1410	10652	5648	4910	11069	17358	82311	891886
Rents 4	215697	2577	7710	0	1709	5059	2636	5628	17932	30445	22088	17695	102220
Royalties 5	1437690	0	0	0	0	0	0	666	0	391	82684	82684	1317126
Other Portfolio Income 6	517645	6874	70765	3511	29555	5023	8902	14699	14602	7953	128068	203321	24374
Other Receipts 7	1078251	10919	22056	4329	132393	72685	105893	106755	48087	58409	121447	110295	284980
Total Receipts 8	178149051	7704705	21122435	9302533	12727654	5498979	7185685	5026360	3541124	7969818	3571279	10160639	84337841
Average Total Receipts 9	4648	1484	769	3493	5253	22354	35224	78537	107307	265661	396809	1128960	28112614
Operating Costs/Operating Income (%)													
Cost of Operations 10	38.9	12.1	63.1	58.1	61.8	71.6	58.8	65.2	55.1	59.0	62.7	36.5	20.7
Salaries and Wages 11	17.1	3.1	9.3	8.7	10.8	8.6	13.2	11.5	13.5	13.3	16.5	20.5	23.6
Taxes Paid 12	6.0	73.0	2.3	1.5	2.4	1.5	3.0	2.2	5.8	1.9	2.1	3.7	3.3
Interest Paid 13	0.5	0.1	0.4	0.5	0.5	0.2	0.8	0.8	1.2	1.2	1.1	2.1	0.3
Depreciation 14	3.1	0.5	1.6	1.6	3.1	1.9	2.3	2.2	4.7	2.8	1.8	2.7	4.2
Amortization and Depletion 15	0.2	0.0	0.0	0.1	0.2	0.1	0.2	0.4	0.5	0.5	0.7	0.7	0.2
Pensions and Other Deferred Comp. 16	1.8	0.0	0.1	0.1	0.2	0.2	0.6	0.2	0.2	0.3	0.5	0.6	3.5
Employee Benefits 17	3.2	0.6	0.4	0.9	0.9	1.0	1.8	1.4	2.5	1.6	2.0	2.7	5.5
Advertising 18	0.5	0.1	0.2	0.1	0.4	0.2	0.3	0.3	0.3	0.1	0.6	0.3	0.8
Other Expenses 19	25.8	9.3	17.8	24.2	18.6	11.4	17.0	17.5	16.5	19.6	16.2	31.0	33.6
Officers' Compensation 20	1.2	2.8	3.3	3.4	2.2	2.2	1.7	0.9	1.1	0.8	0.8	0.5	0.2
Operating Margin 21	1.7	•	1.3	0.8	•	1.1	0.5	•	•	•	•	•	4.0
Operating Margin Before Officers' Comp. 22	2.9	1.3	4.6	4.2	1.2	3.3	2.1	•	•	•	•	•	4.3

Selected Average Balance Sheet ($ in Thousands)

Net Receivables 23	547	0	22	225	625	2228	5142	10910	20389	35526	110995	269197	3604505
Inventories 24	35	0	4	37	18	172	379	1149	2036	2969	5939	29635	134713
Net Property, Plant and Equipment 25	809	0	38	184	715	1869	4529	8965	22792	41766	46739	223641	7115161
Total Assets 26	2480	0	110	721	2037	6532	15366	34907	70791	157431	339643	1083636	19444792
Notes and Loans Payable 27	649	0	75	396	1038	1695	5089	11766	19866	46092	83533	301185	3846853
All Other Liabilities 28	811	0	22	252	503	2760	6538	13709	25704	61092	154328	394501	6026498
Net Worth 29	1020	0	13	72	496	2076	3739	9432	25221	50246	101782	387950	9571441

Selected Financial Ratios (Times to 1)

Current Ratio 30	1.3	•	1.8	1.3	1.5	1.4	1.1	1.3	1.1	1.1	1.0	1.4	1.2
Quick Ratio 31	1.0	•	1.5	0.9	1.3	1.1	0.9	1.0	0.9	0.8	0.8	1.1	1.1
Net Sales to Working Capital 32	23.0	•	32.7	37.6	15.8	17.1	60.9	18.7	32.7	46.9	61.7	8.5	22.0
Coverage Ratio 33	9.2	•	5.1	3.0	1.8	12.8	3.9	1.4	2.1	1.2	5.7	2.8	29.3
Total Asset Turnover 34	1.8	•	6.9	4.8	2.5	3.4	2.3	2.2	1.5	1.7	1.1	1.0	1.4
Inventory Turnover 35	51.0	•	119.4	55.5	182.3	91.7	53.7	43.4	28.3	52.1	38.1	13.2	41.9
Receivables Turnover 36	9.3	•	36.2	13.1	9.2	9.4	7.3	7.9	5.9	7.5	4.5	4.6	8.7
Total Liabilities to Net Worth 37	1.4	•	7.6	8.9	3.1	2.1	3.1	2.7	1.8	2.1	2.3	1.8	1.0
Current Assets to Working Capital 38	4.9	•	2.3	5.0	3.0	3.4	14.8	4.5	9.7	10.9	31.0	3.5	5.2
Current Liabilities to Working Capital 39	3.9	•	1.3	4.0	2.0	2.4	13.8	3.5	8.7	9.9	30.0	2.5	4.2
Working Capital to Net Sales 40	0.0	•	0.0	0.0	0.1	0.1	0.0	0.1	0.0	0.0	0.0	0.1	0.0
Inventory to Working Capital 41	0.2	•	0.2	0.7	0.1	0.1	0.6	0.3	0.6	0.6	1.6	0.3	0.1
Total Receipts to Cash Flow 42	4.1	17.8	6.5	4.4	7.1	11.6	6.6	7.0	8.8	6.5	6.2	3.6	2.9
Cost of Goods to Cash Flow 43	1.6	2.2	4.1	2.6	4.4	8.3	3.9	4.5	4.8	3.8	3.9	1.3	0.6
Cash Flow to Total Debt 44	0.8	•	1.2	1.2	0.5	0.4	0.5	0.4	0.3	0.4	0.2	0.4	0.9

Selected Financial Factors (in Percentages)

Debt Ratio 45	58.9	•	88.3	89.9	75.6	68.2	75.7	73.0	64.4	68.1	70.0	64.2	50.8
Return on Total Assets 46	8.8	•	15.8	6.9	2.4	9.8	6.9	2.5	3.6	2.5	6.5	6.1	10.8
Return on Equity Before Income Taxes 47	19.0	•	108.5	45.7	4.4	28.6	21.1	2.5	5.3	1.4	18.0	11.0	21.1
Return on Equity After Income Taxes 48	12.2	•	104.9	41.6	2.3	23.7	17.7	•	2.8	•	12.6	6.5	13.3
Profit Margin (Before Income Tax) 49	4.3	•	1.8	0.9	0.4	2.7	2.3	0.3	1.3	0.3	5.1	4.0	7.4
Profit Margin (After Income Tax) 50	2.8	•	1.8	0.9	0.2	2.2	1.9	•	0.7	•	3.6	2.3	4.7

Table II

Corporations with Net Income

OTHER TRANSPORTATION AND SUPPORT ACTIVITIES

MONEY AMOUNTS AND SIZE OF ASSETS IN THOUSANDS OF DOLLARS

Item Description for Accounting Period 7/04 Through 6/05	Total	Zero Assets	Under 500	500 to 1,000	1,000 to 5,000	5,000 to 10,000	10,000 to 25,000	25,000 to 50,000	50,000 to 100,000	100,000 to 250,000	250,000 to 500,000	500,000 to 2,500,000	2,500,000 and over
Number of Enterprises 1	19851	1725	15093	1287	1283	228	146	38	21	14	0	0	0
Revenues ($ in Thousands)													
Net Sales 2	137296911	813175	17355346	4745887	9558827	4901654	5547642	3406982	2260987	5379921	0	0	0
Interest 3	1000394	115	2778	2236	8739	1388	8968	3673	4457	3631	0	0	0
Rents 4	171772	1664	4230	0	1709	4093	1422	3013	16822	15229	0	0	0
Royalties 5	142244	0	0	0	0	0	0	379	0	391	0	0	0
Other Portfolio Income 6	476441	6874	52293	3511	27688	4953	6753	10697	5759	7574	0	0	0
Other Receipts 7	842387	2706	13861	2652	107673	26270	79265	98741	37929	52379	0	0	0
Total Receipts 8	141216149	824534	17428508	4754286	9704636	4938358	5644050	3523485	2325954	5459125	0	0	0
Average Total Receipts 9	7114	478	1155	3694	7564	21659	38658	92723	110760	389938	•	•	•
Operating Costs/Operating Income (%)													
Cost of Operations 10	40.4	41.4	69.8	52.2	67.5	70.6	59.2	74.3	54.1	65.9	•	•	•
Salaries and Wages 11	17.8	11.0	6.6	8.2	9.4	8.1	13.5	9.3	11.0	11.3	•	•	•
Taxes Paid 12	3.0	2.1	1.9	1.7	2.1	1.6	3.2	2.1	7.5	2.0	•	•	•
Interest Paid 13	0.4	0.0	0.3	0.4	0.4	0.2	0.6	0.4	0.7	0.3	•	•	•
Depreciation 14	3.3	2.0	1.1	1.9	2.5	1.9	1.8	1.4	3.9	1.8	•	•	•
Amortization and Depletion 15	0.2	0.0	0.0	0.1	0.2	0.1	0.1	0.2	0.2	0.2	•	•	•
Pensions and Other Deferred Comp. 16	2.2	0.2	0.1	0.1	0.2	0.1	0.5	0.2	0.3	0.3	•	•	•
Employee Benefits 17	3.6	2.3	0.4	0.8	0.9	0.8	1.8	1.2	2.4	1.6	•	•	•
Advertising 18	0.6	0.4	0.2	0.1	0.4	0.2	0.2	0.2	0.3	0.1	•	•	•
Other Expenses 19	23.8	31.1	13.3	25.9	12.4	11.2	14.6	10.2	16.5	14.2	•	•	•
Officers' Compensation 20	1.0	1.9	2.8	4.2	2.2	2.3	1.8	0.8	1.2	0.7	•	•	•
Operating Margin 21	3.7	7.5	3.6	4.2	1.7	2.9	2.6	•	1.8	1.6	•	•	•
Operating Margin Before Officers' Comp. 22	4.8	9.4	6.4	8.5	3.9	5.2	4.4	0.5	3.0	2.3	•	•	•

Selected Average Balance Sheet ($ in Thousands)

Net Receivables **23**	850	0	24	185	858	2321	5462	13040	21962	46920
Inventories **24**	47	0	4	4	14	122	298	1183	2350	1050
Net Property, Plant and Equipment **25**	1313	0	27	173	540	1827	4159	6371	20687	38075
Total Assets **26**	3836	0	104	688	2232	6549	15173	36053	71349	167519
Notes and Loans Payable **27**	807	0	45	257	721	1370	4216	6188	15202	26986
All Other Liabilities **28**	1231	0	24	224	644	2726	5742	13744	24630	62219
Net Worth **29**	1797	0	35	208	867	2452	5214	16121	31518	78315

Selected Financial Ratios (Times to 1)

Current Ratio **30**	1.3	•	2.0	1.7	1.6	1.5	1.3	1.6	1.4	1.5
Quick Ratio **31**	1.1	•	1.7	1.5	1.4	1.2	1.1	1.2	1.2	1.2
Net Sales to Working Capital **32**	18.1	•	40.1	23.0	16.3	15.4	19.6	11.3	11.7	14.5
Coverage Ratio **33**	17.6	302.4	15.6	11.3	8.6	17.8	8.3	9.8	7.3	10.6
Total Asset Turnover **34**	1.8	•	11.1	5.4	3.3	3.3	2.5	2.5	1.5	2.3
Inventory Turnover **35**	59.5	•	190.8	439.4	362.8	124.2	75.4	56.3	24.8	241.2
Receivables Turnover **36**	9.1	•	55.1	12.0	10.0	9.4	8.1	7.7	5.5	8.9
Total Liabilities to Net Worth **37**	1.1	•	2.0	2.3	1.6	1.7	1.9	1.2	1.3	1.1
Current Assets to Working Capital **38**	3.9	•	2.0	2.4	2.8	3.2	4.6	2.8	3.8	3.0
Current Liabilities to Working Capital **39**	2.9	•	1.0	1.4	1.8	2.2	3.6	1.8	2.8	2.0
Working Capital to Net Sales **40**	0.1	•	0.0	0.0	0.1	0.1	0.1	0.1	0.1	0.1
Inventory to Working Capital **41**	0.1	•	0.1	0.1	0.0	0.1	0.2	0.1	0.2	0.0
Total Receipts to Cash Flow **42**	4.1	3.4	7.0	3.7	8.2	10.9	6.4	10.1	7.0	7.1
Cost of Goods to Cash Flow **43**	1.6	1.4	4.9	2.0	5.5	7.7	3.8	7.5	3.8	4.7
Cash Flow to Total Debt **44**	0.8	•	2.4	2.1	0.7	0.5	0.6	0.4	0.4	0.6

Selected Financial Factors (in Percentages)

Debt Ratio **45**	53.1	•	66.6	69.8	61.2	62.6	65.6	55.3	55.8	53.3
Return on Total Assets **46**	12.9	•	47.6	26.0	12.4	12.8	12.4	8.7	8.2	7.7
Return on Equity Before Income Taxes **47**	25.9	•	133.3	78.6	28.1	32.4	31.7	17.5	16.1	15.0
Return on Equity After Income Taxes **48**	18.4	•	130.9	75.6	25.8	27.9	28.3	13.2	12.9	11.7
Profit Margin (Before Income Tax) **49**	6.7	8.9	4.0	4.4	3.3	3.7	4.4	3.2	4.7	3.1
Profit Margin (After Income Tax) **50**	4.8	8.4	4.0	4.3	3.0	3.2	3.9	2.4	3.8	2.4

Table I

Corporations with and without Net Income

WAREHOUSING AND STORAGE

MONEY AMOUNTS AND SIZE OF ASSETS IN THOUSANDS OF DOLLARS

Item Description for Accounting Period 7/04 Through 6/05	Total	Zero Assets	Under 500	500 to 1,000	1,000 to 5,000	5,000 to 10,000	10,000 to 25,000	25,000 to 50,000	50,000 to 100,000	100,000 to 250,000	250,000 to 500,000	500,000 to 2,500,000	2,500,000 and over
Number of Enterprises 1	7289	289	4688	726	1215	188	112	28	17	17	5	3	0
Revenues ($ in Thousands)													
Net Sales 2	18554733	155574	1620248	1282627	4715795	871751	1946722	673386	1392690	2926289	1163088	1806563	0
Interest 3	228015	1183	67	2461	1596	924	3023	1601	4530	13364	5187	194079	0
Rents 4	22662	0	0	1316	4301	1572	7660	1539	261	626	59	5330	0
Royalties 5	8702	0	0	0	0	0	120	0	7801	0	678	103	0
Other Portfolio Income 6	72745	2346	1964	79	22194	395	13520	330	4683	4674	12511	10046	0
Other Receipts 7	401279	19092	2698	1170	139695	16085	20943	14073	43204	33700	71432	39187	0
Total Receipts 8	19288136	178195	1624977	1287653	4883581	890727	1991988	690929	1453169	2978653	1252955	2055308	0
Average Total Receipts 9	2646	617	347	1774	4019	4738	17786	24676	85481	175215	250591	685103	•
Operating Costs/Operating Income (%)													
Cost of Operations 10	40.8	21.6	52.3	28.6	62.8	47.3	34.4	25.1	41.4	42.4	15.2	6.7	•
Salaries and Wages 11	18.4	28.1	4.4	16.5	13.3	9.6	17.2	20.7	17.2	26.9	26.4	31.8	•
Taxes Paid 12	3.3	3.1	1.3	3.8	2.7	3.1	3.7	4.7	2.8	2.5	7.6	4.7	•
Interest Paid 13	3.3	5.4	0.3	1.8	1.0	2.4	1.7	2.6	2.3	1.6	2.6	19.0	•
Depreciation 14	4.8	3.1	2.2	3.8	4.2	4.4	4.7	6.9	4.1	3.7	8.1	9.5	•
Amortization and Depletion 15	0.7	0.1	0.0	0.0	0.1	0.0	0.1	0.7	0.7	0.3	1.9	4.2	•
Pensions and Other Deferred Comp. 16	0.5	0.2	0.0	0.1	0.3	0.6	0.9	0.6	0.4	0.6	1.4	0.2	•
Employee Benefits 17	2.1	3.5	1.1	1.6	0.7	1.2	2.4	3.4	3.8	3.8	1.7	2.8	•
Advertising 18	0.4	0.1	0.3	0.9	0.1	0.0	0.3	0.2	0.2	0.9	0.6	0.5	•
Other Expenses 19	26.2	46.7	33.7	38.9	16.2	24.7	31.9	32.0	29.2	17.7	38.4	31.1	•
Officers' Compensation 20	1.4	0.5	1.8	2.7	1.4	4.6	2.0	2.6	1.1	0.5	0.6	•	•
Operating Margin 21	•	•	2.5	1.3	•	2.1	0.6	0.4	•	•	•	•	•
Operating Margin Before Officers' Comp. 22	•	•	4.2	4.0	•	6.7	2.7	3.0	•	•	•	•	•

Selected Average Balance Sheet ($ in Thousands)

Net Receivables 23	307	0	22	193	341	449	2459	4730	15495	26497	55494	33081	•
Inventories 24	45	0	3	5	68	263	513	570	2838	2561	2278	2587	•
Net Property, Plant and Equipment 25	987	0	64	264	869	2602	6613	17250	35001	67472	114207	540546	•
Total Assets 26	2660	0	145	705	1922	6365	15143	34252	71459	154576	326701	2177651	•
Notes and Loans Payable 27	1149	0	63	582	633	1969	5841	12769	35361	56968	81995	1175783	•
All Other Liabilities 28	667	0	22	168	493	1552	2505	5740	14368	34998	152416	567222	•
Net Worth 29	844	0	60	-45	796	2844	6798	15742	21730	62609	92289	434646	•

Selected Financial Ratios (Times to 1)

Current Ratio 30	1.2	•	1.6	1.1	1.7	1.4	1.7	1.2	1.6	1.4	0.7	0.7
Quick Ratio 31	0.8	•	1.4	0.9	1.2	1.0	1.2	1.0	1.1	1.0	0.5	0.4
Net Sales to Working Capital 32	24.0	•	17.5	79.1	13.1	12.6	7.1	15.6	8.5	11.4	•	•
Coverage Ratio 33	1.6	1.4	9.0	1.9	1.6	2.8	2.7	2.2	1.4	1.5	2.3	1.2
Total Asset Turnover 34	1.0	•	2.4	2.5	2.0	0.7	1.1	0.7	1.1	1.1	0.7	0.3
Inventory Turnover 35	22.9	•	62.2	97.2	35.6	8.3	11.6	10.6	11.9	28.5	15.5	15.5
Receivables Turnover 36	8.6	•	15.8	11.3	15.0	7.4	7.4	4.0	5.8	8.4	2.7	•
Total Liabilities to Net Worth 37	2.2	•	1.4	•	1.4	1.2	1.2	1.2	2.3	1.5	2.5	4.0
Current Assets to Working Capital 38	6.6	•	2.7	14.1	2.5	3.6	2.4	5.3	2.6	3.4	•	•
Current Liabilities to Working Capital 39	5.6	•	1.7	13.1	1.5	2.6	1.4	4.3	1.6	2.4	•	•
Working Capital to Net Sales 40	0.0	•	0.1	0.0	0.1	0.1	0.1	0.1	0.1	0.1	•	•
Inventory to Working Capital 41	0.5	•	0.1	0.4	0.4	0.1	0.2	0.4	0.3	0.3	•	•
Total Receipts to Cash Flow 42	5.6	4.2	7.9	3.6	9.0	6.3	4.5	4.3	4.3	7.6	3.1	4.6
Cost of Goods to Cash Flow 43	2.3	0.9	4.1	1.0	5.6	3.0	1.5	1.1	1.8	3.2	0.5	0.3
Cash Flow to Total Debt 44	0.3	•	0.5	0.7	0.4	0.2	0.5	0.3	0.4	0.2	0.3	0.1

Selected Financial Factors (in Percentages)

Debt Ratio 45	68.3	58.8	106.4	58.6	55.3	55.1	54.0	69.6	59.5	71.8	80.0
Return on Total Assets 46	4.9	7.4	8.8	3.3	4.9	5.3	4.0	3.8	2.7	4.2	6.2
Return on Equity Before Income Taxes 47	5.7	16.0	•	3.1	7.0	7.5	4.6	3.9	2.3	8.2	4.6
Return on Equity After Income Taxes 48	4.4	14.1	•	2.3	6.0	6.3	2.5	1.1	0.5	6.2	4.5
Profit Margin (Before Income Tax) 49	1.9	2.2	1.7	0.6	4.3	2.9	3.0	1.0	0.8	3.3	3.3
Profit Margin (After Income Tax) 50	1.5	1.6	1.7	0.5	3.7	2.4	1.7	0.3	0.2	2.5	3.2

Table II

Corporations with Net Income

WAREHOUSING AND STORAGE

MONEY AMOUNTS AND SIZE OF ASSETS IN THOUSANDS OF DOLLARS

Item Description for Accounting Period 7/04 Through 6/05	Total	Zero Assets	Under 500	500 to 1000	251 to 500	501 to 1,000	1,001 to 5,000	5,001 to 10,000	10,001 to 25,000	25,001 to 50,000	50,001 to 100,000	100,001 to 250,000	250,001 and over
Number of Enterprises 1	3586	270	1915	433	706	140	76	15	11	0	0	0	0
Revenues ($ in Thousands)													
Net Sales 2	12878024	59315	658403	687690	3821527	840441	1397610	461134	944518	0	0	0	0
Interest 3	213352	790	1	2421	1590	901	2583	1564	796	0	0	0	0
Rents 4	21041	0	0	1316	4301	1132	6891	1158	261	0	0	0	0
Royalties 5	7780	0	0	0	0	0	120	0	7557	0	0	0	0
Other Portfolio Income 6	60229	0	0	79	18148	278	13048	152	1768	0	0	0	0
Other Receipts 7	253965	13098	2694	842	38170	15858	15047	6125	24224	0	0	0	0
Total Receipts 8	13434391	73203	661098	692348	3883736	858610	1435299	470133	979124	0	0	0	0
Average Total Receipts 9	3746	271	345	1599	5501	6133	18886	31342	89011	•	•	•	•
Operating Costs/Operating Income (%)													
Cost of Operations 10	38.6	•	20.8	22.4	68.8	48.3	33.8	33.3	54.7	•	•	•	•
Salaries and Wages 11	17.6	38.2	2.5	20.1	8.3	9.4	16.8	17.6	11.7	•	•	•	•
Taxes Paid 12	3.5	0.6	0.7	3.9	1.6	2.9	3.6	4.3	2.9	•	•	•	•
Interest Paid 13	3.8	1.0	0.1	1.8	0.8	2.1	1.4	1.9	1.7	•	•	•	•
Depreciation 14	4.4	0.5	1.2	1.1	1.8	4.3	3.7	5.0	3.9	•	•	•	•
Amortization and Depletion 15	0.9	0.2	0.0	0.0	0.1	0.0	0.1	0.4	0.6	•	•	•	•
Pensions and Other Deferred Comp. 16	0.5	•	0.0	0.1	0.3	0.6	0.6	0.6	0.5	•	•	•	•
Employee Benefits 17	1.7	•	0.4	0.9	0.7	1.2	2.2	3.6	2.5	•	•	•	•
Advertising 18	0.3	•	0.1	0.7	0.1	0.0	0.3	0.2	0.2	•	•	•	•
Other Expenses 19	25.9	53.1	59.8	38.4	13.2	23.0	31.7	24.9	17.7	•	•	•	•
Officers' Compensation 20	1.4	•	0.0	2.8	1.4	4.4	2.0	1.7	1.3	•	•	•	•
Operating Margin 21	1.6	6.4	14.4	7.6	2.7	3.6	3.7	6.7	2.2	•	•	•	•
Operating Margin Before Officers' Comp. 22	2.9	6.4	14.4	10.4	4.2	8.1	5.7	8.3	3.5	•	•	•	•

Selected Average Balance Sheet ($ in Thousands)

Net Receivables 23	451	0	32	221	445	551	2634	4841	17014
Inventories 24	70	0	5	3	105	342	575	749	3913
Net Property, Plant and Equipment 25	1456	0	34	167	912	2806	6268	19766	37093
Total Assets 26	4137	0	101	691	2015	6299	15060	36322	73727
Notes and Loans Payable 27	1731	0	45	468	677	2160	5146	11906	32788
All Other Liabilities 28	1067	0	18	96	422	1994	2645	5132	13945
Net Worth 29	1339	0	38	127	916	2145	7268	19284	26994

Selected Financial Ratios (Times to 1)

Current Ratio 30	1.2	•	1.2	1.7	2.2	1.4	1.9	1.8	1.6
Quick Ratio 31	0.8	•	1.1	1.6	1.5	1.0	1.3	1.4	1.1
Net Sales to Working Capital 32	20.8	•	36.8	11.2	10.3	14.6	6.0	7.4	7.6
Coverage Ratio 33	2.6	30.0	163.2	5.6	6.5	3.8	5.4	5.7	4.4
Total Asset Turnover 34	0.9	•	3.4	2.3	2.7	1.0	1.2	0.8	1.2
Inventory Turnover 35	19.8	•	14.9	136.0	35.4	8.5	10.8	13.7	12.0
Receivables Turnover 36	8.6	•	9.2	10.6	16.1	8.5	7.5	5.1	5.0
Total Liabilities to Net Worth 37	2.1	•	1.7	4.4	1.2	1.9	1.1	0.9	1.7
Current Assets to Working Capital 38	6.3	•	5.7	2.3	1.9	3.8	2.1	2.2	2.5
Current Liabilities to Working Capital 39	5.3	•	4.7	1.3	0.9	2.8	1.1	1.2	1.5
Working Capital to Net Sales 40	0.0	•	0.0	0.1	0.1	0.1	0.2	0.1	0.1
Inventory to Working Capital 41	0.4	•	0.2	0.0	0.3	0.1	0.2	0.2	0.4
Total Receipts to Cash Flow 42	4.9	2.6	4.3	3.6	7.9	6.2	3.9	3.9	5.4
Cost of Goods to Cash Flow 43	1.9	•	0.9	0.8	5.4	3.0	1.3	1.3	3.0
Cash Flow to Total Debt 44	0.3	•	1.3	0.8	0.6	0.2	0.6	0.5	0.3

Selected Financial Factors (in Percentages)

Debt Ratio 45	67.6	•	62.4	81.6	54.5	65.9	51.7	46.9	63.4
Return on Total Assets 46	8.4	•	50.5	23.3	13.9	7.5	9.5	8.9	8.7
Return on Equity Before Income Taxes 47	15.8	•	133.5	103.7	25.8	16.3	16.1	13.7	18.4
Return on Equity After Income Taxes 48	14.1	•	126.1	103.1	24.7	14.4	14.4	10.6	15.1
Profit Margin (Before Income Tax) 49	5.9	29.8	14.8	8.3	4.4	5.8	6.3	8.6	5.8
Profit Margin (After Income Tax) 50	5.3	28.2	14.0	8.2	4.2	5.1	5.7	6.7	4.7

Table I

Corporations with and without Net Income

NEWSPAPER PUBLISHERS

MONEY AMOUNTS AND SIZE OF ASSETS IN THOUSANDS OF DOLLARS

Item Description for Accounting Period 7/04 Through 6/05	Total	Zero Assets	Under 500	500 to 1,000	1,000 to 5,000	5,000 to 10,000	10,000 to 25,000	25,000 to 50,000	50,000 to 100,000	100,000 to 250,000	250,000 to 500,000	500,000 to 2,500,000	2,500,000 and over
Number of Enterprises 1	7668	531	5810	614	430	86	82	40	25	14	11	16	9
Revenues ($ in Thousands)													
Net Sales 2	54286101	1738646	2515263	775776	2460653	947297	1492564	1187921	1574370	1710103	2456675	10613244	26813589
Interest 3	327571	103	290	626	1212	1105	4656	1568	3424	7490	6513	122227	178357
Rents 4	160536	0	10	0	10	1521	1087	2835	5036	6160	8311	22154	113410
Royalties 5	433922	0	0	0	0	26	10	1356	35	0	1759	92885	337851
Other Portfolio Income 6	564346	99193	3546	197	9825	29708	9158	3713	21644	9645	21406	92917	263398
Other Receipts 7	1787064	151433	6318	298	43809	14035	21739	74565	31064	21245	71748	463487	887323
Total Receipts 8	57559540	1989375	2525427	776897	2515509	993692	1529214	1271958	1635573	1754643	2566412	11406914	28593928
Average Total Receipts 9	7506	3746	435	1265	5850	11555	18649	31799	65423	125332	233310	712932	3177103
Operating Costs/Operating Income (%)													
Cost of Operations 10	26.4	49.5	32.8	34.1	40.8	19.1	28.4	29.7	34.0	27.1	15.2	16.7	27.2
Salaries and Wages 11	22.7	22.9	17.1	19.4	13.4	36.1	26.3	26.8	21.8	24.0	27.5	25.8	21.6
Taxes Paid 12	3.5	4.0	2.7	4.3	3.3	3.9	3.9	3.9	3.3	3.9	3.7	3.9	3.4
Interest Paid 13	3.2	3.5	0.8	1.0	0.9	1.2	1.2	2.3	2.6	2.4	3.8	4.9	3.2
Depreciation 14	4.3	2.9	0.9	2.2	3.5	1.8	4.4	4.7	5.2	5.9	6.9	5.0	4.2
Amortization and Depletion 15	2.3	0.0	0.4	1.1	0.2	1.1	0.7	2.7	1.4	3.0	5.1	5.4	1.6
Pensions and Other Deferred Comp. 16	1.4	0.1	0.5	0.3	0.1	0.8	1.2	1.3	1.0	2.0	2.3	1.9	1.6
Employee Benefits 17	3.1	1.7	1.0	3.5	1.0	3.3	3.4	3.4	2.7	3.8	2.7	3.5	3.3
Advertising 18	1.6	0.1	1.9	0.6	2.0	0.7	1.2	1.6	1.2	1.8	1.7	1.9	1.7
Other Expenses 19	25.1	20.1	34.7	23.0	30.4	25.5	21.9	24.3	19.4	23.4	31.0	24.2	24.5
Officers' Compensation 20	1.8	1.1	7.3	5.9	2.6	3.4	3.3	2.1	2.1	1.6	1.2	1.5	1.2
Operating Margin 21	4.6	•	0.0	4.6	1.8	3.2	4.1	•	5.2	1.1	•	5.4	6.7
Operating Margin Before Officers' Comp. 22	6.4	7.3	7.3	10.5	4.4	6.7	7.4	•	7.2	2.6	0.2	6.9	7.9

Selected Average Balance Sheet ($ in Thousands)

Item													
Net Receivables 23	1131	0	27	116	475	1205	2392	4263	7318	15680	27521	91937	622086
Inventories 24	88	0	0	9	21	108	241	478	849	2376	4061	9847	39628
Net Property, Plant and Equipment 25	2031	0	18	104	916	1108	4155	9552	19759	43332	91762	216679	956840
Total Assets 26	11811	0	83	670	2460	6430	15580	36421	65915	149636	387384	1239992	6636558
Notes and Loans Payable 27	3157	0	28	351	834	1270	4234	12148	21913	45884	122822	482555	1363371
All Other Liabilities 28	2643	0	67	49	675	1730	3672	6966	15412	24915	90136	24386	1856899
Net Worth 29	6010	0	-12	270	951	3431	7673	17307	28590	78838	174426	733051	3166287

Selected Financial Ratios (Times to 1)

Item													
Current Ratio 30	1.1	•	0.7	2.4	1.2	1.9	1.9	1.4	1.1	2.6	2.0	1.3	1.0
Quick Ratio 31	0.8	•	0.7	2.3	1.1	1.6	1.6	1.2	0.8	2.0	1.5	1.1	0.7
Net Sales to Working Capital 32	30.5	•	•	9.8	43.8	8.7	6.9	9.8	41.6	4.3	6.4	14.9	•
Coverage Ratio 33	4.7	3.5	1.5	5.6	5.3	8.0	6.4	2.8	4.5	2.5	1.9	3.6	5.9
Total Asset Turnover 34	0.6	•	5.2	1.9	2.3	1.7	1.2	0.8	1.0	0.8	0.6	0.5	0.5
Inventory Turnover 35	21.2	•	474.7	48.8	109.2	19.5	21.5	18.5	25.2	13.9	8.3	11.2	20.4
Receivables Turnover 36	6.3	•	17.2	11.1	13.6	7.7	7.3	6.9	9.5	7.5	9.7	7.0	4.8
Total Liabilities to Net Worth 37	1.0	•	•	1.5	1.6	0.9	1.0	1.1	1.3	0.9	1.2	0.7	1.0
Current Assets to Working Capital 38	8.8	•	•	1.7	6.7	2.1	2.1	3.4	12.3	1.6	2.0	4.2	•
Current Liabilities to Working Capital 39	7.8	•	•	0.7	5.7	1.1	1.1	2.4	11.3	0.6	1.0	3.2	•
Working Capital to Net Sales 40	0.0	•	0.1	0.0	0.0	0.1	0.1	0.1	0.0	0.2	0.2	0.1	•
Inventory to Working Capital 41	0.4	•	•	0.1	0.2	0.1	0.1	0.2	0.7	0.1	0.2	0.2	•
Total Receipts to Cash Flow 42	3.1	3.2	4.9	4.4	3.2	3.5	3.9	3.9	4.1	4.2	3.5	3.0	2.9
Cost of Goods to Cash Flow 43	0.8	2.4	1.0	1.5	1.3	0.7	1.1	1.2	1.4	1.1	0.5	0.5	0.8
Cash Flow to Total Debt 44	0.4	•	1.4	0.7	1.2	1.0	0.6	0.4	0.4	0.4	0.3	0.4	0.3

Selected Financial Factors (in Percentages)

Item													
Debt Ratio 45	49.1	•	114.0	59.7	61.3	46.6	50.7	52.5	56.6	47.3	55.0	40.9	50.4
Return on Total Assets 46	8.9	•	6.2	11.0	11.4	15.9	9.0	5.2	11.1	4.9	4.2	9.5	8.7
Return on Equity Before Income Taxes 47	13.7	•	•	22.4	24.0	26.0	15.5	7.1	19.9	5.6	4.3	11.7	14.5
Return on Equity After Income Taxes 48	9.4	•	•	21.5	23.4	25.8	13.6	5.8	16.3	4.5	2.6	7.5	9.6
Profit Margin (Before Income Tax) 49	11.6	8.6	0.4	4.8	4.0	8.1	6.5	4.1	9.0	3.6	3.4	12.9	15.5
Profit Margin (After Income Tax) 50	7.9	8.5	0.1	4.6	3.9	8.0	5.7	3.4	7.4	2.9	2.0	8.3	10.2

253

Table II

Corporations with Net Income

NEWSPAPER PUBLISHERS

MONEY AMOUNTS AND SIZE OF ASSETS IN THOUSANDS OF DOLLARS

Item Description for Accounting Period 7/04 Through 6/05	Total	Zero Assets	Under 500	500 to 1,000	1,000 to 5,000	5,000 to 10,000	10,000 to 25,000	25,000 to 50,000	50,000 to 100,000	100,000 to 250,000	250,000 to 500,000	500,000 to 2,500,000	2,500,000 and over
Number of Enterprises **1**	5396	231	4182	484	271	73	63	30	22	10	7	0	0
Revenues ($ in Thousands)													
Net Sales **2**	43915651	1702627	1496544	714106	1024773	821787	1230726	881803	1407504	1051829	1470079	0	0
Interest **3**	316200	101	286	91	980	31	2274	1179	2591	6196	4823	0	0
Rents **4**	116932	0	10	0	0	1521	725	2618	5024	6160	6627	0	0
Royalties **5**	412149	0	0	0	0	0	0	1314	35	0	1725	0	0
Other Portfolio Income **6**	516257	3541	0	0	9737	29666	8147	2113	21628	9528	5523	0	0
Other Receipts **7**	1645926	151399	1568	57	42729	13958	21905	72655	30505	19708	7858	0	0
Total Receipts **8**	46923115	1953320	1501949	714254	1078219	866963	1263777	961682	1467287	1093421	1499635	0	0
Average Total Receipts **9**	8696	8456	359	1476	3979	11876	20060	32056	66695	109342	213805	•	•
Operating Costs/Operating Income (%)													
Cost of Operations **10**	27.0	50.5	31.8	34.3	33.4	19.5	29.9	26.7	32.3	30.8	21.0	•	•
Salaries and Wages **11**	22.3	23.4	14.1	18.1	14.8	38.3	24.4	29.4	21.9	16.4	24.6	•	•
Taxes Paid **12**	3.7	4.0	2.7	4.4	3.2	4.2	3.9	4.0	3.4	4.1	3.9	•	•
Interest Paid **13**	3.2	3.6	1.2	1.1	1.5	0.8	1.2	1.5	2.2	2.6	2.0	•	•
Depreciation **14**	4.4	2.9	1.1	2.2	5.0	1.7	4.1	4.6	4.8	7.1	6.2	•	•
Amortization and Depletion **15**	2.1	0.0	0.1	1.2	0.1	0.4	0.6	2.1	1.2	2.9	5.1	•	•
Pensions and Other Deferred Comp. **16**	1.3	0.1	0.9	0.3	0.1	0.9	1.1	1.4	1.1	1.0	1.5	•	•
Employee Benefits **17**	3.1	1.8	1.0	3.6	2.1	3.3	3.4	3.5	2.8	3.0	1.5	•	•
Advertising **18**	1.6	0.1	0.7	0.5	0.7	0.2	1.0	1.5	1.2	0.8	1.4	•	•
Other Expenses **19**	22.2	18.4	32.1	22.9	25.4	22.1	19.6	24.3	19.9	24.0	22.8	•	•
Officers' Compensation **20**	1.8	0.8	7.3	6.1	4.8	3.9	3.5	2.4	2.2	1.8	1.5	•	•
Operating Margin **21**	7.4	•	7.0	5.4	8.9	4.8	7.4	•	7.0	5.6	8.5	•	•
Operating Margin Before Officers' Comp. **22**	9.2	•	14.4	11.5	13.6	8.6	10.9	1.0	9.2	7.4	10.0	•	•

Selected Average Balance Sheet ($ in Thousands)

Net Receivables 23	1403	0	22	127	452	1385	2280	4575	7432	13559	28132
Inventories 24	93	0	0	11	31	86	244	484	796	1732	2998
Net Property, Plant and Equipment 25	2510	0	23	122	1031	1244	4247	9474	19796	48605	70385
Total Assets 26	14809	0	71	648	2543	5992	15541	35448	66387	153928	338295
Notes and Loans Payable 27	3587	0	16	253	1061	914	3190	9210	20222	36968	69214
All Other Liabilities 28	2973	0	44	39	433	2021	3439	7804	16216	21552	90847
Net Worth 29	8249	0	10	357	1049	3056	8912	18434	29948	95407	178234

Selected Financial Ratios (Times to 1)

Current Ratio 30	1.1	•	1.5	2.7	1.4	2.2	2.1	1.6	1.1	3.0	1.7
Quick Ratio 31	0.8	•	1.5	2.5	1.2	1.9	1.7	1.3	0.8	2.3	1.3
Net Sales to Working Capital 32	29.8	•	33.2	10.5	20.5	7.2	6.6	7.2	40.1	3.2	8.6
Coverage Ratio 33	5.9	3.6	7.1	6.0	10.1	13.5	9.4	5.9	6.0	4.7	6.2
Total Asset Turnover 34	0.5	•	5.0	2.3	1.5	1.9	1.3	0.8	1.0	0.7	0.6
Inventory Turnover 35	23.5	•	50083.1	45.6	40.9	25.4	24.0	16.2	25.9	18.7	14.7
Receivables Turnover 36	5.9	•	17.4	11.7	10.3	9.3	8.3	6.6	10.0	7.6	9.3
Total Liabilities to Net Worth 37	0.8	•	5.9	0.8	1.4	1.0	0.7	0.9	1.2	0.6	0.9
Current Assets to Working Capital 38	9.2	•	3.0	1.6	3.7	1.9	1.9	2.8	12.4	1.5	2.3
Current Liabilities to Working Capital 39	8.2	•	2.0	0.6	2.7	0.9	0.9	1.8	11.4	0.5	1.3
Working Capital to Net Sales 40	0.0	•	0.0	0.1	0.0	0.1	0.2	0.1	0.0	0.3	0.1
Inventory to Working Capital 41	0.3	•	0.0	0.1	0.2	0.1	0.1	0.1	0.6	0.1	0.1
Total Receipts to Cash Flow 42	3.0	5.1	2.8	4.3	2.9	3.7	3.7	3.4	3.7	3.3	3.3
Cost of Goods to Cash Flow 43	0.8	2.6	0.9	1.5	1.0	0.7	1.1	0.9	1.2	1.0	0.7
Cash Flow to Total Debt 44	0.4	•	2.1	1.2	0.9	1.0	0.8	0.5	0.5	0.5	0.4

Selected Financial Factors (in Percentages)

Debt Ratio 45	44.3	•	85.5	45.0	58.8	49.0	42.7	48.0	54.9	38.0	47.3
Return on Total Assets 46	10.3	•	43.3	14.8	23.2	20.8	14.1	7.6	13.0	8.2	7.6
Return on Equity Before Income Taxes 47	15.4	•	255.6	22.4	50.8	37.7	22.0	12.1	23.9	10.4	12.2
Return on Equity After Income Taxes 48	10.9	•	237.4	21.5	49.9	37.4	19.9	10.6	20.1	9.2	9.5
Profit Margin (Before Income Tax) 49	15.6	9.2	7.4	5.4	14.1	10.2	10.0	7.6	11.2	9.5	10.3
Profit Margin (After Income Tax) 50	11.0	9.1	6.9	5.2	13.8	10.2	9.1	6.6	9.4	8.3	8.1

Table I

Corporations with and without Net Income

PERIODICAL PUBLISHERS

MONEY AMOUNTS AND SIZE OF ASSETS IN THOUSANDS OF DOLLARS

Item Description for Accounting Period 7/04 Through 6/05	Total	Zero Assets	Under 500	500 to 1,000	1,000 to 5,000	5,000 to 10,000	10,000 to 25,000	25,000 to 50,000	50,000 to 100,000	100,000 to 250,000	250,000 to 500,000	500,000 to 2,500,000	2,500,000 and over
Number of Enterprises 1	7788	1215	4730	799	830	75	66	28	14	10	12	8	0
Revenues ($ in Thousands)													
Net Sales 2	23482937	894856	1794847	1007881	6090305	796707	1581978	1335243	1019695	1462423	1739467	5759534	0
Interest 3	232264	702	274	2666	3261	1892	1908	1670	2937	4499	71104	141352	0
Rents 4	39954	0	1222	0	1733	120	562	4991	2686	260	12928	15452	0
Royalties 5	309819	299	0	0	0	20	0	113	1095	963	108144	199185	0
Other Portfolio Income 6	138216	0	0	5	10215	308	4365	9048	6253	560	55138	52323	0
Other Receipts 7	372492	-12103	2880	10432	68650	64041	22335	26715	10946	75001	34084	69510	0
Total Receipts 8	24575682	883754	1799223	1020984	6174164	863088	1611148	1377780	1043612	1543706	2020865	6237356	0
Average Total Receipts 9	3156	727	380	1278	7439	11508	24411	49206	74544	154371	168405	779670	·
Operating Costs/Operating Income (%)													
Cost of Operations 10	41.2	14.3	31.6	28.2	57.6	51.5	40.8	37.2	48.8	39.2	35.5	33.9	·
Salaries and Wages 11	18.0	57.1	23.2	16.8	11.7	16.2	16.5	21.8	12.9	16.9	21.8	16.8	·
Taxes Paid 12	2.6	10.9	2.8	3.1	2.2	2.4	2.2	2.4	1.9	3.4	2.7	1.8	·
Interest Paid 13	3.1	0.0	0.0	1.2	0.4	2.0	1.1	1.1	1.2	4.8	8.4	7.2	·
Depreciation 14	1.6	0.9	0.9	0.7	0.7	2.0	1.7	2.3	2.3	2.0	4.3	2.0	·
Amortization and Depletion 15	2.4	0.6	0.1	1.4	0.9	1.3	1.0	2.1	1.4	3.9	3.9	5.1	·
Pensions and Other Deferred Comp. 16	0.7	0.9	0.2	0.9	0.4	1.7	0.5	0.4	0.8	1.2	2.0	0.6	·
Employee Benefits 17	1.7	3.8	1.5	1.7	1.3	1.0	1.8	1.9	1.5	2.3	2.4	1.6	·
Advertising 18	2.0	4.6	1.3	0.1	1.2	1.8	1.7	1.7	2.3	2.6	4.8	2.3	·
Other Expenses 19	25.3	17.4	34.7	28.7	16.0	21.3	24.2	24.6	20.5	25.4	27.8	33.7	·
Officers' Compensation 20	3.5	2.6	6.3	13.0	3.6	3.0	3.7	3.6	1.8	3.3	3.7	1.2	·
Operating Margin 21	·	·	·	4.1	4.2	·	4.8	0.9	4.5	·	·	·	·
Operating Margin Before Officers' Comp. 22	1.4	·	·	7.7	17.2	·	8.5	4.4	6.3	·	·	·	·

Selected Average Balance Sheet ($ in Thousands)

Net Receivables 23	•	376	0	5	225	1044	985	3212	5716	10815	21714	23860	94893
Inventories 24	•	64	0	4	16	64	392	781	1019	2515	3883	3462	23758
Net Property, Plant and Equipment 25	•	200	0	7	65	218	1136	2122	4318	7695	19956	16912	54524
Total Assets 26	•	2912	0	59	654	2589	7625	15550	35540	71180	169417	362083	1262728
Notes and Loans Payable 27	•	1136	0	42	181	538	3476	4096	9713	15208	68996	136972	588676
All Other Liabilities 28	•	1190	0	9	324	1766	1408	8129	16022	35194	73971	86501	517441
Net Worth 29	•	586	0	7	149	285	2741	3325	9804	20778	26451	138609	156611

Selected Financial Ratios (Times to 1)

Current Ratio 30	•	1.0	•	1.2	1.1	1.2	2.3	1.2	1.5	1.3	1.2	1.4	0.5
Quick Ratio 31	•	0.7	•	0.7	1.0	1.0	1.8	0.8	1.1	0.8	0.9	1.0	0.4
Net Sales to Working Capital 32	•	•	•	44.1	71.9	34.4	5.3	22.1	7.7	9.4	13.9	4.5	•
Coverage Ratio 33	•	1.9	•	5.4	1.9	14.2	2.8	7.1	1.5	4.4	6.7	1.2	1.4
Total Asset Turnover 34	•	1.0	•	6.4	1.9	2.8	1.4	1.5	1.3	1.0	1.2	0.9	0.6
Inventory Turnover 35	•	19.3	•	29.3	21.8	66.1	14.0	12.5	17.4	14.1	14.8	14.9	10.3
Receivables Turnover 36	•	7.9	•	31.3	6.3	7.5	10.6	7.3	8.3	7.6	6.9	5.0	7.4
Total Liabilities to Net Worth 37	•	4.0	•	6.9	3.4	8.1	1.8	3.7	2.6	2.4	5.4	1.6	7.1
Current Assets to Working Capital 38	•	5.6	•	20.7	7.5	1.8	7.5	2.9	4.1	5.7	3.4	•	•
Current Liabilities to Working Capital 39	•	4.6	•	19.7	6.5	0.8	6.5	1.9	3.1	4.7	2.4	•	•
Working Capital to Net Sales 40	•	0.0	•	0.0	0.0	0.2	0.0	0.1	0.1	0.1	0.2	•	•
Inventory to Working Capital 41	•	•	•	1.1	0.3	0.2	0.7	0.4	0.4	0.1	•	•	•
Total Receipts to Cash Flow 42	•	4.1	•	3.4	3.3	5.4	4.3	3.6	3.8	4.0	4.5	5.0	3.1
Cost of Goods to Cash Flow 43	•	1.7	•	1.1	0.9	3.1	2.2	1.5	1.4	2.0	1.8	1.8	1.0
Cash Flow to Total Debt 44	•	0.3	•	2.2	0.8	0.6	0.5	0.5	0.5	0.4	0.2	0.1	0.2

Selected Financial Factors (in Percentages)

Debt Ratio 45	•	79.9	87.4	77.2	89.0	64.1	78.6	72.4	70.8	84.4	61.7	87.6	•
Return on Total Assets 46	•	6.1	•	12.9	16.9	8.4	11.8	6.7	8.0	4.9	3.1	5.8	•
Return on Equity Before Income Taxes 47	•	14.3	•	46.1	142.8	15.7	47.5	18.8	23.4	5.2	13.7	•	•
Return on Equity After Income Taxes 48	•	9.7	•	45.8	140.9	11.9	44.0	10.8	17.5	6.7	•	•	•
Profit Margin (Before Income Tax) 49	•	2.8	•	5.4	5.5	4.0	6.6	3.9	6.7	0.9	3.0	•	•
Profit Margin (After Income Tax) 50	•	1.9	•	5.4	5.5	3.1	6.1	2.2	5.0	1.5	•	•	•

Table II

Corporations with Net Income

PERIODICAL PUBLISHERS

MONEY AMOUNTS AND SIZE OF ASSETS IN THOUSANDS OF DOLLARS

Item Description for Accounting Period 7/04 Through 6/05	Total	Zero Assets	Under 500	500 to 1,000	1,000 to 5,000	5,000 to 10,000	10,000 to 25,000	25,000 to 50,000	50,000 to 100,000	100,000 to 250,000	250,000 to 500,000	500,000 to 2,500,000	2,500,000 and over
Number of Enterprises 1	3385	456	1628	433	733	52	40	19	9	6	5	4	0
Revenues ($ in Thousands)													
Net Sales 2	15560265	40798	461471	622426	5745078	637274	1162368	909336	817052	926538	843506	3394420	0
Interest 3	29417	242	0	2466	1037	1353	1355	1637	2604	3730	10871	4123	0
Rents 4	22919	0	0	0	0	120	555	4991	0	152	3084	14018	0
Royalties 5	62273	0	0	0	0	20	0	88	516	391	17541	43717	0
Other Portfolio Income 6	94365	0	0	0	3030	288	3916	3477	1336	560	54295	27464	0
Other Receipts 7	298347	2215	0	1286	68185	67929	17942	15877	7221	63035	13980	40673	0
Total Receipts 8	16067586	43255	461471	626178	5817330	706984	1186136	935406	828729	994406	943277	3524415	0
Average Total Receipts 9	4747	95	283	1446	7936	13596	29653	49232	92081	165734	188655	881104	•
Operating Costs/Operating Income (%)													
Cost of Operations 10	44.6	51.5	1.1	35.7	58.0	49.7	41.4	31.6	48.7	34.1	30.0	38.3	•
Salaries and Wages 11	13.6	12.1	5.7	11.0	11.3	15.1	15.4	21.1	14.0	14.9	22.7	13.2	•
Taxes Paid 12	2.2	1.6	2.5	2.5	2.1	2.5	2.3	2.6	1.8	3.7	3.8	1.6	•
Interest Paid 13	1.0	0.4	0.0	0.2	0.3	0.3	0.6	0.8	1.1	0.8	1.7	2.7	•
Depreciation 14	1.2	1.4	1.0	0.6	0.6	2.3	1.7	2.9	1.2	2.2	1.8	1.2	•
Amortization and Depletion 15	1.6	0.0	•	•	0.6	1.3	0.7	1.4	1.5	1.6	0.8	4.4	•
Pensions and Other Deferred Comp. 16	0.8	•	0.0	1.5	0.3	2.0	0.5	0.5	0.8	1.7	3.7	0.8	•
Employee Benefits 17	1.6	1.6	•	1.9	1.2	1.0	1.7	2.3	1.5	2.7	2.3	1.7	•
Advertising 18	1.7	4.5	1.4	0.0	2.2	2.2	1.1	1.9	2.8	2.4	2.3	2.2	•
Other Expenses 19	22.5	17.9	54.8	14.1	15.6	22.8	20.2	25.3	16.8	27.5	28.5	29.8	•
Officers' Compensation 20	3.2	5.8	5.3	16.0	3.3	3.8	4.2	2.8	1.6	3.4	2.2	0.6	•
Operating Margin 21	6.1	3.1	28.2	16.3	5.5	•	10.3	6.9	8.2	4.9	0.3	3.3	•
Operating Margin Before Officers' Comp. 22	9.3	8.9	33.4	32.3	8.8	0.9	14.5	9.7	9.8	8.3	2.5	4.0	•

Selected Average Balance Sheet ($ in Thousands)

Net Receivables 23	598	0	0	274	1152	1198	3675	6983	13519	22855	19288	90951
Inventories 24	111	0	12	9	59	564	803	1031	3757	5735	2000	38913
Net Property, Plant and Equipment 25	285	0	4	49	189	1582	2525	5662	6327	20654	10709	68045
Total Assets 26	3493	15	556	•	2671	8106	16177	35620	74314	154958	360759	1112814
Notes and Loans Payable 27	762	4	39	•	385	2481	3143	7908	10909	27341	51547	336849
All Other Liabilities 28	1522	1	373	•	1745	1564	8775	14731	40035	73861	95804	428734
Net Worth 29	1209	10	144	•	541	4060	4259	12982	23370	53756	213407	347231

Selected Financial Ratios (Times to 1)

Current Ratio 30	1.2	•	16.4	1.3	1.2	2.3	1.2	1.9	1.4	1.6	1.3	0.7
Quick Ratio 31	0.9	•	16.4	1.2	1.0	1.8	1.0	1.2	0.9	1.2	0.9	0.4
Net Sales to Working Capital 32	18.4	•	26.9	13.4	24.1	5.4	17.6	5.3	8.3	5.8	4.1	•
Coverage Ratio 33	10.5	22.1	651.0	70.8	23.0	26.3	22.7	13.9	10.0	17.2	8.5	4.1
Total Asset Turnover 34	1.3	•	18.8	2.6	2.9	1.5	1.8	1.3	1.2	1.0	0.5	0.8
Inventory Turnover 35	18.4	•	0.3	55.9	77.6	10.8	15.0	14.7	11.8	9.2	25.3	8.4
Receivables Turnover 36	8.2	•	30.3	5.2	8.2	10.4	7.5	•	•	6.6	6.9	10.0
Total Liabilities to Net Worth 37	1.9	•	0.5	2.9	3.9	1.0	2.8	1.7	2.2	1.9	0.7	2.2
Current Assets to Working Capital 38	5.7	•	1.1	4.5	5.3	1.8	5.4	2.2	3.5	2.6	4.1	•
Current Liabilities to Working Capital 39	4.7	•	0.1	3.5	4.3	0.8	4.4	1.2	2.5	1.6	3.1	•
Working Capital to Net Sales 40	0.1	•	0.0	0.1	0.0	0.2	0.1	0.2	0.1	0.2	0.2	•
Inventory to Working Capital 41	0.5	•	•	0.2	0.2	0.3	0.5	0.1	0.3	0.3	0.0	•
Total Receipts to Cash Flow 42	3.5	3.9	1.3	3.7	5.2	3.5	3.3	3.1	4.1	2.7	3.0	2.9
Cost of Goods to Cash Flow 43	1.6	2.0	0.0	1.3	3.0	1.7	1.4	1.0	2.0	0.9	0.9	1.1
Cash Flow to Total Debt 44	0.6	•	42.6	0.9	0.7	0.9	0.7	0.7	0.4	0.6	0.4	0.4

Selected Financial Factors (in Percentages)

Debt Ratio 45	65.4	•	34.8	74.0	79.7	49.9	73.7	63.6	68.6	65.3	40.8	68.8
Return on Total Assets 46	14.1	•	529.6	44.3	20.8	12.6	23.0	14.1	13.0	13.3	6.8	8.6
Return on Equity Before Income Taxes 47	36.7	•	810.9	168.3	98.4	24.2	83.5	36.0	37.2	36.2	10.2	20.8
Return on Equity After Income Taxes 48	32.0	•	810.9	167.7	97.3	20.5	79.1	34.3	29.1	28.1	6.6	14.5
Profit Margin (Before Income Tax) 49	9.7	9.2	28.2	16.9	6.8	8.0	12.2	9.8	9.6	12.6	12.9	8.5
Profit Margin (After Income Tax) 50	8.4	8.0	28.2	16.8	6.7	6.8	11.6	9.3	7.5	9.8	8.4	5.9

Table I

Corporations with and without Net Income

BOOK PUBLISHERS

MONEY AMOUNTS AND SIZE OF ASSETS IN THOUSANDS OF DOLLARS

Item Description for Accounting Period 7/04 Through 6/05	Total	Zero Assets	Under 500	500 to 1,000	1,000 to 5,000	5,000 to 10,000	10,000 to 25,000	25,000 to 50,000	50,000 to 100,000	100,000 to 250,000	250,000 to 500,000	500,000 to 2,500,000	2,500,000 and over
Number of Enterprises **1**	6109	1669	3516	395	384	45	57	14	5	8	6	5	5
Revenues ($ in Thousands)													
Net Sales **2**	26127976	24320	426021	251874	925910	787813	1152432	553602	464383	751199	1514842	4173017	15102564
Interest **3**	802028	1	464	635	1634	10	589	1169	738	7048	4572	18562	766605
Rents **4**	62788	0	0	477	0	0	1012	348	1542	52	0	6879	52478
Royalties **5**	443565	0	0	0	45	215	3646	1597	2168	6193	10908	55891	362901
Other Portfolio Income **6**	670478	9	0	0	5724	10049	3423	680	531	852	3831	130030	515348
Other Receipts **7**	887890	824	23337	232	623	1967	12263	8194	11964	70175	51355	110460	596499
Total Receipts **8**	28994725	25154	449822	253218	933936	800054	1173365	565590	481326	835519	1585508	4494839	17396395
Average Total Receipts **9**	4746	15	128	641	2432	17779	20585	40399	96265	104440	264251	898968	3479279
Operating Costs/Operating Income (%)													
Cost of Operations **10**	28.7	53.0	59.0	41.2	37.3	6.3	46.6	33.6	41.8	46.7	33.5	39.6	21.9
Salaries and Wages **11**	21.7	2.5	13.9	9.1	9.9	42.1	16.1	22.4	14.5	20.0	17.7	18.3	23.8
Taxes Paid **12**	2.7	1.4	2.0	1.9	1.5	4.3	2.1	2.5	1.4	2.3	1.8	2.1	3.0
Interest Paid **13**	6.9	•	0.4	12.8	1.2	0.9	1.0	1.2	0.5	4.7	6.2	5.2	9.2
Depreciation **14**	4.2	•	0.9	0.6	0.8	3.3	1.5	3.1	0.7	1.0	1.0	5.0	5.2
Amortization and Depletion **15**	3.0	•	0.0	13.4	0.3	0.1	1.3	2.2	1.1	2.4	6.0	2.3	3.4
Pensions and Other Deferred Comp. **16**	1.2	1.0	1.0	•	2.3	1.0	0.6	1.4	0.4	1.2	0.5	1.5	1.2
Employee Benefits **17**	2.6	1.8	1.0	•	0.5	3.9	1.4	1.9	0.9	2.3	1.6	4.0	2.7
Advertising **18**	2.9	0.7	1.2	1.8	0.6	1.0	3.4	3.8	21.9	4.0	1.9	3.0	2.6
Other Expenses **19**	28.0	52.7	16.2	41.4	21.0	30.4	19.2	21.2	18.0	14.0	32.2	20.8	31.9
Officers' Compensation **20**	2.4	12.3	8.1	12.3	12.9	3.9	4.2	2.9	1.7	2.7	1.0	2.0	1.4
Operating Margin **21**	•	•	•	•	11.7	2.7	2.7	3.8	•	•	•	•	•
Operating Margin Before Officers' Comp. **22**	•	•	4.5	•	24.5	6.6	6.9	6.8	•	1.3	•	•	•

Selected Average Balance Sheet ($ in Thousands)

Net Receivables 23	840	0	7	125	353	3351	3593	5664	14770	26588	52730	190926	585228
Inventories 24	493	0	10	268	465	778	3763	9041	16093	16326	24156	118112	274273
Net Property, Plant and Equipment 25	457	0	20	6	248	1761	1177	4550	7354	2806	12010	137479	318717
Total Assets 26	9164	0	55	823	2122	7232	15230	35841	67328	148557	359252	1439016	8415379
Notes and Loans Payable 27	3082	0	13	1276	609	3126	3552	5532	7904	137368	208644	589612	2457333
All Other Liabilities 28	2873	0	17	277	313	1795	5892	10484	29150	39474	119982	413702	2689543
Net Worth 29	3209	0	25	-729	1201	2312	5787	19824	30273	-28285	30628	435702	3268504

Selected Financial Ratios (Times to 1)

Current Ratio 30	1.2	•	1.1	1.3	2.2	2.1	1.6	2.1	1.9	1.2	1.1	1.6	1.1
Quick Ratio 31	0.5	•	0.8	0.3	1.2	1.7	0.8	0.9	0.6	0.7	0.8	1.0	0.4
Net Sales to Working Capital 32	7.9	•	44.8	4.1	4.7	6.9	5.2	3.3	3.4	9.9	17.6	4.9	11.0
Coverage Ratio 33	2.0	•	6.4	•	11.5	5.9	5.5	5.9	6.0	3.2	1.2	1.9	2.0
Total Asset Turnover 34	0.5	•	2.2	0.8	1.1	2.4	1.3	1.1	1.4	0.6	0.7	0.6	0.4
Inventory Turnover 35	2.5	•	7.3	1.0	1.9	1.4	2.5	1.5	2.4	2.7	3.5	2.8	2.4
Receivables Turnover 36	3.8	•	30.1	8.7	6.3	5.1	5.6	5.6	5.2	3.1	5.2	5.2	3.1
Total Liabilities to Net Worth 37	1.9	•	1.2	•	0.8	2.1	1.6	0.8	1.2	•	10.7	2.3	1.6
Current Assets to Working Capital 38	5.6	•	11.9	3.9	1.8	1.9	2.8	1.9	2.1	6.0	8.9	2.6	9.4
Current Liabilities to Working Capital 39	4.6	•	10.9	2.9	0.8	0.9	1.8	0.9	1.1	5.0	7.9	1.6	8.4
Working Capital to Net Sales 40	0.1	•	0.0	0.2	0.2	0.1	0.2	0.3	0.3	0.1	0.1	0.2	0.1
Inventory to Working Capital 41	0.9	•	3.2	2.9	0.6	0.1	1.0	0.7	0.7	1.6	1.8	0.7	1.0
Total Receipts to Cash Flow 42	3.3	3.0	6.6	36.3	3.4	3.5	4.8	4.2	6.0	4.9	3.2	4.8	2.8
Cost of Goods to Cash Flow 43	1.0	1.6	3.9	14.9	1.3	0.2	2.2	1.4	2.5	2.3	1.1	1.9	0.6
Cash Flow to Total Debt 44	0.2	•	0.6	0.0	0.8	1.0	0.4	0.6	0.4	0.1	0.2	0.2	0.2

Selected Financial Factors (in Percentages)

Debt Ratio 45	65.0	•	55.4	188.5	43.4	68.0	62.0	44.7	55.0	119.0	91.5	69.7	61.2
Return on Total Assets 46	6.4	•	5.1	•	15.6	12.5	7.3	7.9	3.9	9.3	5.3	5.6	6.5
Return on Equity Before Income Taxes 47	9.2	•	9.6	30.1	25.1	32.4	15.6	11.8	7.2	•	11.3	8.5	8.3
Return on Equity After Income Taxes 48	6.5	•	9.2	30.1	24.7	31.7	12.6	9.6	5.7	•	4.6	6.5	5.7
Profit Margin (Before Income Tax) 49	6.9	2.0	•	12.5	4.3	4.5	5.9	2.3	10.1	•	1.4	4.5	9.0
Profit Margin (After Income Tax) 50	4.9	1.9	•	12.3	4.2	3.6	4.8	1.9	6.8	•	0.6	3.4	6.2

Table II

Corporations with Net Income

BOOK PUBLISHERS

MONEY AMOUNTS AND SIZE OF ASSETS IN THOUSANDS OF DOLLARS

Item Description for Accounting Period 7/04 Through 6/05	Total	Zero Assets	Under 500	500 to 1,000	1,000 to 5,000	5,000 to 10,000	10,000 to 25,000	25,000 to 50,000	50,000 to 100,000	100,000 to 250,000	250,000 to 500,000	500,000 to 2,500,000	2,500,000 and over
Number of Enterprises **1**	2185	233	1441	65	330	0	44	10	0	5	0	0	0

Revenues ($ in Thousands)

	Total	Zero Assets	Under 500	500 to 1,000	1,000 to 5,000	5,000 to 10,000	10,000 to 25,000	25,000 to 50,000	50,000 to 100,000	100,000 to 250,000	250,000 to 500,000	500,000 to 2,500,000	2,500,000 and over
Net Sales **2**	17376649	23789	155501	48299	832951	0	945295	425288	0	446080	0	0	0
Interest **3**	320740	0	463	635	1620	0	444	679	0	6649	0	0	0
Rents **4**	52169	0	0	0	0	0	816	311	0	28	0	0	0
Royalties **5**	346059	0	0	0	15	0	648	1552	0	0	0	0	0
Other Portfolio Income **6**	666380	0	0	0	5724	0	2865	615	0	0	0	0	0
Other Receipts **7**	770681	606	0	0	582	0	9067	7216	0	60170	0	0	0
Total Receipts **8**	19532678	24395	155964	48934	840892	0	959135	435661	0	512927	0	0	0
Average Total Receipts **9**	8939	105	108	753	2548	•	21799	43566	•	102585	•	•	•

Operating Costs/Operating Income (%)

	Total	Zero Assets	Under 500	500 to 1,000	1,000 to 5,000	5,000 to 10,000	10,000 to 25,000	25,000 to 50,000	50,000 to 100,000	100,000 to 250,000	250,000 to 500,000	500,000 to 2,500,000	2,500,000 and over
Cost of Operations **10**	26.1	53.2	9.2	18.4	38.3	•	45.7	35.1	•	46.3	•	•	•
Salaries and Wages **11**	21.3	1.3	14.9	1.6	9.3	•	15.1	21.6	•	17.9	•	•	•
Taxes Paid **12**	2.8	0.1	2.8	3.4	1.4	•	2.0	2.4	•	2.5	•	•	•
Interest Paid **13**	3.2	•	0.2	2.7	1.3	•	0.9	0.7	•	5.7	•	•	•
Depreciation **14**	3.3	•	1.3	•	0.8	•	1.4	2.7	•	0.4	•	•	•
Amortization and Depletion **15**	2.6	•	•	•	0.3	•	0.6	2.8	•	3.3	•	•	•
Pensions and Other Deferred Comp. **16**	1.3	•	2.8	•	2.3	•	0.6	0.4	•	1.0	•	•	•
Employee Benefits **17**	2.1	•	1.6	1.6	0.5	•	1.2	1.8	•	1.7	•	•	•
Advertising **18**	3.4	0.7	0.3	2.8	0.6	•	3.2	4.4	•	4.9	•	•	•
Other Expenses **19**	31.6	32.8	26.1	23.6	19.6	•	19.1	18.2	•	9.3	•	•	•
Officers' Compensation **20**	2.9	•	19.3	44.9	12.0	•	4.6	3.1	•	3.2	•	•	•
Operating Margin **21**	•	11.9	21.6	0.8	13.7	•	5.5	6.6	•	3.6	•	•	•
Operating Margin Before Officers' Comp. **22**	2.4	11.9	40.8	45.8	25.7	•	10.2	9.7	•	6.9	•	•	•

Selected Average Balance Sheet ($ in Thousands)

Net Receivables 23	1607	0	2	12	392	3791	6734	26994
Inventories 24	922	0	15	23	329	3700	9054	16509
Net Property, Plant and Equipment 25	930	0	22	0	287	1189	4312	1067
Total Assets 26	18377	0	79	638	2105	14916	35972	161431
Notes and Loans Payable 27	4775	0	3	396	666	2845	4394	114887
All Other Liabilities 28	4938	0	11	20	317	5872	8907	23564
Net Worth 29	8665	0	66	223	1121	6199	22671	22980

Selected Financial Ratios (Times to 1)

Current Ratio 30	1.3		4.6	0.1	2.3	1.7	2.4	1.2
Quick Ratio 31	0.5		3.2	0.1	1.4	0.9	1.0	0.7
Net Sales to Working Capital 32	6.0		2.8		4.7	4.8	2.9	8.4
Coverage Ratio 33	4.8		104.9	1.8	12.6	8.5	13.4	4.3
Total Asset Turnover 34	0.4		1.4	1.2	1.2	1.4	1.2	0.6
Inventory Turnover 35	2.2		0.7	5.9	2.9	2.7	1.6	2.5
Receivables Turnover 36	4.2		105.1	33.4	6.3	5.9	5.6	
Total Liabilities to Net Worth 37	1.1		0.2	1.9	0.9	1.4	0.6	6.0
Current Assets to Working Capital 38	4.9		1.3		1.8	2.4	1.7	5.8
Current Liabilities to Working Capital 39	3.9		0.3		0.8	1.4	0.7	4.8
Working Capital to Net Sales 40	0.2		0.4		0.2	0.2	0.3	0.1
Inventory to Working Capital 41	0.7		0.4		0.5	0.9	0.5	1.6
Total Receipts to Cash Flow 42	2.6	2.1	2.4	4.0	3.3	4.3	4.2	4.0
Cost of Goods to Cash Flow 43	0.7	1.1	0.2	0.7	1.3	2.0	1.5	1.9
Cash Flow to Total Debt 44	0.3		3.2	0.4	0.8	0.6	0.8	0.2

Selected Financial Factors (in Percentages)

Debt Ratio 45	52.9		17.2	65.0	46.7	58.4	37.0	85.8
Return on Total Assets 46	6.7		30.0	5.7	19.0	11.4	11.4	13.7
Return on Equity Before Income Taxes 47	11.2		35.9	7.1	32.9	24.1	16.8	74.3
Return on Equity After Income Taxes 48	8.5		35.5	6.1	32.4	20.5	14.0	52.6
Profit Margin (Before Income Tax) 49	12.2	14.5	21.9	2.1	14.6	7.0	8.9	19.1
Profit Margin (After Income Tax) 50	9.2	14.4	21.6	1.8	14.4	5.9	7.5	13.5

Table I

Corporations with and without Net Income

DATABASE, DIRECTORY, AND OTHER PUBLISHERS

MONEY AMOUNTS AND SIZE OF ASSETS IN THOUSANDS OF DOLLARS

Item Description for Accounting Period 7/04 Through 6/05	Total	Zero Assets	Under 500	500 to 1,000	1,000 to 5,000	5,000 to 10,000	10,000 to 25,000	25,000 to 50,000	50,000 to 100,000	100,000 to 250,000	250,000 to 500,000	500,000 to 2,500,000	2,500,000 and over
Number of Enterprises **1**	4083	311	3139	333	165	58	36	15	6	11	0	5	4
Revenues ($ in Thousands)													
Net Sales **2**	22381619	288509	231607	788179	1262761	1158814	927867	712524	373864	1060145	0	3038285	12539064
Interest **3**	456711	195	1938	343	128	190	7439	453	63	4315	0	6879	434767
Rents **4**	55861	0	0	0	0	0	31	844	35	0	0	0	54952
Royalties **5**	289052	0	0	0	0	0	91	53	5	9692	0	13914	265296
Other Portfolio Income **6**	179040	2521	7780	0	121	0	1945	7510	43	1392	0	119378	38349
Other Receipts **7**	619229	33903	142	4168	26713	4284	7289	-447	10641	50395	0	242728	239414
Total Receipts **8**	23981512	325128	241467	792690	1289723	1163288	944662	720937	384651	1125939	0	3421184	13571842
Average Total Receipts **9**	5874	1045	77	2380	7817	20057	26241	48062	64108	102358	•	684237	3392960
Operating Costs/Operating Income (%)													
Cost of Operations **10**	29.7	1.3	8.3	22.7	36.1	46.8	43.5	35.4	57.3	22.4	•	16.7	30.5
Salaries and Wages **11**	20.9	27.0	12.2	23.5	18.5	29.4	18.6	22.9	9.9	24.0	•	35.1	16.8
Taxes Paid **12**	3.1	1.1	3.5	4.0	2.4	3.1	2.6	3.2	1.1	2.1	•	2.9	3.3
Interest Paid **13**	8.0	12.4	0.6	0.5	0.2	0.3	0.8	1.1	2.0	3.2	•	5.2	12.2
Depreciation **14**	2.6	1.5	1.7	0.9	1.5	1.2	2.4	1.9	5.6	2.6	•	2.4	2.9
Amortization and Depletion **15**	5.2	14.1	2.3	0.0	0.5	0.0	0.9	0.8	2.3	6.1	•	3.9	7.1
Pensions and Other Deferred Comp. **16**	0.9	0.1	•	0.4	0.1	0.4	0.5	0.8	0.1	0.1	•	0.2	1.5
Employee Benefits **17**	1.9	3.1	2.2	0.9	0.1	2.4	1.4	2.1	1.5	3.0	•	3.7	1.6
Advertising **18**	2.5	2.1	0.3	1.2	2.7	0.8	3.9	4.0	1.1	2.9	•	2.5	2.6
Other Expenses **19**	27.9	49.4	42.8	43.2	16.0	10.7	21.1	17.6	16.9	40.9	•	27.1	29.5
Officers' Compensation **20**	2.8	1.2	33.3	8.5	15.1	3.6	3.6	1.9	0.6	1.4	•	1.0	1.3
Operating Margin **21**	•	•	•	•	6.8	1.3	0.8	8.4	1.6	•	•	•	•
Operating Margin Before Officers' Comp. **22**	•	26.0	•	2.6	21.8	4.9	4.4	10.3	2.2	2.9	•	•	0.3

Selected Average Balance Sheet ($ in Thousands)

Net Receivables 23	1185	0	5	294	1162	6710	4480	9604	18298	41821	•	182828	588509
Inventories 24	621	0	1	15	41	244	1242	2681	1631	4382	•	2953	584877
Net Property, Plant and Equipment 25	561	0	6	68	384	619	1970	3261	11129	9770	•	57477	392254
Total Assets 26	9380	49	679	2557	8778	15853	36327	85207	199545	•	835930	7246301
Notes and Loans Payable 27	6085	0	60	37	161	1110	4192	7167	32426	73085	•	652022	5009139
All Other Liabilities 28	2190	0	8	549	1033	7160	6722	18570	18898	70673	•	317658	1287518
Net Worth 29	1105	0	-18	94	1363	508	4939	10590	33883	55787	•	-133750	949644

Selected Financial Ratios (Times to 1)

Current Ratio 30	1.1	•	0.5	0.9	2.3	1.1	1.3	2.0	1.4	0.9	•	1.1	1.1
Quick Ratio 31	0.7	•	0.4	0.8	2.1	1.0	0.9	1.5	1.1	0.7	•	0.8	0.5
Net Sales to Working Capital 32	22.6	•	•	6.4	49.9	12.6	4.4	7.1	•	•	40.9	22.4
Coverage Ratio 33	1.2	0.9	•	•	50.6	6.5	4.3	9.9	3.3	0.2	•	3.4	0.9
Total Asset Turnover 34	0.6	•	1.5	3.5	3.0	2.3	1.6	1.3	0.7	0.5	•	0.7	0.4
Inventory Turnover 35	2.6	•	7.0	35.2	68.0	38.4	9.0	6.3	21.9	4.9	•	34.4	1.6
Receivables Turnover 36	4.6	•	17.2	8.5	9.8	5.3	7.0	4.6	3.5	2.6	•	4.0	4.6
Total Liabilities to Net Worth 37	7.5	•	•	6.2	•	16.3	2.2	2.4	1.5	2.6	•	•	6.6
Current Assets to Working Capital 38	9.9	•	•	1.8	19.4	4.7	2.0	3.7	•	•	19.5	10.4
Current Liabilities to Working Capital 39	8.9	•	•	0.8	18.4	3.7	1.0	2.7	•	•	18.5	9.4
Working Capital to Net Sales 40	0.0	•	•	0.2	0.0	0.1	0.2	0.1	•	•	0.0	0.0
Inventory to Working Capital 41	2.5	•	•	0.0	0.6	0.7	0.2	0.2	•	•	0.3	4.0
Total Receipts to Cash Flow 42	4.7	2.2	2.9	8.1	4.9	10.5	4.8	4.4	5.5	2.8	•	2.8	5.8
Cost of Goods to Cash Flow 43	1.4	0.0	0.2	1.8	1.8	4.9	2.1	1.5	3.1	0.6	•	0.5	1.8
Cash Flow to Total Debt 44	0.1	•	0.4	0.5	1.3	0.2	0.5	0.4	0.2	0.2	•	0.2	0.1

Selected Financial Factors (in Percentages)

Debt Ratio 45	88.2	•	135.9	86.2	46.7	94.2	68.8	70.8	60.2	72.0	•	116.0	86.9
Return on Total Assets 46	5.8	•	•	•	27.1	4.5	5.4	14.0	4.7	0.4	•	12.9	4.8
Return on Equity Before Income Taxes 47	9.0	•	12.5	•	49.9	65.7	13.4	43.1	8.3	•	•
Return on Equity After Income Taxes 48	5.2	•	16.6	•	49.2	63.7	12.6	38.1	7.9	•	•
Profit Margin (Before Income Tax) 49	1.8	•	•	•	8.9	1.7	2.6	9.6	4.5	•	•	12.5	•
Profit Margin (After Income Tax) 50	1.0	•	•	•	8.8	1.6	2.4	8.5	4.3	•	•	9.1	•

Table II

Corporations with Net Income

DATABASE, DIRECTORY, AND OTHER PUBLISHERS

MONEY AMOUNTS AND SIZE OF ASSETS IN THOUSANDS OF DOLLARS

Item Description for Accounting Period 7/04 Through 6/05	Total	Zero Assets	Under 500	500 to 1,000	1,000 to 5,000	5,000 to 10,000	10,000 to 25,000	25,000 to 50,000	50,000 to 100,000	100,000 to 250,000	250,000 to 500,000	500,000 to 2,500,000	2,500,000 and over
Number of Enterprises **1**	1593	10	1206	122	146	0	26	12	0	7	0	5	0

Revenues ($ in Thousands)

	Total	Zero Assets	Under 500	500 to 1,000	1,000 to 5,000	5,000 to 10,000	10,000 to 25,000	25,000 to 50,000	50,000 to 100,000	100,000 to 250,000	250,000 to 500,000	500,000 to 2,500,000	2,500,000 and over
Net Sales **2**	9235671	9303	167736	159458	1197388	0	634259	570060	0	509443	0	4679053	0
Interest **3**	12482	24	130	342	99	0	417	453	0	3090	0	7726	0
Rents **4**	2826	0	0	0	0	0	28	844	0	0	0	1920	0
Royalties **5**	166858	0	0	0	0	0	91	0	0	17	0	166745	0
Other Portfolio Income **6**	162260	2309	7780	0	121	0	1636	7489	0	730	0	142149	0
Other Receipts **7**	203691	4865	143	4163	5565	0	6614	-512	0	38984	0	136622	0
Total Receipts **8**	9783788	16501	175789	163963	1203173	0	643045	578334	0	552264	0	5134215	0
Average Total Receipts **9**	6142	1650	146	1344	8241	•	24732	48194	•	78895	•	1026843	•

Operating Costs/Operating Income (%)

	Total	Zero Assets	Under 500	500 to 1,000	1,000 to 5,000	5,000 to 10,000	10,000 to 25,000	25,000 to 50,000	50,000 to 100,000	100,000 to 250,000	250,000 to 500,000	500,000 to 2,500,000	2,500,000 and over
Cost of Operations **10**	33.1	41.1	7.2	45.4	34.0	•	38.3	26.4	•	30.4	•	29.9	•
Salaries and Wages **11**	22.3	4.2	5.0	15.0	18.7	•	20.2	25.9	•	20.4	•	22.9	•
Taxes Paid **12**	3.0	2.8	3.3	4.6	2.3	•	2.3	2.9	•	2.0	•	3.3	•
Interest Paid **13**	2.9	0.8	0.2	0.0	0.2	•	0.6	0.5	•	5.1	•	4.8	•
Depreciation **14**	1.8	0.9	0.8	0.7	1.4	•	2.3	1.5	•	2.8	•	2.1	•
Amortization and Depletion **15**	2.1	0.0	•	•	0.4	•	0.9	0.7	•	7.2	•	3.0	•
Pensions and Other Deferred Comp. **16**	0.6	1.0	•	2.0	0.2	•	0.5	0.8	•	0.0	•	0.8	•
Employee Benefits **17**	2.1	•	3.0	1.9	0.1	•	1.5	2.5	•	3.0	•	2.5	•
Advertising **18**	2.0	0.8	0.0	0.3	1.8	•	2.1	4.9	•	1.0	•	2.3	•
Other Expenses **19**	20.9	13.4	22.7	15.3	14.0	•	21.0	19.4	•	23.4	•	25.4	•
Officers' Compensation **20**	4.8	23.6	43.7	15.5	15.8	•	4.9	1.9	•	0.5	•	1.6	•
Operating Margin **21**	4.4	11.5	14.1	•	11.1	•	5.3	12.6	•	4.2	•	1.4	•
Operating Margin Before Officers' Comp. **22**	9.2	35.0	57.8	14.8	26.9	•	10.1	14.5	•	4.7	•	3.0	•

Selected Average Balance Sheet ($ in Thousands)

Net Receivables 23	1880	0	0	64	1226	·	3778	9272	17476	·	406055
Inventories 24	279	0	1	0	24	·	1414	1436	2800	·	42612
Net Property, Plant and Equipment 25	489	0	0	2	394	·	1904	2496	11273	·	104242
Total Assets 26	6612	0	66	729	2731	·	16083	35083	204126	·	1389231
Notes and Loans Payable 27	3106	0	22	10	182	·	2641	4757	87385	·	804802
All Other Liabilities 28	2044	0	18	225	758	·	7251	18933	23605	·	418117
Net Worth 29	1462	0	27	494	1790	·	6191	11393	93135	·	166312

Selected Financial Ratios (Times to 1)

Current Ratio 30	1.3	·	11.7	1.8	3.0	·	1.2	2.4	1.8	·	1.1
Quick Ratio 31	1.0	·	8.2	1.1	2.8	·	0.8	1.9	1.2	·	0.9
Net Sales to Working Capital 32	9.4	·	4.8	6.9	5.4	·	17.7	3.6	5.2	·	16.2
Coverage Ratio 33	4.6	109.8	80.0	170.2	67.7	·	11.4	31.7	3.4	·	3.4
Total Asset Turnover 34	0.9	·	2.1	1.8	3.0	·	1.5	1.4	0.4	·	0.7
Inventory Turnover 35	6.9	·	10.5	·	115.8	·	6.6	8.7	7.9	·	6.6
Receivables Turnover 36	2.9	·	2431.0	3.5	10.6	·	7.8	·	·	·	·
Total Liabilities to Net Worth 37	3.5	·	1.5	0.5	0.5	·	1.6	2.1	1.2	·	7.4
Current Assets to Working Capital 38	4.6	·	1.1	2.2	1.5	·	7.0	1.7	2.3	·	9.7
Current Liabilities to Working Capital 39	3.6	·	0.1	1.2	0.5	·	6.0	0.7	1.3	·	8.7
Working Capital to Net Sales 40	0.1	·	0.2	0.1	0.2	·	0.1	0.3	0.2	·	0.1
Inventory to Working Capital 41	0.3	·	0.0	·	0.0	·	1.2	0.1	0.2	·	0.7
Total Receipts to Cash Flow 42	4.2	1.0	2.7	7.8	4.7	·	4.1	3.4	3.0	·	3.9
Cost of Goods to Cash Flow 43	1.4	0.4	0.2	3.5	1.6	·	1.6	0.9	0.9	·	1.2
Cash Flow to Total Debt 44	0.3	·	1.3	0.7	1.8	·	0.6	0.6	0.2	·	0.2

Selected Financial Factors (in Percentages)

Debt Ratio 45	77.9	·	59.9	32.2	34.4	·	61.5	67.5	54.4	·	88.0
Return on Total Assets 46	11.7	·	40.1	3.8	35.2	·	11.0	19.6	6.3	·	11.0
Return on Equity Before Income Taxes 47	41.5	·	98.6	5.6	52.8	·	26.1	58.6	9.8	·	64.8
Return on Equity After Income Taxes 48	34.0	·	91.5	4.8	52.3	·	25.2	52.7	8.5	·	46.6
Profit Margin (Before Income Tax) 49	10.5	88.8	18.9	2.1	11.5	·	6.6	14.1	12.6	·	11.5
Profit Margin (After Income Tax) 50	8.6	88.8	17.5	1.8	11.4	·	6.4	12.6	10.9	·	8.3

Table I

Corporations with and without Net Income

SOFTWARE PUBLISHERS

MONEY AMOUNTS AND SIZE OF ASSETS IN THOUSANDS OF DOLLARS

Item Description for Accounting Period 7/04 Through 6/05	Total	Zero Assets	Under 500	500 to 1,000	1,000 to 5,000	5,000 to 10,000	10,000 to 25,000	25,000 to 50,000	50,000 to 100,000	100,000 to 250,000	250,000 to 500,000	500,000 to 2,500,000	2,500,000 and over
Number of Enterprises 1	10093	733	6839	1156	635	263	216	86	44	47	31	29	12
Revenues ($ in Thousands)													
Net Sales 2	83120151	937084	1638593	2510261	1904733	2114966	2904074	2417868	2466407	4057391	5058956	12294936	44814882
Interest 3	1134797	3883	1574	1167	4992	10194	19446	12459	21159	50976	72581	202598	733767
Rents 4	67987	180	0	10	37	4275	929	1863	1430	3906	10765	34444	10150
Royalties 5	5469874	4597	0	30081	2949	50844	32379	22888	58641	206095	42165	1108148	3911088
Other Portfolio Income 6	5090521	70160	1807	36	14317	16644	25880	15866	72065	14946	95263	221114	4542424
Other Receipts 7	9773273	37566	-48936	8667	37666	65560	77141	47595	7397	103535	113429	451777	8871872
Total Receipts 8	104656603	1053470	1593038	2550222	1964694	2262483	3059849	2518539	2627099	4436849	5393159	14313017	62884183
Average Total Receipts 9	10369	1437	233	2206	3094	8603	14166	29285	59707	94401	173973	493552	5240349
Operating Costs/Operating Income (%)													
Cost of Operations 10	19.5	32.8	7.2	37.9	20.1	17.1	26.5	23.5	15.7	18.6	21.0	28.0	15.8
Salaries and Wages 11	36.3	33.3	36.7	29.1	50.4	45.2	44.4	34.6	40.0	40.9	37.4	39.4	33.6
Taxes Paid 12	3.4	4.7	4.3	3.2	5.0	4.2	4.2	5.4	3.8	3.5	3.6	2.7	3.2
Interest Paid 13	1.7	2.1	3.2	1.3	2.0	0.9	0.9	1.0	0.8	0.9	0.3	1.8	2.0
Depreciation 14	3.1	1.3	1.9	1.7	3.8	3.7	3.0	3.5	2.9	2.8	3.3	3.9	3.1
Amortization and Depletion 15	2.0	3.5	0.6	1.3	2.0	1.3	1.7	2.1	3.7	2.4	2.2	3.6	1.5
Pensions and Other Deferred Comp. 16	0.5	0.4	0.6	2.4	0.5	0.5	0.2	0.5	0.4	0.9	0.8	0.7	0.2
Employee Benefits 17	3.3	3.1	3.2	2.0	4.5	3.1	3.5	3.2	2.7	3.1	3.2	4.1	3.1
Advertising 18	5.1	0.6	2.0	1.6	2.3	1.9	2.3	2.0	2.1	2.5	1.8	5.5	6.7
Other Expenses 19	32.3	32.5	46.2	22.1	32.3	45.9	33.5	30.0	32.3	38.6	25.8	25.1	33.8
Officers' Compensation 20	2.5	2.6	13.4	6.7	7.1	6.1	5.3	3.9	3.5	2.5	2.2	2.6	1.2
Operating Margin 21	•	•	•	•	•	•	•	•	•	•	•	•	•
Operating Margin Before Officers' Comp. 22	•	•	•	•	•	•	•	•	•	•	0.6	•	•

Selected Average Balance Sheet ($ in Thousands)

Line item	1	2	3	4	5	6	7	8	9	10	11	12	13
Net Receivables 23	2352	0	10	213	502	1602	3165	7110	14280	25982	56272	157878	1100880
Inventories 24	122	0	3	29	50	211	147	219	517	963	1418	14910	41443
Net Property, Plant and Equipment 25	935	0	7	51	245	761	912	2105	4450	6745	19082	54207	493440
Total Assets 26	16544	0	78	722	2370	7440	15572	34784	70190	163312	348900	1019516	8720930
Notes and Loans Payable 27	1313	0	105	396	1887	1731	1757	5401	11324	14610	9531	117436	390663
All Other Liabilities 28	6402	0	108	563	1146	3602	8443	12702	27418	59263	94075	329207	3515148
Net Worth 29	8829	0	-136	-236	-664	2108	5371	16682	31448	89440	245294	572873	4815118

Selected Financial Ratios (Times to 1)

Line item	1	2	3	4	5	6	7	8	9	10	11	12	13
Current Ratio 30	1.2	•	1.0	1.0	1.2	1.5	1.7	1.7	1.7	1.7	2.6	1.6	0.9
Quick Ratio 31	0.8	•	0.8	0.8	1.0	1.3	1.4	1.4	1.4	1.2	2.0	1.1	0.6
Net Sales to Working Capital 32	7.7	•	•	510.9	11.0	4.3	3.0	3.2	3.2	2.6	1.5	2.6	•
Coverage Ratio 33	12.0	•	•	•	•	•	•	•	•	•	16.3	0.8	21.1
Total Asset Turnover 34	0.5	•	3.1	3.0	1.3	1.1	0.9	0.8	0.8	0.5	0.5	0.4	0.4
Inventory Turnover 35	13.1	•	6.6	28.3	12.0	6.5	24.2	30.2	17.0	16.7	24.2	8.0	14.2
Receivables Turnover 36	3.9	•	28.7	13.2	5.4	5.5	4.4	4.1	4.3	3.2	2.8	2.9	4.0
Total Liabilities to Net Worth 37	0.9	•	•	•	•	2.5	1.9	1.1	1.2	0.8	0.4	0.8	0.8
Current Assets to Working Capital 38	6.3	•	•	136.2	5.6	2.9	2.5	2.4	2.4	2.5	1.6	2.7	•
Current Liabilities to Working Capital 39	5.3	•	•	135.2	4.6	1.9	1.5	1.4	1.4	1.5	0.6	1.7	•
Working Capital to Net Sales 40	0.1	•	•	0.0	0.1	0.2	0.3	0.3	0.3	0.4	0.7	0.4	•
Inventory to Working Capital 41	0.1	•	•	6.9	•	0.2	0.0	0.0	0.0	0.0	0.0	0.1	•
Total Receipts to Cash Flow 42	2.2	•	5.4	10.5	5.5	5.5	12.1	5.1	4.2	3.8	4.0	5.4	1.5
Cost of Goods to Cash Flow 43	0.4	•	1.8	4.0	0.9	0.9	3.2	0.7	0.7	0.7	0.8	1.5	0.2
Cash Flow to Total Debt 44	0.5	•	0.2	0.2	0.3	0.3	0.1	0.3	0.3	0.3	0.4	0.2	0.6

Selected Financial Factors (in Percentages)

Line item	1	2	3	4	5	6	7	8	9	10	11	12	13
Debt Ratio 45	46.6	•	274.8	132.7	128.0	71.7	65.5	52.0	55.2	45.2	29.7	43.8	44.8
Return on Total Assets 46	10.0	•	•	•	•	•	•	•	•	•	2.5	0.6	17.7
Return on Equity Before Income Taxes 47	17.1	•	39.0	71.8	121.9	•	•	•	•	•	3.3	•	30.6
Return on Equity After Income Taxes 48	11.2	•	39.1	72.8	127.9	•	•	•	•	•	2.4	•	22.1
Profit Margin (Before Income Tax) 49	18.4	•	•	•	•	•	•	•	•	•	5.0	•	39.5
Profit Margin (After Income Tax) 50	12.0	•	•	•	•	•	•	•	•	•	3.6	•	28.5

Table II

Corporations with Net Income

SOFTWARE PUBLISHERS

MONEY AMOUNTS AND SIZE OF ASSETS IN THOUSANDS OF DOLLARS

Item Description for Accounting Period 7/04 Through 6/05	Total	Zero Assets	Under 500	500 to 1,000	1,000 to 5,000	5,000 to 10,000	10,000 to 25,000	25,000 to 50,000	50,000 to 100,000	100,000 to 250,000	250,000 to 500,000	500,000 to 2,500,000	2,500,000 and over
Number of Enterprises **1**	3651	20	2465	639	250	100	64	38	15	20	0	15	0
Revenues ($ in Thousands)													
Net Sales **2**	63463429	685772	1029454	1877005	1196176	1229252	1335651	1515177	1116224	1721366	0	6826979	0
Interest **3**	886931	2001	209	99	1438	1491	3136	5833	5066	20577	0	134079	0
Rents **4**	36307	0	0	0	0	3020	0	59	0	2703	0	9632	0
Royalties **5**	4968648	0	0	0	0	49384	25519	10565	2731	105793	0	839804	0
Other Portfolio Income **6**	4893393	69728	1676	0	12560	7383	9006	228	1013	6660	0	182660	0
Other Receipts **7**	9156805	32726	33692	4853	33179	43278	29098	35593	-9951	103663	0	58842	0
Total Receipts **8**	83405513	790227	1065031	1881957	1243353	1333808	1402410	1567455	1115083	1960762	0	8051996	0
Average Total Receipts **9**	22845	39511	432	2945	4973	13338	21913	41249	74339	98038	•	536800	•
Operating Costs/Operating Income (%)													
Cost of Operations **10**	19.9	39.5	2.7	46.5	13.2	16.3	30.1	23.3	11.9	10.8	•	38.0	•
Salaries and Wages **11**	31.0	20.8	26.7	16.0	34.0	26.2	27.9	27.5	35.1	41.5	•	29.5	•
Taxes Paid **12**	3.1	4.3	3.4	2.3	3.7	2.8	3.1	6.3	4.4	3.5	•	1.7	•
Interest Paid **13**	1.8	2.1	0.7	0.4	1.1	0.6	0.3	0.9	0.8	0.6	•	2.5	•
Depreciation **14**	2.8	1.0	1.8	1.3	2.6	3.0	1.8	2.8	2.9	2.6	•	2.9	•
Amortization and Depletion **15**	1.4	0.9	0.3	0.2	0.1	0.1	0.7	0.9	1.1	2.1	•	1.9	•
Pensions and Other Deferred Comp. **16**	0.4	0.6	0.8	3.2	0.7	0.4	0.3	0.6	0.7	0.8	•	0.4	•
Employee Benefits **17**	2.9	2.3	2.8	1.0	3.7	1.8	2.3	2.6	2.4	3.1	•	3.2	•
Advertising **18**	5.9	0.4	0.3	1.8	2.1	1.5	1.5	1.6	1.3	1.0	•	7.5	•
Other Expenses **19**	30.8	26.8	39.3	14.2	17.3	40.8	21.0	20.7	22.3	34.5	•	21.9	•
Officers' Compensation **20**	1.9	1.1	10.0	6.4	5.1	4.7	4.0	2.7	2.8	2.7	•	1.3	•
Operating Margin **21**	•	0.3	11.0	6.5	16.4	1.8	6.9	9.9	14.4	•	•	•	•
Operating Margin Before Officers' Comp. **22**	•	1.4	21.0	13.0	21.5	6.5	10.9	12.7	17.1	•	•	•	•

Selected Average Balance Sheet ($ in Thousands)

Net Receivables 23	4561	0	5	287	740	1883	4173	8319	17263	23128	189097
Inventories 24	282	0	3	48	102	356	213	151	160	414	26548
Net Property, Plant and Equipment 25	1894	0	8	61	198	781	1039	2569	4881	6867	39104
Total Assets 26	33910	0	53	697	2320	7721	15330	34160	68013	149330	1034406
Notes and Loans Payable 27	2315	0	65	206	1994	767	1463	6548	15655	7266	158804
All Other Liabilities 28	13482	0	11	445	837	4421	7863	12707	32008	74282	304065
Net Worth 29	18113	0	-23	46	-512	2533	6004	14905	20351	67782	571537

Selected Financial Ratios (Times to 1)

Current Ratio 30	1.0	•	0.9	1.8	1.6	1.3	1.4	1.7	1.6	1.7	1.5
Quick Ratio 31	0.7	•	0.9	1.5	1.4	1.0	1.1	1.4	1.4	1.3	1.1
Net Sales to Working Capital 32	70.3	•	•	10.9	7.4	9.7	6.7	4.1	4.4	2.6	3.0
Coverage Ratio 33	18.9	8.6	21.0	19.0	19.3	17.0	43.7	15.2	18.4	20.3	4.3
Total Asset Turnover 34	0.5	•	7.9	4.2	2.1	1.6	1.4	1.2	1.1	0.6	0.4
Inventory Turnover 35	12.2	•	3.7	28.7	6.2	5.6	29.6	61.4	55.2	22.5	6.5
Receivables Turnover 36	4.3	•	39.5	13.7	9.1	8.3	5.3	5.5	5.1	3.2	3.2
Total Liabilities to Net Worth 37	0.9	•	•	14.0	•	2.0	1.6	1.3	2.3	1.2	0.8
Current Assets to Working Capital 38	50.9	•	•	2.3	2.6	4.4	3.4	2.4	2.6	2.4	3.1
Current Liabilities to Working Capital 39	49.9	•	•	1.3	1.6	3.4	2.4	1.4	1.6	1.4	2.1
Working Capital to Net Sales 40	0.0	•	•	0.1	0.1	0.1	0.2	0.2	0.2	0.4	0.3
Inventory to Working Capital 41	1.2	•	•	0.2	0.1	0.6	0.1	0.0	0.0	0.0	0.2
Total Receipts to Cash Flow 42	1.7	3.1	2.0	5.8	3.1	2.1	3.4	3.2	3.0	2.4	4.0
Cost of Goods to Cash Flow 43	0.3	1.2	0.1	2.7	0.4	0.3	1.0	0.7	0.4	0.3	1.5
Cash Flow to Total Debt 44	0.6	•	2.8	0.8	0.5	1.1	0.6	0.6	0.5	0.4	0.2

Selected Financial Factors (in Percentages)

Debt Ratio 45	46.6	•	143.6	93.3	122.1	67.2	60.8	56.4	70.1	54.6	44.7
Return on Total Assets 46	17.3	•	119.9	30.2	44.3	17.3	16.7	16.7	16.4	6.8	4.7
Return on Equity Before Income Taxes 47	30.7	•	•	430.9	•	49.8	41.6	35.9	51.8	14.2	6.4
Return on Equity After Income Taxes 48	22.7	•	•	421.6	•	46.6	34.4	30.9	46.1	11.9	4.9
Profit Margin (Before Income Tax) 49	32.0	15.5	14.4	6.8	20.4	10.3	12.0	13.4	14.2	11.2	8.1
Profit Margin (After Income Tax) 50	23.7	13.3	14.4	6.6	18.3	9.6	9.9	11.5	12.6	9.3	6.2

Table I

Corporations with and without Net Income

MOTION PICTURE AND VIDEO INDUSTRIES (EXCEPT VIDEO RENTAL)

MONEY AMOUNTS AND SIZE OF ASSETS IN THOUSANDS OF DOLLARS

Item Description for Accounting Period 7/04 Through 6/05	Total	Zero Assets	Under 500	500 to 1,000	1,000 to 5,000	5,000 to 10,000	10,000 to 25,000	25,000 to 50,000	50,000 to 100,000	100,000 to 250,000	250,000 to 500,000	500,000 to 2,500,000	2,500,000 and over
Number of Enterprises 1	26069	3720	20119	958	967	106	97	40	22	15	6	12	7
Revenues ($ in Thousands)													
Net Sales 2	70555152	1608939	6120103	1922809	2729256	1418474	1568552	1231319	885367	979255	1441382	4730916	45918779
Interest 3	8453755	13880	3817	435	2429	3926	1105	3071	2234	8292	5570	62987	8346010
Rents 4	291445	221	0	0	0	208	2938	471	282	5796	1497	7538	272494
Royalties 5	997154	5072	24769	0	2293	103	949	291	0	8456	0	46152	909069
Other Portfolio Income 6	1838600	12883	12570	958	11738	1544	2378	22467	246	1260198	17344	9874	486398
Other Receipts 7	1835745	74448	69917	1162	52453	27314	113756	53308	10456	-54025	77325	329469	1080165
Total Receipts 8	83971851	1715443	6231176	1925364	2798169	1451569	1689678	1310927	898585	2207972	1543118	5186936	57012915
Average Total Receipts 9	3221	461	310	2010	2894	13694	17419	32773	40845	147198	257186	432245	8144702
Operating Costs/Operating Income (%)													
Cost of Operations 10	30.3	9.6	36.1	29.5	54.4	47.2	39.6	43.7	33.9	15.7	23.2	41.1	27.0
Salaries and Wages 11	10.6	11.2	3.3	20.5	9.1	14.2	12.6	10.5	8.8	8.1	12.2	11.5	11.0
Taxes Paid 12	2.3	3.9	1.7	2.8	1.9	1.6	3.5	2.6	2.2	1.8	2.1	2.2	2.3
Interest Paid 13	14.6	3.9	0.3	1.2	1.1	1.5	1.3	2.6	2.1	4.3	2.5	4.0	21.4
Depreciation 14	6.5	6.3	1.8	8.1	4.1	6.1	7.1	4.4	9.6	3.6	5.8	4.2	7.5
Amortization and Depletion 15	11.4	0.9	0.2	0.8	0.4	0.3	4.0	2.5	16.8	18.3	7.7	9.6	15.3
Pensions and Other Deferred Comp. 16	1.0	1.6	2.3	1.6	0.3	0.0	0.2	0.1	0.1	0.0	0.5	0.1	1.0
Employee Benefits 17	1.1	0.7	0.9	1.9	0.6	1.4	1.6	1.1	0.6	0.3	1.3	1.4	1.1
Advertising 18	4.4	1.6	0.3	1.3	0.6	0.5	0.7	0.6	1.9	0.9	0.9	1.9	6.2
Other Expenses 19	24.2	62.7	23.9	23.9	23.2	18.5	21.7	25.2	25.8	37.9	34.0	21.3	22.8
Officers' Compensation 20	3.8	2.6	27.6	5.9	7.3	8.0	10.6	6.2	2.1	1.1	9.4	1.0	0.2
Operating Margin 21	•	•	1.6	2.5	•	0.7	•	0.3	•	8.0	0.5	1.7	•
Operating Margin Before Officers' Comp. 22	•	29.2	•	8.4	4.3	8.7	7.8	6.5	9.1	9.9	2.7		•

Selected Average Balance Sheet ($ in Thousands)

Net Receivables 23	726	0	5	85	186	2483	1557	5265	7051	9475	14705	96940	2341348
Inventories 24	326	0	2	18	114	355	542	831	1974	11157	17230	7027	1115372
Net Property, Plant and Equipment 25	662	0	12	465	382	2374	3606	8022	14916	18080	117803	149809	1740570
Total Assets 26	26459	0	50	833	1890	7553	15338	34542	73427	145878	383162	1079849	94770024
Notes and Loans Payable 27	7730	0	155	709	1250	2404	5427	17477	26942	69594	77614	280425	27082808
All Other Liabilities 28	2205	0	14	64	435	3060	4118	8959	22856	30739	127292	219087	7324449
Net Worth 29	16523	0	-119	59	205	2088	5793	8106	23630	45545	178256	580337	60362768

Selected Financial Ratios (Times to 1)

Current Ratio 30	1.9	•	2.0	1.5	1.3	1.2	1.2	1.1	3.4	0.8	1.9	1.9
Quick Ratio 31	0.9	•	1.7	1.3	0.8	0.7	0.9	0.6	1.6	0.3	0.7	0.9
Net Sales to Working Capital 32	1.8	•	19.6	33.6	15.4	24.7	16.7	13.4	1.6	•	2.5	1.3
Coverage Ratio 33	1.6	1.4	14.0	3.2	0.6	3.1	4.7	3.6	31.9	4.0	3.8	1.4
Total Asset Turnover 34	0.1	•	6.1	2.4	1.5	1.8	1.1	0.9	0.4	0.6	0.4	0.1
Inventory Turnover 35	2.5	•	51.1	33.1	13.4	17.8	11.8	16.2	6.9	3.2	23.1	1.6
Receivables Turnover 36	4.1	•	48.5	35.1	16.5	6.2	11.6	6.3	6.1	13.7	5.6	3.1
Total Liabilities to Net Worth 37	0.6	•	•	13.1	8.2	2.6	1.6	3.3	2.2	1.1	0.9	0.6
Current Assets to Working Capital 38	2.1	•	2.0	3.1	3.9	7.5	5.7	5.5	1.4	•	2.1	2.1
Current Liabilities to Working Capital 39	1.1	•	1.0	2.1	2.9	6.5	4.7	4.5	0.4	•	1.1	1.1
Working Capital to Net Sales 40	0.6	•	0.1	0.0	0.1	0.0	0.1	0.1	0.6	•	0.4	0.8
Inventory to Working Capital 41	0.3	•	0.1	0.3	0.7	0.2	0.6	0.2	0.2	•	0.1	0.3
Total Receipts to Cash Flow 42	3.8	2.2	4.2	5.0	5.9	5.6	4.8	4.5	0.6	6.9	3.9	4.1
Cost of Goods to Cash Flow 43	1.2	0.2	1.5	1.5	3.2	2.7	1.9	2.0	0.1	1.6	1.6	1.1
Cash Flow to Total Debt 44	0.1	•	0.4	0.5	0.3	0.4	0.4	0.3	1.1	0.2	0.2	0.0

Selected Financial Factors (in Percentages)

Debt Ratio 45	37.5	•	338.1	92.9	89.2	72.3	62.2	76.5	67.8	68.8	53.5	46.3	36.3
Return on Total Assets 46	2.4	•	22.2	9.2	1.1	8.0	6.6	8.4	•	61.6	6.1	5.5	2.1
Return on Equity Before Income Taxes 47	1.5	•	•	•	•	19.5	13.7	25.8	•	191.2	9.8	7.6	0.9
Return on Equity After Income Taxes 48	1.2	•	•	•	88.9	19.1	13.1	25.2	•	190.9	8.1	5.8	0.7
Profit Margin (Before Income Tax) 49	8.9	1.7	3.4	2.6	•	3.0	4.9	6.8	•	133.4	7.3	11.1	8.5
Profit Margin (After Income Tax) 50	7.2	1.3	3.3	2.6	•	3.0	4.7	6.6	•	133.2	6.0	8.6	6.2

263

Table II
Corporations with Net Income

MOTION PICTURE AND VIDEO INDUSTRIES (EXCEPT VIDEO RENTAL)

MONEY AMOUNTS AND SIZE OF ASSETS IN THOUSANDS OF DOLLARS

Item Description for Accounting Period 7/04 Through 6/05	Total	Zero Assets	Under 500	500 to 1,000	1,000 to 5,000	5,000 to 10,000	10,000 to 25,000	25,000 to 50,000	50,000 to 100,000	100,000 to 250,000	250,000 to 500,000	500,000 to 2,500,000	2,500,000 and over
Number of Enterprises 1	13346	2300	10487	0	291	65	43	0	0	9	0	0	9
Revenues ($ in Thousands)													
Net Sales 2	61639829	1589627	4366076	0	1516019	1175923	1019857	0	0	774412	0	0	4064719
Interest 3	8417512	12288	774	0	1129	187	819	0	0	7271	0	0	58992
Rents 4	284865	221	0	0	0	177	2783	0	0	5716	0	0	1336
Royalties 5	231155	0	0	0	2293	0	158	0	0	3187	0	0	25121
Other Portfolio Income 6	1815478	12883	12391	0	643	229	1434	0	0	1260140	0	0	9594
Other Receipts 7	1633294	78854	68849	0	47294	24523	105024	0	0	-52319	0	0	303477
Total Receipts 8	74022133	1693873	4448090	0	1567378	1201039	1130075	0	0	1998407	0	0	4463239
Average Total Receipts 9	5546	736	424	•	5386	18478	26281	•	•	222045	•	•	495915
Operating Costs/Operating Income (%)													
Cost of Operations 10	29.2	9.6	36.6	•	34.0	49.9	39.6	•	•	14.1	•	•	41.4
Salaries and Wages 11	10.4	11.2	3.1	•	12.4	14.9	11.5	•	•	9.2	•	•	11.9
Taxes Paid 12	2.3	3.8	1.6	•	2.3	1.5	3.9	•	•	2.1	•	•	2.1
Interest Paid 13	16.2	3.8	0.1	•	0.5	0.9	0.9	•	•	3.1	•	•	2.4
Depreciation 14	5.5	6.3	1.2	•	4.0	6.4	7.9	•	•	3.2	•	•	4.1
Amortization and Depletion 15	12.4	0.9	0.3	•	0.6	0.4	1.3	•	•	8.2	•	•	9.0
Pensions and Other Deferred Comp. 16	1.0	1.6	2.2	•	0.4	0.0	0.2	•	•	0.0	•	•	0.1
Employee Benefits 17	1.1	0.6	0.8	•	0.5	1.5	0.8	•	•	0.2	•	•	1.5
Advertising 18	4.3	1.6	0.3	•	0.8	0.6	0.7	•	•	1.0	•	•	2.0
Other Expenses 19	22.9	59.2	19.2	•	24.6	8.8	17.1	•	•	42.9	•	•	20.6
Officers' Compensation 20	3.0	2.6	24.5	•	11.0	8.0	14.0	•	•	0.8	•	•	1.1
Operating Margin 21	•	10.1		•	8.8	7.2	2.2	•	•	15.2	•	•	3.8
Operating Margin Before Officers' Comp. 22	•	1.5	34.6	•	19.8	15.2	16.2	•	•	15.9	•	•	5.0

Selected Average Balance Sheet ($ in Thousands)

	1	2	3	4	5	6	7	8
Net Receivables 23	1316	0	7	226	3654	2362	14393	121372
Inventories 24	601	0	2	106	139	345	5295	9641
Net Property, Plant and Equipment 25	948	0	6	443	2876	4334	28983	159772
Total Assets 26	50512	0	45	1708	8371	14818	146173	1164516
Notes and Loans Payable 27	14219	0	18	472	2565	4418	48107	202315
All Other Liabilities 28	4038	0	8	584	2190	4727	20028	269766
Net Worth 29	32255	0	19	653	3616	5673	78038	692435

Selected Financial Ratios (Times to 1)

	1	2	3	4	5	6	7	8
Current Ratio 30	2.1		3.6	1.4	1.2	1.6	4.2	2.3
Quick Ratio 31	1.0		3.4	1.1	1.1	1.2	2.3	1.0
Net Sales to Working Capital 32	1.5		17.3	18.2	25.1	9.2	1.6	2.2
Coverage Ratio 33	1.7	2.4	132.7	25.2	11.9	15.7	56.4	6.6
Total Asset Turnover 34	0.1		9.3	3.0	2.2	1.6	0.6	0.4
Inventory Turnover 35	2.2		66.0	16.7	65.0	27.2	2.3	19.4
Receivables Turnover 36	3.9		48.7	18.8		11.7	8.0	
Total Liabilities to Net Worth 37	0.6		1.3	1.6	1.3	1.6	0.9	0.7
Current Assets to Working Capital 38	2.0		1.4	3.3	6.0	2.7	1.3	1.8
Current Liabilities to Working Capital 39	1.0		0.4	2.3	5.0	1.7	0.3	0.8
Working Capital to Net Sales 40	0.7		0.1	0.1	0.0	0.1	0.6	0.5
Inventory to Working Capital 41	0.2		0.0	0.6	0.2	0.1	0.2	0.0
Total Receipts to Cash Flow 42	3.6		3.6	3.5	7.1	4.0	0.5	3.6
Cost of Goods to Cash Flow 43	1.1	0.2	1.3	1.2	3.6	1.6	0.1	1.5
Cash Flow to Total Debt 44	0.1		4.5	1.4	0.5	0.6	2.6	0.3

Selected Financial Factors (in Percentages)

	1	2	3	4	5	6	7	8
Debt Ratio 45	36.1		57.4	61.8	56.8	61.7	46.6	40.5
Return on Total Assets 46	2.6		112.0	38.7	21.9	22.3	103.8	6.1
Return on Equity Before Income Taxes 47	1.7		260.8	97.2	46.4	54.4	190.9	8.7
Return on Equity After Income Taxes 48	1.4		257.4	94.4	46.1	53.1	190.6	6.8
Profit Margin (Before Income Tax) 49	11.8	5.5	12.0	12.2	9.3	13.0	173.1	13.4
Profit Margin (After Income Tax) 50	9.8	5.1	11.8	11.8	9.2	12.7	172.9	10.4

Table I

Corporations with and without Net Income

SOUND RECORDING INDUSTRIES

MONEY AMOUNTS AND SIZE OF ASSETS IN THOUSANDS OF DOLLARS

Item Description for Accounting Period 7/04 Through 6/05	Total	Zero Assets	Under 500	500 to 1,000	1,000 to 5,000	5,000 to 10,000	10,000 to 25,000	25,000 to 50,000	50,000 to 100,000	100,000 to 250,000	250,000 to 500,000	500,000 to 2,500,000	2,500,000 and over
Number of Enterprises **1**	8317	2016	5901	57	253	56	18	7	6	0	0	0	3
Revenues ($ in Thousands)													
Net Sales **2**	7488394	96371	1545765	32821	132728	92434	172578	148822	1095079	0	0	0	4171797
Interest **3**	361484	0	23	57	199	1168	1439	722	32709	0	0	0	325168
Rents **4**	8126	0	0	613	0	0	188	317	244	0	0	0	6764
Royalties **5**	1754694	320	0	0	39614	1	14650	48776	554522	0	0	0	1096812
Other Portfolio Income **6**	536157	38191	0	0	34	52	3270	556	2694	0	0	0	491360
Other Receipts **7**	974888	1987	18546	169	23051	1300	18712	3918	13197	0	0	0	894006
Total Receipts **8**	11123743	136869	1564334	33660	195626	94955	210837	203111	1698445	0	0	0	6985907
Average Total Receipts **9**	1337	68	265	591	773	1696	11713	29016	283074	•	•	•	2328636
Operating Costs/Operating Income (%)													
Cost of Operations **10**	47.2	42.9	6.6	45.1	3.2	62.6	48.6	42.9	45.4	•	•	•	64.1
Salaries and Wages **11**	16.0	1.4	10.7	12.9	12.1	3.3	15.9	15.3	15.4	•	•	•	18.9
Taxes Paid **12**	4.3	0.5	2.1	2.1	3.8	1.7	2.5	1.9	2.6	•	•	•	5.9
Interest Paid **13**	7.9	8.9	1.1	5.5	0.3	1.1	2.0	3.9	4.5	•	•	•	12.1
Depreciation **14**	7.1	20.4	3.4	1.1	6.1	3.3	5.8	1.5	10.7	•	•	•	7.7
Amortization and Depletion **15**	3.2	0.1	0.2	•	20.1	0.2	1.1	2.8	3.4	•	•	•	4.0
Pensions and Other Deferred Comp. **16**	0.9	•	3.2	•	1.3	0.1	0.6	0.7	•	•	•	•	0.3
Employee Benefits **17**	2.9	•	1.7	•	•	0.7	1.4	1.7	0.6	•	•	•	4.3
Advertising **18**	5.5	8.2	0.4	2.2	10.9	1.0	3.9	2.8	4.7	•	•	•	7.7
Other Expenses **19**	38.1	28.1	53.0	30.8	85.1	14.3	38.0	51.1	61.9	•	•	•	25.2
Officers' Compensation **20**	4.4	14.5	9.2	•	4.5	1.5	4.9	9.6	1.8	•	•	•	1.2
Operating Margin **21**	•	•	3.2	•	•	10.4	•	•	•	•	•	•	•
Operating Margin Before Officers' Comp. **22**	•	•	17.7	0.3	•	11.9	•	•	•	•	•	•	•

Selected Average Balance Sheet ($ in Thousands)

Net Receivables 23	552	0	10	347	204	254	2094	1712	34634	•	1396373
Inventories 24	77	0	7	448	8	43	1564	1461	5083	•	165260
Net Property, Plant and Equipment 25	237	0	21	146	152	1053	2246	3677	15737	•	527840
Total Assets 26	4538	0	70	722	1671	6605	15145	34997	376502	•	11240976
Notes and Loans Payable 27	820	0	158	1070	601	5243	12012	13772	137943	•	1413321
All Other Liabilities 28	1502	0	24	14	162	778	26904	12917	118962	•	3660858
Net Worth 29	2216	0	-111	-362	908	584	-23772	8309	119596	•	6166797

Selected Financial Ratios (Times to 1)

Current Ratio 30	0.4	•	1.7	41.6	2.8	7.3	0.3	1.0	1.0	•	0.3
Quick Ratio 31	0.3	•	1.3	25.5	2.0	1.3	0.2	0.5	0.5	•	0.2
Net Sales to Working Capital 32	•	•	13.6	1.0	1.2	0.4	•	91.4	91.4	•	•
Coverage Ratio 33	2.5	4.6	•	5.0	1.0	13.1	•	1.9	1.9	•	2.4
Total Asset Turnover 34	0.2	•	3.8	0.8	0.3	0.2	0.6	0.6	0.5	•	0.1
Inventory Turnover 35	5.5	•	2.4	0.6	2.0	24.2	3.0	6.2	16.3	•	5.4
Receivables Turnover 36	1.9	•	41.7	0.9	2.5	4.9	3.5	11.9	9.5	•	•
Total Liabilities to Net Worth 37	1.0	•	•	•	0.8	10.3	•	3.2	2.1	•	0.8
Current Assets to Working Capital 38	•	•	2.5	1.0	1.6	1.2	•	•	47.5	•	•
Current Liabilities to Working Capital 39	•	•	1.5	0.0	0.6	0.2	•	•	46.5	•	•
Working Capital to Net Sales 40	•	•	0.1	1.0	0.8	2.5	•	•	0.0	•	•
Inventory to Working Capital 41	•	•	0.3	0.4	0.0	0.0	•	•	3.4	•	•
Total Receipts to Cash Flow 42	2.3	1.9	2.2	4.2	1.2	3.9	3.3	2.0	1.6	•	2.6
Cost of Goods to Cash Flow 43	1.1	0.8	0.1	1.9	0.0	2.4	1.6	0.9	0.7	•	1.7
Cash Flow to Total Debt 44	0.2	•	0.7	0.1	0.6	0.1	0.1	0.4	0.4	•	0.1

Selected Financial Factors (in Percentages)

Debt Ratio 45	51.2	•	260.0	150.2	45.7	91.2	257.0	76.3	68.2	•	45.1
Return on Total Assets 46	3.9	•	20.8	•	0.1	3.5	•	4.6	4.3	•	3.7
Return on Equity Before Income Taxes 47	4.8	•	•	10.1	•	36.9	1.0	9.4	6.4	•	3.9
Return on Equity After Income Taxes 48	4.7	•	•	10.4	•	26.8	1.2	6.0	6.4	•	3.9
Profit Margin (Before Income Tax) 49	11.8	31.6	4.4	•	13.0	•	3.7	•	4.2	•	17.5
Profit Margin (After Income Tax) 50	11.5	31.6	4.4	•	9.5	•	2.4	•	4.2	•	17.2

Table II

Corporations with Net Income

SOUND RECORDING INDUSTRIES

MONEY AMOUNTS AND SIZE OF ASSETS IN THOUSANDS OF DOLLARS

Item Description for Accounting Period 7/04 Through 6/05	Total	Zero Assets	Under 500	500 to 1,000	1,000 to 5,000	5,000 to 10,000	10,000 to 25,000	25,000 to 50,000	50,000 to 100,000	100,000 to 250,000	250,000 to 500,000	500,000 to 2,500,000	2,500,000 and over
Number of Enterprises **1**	4796	841	3660	0	209	12	8	0	0	0	0	0	0
Revenues ($ in Thousands)													
Net Sales **2**	5501014	90975	1409432	0	128664	84533	108870	0	0	0	0	0	0
Interest **3**	353252	0	23	0	199	1168	534	0	0	0	0	0	0
Rents **4**	1240	0	0	0	0	0	87	0	0	0	0	0	0
Royalties **5**	1228011	0	0	0	39614	0	12496	0	0	0	0	0	0
Other Portfolio Income **6**	534255	38191	0	0	34	52	2050	0	0	0	0	0	0
Other Receipts **7**	768852	0	23583	0	23051	1300	5524	0	0	0	0	0	0
Total Receipts **8**	8386624	129166	1433038	0	191562	87053	129561	0	0	0	0	0	0
Average Total Receipts **9**	1749	154	392	•	917	7254	16195	•	•	•	•	•	•
Operating Costs/Operating Income (%)													
Cost of Operations **10**	45.0	45.4	2.6	•	3.1	63.4	55.3	•	•	•	•	•	•
Salaries and Wages **11**	14.6	•	9.7	•	7.2	2.6	10.4	•	•	•	•	•	•
Taxes Paid **12**	4.7	0.4	2.0	•	3.2	1.7	1.3	•	•	•	•	•	•
Interest Paid **13**	9.1	9.2	1.2	•	0.3	0.7	0.8	•	•	•	•	•	•
Depreciation **14**	4.1	15.9	2.8	•	1.0	1.4	0.8	•	•	•	•	•	•
Amortization and Depletion **15**	2.1	•	0.1	•	0.0	0.0	0.8	•	•	•	•	•	•
Pensions and Other Deferred Comp. **16**	1.0	•	3.5	•	1.4	0.1	0.1	•	•	•	•	•	•
Employee Benefits **17**	3.1	•	1.3	•	•	0.8	0.7	•	•	•	•	•	•
Advertising **18**	5.0	•	0.1	•	0.1	1.1	5.9	•	•	•	•	•	•
Other Expenses **19**	34.6	21.5	47.2	•	47.3	9.2	30.8	•	•	•	•	•	•
Officers' Compensation **20**	4.6	•	15.0	•	4.6	1.4	4.1	•	•	•	•	•	•
Operating Margin **21**	•	7.6	14.5	•	31.9	17.6	•	•	•	•	•	•	•
Operating Margin Before Officers' Comp. **22**	•	7.6	29.5	•	36.5	19.0	•	•	•	•	•	•	•

Selected Average Balance Sheet ($ in Thousands)

Net Receivables 23	359	0	2	•	247	1027	2595
Inventories 24	64	0	0	•	5	169	2547
Net Property, Plant and Equipment 25	71	0	25	•	42	58	552
Total Assets 26	5841	0	72	•	1407	6491	15972
Notes and Loans Payable 27	386	0	32	•	690	0	6885
All Other Liabilities 28	1615	0	23	•	195	2000	4900
Net Worth 29	3840	0	18	•	522	4491	4188

Selected Financial Ratios (Times to 1)

Current Ratio 30	0.2	•	3.9	•	2.4	2.1	1.3
Quick Ratio 31	0.1	•	3.5	•	1.9	1.9	0.6
Net Sales to Working Capital 32	•	•	11.1	•	1.5	3.1	5.2
Coverage Ratio 33	3.8	6.4	14.5	•	313.0	31.4	10.5
Total Asset Turnover 34	0.2	•	5.3	•	0.4	1.1	0.9
Inventory Turnover 35	8.1	•	•	•	4.0	26.5	3.0
Receivables Turnover 36	5.2	•	238.8	•	2.5	•	4.1
Total Liabilities to Net Worth 37	0.5	•	3.1	•	1.7	0.4	2.8
Current Assets to Working Capital 38	•	•	1.3	•	1.7	1.9	4.0
Current Liabilities to Working Capital 39	•	•	0.3	•	0.7	0.9	3.0
Working Capital to Net Sales 40	•	•	0.1	•	0.7	0.3	0.2
Inventory to Working Capital 41	•	•	•	•	0.0	0.1	0.9
Total Receipts to Cash Flow 42	1.8	1.4	1.8	•	0.8	3.5	2.8
Cost of Goods to Cash Flow 43	0.8	0.6	0.0	•	0.0	2.2	1.6
Cash Flow to Total Debt 44	0.3	•	3.9	•	0.9	1.0	0.4

Selected Financial Factors (in Percentages)

Debt Ratio 45	34.3	•	75.4	•	62.9	30.8	73.8
Return on Total Assets 46	6.8	•	92.7	•	35.4	23.0	7.5
Return on Equity Before Income Taxes 47	7.7	•	350.8	•	95.2	32.2	25.8
Return on Equity After Income Taxes 48	7.5	•	349.2	•	92.0	26.1	22.1
Profit Margin (Before Income Tax) 49	25.6	49.6	16.2	•	80.7	20.5	7.9
Profit Margin (After Income Tax) 50	25.2	49.6	16.1	•	78.1	16.6	6.8

Table I

Corporations with and without Net Income

BROADCASTING (EXCEPT INTERNET)

MONEY AMOUNTS AND SIZE OF ASSETS IN THOUSANDS OF DOLLARS

Item Description for Accounting Period 7/04 Through 6/05	Total	Zero Assets	Under 500	500 to 1,000	1,000 to 5,000	5,000 to 10,000	10,000 to 25,000	25,000 to 50,000	50,000 to 100,000	100,000 to 250,000	250,000 to 500,000	500,000 to 2,500,000	2,500,000 and over
Number of Enterprises 1	6524	1018	3789	644	635	173	106	43	28	36	12	27	13
Revenues ($ in Thousands)													
Net Sales 2	88344102	28447	721949	942899	1840354	869971	1210782	734073	851807	3035359	1574641	8322584	68211237
Interest 3	2024852	28	365	88	5621	2832	3005	14459	16373	67804	29639	473879	1410758
Rents 4	386381	0	0	453	4676	2332	2194	1119	779	12639	6080	14720	341390
Royalties 5	2985306	0	0	0	0	3	0	1	159	2	31906	201207	2752027
Other Portfolio Income 6	2953970	10189	5	2378	7924	34684	29626	25832	80034	171243	11580	591987	1988490
Other Receipts 7	2706947	-30074	2038	127783	157857	9459	20652	24281	75845	19629	31987	141944	2125546
Total Receipts 8	99401558	8590	724357	1073601	2016432	919281	1266259	799765	1024997	3306676	1685833	9746321	76829448
Average Total Receipts 9	15236	8	191	1667	3175	5314	11946	18599	36607	91852	140486	360975	5909958
Operating Costs/Operating Income (%)													
Cost of Operations 10	27.2	8.1	22.2	3.7	36.1	41.3	22.2	18.4	9.4	45.5	13.5	11.7	29.0
Salaries and Wages 11	14.2	21.3	29.2	45.9	23.5	13.3	21.0	16.7	26.3	11.3	22.1	22.5	12.1
Taxes Paid 12	2.5	2.4	3.7	6.2	4.1	2.5	4.2	5.3	3.4	2.0	5.0	4.1	2.1
Interest Paid 13	6.7	436.2	1.6	2.1	3.1	2.6	2.5	3.3	12.6	5.6	13.5	15.8	5.6
Depreciation 14	6.2	1.1	3.0	2.3	3.8	5.1	6.5	8.2	6.4	7.2	13.5	7.9	5.9
Amortization and Depletion 15	7.6	0.0	1.5	0.1	2.6	4.5	3.9	4.9	11.5	3.9	8.9	16.4	7.0
Pensions and Other Deferred Comp. 16	0.4	•	0.0	•	0.3	0.1	0.9	0.2	0.5	0.3	0.3	0.4	0.4
Employee Benefits 17	1.9	4.6	1.2	1.7	1.6	0.7	1.3	1.6	1.6	1.0	2.4	1.5	2.0
Advertising 18	2.3	0.2	2.1	1.1	1.3	5.5	2.1	3.0	2.9	1.4	1.9	2.8	2.3
Other Expenses 19	41.3	129.8	38.1	43.3	32.1	22.3	29.0	46.8	35.5	25.9	27.8	64.5	40.2
Officers' Compensation 20	1.3	20.5	7.5	3.1	6.7	4.4	4.3	2.3	3.6	1.2	2.4	1.5	0.9
Operating Margin 21	•	•	•	•	•	•	2.0	•	•	•	•	•	•
Operating Margin Before Officers' Comp. 22	•	•	2.1	•	•	•	6.3	•	•	•	•	•	•

Selected Average Balance Sheet ($ in Thousands)

Net Receivables 23	2706	0	22	286	650	621	2012	2637	5963	15980	24838	67174	1052641
Inventories 24	206	0	0	2	48	10	399	627	285	2968	1150	318	85024
Net Property, Plant and Equipment 25	5005	0	25	112	466	1557	3607	4336	10878	27617	83056	109928	2007026
Total Assets 26	36108	0	91	704	2143	6866	15407	35170	70308	161356	359722	1262393	14069317
Notes and Loans Payable 27	15447	0	127	642	2130	5199	6277	9894	39162	54973	231422	547239	5839498
All Other Liabilities 28	8414	0	18	954	449	2719	2835	9336	17525	51152	67767	448721	2883727
Net Worth 29	12247	0	-55	-892	-436	-1051	6295	15940	13622	55230	60533	266433	5346092

Selected Financial Ratios (Times to 1)

Current Ratio 30	1.2	•	2.0	0.4	1.8	1.1	1.6	1.3	0.7	1.2	0.8	2.3	1.1
Quick Ratio 31	0.9	•	1.9	0.4	1.6	1.0	1.2	0.9	0.5	0.9	0.6	2.1	0.8
Net Sales to Working Capital 32	14.2	•	9.6	•	5.4	17.7	5.7	7.9	•	13.5	•	2.9	21.2
Coverage Ratio 33	1.1	•	•	3.2	•	2.3	3.6	0.4	1.5	1.6	0.7	•	2.0
Total Asset Turnover 34	0.4	•	2.1	2.1	1.4	0.7	0.7	0.5	0.4	0.5	0.4	0.2	0.4
Inventory Turnover 35	17.9	•	•	26.7	22.0	207.6	6.4	5.0	10.0	12.9	15.4	113.5	17.9
Receivables Turnover 36	5.1	•	8.9	7.2	5.3	7.9	5.1	7.0	5.1	5.2	4.4	5.2	5.0
Total Liabilities to Net Worth 37	1.9	•	•	•	•	•	1.4	1.2	4.2	1.9	4.9	3.7	1.6
Current Assets to Working Capital 38	6.0	•	2.0	•	2.2	12.6	2.6	4.3	•	6.6	•	1.8	8.4
Current Liabilities to Working Capital 39	5.0	•	1.0	•	1.2	11.6	1.6	3.3	•	5.6	•	0.8	7.4
Working Capital to Net Sales 40	0.1	•	0.1	•	0.2	0.2	0.1	0.2	0.1	0.1	•	0.3	0.0
Inventory to Working Capital 41	0.2	•	•	•	0.1	0.0	0.2	0.3	•	0.5	•	0.0	0.2
Total Receipts to Cash Flow 42	2.7	•	4.4	2.5	4.3	5.0	3.3	2.6	3.6	4.6	5.1	3.6	2.4
Cost of Goods to Cash Flow 43	0.7	•	1.0	0.1	1.6	2.1	0.7	0.5	0.3	2.1	0.7	0.4	0.7
Cash Flow to Total Debt 44	0.2	•	0.3	0.4	0.3	0.1	0.4	0.3	0.2	0.2	0.1	0.1	0.2

Selected Financial Factors (in Percentages)

Debt Ratio 45	66.1	•	160.2	226.7	120.4	115.3	59.1	54.7	80.6	65.8	83.2	78.9	62.0
Return on Total Assets 46	2.9	•	13.8	•	4.3	6.7	0.7	8.5	4.8	3.3	•	•	4.1
Return on Equity Before Income Taxes 47	1.1	•	34.1	•	36.4	11.9	•	15.5	5.3	•	•	•	5.3
Return on Equity After Income Taxes 48	•	•	36.3	•	39.5	9.1	•	9.4	3.5	•	•	•	3.2
Profit Margin (Before Income Tax) 49	1.0	•	•	4.5	3.3	6.6	•	6.9	3.5	•	•	•	5.4
Profit Margin (After Income Tax) 50	•	•	•	3.8	2.1	5.0	•	4.2	2.3	•	•	•	3.2

Table II

Corporations with Net Income

BROADCASTING (EXCEPT INTERNET)

MONEY AMOUNTS AND SIZE OF ASSETS IN THOUSANDS OF DOLLARS

Item Description for Accounting Period 7/04 Through 6/05	Total	Zero Assets	Under 500	500 to 1,000	1,000 to 5,000	5,000 to 10,000	10,000 to 25,000	25,000 to 50,000	50,000 to 100,000	100,000 to 250,000	250,000 to 500,000	500,000 to 2,500,000	2,500,000 and over
Number of Enterprises **1**	3759	909	2144	215	243	102	66	23	16	19	0	12	9
Revenues ($ in Thousands)													
Net Sales **2**	74053963	27321	510298	481187	1112926	789545	988680	483634	633189	1366108	0	4333673	63327402
Interest **3**	1333005	27	0	23	1202	2370	2280	1417	1867	52396	0	28617	1242805
Rents **4**	366070	0	0	0	2087	2281	1948	309	319	13245	0	4717	341163
Royalties **5**	2953334	0	0	0	0	3	0	0	96	0	0	201207	2752027
Other Portfolio Income **6**	2588859	9984	5	0	567	34684	28022	9200	78541	160083	0	505991	1762783
Other Receipts **7**	2076989	159	2676	127317	120079	4421	13876	24945	15196	18351	0	51777	1698194
Total Receipts **8**	83373220	37491	512979	608527	1236861	833304	1034806	519505	729208	1610183	0	5125982	71124374
Average Total Receipts **9**	22180	41	239	2830	5090	8170	15679	22587	45576	84746	•	427165	7902708
Operating Costs/Operating Income (%)													
Cost of Operations **10**	29.7	8.4	31.4	0.1	42.6	44.5	21.4	25.7	10.9	14.7	•	16.2	31.1
Salaries and Wages **11**	12.6	0.4	20.9	45.3	14.7	9.5	20.0	12.5	23.8	17.5	•	19.9	11.5
Taxes Paid **12**	2.4	0.4	2.4	5.0	3.4	2.1	3.9	2.6	3.1	3.6	•	4.9	2.1
Interest Paid **13**	4.5	•	1.6	1.5	0.9	1.8	1.9	2.0	2.6	6.0	•	7.2	4.5
Depreciation **14**	4.0	0.7	1.7	2.2	1.1	4.2	4.0	5.1	4.6	9.0	•	5.3	3.9
Amortization and Depletion **15**	6.9	•	•	0.1	0.1	3.9	3.1	2.3	9.2	4.2	•	10.9	7.0
Pensions and Other Deferred Comp. **16**	0.4	•	0.0	0.5	0.5	0.1	1.0	0.2	0.6	0.6	•	0.3	0.4
Employee Benefits **17**	1.9	0.0	0.5	0.6	2.2	0.5	1.3	1.0	1.6	1.9	•	1.3	2.0
Advertising **18**	2.2	0.2	0.7	1.4	0.6	5.8	1.8	1.8	3.2	1.8	•	2.8	2.2
Other Expenses **19**	37.8	72.7	27.8	42.7	25.1	15.4	27.2	34.5	26.6	34.4	•	26.9	39.5
Officers' Compensation **20**	1.2	21.4	4.9	4.3	8.6	2.3	3.9	1.9	2.9	2.3	•	1.0	0.9
Operating Margin **21**	•	•	8.1	•	0.4	10.1	10.3	10.4	11.1	3.9	•	3.3	•
Operating Margin Before Officers' Comp. **22**	•	17.2	13.0	1.1	9.0	12.3	14.2	12.3	13.9	6.2	•	4.4	•

Selected Average Balance Sheet ($ in Thousands)

Net Receivables 23	3581	0	33	570	660	953	2673	2748	7165	16871	63911	1288396
Inventories 24	303	0	0	0	24	13	158	1020	472	5648	92	108591
Net Property, Plant and Equipment 25	6102	0	12	23	195	2181	3188	4027	12228	33740	68170	2297776
Total Assets 26	49587	0	98	807	1477	6430	15586	34270	68681	174762	1272902	18165286
Notes and Loans Payable 27	17552	0	71	298	1865	4289	5660	7734	33840	53307	309662	6560838
All Other Liabilities 28	10146	0	7	2097	379	3330	2760	5581	13713	38261	298558	3600266
Net Worth 29	21889	0	20	-1588	-767	-1189	7166	20955	21128	83194	664683	8004181

Selected Financial Ratios (Times to 1)

Current Ratio 30	1.3	•	7.9	0.4	3.5	0.7	1.9	2.6	0.6	2.2	3.9	1.2
Quick Ratio 31	0.9	•	7.6	0.4	3.2	0.6	1.4	1.7	0.4	1.6	3.6	0.8
Net Sales to Working Capital 32	13.5	•	4.3	•	4.1	•	4.9	2.9	•	2.8	2.3	21.4
Coverage Ratio 33	3.0	•	6.4	16.9	14.0	9.6	8.9	10.0	11.3	4.6	4.0	2.7
Total Asset Turnover 34	0.4	•	2.4	2.8	3.1	1.2	1.0	0.6	0.6	0.4	0.3	0.4
Inventory Turnover 35	19.3	•	•	•	80.4	271.4	20.2	5.3	9.1	1.9	634.5	20.2
Receivables Turnover 36	6.0	•	7.8	5.6	6.9	7.8	5.3	8.2	7.5	5.6	6.8	5.9
Total Liabilities to Net Worth 37	1.3	•	4.0	•	•	•	1.2	0.6	2.3	1.1	0.9	1.3
Current Assets to Working Capital 38	4.9	•	1.1	•	1.4	•	2.1	1.6	•	1.8	1.3	7.2
Current Liabilities to Working Capital 39	3.9	•	0.1	•	0.4	•	1.1	0.6	•	0.8	0.3	6.2
Working Capital to Net Sales 40	0.1	•	0.2	•	0.2	•	0.2	0.3	•	0.4	0.4	0.0
Inventory to Working Capital 41	0.2	•	•	•	0.0	•	0.1	0.1	•	0.2	0.0	0.3
Total Receipts to Cash Flow 42	2.3	1.6	3.2	1.6	2.9	3.8	2.7	2.0	2.6	2.4	2.3	2.3
Cost of Goods to Cash Flow 43	0.7	0.1	1.0	0.0	1.2	1.7	0.6	0.5	0.3	0.4	0.4	0.7
Cash Flow to Total Debt 44	0.3	•	0.9	0.6	0.7	0.3	0.7	0.8	0.3	0.3	0.3	0.3

Selected Financial Factors (in Percentages)

Debt Ratio 45	55.9	•	79.8	296.8	151.9	118.5	54.0	38.9	69.2	52.4	47.8	55.9
Return on Total Assets 46	5.4	•	24.7	68.6	38.4	21.0	16.2	12.1	16.6	11.3	8.1	4.7
Return on Equity Before Income Taxes 47	8.3	•	103.2	•	•	•	31.2	17.8	49.1	18.6	11.6	6.6
Return on Equity After Income Taxes 48	6.2	•	92.7	•	•	•	27.8	15.0	42.3	15.4	9.9	4.6
Profit Margin (Before Income Tax) 49	9.2	33.0	8.6	23.3	11.5	15.6	14.9	17.7	26.2	21.5	21.3	7.5
Profit Margin (After Income Tax) 50	6.9	33.0	7.7	21.8	10.7	14.3	13.3	15.0	22.6	17.9	18.3	5.2

Table I

Corporations with and without Net Income

INTERNET PUBLISHING AND BROADCASTING

MONEY AMOUNTS AND SIZE OF ASSETS IN THOUSANDS OF DOLLARS

Item Description for Accounting Period 7/04 Through 6/05	Total	Zero Assets	Under 500	500 to 1,000	1,000 to 5,000	5,000 to 10,000	10,000 to 25,000	25,000 to 50,000	50,000 to 100,000	100,000 to 250,000	250,000 to 500,000	500,000 to 2,500,000	2,500,000 and over
Number of Enterprises 1	4163	864	3118	47	55	38	15	10	7	7	3	0	0
Revenues ($ in Thousands)													
Net Sales 2	9668757	50781	275184	22880	376386	348861	232732	480450	280677	487151	7113654	0	0
Interest 3	14469	668	1	6	334	911	603	3348	1444	2181	4973	0	0
Rents 4	37534	0	0	0	333	1240	46	0	0	0	35915	0	0
Royalties 5	104826	0	49	0	0	0	4862	1824	229	0	97861	0	0
Other Portfolio Income 6	273039	0	1	0	0	72	17	11	60	75	272804	0	0
Other Receipts 7	103024	2808	441	2843	671	1698	4080	1974	48465	-1342	41387	0	0
Total Receipts 8	10201649	54257	275676	25729	377724	352782	242340	487607	330875	488065	7566594	0	0
Average Total Receipts 9	2451	63	88	547	6868	9284	16156	48761	47268	69724	2522198	•	•
Operating Costs/Operating Income (%)													
Cost of Operations 10	24.1	•	16.9	•	38.5	42.8	24.3	47.0	31.0	21.4	21.4	•	•
Salaries and Wages 11	22.9	51.5	29.8	126.2	21.9	27.2	25.4	20.1	28.4	32.6	21.2	•	•
Taxes Paid 12	3.0	5.0	3.0	18.6	2.4	4.4	2.6	1.2	4.5	4.4	2.8	•	•
Interest Paid 13	5.9	0.1	4.5	•	0.8	0.3	1.5	0.5	0.6	1.9	7.5	•	•
Depreciation 14	6.0	0.2	2.9	8.7	0.8	3.7	2.5	3.5	5.3	8.7	6.6	•	•
Amortization and Depletion 15	3.6	5.9	0.1	3.4	1.1	2.7	0.6	1.3	3.8	6.6	3.9	•	•
Pensions and Other Deferred Comp. 16	0.7	0.0	•	•	0.0	0.1	0.1	0.0	1.0	0.1	0.9	•	•
Employee Benefits 17	2.0	•	3.3	6.5	1.5	3.1	1.8	1.1	1.7	2.6	2.0	•	•
Advertising 18	1.2	1.9	1.2	6.1	2.4	5.8	5.2	1.5	1.1	2.1	0.6	•	•
Other Expenses 19	27.6	122.0	46.6	112.0	25.9	22.0	19.7	25.6	39.0	24.7	26.4	•	•
Officers' Compensation 20	2.1	•	6.8	10.3	4.2	10.7	5.0	2.5	3.1	2.5	1.1	•	•
Operating Margin 21	1.0	•	•	•	0.4	•	11.3	•	•	•	5.5	•	•
Operating Margin Before Officers' Comp. 22	3.1	•	•	•	4.6	•	16.3	•	•	•	6.6	•	•

Selected Average Balance Sheet ($ in Thousands)

Net Receivables 23	433	0	13	57	889	1025	2670	7382	24171	18850	418529
Inventories 24	34	0	0	0	80	65	357	221	54	680	80803
Net Property, Plant and Equipment 25	358	0	17	101	135	413	1090	4577	2846	7191	425430
Total Assets 26	4500	0	56	828	3291	6378	14596	36109	72548	128707	5369458
Notes and Loans Payable 27	1513	0	41	2	1222	284	3463	3527	3789	17698	1951744
All Other Liabilities 28	1260	0	16	1020	1307	2748	3749	19243	18502	41604	1433247
Net Worth 29	1727	0	-1	-193	762	3346	7384	13339	50258	69405	1984468

Selected Financial Ratios (Times to 1)

Current Ratio 30	1.1		0.6	0.3	1.8	1.6	2.1	1.6	3.6	1.7	0.9
Quick Ratio 31	0.9		0.6	0.3	1.5	1.5	1.8	1.3	3.1	1.3	0.7
Net Sales to Working Capital 32	20.5				6.0	5.3	3.2	6.6	1.1	3.0	
Coverage Ratio 33	2.1				2.0		11.3				2.6
Total Asset Turnover 34	0.5		1.6	0.6	2.1	1.4	1.1	1.3	0.6	0.5	0.4
Inventory Turnover 35	16.5		100.9		32.8	60.4	10.6	102.3	231.7	21.9	6.3
Receivables Turnover 36	8.4		10.0	3.1	9.1	10.3	5.3	8.0	2.0	2.8	6.3
Total Liabilities to Net Worth 37	1.6				3.3	0.9	1.0	1.7	0.4	0.9	1.7
Current Assets to Working Capital 38	8.0				2.2	2.6	1.9	2.8	1.4	2.5	
Current Liabilities to Working Capital 39	7.0				1.2	1.6	0.9	1.8	0.4	1.5	
Working Capital to Net Sales 40	0.0				0.2	0.2	0.3	0.2	0.9	0.3	
Inventory to Working Capital 41	0.6				0.1	0.0	0.1	0.0	0.0	0.0	
Total Receipts to Cash Flow 42	3.5	3.3	3.9		4.1		3.2	5.0	2.9	7.6	3.1
Cost of Goods to Cash Flow 43	0.9		0.7		1.6		0.8	2.3	0.9	1.6	0.7
Cash Flow to Total Debt 44	0.2		0.4		0.7		0.7	0.4	0.6	0.2	0.2

Selected Financial Factors (in Percentages)

Debt Ratio 45	61.6		102.2	123.4	76.8	47.5	49.4	63.1	30.7	46.1	63.0
Return on Total Assets 46	6.4				3.3		18.0				8.5
Return on Equity Before Income Taxes 47	8.7		1059.1	451.7	7.1		32.4				14.1
Return on Equity After Income Taxes 48	4.6		1059.6	451.7			29.9				9.5
Profit Margin (Before Income Tax) 49	6.5			0.8			15.4				11.8
Profit Margin (After Income Tax) 50	3.4						14.3				7.9

Table II

Corporations with Net Income

INTERNET PUBLISHING AND BROADCASTING

MONEY AMOUNTS AND SIZE OF ASSETS IN THOUSANDS OF DOLLARS

Item Description for Accounting Period 7/04 Through 6/05	Total	Zero Assets	Under 500	500 to 1,000	1,000 to 5,000	5,000 to 10,000	10,000 to 25,000	25,000 to 50,000	50,000 to 100,000	100,000 to 250,000	250,000 to 500,000	500,000 to 2,500,000	2,500,000 and over
Number of Enterprises **1**	2311	389	1853	0	47	4	9	6	0	4	0	0	0
Revenues ($ in Thousands)													
Net Sales **2**	8452052	1748	141768	0	357848	94183	145620	493542	0	7217342	0	0	0
Interest **3**	8737	0	3	0	127	173	316	3096	0	5021	0	0	0
Rents **4**	36294	0	0	0	333	0	46	0	0	35915	0	0	0
Royalties **5**	102724	0	0	0	0	0	4862	0	0	97861	0	0	0
Other Portfolio Income **6**	272887	0	0	0	0	72	0	10	0	272804	0	0	0
Other Receipts **7**	43294	0	30	0	23	400	313	891	0	41641	0	0	0
Total Receipts **8**	8915988	1748	141801	0	358331	94828	151157	497539	0	7670584	0	0	0
Average Total Receipts **9**	3858	4	77	•	7624	23707	16795	82923	•	1917646	•	•	•
Operating Costs/Operating Income (%)													
Cost of Operations **10**	24.8	•	30.7	•	39.1	38.9	27.1	57.2	•	21.5	•	•	•
Salaries and Wages **11**	20.4	•	13.3	•	18.9	11.4	15.9	12.9	•	21.3	•	•	•
Taxes Paid **12**	2.7	•	1.8	•	2.2	1.6	2.3	1.3	•	2.8	•	•	•
Interest Paid **13**	6.5	•	0.7	•	0.7	0.0	1.3	0.3	•	7.5	•	•	•
Depreciation **14**	5.8	•	0.7	•	0.6	0.7	1.9	1.8	•	6.6	•	•	•
Amortization and Depletion **15**	3.4	•	0.0	•	0.8	0.1	0.3	0.4	•	3.9	•	•	•
Pensions and Other Deferred Comp. **16**	0.8	•	•	•	0.0	0.1	0.0	0.0	•	0.9	•	•	•
Employee Benefits **17**	1.8	•	0.6	•	1.2	0.5	1.1	0.5	•	2.0	•	•	•
Advertising **18**	0.8	25.8	0.8	•	2.4	4.8	1.5	0.8	•	0.6	•	•	•
Other Expenses **19**	25.0	•	32.5	•	18.5	9.3	13.4	15.3	•	26.3	•	•	•
Officers' Compensation **20**	1.5	•	8.9	•	3.5	9.8	4.2	1.0	•	1.2	•	•	•
Operating Margin **21**	6.7	74.2	9.9	•	12.0	22.7	31.1	8.4	•	5.5	•	•	•
Operating Margin Before Officers' Comp. **22**	8.2	74.2	18.7	•	15.5	32.5	35.2	9.4	•	6.7	•	•	•

Selected Average Balance Sheet ($ in Thousands)

Net Receivables 23	637	0	2	•	941	997	2771	13784	•	328234
Inventories 24	57	0	0	•	182	2	98	15	•	60608
Net Property, Plant and Equipment 25	578	0	10	•	101	186	1055	2270	•	322505
Total Assets 26	7187	0	20	•	3281	6497	13111	46376	•	3999112
Notes and Loans Payable 27	2606	0	10	•	1235	2	2973	2020	•	1477134
All Other Liabilities 28	2033	0	4	•	982	2900	2482	26829	•	1112414
Net Worth 29	2548	0	6	•	1064	3595	7656	17526	•	1409563

Selected Financial Ratios (Times to 1)

Current Ratio 30	1.0	•	1.6	•	2.3	2.2	2.4	1.9	•	0.9
Quick Ratio 31	0.8	•	1.6	•	1.9	1.9	2.0	1.5	•	0.7
Net Sales to Working Capital 32	885.0	•	32.6	•	5.5	7.3	3.0	5.3	•	•
Coverage Ratio 33	2.9	•	14.3	•	18.3	1469.1	28.1	32.3	•	2.6
Total Asset Turnover 34	0.5	•	3.9	•	2.3	3.6	1.2	1.8	•	0.5
Inventory Turnover 35	15.9	•	102.5	•	16.4	4583.4	45.0	3189.9	•	6.4
Receivables Turnover 36	9.2	•	41.6	•	15.4	13.7	6.0	9.5	•	•
Total Liabilities to Net Worth 37	1.8	•	2.0	•	2.1	0.8	0.7	1.6	•	1.8
Current Assets to Working Capital 38	287.9	•	2.5	•	1.8	1.8	1.7	2.1	•	•
Current Liabilities to Working Capital 39	286.9	•	1.5	•	0.8	0.8	0.7	1.1	•	•
Working Capital to Net Sales 40	0.0	•	0.0	•	0.2	0.1	0.3	0.2	•	•
Inventory to Working Capital 41	26.5	•	0.1	•	0.1	•	0.0	0.0	•	•
Total Receipts to Cash Flow 42	3.2	1.3	2.4	•	3.5	3.1	2.2	4.3	•	3.2
Cost of Goods to Cash Flow 43	0.8	•	0.7	•	1.4	1.2	0.6	2.5	•	0.7
Cash Flow to Total Debt 44	0.2	•	2.4	•	1.0	2.6	1.4	0.7	•	0.2

Selected Financial Factors (in Percentages)

Debt Ratio 45	64.5	•	67.2	•	67.6	44.7	41.6	62.2	•	64.8
Return on Total Assets 46	9.5	•	41.6	•	29.8	84.8	44.6	16.8	•	8.7
Return on Equity Before Income Taxes 47	17.4	•	118.0	•	87.0	153.1	73.7	43.2	•	15.0
Return on Equity After Income Taxes 48	12.3	•	117.8	•	74.2	115.4	69.8	36.1	•	10.1
Profit Margin (Before Income Tax) 49	12.1	74.3	9.9	•	12.2	23.4	34.9	9.2	•	11.7
Profit Margin (After Income Tax) 50	8.6	74.3	9.9	•	10.4	17.6	33.0	7.7	•	7.9

Table I

Corporations with and without Net Income

TELECOMMUNICATIONS

MONEY AMOUNTS AND SIZE OF ASSETS IN THOUSANDS OF DOLLARS

Item Description for Accounting Period 7/04 Through 6/05	Total	Zero Assets	Under 500	500 to 1,000	1,000 to 5,000	5,000 to 10,000	10,000 to 25,000	25,000 to 50,000	50,000 to 100,000	100,000 to 250,000	250,000 to 500,000	500,000 to 2,500,000	2,500,000 and over
Number of Enterprises **1**	18655	4033	11114	945	1306	333	404	203	116	84	35	46	36
Revenues ($ in Thousands)													
Net Sales **2**	375460410	7393495	6386877	1336088	6374925	3941324	5252095	4965347	6031048	9583898	6948130	21294179	295953005
Interest **3**	12741077	75336	1375	1746	8728	8222	27919	25596	37702	82436	59888	236424	12175707
Rents **4**	10194457	0	0	2581	2757	3206	6526	8475	9113	28304	20544	41396	10071554
Royalties **5**	1503048	12384	0	0	5627	0	346	2514	5371	4	13688	1770	1461345
Other Portfolio Income **6**	9966954	75893	972	6	38881	55383	98761	98200	120237	70185	151997	1756669	7499770
Other Receipts **7**	13500910	234489	133262	19998	84942	38402	297479	262615	95241	261959	175263	449562	11447695
Total Receipts **8**	423366856	7791597	6522486	1360419	6515860	4046537	5683126	5362747	6298712	10026786	7369510	23780000	338609076
Average Total Receipts **9**	22695	1932	587	1440	4989	12152	14067	26417	54299	119366	210557	516957	9405808
Operating Costs/Operating Income (%)													
Cost of Operations **10**	22.7	5.2	61.3	38.5	66.3	64.6	52.1	40.1	43.7	48.2	37.2	41.8	16.9
Salaries and Wages **11**	14.3	15.4	8.5	14.7	12.2	12.8	11.4	11.9	14.6	13.3	14.5	14.1	14.6
Taxes Paid **12**	3.0	2.6	1.4	4.2	2.0	1.7	2.5	2.6	2.5	2.0	2.6	2.3	3.2
Interest Paid **13**	8.8	14.3	1.1	3.8	0.8	0.7	2.5	3.4	3.6	3.1	5.6	18.1	9.1
Depreciation **14**	16.8	27.0	1.4	3.1	3.9	5.2	9.3	12.7	14.5	10.0	18.3	18.6	17.6
Amortization and Depletion **15**	1.7	4.1	0.2	0.9	0.7	0.6	1.0	1.9	1.8	1.5	1.7	2.6	1.6
Pensions and Other Deferred Comp. **16**	1.2	0.9	0.9	0.0	0.1	0.2	0.3	0.3	0.1	0.3	0.6	0.3	1.4
Employee Benefits **17**	2.6	1.3	0.4	2.7	1.1	0.5	1.0	1.1	1.4	1.4	1.9	1.9	2.9
Advertising **18**	2.2	1.9	1.6	0.8	1.0	0.6	1.1	1.0	1.8	1.2	1.9	3.1	2.2
Other Expenses **19**	42.4	109.1	17.1	32.3	15.5	17.6	27.8	33.7	27.8	24.8	28.6	27.5	44.9
Officers' Compensation **20**	0.6	0.7	7.2	5.2	3.2	2.6	2.1	1.7	1.2	1.0	1.3	0.8	0.2
Operating Margin **21**	•	•	•	•	•	•	•	•	•	•	•	•	•
Operating Margin Before Officers' Comp. **22**	6.2	•	•	•	•	•	•	•	•	•	•	•	•

Selected Average Balance Sheet ($ in Thousands)

Net Receivables 23	6049	0	8	121	450	1360	1958	3804	7992	21327	36797	111005	2803686
Inventories 24	323	0	5	20	93	140	434	715	1363	2889	3392	12973	120971
Net Property, Plant and Equipment 25	15283	0	24	112	797	2378	5463	13411	27541	48844	133247	314581	6987465
Total Assets 26	65057	0	87	736	2340	7227	15872	35323	70708	151704	357127	1179248	30700818
Notes and Loans Payable 27	20506	0	107	610	965	3172	5093	12112	24862	58778	138794	516932	9374324
All Other Liabilities 28	19000	0	139	382	1085	3123	4435	10501	19256	40854	78965	346610	8933371
Net Worth 29	25551	0	-158	-257	290	932	6345	12710	26590	52071	139369	315706	12388123

Selected Financial Ratios (Times to 1)

Current Ratio 30	0.9	·	1.0	1.1	1.1	1.2	1.5	1.5	1.1	1.4	1.6	1.0	0.9
Quick Ratio 31	0.7	·	0.8	0.6	0.8	0.9	1.1	1.1	0.8	1.1	1.2	0.8	0.7
Net Sales to Working Capital 32	·	·	1672.0	40.8	67.7	21.4	6.8	6.3	20.4	6.6	5.1	·	·
Coverage Ratio 33	0.6	·	2.0	·	·	·	·	0.3	·	0.4	·	·	1.0
Total Asset Turnover 34	0.3	·	6.6	1.9	2.1	1.6	0.8	0.7	0.7	0.8	0.6	0.4	0.3
Inventory Turnover 35	14.1	·	71.0	27.8	34.6	54.5	15.6	13.7	16.7	19.1	21.8	14.9	11.5
Receivables Turnover 36	3.9	·	52.0	14.6	10.1	10.0	6.3	6.5	6.0	5.1	4.7	4.0	3.5
Total Liabilities to Net Worth 37	1.5	·	·	7.1	6.8	1.5	1.8	1.7	1.9	1.6	2.7	1.5	1.5
Current Assets to Working Capital 38	·	·	144.7	14.5	15.8	6.8	3.2	3.1	9.3	3.3	2.6	·	·
Current Liabilities to Working Capital 39	·	·	143.7	13.5	14.8	5.8	2.2	2.1	8.3	2.3	1.6	·	·
Working Capital to Net Sales 40	·	·	0.0	0.0	0.0	0.0	0.1	0.2	0.0	0.2	0.2	·	·
Inventory to Working Capital 41	·	·	14.2	0.8	1.5	0.3	0.2	0.2	0.6	0.2	0.1	·	·
Total Receipts to Cash Flow 42	3.3	15.5	8.2	4.3	16.4	11.2	5.5	3.9	9.7	5.7	8.1	·	2.8
Cost of Goods to Cash Flow 43	0.7	0.8	5.0	1.6	10.9	7.2	2.8	1.6	4.3	2.8	3.0	·	0.5
Cash Flow to Total Debt 44	0.2	·	0.3	0.3	0.1	0.2	0.3	0.3	0.1	0.2	0.1	·	0.2

Selected Financial Factors (in Percentages)

Debt Ratio 45	60.7	·	281.5	134.9	87.6	87.1	60.0	64.0	62.4	65.7	61.0	73.2	59.6
Return on Total Assets 46	1.7	15.0	·	·	·	·	·	0.7	·	0.8	·	·	2.4
Return on Equity Before Income Taxes 47	·	24.7	·	·	·	·	·	·	·	·	·	·	·
Return on Equity After Income Taxes 48	·	25.4	·	·	·	·	·	·	·	·	·	·	·
Profit Margin (Before Income Tax) 49	1.1	1.1	·	·	·	·	·	·	·	·	·	·	·
Profit Margin (After Income Tax) 50	·	1.1	·	·	·	·	·	·	·	·	·	·	·

Table II

Corporations with Net Income

TELECOMMUNICATIONS

MONEY AMOUNTS AND SIZE OF ASSETS IN THOUSANDS OF DOLLARS

Item Description for Accounting Period 7/04 Through 6/05	Total	Zero Assets	Under 500	500 to 1,000	1,000 to 5,000	5,000 to 10,000	10,000 to 25,000	25,000 to 50,000	50,000 to 100,000	100,000 to 250,000	250,000 to 500,000	500,000 to 2,500,000	2,500,000 and over
Number of Enterprises 1	8340	988	5536	514	634	175	234	117	59	42	9	17	15
Revenues ($ in Thousands)													
Net Sales 2	209755642	535285	3374748	807469	4578993	1345187	3381298	2600115	2759160	4994370	1771495	6416055	177191466
Interest 3	8000178	1247	444	428	5561	5617	19130	13320	17433	25256	14049	37547	7860146
Rents 4	8644509	0	0	0	1921	3180	5756	5052	7610	16152	11414	37100	8556325
Royalties 5	1423308	12384	0	0	5627	0	346	0	0	4	10972	0	1393976
Other Portfolio Income 6	5531623	19890	972	6	36481	55143	89959	87445	107994	52913	88939	478007	4513875
Other Receipts 7	9214443	155909	20118	2108	79787	28285	224485	124680	83190	62305	99860	194506	8139209
Total Receipts 8	242569703	724715	3396282	810011	4708370	1437412	3720974	2830612	2975387	5151000	1996729	7163215	207654997
Average Total Receipts 9	29085	734	613	1576	7426	8214	15902	24193	50430	122643	221859	421366	13843666
Operating Costs/Operating Income (%)													
Cost of Operations 10	14.3	14.3	41.2	26.4	65.4	48.1	49.7	31.3	41.4	47.5	25.5	34.7	9.1
Salaries and Wages 11	15.5	22.4	13.3	14.2	9.6	7.5	8.3	9.0	7.3	11.0	15.6	10.7	16.4
Taxes Paid 12	3.4	3.6	2.0	5.1	1.6	2.2	2.5	2.8	2.3	2.1	3.3	1.9	3.6
Interest Paid 13	7.2	1.7	0.6	0.5	0.5	0.8	1.8	2.7	2.6	1.9	4.1	10.0	7.9
Depreciation 14	14.9	15.9	0.8	2.6	3.1	7.2	7.4	12.3	10.8	9.1	14.1	12.2	16.0
Amortization and Depletion 15	0.8	4.1	0.3	0.3	0.1	0.7	0.4	1.2	1.0	0.8	2.3	2.6	0.8
Pensions and Other Deferred Comp. 16	1.7	0.1	1.1	0.0	0.1	0.5	0.3	0.3	0.2	0.3	0.7	0.2	2.0
Employee Benefits 17	2.8	2.2	0.4	1.7	1.0	0.5	0.7	0.9	1.1	1.2	2.2	1.9	3.1
Advertising 18	1.7	0.3	2.7	0.5	1.2	0.3	1.2	0.7	1.2	0.8	1.7	2.1	1.8
Other Expenses 19	44.4	42.3	16.1	23.6	12.8	24.5	25.0	31.9	26.5	18.2	27.5	24.4	48.5
Officers' Compensation 20	0.5	4.7	10.6	2.2	3.1	2.2	1.9	1.8	1.2	0.9	1.2	0.8	0.2
Operating Margin 21	•	•	10.9	23.0	1.4	5.5	1.0	5.2	4.4	6.1	1.8	•	•
Operating Margin Before Officers' Comp. 22	•	•	21.5	25.2	4.5	7.6	2.9	7.0	5.6	7.1	3.0	•	•

Selected Average Balance Sheet ($ in Thousands)

Net Receivables 23	10438	0	10	98	519	922	2004	2965	6882	16651	28547	130284	5471008
Inventories 24	384	0	4	16	129	114	395	507	1500	3070	1496	15000	162389
Net Property, Plant and Equipment 25	22396	0	11	105	1088	2746	6029	14055	27465	49415	107335	209085	11615297
Total Assets 26	92986	0	84	787	2808	7345	16319	35351	70604	151761	333128	1159424	48691316
Notes and Loans Payable 27	26632	0	72	136	746	1502	3655	10684	17296	36352	85191	486773	13814215
All Other Liabilities 28	27850	0	21	317	901	1643	3254	5975	14652	33083	87061	346786	14715514
Net Worth 29	38505	0	-9	333	1161	4200	9409	18692	38656	82326	160876	325864	20161587

Selected Financial Ratios (Times to 1)

Current Ratio 30	0.9	•	2.6	1.9	1.5	2.4	2.0	1.8	1.7	2.4	1.5	0.9	0.8
Quick Ratio 31	0.7	•	2.4	0.7	1.1	1.7	1.5	1.3	1.3	1.4	1.2	0.7	0.7
Net Sales to Working Capital 32	•	•	19.3	5.3	15.7	4.1	4.6	4.6	5.0	3.5	8.7	•	•
Coverage Ratio 33	2.2	15.3	20.7	46.2	10.1	16.1	7.2	6.3	5.7	6.1	4.6	2.1	2.0
Total Asset Turnover 34	0.3	•	7.3	2.0	2.6	1.0	0.9	0.6	0.7	0.8	0.6	0.3	0.2
Inventory Turnover 35	9.4	•	67.1	26.5	36.5	32.4	18.2	13.7	12.9	18.4	33.5	8.7	6.6
Receivables Turnover 36	3.1	•	51.0	24.9	12.8	11.1	7.4	8.0	7.1	7.2	6.8	4.2	2.8
Total Liabilities to Net Worth 37	1.4	•	•	1.4	1.4	0.7	0.7	0.9	0.8	0.8	1.1	2.6	1.4
Current Assets to Working Capital 38	•	•	1.6	2.2	3.0	1.7	2.0	2.3	2.4	1.7	3.0	•	•
Current Liabilities to Working Capital 39	•	•	0.6	1.2	2.0	0.7	1.0	1.3	1.4	0.7	2.0	•	•
Working Capital to Net Sales 40	•	•	0.1	0.2	0.1	0.2	0.2	0.2	0.2	0.3	0.1	•	•
Inventory to Working Capital 41	•	•	0.1	0.1	0.3	0.1	0.1	0.1	0.2	0.1	0.1	•	•
Total Receipts to Cash Flow 42	2.2	2.4	4.4	2.4	7.5	3.3	3.3	2.5	3.3	4.1	3.1	4.0	2.0
Cost of Goods to Cash Flow 43	0.3	0.3	1.8	0.6	4.9	1.6	1.7	0.8	1.3	2.0	0.8	1.4	0.2
Cash Flow to Total Debt 44	0.2	•	1.5	1.5	0.6	0.7	0.6	0.5	0.4	0.4	0.4	0.1	0.2

Selected Financial Factors (in Percentages)

Debt Ratio 45	58.6	•	111.1	57.7	58.6	42.8	42.3	47.1	45.2	45.8	51.7	71.9	58.6
Return on Total Assets 46	4.2	•	88.5	47.5	12.1	13.7	11.3	10.5	9.8	8.9	11.1	6.7	3.9
Return on Equity Before Income Taxes 47	5.6	•	•	109.7	26.4	22.4	16.9	16.7	14.7	13.8	17.9	12.2	4.7
Return on Equity After Income Taxes 48	4.2	•	•	108.7	23.4	17.3	13.4	13.3	10.7	11.2	13.1	11.3	3.5
Profit Margin (Before Income Tax) 49	8.5	23.9	11.6	23.3	4.2	12.3	11.0	14.0	12.2	9.5	14.6	10.6	8.1
Profit Margin (After Income Tax) 50	6.4	20.7	11.5	23.1	3.8	9.5	8.7	11.2	8.9	7.7	10.7	9.7	5.9

Table I

Corporations with and without Net Income

INTERNET SERVICE PROVIDERS, WEB PORTALS, AND D.P. SERVICES

MONEY AMOUNTS AND SIZE OF ASSETS IN THOUSANDS OF DOLLARS

Item Description for Accounting Period 7/04 Through 6/05	Total	Zero Assets	Under 500	500 to 1,000	1,000 to 5,000	5,000 to 10,000	10,000 to 25,000	25,000 to 50,000	50,000 to 100,000	100,000 to 250,000	250,000 to 500,000	500,000 to 2,500,000	2,500,000 and over
Number of Enterprises 1	15754	2757	11859	231	650	67	96	29	23	16	8	9	9
Revenues ($ in Thousands)													
Net Sales 2	83627448	709197	3371289	331478	1562671	580771	2298674	1501395	1216848	1459586	1367847	5670373	63557317
Interest 3	4766812	1568	1807	429	1362	4077	7221	5368	8576	8856	9682	57160	4660704
Rents 4	757234	3026	2473	0	21	1383	1468	7	776	2742	12633	283	732422
Royalties 5	10181461	0	0	0	0	0	14531	382	0	11195	0	2835	10152518
Other Portfolio Income 6	1597241	76080	690	908	10103	33408	18643	475	15763	3767	14362	18665	1404377
Other Receipts 7	3640697	43601	15266	978	5507	7406	67329	58462	14704	56028	85943	-935	3286414
Total Receipts 8	104570893	833472	3391525	333793	1579664	627045	2407866	1566089	1256667	1542174	1490467	5748381	83793752
Average Total Receipts 9	6638	302	286	1445	2430	9359	25082	54003	54638	96386	186308	638709	9310417
Operating Costs/Operating Income (%)													
Cost of Operations 10	15.5	35.0	27.8	15.1	33.6	28.9	47.6	51.6	15.8	17.7	17.0	19.5	11.6
Salaries and Wages 11	22.8	36.4	13.5	45.1	26.7	32.3	22.2	16.6	35.9	36.3	33.0	24.9	22.0
Taxes Paid 12	2.8	3.2	2.1	4.4	3.7	3.9	2.7	2.4	4.2	3.6	2.4	2.3	2.8
Interest Paid 13	8.0	0.6	0.6	2.9	2.2	1.1	2.3	1.6	1.7	3.0	1.8	2.5	9.9
Depreciation 14	5.5	3.3	2.9	7.3	6.6	5.0	4.6	4.2	6.4	7.6	5.8	6.4	5.5
Amortization and Depletion 15	6.4	4.1	0.5	2.8	1.8	5.6	2.7	1.1	2.8	2.9	1.2	5.2	7.5
Pensions and Other Deferred Comp. 16	0.6	0.2	0.3	0.0	0.2	0.3	0.4	0.2	0.8	0.4	1.9	0.2	0.7
Employee Benefits 17	2.3	1.5	0.4	3.3	1.4	2.7	2.1	2.5	3.3	2.4	3.0	2.2	2.4
Advertising 18	5.4	4.5	4.1	0.8	5.2	1.8	1.0	4.1	7.0	0.6	0.4	6.8	5.8
Other Expenses 19	53.6	33.9	33.9	35.6	31.2	40.4	24.1	22.4	26.4	43.5	37.3	33.3	55.3
Officers' Compensation 20	1.8	2.0	10.3	4.4	4.8	5.4	4.0	2.0	4.0	1.2	1.6	1.2	1.2
Operating Margin 21	•	•	3.6	•	•	•	•	•	•	•	•	•	•
Operating Margin Before Officers' Comp. 22	•	14.0	•	•	•	•	•	•	•	•	•	•	•

Selected Average Balance Sheet ($ in Thousands)

Net Receivables 23	2103	0	3	108	404	924	2737	5873	7957	13872	53981	78877	3418708
Inventories 24	310	0	1	33	13	62	208	566	373	249	1317	5343	527056
Net Property, Plant and Equipment 25	1083	0	9	94	668	987	2624	5451	7855	24015	55297	140317	1527148
Total Assets 26	19963	0	52	604	1794	7090	16050	35523	70738	157781	296568	950049	32717823
Notes and Loans Payable 27	2463	0	60	741	1413	2237	5688	22758	12382	38026	73820	297219	3498475
All Other Liabilities 28	10222	0	22	615	808	5014	6156	13504	20860	45921	70252	217944	17228592
Net Worth 29	7278	0	-31	-752	-428	-160	4206	-740	37496	73834	152495	434886	11990756

Selected Financial Ratios (Times to 1)

Current Ratio 30	1.1	·	1.0	0.4	0.8	1.1	1.6	1.2	2.2	1.7	1.4	1.1	1.1
Quick Ratio 31	0.5	·	0.6	0.3	0.7	1.0	1.2	0.9	1.8	1.2	1.2	0.9	0.4
Net Sales to Working Capital 32	6.2	·	·	·	·	15.5	6.9	15.5	2.9	3.8	6.0	18.5	5.3
Coverage Ratio 33	1.2	7.7	·	·	·	·	·	·	·	·	2.9	·	1.9
Total Asset Turnover 34	0.3	·	5.5	2.4	1.3	1.2	1.5	1.5	0.7	0.6	0.6	0.7	0.2
Inventory Turnover 35	2.7	·	83.1	6.7	60.5	40.3	54.9	47.3	22.4	64.7	22.0	23.0	1.6
Receivables Turnover 36	2.8	·	63.8	9.1	6.5	8.9	8.6	8.6	7.0	5.6	4.9	7.1	2.3
Total Liabilities to Net Worth 37	1.7	·	·	·	2.8	·	2.8	·	0.9	1.1	0.9	1.2	1.7
Current Assets to Working Capital 38	8.8	·	·	·	8.1	·	2.8	5.7	1.9	2.4	3.3	7.9	9.3
Current Liabilities to Working Capital 39	7.8	·	·	·	7.1	7.1	1.8	4.7	0.9	1.4	2.3	6.9	8.3
Working Capital to Net Sales 40	0.2	·	·	·	·	0.1	0.1	0.1	0.4	0.3	0.2	0.1	0.2
Inventory to Working Capital 41	0.4	·	·	·	·	0.0	0.1	0.2	0.0	0.0	0.1	0.1	0.4
Total Receipts to Cash Flow 42	2.3	·	2.9	21.0	10.4	9.2	9.9	6.5	6.2	4.7	3.8	4.0	1.8
Cost of Goods to Cash Flow 43	0.4	·	0.8	3.2	3.5	2.7	4.7	3.4	1.0	0.8	0.6	0.8	0.6
Cash Flow to Total Debt 44	0.2	·	1.2	0.1	0.1	0.2	0.2	0.2	0.3	0.2	0.3	0.3	0.2

Selected Financial Factors (in Percentages)

Debt Ratio 45	63.5	·	159.3	224.4	123.8	102.3	73.8	102.1	47.0	53.2	48.6	54.2	63.4
Return on Total Assets 46	2.5	·	26.7	·	·	·	·	·	·	·	3.0	·	4.0
Return on Equity Before Income Taxes 47	1.1	·	·	40.3	91.7	1048.4	·	310.2	·	·	·	3.9	5.0
Return on Equity After Income Taxes 48	·	·	·	40.3	93.3	1103.7	·	352.1	·	·	·	0.7	3.7
Profit Margin (Before Income Tax) 49	1.5	4.2	·	·	·	·	·	·	·	·	3.5	·	8.6
Profit Margin (After Income Tax) 50	·	4.1	·	·	·	·	·	·	·	·	3.5	·	6.4

Table II

Corporations with Net Income

INTERNET SERVICE PROVIDERS, WEB PORTALS, AND D.P. SERVICES

MONEY AMOUNTS AND SIZE OF ASSETS IN THOUSANDS OF DOLLARS

Item Description for Accounting Period 7/04 Through 6/05	Total	Zero Assets	Under 500	500 to 1,000	1,000 to 5,000	5,000 to 10,000	10,000 to 25,000	25,000 to 50,000	50,000 to 100,000	100,000 to 250,000	250,000 to 500,000	500,000 to 2,500,000	2,500,000 and over
Number of Enterprises 1	7073	1185	5519	68	192	25	40	14	12	5	0	3	0
Revenues ($ in Thousands)													
Net Sales 2	67624283	352227	2051409	222270	442827	305378	1485187	689504	678685	441250	0	286796	0
Interest 3	1136661	548	149	0	296	2980	2450	1066	2947	760	0	16286	0
Rents 4	457974	43	2473	0	0	0	1188	0	776	13	0	0	0
Royalties 5	10164977	0	0	0	0	0	14190	0	0	10661	0	0	0
Other Portfolio Income 6	1334489	798	662	897	9181	33387	16310	194	14759	885	0	3271	0
Other Receipts 7	3136814	30129	6253	118	4240	6749	48628	441	13721	14572	0	3267	0
Total Receipts 8	83855198	383745	2060946	223285	456544	348494	1567953	691205	710888	468141	0	2883620	0
Average Total Receipts 9	11856	324	373	3284	2378	13940	39199	49372	59241	93628	·	961207	·
Operating Costs/Operating Income (%)													
Cost of Operations 10	10.4	50.3	27.2	20.4	36.4	25.1	52.1	36.4	14.4	23.4	·	21.1	·
Salaries and Wages 11	21.5	17.2	13.2	39.8	18.0	19.1	14.7	19.5	24.8	29.4	·	19.8	·
Taxes Paid 12	2.9	1.7	1.8	3.7	3.2	2.8	2.3	2.4	4.3	2.9	·	1.7	·
Interest Paid 13	3.6	0.1	0.3	2.0	1.0	0.5	0.3	1.6	1.2	1.4	·	0.8	·
Depreciation 14	4.2	1.1	2.3	5.0	4.7	2.1	2.2	3.1	4.4	4.4	·	5.8	·
Amortization and Depletion 15	7.2	0.2	0.0	·	0.6	0.4	0.3	1.1	0.9	2.4	·	5.5	·
Pensions and Other Deferred Comp. 16	0.7	0.4	0.2	0.0	0.1	0.4	0.6	0.2	1.4	0.7	·	0.2	·
Employee Benefits 17	2.3	2.5	0.1	4.1	0.7	1.0	1.7	3.4	2.7	3.9	·	1.5	·
Advertising 18	6.0	0.3	4.2	0.3	5.1	1.3	0.5	1.3	8.2	0.3	·	11.5	·
Other Expenses 19	54.1	18.4	27.4	18.6	14.5	27.4	18.3	21.6	21.6	28.5	·	24.3	·
Officers' Compensation 20	1.2	0.6	7.5	0.2	8.0	4.1	4.2	2.2	6.2	1.0	·	0.4	·
Operating Margin 21	·	7.3	15.8	5.8	7.8	15.9	2.8	7.0	9.8	1.8	·	7.5	·
Operating Margin Before Officers' Comp. 22	·	7.9	23.3	6.1	15.8	19.9	7.0	9.3	16.0	2.8	·	7.9	·

Selected Average Balance Sheet ($ in Thousands)

Net Receivables 23	4030	0	4	221	312	693	3382	5476	5722	10001	83930
Inventories 24	659	0	0	1	6	32	176	175	205	702	1261
Net Property, Plant and Equipment 25	1268	0	11	62	459	480	2072	5319	8534	10354	130375
Total Assets 26	34163	0	61	544	1539	7162	16632	34851	67427	122016	832932
Notes and Loans Payable 27	3846	0	32	970	998	2525	4445	11258	9133	34240	110910
All Other Liabilities 28	15458	0	19	938	263	2682	6529	14919	20596	26540	183029
Net Worth 29	14859	0	10	-1363	279	1954	5658	8674	37698	61236	538992

Selected Financial Ratios (Times to 1)

Current Ratio 30	1.2	•	2.1	0.5	1.4	1.9	1.4	1.1	2.3	1.4	1.9
Quick Ratio 31	0.7	•	1.3	0.3	1.2	1.5	1.2	0.8	1.9	0.8	1.7
Net Sales to Working Capital 32	6.0	•	17.5	•	11.5	6.7	12.3	21.8	3.2	6.7	5.0
Coverage Ratio 33	4.1	184.4	64.3	4.1	12.3	65.2	26.8	5.5	12.7	6.7	10.8
Total Asset Turnover 34	0.3	•	6.1	6.0	1.5	1.7	2.2	1.4	0.8	0.7	1.1
Inventory Turnover 35	1.5	•	406.0	737.2	134.8	95.8	109.9	102.7	39.8	29.5	159.5
Receivables Turnover 36	2.8	•	55.0	11.6	6.7	12.1	10.4	9.6	9.7	3.1	
Total Liabilities to Net Worth 37	1.3	•	5.1	•	4.5	2.7	1.9	3.0	0.8	1.0	0.5
Current Assets to Working Capital 38	5.8	•	1.9	•	3.3	2.1	3.3	8.7	1.8	3.3	2.1
Current Liabilities to Working Capital 39	4.8	•	0.9	•	2.3	1.1	2.3	7.7	0.8	2.3	1.1
Working Capital to Net Sales 40	0.2	•	0.1	0.1	0.1	0.1	0.1	0.0	0.3	0.1	0.2
Inventory to Working Capital 41	0.4	•	0.0	0.0	0.0	•	0.1	0.1	0.0	0.1	0.0
Total Receipts to Cash Flow 42	1.7	3.1	2.4	6.0	5.1	2.3	4.3	3.7	3.3	3.2	3.4
Cost of Goods to Cash Flow 43	0.2	1.6	0.7	1.2	1.9	0.6	2.2	1.4	0.5	0.8	0.7
Cash Flow to Total Debt 44	0.3	•	3.0	0.3	0.4	1.0	0.8	0.5	0.6	0.5	1.0

Selected Financial Factors (in Percentages)

Debt Ratio 45	56.5	•	83.7	350.4	81.9	72.7	66.0	75.1	44.1	49.8	35.3
Return on Total Assets 46	4.2	•	100.4	49.9	17.8	51.9	19.4	12.5	13.2	6.7	10.3
Return on Equity Before Income Taxes 47	7.3	•	606.9	•	90.1	187.3	54.8	41.2	21.7	11.3	14.4
Return on Equity After Income Taxes 48	5.9	•	601.6	•	82.2	175.2	49.8	33.8	20.4	9.1	14.2
Profit Margin (Before Income Tax) 49	11.4	16.2	16.2	6.3	10.9	30.0	8.4	7.3	14.5	7.8	8.2
Profit Margin (After Income Tax) 50	9.2	14.7	16.1	6.3	9.9	28.0	7.6	6.0	13.6	6.3	8.0

Table I

Corporations with and without Net Income

OTHER INFORMATION SERVICES, NEWS SYNDICATES, LIBRARIES

MONEY AMOUNTS AND SIZE OF ASSETS IN THOUSANDS OF DOLLARS

Item Description for Accounting Period 7/04 Through 6/05	Total	Zero Assets	Under 500	500 to 1,000	1,000 to 5,000	5,000 to 10,000	10,000 to 25,000	25,000 to 50,000	50,000 to 100,000	100,000 to 250,000	250,000 to 500,000	500,000 to 2,500,000	2,500,000 and over
Number of Enterprises **1**	8637	649	7224	186	359	91	52	24	14	14	10	14	0
Revenues ($ in Thousands)													
Net Sales **2**	19765154	336815	1476088	202662	888856	1428262	841869	853595	894650	1521326	2329872	8991159	0
Interest **3**	164612	371	377	41	3796	1538	4281	5338	3697	10933	13869	120374	0
Rents **4**	13410	0	1646	0	1954	300	540	136	235	568	0	8031	0
Royalties **5**	106106	0	259	0	2312	0	155	21	2747	5	4430	96177	0
Other Portfolio Income **6**	206328	0	8	3	29323	101	12398	2523	243	1696	15737	144296	0
Other Receipts **7**	705091	2030	28812	-2	17433	1972	29510	11708	35157	28819	-171	549819	0
Total Receipts **8**	20960701	339216	1507190	202704	943674	1432173	888753	873321	936729	1563347	2363737	9909856	0
Average Total Receipts **9**	2427	523	209	1090	2629	15738	17091	36388	66909	111668	236374	707847	•
Operating Costs/Operating Income (%)													
Cost of Operations **10**	22.8	55.1	40.2	0.6	22.4	39.1	22.6	23.5	7.3	18.6	17.6	20.2	•
Salaries and Wages **11**	26.4	11.0	9.7	66.2	32.4	24.6	29.6	25.3	34.4	29.6	29.2	26.2	•
Taxes Paid **12**	3.0	1.5	3.0	5.2	3.8	4.3	3.3	2.9	2.8	2.8	3.4	2.6	•
Interest Paid **13**	2.9	0.0	2.3	2.6	1.1	0.4	1.2	1.5	2.5	1.8	3.1	4.1	•
Depreciation **14**	3.7	3.1	1.3	12.6	4.3	1.5	4.9	3.8	3.1	5.3	3.5	3.8	•
Amortization and Depletion **15**	2.3	0.3	0.6	1.8	1.3	0.0	2.7	1.3	1.4	2.4	4.3	2.7	•
Pensions and Other Deferred Comp. **16**	0.7	0.1	2.5	•	0.1	1.2	0.7	0.4	0.4	0.5	0.2	0.7	•
Employee Benefits **17**	2.7	0.9	0.8	3.7	1.4	2.4	3.1	1.7	2.8	2.5	2.2	3.4	•
Advertising **18**	2.6	6.5	3.9	1.7	0.6	0.5	11.2	7.2	1.1	3.7	3.1	1.3	•
Other Expenses **19**	33.0	17.6	28.4	60.5	36.6	22.1	29.7	24.5	48.1	37.6	40.7	31.9	•
Officers' Compensation **20**	3.7	2.9	13.9	11.8	8.2	3.1	4.1	5.9	2.1	2.0	2.2	2.1	•
Operating Margin **21**	•	0.9	•	•	•	0.7	•	1.9	•	•	•	0.9	•
Operating Margin Before Officers' Comp. **22**	0.1	3.9	7.2	•	•	3.8	•	7.8	•	•	•	3.0	•

Selected Average Balance Sheet ($ in Thousands)

Net Receivables 23	461	0	7	109	523	2564	1474	7161	11188	21172	56810	158794
Inventories 24	14	0	2	0	7	25	57	39	881	861	60	5260
Net Property, Plant and Equipment 25	208	0	5	326	138	584	1995	3410	5149	18496	21379	62275
Total Assets 26	3081	0	35	742	2076	6186	15700	33724	72524	156991	363807	1173819
Notes and Loans Payable 27	1070	0	131	921	786	2228	3148	5724	13503	36277	68803	425201
All Other Liabilities 28	1130	0	151	512	851	2576	6874	16165	23388	48257	99229	378105
Net Worth 29	881	0	-247	-691	438	1382	5679	11835	35633	72458	195775	370513

Selected Financial Ratios (Times to 1)

Current Ratio 30	0.8	•	0.1	0.7	1.3	1.9	1.3	1.6	1.5	1.6	2.3	0.6
Quick Ratio 31	0.7	•	0.1	0.6	1.2	1.8	1.1	1.5	1.2	1.5	2.1	0.4
Net Sales to Working Capital 32	•	•	•	•	7.9	6.6	8.2	5.1	5.0	3.5	3.3	•
Coverage Ratio 33	1.9	53.3	•	•	•	3.2	•	3.8	0.7	•	•	3.8
Total Asset Turnover 34	0.7	•	5.8	1.5	1.2	2.5	1.0	1.1	0.9	0.7	0.6	0.5
Inventory Turnover 35	36.6	•	38.1	76.4	242.2	64.2	212.4	5.3	23.4	690.4	24.7	•
Receivables Turnover 36	4.6	•	21.8	14.4	5.6	6.0	6.9	8.0	5.9	4.6	4.8	3.4
Total Liabilities to Net Worth 37	2.5	•	•	•	3.7	3.5	1.8	1.8	1.0	1.2	0.9	2.2
Current Assets to Working Capital 38	•	•	•	•	4.3	2.1	3.9	2.6	2.8	2.6	1.7	•
Current Liabilities to Working Capital 39	•	•	•	3.3	3.3	1.1	2.9	1.6	1.8	1.6	0.7	•
Working Capital to Net Sales 40	•	•	•	0.1	0.1	0.2	0.1	0.2	0.2	0.3	0.3	•
Inventory to Working Capital 41	•	•	•	0.0	0.0	0.0	0.0	0.0	0.1	0.0	0.0	•
Total Receipts to Cash Flow 42	3.2	5.8	5.1	4.7	4.8	5.8	4.0	2.3	3.6	3.6	2.5	•
Cost of Goods to Cash Flow 43	0.7	3.2	2.1	1.1	1.9	1.3	0.9	0.2	0.7	0.2	0.6	0.5
Cash Flow to Total Debt 44	0.3	0.1	•	0.3	0.7	0.3	0.4	0.8	0.4	0.4	0.3	•

Selected Financial Factors (in Percentages)

Debt Ratio 45	71.4	800.1	193.1	78.9	77.7	63.8	64.9	50.9	53.8	46.2	•	68.4
Return on Total Assets 46	4.2	•	•	•	3.4	•	6.1	1.6	•	•	•	8.7
Return on Equity Before Income Taxes 47	7.0	3.8	•	•	10.6	•	12.7	•	•	•	•	20.3
Return on Equity After Income Taxes 48	0.5	4.1	105.3	•	3.2	•	5.6	•	•	•	•	12.7
Profit Margin (Before Income Tax) 49	2.7	1.7	•	•	0.9	•	4.2	•	•	•	•	11.7
Profit Margin (After Income Tax) 50	0.2	0.5	•	•	0.3	•	1.9	•	•	•	•	7.3

Table II

Corporations with Net Income

OTHER INFORMATION SERVICES, NEWS SYNDICATES, LIBRARIES

MONEY AMOUNTS AND SIZE OF ASSETS IN THOUSANDS OF DOLLARS

Item Description for Accounting Period 7/04 Through 6/05	Total	Zero Assets	Under 500	500 to 1,000	1,000 to 5,000	5,000 to 10,000	10,000 to 25,000	25,000 to 50,000	50,000 to 100,000	100,000 to 250,000	250,000 to 500,000	500,000 to 2,500,000	2,500,000 and over
Number of Enterprises **1**	3543	331	2952	0	131	69	21	11	8	6	4	9	0

Revenues ($ in Thousands)

Net Sales **2**	13787141	305447	694865	0	497757	1326053	509544	530616	694583	769953	1017551	7440773	0
Interest **3**	129647	247	322	0	3040	1153	1847	2129	1048	5492	3093	111276	0
Rents **4**	10663	0	0	0	1140	300	540	136	0	568	0	7979	0
Royalties **5**	87746	0	0	0	2312	0	120	21	0	5	0	85288	0
Other Portfolio Income **6**	175901	0	3	0	29280	99	11953	1283	243	1691	1326	130023	0
Other Receipts **7**	173577	2026	7223	0	16825	3722	13902	3547	11296	5610	-66	109491	0
Total Receipts **8**	14364675	307720	702413	0	550354	1331327	537906	537732	707170	783319	1021904	7884830	0
Average Total Receipts **9**	4054	930	238	•	4201	19295	25615	48885	88396	130553	255476	876092	•

Operating Costs/Operating Income (%)

Cost of Operations **10**	20.3	58.0	9.1	•	14.4	41.1	24.4	16.5	4.0	5.6	21.7	19.3	•
Salaries and Wages **11**	22.7	7.2	11.7	•	25.2	22.7	20.7	17.2	31.9	30.3	17.7	23.8	•
Taxes Paid **12**	3.0	1.2	3.5	•	3.6	4.4	2.3	2.4	2.6	2.2	3.5	2.8	•
Interest Paid **13**	2.1	0.0	0.2	•	1.6	0.3	0.5	0.4	0.5	2.2	1.0	3.2	•
Depreciation **14**	2.9	1.8	1.2	•	3.6	1.0	2.9	4.7	2.4	6.5	3.2	2.8	•
Amortization and Depletion **15**	2.0	0.4	0.8	•	0.7	0.0	0.4	0.4	0.9	2.5	3.9	2.6	•
Pensions and Other Deferred Comp. **16**	0.8	0.1	3.7	•	0.0	1.3	0.4	0.3	0.5	0.7	0.2	0.7	•
Employee Benefits **17**	2.4	0.7	1.3	•	0.5	2.4	2.9	1.9	2.5	2.4	1.7	2.8	•
Advertising **18**	2.0	7.0	1.2	•	0.8	0.4	8.4	10.5	0.8	3.7	3.6	0.8	•
Other Expenses **19**	29.5	13.4	27.7	•	32.8	19.4	26.1	18.7	48.6	26.9	37.2	30.3	•
Officers' Compensation **20**	3.2	3.2	19.5	•	7.7	2.6	3.4	3.2	1.5	2.1	2.6	1.8	•
Operating Margin **21**	9.2	7.0	20.1	•	9.2	4.3	7.6	23.8	3.7	15.0	3.6	8.9	•
Operating Margin Before Officers' Comp. **22**	12.4	10.2	39.6	•	16.9	6.9	11.1	27.0	5.2	17.1	6.1	10.7	•

Selected Average Balance Sheet ($ in Thousands)

Net Receivables 23	713	0	14	•	256	2751	1858	7788	13996	18381	38664	195699	•
Inventories 24	22	0	0	•	17	6	50	50	37	89	122	8119	•
Net Property, Plant and Equipment 25	322	0	5	•	215	557	2008	5551	5418	30426	19046	72636	•
Total Assets 26	4766	0	46	•	2335	6142	15114	34463	74405	167072	368606	1361255	•
Notes and Loans Payable 27	1406	0	57	•	965	830	2469	4095	7174	53978	57058	435889	•
All Other Liabilities 28	1372	0	17	•	888	2394	8904	13980	30624	43014	51990	386330	•
Net Worth 29	1988	0	-28	•	482	2918	3742	16388	36607	70080	259559	539036	•

Selected Financial Ratios (Times to 1)

Current Ratio 30	0.8	•	1.2	•	1.1	1.9	1.7	1.6	1.6	1.3	2.1	0.6	•
Quick Ratio 31	0.6	•	1.1	•	1.0	1.9	1.3	1.5	1.4	1.2	1.9	0.5	•
Net Sales to Working Capital 32	•	•	53.8	•	58.3	7.6	5.9	5.8	5.2	9.7	6.1	•	•
Coverage Ratio 33	7.6	366.6	137.5	•	13.6	16.4	27.4	60.2	11.4	8.5	5.2	5.8	•
Total Asset Turnover 34	0.8	•	5.1	•	1.6	3.1	1.6	1.4	1.2	0.8	0.7	0.6	•
Inventory Turnover 35	35.2	•	43.8	•	32.9	1242.7	118.1	160.4	94.5	81.0	453.3	19.7	•
Receivables Turnover 36	5.9	•	29.0	•	14.9	6.8	8.1	9.9	6.5	8.0	4.2	4.9	•
Total Liabilities to Net Worth 37	1.4	•	•	•	3.8	1.1	3.0	1.1	1.0	1.4	0.4	1.5	•
Current Assets to Working Capital 38	•	•	6.9	•	19.5	2.1	2.4	2.6	2.7	4.9	1.9	•	•
Current Liabilities to Working Capital 39	•	•	5.9	•	18.5	1.1	1.4	1.6	1.7	3.9	0.9	•	•
Working Capital to Net Sales 40	•	•	0.0	•	0.0	0.1	0.2	0.2	0.2	0.1	0.2	•	•
Inventory to Working Capital 41	•	•	0.2	•	0.3	•	0.0	0.0	•	0.0	0.0	•	•
Total Receipts to Cash Flow 42	2.6	5.0	2.4	•	2.4	4.5	2.8	2.5	2.0	2.6	2.8	2.4	•
Cost of Goods to Cash Flow 43	0.5	2.9	0.2	•	0.3	1.9	0.7	0.4	0.1	0.1	0.6	0.5	•
Cash Flow to Total Debt 44	0.5	•	1.4	•	0.9	1.3	0.7	1.1	1.2	0.5	0.8	0.4	•

Selected Financial Factors (in Percentages)

Debt Ratio 45	58.3	•	161.4	•	79.4	52.5	75.2	52.4	50.8	58.1	29.6	60.4	•
Return on Total Assets 46	12.9	•	109.3	•	34.7	15.8	22.0	35.8	7.0	14.5	3.4	11.4	•
Return on Equity Before Income Taxes 47	26.9	•	•	•	155.8	31.3	85.6	74.1	13.1	30.5	3.9	23.8	•
Return on Equity After Income Taxes 48	19.9	•	•	•	140.4	26.7	82.5	62.9	11.9	22.9	2.7	15.7	•
Profit Margin (Before Income Tax) 49	13.7	7.8	21.2	•	19.8	4.7	13.2	25.2	5.5	16.6	4.0	15.5	•
Profit Margin (After Income Tax) 50	10.2	6.6	20.2	•	17.8	4.0	12.7	21.4	5.0	12.5	2.8	10.3	•

Table I
Corporations with and without Net Income

CREDIT INTERMEDIATION

MONEY AMOUNTS AND SIZE OF ASSETS IN THOUSANDS OF DOLLARS

Item Description for Accounting Period 7/04 Through 6/05		Total	Zero Assets	Under 500	500 to 1,000	1,000 to 5,000	5,000 to 10,000	10,000 to 25,000	25,000 to 50,000	50,000 to 100,000	100,000 to 250,000	250,000 to 500,000	500,000 to 2,500,000	2,500,000 and over
Number of Enterprises	1	58322	6690	38323	3592	3895	1375	1029	804	797	887	419	376	136
Revenues ($ in Thousands)														
Net Sales	2	472705946	37864797	13886282	3932137	5715872	3805900	5589120	5529249	6089293	12372736	11360101	36021568	330538893
Interest	3	281124509	22670304	90889	45194	213158	207225	347726	934979	1798790	5438760	5825771	15589718	227961995
Rents	4	1715817	144131	1272	12	6383	937	7133	8248	9681	23776	23155	228470	1262618
Royalties	5	507909	0	1786	0	45	99	0	230	20	27988	145	12114	465483
Other Portfolio Income	6	17991717	2313728	21687	31900	60468	109155	82496	518247	179927	270737	579762	1797152	12028460
Other Receipts	7	171365994	12736634	13770648	3885031	5435818	3488484	5151765	4067545	4100875	6611475	4931268	18394114	88822337
Total Receipts	8	472705946	37864797	13886282	3932137	5715872	3805900	5589120	5529249	6089293	12372736	11360101	36021568	330538893
Average Total Receipts	9	8105	5660	362	1095	1467	2768	5432	6877	7640	13949	27112	95802	2430433
Operating Costs/Operating Income (%)														
Cost of Operations	10	2.4	0.4	8.3	14.8	3.5	12.7	11.1	3.6	4.1	4.8	0.7	1.3	2.0
Salaries and Wages	11	10.8	11.7	29.8	16.2	29.0	22.8	29.4	25.1	22.3	18.0	19.3	15.7	7.6
Taxes Paid	12	1.5	1.8	3.0	2.7	3.3	3.0	3.0	2.9	3.1	2.8	3.0	2.2	1.1
Interest Paid	13	43.6	44.3	7.8	4.5	47.0	9.2	7.6	11.9	15.2	18.8	23.4	20.1	51.7
Depreciation	14	3.0	1.8	1.2	1.0	1.8	2.0	1.5	2.2	2.9	2.8	3.8	3.0	3.3
Amortization and Depletion	15	0.6	0.4	0.1	0.2	0.2	0.2	0.3	0.7	0.7	1.1	1.1	1.1	0.6
Pensions and Other Deferred Comp.	16	0.5	0.4	0.2	0.2	0.4	0.3	0.4	0.6	0.7	1.0	1.1	1.3	0.4
Employee Benefits	17	1.0	0.8	0.7	0.5	1.0	1.0	1.2	1.7	1.9	2.0	2.1	1.7	0.8
Advertising	18	1.5	0.3	3.0	1.2	1.4	1.4	2.6	2.3	2.2	1.8	1.4	3.3	1.3
Other Expenses	19	21.9	30.4	40.2	42.7	38.2	33.8	37.0	32.8	28.7	27.8	24.8	32.2	17.5
Officers' Compensation	20	1.4	1.5	7.9	5.4	6.0	6.1	5.3	5.0	6.7	4.8	3.3	1.7	0.5
Operating Margin	21	11.7	6.2	•	10.7	•	7.4	0.6	11.3	11.5	14.2	15.9	16.4	13.2
Operating Margin Before Officers' Comp.	22	13.1	7.6	5.7	16.1	•	13.5	5.9	16.3	18.1	19.0	19.3	18.1	13.7

Selected Average Balance Sheet ($ in Thousands)

Net Receivables 23	13494	0	16	219	864	2894	6691	15149	29929	58558	95736	265049	3997436
Inventories 24	•	•	•	•	•	•	•	•	•	•	•	•	•
Net Property, Plant and Equipment 25	795	0	15	49	187	157	479	839	1415	3000	5546	13294	238427
Total Assets 26	79133	0	91	681	2055	7003	16211	35939	71165	157217	351642	1001699	28131773
Notes and Loans Payable 27	47627	0	38	224	1179	4367	6572	8904	10490	23681	63155	259998	19098355
All Other Liabilities 28	26743	0	149	117	1479	1955	7454	23869	50837	112902	246118	594243	7728624
Net Worth 29	4762	0	-95	341	-602	680	2185	3166	9838	20634	42368	147458	1304793

Selected Financial Ratios (Times to 1)

Current Ratio 30	0.5	•	0.5	3.2	0.9	1.3	1.1	0.9	0.8	0.7	0.6	0.6	0.5
Quick Ratio 31	0.4	•	0.5	2.8	0.8	1.1	0.9	0.9	0.8	0.7	0.5	0.5	0.4
Net Sales to Working Capital 32	•	•	•	2.8	•	3.2	7.4	•	•	•	•	•	•
Coverage Ratio 33	1.3	1.1	0.7	3.4	0.3	1.8	1.1	1.9	1.7	1.6	1.6	1.8	1.2
Total Asset Turnover 34	0.1	•	4.0	1.6	0.7	0.4	0.3	0.2	0.1	0.1	0.1	0.1	0.1
Inventory Turnover 35	•	•	•	•	•	•	•	•	•	•	•	•	•
Receivables Turnover 36	•	•	•	•	•	•	•	•	•	•	•	•	•
Total Liabilities to Net Worth 37	15.6	•	•	1.0	•	9.3	6.4	10.4	6.2	6.6	7.3	5.8	20.6
Current Assets to Working Capital 38	•	•	•	1.4	5.0	14.3	•	•	•	•	•	•	•
Current Liabilities to Working Capital 39	•	•	•	0.4	4.0	13.3	•	•	•	•	•	•	•
Working Capital to Net Sales 40	•	•	•	0.4	0.3	0.1	•	•	•	•	•	•	•
Inventory to Working Capital 41	•	•	•	0.0	0.0	0.0	•	•	•	•	•	•	•
Total Receipts to Cash Flow 42	3.3	3.3	3.2	2.1	2.7	2.7	3.0	2.6	2.7	2.6	2.7	2.2	3.5
Cost of Goods to Cash Flow 43	0.1	0.0	0.3	0.3	0.3	0.1	0.3	0.1	0.1	0.0	0.0	0.0	0.1
Cash Flow to Total Debt 44	0.0	•	0.6	1.5	•	0.2	0.1	0.1	0.0	0.0	0.0	0.1	0.0

Selected Financial Factors (in Percentages)

Debt Ratio 45	94.0	•	205.4	50.0	129.3	90.3	86.5	91.2	86.2	86.9	88.0	85.3	95.4
Return on Total Assets 46	5.6	•	22.7	24.4	9.1	6.5	2.7	4.4	2.7	2.8	3.0	3.5	5.6
Return on Equity Before Income Taxes 47	19.0	8.2	34.3	83.7	29.6	•	1.1	23.6	8.0	8.9	9.6	10.4	23.5
Return on Equity After Income Taxes 48	12.8	8.7	33.4	84.6	26.3	•	20.6	6.4	6.8	7.2	•	•	15.9
Profit Margin (Before Income Tax) 49	11.2	6.1	•	10.7	•	7.3	0.5	10.9	10.3	13.1	15.0	16.0	12.6
Profit Margin (After Income Tax) 50	7.5	4.2	•	10.4	•	6.5	•	9.5	8.3	9.4	10.6	11.1	8.6

Table II

Corporations with Net Income

CREDIT INTERMEDIATION

MONEY AMOUNTS AND SIZE OF ASSETS IN THOUSANDS OF DOLLARS

Item Description for Accounting Period 7/04 Through 6/05	Total	Zero Assets	Under 500	500 to 1,000	1,000 to 5,000	5,000 to 10,000	10,000 to 25,000	25,000 to 50,000	50,000 to 100,000	100,000 to 250,000	250,000 to 500,000	500,000 to 2,500,000	2,500,000 and over
Number of Enterprises 1	35911	1686	23893	2930	2758	1005	778	605	642	779	371	341	122
Revenues ($ in Thousands)													
Net Sales 2	442237214	28149244	11172718	3369035	4501890	2586321	4648507	4582798	4977726	10853355	9824381	33077138	324494102
Interest 3	267931520	16620504	19663	45104	135586	166384	276949	723326	1490777	4800810	5239925	13988048	224424045
Rents 4	1289256	75897	1272	12	3818	701	6249	6907	8657	16054	21092	217481	931116
Royalties 5	507683	0	1786	0	0	53	0	230	20	27988	10	12114	465483
Other Portfolio Income 6	16002319	1181312	26892	34459	43947	105899	42371	496556	120594	223939	478648	1425389	11822313
Other Receipts 7	156506436	10271531	11123105	3289460	4318139	2313284	4322938	3355779	3357678	5784564	4084706	17434106	86851145
Total Receipts 8	442237214	28149244	11172718	3369035	4501890	2586321	4648507	4582798	4977726	10853355	9824381	33077138	324494102
Average Total Receipts 9	12315	16696	468	1150	1632	2573	5975	7575	7753	13932	26481	97000	2659788
Operating Costs/Operating Income (%)													
Cost of Operations 10	2.4	0.2	7.9	17.2	1.9	12.9	12.4	3.7	3.9	4.1	0.4	1.3	2.1
Salaries and Wages 11	10.2	11.8	29.2	17.1	27.9	21.1	27.5	23.1	20.0	17.8	18.6	15.5	7.4
Taxes Paid 12	1.5	2.0	2.7	2.9	3.2	2.9	2.8	2.8	2.8	2.9	3.1	2.2	1.1
Interest Paid 13	43.6	44.6	0.5	4.4	4.2	8.7	6.9	9.9	14.8	17.7	22.0	17.2	51.9
Depreciation 14	2.8	1.3	0.8	1.0	1.1	2.1	1.1	1.7	2.5	2.6	3.2	2.9	3.0
Amortization and Depletion 15	0.5	0.5	0.1	0.2	0.2	0.2	0.3	0.3	0.6	0.5	0.7	1.2	0.5
Pensions and Other Deferred Comp. 16	0.5	0.4	0.2	0.3	0.5	0.4	0.4	0.6	0.8	1.0	1.1	1.1	0.4
Employee Benefits 17	0.9	0.8	0.3	0.5	1.2	1.1	1.0	1.6	1.9	2.1	2.2	1.7	0.8
Advertising 18	1.4	0.4	1.9	0.9	3.6	1.2	2.6	2.0	1.9	1.8	1.5	3.4	1.2
Other Expenses 19	20.5	23.9	38.5	34.8	33.1	25.7	27.4	25.6	25.7	25.7	22.8	32.3	17.5
Officers' Compensation 20	1.3	1.0	6.4	5.9	5.7	6.4	4.9	5.0	6.7	4.9	3.5	1.8	0.5
Operating Margin 21	14.4	13.1	11.5	14.9	17.4	17.5	12.6	23.9	18.5	18.9	20.9	19.3	13.5
Operating Margin Before Officers' Comp. 22	15.7	14.1	17.9	20.8	23.1	23.8	17.5	28.9	25.2	23.9	24.4	21.1	14.1

Selected Average Balance Sheet ($ in Thousands)

Net Receivables 23	19397	0	13	193	930	3261	7054	15021	30112	59426	96106	233868	4051159
Inventories 24	•	•	•	•	•	•	•	•	•	•	•	•	•
Net Property, Plant and Equipment 25	1208	0	14	52	175	137	382	794	1375	2898	5563	13683	259246
Total Assets 26	121639	0	103	694	2075	7000	16226	35991	71705	158416	352032	971930	3205282
Notes and Loans Payable 27	73498	0	25	153	1134	3860	6482	8176	9492	19690	48679	208845	20579010
All Other Liabilities 28	40677	0	18	384	269	1569	7852	23221	51727	117837	261428	614296	8239601
Net Worth 29	7464	0	60	156	672	1570	1892	4594	10486	20889	41925	148789	1386671

Selected Financial Ratios (Times to 1)

Current Ratio 30	0.5	•	3.7	3.4	2.4	1.5	1.1	0.9	0.8	0.7	0.6	0.5	0.5
Quick Ratio 31	0.4	•	3.4	2.9	2.2	1.3	1.0	0.9	0.8	0.7	0.5	0.5	0.4
Net Sales to Working Capital 32	•	•	10.1	2.7	2.1	1.7	7.8	•	•	•	•	•	•
Coverage Ratio 33	1.3	1.3	25.4	4.4	5.2	3.0	2.8	3.4	2.2	2.0	1.9	2.1	1.3
Total Asset Turnover 34	0.1	•	4.5	1.7	0.8	0.4	0.4	0.2	0.1	0.1	0.1	0.1	0.1
Inventory Turnover 35	•	•	•	•	•	•	•	•	•	•	•	•	•
Receivables Turnover 36	•	•	•	•	•	•	•	•	•	•	•	•	•
Total Liabilities to Net Worth 37	15.3	•	0.7	3.4	2.1	3.5	7.6	6.8	5.8	6.6	7.4	5.5	20.8
Current Assets to Working Capital 38	•	•	1.4	1.4	1.7	2.9	14.1	•	•	•	•	•	•
Current Liabilities to Working Capital 39	•	•	0.4	0.4	0.7	1.9	13.1	•	•	•	•	•	•
Working Capital to Net Sales 40	•	•	0.1	0.4	0.5	0.6	0.1	•	•	•	•	•	•
Inventory to Working Capital 41	•	•	•	•	•	•	0.0	•	•	•	•	•	•
Total Receipts to Cash Flow 42	3.1	3.2	2.3	2.3	2.2	2.5	2.7	2.2	2.4	2.4	2.5	2.1	3.5
Cost of Goods to Cash Flow 43	0.1	0.0	0.2	0.4	0.0	0.3	0.3	0.1	0.1	0.1	0.0	0.0	0.1
Cash Flow to Total Debt 44	0.0	•	4.7	0.9	0.5	0.2	0.2	0.1	0.1	0.0	0.0	0.1	0.0

Selected Financial Factors (in Percentages)

Debt Ratio 45	93.9	•	42.2	77.4	67.6	77.6	88.3	87.2	85.4	86.8	88.1	84.7	95.4
Return on Total Assets 46	5.8	•	54.3	31.8	16.9	9.5	7.1	7.0	3.5	3.1	3.1	3.6	5.7
Return on Equity Before Income Taxes 47	23.0	•	90.2	109.2	42.2	28.3	39.2	38.6	12.7	11.9	12.5	12.3	25.0
Return on Equity After Income Taxes 48	16.5	•	88.9	106.9	41.0	26.3	36.0	35.9	10.9	9.1	9.3	8.8	17.0
Profit Margin (Before Income Tax) 49	13.9	13.1	11.5	14.9	17.4	17.2	12.4	23.4	17.1	17.9	19.8	18.8	13.0
Profit Margin (After Income Tax) 50	10.0	10.6	11.4	14.6	16.9	16.0	11.4	21.8	14.7	13.6	14.7	13.5	8.9

Table I

Corporations with and without Net Income

COMMERCIAL BANKING

MONEY AMOUNTS AND SIZE OF ASSETS IN THOUSANDS OF DOLLARS

Item Description for Accounting Period 7/04 Through 6/05	Total	Zero Assets	Under 500	500 to 1,000	1,000 to 5,000	5,000 to 10,000	10,000 to 25,000	25,000 to 50,000	50,000 to 100,000	100,000 to 250,000	250,000 to 500,000	500,000 to 2,500,000	2,500,000 and over
Number of Enterprises **1**	1940	271	0	35	48	0	220	350	434	385	116	54	8
Revenues ($ in Thousands)													
Net Sales **2**	47271991	33912332	0	57870	25681	0	215939	1160946	1682513	3395260	2299355	3003841	1507108
Interest **3**	28105243	20494719	0	162	5861	0	115609	394545	973012	2023011	1296150	1904867	892500
Rents **4**	336799	140319	0	0	4	0	1672	2598	5895	7273	3561	35154	140318
Royalties **5**	1781	0	0	0	0	0	0	0	4	184	0	1566	26
Other Portfolio Income **6**	3041133	2082598	0	5769	2568	0	10503	412921	75229	123504	102580	115915	109231
Other Receipts **7**	15787035	11194696	0	51939	17248	0	88155	350882	628373	1241288	897064	946339	365033
Total Receipts **8**	47271991	33912332	0	57870	25681	0	215939	1160946	1682513	3395260	2299355	3003841	1507108
Average Total Receipts **9**	24367	125138	•	1653	535	•	982	3317	3877	8819	19822	55627	188388
Operating Costs/Operating Income (%)													
Cost of Operations **10**	•	•	•	•	•	•	•	•	•	•	•	•	•
Salaries and Wages **11**	12.0	10.9	•	19.0	7.6	•	15.2	8.8	15.3	15.3	15.9	17.1	13.3
Taxes Paid **12**	2.1	1.7	•	2.0	2.1	•	3.3	2.0	3.4	3.2	3.1	3.0	3.7
Interest Paid **13**	44.4	46.8	•	0.2	8644.6	•	18.4	12.1	22.1	22.3	22.0	22.0	26.5
Depreciation **14**	2.6	1.8	•	0.1	0.6	•	5.0	2.8	4.0	3.4	3.7	4.1	10.4
Amortization and Depletion **15**	0.4	0.2	•	0.0	•	•	0.8	0.6	0.8	1.5	0.3	0.4	0.6
Pensions and Other Deferred Comp. **16**	0.5	0.4	•	2.4	0.1	•	0.7	0.5	0.8	0.8	0.8	0.9	1.3
Employee Benefits **17**	1.3	0.8	•	5.1	0.4	•	3.9	2.0	3.0	2.5	2.5	2.8	1.6
Advertising **18**	0.4	0.2	•	2.6	0.2	•	1.1	0.8	1.1	1.1	0.8	0.9	0.8
Other Expenses **19**	28.3	30.8	•	34.8	127.9	•	28.6	27.9	24.2	22.9	20.1	19.0	15.9
Officers' Compensation **20**	2.6	1.1	•	8.9	4.0	•	13.8	7.5	10.1	7.1	5.7	3.1	4.8
Operating Margin **21**	5.6	5.3	•	24.9	•	•	9.1	34.9	15.1	19.9	24.9	26.7	21.2
Operating Margin Before Officers' Comp. **22**	8.1	6.5	•	33.7	•	•	22.9	42.4	25.2	27.0	30.6	29.8	26.0

Selected Average Balance Sheet ($ in Thousands)

Item													
Net Receivables 23	61343	0	•	318	859	•	9470	20947	41240	90010	194731	421410	1446060
Inventories 24	•	•	•	•	•	•	•	•	•	•	•	•	•
Net Property, Plant and Equipment 25	1748	0	•	0	720	•	301	732	1298	2630	5859	11411	20268
Total Assets 26	118457		•	892	2619	•	17431	36755	70352	152922	349018	898312	4299503
Notes and Loans Payable 27	4973	0	•	11	14	•	173	427	1525	5088	14246	58101	256083
All Other Liabilities 28	103634	0	•	1264	84625	•	18857	34337	60032	132029	300787	744037	3583678
Net Worth 29	9850	0	•	-383	-82019	•	-1599	1991	8795	15805	33986	96174	459742

Selected Financial Ratios (Times to 1)

Item													
Current Ratio 30	0.9	•	•	5.8	0.0	•	1.1	1.1	1.0	0.9	0.9	0.8	1.0
Quick Ratio 31	0.9	•	•	4.7	0.0	•	1.1	1.0	1.0	0.9	0.9	0.8	0.8
Net Sales to Working Capital 32	•	•	2.3	•	0.5	1.5	7.6	•	•	•	•	•	•
Coverage Ratio 33	1.1	1.1	•	106.9	•	1.4	3.7	1.5	1.8	2.0	2.1	1.8	
Total Asset Turnover 34	0.2	•	•	1.9	0.2	•	0.1	0.1	0.1	0.1	0.1	0.1	0.0
Inventory Turnover 35	•	•	•	•	•	•	•	•	•	•	•	•	•
Receivables Turnover 36	•	•	•	•	•	•	•	•	•	•	•	•	•
Total Liabilities to Net Worth 37	11.0	•	•	•	•	•	17.5	7.0	8.7	9.3	8.3	8.4	•
Current Assets to Working Capital 38	1.2	•	•	•	•	8.3	14.5	119.8	•	•	•	•	•
Current Liabilities to Working Capital 39	0.2	•	•	•	•	7.3	13.5	118.8	•	•	•	•	•
Working Capital to Net Sales 40	0.4	•	•	•	•	2.0	0.7	0.1	•	•	•	•	•
Inventory to Working Capital 41	•	•	•	•	•	•	•	•	•	•	•	•	•
Total Receipts to Cash Flow 42	3.6	3.4	•	1.9	•	3.1	1.7	2.8	2.5	2.4	2.4	3.0	•
Cost of Goods to Cash Flow 43	•	•	•	•	•	•	•	•	•	•	•	•	•
Cash Flow to Total Debt 44	0.1	•	0.7	•	•	0.0	0.1	0.0	0.0	0.0	0.0	0.0	0.0

Selected Financial Factors (in Percentages)

Item													
Debt Ratio 45	91.7	•	•	143.0	3231.2	•	109.2	94.6	87.5	89.7	90.3	89.3	89.3
Return on Total Assets 46	10.1	•	•	46.2	•	•	1.4	4.1	1.9	2.3	2.5	2.9	2.1
Return on Equity Before Income Taxes 47	12.0	•	•	•	56.7	•	55.3	5.1	9.7	12.9	14.1	•	8.6
Return on Equity After Income Taxes 48	5.8	•	•	•	56.7	•	51.9	3.7	7.3	9.7	10.1	•	5.9
Profit Margin (Before Income Tax) 49	4.9	5.3	•	24.7	•	6.7	33.2	11.5	17.3	22.0	24.4	20.9	
Profit Margin (After Income Tax) 50	2.3	3.7	•	23.2	•	4.9	31.1	8.3	13.1	16.6	17.4	14.3	

Table II

Corporations with Net Income

COMMERCIAL BANKING

MONEY AMOUNTS AND SIZE OF ASSETS IN THOUSANDS OF DOLLARS

Item Description for Accounting Period 7/04 Through 6/05	Total	Zero Assets	Under 500	500 to 1,000	1,000 to 5,000	5,000 to 10,000	10,000 to 25,000	25,000 to 50,000	50,000 to 100,000	100,000 to 250,000	250,000 to 500,000	500,000 to 2,500,000	2,500,000 and over
Number of Enterprises **1**	1508	164	0	0	0	0	162	257	351	355	112	54	8
Revenues ($ in Thousands)													
Net Sales **2**	37611614	25072933	0	0	0	0	185097	983052	1452040	3096348	2237128	3003841	1507108
Interest **3**	21996475	14860648	0	0	0	0	93705	300569	793222	1899359	1247219	1904867	892500
Rents **4**	267674	72968	0	0	0	0	1629	2400	5376	6357	3472	35154	140318
Royalties **5**	1781	0	0	0	0	0	0	0	4	184	0	1566	26
Other Portfolio Income **6**	1908034	968255	0	0	0	0	9700	408966	70220	115058	102047	115915	109231
Other Receipts **7**	13437650	9171062	0	0	0	0	80063	271117	583218	1075390	884390	946339	365033
Total Receipts **8**	37611614	25072933	0	0	0	0	185097	983052	1452040	3096348	2237128	3003841	1507108
Average Total Receipts **9**	24941	152884	•	•	•	•	1143	3825	4137	8722	19974	55627	188388
Operating Costs/Operating Income (%)													
Cost of Operations **10**	•	•	•	•	•	•	•	•	•	•	•	•	•
Salaries and Wages **11**	12.5	11.4	•	•	•	•	13.0	7.1	13.8	15.4	15.6	17.1	13.3
Taxes Paid **12**	2.3	1.9	•	•	•	•	2.9	1.8	3.3	3.3	3.1	3.0	3.7
Interest Paid **13**	39.0	47.6	•	•	•	•	17.8	11.0	21.6	22.8	22.0	22.0	26.5
Depreciation **14**	2.3	1.3	•	•	•	•	2.4	1.8	3.5	3.4	3.7	4.1	10.4
Amortization and Depletion **15**	0.3	0.2	•	•	•	•	0.2	0.2	0.5	0.4	0.3	0.4	0.6
Pensions and Other Deferred Comp. **16**	0.5	0.4	•	•	•	•	0.8	0.5	0.8	0.8	0.8	0.9	1.3
Employee Benefits **17**	1.4	0.8	•	•	•	•	3.7	1.8	2.8	2.6	2.6	2.8	1.6
Advertising **18**	0.5	0.3	•	•	•	•	0.8	0.5	1.0	1.1	0.8	0.9	0.8
Other Expenses **19**	22.9	24.6	•	•	•	•	23.7	21.5	21.1	19.7	19.4	19.0	15.9
Officers' Compensation **20**	2.5	0.8	•	•	•	•	12.7	6.8	9.6	7.2	5.6	3.1	4.8
Operating Margin **21**	15.8	10.7	•	•	•	•	22.1	47.0	21.7	23.2	26.0	26.7	21.2
Operating Margin Before Officers' Comp. **22**	18.3	11.5	•	•	•	•	34.8	53.8	31.4	30.4	31.7	29.8	26.0

Selected Average Balance Sheet ($ in Thousands)

	1	2	3	4	5	6	7	8	9
Net Receivables 23	73012	0	9292	20872	41617	91590	193810	421410	1446060
Inventories 24									
Net Property, Plant and Equipment 25	1979	0	194	562	1215	2657	5892	11411	20268
Total Assets 26	142007		17520	36668	71079	154525	348714	898312	4299503
Notes and Loans Payable 27	6116	0	142	418	1589	4979	14113	58101	256083
All Other Liabilities 28	122532	0	21644	34863	61017	133579	300706	744037	3583678
Net Worth 29	13359	0	-4266	1388	8473	15967	33895	96174	459742

Selected Financial Ratios (Times to 1)

	1	2	3	4	5	6	7	8	9
Current Ratio 30	0.9		1.1	1.1	1.0	1.0	0.9	0.8	1.0
Quick Ratio 31	0.9		1.1	1.1	1.0	0.9	0.9	0.8	0.8
Net Sales to Working Capital 32			0.9	1.6	3.3	1.9	2.0		
Coverage Ratio 33	1.4	1.2	2.1	5.1	1.8	1.9	2.0	2.1	1.8
Total Asset Turnover 34	0.2		0.1	0.1	0.1	0.1	0.1	0.1	0.0
Inventory Turnover 35									
Receivables Turnover 36									
Total Liabilities to Net Worth 37	9.6			25.4	7.4	8.7	9.3	8.3	8.4
Current Assets to Working Capital 38	13.2			13.9	49.2				
Current Liabilities to Working Capital 39	12.2			12.9	48.2				
Working Capital to Net Sales 40	1.1			0.6	0.3				
Inventory to Working Capital 41									
Total Receipts to Cash Flow 42	3.0	3.4	2.4	1.5	2.5	2.5	2.4	2.4	3.0
Cost of Goods to Cash Flow 43									
Cash Flow to Total Debt 44	0.1		0.0	0.1	0.0	0.0	0.0	0.0	0.0

Selected Financial Factors (in Percentages)

	1	2	3	4	5	6	7	8	9
Debt Ratio 45	90.6		124.3	96.2	88.1	89.7	90.3	89.3	89.3
Return on Total Assets 46	9.5		2.4	5.9	2.3	2.4	2.6	2.9	2.1
Return on Equity Before Income Taxes 47	27.9			124.7	8.7	11.2	13.6	14.1	8.6
Return on Equity After Income Taxes 48	22.0			118.0	6.9	8.7	10.3	10.1	5.9
Profit Margin (Before Income Tax) 49	14.9	10.6	19.6	45.2	17.8	20.6	23.1	24.4	20.9
Profit Margin (After Income Tax) 50	11.8	8.5	17.5	42.8	14.1	15.9	17.5	17.4	14.3

Table I

Corporations with and without Net Income

SAVINGS INSTITUTIONS AND OTHER DEPOSITORY CREDIT

MONEY AMOUNTS AND SIZE OF ASSETS IN THOUSANDS OF DOLLARS

Item Description for Accounting Period 7/04 Through 6/05	Total	Zero Assets	Under 500	500 to 1,000	1,000 to 5,000	5,000 to 10,000	10,000 to 25,000	25,000 to 50,000	50,000 to 100,000	100,000 to 250,000	250,000 to 500,000	500,000 to 2,500,000	2,500,000 and over
Number of Enterprises 1	1346	46	0	0	63	0	63	131	188	343	222	209	59
Revenues ($ in Thousands)													
Net Sales 2	78115905	2610123	0	0	76178	0	65740	315163	738948	3169994	4514658	11236434	55360820
Interest 3	51366918	1902772	0	0	95	0	48924	239169	605478	2467528	3416877	7972061	34706692
Rents 4	810745	3793	0	0	0	0	714	639	1652	7387	9234	98385	688931
Royalties 5	3716	0	0	0	0	0	0	8	0	0	10	3461	237
Other Portfolio Income 6	3641097	214424	0	0	11191	0	1283	5414	26054	101458	199739	600684	2473845
Other Receipts 7	22293429	489134	0	0	64892	0	14819	69933	105764	593621	888798	2561843	17491115
Total Receipts 8	78115905	2610123	0	0	76178	0	65740	315163	738948	3169994	4514658	11236434	55360820
Average Total Receipts 9	58036	56742	•	•	1209	•	1043	2406	3931	9242	20336	53763	938319
Operating Costs/Operating Income (%)													
Cost of Operations 10	0.3	0.0	•	•	1.9	•	•	•	0.4	•	0.0	0.4	0.3
Salaries and Wages 11	17.5	18.0	•	•	28.3	•	15.3	17.9	14.0	17.1	15.9	16.7	17.9
Taxes Paid 12	2.7	2.6	•	•	4.0	•	3.6	3.0	3.3	3.2	2.9	2.6	2.7
Interest Paid 13	31.3	28.0	•	•	230.8	•	28.9	28.4	31.5	29.9	30.6	31.1	29.5
Depreciation 14	4.0	2.0	•	•	0.8	•	3.8	2.8	3.1	3.1	4.1	3.2	4.3
Amortization and Depletion 15	1.2	2.9	•	•	•	•	0.7	0.2	0.2	0.2	0.2	0.7	1.4
Pensions and Other Deferred Comp. 16	1.1	1.3	•	•	•	•	2.0	1.5	2.0	1.7	1.7	1.7	0.9
Employee Benefits 17	2.3	1.8	•	•	5.2	•	3.3	2.8	2.6	2.8	2.5	2.4	2.3
Advertising 18	1.4	1.0	•	•	0.2	•	1.1	1.3	1.1	1.5	1.5	1.3	1.5
Other Expenses 19	18.2	20.8	•	•	127.3	•	22.1	24.4	20.6	19.5	19.8	17.9	17.7
Officers' Compensation 20	1.7	4.5	•	•	4.7	•	10.7	7.0	7.4	5.4	3.5	2.4	0.9
Operating Margin 21	18.3	17.1	•	•	•	•	8.6	10.6	13.9	15.5	17.5	19.4	20.7
Operating Margin Before Officers' Comp. 22	20.0	21.6	•	•	•	•	19.3	17.6	21.3	21.0	20.9	21.9	21.6

Selected Average Balance Sheet ($ in Thousands)

Net Receivables 23	66208	0	•	940	•	1102	3530	5056	16775	27433	74051	1021295
Inventories 24	•	•	•	•	•	•	•	•	•	•	•	•
Net Property, Plant and Equipment 25	10593	0	•	572	•	469	545	1313	3034	5589	13316	149290
Total Assets 26	930970	0	•	2446	•	18016	37114	73485	162509	352896	968855	15193970
Notes and Loans Payable 27	237427	0	•	2675	•	1418	2105	4402	14295	30074	116673	4783916
All Other Liabilities 28	678406	0	•	10589	•	13527	29749	59130	129632	285729	740724	10643908
Net Worth 29	15136	0	•	-10818	•	3070	5260	9953	18582	37093	111458	-233853

Selected Financial Ratios (Times to 1)

Current Ratio 30	0.2	•	•	1.6	•	0.4	0.4	0.3	0.3	0.3	0.3	0.2
Quick Ratio 31	0.2	•	•	1.6	•	0.4	0.3	0.3	0.3	0.3	0.2	0.1
Net Sales to Working Capital 32	•	•	•	1.8	•	•	•	•	•	•	•	•
Coverage Ratio 33	1.6	1.6	•	•	•	1.3	1.3	1.4	1.5	1.5	1.6	1.7
Total Asset Turnover 34	0.1	•	•	0.5	•	0.1	0.1	0.1	0.1	0.1	0.1	0.1
Inventory Turnover 35	•	•	•	•	•	•	•	•	•	•	•	•
Receivables Turnover 36	•	•	•	•	•	•	•	•	•	•	•	•
Total Liabilities to Net Worth 37	60.5	•	•	•	•	4.9	6.1	6.4	7.7	7.7	8.5	7.7
Current Assets to Working Capital 38	•	•	•	2.7	•	•	•	•	•	•	•	•
Current Liabilities to Working Capital 39	•	•	•	1.7	•	•	•	•	•	•	•	•
Working Capital to Net Sales 40	•	•	•	0.6	•	•	•	•	•	•	•	•
Inventory to Working Capital 41	•	•	•	•	•	•	•	•	•	•	•	•
Total Receipts to Cash Flow 42	3.2	2.8	•	•	•	3.5	3.3	3.2	3.1	2.9	3.0	3.1
Cost of Goods to Cash Flow 43	0.0	0.0	•	•	•	•	•	•	•	•	•	•
Cash Flow to Total Debt 44	0.0	•	•	0.0	•	0.0	0.0	0.0	0.0	0.0	0.0	0.0

Selected Financial Factors (in Percentages)

Debt Ratio 45	98.4	•	•	542.2	•	83.0	85.8	86.5	88.6	89.5	88.5	101.5
Return on Total Assets 46	3.1	•	•	•	•	2.1	2.5	2.4	2.5	2.7	2.8	3.1
Return on Equity Before Income Taxes 47	68.8	•	•	33.9	•	2.7	4.5	5.0	7.2	9.1	9.0	•
Return on Equity After Income Taxes 48	44.2	•	•	33.9	•	1.5	2.8	3.1	4.7	6.2	6.2	•
Profit Margin (Before Income Tax) 49	17.9	16.9	•	•	•	8.1	9.7	12.7	14.5	16.6	18.7	20.6
Profit Margin (After Income Tax) 50	11.5	12.0	•	•	•	4.4	6.1	7.7	9.5	11.2	12.8	13.8

Table II

Corporations with Net Income

SAVINGS INSTITUTIONS AND OTHER DEPOSITORY CREDIT

MONEY AMOUNTS AND SIZE OF ASSETS IN THOUSANDS OF DOLLARS

Item Description for Accounting Period 7/04 Through 6/05	Total	Zero Assets	Under 500	500 to 1,000	1,000 to 5,000	5,000 to 10,000	10,000 to 25,000	25,000 to 50,000	50,000 to 100,000	100,000 to 250,000	250,000 to 500,000	500,000 to 2,500,000	2,500,000 and over
Number of Enterprises 1	1132	19	3	0	0	11	52	108	168	309	208	200	54
Revenues ($ in Thousands)													
Net Sales 2	72387525	2121225	17503	0	0	7177	57615	278611	674506	2902397	4154784	10800280	51373427
Interest 3	47727504	1502522	2083	0	0	3284	45390	210088	556101	2259234	3234573	7614096	32300132
Rents 4	475560	2917	0	0	0	10	274	588	1522	6932	8615	97274	357428
Royalties 5	3716	0	0	0	0	0	0	8	0	0	10	3461	237
Other Portfolio Income 6	3385832	200674	12227	0	0	3509	1124	4198	21485	83163	169696	579014	2310744
Other Receipts 7	2079913	415112	3193	0	0	374	10827	63729	95398	553068	741890	2506435	16404886
Total Receipts 8	72387525	2121225	17503	0	0	7177	57615	278611	674506	2902397	4154784	10800280	51373427
Average Total Receipts 9	63947	111643	5834	•	•	652	1108	2580	4015	9393	19975	54001	951360
Operating Costs/Operating Income (%)													
Cost of Operations 10	0.3	0.1	8.1	•	•	•	•	•	0.4	•	0.0	0.4	0.3
Salaries and Wages 11	17.0	14.4	3.6	•	•	21.7	15.2	17.8	13.4	16.8	15.9	16.2	17.4
Taxes Paid 12	2.8	2.5	0.9	•	•	3.1	3.7	2.9	3.3	3.3	3.0	2.6	2.8
Interest Paid 13	29.4	22.0	13.6	•	•	17.5	28.3	27.8	30.4	29.7	30.1	30.9	29.3
Depreciation 14	3.4	1.8	0.8	•	•	1.0	2.1	2.8	3.1	3.0	2.7	3.3	3.6
Amortization and Depletion 15	0.7	3.5	0.5	•	•	•	0.1	0.1	0.1	0.2	0.2	0.7	0.6
Pensions and Other Deferred Comp. 16	1.0	1.1	•	•	•	0.1	2.0	1.5	1.8	1.7	1.7	1.6	0.8
Employee Benefits 17	2.1	1.5	0.9	•	•	2.6	3.0	2.6	2.6	2.7	2.6	2.3	2.1
Advertising 18	1.4	1.0	0.0	•	•	0.5	1.1	1.3	1.1	1.2	1.5	1.3	1.4
Other Expenses 19	17.6	15.9	9.5	•	•	14.3	18.6	20.4	18.0	17.5	19.1	17.1	17.7
Officers' Compensation 20	1.6	1.6	0.6	•	•	0.8	10.0	7.0	7.2	5.4	3.4	2.4	0.9
Operating Margin 21	22.7	34.7	61.5	•	•	38.3	16.1	15.8	18.5	18.5	19.8	21.1	23.1
Operating Margin Before Officers' Comp. 22	24.3	36.3	62.1	•	•	39.1	26.1	22.8	25.7	23.9	23.2	23.5	24.0

Selected Average Balance Sheet ($ in Thousands)

Item													
Net Receivables 23	61841	0	597	•	•	-9	710	3494	5236	16809	27394	73258	799346
Inventories 24	•	•	•	•	•	•	•	•	•	•	•	•	•
Net Property, Plant and Equipment 25	11565	0	53	•	•	42	215	545	1319	3009	5600	13396	148620
Total Assets 26	1013608	0	1930	•	•	6175	18180	37723	73969	164300	352977	959830	15069075
Notes and Loans Payable 27	250581	0	633	•	•	0	974	2144	4302	13835	27640	113592	4627927
All Other Liabilities 28	746268	0	21073	•	•	4988	14294	29567	59451	131750	287642	737809	10789465
Net Worth 29	16759	0	-19776	•	•	1188	2912	6012	10216	18715	37695	108429	-348316

Selected Financial Ratios (Times to 1)

Item													
Current Ratio 30	0.2	•	0.0	•	•	0.2	0.3	0.4	0.3	0.3	0.3	0.3	0.2
Quick Ratio 31	0.2	•	0.0	•	•	0.2	0.3	0.3	0.3	0.3	0.3	0.2	0.1
Net Sales to Working Capital 32	•	•	•	•	•	•	•	•	•	•	•	•	•
Coverage Ratio 33	1.8	2.6	5.5	•	•	3.2	1.6	1.5	1.6	1.6	1.6	1.7	1.8
Total Asset Turnover 34	0.1	•	3.0	•	•	0.1	0.1	0.1	0.1	0.1	0.1	0.1	0.1
Inventory Turnover 35	•	•	•	•	•	•	•	•	•	•	•	•	•
Receivables Turnover 36	•	•	•	•	•	•	•	•	•	•	•	•	•
Total Liabilities to Net Worth 37	59.5	•	•	•	•	4.2	5.2	5.3	6.2	7.8	8.4	7.9	•
Current Assets to Working Capital 38	•	•	•	•	•	•	•	•	•	•	•	•	•
Current Liabilities to Working Capital 39	•	•	•	•	•	•	•	•	•	•	•	•	•
Working Capital to Net Sales 40	•	•	•	•	•	•	•	•	•	•	•	•	•
Inventory to Working Capital 41	•	•	•	•	•	•	•	•	•	•	•	•	•
Total Receipts to Cash Flow 42	2.9	2.1	2.6	•	•	1.9	3.1	3.0	3.0	2.8	2.9	2.9	•
Cost of Goods to Cash Flow 43	0.0	0.0	0.2	•	•	0.0	0.0	0.0	0.0	0.0	0.0	0.0	0.0
Cash Flow to Total Debt 44	0.0	•	0.1	•	•	0.1	0.0	0.0	0.0	0.0	0.0	0.0	0.0

Selected Financial Factors (in Percentages)

Item													
Debt Ratio 45	98.3	•	1124.8	•	•	80.8	84.0	84.1	86.2	88.6	89.3	88.7	102.3
Return on Total Assets 46	3.3	•	227.0	•	•	5.9	2.7	2.6	2.7	2.8	2.9	3.3	•
Return on Equity Before Income Taxes 47	85.4	•	•	•	•	21.0	6.0	6.5	6.9	8.8	10.0	10.1	3.3
Return on Equity After Income Taxes 48	59.0	•	•	•	•	20.5	4.4	4.8	4.7	6.0	6.9	7.0	•
Profit Margin (Before Income Tax) 49	22.4	34.6	61.5	•	•	38.3	15.7	15.1	17.4	17.5	18.8	20.3	23.0
Profit Margin (After Income Tax) 50	15.5	28.5	60.7	•	•	37.2	11.6	12.0	13.0	14.1	15.6	•	•

Table I

Corporations with and without Net Income

CREDIT CARD ISSUING AND OTHER CONSUMER CREDIT

MONEY AMOUNTS AND SIZE OF ASSETS IN THOUSANDS OF DOLLARS

Item Description for Accounting Period 7/04 Through 6/05	Total	Zero Assets	Under 500	500 to 1,000	1,000 to 5,000	5,000 to 10,000	10,000 to 25,000	25,000 to 50,000	50,000 to 100,000	100,000 to 250,000	250,000 to 500,000	500,000 to 2,500,000	2,500,000 and over
Number of Enterprises **1**	6641	663	2720	805	1397	601	223	79	43	38	18	35	18
Revenues ($ in Thousands)													
Net Sales **2**	92831900	201974	127879	434195	1601656	1123051	986799	787513	751217	1632671	1200780	7645053	76339111
Interest **3**	32905459	100257	33345	9420	102109	104774	52614	118118	57617	400451	349590	2554579	29022585
Rents **4**	293010	0	0	0	115	27	596	693	176	93	0	42353	248957
Royalties **5**	34919	0	0	0	45	1	0	0	0	27754	0	7087	32
Other Portfolio Income **6**	3890792	1771	116	75	1398	45988	2390	14902	4813	10408	2794	396061	3410078
Other Receipts **7**	55707720	99946	94418	424700	1497989	972261	931199	653800	688611	1193965	848396	4464973	43657459
Total Receipts **8**	92831900	201974	127879	434195	1601656	1123051	986799	787513	751217	1632671	1200780	7645053	76339111
Average Total Receipts **9**	13979	305	47	539	1146	1869	4425	9969	17470	42965	66710	218430	4241062
Operating Costs/Operating Income (%)													
Cost of Operations **10**	6.3	•	•	•	•	•	0.9	0.4	1.4	0.1	0.1	0.0	7.6
Salaries and Wages **11**	9.0	20.5	12.5	12.1	19.3	14.0	17.7	20.5	16.7	15.7	18.0	9.1	8.1
Taxes Paid **12**	1.3	1.1	2.8	3.6	2.6	2.8	2.3	2.4	2.2	2.9	2.4	1.1	1.1
Interest Paid **13**	19.1	27.2	2.5	28.5	7.5	17.1	11.2	13.7	13.1	12.2	14.7	20.1	19.7
Depreciation **14**	8.1	0.4	1.1	2.0	1.9	3.8	1.8	2.6	4.9	3.0	4.6	2.4	9.3
Amortization and Depletion **15**	1.2	0.8	0.2	1.2	0.1	0.4	0.7	0.3	1.0	1.7	0.7	2.0	1.1
Pensions and Other Deferred Comp. **16**	0.5	0.1	•	•	0.2	0.3	0.5	0.9	0.5	0.2	0.1	0.3	0.6
Employee Benefits **17**	0.9	0.3	0.0	0.0	0.7	0.7	1.2	1.2	1.6	1.3	0.2	0.7	1.0
Advertising **18**	2.9	0.4	2.5	0.7	7.7	1.4	1.5	2.6	2.5	1.8	2.9	2.1	3.0
Other Expenses **19**	38.6	37.2	68.3	25.4	46.9	44.0	42.4	30.4	29.2	40.0	45.4	47.9	37.4
Officers' Compensation **20**	1.0	0.9	3.4	5.3	3.8	6.9	6.0	4.2	5.6	3.9	0.7	0.9	0.6
Operating Margin **21**	11.0	11.1	6.6	21.2	9.3	8.7	13.8	20.7	21.2	17.3	10.2	13.4	10.5
Operating Margin Before Officers' Comp. **22**	12.0	12.0	10.1	26.4	13.1	15.6	19.8	24.9	26.8	21.2	10.9	14.3	11.1

Selected Average Balance Sheet ($ in Thousands)

Net Receivables 23	50724	0	26	391	1214	4428	11627	24752	45394	98529	186235	578667	16570494
Inventories 24	•	•	•	•	•	•	•	•	•	•	•	•	•
Net Property, Plant and Equipment 25	3092	0	3	34	73	127	287	1210	1804	2821	5913	8035	1088075
Total Assets 26	91184		79	684	1821	6410	15598	35702	72124	152732	352751	1011379	30079850
Notes and Loans Payable 27	48134	0	37	283	950	4501	9621	23248	42740	93756	255732	607711	15557843
All Other Liabilities 28	28939	0	11	63	214	772	2391	4599	18255	21490	41355	182236	10095463
Net Worth 29	14111	0	30	338	657	1137	3586	7855	11129	37486	55664	221432	4426544

Selected Financial Ratios (Times to 1)

Current Ratio 30	2.1	•	4.8	2.4	3.1	2.5	2.2	2.0	2.2	2.7	1.0	1.8	2.1
Quick Ratio 31	2.0	•	3.3	2.1	3.1	2.2	2.0	1.9	2.0	2.4	1.0	1.6	2.0
Net Sales to Working Capital 32	0.5	•	1.2	1.4	1.1	0.6	0.6	0.7	0.6	0.6	9.1	0.6	0.4
Coverage Ratio 33	1.6	1.4	3.6	1.7	2.2	1.5	2.2	2.5	2.6	2.4	1.7	1.7	1.5
Total Asset Turnover 34	0.2	•	0.6	0.8	0.6	0.3	0.3	0.3	0.2	0.3	0.2	0.2	0.1
Inventory Turnover 35	•	•	•	•	•	•	•	•	•	•	•	•	•
Receivables Turnover 36	•	•	•	•	•	•	•	•	•	•	•	•	•
Total Liabilities to Net Worth 37	5.5	•	1.6	1.0	1.8	4.6	3.3	3.5	5.5	3.1	5.3	3.6	5.8
Current Assets to Working Capital 38	1.9	•	1.3	1.7	1.5	1.7	1.9	2.0	1.9	1.6	27.6	2.2	1.9
Current Liabilities to Working Capital 39	0.9	•	0.3	0.7	0.5	0.7	0.9	1.0	0.9	0.6	26.6	1.2	0.9
Working Capital to Net Sales 40	2.2	1.4	0.9	0.7	0.9	1.8	1.6	1.4	1.7	1.8	0.1	1.6	2.4
Inventory to Working Capital 41	0.0	•	0.0	•	0.0	0.0	0.0	•	0.0	0.0	0.0	0.0	0.0
Total Receipts to Cash Flow 42	2.1	2.1	1.4	2.3	2.0	2.1	1.9	2.2	2.1	1.9	2.0	1.7	2.2
Cost of Goods to Cash Flow 43	0.1	•	•	•	•	0.0	0.0	0.0	0.0	0.0	0.0	0.0	0.2
Cash Flow to Total Debt 44	0.1	•	0.7	0.7	0.5	0.2	0.2	0.2	0.1	0.2	0.1	0.2	0.1

Selected Financial Factors (in Percentages)

Debt Ratio 45	84.5	•	61.8	50.6	63.9	82.3	77.0	78.0	84.6	75.5	84.2	78.1	85.3
Return on Total Assets 46	4.7	•	5.4	39.2	10.6	7.5	7.1	9.6	8.3	8.3	4.7	7.2	4.3
Return on Equity Before Income Taxes 47	11.1	•	10.1	33.8	16.2	14.2	16.9	26.3	33.2	19.8	12.2	13.2	10.3
Return on Equity After Income Taxes 48	8.0	11.1	9.6	32.0	15.2	12.7	15.7	23.9	31.0	14.9	9.8	9.5	7.2
Profit Margin (Before Income Tax) 49	11.2	11.1	6.5	21.2	9.3	8.7	13.7	20.7	21.2	17.3	10.2	13.3	10.7
Profit Margin (After Income Tax) 50	8.1	•	6.2	20.0	8.7	7.7	12.7	18.8	19.8	13.0	8.2	9.7	7.5

Table II

Corporations with Net Income

CREDIT CARD ISSUING AND OTHER CONSUMER CREDIT

MONEY AMOUNTS AND SIZE OF ASSETS IN THOUSANDS OF DOLLARS

Item Description for Accounting Period 7/04 Through 6/05	Total	Zero Assets	Under 500	500 to 1,000	1,000 to 5,000	5,000 to 10,000	10,000 to 25,000	25,000 to 50,000	50,000 to 100,000	100,000 to 250,000	250,000 to 500,000	500,000 to 2,500,000	2,500,000 and over
Number of Enterprises **1**	4359	248	1453	0	1026	456	184	66	37	30	8	30	0
Revenues ($ in Thousands)													
Net Sales **2**	89649303	188991	72530	0	1392876	724921	875624	731717	699622	1406905	949931	6703372	0
Interest **3**	32003631	99354	177	0	62721	101788	39559	115875	48365	249164	244921	2229700	0
Rents **4**	292741	0	0	0	8	27	541	586	176	93	0	42353	0
Royalties **5**	34873	0	0	0	0	1	0	0	0	27754	0	7087	0
Other Portfolio Income **6**	3497698	1700	116	0	703	45688	1194	14056	4813	7616	1021	47482	0
Other Receipts **7**	53820360	87937	72237	0	1329444	577417	834330	601200	646268	1122278	703989	4376750	0
Total Receipts **8**	89649303	188991	72530	0	1392876	724921	875624	731717	699622	1406905	949931	6703372	0
Average Total Receipts **9**	20566	762	50	•	1358	1590	4759	11087	18909	46897	118741	223446	•
Operating Costs/Operating Income (%)													
Cost of Operations **10**	6.5	•	•	•	•	•	1.0	0.4	1.5	0.1	0.1	0.0	
Salaries and Wages **11**	8.9	0.1	14.5	•	16.4	11.7	17.5	20.3	17.3	16.3	18.5	9.8	
Taxes Paid **12**	1.3	0.8	0.7	•	2.6	2.3	2.2	2.4	2.3	3.1	2.5	1.2	
Interest Paid **13**	18.4	28.2	1.8	•	5.9	17.1	10.4	13.1	11.8	8.1	7.8	12.1	
Depreciation **14**	7.5	0.2	0.6	•	0.7	4.9	1.1	1.4	2.5	2.3	4.3	1.8	
Amortization and Depletion **15**	1.2	0.6	0.3	•	0.1	0.4	0.7	0.3	1.1	1.1	0.8	2.2	
Pensions and Other Deferred Comp. **16**	0.6	•	•	•	0.1	0.2	0.5	1.0	0.6	0.2	0.1	0.2	
Employee Benefits **17**	0.9	0.3	0.0	•	0.7	0.5	1.3	1.2	1.7	1.3	0.2	0.8	
Advertising **18**	2.9	0.0	0.2	•	7.3	0.8	1.4	2.7	2.1	2.0	3.6	2.4	
Other Expenses **19**	38.7	29.6	41.4	•	42.5	36.3	39.8	29.2	28.3	36.5	47.4	50.6	
Officers' Compensation **20**	0.9	•	0.2	•	3.1	5.5	6.2	4.1	6.0	4.4	0.8	1.0	
Operating Margin **21**	12.1	40.2	40.3	•	20.6	20.3	18.0	23.9	24.8	24.8	14.0	17.9	
Operating Margin Before Officers' Comp. **22**	13.0	40.2	40.5	•	23.7	25.9	24.1	28.0	30.9	29.2	14.8	18.9	

Selected Average Balance Sheet ($ in Thousands)

Net Receivables 23	74372	0	1	•	1327	4560	12256	24914	45783	99741	283114	539601
Inventories 24	•	•	•	•	•	•	•	•	•	•	•	•
Net Property, Plant and Equipment 25	4639	0	0	•	23	121	213	1403	1900	2449	8579	6174
Total Assets 26	134349	0	56	•	1930	6408	15695	35737	72031	154313	380301	944468
Notes and Loans Payable 27	69855	0	1	•	874	4324	9547	23508	41115	81665	253099	482958
All Other Liabilities 28	43692	0	3	•	262	884	2165	4982	12212	23238	44383	205526
Net Worth 29	20802	0	52	•	794	1201	3983	7247	18704	49410	82819	255984

Selected Financial Ratios (Times to 1)

Current Ratio 30	2.1	•	4.1	•	3.2	2.6	2.2	1.9	2.1	3.0	1.3	1.6
Quick Ratio 31	2.0	•	3.3	•	3.1	2.4	2.1	1.8	2.0	2.5	1.3	1.4
Net Sales to Working Capital 32	0.5	•	3.7	•	1.3	0.5	0.6	0.8	0.7	0.6	1.6	0.8
Coverage Ratio 33	1.7	2.4	23.4	•	4.5	2.2	2.7	2.8	3.1	4.1	2.8	2.5
Total Asset Turnover 34	0.2	•	0.9	•	0.7	0.2	0.3	0.3	0.3	0.3	0.3	0.2
Inventory Turnover 35	•	•	•	•	•	•	•	•	•	•	•	•
Receivables Turnover 36	•	•	•	•	•	•	•	•	•	•	•	•
Total Liabilities to Net Worth 37	5.5	•	0.1	•	1.4	4.3	2.9	3.9	2.9	2.1	3.6	2.7
Current Assets to Working Capital 38	1.9	•	1.3	•	1.4	1.6	1.8	2.1	1.9	1.5	4.2	2.6
Current Liabilities to Working Capital 39	0.9	•	0.3	•	0.4	0.6	0.8	1.1	0.9	0.5	3.2	1.6
Working Capital to Net Sales 40	2.2	•	0.3	•	0.8	2.1	1.6	1.2	1.5	1.8	0.6	1.2
Inventory to Working Capital 41	0.0	•	•	•	0.0	0.0	0.0	•	0.0	0.0	•	•
Total Receipts to Cash Flow 42	2.0	1.4	1.3	•	1.7	1.9	1.8	2.1	2.0	1.8	1.8	1.5
Cost of Goods to Cash Flow 43	0.1	•	•	•	•	0.0	0.0	0.0	0.0	0.0	0.0	0.0
Cash Flow to Total Debt 44	0.1	•	9.2	•	0.7	0.2	0.2	0.2	0.2	0.3	0.2	0.2

Selected Financial Factors (in Percentages)

Debt Ratio 45	84.5	•	7.6	•	58.8	81.3	74.6	79.7	74.0	68.0	78.2	72.9
Return on Total Assets 46	4.7	•	37.2	•	18.6	9.3	8.6	11.5	9.6	10.0	6.8	7.1
Return on Equity Before Income Taxes 47	12.2	•	38.6	•	35.2	26.9	21.4	36.5	25.1	23.5	20.1	15.5
Return on Equity After Income Taxes 48	8.9	•	38.0	•	34.1	25.0	20.0	33.3	23.6	18.8	16.6	11.9
Profit Margin (Before Income Tax) 49	12.3	40.2	40.2	•	20.6	20.3	17.9	23.9	24.8	24.8	14.0	17.8
Profit Margin (After Income Tax) 50	9.0	26.3	39.6	•	20.0	18.9	16.8	21.8	23.3	19.9	11.6	13.6

Table I

Corporations with and without Net Income

REAL ESTATE CREDIT INCL. MORTGAGE BANKERS AND ORIGINATORS

MONEY AMOUNTS AND SIZE OF ASSETS IN THOUSANDS OF DOLLARS

Item Description for Accounting Period 7/04 Through 6/05	Total	Zero Assets	Under 500	500 to 1,000	1,000 to 5,000	5,000 to 10,000	10,000 to 25,000	25,000 to 50,000	50,000 to 100,000	100,000 to 250,000	250,000 to 500,000	500,000 to 2,500,000	2,500,000 and over
Number of Enterprises **1**	17257	2594	11540	956	1097	506	280	123	59	43	26	22	9
Revenues ($ in Thousands)													
Net Sales **2**	40895810	496252	4995367	983049	1599483	1163018	2183300	1755447	1507558	1657153	1801334	3430401	19323449
Interest **3**	8417149	65444	5345	930	53382	39739	87547	119070	63042	194744	369095	957993	6460820
Rents **4**	50558	13	0	0	3977	716	3811	1624	18	6778	8474	7307	17840
Royalties **5**	116	0	0	0	0	98	0	18	0	0	0	0	0
Other Portfolio Income **6**	3736053	116	1394	21219	4039	25873	56221	33957	69673	31805	240551	419636	2831573
Other Receipts **7**	28691934	430679	498628	960900	1538085	1096592	2035721	1600778	1374825	1423826	1183214	2045465	10013216
Total Receipts **8**	40895810	496252	4995367	983049	1599483	1163018	2183300	1755447	1507558	1657153	1801334	3430401	19323449
Average Total Receipts **9**	2370	191	433	1028	1458	2298	7798	14272	25552	38538	69282	155927	2147050
Operating Costs/Operating Income (%)													
Cost of Operations **10**	2.4	0.4	1.0	0.1	3.2	3.5	8.1	7.8	5.4	2.2	4.1	0.1	1.8
Salaries and Wages **11**	30.4	25.1	35.8	31.0	39.8	39.9	37.2	36.4	37.1	33.3	28.7	28.3	26.1
Taxes Paid **12**	3.5	5.5	3.7	5.0	3.8	3.7	3.8	3.6	3.2	3.4	4.0	3.9	3.1
Interest Paid **13**	13.6	9.3	0.3	1.4	5.4	7.5	7.1	10.5	6.1	11.2	16.3	16.6	19.9
Depreciation **14**	1.8	0.7	0.8	0.7	1.2	1.0	0.9	1.5	1.2	1.3	4.4	2.2	2.2
Amortization and Depletion **15**	0.4	0.7	0.2	0.0	0.1	0.3	0.1	1.1	0.8	1.0	0.9	0.3	0.4
Pensions and Other Deferred Comp. **16**	0.4	0.2	0.1	0.8	0.8	0.6	0.4	0.3	0.2	1.2	0.4	0.2	0.4
Employee Benefits **17**	1.6	0.8	0.9	1.0	1.6	0.9	1.0	1.6	1.3	1.5	1.9	1.9	1.9
Advertising **18**	2.3	1.5	3.5	1.5	2.3	2.6	3.6	3.3	4.0	4.2	1.5	3.8	1.3
Other Expenses **19**	26.0	46.9	42.8	28.0	28.9	29.9	27.2	36.3	30.4	25.6	28.3	27.3	18.8
Officers' Compensation **20**	3.5	7.4	7.4	14.2	9.4	4.5	4.8	3.8	6.4	4.1	2.7	2.4	1.1
Operating Margin **21**	14.0	1.5	3.5	16.4	3.4	5.4	5.8	•	3.8	11.0	6.8	12.8	23.0
Operating Margin Before Officers' Comp. **22**	17.5	9.0	10.9	30.6	12.8	10.0	10.5	•	10.3	15.0	9.5	15.2	24.1

Selected Average Balance Sheet ($ in Thousands)

Net Receivables 23	1352	0	14	63	704	2214	3060	4827	11724	26540	53933	248673	1228689
Inventories 24	•	•	•	•	•	•	•	•	•	•	•	•	•
Net Property, Plant and Equipment 25	176	0	16	38	218	131	537	1031	1598	3026	5872	12471	176053
Total Assets 26	13958	0	100	645	2315	7399	15668	33773	69799	159497	338078	1055033	20143953
Notes and Loans Payable 27	7668	0	31	77	1429	4382	8689	20658	37607	94316	206335	605213	10908373
All Other Liabilities 28	4903	0	20	171	271	1874	4055	15409	21369	46021	94244	332878	7436604
Net Worth 29	1387	0	48	397	615	1143	2924	-2294	10823	19161	37500	116943	1798975

Selected Financial Ratios (Times to 1)

Current Ratio 30	0.4	•	4.5	2.3	1.3	0.7	0.7	0.5	0.5	0.6	0.5	0.5	0.3
Quick Ratio 31	0.3	•	4.1	2.0	1.1	0.6	0.5	0.3	0.4	0.4	0.4	0.5	0.2
Net Sales to Working Capital 32	•	•	9.0	3.9	6.4	•	•	•	•	•	•	•	•
Coverage Ratio 33	2.0	1.2	11.6	13.1	1.6	1.7	1.8	0.4	1.6	1.9	1.4	1.8	2.2
Total Asset Turnover 34	0.2	•	4.3	1.6	0.6	0.3	0.5	0.4	0.4	0.2	0.2	0.1	0.1
Inventory Turnover 35	•	•	•	•	•	•	•	•	•	•	•	•	•
Receivables Turnover 36	•	•	•	•	•	•	•	•	•	•	•	•	•
Total Liabilities to Net Worth 37	9.1	•	1.1	0.6	2.8	5.5	4.4	•	5.4	7.3	8.0	8.0	10.2
Current Assets to Working Capital 38	•	•	1.3	1.8	4.8	•	•	•	•	•	•	•	•
Current Liabilities to Working Capital 39	•	•	0.3	0.8	3.8	•	•	•	•	•	•	•	•
Working Capital to Net Sales 40	•	•	0.1	0.3	0.2	•	•	•	•	•	•	•	•
Inventory to Working Capital 41	•	•	•	•	•	•	•	•	•	•	•	•	•
Total Receipts to Cash Flow 42	2.9	2.3	2.5	2.7	3.7	3.5	3.5	4.0	3.3	3.0	3.2	2.7	2.8
Cost of Goods to Cash Flow 43	0.1	0.0	0.0	0.1	0.1	0.3	0.3	0.3	0.2	0.1	0.1	0.0	0.1
Cash Flow to Total Debt 44	0.1	•	1.5	0.2	0.1	0.2	0.1	0.1	0.1	0.1	0.1	0.1	0.0

Selected Financial Factors (in Percentages)

Debt Ratio 45	90.1	•	51.5	38.5	73.5	84.5	81.3	106.8	84.5	88.0	88.9	88.9	91.1
Return on Total Assets 46	4.7	•	16.6	28.2	5.5	3.9	6.4	1.7	3.6	5.2	4.7	4.4	4.6
Return on Equity Before Income Taxes 47	23.9	•	31.3	42.4	7.9	9.9	15.3	40.0	8.9	20.8	12.5	17.4	27.5
Return on Equity After Income Taxes 48	18.2	•	30.9	41.7	7.1	9.1	13.7	43.3	7.8	18.3	6.3	11.4	20.9
Profit Margin (Before Income Tax) 49	14.0	1.5	3.5	16.4	3.3	4.9	5.7	•	3.8	10.3	6.8	13.1	23.0
Profit Margin (After Income Tax) 50	10.6	0.1	3.5	16.1	3.0	5.1	5.1	•	3.3	9.1	3.4	8.5	17.5

Table II

Corporations with Net Income

REAL ESTATE CREDIT INCL. MORTGAGE BANKERS AND ORIGINATORS

MONEY AMOUNTS AND SIZE OF ASSETS IN THOUSANDS OF DOLLARS

Item Description for Accounting Period 7/04 Through 6/05	Total	Zero Assets	Under 500	500 to 1,000	1,000 to 5,000	5,000 to 10,000	10,000 to 25,000	25,000 to 50,000	50,000 to 100,000	100,000 to 250,000	250,000 to 500,000	500,000 to 2,500,000	2,500,000 and over
Number of Enterprises **1**	9758	686	6690	838	761	379	206	85	40	32	0	15	0
Revenues ($ in Thousands)													
Net Sales **2**	35755631	362829	4063198	960853	1213814	726136	1710870	1242575	1016304	1375222	0	2723279	0
Interest **3**	7752128	57033	4496	930	38770	23320	68492	64075	37855	141744	0	679584	0
Rents **4**	40759	13	0	0	2941	485	3465	651	0	799	0	7268	0
Royalties **5**	70	0	0	0	0	52	0	18	0	0	0	0	0
Other Portfolio Income **6**	3561884	116	1394	21219	3724	25397	24644	28459	21435	14652	0	419624	0
Other Receipts **7**	24400790	305667	4057308	938704	1168379	676882	1614269	1149372	957014	1218027	0	1616803	0
Total Receipts **8**	35755631	362829	4063198	960853	1213814	726136	1710870	1242575	1016304	1375222	0	2723279	0
Average Total Receipts **9**	3664	529	607	1147	1595	1916	8305	14619	25408	42976	•	181552	•
Operating Costs/Operating Income (%)													
Cost of Operations **10**	2.4	0.6	0.8	0.1	2.4	3.8	8.7	8.7	7.8	2.5	•	0.1	•
Salaries and Wages **11**	29.1	27.8	36.1	31.4	41.8	34.8	35.4	33.6	32.7	31.8	•	24.7	•
Taxes Paid **12**	3.5	6.1	3.8	4.9	3.8	4.2	3.6	3.5	3.1	3.5	•	4.0	•
Interest Paid **13**	13.6	9.6	0.3	1.4	3.9	9.5	6.7	7.2	6.2	8.3	•	11.9	•
Depreciation **14**	1.8	0.9	0.7	0.7	1.3	0.6	0.8	1.2	0.8	1.1	•	2.3	•
Amortization and Depletion **15**	0.3	0.7	0.1	0.0	0.0	0.2	0.1	0.2	0.4	1.1	•	0.4	•
Pensions and Other Deferred Comp. **16**	0.4	0.2	0.2	0.8	1.0	0.9	0.3	0.3	0.3	1.4	•	0.3	•
Employee Benefits **17**	1.5	1.0	0.3	1.0	1.4	1.2	0.7	1.3	1.3	1.4	•	1.7	•
Advertising **18**	2.0	0.5	2.1	1.4	2.4	2.7	3.7	2.4	3.2	4.8	•	4.2	•
Other Expenses **19**	23.1	22.9	41.5	25.5	25.0	21.4	26.0	22.8	24.7	23.6	•	25.2	•
Officers' Compensation **20**	2.9	9.9	4.7	14.5	8.3	4.6	4.3	4.4	6.9	4.5	•	2.4	•
Operating Margin **21**	19.3	19.8	9.5	18.3	8.6	16.0	9.7	14.4	12.5	16.0	•	22.7	•
Operating Margin Before Officers' Comp. **22**	22.2	29.7	14.2	32.8	16.9	20.6	14.0	18.8	19.4	20.5	•	25.2	•

Selected Average Balance Sheet ($ in Thousands)

Net Receivables 23	2009	0	16	71	807	2751	3341	4366	13721	27838	207582
Inventories 24	•	•									•
Net Property, Plant and Equipment 25	261	0	12	41	294	102	495	979	964	2719	13794
Total Assets 26	22368	0	117	649	2409	7290	15472	33563	68390	160300	1110216
Notes and Loans Payable 27	11856	0	22	87	1530	3367	8597	17893	40050	79948	566404
All Other Liabilities 28	8226	0	30	190	258	2026	3759	9415	16926	52958	426164
Net Worth 29	2286	0	65	372	622	1898	3115	6255	11414	27394	117648

Selected Financial Ratios (Times to 1)

Current Ratio 30	0.4	•	3.7	2.3	1.3	0.9	0.7	0.5	0.6	0.6	0.4
Quick Ratio 31	0.3	•	3.5	2.1	1.2	0.9	0.5	0.3	0.4	0.4	0.4
Net Sales to Working Capital 32	•	•	11.9	3.8	6.0	•	•	•	•	•	•
Coverage Ratio 33	2.4	3.1	39.1	14.2	3.2	2.6	2.4	3.0	3.0	2.9	2.9
Total Asset Turnover 34	0.2	•	5.2	1.8	0.7	0.3	0.5	0.4	0.4	0.3	0.2
Inventory Turnover 35	•	•	•	•	•	•	•	•	•	•	•
Receivables Turnover 36	•	•	•	•	•	•	•	•	•	•	•
Total Liabilities to Net Worth 37	8.8	•	0.8	0.7	2.9	2.8	4.0	4.4	5.0	4.9	8.4
Current Assets to Working Capital 38	•	•	1.4	1.8	4.2	•	•	•	•	•	•
Current Liabilities to Working Capital 39	•	•	0.4	0.8	3.2	•	•	•	•	•	•
Working Capital to Net Sales 40	•	•	0.1	0.3	0.2	•	•	•	•	•	•
Inventory to Working Capital 41	•	•	•	•	•	•	•	•	•	•	•
Total Receipts to Cash Flow 42	2.7	2.4	2.2	2.7	3.5	3.2	3.2	3.0	2.9	2.8	2.2
Cost of Goods to Cash Flow 43	0.1	0.0	0.0	0.0	0.1	0.1	0.3	0.3	0.2	0.1	0.0
Cash Flow to Total Debt 44	0.1	•	5.4	1.5	0.3	0.1	0.2	0.2	0.2	0.1	0.1

Selected Financial Factors (in Percentages)

Debt Ratio 45	89.8	•	44.3	42.6	74.2	74.0	79.9	81.4	83.3	82.9	89.4
Return on Total Assets 46	5.4	•	50.8	34.7	8.2	6.5	8.8	9.4	6.9	6.4	5.7
Return on Equity Before Income Taxes 47	30.8	•	88.9	56.2	21.9	15.4	25.7	33.5	27.5	24.7	35.6
Return on Equity After Income Taxes 48	24.8	•	88.4	55.4	20.8	14.7	23.6	32.1	26.0	22.4	26.8
Profit Margin (Before Income Tax) 49	19.2	19.8	9.5	18.3	8.5	15.2	9.6	14.3	12.4	15.8	23.0
Profit Margin (After Income Tax) 50	15.4	17.9	9.5	18.0	8.1	14.6	8.9	13.7	11.7	14.3	17.4

Table I

Corporations with and without Net Income

INTL. TRADE, SECONDARY FINANCING, OTHER NONDEPOSITORY CREDIT

MONEY AMOUNTS AND SIZE OF ASSETS IN THOUSANDS OF DOLLARS

Item Description for Accounting Period 7/04 Through 6/05	Total	Zero Assets	Under 500	500 to 1,000	1,000 to 5,000	5,000 to 10,000	10,000 to 25,000	25,000 to 50,000	50,000 to 100,000	100,000 to 250,000	250,000 to 500,000	500,000 to 2,500,000	2,500,000 and over
Number of Enterprises **1**	6865	994	4512	554	397	54	102	54	33	56	28	42	38
Revenues ($ in Thousands)													
Net Sales **2**	172478137	153778	624043	174468	408101	289629	703937	418528	279810	813801	631311	2517782	165462949
Interest **3**	15878375	62342	42486	29991	26551	28744	21222	34634	62905	302413	305454	1485037	156381595
Rents **4**	70993	0	0	12	555	0	80	2284	148	2099	1522	13459	50827
Royalties **5**	6635	0	1786	0	0	0	0	31	16	50	135	0	4618
Other Portfolio Income **6**	2391666	862	2564	4586	2121	26229	5287	11041	984	3324	534	186830	2147301
Other Receipts **7**	11225468	90568	577207	139879	378874	234656	677348	370538	215757	505915	323666	832456	6878608
Total Receipts **8**	172478137	153778	624043	174468	408101	289629	703937	418528	279810	813801	631311	2517782	165462949
Average Total Receipts **9**	25124	155	138	315	1028	5364	6901	7751	8479	14532	22547	59947	4354288
Operating Costs/Operating Income (%)													
Cost of Operations **10**	0.4	28.2	•	•	•	9.7	30.8	3.7	18.7	1.9	•	0.4	0.1
Salaries and Wages **11**	1.6	4.4	21.4	21.0	41.7	16.6	14.1	25.9	13.1	17.3	18.2	8.3	1.0
Taxes Paid **12**	0.2	1.4	3.7	5.2	2.7	6.1	1.7	2.9	5.6	1.0	2.1	1.2	0.1
Interest Paid **13**	78.9	37.1	0.7	15.5	8.4	14.6	6.1	16.0	21.6	18.6	32.6	34.2	81.3
Depreciation **14**	0.5	0.0	1.9	1.1	4.8	2.4	1.2	1.6	1.0	2.0	2.1	5.1	0.4
Amortization and Depletion **15**	0.1	0.2	0.3	0.1	0.0	0.2	0.2	0.5	0.2	1.1	0.5	0.5	0.1
Pensions and Other Deferred Comp. **16**	0.1	0.0	0.0	0.0	0.2	0.0	0.2	0.6	1.1	0.7	1.2	1.2	0.1
Employee Benefits **17**	0.1	0.1	0.0	1.1	0.8	1.2	1.2	1.7	1.6	1.4	2.2	0.7	0.1
Advertising **18**	0.1	0.0	0.6	5.0	1.1	0.2	0.8	1.1	0.7	0.7	1.1	0.5	0.0
Other Expenses **19**	7.4	41.5	60.2	40.1	36.7	32.0	85.5	37.9	28.8	39.1	36.5	20.1	6.1
Officers' Compensation **20**	0.4	11.5	4.7	11.3	3.1	11.0	4.6	3.6	5.0	3.1	2.1	0.9	0.3
Operating Margin **21**	10.2	•	6.6	•	0.5	6.0	•	4.5	2.5	13.2	0.5	27.0	10.3
Operating Margin Before Officers' Comp. **22**	10.6	•	11.3	11.0	3.6	17.0	•	8.1	7.5	16.4	2.6	27.9	10.6

Selected Average Balance Sheet ($ in Thousands)

	1	2	3	4	5	6	7	8	9	10	11	12	13
Net Receivables 23	30434	0	15	378	689	1329	7903	20350	54011	105642	213519	757949	4234035
Inventories 24	•	•	•	•	•	•	•	•	•	•	•	•	•
Net Property, Plant and Equipment 25	300	0	5	10	450	770	473	568	961	1315	3007	8016	31607
Total Assets 26	320318	0	72	604	2018	6815	15689	35448	73423	156501	354750	1220715	55822411
Notes and Loans Payable 27	285767	0	29	429	2117	6034	9005	21864	48292	92254	224925	741293	50367361
All Other Liabilities 28	19903	0	6	59	115	1312	3015	7187	8240	16830	25283	188271	3314085
Net Worth 29	14648	0	36	116	-214	-531	3669	6397	16891	47417	104542	291151	2140965

Selected Financial Ratios (Times to 1)

	1	2	3	4	5	6	7	8	9	10	11	12	13
Current Ratio 30	0.4	•	8.0	4.5	1.6	0.9	1.5	1.5	1.4	1.4	1.3	1.3	0.4
Quick Ratio 31	0.3	•	5.2	3.6	1.2	0.7	1.3	1.2	1.4	1.4	1.1	1.2	0.3
Net Sales to Working Capital 32	•	•	2.8	0.7	2.3	•	1.9	0.9	0.5	0.4	0.4	0.3	•
Coverage Ratio 33	1.1	0.3	10.4	1.0	1.1	1.4	1.3	1.3	1.1	1.7	1.0	1.8	1.1
Total Asset Turnover 34	0.1	•	1.9	0.5	0.5	0.8	0.4	0.2	0.1	0.1	0.1	0.0	0.1
Inventory Turnover 35	•	•	•	•	•	•	•	•	•	•	•	•	•
Receivables Turnover 36	•	•	•	•	•	•	•	•	•	•	•	•	•
Total Liabilities to Net Worth 37	20.9	•	1.0	4.2	•	3.3	•	4.5	3.3	2.3	2.4	3.2	25.1
Current Assets to Working Capital 38	•	•	1.1	1.3	2.7	•	3.0	3.2	3.3	3.4	4.5	4.0	•
Current Liabilities to Working Capital 39	•	•	0.1	0.3	1.7	•	2.0	2.2	2.3	2.4	3.5	3.0	•
Working Capital to Net Sales 40	•	•	0.4	1.4	0.4	0.5	0.5	1.1	2.1	2.3	2.5	3.7	•
Inventory to Working Capital 41	•	•	•	•	•	0.0	0.0	•	0.0	0.0	0.0	0.0	•
Total Receipts to Cash Flow 42	5.8	•	1.7	3.8	3.1	2.8	2.8	2.8	3.5	2.0	2.9	2.2	6.2
Cost of Goods to Cash Flow 43	0.0	•	•	•	•	0.3	0.9	0.1	0.7	0.0	•	0.0	0.0
Cash Flow to Total Debt 44	0.0	•	2.3	0.2	0.2	0.3	0.2	0.1	0.0	0.1	0.0	0.0	0.0

Selected Financial Factors (in Percentages)

	1	2	3	4	5	6	7	8	9	10	11	12	13
Debt Ratio 45	95.4	•	49.2	80.8	110.6	107.8	76.6	82.0	77.0	69.7	70.5	76.1	96.2
Return on Total Assets 46	6.9	•	14.0	7.9	4.5	16.2	•	4.5	2.7	3.0	2.1	3.0	7.1
Return on Equity Before Income Taxes 47	15.9	•	24.9	•	•	•	•	5.4	1.1	4.0	0.1	5.5	19.0
Return on Equity After Income Taxes 48	10.2	•	23.7	•	•	•	•	3.1	0.3	2.5	•	3.8	12.4
Profit Margin (Before Income Tax) 49	9.3	•	6.6	0.5	6.0	•	•	4.5	2.2	13.2	0.5	26.7	9.4
Profit Margin (After Income Tax) 50	6.0	•	6.2	0.3	2.3	•	•	2.6	0.6	8.3	•	18.5	6.1

Table II

Corporations with Net Income

INTL. TRADE, SECONDARY FINANCING, OTHER NONDEPOSITORY CREDIT

MONEY AMOUNTS AND SIZE OF ASSETS IN THOUSANDS OF DOLLARS

Item Description for Accounting Period 7/04 Through 6/05	Total	Zero Assets	Under 500	500 to 1,000	1,000 to 5,000	5,000 to 10,000	10,000 to 25,000	25,000 to 50,000	50,000 to 100,000	100,000 to 250,000	250,000 to 500,000	500,000 to 2,500,000	2,500,000 and over
Number of Enterprises **1**	4070	522	2702	341	231	24	70	38	21	40	18	31	31
Revenues ($ in Thousands)													
Net Sales **2**	170075538	136726	501775	146699	253729	280632	588835	353354	239003	733186	403306	1947296	16449096
Interest **3**	157137248	58351	11042	29892	12100	26910	15240	17681	40644	241702	210578	963057	155510050
Rents **4**	67103	0	0	12	40	0	80	2272	148	1873	1344	10507	50827
Royalties **5**	6500	0	1786	0	0	0	0	31	16	50	0	0	4618
Other Portfolio Income **6**	2379212	0	2564	4586	791	26229	1803	8697	233	3211	311	185329	2145457
Other Receipts **7**	10485475	78375	486383	112209	240798	227493	571712	324673	197962	486350	191073	788403	6780044
Total Receipts **8**	170075538	136726	501775	146699	253729	280632	588835	353354	239003	733186	403306	1947296	16449096
Average Total Receipts **9**	41788	262	186	430	1098	11693	8412	9299	11381	18330	22406	62816	5306161
Operating Costs/Operating Income (%)													
Cost of Operations **10**	0.4	31.7	*	*	*	10.0	36.8	4.4	21.9	2.1	*	0.6	0.1
Salaries and Wages **11**	1.5	0.5	19.3	24.7	32.9	17.1	12.9	25.7	12.8	17.5	13.2	9.3	1.0
Taxes Paid **12**	0.2	1.1	3.2	5.8	3.3	3.7	1.5	2.9	1.7	1.0	1.7	1.4	0.1
Interest Paid **13**	79.2	36.8	0.6	2.8	9.4	8.3	5.2	9.3	12.7	15.5	28.2	24.9	81.3
Depreciation **14**	0.5	0.0	2.1	1.2	1.6	2.5	0.9	1.8	1.0	2.1	1.7	6.1	0.4
Amortization and Depletion **15**	0.1	0.0	0.3	0.1	0.0	0.1	0.2	0.6	0.2	1.0	0.1	0.6	0.1
Pensions and Other Deferred Comp. **16**	0.1	*	0.0	*	0.3	0.0	0.1	0.6	0.3	0.7	2.7	1.1	0.1
Employee Benefits **17**	0.1	*	0.0	0.1	1.0	1.2	0.8	1.7	1.4	1.2	1.7	0.8	0.1
Advertising **18**	0.1	0.0	0.6	5.9	1.3	0.2	0.6	1.2	0.7	0.7	0.7	0.6	0.0
Other Expenses **19**	6.8	7.4	57.8	38.6	30.3	30.9	22.8	31.0	22.2	37.8	30.7	17.8	6.1
Officers' Compensation **20**	0.4	10.8	4.2	8.8	3.8	11.3	3.1	3.6	4.6	3.3	1.5	1.1	0.3
Operating Margin **21**	10.8	11.7	11.8	11.9	16.0	14.5	15.1	17.2	20.4	17.0	17.7	35.8	10.3
Operating Margin Before Officers' Comp. **22**	11.1	22.5	16.0	20.7	19.8	25.8	18.2	20.8	25.0	20.3	19.3	36.9	10.6

Selected Average Balance Sheet ($ in Thousands)

Net Receivables 23	40347	0	·	19	286	607	2200	9346	20908	56519	109172	233884	619628	4304907
Inventories 24	·												·	
Net Property, Plant and Equipment 25	461	0	·	8	17	569	978	334	563	1218	1706	2099	10290	38744
Total Assets 26	521912	0	·	97	627	1676	6506	16074	34450	73358	156339	363374	1046201	6901953
Notes and Loans Payable 27	465963	0	·	35	219	2422	1387	9014	18332	46255	96865	225797	602375	60219225
All Other Liabilities 28	32126	0	·	9	17	15	2387	2899	7890	4425	12428	33942	101052	4058953
Net Worth 29	23822	0	·	53	391	-761	2733	4160	8228	22678	47047	103634	342774	2623776

Selected Financial Ratios (Times to 1)

Current Ratio 30	0.4	·	7.1	8.9	3.6	1.5	1.6	1.7	1.7	1.4	1.3	1.6	0.4
Quick Ratio 31	0.3	·	4.8	6.1	3.0	1.2	1.4	1.4	1.7	1.3	1.1	1.5	0.3
Net Sales to Working Capital 32	·	·	2.8	0.8	1.9	8.4	1.8	0.8	0.4	0.6	0.4	0.2	0.3
Coverage Ratio 33	1.1	1.3	19.4	5.2	2.7	2.7	3.9	2.8	2.6	2.1	1.6	2.4	1.1
Total Asset Turnover 34	0.1	·	1.9	0.7	0.7	1.8	0.5	0.3	0.2	0.1	0.1	0.1	
Inventory Turnover 35	·	·	·	·	·	·	·	·	·	·	·	·	·
Receivables Turnover 36	·	·	·	·	·	·	·	·	·	·	·	·	·
Total Liabilities to Net Worth 37	20.9	·	0.8	0.6		1.4	2.9	3.2	2.2	2.3	2.5	2.1	24.5
Current Assets to Working Capital 38	·	·	1.2	1.1	1.4	3.2	2.7	2.5	2.3	3.6	4.5	2.6	
Current Liabilities to Working Capital 39	·	·	0.2	0.1	0.4	2.2	1.7	1.5	1.3	2.6	3.5	1.6	
Working Capital to Net Sales 40	·	·	0.4	1.2	0.5	0.1	0.5	1.2	2.3	1.8	2.9	4.5	
Inventory to Working Capital 41	·	·	·	·	·	0.0	0.0	·	·	0.0	·	0.0	
Total Receipts to Cash Flow 42	5.8	5.3	1.6	2.9	2.4	2.3	2.8	2.4	2.5	1.9	2.1	1.9	6.2
Cost of Goods to Cash Flow 43	0.0	1.7	·	·	0.2	1.0	0.1	0.6	0.0	·	0.0	0.0	
Cash Flow to Total Debt 44	0.0	·	2.6	0.6	1.3	0.3	0.1	0.1	0.1	0.0	0.0	0.0	

Selected Financial Factors (in Percentages)

Debt Ratio 45	95.4	·	45.8	37.6	145.4	58.0	74.1	76.1	69.1	69.9	71.5	67.2	96.1
Return on Total Assets 46	7.1	·	23.8	10.1	16.7	41.1	10.6	7.2	5.1	3.8	2.8	3.6	7.2
Return on Equity Before Income Taxes 47	17.3	·	41.7	13.0	·	62.1	30.3	19.4	10.2	6.6	3.8	6.5	19.1
Return on Equity After Income Taxes 48	11.4	·	40.3	12.4	·	45.8	26.8	16.9	9.3	4.5	2.5	4.6	12.4
Profit Margin (Before Income Tax) 49	9.9	11.7	11.8	11.9	16.0	14.5	15.0	17.2	20.4	17.0	17.7	35.4	9.4
Profit Margin (After Income Tax) 50	6.5	10.3	11.4	11.3	15.7	10.7	13.3	14.9	18.4	11.5	11.7	24.8	6.1

Table I

Corporations with and without Net Income

ACTIVITIES RELATED TO CREDIT INTERMEDIATION

MONEY AMOUNTS AND SIZE OF ASSETS IN THOUSANDS OF DOLLARS

Item Description for Accounting Period 7/04 Through 6/05	Total	Zero Assets	Under 500	500 to 1,000	1,000 to 5,000	5,000 to 10,000	10,000 to 25,000	25,000 to 50,000	50,000 to 100,000	100,000 to 250,000	250,000 to 500,000	500,000 to 2,500,000	2,500,000 and over
Number of Enterprises **1**	24273	2122	19543	1240	893	181	140	66	39	21	9	14	4
Revenues ($ in Thousands)													
Net Sales **2**	41112202	490338	8134462	2282555	2004773	1195738	1433405	1091653	1129246	1703857	912663	8188057	12545456
Interest **3**	1546365	44772	7341	4691	25160	24211	21810	29443	36735	50614	88604	715180	497804
Rents **4**	153712	0	1272	0	1732	179	260	411	1793	146	364	31812	115745
Royalties **5**	460743	0	0	0	0	0	0	173	0	0	0	0	460570
Other Portfolio Income **6**	1290975	13957	16577	251	39151	4782	6813	40013	3172	239	33563	78027	1054432
Other Receipts **7**	37660407	431609	8109272	2277613	1938730	1166566	1404522	1021613	1087546	1652858	790132	7363038	10416905
Total Receipts **8**	41112202	490338	8134462	2282555	2004773	1195738	1433405	1091653	1129246	1703857	912663	8188057	12545456
Average Total Receipts **9**	1694	231	416	1841	2245	6606	10239	16540	28955	81136	101407	584861	3136364
Operating Costs/Operating Income (%)													
Cost of Operations **10**	9.3	18.5	13.5	25.4	7.5	34.5	15.3	4.0	8.9	31.4	•	4.8	1.7
Salaries and Wages **11**	19.8	19.0	27.0	10.1	25.9	16.0	35.6	29.1	24.5	12.4	28.9	17.0	15.5
Taxes Paid **12**	2.6	2.8	2.6	1.4	3.5	1.7	2.9	3.0	2.5	1.7	3.1	1.9	3.2
Interest Paid **13**	3.2	3.5	0.7	0.6	2.5	1.5	4.0	6.3	6.5	5.1	10.4	1.6	5.1
Depreciation **14**	2.1	3.5	1.4	0.9	1.6	1.2	1.8	2.2	2.5	2.9	1.4	2.5	2.5
Amortization and Depletion **15**	1.3	0.1	0.1	0.1	0.5	0.1	0.3	0.5	0.7	1.5	8.5	1.7	1.9
Pensions and Other Deferred Comp. **16**	0.9	0.2	0.3	0.0	0.5	0.1	0.3	0.5	0.5	0.9	0.6	2.3	0.9
Employee Benefits **17**	1.4	0.4	0.6	0.2	1.5	1.2	0.9	1.6	0.9	1.3	2.2	1.6	2.1
Advertising **18**	4.7	2.1	2.9	0.8	1.8	0.5	2.9	3.0	2.2	1.9	0.6	8.5	6.2
Other Expenses **19**	40.5	32.8	36.6	52.7	34.3	27.4	26.5	34.4	37.9	38.4	19.9	47.7	42.7
Officers' Compensation **20**	2.9	1.1	8.5	1.1	5.8	5.6	4.4	4.6	2.4	1.5	2.3	0.9	0.3
Operating Margin **21**	11.4	16.1	5.9	6.7	14.8	10.2	5.1	10.7	10.5	1.0	22.1	9.7	17.8
Operating Margin Before Officers' Comp. **22**	14.3	17.3	14.4	7.8	20.6	15.7	9.5	15.3	12.8	2.5	24.3	10.6	18.1

Selected Average Balance Sheet ($ in Thousands)

Net Receivables 23	402	0	15	154	585	305	3400	11186	14844	34862	77947	276270	401487
Inventories 24	•	•	•	•	•	•	•	•	•	•	•	•	•
Net Property, Plant and Equipment 25	128	0	18	86	155	173	962	1416	2927	14133	6672	50515	271232
Total Assets 26	3580	0	91	738	2060	7807	16041	34551	69956	162396	381808	1125727	12774082
Notes and Loans Payable 27	1431	0	43	214	769	4181	8128	17813	31300	64691	207497	322725	5225097
All Other Liabilities 28	1323	0	15	103	434	1463	4955	9533	26393	52936	99743	488364	4962474
Net Worth 29	826	0	33	421	858	2162	2959	7205	12263	44769	74567	314639	2586512

Selected Financial Ratios (Times to 1)

Current Ratio 30	0.6	•	2.8	5.1	2.5	1.1	0.8	1.1	0.8	1.1	1.2	1.0	0.3
Quick Ratio 31	0.4	•	2.6	4.5	2.2	0.4	0.6	1.0	0.7	0.9	1.2	0.8	0.1
Net Sales to Working Capital 32	•	•	12.3	3.9	2.7	19.3	•	6.5	•	12.3	5.1	•	•
Coverage Ratio 33	4.3	6.1	9.8	13.2	6.9	7.7	2.3	2.7	2.6	1.2	3.1	7.2	4.0
Total Asset Turnover 34	0.5	•	4.6	2.5	1.1	0.8	0.6	0.5	0.4	0.5	0.3	0.5	0.2
Inventory Turnover 35	•	•	•	•	•	•	•	•	•	•	•	•	•
Receivables Turnover 36	•	•	•	•	•	•	•	•	•	•	•	•	•
Total Liabilities to Net Worth 37	3.3	•	1.7	0.8	1.4	2.6	4.4	3.8	4.7	2.6	4.1	2.6	3.9
Current Assets to Working Capital 38	•	•	1.6	1.2	1.7	10.7	•	7.7	•	9.2	5.9	•	•
Current Liabilities to Working Capital 39	•	•	0.6	0.2	0.7	9.7	•	6.7	•	8.2	4.9	•	•
Working Capital to Net Sales 40	•	•	0.1	0.3	0.4	0.1	•	0.2	•	0.1	0.2	•	•
Inventory to Working Capital 41	•	•	•	•	•	0.1	•	0.0	•	0.1	0.0	•	•
Total Receipts to Cash Flow 42	2.1	2.4	2.8	1.8	2.3	2.9	3.6	2.7	2.2	2.8	2.6	1.9	1.8
Cost of Goods to Cash Flow 43	0.2	0.4	0.4	0.5	0.2	1.0	0.6	0.1	0.2	0.9	0.1	0.1	0.0
Cash Flow to Total Debt 44	0.3	•	2.6	3.2	0.8	0.4	0.2	0.2	0.2	0.3	0.1	0.4	0.2

Selected Financial Factors (in Percentages)

Debt Ratio 45	76.9	•	63.4	42.9	58.4	72.3	81.6	79.1	82.5	72.4	80.5	72.1	79.8
Return on Total Assets 46	6.5	•	30.2	18.1	18.8	9.9	5.8	8.1	6.9	3.0	8.6	5.8	5.0
Return on Equity Before Income Taxes 47	21.8	•	74.2	29.3	38.6	31.0	17.4	24.3	24.3	1.8	30.0	18.0	18.5
Return on Equity After Income Taxes 48	16.8	•	72.3	29.2	37.6	30.1	15.8	22.4	22.7	•	26.3	12.4	12.3
Profit Margin (Before Income Tax) 49	10.6	17.7	5.9	6.7	14.7	10.2	5.0	10.6	10.3	1.0	22.0	9.7	15.3
Profit Margin (After Income Tax) 50	8.2	16.4	5.8	6.7	14.4	9.8	4.6	9.8	9.6	•	19.3	6.7	10.1

289

Table II

Corporations with Net Income

ACTIVITIES RELATED TO CREDIT INTERMEDIATION

MONEY AMOUNTS AND SIZE OF ASSETS IN THOUSANDS OF DOLLARS

Item Description for Accounting Period 7/04 Through 6/05	Total	Zero Assets	Under 500	500 to 1,000	1,000 to 5,000	5,000 to 10,000	10,000 to 25,000	25,000 to 50,000	50,000 to 100,000	100,000 to 250,000	250,000 to 500,000	500,000 to 2,500,000	2,500,000 and over
Number of Enterprises **1**	15083	46	13045	912	740	0	103	51	25	12	0	11	4
Revenues ($ in Thousands)													
Net Sales **2**	36757603	266539	6517713	1763219	1641471	0	1230467	993489	896252	1339297	0	7899068	12545456
Interest **3**	1314533	42595	1866	4684	22394	0	14563	15038	14589	9607	0	596743	497804
Rents **4**	145419	0	1272	0	829	0	260	411	1435	0	0	24925	115745
Royalties **5**	460743	0	0	0	0	0	0	173	0	0	0	0	460570
Other Portfolio Income **6**	1269657	10568	10591	251	38729	0	3907	32180	2407	239	0	78027	1054432
Other Receipts **7**	33567251	213376	6503984	1758284	1579519	0	1211737	945687	877821	1329451	0	7199373	10416905
Total Receipts **8**	36757603	266539	6517713	1763219	1641471	0	1230467	993489	896252	1339297	0	7899068	12545456
Average Total Receipts **9**	2437	5794	500	1933	2218	•	11946	19480	35850	111608	•	718097	3136364
Operating Costs/Operating Income (%)													
Cost of Operations **10**	8.2	2.4	13.0	32.8	3.4	•	16.6	4.4	5.5	29.2	•	4.7	1.7
Salaries and Wages **11**	19.4	19.4	26.0	9.8	26.5	•	33.6	28.3	24.7	12.7	•	17.0	15.5
Taxes Paid **12**	2.5	3.3	2.0	1.3	3.1	•	2.7	2.9	2.2	1.7	•	1.8	3.2
Interest Paid **13**	2.8	6.1	0.5	0.3	2.1	•	3.1	4.9	4.5	0.6	•	1.0	5.1
Depreciation **14**	1.9	0.8	0.7	1.0	1.3	•	1.3	2.1	2.7	1.7	•	2.5	2.5
Amortization and Depletion **15**	1.2	0.1	0.1	0.1	0.5	•	0.3	0.4	0.7	0.2	•	1.7	1.9
Pensions and Other Deferred Comp. **16**	0.8	0.3	0.3	0.0	0.6	•	0.3	0.5	0.6	0.5	•	1.6	0.9
Employee Benefits **17**	1.4	0.7	0.3	0.2	1.5	•	0.8	1.6	0.9	1.4	•	1.6	2.1
Advertising **18**	4.7	2.6	2.0	0.3	1.7	•	3.2	2.9	2.5	2.2	•	8.4	6.2
Other Expenses **19**	39.8	20.6	35.2	41.9	31.6	•	23.8	29.9	38.8	41.1	•	48.6	42.7
Officers' Compensation **20**	2.6	1.4	7.7	1.1	6.3	•	4.5	4.7	2.3	0.8	•	0.8	0.3
Operating Margin **21**	14.6	42.3	12.3	11.1	21.4	•	9.9	17.5	14.6	7.8	•	10.1	17.8
Operating Margin Before Officers' Comp. **22**	17.2	43.7	20.0	12.3	27.7	•	14.4	22.1	16.9	8.7	•	11.0	18.1

Selected Average Balance Sheet ($ in Thousands)

Net Receivables 23	561	0	12	91	607	•	3379	10519	16616	27865	•	348264	401487
Inventories 24	•	•	•	•	•	•	•	•	•	•	•	•	•
Net Property, Plant and Equipment 25	176	0	18	92	140	•	876	1568	4001	12967	•	59943	271232
Total Assets 26	5208	0	103	760	2058	•	15920	34433	68711	147339	•	1230338	12774082
Notes and Loans Payable 27	1980	0	27	136	686	•	7872	16438	28761	34406	•	336535	5225097
All Other Liabilities 28	1970	0	12	116	370	•	4692	9156	23280	64571	•	549478	4962474
Net Worth 29	1259	0	64	508	1002	•	3356	8838	16670	48362	•	344326	2586512

Selected Financial Ratios (Times to 1)

Current Ratio 30	0.5	•	4.5	4.2	3.0	•	0.8	1.1	0.8	0.8	•	1.1	0.3
Quick Ratio 31	0.4	•	4.2	3.8	2.7	•	0.5	0.9	0.7	0.6	•	0.8	0.1
Net Sales to Working Capital 32	•	•	10.4	4.2	2.4	•	•	17.7	•	•	•	23.1	•
Coverage Ratio 33	5.9	8.5	23.5	37.1	11.4	•	4.2	4.5	4.2	14.3	•	11.1	4.0
Total Asset Turnover 34	0.5	•	4.9	2.5	1.1	•	0.8	0.6	0.5	0.8	•	0.6	0.2
Inventory Turnover 35	•	•	•	•	•	•	•	•	•	•	•	•	•
Receivables Turnover 36	•	•	•	•	•	•	•	•	•	•	•	•	•
Total Liabilities to Net Worth 37	3.1	•	0.6	0.5	1.1	•	3.7	2.9	3.1	2.0	•	2.6	3.9
Current Assets to Working Capital 38	•	•	1.3	1.3	1.5	•	17.8	17.8	•	•	•	20.7	•
Current Liabilities to Working Capital 39	•	•	0.3	0.3	0.5	•	16.8	•	•	•	•	19.7	•
Working Capital to Net Sales 40	•	•	0.1	0.2	0.4	•	0.1	•	•	•	•	0.0	•
Inventory to Working Capital 41	•	•	•	•	•	•	0.0	•	•	•	•	0.0	•
Total Receipts to Cash Flow 42	2.0	1.8	2.5	2.1	2.1	•	3.3	2.3	2.0	2.1	•	1.8	1.8
Cost of Goods to Cash Flow 43	0.2	0.0	0.3	0.7	0.1	•	0.5	0.1	0.1	0.6	•	0.1	0.0
Cash Flow to Total Debt 44	0.3	•	5.2	3.7	1.0	•	0.3	0.3	0.3	0.5	•	0.4	0.2

Selected Financial Factors (in Percentages)

Debt Ratio 45	75.8	•	37.6	33.2	51.3	•	78.9	74.3	75.7	67.2	•	72.0	79.8
Return on Total Assets 46	7.7	•	62.6	29.1	25.2	•	9.7	12.6	9.9	6.4	•	6.5	5.0
Return on Equity Before Income Taxes 47	26.6	•	96.0	42.4	47.3	•	35.1	38.3	31.1	18.1	•	21.0	18.5
Return on Equity After Income Taxes 48	21.4	•	94.5	42.2	46.3	•	33.2	36.4	29.3	13.9	•	14.5	12.3
Profit Margin (Before Income Tax) 49	13.8	45.2	12.3	11.1	21.4	•	9.9	17.4	14.5	7.8	•	10.1	15.3
Profit Margin (After Income Tax) 50	11.1	42.8	12.1	11.1	20.9	•	9.3	16.5	13.6	6.0	•	7.0	10.1

Table I

Corporations with and without Net Income

INVESTMENT BANKING AND SECURITIES DEALING

MONEY AMOUNTS AND SIZE OF ASSETS IN THOUSANDS OF DOLLARS

Item Description for Accounting Period 7/04 Through 6/05	Total	Zero Assets	Under 500	500 to 1,000	1,000 to 5,000	5,000 to 10,000	10,000 to 25,000	25,000 to 50,000	50,000 to 100,000	100,000 to 250,000	250,000 to 500,000	500,000 to 2,500,000	2,500,000 and over
Number of Enterprises 1	2886	444	2001	57	253	17	47	17	15	5	6	11	12
Revenues ($ in Thousands)													
Net Sales 2	117660014	208805	430024	4285	219281	103207	350435	448441	293554	40784	311406	2154011	113095780
Interest 3	69385045	15608	25875	459	7258	1751	2831	4472	6727	6017	34168	183463	69096416
Rents 4	977748	4231	0	0	0	0	104	790	42	0	261	0	972321
Royalties 5	2254	0	0	0	0	0	0	0	0	0	0	0	2254
Other Portfolio Income 6	3703050	7796	0	3382	1566	1053	8456	5393	13478	12144	422	315601	3333760
Other Receipts 7	43591917	181170	404149	444	210457	100403	339044	437786	273307	22623	276816	1654686	39691029
Total Receipts 8	117660014	208805	430024	4285	219281	103207	350435	448441	293554	40784	311406	2154011	113095780
Average Total Receipts 9	40769	470	215	75	867	6071	7456	26379	19570	8157	51901	195819	9424648
Operating Costs/Operating Income (%)													
Cost of Operations 10	0.2	•	•	•	2.5	•	1.8	0.0	0.6	•	•	•	0.2
Salaries and Wages 11	19.1	22.4	9.4	•	45.8	26.2	49.8	23.8	35.8	10.5	26.2	21.3	18.9
Taxes Paid 12	1.0	0.8	3.3	1.7	3.7	2.4	2.9	1.8	3.0	4.9	3.1	2.1	0.9
Interest Paid 13	45.5	47.7	6.4	0.3	3.4	0.3	1.1	1.2	2.1	0.5	10.7	14.9	46.9
Depreciation 14	1.9	0.6	0.2	3.9	1.5	1.8	2.2	2.1	1.3	0.3	4.2	1.3	1.9
Amortization and Depletion 15	0.3	0.1	0.1	0.1	1.4	0.0	1.3	0.2	0.2	0.0	0.3	0.4	0.3
Pensions and Other Deferred Comp. 16	0.6	0.0	0.0	•	1.8	1.8	0.7	0.4	1.4	2.9	0.4	1.1	0.5
Employee Benefits 17	0.9	0.2	0.6	•	3.2	2.0	2.4	1.3	2.5	0.5	1.2	0.5	0.9
Advertising 18	0.2	0.1	5.2	•	0.4	0.1	0.5	0.5	0.5	0.1	0.5	1.2	0.2
Other Expenses 19	22.0	24.0	37.0	15.4	59.4	21.6	23.2	57.2	44.5	20.2	33.9	27.0	21.5
Officers' Compensation 20	2.4	1.2	1.4	•	15.7	33.3	6.3	5.6	16.2	50.5	3.7	3.3	2.3
Operating Margin 21	6.0	2.8	36.3	78.6	•	10.7	7.5	5.8	•	9.4	15.7	26.9	5.5
Operating Margin Before Officers' Comp. 22	8.4	4.0	37.7	78.6	•	44.0	13.9	11.4	8.1	59.9	19.5	30.2	7.8

Selected Average Balance Sheet ($ in Thousands)

Item												
Net Receivables 23	200809	0	0	457	147	2270	7377	15352	41455	127207	83263	48088985
Inventories 24	•	•	•	•	•	•	•	•	•	•	•	•
Net Property, Plant and Equipment 25	4644	0	1	45	420	493	1989	857	179	9531	8733	1096589
Total Assets 26	960093	48	672	1784	7214	17162	36236	68985	132648	336050	1018929	229481369
Notes and Loans Payable 27	150185	3	303	190	4616	2504	7959	17183	24765	66877	112294	35917591
All Other Liabilities 28	748442	1	0	438	2942	5011	8321	15612	7754	210335	331691	179523526
Net Worth 29	61466	44	369	1156	-344	9647	19956	36190	100129	58839	574945	14040252

Selected Financial Ratios (Times to 1)

Item													
Current Ratio 30	0.8	•	31.6	•	5.0	1.1	1.8	1.5	1.8	134.1	1.1	1.3	0.8
Quick Ratio 31	0.4	•	31.6	•	4.5	0.7	1.2	0.9	1.1	102.9	0.7	1.0	0.4
Net Sales to Working Capital 32	•	•	12.9	0.1	1.1	23.4	1.7	1.2	0.1	2.7	1.7	4.0	•
Coverage Ratio 33	1.1	•	6.6	307.0	•	40.2	7.2	5.3	18.6	2.5	2.8	1.1	•
Total Asset Turnover 34	0.0	•	4.5	0.1	0.5	0.8	0.4	0.7	0.3	0.1	0.2	0.2	0.0
Inventory Turnover 35	•	•	•	•	•	•	•	•	•	•	•	•	•
Receivables Turnover 36	•	•	•	•	•	•	•	•	•	•	•	•	•
Total Liabilities to Net Worth 37	14.6	•	0.1	0.8	0.5	0.8	•	0.8	0.9	0.3	4.7	0.8	15.3
Current Assets to Working Capital 38	•	•	1.0	1.0	1.2	3.1	2.2	2.3	1.0	12.3	4.0	•	•
Current Liabilities to Working Capital 39	•	•	0.0	0.0	0.2	2.1	1.2	1.3	0.0	11.3	3.0	•	•
Working Capital to Net Sales 40	•	•	0.1	6.9	0.9	0.3	0.6	0.8	7.6	0.4	0.6	•	•
Inventory to Working Capital 41	•	•	•	•	0.0	0.0	•	•	•	•	•	•	•
Total Receipts to Cash Flow 42	4.1	4.4	1.5	6.2	8.7	4.0	1.7	3.5	•	2.2	2.6	4.2	•
Cost of Goods to Cash Flow 43	0.0	•	0.0	0.2	0.2	0.1	0.0	0.0	•	•	0.0	0.0	•
Cash Flow to Total Debt 44	0.0	•	36.3	0.0	0.2	1.0	0.2	0.2	•	0.1	0.2	0.0	•

Selected Financial Factors (in Percentages)

Item													
Debt Ratio 45	93.6	•	8.4	45.1	35.2	104.8	43.8	44.9	47.5	24.5	82.5	43.6	93.9
Return on Total Assets 46	2.2	•	191.8	8.8	•	9.2	3.6	4.7	•	0.6	4.1	8.0	2.2
Return on Equity Before Income Taxes 47	4.3	•	177.8	16.0	•	•	5.5	7.0	•	0.8	13.8	9.0	4.1
Return on Equity After Income Taxes 48	2.9	•	176.2	13.4	•	•	4.1	6.8	•	0.4	9.0	9.0	2.8
Profit Margin (Before Income Tax) 49	6.5	2.8	36.3	78.6	10.6	5.3	7.1	5.3	9.4	15.6	26.5	6.6	6.1
Profit Margin (After Income Tax) 50	4.4	•	36.0	65.8	9.4	5.3	5.1	4.8	10.2	19.5	26.5	6.1	4.1

Table II

Corporations with Net Income

INVESTMENT BANKING AND SECURITIES DEALING

MONEY AMOUNTS AND SIZE OF ASSETS IN THOUSANDS OF DOLLARS

Item Description for Accounting Period 7/04 Through 6/05	Total	Zero Assets	Under 500	500 to 1,000	1,000 to 5,000	5,000 to 10,000	10,000 to 25,000	25,000 to 50,000	50,000 to 100,000	100,000 to 250,000	250,000 to 500,000	500,000 to 2,500,000	2,500,000 and over
Number of Enterprises **1**	2290	0	1587	57	136	14	25	10	7	0	3	11	0
Revenues ($ in Thousands)													
Net Sales **2**	116143401	0	429806	4285	241585	87402	300538	281593	200155	0	258079	2154011	0
Interest **3**	68537601	0	25875	459	1412	1711	2666	3028	6431	0	11761	183463	0
Rents **4**	831721	0	0	0	0	0	104	0	42	0	0	261	0
Royalties **5**	2144	0	0	0	0	0	0	0	0	0	0	0	0
Other Portfolio Income **6**	3682907	0	0	3382	1294	1032	7620	2187	11383	0	422	315601	0
Other Receipts **7**	43089028	0	403931	444	238879	84659	290148	276378	182299	0	245896	1654686	0
Total Receipts **8**	116143401	0	429806	4285	241585	87402	300538	281593	200155	0	258079	2154011	0
Average Total Receipts **9**	50718	•	271	75	1776	6243	12022	28159	28594	•	86026	195819	•
Operating Costs/Operating Income (%)													
Cost of Operations **10**	0.2	•	•	•	2.3	•	2.1	•	0.8	•	•	•	•
Salaries and Wages **11**	19.2	•	9.4	•	33.9	9.7	44.6	28.2	36.7	•	28.1	21.3	•
Taxes Paid **12**	1.0	•	3.3	1.7	2.8	1.9	2.7	2.0	3.4	•	3.6	2.1	•
Interest Paid **13**	45.3	•	6.4	0.3	0.8	0.3	0.9	1.3	2.1	•	1.5	14.9	•
Depreciation **14**	1.8	•	0.1	3.9	1.1	0.6	1.6	0.7	0.8	•	4.8	1.3	•
Amortization and Depletion **15**	0.3	•	0.1	0.1	•	0.0	0.5	0.2	0.2	•	0.3	0.4	•
Pensions and Other Deferred Comp. **16**	0.6	•	0.0	•	0.7	2.0	0.7	0.6	1.6	•	0.5	1.1	•
Employee Benefits **17**	0.9	•	0.6	•	1.8	1.5	2.6	1.3	1.2	•	1.4	0.5	•
Advertising **18**	0.2	•	5.2	•	0.3	0.1	0.5	0.6	0.6	•	0.6	1.2	•
Other Expenses **19**	21.9	•	35.8	15.4	41.0	14.3	20.6	36.5	33.5	•	34.7	27.0	•
Officers' Compensation **20**	2.4	•	1.4	•	9.9	37.7	4.5	8.3	9.9	•	3.4	3.3	•
Operating Margin **21**	6.3	•	37.8	78.6	5.5	31.8	18.7	20.4	9.0	•	21.1	26.9	•
Operating Margin Before Officers' Comp. **22**	8.7	•	39.1	78.6	15.3	69.6	23.2	28.7	18.9	•	24.6	30.2	•

Selected Average Balance Sheet ($ in Thousands)

	1	2	3	4	5	6	7	8	9	10	11	12
Net Receivables **23**	252391	•	0	0	620	108	3622	8295	1601	•	174808	83263
Inventories **24**	•	•	•	•	•	•	•	•	•	•	•	•
Net Property, Plant and Equipment **25**	5824	•	0	57	188	737	659	697	•	•	17984	8733
Total Assets **26**	1200360	•	47	672	1625	7200	17760	38609	61944	•	346642	1018929
Notes and Loans Payable **27**	188850	•	2	303	334	0	2392	8628	15220	•	38586	112294
All Other Liabilities **28**	934966	•	0	0	595	2632	5072	11510	20199	•	195125	331691
Net Worth **29**	76544	•	45	369	696	4568	10296	18472	26525	•	112931	574945

Selected Financial Ratios (Times to 1)

	1	2	3	4	5	6	7	8	9	10	11	12
Current Ratio **30**	0.8	•	40.2	•	8.8	1.3	1.9	1.2	1.3	•	1.2	1.3
Quick Ratio **31**	0.4	•	40.2	•	8.5	0.8	1.7	0.6	0.7	•	1.1	1.0
Net Sales to Working Capital **32**	•	•	30.3	0.1	1.6	9.5	2.8	7.1	3.2	•	2.3	1.7
Coverage Ratio **33**	1.2	•	6.9	307.0	8.0	112.3	20.8	16.1	4.5	•	15.1	2.8
Total Asset Turnover **34**	0.0	•	5.8	0.1	1.1	0.9	0.7	0.7	0.5	•	0.2	0.2
Inventory Turnover **35**	•	•	•	•	•	•	•	•	•	•	•	•
Receivables Turnover **36**	•	•	•	•	•	•	•	•	•	•	•	•
Total Liabilities to Net Worth **37**	14.7	•	0.0	0.8	1.3	0.6	0.7	1.1	1.3	•	2.1	0.8
Current Assets to Working Capital **38**	•	•	1.0	1.0	1.1	4.9	2.2	6.2	3.9	•	6.3	4.0
Current Liabilities to Working Capital **39**	•	•	0.0	0.1	0.1	3.9	1.2	5.2	2.9	•	5.3	3.0
Working Capital to Net Sales **40**	•	•	0.0	6.9	0.6	0.1	0.4	0.1	0.3	•	0.4	0.6
Inventory to Working Capital **41**	•	•	•	•	•	•	•	•	•	•	•	•
Total Receipts to Cash Flow **42**	4.1	•	1.5	6.2	2.4	2.3	2.9	1.8	3.0	•	1.9	2.6
Cost of Goods to Cash Flow **43**	0.0	•	0.0	0.1	0.1	•	0.1	•	0.0	•	•	•
Cash Flow to Total Debt **44**	0.0	•	84.6	0.0	0.8	1.0	0.5	0.8	0.3	•	0.2	0.2

Selected Financial Factors (in Percentages)

	1	2	3	4	5	6	7	8	9	10	11	12
Debt Ratio **45**	93.6	•	4.7	45.1	57.2	36.6	42.0	52.2	57.2	•	67.4	43.6
Return on Total Assets **46**	2.2	•	255.4	8.8	6.8	27.8	13.0	15.2	4.4	•	5.6	8.0
Return on Equity Before Income Taxes **47**	4.6	•	229.2	16.0	13.9	43.5	21.4	29.9	8.0	•	16.0	9.0
Return on Equity After Income Taxes **48**	3.2	•	227.1	13.4	13.0	41.5	19.0	29.5	6.0	•	11.0	6.6
Profit Margin (Before Income Tax) **49**	6.9	•	37.8	78.6	5.4	31.8	18.3	19.6	7.4	•	21.0	26.5
Profit Margin (After Income Tax) **50**	4.8	•	37.4	65.8	5.1	30.4	16.3	19.4	5.6	•	14.4	19.5

Table I

Corporations with and without Net Income

SECURITIES BROKERAGE

MONEY AMOUNTS AND SIZE OF ASSETS IN THOUSANDS OF DOLLARS

Item Description for Accounting Period 7/04 Through 6/05		Total	Zero Assets	Under 500	500 to 1,000	1,000 to 5,000	5,000 to 10,000	10,000 to 25,000	25,000 to 50,000	50,000 to 100,000	100,000 to 250,000	250,000 to 500,000	500,000 to 2,500,000	2,500,000 and over
Number of Enterprises	1	8459	1858	5069	437	750	132	86	36	18	18	9	20	26
Revenues ($ in Thousands)														
Net Sales	2	118417494	476347	2499550	1126580	2395880	1258359	1980301	1052471	750153	1006015	1516607	6683091	97672140
Interest	3	39237304	28826	1107	2397	5666	7419	15267	19983	5879	29575	43371	453738	38624077
Rents	4	581217	11635	0	0	884	642	217	908	923	69	2190	19944	543806
Royalties	5	78884	0	0	0	0	0	0	5	232	4662	1245	0	72739
Other Portfolio Income	6	2375981	20968	1949	2510	12944	26706	7266	19072	38366	32746	20610	166133	2026712
Other Receipts	7	76144108	414918	2496494	1121673	2376386	1223592	1957551	1012503	704753	938963	1449191	6043276	56404806
Total Receipts	8	118417494	476347	2499550	1126580	2395880	1258359	1980301	1052471	750153	1006015	1516607	6683091	97672140
Average Total Receipts	9	13999	256	493	2578	3195	9533	23027	29235	41675	55890	168512	334155	3756621
Operating Costs/Operating Income (%)														
Cost of Operations	10	1.9	•	•	•	0.3	5.8	4.9	0.6	11.1	0.5	0.3	0.4	1.9
Salaries and Wages	11	21.7	13.5	19.6	23.2	30.6	16.2	27.7	31.9	36.6	35.6	46.1	27.2	20.4
Taxes Paid	12	1.7	2.2	2.2	2.2	2.7	2.3	2.2	2.8	3.2	3.0	3.0	1.9	1.6
Interest Paid	13	27.6	2.5	0.5	0.0	0.3	0.3	0.4	1.1	0.9	2.1	1.7	6.3	32.9
Depreciation	14	1.4	0.1	0.8	1.1	0.6	0.8	0.7	1.6	1.1	2.0	1.7	1.5	1.5
Amortization and Depletion	15	0.7	3.8	0.0	0.1	0.0	0.3	0.1	0.2	0.1	0.5	0.1	3.4	0.6
Pensions and Other Deferred Comp.	16	0.6	2.4	1.0	•	0.9	0.2	0.5	0.6	0.4	0.9	0.4	0.4	0.6
Employee Benefits	17	1.3	1.3	1.1	1.6	1.2	1.4	1.3	1.3	1.0	1.9	2.7	1.1	1.3
Advertising	18	0.7	1.2	2.0	0.1	0.4	0.4	0.3	1.1	0.8	0.4	0.4	0.8	0.7
Other Expenses	19	30.9	60.4	57.2	62.7	38.5	62.7	50.7	40.2	25.4	28.7	27.7	48.3	27.6
Officers' Compensation	20	5.3	4.6	10.1	8.5	13.1	5.6	6.5	7.5	9.5	13.5	3.9	3.8	4.9
Operating Margin	21	6.2	7.9	5.6	0.5	11.5	3.9	4.6	11.0	9.9	10.8	12.1	5.0	6.0
Operating Margin Before Officers' Comp.	22	11.5	12.5	15.7	9.0	24.6	9.6	11.1	18.5	19.4	24.4	16.0	8.7	11.0

Selected Average Balance Sheet ($ in Thousands)

Item													
Net Receivables 23	30523	0	14	85	275	1303	2065	7396	14490	31852	85875	248225	9642170
Inventories 24	•	•	•	•	•	•	•	•	•	•	•	•	•
Net Property, Plant and Equipment 25	600	0	3	30	84	389	531	1505	2297	6121	7480	15867	165057
Total Assets 26	209112	0	98	705	2032	7452	15598	37019	60273	165733	374799	1383030	66453463
Notes and Loans Payable 27	44496	0	83	21	114	562	1810	6587	6383	6303	57534	202859	14253912
All Other Liabilities 28	152851	0	35	333	770	3239	5437	17286	28106	89847	190940	791038	48880215
Net Worth 29	11765	0	-20	351	1148	3651	8352	13147	25784	69583	126325	389132	3319336

Selected Financial Ratios (Times to 1)

Item													
Current Ratio 30	1.1	•	0.9	1.6	3.7	1.4	1.8	1.4	1.2	1.3	1.2	1.0	1.1
Quick Ratio 31	0.3	•	0.6	1.1	2.6	1.1	1.3	1.0	0.9	0.8	0.8	0.5	0.3
Net Sales to Working Capital 32	1.2	•	•	15.2	2.9	8.6	5.6	3.9	7.4	2.1	5.5	•	1.1
Coverage Ratio 33	1.2	4.1	12.9	11.5	43.4	13.3	13.5	10.9	10.3	6.5	8.0	1.9	1.2
Total Asset Turnover 34	0.1	•	5.1	3.7	1.6	1.3	1.5	0.8	0.7	0.3	0.4	0.2	0.1
Inventory Turnover 35	•	•	•	•	•	•	•	•	•	•	•	•	•
Receivables Turnover 36	•	•	•	•	•	•	•	•	•	•	•	•	•
Total Liabilities to Net Worth 37	16.8	•	•	1.0	0.8	1.0	0.9	1.8	1.3	1.4	2.0	2.6	19.0
Current Assets to Working Capital 38	13.1	•	2.6	1.4	3.5	2.3	3.4	6.7	4.0	7.6	•	2.0	13.1
Current Liabilities to Working Capital 39	12.1	•	1.6	0.4	2.5	1.3	2.4	5.7	3.0	6.6	•	1.0	12.1
Working Capital to Net Sales 40	0.8	•	0.1	0.3	0.1	0.1	0.2	0.3	0.1	0.5	0.2	•	0.9
Inventory to Working Capital 41	0.0	•	•	•	0.0	0.0	0.0	0.0	0.0	•	0.0	•	•
Total Receipts to Cash Flow 42	3.1	1.6	1.7	2.2	1.6	1.9	2.2	3.1	2.9	1.6	2.1	•	3.4
Cost of Goods to Cash Flow 43	0.1	•	•	0.0	0.1	0.1	0.0	0.0	0.0	0.0	0.0	0.0	0.1
Cash Flow to Total Debt 44	0.0	•	2.4	1.7	4.2	1.6	1.7	0.6	0.4	0.2	0.2	0.2	0.0

Selected Financial Factors (in Percentages)

Item													
Debt Ratio 45	94.4	•	120.8	50.3	43.5	51.0	46.5	64.5	57.2	58.0	66.3	71.9	95.0
Return on Total Assets 46	2.3	•	30.4	2.0	18.4	5.2	7.2	9.3	6.7	4.7	6.0	2.9	2.2
Return on Equity Before Income Taxes 47	7.4	•	•	3.6	31.9	9.9	12.5	23.8	14.2	9.5	15.6	4.7	6.9
Return on Equity After Income Taxes 48	5.3	•	•	1.9	30.8	6.4	9.1	17.3	9.4	7.1	9.8	2.7	4.8
Profit Margin (Before Income Tax) 49	6.2	7.8	5.6	0.5	11.5	3.8	4.5	10.7	8.8	11.8	11.7	5.5	6.1
Profit Margin (After Income Tax) 50	4.4	6.2	5.3	0.3	11.1	2.5	3.3	7.8	5.8	8.8	7.4	3.1	4.3

Table II
Corporations with Net Income

SECURITIES BROKERAGE

MONEY AMOUNTS AND SIZE OF ASSETS IN THOUSANDS OF DOLLARS

Item Description for Accounting Period 7/04 Through 6/05	Total	Zero Assets	Under 500	500 to 1,000	1,000 to 5,000	5,000 to 10,000	10,000 to 25,000	25,000 to 50,000	50,000 to 100,000	100,000 to 250,000	250,000 to 500,000	500,000 to 2,500,000	2,500,000 and over
Number of Enterprises **1**	5845	1182	3616	287	540	75	59	20	11	0	0	16	21
Revenues ($ in Thousands)													
Net Sales **2**	105850739	302972	1979425	501417	1911559	1234912	1699828	649101	537202	0	0	6121638	88756561
Interest **3**	33849168	26492	1081	411	769	6497	9551	11913	2963	0	0	375818	33355982
Rents **4**	322439	11635	0	0	884	642	194	123	0	0	0	15217	291554
Royalties **5**	78875	0	0	0	0	0	0	5	232	0	0	0	72730
Other Portfolio Income **6**	1738940	20459	1724	2510	3401	25291	4779	7273	38236	0	0	117203	1503794
Other Receipts **7**	69861317	244386	1976620	498496	1906505	1202482	1685304	629787	495771	0	0	5613400	53532501
Total Receipts **8**	105850739	302972	1979425	501417	1911559	1234912	1699828	649101	537202	0	0	6121638	88756561
Average Total Receipts **9**	18110	256	547	1747	3540	16465	28811	32455	48837	·	·	382602	4226503
Operating Costs/Operating Income (%)													
Cost of Operations **10**	2.0	·	·	·	0.4	4.9	3.1	0.7	12.3	·	·	0.4	2.1
Salaries and Wages **11**	22.2	9.3	17.4	12.0	28.8	14.1	26.5	26.6	39.2	·	·	27.3	21.4
Taxes Paid **12**	1.8	2.2	1.8	2.5	2.8	2.2	2.1	3.2	3.6	·	·	1.9	1.7
Interest Paid **13**	25.8	3.8	0.4	0.1	0.2	0.2	0.2	0.7	0.8	·	·	4.9	30.4
Depreciation **14**	1.4	·	0.8	0.9	0.5	0.6	0.6	1.5	1.3	·	·	1.5	1.5
Amortization and Depletion **15**	0.7	0.0	0.0	·	0.0	0.3	0.1	0.1	0.1	·	·	3.5	0.6
Pensions and Other Deferred Comp. **16**	0.7	1.5	0.8	·	0.8	0.2	0.5	0.4	0.4	·	·	0.4	0.7
Employee Benefits **17**	1.4	1.4	0.9	1.2	1.2	1.2	1.1	1.0	1.2	·	·	1.0	1.4
Advertising **18**	0.7	1.8	2.1	0.0	0.5	0.3	0.2	1.3	0.7	·	·	0.9	0.7
Other Expenses **19**	29.9	52.5	55.6	69.6	33.7	60.3	50.0	32.6	16.2	·	·	47.2	27.1
Officers' Compensation **20**	5.6	6.9	7.2	3.8	13.8	5.0	6.0	7.1	6.0	·	·	3.9	5.4
Operating Margin **21**	7.9	20.6	13.0	9.9	17.4	10.5	9.7	24.8	18.4	·	·	7.1	7.0
Operating Margin Before Officers' Comp. **22**	13.4	27.5	20.2	13.7	31.2	15.5	15.7	31.9	24.3	·	·	11.0	12.4

Selected Average Balance Sheet ($ in Thousands)

Net Receivables 23	38103	0	14	94	226	2014	2274	8224	15746	•	290560	10290983
Inventories 24	•	•	•	•	•	•	•	•	•	•	•	•
Net Property, Plant and Equipment 25	830	0	4	21	56	591	496	1793	1642	•	19431	200050
Total Assets 26	255487	0	74	704	2073	8058	15660	37085	60416	•	1350288	69643654
Notes and Loans Payable 27	59215	0	35	11	38	381	1241	2610	6353	•	157586	16322772
All Other Liabilities 28	181352	0	19	188	780	2917	5604	17258	31615	•	768745	49680811
Net Worth 29	14920	0	20	505	1254	4760	8815	17216	22448	•	423957	3640071

Selected Financial Ratios (Times to 1)

Current Ratio 30	1.1	•	3.3	2.0	4.0	1.9	1.9	1.6	0.9	•	1.0	1.1
Quick Ratio 31	0.4	•	3.2	1.5	3.4	1.7	1.5	1.4	0.7	•	0.6	0.7
Net Sales to Working Capital 32	1.2	•	16.5	9.1	3.2	6.2	6.1	3.2	•	•	•	1.0
Coverage Ratio 33	1.3	6.4	30.8	103.5	111.6	51.8	39.6	35.0	22.5	•	•	•
Total Asset Turnover 34	0.1	•	7.4	2.5	1.7	2.0	1.8	0.9	0.8	•	0.3	0.1
Inventory Turnover 35	•	•	•	•	•	•	•	•	•	•	•	•
Receivables Turnover 36	•	•	•	•	•	•	•	•	•	•	•	•
Total Liabilities to Net Worth 37	16.1	•	2.7	0.4	0.7	0.7	0.8	1.2	2.2	•	•	1.7
Current Assets to Working Capital 38	11.4	•	1.4	2.0	1.3	2.1	2.1	2.8	•	•	•	11.5
Current Liabilities to Working Capital 39	10.4	•	0.4	1.0	0.3	1.1	1.1	1.8	•	•	•	10.5
Working Capital to Net Sales 40	0.8	•	0.1	0.1	0.3	0.2	0.2	0.3	•	•	•	1.0
Inventory to Working Capital 41	0.0	•	•	•	0.0	0.0	•	•	•	•	•	•
Total Receipts to Cash Flow 42	3.0	1.5	1.5	1.3	2.1	1.5	1.7	1.9	3.1	•	2.1	3.3
Cost of Goods to Cash Flow 43	0.1	•	0.0	0.0	0.0	0.1	0.1	0.0	0.4	•	0.0	0.1
Cash Flow to Total Debt 44	0.0	•	6.5	6.6	2.1	3.3	2.4	0.9	0.4	•	0.2	0.0

Selected Financial Factors (in Percentages)

Debt Ratio 45	94.2	•	73.1	28.3	39.5	40.9	43.7	53.6	62.8	•	68.6	94.8
Return on Total Assets 46	2.4	•	99.2	24.7	29.8	21.9	18.1	22.1	14.2	•	3.5	2.3
Return on Equity Before Income Taxes 47	9.6	•	356.5	34.2	48.9	36.3	31.4	46.3	36.6	•	6.9	8.2
Return on Equity After Income Taxes 48	7.2	•	346.6	32.3	47.5	31.6	26.7	37.4	27.7	•	4.5	5.9
Profit Margin (Before Income Tax) 49	7.9	20.6	13.0	9.9	17.3	10.5	9.6	24.6	16.8	•	7.6	7.1
Profit Margin (After Income Tax) 50	5.9	18.0	12.7	9.3	16.8	9.1	8.2	19.8	12.7	•	5.0	5.1

Table I
Corporations with and without Net Income

COMMODITY CONTRACTS DEALING AND BROKERAGE

MONEY AMOUNTS AND SIZE OF ASSETS IN THOUSANDS OF DOLLARS

Item Description for Accounting Period 7/04 Through 6/05	Total	Zero Assets	Under 500	500 to 1,000	1,000 to 5,000	5,000 to 10,000	10,000 to 25,000	25,000 to 50,000	50,000 to 100,000	100,000 to 250,000	250,000 to 500,000	500,000 to 2,500,000	2,500,000 and over
Number of Enterprises **1**	2553	4	2206	112	110	31	39	18	10	16	0	3	4
Revenues ($ in Thousands)													
Net Sales **2**	4169719	48957	315887	57168	213806	100645	616195	311417	243906	353616	0	289325	1618796
Interest **3**	499354	1111	1705	0	125	506	659	548	2813	14131	0	644	477114
Rents **4**	10579	0	0	1992	0	392	0	4605	20	84	0	0	3486
Royalties **5**	7068	0	0	0	0	0	0	7068	0	0	0	0	0
Other Portfolio Income **6**	67816	0	1051	1	942	2423	8709	756	1847	3853	0	0	48232
Other Receipts **7**	3584902	47846	313131	55175	212739	97324	606827	298440	239226	335548	0	288681	1089964
Total Receipts **8**	4169719	48957	315887	57168	213806	100645	616195	311417	243906	353616	0	289325	1618796
Average Total Receipts **9**	1633	12239	143	510	1944	3247	15800	17301	24391	22101	•	96442	404699
Operating Costs/Operating Income (%)													
Cost of Operations **10**	18.5	20.2	•	•	64.0	23.3	53.4	74.9	•	10.9	•	•	•
Salaries and Wages **11**	18.6	12.5	7.3	13.1	1.8	21.3	10.5	21.5	12.1	19.4	•	38.5	23.1
Taxes Paid **12**	1.8	0.5	2.4	3.8	1.7	2.5	1.4	1.7	2.0	2.4	•	0.8	1.8
Interest Paid **13**	14.0	1.6	1.2	4.1	7.3	1.7	0.7	0.7	1.1	6.1	•	30.0	27.4
Depreciation **14**	1.6	0.4	0.4	21.3	0.1	4.4	0.6	1.7	0.8	1.5	•	0.3	1.9
Amortization and Depletion **15**	0.4	0.0	0.0	0.0	1.9	0.4	0.0	0.0	0.3	0.1	•	0.2	0.7
Pensions and Other Deferred Comp. **16**	0.5	0.1	1.1	0.2	•	0.1	0.3	0.4	0.4	0.9	•	0.1	0.5
Employee Benefits **17**	1.2	0.6	0.5	3.6	0.1	1.2	0.5	1.2	1.2	1.0	•	0.8	1.9
Advertising **18**	0.2	0.3	0.7	•	0.0	0.3	0.3	0.2	0.9	0.1	•	0.3	0.1
Other Expenses **19**	31.9	25.8	63.5	22.8	9.7	35.5	24.9	20.2	49.6	36.6	•	24.7	31.4
Officers' Compensation **20**	4.8	0.2	17.5	22.3	3.1	5.1	8.4	1.5	5.7	3.6	•	1.1	2.2
Operating Margin **21**	6.4	37.7	5.5	8.8	10.4	4.2	•	•	26.1	17.3	•	3.1	9.0
Operating Margin Before Officers' Comp. **22**	11.2	37.9	22.9	31.2	13.4	9.3	7.3	•	31.7	21.0	•	4.2	11.2

Selected Average Balance Sheet ($ in Thousands)

Net Receivables **23**	2448	0	22	291	608	139	4849	5949	15959	44094	·	502351	·	857762
Inventories **24**	·	·	·	·	·	·	·	·	·	·	·	·	·	·
Net Property, Plant and Equipment **25**	103	0	3	326	24	1022	442	820	736	6490	·	776	·	9708
Total Assets **26**	15430	101	856	2407	6716	15677	33970	65937	175096	·	·	1006652	·	7724780
Notes and Loans Payable **27**	2200	0	28	343	307	5214	6812	12511	31336	·	·	509312	·	697738
All Other Liabilities **28**	12263	0	9	293	3432	6700	12591	32193	125190	·	·	796034	·	6457988
Net Worth **29**	967	0	63	220	2977	3763	14567	21232	18570	·	·	-298694	·	569054

Selected Financial Ratios (Times to 1)

Current Ratio **30**	1.2	·	5.3	0.8	0.7	1.5	1.2	1.4	1.1	0.9	·	0.8	·	1.3
Quick Ratio **31**	0.7	·	4.4	0.8	0.6	1.1	0.9	0.9	0.9	0.6	·	0.6	·	0.6
Net Sales to Working Capital **32**	0.9	·	2.6	·	1.9	7.9	3.6	4.0	·	·	·	·	·	0.3
Coverage Ratio **33**	1.4	25.1	5.5	3.1	2.4	3.4	·	·	25.7	3.8	·	1.1	·	1.3
Total Asset Turnover **34**	0.1	·	1.4	0.6	0.8	0.5	1.0	0.5	0.4	0.1	·	0.1	·	0.1
Inventory Turnover **35**	·	·	·	·	·	·	·	·	·	·	·	·	·	·
Receivables Turnover **36**	·	·	·	·	·	·	·	·	·	·	·	·	·	·
Total Liabilities to Net Worth **37**	15.0	·	0.6	2.9	·	1.3	3.2	1.3	2.1	8.4	·	·	·	12.6
Current Assets to Working Capital **38**	6.8	·	1.2	·	3.0	5.7	3.8	7.8	·	·	·	·	·	5.0
Current Liabilities to Working Capital **39**	5.8	·	0.2	·	2.0	4.7	2.8	6.8	·	·	·	·	·	4.0
Working Capital to Net Sales **40**	1.1	·	0.4	·	0.5	0.1	0.3	0.3	·	·	·	·	·	3.1
Inventory to Working Capital **41**	0.0	·	·	·	·	·	0.0	·	·	·	·	·	·	·
Total Receipts to Cash Flow **42**	2.9	1.6	1.6	3.9	3.0	4.6	·	1.4	·	·	·	3.7	·	2.7
Cost of Goods to Cash Flow **43**	0.5	0.3	·	3.3	0.7	2.5	·	0.3	·	·	·	·	·	·
Cash Flow to Total Debt **44**	0.0	·	2.5	0.2	0.3	0.3	·	0.4	0.1	·	·	·	·	0.0

Selected Financial Factors (in Percentages)

Debt Ratio **45**	93.7	·	36.9	74.3	132.9	55.7	76.0	57.1	67.8	89.4	·	129.7	·	92.6
Return on Total Assets **46**	2.1	·	9.5	7.7	14.3	2.8	·	·	10.0	2.9	·	3.2	·	1.9
Return on Equity Before Income Taxes **47**	10.6	·	12.3	20.5	4.4	·	·	·	29.9	20.5	·	·	·	6.3
Return on Equity After Income Taxes **48**	6.7	·	12.0	19.7	·	2.4	·	·	22.0	14.7	·	·	·	4.2
Profit Margin (Before Income Tax) **49**	6.3	37.7	5.5	8.8	10.4	4.1	·	·	26.1	17.2	·	3.1	·	8.8
Profit Margin (After Income Tax) **50**	4.0	28.1	5.3	9.7	2.2	·	·	·	19.2	12.4	·	2.5	·	5.9

Table II

Corporations with Net Income

COMMODITY CONTRACTS DEALING AND BROKERAGE

MONEY AMOUNTS AND SIZE OF ASSETS IN THOUSANDS OF DOLLARS

Item Description for Accounting Period 7/04 Through 6/05	Total	Zero Assets	Under 500	500 to 1,000	1,000 to 5,000	5,000 to 10,000	10,000 to 25,000	25,000 to 50,000	50,000 to 100,000	100,000 to 250,000	250,000 to 500,000	500,000 to 2,500,000	2,500,000 and over
Number of Enterprises 1	1783	0	1512	112	84	15	26	7	6	0	0	0	4
Revenues ($ in Thousands)													
Net Sales 2	3908216	0	305465	57168	197436	95776	622329	326918	190114	0	0	0	1618796
Interest 3	493342	0	1705	0	62	374	648	376	1618	0	0	0	477114
Rents 4	10579	0	0	1992	0	392	0	4605	20	0	0	0	3486
Royalties 5	7068	0	0	0	0	0	0	7068	0	0	0	0	0
Other Portfolio Income 6	66030	0	1051	1	916	2423	8446	299	1847	0	0	0	48232
Other Receipts 7	3331197	0	302709	55175	196458	92587	613235	314570	186629	0	0	0	1089964
Total Receipts 8	3908216	0	305465	57168	197436	95776	622329	326918	190114	0	0	0	1618796
Average Total Receipts 9	2192	•	202	510	2350	6385	23936	46703	31686	•	•	•	404699
Operating Costs/Operating Income (%)													
Cost of Operations 10	18.4	•	•	•	69.3	13.0	52.9	61.9	•	•	•	•	•
Salaries and Wages 11	17.8	•	5.0	13.1	1.6	11.4	8.2	13.7	10.1	•	•	•	23.1
Taxes Paid 12	1.7	•	1.8	3.8	1.8	2.1	1.2	1.3	2.0	•	•	•	1.8
Interest Paid 13	12.3	•	1.3	4.1	0.2	0.7	0.3	0.4	0.8	•	•	•	27.4
Depreciation 14	1.6	•	0.3	21.3	0.2	2.2	0.5	1.3	1.0	•	•	•	1.9
Amortization and Depletion 15	0.3	•	•	0.0	•	•	0.0	0.0	0.3	•	•	•	0.7
Pensions and Other Deferred Comp. 16	0.4	•	0.2	0.2	•	0.1	0.3	0.4	0.3	•	•	•	0.5
Employee Benefits 17	1.3	•	0.5	3.6	0.1	1.3	0.4	1.1	1.1	•	•	•	1.9
Advertising 18	0.2	•	0.6	•	0.0	0.1	0.3	0.2	1.0	•	•	•	0.1
Other Expenses 19	27.8	•	48.7	22.8	7.2	26.1	20.7	14.7	40.6	•	•	•	31.4
Officers' Compensation 20	4.5	•	14.9	22.3	3.3	3.2	7.8	1.2	5.6	•	•	•	2.2
Operating Margin 21	13.6	•	26.7	8.8	16.3	39.9	7.4	3.9	37.2	•	•	•	9.0
Operating Margin Before Officers' Comp. 22	18.2	•	41.6	31.2	19.7	43.1	15.2	5.1	42.8	•	•	•	11.2

Selected Average Balance Sheet ($ in Thousands)

Net Receivables 23	3223	32	291	419	96	4031	13538	25096	857762
Inventories 24	•	•	•	•	•	•	•	1124	•
Net Property, Plant and Equipment 25	138	5	326	31	1924	393	1695	•	9708
Total Assets 26	20548	136	856	1938	6594	15688	30676	60025	7724780
Notes and Loans Payable 27	1945	41	343	124	32	2898	5839	11067	697738
All Other Liabilities 28	16839	10	293	1235	2698	8023	20612	26212	6457988
Net Worth 29	1764	84	220	578	3863	4768	4225	22747	569054

Selected Financial Ratios (Times to 1)

Current Ratio 30	1.2	6.0	0.8	1.4	1.5	1.3	1.2	1.4	1.3
Quick Ratio 31	0.7	4.9	0.8	1.2	1.1	0.9	1.1	1.2	0.6
Net Sales to Working Capital 32	0.8	2.4	•	4.4	4.9	9.7	14.3	2.5	0.3
Coverage Ratio 33	2.1	22.0	3.1	104.3	59.7	23.7	9.7	47.9	1.3
Total Asset Turnover 34	0.1	1.5	0.6	1.2	1.0	1.5	1.5	0.5	0.1
Inventory Turnover 35	•	•	•	•	•	•	•	•	•
Receivables Turnover 36	•	•	•	•	•	•	•	•	•
Total Liabilities to Net Worth 37	10.6	0.6	2.9	2.4	0.7	2.3	6.3	1.6	12.6
Current Assets to Working Capital 38	5.9	1.2	•	3.5	3.1	4.9	7.1	3.6	5.0
Current Liabilities to Working Capital 39	4.9	0.2	•	2.5	2.1	3.9	6.1	2.6	4.0
Working Capital to Net Sales 40	1.3	0.4	•	0.2	0.2	0.1	0.1	0.4	3.1
Inventory to Working Capital 41	0.0	•	•	•	•	•	0.0	•	•
Total Receipts to Cash Flow 42	2.6	1.4	3.9	4.3	1.6	3.7	6.0	1.3	2.7
Cost of Goods to Cash Flow 43	0.5	•	•	3.0	0.2	2.0	3.7	•	•
Cash Flow to Total Debt 44	0.0	2.8	0.2	0.4	1.5	0.6	0.3	0.6	0.0

Selected Financial Factors (in Percentages)

Debt Ratio 45	91.4	38.0	74.3	70.2	41.4	69.6	86.2	62.1	92.6
Return on Total Assets 46	2.8	41.6	7.7	20.0	39.2	11.7	6.5	20.1	1.9
Return on Equity Before Income Taxes 47	16.8	64.0	20.5	66.4	65.8	37.0	42.6	51.9	6.3
Return on Equity After Income Taxes 48	13.8	63.7	19.7	63.5	62.6	35.2	38.4	39.5	4.2
Profit Margin (Before Income Tax) 49	13.5	26.7	8.8	16.3	39.8	7.4	3.9	37.2	8.8
Profit Margin (After Income Tax) 50	11.1	26.5	8.5	15.6	37.9	7.0	3.5	28.4	5.9

Table I

Corporations with and without Net Income

SECURITIES & COMMODITY EXCHANGES, OTHER FINANCIAL INVESTMENT

MONEY AMOUNTS AND SIZE OF ASSETS IN THOUSANDS OF DOLLARS

Item Description for Accounting Period 7/04 Through 6/05	Total	Zero Assets	Under 500	500 to 1,000	1,000 to 5,000	5,000 to 10,000	10,000 to 25,000	25,000 to 50,000	50,000 to 100,000	100,000 to 250,000	250,000 to 500,000	500,000 to 2,500,000	2,500,000 and over
Number of Enterprises 1	36536	7453	24560	1059	2332	353	421	137	83	63	21	39	16
Revenues ($ in Thousands)													
Net Sales 2	81356783	1076909	8147142	907651	4712181	2862955	4234016	2466711	2038205	3992692	1610697	13524057	35783567
Interest 3	7424532	67529	2531	6692	42644	9997	46662	30937	43378	128149	94341	275249	6676423
Rents 4	60248	18	9785	177	2244	305	4259	317	55	3462	7331	10473	21821
Royalties 5	183797	0	93933	0	43	0	176	23	8631	18913	60478	1601	0
Other Portfolio Income 6	237099	14259	16184	62315	123698	13634	76938	46754	88959	328170	42611	556566	977011
Other Receipts 7	71341107	995103	8024709	838467	4543552	2839019	4105981	2388680	1897182	3513998	1405936	12680168	28108312
Total Receipts 8	81356783	1076909	8147142	907651	4712181	2862955	4234016	2466711	2038205	3992692	1610697	13524057	35783567
Average Total Receipts 9	2227	144	332	857	2021	8110	10057	18005	24557	63376	76700	346771	2236473
Operating Costs/Operating Income (%)													
Cost of Operations 10	0.7	0.3	1.7	0.0	1.2	3.5	0.6	3.0	0.8	0.9	•	0.1	0.2
Salaries and Wages 11	21.9	12.2	22.5	25.8	29.0	38.7	26.7	26.4	25.3	28.5	15.2	24.8	17.0
Taxes Paid 12	2.3	3.2	2.8	3.3	2.9	2.2	2.1	2.9	2.6	2.9	3.8	2.3	2.0
Interest Paid 13	5.1	8.9	0.5	0.6	1.6	1.1	2.8	2.5	3.0	3.4	6.8	2.0	8.8
Depreciation 14	2.1	1.2	1.0	1.0	3.5	1.6	2.3	2.6	2.5	3.4	5.0	2.5	1.8
Amortization and Depletion 15	0.9	0.9	0.3	0.3	0.7	0.4	0.7	0.7	0.9	1.0	4.0	1.8	0.6
Pensions and Other Deferred Comp. 16	1.2	2.7	3.2	1.0	1.8	1.6	0.8	1.0	1.2	0.9	1.1	1.7	0.5
Employee Benefits 17	2.5	2.6	2.2	1.4	1.7	1.4	1.3	1.7	1.5	1.2	2.2	2.8	3.1
Advertising 18	2.5	1.0	1.2	1.5	0.4	0.3	0.5	1.5	0.8	0.8	0.7	2.3	4.0
Other Expenses 19	33.9	46.4	28.8	26.3	32.4	26.2	32.2	27.3	32.9	24.2	35.2	35.5	36.8
Officers' Compensation 20	10.4	24.8	24.7	9.0	21.4	17.0	16.5	16.5	18.8	12.0	7.4	9.6	3.5
Operating Margin 21	16.6	•	11.0	29.8	3.6	5.9	13.4	14.0	9.6	20.7	18.6	14.8	21.9
Operating Margin Before Officers' Comp. 22	27.0	20.7	35.7	38.8	24.9	22.9	29.9	30.5	28.4	32.7	26.0	24.4	25.3

Selected Average Balance Sheet ($ in Thousands)

Net Receivables 23	1070	0	6	54	223	642	1649	4028	8265	12672	47073	89596	1933980
Inventories 24	•	•	•	•	•	•	•	•	•	•	•	•	•
Net Property, Plant and Equipment 25	223	0	11	27	334	542	1152	2062	3433	10443	24654	46862	176750
Total Assets 26	10888	0	71	749	2168	6982	15430	34767	68852	156998	351650	1087468	19442992
Notes and Loans Payable 27	4406	0	29	521	892	3665	4514	9870	16374	41065	122901	170764	8742478
All Other Liabilities 28	2947	0	22	216	473	1290	2649	7756	15678	38419	98460	345254	5245145
Net Worth 29	3535	0	20	12	802	2027	8266	17141	36800	77514	130289	571449	5455370

Selected Financial Ratios (Times to 1)

Current Ratio 30	1.0	•	1.7	1.3	1.9	0.8	2.1	1.8	1.7	1.4	1.6	1.7	1.0
Quick Ratio 31	0.7	•	1.6	1.1	1.5	0.5	1.5	1.3	1.4	0.8	1.5	1.0	0.6
Net Sales to Working Capital 32	13.7	•	21.1	9.4	4.8	•	3.2	2.8	2.4	4.0	1.7	2.1	•
Coverage Ratio 33	4.2	0.5	21.4	46.9	3.2	6.4	5.8	6.5	4.1	5.5	3.7	8.5	3.5
Total Asset Turnover 34	0.2	•	4.6	1.1	0.9	1.2	0.7	0.5	0.4	0.4	0.2	0.3	0.1
Inventory Turnover 35	•	•	•	•	•	•	•	•	•	•	•	•	•
Receivables Turnover 36	•	•	•	•	•	•	•	•	•	•	•	•	•
Total Liabilities to Net Worth 37	2.1	•	2.6	60.6	1.7	2.4	0.9	1.0	0.9	1.0	1.7	0.9	2.6
Current Assets to Working Capital 38	27.8	•	2.4	4.2	2.2	•	1.9	2.3	2.5	3.7	2.8	2.5	•
Current Liabilities to Working Capital 39	26.8	•	1.4	3.2	1.2	•	0.9	1.3	1.5	2.7	1.8	1.5	•
Working Capital to Net Sales 40	0.1	•	0.0	0.1	0.2	0.3	0.3	0.4	0.4	0.3	0.6	0.5	•
Inventory to Working Capital 41	0.0	•	•	0.0	0.0	•	0.0	0.0	0.0	0.0	0.0	0.0	•
Total Receipts to Cash Flow 42	2.2	2.6	2.9	2.1	3.7	3.6	2.4	2.8	2.6	2.5	2.3	2.2	1.8
Cost of Goods to Cash Flow 43	0.0	0.0	0.0	0.0	0.0	0.1	0.0	0.1	0.0	0.0	0.0	0.0	0.0
Cash Flow to Total Debt 44	0.1	•	2.2	0.5	0.4	0.4	0.6	0.4	0.3	0.3	0.2	0.3	0.1

Selected Financial Factors (in Percentages)

Debt Ratio 45	67.5	•	72.0	98.4	63.0	71.0	46.4	50.7	46.6	50.6	62.9	47.5	71.9
Return on Total Assets 46	4.4	•	53.8	34.7	4.6	8.1	10.4	8.5	4.4	7.6	5.4	5.3	3.5
Return on Equity Before Income Taxes 47	10.3	•	183.0	2094.4	8.6	23.4	16.1	14.6	6.2	12.6	10.7	8.9	9.0
Return on Equity After Income Taxes 48	7.4	•	179.9	1950.8	6.2	20.9	15.1	12.3	5.0	10.9	7.3	5.6	6.0
Profit Margin (Before Income Tax) 49	16.3	•	11.0	29.7	3.4	5.9	13.2	13.9	9.3	15.4	18.1	14.7	21.9
Profit Margin (After Income Tax) 50	11.7	•	10.9	27.7	2.4	5.2	12.4	11.7	7.5	13.4	12.4	9.3	14.7

Table II

Corporations with Net Income

SECURITIES & COMMODITY EXCHANGES, OTHER FINANCIAL INVESTMENT

MONEY AMOUNTS AND SIZE OF ASSETS IN THOUSANDS OF DOLLARS

Item Description for Accounting Period 7/04 Through 6/05	Total	Zero Assets	Under 500	500 to 1,000	1,000 to 5,000	5,000 to 10,000	10,000 to 25,000	25,000 to 50,000	50,000 to 100,000	100,000 to 250,000	250,000 to 500,000	500,000 to 2,500,000	2,500,000 and over
Number of Enterprises 1	20200	2459	15276	764	1118	142	222	81	41	44	0	25	0
Revenues ($ in Thousands)													
Net Sales 2	70086045	755557	7167937	891551	3921210	1159133	3470545	2097336	1565651	2984448	0	9473519	0
Interest 3	7152055	63198	1858	4024	33227	6261	22943	21053	18168	80284	0	159204	0
Rents 4	52265	18	6637	177	248	295	2763	172	48	2963	0	9591	0
Royalties 5	173776	0	93933	0	43	0	143	23	1	18913	0	242	0
Other Portfolio Income 6	1974734	11865	15665	58604	105661	10266	57369	36919	43945	118219	0	504060	0
Other Receipts 7	6073215	680476	7049644	828746	3782031	1142311	3387327	2039169	1503489	2766069	0	8800422	0
Total Receipts 8	70086045	755557	7167937	891551	3921210	1159133	3470545	2097336	1565651	2984448	0	9473519	0
Average Total Receipts 9	3470	307	469	1167	3507	8163	15633	25893	38187	67874	·	378941	·
Operating Costs/Operating Income (%)													
Cost of Operations 10	0.6	·	1.9	·	0.9	3.4	0.2	3.4	0.7	1.1	·	0.0	·
Salaries and Wages 11	19.3	12.4	20.0	23.4	26.7	19.7	24.2	22.5	20.6	29.6	·	21.0	·
Taxes Paid 12	2.2	3.0	2.8	3.0	2.5	2.1	2.0	2.8	2.5	2.8	·	2.0	·
Interest Paid 13	5.3	9.1	0.4	0.3	1.0	1.7	1.2	1.3	2.0	3.1	·	1.5	·
Depreciation 14	1.7	0.4	0.8	0.6	2.6	1.1	1.6	1.4	1.4	3.0	·	1.4	·
Amortization and Depletion 15	0.8	0.0	0.3	0.3	0.3	0.0	0.7	0.3	0.5	1.1	·	2.4	·
Pensions and Other Deferred Comp. 16	1.0	1.1	3.1	1.0	2.0	1.0	0.8	0.7	1.2	0.8	·	1.1	·
Employee Benefits 17	2.3	2.9	2.3	1.3	1.6	0.7	1.2	1.5	0.8	0.9	·	1.2	·
Advertising 18	2.6	0.9	0.7	1.4	0.4	0.2	0.6	1.7	0.8	0.9	·	2.3	·
Other Expenses 19	32.4	23.3	26.7	22.6	25.9	24.9	24.2	24.5	26.5	17.3	·	34.9	·
Officers' Compensation 20	9.3	30.9	25.5	8.6	18.9	16.5	17.3	15.7	22.6	13.9	·	5.6	·
Operating Margin 21	22.5	16.0	15.5	37.6	17.2	28.5	26.1	24.1	20.5	25.6	·	26.6	·
Operating Margin Before Officers' Comp. 22	31.8	46.9	40.9	46.1	36.1	45.1	43.4	39.8	43.0	39.4	·	32.2	·

Selected Average Balance Sheet ($ in Thousands)

Net Receivables 23	1778	0	8	73	268	991	2208	3892	10911	14409	80310
Inventories 24	•	•	•	•	•	•	•	•	•	•	•
Net Property, Plant and Equipment 25	280	0	14	19	337	466	1197	1421	2546	10070	30354
Total Assets 26	17662	0	84	726	2172	6915	15349	34375	68425	153951	1033256
Notes and Loans Payable 27	7271	0	26	315	457	3032	3754	6899	15465	35992	122284
All Other Liabilities 28	4856	0	29	57	538	829	3403	9059	17085	34137	343218
Net Worth 29	5535	0	29	354	1177	3054	8192	18417	35876	83822	567754

Selected Financial Ratios (Times to 1)

Current Ratio 30	1.0	•	1.7	3.3	2.9	1.9	2.2	1.6	1.3	1.6	1.6
Quick Ratio 31	0.7	•	1.6	3.0	2.3	1.6	1.5	1.2	1.0	0.9	1.2
Net Sales to Working Capital 32	70.9	•	23.4	4.1	4.6	7.0	4.0	4.6	7.2	3.1	2.7
Coverage Ratio 33	5.3	2.8	40.4	148.1	17.6	17.3	21.9	19.6	11.2	9.2	19.2
Total Asset Turnover 34	0.2	•	5.6	1.6	1.6	1.2	1.0	0.8	0.6	0.4	0.4
Inventory Turnover 35	•	•	•	•	•	•	•	•	•	•	•
Receivables Turnover 36	•	•	•	•	•	•	•	•	•	•	•
Total Liabilities to Net Worth 37	2.2	•	1.9	1.1	0.8	1.3	0.9	0.9	0.9	0.8	0.8
Current Assets to Working Capital 38	153.7	•	2.4	1.4	1.5	2.2	1.8	2.8	4.8	2.8	2.7
Current Liabilities to Working Capital 39	152.7	•	1.4	0.4	0.5	1.2	0.8	1.8	3.8	1.8	1.7
Working Capital to Net Sales 40	0.0	•	0.0	0.2	0.2	0.1	0.3	0.2	0.1	0.3	0.4
Inventory to Working Capital 41	0.0	•	•	•	•	•	0.0	•	0.0	0.0	0.0
Total Receipts to Cash Flow 42	2.0	2.7	2.7	1.9	2.8	2.0	2.2	2.3	2.3	2.6	1.8
Cost of Goods to Cash Flow 43	0.0	•	0.0	0.0	0.0	0.1	0.0	0.1	0.0	0.0	0.0
Cash Flow to Total Debt 44	0.1	•	3.2	1.6	1.3	1.1	1.0	0.7	0.5	0.4	0.5

Selected Financial Factors (in Percentages)

Debt Ratio 45	68.7	•	65.6	51.2	45.8	55.8	46.6	46.4	47.6	45.6	45.1
Return on Total Assets 46	5.5	•	88.5	60.8	29.4	35.7	27.7	19.4	12.4	12.6	10.3
Return on Equity Before Income Taxes 47	14.1	•	251.3	123.8	51.1	76.2	49.5	34.4	21.6	20.6	17.8
Return on Equity After Income Taxes 48	10.8	•	247.9	116.9	47.6	72.1	47.7	30.6	19.1	18.4	12.6
Profit Margin (Before Income Tax) 49	22.5	16.0	15.5	37.6	17.1	28.5	26.0	24.5	20.3	25.4	26.7
Profit Margin (After Income Tax) 50	17.2	14.0	15.3	35.5	16.0	27.0	25.0	21.8	17.9	22.7	18.9

Table I

Corporations with and without Net Income

LIFE INSURANCE

MONEY AMOUNTS AND SIZE OF ASSETS IN THOUSANDS OF DOLLARS

Item Description for Accounting Period 7/04 Through 6/05	Total	Zero Assets	Under 500	500 to 1,000	1,000 to 5,000	5,000 to 10,000	10,000 to 25,000	25,000 to 50,000	50,000 to 100,000	100,000 to 250,000	250,000 to 500,000	500,000 to 2,500,000	2,500,000 and over
Number of Enterprises 1	1241	51	303	103	240	77	93	59	47	49	51	69	99
Revenues ($ in Thousands)													
Net Sales 2	862569092	23571339	39067	36149	220318	235640	667186	2757193	1399722	3754146	5796410	19135347	804956575
Interest 3	145733785	2625001	978	1758	14744	19709	47279	120278	118908	305623	758485	3248615	138472407
Rents 4	3412107	53467	0	0	182	529	2536	1689	6704	11347	14490	37444	3283718
Royalties 5	7148	0	0	0	0	0	0	0	0	404	0	1	6743
Other Portfolio Income 6	19005784	1922095	448	217	4985	8582	12860	15067	19515	85490	64057	303915	16568551
Other Receipts 7	694410268	18970776	37641	34174	200407	206820	604511	2620159	1254595	3351282	4959378	15545372	646625156
Total Receipts 8	862569092	23571339	39067	36149	220318	235640	667186	2757193	1399722	3754146	5796410	19135347	804956575
Average Total Receipts 9	695060	462183	129	351	918	3060	7174	46732	29781	76615	113655	277324	8130874
Operating Costs/Operating Income (%)													
Cost of Operations 10	45.7	74.6	31.0	19.0	37.2	33.2	39.7	85.2	42.8	35.0	41.7	48.4	44.8
Salaries and Wages 11	2.1	0.5	•	•	•	•	0.3	0.2	1.2	0.4	0.6	1.1	2.2
Taxes Paid 12	0.8	0.5	0.9	0.9	1.0	1.0	1.7	0.4	1.4	1.3	1.4	1.3	0.8
Interest Paid 13	2.2	0.3	0.3	0.3	0.1	0.4	0.6	0.1	0.2	0.2	0.6	0.4	2.3
Depreciation 14	0.6	0.0	0.0	0.0	0.1	0.2	0.4	0.1	0.4	0.3	0.3	0.4	0.6
Amortization and Depletion 15	1.0	0.5	0.5	0.5	1.0	0.9	1.7	0.8	1.7	2.0	2.2	2.2	1.0
Pensions and Other Deferred Comp. 16	0.3	0.3	•	•	0.7	0.5	0.4	0.1	1.4	0.5	0.4	0.7	0.3
Employee Benefits 17	0.3	0.1	•	•	0.2	0.1	0.2	0.1	1.1	0.2	0.2	0.3	0.3
Advertising 18	0.3	0.0	•	0.0	0.1	0.1	0.2	0.0	2.8	0.1	0.4	0.7	0.3
Other Expenses 19	43.1	25.7	66.1	42.1	45.2	53.1	54.0	10.7	40.8	57.2	47.5	39.9	43.7
Officers' Compensation 20	0.1	0.0	•	•	•	•	0.2	0.0	0.1	0.0	0.1	0.1	0.1
Operating Margin 21	3.6	•	1.1	37.2	14.5	10.6	0.6	2.3	6.1	2.6	4.7	4.7	3.7
Operating Margin Before Officers' Comp. 22	3.7	•	1.1	37.2	14.5	10.6	0.8	2.4	6.2	2.7	4.8	4.8	3.9

Selected Average Balance Sheet ($ in Thousands)

Net Receivables **23**	66401	0	8	82	139	279	900	1064	1197	1265	3757	9856	820220
Inventories **24**	•	•	•	•	•	•	•	•	•	•	•	•	•
Net Property, Plant and Equipment **25**	41509	0	0	0	11	62	139	187	749	853	1853	5742	514277
Total Assets **26**	3697474	184	745	2457	6935	16538	36437	70390	157970	357841	1185081	•	45177291
Notes and Loans Payable **27**	104578	0	0	0	0	36	110	22	1424	4475	3973	•	1305032
All Other Liabilities **28**	3070167	182	450	1699	244	10716	24762	48892	129649	286333	968106	•	37545848
Net Worth **29**	522728	1	295	758	6691	5785	11565	21476	26897	67033	213002	•	6326411

Selected Financial Ratios (Times to 1)

Current Ratio **30**	0.8	•	5.0	12.7	4.4	3.9	3.1	2.3	2.5	1.7	1.6	1.4	0.8
Quick Ratio **31**	0.6	•	4.0	9.2	3.5	2.9	2.2	1.8	1.8	1.4	1.3	1.0	0.6
Net Sales to Working Capital **32**	•	•	1.0	0.6	0.8	1.3	1.2	5.2	1.6	3.6	2.3	3.3	•
Coverage Ratio **33**	2.8	•	4.7	145.2	165.1	28.8	2.0	34.1	27.2	14.0	9.0	13.3	2.8
Total Asset Turnover **34**	0.2	•	0.7	0.5	0.4	0.4	0.4	1.3	0.4	0.5	0.3	0.2	0.2
Inventory Turnover **35**	•	•	•	•	•	•	•	•	•	•	•	•	•
Receivables Turnover **36**	•	•	•	•	•	•	•	•	•	•	•	•	•
Total Liabilities to Net Worth **37**	6.1	136.4	•	1.5	2.2	0.0	1.9	2.2	2.3	4.9	4.3	4.6	6.1
Current Assets to Working Capital **38**	•	•	1.2	1.1	1.3	1.3	1.5	1.8	1.7	2.5	2.6	3.5	6.1
Current Liabilities to Working Capital **39**	•	•	0.2	0.1	0.3	0.3	0.5	0.7	0.8	1.5	1.6	2.6	•
Working Capital to Net Sales **40**	•	•	1.0	1.7	0.8	1.3	0.8	0.7	0.6	0.3	0.4	0.3	•
Inventory to Working Capital **41**	•	•	•	•	•	•	0.6	0.6	0.0	0.0	0.3	0.3	•
Total Receipts to Cash Flow **42**	2.2	4.4	1.5	1.3	1.7	1.6	1.9	8.0	2.2	1.7	2.0	2.3	2.2
Cost of Goods to Cash Flow **43**	1.0	3.3	0.5	0.2	0.6	0.5	0.8	6.8	1.0	0.6	0.8	1.1	1.0
Cash Flow to Total Debt **44**	0.1	•	0.5	0.6	0.3	7.7	0.4	0.2	0.3	0.3	0.2	0.1	0.1

Selected Financial Factors (in Percentages)

Debt Ratio **45**	85.9	•	99.3	60.4	69.2	65.0	68.3	69.5	83.0	81.3	82.0	•	86.0
Return on Total Assets **46**	1.1	•	1.0	17.6	5.4	0.5	3.0	2.7	1.3	1.7	1.1	•	1.2
Return on Equity Before Income Taxes **47**	5.3	•	104.7	44.1	17.4	4.8	0.7	9.1	8.4	7.3	8.0	5.7	5.3
Return on Equity After Income Taxes **48**	3.6	•	10.1	42.0	14.6	3.5	•	6.0	5.4	3.9	5.6	2.6	3.7
Profit Margin (Before Income Tax) **49**	4.0	•	1.1	37.1	14.4	10.4	0.6	2.3	6.0	2.6	4.7	4.3	4.1
Profit Margin (After Income Tax) **50**	2.7	•	0.1	35.3	12.1	7.7	•	1.5	3.9	1.4	3.3	2.0	2.8

Table II

Corporations with Net Income

LIFE INSURANCE

MONEY AMOUNTS AND SIZE OF ASSETS IN THOUSANDS OF DOLLARS

Item Description for Accounting Period 7/04 Through 6/05	Total	Zero Assets	Under 500	500 to 1,000	1,000 to 5,000	5,000 to 10,000	10,000 to 25,000	25,000 to 50,000	50,000 to 100,000	100,000 to 250,000	250,000 to 500,000	500,000 to 2,500,000	2,500,000 and over
Number of Enterprises **1**	920	34	188	94	184	56	69	50	38	34	42	51	80
Revenues ($ in Thousands)													
Net Sales **2**	734038162	19435065	28478	33243	163355	184655	533865	669813	1256433	1937558	4934124	14768000	69093574
Interest **3**	117281629	1884552	1083	1694	10851	13966	36006	74334	95545	207774	651960	2692162	11161703
Rents **4**	2538609	8185	0	0	182	342	1579	1566	3879	7881	14143	28903	2471949
Royalties **5**	5228	0	0	0	0	0	0	0	0	38	0	1	5189
Other Portfolio Income **6**	16891773	1915228	507	217	4387	7592	10487	13434	18648	27664	48821	235186	14609600
Other Receipts **7**	597320923	15627100	26888	31332	147935	162755	485793	580479	1138361	1694201	4219200	11811748	561395133
Total Receipts **8**	734038162	19435065	28478	33243	163355	184655	533865	669813	1256433	1937558	4934124	14768000	69093574
Average Total Receipts **9**	797868	571620	151	354	888	3297	7737	13396	33064	56987	117479	289569	8626170
Operating Costs/Operating Income (%)													
Cost of Operations **10**	45.4	75.8	19.1	19.2	29.6	34.2	43.1	42.5	41.7	42.6	44.0	46.8	44.6
Salaries and Wages **11**	2.2	0.0	*	*	*	*	0.2	0.7	1.4	0.7	0.4	0.3	2.3
Taxes Paid **12**	0.8	0.1	1.2	0.9	1.1	1.0	1.6	1.3	1.3	1.6	1.2	1.4	0.8
Interest Paid **13**	2.2	0.0	0.0	0.1	0.1	0.2	0.3	0.2	0.2	0.3	0.5	0.2	2.4
Depreciation **14**	0.6	0.0	0.4	*	0.1	0.1	0.4	0.1	0.2	0.4	0.2	0.4	0.7
Amortization and Depletion **15**	1.0	0.3	0.7	0.5	0.9	0.8	1.7	1.6	1.6	3.0	1.8	2.5	1.0
Pensions and Other Deferred Comp. **16**	0.3	0.1	*	*	0.9	0.6	0.4	0.6	1.4	0.8	0.4	0.6	0.3
Employee Benefits **17**	0.3	0.0	0.2	*	0.2	0.1	0.2	0.3	0.9	0.2	0.1	0.2	0.3
Advertising **18**	0.3	0.0	0.0	0.0	0.1	0.1	0.1	0.1	2.6	0.2	0.2	0.8	0.3
Other Expenses **19**	41.9	23.2	49.8	37.1	40.4	44.3	35.4	35.0	38.6	42.0	44.8	36.9	42.5
Officers' Compensation **20**	0.2	*	*	*	*	*	0.2	0.1	0.1	0.1	0.0	0.1	0.2
Operating Margin **21**	4.7	0.3	28.4	42.1	26.8	18.6	16.5	17.5	9.8	8.1	6.3	9.8	4.7
Operating Margin Before Officers' Comp. **22**	4.9	0.3	28.4	42.1	26.8	18.6	16.7	17.6	10.0	8.2	6.3	9.9	4.8

Selected Average Balance Sheet ($ in Thousands)

Net Receivables 23	83399	0	9	77	129	368	824	1251	1456	719	3284	3448	952005
Inventories 24	•	•	•	•	•	•	•	•	•	•	•	•	•
Net Property, Plant and Equipment 25	44482	0	10	0	2	33	101	211	414	403	1623	6019	506212
Total Assets 26	4225627	0	259	743	2474	6768	16540	36531	70883	160010	359625	1258726	47452794
Notes and Loans Payable 27	127450	0	0	0	0	0	43	130	27	1092	2246	2402	1462370
All Other Liabilities 28	3474281	0	190	385	1204	-1798	10214	23752	47181	126927	286049	1022711	39049652
Net Worth 29	623897	0	69	358	1269	8566	6282	12649	23675	31991	71329	233613	6940772

Selected Financial Ratios (Times to 1)

Current Ratio 30	0.7	•	•	6.3	11.9	4.8	5.2	4.3	2.0	3.0	1.9	1.5	1.4	0.7
Quick Ratio 31	0.5	•	•	5.4	8.4	3.8	3.6	3.2	1.5	2.4	1.6	1.2	1.0	0.5
Net Sales to Working Capital 32	•			0.8	0.6	0.7	1.2	1.2	1.8	1.6	2.4	2.6	3.2	•
Coverage Ratio 33	3.3	30.8	674.8	341.7	256.8	79.7	65.2	87.6	41.7	29.9	13.0	53.6	3.2	
Total Asset Turnover 34	0.2		0.6	0.5	0.4	0.5	0.5	0.4	0.5	0.4	0.3	0.2	0.2	
Inventory Turnover 35	•		•	•	•	•	•	•	•	•	•	•	•	
Receivables Turnover 36	•		•	•	•	•	•	•	•	•	•	•	•	
Total Liabilities to Net Worth 37	5.8	2.8	1.1	0.9	1.6	1.9	2.0	4.0	4.0	4.4	5.8			
Current Assets to Working Capital 38	•	1.2	1.1	1.3	1.3	2.0	1.5	2.2	2.9	3.2				
Current Liabilities to Working Capital 39	•	0.2	0.1	0.3	0.3	1.0	0.5	1.2	1.9	2.2				
Working Capital to Net Sales 40	•	1.2	1.6	1.3	0.8	0.9	0.5	0.6	0.4	0.4	0.3			
Inventory to Working Capital 41	•	•	•	•	•	•	0.0	0.0	0.0	•				
Total Receipts to Cash Flow 42	2.2	4.3	1.3	1.5	1.7	2.0	2.0	2.2	2.1	2.0	2.2	2.2	2.2	
Cost of Goods to Cash Flow 43	1.0	3.2	0.2	0.5	0.6	0.9	0.8	0.9	0.9	0.9	1.0	1.0		
Cash Flow to Total Debt 44	0.1	•	0.6	0.7	0.5	0.4	0.3	0.3	0.2	0.2	0.1	0.1		

Selected Financial Factors (in Percentages)

Debt Ratio 45	85.2	•	73.4	51.8	48.7	•	62.0	65.4	66.6	80.0	80.2	81.4	85.4
Return on Total Assets 46	1.4	•	16.6	20.1	9.6	9.1	6.4	4.7	4.7	2.9	2.2	2.2	1.4
Return on Equity Before Income Taxes 47	6.6	•	62.5	41.5	18.6	7.1	20.2	18.2	13.7	14.2	10.2	11.8	6.4
Return on Equity After Income Taxes 48	4.7	•	59.5	39.6	16.4	5.8	16.0	14.9	10.3	10.2	7.6	8.0	4.5
Profit Margin (Before Income Tax) 49	5.1	0.3	28.4	42.0	26.6	18.5	16.4	17.2	9.8	8.0	6.2	9.5	5.1
Profit Margin (After Income Tax) 50	3.7	0.2	27.0	40.1	23.5	15.1	13.0	14.0	7.4	5.7	4.6	6.4	3.6

Table I

Corporations with and without Net Income

LIFE INSURANCE, STOCK COMPANIES (FORM 1120L)

MONEY AMOUNTS AND SIZE OF ASSETS IN THOUSANDS OF DOLLARS

Item Description for Accounting Period 7/04 Through 6/05	Total	Zero Assets	Under 500	500 to 1,000	1,000 to 5,000	5,000 to 10,000	10,000 to 25,000	25,000 to 50,000	50,000 to 100,000	100,000 to 250,000	250,000 to 500,000	500,000 to 2,500,000	2,500,000 and over
Number of Enterprises **1**	1177	46	293	103	230	77	93	52	47	44	43	58	91
Revenues ($ in Thousands)													
Net Sales **2**	772437778	23571249	38947	36149	198877	235640	667186	2678386	1399722	3551241	5124677	16578251	718357454
Interest **3**	127244290	2624986	958	1758	13476	19709	47279	105306	118908	268606	620167	2586047	120837090
Rents **4**	2443564	53467	0	0	182	529	2536	1689	6704	9154	10041	31219	2328042
Royalties **5**	4354	0	0	0	0	0	0	0	0	38	0	0	4316
Other Portfolio Income **6**	16424117	1922095	446	217	4651	8582	12860	13914	19515	78356	48013	250434	14065034
Other Receipts **7**	626321453	18970701	37543	34174	180568	206820	604511	2557477	1254595	3195087	446456	13710551	581122972
Total Receipts **8**	772437778	23571249	38947	36149	198877	235640	667186	2678386	1399722	3551241	5124677	16578251	718357454
Average Total Receipts **9**	656277	512418	133	351	865	3060	7174	51507	29781	80710	119179	285832	7894038
Operating Costs/Operating Income (%)													
Cost of Operations **10**	46.0	74.6	30.8	19.0	34.2	33.2	39.7	86.1	42.8	34.0	41.2	49.0	45.0
Salaries and Wages **11**	2.2	0.5	•	•	•	•	0.3	0.2	1.2	0.5	0.7	1.3	2.3
Taxes Paid **12**	0.8	0.5	0.9	0.9	1.1	1.0	1.7	0.3	1.4	1.2	1.3	1.3	0.8
Interest Paid **13**	2.3	0.3	0.3	0.3	0.1	0.4	0.6	0.1	0.2	0.2	0.7	0.3	2.5
Depreciation **14**	0.6	0.0	0.0	0.0	0.1	0.2	0.4	0.0	0.4	0.3	0.3	0.4	0.7
Amortization and Depletion **15**	0.9	0.5	0.5	0.5	0.9	0.9	1.7	0.7	1.7	2.0	2.0	2.1	0.9
Pensions and Other Deferred Comp. **16**	0.3	0.3	•	•	0.7	0.5	0.4	0.1	1.4	0.5	0.4	0.6	0.3
Employee Benefits **17**	0.3	0.1	•	•	0.2	0.1	0.2	0.1	1.1	0.2	0.2	0.3	0.3
Advertising **18**	0.3	0.0	•	0.0	0.1	0.1	0.2	0.0	2.8	0.1	0.4	0.7	0.3
Other Expenses **19**	42.5	25.7	66.1	42.1	46.2	53.1	54.0	10.1	40.8	58.3	47.8	39.3	43.1
Officers' Compensation **20**	0.1	0.0	•	0.0	0.1	•	0.2	0.0	0.1	0.0	0.1	0.1	0.1
Operating Margin **21**	3.6	•	1.3	37.2	16.5	10.6	0.6	2.3	6.1	2.7	5.1	4.6	3.7
Operating Margin Before Officers' Comp. **22**	3.7	•	1.3	37.2	16.5	10.6	0.8	2.3	6.2	2.8	5.1	4.8	3.9

Selected Average Balance Sheet ($ in Thousands)

Net Receivables 23	66613	0	8	82	144	279	900	1205	1197	1387	4071	11499	848709
Inventories 24	•	•	•	•	•	•	•	•	•	•	•	•	•
Net Property, Plant and Equipment 25	42788	0	0	0	3	62	139	192	749	763	1978	5947	547634
Total Assets 26	3492558	176	745	2443	6935	16538	35545	70390	157285	354092	•	1194851	44081037
Notes and Loans Payable 27	107483	0	0	0	0	36	125	22	1586	5307	4724	•	1383784
All Other Liabilities 28	2873692	182	450	1702	244	10716	23516	48892	126681	275773	962083	•	36308524
Net Worth 29	511383	-6	295	741	6691	5785	11904	21476	29019	73012	228044	•	6388729

Selected Financial Ratios (Times to 1)

Current Ratio 30	0.8	•	4.9	12.7	4.5	3.9	3.1	2.5	2.5	1.6	2.0	1.3	0.8
Quick Ratio 31	0.6	•	3.8	9.2	3.7	2.9	2.2	1.9	1.8	1.3	1.5	0.9	0.6
Net Sales to Working Capital 32	•	•	1.1	0.6	0.7	1.3	1.2	5.3	1.6	4.0	1.9	4.1	•
Coverage Ratio 33	2.7	•	5.5	145.2	184.4	28.8	2.0	33.0	27.2	14.4	8.8	14.8	2.7
Total Asset Turnover 34	0.2	•	0.8	0.5	0.4	0.4	0.4	1.4	0.4	0.5	0.3	0.2	0.2
Inventory Turnover 35	•	•	•	•	•	•	•	•	•	•	•	•	•
Receivables Turnover 36	•	•	•	•	•	•	•	•	•	•	•	•	•
Total Liabilities to Net Worth 37	5.8	•	•	1.5	2.3	0.0	1.9	2.0	2.3	4.4	3.8	4.2	5.9
Current Assets to Working Capital 38	•	•	1.3	1.1	1.3	1.3	1.5	1.7	1.7	2.6	2.0	4.1	•
Current Liabilities to Working Capital 39	•	•	0.3	0.1	0.3	0.3	0.5	0.7	0.7	1.6	1.0	3.1	•
Working Capital to Net Sales 40	•	•	0.9	1.7	1.4	0.8	0.8	0.2	0.6	0.2	0.5	0.2	•
Inventory to Working Capital 41	•	•	•	•	•	•	•	•	0.0	0.0	•	0.0	•
Total Receipts to Cash Flow 42	2.2	4.4	1.5	1.3	1.7	1.6	1.9	8.4	2.2	1.7	1.9	2.3	2.2
Cost of Goods to Cash Flow 43	1.0	3.3	0.5	0.2	0.6	0.5	0.8	7.2	1.0	0.6	0.8	1.1	1.0
Cash Flow to Total Debt 44	0.1	•	0.5	0.6	0.3	7.7	0.4	0.3	0.3	0.4	0.2	0.1	0.1

Selected Financial Factors (in Percentages)

Debt Ratio 45	85.4	•	103.5	60.4	69.7	65.0	66.5	69.5	81.6	79.4	80.9	•	85.5
Return on Total Assets 46	1.2	1.2	•	17.6	5.8	0.5	3.3	2.7	1.5	1.9	1.1	•	1.2
Return on Equity Before Income Taxes 47	5.1	•	•	44.1	19.1	4.8	0.7	9.7	8.4	7.4	8.3	5.4	5.2
Return on Equity After Income Taxes 48	3.5	•	•	42.0	16.1	3.5	•	6.4	5.4	4.0	5.9	2.3	3.6
Profit Margin (Before Income Tax) 49	4.0	•	1.3	37.1	16.3	10.4	0.6	2.2	6.0	2.7	5.1	4.3	4.2
Profit Margin (After Income Tax) 50	2.7	•	0.4	35.3	13.8	7.7	•	1.5	3.9	1.4	3.6	1.8	2.9

Table II
Corporations with Net Income

LIFE INSURANCE, STOCK COMPANIES (FORM 1120L)

MONEY AMOUNTS AND SIZE OF ASSETS IN THOUSANDS OF DOLLARS

Item Description for Accounting Period 7/04 Through 6/05	Total	Zero Assets	Under 500	500 to 1000	251 to 500	501 to 1,000	1,001 to 5,000	5,001 to 10,000	10,001 to 25,000	25,001 to 50,000	50,001 to 100,000	100,001 to 250,000	250,001 and over
Number of Enterprises 1	879	0	180	94	184	56	69	0	38	0	0	0	0
Revenues ($ in Thousands)													
Net Sales 2	646050482	0	22603	33243	163355	184655	533865	0	1256433	0	0	0	0
Interest 3	99228750	0	813	1694	10851	13966	36006	0	95545	0	0	0	0
Rents 4	1598623	0	0	0	182	342	1579	0	3879	0	0	0	0
Royalties 5	2801	0	0	0	0	0	0	0	0	0	0	0	0
Other Portfolio Income 6	14326937	0	425	217	4387	7592	10487	0	18648	0	0	0	0
Other Receipts 7	530893371	0	21365	31332	147935	162755	485793	0	1138361	0	0	0	0
Total Receipts 8	646050482	0	22603	33243	163355	184655	533865	0	1256433	0	0	0	0
Average Total Receipts 9	734983	.	126	354	888	3297	7737	.	33064	.	.	.	.
Operating Costs/Operating Income (%)													
Cost of Operations 10	45.9	.	21.7	19.2	29.6	34.2	43.1	.	41.7	.	.	.	.
Salaries and Wages 11	2.3	.	.	.	.	.	0.2	.	1.4	.	.	.	.
Taxes Paid 12	0.8	.	1.1	0.9	1.1	1.0	1.6	.	1.3	.	.	.	.
Interest Paid 13	2.5	.	0.1	0.1	0.1	0.2	0.3	.	0.2	.	.	.	.
Depreciation 14	0.7	.	0.1	.	0.1	0.1	0.4	.	0.2	.	.	.	.
Amortization and Depletion 15	0.9	.	0.6	0.5	0.9	0.8	1.7	.	1.6	.	.	.	.
Pensions and Other Deferred Comp. 16	0.3	.	.	.	0.9	0.6	0.4	.	1.4	.	.	.	.
Employee Benefits 17	0.3	.	.	.	0.2	0.1	0.2	.	0.9	.	.	.	.
Advertising 18	0.3	.	.	0.0	0.1	0.1	0.1	.	2.6	.	.	.	.
Other Expenses 19	41.0	.	44.2	37.1	40.4	44.3	35.4	.	38.6	.	.	.	.
Officers' Compensation 20	0.2	.	.	.	.	.	0.2	.	0.1	.	.	.	.
Operating Margin 21	4.8	.	32.3	42.1	26.8	18.6	16.5	.	9.8	.	.	.	.
Operating Margin Before Officers' Comp. 22	5.0	.	32.3	42.1	26.8	18.6	16.7	.	10.0	.	.	.	.

Selected Average Balance Sheet ($ in Thousands)

Net Receivables 23	82762	9	77	129	368	824	1456
Inventories 24	·	·	·	·	·	·	·
Net Property, Plant and Equipment 25	45612	·	0	2	33	101	414
Total Assets 26	3895892	205	743	2474	6768	16540	70883
Notes and Loans Payable 27	129670	0	0	0	0	43	27
All Other Liabilities 28	3165239	146	385	1204	-1798	10214	47181
Net Worth 29	600982	59	358	1269	8566	6282	23675

Selected Financial Ratios (Times to 1)

Current Ratio 30	0.7	5.6	11.9	4.8	5.2	4.3	3.0
Quick Ratio 31	0.5	4.7	8.4	3.8	3.6	3.2	2.4
Net Sales to Working Capital 32	·	0.8	0.6	0.7	1.2	1.2	1.6
Coverage Ratio 33	3.2	609.4	341.7	256.8	79.7	65.2	41.7
Total Asset Turnover 34	0.2	0.6	0.5	0.4	0.5	0.5	0.5
Inventory Turnover 35	·	·	·	·	·	·	·
Receivables Turnover 36	·	·	·	·	·	·	·
Total Liabilities to Net Worth 37	5.5	2.5	1.1	0.9	·	1.6	2.0
Current Assets to Working Capital 38	·	1.2	1.1	1.3	1.2	1.3	1.5
Current Liabilities to Working Capital 39	·	0.2	0.1	0.3	0.2	0.3	0.5
Working Capital to Net Sales 40	·	1.2	1.6	1.3	0.8	0.9	0.6
Inventory to Working Capital 41	·	·	·	·	·	·	·
Total Receipts to Cash Flow 42	2.2	1.3	1.3	1.5	1.7	2.0	2.2
Cost of Goods to Cash Flow 43	1.0	0.3	0.2	0.5	0.6	0.9	0.9
Cash Flow to Total Debt 44	0.1	0.6	0.7	0.5	·	0.4	0.3

Selected Financial Factors (in Percentages)

Debt Ratio 45	84.6	71.2	51.8	48.7	·	62.0	66.6
Return on Total Assets 46	1.5	19.8	20.1	9.6	9.1	7.8	4.7
Return on Equity Before Income Taxes 47	6.5	68.6	41.5	18.6	7.1	20.2	13.7
Return on Equity After Income Taxes 48	4.6	65.0	39.6	16.4	5.8	16.0	10.3
Profit Margin (Before Income Tax) 49	5.3	32.3	42.0	26.6	18.5	16.4	9.8
Profit Margin (After Income Tax) 50	3.8	30.6	40.1	23.5	15.1	13.0	7.4

Table I

Corporations with and without Net Income

LIFE INSURANCE, MUTUAL COMPANIES (FORM 1120L)

MONEY AMOUNTS AND SIZE OF ASSETS IN THOUSANDS OF DOLLARS

Item Description for Accounting Period 7/04 Through 6/05	Total	Zero Assets	Under 500	500 to 1,000	1,000 to 5,000	5,000 to 10,000	10,000 to 25,000	25,000 to 50,000	50,000 to 100,000	100,000 to 250,000	250,000 to 500,000	500,000 to 2,500,000	2,500,000 and over
Number of Enterprises **1**	64	5	10	0	10	0	0	7	0	5	8	11	8
Revenues ($ in Thousands)													
Net Sales **2**	90131313	91	120	0	21442	0	0	78808	0	202904	671733	2557096	86599120
Interest **3**	18489495	14	20	0	1268	0	0	14973	0	37017	138318	662568	17635317
Rents **4**	968543	0	0	0	0	0	0	0	0	2193	4449	6225	955676
Royalties **5**	2793	0	0	0	0	0	0	0	0	366	0	1	2427
Other Portfolio Income **6**	2581667	0	1	0	334	0	0	1152	0	7135	16044	53481	2503519
Other Receipts **7**	68088815	77	99	0	19840	0	0	62683	0	156193	512922	1834821	65502181
Total Receipts **8**	90131313	91	120	0	21442	0	0	78808	0	202904	671733	2557096	86599120
Average Total Receipts **9**	1408302	18	12	•	2144	•	•	11258	•	40581	83967	232463	10824890
Operating Costs/Operating Income (%)													
Cost of Operations **10**	43.0	86.8	107.5	•	64.6	•	•	57.9	•	52.0	45.3	44.2	43.0
Salaries and Wages **11**	1.0	•	•	•	•	•	•	•	•	•	0.0	•	1.0
Taxes Paid **12**	0.9	1.1	2.5	•	0.8	•	•	2.2	•	2.7	2.1	1.7	0.9
Interest Paid **13**	0.7	•	•	•	0.1	•	•	•	•	0.2	0.1	0.6	0.7
Depreciation **14**	0.4	•	•	•	0.5	•	•	1.3	•	0.5	0.3	0.5	0.4
Amortization and Depletion **15**	1.4	•	•	•	1.5	•	•	2.7	•	2.2	3.9	2.7	1.4
Pensions and Other Deferred Comp. **16**	0.5	•	•	•	0.0	•	•	1.2	•	1.7	0.6	1.0	0.5
Employee Benefits **17**	0.1	•	•	•	0.3	•	•	1.0	•	0.1	0.2	0.2	0.1
Advertising **18**	0.2	•	•	•	•	•	•	0.1	•	0.4	0.2	0.3	0.2
Other Expenses **19**	47.8	23.1	74.2	•	35.9	•	•	30.7	•	39.3	45.1	44.1	48.0
Officers' Compensation **20**	0.1	•	•	•	•	•	•	•	•	•	0.5	•	0.1
Operating Margin **21**	3.8	•	•	•	•	•	•	2.8	•	0.8	1.8	4.8	3.8
Operating Margin Before Officers' Comp. **22**	3.9	•	•	•	•	•	•	2.8	•	0.8	2.3	4.8	3.9

Selected Average Balance Sheet ($ in Thousands)

Net Receivables 23	62502	0	9	14	191	2072	1195	496154
Inventories 24	•	•	•	•	•	•	•	•
Net Property, Plant and Equipment 25	17979	0	182	156	1643	1186	4662	134842
Total Assets 26	7465999	413	2781	43060	163993	377992	1133565	57647182
Notes and Loans Payable 27	51156	0	0	0	0	0	14	409227
All Other Liabilities 28	6683464	192	1634	34012	155767	343094	999862	51620414
Net Worth 29	731379	222	1147	9048	8226	34898	133689	5617541

Selected Financial Ratios (Times to 1)

Current Ratio 30	0.6	58.1	2.6	1.3	2.1	0.8	2.0	0.6
Quick Ratio 31	0.5	55.3	1.6	1.0	1.6	0.7	1.6	0.5
Net Sales to Working Capital 32	•	0.1	2.4	3.8	1.3	•	1.5	•
Coverage Ratio 33	6.5	•	•	•	5.1	16.4	8.5	6.4
Total Asset Turnover 34	0.2	0.0	0.8	0.3	0.2	0.2	0.2	0.2
Inventory Turnover 35	•	•	•	•	•	•	•	•
Receivables Turnover 36	•	•	•	•	•	•	•	•
Total Liabilities to Net Worth 37	9.2	0.9	1.4	3.8	18.9	9.8	7.5	9.3
Current Assets to Working Capital 38	•	1.0	1.6	4.2	1.9	2.0	•	•
Current Liabilities to Working Capital 39	•	0.0	0.6	3.2	0.9	•	1.0	•
Working Capital to Net Sales 40	•	16.2	0.4	0.3	0.7	•	0.7	•
Inventory to Working Capital 41	•	•	•	•	•	•	0.0	•
Total Receipts to Cash Flow 42	2.0	8.3	3.2	3.1	2.8	2.2	2.1	2.0
Cost of Goods to Cash Flow 43	0.9	7.2	2.1	1.8	1.5	1.0	0.9	0.9
Cash Flow to Total Debt 44	0.1	•	0.4	0.1	0.1	0.1	0.1	0.1

Selected Financial Factors (in Percentages)

Debt Ratio 45	90.2	46.3	58.8	79.0	95.0	90.8	88.2	90.3
Return on Total Assets 46	0.8	•	•	0.7	0.2	0.4	1.1	0.8
Return on Equity Before Income Taxes 47	7.2	•	•	3.3	3.6	4.2	8.3	7.2
Return on Equity After Income Taxes 48	4.8	•	•	2.4	2.5	2.9	5.3	4.9
Profit Margin (Before Income Tax) 49	3.8	•	•	2.7	0.7	1.7	4.8	3.7
Profit Margin (After Income Tax) 50	2.5	•	•	1.9	0.5	1.2	3.0	2.5

Table II
Corporations with Net Income

LIFE INSURANCE, MUTUAL COMPANIES (FORM 1120L)

MONEY AMOUNTS AND SIZE OF ASSETS IN THOUSANDS OF DOLLARS

Item Description for Accounting Period 7/04 Through 6/05	Total	Zero Assets	Under 500	500 to 1,000	1,000 to 5,000	5,000 to 10,000	10,000 to 25,000	25,000 to 50,000	50,000 to 100,000	100,000 to 250,000	250,000 to 500,000	500,000 to 2,500,000	2,500,000 and over
Number of Enterprises **1**	41	0	7	0	0	0	0	0	0	0	0	0	0
Revenues ($ in Thousands)													
Net Sales **2**	87987680	0	5874	0	0	0	0	0	0	0	0	0	0
Interest **3**	18052879	0	270	0	0	0	0	0	0	0	0	0	0
Rents **4**	939986	0	0	0	0	0	0	0	0	0	0	0	0
Royalties **5**	2428	0	0	0	0	0	0	0	0	0	0	0	0
Other Portfolio Income **6**	2564834	0	80	0	0	0	0	0	0	0	0	0	0
Other Receipts **7**	66427553	0	5524	0	0	0	0	0	0	0	0	0	0
Total Receipts **8**	87987680	0	5874	0	0	0	0	0	0	0	0	0	0
Average Total Receipts **9**	2146041	·	839	·	·	·	·	·	·	·	·	·	·
Operating Costs/Operating Income (%)													
Cost of Operations **10**	42.4	·	9.2	·	·	·	·	·	·	·	·	·	·
Salaries and Wages **11**	1.0	·	·	·	·	·	·	·	·	·	·	·	·
Taxes Paid **12**	0.9	·	1.8	·	·	·	·	·	·	·	·	·	·
Interest Paid **13**	0.7	·	·	·	·	·	·	·	·	·	·	·	·
Depreciation **14**	0.4	·	1.9	·	·	·	·	·	·	·	·	·	·
Amortization and Depletion **15**	1.4	·	1.3	·	·	·	·	·	·	·	·	·	·
Pensions and Other Deferred Comp. **16**	0.5	·	·	·	·	·	·	·	·	·	·	·	·
Employee Benefits **17**	0.1	·	1.1	·	·	·	·	·	·	·	·	·	·
Advertising **18**	0.2	·	·	·	·	·	·	·	·	·	·	·	·
Other Expenses **19**	48.3	·	71.3	·	·	·	·	·	·	·	·	·	·
Officers' Compensation **20**	0.1	·	·	·	·	·	·	·	·	·	·	·	·
Operating Margin **21**	4.0	·	13.3	·	·	·	·	·	·	·	·	·	·
Operating Margin Before Officers' Comp. **22**	4.1	·	13.3	·	·	·	·	·	·	·	·	·	·

Selected Average Balance Sheet ($ in Thousands)

Net Receivables **23**	97039
Inventories **24**	
Net Property, Plant and Equipment **25**	20256
Total Assets **26**	11294838
Notes and Loans Payable **27**	79853
All Other Liabilities **28**	10099824
Net Worth **29**	1115161

Selected Financial Ratios (Times to 1)

Current Ratio **30**	12.6
Quick Ratio **31**	11.3
Net Sales to Working Capital **32**	0.7
Coverage Ratio **33**	6.6
Total Asset Turnover **34**	0.5
Inventory Turnover **35**	
Receivables Turnover **36**	
Total Liabilities to Net Worth **37**	9.1
Current Assets to Working Capital **38**	1.1
Current Liabilities to Working Capital **39**	0.1
Working Capital to Net Sales **40**	1.4
Inventory to Working Capital **41**	
Total Receipts to Cash Flow **42**	2.0
Cost of Goods to Cash Flow **43**	0.9
Cash Flow to Total Debt **44**	0.1

Selected Financial Factors (in Percentages)

Debt Ratio **45**	90.1
Return on Total Assets **46**	0.9
Return on Equity Before Income Taxes **47**	7.5
Return on Equity After Income Taxes **48**	5.1
Profit Margin (Before Income Tax) **49**	3.9
Profit Margin (After Income Tax) **50**	2.7

304

Table I

Corporations with and without Net Income

MUTUAL PROPERTY AND CASUALTY COMPANIES (FORM 1120-PC)

MONEY AMOUNTS AND SIZE OF ASSETS IN THOUSANDS OF DOLLARS

Item Description for Accounting Period 7/04 Through 6/05	Total	Zero Assets	Under 500	500 to 1,000	1,000 to 5,000	5,000 to 10,000	10,000 to 25,000	25,000 to 50,000	50,000 to 100,000	100,000 to 250,000	250,000 to 500,000	500,000 to 2,500,000	2,500,000 and over
Number of Enterprises **1**	1576	10	102	86	590	162	239	99	76	81	44	63	25
Revenues ($ in Thousands)													
Net Sales **2**	219512054	0	10236	37849	608837	571922	2124827	1695047	1884144	8014737	8377881	40565343	155621231
Interest **3**	12553985	0	282	1756	33902	22111	86064	82034	135657	328843	345694	1548277	9969365
Rents **4**	499320	0	0	49	1367	825	2985	2559	2228	19756	17963	66175	385413
Royalties **5**	395	0	0	0	0	0	0	28	0	0	0	350	17
Other Portfolio Income **6**	6252562	0	187	62	13969	9905	29333	28537	54366	154961	161584	849316	4950341
Other Receipts **7**	200205792	0	9767	35982	559599	539081	2006445	1581889	1691893	7511177	7852640	38101225	140316095
Total Receipts **8**	219512054	0	10236	37849	608837	571922	2124827	1695047	1884144	8014737	8377881	40565343	155621231
Average Total Receipts **9**	139284	0	100	440	1032	3530	8890	17122	24791	98947	190406	643894	6224849
Operating Costs/Operating Income (%)													
Cost of Operations **10**	59.0	•	150.8	45.1	52.8	56.6	57.1	48.8	51.7	57.2	57.9	62.9	58.4
Salaries and Wages **11**	11.8	•	3.8	17.3	13.7	8.1	10.5	16.0	15.6	15.7	15.8	14.0	10.8
Taxes Paid **12**	2.4	•	0.0	2.5	6.7	4.5	2.5	4.3	2.5	2.8	2.2	2.3	2.3
Interest Paid **13**	0.6	•	•	0.4	0.3	0.0	0.1	0.1	0.2	0.2	0.2	0.2	0.8
Depreciation **14**	1.1	•	•	0.6	0.4	0.2	0.5	0.8	1.0	1.3	0.9	1.1	1.1
Amortization and Depletion **15**	0.2	•	•	•	0.1	0.0	0.1	1.0	0.0	0.1	0.2	0.1	0.3
Pensions and Other Deferred Comp. **16**	0.5	•	•	•	0.1	0.1	0.1	0.6	0.3	0.3	0.7	0.6	0.5
Employee Benefits **17**	1.5	•	•	0.1	1.0	0.5	0.5	2.8	1.2	1.6	1.7	1.9	1.3
Advertising **18**	0.3	•	•	0.4	0.3	0.1	0.2	0.3	0.3	0.2	0.2	0.2	0.3
Other Expenses **19**	13.3	•	8.7	33.4	19.0	26.5	22.0	19.7	17.8	12.4	10.2	8.1	14.5
Officers' Compensation **20**	0.2	•	•	3.5	1.7	1.1	0.6	1.0	0.8	0.5	0.5	0.4	0.2
Operating Margin **21**	9.1	•	•	•	4.0	2.2	5.8	4.5	8.4	7.6	9.4	8.3	9.5
Operating Margin Before Officers' Comp. **22**	9.3	•	•	0.2	5.7	3.3	6.4	5.5	9.3	8.2	10.0	8.6	9.7

Selected Average Balance Sheet ($ in Thousands)

Net Receivables 23	27044	0	1	52	78	514	1286	2651	5021	17921	32721	113702	1259241
Inventories 24	•	•	•	•	•	•	•	•	•	•	•	•	•
Net Property, Plant and Equipment 25	4987	•	0	13	55	58	164	330	656	3860	5937	19286	236203
Total Assets 26	330789	115	804	2540	7396	16124	35509	66719	165380	333731	1113279	•	16315580
Notes and Loans Payable 27	9485	0	24	55	5	322	83	384	798	1585	5907	•	572518
All Other Liabilities 28	199392	189	360	1168	7007	11322	24501	38249	105756	213778	698940	•	9692932
Net Worth 29	121912	-74	421	1367	335	4480	10925	28085	58826	118367	408432	•	6050129

Selected Financial Ratios (Times to 1)

Current Ratio 30	0.9	•	0.4	1.7	1.6	0.8	1.0	0.9	0.9	0.9	0.9	0.9	0.9
Quick Ratio 31	0.8	•	0.3	1.7	1.4	0.7	0.9	0.8	0.7	0.8	0.8	0.8	0.8
Net Sales to Working Capital 32	•	•	•	1.6	1.6	•	•	•	•	•	•	•	•
Coverage Ratio 33	13.8	•	•	•	14.4	30.0	57.5	31.7	33.4	42.3	50.7	39.6	11.3
Total Asset Turnover 34	0.4	0.9	0.5	0.5	0.4	0.6	0.5	0.4	0.6	0.6	0.6	0.6	0.4
Inventory Turnover 35	•	•	•	•	•	•	•	•	•	•	•	•	•
Receivables Turnover 36	•	•	•	•	•	•	•	•	•	•	•	•	•
Total Liabilities to Net Worth 37	1.7	•	•	21.1	0.9	2.6	2.3	1.4	1.8	1.8	1.8	1.7	1.7
Current Assets to Working Capital 38	•	•	•	2.3	2.6	•	•	•	•	•	•	•	•
Current Liabilities to Working Capital 39	•	•	•	1.3	1.6	•	•	•	•	•	•	•	•
Working Capital to Net Sales 40	•	•	•	0.6	0.6	•	•	•	•	•	•	•	•
Inventory to Working Capital 41	•	•	•	•	•	•	•	•	•	•	•	•	•
Total Receipts to Cash Flow 42	4.9	•	3.4	4.7	3.6	4.4	3.7	4.4	4.1	5.4	5.4	6.9	4.5
Cost of Goods to Cash Flow 43	2.9	•	1.5	2.5	2.0	2.1	2.2	2.2	2.1	3.1	3.2	4.3	2.6
Cash Flow to Total Debt 44	0.1	•	0.3	0.2	0.1	0.2	0.2	0.2	0.2	0.2	0.2	0.1	0.1

Selected Financial Factors (in Percentages)

Debt Ratio 45	63.1	•	164.6	47.7	46.2	95.5	72.2	69.2	57.9	64.4	64.5	63.3	62.9
Return on Total Assets 46	3.7	•	•	1.5	0.7	3.0	1.9	3.0	4.3	5.0	4.5	•	3.5
Return on Equity Before Income Taxes 47	9.3	•	85.6	2.6	14.1	10.6	7.0	6.1	7.0	11.9	13.7	12.0	8.6
Return on Equity After Income Taxes 48	5.9	•	85.7	•	0.9	6.8	4.6	7.7	4.6	7.7	9.2	8.0	5.5
Profit Margin (Before Income Tax) 49	8.1	•	•	3.4	1.3	5.3	3.9	7.9	7.1	8.5	7.6	•	8.4
Profit Margin (After Income Tax) 50	5.2	•	•	1.2	•	3.4	1.7	5.3	4.6	5.7	5.1	•	5.3

Table II

Corporations with Net Income

MUTUAL PROPERTY AND CASUALTY COMPANIES (FORM 1120-PC)

MONEY AMOUNTS AND SIZE OF ASSETS IN THOUSANDS OF DOLLARS

Item Description for Accounting Period 7/04 Through 6/05		Total	Zero Assets	Under 500	500 to 1,000	1,000 to 5,000	5,000 to 10,000	10,000 to 25,000	25,000 to 50,000	50,000 to 100,000	100,000 to 250,000	250,000 to 500,000	500,000 to 2,500,000	2,500,000 and over
Number of Enterprises	1	1072	0	41	55	392	95	176	68	56	68	0	56	0
Revenues ($ in Thousands)														
Net Sales	2	210483579	0	1911	30314	371782	286219	1580838	1323855	1483006	7283546	0	36096688	0
Interest	3	12006164	0	136	1483	22213	11496	65733	57690	97758	272396	0	1434084	0
Rents	4	493065	0	0	49	610	480	2302	2300	2096	18415	0	64239	0
Royalties	5	379	0	0	0	0	0	0	28	0	0	0	350	0
Other Portfolio Income	6	5863636	0	185	62	7808	9747	21990	22762	45409	135739	0	722992	0
Other Receipts	7	192120335	0	1590	28720	341151	264496	1490813	1241075	1337743	6856996	0	33875023	0
Total Receipts	8	210483579	0	1911	30314	371782	286219	1580838	1323855	1483006	7283546	0	3096688	0
Average Total Receipts	9	196347	•	47	551	948	3013	8982	19468	26482	107111	•	644584	•
Operating Costs/Operating Income (%)														
Cost of Operations	10	58.1	•	•	33.9	40.2	47.2	51.5	44.4	49.4	56.0	•	60.4	•
Salaries and Wages	11	12.0	•	•	21.6	12.9	10.5	11.3	18.0	17.4	16.2	•	15.0	•
Taxes Paid	12	2.4	•	•	1.8	7.8	1.8	2.2	3.8	2.6	2.6	•	2.5	•
Interest Paid	13	0.7	•	•	0.5	0.3	0.1	0.1	0.1	0.1	0.1	•	0.2	•
Depreciation	14	1.1	•	•	0.7	0.4	0.2	0.4	0.8	1.1	1.2	•	1.1	•
Amortization and Depletion	15	0.2	•	•	•	0.0	0.0	0.1	0.1	0.0	0.1	•	0.1	•
Pensions and Other Deferred Comp.	16	0.5	•	•	•	0.0	0.1	0.2	0.8	0.4	0.3	•	0.5	•
Employee Benefits	17	1.4	•	•	0.2	1.2	0.4	0.6	3.2	1.2	1.6	•	1.7	•
Advertising	18	0.3	•	•	0.4	0.2	0.2	0.2	0.4	0.2	0.2	•	0.2	•
Other Expenses	19	13.2	•	17.5	8.2	17.4	25.9	22.0	16.5	13.8	12.1	•	8.2	•
Officers' Compensation	20	0.2	•	•	4.3	1.3	1.0	0.7	1.3	1.0	0.6	•	0.4	•
Operating Margin	21	9.9	•	82.5	28.3	18.2	12.7	10.6	10.6	12.7	8.9	•	9.6	•
Operating Margin Before Officers' Comp.	22	10.1	•	82.5	32.6	19.5	13.7	11.4	11.9	13.7	9.5	•	10.0	•

Selected Average Balance Sheet ($ in Thousands)

Net Receivables 23	37968	•	0	43	64	389	1176	2814	4689	18062	•	112644
Inventories 24	•	•	•	•	•	•	•	•	•	•	•	•
Net Property, Plant and Equipment 25	7179	•	0	20	52	75	150	426	731	4417	•	19976
Total Assets 26	463843	•	137	799	2504	7279	16123	36507	66346	164981	•	1133880
Notes and Loans Payable 27	13875	•	0	37	1	93	421	14	521	936	•	5582
All Other Liabilities 28	275509	•	99	355	952	7679	10258	23419	34974	104323	•	707365
Net Worth 29	174458	•	38	407	1551	-493	5444	13074	30852	59722	•	420933

Selected Financial Ratios (Times to 1)

Current Ratio 30	0.9	•	0.6	1.5	2.0	0.8	1.1	1.0	0.9	0.9	•	0.9
Quick Ratio 31	0.8	•	0.6	1.5	1.8	0.6	1.0	0.9	0.7	0.9	•	0.8
Net Sales to Working Capital 32	•	•	•	3.3	1.1	•	13.2	•	•	•	•	•
Coverage Ratio 33	14.6	•	•	53.6	60.8	131.4	106.7	92.2	92.0	67.7	•	41.8
Total Asset Turnover 34	0.4	•	0.3	0.7	0.4	0.4	0.6	0.5	0.4	0.6	•	0.6
Inventory Turnover 35	•	•	•	•	•	•	•	•	•	•	•	•
Receivables Turnover 36	•	•	•	•	•	•	•	•	•	•	•	•
Total Liabilities to Net Worth 37	1.7	•	2.6	1.0	0.6	•	2.0	1.8	1.2	1.8	•	1.7
Current Assets to Working Capital 38	•	•	•	3.1	2.0	14.5	•	•	•	•	•	•
Current Liabilities to Working Capital 39	•	•	•	2.1	1.0	13.5	•	•	•	•	•	•
Working Capital to Net Sales 40	•	•	•	0.3	1.0	0.1	•	•	•	•	•	•
Inventory to Working Capital 41	•	•	•	•	•	•	•	•	•	•	•	•
Total Receipts to Cash Flow 42	4.7	•	1.0	2.8	2.9	2.7	3.2	3.9	4.1	5.1	•	6.2
Cost of Goods to Cash Flow 43	2.7	•	•	0.9	1.2	1.3	1.6	1.7	2.0	2.9	•	3.8
Cash Flow to Total Debt 44	0.1	•	0.5	0.5	0.3	0.1	0.3	0.2	0.2	0.2	•	0.1

Selected Financial Factors (in Percentages)

Debt Ratio 45	62.4	•	72.1	49.1	38.1	106.8	66.2	64.2	53.5	63.8	•	62.9
Return on Total Assets 46	4.0	•	28.1	19.9	6.7	4.6	5.7	5.3	4.9	5.5	•	5.2
Return on Equity Before Income Taxes 47	10.0	•	100.7	38.3	10.7	•	16.7	14.7	10.4	14.9	•	13.6
Return on Equity After Income Taxes 48	6.6	•	100.4	30.7	8.5	•	12.5	10.5	7.6	10.0	•	9.3
Profit Margin (Before Income Tax) 49	8.9	•	82.5	28.3	17.5	11.0	10.1	9.9	12.1	8.3	•	8.9
Profit Margin (After Income Tax) 50	5.8	•	82.3	22.7	13.9	7.8	7.5	7.0	8.8	5.6	•	6.1

Table I

Corporations with and without Net Income

STOCK PROPERTY AND CASUALTY COMPANIES (FORM 1120-PC)

MONEY AMOUNTS AND SIZE OF ASSETS IN THOUSANDS OF DOLLARS

Item Description for Accounting Period 7/04 Through 6/05	Total	Zero Assets	Under 500	500 to 1,000	1,000 to 5,000	5,000 to 10,000	10,000 to 25,000	25,000 to 50,000	50,000 to 100,000	100,000 to 250,000	250,000 to 500,000	500,000 to 2,500,000	2,500,000 and over
Number of Enterprises **1**	4077	119	1376	520	847	323	272	160	114	132	53	90	71
Revenues ($ in Thousands)													
Net Sales **2**	550628861	715611	57993	28286	868692	1371221	3427329	4988714	7822075	16472559	8299566	78919555	427657259
Interest **3**	25631613	33585	3415	6428	33720	48207	85623	104904	176072	383652	408438	2231730	22115839
Rents **4**	844183	116	0	0	1252	294	992	2608	4273	11677	10849	51454	760669
Royalties **5**	518827	0	0	0	55	0	0	350	1283	2117	0	3934	511089
Other Portfolio Income **6**	7673555	2179	6328	1134	7787	11010	34539	49384	136317	140501	155312	752856	6376206
Other Receipts **7**	51596063	679731	48250	20724	825878	1311710	3306175	4831468	7504130	15934612	7724967	75879581	397893456
Total Receipts **8**	550628861	715611	57993	28286	868692	1371221	3427329	4988714	7822075	16472559	8299566	78919555	427657259
Average Total Receipts **9**	135057	6014	42	54	1026	4245	12600	31179	68615	124792	156596	876884	6023342
Operating Costs/Operating Income (%)													
Cost of Operations **10**	54.4	39.4	48.2	57.5	68.6	44.5	57.4	74.5	66.7	65.0	51.5	67.3	51.2
Salaries and Wages **11**	13.5	15.7	15.1	10.0	14.7	29.3	13.7	10.5	14.0	11.7	14.5	11.1	14.0
Taxes Paid **12**	2.1	1.6	1.2	0.5	1.8	3.4	2.1	2.1	1.8	2.3	2.6	1.9	2.2
Interest Paid **13**	1.2	0.2	0.4	•	0.2	0.6	0.3	0.2	0.3	0.2	0.4	0.6	1.3
Depreciation **14**	0.8	0.5	0.1	•	1.3	0.4	0.3	0.4	0.4	0.6	0.8	0.9	0.8
Amortization and Depletion **15**	0.3	0.3	0.3	0.0	0.1	0.4	0.1	0.1	0.0	0.1	0.3	0.2	0.3
Pensions and Other Deferred Comp. **16**	0.5	0.1	0.0	•	0.0	0.0	0.1	0.1	0.1	0.2	0.2	0.2	0.6
Employee Benefits **17**	3.5	0.7	•	0.4	0.2	7.3	0.5	0.4	0.5	1.1	1.1	1.2	4.2
Advertising **18**	0.4	0.6	0.0	•	0.3	0.4	0.2	0.3	0.3	0.2	0.7	0.4	0.4
Other Expenses **19**	17.5	28.5	25.0	10.5	13.0	12.0	21.1	9.8	10.7	14.6	18.3	12.4	18.8
Officers' Compensation **20**	0.4	0.2	1.0	•	0.8	1.0	0.8	0.7	0.6	0.5	0.5	0.4	0.4
Operating Margin **21**	5.5	12.1	8.7	21.1	0.7	0.7	3.4	0.9	4.5	3.5	9.1	3.3	6.0
Operating Margin Before Officers' Comp. **22**	5.9	12.3	9.7	21.1	1.7	1.7	4.2	1.6	5.1	4.0	9.6	3.8	6.3

Selected Average Balance Sheet ($ in Thousands)

Net Receivables 23	20860	0	1	6	106	409	1511	3303	7941	13498	26732	111801	981895
Inventories 24	•	•	•	•	•	•	•	•	•	•	•	•	•
Net Property, Plant and Equipment 25	3594	0	0	0	13	51	116	362	982	2496	4742	21376	167881
Total Assets 26	355561	0	208	755	2535	7133	16333	36228	71366	156290	342619	1180919	18042892
Notes and Loans Payable 27	25628	0	1	10	44	54	425	580	2742	7451	14359	70342	1349724
All Other Liabilities 28	189803	0	206	756	2040	5428	10959	30339	53017	99803	208329	725146	9384645
Net Worth 29	140130	0	1	-11	451	1651	4949	5310	15607	49036	119931	385431	7308524

Selected Financial Ratios (Times to 1)

Current Ratio 30	0.9	•	0.8	0.6	0.9	0.8	1.0	0.9	0.9	1.0	0.9	0.8	0.9
Quick Ratio 31	0.7	•	0.6	0.4	0.7	0.6	0.8	0.7	0.7	0.8	0.8	0.7	0.7
Net Sales to Working Capital 32	•	•	•	•	•	•	1133.1	•	•	•	•	•	•
Coverage Ratio 33	5.7	51.7	18.5	•	2.0	12.9	3.8	16.8	15.2	23.0	6.1	•	5.4
Total Asset Turnover 34	0.4	•	0.2	0.1	0.6	0.8	0.9	1.0	0.8	0.5	0.7	•	0.3
Inventory Turnover 35	•	•	•	•	•	•	•	•	•	•	•	•	•
Receivables Turnover 36	•	•	•	•	•	•	•	•	•	•	•	•	•
Total Liabilities to Net Worth 37	1.5	•	155.2	•	4.6	3.3	2.3	5.8	3.6	2.2	1.9	2.1	1.5
Current Assets to Working Capital 38	•	•	•	•	•	•	780.0	•	•	•	•	•	•
Current Liabilities to Working Capital 39	•	•	•	•	•	•	779.0	•	•	•	•	•	•
Working Capital to Net Sales 40	•	•	•	•	•	•	0.0	•	•	•	•	•	•
Inventory to Working Capital 41	•	•	•	•	•	•	1.7	•	•	•	•	•	•
Total Receipts to Cash Flow 42	4.7	2.5	3.6	3.3	9.4	4.3	9.7	10.4	7.7	6.0	4.0	7.0	4.4
Cost of Goods to Cash Flow 43	2.6	1.0	1.8	1.9	6.5	2.5	4.3	7.8	5.2	3.9	2.1	4.7	2.2
Cash Flow to Total Debt 44	0.1	•	0.1	0.0	0.1	0.3	0.1	0.1	0.2	0.2	0.2	0.2	0.1

Selected Financial Factors (in Percentages)

Debt Ratio 45	60.6	•	99.4	101.4	82.2	76.9	69.7	85.3	78.1	68.6	65.0	67.4	59.5
Return on Total Assets 46	2.5	•	1.4	•	0.7	2.6	0.8	4.4	2.9	4.2	2.9	•	2.4
Return on Equity Before Income Taxes 47	5.2	•	210.4	•	1.4	8.1	4.1	18.9	8.6	11.6	7.3	•	4.9
Return on Equity After Income Taxes 48	3.3	•	117.9	•	•	3.7	•	11.4	4.8	7.2	3.5	•	3.2
Profit Margin (Before Income Tax) 49	5.4	12.0	6.7	20.9	0.6	3.2	0.7	4.3	3.4	8.8	3.2	•	6.0
Profit Margin (After Income Tax) 50	3.4	8.2	3.7	17.9	1.5	2.6	•	1.9	5.5	3.2	1.5	•	3.9

Table II
Corporations with Net Income

STOCK PROPERTY AND CASUALTY COMPANIES (FORM 1120-PC)

MONEY AMOUNTS AND SIZE OF ASSETS IN THOUSANDS OF DOLLARS

Item Description for Accounting Period 7/04 Through 6/05	Total	Zero Assets	Under 500	500 to 1,000	1,000 to 5,000	5,000 to 10,000	10,000 to 25,000	25,000 to 50,000	50,000 to 100,000	100,000 to 250,000	250,000 to 500,000	500,000 to 2,500,000	2,500,000 and over
Number of Enterprises **1**	3170	56	1050	489	704	196	203	111	85	100	44	70	62
Revenues ($ in Thousands)													
Net Sales **2**	51436138	689671	30511	24273	367831	1045583	2619447	3822674	5818545	13212211	6729317	71178747	408821328
Interest **3**	22675087	33157	3157	6291	29519	32187	68147	65403	130996	278026	344917	1643021	20040266
Rents **4**	794084	116	0	0	1252	294	874	2378	3312	7722	10849	40204	727085
Royalties **5**	513307	0	0	0	55	0	0	350	0	1784	0	29	511089
Other Portfolio Income **6**	7155538	2119	6138	1048	7581	8282	29527	46032	123666	109341	146268	641382	6034155
Other Receipts **7**	483222122	654279	21216	16934	329424	1004820	2520899	3708511	5560571	12815338	6227283	68854111	381508733
Total Receipts **8**	514360138	689671	30511	24273	367831	1045583	2619447	3822674	5818545	13212211	6729317	71178747	408821328
Average Total Receipts **9**	162259	12316	29	50	522	5335	12904	34439	68453	132122	152939	1016839	6593892
Operating Costs/Operating Income (%)													
Cost of Operations **10**	53.0	37.8	19.5	38.1	44.9	32.4	51.2	65.9	61.7	60.8	43.2	66.8	50.4
Salaries and Wages **11**	13.5	16.1	6.3	10.6	10.9	30.5	14.4	10.1	14.8	11.7	16.3	10.8	14.0
Taxes Paid **12**	2.1	1.5	0.7	0.5	1.3	3.9	2.3	1.9	2.1	2.4	2.7	1.9	2.1
Interest Paid **13**	1.0	0.2	.	.	0.1	0.2	0.3	0.2	0.3	0.3	0.4	0.5	1.2
Depreciation **14**	0.8	0.5	0.1	.	0.2	0.2	0.3	0.5	0.5	0.7	0.9	0.8	0.8
Amortization and Depletion **15**	0.3	0.3	0.0	0.0	0.1	0.5	0.1	0.1	0.0	0.1	0.3	0.1	0.3
Pensions and Other Deferred Comp. **16**	0.5	0.1	.	0.0	.	0.1	0.1	0.1	0.1	0.2	0.3	0.2	0.6
Employee Benefits **17**	3.6	0.7	.	.	0.2	9.3	0.5	0.4	0.7	1.2	1.2	1.1	4.3
Advertising **18**	0.4	0.7	0.0	.	0.1	0.3	0.2	0.3	0.3	0.3	0.8	0.5	0.4
Other Expenses **19**	17.4	27.4	27.2	11.1	15.3	8.8	21.1	10.7	10.1	15.7	19.3	11.6	18.6
Officers' Compensation **20**	0.4	0.1	0.9	.	0.3	1.1	0.9	0.9	0.7	0.5	0.6	0.4	0.4
Operating Margin **21**	7.0	14.6	45.3	39.6	26.5	12.6	8.7	9.0	8.7	6.4	13.9	5.3	7.0
Operating Margin Before Officers' Comp. **22**	7.3	14.7	46.2	39.6	26.9	13.7	9.6	9.8	9.4	6.9	14.5	5.7	7.4

Selected Average Balance Sheet ($ in Thousands)

Net Receivables **23**	22698	•	0	1	6	72	386	1629	3857	9086	14523	29371	117408	956872
Inventories **24**	•	•	•	•	•	•	•	•	•	•	•	•	•	•
Net Property, Plant and Equipment **25**	4306	•	0	0	0	83	99	402	1036	2764	5682	21395	•	184679
Total Assets **26**	399949		233	751	2474	7248	16732	35452	72256	156387	345294	1206845		18310964
Notes and Loans Payable **27**	26605	0	0	3	7	72	411	525	2787	6889	12701	61244		1264585
All Other Liabilities **28**	205342	0	207	562	1533	4239	10071	22910	44516	96438	195930	688293		9253477
Net Worth **29**	168002	0	26	187	934	2937	6250	12017	24953	53060	136663	457308		7792902

Selected Financial Ratios (Times to 1)

Current Ratio **30**	0.9	•	0.8	1.1	1.1	1.1	1.1	1.2	1.0	0.8	1.0	0.9	1.0	0.9
Quick Ratio **31**	0.8	0.7	•	•	0.9	0.9	1.0	1.0	0.8	0.7	0.9	0.7
Net Sales to Working Capital **32**	•	•	•	2.9	19.9	19.6	13.8	9.4	•	•	102.9	0.7
Coverage Ratio **33**	7.9	67.5	•	65.5	317.0	45.2	34.1	29.7	25.7	33.9	12.4	7.0
Total Asset Turnover **34**	0.4	0.1	0.1	0.2	0.7	1.0	0.8	0.9	0.8	0.4	0.8	0.4
Inventory Turnover **35**	•	•	•	•	•	•	•	•	•	•	•	•
Receivables Turnover **36**	•	•	•	•	•	•	•	•	•	•	•	•
Total Liabilities to Net Worth **37**	1.4	8.0	3.0	1.5	1.7	2.0	1.9	1.9	1.5	1.6	1.3
Current Assets to Working Capital **38**	•	•	8.7	16.8	14.9	9.4	6.7	64.2
Current Liabilities to Working Capital **39**	•	•	7.7	15.8	13.9	8.4	5.7	63.2
Working Capital to Net Sales **40**	•	•	0.3	0.1	0.1	0.1	0.1	0.0
Inventory to Working Capital **41**	•	•	•	0.0	0.0	0.0	0.0
Total Receipts to Cash Flow **42**	4.4	2.5	1.6	2.0	2.5	5.3	3.5	5.4	6.2	4.9	6.2	3.3	6.4	4.2
Cost of Goods to Cash Flow **43**	2.3	0.9	0.3	0.8	1.1	1.7	1.8	3.6	3.8	3.0	1.4	2.1
Cash Flow to Total Debt **44**	0.2	0.1	0.0	0.0	0.1	0.2	0.4	0.3	0.2	0.2	0.2	0.1

Selected Financial Factors (in Percentages)

Debt Ratio **45**	58.0	•	88.8	75.2	62.3	59.5	62.6	66.1	65.5	66.1	60.4	62.1	57.4
Return on Total Assets **46**	3.2	•	5.2	2.6	5.6	9.3	6.8	8.7	8.4	5.5	6.2	4.8	3.0
Return on Equity Before Income Taxes **47**	6.7	•	46.5	10.5	14.8	22.6	17.6	25.0	23.4	15.6	15.3	11.5	6.0
Return on Equity After Income Taxes **48**	4.6	•	40.3	9.6	11.9	15.3	13.0	17.8	17.1	11.0	10.7	7.4	4.1
Profit Margin (Before Income Tax) **49**	6.9	14.6	41.5	39.3	26.4	12.4	8.5	8.7	8.5	6.3	13.7	5.2	7.0
Profit Margin (After Income Tax) **50**	4.8	10.6	35.9	35.9	21.2	8.4	6.3	6.2	4.4	6.2	9.6	3.3	4.9

Table I

Corporations with and without Net Income

INSURANCE AGENCIES AND BROKERAGES

MONEY AMOUNTS AND SIZE OF ASSETS IN THOUSANDS OF DOLLARS

Item Description for Accounting Period 7/04 Through 6/05	Total	Zero Assets	Under 500	500 to 1,000	1,000 to 5,000	5,000 to 10,000	10,000 to 25,000	25,000 to 50,000	50,000 to 100,000	100,000 to 250,000	250,000 to 500,000	500,000 to 2,500,000	2,500,000 and over
Number of Enterprises **1**	83944	11331	63455	4489	3756	494	254	89	33	21	7	8	6
Revenues ($ in Thousands)													
Net Sales **2**	83455370	1541834	22112618	5447741	15143638	3690093	4032595	2945366	2288379	2950913	852643	2677228	19772321
Interest **3**	572632	4084	13390	14739	15322	13289	13930	10876	16016	34765	5420	12056	418744
Rents **4**	73857	0	14569	4715	5408	17263	4433	1231	787	6156	196	515	18583
Royalties **5**	15766	0	10958	0	0	50	418	294	0	0	0	0	4045
Other Portfolio Income **6**	863195	62732	31911	31183	18037	19982	28877	17613	6805	25862	74	45935	574185
Other Receipts **7**	81929920	1475018	22044790	5397104	15104871	3639509	3984937	2915352	2264771	2884130	846953	2618722	18756764
Total Receipts **8**	83455370	1541834	22112618	5447741	15143638	3690093	4032595	2945366	2288379	2950913	852643	2677228	19772321
Average Total Receipts **9**	994	136	348	1214	4032	7470	15876	33094	69345	140520	121806	334654	3295387
Operating Costs/Operating Income (%)													
Cost of Operations **10**	10.2	2.9	12.6	8.6	8.5	12.9	17.6	21.1	24.3	3.5	9.4	•	6.8
Salaries and Wages **11**	28.9	27.5	23.8	25.3	29.4	27.7	30.1	29.9	29.3	35.1	34.5	27.7	34.2
Taxes Paid **12**	3.1	3.0	2.7	3.2	3.1	3.1	2.6	2.8	1.8	2.3	3.0	3.3	3.7
Interest Paid **13**	1.4	1.2	0.5	1.3	0.6	0.7	0.8	0.9	0.5	1.1	4.7	1.5	3.5
Depreciation **14**	1.4	1.4	1.0	1.0	1.8	1.6	1.5	1.9	1.3	1.3	2.0	1.5	1.4
Amortization and Depletion **15**	0.9	1.8	0.5	1.0	0.5	0.5	0.6	0.6	0.4	0.7	2.1	3.5	1.6
Pensions and Other Deferred Comp. **16**	2.0	0.8	1.5	1.6	1.3	1.2	1.4	1.2	1.0	0.4	0.5	0.7	4.1
Employee Benefits **17**	1.9	1.9	1.4	2.1	1.7	1.5	2.1	2.0	1.4	1.9	2.6	3.4	2.5
Advertising **18**	0.9	1.7	1.4	1.2	0.8	0.6	1.3	0.7	0.4	0.8	0.6	0.7	0.5
Other Expenses **19**	27.2	31.5	25.8	22.7	24.7	29.8	25.6	25.6	32.3	42.8	27.7	31.7	28.3
Officers' Compensation **20**	12.0	13.3	14.9	18.9	18.9	12.9	8.0	7.3	3.7	2.4	5.9	6.1	6.3
Operating Margin **21**	10.0	12.9	13.9	13.1	8.8	7.6	8.2	6.1	3.6	7.7	6.9	19.9	7.0
Operating Margin Before Officers' Comp. **22**	22.1	26.2	28.8	32.0	27.7	20.5	16.3	13.4	7.3	10.0	12.9	26.0	13.3

Selected Average Balance Sheet ($ in Thousands)

	1	2	3	4	5	6	7	8	9	10	11	12	13
Net Receivables 23	338	0	6	110	444	1579	4033	9361	14817	39547	118318	141199	3319160
Inventories 24	•	•	•	•	•	•	•	•	•	•	•	•	•
Net Property, Plant and Equipment 25	54	0	11	70	186	533	863	2524	3542	6947	5234	19388	281991
Total Assets 26	1393	0	80	762	2256	6914	15077	35141	65131	136596	338764	1000746	12356305
Notes and Loans Payable 27	180	0	27	259	539	1219	2636	5794	8086	26556	100827	204176	874154
All Other Liabilities 28	759	0	26	232	1192	4562	9439	22589	44761	93278	157536	308806	7147822
Net Worth 29	453	0	27	271	525	1134	3001	6758	12284	16762	80400	487764	4334328

Selected Financial Ratios (Times to 1)

	1	2	3	4	5	6	7	8	9	10	11	12	13
Current Ratio 30	1.1	•	1.3	1.3	1.2	1.1	1.1	1.1	1.0	1.0	1.1	1.0	1.0
Quick Ratio 31	0.9	•	1.2	1.2	1.1	1.0	0.9	0.9	0.9	0.8	0.9	0.7	0.9
Net Sales to Working Capital 32	30.3	•	38.3	12.3	19.3	13.9	13.4	20.2	46.3	•	11.2	32.3	412.2
Coverage Ratio 33	8.4	11.4	27.7	11.3	16.2	12.3	11.7	7.7	8.8	8.1	2.5	14.1	3.5
Total Asset Turnover 34	0.7	•	4.3	1.6	1.8	1.1	1.1	0.9	1.1	1.0	0.4	0.3	0.3
Inventory Turnover 35	•	•	•	•	•	•	•	•	•	•	•	•	•
Receivables Turnover 36	•	•	•	•	•	•	•	•	•	•	•	•	•
Total Liabilities to Net Worth 37	2.1	•	2.0	1.8	3.3	4.0	4.2	4.2	4.3	7.1	3.2	1.1	1.9
Current Assets to Working Capital 38	19.3	•	4.4	4.0	6.9	9.0	9.6	14.4	29.7	•	16.3	35.5	595.3
Current Liabilities to Working Capital 39	18.3	•	3.4	3.0	5.9	8.0	8.6	13.4	28.7	•	15.3	34.5	594.3
Working Capital to Net Sales 40	0.0	•	0.0	0.1	0.1	0.1	0.1	0.0	0.0	•	0.1	0.0	0.0
Inventory to Working Capital 41	0.0	•	•	•	•	0.0	0.0	0.0	0.1	•	•	•	0.0
Total Receipts to Cash Flow 42	3.1	3.0	2.9	3.3	3.4	3.2	3.3	3.6	3.0	2.1	3.1	2.1	3.5
Cost of Goods to Cash Flow 43	0.3	0.1	0.4	0.3	0.3	0.4	0.6	0.8	0.7	0.1	0.3	•	0.2
Cash Flow to Total Debt 44	0.3	•	2.3	0.7	0.7	0.4	0.4	0.3	0.4	0.6	0.2	0.3	0.1

Selected Financial Factors (in Percentages)

	1	2	3	4	5	6	7	8	9	10	11	12	13
Debt Ratio 45	67.5	•	66.5	64.4	76.7	83.6	80.1	80.8	81.1	87.7	76.3	51.3	64.9
Return on Total Assets 46	8.5	•	62.3	22.8	16.7	8.9	9.4	6.5	4.2	8.9	4.2	7.2	3.3
Return on Equity Before Income Taxes 47	23.0	•	179.5	58.4	67.5	49.8	43.2	29.6	20.0	63.8	10.5	13.7	6.7
Return on Equity After Income Taxes 48	19.9	•	176.2	57.1	64.5	41.8	37.8	23.4	14.9	52.4	7.4	9.2	4.3
Profit Margin (Before Income Tax) 49	10.5	12.9	13.9	13.1	8.8	7.5	8.2	6.0	3.5	7.6	6.9	20.0	8.8
Profit Margin (After Income Tax) 50	9.1	11.2	13.6	12.8	8.4	6.4	7.2	4.8	2.6	6.3	4.9	13.4	5.7

Table II
Corporations with Net Income

INSURANCE AGENCIES AND BROKERAGES

MONEY AMOUNTS AND SIZE OF ASSETS IN THOUSANDS OF DOLLARS

Item Description for Accounting Period 7/04 Through 6/05	Total	Zero Assets	Under 500	500 to 1,000	1,000 to 5,000	5,000 to 10,000	10,000 to 25,000	25,000 to 50,000	50,000 to 100,000	100,000 to 250,000	250,000 to 500,000	500,000 to 2,500,000	2,500,000 and over
Number of Enterprises 1	67763	7692	51983	4036	3316	389	211	78	25	16	0	0	0
Revenues ($ in Thousands)													
Net Sales 2	74871356	1387110	18663151	5038248	13774539	2832517	3569190	2838903	2108054	2616075	0	0	0
Interest 3	497036	3311	11637	12933	15273	9219	9856	8938	12368	31026	0	0	0
Rents 4	58426	0	6634	4189	4750	17263	3589	1031	787	6156	0	0	0
Royalties 5	15766	0	10958	0	0	50	418	294	0	0	0	0	0
Other Portfolio Income 6	796534	53624	26624	31163	15958	15312	21994	17547	5243	10753	0	0	0
Other Receipts 7	73503594	1330175	18607298	4989963	13738558	2790673	3533333	2811093	2089656	2568140	0	0	0
Total Receipts 8	74871356	1387110	18663151	5038248	13774539	2832517	3569190	2838903	2108054	2616075	0	0	0
Average Total Receipts 9	1105	180	359	1248	4154	7282	16916	36396	84322	163505	.	.	.
Operating Costs/Operating Income (%)													
Cost of Operations 10	9.9	1.0	11.8	8.9	9.0	5.3	19.3	21.5	23.4	3.8	.	.	.
Salaries and Wages 11	29.1	27.1	24.5	25.5	28.1	28.3	29.0	29.2	28.4	33.2	.	.	.
Taxes Paid 12	3.0	2.5	2.6	3.3	3.0	3.3	2.5	2.6	1.7	2.1	.	.	.
Interest Paid 13	1.4	1.3	0.5	1.2	0.5	0.5	0.5	0.7	0.3	0.9	.	.	.
Depreciation 14	1.3	1.3	0.9	0.9	1.5	1.2	1.4	1.7	1.3	1.2	.	.	.
Amortization and Depletion 15	0.9	0.0	0.5	0.9	0.4	0.3	0.4	0.6	0.3	0.5	.	.	.
Pensions and Other Deferred Comp. 16	1.9	0.9	1.3	1.7	1.2	1.5	1.2	1.2	1.0	0.3	.	.	.
Employee Benefits 17	1.9	2.0	1.3	2.1	1.6	1.8	1.9	2.0	1.2	1.6	.	.	.
Advertising 18	0.9	1.8	1.5	1.1	0.7	0.6	1.0	0.7	0.3	0.9	.	.	.
Other Expenses 19	26.1	27.8	24.0	21.0	24.0	29.6	23.5	23.4	30.6	42.6	.	.	.
Officers' Compensation 20	11.3	12.4	14.0	18.9	19.4	14.3	8.1	7.4	3.8	1.7	.	.	.
Operating Margin 21	12.3	21.9	17.1	14.4	10.6	13.4	11.1	8.9	7.7	11.1	.	.	.
Operating Margin Before Officers' Comp. 22	23.6	34.3	31.1	33.3	30.0	27.8	19.2	16.2	11.5	12.8	.	.	.

Selected Average Balance Sheet ($ in Thousands)

Net Receivables 23	333	0	6	117	396	1520	4210	10130	15143	39720
Inventories 24		0								
Net Property, Plant and Equipment 25	61	0	12	74	168	545	867	2729	4197	7659
Total Assets 26	1557	0	86	760	2178	7043	14909	35293	65867	140534
Notes and Loans Payable 27	189	0	25	248	444	716	2035	5454	6430	28991
All Other Liabilities 28	812	0	23	229	1135	4712	9651	23478	39045	83775
Net Worth 29	556	0	37	282	598	1615	3222	6361	20392	27768

Selected Financial Ratios (Times to 1)

Current Ratio 30	1.1		1.5	1.3	1.2	1.2	1.1	1.1	1.3	1.1
Quick Ratio 31	1.0		1.4	1.2	1.0	1.0	1.0	0.9	1.1	0.9
Net Sales to Working Capital 32	20.8		25.0	14.9	8.2	12.0	13.6	13.6	9.1	35.1
Coverage Ratio 33	10.1	17.7	34.4	13.1	26.7	20.2	21.6	13.3	28.1	12.8
Total Asset Turnover 34	0.7		4.2	1.6	1.9	1.0	1.1	1.0	1.3	1.2
Inventory Turnover 35										
Receivables Turnover 36										
Total Liabilities to Net Worth 37	1.8		1.3	1.7	2.6	7.7	3.6	4.5	2.2	4.1
Current Assets to Working Capital 38	12.5		3.0	4.3	5.2	6.3	7.7	9.3	5.0	18.0
Current Liabilities to Working Capital 39	11.5		2.0	3.3	4.2	5.3	6.7	8.3	4.0	17.0
Working Capital to Net Sales 40	0.0		0.0	0.1	0.1	0.1	0.1	0.1	0.1	0.0
Inventory to Working Capital 41	0.0					0.0	0.0	0.0	0.0	0.0
Total Receipts to Cash Flow 42	3.0	2.5	2.7	3.3	3.2	2.6	3.2	3.5	2.8	2.0
Cost of Goods to Cash Flow 43	0.3	0.0	0.3	0.3	0.3	0.1	0.6	0.7	0.6	0.1
Cash Flow to Total Debt 44	0.4		2.7	0.8	0.8	0.5	0.5	0.4	0.7	0.7

Selected Financial Factors (in Percentages)

Debt Ratio 45	64.3		56.7	62.8	72.5	77.1	78.4	82.0	69.0	80.2
Return on Total Assets 46	10.0		73.6	25.6	21.2	14.4	13.1	9.8	10.2	13.9
Return on Equity Before Income Taxes 47	25.4		165.2	63.5	73.2	60.6	57.8	50.5	31.6	64.7
Return on Equity After Income Taxes 48	22.3		162.2	62.1	70.2	53.5	51.8	43.1	27.6	55.7
Profit Margin (Before Income Tax) 49	12.8	21.9	17.1	14.4	10.6	13.4	11.0	8.8	7.6	11.0
Profit Margin (After Income Tax) 50	11.2	20.1	16.8	14.0	10.1	11.9	9.9	7.5	6.7	9.5

Table I

Corporations with and without Net Income

OTHER INSURANCE RELATED ACTIVITIES

MONEY AMOUNTS AND SIZE OF ASSETS IN THOUSANDS OF DOLLARS

Item Description for Accounting Period 7/04 Through 6/05	Total	Zero Assets	Under 500	500 to 1,000	1,000 to 5,000	5,000 to 10,000	10,000 to 25,000	25,000 to 50,000	50,000 to 100,000	100,000 to 250,000	250,000 to 500,000	500,000 to 2,500,000	2,500,000 and over
Number of Enterprises **1**	13239	1216	10746	284	640	129	104	46	25	21	13	11	4
Revenues ($ in Thousands)													
Net Sales **2**	4589192	135281	4726357	420495	2988983	2510986	2959373	1508303	2200150	2890019	3689896	5489232	16372917
Interest **3**	974973	1336	2925	963	9133	6235	10019	9689	17975	20043	50858	200531	645267
Rents **4**	107209	0	5142	6913	9204	307	1131	3505	1590	9279	2419	975	66744
Royalties **5**	22422	0	0	0	0	0	0	0	0	2005	20417	0	0
Other Portfolio Income **6**	389778	28083	132	218	11977	44747	9454	6503	14899	4506	12671	39341	217247
Other Receipts **7**	44397610	105862	4718158	412401	2958669	2459697	2938769	1488606	2165686	2854186	3603531	5248385	15443659
Total Receipts **8**	45891992	135281	4726357	420495	2988983	2510986	2959373	1508303	2200150	2890019	3689896	5489232	16372917
Average Total Receipts **9**	3466	111	440	1481	4670	19465	28456	32789	88006	137620	283838	499021	4093229
Operating Costs/Operating Income (%)													
Cost of Operations **10**	39.5	10.8	5.0	•	11.5	12.9	15.9	29.6	27.6	33.2	41.1	42.7	66.4
Salaries and Wages **11**	16.4	26.6	31.2	23.0	27.4	7.9	20.7	26.6	15.2	21.3	23.9	16.1	7.2
Taxes Paid **12**	1.8	3.0	2.5	2.6	3.8	0.8	2.2	2.1	1.8	1.9	2.5	1.6	1.2
Interest Paid **13**	1.2	0.9	0.3	0.0	0.6	0.1	0.6	0.5	1.2	1.9	0.6	3.2	1.3
Depreciation **14**	1.2	1.1	0.8	1.9	1.8	0.8	1.0	1.6	1.5	1.8	1.5	2.5	0.6
Amortization and Depletion **15**	0.7	1.6	0.1	0.0	0.5	0.1	0.2	0.7	1.0	1.0	1.4	2.3	0.4
Pensions and Other Deferred Comp. **16**	0.6	0.3	1.5	0.7	1.3	0.2	0.3	0.5	0.9	0.3	0.4	0.1	0.6
Employee Benefits **17**	1.7	1.8	1.9	1.5	2.8	1.0	1.4	1.8	1.5	6.7	2.3	2.5	0.5
Advertising **18**	0.4	2.0	0.3	0.5	1.1	0.1	0.3	0.9	0.4	0.4	0.4	0.6	0.2
Other Expenses **19**	29.7	82.4	42.8	68.0	37.9	70.4	51.2	37.6	41.5	24.2	22.3	36.1	11.1
Officers' Compensation **20**	2.3	4.5	8.3	9.2	9.7	1.5	2.6	1.9	3.0	1.7	1.3	0.4	0.0
Operating Margin **21**	4.4	•	5.3	•	1.6	4.2	3.5	•	4.6	5.7	2.4	•	10.5
Operating Margin Before Officers' Comp. **22**	6.7	•	13.6	1.7	11.3	5.7	6.2	•	7.6	7.4	3.7	•	10.5

Selected Average Balance Sheet ($ in Thousands)

Net Receivables 23	446	0	6	81	632	863	3258	6603	11406	17052	78190	193058	217110
Inventories 24	•	•	•	•	•	•	•	•	•	•	•	•	•
Net Property, Plant and Equipment 25	180	0	14	152	298	314	852	2546	3545	10761	13630	72101	115419
Total Assets 26	4576	0	65	830	2620	7778	15631	34434	70632	159948	352895	1187068	7747104
Notes and Loans Payable 27	1066	0	43	6	606	3030	3314	4527	13522	47741	33890	275816	1876324
All Other Liabilities 28	1895	0	14	126	1980	4219	7359	22579	32868	116257	204346	576299	2256645
Net Worth 29	1616	0	9	699	35	529	4958	7328	24242	-4050	114659	334952	3614136

Selected Financial Ratios (Times to 1)

Current Ratio 30	1.2	•	3.5	4.3	1.3	1.3	1.4	1.0	1.2	1.0	1.0	1.8	0.9
Quick Ratio 31	0.9	•	3.0	2.1	1.2	1.2	1.0	0.7	0.9	0.8	0.6	1.3	0.7
Net Sales to Working Capital 32	15.5	•	14.0	3.7	9.4	19.0	9.8	•	13.2	45.2	446.3	2.7	•
Coverage Ratio 33	4.6	•	16.3	•	3.7	32.9	6.8	•	4.7	4.0	5.0	•	9.2
Total Asset Turnover 34	0.8	•	6.7	1.8	1.8	2.5	1.8	1.0	1.2	0.9	0.8	0.4	0.5
Inventory Turnover 35	•	•	•	•	•	•	•	•	•	•	•	•	•
Receivables Turnover 36	•	•	•	•	•	•	•	•	•	•	•	•	•
Total Liabilities to Net Worth 37	1.8	•	6.3	0.2	74.7	13.7	2.2	3.7	1.9	2.1	•	2.5	1.1
Current Assets to Working Capital 38	6.4	•	1.4	1.3	3.9	4.1	3.7	•	5.1	21.5	303.2	2.3	•
Current Liabilities to Working Capital 39	5.4	•	0.4	0.3	2.9	3.1	2.7	•	4.1	20.5	302.2	1.3	•
Working Capital to Net Sales 40	0.1	•	0.1	0.3	0.1	0.1	0.1	•	0.1	0.0	0.0	0.4	•
Inventory to Working Capital 41	0.0	•	•	•	0.0	0.0	0.0	•	•	1.0	7.6	0.0	•
Total Receipts to Cash Flow 42	3.2	4.7	2.4	1.8	3.0	1.4	1.9	3.5	2.3	3.7	4.7	4.0	4.8
Cost of Goods to Cash Flow 43	1.3	0.5	0.1	•	0.3	0.2	0.3	1.0	0.6	1.2	1.9	1.7	3.2
Cash Flow to Total Debt 44	0.4	•	3.3	6.2	0.6	1.9	1.4	0.3	0.8	0.2	0.3	0.1	0.2

Selected Financial Factors (in Percentages)

Debt Ratio 45	64.7	•	86.4	15.8	98.7	93.2	68.3	78.7	65.7	102.5	67.5	71.8	53.3
Return on Total Assets 46	4.2	•	38.1	•	3.9	10.8	7.4	•	7.2	6.5	2.3	•	6.2
Return on Equity Before Income Taxes 47	9.3	•	262.5	•	212.4	153.8	19.9	•	16.5	•	5.7	•	11.9
Return on Equity After Income Taxes 48	4.9	•	257.1	•	159.4	142.4	16.6	•	11.9	•	5.7	•	8.2
Profit Margin (Before Income Tax) 49	4.3	•	5.3	•	1.6	4.2	3.5	•	4.6	5.7	0.1	2.3	10.5
Profit Margin (After Income Tax) 50	2.3	•	5.2	•	1.2	3.9	2.9	•	3.3	4.2	0.1	2.3	7.2

Table II

Corporations with Net Income

OTHER INSURANCE RELATED ACTIVITIES

MONEY AMOUNTS AND SIZE OF ASSETS IN THOUSANDS OF DOLLARS

Item Description for Accounting Period 7/04 Through 6/05	Total	Zero Assets	Under 500	500 to 1,000	1,000 to 5,000	5,000 to 10,000	10,000 to 25,000	25,000 to 50,000	50,000 to 100,000	100,000 to 250,000	250,000 to 500,000	500,000 to 2,500,000	2,500,000 and over
Number of Enterprises **1**	8110	29	7315	130	403	86	70	22	20	14	10	7	4
Revenues ($ in Thousands)													
Net Sales **2**	39099558	87170	3702331	305719	1816483	710596	2077595	1090025	2026319	2630983	3536563	4742856	16372917
Interest **3**	858374	560	2496	0	4732	689	7779	2888	11110	6758	19203	156891	645267
Rents **4**	97356	0	5142	2358	8107	41	829	7	1558	9279	2419	873	66744
Royalties **5**	22422	0	0	0	0	0	0	0	0	2005	20417	0	0
Other Portfolio Income **6**	374955	26347	56	0	11463	43146	7520	3828	11305	4402	10650	38991	217247
Other Receipts **7**	37746451	60263	3694637	303361	1792181	666720	2061467	1083302	2002346	2608539	3483874	4546101	15443659
Total Receipts **8**	39099558	87170	3702331	305719	1816483	710596	2077595	1090025	2026319	2630983	3536563	4742856	16372917
Average Total Receipts **9**	4821	3006	506	2352	4507	8263	29680	49547	101316	187927	353656	677551	4093229
Operating Costs/Operating Income (%)													
Cost of Operations **10**	44.1	•	6.3	•	2.0	15.1	17.7	37.4	29.1	36.4	42.8	45.5	66.4
Salaries and Wages **11**	16.2	27.0	32.0	20.8	33.5	24.8	24.1	22.4	13.3	19.6	24.9	14.7	7.2
Taxes Paid **12**	1.8	3.4	2.6	2.5	3.5	2.6	2.6	1.6	1.7	1.8	2.4	1.5	1.2
Interest Paid **13**	1.0	0.4	0.2	0.0	0.6	0.3	0.4	0.2	1.2	1.4	0.6	1.5	1.3
Depreciation **14**	1.1	1.0	0.8	1.0	2.1	1.4	1.1	0.9	1.4	1.6	1.6	2.1	0.6
Amortization and Depletion **15**	0.7	2.3	0.0	0.0	0.7	0.2	0.1	0.2	1.0	0.8	1.4	2.3	0.4
Pensions and Other Deferred Comp. **16**	0.5	0.4	1.2	1.0	0.4	0.5	0.4	0.2	0.8	0.3	0.4	0.1	0.6
Employee Benefits **17**	1.7	0.4	2.0	2.1	2.2	2.7	1.6	0.9	1.4	6.9	2.4	2.3	0.5
Advertising **18**	0.3	0.2	0.2	0.3	1.1	0.3	0.4	0.3	0.3	0.3	0.4	0.5	0.2
Other Expenses **19**	20.5	26.2	37.7	28.4	39.6	26.0	41.4	25.7	39.5	21.8	14.2	16.7	11.1
Officers' Compensation **20**	1.7	2.5	7.9	9.9	5.8	3.0	2.9	1.8	2.8	1.1	1.3	0.2	0.0
Operating Margin **21**	10.2	36.3	9.0	34.0	8.5	23.0	7.3	8.4	7.6	8.2	7.5	12.5	10.5
Operating Margin Before Officers' Comp. **22**	11.9	38.8	16.9	43.9	14.3	26.0	10.2	10.2	10.4	9.3	8.9	12.7	10.5

Selected Average Balance Sheet ($ in Thousands)

Net Receivables 23	623	·	0	8	·	59	681	662	3291	6651	8700	19881	101647	277023	217110
Inventories 24	·	·	·	·	·	·	·	·	·	·	·	·	·	·	·
Net Property, Plant and Equipment 25	199	·	0	14	·	130	381	266	879	2572	3736	12214	17545	45286	115419
Total Assets 26	6053	·	0	75	·	903	3029	7602	15294	33212	72059	157499	356223	935467	7747104
Notes and Loans Payable 27	1415	·	0	31	·	12	485	3869	2602	3311	15881	43172	44053	227636	1876324
All Other Liabilities 28	2044	·	0	9	·	113	1969	1763	6716	20918	28198	66531	223796	266541	2256645
Net Worth 29	2594	·	0	36	·	779	575	1970	5976	8982	27980	47796	88374	441290	3614136

Selected Financial Ratios (Times to 1)

Current Ratio 30	1.1	·	3.7	7.6	1.5	2.8	1.6	1.2	1.3	0.9	1.1	1.6	0.9
Quick Ratio 31	0.9	·	3.4	3.8	1.4	2.4	1.2	0.9	0.9	0.6	0.6	1.5	0.7
Net Sales to Working Capital 32	21.3	·	13.2	3.5	6.6	4.7	7.6	13.2	15.6	·	28.4	4.6	·
Coverage Ratio 33	11.1	89.0	37.2	14.9	71.9	20.2	50.9	7.3	7.0	13.5	9.4	9.2	
Total Asset Turnover 34	0.8	·	6.7	2.6	1.5	1.9	1.5	1.4	1.2	1.0	0.7	0.5	
Inventory Turnover 35	·	·	·	·	·	·	·	·	·	·	·	·	·
Receivables Turnover 36	·	·	·	·	·	·	·	·	·	·	·	·	·
Total Liabilities to Net Worth 37	1.3	·	1.1	0.2	4.3	2.9	1.6	2.7	1.6	2.3	3.0	1.1	1.1
Current Assets to Working Capital 38	7.8	·	1.4	1.2	3.1	1.6	2.7	5.9	4.9	18.7	2.6	·	
Current Liabilities to Working Capital 39	6.8	·	0.4	0.2	2.1	0.6	1.7	4.9	3.9	17.7	1.6	·	
Working Capital to Net Sales 40	0.0	·	0.1	0.3	0.2	0.2	0.1	0.1	0.0	0.0	0.2	·	
Inventory to Working Capital 41	0.1	·	·	·	0.0	0.0	0.0	·	·	0.5	·		
Total Receipts to Cash Flow 42	3.5	3.4	2.4	1.7	2.3	2.6	2.2	3.1	2.2	3.7	5.4	3.8	4.8
Cost of Goods to Cash Flow 43	1.6	·	0.2	0.0	0.0	0.4	0.4	1.2	0.6	1.3	2.3	1.7	3.2
Cash Flow to Total Debt 44	0.4	·	5.3	10.9	0.8	0.6	1.5	0.7	1.0	0.5	0.2	0.4	0.2

Selected Financial Factors (in Percentages)

Debt Ratio 45	57.1	·	52.7	13.8	81.0	74.1	60.9	73.0	61.2	69.7	75.2	52.8	53.3
Return on Total Assets 46	8.9	·	62.4	88.6	13.4	25.3	14.7	12.7	12.3	11.3	8.0	10.0	6.2
Return on Equity Before Income Taxes 47	18.8	·	128.2	102.7	65.8	96.1	35.7	46.2	27.3	32.0	29.9	18.9	11.9
Return on Equity After Income Taxes 48	14.3	·	126.2	100.0	60.8	91.6	31.5	41.0	22.2	25.6	20.5	12.7	8.2
Profit Margin (Before Income Tax) 49	10.1	36.3	9.0	34.0	8.4	22.9	7.2	8.4	7.5	8.1	7.5	12.3	10.5
Profit Margin (After Income Tax) 50	7.7	24.3	8.9	33.1	7.8	21.8	6.4	7.4	6.1	6.5	5.1	8.2	7.2

Table I

Corporations with and without Net Income

OPEN-END INVESTMENT FUNDS (FORM 1120-RIC)

MONEY AMOUNTS AND SIZE OF ASSETS IN THOUSANDS OF DOLLARS

Item Description for Accounting Period 7/04 Through 6/05		Total	Zero Assets	Under 500	500 to 1,000	1,000 to 5,000	5,000 to 10,000	10,000 to 25,000	25,000 to 50,000	50,000 to 100,000	100,000 to 250,000	250,000 to 500,000	500,000 to 2,500,000	2,500,000 and over
Number of Enterprises	1	10896	760	30	84	320	290	707	925	1360	2092	1486	2155	688
Revenues ($ in Thousands)														
Net Sales	2	220664884	2827333	284	3540	25049	61279	334475	977994	3113283	10621892	15516126	62889650	124293978
Interest	3	94242109	1932210	263	738	6820	18838	110530	276180	1018699	3307723	5859501	25275678	56434929
Rents	4	0	0	0	0	0	0	0	0	0	0	0	0	0
Royalties	5	0	0	0	0	0	0	0	0	0	0	0	0	0
Other Portfolio Income	6	41394498	307618	0	2248	6223	24427	125912	394732	1170999	4162439	5061499	16159048	13979352
Other Receipts	7	85028277	587505	21	554	12006	18014	98033	307082	923585	3151730	4595126	21454924	53879697
Total Receipts	8	220664884	2827333	284	3540	25049	61279	334475	977994	3113283	10621892	15516126	62889650	124293978
Average Total Receipts	9	20252	3720	9	42	78	211	473	1057	2289	5077	10442	29183	180660
Operating Costs/Operating Income (%)														
Cost of Operations	10	•	•	•	•	•	•	•	•	•	•	•	•	•
Salaries and Wages	11	0.0	0.0	6.7	0.2	0.3	0.3	0.2	0.1	0.1	0.1	0.0	0.1	0.0
Taxes Paid	12	0.2	0.2	0.6	1.4	0.3	0.3	0.6	0.6	0.4	0.4	0.3	0.2	0.2
Interest Paid	13	0.3	0.1	•	0.1	0.2	•	0.0	0.3	0.6	0.3	0.4	0.3	0.2
Depreciation	14	0.0	0.0	•	•	•	•	•	0.0	0.0	0.0	0.0	0.0	0.0
Amortization and Depletion	15	0.0	0.0	•	0.7	1.2	0.3	0.2	0.0	0.0	0.0	0.0	0.0	0.0
Pensions and Other Deferred Comp.	16	•	•	•	•	•	•	•	•	•	•	•	•	•
Employee Benefits	17	•	•	•	•	•	•	•	•	•	•	•	•	•
Advertising	18	0.0	•	•	•	•	•	•	•	0.0	0.0	0.0	0.0	0.0
Other Expenses	19	26.1	26.8	21.1	56.4	47.2	34.8	37.9	33.1	28.1	27.1	26.0	26.1	25.8
Officers' Compensation	20	0.0	•	•	•	•	•	0.0	0.0	0.1	0.0	0.0	0.0	0.0
Operating Margin	21	73.4	72.9	78.9	35.6	50.0	64.2	61.4	65.8	70.7	72.1	73.3	73.3	73.8
Operating Margin Before Officers' Comp.	22	73.4	72.9	78.9	35.6	50.0	64.2	61.5	65.8	70.7	72.1	73.3	73.3	73.8

Selected Average Balance Sheet ($ in Thousands)

Net Receivables 23	13367	0	4	5	37	65	236	556	1117	2722	5080	17142	135508
Inventories 24	•	•	•	•	•	•	•	•	•	•	•	•	•
Net Property, Plant and Equipment 25	2	0	0	0	0	0	4	0	0	0	0	8	2
Total Assets 26	841724		174	700	2771	7237	17273	36980	72367	166559	361034	1081440	8441999
Notes and Loans Payable 27	805		0	0	0	0	8	86	276	330	1072	1592	3765
All Other Liabilities 28	39932		14	24	99	173	537	1512	2782	7894	19523	74258	325432
Net Worth 29	800987		160	676	2672	7064	16728	35382	69308	158334	340439	1005589	8112802

Selected Financial Ratios (Times to 1)

Current Ratio 30	3.2	6.9	6.2	2.1	8.5	5.4	4.4	5.3	4.9	3.7	2.8	3.3
Quick Ratio 31	3.0	6.3	5.1	1.9	8.3	4.9	4.1	4.8	4.5	3.4	2.5	3.0
Net Sales to Working Capital 32	0.2	0.1	0.3	0.7	0.2	0.2	0.2	0.2	0.2	0.2	0.2	0.2
Coverage Ratio 33	244.3	672.2	•	632.0	308.3	3438.5	138.1	75.4	172.1	129.7	187.5	332.1
Total Asset Turnover 34	0.0	•	0.1	•	0.0	0.0	0.0	0.0	0.0	0.0	0.0	0.0
Inventory Turnover 35	•	•	•	•	•	•	•	•	•	•	•	•
Receivables Turnover 36	•	•	•	•	•	•	•	•	•	•	•	•
Total Liabilities to Net Worth 37	0.1	0.1	0.0	0.0	0.0	0.0	0.0	0.0	0.0	0.1	0.1	0.0
Current Assets to Working Capital 38	1.4	1.2	1.2	1.9	1.1	1.2	1.3	1.2	1.3	1.4	1.6	1.4
Current Liabilities to Working Capital 39	0.4	0.2	0.2	0.9	0.1	0.2	0.3	0.2	0.2	0.4	0.6	0.4
Working Capital to Net Sales 40	4.4	8.4	3.0	1.4	6.1	4.8	4.8	5.3	6.1	5.2	4.4	4.2
Inventory to Working Capital 41	•	•	•	•	•	•	•	•	•	•	•	•
Total Receipts to Cash Flow 42	1.1	1.0	3.5	1.4	1.5	1.2	1.3	1.2	1.2	1.1	1.1	1.1
Cost of Goods to Cash Flow 43	•	•	•	•	•	•	•	•	•	•	•	•
Cash Flow to Total Debt 44	0.5	0.7	0.5	0.6	0.8	0.7	0.5	0.6	0.5	0.5	0.3	0.5

Selected Financial Factors (in Percentages)

Debt Ratio 45	4.8	7.8	3.5	3.6	2.4	3.2	4.3	4.2	4.9	5.7	7.0	3.9
Return on Total Assets 46	1.5	4.3	2.1	1.4	1.6	1.2	1.3	1.5	1.4	1.5	1.5	1.5
Return on Equity Before Income Taxes 47	1.6	4.7	2.2	1.5	1.7	1.2	1.4	1.5	1.6	1.6	1.7	1.5
Return on Equity After Income Taxes 48	1.6	4.7	2.2	1.5	1.7	1.2	1.4	1.5	1.5	1.6	1.7	1.5
Profit Margin (Before Income Tax) 49	62.1	67.2	78.9	35.6	50.0	55.7	42.1	46.2	46.9	51.1	57.0	67.8
Profit Margin (After Income Tax) 50	62.1	67.2	78.9	35.6	50.0	55.7	42.1	46.2	46.9	51.1	57.0	67.8

Table II

Corporations with Net Income

OPEN-END INVESTMENT FUNDS (FORM 1120-RIC)

MONEY AMOUNTS AND SIZE OF ASSETS IN THOUSANDS OF DOLLARS

Item Description for Accounting Period 7/04 Through 6/05	Total	Zero Assets	Under 500	500 to 1,000	1,000 to 5,000	5,000 to 10,000	10,000 to 25,000	25,000 to 50,000	50,000 to 100,000	100,000 to 250,000	250,000 to 500,000	500,000 to 2,500,000	2,500,000 and over
Number of Enterprises 1	8290	503	23	61	206	213	473	654	1019	1573	1167	1795	603
Revenues ($ in Thousands)													
Net Sales 2	205704688	2743858	283	3291	20150	52729	295397	836405	2641824	9198978	13742607	57688527	118480640
Interest 3	93747358	1928114	262	597	6276	18015	104535	265602	996533	3258099	5795846	25142439	56231039
Rents 4	0	0	0	0	0	0	0	0	0	0	0	0	0
Royalties 5	0	0	0	0	0	0	0	0	0	0	0	0	0
Other Portfolio Income 6	32093573	272668	0	2248	6153	19163	97574	276638	843520	3161822	3748610	12754522	10910654
Other Receipts 7	79863757	543076	21	446	7721	15551	93288	294165	801771	2779057	4198151	19791566	51338947
Total Receipts 8	205704688	2743858	283	3291	20150	52729	295397	836405	2641824	9198978	13742607	57688527	118480640
Average Total Receipts 9	24814	5455	12	54	98	248	625	1279	2593	5848	11776	32138	196485
Operating Costs/Operating Income (%)													
Cost of Operations 10	•	•	•	•	•	•	•	•	•	•	•	•	•
Salaries and Wages 11	0.0	0.0	•	7.2	0.0	0.1	0.1	0.1	0.1	0.1	0.0	0.1	0.0
Taxes Paid 12	0.2	0.1	•	0.6	0.3	0.2	0.2	0.6	0.3	0.3	0.2	0.2	0.2
Interest Paid 13	0.2	0.1	•	0.1	•	•	0.0	0.1	0.4	0.2	0.4	0.3	0.1
Depreciation 14	0.0	0.0	•	•	•	•	•	0.0	0.0	0.0	0.0	0.0	0.0
Amortization and Depletion 15	0.0	0.0	•	0.7	1.5	0.4	0.2	0.0	0.0	0.0	0.0	0.0	0.0
Pensions and Other Deferred Comp. 16	•	•	•	•	•	•	•	•	•	•	•	•	•
Employee Benefits 17	•	•	•	•	•	•	•	•	•	•	•	•	•
Advertising 18	0.0	•	•	•	•	•	•	•	0.0	0.0	0.0	0.0	0.0
Other Expenses 19	23.1	23.8	18.0	47.5	24.5	21.8	24.2	25.1	23.0	21.9	22.0	22.7	23.6
Officers' Compensation 20	0.0	•	•	•	•	•	0.0	0.0	0.1	0.0	0.0	0.0	0.0
Operating Margin 21	76.4	75.9	82.0	43.9	73.7	77.4	75.4	74.1	76.1	77.4	77.4	76.7	76.1
Operating Margin Before Officers' Comp. 22	76.4	75.9	82.0	43.9	73.7	77.4	75.4	74.2	76.2	77.4	76.7	76.7	76.1

Selected Average Balance Sheet ($ in Thousands)

Item													
Net Receivables 23	15715	0	0	3	46	50	222	537	1136	2554	5446	16944	145693
Inventories 24	•	•	•	•	•	•	•	•	•	•	•	•	•
Net Property, Plant and Equipment 25	1	0	0	0	0	0	0	0	0	0	•	1	2
Total Assets 26	974060	176	704	2710	7122	17375	36993	72203	167607	360836	1088518	8836176	
Notes and Loans Payable 27	914	0	0	0	0	2	25	257	329	1131	1710	3970	
All Other Liabilities 28	45328	11	18	114	154	502	1456	2630	7726	19806	76250	331192	
Net Worth 29	927817	165	686	2596	6968	16871	35512	69316	159552	339899	1010558	8501014	

Selected Financial Ratios (Times to 1)

Item													
Current Ratio 30	3.0	•	10.4	6.6	2.3	8.9	4.9	3.6	4.8	4.5	3.3	2.5	3.1
Quick Ratio 31	2.7	•	9.5	5.4	2.1	8.7	4.2	3.3	4.3	4.1	3.0	2.3	2.8
Net Sales to Working Capital 32	0.3	•	0.1	0.5	0.7	0.2	0.3	0.4	0.3	0.2	0.2	0.3	0.3
Coverage Ratio 33	356.1	882.4	•	723.5	•	26546.1	801.9	160.5	267.2	166.0	233.3	563.2	
Total Asset Turnover 34	0.0	•	0.1	0.1	0.0	0.0	0.0	0.0	0.0	0.0	0.0	0.0	0.0
Inventory Turnover 35	•	•	•	•	•	•	•	•	•	•	•	•	•
Receivables Turnover 36	•	•	•	•	•	•	•	•	•	•	•	•	•
Total Liabilities to Net Worth 37	0.0	•	0.1	0.0	0.0	0.0	0.0	0.0	0.0	0.1	0.1	0.1	0.0
Current Assets to Working Capital 38	1.5	•	1.1	1.2	1.8	1.1	1.3	1.4	1.3	1.3	1.4	1.6	1.5
Current Liabilities to Working Capital 39	0.5	•	0.1	0.2	0.8	0.1	0.3	0.4	0.3	0.3	0.4	0.6	0.5
Working Capital to Net Sales 40	3.6	•	8.5	1.9	1.5	4.9	3.0	2.9	4.0	4.7	4.0	3.6	3.6
Inventory to Working Capital 41	•	•	•	•	•	•	•	•	•	•	•	•	•
Total Receipts to Cash Flow 42	1.1	1.1	1.0	4.3	1.5	1.6	1.3	1.3	1.2	1.2	1.1	1.1	1.1
Cost of Goods to Cash Flow 43	•	•	•	•	•	•	•	•	•	•	•	•	•
Cash Flow to Total Debt 44	0.5	•	1.1	0.7	0.6	1.0	1.0	0.6	0.8	0.6	0.5	0.4	0.6

Selected Financial Factors (in Percentages)

Item													
Debt Ratio 45	4.7	•	6.4	2.5	4.2	2.2	2.9	4.0	4.0	4.8	5.8	7.2	3.8
Return on Total Assets 46	1.8	•	5.7	3.4	2.7	2.7	2.3	2.3	2.2	2.1	2.0	1.9	1.6
Return on Equity Before Income Taxes 47	1.8	•	6.1	3.5	2.8	2.8	2.3	2.3	2.2	2.2	2.1	2.1	1.7
Return on Equity After Income Taxes 48	1.8	•	6.1	3.5	2.8	2.8	2.3	2.3	2.2	2.2	2.1	2.1	1.7
Profit Margin (Before Income Tax) 49	68.7	71.2	82.0	43.9	73.7	77.4	62.9	65.0	59.6	59.0	61.8	64.9	72.4
Profit Margin (After Income Tax) 50	68.7	71.2	82.0	43.9	73.7	77.4	62.9	65.0	59.6	59.0	61.8	64.9	72.4

Table I

Corporations with and without Net Income

REAL ESTATE INVESTMENT TRUSTS (FORM 1120-REIT)

MONEY AMOUNTS AND SIZE OF ASSETS IN THOUSANDS OF DOLLARS

Item Description for Accounting Period 7/04 Through 6/05	Total	Zero Assets	Under 500	500 to 1,000	1,000 to 5,000	5,000 to 10,000	10,000 to 25,000	25,000 to 50,000	50,000 to 100,000	100,000 to 250,000	250,000 to 500,000	500,000 to 2,500,000	2,500,000 and over
Number of Enterprises **1**	1123	80	35	14	53	35	100	84	112	151	125	219	115
Revenues ($ in Thousands)													
Net Sales **2**	80674630	3510178	882	78756	590981	54868	243447	1495986	1128028	3038401	3915992	20730990	45886119
Interest **3**	30269205	450318	23	556	4639	2128	26343	110603	305086	597866	1044287	6818887	20908470
Rents **4**	33229580	648969	1292	2822	52139	34027	159240	277975	507933	1449042	2140891	10169859	17785390
Royalties **5**	0	0	0	0	0	0	0	0	0	0	0	0	0
Other Portfolio Income **6**	9204088	2208190	218	0	528672	6658	42963	1080329	249734	791041	407851	1547988	2240446
Other Receipts **7**	7971757	202701	-651	75378	5531	12055	14901	27079	65275	200452	322963	2194256	4851813
Total Receipts **8**	80674630	3510178	882	78756	590981	54868	243447	1495986	1128028	3038401	3915992	20730990	45886119
Average Total Receipts **9**	71838	43877	25	5625	11151	1568	2434	17809	10072	20122	31328	94662	399010
Operating Costs/Operating Income (%)													
Cost of Operations **10**	•	•	•	•	•	•	•	•	•	•	•	•	•
Salaries and Wages **11**	2.1	9.2	•	•	1.6	1.2	1.1	0.2	1.5	0.8	1.4	2.1	1.8
Taxes Paid **12**	2.8	1.7	17.9	0.0	0.6	2.5	3.6	1.8	3.1	2.4	4.0	3.4	2.6
Interest Paid **13**	11.8	7.4	4.8	0.4	2.3	19.6	8.0	8.0	20.7	8.2	8.3	12.1	12.7
Depreciation **14**	7.3	2.5	5.1	•	1.3	2.9	4.7	1.5	6.1	5.7	6.7	8.4	7.7
Amortization and Depletion **15**	0.9	0.2	0.2	•	1.9	0.8	1.3	0.2	0.6	0.6	0.5	0.9	1.0
Pensions and Other Deferred Comp. **16**	•	•	•	•	•	•	•	•	•	•	•	•	•
Employee Benefits **17**	•	•	•	•	•	•	•	•	•	•	•	•	•
Advertising **18**	0.2	0.1	15.9	•	0.0	0.2	0.3	0.1	0.2	0.2	0.2	0.3	0.2
Other Expenses **19**	15.6	9.0	1362.0	7.7	6.1	33.1	30.6	12.9	21.4	26.9	26.9	16.2	14.1
Officers' Compensation **20**	0.6	1.0	•	•	4.9	•	0.2	0.0	0.2	0.3	0.4	0.7	0.5
Operating Margin **21**	58.7	69.0	•	91.9	81.2	39.8	50.2	75.3	46.1	55.0	51.6	56.0	59.4
Operating Margin Before Officers' Comp. **22**	59.3	70.0	•	91.9	86.1	39.8	50.3	75.4	46.3	55.3	52.0	56.7	60.0

Selected Average Balance Sheet ($ in Thousands)

Item	1	2	3	4	5	6	7	8	9	10	11	12	13
Net Receivables 23	53841	0	0	3	2	43	274	1755	1839	12536	6357	45922	411625
Inventories 24	•	•	•	•	•	•	•	•	•	•	•	•	•
Net Property, Plant and Equipment 25	207087	0	44	0	347	1882	4900	10107	22969	47586	88070	316384	1226777
Total Assets 26	990493	•	125	754	2211	7148	17237	37465	71860	168288	348637	1183314	6703351
Notes and Loans Payable 27	185762	0	83	25	427	3673	4183	6290	19003	35592	58975	213758	1268021
All Other Liabilities 28	140967	0	1	22	132	1003	285	1598	2566	6323	14742	105232	1147564
Net Worth 29	663764	0	41	707	1653	2473	12768	29577	50291	126373	274920	864325	4287766

Selected Financial Ratios (Times to 1)

Item	1	2	3	4	5	6	7	8	9	10	11	12	13
Current Ratio 30	1.0	•	2.4	6.4	2.5	0.9	2.6	2.9	1.6	3.6	4.3	2.1	0.8
Quick Ratio 31	0.9	•	2.1	6.4	2.1	0.3	1.5	2.5	1.2	2.9	3.2	1.6	0.7
Net Sales to Working Capital 32	•	•	7.3	28.4	76.1	•	1.6	5.8	4.1	1.1	1.0	1.2	•
Coverage Ratio 33	6.0	10.4	•	238.3	35.8	3.0	7.1	10.5	3.2	7.7	7.2	5.6	5.7
Total Asset Turnover 34	0.1	0.2	•	7.5	5.0	0.2	0.1	0.5	0.1	0.1	0.1	0.1	0.1
Inventory Turnover 35	•	•	•	•	•	•	•	•	•	•	•	•	•
Receivables Turnover 36	•	•	•	•	•	•	•	•	•	•	•	•	•
Total Liabilities to Net Worth 37	0.5	•	2.1	0.1	0.3	1.9	0.3	0.3	0.4	0.3	0.3	0.4	0.6
Current Assets to Working Capital 38	•	•	1.7	1.2	1.7	•	1.6	1.5	2.8	1.4	1.3	1.9	•
Current Liabilities to Working Capital 39	•	•	0.7	0.2	0.7	•	0.6	0.5	1.8	0.4	0.3	0.9	•
Working Capital to Net Sales 40	•	0.1	0.0	0.0	•	0.6	0.2	0.2	0.9	0.3	1.0	0.9	•
Inventory to Working Capital 41	•	•	•	•	•	•	•	•	•	•	•	•	•
Total Receipts to Cash Flow 42	1.7	7.8	1.0	14.4	1.8	1.9	6.7	2.3	1.8	1.6	1.7	1.5	•
Cost of Goods to Cash Flow 43	•	•	•	•	•	•	•	•	•	•	•	•	•
Cash Flow to Total Debt 44	0.1	•	118.3	1.4	0.2	0.3	•	0.2	0.3	0.3	0.2	•	0.1

Selected Financial Factors (in Percentages)

Item	1	2	3	4	5	6	7	8	9	10	11	12	13
Debt Ratio 45	33.0	67.3	•	6.3	25.3	65.4	25.9	21.1	30.0	24.9	21.1	27.0	36.0
Return on Total Assets 46	5.1	•	•	688.7	421.0	13.0	8.1	39.6	9.4	7.5	5.4	5.4	4.3
Return on Equity Before Income Taxes 47	6.3	•	•	731.7	547.5	25.2	9.4	45.4	9.2	8.8	5.9	6.1	5.5
Return on Equity After Income Taxes 48	6.3	•	•	731.7	546.9	25.2	9.4	45.4	9.2	8.7	5.9	5.9	5.5
Profit Margin (Before Income Tax) 49	58.6	69.0	•	91.9	81.2	39.8	49.2	75.3	46.1	55.0	51.6	56.0	59.4
Profit Margin (After Income Tax) 50	58.6	68.8	•	91.9	81.1	39.8	49.1	75.3	46.0	54.9	51.6	55.9	59.4

Table II

Corporations with Net Income

REAL ESTATE INVESTMENT TRUSTS (FORM 1120-REIT)

MONEY AMOUNTS AND SIZE OF ASSETS IN THOUSANDS OF DOLLARS

Item Description for Accounting Period 7/04 Through 6/05	Total	Zero Assets	Under 500	500 to 1,000	1,000 to 5,000	5,000 to 10,000	10,000 to 25,000	25,000 to 50,000	50,000 to 100,000	100,000 to 250,000	250,000 to 500,000	500,000 to 2,500,000	2,500,000 and over
Number of Enterprises **1**	939	58	11	0	42	21	78	60	97	127	115	209	0
Revenues ($ in Thousands)													
Net Sales **2**	78112242	2810074	414	0	586307	49958	230880	1381554	1059507	2755579	3693647	19960418	0
Interest **3**	29993364	431306	4	0	4621	2032	25129	105886	297627	582421	1033971	6610911	0
Rents **4**	31014961	59733	227	0	45131	28549	138308	162945	446578	1190506	1925952	9597549	0
Royalties **5**	0	0	0	0	0	0	0	0	0	0	0	0	0
Other Portfolio Income **6**	9140063	2173425	170	0	528642	6658	42943	1078905	248346	770372	407498	1542659	0
Other Receipts **7**	7963854	145610	13	0	7913	12719	24500	33818	66956	212280	326226	2209299	0
Total Receipts **8**	78112242	2810074	414	0	586307	49958	230880	1381554	1059507	2755579	3693647	19960418	0
Average Total Receipts **9**	83187	48450	38	•	13960	2379	2960	23026	10923	21697	32119	95504	•
Operating Costs/Operating Income (%)													
Cost of Operations **10**	•	•	•	•	•	•	•	•	•	•	•	•	•
Salaries and Wages **11**	1.7	0.0	•	•	1.6	•	1.0	0.2	1.4	0.5	1.4	1.9	•
Taxes Paid **12**	2.7	0.0	8.5	•	0.6	1.3	2.9	1.0	3.0	1.8	4.1	3.3	•
Interest Paid **13**	11.3	1.5	7.0	•	2.4	20.2	5.4	1.9	20.3	6.1	8.4	11.1	•
Depreciation **14**	7.1	0.2	4.1	•	1.1	1.7	3.5	1.2	5.8	4.1	7.0	7.7	•
Amortization and Depletion **15**	0.9	0.1	•	•	1.9	0.9	0.6	0.2	0.6	0.5	0.5	0.9	•
Pensions and Other Deferred Comp. **16**	•	•	•	•	•	•	•	•	•	•	•	•	•
Employee Benefits **17**	•	•	•	•	•	•	•	•	•	•	•	•	•
Advertising **18**	0.2	0.0	•	•	0.0	•	0.3	0.1	0.1	0.1	0.3	0.3	•
Other Expenses **19**	14.1	7.4	62.3	•	5.2	23.8	23.8	5.5	13.9	24.1	22.2	14.6	•
Officers' Compensation **20**	0.6	•	•	•	5.0	•	0.2	0.0	0.3	0.3	0.4	0.7	•
Operating Margin **21**	61.5	90.7	17.9	•	82.3	52.2	62.4	89.9	54.7	62.5	55.8	59.6	•
Operating Margin Before Officers' Comp. **22**	62.1	90.7	17.9	•	87.2	52.2	62.6	90.0	54.9	62.9	56.1	60.3	•

Selected Average Balance Sheet ($ in Thousands)

Net Receivables 23	63802	0	0	•	3	72	200	2431	2117	14869	6799	47456
Inventories 24	•	•	•	•	•	•	•	•	•	•	•	•
Net Property, Plant and Equipment 25	234777	46	0	•	438	2157	4571	10056	22820	39700	91115	303817
Total Assets 26	1156934	183	0	•	2061	6609	16988	37019	72633	168661	349996	1177898
Notes and Loans Payable 27	211038	31	0	•	535	4928	4210	4039	17470	27106	55714	200210
All Other Liabilities 28	163152	1	0	•	163	1655	121	1812	2760	6203	15018	88098
Net Worth 29	782743	150	0	•	1363	26	12657	31169	52403	135351	279264	889590

Selected Financial Ratios (Times to 1)

Current Ratio 30	1.0	•	8.6	•	2.5	0.9	2.6	5.6	1.8	4.9	4.4	2.5
Quick Ratio 31	0.9	•	7.2	•	2.0	0.3	1.4	5.4	1.7	4.0	3.2	1.9
Net Sales to Working Capital 32	•	•	3.4	83.3	•	1.9	5.1	3.7	0.9	1.0	1.0	1.0
Coverage Ratio 33	6.4	60.4	3.6	36.0	3.6	12.4	48.7	3.7	11.2	7.6	6.3	•
Total Asset Turnover 34	0.1	•	0.2	6.8	0.4	0.2	0.6	0.2	0.1	0.1	0.1	•
Inventory Turnover 35	•	•	•	•	•	•	•	•	•	•	•	•
Receivables Turnover 36	•	•	•	•	•	•	•	•	•	•	•	•
Total Liabilities to Net Worth 37	0.5	0.2	0.5	249.5	0.3	0.2	0.4	0.2	0.3	0.3	•	•
Current Assets to Working Capital 38	•	•	•	•	1.1	1.7	1.6	1.2	2.2	1.3	1.3	1.7
Current Liabilities to Working Capital 39	•	•	•	•	0.1	0.7	0.6	0.2	1.2	0.3	0.3	0.7
Working Capital to Net Sales 40	•	•	•	•	0.3	0.0	0.5	0.2	0.3	1.1	1.0	1.0
Inventory to Working Capital 41	•	•	•	•	•	•	•	•	•	•	•	•
Total Receipts to Cash Flow 42	1.6	4.8	4.2	15.5	1.6	1.7	6.0	2.3	1.7	1.6	•	•
Cost of Goods to Cash Flow 43	•	•	•	•	•	•	•	•	•	•	•	•
Cash Flow to Total Debt 44	0.1	•	0.3	1.3	0.2	0.4	0.7	0.2	0.4	0.3	0.2	•

Selected Financial Factors (in Percentages)

Debt Ratio 45	32.3	•	18.0	•	33.9	99.6	25.5	15.8	27.9	19.7	20.2	24.5
Return on Total Assets 46	5.2	•	5.2	•	573.0	26.0	11.6	57.1	11.3	8.8	5.9	5.7
Return on Equity Before Income Taxes 47	6.5	•	4.6	4707.0	842.7	66.4	14.3	66.4	11.4	10.0	6.4	6.4
Return on Equity After Income Taxes 48	6.5	•	4.6	4707.0	841.9	66.4	14.3	66.4	11.4	10.0	6.4	6.4
Profit Margin (Before Income Tax) 49	61.5	90.7	18.1	82.3	52.2	89.9	61.3	54.6	62.5	55.8	59.6	•
Profit Margin (After Income Tax) 50	61.5	90.4	18.1	82.2	52.2	89.9	61.3	54.6	62.5	55.7	59.5	•

Table I

Corporations with and without Net Income

OTHER FINANCIAL VEHICLES

MONEY AMOUNTS AND SIZE OF ASSETS IN THOUSANDS OF DOLLARS

Item Description for Accounting Period 7/04 Through 6/05	Total	Zero Assets	Under 500	500 to 1,000	1,000 to 5,000	5,000 to 10,000	10,000 to 25,000	25,000 to 50,000	50,000 to 100,000	100,000 to 250,000	250,000 to 500,000	500,000 to 2,500,000	2,500,000 and over
Number of Enterprises 1	14160	3737	8239	607	1031	90	123	59	26	46	46	106	50
Revenues ($ in Thousands)													
Net Sales 2	15266425	779423	300711	209472	298789	94635	302102	188679	98665	362728	933538	4118686	7578999
Interest 3	10483027	134439	67556	78806	41395	12465	30581	55050	51527	222018	775263	3396347	5617581
Rents 4	53404	4601	0	5378	2032	2	3829	4577	1899	31086	0	0	0
Royalties 5	11788	2403	0	0	0	0	278	78	9028	0	0	0	0
Other Portfolio Income 6	1390074	431718	18171	10265	45873	2650	51700	36814	24308	56715	41417	365800	304639
Other Receipts 7	3328132	206262	214984	115023	209489	79518	215714	92160	11903	52909	116858	356539	1656779
Total Receipts 8	15266425	779423	300711	209472	298789	94635	302102	188679	98665	362728	933538	4118686	7578999
Average Total Receipts 9	1078	209	36	345	290	1052	2456	3198	3795	7885	20294	38856	151580
Operating Costs/Operating Income (%)													
Cost of Operations 10	0.2	0.0	0.2	•	•	11.9	1.8	5.8	0.4	•	•	0.0	•
Salaries and Wages 11	0.7	0.4	4.8	9.9	2.0	14.7	9.1	5.9	3.3	0.2	0.0	0.0	0.0
Taxes Paid 12	0.6	1.8	3.7	2.3	2.9	2.9	1.8	3.4	2.1	1.5	0.4	0.5	0.0
Interest Paid 13	43.0	9.6	22.7	32.4	13.7	20.9	9.2	28.6	40.0	65.4	46.1	40.2	50.7
Depreciation 14	0.9	1.0	0.4	5.4	0.6	1.2	1.0	1.0	2.4	14.0	6.3	•	0.0
Amortization and Depletion 15	0.4	0.2	1.8	•	0.5	0.0	2.9	1.4	0.5	0.1	0.2	0.8	0.0
Pensions and Other Deferred Comp. 16	0.0	•	0.0	•	0.9	0.2	0.2	0.1	0.2	0.0	•	•	3.5
Employee Benefits 17	2.0	2.2	5.2	2.0	0.7	0.9	0.9	0.4	0.2	0.0	0.0	0.0	•
Advertising 18	0.1	0.1	5.2	0.1	0.1	0.1	0.8	0.4	0.3	0.0	0.0	0.5	•
Other Expenses 19	16.9	26.4	98.5	48.1	44.0	79.9	75.6	43.4	15.4	34.9	7.6	10.3	10.9
Officers' Compensation 20	0.9	0.6	13.8	1.8	15.0	2.8	9.4	3.1	0.4	0.1	0.0	0.0	0.0
Operating Margin 21	34.3	57.7	•	19.5	•	•	6.7	34.7	•	•	39.4	48.2	34.8
Operating Margin Before Officers' Comp. 22	35.2	58.3	•	34.5	•	9.7	35.1	•	•	39.4	48.2	34.8	

Selected Average Balance Sheet ($ in Thousands)

Net Receivables 23	5605	0	2	33	156	65	1211	5762	3642	40668	56933	209946	1036602
Inventories 24	•	•	•	•	•	•	•	•	•	•	•	•	•
Net Property, Plant and Equipment 25	24	0	7	102	11	29	837	1190	295	549	57	2	0
Total Assets 26	32239	0	92	696	1932	6449	15724	35655	70054	164450	354737	1068261	6195538
Notes and Loans Payable 27	18002	0	50	227	1407	3515	5376	16515	23744	85111	168210	463001	3792050
All Other Liabilities 28	3952	0	23	92	121	792	2192	12402	7197	49035	37778	151174	686362
Net Worth 29	10285	0	19	377	404	2143	8155	6739	39113	30304	148749	454087	1717126

Selected Financial Ratios (Times to 1)

Current Ratio 30	0.5	•	4.5	3.4	2.4	1.7	1.9	2.9	1.2	1.1	1.1	0.7	0.4
Quick Ratio 31	0.4	•	3.7	1.7	2.2	1.1	1.4	2.3	0.8	1.0	1.1	0.6	0.4
Net Sales to Working Capital 32	•	•	1.9	1.4	0.7	1.2	1.1	0.3	1.1	1.0	2.6	•	•
Coverage Ratio 33	1.8	6.6	•	0.8	2.3	•	1.2	1.2	1.8	0.7	1.9	2.2	1.7
Total Asset Turnover 34	0.0	•	0.4	0.5	0.1	0.2	0.2	0.1	0.1	0.0	0.1	0.0	0.0
Inventory Turnover 35	•	•	•	•	•	•	•	•	•	•	•	•	•
Receivables Turnover 36	•	•	•	•	•	•	•	•	•	•	•	•	•
Total Liabilities to Net Worth 37	2.1	•	4.0	0.8	3.8	2.0	0.9	4.3	0.8	4.4	1.4	1.4	2.6
Current Assets to Working Capital 38	•	•	1.3	1.4	1.7	2.4	2.1	1.5	5.3	8.2	10.9	•	•
Current Liabilities to Working Capital 39	•	•	0.3	0.4	0.7	1.4	1.1	0.5	4.3	7.2	9.9	•	•
Working Capital to Net Sales 40	•	•	0.5	0.7	1.5	0.8	0.9	3.0	0.9	1.0	0.4	•	•
Inventory to Working Capital 41	•	•	•	•	•	•	•	0.0	0.1	0.0	0.0	•	•
Total Receipts to Cash Flow 42	2.2	2.3	5.5	3.5	2.1	2.4	2.0	3.0	3.6	22.2	2.2	1.7	2.2
Cost of Goods to Cash Flow 43	0.0	0.0	0.0	0.0	0.3	0.3	0.0	0.2	0.0	•	•	0.0	•
Cash Flow to Total Debt 44	0.0	•	0.1	0.3	0.1	0.1	0.2	0.0	0.0	0.0	0.0	0.0	0.0

Selected Financial Factors (in Percentages)

Debt Ratio 45	68.1	•	79.9	45.8	79.1	66.8	48.1	81.1	44.2	81.6	58.1	57.5	72.3
Return on Total Assets 46	2.6	•	•	13.2	4.8	•	•	3.2	3.9	2.3	4.9	3.2	2.1
Return on Equity Before Income Taxes 47	3.6	•	•	•	13.2	•	•	3.3	3.1	•	5.4	4.1	3.1
Return on Equity After Income Taxes 48	2.2	•	•	•	10.3	•	•	1.1	1.7	•	3.6	2.7	2.0
Profit Margin (Before Income Tax) 49	34.3	53.6	•	•	18.3	•	•	6.9	32.4	•	39.7	47.8	35.5
Profit Margin (After Income Tax) 50	21.5	34.6	•	•	14.3	•	•	2.3	18.0	•	26.0	31.6	23.1

Table II

Corporations with Net Income

OTHER FINANCIAL VEHICLES

MONEY AMOUNTS AND SIZE OF ASSETS IN THOUSANDS OF DOLLARS

Item Description for Accounting Period 7/04 Through 6/05	Total	Zero Assets	Under 500	500 to 1,000	1,000 to 5,000	5,000 to 10,000	10,000 to 25,000	25,000 to 50,000	50,000 to 100,000	100,000 to 250,000	250,000 to 500,000	500,000 to 2,500,000	2,500,000 and over
Number of Enterprises **1**	4966	1069	2887	0	521	52	54	24	11	15	28	73	0
Revenues ($ in Thousands)													
Net Sales **2**	11251432	758997	246905	0	259866	79541	241463	84557	77459	160490	605909	3087571	0
Interest **3**	7064398	123852	44723	0	15282	9310	16110	27101	29755	60834	516440	2460435	0
Rents **4**	9871	289	0	0	1202	2	1911	4577	1874	17	0	0	0
Royalties **5**	11432	2403	0	0	0	0	0	0	9028	0	0	0	0
Other Portfolio Income **6**	1200236	422403	18171	0	29776	2561	38679	30627	23029	53593	32166	300008	0
Other Receipts **7**	2965495	210050	184011	0	213606	67668	184763	22252	13773	4046	57303	327128	0
Total Receipts **8**	11251432	758997	246905	0	259866	79541	241463	84557	77459	160490	605909	3087571	0
Average Total Receipts **9**	2266	710	86	•	499	1530	4472	3523	7042	10699	21640	42295	•
Operating Costs/Operating Income (%)													
Cost of Operations **10**	0.1	0.1	•	•	•	•	2.2	•	0.5	•	•	0.0	•
Salaries and Wages **11**	0.6	0.0	4.8	•	0.1	15.5	8.2	2.8	3.9	0.5	0.0	0.0	•
Taxes Paid **12**	0.6	1.5	2.9	•	2.5	2.9	2.0	3.7	2.7	1.7	0.0	0.6	•
Interest Paid **13**	29.1	8.0	16.5	•	4.1	10.1	5.0	20.5	21.9	38.9	32.2	22.8	•
Depreciation **14**	0.1	1.0	0.3	•	0.2	1.2	0.9	1.7	0.5	0.3	0.3	•	•
Amortization and Depletion **15**	0.4	0.1	0.3	•	0.0	0.0	2.1	1.0	0.7	0.0	0.2	1.0	•
Pensions and Other Deferred Comp. **16**	0.0	•	•	•	1.1	0.1	0.2	0.0	0.3	0.0	•	•	•
Employee Benefits **17**	2.5	0.2	2.0	•	0.0	1.0	0.7	0.3	0.2	0.0	0.0	0.0	•
Advertising **18**	0.0	0.1	0.5	•	0.0	0.1	0.7	0.0	0.4	0.0	•	0.0	•
Other Expenses **19**	9.4	10.6	46.8	•	18.6	11.8	30.1	20.0	9.3	21.5	4.2	3.6	•
Officers' Compensation **20**	0.8	0.3	8.1	•	13.8	2.5	11.1	4.0	0.5	0.3	0.0	0.0	•
Operating Margin **21**	56.4	78.0	17.9	•	59.7	54.8	36.7	45.9	59.2	36.8	63.0	72.0	•
Operating Margin Before Officers' Comp. **22**	57.2	78.3	25.9	•	73.5	57.3	47.9	49.9	59.7	37.1	63.0	72.0	•

Selected Average Balance Sheet ($ in Thousands)

Net Receivables 23	13157	0	5	296	33	1878	5573	7664	27357	59929	255182	•
Inventories 24	•	•	•	•	•	•	•	•	•	•	•	•
Net Property, Plant and Equipment 25	29	0	6	13	35	417	2800	375	1685	45	0	•
Total Assets 26	60554		45	1642	6485	15615	34355	68503	165620	378252	1050399	•
Notes and Loans Payable 27	25004	0	12	501	2817	4193	11674	16793	77930	129159	309091	•
All Other Liabilities 28	8177	0	1	159	727	2210	4735	6709	52762	5102	111618	•
Net Worth 29	27373	0	32	983	2941	9212	17946	45001	34928	243990	629690	•

Selected Financial Ratios (Times to 1)

Current Ratio 30	0.8	•	31.2	•	7.4	6.4	1.9	2.1	1.8	1.3	2.3	1.3
Quick Ratio 31	0.7	•	28.4	•	7.2	1.6	1.4	1.5	1.6	0.8	2.2	1.1
Net Sales to Working Capital 32	•	•	3.8	•	0.8	1.0	2.3	0.6	1.2	0.7	0.5	0.6
Coverage Ratio 33	3.0	10.2	2.1	•	15.4	6.2	8.3	3.4	3.6	1.9	3.0	4.2
Total Asset Turnover 34	0.0	•	1.9	•	0.3	0.2	0.3	0.1	0.1	0.1	0.1	0.0
Inventory Turnover 35	•	•	•	•	•	•	•	•	•	•	•	•
Receivables Turnover 36	•	•	•	•	•	•	•	•	•	•	•	•
Total Liabilities to Net Worth 37	1.2	•	0.4	•	0.7	1.2	0.7	0.9	0.5	3.7	0.6	0.7
Current Assets to Working Capital 38	•	•	1.0	•	1.2	1.2	2.1	1.9	2.3	4.1	1.8	5.0
Current Liabilities to Working Capital 39	•	•	0.0	•	0.2	0.2	1.1	0.9	1.3	3.1	0.8	4.0
Working Capital to Net Sales 40	•	•	0.3	•	1.2	1.0	0.4	1.7	0.8	1.5	2.2	1.7
Inventory to Working Capital 41	•	•	•	•	•	•	•	•	•	•	0.0	•
Total Receipts to Cash Flow 42	1.7	2.1	2.1	•	1.5	1.6	1.8	2.8	2.4	3.4	1.6	1.3
Cost of Goods to Cash Flow 43	0.0	0.0	•	•	•	•	0.0	•	0.0	•	•	•
Cash Flow to Total Debt 44	0.0	•	3.1	•	0.5	0.3	0.4	0.1	0.1	0.0	0.1	0.1

Selected Financial Factors (in Percentages)

Debt Ratio 45	54.8	•	28.9	•	40.2	54.6	41.0	47.8	34.3	78.9	35.5	40.1
Return on Total Assets 46	3.2	•	65.4	•	19.1	14.7	11.8	7.1	8.2	4.9	5.5	3.8
Return on Equity Before Income Taxes 47	4.7	•	47.8	•	29.9	27.2	17.6	9.5	9.1	11.3	5.6	4.8
Return on Equity After Income Taxes 48	3.3	•	44.8	•	27.5	24.2	15.0	7.6	6.2	8.7	3.8	3.4
Profit Margin (Before Income Tax) 49	57.0	73.8	17.8	•	58.9	52.4	36.2	48.4	57.9	36.8	63.4	72.0
Profit Margin (After Income Tax) 50	39.7	55.3	16.7	•	54.3	46.5	30.8	38.5	39.5	28.5	42.4	50.4

Table I

Corporations with and without Net Income

LESSORS OF BUILDINGS

MONEY AMOUNTS AND SIZE OF ASSETS IN THOUSANDS OF DOLLARS

Item Description for Accounting Period 7/04 Through 6/05	Total	Zero Assets	Under 500	500 to 1,000	1,000 to 5,000	5,000 to 10,000	10,000 to 25,000	25,000 to 50,000	50,000 to 100,000	100,000 to 250,000	250,000 to 500,000	500,000 to 2,500,000	2,500,000 and over
Number of Enterprises 1	215964	17422	118866	35895	37125	4030	1868	470	157	87	24	16	3
Revenues ($ in Thousands)													
Net Sales 2	36530060	1928275	4158101	2733950	9538925	3608219	3657071	2235429	1459541	2102072	1485505	2299801	1323173
Interest 3	652352	40168	42933	29421	95955	58180	57262	46199	35798	44476	60087	71084	70789
Rents 4	250994	6116	22826	11342	33902	7035	22132	8114	30435	13236	9	63901	31946
Royalties 5	50359	1	2053	138	8375	305	19583	19339	150	78	336	0	0
Other Portfolio Income 6	3200882	669420	426160	213010	564852	221948	176518	130565	189285	163159	156958	116031	172975
Other Receipts 7	32375473	1212570	3664129	2480039	8835841	3320751	3381576	2031212	1203873	1881123	1268115	2048785	1047463
Total Receipts 8	36530060	1928275	4158101	2733950	9538925	3608219	3657071	2235429	1459541	2102072	1485505	2299801	1323173
Average Total Receipts 9	169	111	35	76	257	895	1958	4756	9296	24162	61896	143738	441058
Operating Costs/Operating Income (%)													
Cost of Operations 10	13.2	6.0	12.8	4.4	11.5	10.0	13.2	10.8	13.1	28.0	23.6	26.3	9.3
Salaries and Wages 11	9.5	2.3	6.4	7.3	12.3	11.7	10.1	11.4	8.9	8.9	8.1	9.8	6.5
Taxes Paid 12	10.8	10.0	9.9	13.8	12.1	15.5	14.1	11.9	9.9	6.2	6.1	3.1	3.4
Interest Paid 13	11.4	11.2	5.8	12.8	9.7	12.7	15.0	12.5	14.2	12.6	11.1	14.6	13.8
Depreciation 14	9.5	9.3	6.9	9.7	8.8	11.8	12.6	10.7	10.9	8.6	7.7	12.0	3.2
Amortization and Depletion 15	0.6	1.0	0.2	1.0	0.5	0.6	0.8	0.7	0.9	1.2	0.6	0.6	0.2
Pensions and Other Deferred Comp. 16	0.3	0.1	0.1	0.1	0.3	0.4	0.3	0.4	0.3	0.2	0.6	0.0	0.0
Employee Benefits 17	1.2	0.2	1.2	1.2	1.3	1.8	1.5	1.5	1.2	0.6	1.1	0.6	0.3
Advertising 18	0.5	0.3	1.0	0.2	0.6	0.5	0.3	0.4	0.5	0.7	1.0	0.4	0.5
Other Expenses 19	32.7	35.6	47.7	34.3	35.2	28.3	31.1	32.8	26.4	23.8	27.3	26.9	14.2
Officers' Compensation 20	2.8	0.7	3.2	7.8	3.1	3.2	2.2	2.4	1.7	2.1	1.4	1.0	0.9
Operating Margin 21	7.4	23.3	4.8	7.3	4.5	3.4	•	4.6	12.0	7.1	11.5	4.5	47.6
Operating Margin Before Officers' Comp. 22	10.2	24.1	8.1	15.1	7.6	6.6	1.0	7.0	13.7	9.2	12.8	5.5	48.6

Selected Average Balance Sheet ($ in Thousands)

Net Receivables 23	41	0	4	19	56	180	393	1336	2846	7928	11022	58490	393124
Inventories 24	•	•	•	•	•	•	•	•	•	•	•	•	•
Net Property, Plant and Equipment 25	764	0	129	517	1458	4629	10240	21639	41605	84845	133829	438233	1645592
Total Assets 26	1168	0	176	701	2026	6792	15050	33951	68512	150843	306910	852426	4864226
Notes and Loans Payable 27	726	0	112	518	1393	4334	9699	18807	39996	85799	149026	483714	1204575
All Other Liabilities 28	95	0	11	31	133	290	1013	3285	5507	23583	34501	142032	853906
Net Worth 29	347	0	53	152	500	2168	4338	11860	23009	41461	123383	226681	2805745

Selected Financial Ratios (Times to 1)

Current Ratio 30	2.0	•	2.1	2.3	1.8	2.3	1.8	2.2	1.8	2.1	2.1	0.9	3.8
Quick Ratio 31	1.4	•	1.6	1.8	1.3	1.9	1.2	1.7	1.3	1.7	1.3	0.8	1.0
Net Sales to Working Capital 32	1.9	•	2.6	1.4	2.1	1.7	2.0	1.5	1.9	1.8	2.1	•	0.4
Coverage Ratio 33	1.6	3.1	1.8	1.6	1.5	1.3	0.9	1.3	1.8	1.7	2.0	1.3	4.4
Total Asset Turnover 34	0.1	•	0.2	0.1	0.1	0.1	0.1	0.1	0.1	0.2	0.2	0.2	0.1
Inventory Turnover 35	•	•	•	•	•	•	•	•	•	•	•	•	•
Receivables Turnover 36	•	•	•	•	•	•	•	•	•	•	•	•	•
Total Liabilities to Net Worth 37	2.4	•	2.3	3.6	3.1	2.1	2.5	1.9	2.0	2.6	1.5	2.8	0.7
Current Assets to Working Capital 38	2.0	•	1.9	1.8	2.3	1.8	2.3	1.8	2.2	1.9	1.9	•	1.4
Current Liabilities to Working Capital 39	1.0	•	0.9	0.8	1.3	0.8	1.3	0.8	1.2	0.9	0.9	•	0.4
Working Capital to Net Sales 40	0.5	•	0.4	0.7	0.5	0.6	0.5	0.7	0.5	0.5	0.5	•	2.5
Inventory to Working Capital 41	0.0	•	•	•	0.0	0.0	0.0	0.0	0.0	0.0	0.0	•	0.0
Total Receipts to Cash Flow 42	4.3	3.9	3.7	3.9	4.3	4.8	5.3	3.8	4.4	6.0	4.2	6.5	2.2
Cost of Goods to Cash Flow 43	0.6	0.2	0.5	0.2	0.5	0.5	0.7	0.4	0.6	1.7	1.0	1.7	0.2
Cash Flow to Total Debt 44	0.0	0.0	0.1	0.0	0.0	0.0	0.0	0.1	0.0	0.0	0.1	0.0	0.1

Selected Financial Factors (in Percentages)

Debt Ratio 45	70.3	•	69.9	78.3	75.3	68.1	71.2	65.1	66.4	72.5	73.4	59.8	42.3
Return on Total Assets 46	2.7	•	2.1	2.2	1.8	2.1	1.8	2.3	3.5	3.5	4.5	3.2	5.6
Return on Equity Before Income Taxes 47	3.6	•	3.2	3.6	2.3	1.3	•	1.7	4.8	5.5	5.7	2.9	7.5
Return on Equity After Income Taxes 48	2.1	•	2.0	2.7	1.3	0.4	•	0.4	3.0	3.4	3.9	1.2	6.2
Profit Margin (Before Income Tax) 49	7.4	23.3	4.8	7.2	4.4	3.2	•	4.2	12.0	9.4	11.4	4.5	47.6
Profit Margin (After Income Tax) 50	4.4	14.1	3.0	5.4	2.5	1.1	•	0.9	7.4	5.8	7.7	1.9	39.3

Table II

Corporations with Net Income

LESSORS OF BUILDINGS

MONEY AMOUNTS AND SIZE OF ASSETS IN THOUSANDS OF DOLLARS

Item Description for Accounting Period 7/04 Through 6/05	Total	Zero Assets	Under 500	500 to 1,000	1,000 to 5,000	5,000 to 10,000	10,000 to 25,000	25,000 to 50,000	50,000 to 100,000	100,000 to 250,000	250,000 to 500,000	500,000 to 2,500,000	2,500,000 and over
Number of Enterprises **1**	48669	4748	24280	8255	9204	1269	570	190	77	49	14	9	3
Revenues ($ in Thousands)													
Net Sales **2**	23475379	1545025	2943380	1883262	6265773	1875571	1919655	1300410	1032964	1187804	797901	1400462	1323173
Interest **3**	491285	31885	30911	18547	71675	33451	38115	29052	29655	36507	41025	59673	70789
Rents **4**	216703	5735	22600	4755	14485	6365	16513	7183	30273	12940	9	63901	31946
Royalties **5**	14699	1	50	138	4877	305	8729	90	96	78	336	0	0
Other Portfolio Income **6**	2968662	655548	361698	189493	538961	200427	157358	117465	174518	140984	155496	103736	172975
Other Receipts **7**	19784030	851856	2528121	1670329	5635775	1635023	1698940	1146620	798422	997295	601035	1173152	1047463
Total Receipts **8**	23475379	1545025	2943380	1883262	6265773	1875571	1919655	1300410	1032964	1187804	797901	1400462	1323173
Average Total Receipts **9**	482	325	121	228	681	1478	3368	6844	13415	24241	56993	155607	441058
Operating Costs/Operating Income (%)													
Cost of Operations **10**	11.7	7.2	12.3	5.9	12.9	2.4	17.6	10.7	9.9	17.0	0.5	28.9	9.3
Salaries and Wages **11**	8.2	1.4	6.1	8.2	11.5	10.6	6.9	8.9	6.7	7.0	5.0	9.2	6.5
Taxes Paid **12**	7.5	6.8	7.0	9.8	7.2	11.7	8.1	8.8	8.4	7.0	7.4	3.9	3.4
Interest Paid **13**	8.5	6.8	3.5	9.0	5.4	11.4	10.1	9.3	12.2	14.1	11.6	12.3	13.8
Depreciation **14**	6.6	6.5	4.1	6.9	4.8	8.4	8.5	8.1	8.9	9.7	8.3	11.7	3.2
Amortization and Depletion **15**	0.5	0.9	0.1	0.9	0.4	0.5	0.6	0.5	0.8	0.8	1.0	0.4	0.2
Pensions and Other Deferred Comp. **16**	0.2	0.1	0.1	0.2	0.3	0.5	0.2	0.4	0.2	0.1	0.1	0.1	0.0
Employee Benefits **17**	0.8	0.1	1.3	1.3	0.9	1.3	0.9	1.0	0.7	0.5	0.2	0.3	0.3
Advertising **18**	0.6	0.3	1.0	0.2	0.7	0.8	0.3	0.3	0.5	0.6	0.5	0.2	0.5
Other Expenses **19**	28.1	26.3	39.4	25.4	33.1	26.3	24.1	26.8	21.6	21.3	34.6	16.2	14.2
Officers' Compensation **20**	3.2	0.5	3.3	9.5	3.4	4.4	2.9	2.6	1.5	1.6	2.0	0.9	0.9
Operating Margin **21**	24.1	43.2	21.9	22.7	19.6	21.7	19.8	22.5	28.6	20.4	28.5	15.9	47.6
Operating Margin Before Officers' Comp. **22**	27.3	43.7	25.2	32.2	23.0	26.1	22.7	25.1	30.1	22.0	30.5	16.8	48.6

Selected Average Balance Sheet ($ in Thousands)

Net Receivables 23	91	0	6	23	93	143	500	1474	2874	6976	13260	62019	393124
Inventories 24	•	•	•	•	•	•	•	•	•	•	•	•	•
Net Property, Plant and Equipment 25	991	0	101	458	1153	4311	9063	19804	39208	81944	131488	353495	1645592
Total Assets 26	1845	0	171	693	1969	6861	15294	33651	69927	145460	328013	699238	4864226
Notes and Loans Payable 27	877	0	81	453	992	3464	8320	16695	37235	75646	146753	366298	1204575
All Other Liabilities 28	204	0	15	39	207	307	1198	2526	6951	15850	32261	161074	853906
Net Worth 29	765	0	75	202	771	3089	5775	14430	25742	53964	148999	171866	2805745

Selected Financial Ratios (Times to 1)

Current Ratio 30	2.4	•	2.6	2.9	2.4	2.2	2.0	2.6	1.8	2.6	2.3	1.2	3.8
Quick Ratio 31	1.6	•	2.1	2.6	1.9	1.8	1.4	2.0	1.4	2.0	1.5	0.9	1.0
Net Sales to Working Capital 32	2.2	•	4.6	3.0	2.8	2.7	2.3	1.7	2.5	1.7	1.6	8.5	0.4
Coverage Ratio 33	3.9	7.4	7.3	3.5	4.6	2.9	2.9	3.4	3.3	2.7	3.5	2.3	4.4
Total Asset Turnover 34	0.3	•	0.7	0.3	0.3	0.2	0.2	0.2	0.2	0.2	0.2	0.2	0.1
Inventory Turnover 35	•	•	•	•	•	•	•	•	•	•	•	•	•
Receivables Turnover 36	•	•	•	•	•	•	•	•	•	•	•	•	•
Total Liabilities to Net Worth 37	1.4	•	1.3	2.4	1.6	1.2	1.6	1.3	1.7	1.7	1.2	3.1	0.7
Current Assets to Working Capital 38	1.7	•	1.6	1.5	1.7	1.8	2.0	1.6	2.2	1.6	1.8	7.1	1.4
Current Liabilities to Working Capital 39	0.7	•	0.6	0.5	0.7	0.8	1.0	0.6	1.2	0.6	0.8	6.1	0.4
Working Capital to Net Sales 40	0.5	•	0.2	0.3	0.4	0.4	0.4	0.6	0.4	0.6	0.6	0.1	2.5
Inventory to Working Capital 41	0.0	•	0.0	0.0	0.0	0.0	0.0	0.0	0.0	0.0	0.0	0.1	0.0
Total Receipts to Cash Flow 42	3.0	3.0	2.8	3.0	3.1	3.0	3.2	2.8	3.2	3.8	2.5	4.7	2.2
Cost of Goods to Cash Flow 43	0.4	0.2	0.3	0.2	0.4	0.1	0.6	0.3	0.3	0.7	0.0	1.4	0.2
Cash Flow to Total Debt 44	0.1	•	0.4	0.2	0.2	0.2	0.1	0.1	0.1	0.1	0.1	0.1	0.1

Selected Financial Factors (in Percentages)

Debt Ratio 45	58.6	•	56.2	70.9	60.8	55.0	62.2	57.1	63.2	62.9	54.6	75.4	42.3
Return on Total Assets 46	8.5	•	17.9	10.4	8.6	7.1	6.5	6.4	7.8	6.4	6.9	6.3	5.6
Return on Equity Before Income Taxes 47	15.3	•	35.3	25.6	17.2	10.3	11.4	10.6	14.8	11.0	10.9	14.3	7.5
Return on Equity After Income Taxes 48	12.4	•	31.1	22.6	14.7	8.3	8.9	7.9	11.5	8.2	8.2	10.4	6.2
Profit Margin (Before Income Tax) 49	24.3	43.1	21.9	22.6	21.5	19.6	22.3	28.4	28.4	24.6	28.4	15.8	47.6
Profit Margin (After Income Tax) 50	19.6	31.6	19.3	20.0	16.6	17.3	15.3	16.7	22.1	18.2	21.5	11.5	39.3

Table I

Corporations with and without Net Income

LESSORS OF MINIWAREHOUSES, SELF-STORAGE, OTHER REAL ESTATE

MONEY AMOUNTS AND SIZE OF ASSETS IN THOUSANDS OF DOLLARS

Item Description for Accounting Period 7/04 Through 6/05	Total	Zero Assets	Under 500	500 to 1,000	1,000 to 5,000	5,000 to 10,000	10,000 to 25,000	25,000 to 50,000	50,000 to 100,000	100,000 to 250,000	250,000 to 500,000	500,000 to 2,500,000	2,500,000 and over
Number of Enterprises **1**	59828	7383	35974	7557	7319	874	487	124	57	31	12	8	0
Revenues ($ in Thousands)													
Net Sales **2**	11468691	625761	2306800	974077	2437074	701078	925395	617226	723786	499114	564627	1093752	0
Interest **3**	367997	16760	14672	22525	36503	19369	23036	17558	25757	34798	65342	91678	0
Rents **4**	165693	1845	2559	1475	7835	1896	10167	4942	12815	1209	0	120951	0
Royalties **5**	55118	0	401	4964	6602	7279	24733	2187	8953	0	0	0	0
Other Portfolio Income **6**	1530258	241083	132403	217455	337416	74974	101806	46040	72847	28065	34821	243351	0
Other Receipts **7**	9349625	366073	2156765	727658	2048718	597560	765653	546499	603414	435042	464464	637772	0
Total Receipts **8**	11468691	625761	2306800	974077	2437074	701078	925395	617226	723786	499114	564627	1093752	0
Average Total Receipts **9**	192	85	64	129	333	802	1900	4978	12698	16100	47052	136719	•
Operating Costs/Operating Income (%)													
Cost of Operations **10**	6.3	7.0	0.9	4.3	7.6	12.6	12.0	3.4	4.9	5.2	8.9	8.8	•
Salaries and Wages **11**	10.9	7.7	19.2	4.0	9.9	6.0	13.3	19.0	8.3	12.0	5.1	4.3	•
Taxes Paid **12**	6.4	6.7	5.9	5.8	8.0	7.6	6.3	6.1	3.8	6.7	2.6	7.2	•
Interest Paid **13**	10.2	3.7	3.8	6.5	7.6	11.4	12.7	12.2	8.6	23.0	12.6	26.1	•
Depreciation **14**	7.3	2.9	4.8	4.8	7.0	7.5	8.2	9.4	7.2	12.0	8.7	13.4	•
Amortization and Depletion **15**	0.6	0.1	0.0	0.1	0.2	0.8	0.9	1.3	0.6	1.4	0.7	1.8	•
Pensions and Other Deferred Comp. **16**	1.1	0.0	0.8	0.1	3.6	1.3	0.4	0.2	0.2	0.5	0.1	0.1	•
Employee Benefits **17**	0.8	0.6	1.4	0.5	0.3	0.8	1.0	1.7	0.7	0.8	0.1	0.9	•
Advertising **18**	1.0	0.1	1.5	1.9	1.0	0.2	1.1	0.8	1.0	0.4	0.8	0.4	•
Other Expenses **19**	37.9	50.0	43.8	30.0	35.4	35.5	28.8	28.8	43.8	31.9	60.5	33.0	•
Officers' Compensation **20**	6.2	0.2	11.8	1.5	7.3	11.3	3.6	6.4	2.7	2.8	4.8	3.3	•
Operating Margin **21**	11.3	21.1	6.0	40.5	11.9	5.0	11.7	10.6	18.3	3.3	•	0.8	•
Operating Margin Before Officers' Comp. **22**	17.5	21.2	17.8	42.1	19.3	16.3	15.2	17.1	21.1	6.1	•	4.1	•

Selected Average Balance Sheet ($ in Thousands)

Net Receivables 23	49	•	0	4	6	83	294	544	1095	4559	7976	65439	19537
Inventories 24	•	•	•	•	•	•	•	•	•	•	•	•	•
Net Property, Plant and Equipment 25	521	0	106	431	1045	3317	6798	14341	27517	64430	112182	441052	
Total Assets 26	1055	0	160	690	1870	7231	15446	34455	68048	148564	379392	914362	
Notes and Loans Payable 27	552	0	84	371	1141	3863	8533	17939	28089	79133	109240	471217	
All Other Liabilities 28	121	0	21	41	186	821	1914	3456	13412	10746	78036	86952	
Net Worth 29	382	0	55	278	543	2547	4999	13060	26548	58685	192116	356193	

Selected Financial Ratios (Times to 1)

Current Ratio 30	2.1	•	1.4	2.7	1.5	3.7	1.5	1.5	1.9	1.5	2.7	2.9	4.4
Quick Ratio 31	1.2	•	0.9	1.5	1.0	1.9	0.9	1.2	1.1	2.0	2.0	1.8	
Net Sales to Working Capital 32	1.6	•	7.8	1.3	3.0	0.7	1.7	1.5	2.4	1.3	0.6	0.7	
Coverage Ratio 33	2.1	6.7	2.5	7.2	2.6	1.4	1.9	1.8	3.1	1.1	0.6	1.0	
Total Asset Turnover 34	0.2	•	0.4	0.2	0.2	0.1	0.1	0.1	0.2	0.1	0.1	0.1	
Inventory Turnover 35	•	•	•	•	•	•	•	•	•	•	•	•	
Receivables Turnover 36	•	•	•	•	•	•	•	•	•	•	•	•	
Total Liabilities to Net Worth 37	1.8	•	1.9	1.5	2.4	1.8	2.1	1.6	1.6	1.5	1.0	1.6	
Current Assets to Working Capital 38	1.9	•	3.8	1.6	3.0	1.4	2.9	2.2	2.9	1.6	1.5	1.3	
Current Liabilities to Working Capital 39	0.9	•	2.8	0.6	2.0	0.4	1.9	1.2	1.9	0.6	0.5	0.3	
Working Capital to Net Sales 40	0.6	•	0.1	0.8	0.3	1.4	0.6	0.7	0.4	0.8	1.6	1.5	
Inventory to Working Capital 41	0.0	•	•	0.0	0.0	•	0.0	0.0	0.0	0.0	0.0	0.0	
Total Receipts to Cash Flow 42	3.4	10.1	3.1	2.5	3.1	4.4	3.8	4.1	2.1	4.0	2.0	12.1	
Cost of Goods to Cash Flow 43	0.2	0.7	0.0	0.1	0.2	0.6	0.5	0.1	0.1	0.2	0.2	1.1	
Cash Flow to Total Debt 44	0.1	•	0.2	0.1	0.1	0.0	0.0	0.1	0.1	0.0	0.1	0.0	

Selected Financial Factors (in Percentages)

Debt Ratio 45	63.8	•	65.4	59.8	71.0	64.8	67.6	62.1	61.0	60.5	49.4	61.0	
Return on Total Assets 46	3.9	•	3.9	8.8	3.5	1.8	3.0	3.3	5.0	2.9	1.0	4.0	
Return on Equity Before Income Taxes 47	5.6	•	6.8	18.8	7.3	1.4	4.3	3.9	8.7	0.9	•	0.3	
Return on Equity After Income Taxes 48	3.7	•	5.7	15.8	5.1	3.0	2.6	6.5	0.1	1.6	•	0.3	
Profit Margin (Before Income Tax) 49	11.1	20.9	5.9	40.5	11.9	4.4	11.3	10.3	18.2	3.3	•	0.8	
Profit Margin (After Income Tax) 50	7.3	10.6	4.9	34.1	8.4	•	7.8	6.8	13.7	0.2	•		

Table II

Corporations with Net Income

LESSORS OF MINIWAREHOUSES, SELF-STORAGE, OTHER REAL ESTATE

MONEY AMOUNTS AND SIZE OF ASSETS IN THOUSANDS OF DOLLARS

Item Description for Accounting Period 7/04 Through 6/05	Total	Zero Assets	Under 500	500 to 1,000	1,000 to 5,000	5,000 to 10,000	10,000 to 25,000	25,000 to 50,000	50,000 to 100,000	100,000 to 250,000	250,000 to 500,000	500,000 to 2,500,000	2,500,000 and over
Number of Enterprises **1**	21978	2509	13408	3170	2337	258	183	58	32	15	0	0	0
Revenues ($ in Thousands)													
Net Sales **2**	8191886	549122	1793897	913552	1722123	534265	689047	454302	594029	359623	0	0	0
Interest **3**	184878	14111	10852	15757	24219	17597	16230	14861	17521	8395	0	0	0
Rents **4**	31481	1606	0	1475	3740	1607	7775	1255	12815	1209	0	0	0
Royalties **5**	53148	0	7	4964	6602	7279	24452	890	8953	0	0	0	0
Other Portfolio Income **6**	1376684	235771	127088	217404	317611	67052	94209	39510	71585	17845	0	0	0
Other Receipts **7**	6545695	297634	1655950	673952	1369951	440730	546381	397786	483155	332174	0	0	0
Total Receipts **8**	8191886	549122	1793897	913552	1722123	534265	689047	454302	594029	359623	0	0	0
Average Total Receipts **9**	373	219	134	288	737	2071	3765	7833	18563	23975	·	·	·
Operating Costs/Operating Income (%)													
Cost of Operations **10**	4.8	1.3	1.2	3.7	7.9	13.5	11.3	1.7	1.4	7.2	·	·	·
Salaries and Wages **11**	8.8	1.2	15.1	3.9	6.9	3.2	11.8	19.0	7.4	13.8	·	·	·
Taxes Paid **12**	5.6	5.7	5.6	5.4	4.8	5.9	5.0	6.3	4.0	7.3	·	·	·
Interest Paid **13**	5.6	3.4	2.7	6.4	6.0	6.6	8.4	8.7	5.7	12.1	·	·	·
Depreciation **14**	4.4	2.0	2.9	4.1	3.4	3.9	5.1	6.3	4.6	12.4	·	·	·
Amortization and Depletion **15**	0.3	0.1	0.0	0.2	0.2	0.4	0.7	0.3	0.6	0.7	·	·	·
Pensions and Other Deferred Comp. **16**	0.4	·	1.0	·	0.3	1.1	0.3	0.2	0.2	0.6	·	·	·
Employee Benefits **17**	0.8	0.5	1.6	0.5	0.4	0.4	0.8	2.2	0.2	1.0	·	·	·
Advertising **18**	0.8	0.1	0.9	2.0	0.7	0.2	0.6	0.8	0.8	0.4	·	·	·
Other Expenses **19**	29.5	19.6	32.6	27.9	32.5	20.9	18.8	21.8	45.7	22.3	·	·	·
Officers' Compensation **20**	4.6	0.0	11.4	1.1	3.5	3.6	2.3	7.0	2.2	3.2	·	·	·
Operating Margin **21**	34.4	66.0	25.0	45.0	33.5	40.4	34.8	25.7	27.1	19.0	·	·	·
Operating Margin Before Officers' Comp. **22**	39.0	66.0	36.4	46.1	37.0	44.0	37.2	32.8	29.3	22.1	·	·	·

Selected Average Balance Sheet ($ in Thousands)

Net Receivables 23	47	0	8	11	42	720	601	1969	5508	8915
Inventories 24	•	•	•	•	•	•	•	•	•	•
Net Property, Plant and Equipment 25	426	0	101	314	817	2167	5264	10964	22356	72411
Total Assets 26	1078	0	161	679	1946	6665	15293	34133	67416	152125
Notes and Loans Payable 27	392	0	51	215	995	2494	6614	14268	20973	72064
All Other Liabilities 28	118	0	19	55	246	1125	2157	3353	10263	13559
Net Worth 29	568	0	91	409	706	3046	6521	16511	36180	66502

Selected Financial Ratios (Times to 1)

Current Ratio 30	2.7	•	1.5	4.2	2.4	3.4	1.8	2.4	1.9	2.0
Quick Ratio 31	1.6	•	1.3	2.7	1.3	2.7	1.2	1.7	1.3	1.5
Net Sales to Working Capital 32	1.9	•	10.9	1.5	2.8	1.4	2.0	1.5	2.2	1.9
Coverage Ratio 33	7.2	20.6	10.2	8.0	6.6	7.0	5.1	3.9	5.7	2.6
Total Asset Turnover 34	0.3	•	0.8	0.4	0.4	0.3	0.2	0.2	0.3	0.2
Inventory Turnover 35	•	•	•	•	•	•	•	•	•	•
Receivables Turnover 36	•	•	•	•	•	•	•	•	•	•
Total Liabilities to Net Worth 37	0.9	•	0.8	0.7	1.8	1.2	1.3	1.1	0.9	1.3
Current Assets to Working Capital 38	1.6	•	3.0	1.3	1.7	1.4	2.2	1.7	2.1	2.0
Current Liabilities to Working Capital 39	0.6	•	2.0	0.3	0.7	0.4	1.2	0.7	1.1	1.0
Working Capital to Net Sales 40	0.5	•	0.1	0.6	0.4	0.7	0.5	0.6	0.5	0.5
Inventory to Working Capital 41	0.0	•	•	0.1	0.1	•	0.0	0.0	0.0	0.0
Total Receipts to Cash Flow 42	2.3	2.4	2.4	2.0	2.2	2.0	2.6	3.1	1.7	3.1
Cost of Goods to Cash Flow 43	0.1	0.0	0.0	0.1	0.2	0.3	0.3	0.1	0.0	0.2
Cash Flow to Total Debt 44	0.3	•	0.8	0.4	0.3	0.3	0.2	0.1	0.3	0.1

Selected Financial Factors (in Percentages)

Debt Ratio 45	47.3	•	43.4	39.8	63.7	54.3	57.4	51.6	46.3	56.3
Return on Total Assets 46	13.8	•	23.0	21.8	14.9	14.4	10.6	7.9	9.0	4.9
Return on Equity Before Income Taxes 47	22.5	•	36.7	31.7	34.9	27.0	20.0	12.2	13.9	6.8
Return on Equity After Income Taxes 48	19.0	•	34.9	26.9	29.7	22.8	17.2	9.9	11.0	5.3
Profit Margin (Before Income Tax) 49	34.3	66.0	24.9	45.0	33.4	39.7	34.6	25.6	27.0	18.9
Profit Margin (After Income Tax) 50	28.9	54.3	23.7	38.1	28.5	33.5	29.9	20.9	21.5	14.7

Table I

Corporations with and without Net Income

OFFICES OF REAL ESTATE AGENTS AND BROKERS

MONEY AMOUNTS AND SIZE OF ASSETS IN THOUSANDS OF DOLLARS

Item Description for Accounting Period 7/04 Through 6/05	Total	Zero Assets	Under 500	500 to 1,000	1,000 to 5,000	5,000 to 10,000	10,000 to 25,000	25,000 to 50,000	50,000 to 100,000	100,000 to 250,000	250,000 to 500,000	500,000 to 2,500,000	2,500,000 and over
Number of Enterprises **1**	97035	15957	75324	3096	2263	251	89	26	13	10	0	6	0
Revenues ($ in Thousands)													
Net Sales **2**	59232010	1279244	32103600	3990145	10211021	1302848	2105191	1235935	1353651	1248548	0	4401828	0
Interest **3**	183615	1867	16148	10024	25194	8191	6765	4684	4294	22930	0	83518	0
Rents **4**	304759	1961	29524	7782	56013	12963	11412	1152	66	16840	0	167047	0
Royalties **5**	6080	640	0	0	9	0	0	0	669	0	0	4762	0
Other Portfolio Income **6**	257831	61306	17384	14812	49176	18439	2724	802	592	25149	0	67452	0
Other Receipts **7**	58479725	1213470	32040544	3957527	10080629	1263255	2084290	1229297	1348030	1183629	0	4079049	0
Total Receipts **8**	59232010	1279244	32103600	3990145	10211021	1302848	2105191	1235935	1353651	1248548	0	4401828	0
Average Total Receipts **9**	610	80	426	1289	4512	5191	23654	47536	104127	124855	·	733638	·
Operating Costs/Operating Income (%)													
Cost of Operations **10**	16.8	1.7	15.3	4.9	18.9	31.5	40.7	26.9	42.9	54.6	·	0.5	·
Salaries and Wages **11**	28.3	26.6	23.6	23.8	38.5	30.5	25.3	29.4	12.4	10.2	·	54.1	·
Taxes Paid **12**	1.7	1.4	1.4	2.1	1.4	2.1	1.5	1.9	1.5	1.6	·	4.8	·
Interest Paid **13**	0.9	0.9	0.3	0.8	0.8	3.4	1.2	1.0	0.9	2.2	·	4.0	·
Depreciation **14**	1.1	1.0	0.9	1.0	0.7	1.7	1.4	1.5	2.0	1.8	·	1.9	·
Amortization and Depletion **15**	0.2	0.5	0.0	0.1	0.1	0.1	1.3	0.2	0.2	0.1	·	1.0	·
Pensions and Other Deferred Comp. **16**	1.0	0.2	1.5	1.1	0.4	0.3	0.1	0.1	0.3	0.6	·	0.1	·
Employee Benefits **17**	0.6	0.2	0.5	0.9	0.7	0.9	0.6	0.5	0.9	0.4	·	1.5	·
Advertising **18**	3.4	2.5	4.0	5.8	2.3	2.0	3.1	2.4	3.0	2.1	·	0.9	·
Other Expenses **19**	27.6	30.6	30.3	42.0	22.6	16.9	13.8	22.7	19.2	11.1	·	24.0	·
Officers' Compensation **20**	8.3	10.0	11.3	9.3	4.9	3.1	2.0	3.8	5.0	1.1	·	2.0	·
Operating Margin **21**	10.1	24.3	10.7	8.4	8.7	7.4	9.0	9.6	11.8	14.1	·	5.5	·
Operating Margin Before Officers' Comp. **22**	18.4	34.4	22.0	17.6	13.6	10.5	11.0	13.4	16.7	15.3	·	7.4	·

Selected Average Balance Sheet ($ in Thousands)

Net Receivables 23	35	•	3	48	128	788	1622	4190	2523	33103	322488
Inventories 24	•	0	•	•	•	•	•	•	•	•	•
Net Property, Plant and Equipment 25	63	0	21	212	373	3148	4171	5360	13159	22459	216401
Total Assets 26	301	0	77	743	1971	7670	15064	33923	72174	173399	1627837
Notes and Loans Payable 27	116	0	36	274	1029	4441	7956	15259	23643	40521	401615
All Other Liabilities 28	85	0	15	144	411	771	3228	6354	13784	36763	750500
Net Worth 29	100	0	25	325	531	2459	3880	12310	34746	96114	475722

Selected Financial Ratios (Times to 1)

Current Ratio 30	1.5	•	1.9	2.0	2.3	1.2	1.4	1.7	1.2	2.8	1.0
Quick Ratio 31	1.1	•	1.5	1.3	1.4	0.7	0.9	0.9	0.6	2.2	0.8
Net Sales to Working Capital 32	13.5	•	22.7	8.5	8.1	11.2	12.5	6.2	25.6	1.7	•
Coverage Ratio 33	12.8	26.9	42.3	12.1	11.9	3.2	8.2	10.5	14.1	7.3	2.4
Total Asset Turnover 34	2.0	•	5.5	1.7	2.3	0.7	1.6	1.4	1.4	0.7	0.5
Inventory Turnover 35	•	•	•	•	•	•	•	•	•	•	•
Receivables Turnover 36	•	•	•	•	•	•	•	•	•	•	•
Total Liabilities to Net Worth 37	2.0	•	2.0	1.3	2.7	2.1	2.9	1.8	1.1	0.8	2.4
Current Assets to Working Capital 38	2.9	•	2.1	2.0	1.8	5.2	3.6	2.4	6.9	1.5	•
Current Liabilities to Working Capital 39	1.9	•	1.1	1.0	0.8	4.2	2.6	1.4	5.9	0.5	•
Working Capital to Net Sales 40	0.1	•	0.0	0.1	0.1	0.1	0.1	0.2	0.0	0.6	•
Inventory to Working Capital 41	0.0	•	•	0.0	0.0	0.0	0.0	0.1	•	•	•
Total Receipts to Cash Flow 42	3.0	2.2	2.7	2.3	3.6	4.8	5.3	3.6	3.6	4.5	4.1
Cost of Goods to Cash Flow 43	0.5	0.0	0.4	0.1	0.7	1.5	2.2	1.0	1.5	2.5	0.0
Cash Flow to Total Debt 44	1.0	•	3.0	1.4	0.9	0.2	0.4	0.6	0.8	0.4	0.2

Selected Financial Factors (in Percentages)

Debt Ratio 45	66.8	•	67.1	56.2	73.1	67.9	74.2	63.7	51.9	44.6	70.8
Return on Total Assets 46	22.2	•	60.6	15.9	21.8	7.3	16.0	14.8	18.2	11.7	4.3
Return on Equity Before Income Taxes 47	61.7	•	179.9	33.3	74.2	15.7	54.6	36.9	35.2	18.2	8.5
Return on Equity After Income Taxes 48	59.7	•	179.0	31.8	72.3	14.3	52.7	34.6	34.2	17.5	5.3
Profit Margin (Before Income Tax) 49	10.1	24.3	10.7	8.4	8.7	7.4	9.0	9.6	11.7	14.0	5.5
Profit Margin (After Income Tax) 50	9.7	23.5	10.7	8.0	8.5	6.8	8.6	9.0	11.4	13.5	3.5

Table II

Corporations with Net Income

OFFICES OF REAL ESTATE AGENTS AND BROKERS

MONEY AMOUNTS AND SIZE OF ASSETS IN THOUSANDS OF DOLLARS

Item Description for Accounting Period 7/04 Through 6/05	Total	Zero Assets	Under 500	500 to 1,000	1,000 to 5,000	5,000 to 10,000	10,000 to 25,000	25,000 to 50,000	50,000 to 100,000	100,000 to 250,000	250,000 to 500,000	500,000 to 2,500,000	2,500,000 and over
Number of Enterprises 1	66641	9390	52962	2251	1788	136	68	23	0	0	0	0	0
Revenues ($ in Thousands)													
Net Sales 2	51575816	852917	27703917	3273040	9767534	851419	1867121	1226837	0	0	0	0	0
Interest 3	124718	591	7757	9465	18687	4288	3799	2808	0	0	0	0	0
Rents 4	219932	0	11088	3075	21530	376	6900	1152	0	0	0	0	0
Royalties 5	1342	640	0	0	9	0	0	0	0	0	0	0	0
Other Portfolio Income 6	187069	61231	11675	10716	7726	14702	2537	802	0	0	0	0	0
Other Receipts 7	51042755	790455	27673397	3249784	9719582	832053	1853885	1222075	0	0	0	0	0
Total Receipts 8	51575816	852917	27703917	3273040	9767534	851419	1867121	1226837	0	0	0	0	0
Average Total Receipts 9	774	91	523	1454	5463	6260	27458	53341	.	.	.	.	.
Operating Costs/Operating Income (%)													
Cost of Operations 10	17.4	1.2	16.1	4.3	19.7	13.3	40.3	27.1	.	.	.	.	.
Salaries and Wages 11	28.4	9.8	24.2	22.2	38.9	40.5	26.2	29.6	.	.	.	.	.
Taxes Paid 12	1.6	1.6	1.3	1.4	1.2	2.2	1.4	1.9	.	.	.	.	.
Interest Paid 13	0.7	1.1	0.2	0.7	0.6	1.5	0.8	0.8	.	.	.	.	.
Depreciation 14	1.0	1.0	0.9	1.0	0.6	1.0	1.2	1.1	.	.	.	.	.
Amortization and Depletion 15	0.2	0.2	0.0	0.1	0.1	0.1	1.4	0.2	.	.	.	.	.
Pensions and Other Deferred Comp. 16	0.8	.	1.2	1.3	0.4	0.5	0.1	0.1	.	.	.	.	.
Employee Benefits 17	0.5	0.0	0.4	0.3	0.6	1.1	0.4	0.5	.	.	.	.	.
Advertising 18	3.3	2.8	4.0	3.6	2.4	2.6	2.8	2.4	.	.	.	.	.
Other Expenses 19	25.1	27.7	26.7	41.7	21.4	19.8	12.1	22.7	.	.	.	.	.
Officers' Compensation 20	8.5	11.8	11.4	11.1	4.7	4.0	1.8	3.8	.	.	.	.	.
Operating Margin 21	12.6	42.9	13.5	12.3	9.4	13.2	11.5	9.7	.	.	.	.	.
Operating Margin Before Officers' Comp. 22	21.1	54.6	25.0	23.3	14.1	17.3	13.3	13.5	.	.	.	.	.

Selected Average Balance Sheet ($ in Thousands)

Item								
Net Receivables 23	43	·	0	·	37	135	1028	1331	4723
Inventories 24	·	·	·	·	·	·	·	·	·
Net Property, Plant and Equipment 25	62	·	0	20	192	323	821	3666	3877
Total Assets 26	339	·	0	76	732	1955	7085	15030	34113
Notes and Loans Payable 27	111	·	0	29	237	1002	2605	5879	12385
All Other Liabilities 28	102	·	0	13	112	424	673	3628	7105
Net Worth 29	127	·	0	34	383	530	3806	5523	14623

Selected Financial Ratios (Times to 1)

Item								
Current Ratio 30	1.6	·	2.4	2.8	2.5	3.3	1.3	1.7
Quick Ratio 31	1.2	·	2.1	1.6	1.4	1.7	0.8	0.9
Net Sales to Working Capital 32	13.4	·	22.1	6.9	8.6	2.9	16.3	6.6
Coverage Ratio 33	19.7	39.9	58.9	18.2	17.8	9.6	15.7	12.5
Total Asset Turnover 34	2.3	·	6.9	2.0	2.8	0.9	1.8	1.6
Inventory Turnover 35	·	·	·	·	·	·	·	·
Receivables Turnover 36	·	·	·	·	·	·	·	1.3
Total Liabilities to Net Worth 37	1.7	·	1.2	0.9	2.7	0.9	1.7	1.3
Current Assets to Working Capital 38	2.7	·	1.7	1.6	1.7	1.4	4.2	2.5
Current Liabilities to Working Capital 39	1.7	·	0.7	0.6	0.7	0.4	3.2	1.5
Working Capital to Net Sales 40	0.1	·	0.0	0.1	0.1	0.3	0.1	0.2
Inventory to Working Capital 41	0.0	·	·	0.0	0.0	·	0.0	0.0
Total Receipts to Cash Flow 42	3.0	1.7	2.8	2.0	3.6	3.4	4.9	3.6
Cost of Goods to Cash Flow 43	0.5	0.0	0.4	0.1	0.7	0.5	2.0	1.0
Cash Flow to Total Debt 44	1.2	·	4.5	2.1	1.1	0.6	0.8

Selected Financial Factors (in Percentages)

Item								
Debt Ratio 45	62.7	·	55.1	47.7	72.9	46.3	63.3	57.1
Return on Total Assets 46	30.4	·	94.3	25.8	27.8	13.1	22.4	16.5
Return on Equity Before Income Taxes 47	77.2	·	206.6	46.6	96.8	21.8	57.0	35.4
Return on Equity After Income Taxes 48	75.0	·	205.6	44.9	94.5	20.2	55.4	33.2
Profit Margin (Before Income Tax) 49	12.6	42.9	13.5	12.3	9.4	13.2	11.5	9.7
Profit Margin (After Income Tax) 50	12.3	41.7	13.5	11.8	9.2	12.3	11.1	9.1

Table I

Corporations with and without Net Income

OTHER REAL ESTATE ACTIVITIES

MONEY AMOUNTS AND SIZE OF ASSETS IN THOUSANDS OF DOLLARS

Item Description for Accounting Period 7/04 Through 6/05	Total	Zero Assets	Under 500	500 to 1,000	1,000 to 5,000	5,000 to 10,000	10,000 to 25,000	25,000 to 50,000	50,000 to 100,000	100,000 to 250,000	250,000 to 500,000	500,000 to 2,500,000	2,500,000 and over
Number of Enterprises **1**	178807	31059	125121	8854	10863	1422	1000	278	131	63	12	5	0
Revenues ($ in Thousands)													
Net Sales **2**	53271107	2013675	20031680	3368399	8736004	3520173	4391048	3529668	1807601	2656988	733712	2482158	0
Interest **3**	827179	38989	68310	52886	94491	38879	77369	78652	83396	60031	46845	187331	0
Rents **4**	1425163	44673	201366	183368	231409	120737	177646	154031	136019	111847	18242	45825	0
Royalties **5**	37943	69	2765	0	19550	2013	3358	107	9665	415	0	0	0
Other Portfolio Income **6**	2274109	474801	140326	110841	334807	134070	238451	101971	132970	178518	152985	274367	0
Other Receipts **7**	48706713	1455143	19618913	3021304	8055747	3224474	3894224	3194907	1445551	2306177	515640	1974635	0
Total Receipts **8**	53271107	2013675	20031680	3368399	8736004	3520173	4391048	3529668	1807601	2656988	733712	2482158	0
Average Total Receipts **9**	298	65	160	380	804	2476	4391	12697	13798	42174	61143	496432	·
Operating Costs/Operating Income (%)													
Cost of Operations **10**	11.6	11.2	4.8	13.0	13.3	12.5	17.8	30.3	28.0	8.5	26.0	8.0	·
Salaries and Wages **11**	24.2	11.9	28.5	18.9	23.6	22.2	21.2	15.4	15.2	35.8	8.7	27.1	·
Taxes Paid **12**	3.7	3.9	3.4	3.8	6.1	3.0	3.5	2.5	4.2	2.0	3.5	1.1	·
Interest Paid **13**	3.2	5.0	1.0	2.6	4.0	4.2	5.0	4.0	10.0	3.7	4.2	4.8	·
Depreciation **14**	2.3	2.8	1.7	2.3	2.3	1.8	3.0	2.7	4.3	3.5	1.2	2.6	·
Amortization and Depletion **15**	0.3	0.3	0.2	0.1	0.2	0.3	0.4	0.4	0.5	0.6	0.1	0.6	·
Pensions and Other Deferred Comp. **16**	0.6	0.5	0.9	1.1	0.6	0.6	0.5	0.2	0.3	0.5	0.5	0.2	·
Employee Benefits **17**	1.6	0.5	1.8	2.3	1.4	1.0	1.3	1.1	1.1	1.6	0.6	3.2	·
Advertising **18**	0.9	0.9	0.8	0.7	0.3	1.1	1.0	1.4	1.7	1.9	0.1	0.6	·
Other Expenses **19**	34.2	47.4	36.7	41.0	31.0	41.5	28.2	27.0	25.6	34.7	14.6	27.5	·
Officers' Compensation **20**	7.9	7.0	11.8	10.0	7.3	4.8	5.3	2.4	3.2	4.0	3.6	2.1	·
Operating Margin **21**	9.6	8.6	8.3	3.8	10.1	6.9	13.0	12.5	5.9	3.2	37.0	22.1	·
Operating Margin Before Officers' Comp. **22**	17.5	15.6	20.2	13.9	17.3	11.6	18.3	14.9	9.2	7.1	40.6	24.3	·

Selected Average Balance Sheet ($ in Thousands)

Net Receivables 23	48	0	5	64	106	576	1128	2178	6011	11581	14903	420096	•
Inventories 24	•	•	•	•	•	•	•	•	•	•	•	•	•
Net Property, Plant and Equipment 25	150	0	22	222	636	1575	3986	10845	20661	30019	44892	169906	•
Total Assets 26	561	0	85	678	2088	6631	14984	35464	69884	141767	333666	912425	•
Notes and Loans Payable 27	263	0	60	421	1019	3068	7224	15974	34210	41766	45211	224594	•
All Other Liabilities 28	135	0	21	121	530	1517	2687	9762	15065	43392	99519	233304	•
Net Worth 29	162	0	4	136	538	2046	5073	9728	20609	56610	188937	454527	•

Selected Financial Ratios (Times to 1)

Current Ratio 30	1.6	•	2.0	1.7	1.5	1.5	1.6	1.6	1.2	1.6	0.7	2.4	•
Quick Ratio 31	1.0	•	1.4	1.2	1.0	0.9	0.9	0.9	0.8	1.1	0.7	2.0	•
Net Sales to Working Capital 32	3.8	•	7.2	3.4	3.1	3.5	2.1	3.3	3.5	2.1	•	1.5	•
Coverage Ratio 33	4.0	2.7	9.2	2.5	3.4	2.5	3.6	4.1	1.3	1.8	9.8	5.6	•
Total Asset Turnover 34	0.5	•	1.9	0.6	0.4	0.4	0.3	0.4	0.2	0.3	0.2	0.5	•
Inventory Turnover 35	•	•	•	•	•	•	•	•	•	•	•	•	•
Receivables Turnover 36	•	•	•	•	•	•	•	•	•	•	•	•	•
Total Liabilities to Net Worth 37	2.5	•	20.0	4.0	2.9	2.2	2.0	2.6	2.4	1.5	0.8	1.0	•
Current Assets to Working Capital 38	2.6	•	2.0	2.4	2.9	2.9	2.5	2.7	5.1	2.6	•	1.7	•
Current Liabilities to Working Capital 39	1.6	•	1.0	1.4	1.9	1.9	1.5	1.7	4.1	1.6	•	0.7	•
Working Capital to Net Sales 40	0.3	•	0.1	0.3	0.3	0.3	0.5	0.3	0.3	0.5	•	0.7	•
Inventory to Working Capital 41	0.0	•	•	•	0.0	•	0.0	0.0	0.1	0.1	•	0.1	•
Total Receipts to Cash Flow 42	3.0	3.9	2.7	3.0	3.1	4.7	3.2	3.1	4.3	3.9	2.1	2.2	•
Cost of Goods to Cash Flow 43	0.3	0.4	0.1	0.4	0.4	0.6	0.6	1.0	1.2	0.3	0.6	0.2	•
Cash Flow to Total Debt 44	0.2	•	0.7	0.2	0.2	0.1	0.1	0.2	0.1	0.1	0.2	0.5	•

Selected Financial Factors (in Percentages)

Debt Ratio 45	71.0	•	95.2	79.9	74.2	69.1	66.1	72.6	70.5	60.1	43.4	50.2	•
Return on Total Assets 46	6.7	•	17.6	3.6	5.4	4.0	5.2	5.9	2.6	2.0	7.5	14.6	•
Return on Equity Before Income Taxes 47	17.3	•	328.6	10.8	14.8	7.8	11.2	16.2	2.1	2.3	11.9	24.1	•
Return on Equity After Income Taxes 48	14.5	•	317.7	7.3	13.2	5.5	9.7	14.8	0.6	1.0	9.7	15.7	•
Profit Margin (Before Income Tax) 49	9.4	8.5	8.3	3.8	9.9	6.4	12.9	12.4	3.1	3.0	36.9	22.1	•
Profit Margin (After Income Tax) 50	7.9	3.4	8.1	2.6	8.8	4.5	11.2	11.4	0.9	1.4	29.9	14.4	•

325

Table II
Corporations with Net Income

OTHER REAL ESTATE ACTIVITIES

MONEY AMOUNTS AND SIZE OF ASSETS IN THOUSANDS OF DOLLARS

Item Description for Accounting Period 7/04 Through 6/05	Total	Zero Assets	Under 500	500 to 1,000	1,000 to 5,000	5,000 to 10,000	10,000 to 25,000	25,000 to 50,000	50,000 to 100,000	100,000 to 250,000	250,000 to 500,000	500,000 to 2,500,000	2,500,000 and over
Number of Enterprises **1**	83302	10417	62943	3894	4803	538	466	137	0	0	0	5	0
Revenues ($ in Thousands)													
Net Sales **2**	41742651	1426927	16038454	2031906	7193134	2484839	3333866	2476537	0	0	0	2482158	0
Interest **3**	602615	19168	27258	45920	77958	31549	64603	39195	0	0	0	187331	0
Rents **4**	941513	36650	106807	144027	133071	85108	121527	109803	0	0	0	45825	0
Royalties **5**	37591	0	2765	0	19541	2013	3358	107	0	0	0	0	0
Other Portfolio Income **6**	2041346	448908	122326	109287	308151	117413	225313	82913	0	0	0	274367	0
Other Receipts **7**	38119586	922201	15779298	1732672	6654413	2248756	2919065	2244519	0	0	0	1974635	0
Total Receipts **8**	41742651	1426927	16038454	2031906	7193134	2484839	3333866	2476537	0	0	0	2482158	0
Average Total Receipts **9**	501	137	255	522	1498	4619	7154	18077	·	·	·	496432	·
Operating Costs/Operating Income (%)													
Cost of Operations **10**	11.5	6.1	5.1	17.3	13.5	15.0	16.0	30.7	·	·	·	8.0	·
Salaries and Wages **11**	22.6	3.7	28.0	9.6	22.7	10.6	20.3	14.0	·	·	·	27.1	·
Taxes Paid **12**	3.4	2.7	3.1	2.5	6.3	2.5	3.1	2.3	·	·	·	1.1	·
Interest Paid **13**	2.2	4.2	0.7	1.6	2.1	4.1	3.9	2.5	·	·	·	4.8	·
Depreciation **14**	1.8	2.9	1.3	1.5	2.0	1.0	2.2	1.9	·	·	·	2.6	·
Amortization and Depletion **15**	0.3	0.3	0.2	0.1	0.2	0.2	0.3	0.3	·	·	·	0.6	·
Pensions and Other Deferred Comp. **16**	0.7	0.5	1.0	1.7	0.6	0.3	0.5	0.2	·	·	·	0.2	·
Employee Benefits **17**	1.3	0.1	1.3	1.9	1.2	0.7	0.9	1.0	·	·	·	3.2	·
Advertising **18**	0.8	0.8	0.8	0.6	0.2	0.5	0.7	1.5	·	·	·	0.6	·
Other Expenses **19**	27.4	20.0	31.1	29.0	23.7	40.2	22.5	18.1	·	·	·	27.5	·
Officers' Compensation **20**	7.2	6.4	10.8	6.7	7.6	3.4	4.3	2.5	·	·	·	2.1	·
Operating Margin **21**	21.0	52.4	16.6	27.5	19.8	21.7	25.4	25.1	·	·	·	22.1	·
Operating Margin Before Officers' Comp. **22**	28.1	58.8	27.4	34.2	27.4	25.0	29.7	27.6	·	·	·	24.3	·

Selected Average Balance Sheet ($ in Thousands)

Net Receivables 23	72	0	6	56	149	935	1468	2432	•	420096
Inventories 24	•	0	•	•	•	•	•	•	•	•
Net Property, Plant and Equipment 25	125	0	18	199	536	739	3167	8863	•	169906
Total Assets 26	609	0	93	688	2091	6573	15215	35423	•	912425
Notes and Loans Payable 27	225	0	39	286	891	2630	6278	13671	•	224594
All Other Liabilities 28	139	0	20	105	361	1548	2953	7801	•	233304
Net Worth 29	245	0	34	297	839	2395	5985	13951	•	454527

Selected Financial Ratios (Times to 1)

Current Ratio 30	1.9	•	2.6	2.4	2.3	2.1	1.8	1.8	•	2.4
Quick Ratio 31	1.3	•	1.9	1.8	1.4	1.4	1.0	1.1	•	2.0
Net Sales to Working Capital 32	4.0	•	7.7	2.7	2.8	3.5	2.6	3.6	•	1.5
Coverage Ratio 33	10.5	13.5	25.6	18.1	10.2	6.3	7.5	11.2	•	5.6
Total Asset Turnover 34	0.8	•	2.7	0.8	0.7	0.7	0.5	0.5	•	0.5
Inventory Turnover 35	•	•	•	•	•	•	•	•	•	•
Receivables Turnover 36	•	•	•	•	•	•	•	•	•	•
Total Liabilities to Net Worth 37	1.5	•	1.7	1.3	1.5	1.7	1.5	1.5	•	1.0
Current Assets to Working Capital 38	2.1	•	1.6	1.7	1.8	1.9	2.3	2.3	•	1.7
Current Liabilities to Working Capital 39	1.1	•	0.6	0.7	0.8	0.9	1.3	1.3	•	0.7
Working Capital to Net Sales 40	0.2	•	0.1	0.4	0.4	0.3	0.4	0.3	•	0.7
Inventory to Working Capital 41	0.0	•	•	0.0	0.0	•	0.0	0.0	•	0.1
Total Receipts to Cash Flow 42	2.6	2.5	2.5	2.3	2.8	3.6	2.6	2.7	•	2.2
Cost of Goods to Cash Flow 43	0.3	0.2	0.1	0.4	0.4	0.5	0.4	0.8	•	0.2
Cash Flow to Total Debt 44	0.5	•	1.8	0.6	0.4	0.3	0.3	0.3	•	0.5

Selected Financial Factors (in Percentages)

Debt Ratio 45	59.7	•	63.5	56.9	59.9	63.6	60.7	60.6	•	50.2
Return on Total Assets 46	19.0	•	47.3	22.0	15.7	18.1	13.7	14.0	•	14.6
Return on Equity Before Income Taxes 47	42.7	•	124.4	48.3	35.2	41.8	30.3	32.4	•	24.1
Return on Equity After Income Taxes 48	38.8	•	121.8	44.7	32.9	36.6	27.6	30.4	•	15.7
Profit Margin (Before Income Tax) 49	20.9	52.3	16.6	27.5	19.7	21.7	25.3	25.0	•	22.1
Profit Margin (After Income Tax) 50	19.0	45.1	16.2	25.4	18.4	19.0	23.1	23.4	•	14.4

Table I

Corporations with and without Net Income

AUTOMOTIVE EQUIPMENT RENTAL AND LEASING

MONEY AMOUNTS AND SIZE OF ASSETS IN THOUSANDS OF DOLLARS

Item Description for Accounting Period 7/04 Through 6/05	Total	Zero Assets	Under 500	500 to 1,000	1,000 to 5,000	5,000 to 10,000	10,000 to 25,000	25,000 to 50,000	50,000 to 100,000	100,000 to 250,000	250,000 to 500,000	500,000 to 2,500,000	2,500,000 and over
Number of Enterprises 1	7336	666	4549	745	1068	82	134	51	20	10	3	3	5
Revenues ($ in Thousands)													
Net Sales 2	32916544	101601	1422817	518025	1350512	395441	1899393	1014638	1042547	965405	721264	1473088	22011813
Interest 3	769017	36	1489	219	711	2938	3420	1344	3929	9166	421	2622	742724
Rents 4	190302	108	1089	422	899	0	2908	1483	1426	55	923	530	180460
Royalties 5	15218	0	0	0	0	0	0	0	0	0	0	0	15218
Other Portfolio Income 6	1939353	18033	29877	4614	115592	37753	196557	104102	66378	135730	91844	3852	1135019
Other Receipts 7	30002654	83424	1390362	512770	1233310	354750	1696508	907709	970814	820454	628076	1466084	19938392
Total Receipts 8	32916544	101601	1422817	518025	1350512	395441	1899393	1014638	1042547	965405	721264	1473088	22011813
Average Total Receipts 9	4487	153	313	695	1265	4822	14175	19895	52127	96540	240421	491029	4402363
Operating Costs/Operating Income (%)													
Cost of Operations 10	18.3	31.9	71.0	34.5	13.4	31.6	35.0	29.6	46.0	31.2	0.9	0.1	12.4
Salaries and Wages 11	12.6	4.9	2.3	8.4	12.9	6.2	8.8	7.3	7.8	6.0	6.9	4.3	15.3
Taxes Paid 12	2.6	0.8	0.8	1.8	3.0	2.9	2.0	2.0	1.7	2.9	0.9	0.3	3.0
Interest Paid 13	5.8	4.2	1.8	3.1	4.4	6.5	5.1	5.0	3.9	4.7	2.8	4.2	6.6
Depreciation 14	41.6	26.9	7.2	17.5	32.3	31.7	31.5	44.1	25.0	41.8	78.4	86.6	42.6
Amortization and Depletion 15	0.1	0.1	0.0	0.0	0.1	0.1	0.1	0.0	0.1	0.1	0.1	0.4	0.1
Pensions and Other Deferred Comp. 16	0.3	0.1	0.0	0.4	0.4	0.1	0.1	0.1	0.4	0.1	0.1	0.2	0.4
Employee Benefits 17	1.4	0.6	0.5	0.3	0.3	0.5	0.7	0.8	0.5	0.9	0.7	0.4	1.9
Advertising 18	0.9	0.1	0.2	3.7	2.3	1.6	0.9	0.6	0.6	0.5	0.3	0.1	0.9
Other Expenses 19	31.9	6.7	13.4	16.9	29.1	194.9	13.8	13.8	15.3	14.3	20.6	5.6	37.0
Officers' Compensation 20	0.8	0.2	2.7	4.4	2.7	1.0	1.6	1.5	1.2	1.3	0.6	0.4	0.4
Operating Margin 21	•	23.6	9.7	•	•	•	0.4	•	•	•	•	•	•
Operating Margin Before Officers' Comp. 22	•	23.8	2.7	14.1	1.9	•	2.0	•	•	•	•	•	•

Selected Average Balance Sheet ($ in Thousands)

Net Receivables 23	463	0	20	29	413	413	1542	4107	7508	33991	23512	35752	344073
Inventories 24	•	•	•	•	•	•	•	•	•	•	•	•	•
Net Property, Plant and Equipment 25	4022	0	64	433	1603	4172	10077	21168	42254	102939	369270	654351	3892511
Total Assets 26	6024	0	128	798	2358	6866	16076	35556	72341	150448	353497	1238504	5648195
Notes and Loans Payable 27	3005	0	105	396	1608	4602	10879	24170	51192	109365	281150	1098172	2046184
All Other Liabilities 28	1777	0	15	21	176	1229	1727	4842	6369	18602	33452	127185	2277388
Net Worth 29	1243	0	8	381	574	1036	3470	6543	14780	22482	38895	13147	1324623

Selected Financial Ratios (Times to 1)

Current Ratio 30	0.4	•	1.4	2.2	1.6	0.8	0.8	0.7	1.7	0.7	0.2	0.1	0.3
Quick Ratio 31	0.3	•	0.9	1.5	1.5	0.7	0.5	0.5	1.0	0.6	0.1	0.0	0.2
Net Sales to Working Capital 32	•	•	19.7	3.8	5.7	•	•	6.9	•	•	•	•	•
Coverage Ratio 33	•	6.6	1.0	4.2	0.8	•	1.1	0.0	0.4	0.2	•	0.4	•
Total Asset Turnover 34	0.7	•	2.4	0.9	0.5	0.7	0.9	0.6	0.7	0.6	0.7	0.4	0.8
Inventory Turnover 35	•	•	•	•	•	•	•	•	•	•	•	•	•
Receivables Turnover 36	•	•	•	•	•	•	•	•	•	•	•	•	•
Total Liabilities to Net Worth 37	3.8	•	15.5	3.1	5.6	3.6	4.4	3.9	5.7	8.1	•	93.2	3.3
Current Assets to Working Capital 38	•	•	3.2	1.9	2.7	•	•	2.5	•	•	•	•	•
Current Liabilities to Working Capital 39	•	•	2.2	0.9	1.7	•	•	1.5	•	•	•	•	•
Working Capital to Net Sales 40	•	•	0.1	0.3	0.2	•	•	0.1	•	•	•	•	•
Inventory to Working Capital 41	•	•	0.5	0.2	0.0	•	•	0.5	•	•	•	•	•
Total Receipts to Cash Flow 42	70.4	4.6	17.1	5.4	8.1	9.3	11.4	30.3	18.0	25.6	17.0	369.2	•
Cost of Goods to Cash Flow 43	12.9	1.5	12.1	1.9	1.1	2.9	4.0	8.9	8.3	8.0	0.2	0.4	•
Cash Flow to Total Debt 44	0.0	•	0.2	0.3	0.1	0.1	0.1	0.0	0.1	0.0	0.0	0.0	•

Selected Financial Factors (in Percentages)

Debt Ratio 45	79.4	•	93.9	52.3	75.7	84.9	78.4	81.6	79.6	85.1	89.0	98.9	76.5
Return on Total Assets 46	•	•	4.4	11.1	1.9	•	4.9	0.1	1.1	0.5	•	0.6	•
Return on Equity Before Income Taxes 47	•	•	•	17.8	•	1.7	•	•	•	•	•	•	•
Return on Equity After Income Taxes 48	•	•	•	17.2	•	1.0	•	•	•	•	•	•	•
Profit Margin (Before Income Tax) 49	•	23.6	9.7	•	•	0.4	•	•	•	•	•	•	•
Profit Margin (After Income Tax) 50	•	23.2	9.4	•	•	0.2	•	•	•	•	•	•	•

Table II
Corporations with Net Income

AUTOMOTIVE EQUIPMENT RENTAL AND LEASING

MONEY AMOUNTS AND SIZE OF ASSETS IN THOUSANDS OF DOLLARS

Item Description for Accounting Period 7/04 Through 6/05	Total	Zero Assets	Under 500	500 to 1,000	1,000 to 5,000	5,000 to 10,000	10,000 to 25,000	25,000 to 50,000	50,000 to 100,000	100,000 to 250,000	250,000 to 500,000	500,000 to 2,500,000	2,500,000 and over
Number of Enterprises 1	2709	0	1318	542	435	33	66	0	12	4	0	0	0
Revenues ($ in Thousands)													
Net Sales 2	13231976	0	294681	351403	705510	178967	1232557	0	764140	313078	0	0	0
Interest 3	385796	0	219	219	697	2445	1425	0	701	8181	0	0	0
Rents 4	87777	0	220	422	899	0	2548	0	1426	0	0	0	0
Royalties 5	0	0	0	0	0	0	0	0	0	0	0	0	0
Other Portfolio Income 6	604293	0	22034	4614	88729	25145	104229	0	31422	43470	0	0	0
Other Receipts 7	12154110	0	272208	346148	615185	151377	1124355	0	730591	261427	0	0	0
Total Receipts 8	13231976	0	294681	351403	705510	178967	1232557	0	764140	313078	0	0	0
Average Total Receipts 9	4884	·	224	648	1622	5423	18675	·	63678	78270	·	·	·
Operating Costs/Operating Income (%)													
Cost of Operations 10	22.5	·	46.3	37.1	20.4	25.2	37.5	·	60.2	26.6	·	·	·
Salaries and Wages 11	10.4	·	1.1	5.7	9.3	6.6	8.4	·	7.1	10.6	·	·	·
Taxes Paid 12	3.1	·	0.8	1.3	3.0	2.3	2.0	·	1.6	3.1	·	·	·
Interest Paid 13	5.0	·	2.0	2.1	4.3	4.2	5.1	·	2.5	2.9	·	·	·
Depreciation 14	18.1	·	21.3	15.6	34.4	25.0	25.7	·	13.1	29.1	·	·	·
Amortization and Depletion 15	0.1	·	0.0	0.0	0.1	0.0	0.1	·	0.1	0.0	·	·	·
Pensions and Other Deferred Comp. 16	0.3	·	·	·	0.7	0.0	0.2	·	0.5	0.2	·	·	·
Employee Benefits 17	1.4	·	·	0.1	0.4	0.6	0.6	·	0.4	0.7	·	·	·
Advertising 18	0.6	·	0.1	1.2	0.8	1.4	0.8	·	0.4	0.4	·	·	·
Other Expenses 19	32.8	·	21.2	16.7	18.1	15.3	12.6	·	10.9	19.8	·	·	·
Officers' Compensation 20	0.9	·	·	4.4	3.3	1.2	1.4	·	1.0	1.0	·	·	·
Operating Margin 21	4.9	·	7.3	15.9	5.2	18.4	5.8	·	2.1	5.4	·	·	·
Operating Margin Before Officers' Comp. 22	5.8	·	7.3	20.3	8.5	19.5	7.2	·	3.1	6.4	·	·	·

Selected Average Balance Sheet ($ in Thousands)

Net Receivables 23	553	55	25	475	568	1701	•	8428	68355
Inventories 24	•	•	•	•	•	•	•	•	•
Net Property, Plant and Equipment 25	2739	43	393	1700	3191	8959	•	36920	77938
Total Assets 26	5503	161	834	2377	7380	16045	•	68409	156028
Notes and Loans Payable 27	2599	79	270	1574	3441	9551	•	44728	111042
All Other Liabilities 28	1606	35	11	220	1863	2044	•	6596	12986
Net Worth 29	1298	47	552	583	2077	4450	•	17084	32001

Selected Financial Ratios (Times to 1)

Current Ratio 30	0.6	1.2	3.2	1.8	1.0	1.0	•	1.6	2.8
Quick Ratio 31	0.4	1.1	2.1	1.7	0.8	0.6	•	0.9	2.7
Net Sales to Working Capital 32	•	13.4	2.3	6.2	120.9	•	•	7.8	1.6
Coverage Ratio 33	2.0	4.7	8.7	2.2	5.4	2.1	•	1.8	2.8
Total Asset Turnover 34	0.9	1.4	0.8	0.7	0.7	1.2	•	0.9	0.5
Inventory Turnover 35	•	•	•	•	•	•	•	•	•
Receivables Turnover 36	•	•	•	•	•	•	•	•	•
Total Liabilities to Net Worth 37	3.2	2.4	0.5	3.1	2.6	2.6	•	3.0	3.9
Current Assets to Working Capital 38	•	5.5	1.4	2.3	85.9	•	•	2.6	1.5
Current Liabilities to Working Capital 39	•	4.5	0.4	1.3	84.9	•	•	1.6	0.5
Working Capital to Net Sales 40	•	0.1	0.4	0.2	0.0	•	•	0.1	0.6
Inventory to Working Capital 41	•	•	0.2	0.1	1.6	•	•	0.8	0.0
Total Receipts to Cash Flow 42	4.2	6.4	4.3	6.6	4.0	7.3	•	13.1	5.8
Cost of Goods to Cash Flow 43	0.9	3.0	1.6	1.3	1.0	2.7	•	7.9	1.5
Cash Flow to Total Debt 44	0.3	0.3	0.5	0.1	0.3	0.2	•	0.1	0.1

Selected Financial Factors (in Percentages)

Debt Ratio 45	76.4	70.6	33.8	75.5	71.9	72.3	•	75.0	79.5
Return on Total Assets 46	8.8	12.8	14.0	6.5	16.5	12.7	•	4.3	4.2
Return on Equity Before Income Taxes 47	18.6	34.2	18.7	14.4	48.0	24.5	•	7.9	13.1
Return on Equity After Income Taxes 48	15.5	33.4	18.1	13.7	39.7	23.5	•	7.1	12.5
Profit Margin (Before Income Tax) 49	4.9	7.3	15.9	5.2	18.4	5.8	•	2.1	5.4
Profit Margin (After Income Tax) 50	4.1	7.1	15.4	4.9	15.2	5.6	•	1.9	5.1

Table I

Corporations with and without Net Income

OTHER CONSUMER GOODS AND GENERAL RENTAL CENTERS

MONEY AMOUNTS AND SIZE OF ASSETS IN THOUSANDS OF DOLLARS

Item Description for Accounting Period 7/04 Through 6/05	Total	Zero Assets	Under 500	500 to 1,000	1,000 to 5,000	5,000 to 10,000	10,000 to 25,000	25,000 to 50,000	50,000 to 100,000	100,000 to 250,000	250,000 to 500,000	500,000 to 2,500,000	2,500,000 and over
Number of Enterprises 1	12828	529	11009	704	384	127	46	12	5	3	5	4	0
Revenues ($ in Thousands)													
Net Sales 2	16646354	89310	3119533	1652827	639365	1001984	795153	361146	330007	245042	1960851	6451137	0
Interest 3	20938	48	382	53	1615	368	863	189	403	2257	1071	13688	0
Rents 4	9001	0	5346	0	0	380	1700	0	0	0	1576	0	0
Royalties 5	55407	0	0	0	0	0	0	0	0	0	33	55374	0
Other Portfolio Income 6	66338	218	23042	2917	10840	137	13720	3657	2264	901	382	8262	0
Other Receipts 7	16494670	89044	3090763	1649857	626910	1001099	778870	357300	327340	241884	1957789	6373813	0
Total Receipts 8	16646354	89310	3119533	1652827	639365	1001984	795153	361146	330007	245042	1960851	6451137	0
Average Total Receipts 9	1298	169	283	2348	1665	7890	17286	30096	66001	81681	392170	1612784	•
Operating Costs/Operating Income (%)													
Cost of Operations 10	23.9	45.9	25.3	24.6	36.5	36.5	38.4	38.8	18.4	•	15.1	20.8	
Salaries and Wages 11	20.8	11.2	20.3	26.1	19.6	16.6	16.0	15.7	18.0	23.4	20.0	21.7	
Taxes Paid 12	3.9	4.8	4.3	4.2	3.3	5.4	3.6	2.7	2.5	2.5	4.7	3.5	
Interest Paid 13	1.7	2.4	1.3	1.3	4.3	1.2	1.8	2.7	3.6	3.1	2.6	1.4	
Depreciation 14	13.8	6.5	7.9	10.0	6.8	12.7	13.7	17.8	17.6	10.5	21.2	15.9	
Amortization and Depletion 15	1.6	0.0	0.5	0.2	0.5	0.6	0.5	0.2	1.1	1.8	5.0	2.0	
Pensions and Other Deferred Comp. 16	0.1	0.4	0.1	0.3	0.0	0.5	0.2	0.1	0.1	0.5	0.1	0.0	
Employee Benefits 17	1.3	1.2	0.9	0.5	0.8	2.5	1.8	1.5	1.8	1.1	1.4	1.4	
Advertising 18	3.1	0.2	2.1	3.1	1.1	3.0	1.3	1.3	18.5	0.4	5.6	2.8	
Other Expenses 19	26.8	34.1	29.8	26.8	25.9	18.4	22.9	17.3	21.1	53.0	23.3	28.0	
Officers' Compensation 20	2.1	2.1	4.8	4.2	2.9	3.6	1.9	2.7	1.5	1.4	1.5	0.3	
Operating Margin 21	0.8	•	2.5	•	•	•	•	•	•	2.4	•	2.1	
Operating Margin Before Officers' Comp. 22	2.9	•	7.4	2.9	1.1	2.6	•	2.1	•	3.8	1.0	2.4	

Selected Average Balance Sheet ($ in Thousands)

Net Receivables 23	52	•	0	6	47	107	430	2558	3009	8670	6870	3803	59207 •
Inventories 24	•	•	•	•	•	•	•	•	•	•	•	•	• •
Net Property, Plant and Equipment 25	494	•	0	54	469	1318	3341	6151	16323	38547	17914	137828	766141 •
Total Assets 26	1172	•	0	103	754	1936	5505	14386	33414	72451	157820	353143	2066560 •
Notes and Loans Payable 27	514	•	0	86	496	2075	1943	11023	14747	37303	85420	106514	648065 •
All Other Liabilities 28	245	•	0	11	84	171	693	4057	6155	12861	13950	111355	470318 •
Net Worth 29	413	•	0	5	175	-310	2869	-694	12512	22287	58450	135274	948178 •

Selected Financial Ratios (Times to 1)

Current Ratio 30	0.9	•	1.9	1.3	2.4	3.1	0.7	1.1	1.1	1.1	0.9	0.6	• •
Quick Ratio 31	0.5	•	1.3	1.0	1.1	1.0	0.5	0.8	0.9	0.5	0.4	0.3	• •
Net Sales to Working Capital 32	•	•	14.3	38.0	6.5	6.0	•	28.8	63.5	27.2	•	•	• •
Coverage Ratio 33	1.5	•	3.0	0.0	0.6	0.2	•	0.8	•	1.8	0.8	2.5	• •
Total Asset Turnover 34	1.1	•	2.8	3.1	0.9	1.4	1.2	0.9	0.9	0.5	1.1	0.8	• •
Inventory Turnover 35	•	•	•	•	•	•	•	•	•	•	•	•	• •
Receivables Turnover 36	•	•	•	•	•	•	•	•	•	•	•	•	• •
Total Liabilities to Net Worth 37	1.8	•	18.6	3.3	0.9	•	1.7	2.3	1.7	1.6	1.2	•	• •
Current Assets to Working Capital 38	•	•	2.1	4.0	1.7	1.5	8.0	17.4	8.0	•	•	•	• •
Current Liabilities to Working Capital 39	•	•	1.1	3.0	0.7	0.5	7.0	16.4	7.0	•	•	•	• •
Working Capital to Net Sales 40	•	•	0.1	0.0	0.2	0.2	0.0	0.0	0.0	•	•	•	• •
Inventory to Working Capital 41	•	•	0.5	0.6	0.9	0.5	1.6	0.1	3.9	•	•	•	• •
Total Receipts to Cash Flow 42	5.9	5.4	5.0	6.9	6.7	12.3	7.5	8.0	11.3	3.2	7.9	5.2	• •
Cost of Goods to Cash Flow 43	1.4	2.5	1.3	1.7	2.4	4.5	2.9	3.1	2.1	•	1.2	1.1	• •
Cash Flow to Total Debt 44	0.3	•	0.6	0.6	0.1	0.2	0.2	0.2	0.1	0.3	0.2	0.3	• •

Selected Financial Factors (in Percentages)

Debt Ratio 45	64.7	•	94.9	76.9	116.0	47.9	104.8	62.6	69.2	63.0	61.7	54.1	• •
Return on Total Assets 46	2.8	•	10.6	0.2	2.2	0.3	1.8	•	2.8	•	2.3	2.8	• •
Return on Equity Before Income Taxes 47	2.5	•	138.0	9.8	•	50.3	•	•	•	3.4	•	3.6	• •
Return on Equity After Income Taxes 48	0.9	•	134.3	13.5	•	56.1	•	•	•	3.3	•	2.3	• •
Profit Margin (Before Income Tax) 49	0.8	•	2.5	•	•	•	•	•	•	2.4	•	2.1	• •
Profit Margin (After Income Tax) 50	0.3	2.5	2.5	•	•	•	•	•	•	2.3	•	1.3	• •

329

Table II

Corporations with Net Income

OTHER CONSUMER GOODS AND GENERAL RENTAL CENTERS

MONEY AMOUNTS AND SIZE OF ASSETS IN THOUSANDS OF DOLLARS

Item Description for Accounting Period 7/04 Through 6/05	Total	Zero Assets	Under 500	500 to 1,000	1,000 to 5,000	5,000 to 10,000	10,000 to 25,000	25,000 to 50,000	50,000 to 100,000	100,000 to 250,000	250,000 to 500,000	500,000 to 2,500,000	2,500,000 and over
Number of Enterprises 1	5943	0	5448	271	154	0	0	4	0	3	0	0	0
Revenues ($ in Thousands)													
Net Sales 2	10680915	0	2190205	848634	455147	0	0	206173	0	1126294	0	0	0
Interest 3	15366	0	256	53	1615	0	0	189	0	149	0	0	0
Rents 4	3237	0	0	0	0	0	0	0	0	1538	0	0	0
Royalties 5	31933	0	0	0	0	0	0	0	0	33	0	0	0
Other Portfolio Income 6	28800	0	7162	795	10840	0	0	2	0	382	0	0	0
Other Receipts 7	10601579	0	2182787	847786	442692	0	0	205982	0	1124192	0	0	0
Total Receipts 8	10680915	0	2190205	848634	455147	0	0	206173	0	1126294	0	0	0
Average Total Receipts 9	1797	·	402	3131	2956	·	·	51543	·	375431	·	·	·
Operating Costs/Operating Income (%)													
Cost of Operations 10	23.3	·	22.9	37.0	41.4	·	·	53.0	·	4.5	·	·	·
Salaries and Wages 11	20.2	·	19.5	16.7	18.9	·	·	13.7	·	22.6	·	·	·
Taxes Paid 12	4.0	·	4.5	3.8	3.4	·	·	1.9	·	5.5	·	·	·
Interest Paid 13	1.1	·	0.8	0.9	1.1	·	·	0.6	·	0.7	·	·	·
Depreciation 14	13.9	·	5.0	6.8	5.2	·	·	5.9	·	20.4	·	·	·
Amortization and Depletion 15	1.7	·	0.1	0.0	0.6	·	·	0.2	·	7.0	·	·	·
Pensions and Other Deferred Comp. 16	0.2	·	0.2	0.5	0.0	·	·	0.1	·	0.1	·	·	·
Employee Benefits 17	1.4	·	1.0	1.0	0.6	·	·	1.4	·	0.7	·	·	·
Advertising 18	1.6	·	2.3	0.7	0.5	·	·	1.3	·	0.3	·	·	·
Other Expenses 19	24.8	·	29.7	25.7	18.7	·	·	12.5	·	31.0	·	·	·
Officers' Compensation 20	2.2	·	5.2	4.4	3.8	·	·	3.5	·	2.4	·	·	·
Operating Margin 21	5.7	·	8.7	2.6	5.7	·	·	6.0	·	4.8	·	·	·
Operating Margin Before Officers' Comp. 22	7.9	·	13.9	7.0	9.6	·	·	9.5	·	7.2	·	·	·

Selected Average Balance Sheet ($ in Thousands)

Net Receivables 23	55	9	20	264	6481	9193
Inventories 24						
Net Property, Plant and Equipment 25	541	57	484	805	10490	162501
Total Assets 26	1114	136	913	1966	33680	312678
Notes and Loans Payable 27	371	46	346	803	6600	45776
All Other Liabilities 28	210	18	99	269	6398	80076
Net Worth 29	534	73	468	894	20681	186825

Selected Financial Ratios (Times to 1)

Current Ratio 30	0.9	3.0	2.8	2.7	3.1	0.4
Quick Ratio 31	0.5	2.1	2.3	1.5	2.1	0.2
Net Sales to Working Capital 32		8.7	12.1	5.6	3.7	
Coverage Ratio 33	6.0	11.8	3.8	6.0	10.6	8.0
Total Asset Turnover 34	1.6	3.0	3.4	1.5	1.5	1.2
Inventory Turnover 35						
Receivables Turnover 36						
Total Liabilities to Net Worth 37	1.1	0.9	1.0	1.2	0.6	0.7
Current Assets to Working Capital 38		1.5	1.6	1.6	1.5	1.5
Current Liabilities to Working Capital 39		0.5	0.6	0.6	0.5	0.5
Working Capital to Net Sales 40		0.1	0.1	0.2	0.3	0.3
Inventory to Working Capital 41		0.3	0.0	0.6	0.3	0.3
Total Receipts to Cash Flow 42	5.0	3.7	5.7	5.2	6.3	4.7
Cost of Goods to Cash Flow 43	1.2	0.8	2.1	2.2	3.3	0.2
Cash Flow to Total Debt 44	0.6	1.7	1.2	0.5	0.6	0.6

Selected Financial Factors (in Percentages)

Debt Ratio 45	52.1	46.5	48.8	54.5	38.6	40.2
Return on Total Assets 46	11.0	28.1	11.9	10.4	10.1	6.6
Return on Equity Before Income Taxes 47	19.1	48.1	17.1	19.0	14.9	9.7
Return on Equity After Income Taxes 48	16.5	47.6	12.1	15.8	14.8	6.9
Profit Margin (Before Income Tax) 49	5.7	8.7	2.6	5.7	6.0	4.8
Profit Margin (After Income Tax) 50	4.9	8.6	1.8	4.8	5.9	3.4

Table I

Corporations with and without Net Income

COMMERCIAL AND INDUSTRIAL MACHINERY AND EQUIPMENT RENTAL

MONEY AMOUNTS AND SIZE OF ASSETS IN THOUSANDS OF DOLLARS

Item Description for Accounting Period 7/04 Through 6/05	Total	Zero Assets	Under 500	500 to 1,000	1,000 to 5,000	5,000 to 10,000	10,000 to 25,000	25,000 to 50,000	50,000 to 100,000	100,000 to 250,000	250,000 to 500,000	500,000 to 2,500,000	2,500,000 and over
Number of Enterprises **1**	30836	3032	20478	3025	3284	529	259	102	46	30	18	24	9
Revenues ($ in Thousands)													
Net Sales **2**	42639036	663954	3089421	2535127	3897285	3889961	2877714	2239887	1505063	2123253	2741586	5688433	11387352
Interest **3**	1330867	2704	6890	3553	9694	5389	15595	14201	35063	23601	117626	386675	709878
Rents **4**	25267	751	0	277	1530	281	1235	10005	336	215	1205	9433	0
Royalties **5**	14103	0	0	0	0	368	48	252	0	4851	0	0	8584
Other Portfolio Income **6**	2806282	113577	116212	61814	149568	43048	119803	103151	113718	62443	270851	233460	1418640
Other Receipts **7**	38462517	546922	2966319	2469483	3736493	3840875	2741033	2112278	1355946	2032143	2351904	5058865	9250250
Total Receipts **8**	42639036	663954	3089421	2535127	3897285	3889961	2877714	2239887	1505063	2123253	2741586	5688433	11387352
Average Total Receipts **9**	1383	219	151	838	1187	7353	11111	21960	32719	70775	152310	237018	1265261
Operating Costs/Operating Income (%)													
Cost of Operations **10**	25.3	29.5	20.0	31.6	38.2	43.3	35.8	37.2	35.3	31.5	24.5	17.1	11.3
Salaries and Wages **11**	11.5	4.4	16.1	12.0	11.4	9.5	10.2	8.7	9.5	8.7	9.7	10.4	13.9
Taxes Paid **12**	2.1	1.2	3.7	2.7	2.7	3.5	2.2	1.5	1.8	1.6	1.7	1.5	1.6
Interest Paid **13**	8.1	6.9	2.1	2.4	3.9	2.4	3.8	3.6	6.1	7.4	9.1	13.1	14.2
Depreciation **14**	24.4	11.1	15.2	12.1	14.8	15.3	20.3	26.6	21.3	26.2	37.5	32.3	30.4
Amortization and Depletion **15**	0.8	1.8	0.0	0.0	0.1	0.2	0.2	0.7	0.6	0.5	1.6	1.1	1.4
Pensions and Other Deferred Comp. **16**	0.5	0.0	0.2	0.5	0.6	1.9	0.4	0.3	0.2	0.4	0.1	0.2	0.7
Employee Benefits **17**	1.5	0.6	1.3	0.4	1.4	0.8	1.4	0.8	2.1	1.3	1.0	2.4	2.1
Advertising **18**	0.4	0.1	0.8	0.5	0.3	0.4	0.4	0.5	0.4	0.4	0.4	0.3	0.4
Other Expenses **19**	24.1	123.0	32.0	22.6	25.1	17.9	23.7	16.4	20.6	23.4	21.4	26.4	20.2
Officers' Compensation **20**	2.1	0.2	8.4	3.8	3.6	3.9	2.7	1.6	1.4	1.8	0.6	0.7	0.3
Operating Margin **21**	•	•	0.2	11.3	•	0.8	•	2.3	0.9	•	•	•	3.8
Operating Margin Before Officers' Comp. **22**	1.2	•	8.6	15.1	1.6	4.7	3.8	3.8	2.2	•	•	•	4.1

Selected Average Balance Sheet ($ in Thousands)

Net Receivables 23	663	0	17	85	391	883	2296	5558	12186	20754	58380	164670	1193198
Inventories 24	•	0	•	•	•	•	•	•	•	•	•	•	•
Net Property, Plant and Equipment 25	1392	0	53	290	904	4261	7588	15453	25211	71136	147450	270296	2194514
Total Assets 26	3961	0	115	700	2018	7243	15378	35112	67910	166346	312026	1022446	6819970
Notes and Loans Payable 27	1935	0	70	536	1270	4590	8235	16588	40562	93887	137871	425249	3202660
All Other Liabilities 28	1083	0	14	59	352	806	2636	6384	13700	32336	97624	215359	2387149
Net Worth 29	943	0	31	104	396	1847	4507	12140	13649	40123	76531	381839	1230161

Selected Financial Ratios (Times to 1)

Current Ratio 30	1.1	•	2.2	2.2	1.9	1.4	1.5	1.3	1.5	1.1	1.0	1.6	0.9
Quick Ratio 31	0.8	•	2.0	1.9	1.2	1.0	0.9	0.9	1.1	0.8	0.7	1.2	0.6
Net Sales to Working Capital 32	13.8	•	6.3	5.9	3.1	12.0	7.0	7.2	4.7	14.3	61.2	2.6	•
Coverage Ratio 33	0.9	•	1.1	5.7	0.5	1.3	0.7	1.6	1.1	0.6	0.1	0.6	1.2
Total Asset Turnover 34	0.3	•	1.3	1.2	0.6	1.0	0.7	0.6	0.5	0.4	0.5	0.2	0.2
Inventory Turnover 35	•	•	•	•	•	•	•	•	•	•	•	•	•
Receivables Turnover 36	•	•	•	•	•	•	•	•	•	•	•	•	•
Total Liabilities to Net Worth 37	3.2	•	2.7	5.7	4.1	2.9	2.4	1.9	4.0	3.1	3.1	1.7	4.5
Current Assets to Working Capital 38	11.3	•	1.8	1.8	2.2	3.4	3.2	3.9	2.9	9.3	36.7	2.8	•
Current Liabilities to Working Capital 39	10.3	•	0.8	0.8	1.2	2.4	2.2	2.9	1.9	8.3	35.7	1.8	•
Working Capital to Net Sales 40	0.1	•	0.2	0.2	0.3	0.1	0.1	0.1	0.2	0.1	0.0	0.4	•
Inventory to Working Capital 41	0.7	•	0.1	0.2	0.2	0.2	0.6	0.6	0.4	0.7	4.5	0.2	•
Total Receipts to Cash Flow 42	10.5	•	5.3	3.9	9.3	8.7	12.2	8.1	9.4	9.7	30.3	14.5	10.9
Cost of Goods to Cash Flow 43	2.7	•	1.1	1.2	3.6	3.8	4.4	3.0	3.3	3.1	7.4	2.5	1.2
Cash Flow to Total Debt 44	0.0	•	0.3	0.4	0.1	0.2	0.1	0.1	0.1	0.1	0.0	0.0	0.0

Selected Financial Factors (in Percentages)

Debt Ratio 45	76.2	•	72.8	85.1	80.4	74.5	70.7	65.4	79.9	75.9	75.5	62.7	82.0
Return on Total Assets 46	2.5	•	3.1	16.4	1.1	3.3	2.0	3.6	3.4	1.9	0.7	1.9	3.2
Return on Equity Before Income Taxes 47	•	•	0.9	90.9	•	3.2	•	4.1	2.1	•	•	•	3.4
Return on Equity After Income Taxes 48	•	•	0.3	87.7	•	1.7	•	3.0	0.8	•	•	•	3.0
Profit Margin (Before Income Tax) 49	•	•	0.2	11.3	•	0.8	•	2.3	0.9	•	•	•	3.3
Profit Margin (After Income Tax) 50	•	•	0.1	10.9	•	0.4	•	1.7	0.3	•	•	•	2.9

Table II

Corporations with Net Income

COMMERCIAL AND INDUSTRIAL MACHINERY AND EQUIPMENT RENTAL

MONEY AMOUNTS AND SIZE OF ASSETS IN THOUSANDS OF DOLLARS

Item Description for Accounting Period 7/04 Through 6/05	Total	Zero Assets	Under 500	500 to 1,000	1,000 to 5,000	5,000 to 10,000	10,000 to 25,000	25,000 to 50,000	50,000 to 100,000	100,000 to 250,000	250,000 to 500,000	500,000 to 2,500,000	2,500,000 and over
Number of Enterprises 1	12994	1266	8195	1749	1235	300	127	59	20	14	8	17	4
Revenues ($ in Thousands)													
Net Sales 2	25469101	274411	2177102	1810409	2508360	2837619	1781528	1715519	806004	1162097	1161187	3656836	5578029
Interest 3	846510	1332	5194	1185	3881	2330	13917	8623	22945	9778	55718	286815	434793
Rents 4	21922	751	0	186	1367	281	882	7601	0	215	1205	9433	0
Royalties 5	8103	0	0	0	0	368	0	252	0	4851	0	0	2633
Other Portfolio Income 6	1666127	45735	47619	59863	116415	33736	74860	75447	57484	53117	25709	161678	914468
Other Receipts 7	22926439	226593	2124289	1749175	2386697	2800904	1691869	1623596	725575	1094136	1078555	3198910	4226135
Total Receipts 8	25469101	274411	2177102	1810409	2508360	2837619	1781528	1715519	806004	1162097	1161187	3656836	5578029
Average Total Receipts 9	1960	217	266	1035	2031	9459	14028	29077	40300	83007	145148	215108	1394507
Operating Costs/Operating Income (%)													
Cost of Operations 10	27.2	44.9	18.4	19.8	40.2	36.6	36.4	42.4	42.3	31.7	41.0	13.9	16.7
Salaries and Wages 11	11.4	1.7	19.5	13.8	9.5	10.4	9.3	7.2	8.7	9.7	7.4	10.2	13.7
Taxes Paid 12	2.3	0.9	3.7	3.1	2.6	3.8	2.0	1.3	1.7	1.7	1.5	1.2	2.3
Interest Paid 13	6.5	6.1	1.7	2.1	3.1	2.2	2.8	2.8	4.5	4.0	4.7	10.2	14.4
Depreciation 14	17.5	12.5	9.8	13.7	9.9	15.6	16.0	19.8	16.5	21.2	19.6	25.3	19.9
Amortization and Depletion 15	0.5	0.5	0.0	0.0	0.0	0.3	0.0	0.6	0.2	0.3	1.1	1.0	0.8
Pensions and Other Deferred Comp. 16	0.4	0.1	0.0	0.4	0.4	0.4	0.5	0.3	0.3	0.4	0.0	0.3	0.5
Employee Benefits 17	1.2	0.2	1.7	0.4	1.0	0.8	1.2	0.8	0.9	1.2	1.0	2.0	1.4
Advertising 18	0.4	0.1	0.5	0.6	0.2	0.5	0.4	0.4	0.5	0.6	0.4	0.3	0.4
Other Expenses 19	20.8	11.1	26.3	23.4	19.7	19.3	20.7	13.4	12.2	18.3	13.9	30.5	18.6
Officers' Compensation 20	2.5	0.2	7.1	4.1	4.1	4.7	2.9	1.4	1.1	2.5	0.6	0.7	0.2
Operating Margin 21	9.4	21.9	11.2	18.6	9.2	5.4	7.8	9.6	11.2	8.3	8.6	4.5	11.1
Operating Margin Before Officers' Comp. 22	11.9	22.1	18.3	22.7	13.3	10.1	10.7	11.0	12.2	10.8	9.2	5.2	11.3

Selected Average Balance Sheet ($ in Thousands)

Net Receivables 23	810	•	30	69	736	1102	2563	5762	16770	14277	101390	144474	1111325
Inventories 24	•	•	•	•	•	•	•	•	•	•	•	•	•
Net Property, Plant and Equipment 25	1402	0	75	313	762	4021	6628	12246	27483	62491	58867	172898	2128573
Total Assets 26	5003	0	152	726	2042	7356	15378	34369	70530	159254	318771	989627	7692821
Notes and Loans Payable 27	2090	0	71	336	866	3283	7014	15842	44860	52498	98110	354739	3414727
All Other Liabilities 28	1463	0	16	43	279	872	2912	7204	9054	42829	78523	242096	2971767
Net Worth 29	1450	0	66	348	896	3200	5453	11323	16616	63928	142138	392793	1306327

Selected Financial Ratios (Times to 1)

Current Ratio 30	1.0	•	2.5	2.3	1.6	1.7	1.3	2.8	1.8	2.6	1.8	0.5
Quick Ratio 31	0.7	•	2.2	1.9	1.3	1.1	0.8	2.1	1.1	1.9	1.4	0.4
Net Sales to Working Capital 32	•	•	7.1	6.5	10.1	5.4	10.8	2.3	3.7	1.5	2.0	•
Coverage Ratio 33	2.4	4.6	7.4	9.9	3.5	3.8	4.5	3.5	3.1	2.8	1.5	1.7
Total Asset Turnover 34	0.4	•	1.7	1.4	1.0	0.9	0.8	0.6	0.5	0.5	0.2	0.2
Inventory Turnover 35	•	•	•	•	•	•	•	•	•	•	•	•
Receivables Turnover 36	•	•	•	•	•	•	•	•	•	•	•	•
Total Liabilities to Net Worth 37	2.5	•	1.3	1.1	1.3	1.8	2.0	3.2	1.5	1.2	1.5	4.9
Current Assets to Working Capital 38	•	•	1.7	1.8	2.5	2.4	4.8	1.6	2.3	1.6	2.2	•
Current Liabilities to Working Capital 39	•	•	0.7	0.8	1.5	1.4	3.8	0.6	1.3	0.6	1.2	•
Working Capital to Net Sales 40	•	•	0.1	0.2	0.1	0.2	0.1	0.4	0.3	0.7	0.5	•
Inventory to Working Capital 41	•	•	0.0	0.2	0.2	0.5	0.9	0.3	0.1	0.2	0.1	•
Total Receipts to Cash Flow 42	5.4	3.3	3.7	3.1	6.1	6.7	5.9	5.0	5.7	5.6	6.5	6.6
Cost of Goods to Cash Flow 43	1.5	1.5	0.7	0.6	2.2	2.4	2.5	2.1	1.8	2.3	0.9	1.1
Cash Flow to Total Debt 44	0.1	•	0.8	0.9	0.4	0.2	0.2	0.2	0.2	0.1	0.1	0.0

Selected Financial Factors (in Percentages)

Debt Ratio 45	71.0	•	56.7	52.1	56.5	64.5	67.1	76.4	59.9	55.4	60.3	83.0
Return on Total Assets 46	6.2	•	22.6	29.5	9.7	9.6	10.5	9.0	6.5	6.0	3.3	4.5
Return on Equity Before Income Taxes 47	12.6	•	45.2	55.4	15.9	20.0	24.6	27.0	11.1	8.7	2.7	11.2
Return on Equity After Income Taxes 48	11.5	•	44.4	53.7	14.4	18.6	22.7	24.7	8.1	6.6	2.3	10.3
Profit Margin (Before Income Tax) 49	9.4	21.9	11.2	18.6	5.4	7.8	9.6	11.1	8.5	8.6	5.0	10.5
Profit Margin (After Income Tax) 50	8.5	20.6	11.0	18.0	4.9	7.2	8.8	10.2	6.3	6.5	4.1	9.6

Table I

Corporations with and without Net Income

LESSORS OF NONFINAN. INTANGIBLE ASSETS (EX. COPYRIGHTED WORKS)

MONEY AMOUNTS AND SIZE OF ASSETS IN THOUSANDS OF DOLLARS

Item Description for Accounting Period 7/04 Through 6/05	Total	Zero Assets	Under 500	500 to 1,000	1,000 to 5,000	5,000 to 10,000	10,000 to 25,000	25,000 to 50,000	50,000 to 100,000	100,000 to 250,000	250,000 to 500,000	500,000 to 2,500,000	2,500,000 and over
Number of Enterprises **1**	1154	17	903	182	19	6	8	5	11	0	3	0	0
Revenues ($ in Thousands)													
Net Sales **2**	1125688	8768	63140	0	105038	37316	84507	148647	460899	0	217375	0	0
Interest **3**	23639	459	0	0	1478	433	290	384	5806	0	14789	0	0
Rents **4**	3503	0	0	0	0	51	210	98	0	0	3144	0	0
Royalties **5**	541695	8309	24434	0	0	15131	7196	45686	296653	0	144286	0	0
Other Portfolio Income **6**	2621	0	0	0	230	7	1409	19	953	0	5	0	0
Other Receipts **7**	554230	0	38706	0	103330	21694	75402	102460	157487	0	55151	0	0
Total Receipts **8**	1125688	8768	63140	0	105038	37316	84507	148647	460899	0	217375	0	0
Average Total Receipts **9**	975	516	70	0	5528	6219	10563	29729	41900	·	72458	·	·
Operating Costs/Operating Income (%)													
Cost of Operations **10**	5.7	·	0.5	·	1.6	2.2	6.3	20.1	5.7	·	·	·	·
Salaries and Wages **11**	15.1	0.1	13.2	·	29.3	12.5	17.0	10.3	16.5	·	9.1	·	·
Taxes Paid **12**	3.2	0.0	8.3	·	3.3	2.9	2.7	6.3	2.0	·	2.2	·	·
Interest Paid **13**	2.7	·	1.3	·	0.2	0.6	3.0	3.8	2.0	·	5.5	·	·
Depreciation **14**	2.8	·	·	·	0.4	0.5	2.4	0.6	1.5	·	9.5	·	·
Amortization and Depletion **15**	4.8	53.5	10.7	·	1.1	12.4	1.9	11.8	3.5	·	0.5	·	·
Pensions and Other Deferred Comp. **16**	0.1	·	·	·	·	0.0	0.5	0.1	0.0	·	0.3	·	·
Employee Benefits **17**	1.5	·	·	·	1.8	0.1	0.5	0.9	2.3	·	1.1	·	·
Advertising **18**	2.8	·	0.6	·	1.3	0.9	3.4	1.8	5.2	·	0.0	·	·
Other Expenses **19**	29.0	5.9	65.6	·	28.3	21.7	28.0	40.1	31.0	·	9.5	·	·
Officers' Compensation **20**	6.3	·	26.4	·	19.9	·	13.2	2.5	1.2	·	5.8	·	·
Operating Margin **21**	26.1	40.5	·	·	12.7	46.1	21.1	1.7	29.0	·	56.5	·	·
Operating Margin Before Officers' Comp. **22**	32.4	40.5	40.5	·	32.6	46.1	34.2	4.3	30.2	·	62.3	·	·

Selected Average Balance Sheet ($ in Thousands)

Item										
Net Receivables 23	129	0	0	2170	72	3037	3398	72	2543	5858
Inventories 24	•	•	•	•	•	•	•	•	•	•
Net Property, Plant and Equipment 25	297	0	0	158	228	2836	1094	228	1407	98342
Total Assets 26	2566	0	539	2830	7464	18450	34464	1094	83404	486655
Notes and Loans Payable 27	374	0	0	0	979	4940	23778		13403	33663
All Other Liabilities 28	477	0	110	714	1236	1747	5997		12897	81592
Net Worth 29	1715	0	-56	2116	5249	11762	4689		57104	371400

Selected Financial Ratios (Times to 1)

Item										
Current Ratio 30	1.4		0.4	3.5	2.4	2.7	1.6	2.2	0.7	
Quick Ratio 31	0.8		0.4	3.4	1.2	1.8	1.5	0.6	0.6	
Net Sales to Working Capital 32	8.7			3.1	3.5	2.2	6.6	4.5		
Coverage Ratio 33	10.6			55.2	73.9	8.0	1.4	15.6	11.2	
Total Asset Turnover 34	0.4	0.9		2.0	0.8	0.6	0.9	0.5	0.1	
Inventory Turnover 35	•	•	•	•	•	•	•	•	•	
Receivables Turnover 36	•	•	•	•	•	•	•	•	•	
Total Liabilities to Net Worth 37	0.5			0.3	0.4	0.6	6.3	0.5	0.3	
Current Assets to Working Capital 38	3.5			1.4	1.7	1.6	2.6	1.9		
Current Liabilities to Working Capital 39	2.5			0.4	0.7	0.6	1.6	0.9		
Working Capital to Net Sales 40	0.1			0.3	0.3	0.5	0.2	0.2		
Inventory to Working Capital 41	0.1				0.0	0.0	0.1	0.0		
Total Receipts to Cash Flow 42	1.9	2.2	2.6	2.6	1.5	2.2	2.5	1.7	1.6	
Cost of Goods to Cash Flow 43	0.1	0.0		0.0	0.0	0.0	0.1	0.5	0.1	
Cash Flow to Total Debt 44	0.6		0.2	2.9	1.9	0.7	0.4	0.9	0.4	

Selected Financial Factors (in Percentages)

Item								
Debt Ratio 45	33.2	174.9	25.2	29.7	36.2	86.4	31.5	23.7
Return on Total Assets 46	10.9		25.3	38.9	13.7	4.7	15.5	9.2
Return on Equity Before Income Taxes 47	14.8	33.1	33.2	54.6	18.8	10.8	21.2	11.0
Return on Equity After Income Taxes 48	10.9	33.1	33.2	38.9	16.9		17.7	7.2
Profit Margin (Before Income Tax) 49	26.0	40.5	12.7	46.1	21.0	1.7	28.8	56.5
Profit Margin (After Income Tax) 50	19.1	26.6	12.7	32.8	18.9		24.1	36.7

Table II
Corporations with Net Income

REAL ESTATE AND RENTAL AND LEASING
533110

LESSORS OF NONFINAN. INTANGIBLE ASSETS (EX. COPYRIGHTED WORKS)

MONEY AMOUNTS AND SIZE OF ASSETS IN THOUSANDS OF DOLLARS

Item Description for Accounting Period 7/04 Through 6/05	Total	Zero Assets	Under 500	500 to 1,000	1,000 to 5,000	5,000 to 10,000	10,000 to 25,000	25,000 to 50,000	50,000 to 100,000	100,000 to 250,000	250,000 to 500,000	500,000 to 2,500,000	2,500,000 and over
Number of Enterprises **1**	289	0	247	0	19	0	0	0	6	0	3	0	0
Revenues ($ in Thousands)													
Net Sales **2**	1025158	0	29659	0	105038	0	0	0	444739	0	217375	0	0
Interest **3**	23586	0	0	0	1478	0	0	0	5789	0	14789	0	0
Rents **4**	3503	0	0	0	0	0	0	0	0	0	3144	0	0
Royalties **5**	528005	0	24434	0	0	0	0	0	282963	0	144286	0	0
Other Portfolio Income **6**	2311	0	0	0	230	0	0	0	649	0	5	0	0
Other Receipts **7**	467753	0	5225	0	103330	0	0	0	155338	0	55151	0	0
Total Receipts **8**	1025158	0	29659	0	105038	0	0	0	444739	0	217375	0	0
Average Total Receipts **9**	3547	.	120	.	5528	.	.	.	74123	.	72458	.	.
Operating Costs/Operating Income (%)													
Cost of Operations **10**	6.0	.	1.2	.	1.6	.	.	.	5.9	.	.	.	.
Salaries and Wages **11**	15.5	.	28.1	.	29.3	.	.	.	16.7	.	9.1	.	.
Taxes Paid **12**	3.0	.	6.0	.	3.3	.	.	.	2.0	.	2.2	.	.
Interest Paid **13**	2.1	.	.	.	0.2	.	.	.	1.3	.	5.5	.	.
Depreciation **14**	2.9	.	.	.	0.4	.	.	.	1.5	.	9.5	.	.
Amortization and Depletion **15**	2.2	.	.	.	1.1	.	.	.	2.4	.	0.5	.	.
Pensions and Other Deferred Comp. **16**	0.1	.	.	.	.	.	.	.	0.0	.	0.3	.	.
Employee Benefits **17**	1.6	.	.	.	1.8	.	.	.	2.4	.	1.1	.	.
Advertising **18**	2.9	.	1.3	.	1.3	.	.	.	5.4	.	0.0	.	.
Other Expenses **19**	24.7	.	7.0	.	28.3	.	.	.	30.7	.	9.5	.	.
Officers' Compensation **20**	5.9	.	56.1	.	19.9	.	.	.	0.8	.	5.8	.	.
Operating Margin **21**	33.0	.	0.4	.	12.7	.	.	.	30.8	.	56.5	.	.
Operating Margin Before Officers' Comp. **22**	38.9	.	56.5	.	32.6	.	.	.	31.6	.	62.3	.	.

Selected Average Balance Sheet ($ in Thousands)

Net Receivables 23	404	15	2170	4324	5858
Inventories 24					
Net Property, Plant and Equipment 25	1140	0	158	2540	98342
Total Assets 26	8262	124	2830	102585	486655
Notes and Loans Payable 27	982	0	0	22890	33663
All Other Liabilities 28	1194	101	714	3224	81592
Net Worth 29	6085	22	2116	76471	371400

Selected Financial Ratios (Times to 1)

Current Ratio 30	1.9	1.2	3.5	2.3	0.7
Quick Ratio 31	1.1	1.2	3.4	0.6	0.6
Net Sales to Working Capital 32	5.6	5.4	3.1	4.2	
Coverage Ratio 33	17.0		55.2	24.2	11.2
Total Asset Turnover 34	0.4	1.0	2.0	0.7	0.1
Inventory Turnover 35					
Receivables Turnover 36					
Total Liabilities to Net Worth 37	0.4	4.5	0.3	0.3	0.3
Current Assets to Working Capital 38	2.2	5.5	1.4	1.7	
Current Liabilities to Working Capital 39	1.2	4.5	0.4	0.7	
Working Capital to Net Sales 40	0.2	0.2	0.3	0.2	
Inventory to Working Capital 41	0.0	0.0		0.0	
Total Receipts to Cash Flow 42	1.8	13.7	2.6	1.7	1.6
Cost of Goods to Cash Flow 43	0.1	0.2	0.0	0.1	
Cash Flow to Total Debt 44	0.9	0.1	2.9	1.7	0.4

Selected Financial Factors (in Percentages)

Debt Ratio 45	26.3	81.9	25.2	25.5	23.7
Return on Total Assets 46	15.0	0.4	25.3	23.1	9.2
Return on Equity Before Income Taxes 47	19.2	2.1	33.2	29.7	11.0
Return on Equity After Income Taxes 48	14.8	1.8	33.2	25.0	7.2
Profit Margin (Before Income Tax) 49	33.0	0.4	12.7	30.7	56.5
Profit Margin (After Income Tax) 50	25.3	0.3	12.7	25.7	36.7

Table I

Corporations with and without Net Income

LEGAL SERVICES

MONEY AMOUNTS AND SIZE OF ASSETS IN THOUSANDS OF DOLLARS

Item Description for Accounting Period 7/04 Through 6/05	Total	Zero Assets	Under 500	500 to 1,000	1,000 to 5,000	5,000 to 10,000	10,000 to 25,000	25,000 to 50,000	50,000 to 100,000	100,000 to 250,000	250,000 to 500,000	500,000 to 2,500,000	2,500,000 and over
Number of Enterprises 1	99464	13931	81065	2481	1685	170	95	24	8	4	0	0	0
Revenues ($ in Thousands)													
Net Sales 2	71541661	1526378	43341943	5926258	8312197	5007966	4011949	2234060	512406	608504	0	0	0
Interest 3	53377	256	31675	5833	3369	4456	3675	2074	1258	780	0	0	0
Rents 4	86623	153	36881	19547	19137	6986	3174	744	0	0	0	0	0
Royalties 5	6903	1	6875	0	0	0	18	10	0	0	0	0	0
Other Portfolio Income 6	108862	5069	87432	4832	237	8075	1403	716	369	727	0	0	0
Other Receipts 7	3001664	22572	1517531	653742	388423	54823	125181	218766	2514	18114	0	0	0
Total Receipts 8	74799090	1554429	45082337	6610212	8723363	5082306	4145400	2456370	516547	628125	0	0	0
Average Total Receipts 9	752	112	556	2664	5177	29896	43636	102349	64568	157031	•	•	•
Operating Costs/Operating Income (%)													
Cost of Operations 10	4.3	5.2	5.0	5.6	3.4	0.5	4.8	0.4	3.6	•	•	•	•
Salaries and Wages 11	28.7	14.8	23.3	27.9	31.2	50.5	45.4	54.5	32.9	34.0	•	•	•
Taxes Paid 12	3.6	3.6	3.7	3.9	3.2	3.6	3.1	3.4	3.2	2.5	•	•	•
Interest Paid 13	0.4	0.3	0.3	0.3	0.4	0.3	0.5	0.3	1.3	0.4	•	•	•
Depreciation 14	1.1	0.7	1.0	1.3	1.0	1.7	1.7	1.8	2.0	1.7	•	•	•
Amortization and Depletion 15	0.1	0.0	0.0	0.1	0.0	0.0	0.0	0.1	0.8	1.7	•	•	•
Pensions and Other Deferred Comp. 16	2.1	2.8	1.8	2.9	2.4	2.3	2.6	3.1	0.3	0.6	•	•	•
Employee Benefits 17	1.8	0.9	1.7	2.2	1.3	2.2	2.1	2.1	2.2	1.7	•	•	•
Advertising 18	1.6	1.9	1.5	3.2	2.0	0.9	0.6	0.7	2.0	0.9	•	•	•
Other Expenses 19	28.8	39.6	32.3	24.9	19.0	21.5	23.1	24.1	28.6	36.9	•	•	•
Officers' Compensation 20	23.2	21.5	23.0	34.1	30.7	15.0	15.0	13.9	5.7	1.5	•	•	•
Operating Margin 21	4.5	8.6	6.4	•	5.3	1.6	1.0	•	17.4	18.1	•	•	•
Operating Margin Before Officers' Comp. 22	27.6	30.1	29.4	27.7	36.0	16.5	16.1	9.5	23.0	19.6	•	•	•

Selected Average Balance Sheet ($ in Thousands)

Net Receivables 23	8	0	2	46	100	275	921	3619	6511	20332
Inventories 24	1	0	0	2	7	39	145	392	0	0
Net Property, Plant and Equipment 25	26	0	16	71	200	1895	2579	5778	3301	6264
Total Assets 26	156	0	74	726	1783	7561	14898	34096	61727	170592
Notes and Loans Payable 27	56	0	38	276	304	2640	4669	6982	11741	29560
All Other Liabilities 28	73	0	35	260	945	2996	7434	15809	24280	95798
Net Worth 29	27	0	1	190	534	1926	2795	11305	25706	45234

Selected Financial Ratios (Times to 1)

Current Ratio 30	1.2	.	1.0	1.1	1.5	1.2	1.2	1.2	1.6	1.0
Quick Ratio 31	0.7	.	0.7	0.6	0.8	0.7	0.7	0.7	0.9	0.4
Net Sales to Working Capital 32	53.9	.	3236.3	41.5	11.9	35.1	26.1	35.5	4.2	.
Coverage Ratio 33	26.2	32.5	30.8	16.0	28.9	12.8	9.4	17.7	14.9	55.0
Total Asset Turnover 34	4.6	.	7.2	3.3	2.8	3.9	2.8	2.7	1.0	0.9
Inventory Turnover 35	57.0	.	174.1	73.8	23.0	3.7	13.9	0.8	.	.
Receivables Turnover 36	84.4	.	219.8	63.4	43.2	104.9	44.3	21.2	10.1	8.6
Total Liabilities to Net Worth 37	4.7	.	70.8	2.8	2.3	2.9	4.3	2.0	1.4	2.8
Current Assets to Working Capital 38	7.2	.	244.3	7.9	3.2	5.7	6.1	7.1	2.6	.
Current Liabilities to Working Capital 39	6.2	.	243.3	6.9	2.2	4.7	5.1	6.1	1.6	.
Working Capital to Net Sales 40	0.0	.	0.0	0.0	0.1	0.0	0.0	0.0	0.2	.
Inventory to Working Capital 41	0.0	.	0.5	0.1	.	.	0.1	0.1	.	.
Total Receipts to Cash Flow 42	3.2	2.4	2.8	4.3	4.1	5.5	4.7	4.6	2.3	1.8
Cost of Goods to Cash Flow 43	0.1	0.1	0.1	0.2	0.1	0.0	0.2	0.0	0.1	.
Cash Flow to Total Debt 44	1.7	.	2.6	1.0	1.0	1.0	0.7	0.9	0.8	0.7

Selected Financial Factors (in Percentages)

Debt Ratio 45	82.5	.	98.6	73.9	70.1	74.5	81.2	66.8	58.4	73.5
Return on Total Assets 46	43.3	.	76.9	18.0	29.5	13.0	13.8	16.2	20.4	19.2
Return on Equity Before Income Taxes 47	238.3	.	5338.4	64.5	95.0	47.0	65.6	46.2	45.7	71.2
Return on Equity After Income Taxes 48	233.3	.	5278.8	62.6	94.1	40.9	58.7	39.7	42.9	70.2
Profit Margin (Before Income Tax) 49	9.0	10.4	10.3	5.1	10.3	3.1	4.3	5.6	18.3	21.2
Profit Margin (After Income Tax) 50	8.8	10.1	10.1	5.0	10.2	2.7	3.9	4.8	17.2	20.9

Table II
Corporations with Net Income

LEGAL SERVICES

MONEY AMOUNTS AND SIZE OF ASSETS IN THOUSANDS OF DOLLARS

Item Description for Accounting Period 7/04 Through 6/05	Total	Zero Assets	Under 500	500 to 1,000	1,000 to 5,000	5,000 to 10,000	10,000 to 25,000	25,000 to 50,000	50,000 to 100,000	100,000 to 250,000	250,000 to 500,000	500,000 to 2,500,000	2,500,000 and over
Number of Enterprises 1	68266	8242	56979	1709	1097	137	71	0	0	4	0	0	0
Revenues ($ in Thousands)													
Net Sales 2	55822296	755354	33734963	3941037	6858299	4423932	3337637	0	0	608504	0	0	0
Interest 3	31418	256	16471	2529	1631	3792	3118	0	0	780	0	0	0
Rents 4	65874	153	36161	214	18744	6986	2982	0	0	0	0	0	0
Royalties 5	27	1	0	0	0	0	16	0	0	0	0	0	0
Other Portfolio Income 6	50190	5069	30284	4150	211	8075	810	0	0	727	0	0	0
Other Receipts 7	2240729	20532	1412041	301855	104634	51256	116268	0	0	18114	0	0	0
Total Receipts 8	58216534	781365	35229920	4249785	6983519	4494041	3460831	0	0	628125	0	0	0
Average Total Receipts 9	853	95	618	2487	6366	32803	48744	•	•	157031	•	•	•
Operating Costs/Operating Income (%)													
Cost of Operations 10	4.9	•	5.6	8.5	4.1	0.6	5.5	•	•	•	•	•	•
Salaries and Wages 11	27.8	15.0	21.8	23.1	30.3	51.8	42.9	•	•	34.0	•	•	•
Taxes Paid 12	3.5	2.9	3.7	3.4	3.1	3.5	3.0	•	•	2.5	•	•	•
Interest Paid 13	0.3	0.2	0.3	0.3	0.3	0.3	0.4	•	•	0.4	•	•	•
Depreciation 14	1.1	0.8	0.9	1.3	1.0	1.7	1.7	•	•	1.7	•	•	•
Amortization and Depletion 15	0.1	•	0.0	0.1	0.0	0.0	0.0	•	•	1.7	•	•	•
Pensions and Other Deferred Comp. 16	2.0	1.1	1.7	3.3	2.0	2.2	2.6	•	•	0.6	•	•	•
Employee Benefits 17	1.5	0.5	1.5	1.5	0.8	2.1	2.1	•	•	1.7	•	•	•
Advertising 18	1.7	2.9	1.5	4.7	2.2	0.7	0.7	•	•	0.9	•	•	•
Other Expenses 19	27.7	32.8	30.9	24.0	19.3	22.0	22.9	•	•	36.9	•	•	•
Officers' Compensation 20	21.0	21.8	21.7	29.7	25.3	13.1	16.1	•	•	1.5	•	•	•
Operating Margin 21	8.5	22.1	10.5	0.2	11.5	2.0	2.0	•	•	18.1	•	•	•
Operating Margin Before Officers' Comp. 22	29.5	43.9	32.2	29.8	36.8	15.1	18.1	•	•	19.6	•	•	•

Selected Average Balance Sheet ($ in Thousands)

Net Receivables 23	10	0	2	49	121	340	989	20332
Inventories 24	1	0	0	0	11	48	155	0
Net Property, Plant and Equipment 25	29	0	16	62	270	2197	2726	6264
Total Assets 26	168	0	83	712	1525	7463	15201	170592
Notes and Loans Payable 27	51	0	31	182	371	2566	4571	29560
All Other Liabilities 28	73	0	36	326	642	2446	7290	95798
Net Worth 29	44	0	16	205	512	2450	3339	45234

Selected Financial Ratios (Times to 1)

Current Ratio 30	1.3	•	1.2	1.4	1.4	1.2	1.3	1.0
Quick Ratio 31	0.8	•	0.9	0.8	0.9	0.8	0.8	0.4
Net Sales to Working Capital 32	38.3	129.9	67.3	15.5	23.9	46.9	23.1	•
Coverage Ratio 33	42.5	•	54.1	26.2	39.1	15.3	16.5	55.0
Total Asset Turnover 34	4.9	•	7.2	3.2	4.1	4.3	3.1	0.9
Inventory Turnover 35	65.1	•	153.4	83490.0	23.0	3.7	16.7	•
Receivables Turnover 36	80.4	•	203.6	72.7	43.7	99.3	44.1	8.6
Total Liabilities to Net Worth 37	2.8	•	4.1	2.5	2.0	2.0	3.6	2.8
Current Assets to Working Capital 38	4.8	•	5.3	3.7	3.7	6.2	5.0	•
Current Liabilities to Working Capital 39	3.8	•	4.3	2.7	2.7	5.2	4.0	•
Working Capital to Net Sales 40	0.0	•	0.0	0.1	0.0	0.0	0.0	•
Inventory to Working Capital 41	0.0	•	0.0	0.0	•	•	0.1	•
Total Receipts to Cash Flow 42	2.9	1.9	2.5	3.8	3.6	5.2	4.4	1.8
Cost of Goods to Cash Flow 43	0.1	•	0.1	0.3	0.1	0.0	0.2	•
Cash Flow to Total Debt 44	2.3	•	3.5	1.2	1.7	1.2	0.9	0.7

Selected Financial Factors (in Percentages)

Debt Ratio 45	73.7	•	80.5	71.2	66.4	67.2	78.0	73.5
Return on Total Assets 46	63.9	•	108.9	26.9	56.0	16.8	18.8	19.2
Return on Equity Before Income Taxes 47	237.3	•	547.9	90.1	162.6	47.7	80.5	71.2
Return on Equity After Income Taxes 48	232.8	•	542.5	87.5	161.2	41.8	72.9	70.2
Profit Margin (Before Income Tax) 49	12.8	25.5	14.9	8.0	13.3	3.6	5.7	21.2
Profit Margin (After Income Tax) 50	12.6	24.9	14.7	7.8	13.2	3.2	5.2	20.9

ACCOUNTING, TAX PREPARATION, BOOKKEEPING, AND PAYROLL SERVICES

Table I

Corporations with and without Net Income

MONEY AMOUNTS AND SIZE OF ASSETS IN THOUSANDS OF DOLLARS

Item Description for Accounting Period 7/04 Through 6/05	Total	Zero Assets	Under 500	500 to 1,000	1,000 to 5,000	5,000 to 10,000	10,000 to 25,000	25,000 to 50,000	50,000 to 100,000	100,000 to 250,000	250,000 to 500,000	500,000 to 2,500,000	2,500,000 and over
Number of Enterprises **1**	65260	11536	52489	459	675	31	40	15	10	0	5	0	0

Revenues ($ in Thousands)

	Total	Zero Assets	Under 500	500 to 1,000	1,000 to 5,000	5,000 to 10,000	10,000 to 25,000	25,000 to 50,000	50,000 to 100,000	100,000 to 250,000	250,000 to 500,000	500,000 to 2,500,000	2,500,000 and over
Net Sales **2**	27154888	745360	15033268	1236556	2433276	329640	413506	2129662	530957	0	4302663	0	0
Interest **3**	423436	1466	10617	5240	2159	429	2581	3141	13727	0	384076	0	0
Rents **4**	22142	0	3919	8899	0	1307	62	0	1754	0	6202	0	0
Royalties **5**	543372	0	0	0	0	0	2022	0	7999	0	533352	0	0
Other Portfolio Income **6**	238419	0	61739	11423	259	299	19157	161	1290	0	144092	0	0
Other Receipts **7**	1777900	113697	93911	10373	9709	7484	208677	11022	48030	0	1274994	0	0
Total Receipts **8**	30160157	860523	15203454	1272491	2445403	339159	646005	2143986	603757	0	6645379	0	0
Average Total Receipts **9**	462	75	290	2772	3623	10941	16150	142932	60376	•	1329076	•	•

Operating Costs/Operating Income (%)

	Total	Zero Assets	Under 500	500 to 1,000	1,000 to 5,000	5,000 to 10,000	10,000 to 25,000	25,000 to 50,000	50,000 to 100,000	100,000 to 250,000	250,000 to 500,000	500,000 to 2,500,000	2,500,000 and over
Cost of Operations **10**	10.1	0.1	2.4	21.3	0.4	17.5	60.8	82.4	1.8	•	1.0	•	•
Salaries and Wages **11**	32.5	33.7	30.4	36.6	39.9	44.6	35.4	7.4	50.7	•	43.3	•	•
Taxes Paid **12**	4.5	3.7	4.4	4.8	3.8	5.3	4.7	4.4	2.9	•	5.6	•	•
Interest Paid **13**	1.4	1.3	0.4	0.7	0.7	0.4	1.0	0.4	2.7	•	6.0	•	•
Depreciation **14**	1.7	1.4	1.3	2.3	1.0	3.3	1.5	0.1	3.5	•	3.8	•	•
Amortization and Depletion **15**	0.8	0.2	0.3	0.0	0.4	0.3	0.5	0.0	1.0	•	3.6	•	•
Pensions and Other Deferred Comp. **16**	1.9	0.4	2.2	4.9	1.3	0.4	1.1	0.1	2.3	°	1.5	•	•
Employee Benefits **17**	2.5	2.4	2.4	3.2	2.3	3.2	4.6	2.7	3.4	•	2.5	•	•
Advertising **18**	1.9	3.2	1.0	0.2	7.3	0.8	0.7	0.0	2.1	•	3.5	•	•
Other Expenses **19**	29.7	42.1	26.2	16.6	21.9	18.1	34.2	1.4	34.7	•	61.7	•	•
Officers' Compensation **20**	15.2	21.7	22.3	11.7	15.0	7.5	9.2	0.7	0.8	•	0.7	•	•
Operating Margin **21**	•	•	6.9	•	5.9	•	•	0.2	•	•	•	•	•
Operating Margin Before Officers' Comp. **22**	13.0	11.4	29.1	9.3	20.8	6.3	•	1.0	•	•	1.0	•	•

Selected Average Balance Sheet ($ in Thousands)

Net Receivables 23	34	0	4	221	213	514	2286	6204	10571 · · 290122
Inventories 24	2	0	0	0	56	9	2899	561	· · 15769
Net Property, Plant and Equipment 25	21	0	8	369	336	544	402	1099	6806 · · 79217
Total Assets 26	301	54	799	1772	7726	14699	38623	83216	2606729
Notes and Loans Payable 27	166	25	631	533	1974	1872	8558	16188	1696026
All Other Liabilities 28	90	17	205	950	6558	14131	26049	46897	526250
Net Worth 29	45	12	-37	289	-806	-1304	4015	20131	384453

Selected Financial Ratios (Times to 1)

Current Ratio 30	0.9	·	1.1	0.7	0.6	1.1	1.3	0.8	1.2 · 0.8
Quick Ratio 31	0.7	·	0.9	0.6	0.6	0.5	0.9	0.6	0.5 · 0.7
Net Sales to Working Capital 32	·	·	188.5	·	28.2	4.0	·	6.5	· ·
Coverage Ratio 33	7.3	4.9	20.0	1.7	10.4	5.0	3.7	3.3	3.8 · 4.6
Total Asset Turnover 34	1.4	·	5.4	3.4	2.0	1.4	0.7	3.7	0.6 · 0.3
Inventory Turnover 35	21.0	·	196.1	·	88.2	33.0	675.4	40.4	· · 0.5
Receivables Turnover 36	8.9	·	61.0	19.1	13.8	10.6	4.3	18.3	5.8 · 1.9
Total Liabilities to Net Worth 37	5.7	·	3.4	·	5.1	·	·	8.6	3.1 · 5.8
Current Assets to Working Capital 38	·	·	15.5	·	17.6	4.4	·	5.6	· ·
Current Liabilities to Working Capital 39	·	·	14.5	·	16.6	3.4	·	4.6	· ·
Working Capital to Net Sales 40	·	·	0.0	·	0.0	0.3	·	0.2	· ·
Inventory to Working Capital 41	·	·	0.0	·	0.1	0.0	·	0.1	· ·
Total Receipts to Cash Flow 42	3.1	2.9	3.7	8.8	6.8	3.3	48.7	2.8	1.3
Cost of Goods to Cash Flow 43	0.3	0.0	0.1	1.9	0.0	1.2	2.0	40.1	0.1 · 0.0
Cash Flow to Total Debt 44	0.5	1.9	0.4	0.6	0.2	0.2	0.1	0.3	0.3

Selected Financial Factors (in Percentages)

Debt Ratio 45	85.1	·	77.2	104.7	83.7	110.4	108.9	89.6	75.8 · 85.3
Return on Total Assets 46	14.1	·	45.1	4.0	14.3	2.8	2.5	4.7	6.6 · 9.0
Return on Equity Before Income Taxes 47	82.0	·	188.1	·	79.5	·	·	31.5	20.2 · 47.9
Return on Equity After Income Taxes 48	67.8	·	183.5	·	72.8	·	·	29.5	12.7 · 29.9
Profit Margin (Before Income Tax) 49	8.8	5.1	8.0	0.5	6.4	1.6	0.9	2.6	7.7 · 21.4
Profit Margin (After Income Tax) 50	7.3	4.8	7.8	0.4	5.8	1.5	0.8	0.8	4.8 · 13.4

Table II

Corporations with Net Income

ACCOUNTING, TAX PREPARATION, BOOKKEEPING, AND PAYROLL SERVICES

MONEY AMOUNTS AND SIZE OF ASSETS IN THOUSANDS OF DOLLARS

Item Description for Accounting Period 7/04 Through 6/05	Total	Zero Assets	Under 500	500 to 1,000	1,000 to 5,000	5,000 to 10,000	10,000 to 25,000	25,000 to 50,000	50,000 to 100,000	100,000 to 250,000	250,000 to 500,000	500,000 to 2,500,000	2,500,000 and over
Number of Enterprises 1	48363	7556	39906	339	488	27	0	10	6	0	0	0	0
Revenues ($ in Thousands)													
Net Sales 2	20962352	570690	10966085	778067	1968236	204707	0	1942625	408280	0	0	0	0
Interest 3	406642	1465	4949	1842	1030	349	0	194	11246	0	0	0	0
Rents 4	16469	0	0	8512	0	0	0	0	1754	0	0	0	0
Royalties 5	540334	0	0	0	0	0	0	0	7999	0	0	0	0
Other Portfolio Income 6	225885	0	61388	18	231	0	0	62	1284	0	0	0	0
Other Receipts 7	1407474	7421	54975	9897	4648	3869	0	11242	48030	0	0	0	0
Total Receipts 8	23559156	579576	11087397	798336	1974145	208925	0	1954123	478593	0	0	0	0
Average Total Receipts 9	487	77	278	2355	4045	7738	•	195412	79766	•	•	•	•
Operating Costs/Operating Income (%)													
Cost of Operations 10	11.8	•	1.5	27.4	0.2	25.3	•	90.3	0.6	•	•	•	•
Salaries and Wages 11	28.7	12.5	26.4	28.4	41.3	39.8	•	1.4	52.5	•	•	•	•
Taxes Paid 12	4.4	3.8	4.1	5.2	3.6	5.6	•	4.3	2.4	•	•	•	•
Interest Paid 13	1.6	0.4	0.4	0.9	0.5	0.5	•	0.1	2.9	•	•	•	•
Depreciation 14	1.6	0.9	1.2	2.0	0.7	1.4	•	0.1	2.9	•	•	•	•
Amortization and Depletion 15	0.9	0.0	0.3	0.1	0.2	0.3	•	0.0	0.4	•	•	•	•
Pensions and Other Deferred Comp. 16	1.7	0.6	2.0	5.0	1.2	0.1	•	0.1	3.0	•	•	•	•
Employee Benefits 17	2.1	2.7	2.1	1.9	2.3	2.8	•	1.2	4.1	•	•	•	•
Advertising 18	2.2	0.5	1.1	0.2	8.9	1.0	•	0.0	2.5	•	•	•	•
Other Expenses 19	29.3	35.0	25.9	16.9	22.4	14.4	•	1.1	32.8	•	•	•	•
Officers' Compensation 20	14.8	26.7	23.6	12.4	10.4	1.7	•	0.7	0.4	•	•	•	•
Operating Margin 21	0.8	16.8	11.3	•	8.3	7.2	•	0.7	•	•	•	•	•
Operating Margin Before Officers' Comp. 22	15.6	43.5	34.8	12.1	18.7	8.9	•	1.4	•	•	•	•	•

Selected Average Balance Sheet ($ in Thousands)

Net Receivables 23	39	0	3	201	192	471	6011	15530
Inventories 24	3	0	0	0	0	10	4292	1117
Net Property, Plant and Equipment 25	22	0	8	394	383	313	887	8528
Total Assets 26	346	0	50	819	1766	7898	38814	82310
Notes and Loans Payable 27	204	0	22	623	374	804	12198	17374
All Other Liabilities 28	78	0	8	163	615	7107	17864	42945
Net Worth 29	64	0	21	33	777	-14	8752	21990

Selected Financial Ratios (Times to 1)

Current Ratio 30	0.9	•	1.7	0.7	0.6	1.1	1.0	1.3
Quick Ratio 31	0.8	•	1.4	0.7	0.6	0.5	0.6	0.6
Net Sales to Working Capital 32	•	•	29.4	•	•	14.3	1876.9	6.2
Coverage Ratio 33	9.3	43.7	31.3	3.7	19.2	18.2	14.7	5.4
Total Asset Turnover 34	1.3	•	5.4	2.8	2.3	1.0	5.0	0.8
Inventory Turnover 35	19.1	•	91.1	•	299.5	184.0	40.9	0.3
Receivables Turnover 36	7.9	•	60.4	22.7	23.1	14.3	26.0	•
Total Liabilities to Net Worth 37	4.4	•	1.4	23.8	1.3	•	3.4	2.7
Current Assets to Working Capital 38	•	•	2.4	•	•	13.5	265.8	4.4
Current Liabilities to Working Capital 39	•	•	1.4	•	•	12.5	264.8	3.4
Working Capital to Net Sales 40	•	•	0.0	•	•	0.1	0.0	0.2
Inventory to Working Capital 41	•	•	•	•	•	0.0	50.5	0.1
Total Receipts to Cash Flow 42	2.8	2.3	3.2	6.7	3.8	4.7	45.5	2.5
Cost of Goods to Cash Flow 43	0.3	•	0.0	1.8	0.0	1.2	41.1	0.0
Cash Flow to Total Debt 44	0.6	•	2.8	0.4	1.1	0.2	0.1	0.5

Selected Financial Factors (in Percentages)

Debt Ratio 45	81.5	•	59.1	96.0	56.0	100.2	77.5	73.3
Return on Total Assets 46	18.5	•	69.5	9.0	20.7	9.4	7.0	12.9
Return on Equity Before Income Taxes 47	89.5	•	164.4	162.4	44.7	•	28.9	39.2
Return on Equity After Income Taxes 48	76.1	•	160.8	156.8	41.2	•	27.5	27.8
Profit Margin (Before Income Tax) 49	13.2	18.4	12.4	2.3	8.6	9.3	1.3	12.7
Profit Margin (After Income Tax) 50	11.2	18.0	12.1	2.3	7.9	9.1	1.2	9.0

Table I

Corporations with and without Net Income

ARCHITECTURAL, ENGINEERING, AND RELATED SERVICES

MONEY AMOUNTS AND SIZE OF ASSETS IN THOUSANDS OF DOLLARS

Item Description for Accounting Period 7/04 Through 6/05	Total	Zero Assets	Under 500	500 to 1,000	1,000 to 5,000	5,000 to 10,000	10,000 to 25,000	25,000 to 50,000	50,000 to 100,000	100,000 to 250,000	250,000 to 500,000	500,000 to 2,500,000	2,500,000 and over
Number of Enterprises 1	92788	9947	75473	3099	3374	447	246	74	55	41	16	13	3
Revenues ($ in Thousands)													
Net Sales 2	151619487	1510168	51371540	6256306	20551470	7959072	8141375	5338375	6176711	10335228	4878387	15789427	13311427
Interest 3	363553	1249	16005	5419	10784	12962	8597	5882	6097	50735	46439	140449	58935
Rents 4	168714	1060	1775	1446	7525	2558	4023	2645	10696	5419	14827	36030	80710
Royalties 5	153529	15435	0	0	2967	0	10653	862	230	14850	382	8651	99499
Other Portfolio Income 6	423572	24027	23490	46114	53141	29118	28185	6337	9784	63483	17357	106968	15567
Other Receipts 7	1120480	53532	109971	127235	187199	35679	5618	25933	65295	51342	65028	181374	212276
Total Receipts 8	153849335	1605471	51522781	6436520	20813086	8039389	8198451	5380034	6268813	10521057	5022420	16262899	13778414
Average Total Receipts 9	1658	161	683	2077	6169	17985	33327	72703	113978	256611	313901	1250992	4592805
Operating Costs/Operating Income (%)													
Cost of Operations 10	40.5	17.3	27.5	25.1	33.7	36.7	43.3	43.8	45.4	47.5	49.5	66.8	67.9
Salaries and Wages 11	19.9	24.6	20.6	26.1	25.0	27.8	20.9	18.0	20.2	19.6	19.2	7.4	16.8
Taxes Paid 12	3.1	3.4	3.3	4.0	3.9	3.5	3.5	3.1	2.5	2.6	2.1	2.4	1.3
Interest Paid 13	0.8	1.3	0.4	0.7	0.6	0.7	0.5	0.3	0.7	0.8	3.8	1.4	1.0
Depreciation 14	1.7	2.9	1.3	2.9	2.2	2.1	2.0	1.6	2.4	1.9	4.1	1.0	0.8
Amortization and Depletion 15	0.3	0.3	0.0	0.3	0.1	0.4	0.2	0.1	0.3	0.6	1.1	0.5	0.3
Pensions and Other Deferred Comp. 16	1.1	0.3	1.2	0.8	1.5	1.4	1.2	1.4	1.0	1.3	0.7	1.0	0.2
Employee Benefits 17	2.4	6.3	1.9	1.5	2.6	2.6	2.7	2.4	1.9	2.9	2.6	2.3	3.7
Advertising 18	0.3	0.3	0.4	0.4	0.3	0.3	0.3	0.3	0.3	0.2	0.2	0.1	0.0
Other Expenses 19	20.4	41.1	23.4	23.6	20.2	18.4	19.4	22.0	20.6	22.6	17.0	16.6	10.4
Officers' Compensation 20	8.0	8.2	15.6	13.5	7.1	5.0	4.6	4.0	2.0	2.0	1.0	2.0	0.4
Operating Margin 21	1.6	•	4.4	1.1	2.8	1.1	1.4	2.9	2.7	•	•	•	•
Operating Margin Before Officers' Comp. 22	9.6	2.2	19.9	14.6	10.0	6.2	6.0	6.9	4.8	0.0	0.4	•	•

Selected Average Balance Sheet ($ in Thousands)

Net Receivables 23	186	0	8	126	697	2486	7034	14877	25558	46539	71078	285239	619718
Inventories 24	23	0	1	23	57	178	635	1687	2413	4499	8470	17268	256018
Net Property, Plant and Equipment 25	90	0	26	174	410	1173	2355	4638	9497	17216	35479	43584	224332
Total Assets 26	700	0	74	691	2010	6962	15271	34940	69345	165120	341989	1107248	3517672
Notes and Loans Payable 27	210	0	44	232	701	3304	3721	5815	13726	42390	136765	313917	520176
All Other Liabilities 28	253	0	24	116	548	2352	6514	17496	26669	59257	90384	452961	1402190
Net Worth 29	237	0	5	344	761	1306	5036	11629	28950	63474	114839	340370	1595306

Selected Financial Ratios (Times to 1)

Current Ratio 30	1.4	•	1.2	2.3	1.8	1.4	1.5	1.5	1.5	1.5	1.4	1.4	1.3
Quick Ratio 31	1.0	•	1.0	1.5	1.5	1.2	1.2	1.1	1.1	1.1	1.1	0.8	0.6
Net Sales to Working Capital 32	14.0	•	139.7	9.5	9.9	16.1	8.9	9.0	7.9	8.0	8.6	7.9	12.2
Coverage Ratio 33	5.1	1.2	13.8	6.8	7.8	4.0	11.7	4.9	7.3	0.8	1.4	2.0	2.2
Total Asset Turnover 34	2.3	•	9.2	2.9	3.0	2.6	2.1	2.2	1.6	1.5	0.9	1.1	1.3
Inventory Turnover 35	28.8	•	222.2	22.1	36.3	36.7	18.7	22.5	21.1	26.6	17.8	47.0	11.8
Receivables Turnover 36	9.2	•	79.1	14.2	8.3	7.4	5.0	5.2	4.8	6.0	4.3	5.0	7.0
Total Liabilities to Net Worth 37	2.0	•	12.4	1.0	1.6	4.3	2.0	2.0	1.4	1.6	2.0	2.3	1.2
Current Assets to Working Capital 38	3.3	•	7.3	1.8	2.2	3.6	3.2	3.0	3.0	3.1	3.8	3.8	4.3
Current Liabilities to Working Capital 39	2.3	•	6.3	0.8	1.2	2.6	2.2	2.0	2.0	2.1	2.8	2.8	3.3
Working Capital to Net Sales 40	0.1	•	0.0	0.1	0.1	0.1	0.1	0.1	0.1	0.1	0.1	0.1	0.1
Inventory to Working Capital 41	0.2	•	0.1	0.1	0.2	0.2	0.2	0.2	0.2	0.2	0.2	0.1	0.8
Total Receipts to Cash Flow 42	5.1	2.8	4.1	4.6	4.9	6.3	4.6	5.7	4.8	5.8	7.9	6.6	11.1
Cost of Goods to Cash Flow 43	2.1	0.5	1.1	1.1	1.7	2.3	2.0	2.5	2.2	2.8	3.9	4.4	7.6
Cash Flow to Total Debt 44	0.7	•	2.4	1.3	1.0	0.5	0.7	0.6	0.4	0.6	0.2	0.2	0.2

Selected Financial Factors (in Percentages)

Debt Ratio 45	66.2	•	92.5	50.3	62.1	81.2	66.7	67.0	58.3	61.6	66.4	69.3	54.6
Return on Total Assets 46	9.0	•	46.5	13.7	14.3	7.2	8.2	5.6	8.0	1.0	4.8	3.1	2.6
Return on Equity Before Income Taxes 47	21.5	•	577.2	23.5	32.8	29.0	22.6	13.5	16.5	•	4.1	5.0	3.1
Return on Equity After Income Taxes 48	18.7	•	569.9	22.2	30.2	22.7	18.1	9.0	12.5	•	2.2	2.6	1.4
Profit Margin (Before Income Tax) 49	3.1	0.3	4.7	4.0	4.1	2.1	3.6	2.1	4.3	•	1.5	1.4	1.1
Profit Margin (After Income Tax) 50	2.7	•	4.6	3.8	1.7	1.4	2.9	3.2		•	0.8	0.7	0.5

Table II

Corporations with Net Income

ARCHITECTURAL, ENGINEERING, AND RELATED SERVICES

MONEY AMOUNTS AND SIZE OF ASSETS IN THOUSANDS OF DOLLARS

Item Description for Accounting Period 7/04 Through 6/05	Total	Zero Assets	Under 500	500 to 1,000	1,000 to 5,000	5,000 to 10,000	10,000 to 25,000	25,000 to 50,000	50,000 to 100,000	100,000 to 250,000	250,000 to 500,000	500,000 to 2,500,000	2,500,000 and over
Number of Enterprises **1**	61298	4498	52163	1597	2433	285	180	0	43	25	10	0	0
Revenues ($ in Thousands)													
Net Sales **2**	121382921	582105	43160354	445064l	17219505	5733976	6279544	0	5379240	6725854	3595854	0	0
Interest **3**	260445	242	12424	4488	8187	11191	6643	0	5586	30580	37205	0	0
Rents **4**	144732	16	19	1429	6862	2528	2745	0	9681	3786	9638	0	0
Royalties **5**	114667	0	0	0	2946	0	8570	0	230	876	382	0	0
Other Portfolio Income **6**	277552	16408	21960	42512	37899	16161	26289	0	9179	6897	14861	0	0
Other Receipts **7**	918133	18948	65740	93118	160728	16447	55832	0	52920	28670	62240	0	0
Total Receipts **8**	123098450	617719	43260497	4592188	17436127	5780303	6379623	0	5456836	6796663	3720180	0	0
Average Total Receipts **9**	2008	137	829	2876	7167	20282	35442	•	126903	271867	372018	•	•
Operating Costs/Operating Income (%)													
Cost of Operations **10**	39.5	30.0	28.9	24.2	33.8	29.7	42.6	•	46.4	41.4	48.8	•	•
Salaries and Wages **11**	19.9	19.3	19.5	24.9	25.5	30.0	20.9	•	19.8	20.9	18.8	•	•
Taxes Paid **12**	3.0	3.1	3.1	3.6	3.9	3.8	3.4	•	2.5	2.8	2.0	•	•
Interest Paid **13**	0.6	0.4	0.3	0.3	0.5	0.5	0.5	•	0.5	0.8	3.0	•	•
Depreciation **14**	1.4	1.3	1.0	2.3	1.8	2.0	1.9	•	1.7	1.6	4.1	•	•
Amortization and Depletion **15**	0.2	0.2	0.0	0.2	0.1	0.1	0.1	•	0.2	0.4	1.1	•	•
Pensions and Other Deferred Comp. **16**	1.2	0.4	1.3	0.7	1.5	1.6	1.2	•	1.0	1.6	0.8	•	•
Employee Benefits **17**	2.3	0.9	1.6	1.2	2.5	2.5	2.6	•	1.8	2.6	2.2	•	•
Advertising **18**	0.3	0.4	0.4	0.3	0.2	0.4	0.3	•	0.2	0.2	0.2	•	•
Other Expenses **19**	19.3	25.0	21.4	21.3	18.1	19.4	18.1	•	19.8	22.6	16.5	•	•
Officers' Compensation **20**	8.2	7.7	15.6	15.3	6.4	5.5	4.5	•	2.0	2.3	1.0	•	•
Operating Margin **21**	4.3	11.2	6.8	5.7	5.6	4.5	3.9	•	3.9	2.8	1.5	•	•
Operating Margin Before Officers' Comp. **22**	12.5	19.0	22.4	21.0	12.0	10.0	8.4	•	5.9	5.0	2.5	•	•

Selected Average Balance Sheet ($ in Thousands)

Net Receivables 23	208	0	5	140	713	2906	7105	•	28277	51928	74762
Inventories 24	25	0	1	18	63	182	540	•	2560	4992	6697
Net Property, Plant and Equipment 25	89	0	25	143	389	1229	2346	•	8763	16600	26985
Total Assets 26	722	0	72	695	1985	7134	15278	•	68559	159870	367675
Notes and Loans Payable 27	181	0	36	155	560	1250	3582	•	12322	28636	136592
All Other Liabilities 28	253	0	18	143	516	2444	6489	•	26251	62086	93916
Net Worth 29	288	0	18	396	908	3439	5207	•	29986	69148	137166

Selected Financial Ratios (Times to 1)

Current Ratio 30	1.5	•	1.4	2.0	2.0	2.1	1.5	•	1.6	1.5	1.3
Quick Ratio 31	1.1	•	1.3	1.6	1.7	1.8	1.2	•	1.2	1.2	1.0
Net Sales to Working Capital 32	13.4	•	72.0	15.0	10.6	8.3	9.5	•	7.3	7.8	11.8
Coverage Ratio 33	11.0	48.1	24.4	29.5	15.8	11.2	12.5	•	11.8	5.9	2.6
Total Asset Turnover 34	2.7	•	11.5	4.0	3.6	2.8	2.3	•	1.8	1.7	1.0
Inventory Turnover 35	31.8	•	437.0	36.9	38.0	32.9	27.5	•	22.7	22.3	26.2
Receivables Turnover 36	10.2	•	149.3	14.7	9.0	7.0	5.3	•	5.3	5.8	5.3
Total Liabilities to Net Worth 37	1.5	•	3.1	0.8	1.2	1.1	1.9	•	1.3	1.3	1.7
Current Assets to Working Capital 38	2.8	•	3.2	2.0	2.0	1.9	3.1	•	2.7	2.8	4.8
Current Liabilities to Working Capital 39	1.8	•	2.2	1.0	1.0	0.9	2.1	•	1.7	1.8	3.8
Working Capital to Net Sales 40	0.1	•	0.0	0.1	0.1	0.1	0.1	•	0.1	0.1	0.1
Inventory to Working Capital 41	0.2	•	0.0	0.1	0.1	0.1	0.2	•	0.2	0.1	0.3
Total Receipts to Cash Flow 42	4.7	2.8	4.0	4.1	4.7	4.9	5.1	•	4.6	4.4	6.6
Cost of Goods to Cash Flow 43	1.8	0.8	1.2	1.0	1.6	1.5	2.2	•	2.2	1.8	3.2
Cash Flow to Total Debt 44	1.0	•	3.8	2.3	1.4	1.1	0.7	•	0.7	0.7	0.2

Selected Financial Factors (in Percentages)

Debt Ratio 45	60.1	•	75.6	42.9	54.2	51.8	65.9	•	56.3	56.7	62.7
Return on Total Assets 46	17.5	•	84.8	36.9	26.0	16.4	13.6	•	10.8	7.9	7.8
Return on Equity Before Income Taxes 47	39.9	•	333.6	62.5	53.3	30.9	36.7	•	22.6	15.1	13.0
Return on Equity After Income Taxes 48	36.4	•	330.3	60.5	50.2	27.2	30.8	•	17.5	11.0	10.5
Profit Margin (Before Income Tax) 49	5.8	17.3	7.1	8.9	6.8	5.3	5.5	•	5.4	3.9	5.0
Profit Margin (After Income Tax) 50	5.3	16.4	7.0	8.6	6.4	4.7	4.6	•	4.2	2.8	4.0

Table I

Corporations with and without Net Income

SPECIALIZED DESIGN SERVICES

MONEY AMOUNTS AND SIZE OF ASSETS IN THOUSANDS OF DOLLARS

Item Description for Accounting Period 7/04 Through 6/05	Total	Zero Assets	Under 500	500 to 1,000	1,000 to 5,000	5,000 to 10,000	10,000 to 25,000	25,000 to 50,000	50,000 to 100,000	100,000 to 250,000	250,000 to 500,000	500,000 to 2,500,000	2,500,000 and over
Number of Enterprises 1	43575	4682	36900	930	932	94	22	7	5	0	3	0	0
Revenues ($ in Thousands)													
Net Sales 2	19254271	263545	10104668	1732044	3629177	1043057	519675	185732	557934	0	1218439	0	0
Interest 3	19953	591	3063	869	1300	512	510	436	1256	0	11416	0	0
Rents 4	11474	0	0	7703	0	3462	0	0	308	0	0	0	0
Royalties 5	70728	0	0	0	54534	0	10118	0	6076	0	0	0	0
Other Portfolio Income 6	9859	494	109	291	14	272	1829	154	2069	0	4627	0	0
Other Receipts 7	254711	3	12094	79404	7180	2162	10052	6437	10860	0	126519	0	0
Total Receipts 8	19620996	264633	10119934	1820311	3692205	1049465	542184	192759	578503	0	1361001	0	0
Average Total Receipts 9	450	57	274	1957	3962	11165	24645	27537	115701	·	453667	·	·
Operating Costs/Operating Income (%)													
Cost of Operations 10	45.4	16.5	37.9	62.1	62.8	61.3	57.3	66.2	60.0	·	10.3	·	·
Salaries and Wages 11	13.9	16.0	10.8	11.3	10.5	10.2	18.3	15.3	12.7	·	54.7	·	·
Taxes Paid 12	2.7	3.0	2.6	3.2	2.2	2.3	2.5	2.3	2.7	·	4.9	·	·
Interest Paid 13	0.5	0.1	0.5	0.3	0.1	0.7	0.3	1.3	0.9	·	0.9	·	·
Depreciation 14	2.1	0.7	1.9	2.4	0.9	1.5	2.1	2.0	3.3	·	7.2	·	·
Amortization and Depletion 15	0.1	0.0	0.1	0.0	0.0	0.1	0.0	0.8	1.5	·	0.1	·	·
Pensions and Other Deferred Comp. 16	0.9	0.2	1.0	0.9	1.0	0.4	0.8	2.2	0.5	·	0.4	·	·
Employee Benefits 17	1.2	1.7	0.8	0.4	0.8	1.2	1.3	1.2	1.9	·	5.6	·	·
Advertising 18	1.0	0.7	1.0	0.4	1.2	0.3	0.4	0.4	2.1	·	1.2	·	·
Other Expenses 19	22.6	34.0	29.7	10.4	13.4	11.9	9.8	9.9	19.2	·	23.2	·	·
Officers' Compensation 20	8.1	15.1	10.1	8.5	5.1	10.6	4.1	5.1	1.8	·	1.4	·	·
Operating Margin 21	1.5	11.9	3.5	0.2	2.0	·	3.1	·	·	·	·	·	·
Operating Margin Before Officers' Comp. 22	9.7	27.1	13.6	8.7	7.1	10.0	7.2	·	·	·	·	·	·

Selected Average Balance Sheet ($ in Thousands)

Net Receivables 23	36	0	11	152	323	1618	4211	6868	20732	•	108542
Inventories 24	19	0	5	179	393	258	1139	1084	6950	•	5738
Net Property, Plant and Equipment 25	36	0	14	138	395	972	1769	2772	21647	•	95475
Total Assets 26	183	0	63	630	1721	6813	15419	34632	119115	•	547504
Notes and Loans Payable 27	55	0	37	171	475	1121	1843	4379	52697	•	388
All Other Liabilities 28	74	0	28	241	912	5485	6058	9822	5686	•	124379
Net Worth 29	54	0	-2	218	335	206	7517	20430	60732	•	422737

Selected Financial Ratios (Times to 1)

Current Ratio 30	1.5	•	1.2	1.5	1.4	0.8	2.1	1.8	2.7	•	3.5
Quick Ratio 31	1.0	•	0.9	0.8	0.6	0.6	1.6	1.2	1.4	•	2.6
Net Sales to Working Capital 32	11.3	•	35.3	11.9	11.2	•	3.9	3.3	3.1	•	1.8
Coverage Ratio 33	8.2	164.7	7.7	19.6	27.8	1.1	26.9	•	•	•	3.1
Total Asset Turnover 34	2.4	•	4.4	3.0	2.3	1.6	1.5	0.8	0.9	•	0.7
Inventory Turnover 35	10.8	•	22.1	6.5	6.2	26.3	11.9	16.2	9.6	•	7.3
Receivables Turnover 36	12.9	•	24.4	13.6	10.7	8.0	7.6	2.7	•	•	•
Total Liabilities to Net Worth 37	2.4	•	1.9	4.1	32.0	1.1	0.7	1.0	•	•	0.3
Current Assets to Working Capital 38	3.1	•	5.4	3.0	3.6	•	1.9	2.3	1.6	•	1.4
Current Liabilities to Working Capital 39	2.1	•	4.4	2.0	2.6	•	0.9	1.3	0.6	•	0.4
Working Capital to Net Sales 40	0.1	•	0.0	0.1	0.1	•	0.3	0.3	0.3	•	0.6
Inventory to Working Capital 41	0.6	•	0.9	1.2	1.4	•	0.3	0.1	0.2	•	0.0
Total Receipts to Cash Flow 42	4.8	2.4	3.7	7.5	7.6	12.4	7.0	32.6	8.1	•	5.8
Cost of Goods to Cash Flow 43	2.2	0.4	1.4	4.7	4.8	7.6	4.0	21.6	4.9	•	0.6
Cash Flow to Total Debt 44	0.7	•	1.1	0.6	0.4	0.1	0.4	0.1	0.2	•	0.6

Selected Financial Factors (in Percentages)

Debt Ratio 45	70.6	•	103.0	65.4	80.5	97.0	51.2	41.0	49.0	•	22.8
Return on Total Assets 46	9.5	•	18.1	16.4	8.8	1.2	12.0	•	•	•	2.0
Return on Equity Before Income Taxes 47	28.3	•	•	45.0	43.6	2.1	23.6	•	•	•	1.7
Return on Equity After Income Taxes 48	26.3	•	•	41.1	42.3	•	21.2	•	•	•	1.7
Profit Margin (Before Income Tax) 49	3.4	12.4	3.6	5.3	3.8	0.0	7.5	•	•	•	1.8
Profit Margin (After Income Tax) 50	3.2	12.2	3.5	4.8	3.6	•	6.7	•	•	•	1.8

Table II

Corporations with Net Income

SPECIALIZED DESIGN SERVICES

MONEY AMOUNTS AND SIZE OF ASSETS IN THOUSANDS OF DOLLARS

Item Description for Accounting Period 7/04 Through 6/05	Total	Zero Assets	Under 500	500 to 1,000	1,000 to 5,000	5,000 to 10,000	10,000 to 25,000	25,000 to 50,000	50,000 to 100,000	100,000 to 250,000	250,000 to 500,000	500,000 to 2,500,000	2,500,000 and over
Number of Enterprises 1	27480	2487	23376	815	734	43	0	0	0	0	0	0	0
Revenues ($ in Thousands)													
Net Sales 2	14068695	206430	6938136	1532282	3156306	572654	0	0	0	0	0	0	0
Interest 3	5832	243	2769	198	1214	422	0	0	0	0	0	0	0
Rents 4	7705	0	0	7703	0	0	0	0	0	0	0	0	0
Royalties 5	9509	0	0	0	0	0	0	0	0	0	0	0	0
Other Portfolio Income 6	2231	0	106	171	14	3	0	0	0	0	0	0	0
Other Receipts 7	112974	0	11712	79404	5881	20	0	0	0	0	0	0	0
Total Receipts 8	14206946	206673	6952723	1619758	3163415	573099	0	0	0	0	0	0	0
Average Total Receipts 9	517	83	297	1987	4310	13328	•	•	•	•	•	•	•
Operating Costs/Operating Income (%)													
Cost of Operations 10	43.5	14.3	33.3	62.7	63.3	61.3	•	•	•	•	•	•	•
Salaries and Wages 11	12.1	17.3	9.9	11.9	10.0	10.1	•	•	•	•	•	•	•
Taxes Paid 12	2.6	3.2	2.6	3.4	1.9	2.5	•	•	•	•	•	•	•
Interest Paid 13	0.4	0.1	0.5	0.3	0.1	0.4	•	•	•	•	•	•	•
Depreciation 14	1.5	0.5	1.4	2.6	0.9	1.3	•	•	•	•	•	•	•
Amortization and Depletion 15	0.1	0.0	0.1	0.0	0.0	0.1	•	•	•	•	•	•	•
Pensions and Other Deferred Comp. 16	0.9	0.3	1.0	0.4	1.1	0.7	•	•	•	•	•	•	•
Employee Benefits 17	1.2	1.6	0.9	0.3	0.8	2.2	•	•	•	•	•	•	•
Advertising 18	1.0	0.4	1.2	0.4	1.2	0.4	•	•	•	•	•	•	•
Other Expenses 19	22.6	28.2	30.1	10.9	11.1	12.7	•	•	•	•	•	•	•
Officers' Compensation 20	6.8	11.6	8.8	6.8	5.0	4.6	•	•	•	•	•	•	•
Operating Margin 21	7.3	22.6	10.2	0.3	4.6	3.7	•	•	•	•	•	•	•
Operating Margin Before Officers' Comp. 22	14.1	34.2	18.9	7.1	9.6	8.2	•	•	•	•	•	•	•

Selected Average Balance Sheet ($ in Thousands)

Net Receivables 23	34	0	13	144	331	2144
Inventories 24	17	0	1	188	316	426
Net Property, Plant and Equipment 25	29	0	14	150	253	556
Total Assets 26	161	0	64	630	1609	5745
Notes and Loans Payable 27	53	0	34	194	337	1248
All Other Liabilities 28	60	0	20	237	916	3727
Net Worth 29	49	0	9	199	357	770

Selected Financial Ratios (Times to 1)

Current Ratio 30	1.6	•	1.6	1.4	1.4	1.1
Quick Ratio 31	1.0	•	1.5	0.7	0.7	0.6
Net Sales to Working Capital 32	13.0	•	19.1	13.4	10.8	48.9
Coverage Ratio 33	22.0	343.6	20.7	19.8	42.3	9.9
Total Asset Turnover 34	3.2	•	4.6	3.0	2.7	2.3
Inventory Turnover 35	13.1	•	86.5	6.3	8.6	19.1
Receivables Turnover 36	15.3	•	22.0	15.8	12.9	7.9
Total Liabilities to Net Worth 37	2.3	•	5.8	2.2	3.5	6.5
Current Assets to Working Capital 38	2.8	•	2.7	3.2	3.3	16.4
Current Liabilities to Working Capital 39	1.8	•	1.7	2.2	2.3	15.4
Working Capital to Net Sales 40	0.1	•	0.1	0.1	0.1	0.0
Inventory to Working Capital 41	0.6	•	0.1	1.5	1.2	1.8
Total Receipts to Cash Flow 42	3.8	2.2	2.9	6.9	8.1	9.2
Cost of Goods to Cash Flow 43	1.7	0.3	1.0	4.3	5.1	5.6
Cash Flow to Total Debt 44	1.2	•	1.9	0.6	0.4	0.3

Selected Financial Factors (in Percentages)

Debt Ratio 45	69.9	•	85.2	68.5	77.8	86.6
Return on Total Assets 46	27.4	•	50.6	18.9	13.2	9.6
Return on Equity Before Income Taxes 47	86.9	324.8	324.8	56.9	58.2	64.6
Return on Equity After Income Taxes 48	83.4	•	319.9	52.0	56.6	48.8
Profit Margin (Before Income Tax) 49	8.2	22.7	10.4	6.0	4.8	3.7
Profit Margin (After Income Tax) 50	7.9	22.6	10.2	5.5	4.7	2.8

Table I

Corporations with and without Net Income

COMPUTER SYSTEMS DESIGN AND RELATED SERVICES

PROFESSIONAL, SCIENTIFIC, AND TECHNICAL SERVICES 541515

MONEY AMOUNTS AND SIZE OF ASSETS IN THOUSANDS OF DOLLARS

Item Description for Accounting Period 7/04 Through 6/05	Total	Zero Assets	Under 500	500 to 1,000	1,000 to 5,000	5,000 to 10,000	10,000 to 25,000	25,000 to 50,000	50,000 to 100,000	100,000 to 250,000	250,000 to 500,000	500,000 to 2,500,000	2,500,000 and over
Number of Enterprises **1**	99403	21478	69973	2952	3388	630	409	364	79	75	26	23	6
Revenues ($ in Thousands)													
Net Sales **2**	130406236	5333957	22570783	6967862	18493495	6698340	8144134	5515289	5103210	8810183	6217363	13693314	22858307
Interest **3**	1107515	52731	6015	4938	14737	21203	30538	24817	17102	73754	42181	173431	646068
Rents **4**	184112	1790	11153	0	297	1123	3824	1508	5014	9255	5321	45041	99784
Royalties **5**	1714340	8018	1277	14459	11411	2550	12761	25618	14030	42066	77469	882929	621751
Other Portfolio Income **6**	1058112	342290	32492	53345	84673	15553	103784	20215	13250	58121	38341	48317	247730
Other Receipts **7**	1710294	47975	110395	56208	125621	120714	144431	60679	49863	400602	190147	268979	134684
Total Receipts **8**	136180609	5786761	22732115	7096812	18730234	6859483	8439472	5648126	5202469	9393981	6570822	15112011	24608324
Average Total Receipts **9**	1370	269	325	2404	5528	10888	20634	15517	65854	125253	252724	657044	4101387
Operating Costs/Operating Income (%)													
Cost of Operations **10**	31.6	19.5	25.2	41.8	39.5	28.3	46.6	37.2	38.8	34.1	38.7	45.9	12.5
Salaries and Wages **11**	28.3	37.6	22.6	20.9	28.4	35.7	26.8	30.6	30.7	30.3	27.7	26.5	31.5
Taxes Paid **12**	4.0	3.6	3.6	3.3	3.5	3.9	3.1	3.2	3.1	3.1	3.2	3.5	7.1
Interest Paid **13**	1.6	3.3	0.7	0.5	0.6	1.0	0.9	1.1	0.8	1.9	1.3	1.8	3.8
Depreciation **14**	2.4	1.9	1.3	0.9	1.6	2.1	2.9	2.7	2.8	3.5	3.8	2.5	3.4
Amortization and Depletion **15**	1.5	0.9	0.1	0.4	0.6	1.4	0.9	0.9	1.5	2.5	2.7	2.1	3.2
Pensions and Other Deferred Comp. **16**	0.8	0.8	1.3	0.8	0.7	1.7	0.5	0.5	0.3	0.3	0.6	0.6	0.7
Employee Benefits **17**	2.4	2.1	1.6	2.0	2.0	2.9	2.5	2.5	2.8	2.5	3.4	3.2	2.5
Advertising **18**	0.7	0.7	0.7	0.8	0.9	1.2	0.9	1.4	0.8	0.7	0.6	0.6	0.2
Other Expenses **19**	25.5	31.8	23.9	21.7	19.8	25.7	21.7	24.5	21.4	24.9	20.5	23.8	36.5
Officers' Compensation **20**	5.4	4.5	15.3	10.8	6.3	4.7	3.5	3.0	2.4	1.7	1.5	0.9	0.8
Operating Margin **21**	•	3.7	•	•	•	•	•	•	•	•	•	•	•
Operating Margin Before Officers' Comp. **22**	1.2	•	19.0	6.9	2.4	•	•	•	•	•	•	•	•

Selected Average Balance Sheet ($ in Thousands)

Line Item													
Net Receivables 23	306	0	9	222	727	1603	4014	3594	16136	25387	68872	159093	2338756
Inventories 24	15	0	2	47	54	166	333	231	1245	2288	4473	5682	31711
Net Property, Plant and Equipment 25	85	0	9	60	190	541	1239	985	4528	9270	17729	78312	414446
Total Assets 26	1224	0	55	681	2129	7337	14928	12626	70637	162120	364594	989264	7226651
Notes and Loans Payable 27	297	0	47	225	594	1672	2683	2330	12913	35745	33325	202566	1880852
All Other Liabilities 28	433	0	25	284	853	2706	6471	4995	25266	42745	140390	264424	2733894
Net Worth 29	495	0	-18	172	682	2960	5774	5301	32458	83630	190879	522274	2611906

Selected Financial Ratios (Times to 1)

Line Item													
Current Ratio 30	1.4	•	1.1	1.8	1.6	1.6	1.6	1.6	1.4	2.0	1.6	2.0	1.1
Quick Ratio 31	1.2	•	1.0	1.4	1.4	1.4	1.3	1.3	1.1	1.5	1.4	1.6	1.0
Net Sales to Working Capital 32	6.9	•	67.9	10.9	10.0	5.8	5.1	5.1	6.1	3.0	3.9	2.6	15.1
Coverage Ratio 33	1.3	1.5	7.0	•	•	•	•	•	•	1.7	2.2	0.8	2.5
Total Asset Turnover 34	1.1	•	5.9	3.5	2.6	1.4	1.3	1.2	0.9	0.7	0.7	0.6	0.5
Inventory Turnover 35	27.7	•	42.6	20.8	40.2	18.1	27.8	24.4	20.1	17.5	20.7	48.1	15.0
Receivables Turnover 36	4.4	•	34.2	11.7	8.0	6.9	5.2	4.3	4.0	5.4	3.3	3.8	1.7
Total Liabilities to Net Worth 37	1.5	•	•	3.0	2.1	1.5	1.6	1.4	1.2	0.9	0.9	0.9	1.8
Current Assets to Working Capital 38	3.3	•	7.9	2.3	2.8	2.6	2.6	2.7	3.4	2.0	2.6	2.0	12.7
Current Liabilities to Working Capital 39	2.3	•	6.9	1.3	1.8	1.6	1.6	1.7	2.4	1.0	1.6	1.0	11.7
Working Capital to Net Sales 40	0.1	•	0.0	0.1	0.1	0.2	0.2	0.2	0.2	0.3	0.3	0.4	0.1
Inventory to Working Capital 41	0.1	•	0.3	0.2	0.1	0.1	0.1	0.1	0.1	0.1	0.1	0.0	0.1
Total Receipts to Cash Flow 42	4.6	4.2	4.1	6.6	7.3	6.1	9.6	6.3	7.0	4.7	5.6	5.2	2.7
Cost of Goods to Cash Flow 43	1.5	0.8	1.0	2.7	2.9	1.7	4.5	2.3	2.7	1.6	2.2	2.4	0.3
Cash Flow to Total Debt 44	0.4	•	1.1	0.7	0.5	0.4	0.2	0.3	0.2	0.3	0.2	0.2	0.3

Selected Financial Factors (in Percentages)

Line Item													
Debt Ratio 45	59.6	•	132.7	74.7	68.0	59.7	61.3	58.0	54.0	48.4	47.6	47.2	63.9
Return on Total Assets 46	2.2	•	30.7	•	•	•	•	•	•	2.3	1.9	0.9	5.0
Return on Equity Before Income Taxes 47	1.1	•	•	•	•	•	•	•	•	1.8	2.0	•	8.3
Return on Equity After Income Taxes 48	•	•	•	•	•	•	•	•	•	0.3	0.2	•	5.6
Profit Margin (Before Income Tax) 49	0.4	1.7	4.4	•	•	•	•	•	•	1.3	1.6	•	5.7
Profit Margin (After Income Tax) 50	•	0.4	4.3	•	•	•	•	•	•	0.2	0.2	•	3.8

343

Table II

Corporations with Net Income

COMPUTER SYSTEMS DESIGN AND RELATED SERVICES

MONEY AMOUNTS AND SIZE OF ASSETS IN THOUSANDS OF DOLLARS

Item Description for Accounting Period 7/04 Through 6/05	Total	Zero Assets	Under 500	500 to 1,000	1,000 to 5,000	5,000 to 10,000	10,000 to 25,000	25,000 to 50,000	50,000 to 100,000	100,000 to 250,000	250,000 to 500,000	500,000 to 2,500,000	2,500,000 and over
Number of Enterprises **1**	53437	6530	42152	2023	2025	377	175	52	36	40	0	9	0
Revenues ($ in Thousands)													
Net Sales **2**	93363984	3894453	14956432	5653997	15596179	5289669	5113452	3305586	3074074	5475419	0	7898980	0
Interest **3**	699366	48056	3917	3871	5592	4268	8781	12563	4230	38772	0	57802	0
Rents **4**	73630	630	0	0	128	949	2422	849	4847	8647	0	42272	0
Royalties **5**	195716	7776	1277	0	10750	2480	9168	23433	7424	40831	0	0	0
Other Portfolio Income **6**	912889	340841	27751	50074	55567	12490	93502	17741	10774	46101	0	20618	0
Other Receipts **7**	987483	38085	77974	18158	94629	95844	64378	40128	27468	84372	0	258735	0
Total Receipts **8**	96233068	4329841	15067351	5726800	15762845	5405700	5291703	3400300	3128817	5694142	0	8278407	0
Average Total Receipts **9**	1801	663	357	2831	7784	14339	30238	65390	86912	142354	·	919823	·
Operating Costs/Operating Income (%)													
Cost of Operations **10**	29.1	16.8	22.0	45.8	42.2	31.2	51.8	35.3	45.7	37.6	·	42.0	·
Salaries and Wages **11**	25.5	35.9	20.4	18.5	23.1	28.7	17.6	25.5	23.7	23.0	·	23.6	·
Taxes Paid **12**	4.1	3.4	3.1	3.1	3.1	3.2	2.4	3.1	3.2	2.9	·	3.6	·
Interest Paid **13**	1.4	4.1	0.4	0.3	0.4	0.5	0.5	0.6	0.6	1.9	·	1.3	·
Depreciation **14**	2.0	1.0	1.3	0.8	1.0	1.2	1.9	1.7	2.1	2.5	·	2.3	·
Amortization and Depletion **15**	1.1	0.6	0.1	0.0	0.2	0.3	0.4	0.4	0.4	1.8	·	1.2	·
Pensions and Other Deferred Comp. **16**	0.9	0.5	1.4	0.9	0.8	2.2	0.6	0.5	0.3	0.4	·	0.7	·
Employee Benefits **17**	2.1	1.6	1.5	1.5	1.5	2.4	2.0	2.2	2.5	2.0	·	3.5	·
Advertising **18**	0.5	0.7	0.5	0.7	0.7	0.9	0.5	1.0	0.5	0.7	·	0.1	·
Other Expenses **19**	22.2	30.1	21.1	14.4	14.7	17.8	13.4	22.3	12.8	20.4	·	19.1	·
Officers' Compensation **20**	5.0	2.5	15.3	9.8	5.6	4.1	3.0	2.4	2.0	1.5	·	0.6	·
Operating Margin **21**	6.3	2.7	12.9	4.3	6.7	7.6	5.9	5.0	6.2	5.4	·	2.1	·
Operating Margin Before Officers' Comp. **22**	11.3	5.2	28.2	14.1	12.3	11.7	8.9	7.4	8.2	6.8	·	2.7	·

Selected Average Balance Sheet ($ in Thousands)

Net Receivables 23	317	0	10	230	921	1880	5459	13216	20099	26444	196362
Inventories 24	15	0	2	49	59	187	358	1017	1287	2305	1856
Net Property, Plant and Equipment 25	99	0	8	65	192	478	1280	3092	5166	7532	107202
Total Assets 26	1249	0	61	665	2147	7398	15124	34881	70700	162852	981497
Notes and Loans Payable 27	217	0	23	164	438	1194	2523	6341	14323	38009	213842
All Other Liabilities 28	367	0	13	214	792	2403	7161	16758	23648	40507	259539
Net Worth 29	666	0	25	286	917	3801	5440	11782	32730	84337	508115

Selected Financial Ratios (Times to 1)

Current Ratio 30	1.7	•	2.7	2.3	1.8	1.7	1.5	1.5	1.4	2.0	2.3
Quick Ratio 31	1.5	•	2.4	1.9	1.6	1.4	1.3	1.3	1.0	1.6	1.9
Net Sales to Working Capital 32	6.5	•	12.5	9.3	10.7	7.5	7.5	7.4	8.2	3.3	3.1
Coverage Ratio 33	7.8	4.4	38.0	22.0	23.2	22.1	20.8	13.3	14.1	6.0	7.2
Total Asset Turnover 34	1.4	•	5.8	4.2	3.6	1.9	1.9	1.8	1.2	0.8	0.9
Inventory Turnover 35	33.1	•	50.6	26.1	55.0	23.4	42.2	22.1	30.3	22.3	198.6
Receivables Turnover 36	4.9	•	37.9	13.3	9.2	8.6	5.8	4.7	4.7	6.3	•
Total Liabilities to Net Worth 37	0.9	•	1.4	1.3	1.3	0.9	1.8	2.0	1.2	0.9	0.9
Current Assets to Working Capital 38	2.3	•	1.6	1.7	2.3	2.5	2.8	2.9	3.8	2.0	1.8
Current Liabilities to Working Capital 39	1.3	•	0.6	0.7	1.3	1.5	1.8	1.9	2.8	1.0	0.8
Working Capital to Net Sales 40	0.2	•	0.1	0.1	0.1	0.1	0.1	0.1	0.1	0.3	0.3
Inventory to Working Capital 41	0.1	•	0.0	0.2	0.1	0.1	0.1	0.1	0.2	0.1	0.0
Total Receipts to Cash Flow 42	3.6	3.1	3.1	6.3	5.0	4.0	5.4	3.6	5.6	3.9	4.4
Cost of Goods to Cash Flow 43	1.0	0.5	0.7	2.9	2.1	1.2	2.8	1.3	2.6	1.5	1.8
Cash Flow to Total Debt 44	0.8	•	3.2	1.2	1.2	1.0	0.6	0.8	0.4	0.5	0.4

Selected Financial Factors (in Percentages)

Debt Ratio 45	46.7	•	58.8	56.9	57.3	48.6	64.0	66.2	53.7	48.2	48.2
Return on Total Assets 46	15.2	•	81.0	24.8	29.2	19.3	19.1	15.5	10.3	9.6	8.3
Return on Equity Before Income Taxes 47	24.9	•	191.3	55.0	65.4	35.8	50.6	42.3	20.6	15.5	13.8
Return on Equity After Income Taxes 48	21.7	•	188.6	52.7	61.7	32.7	44.3	36.7	18.8	12.7	9.8
Profit Margin (Before Income Tax) 49	9.5	13.9	13.6	5.6	7.8	9.7	9.4	7.8	7.9	9.5	8.0
Profit Margin (After Income Tax) 50	8.3	12.1	13.4	5.4	7.3	8.9	8.2	6.8	7.2	7.8	5.7

Table I
Corporations with and without Net Income

MANAGEMENT, SCIENTIFIC, AND TECHNICAL CONSULTING SERVICES

MONEY AMOUNTS AND SIZE OF ASSETS IN THOUSANDS OF DOLLARS

Item Description for Accounting Period 7/04 Through 6/05		Total	Zero Assets	Under 500	500 to 1,000	1,000 to 5,000	5,000 to 10,000	10,000 to 25,000	25,000 to 50,000	50,000 to 100,000	100,000 to 250,000	250,000 to 500,000	500,000 to 2,500,000	2,500,000 and over
Number of Enterprises	1	227077	41098	174999	4936	4629	674	431	145	75	40	24	21	5
Revenues ($ in Thousands)														
Net Sales	2	151873246	4809729	43539213	19529143	18906051	8219054	8811230	5834787	6494585	6770463	5391805	14404744	9162442
Interest	3	674987	27464	25670	16251	26141	20402	30498	22014	44998	42617	78503	235790	104639
Rents	4	88043	4050	1797	3825	1524	2695	5996	6562	15501	2642	1953	20003	21495
Royalties	5	778408	2449	2200	107	52570	15417	6435	4323	141790	235926	9	317028	150
Other Portfolio Income	6	1190144	503660	111589	45599	87131	29971	48028	35630	25571	15283	85687	199127	2864
Other Receipts	7	4525732	101124	1404476	103550	994133	284293	386810	175189	90702	198414	372724	263073	151252
Total Receipts	8	159130560	5448476	45084945	19698475	20067550	8571832	9288997	6078505	6813147	7265345	5930681	15439765	9442842
Average Total Receipts	9	701	133	258	3991	4335	12718	21552	41921	90842	181634	247112	735227	1888568
Operating Costs/Operating Income (%)														
Cost of Operations	10	25.3	3.6	20.6	8.1	51.9	30.2	33.4	36.2	39.1	48.1	21.9	19.6	5.7
Salaries and Wages	11	25.7	21.2	18.3	26.0	17.6	32.6	27.0	24.0	22.0	24.7	39.1	40.9	43.6
Taxes Paid	12	3.0	3.0	3.0	2.3	2.3	5.0	3.1	3.0	3.1	2.6	3.6	3.7	3.5
Interest Paid	13	0.8	1.6	0.4	0.3	0.4	0.7	1.2	0.8	1.3	1.4	2.0	2.0	1.3
Depreciation	14	1.5	1.9	1.2	0.6	1.2	1.4	2.1	2.3	2.1	1.7	2.4	2.2	2.3
Amortization and Depletion	15	0.4	0.8	0.2	0.1	0.1	0.2	0.4	0.6	0.5	1.0	1.8	1.3	0.4
Pensions and Other Deferred Comp.	16	1.5	1.3	2.2	0.9	0.7	0.8	1.1	0.7	0.7	0.7	0.8	3.2	2.5
Employee Benefits	17	2.0	2.1	1.6	1.9	1.3	2.5	2.1	2.1	3.0	2.4	1.5	3.0	1.9
Advertising	18	0.7	0.5	0.7	0.7	0.6	0.3	0.7	1.4	0.4	0.6	0.5	0.9	0.3
Other Expenses	19	31.2	54.0	31.2	48.2	17.9	17.3	24.7	24.9	25.2	18.1	30.7	35.2	41.1
Officers' Compensation	20	8.4	11.2	16.2	9.5	6.3	8.6	4.6	3.3	2.6	1.5	1.5	3.0	0.5
Operating Margin	21	•	•	4.4	1.4	•	0.4	•	0.8	0.0	•	•	•	•
Operating Margin Before Officers' Comp.	22	7.8	10.0	20.6	10.8	5.9	9.0	4.2	4.1	2.6	•	•	•	•

Selected Average Balance Sheet ($ in Thousands)

Item	1	2	3	4	5	6	7	8	9	10	11	12
Net Receivables 23	100	6	144	531	1915	4081	8260	22147	33779	60880	342171	509417
Inventories 24	6	2	21	52	16	248	668	852	2976	864	14754	1207
Net Property, Plant and Equipment 25	40	8	117	237	715	1817	4872	8209	12282	29372	59236	171361
Total Assets 26	450	52	653	1989	6687	15470	34855	73832	164481	364732	1058422	4260769
Notes and Loans Payable 27	147	40	412	778	1439	5015	8594	20616	34009	84847	419069	536345
All Other Liabilities 28	164	14	203	511	1967	5251	11575	23544	51372	134600	502825	1739712
Net Worth 29	139	-1	38	700	3280	5203	14687	29673	79100	145286	136528	1984712

Selected Financial Ratios (Times to 1)

Item	1	2	3	4	5	6	7	8	9	10	11	12
Current Ratio 30	1.4	•	1.9	2.3	2.0	1.5	1.4	1.6	1.5	1.3	1.5	0.7
Quick Ratio 31	1.1	•	1.5	1.9	1.5	1.2	1.1	1.3	1.2	1.0	1.1	0.4
Net Sales to Working Capital 32	11.3	•	21.9	6.5	6.1	7.3	7.4	6.6	6.7	6.7	3.6	•
Coverage Ratio 33	6.1	9.2	8.0	14.5	7.3	5.2	7.2	4.9	4.3	3.2	•	1.1
Total Asset Turnover 34	1.5	•	6.1	2.1	1.8	1.3	1.2	1.2	1.0	0.6	•	0.4
Inventory Turnover 35	28.4	•	32.6	15.3	40.5	235.2	27.6	21.8	39.8	9.1	56.9	86.0
Receivables Turnover 36	7.3	•	43.3	27.0	7.9	5.3	5.1	4.4	4.7	3.4	2.1	•
Total Liabilities to Net Worth 37	2.2	•	16.1	1.8	1.0	1.4	2.0	1.5	1.1	1.5	6.8	1.1
Current Assets to Working Capital 38	3.6	•	2.2	1.8	3.0	3.3	2.8	2.9	3.9	3.9	3.0	•
Current Liabilities to Working Capital 39	2.6	•	1.2	0.8	2.0	2.3	1.8	1.9	2.9	2.9	2.0	•
Working Capital to Net Sales 40	0.1	0.0	0.0	0.2	0.2	0.1	0.1	0.2	0.1	0.1	0.3	•
Inventory to Working Capital 41	0.1	•	0.1	0.1	0.0	0.1	0.1	0.1	0.1	0.0	0.1	•
Total Receipts to Cash Flow 42	3.3	1.8	2.1	5.3	5.6	3.8	3.9	3.8	3.9	3.4	4.6	2.7
Cost of Goods to Cash Flow 43	0.8	0.1	0.2	2.7	1.7	1.3	1.4	1.5	2.4	0.7	0.9	0.2
Cash Flow to Total Debt 44	0.7	•	3.1	0.6	0.6	0.5	0.5	0.5	0.4	0.2	0.2	0.3

Selected Financial Factors (in Percentages)

Item	1	2	3	4	5	6	7	8	9	10	11	12
Debt Ratio 45	69.2	102.1	94.2	64.8	50.9	66.4	57.9	59.8	51.9	60.2	87.1	53.4
Return on Total Assets 46	7.6	39.9	15.4	12.5	9.8	8.1	6.7	7.3	6.1	6.1	3.8	0.6
Return on Equity Before Income Taxes 47	20.7	•	230.8	33.2	17.3	19.4	13.7	14.4	10.2	9.6	6.6	0.1
Return on Equity After Income Taxes 48	17.0	•	220.9	31.4	14.4	15.7	11.5	10.2	6.8	6.8	3.9	•
Profit Margin (Before Income Tax) 49	4.3	13.0	8.0	2.2	5.7	4.9	4.9	5.0	4.9	4.5	4.3	0.2
Profit Margin (After Income Tax) 50	3.5	11.0	7.8	2.1	5.4	3.9	4.2	3.5	4.0	3.2	2.5	•

Table II

Corporations with Net Income

MANAGEMENT, SCIENTIFIC, AND TECHNICAL CONSULTING SERVICES

MONEY AMOUNTS AND SIZE OF ASSETS IN THOUSANDS OF DOLLARS

Item Description for Accounting Period 7/04 Through 6/05	Total	Zero Assets	Under 500	500 to 1,000	1,000 to 5,000	5,000 to 10,000	10,000 to 25,000	25,000 to 50,000	50,000 to 100,000	100,000 to 250,000	250,000 to 500,000	500,000 to 2,500,000	2,500,000 and over
Number of Enterprises **1**	128385	17207	103777	3343	3184	434	262	81	40	22	0	18	0
Revenues ($ in Thousands)													
Net Sales **2**	114023304	2535498	33443729	18563352	10602502	5817512	6869729	4041195	4467155	4872687	0	13416482	0
Interest **3**	452933	3422	13994	13174	18122	6324	16698	9111	17694	24484	0	217582	0
Rents **4**	70340	201	1567	3825	1277	2610	3764	5302	15399	804	0	18218	0
Royalties **5**	748388	0	2200	107	52452	0	6400	228	139363	230458	0	317028	0
Other Portfolio Income **6**	1070246	493643	89477	26759	84328	27086	27765	31170	18276	13359	0	197091	0
Other Receipts **7**	3556270	49498	1308952	59914	529732	187754	333274	158685	86963	151951	0	249877	0
Total Receipts **8**	119921481	3082262	34859919	18667131	11288413	6041286	7257630	4245691	4744850	5293743	0	14416278	0
Average Total Receipts **9**	934	179	336	5584	3545	13920	27701	52416	118621	240625	•	800904	•
Operating Costs/Operating Income (%)													
Cost of Operations **10**	21.7	6.4	18.9	7.9	30.2	38.3	36.3	36.8	35.0	58.3	•	16.2	•
Salaries and Wages **11**	25.0	23.1	16.2	26.3	22.6	18.3	23.3	22.1	21.7	16.4	•	41.8	•
Taxes Paid **12**	3.0	3.8	2.8	2.3	3.0	3.8	3.0	2.8	3.5	2.2	•	3.8	•
Interest Paid **13**	0.6	1.0	0.2	0.2	0.4	0.3	0.6	0.6	0.9	1.0	•	1.5	•
Depreciation **14**	1.3	0.8	1.0	0.5	1.2	1.2	1.4	1.8	1.5	1.4	•	2.0	•
Amortization and Depletion **15**	0.3	0.2	0.0	0.1	0.1	0.0	0.2	0.3	0.4	0.8	•	1.3	•
Pensions and Other Deferred Comp. **16**	1.5	1.7	1.6	0.9	0.8	0.8	1.0	0.8	0.8	0.5	•	3.3	•
Employee Benefits **17**	2.0	2.4	1.5	2.0	1.6	1.9	2.1	2.2	3.4	1.6	•	3.1	•
Advertising **18**	0.7	0.5	0.8	0.7	1.0	0.2	0.7	1.7	0.3	0.7	•	0.9	•
Other Expenses **19**	28.9	32.6	29.4	47.0	21.9	16.0	21.5	22.3	27.1	14.1	•	23.6	•
Officers' Compensation **20**	8.7	16.3	15.9	9.0	7.9	10.6	4.7	3.2	1.7	0.9	•	3.1	•
Operating Margin **21**	6.3	11.1	11.7	3.2	9.4	8.4	5.2	5.4	3.6	2.1	•	•	•
Operating Margin Before Officers' Comp. **22**	15.0	27.5	27.6	12.2	17.3	19.1	9.9	8.6	5.3	3.1	•	2.5	•

Selected Average Balance Sheet ($ in Thousands)

Net Receivables 23	116	0	6	188	451	2311	4595	9536	27345	32054	252769	•
Inventories 24	8	0	2	25	62	14	337	893	564	3026	14944	•
Net Property, Plant and Equipment 25	46	0	10	119	217	604	1645	4409	7253	11553	56639	•
Total Assets 26	515	0	61	660	1954	6911	15682	35601	73930	158179	1039545	•
Notes and Loans Payable 27	115	0	29	372	468	886	3854	5988	15889	24227	211555	•
All Other Liabilities 28	216	0	13	227	406	1617	5198	12057	28091	42773	562220	•
Net Worth 29	183	0	20	61	1081	4408	6629	17556	29950	91178	265770	•

Selected Financial Ratios (Times to 1)

Current Ratio 30	1.3	•	2.5	1.8	2.5	2.2	1.7	1.5	1.5	1.7	1.2	•
Quick Ratio 31	1.0	•	2.1	1.7	2.0	2.0	1.3	1.2	1.3	1.3	0.8	•
Net Sales to Working Capital 32	14.6	•	13.7	28.9	5.0	6.4	7.2	7.5	8.6	7.7	10.9	•
Coverage Ratio 33	20.8	34.5	71.5	18.2	43.7	37.2	19.6	19.3	11.8	12.2	5.9	•
Total Asset Turnover 34	1.7	•	5.3	8.4	1.7	1.9	1.7	1.4	1.5	1.4	0.7	•
Inventory Turnover 35	22.7	•	24.4	17.5	16.1	370.4	28.3	20.5	69.4	42.6	8.1	•
Receivables Turnover 36	8.2	•	48.1	33.3	6.8	6.2	6.2	5.3	4.5	5.1	2.9	•
Total Liabilities to Net Worth 37	1.8	•	2.0	9.8	0.8	0.6	1.4	1.0	1.5	0.7	2.9	•
Current Assets to Working Capital 38	4.1	•	1.7	2.2	1.7	1.9	2.5	3.0	3.1	2.4	7.3	•
Current Liabilities to Working Capital 39	3.1	•	0.7	1.2	0.7	0.9	1.5	2.0	2.1	1.4	6.3	•
Working Capital to Net Sales 40	0.1	•	0.1	0.0	0.2	0.2	0.1	0.1	0.1	0.1	0.1	•
Inventory to Working Capital 41	0.1	•	0.1	0.1	0.1	0.0	0.1	0.2	0.1	0.1	0.2	•
Total Receipts to Cash Flow 42	2.8	2.2	2.5	2.0	3.2	4.1	3.4	3.6	3.0	4.4	4.1	•
Cost of Goods to Cash Flow 43	0.6	0.1	0.5	0.2	1.0	1.6	1.2	1.3	1.0	2.5	0.7	•
Cash Flow to Total Debt 44	0.9	•	3.1	4.5	1.2	1.3	0.8	0.8	0.8	0.8	0.2	•

Selected Financial Factors (in Percentages)

Debt Ratio 45	64.4	•	67.2	90.7	44.7	36.2	57.7	50.7	59.5	42.4	74.4	•
Return on Total Assets 46	20.9	•	85.0	33.8	27.5	24.4	19.1	15.5	16.2	16.4	6.2	•
Return on Equity Before Income Taxes 47	56.0	•	255.5	343.9	48.6	37.3	43.0	29.8	36.7	26.2	20.2	•
Return on Equity After Income Taxes 48	51.2	•	252.1	334.8	46.9	34.0	38.2	26.5	28.9	21.7	14.3	•
Profit Margin (Before Income Tax) 49	11.5	34.2	15.9	3.8	15.8	12.3	10.9	10.5	9.8	10.8	7.2	•
Profit Margin (After Income Tax) 50	10.6	30.4	15.7	3.7	15.2	11.2	9.7	9.3	7.8	8.9	5.1	•

Table I

Corporations with and without Net Income

SCIENTIFIC RESEARCH AND DEVELOPMENT SERVICES

MONEY AMOUNTS AND SIZE OF ASSETS IN THOUSANDS OF DOLLARS

Item Description for Accounting Period 7/04 Through 6/05	Total	Zero Assets	Under 500	500 to 1,000	1,000 to 5,000	5,000 to 10,000	10,000 to 25,000	25,000 to 50,000	50,000 to 100,000	100,000 to 250,000	250,000 to 500,000	500,000 to 2,500,000	2,500,000 and over
Number of Enterprises 1	10155	1537	5543	1180	1029	307	250	131	74	56	30	13	4
Revenues ($ in Thousands)													
Net Sales 2	33623125	290284	2306733	1553757	2041745	1685107	2075126	1443354	1761060	2954783	2296408	2262428	12952339
Interest 3	601811	5194	1317	2933	9946	14599	25044	36542	51015	103827	105863	122782	122749
Rents 4	40015	45	0	32	1652	302	454	255	1558	2862	1438	18720	12695
Royalties 5	2051460	22156	4	0	3609	21132	14880	9940	53371	67484	503578	258722	1096584
Other Portfolio Income 6	491623	17613	16453	275	32012	31519	37297	40828	5673	104538	82006	21679	101737
Other Receipts 7	2200098	192605	123513	33023	262151	57511	93578	113543	90667	102633	598936	453587	78347
Total Receipts 8	39908132	527897	2448020	1590020	2351115	1810170	2246379	1644462	1963344	3336127	3588229	3137918	14364451
Average Total Receipts 9	3841	343	442	1347	2285	5896	8986	12553	26532	59574	119608	241378	3591113
Operating Costs/Operating Income (%)													
Cost of Operations 10	37.9	19.4	4.4	15.8	28.3	18.8	43.1	32.1	39.5	19.4	26.0	27.3	58.8
Salaries and Wages 11	29.5	81.9	35.4	25.0	37.7	43.8	30.9	45.6	38.5	35.3	51.2	45.9	13.3
Taxes Paid 12	4.1	9.0	4.5	3.6	7.6	4.9	4.7	7.0	6.0	3.7	5.2	5.5	2.3
Interest Paid 13	2.6	2.4	1.2	2.1	2.7	2.3	1.8	2.8	3.1	2.7	6.6	6.4	1.7
Depreciation 14	4.7	7.3	2.7	3.1	5.8	5.4	6.0	8.0	6.1	6.0	9.5	8.1	2.4
Amortization and Depletion 15	2.9	9.1	1.8	0.5	2.5	1.5	3.2	2.5	4.5	4.2	6.8	1.7	2.4
Pensions and Other Deferred Comp. 16	1.4	1.1	1.8	2.5	1.3	1.9	1.1	1.4	2.2	0.9	0.8	0.8	1.5
Employee Benefits 17	2.9	7.9	2.3	2.0	4.5	4.5	3.8	5.0	4.8	4.9	5.3	5.5	0.6
Advertising 18	0.8	1.1	2.2	0.2	1.4	0.9	0.6	1.2	1.2	1.5	1.2	0.4	0.3
Other Expenses 19	49.5	52.3	52.3	41.4	56.7	57.8	51.5	76.9	71.9	59.5	96.0	53.3	28.4
Officers' Compensation 20	5.1	10.7	12.0	10.1	11.9	9.3	6.9	9.5	6.7	5.2	5.6	5.1	0.4
Operating Margin 21	•	•	•	•	•	•	•	•	•	•	•	•	•
Operating Margin Before Officers' Comp. 22	•			3.5							•	•	•

Selected Average Balance Sheet ($ in Thousands)

Net Receivables **23**	788	0	24	105	601	828	1779	2630	5260	12475	23129	50186	913590
Inventories **24**	171	0	0	13	151	162	392	555	1213	2514	4329	14424	200203
Net Property, Plant and Equipment **25**	862	0	17	68	290	1253	2071	3526	6652	16920	55253	138055	506931
Total Assets **26**	7269	0	79	752	2392	6701	15761	34466	70185	156604	363853	819216	5995413
Notes and Loans Payable **27**	1938	0	146	485	973	1727	2139	6134	8678	24833	111841	335595	1420311
All Other Liabilities **28**	1633	0	33	432	824	1743	3460	7664	14152	26798	93438	148577	1340132
Net Worth **29**	3697	0	-99	-165	595	3232	10162	20668	47354	104973	158573	335044	3234970

Selected Financial Ratios (Times to 1)

Current Ratio **30**	2.6	•	1.7	1.1	1.8	2.0	2.8	3.8	3.2	3.7	2.9	2.9	2.2
Quick Ratio **31**	1.7	•	1.0	0.9	1.4	1.8	2.3	2.9	2.0	2.5	1.6	1.4	1.5
Net Sales to Working Capital **32**	1.4	•	13.3	59.8	2.9	2.6	1.3	0.6	0.8	0.8	0.6	0.8	2.4
Coverage Ratio **33**	•	•	•	•	•	•	•	•	•	•	•	•	0.2
Total Asset Turnover **34**	0.5	•	5.2	1.7	0.8	0.8	0.5	0.3	0.3	0.3	0.2	0.2	0.5
Inventory Turnover **35**	7.3	•	78.4	15.9	3.7	6.4	9.1	6.4	7.7	4.1	4.6	3.3	9.5
Receivables Turnover **36**	4.1	•	24.0	9.8	3.7	7.9	4.8	4.4	4.5	4.4	4.1	1.8	3.5
Total Liabilities to Net Worth **37**	1.0	•	•	•	3.0	1.1	0.6	0.7	0.5	0.5	1.3	1.4	0.9
Current Assets to Working Capital **38**	1.6	•	2.4	20.6	2.3	2.0	1.5	1.4	1.5	1.4	1.5	1.5	1.8
Current Liabilities to Working Capital **39**	0.6	•	1.4	19.6	1.3	1.0	0.5	0.4	0.5	0.4	0.5	0.5	0.8
Working Capital to Net Sales **40**	0.7	•	0.1	0.0	0.4	0.4	0.8	1.6	1.3	1.3	1.7	1.2	0.4
Inventory to Working Capital **41**	0.1	•	0.0	0.9	0.2	0.1	0.1	0.0	0.0	0.0	0.0	0.1	0.2
Total Receipts to Cash Flow **42**	6.5	15.9	3.8	3.2	28.8	•	•	•	5.2	4.1	4.5	4.5	
Cost of Goods to Cash Flow **43**	2.5	3.1	0.2	0.5	5.4	•	•	•	1.0	1.1	1.2	2.7	
Cash Flow to Total Debt **44**	0.1	•	0.6	0.4	0.1	0.1	•	0.3	0.2	0.2	0.1	0.1	0.3

Selected Financial Factors (in Percentages)

Debt Ratio **45**	49.1	•	225.2	121.9	75.1	51.8	35.5	40.0	32.5	33.0	56.4	59.1	46.0
Return on Total Assets **46**	•	•	•	•	•	•	•	•	•	•	•	•	0.1
Return on Equity Before Income Taxes **47**	•	•	60.3	33.8	•	•	•	•	•	•	•	•	•
Return on Equity After Income Taxes **48**	•	•	60.5	42.1	•	•	•	•	•	•	•	•	•
Profit Margin (Before Income Tax) **49**	•	•	•	•	•	•	•	•	•	•	•	•	•
Profit Margin (After Income Tax) **50**	•	•	•	•	•	•	•	•	•	•	•	•	•

Table II

Corporations with Net Income

SCIENTIFIC RESEARCH AND DEVELOPMENT SERVICES

MONEY AMOUNTS AND SIZE OF ASSETS IN THOUSANDS OF DOLLARS

Item Description for Accounting Period 7/04 Through 6/05	Total	Zero Assets	Under 500	500 to 1,000	1,000 to 5,000	5,000 to 10,000	10,000 to 25,000	25,000 to 50,000	50,000 to 100,000	100,000 to 250,000	250,000 to 500,000	500,000 to 2,500,000	2,500,000 and over
Number of Enterprises 1	3760	147	2378	679	334	100	54	21	13	16	10	7	0
Revenues ($ in Thousands)													
Net Sales 2	22582280	130083	1976007	1250685	1390066	1121167	1229284	961426	946595	1696871	1441996	10438101	0
Interest 3	173076	1121	27	1725	402	2039	2247	2733	3388	37183	23873	98339	0
Rents 4	19843	41	0	0	1646	48	197	66	0	1368	0	16476	0
Royalties 5	769505	6987	4	0	721	4328	8158	4485	41295	61523	478266	163739	0
Other Portfolio Income 6	331529	2103	8087	16	18017	30683	25546	38535	290	100928	63582	43743	0
Other Receipts 7	1312096	145779	85043	15697	234879	3542	21477	38080	14313	30392	306078	416813	0
Total Receipts 8	25188329	286114	2069168	1268123	1645731	1161807	1286909	1045325	1005881	1928265	2313795	11177211	0
Average Total Receipts 9	6699	1946	870	1868	4927	11618	23832	49777	77375	120517	231380	1596744	•
Operating Costs/Operating Income (%)													
Cost of Operations 10	35.4	1.3	0.1	16.4	22.0	12.2	45.1	34.7	48.9	24.4	30.9	49.2	•
Salaries and Wages 11	20.3	81.4	32.9	23.1	26.6	32.5	13.8	21.4	15.1	22.3	31.2	14.0	•
Taxes Paid 12	3.5	7.8	3.7	3.1	7.2	3.4	3.1	3.3	3.5	2.4	3.0	3.3	•
Interest Paid 13	1.2	0.4	0.1	0.7	0.3	0.2	0.5	0.8	0.3	1.7	2.0	1.8	•
Depreciation 14	2.5	3.3	0.8	1.6	3.6	2.5	2.7	2.9	2.7	4.8	6.3	1.8	•
Amortization and Depletion 15	0.9	0.1	0.0	0.0	1.2	0.1	0.3	0.4	1.1	1.0	4.1	0.8	•
Pensions and Other Deferred Comp. 16	1.5	2.0	2.0	3.0	1.5	2.3	1.2	1.6	3.1	1.1	1.0	1.2	•
Employee Benefits 17	2.3	8.3	1.9	1.8	3.8	4.0	2.6	2.3	3.6	3.2	4.4	1.5	•
Advertising 18	0.5	0.3	2.4	0.2	0.7	0.7	0.3	0.4	0.2	0.4	0.4	0.3	•
Other Expenses 19	27.6	69.2	39.8	23.0	27.3	32.3	18.5	23.0	14.4	34.8	48.4	23.5	•
Officers' Compensation 20	3.1	12.3	7.3	10.1	7.1	3.7	2.9	2.9	2.8	1.4	3.0	1.2	•
Operating Margin 21	1.1	•	9.0	17.1	•	6.2	8.9	6.3	4.2	2.6	•	1.5	•
Operating Margin Before Officers' Comp. 22	4.2	•	16.3	27.2	5.8	9.9	11.8	9.3	7.0	4.0	•	2.7	•

Selected Average Balance Sheet ($ in Thousands)

Net Receivables 23	1179	0	15	147	930	1544	4505	10115	13756	25361	56951	317691
Inventories 24	239	0	0	9	276	65	769	1728	2441	5193	6098	77049
Net Property, Plant and Equipment 25	797	0	14	51	403	1105	2875	5785	7435	25720	60702	184840
Total Assets 26	6920	0	59	806	2715	6253	16487	35625	67391	168866	358140	2143153
Notes and Loans Payable 27	2013	0	9	211	130	392	2373	4433	2372	21275	74658	854930
All Other Liabilities 28	1696	0	14	125	720	1597	4636	9864	15313	27794	85742	557309
Net Worth 29	3210	0	36	470	1865	4264	9478	21328	49705	119797	197740	730915

Selected Financial Ratios (Times to 1)

Current Ratio 30	2.2	•	3.3	4.2	2.7	2.6	2.0	2.2	3.2	3.9	1.7	1.9
Quick Ratio 31	1.4	•	2.7	4.0	1.9	2.4	1.5	1.9	2.5	2.8	1.0	1.1
Net Sales to Working Capital 32	3.2	•	25.5	4.6	3.4	4.4	4.3	3.5	2.4	1.5	1.6	3.5
Coverage Ratio 33	11.4	77.4	205.0	28.8	51.6	55.5	27.5	20.5	39.9	10.8	13.7	5.9
Total Asset Turnover 34	0.9	•	14.0	2.3	1.5	1.8	1.4	1.3	1.1	0.6	0.4	0.7
Inventory Turnover 35	8.9	•	•	35.0	3.3	20.9	13.4	9.2	14.6	5.0	7.3	9.5
Receivables Turnover 36	4.3	•	48.6	11.8	5.7	8.7	5.6	5.1	4.8	5.8	3.9	3.1
Total Liabilities to Net Worth 37	1.2	•	0.6	0.7	0.5	0.5	0.7	0.7	0.4	0.4	0.8	1.9
Current Assets to Working Capital 38	1.9	•	1.4	1.3	1.6	1.6	2.0	1.8	1.5	1.3	2.4	2.1
Current Liabilities to Working Capital 39	0.9	•	0.4	0.3	0.6	0.6	1.0	0.8	0.5	0.3	1.4	1.1
Working Capital to Net Sales 40	0.3	•	0.0	0.2	0.3	0.2	0.2	0.3	0.4	0.7	0.6	0.3
Inventory to Working Capital 41	0.1	•	•	0.0	0.2	0.0	0.2	0.1	0.1	0.1	0.1	0.1
Total Receipts to Cash Flow 42	2.9	1.1	2.2	2.7	2.8	3.1	3.8	3.3	4.5	2.5	1.6	3.4
Cost of Goods to Cash Flow 43	1.0	0.0	0.0	0.4	0.6	0.4	1.7	1.1	2.2	0.6	0.5	1.7
Cash Flow to Total Debt 44	0.6	•	16.7	2.1	1.7	1.8	0.9	1.0	0.9	0.9	0.6	0.3

Selected Financial Factors (in Percentages)

Debt Ratio 45	53.6	•	39.1	41.7	31.3	31.8	42.5	40.1	26.2	29.1	44.8	65.9
Return on Total Assets 46	12.0	•	193.0	43.7	27.1	18.0	19.4	20.3	11.6	11.4	11.2	7.2
Return on Equity Before Income Taxes 47	23.6	•	315.2	72.3	38.6	25.9	32.6	32.3	15.3	14.5	18.8	17.5
Return on Equity After Income Taxes 48	19.9	•	313.9	67.2	37.2	20.9	28.1	27.3	13.4	12.1	14.3	13.5
Profit Margin (Before Income Tax) 49	12.6	33.5	13.7	18.4	17.3	9.8	13.6	15.1	10.4	16.4	25.7	8.6
Profit Margin (After Income Tax) 50	10.7	31.7	13.6	17.2	16.7	8.0	11.7	12.7	9.2	13.7	19.7	6.6

Table I

Corporations with and without Net Income

ADVERTISING AND RELATED SERVICES

MONEY AMOUNTS AND SIZE OF ASSETS IN THOUSANDS OF DOLLARS

Item Description for Accounting Period 7/04 Through 6/05	Total	Zero Assets	Under 500	500 to 1,000	1,000 to 5,000	5,000 to 10,000	10,000 to 25,000	25,000 to 50,000	50,000 to 100,000	100,000 to 250,000	250,000 to 500,000	500,000 to 2,500,000	2,500,000 and over
Number of Enterprises 1	48810	6298	38189	2464	1331	236	174	55	24	21	4	7	7
Revenues ($ in Thousands)													
Net Sales 2	67619012	772311	13228892	5270490	7944130	4019163	6480561	2713573	2215690	4180521	1408201	4807934	14577545
Interest 3	769686	247	3806	3898	10508	4728	5067	3604	3673	8287	17185	44194	664491
Rents 4	78851	74	1380	2879	855	210	679	214	224	214	0	14658	57465
Royalties 5	84911	9	0	0	0	0	36309	14910	0	1100	14284	15093	3205
Other Portfolio Income 6	449771	20000	2763	41669	8151	5331	20097	14231	8816	54015	602	23217	250878
Other Receipts 7	1645622	-7303	165386	158129	-30402	459684	297077	105518	54718	23811	4061	-9394	424337
Total Receipts 8	70647853	785338	13402227	5477065	7933242	4489116	6839790	2852050	2283121	4267948	1144333	4895702	15977921
Average Total Receipts 9	1447	125	351	2223	5960	19022	39309	51855	95130	203236	361083	699386	2282560
Operating Costs/Operating Income (%)													
Cost of Operations 10	36.2	34.8	34.3	54.8	40.9	61.7	55.6	54.0	33.8	56.0	35.8	37.7	3.8
Salaries and Wages 11	20.2	10.7	9.4	19.7	14.1	9.4	11.7	12.9	23.9	14.8	23.8	26.5	40.7
Taxes Paid 12	2.5	2.1	2.3	2.7	1.9	1.2	1.4	1.8	2.0	1.5	2.4	3.0	4.0
Interest Paid 13	3.0	8.2	0.4	0.3	0.4	0.3	0.3	0.7	1.2	1.1	1.2	3.9	10.5
Depreciation 14	1.8	2.4	1.3	1.4	1.3	0.9	1.2	1.5	2.0	1.3	4.9	3.5	2.6
Amortization and Depletion 15	1.2	1.0	0.1	0.0	0.3	0.3	0.2	1.1	1.1	1.1	1.8	2.0	3.6
Pensions and Other Deferred Comp. 16	0.8	0.0	0.8	0.9	0.7	0.7	0.4	0.2	1.0	0.6	0.1	2.0	1.0
Employee Benefits 17	1.3	1.2	0.8	1.1	0.9	0.5	0.9	1.1	1.3	0.8	4.2	2.1	2.0
Advertising 18	4.9	5.3	6.5	1.9	4.7	12.3	14.1	8.4	3.0	0.4	0.6	2.9	0.3
Other Expenses 19	24.1	31.5	31.7	13.4	21.8	13.3	12.1	17.8	27.6	20.5	15.8	17.5	34.9
Officers' Compensation 20	4.9	6.9	9.3	7.5	5.5	4.5	3.0	2.8	2.5	1.7	2.1	2.4	3.1
Operating Margin 21	•	•	3.1	•	7.5	•	•	•	0.8	0.2	7.3	•	•
Operating Margin Before Officers' Comp. 22	4.1	2.7	12.4	3.7	13.0	•	2.2	0.5	3.2	1.9	9.4	•	•

Selected Average Balance Sheet ($ in Thousands)

Net Receivables 23	528	0	15	135	747	2951	6040	12117	17456	45474	83233	285191	2532724
Inventories 24	29	0	4	22	131	286	457	1260	817	830	7500	9995	100329
Net Property, Plant and Equipment 25	121	0	15	154	341	482	1880	3399	4998	13827	70900	95473	361500
Total Assets 26	2143	0	68	715	2418	7351	15258	34965	68988	175544	395403	1175552	10791325
Notes and Loans Payable 27	461	0	43	289	540	757	2788	6309	10882	38922	59631	269275	2175843
All Other Liabilities 28	1026	0	28	228	1078	4853	9663	20403	37016	74563	89351	528676	5225438
Net Worth 29	655	0	-3	198	800	1741	2806	8253	21090	62059	246421	377601	3390044

Selected Financial Ratios (Times to 1)

Current Ratio 30	0.8	·	1.2	1.3	1.5	1.3	1.2	1.1	1.1	1.3	1.5	1.1	0.7
Quick Ratio 31	0.7	·	0.9	1.1	1.4	1.1	1.0	0.9	0.9	1.0	1.4	0.9	0.6
Net Sales to Working Capital 32	·	·	43.6	25.9	10.3	12.9	23.9	31.3	22.0	9.6	7.3	27.7	·
Coverage Ratio 33	2.3	0.7	12.2	1.5	21.8	21.2	15.0	5.1	4.2	3.0	9.5	0.6	1.4
Total Asset Turnover 34	0.6	·	5.1	3.0	2.5	2.3	2.4	1.4	1.3	1.1	0.9	0.6	0.2
Inventory Turnover 35	17.2	·	33.0	52.3	18.6	36.8	45.3	21.1	38.2	134.2	16.8	25.9	0.8
Receivables Turnover 36	2.7	·	25.2	15.7	8.0	8.3	6.6	4.1	5.3	5.3	3.1	2.8	0.8
Total Liabilities to Net Worth 37	2.3	·	2.6	2.6	2.0	3.2	4.4	3.2	2.3	1.8	0.6	2.1	2.2
Current Assets to Working Capital 38	·	·	5.6	5.0	2.8	4.6	7.4	13.7	10.2	4.8	2.9	20.9	·
Current Liabilities to Working Capital 39	·	·	4.6	4.0	1.8	3.6	6.4	12.7	9.2	3.8	1.9	19.9	·
Working Capital to Net Sales 40	·	·	0.0	0.0	0.1	0.1	0.0	0.0	0.0	0.1	0.1	0.0	·
Inventory to Working Capital 41	·	·	0.7	0.3	0.1	0.2	0.3	0.8	0.2	0.1	0.0	0.4	·
Total Receipts to Cash Flow 42	4.3	5.4	3.1	9.8	3.9	5.9	6.9	6.1	3.6	5.0	4.5	8.8	3.4
Cost of Goods to Cash Flow 43	1.6	1.9	1.1	5.4	1.6	3.7	3.8	3.3	1.2	2.8	1.6	3.3	0.1
Cash Flow to Total Debt 44	0.2	1.5	0.4	0.4	0.9	0.5	0.4	0.3	0.5	0.3	0.5	0.1	0.1

Selected Financial Factors (in Percentages)

Debt Ratio 45	69.4	·	104.3	72.2	66.9	76.3	81.6	76.4	69.4	64.6	37.7	67.9	68.6
Return on Total Assets 46	4.5	·	24.3	1.6	19.0	15.6	12.4	5.3	6.6	3.9	9.8	1.4	2.9
Return on Equity Before Income Taxes 47	8.4	·	·	2.0	54.9	62.7	62.7	17.9	16.6	7.4	14.1	·	2.6
Return on Equity After Income Taxes 48	7.1	·	·	0.9	53.4	59.3	58.3	15.5	14.1	5.4	9.9	·	1.6
Profit Margin (Before Income Tax) 49	4.0	·	4.4	0.2	7.4	6.4	4.7	3.0	3.8	2.3	9.9	·	4.3
Profit Margin (After Income Tax) 50	3.4	·	4.3	0.1	7.2	6.1	4.4	2.6	3.2	1.7	6.9	·	2.6

Table II

Corporations with Net Income

ADVERTISING AND RELATED SERVICES

MONEY AMOUNTS AND SIZE OF ASSETS IN THOUSANDS OF DOLLARS

Item Description for Accounting Period 7/04 Through 6/05	Total	Zero Assets	Under 500	500 to 1,000	1,000 to 5,000	5,000 to 10,000	10,000 to 25,000	25,000 to 50,000	50,000 to 100,000	100,000 to 250,000	250,000 to 500,000	500,000 to 2,500,000	2,500,000 and over
Number of Enterprises 1	28302	2181	23484	1219	997	208	137	32	0	12	4	3	0
Revenues ($ in Thousands)													
Net Sales 2	47972766	364976	8052997	3817587	6283031	3934482	4893187	1878155	0	2936243	1408201	2079489	0
Interest 3	622732	59	521	1472	3979	3857	2713	1979	0	4854	17185	10973	0
Rents 4	75683	0	1380	1343	266	0	678	210	0	121	0	14658	0
Royalties 5	56259	0	0	0	0	0	21389	14904	0	1100	14284	1389	0
Other Portfolio Income 6	374992	18869	1959	24285	8145	5014	13879	13397	0	54000	602	19928	0
Other Receipts 7	1081025	14203	134357	138269	125689	26582	197158	57350	0	9416	4061	10841	0
Total Receipts 8	50183457	397907	8191214	3982956	6421110	3969935	5129004	1965995	0	3005734	1444333	2137278	0
Average Total Receipts 9	1773	182	349	3267	6440	19086	37438	61437	*	250478	361083	712426	*
Operating Costs/Operating Income (%)													
Cost of Operations 10	40.3	13.3	37.5	60.7	42.5	61.7	59.4	58.2	*	68.5	35.8	57.2	*
Salaries and Wages 11	18.9	8.6	10.0	12.8	13.7	8.2	12.6	11.5	*	14.0	23.8	13.3	*
Taxes Paid 12	2.5	1.6	2.5	2.0	2.0	1.1	1.6	1.7	*	1.5	2.4	2.7	*
Interest Paid 13	3.0	2.8	0.4	0.2	0.3	0.1	0.2	0.6	*	0.3	1.2	6.3	*
Depreciation 14	1.7	2.0	0.8	1.3	1.2	0.4	1.1	1.3	*	1.1	4.9	4.6	*
Amortization and Depletion 15	0.9	0.1	0.1	0.0	0.1	0.3	0.2	0.9	*	0.4	1.8	1.0	*
Pensions and Other Deferred Comp. 16	0.7	0.1	0.8	1.2	0.4	0.5	0.4	0.2	*	0.6	0.1	0.4	*
Employee Benefits 17	1.1	0.4	0.7	1.0	0.8	0.5	1.0	0.9	*	0.7	4.2	2.5	*
Advertising 18	2.8	9.0	5.1	2.3	0.4	7.0	7.1	4.3	*	0.4	0.6	0.3	*
Other Expenses 19	19.7	35.4	21.0	11.2	24.1	8.9	10.9	15.5	*	7.9	15.8	12.0	*
Officers' Compensation 20	4.9	12.5	10.3	6.7	5.7	3.8	3.2	2.4	*	1.5	2.1	0.7	*
Operating Margin 21	3.6	14.2	10.7	0.4	8.7	7.6	2.4	2.6	*	3.1	7.3	*	*
Operating Margin Before Officers' Comp. 22	8.5	26.7	21.0	7.2	14.4	11.4	5.6	5.0	*	4.6	9.4	*	*

Selected Average Balance Sheet ($ in Thousands)

Net Receivables 23	739	0	14	181	729	3095	6253	13402	52291	83233	203883
Inventories 24	38	0	0	21	90	142	541	1335	1237	4602	15539
Net Property, Plant and Equipment 25	149	0	10	148	320	278	1578	3642	14325	70900	151515
Total Assets 26	2611	0	58	742	2284	7381	15064	34586	174212	395403	1099319
Notes and Loans Payable 27	382	0	28	125	477	694	1698	4065	15308	59631	469923
All Other Liabilities 28	1259	0	24	198	996	4824	9335	20299	81305	89351	487584
Net Worth 29	970	0	5	419	812	1863	4030	10222	77600	246421	141813

Selected Financial Ratios (Times to 1)

Current Ratio 30	0.9	•	1.3	1.9	1.7	1.3	1.2	1.2	1.4	1.5	1.1
Quick Ratio 31	0.8	•	1.2	1.6	1.5	1.2	1.0	1.0	1.2	1.4	0.8
Net Sales to Working Capital 32	•	•	41.2	13.8	9.5	12.0	16.8	15.3	7.6	7.3	24.8
Coverage Ratio 33	3.9	9.3	31.0	21.7	33.2	70.3	32.7	14.5	18.5	9.5	1.2
Total Asset Turnover 34	0.6	•	5.9	4.2	2.8	2.6	2.4	1.7	1.4	0.9	0.6
Inventory Turnover 35	18.0	•	55.5	90.5	29.7	82.3	39.2	25.6	135.4	27.4	25.5
Receivables Turnover 36	2.3	•	25.4	17.1	8.9	9.5	•	4.5	5.5	1.8	•
Total Liabilities to Net Worth 37	1.7	•	9.6	0.8	1.8	3.0	2.7	2.4	1.2	0.6	6.8
Current Assets to Working Capital 38	•	•	4.6	2.2	2.5	4.0	5.6	5.9	3.4	2.9	16.3
Current Liabilities to Working Capital 39	•	•	3.6	1.2	1.5	3.0	4.6	4.9	2.4	1.9	15.3
Working Capital to Net Sales 40	•	•	0.0	0.1	0.1	0.1	0.1	0.1	0.1	0.1	0.0
Inventory to Working Capital 41	•	•	0.3	0.1	0.1	0.1	0.3	0.4	0.1	0.0	0.6
Total Receipts to Cash Flow 42	4.3	2.5	3.4	7.6	3.2	6.8	6.5	5.3	9.7	4.5	8.6
Cost of Goods to Cash Flow 43	1.7	0.3	1.3	4.6	1.4	4.2	3.8	3.1	6.6	1.6	4.9
Cash Flow to Total Debt 44	0.2	•	1.9	1.3	1.3	0.5	0.5	0.5	0.3	0.5	0.1

Selected Financial Factors (in Percentages)

Debt Ratio 45	62.9	•	90.5	43.5	64.5	74.8	73.2	70.4	55.5	37.7	87.1
Return on Total Assets 46	7.5	•	76.3	21.0	31.0	22.1	17.6	14.0	8.1	9.8	5.0
Return on Equity Before Income Taxes 47	15.0	•	779.4	35.5	84.7	86.2	63.9	44.0	17.2	14.1	7.7
Return on Equity After Income Taxes 48	13.5	•	771.5	34.5	82.7	82.6	60.1	40.6	14.4	9.9	7.6
Profit Margin (Before Income Tax) 49	8.6	23.3	12.4	4.7	10.9	8.5	7.2	7.7	5.5	9.9	1.6
Profit Margin (After Income Tax) 50	7.7	22.9	12.3	4.6	10.6	8.1	6.8	7.1	4.6	6.9	1.6

Table I
Corporations with and without Net Income

OTHER PROFESSIONAL, SCIENTIFIC, AND TECHNICAL SERVICES

MONEY AMOUNTS AND SIZE OF ASSETS IN THOUSANDS OF DOLLARS

Item Description for Accounting Period 7/04 Through 6/05	Total	Zero Assets	Under 500	500 to 1,000	1,000 to 5,000	5,000 to 10,000	10,000 to 25,000	25,000 to 50,000	50,000 to 100,000	100,000 to 250,000	250,000 to 500,000	500,000 to 2,500,000	2,500,000 and over
Number of Enterprises 1	92978	12385	74127	3866	1751	453	230	69	39	40	8	6	3
Revenues ($ in Thousands)													
Net Sales 2	68553939	2705098	27071866	6084089	4434919	3928169	6790690	3436486	2503202	5042373	1370692	2068092	3118264
Interest 3	208182	4629	9055	3709	6532	12761	16667	11316	12300	48828	21278	8957	52150
Rents 4	21030	9	2396	101	1007	2167	1426	1769	1547	4547	902	411	4748
Royalties 5	158446	0	27643	0	25	116	7748	100	3880	64456	1772	6497	46208
Other Portfolio Income 6	297283	3121	35929	2382	29157	74156	42606	29258	9564	29908	924	2309	37971
Other Receipts 7	954163	36533	191372	143631	70509	111004	88088	115617	63769	64388	15468	64711	-10930
Total Receipts 8	70193043	2749390	27338261	6233912	4542149	4128373	6947225	3594546	2594262	5254500	1411036	2150977	3248411
Average Total Receipts 9	755	222	369	1612	2594	9113	30205	52095	66520	131362	176380	358496	1082804
Operating Costs/Operating Income (%)													
Cost of Operations 10	26.1	3.6	17.7	28.0	49.9	41.3	45.2	27.2	34.3	31.6	37.4	12.3	8.6
Salaries and Wages 11	22.4	15.1	23.3	18.4	17.7	16.7	16.9	17.0	28.8	28.2	21.4	35.2	37.3
Taxes Paid 12	3.3	1.9	3.5	5.0	2.8	2.1	2.4	2.5	3.7	3.3	2.3	5.0	3.7
Interest Paid 13	1.4	0.4	0.6	0.9	1.2	0.8	0.7	1.1	1.6	2.1	4.5	3.1	9.4
Depreciation 14	2.0	2.1	1.6	1.3	2.4	2.1	1.7	2.3	2.9	2.9	1.7	2.8	3.8
Amortization and Depletion 15	0.9	1.3	0.3	0.3	0.5	0.7	0.4	0.7	0.9	1.8	3.4	2.6	5.1
Pensions and Other Deferred Comp. 16	1.2	0.1	1.2	2.0	0.6	0.8	0.5	0.8	1.2	2.1	0.1	3.2	2.2
Employee Benefits 17	1.6	0.9	1.2	0.9	1.1	1.3	1.6	2.0	2.4	2.9	1.7	2.3	3.5
Advertising 18	0.7	0.6	0.7	0.6	0.9	0.6	0.8	0.5	0.5	1.3	0.4	1.4	0.3
Other Expenses 19	31.6	75.1	33.1	24.3	19.2	28.4	28.6	46.0	24.2	22.8	27.7	27.4	33.4
Officers' Compensation 20	7.7	6.2	11.0	17.8	5.1	7.2	1.9	2.7	2.0	2.8	2.4	1.5	1.4
Operating Margin 21	1.1	•	5.9	0.6	•	•	•	•	•	•	•	3.2	•
Operating Margin Before Officers' Comp. 22	8.8	•	16.9	18.4	3.7	5.3	1.2	•	•	1.1	•	4.7	•

Selected Average Balance Sheet ($ in Thousands)

Net Receivables 23	82	4	104	376	2208	3950	8660	17744	29790	36934	104068	306457
Inventories 24	9	3	44	36	147	598	323	586	1310	5456	4126	3304
Net Property, Plant and Equipment 25	65	20	109	591	693	1973	3398	9613	15856	25952	63093	165754
Total Assets 26	533	75	669	1945	6588	14960	35214	69247	162196	331784	933545	3899532
Notes and Loans Payable 27	209	51	350	1151	4066	3436	7435	16444	34706	143204	365415	1245560
All Other Liabilities 28	161	18	212	477	2565	4534	17446	18283	57370	123192	145434	1243039
Net Worth 29	163	6	107	317	-43	6990	10333	34521	70120	65387	422696	1410932

Selected Financial Ratios (Times to 1)

Current Ratio 30	1.4	•	1.6	1.3	1.7	1.4	1.4	1.7	1.5	1.0	1.6	1.0
Quick Ratio 31	1.1	•	1.2	1.1	1.3	1.0	1.0	1.4	1.1	0.5	1.3	0.7
Net Sales to Working Capital 32	12.6	•	10.7	14.1	4.8	11.6	9.0	4.7	5.8	130.3	5.0	123.4
Coverage Ratio 33	3.6	•	4.5	1.8	5.3	3.1	2.9	1.8	2.2	1.0	3.3	0.8
Total Asset Turnover 34	1.4	•	2.4	1.3	1.3	2.0	1.4	0.9	0.8	0.5	0.4	0.3
Inventory Turnover 35	21.7	•	9.9	34.9	24.4	22.3	42.0	37.5	30.4	11.7	10.3	27.2
Receivables Turnover 36	9.6	•	13.7	4.6	5.5	8.1	5.6	4.4	4.8	4.0	2.8	•
Total Liabilities to Net Worth 37	2.3	•	5.2	5.1	•	1.1	2.4	1.0	1.3	4.1	1.2	1.8
Current Assets to Working Capital 38	3.5	•	2.7	4.4	2.5	3.7	3.6	2.5	3.2	95.0	2.6	69.2
Current Liabilities to Working Capital 39	2.5	•	1.7	3.4	1.5	2.7	2.6	1.5	2.2	94.0	1.6	68.2
Working Capital to Net Sales 40	0.1	•	0.0	0.1	0.2	0.1	0.1	0.2	0.2	0.0	0.2	0.0
Inventory to Working Capital 41	0.2	•	0.4	0.2	0.1	0.3	0.1	0.1	0.0	3.7	0.1	0.4
Total Receipts to Cash Flow 42	3.4	1.5	4.4	6.4	3.9	3.7	2.3	4.8	4.8	4.1	3.3	4.2
Cost of Goods to Cash Flow 43	0.9	0.1	1.2	3.2	1.6	1.7	0.6	1.7	1.5	1.5	0.4	0.4
Cash Flow to Total Debt 44	0.6	•	0.6	0.2	0.3	1.0	0.9	0.4	0.3	0.2	0.2	0.1

Selected Financial Factors (in Percentages)

Debt Ratio 45	69.4	92.3	84.0	83.7	100.7	53.3	70.7	50.1	56.8	80.3	54.7	63.8
Return on Total Assets 46	7.0	•	9.2	2.8	5.3	4.5	4.6	2.7	3.6	2.4	3.8	2.1
Return on Equity Before Income Taxes 47	16.6	436.0	44.9	7.5	•	6.5	10.2	2.5	4.5	0.3	5.9	•
Return on Equity After Income Taxes 48	14.7	430.0	42.2	3.1	•	4.3	4.6	1.0	4.5	0.2	4.9	•
Profit Margin (Before Income Tax) 49	3.7	6.9	3.1	0.9	3.2	1.5	2.1	1.3	2.5	0.1	7.2	•
Profit Margin (After Income Tax) 50	3.2	6.8	2.9	0.4	2.6	1.0	1.0	0.5	1.2	0.1	6.0	•

Table II

Corporations with Net Income

OTHER PROFESSIONAL, SCIENTIFIC, AND TECHNICAL SERVICES

MONEY AMOUNTS AND SIZE OF ASSETS IN THOUSANDS OF DOLLARS

Item Description for Accounting Period 7/04 Through 6/05	Total	Zero Assets	Under 500	500 to 1000	251 to 500	501 to 1,000	1,001 to 5,000	5,001 to 10,000	10,001 to 25,000	25,001 to 50,000	50,001 to 100,000	100,001 to 250,000	250,001 and over
Number of Enterprises **1**	52222	4814	42731	3017	1142	285	138	38	25	25	0	0	0
Revenues ($ in Thousands)													
Net Sales **2**	47008056	1073319	19670820	5123440	3608194	2851232	4344033	2356204	1699604	3382646	0	0	0
Interest **3**	68078	1783	5982	2403	4872	4232	10788	3935	5155	15009	0	0	0
Rents **4**	9659	0	2302	0	920	176	441	1642	1296	1839	0	0	0
Royalties **5**	99496	0	27643	0	0	0	2183	0	0	49446	0	0	0
Other Portfolio Income **6**	174814	2887	27077	988	28577	3852	38981	17868	8154	27867	0	0	0
Other Receipts **7**	754396	32483	227889	126249	45813	101119	52096	34297	26030	34561	0	0	0
Total Receipts **8**	48114499	1110472	19961713	5253080	3688376	2960611	4448522	2413946	1740239	3511368	0	0	0
Average Total Receipts **9**	921	231	467	1741	3230	10388	32236	63525	69610	140455	.	.	.
Operating Costs/Operating Income (%)													
Cost of Operations **10**	26.7	2.6	17.0	22.2	54.0	39.6	46.9	20.5	28.5	38.6	.	.	.
Salaries and Wages **11**	20.2	21.2	21.9	18.4	13.7	16.7	16.7	13.5	28.1	21.8	.	.	.
Taxes Paid **12**	3.3	3.0	3.2	5.4	2.3	2.1	2.6	2.4	3.8	2.7	.	.	.
Interest Paid **13**	0.9	0.4	0.5	0.7	1.2	0.6	0.6	0.7	1.0	1.5	.	.	.
Depreciation **14**	1.5	1.1	1.3	1.0	1.5	1.5	1.3	1.4	2.5	2.6	.	.	.
Amortization and Depletion **15**	0.5	0.4	0.2	0.3	0.3	0.2	0.4	0.4	0.7	1.4	.	.	.
Pensions and Other Deferred Comp. **16**	1.3	0.0	1.3	2.4	0.5	1.0	0.6	0.8	1.8	1.1	.	.	.
Employee Benefits **17**	1.3	0.4	0.9	0.9	0.9	1.0	1.9	1.8	2.7	2.5	.	.	.
Advertising **18**	0.6	0.6	0.6	0.5	0.5	0.5	0.6	0.5	0.4	0.6	.	.	.
Other Expenses **19**	27.0	49.1	29.9	24.2	12.9	22.9	21.3	47.5	24.2	19.3	.	.	.
Officers' Compensation **20**	8.5	9.2	11.3	20.0	4.3	7.4	1.9	1.8	1.6	2.2	.	.	.
Operating Margin **21**	8.4	11.9	11.8	4.1	8.0	6.5	5.1	8.5	4.7	5.7	.	.	.
Operating Margin Before Officers' Comp. **22**	16.8	21.1	23.1	24.1	12.3	14.0	7.1	10.4	6.4	7.9	.	.	.

Selected Average Balance Sheet ($ in Thousands)

Net Receivables 23	83	0	4	87	499	2741	4463	9534	14918	36400	•
Inventories 24	11	0	3	48	42	174	645	101	472	1250	•
Net Property, Plant and Equipment 25	66	0	24	104	445	347	1876	3237	8770	15059	•
Total Assets 26	486	0	94	662	1844	6667	14693	35918	67564	157988	•
Notes and Loans Payable 27	153	0	47	291	1191	1072	3101	6914	10872	31388	•
All Other Liabilities 28	115	0	21	182	479	2636	3507	11402	17116	48019	•
Net Worth 29	218	0	27	189	175	2959	8085	17602	39576	78582	•

Selected Financial Ratios (Times to 1)

Current Ratio 30	1.7	•	1.8	2.0	1.3	1.6	1.4	1.8	1.8	1.9
Quick Ratio 31	1.4	•	1.5	1.5	1.1	1.5	1.0	1.4	1.5	1.5
Net Sales to Working Capital 32	9.6	41.6	21.9	8.0	14.9	5.7	10.5	6.7	4.6	3.9
Coverage Ratio 33	13.6	•	25.6	10.0	9.7	17.2	14.1	16.1	8.1	7.2
Total Asset Turnover 34	1.9	•	4.9	2.6	1.7	1.5	2.1	1.7	1.0	0.9
Inventory Turnover 35	22.3	•	24.9	7.9	40.7	22.8	22.9	126.2	41.0	41.8
Receivables Turnover 36	12.5	•	101.8	17.0	5.5	5.8	8.2	6.8	6.1	4.7
Total Liabilities to Net Worth 37	1.2	•	2.6	2.5	9.5	1.3	0.8	1.0	0.7	1.0
Current Assets to Working Capital 38	2.3	•	2.2	2.0	4.2	2.6	3.3	2.3	2.2	2.1
Current Liabilities to Working Capital 39	1.3	•	1.2	1.0	3.2	1.6	2.3	1.3	1.2	1.1
Working Capital to Net Sales 40	0.1	•	0.0	0.1	0.1	0.2	0.1	0.1	0.2	0.3
Inventory to Working Capital 41	0.1	•	0.2	0.3	0.2	0.1	0.3	0.0	0.0	0.0
Total Receipts to Cash Flow 42	3.0	1.7	2.7	3.8	5.0	3.4	3.8	1.8	3.8	4.0
Cost of Goods to Cash Flow 43	0.8	0.0	0.5	0.8	2.7	1.3	1.8	0.4	1.1	1.5
Cash Flow to Total Debt 44	1.1	•	2.5	1.0	0.4	0.8	1.2	1.9	0.6	0.4

Selected Financial Factors (in Percentages)

Debt Ratio 45	55.1	•	71.9	71.4	90.5	55.6	45.0	51.0	41.4	50.3
Return on Total Assets 46	21.6	•	67.4	19.0	19.4	16.5	17.4	20.3	8.3	9.5
Return on Equity Before Income Taxes 47	44.5	•	230.8	59.8	183.5	34.9	29.4	38.8	12.4	16.4
Return on Equity After Income Taxes 48	42.1	•	228.5	57.8	171.2	32.1	26.2	32.8	10.4	13.0
Profit Margin (Before Income Tax) 49	10.8	15.4	13.3	6.7	10.2	10.3	7.5	11.0	7.2	9.5
Profit Margin (After Income Tax) 50	10.2	14.2	13.2	6.4	9.5	9.5	6.7	9.3	6.0	7.6

Table I

Corporations with and without Net Income

OFFICES OF BANK HOLDING COMPANIES

MONEY AMOUNTS AND SIZE OF ASSETS IN THOUSANDS OF DOLLARS

Item Description for Accounting Period 7/04 Through 6/05	Total	Zero Assets	Under 500	500 to 1,000	1,000 to 5,000	5,000 to 10,000	10,000 to 25,000	25,000 to 50,000	50,000 to 100,000	100,000 to 250,000	250,000 to 500,000	500,000 to 2,500,000	2,500,000 and over
Number of Enterprises **1**	5230	81	0	173	70	0	256	643	1113	1475	722	500	157
Revenues ($ in Thousands)													
Net Sales **2**	169499766	5101792	0	0	0	0	64051	328275	1458341	3371443	3117062	6554893	149494970
Interest **3**	404172047	14570928	0	0	1852	0	122099	604135	2353559	7477767	8962424	18437322	351634155
Rents **4**	27830413	1506148	0	0	0	0	403	2658	13570	41331	55581	193261	26017457
Royalties **5**	316954	34582	0	0	0	0	4	79	485	216	197	431	280960
Other Portfolio Income **6**	33099207	1461911	0	0	10176	0	11428	60403	216043	650131	801782	1571999	28314136
Other Receipts **7**	72467811	3382682	0	0	339	0	78378	390876	910608	2432414	2164913	4201992	58904999
Total Receipts **8**	707386198	26058043	0	0	12367	0	276363	1386426	4952606	13973302	15101959	30959898	614646677
Average Total Receipts **9**	135255	321704	•	0	177	•	1080	2156	4450	9473	20917	61920	3914947
Operating Costs/Operating Income (%)													
Cost of Operations **10**	3.1	8.4	•	•	•	•	•	•	0.4	0.4	0.0	0.1	3.2
Salaries and Wages **11**	61.2	69.3	•	•	•	•	54.0	57.9	50.2	63.8	83.7	81.8	59.6
Taxes Paid **12**	8.4	10.2	•	•	•	•	12.7	13.3	11.0	12.7	15.2	14.1	7.8
Interest Paid **13**	106.8	139.8	•	•	•	•	81.9	96.6	77.2	97.1	115.5	104.5	106.2
Depreciation **14**	23.0	26.7	•	•	•	•	13.9	15.7	13.6	16.7	19.4	18.3	23.4
Amortization and Depletion **15**	4.5	5.9	•	•	•	•	5.4	2.1	1.4	1.5	2.2	2.6	4.7
Pensions and Other Deferred Comp. **16**	4.7	7.4	•	•	•	•	4.1	3.9	3.9	4.1	5.2	5.8	4.6
Employee Benefits **17**	8.7	4.6	•	•	•	•	14.8	14.2	10.0	11.0	11.9	10.5	8.6
Advertising **18**	5.5	12.7	•	•	•	•	3.9	4.5	3.7	4.6	5.4	5.9	5.3
Other Expenses **19**	120.9	163.0	•	•	•	•	113.3	96.4	75.4	84.8	97.1	101.5	122.1
Officers' Compensation **20**	6.5	2.5	•	•	•	•	63.8	49.4	33.4	30.4	25.1	19.8	4.8
Operating Margin **21**	•	•	•	•	•	•	•	•	•	•	•	•	•
Operating Margin Before Officers' Comp. **22**	•	•	•	•	•	•	•	•	•	•	•	•	•

Selected Average Balance Sheet ($ in Thousands)

Net Receivables 23	877446	0	•	0	165	•	9915	21967	45134	99275	216273	565921	25073378
Inventories 24	34	0	•	0	0	•	0	1	6	0	4	13	1020
Net Property, Plant and Equipment 25	17714	0	•	366	46	•	251	603	1611	3323	7056	17897	454695
Total Assets 26	2305814	0	•	575	1920	•	18774	37269	73790	159024	350363	988667	69847886
Notes and Loans Payable 27	395310	0	•	242	0	•	399	920	3430	7627	20883	74806	12733651
All Other Liabilities 28	1609457	0	•	350	369	•	14543	31714	62841	135916	297189	825135	47742555
Net Worth 29	301047	0	•	-18	1550	•	3831	4635	7519	15481	32291	88726	9371679

Selected Financial Ratios (Times to 1)

Current Ratio 30	0.8	•	•	3.2	•	•	1.1	1.0	1.0	1.0	1.0	0.9	0.8
Quick Ratio 31	0.7	•	•	3.2	•	•	1.1	1.0	1.0	0.9	0.9	0.9	0.7
Net Sales to Working Capital 32	•	•	•	•	•	•	0.2	0.5	1.1	•	•	•	•
Coverage Ratio 33	1.6	1.4	•	•	•	•	1.6	1.6	1.7	1.7	1.8	1.9	1.6
Total Asset Turnover 34	0.0	•	•	•	•	•	0.0	0.0	0.0	0.0	0.0	0.0	0.0
Inventory Turnover 35	29.8	•	•	•	•	•	•	0.8	•	36.5	•	1.1	30.2
Receivables Turnover 36	0.0	•	•	•	•	•	0.0	0.0	0.0	0.0	0.0	0.0	0.0
Total Liabilities to Net Worth 37	6.7	•	•	0.2	•	•	3.9	7.0	8.8	9.3	9.9	10.1	6.5
Current Assets to Working Capital 38	•	•	•	1.5	•	•	13.1	30.6	55.1	•	•	•	•
Current Liabilities to Working Capital 39	•	•	•	0.5	•	•	12.1	29.6	54.1	•	•	•	•
Working Capital to Net Sales 40	•	•	•	•	•	•	4.8	2.1	0.9	•	•	•	•
Inventory to Working Capital 41	•	•	•	•	•	•	0.0	0.0	•	•	•	•	•
Total Receipts to Cash Flow 42	0.6	0.5	•	•	•	•	0.6	0.7	0.8	0.6	0.5	0.5	0.6
Cost of Goods to Cash Flow 43	0.0	0.0	•	•	•	•	•	•	0.0	0.0	0.0	0.0	0.0
Cash Flow to Total Debt 44	0.0	•	•	0.3	•	•	0.0	0.0	0.0	0.0	0.0	0.0	0.0

Selected Financial Factors (in Percentages)

Debt Ratio 45	86.9	•	•	19.2	103.1	•	79.6	87.6	89.8	90.3	90.8	91.0	86.6
Return on Total Assets 46	2.4	•	•	•	•	•	1.8	2.1	2.2	2.4	2.5	2.6	2.3
Return on Equity Before Income Taxes 47	6.7	•	•	•	105.7	•	3.4	6.0	8.4	10.7	11.7	14.0	6.2
Return on Equity After Income Taxes 48	4.5	•	•	•	105.7	•	2.8	5.0	6.7	8.2	8.7	10.0	4.0
Profit Margin (Before Income Tax) 49	62.5	58.6	•	•	•	•	51.7	54.8	48.1	72.7	87.6	94.9	60.6
Profit Margin (After Income Tax) 50	41.5	33.7	•	•	•	•	43.1	45.0	38.3	55.7	64.9	67.6	39.8

Table II

Corporations with Net Income

OFFICES OF BANK HOLDING COMPANIES

MONEY AMOUNTS AND SIZE OF ASSETS IN THOUSANDS OF DOLLARS

Item Description for Accounting Period 7/04 Through 6/05	Total	Zero Assets	Under 500	500 to 1,000	1,000 to 5,000	5,000 to 10,000	10,000 to 25,000	25,000 to 50,000	50,000 to 100,000	100,000 to 250,000	250,000 to 500,000	500,000 to 2,500,000	2,500,000 and over
Number of Enterprises **1**	4575	47	0	0	16	0	202	559	1009	1396	690	484	152

Revenues ($ in Thousands)

	Total	Zero Assets	Under 500	500 to 1,000	1,000 to 5,000	5,000 to 10,000	10,000 to 25,000	25,000 to 50,000	50,000 to 100,000	100,000 to 250,000	250,000 to 500,000	500,000 to 2,500,000	2,500,000 and over
Net Sales **2**	167563290	4393085	0	0	0	0	49417	298195	1307679	3222203	2943822	6336926	149003294
Interest **3**	398520512	12557073	0	0	0	0	101356	523233	2086962	7119771	8539663	17903363	349682184
Rents **4**	27568366	1492567	0	0	0	0	297	2216	12689	35961	51484	180032	25793119
Royalties **5**	316702	34582	0	0	0	0	4	79	240	209	197	431	280960
Other Portfolio Income **6**	32622686	1342917	0	0	9700	0	9884	54010	196595	618025	772303	1524140	28093925
Other Receipts **7**	71039594	3200518	0	0	0	0	73770	362082	858648	2325760	2117745	4037354	58063103
Total Receipts **8**	697631150	23020742	0	0	9700	0	234728	1239815	4462813	13321929	14425214	29982246	610916585
Average Total Receipts **9**	152488	489803	•	•	606	•	1162	2218	4423	9543	20906	61947	4019188

Operating Costs/Operating Income (%)

	Total	Zero Assets	Under 500	500 to 1,000	1,000 to 5,000	5,000 to 10,000	10,000 to 25,000	25,000 to 50,000	50,000 to 100,000	100,000 to 250,000	250,000 to 500,000	500,000 to 2,500,000	2,500,000 and over
Cost of Operations **10**	3.2	9.7	•	•	•	•	•	•	0.4	0.4	0.0	0.1	3.2
Salaries and Wages **11**	61.0	74.4	•	•	•	•	49.8	53.5	46.6	62.5	83.2	81.5	59.5
Taxes Paid **12**	8.4	11.2	•	•	•	•	13.4	13.0	10.8	12.7	15.3	14.2	7.8
Interest Paid **13**	105.6	113.4	•	•	•	•	91.4	92.9	77.6	96.1	116.0	103.8	105.8
Depreciation **14**	22.8	29.6	•	•	•	•	11.9	13.7	12.8	16.2	19.4	18.2	23.1
Amortization and Depletion **15**	4.5	6.7	•	•	•	•	0.8	1.3	1.2	1.5	2.0	2.5	4.6
Pensions and Other Deferred Comp. **16**	4.6	8.3	•	•	•	•	5.0	4.0	4.0	4.1	5.3	5.8	4.5
Employee Benefits **17**	8.7	4.8	•	•	•	•	16.1	13.8	10.0	10.9	12.0	10.5	8.6
Advertising **18**	5.5	14.7	•	•	•	•	3.8	4.3	3.6	4.5	5.5	6.0	5.3
Other Expenses **19**	120.1	163.8	•	•	•	•	101.1	85.2	68.1	81.4	94.2	98.8	121.7
Officers' Compensation **20**	6.4	1.5	•	•	•	•	67.2	47.0	33.9	30.1	25.3	19.8	4.7
Operating Margin **21**	•	•	•	•	•	•	•	•	•	•	•	•	•
Operating Margin Before Officers' Comp. **22**	•	•	•	•	•	•	•	•	•	•	•	•	•

Selected Average Balance Sheet ($ in Thousands)

	1	2	3	4	5	6	7	8	9	10	11
Net Receivables 23	995079	0	.	0	10441	22232	45188	99930	216529	571375	25834438
Inventories 24	37	0	.	0	0	0	1	0	4	13	1048
Net Property, Plant and Equipment 25	19759	0	.	0	205	548	1523	3278	7019	17889	463384
Total Assets 26	2605171	0	.	2691	19042	37461	73819	159326	350488	987715	71558455
Notes and Loans Payable 27	447351	0	.	0	370	898	2871	7508	20856	72765	13046460
All Other Liabilities 28	1817474	0	.	1516	15444	32075	62990	136234	297233	826151	48914917
Net Worth 29	340346	0	.	1175	3228	4488	7958	15584	32400	88799	9597078

Selected Financial Ratios (Times to 1)

	1	2	3	4	5	6	7	8	9	10	11
Current Ratio 30	0.8	0.0	.	1.1	1.0	1.0	1.0	1.0	0.9	0.9	0.8
Quick Ratio 31	0.7	0.0	.	1.0	1.0	0.9	1.0	0.9	0.9	0.9	0.7
Net Sales to Working Capital 32	.	.	.	0.2	0.4	0.9	1.0	0.9	.	.	0.7
Coverage Ratio 33	1.6	1.7	.	2.1	1.8	1.8	1.8	1.8	2.0	.	1.6
Total Asset Turnover 34	0.0	0.0	.	0.0	0.0	0.0	0.0	0.0	0.0	0.0	0.0
Inventory Turnover 35	31.3	.	.	.	.	11.2	36.5	0.0	0.0	1.1	30.3
Receivables Turnover 36	0.0	.	.	0.0	0.0	0.0	0.0	0.0	0.0	0.0	0.0
Total Liabilities to Net Worth 37	6.7	1.3	.	4.9	7.3	8.3	9.2	9.8	10.1	.	6.5
Current Assets to Working Capital 38	.	.	.	14.3	25.9	46.1	.	.	.	.	.
Current Liabilities to Working Capital 39	.	.	.	13.3	24.9	45.1	.	.	.	.	.
Working Capital to Net Sales 40	.	.	.	4.8	2.4	1.1	.	.	.	.	.
Inventory to Working Capital 41	.	.	.	0.0	0.0	0.0	.	.	.	.	.
Total Receipts to Cash Flow 42	0.6	0.4	.	0.5	0.6	0.6	0.6	0.8	0.5	0.5	0.6
Cost of Goods to Cash Flow 43	0.0	0.0	.	0.0	0.0	0.0	0.0	0.0	0.0	0.0	0.0
Cash Flow to Total Debt 44	0.0	0.4	.	0.0	0.0	0.0	0.0	0.0	0.0	0.0	0.0

Selected Financial Factors (in Percentages)

	1	2	3	4	5	6	7	8	9	10	11
Debt Ratio 45	86.9	.	.	56.3	83.0	88.0	89.2	90.2	90.8	91.0	86.6
Return on Total Assets 46	2.4	.	.	22.5	2.5	2.4	2.4	2.5	2.6	2.7	2.3
Return on Equity Before Income Taxes 47	6.9	.	.	51.6	7.7	8.7	9.9	11.6	12.6	14.7	6.2
Return on Equity After Income Taxes 48	4.6	.	.	51.6	6.8	7.4	8.1	9.0	9.4	10.5	4.1
Profit Margin (Before Income Tax) 49	64.0	84.2	.	101.2	73.5	60.5	78.4	95.6	99.6	.	61.0
Profit Margin (After Income Tax) 50	42.8	55.4	.	90.0	62.7	49.6	60.7	71.5	71.4	.	40.1

Table I

Corporations with and without Net Income

OFFICES OF OTHER HOLDING COMPANIES

MONEY AMOUNTS AND SIZE OF ASSETS IN THOUSANDS OF DOLLARS

Item Description for Accounting Period 7/04 Through 6/05	Total	Zero Assets	Under 500	500 to 1,000	1,000 to 5,000	5,000 to 10,000	10,000 to 25,000	25,000 to 50,000	50,000 to 100,000	100,000 to 250,000	250,000 to 500,000	500,000 to 2,500,000	2,500,000 and over
Number of Enterprises 1	44569	5670	0	3159	4508	0	874	368	202	155	73	81	27
Revenues ($ in Thousands)													
Net Sales 2	1330243	25144	0	1282	46051	0	99308	67585	96815	39959	137174	86892	723960
Interest 3	5808397	347164	0	44725	56149	0	72467	92699	197338	155237	382407	1428653	2950022
Rents 4	147015	1792	0	3583	15216	0	8770	13343	33721	7166	6311	31958	5289
Royalties 5	358809	2765	0	0	12779	0	6965	7468	4115	3379	59010	255871	3618
Other Portfolio Income 6	6431647	528118	0	199241	484648	0	345097	228087	308263	209034	831628	927487	2000938
Other Receipts 7	7449325	-52046	0	80970	620100	0	952914	430798	488170	427343	457874	2419286	807540
Total Receipts 8	21525236	852937	0	329801	1234943	0	1485521	839980	1128422	842118	1874404	5150147	6491367
Average Total Receipts 9	483	150	•	104	274	•	1700	2283	5586	5433	25677	63582	240421
Operating Costs/Operating Income (%)													
Cost of Operations 10	13.7	12.3	•	68.6	21.7	•	20.4	8.9	43.4	45.9	9.3	0.6	9.1
Salaries and Wages 11	55.9	124.2	•	142.5	56.8	•	72.5	68.1	34.1	82.6	56.9	240.9	20.7
Taxes Paid 12	42.2	108.6	•	290.1	105.0	•	34.6	32.2	26.0	60.8	34.1	185.2	17.1
Interest Paid 13	286.8	399.7	•	3402.0	158.8	•	103.4	168.9	218.4	879.0	235.4	970.9	218.2
Depreciation 14	11.7	15.2	•	207.7	11.3	•	6.8	20.5	38.5	33.7	24.1	17.2	1.8
Amortization and Depletion 15	19.7	9.0	•	101.8	40.1	•	7.6	20.0	20.2	17.0	39.4	143.8	1.1
Pensions and Other Deferred Comp. 16	4.0	0.8	•	2.3	13.9	•	2.7	8.1	1.3	11.6	13.2	11.8	0.2
Employee Benefits 17	13.2	2.1	•	156.6	11.3	•	2.6	4.2	4.7	7.9	13.1	114.5	3.4
Advertising 18	0.9	0.4	•	•	0.2	•	0.2	0.5	0.1	6.0	0.4	1.3	0.9
Other Expenses 19	392.1	2650.2	•	29599.5	887.4	•	524.2	498.7	372.4	1034.9	276.8	842.1	69.9
Officers' Compensation 20	24.6	24.4	•	148.8	83.4	•	33.9	36.8	14.4	66.5	31.5	71.4	1.9
Operating Margin 21	•	•	•	•	•	•	•	•	•	•	•	•	•
Operating Margin Before Officers' Comp. 22	•	•	•	•	•	•	•	•	•	•	•	•	•

Selected Average Balance Sheet ($ in Thousands)

Item													
Net Receivables 23	577	0	•	50	85	•	611	2088	4042	6954	12019	96325	485713
Inventories 24	2	0	•	0	6	•	16	19	14	85	63	89	0
Net Property, Plant and Equipment 25	69	0	•	29	153	•	362	1039	1704	2616	3369	1051	5151
Total Assets 26	8610	712	•	712	2303	•	15771	35160	71492	152432	346240	989945	7036786
Notes and Loans Payable 27	1134	173	•	173	513	•	3659	7887	17097	27023	63497	133032	576080
All Other Liabilities 28	1390	67	•	175	1644	•	22896	5062	17509	31115	141656	1209890	
Net Worth 29	6085	471	•	1614	4378	•	10468	49334	107901	251628	715257	5250816	

Selected Financial Ratios (Times to 1)

Item												
Current Ratio 30	2.3	•	1.3	3.7	•	1.9	2.9	3.5	2.8	1.9	1.5	2.6
Quick Ratio 31	1.9	•	0.9	2.3	•	1.3	1.8	2.1	1.8	1.3	1.2	2.5
Net Sales to Working Capital 32	0.0	•	0.0	0.0	•	0.1	0.0	0.0	0.0	0.1	0.0	0.0
Coverage Ratio 33	3.7	0.4	•	9.0	•	7.6	3.0	2.8	0.9	3.7	4.8	3.5
Total Asset Turnover 34	0.0	•	•	0.0	•	0.0	0.0	0.0	0.0	0.0	0.0	0.0
Inventory Turnover 35	2.2	•	1.7	0.4	•	1.5	0.9	15.0	1.4	2.8	0.1	•
Receivables Turnover 36	0.1	•	0.0	0.1	•	0.2	0.1	0.1	0.0	0.1	0.0	0.1
Total Liabilities to Net Worth 37	0.4	•	0.5	0.4	•	0.5	7.0	0.4	0.4	0.4	0.4	0.3
Current Assets to Working Capital 38	1.8	•	4.7	1.4	•	2.1	1.5	1.4	1.5	2.1	3.2	1.6
Current Liabilities to Working Capital 39	0.8	•	3.7	0.4	•	1.1	0.5	0.4	0.5	1.1	2.2	0.6
Working Capital to Net Sales 40	34.1	•	103.2	45.6	•	13.9	32.5	22.6	67.3	16.1	54.5	34.7
Inventory to Working Capital 41	0.0	•	0.0	0.0	•	0.0	0.0	0.0	0.0	0.0	0.0	•
Total Receipts to Cash Flow 42	0.1	0.1	0.0	0.1	•	0.2	0.2	0.2	0.2	0.3	0.0	0.2
Cost of Goods to Cash Flow 43	0.0	0.0	0.0	0.0	•	0.0	0.1	0.1	0.0	0.0	0.0	0.0
Cash Flow to Total Debt 44	0.1	•	0.2	0.2	•	0.2	0.0	0.1	0.0	0.1	0.2	0.1

Selected Financial Factors (in Percentages)

Item												
Debt Ratio 45	29.3	•	33.8	29.9	•	33.6	87.5	31.0	29.2	27.3	27.7	25.4
Return on Total Assets 46	3.6	•	•	6.4	•	5.6	2.7	4.2	1.3	4.7	5.1	2.9
Return on Equity Before Income Taxes 47	3.7	•	•	8.1	•	7.4	14.2	3.9	•	4.8	5.5	2.7
Return on Equity After Income Taxes 48	2.6	•	•	6.5	•	5.9	10.6	3.1	•	3.2	4.2	2.0
Profit Margin (Before Income Tax) 49	761.0	•	1273.9	•	677.7	339.1	403.9	637.7	3697.5	537.9		
Profit Margin (After Income Tax) 50	533.3	•	1019.5	•	545.1	253.5	317.6	427.9	2769.5	387.9		

Table II

Corporations with Net Income

OFFICES OF OTHER HOLDING COMPANIES

MONEY AMOUNTS AND SIZE OF ASSETS IN THOUSANDS OF DOLLARS

Item Description for Accounting Period 7/04 Through 6/05	Total	Zero Assets	Under 500	500 to 1,000	1,000 to 5,000	5,000 to 10,000	10,000 to 25,000	25,000 to 50,000	50,000 to 100,000	100,000 to 250,000	250,000 to 500,000	500,000 to 2,500,000	2,500,000 and over
Number of Enterprises **1**	14097	824	0	1870	2174	0	415	172	98	76	42	59	22
Revenues ($ in Thousands)													
Net Sales **2**	1107136	14937	0	999	33245	0	87341	15531	51075	29327	76374	72693	723960
Interest **3**	5116809	306522	0	38744	38425	0	50980	62125	67068	97787	313813	1172265	2912624
Rents **4**	98471	1005	0	3583	8667	0	5532	6137	13478	802	6110	30685	5289
Royalties **5**	336675	2703	0	0	12765	0	6782	7368	4114	421	44057	255871	0
Other Portfolio Income **6**	6080224	434793	0	197532	422229	0	299034	201411	276801	189628	818029	903086	2000646
Other Receipts **7**	7888653	521391	0	81229	750508	0	819786	445387	519392	370220	389533	2364317	792231
Total Receipts **8**	20627968	1281351	0	322087	1265839	0	1269455	737959	931928	688185	1647916	4798917	6434750
Average Total Receipts **9**	1463	1555	•	172	582	•	3059	4290	9509	9055	39236	81338	292489
Operating Costs/Operating Income (%)													
Cost of Operations **10**	12.2	•	•	88.1	30.0	•	18.0	19.1	36.7	44.7	10.2	0.7	9.1
Salaries and Wages **11**	41.0	10.2	•	160.5	19.4	•	26.7	168.1	19.2	31.6	31.7	270.7	20.5
Taxes Paid **12**	39.0	126.1	•	227.2	127.4	•	26.2	88.1	32.2	65.9	51.7	148.2	17.0
Interest Paid **13**	238.8	233.6	•	2405.6	104.6	•	42.2	280.6	164.7	206.5	246.6	826.4	209.6
Depreciation **14**	6.4	18.5	•	99.9	8.2	•	3.6	37.1	8.9	7.8	32.1	12.7	1.8
Amortization and Depletion **15**	19.1	6.2	•	72.0	22.7	•	6.5	39.2	9.4	6.5	61.1	170.8	1.1
Pensions and Other Deferred Comp. **16**	2.3	0.0	•	2.9	13.7	•	1.4	9.9	2.2	7.4	3.6	13.6	0.2
Employee Benefits **17**	12.5	0.6	•	69.2	2.6	•	1.5	5.7	6.1	5.7	3.6	136.1	3.4
Advertising **18**	0.8	•	•	•	0.1	•	0.1	0.2	0.0	3.7	0.0	1.3	0.9
Other Expenses **19**	175.7	607.8	•	14569.0	283.4	•	158.6	631.7	180.9	269.9	199.7	621.4	68.9
Officers' Compensation **20**	19.3	2.3	•	155.3	88.1	•	17.5	110.8	18.8	58.9	55.1	73.8	1.7
Operating Margin **21**	•	•	•	•	•	•	•	•	•	•	•	•	•
Operating Margin Before Officers' Comp. **22**	•	•	•	•	•	•	•	•	•	•	•	•	•

Selected Average Balance Sheet ($ in Thousands)

Net Receivables 23	1511	0	•	11	48	•	596	2301	5443	4647	11051	113710	560688
Inventories 24	4	0	•	0	13	•	15	38	7	108	100	73	0
Net Property, Plant and Equipment 25	97	0	•	21	188	•	317	546	928	1536	4310	1232	5661
Total Assets 26	20337	0	•	700	2316	•	15871	35179	73296	149109	348558	983976	7844417
Notes and Loans Payable 27	2093	0	•	65	421	•	2201	5095	16107	23037	41965	144334	573241
All Other Liabilities 28	3622	0	•	75	223	•	1328	45624	5973	14621	28204	117857	1448373
Net Worth 29	14622	0	•	560	1671	•	12342	-15540	51215	111451	278389	721784	5822803

Selected Financial Ratios (Times to 1)

Current Ratio 30	2.4	•	2.3	3.0	•	2.6	3.9	3.1	2.5	2.3	1.7	2.6
Quick Ratio 31	2.1	•	1.4	2.0	•	1.7	2.5	2.1	1.4	1.6	1.4	2.5
Net Sales to Working Capital 32	0.0	•	0.0	0.0	•	0.1	0.0	0.0	0.0	0.0	0.0	0.0
Coverage Ratio 33	6.5	33.6	6.7	30.6	•	28.6	12.6	9.4	9.2	7.0	6.8	3.6
Total Asset Turnover 34	0.0	•	0.0	0.0	•	0.0	0.0	0.0	0.0	0.0	0.0	0.0
Inventory Turnover 35	2.3	•	1.7	0.4	•	2.5	0.4	28.0	1.6	1.9	0.1	0.0
Receivables Turnover 36	0.1	•	0.0	0.4	•	0.3	0.0	0.1	0.0	0.1	0.0	0.1
Total Liabilities to Net Worth 37	0.4	•	0.3	0.4	•	0.3	•	0.4	0.3	0.3	0.4	0.3
Current Assets to Working Capital 38	1.7	•	1.8	1.5	•	1.6	1.4	1.5	1.6	1.8	2.4	1.6
Current Liabilities to Working Capital 39	0.7	•	0.8	0.5	•	0.6	0.4	0.5	0.6	0.8	1.4	0.6
Working Capital to Net Sales 40	34.3	•	207.6	25.4	•	9.1	83.7	20.4	34.5	21.6	76.2	33.5
Inventory to Working Capital 41	0.0	•	0.0	0.1	•	0.0	0.0	0.0	0.0	0.0	•	•
Total Receipts to Cash Flow 42	0.1	0.0	0.0	0.0	•	0.1	0.0	0.1	0.1	0.1	0.0	0.2
Cost of Goods to Cash Flow 43	0.0	•	0.0	0.0	•	0.0	0.0	0.0	0.0	0.0	0.0	0.0
Cash Flow to Total Debt 44	0.2	•	0.5	0.6	•	0.6	0.1	0.3	0.1	0.2	0.2	0.1

Selected Financial Factors (in Percentages)

Debt Ratio 45	28.1	•	20.0	27.8	•	22.2	144.2	30.1	25.3	20.1	26.6	25.8
Return on Total Assets 46	6.0	•	12.3	21.1	•	16.0	9.1	11.0	4.9	9.0	7.0	3.1
Return on Equity Before Income Taxes 47	7.1	•	13.1	28.3	•	19.8	•	14.1	5.9	9.6	8.2	3.0
Return on Equity After Income Taxes 48	5.6	•	12.3	25.1	•	17.3	•	12.4	4.8	7.2	6.3	2.2
Profit Margin (Before Income Tax) 49	1317.8	7615.8	13729.5	3097.1	•	1162.2	3250.6	1381.3	1690.3	1473.9	4782.8	539.0
Profit Margin (After Income Tax) 50	1045.7	5774.4	12874.6	2744.7	•	1011.9	2891.1	1218.0	1390.1	1096.9	3673.6	389.0

Table I

Corporations with and without Net Income

EMPLOYMENT SERVICES

MONEY AMOUNTS AND SIZE OF ASSETS IN THOUSANDS OF DOLLARS

Item Description for Accounting Period 7/04 Through 6/05	Total	Zero Assets	Under 500	500 to 1,000	1,000 to 5,000	5,000 to 10,000	10,000 to 25,000	25,000 to 50,000	50,000 to 100,000	100,000 to 250,000	250,000 to 500,000	500,000 to 2,500,000	2,500,000 and over
Number of Enterprises 1	22647	1487	18510	1246	1089	158	77	25	17	16	10	12	0
Revenues ($ in Thousands)													
Net Sales 2	122947854	740634	19200341	5763463	22628401	4845052	9952894	5091049	6937886	5309595	17490985	24987553	0
Interest 3	165728	1531	2206	3391	4867	404	3148	2024	5202	5834	5859	131262	0
Rents 4	2486	0	0	296	0	0	696	0	538	104	0	852	0
Royalties 5	211755	0	0	0	0	0	0	0	3747	10634	8606	188768	0
Other Portfolio Income 6	290159	0	47115	90	10810	3	19016	18092	3584	78	9001	182367	0
Other Receipts 7	1321378	349117	74550	11731	18558	6964	14588	20133	18031	34417	17462	755831	0
Total Receipts 8	124939360	1091282	19324212	5778971	22662636	4852423	9990342	5131298	6968988	5360662	17531913	2624633	0
Average Total Receipts 9	5517	734	1044	4638	20811	30712	129745	205252	409940	335041	1753191	2187219	•
Operating Costs/Operating Income (%)													
Cost of Operations 10	54.3	44.8	36.5	37.9	57.1	47.5	65.6	41.6	68.9	56.9	62.1	58.7	•
Salaries and Wages 11	24.1	30.2	31.3	39.7	24.0	30.9	17.8	41.1	14.4	23.8	21.7	17.0	•
Taxes Paid 12	6.3	10.1	4.9	7.6	7.0	8.1	6.3	5.8	6.0	4.5	6.5	6.6	•
Interest Paid 13	0.5	0.4	0.3	0.4	0.2	0.3	0.2	0.4	0.5	1.0	0.4	1.1	•
Depreciation 14	0.4	0.2	0.4	0.3	0.3	0.5	0.2	0.5	0.2	0.4	0.4	0.7	•
Amortization and Depletion 15	0.3	0.9	0.1	0.0	0.0	0.1	0.1	0.2	0.4	1.0	0.3	0.9	•
Pensions and Other Deferred Comp. 16	0.2	0.2	0.8	0.1	0.0	0.1	0.1	0.1	0.1	0.0	0.1	0.1	•
Employee Benefits 17	3.2	2.8	5.2	2.1	3.3	2.2	3.7	2.4	3.8	2.1	3.3	1.8	•
Advertising 18	0.3	0.5	0.6	0.5	0.2	0.3	0.2	0.3	0.1	0.5	0.2	0.5	•
Other Expenses 19	8.2	67.9	7.7	8.2	6.4	7.2	5.1	6.4	5.2	10.0	4.2	13.3	•
Officers' Compensation 20	1.4	0.4	4.8	2.2	1.0	1.8	0.5	0.5	0.4	0.4	0.3	0.7	•
Operating Margin 21	0.8	•	7.4	1.0	0.5	1.0	0.2	0.8	0.0	0.0	0.5	•	•
Operating Margin Before Officers' Comp. 22	2.2	•	12.1	3.2	1.5	2.8	0.7	1.3	0.4	0.8	0.8	•	•

Selected Average Balance Sheet ($ in Thousands)

Net Receivables 23	399	0	24	257	883	1811	6094	13135	22390	44306	71274	368885	•
Inventories 24	2	0	0	0	0	5	44	452	27	125	18	2873	•
Net Property, Plant and Equipment 25	71	0	10	53	169	438	1039	2171	5263	4208	19470	50931	•
Total Assets 26	1381	0	90	670	2242	6822	15850	37400	70327	142823	322747	1365551	•
Notes and Loans Payable 27	351	0	59	182	978	5669	3563	12469	16276	57463	80938	172759	•
All Other Liabilities 28	491	0	33	128	850	1293	8134	14791	35021	42920	99029	495507	•
Net Worth 29	540	0	-1	360	413	-140	4154	10140	19030	42439	142780	697285	•

Selected Financial Ratios (Times to 1)

Current Ratio 30	1.3	•	1.2	2.4	1.4	0.7	1.4	1.2	1.3	1.6	1.3	1.3	•
Quick Ratio 31	1.1	•	1.0	2.1	1.2	0.5	1.0	1.0	1.0	1.4	0.9	1.1	•
Net Sales to Working Capital 32	36.2	•	112.5	14.5	53.7	•	42.4	50.3	40.7	13.6	49.3	17.6	•
Coverage Ratio 33	6.0	•	25.5	4.6	4.9	5.3	3.5	5.0	2.0	1.3	3.1	4.6	•
Total Asset Turnover 34	3.9	•	11.5	6.9	9.3	4.5	8.2	5.4	5.8	2.3	5.4	1.5	•
Inventory Turnover 35	1275.5	•	583645.2	•	155662.8	2892.5	1914.9	187.1	10602.9	1511.2	59564.1	425.6	•
Receivables Turnover 36	15.1	•	45.1	25.2	24.4	18.3	23.3	15.2	17.2	7.5	19.9	7.1	•
Total Liabilities to Net Worth 37	1.6	•	•	0.9	4.4	•	2.8	2.7	2.7	2.4	1.3	1.0	•
Current Assets to Working Capital 38	4.5	•	6.4	1.7	3.8	•	3.7	5.4	4.1	2.6	4.6	4.5	•
Current Liabilities to Working Capital 39	3.5	•	5.4	0.7	2.8	•	2.7	4.4	3.1	1.6	3.6	3.5	•
Working Capital to Net Sales 40	0.0	•	0.0	0.1	0.0	•	0.0	0.0	0.0	0.1	0.0	0.1	•
Inventory to Working Capital 41	0.0	•	•	•	0.0	•	0.0	0.1	0.0	0.0	0.0	0.0	•
Total Receipts to Cash Flow 42	10.7	1.9	6.9	12.4	15.4	13.4	20.4	14.7	19.4	11.8	29.2	6.6	•
Cost of Goods to Cash Flow 43	5.8	0.9	2.5	4.7	8.8	6.4	13.4	6.1	13.4	6.7	18.1	3.9	•
Cash Flow to Total Debt 44	0.6	•	1.6	1.2	0.7	0.3	0.5	0.5	0.4	0.3	0.3	0.5	•

Selected Financial Factors (in Percentages)

Debt Ratio 45	60.9	•	101.6	46.3	81.6	102.0	73.8	72.9	72.9	70.3	55.8	48.9	•
Return on Total Assets 46	11.5	•	95.9	11.3	7.7	6.3	6.3	10.8	5.6	3.0	6.2	7.4	•
Return on Equity Before Income Taxes 47	24.5	•	•	16.5	33.3	•	17.3	31.9	10.3	2.0	9.5	11.3	•
Return on Equity After Income Taxes 48	21.0	•	•	16.2	31.4	•	14.2	29.2	5.5	•	6.8	7.4	•
Profit Margin (Before Income Tax) 49	2.4	•	8.0	1.3	0.7	1.1	0.6	1.6	0.5	0.3	0.8	3.8	•
Profit Margin (After Income Tax) 50	2.1	•	8.0	1.3	0.6	1.1	0.5	1.5	0.3	•	0.6	2.5	•

Table II

Corporations with Net Income

EMPLOYMENT SERVICES

MONEY AMOUNTS AND SIZE OF ASSETS IN THOUSANDS OF DOLLARS

Item Description for Accounting Period 7/04 Through 6/05	Total	Zero Assets	Under 500	500 to 1,000	1,000 to 5,000	5,000 to 10,000	10,000 to 25,000	25,000 to 50,000	50,000 to 100,000	100,000 to 250,000	250,000 to 500,000	500,000 to 2,500,000	2,500,000 and over
Number of Enterprises 1	13018	244	11205	715	649	100	51	19	11	9	7	8	0
Revenues ($ in Thousands)													
Net Sales 2	88147664	59292	10968298	4196368	16171634	3055535	7374729	4504775	5810357	3223232	15739439	17044007	0
Interest 3	141887	0	1894	2840	4746	177	2087	1912	1599	5665	4540	116425	0
Rents 4	965	0	0	9	0	0	0	0	0	104	0	852	0
Royalties 5	187634	0	0	0	0	0	0	0	2923	10634	86	173991	0
Other Portfolio Income 6	263059	0	43555	78	5784	3	8839	18092	3381	77	8966	174284	0
Other Receipts 7	870565	780	30246	4366	15054	6359	12323	21070	16918	31079	14778	717594	0
Total Receipts 8	89611774	60072	11043993	4203661	16197218	3062074	7397978	4545849	5835178	3270791	15767809	18227153	0
Average Total Receipts 9	6884	246	986	5879	24957	30621	145058	239255	530471	363421	2252544	2278394	•
Operating Costs/Operating Income (%)													
Cost of Operations 10	56.5	63.6	16.0	30.6	75.1	74.0	68.8	38.8	69.3	54.1	62.4	58.1	•
Salaries and Wages 11	19.8	3.6	37.3	45.8	4.8	5.8	14.7	43.1	14.3	21.6	21.4	15.3	•
Taxes Paid 12	6.5	5.8	5.1	7.9	6.5	8.1	6.2	6.2	6.0	6.8	6.6	6.9	•
Interest Paid 13	0.5	0.2	0.2	0.2	0.1	0.3	0.2	0.2	0.2	1.3	0.4	1.2	•
Depreciation 14	0.4	0.4	0.4	0.2	0.1	0.4	0.2	0.3	0.2	0.4	0.3	0.7	•
Amortization and Depletion 15	0.3	0.1	0.1	0.0	0.0	0.2	0.1	0.1	0.3	0.6	0.3	0.7	•
Pensions and Other Deferred Comp. 16	0.2	•	1.4	0.1	0.0	0.0	0.1	0.1	0.1	0.0	0.1	0.1	•
Employee Benefits 17	3.6	1.9	7.2	1.6	4.0	1.5	3.4	2.4	4.2	2.6	3.5	2.1	•
Advertising 18	0.4	0.2	0.8	0.4	0.2	0.1	0.2	0.3	0.1	0.5	0.1	0.6	•
Other Expenses 19	7.7	18.9	9.2	7.4	6.5	5.2	4.6	5.6	4.5	11.0	3.8	14.5	•
Officers' Compensation 20	1.4	0.7	6.5	1.7	0.9	2.0	0.5	0.4	0.2	0.3	0.2	0.8	•
Operating Margin 21	2.8	4.8	15.9	4.0	1.5	2.4	1.1	2.4	0.6	0.6	0.8	•	•
Operating Margin Before Officers' Comp. 22	4.2	5.5	22.4	5.7	2.5	4.4	1.6	2.8	0.9	1.0	1.0	•	•

Selected Average Balance Sheet ($ in Thousands)

Net Receivables 23	508	0	29	223	997	2724	6915	12146	21691	43285	65795	441288	•
Inventories 24	3	0	0	0	0	0	22	412	23	1	5	4309	•
Net Property, Plant and Equipment 25	72	0	8	63	65	342	1126	2084	4889	4710	24083	45630	•
Total Assets 26	1766	0	93	735	2261	7363	15880	38024	71307	132639	329164	1675187	•
Notes and Loans Payable 27	361	0	45	200	770	2962	3848	11466	10034	54956	109155	182902	•
All Other Liabilities 28	567	0	23	147	967	1473	8038	12461	39236	47196	108555	497220	•
Net Worth 29	839	0	25	388	524	2928	3994	14097	22037	30487	111454	995065	•

Selected Financial Ratios (Times to 1)

Current Ratio 30	1.4	•	1.8	2.3	1.6	1.4	1.4	1.2	1.4	1.4	1.2	1.4	•
Quick Ratio 31	1.2	•	1.6	1.9	1.4	0.9	1.1	0.9	0.9	1.3	0.8	1.2	•
Net Sales to Working Capital 32	26.0	•	32.8	17.5	38.3	20.9	42.0	60.4	42.6	18.9	65.7	11.8	•
Coverage Ratio 33	10.6	40.5	97.2	24.8	13.8	8.6	10.5	16.0	5.5	2.6	3.5	5.9	•
Total Asset Turnover 34	3.8	•	10.5	8.0	11.0	4.1	9.1	6.2	7.4	2.7	6.8	1.3	•
Inventory Turnover 35	1137.5	•	146283.5	•	783997.7	•	4483.9	223.2	16012.7	174238.7	297856.4	287.4	•
Receivables Turnover 36	16.4	•	44.2	34.1	26.3	25.3	22.3	29.4	•	•	6.2	•	
Total Liabilities to Net Worth 37	1.1	•	2.8	0.9	3.3	3.0	1.7	2.2	3.4	2.0	0.7	•	
Current Assets to Working Capital 38	3.4	•	2.2	1.7	2.8	3.4	5.5	3.6	3.2	5.5	3.6	•	
Current Liabilities to Working Capital 39	2.4	•	1.2	0.7	1.8	2.4	4.5	4.5	2.6	2.2	2.6	•	
Working Capital to Net Sales 40	0.0	0.0	0.0	0.1	0.0	0.0	0.0	0.0	0.0	0.1	0.0	0.1	•
Inventory to Working Capital 41	0.0	•	•	0.0	0.0	0.0	0.0	0.1	0.0	0.0	0.0	•	
Total Receipts to Cash Flow 42	9.2	4.1	4.1	9.9	12.8	13.7	18.3	12.6	18.9	8.8	30.8	5.5	•
Cost of Goods to Cash Flow 43	5.2	2.6	0.7	3.0	9.7	10.1	12.6	4.9	13.1	4.7	19.2	3.2	•
Cash Flow to Total Debt 44	0.8	•	3.5	1.7	1.1	0.5	0.7	0.8	0.6	0.4	0.3	0.6	•

Selected Financial Factors (in Percentages)

Debt Ratio 45	52.5	•	73.4	47.2	76.8	60.2	74.8	62.9	69.1	77.0	66.1	40.6	•
Return on Total Assets 46	18.7	•	175.6	35.0	20.0	12.3	14.4	21.8	9.9	9.3	9.3	9.1	•
Return on Equity Before Income Taxes 47	35.8	•	653.2	63.7	79.9	27.4	51.7	55.0	26.3	24.9	19.6	12.8	•
Return on Equity After Income Taxes 48	31.8	•	650.8	63.2	77.4	27.1	46.7	52.5	19.8	18.0	14.7	8.7	•
Profit Margin (Before Income Tax) 49	4.4	6.1	16.6	4.2	1.7	2.6	1.4	3.3	1.1	2.1	1.0	6.0	•
Profit Margin (After Income Tax) 50	3.9	6.1	16.5	4.2	1.6	2.6	1.3	3.1	0.8	1.5	0.7	4.1	•

TRAVEL ARRANGEMENT AND RESERVATION SERVICES

Table I

Corporations with and without Net Income

MONEY AMOUNTS AND SIZE OF ASSETS IN THOUSANDS OF DOLLARS

Item Description for Accounting Period 7/04 Through 6/05	Total	Zero Assets	Under 500	500 to 1,000	1,000 to 5,000	5,000 to 10,000	10,000 to 25,000	25,000 to 50,000	50,000 to 100,000	100,000 to 250,000	250,000 to 500,000	500,000 to 2,500,000	2,500,000 and over
Number of Enterprises **1**	23726	3888	19074	167	407	49	60	30	23	15	9	5	0

Revenues ($ in Thousands)

Item Description for Accounting Period 7/04 Through 6/05	Total	Zero Assets	Under 500	500 to 1,000	1,000 to 5,000	5,000 to 10,000	10,000 to 25,000	25,000 to 50,000	50,000 to 100,000	100,000 to 250,000	250,000 to 500,000	500,000 to 2,500,000	2,500,000 and over
Net Sales **2**	41205076	845885	1404246	469619	2475867	751725	2401783	1490327	2813266	1874563	3166753	10911042	0
Interest **3**	437482	891	676	495	1882	727	3122	4012	5009	4381	37267	379021	0
Rents **4**	34015	937	46	0	271	2081	509	685	2981	839	2929	22738	0
Royalties **5**	14253	0	0	0	0	0	5437	306	2426	0	0	6084	0
Other Portfolio Income **6**	385568	8090	11208	0	451	434	8962	31576	20165	9825	17227	277631	0
Other Receipts **7**	1077278	78670	57264	1	21575	40529	66295	115141	61397	106431	332687	197286	0
Total Receipts **8**	43153672	934473	14073440	470115	2500046	795496	2486108	1642047	2905244	1996039	3556863	11793802	0
Average Total Receipts **9**	1819	240	738	2815	6143	16235	41435	54735	126315	133069	395207	2358760	•

Operating Costs/Operating Income (%)

Item Description for Accounting Period 7/04 Through 6/05	Total	Zero Assets	Under 500	500 to 1,000	1,000 to 5,000	5,000 to 10,000	10,000 to 25,000	25,000 to 50,000	50,000 to 100,000	100,000 to 250,000	250,000 to 500,000	500,000 to 2,500,000	2,500,000 and over
Cost of Operations **10**	60.5	61.2	75.8	53.8	50.3	77.1	70.1	51.1	61.6	41.5	63.4	43.6	•
Salaries and Wages **11**	12.3	8.3	4.9	10.1	23.5	10.8	11.8	16.3	9.3	23.7	17.8	16.3	•
Taxes Paid **12**	1.6	2.3	1.1	1.1	2.5	1.6	1.6	1.9	1.5	3.8	1.8	1.6	•
Interest Paid **13**	0.9	0.3	0.1	0.3	0.2	0.1	0.2	0.3	0.6	1.5	1.8	2.0	•
Depreciation **14**	1.2	1.3	0.7	2.2	1.0	1.0	1.0	1.8	1.2	3.0	1.4	1.4	•
Amortization and Depletion **15**	0.3	0.1	0.0	0.0	0.0	0.8	0.1	0.3	0.6	1.9	0.6	0.3	•
Pensions and Other Deferred Comp. **16**	0.4	•	0.2	0.0	0.3	0.1	0.3	0.4	0.6	0.3	0.8	0.7	•
Employee Benefits **17**	1.0	0.7	0.4	1.3	2.2	0.8	0.9	1.4	1.5	1.9	2.2	1.1	•
Advertising **18**	3.5	1.1	0.9	0.2	1.0	0.7	1.5	2.9	1.4	1.8	3.1	9.4	•
Other Expenses **19**	18.6	25.0	12.6	25.0	17.7	10.0	11.9	31.4	20.8	26.5	20.0	23.5	•
Officers' Compensation **20**	2.1	7.3	2.9	4.9	4.7	2.1	1.4	1.2	1.1	0.8	0.6	1.2	•
Operating Margin **21**	•	•	0.4	1.1	•	•	•	•	•	•	•	•	•
Operating Margin Before Officers' Comp. **22**	•	•	3.3	6.0	1.3	•	0.6	•	0.8	•	•	0.2	•

Selected Average Balance Sheet ($ in Thousands)

	1	2	3	4	5	6	7	8	9	10	11	12
Net Receivables 23	202	0	6	103	513	1690	3559	4200	8682	17305	31915	659435
Inventories 24	5	0	1	0	6	48	67	490	580	570	1481	5577
Net Property, Plant and Equipment 25	92	0	11	112	218	1035	1535	4776	9108	16850	36058	159672
Total Assets 26	1840	0	74	767	2294	7357	15855	35346	70055	154298	340034	6365311
Notes and Loans Payable 27	144	0	39	38	251	1171	1645	11384	7851	18143	104231	134417
All Other Liabilities 28	848	0	27	349	2091	3161	8786	18014	37804	60904	126649	2909323
Net Worth 29	848	0	7	380	-48	3025	5425	5948	24401	75251	109154	3321571

Selected Financial Ratios (Times to 1)

	1	2	3	4	5	6	7	8	9	10	11	12
Current Ratio 30	1.3	•	1.6	1.4	0.8	1.3	1.3	0.9	1.1	1.3	1.1	1.5
Quick Ratio 31	0.9	•	1.3	1.1	0.6	0.9	0.9	0.7	0.8	0.8	0.6	1.1
Net Sales to Working Capital 32	16.3	•	42.1	26.4	•	19.6	16.7	•	73.8	9.2	41.4	5.7
Coverage Ratio 33	4.0	10.8	7.5	5.1	•	7.3	12.7	4.6	6.0	0.7	0.3	5.0
Total Asset Turnover 34	0.9	•	10.0	3.7	2.7	2.1	2.5	1.4	1.7	0.8	1.0	0.3
Inventory Turnover 35	233.4	•	521.7	•	532.3	246.7	421.6	51.8	129.8	91.1	150.7	170.5
Receivables Turnover 36	9.5	•	98.5	54.7	11.2	10.0	11.9	10.0	17.1	7.6	12.1	3.8
Total Liabilities to Net Worth 37	1.2	•	9.3	1.0	•	1.4	1.9	4.9	1.9	1.1	2.1	0.9
Current Assets to Working Capital 38	4.5	•	2.6	3.4	•	4.8	4.7	•	20.8	4.8	14.4	3.0
Current Liabilities to Working Capital 39	3.5	•	1.6	2.4	•	3.8	3.7	•	19.8	3.8	13.4	2.0
Working Capital to Net Sales 40	0.1	•	0.0	0.0	•	0.1	0.1	•	0.0	0.1	0.0	0.2
Inventory to Working Capital 41	0.0	•	0.1	•	•	0.0	0.0	•	0.4	0.0	0.3	0.0
Total Receipts to Cash Flow 42	5.4	4.3	8.6	4.4	8.6	11.3	7.9	3.5	4.7	4.6	6.4	3.5
Cost of Goods to Cash Flow 43	3.3	2.6	6.5	2.3	4.3	8.7	5.5	1.8	2.9	1.9	4.1	1.5
Cash Flow to Total Debt 44	0.3	•	1.3	1.7	0.3	0.3	0.5	0.5	0.6	0.3	0.2	0.2

Selected Financial Factors (in Percentages)

	1	2	3	4	5	6	7	8	9	10	11	12
Debt Ratio 45	53.9	•	90.3	50.4	102.1	58.9	65.8	83.2	65.2	51.2	67.9	47.8
Return on Total Assets 46	3.3	•	10.8	5.5	•	1.7	7.4	2.1	5.9	0.8	0.6	3.3
Return on Equity Before Income Taxes 47	5.3	•	96.4	9.0	314.5	3.5	19.9	9.8	14.2	•	•	5.1
Return on Equity After Income Taxes 48	3.8	•	94.3	8.7	338.5	1.6	16.6	3.1	9.4	•	•	3.8
Profit Margin (Before Income Tax) 49	2.6	2.8	0.9	1.2	•	0.7	2.7	1.2	2.8	•	•	7.8
Profit Margin (After Income Tax) 50	1.9	2.7	0.9	1.2	0.3	0.3	2.2	0.4	1.9	•	•	5.8

Table II

Corporations with Net Income

TRAVEL ARRANGEMENT AND RESERVATION SERVICES

MONEY AMOUNTS AND SIZE OF ASSETS IN THOUSANDS OF DOLLARS

Item Description for Accounting Period 7/04 Through 6/05	Total	Zero Assets	Under 500	500 to 1,000	1,000 to 5,000	5,000 to 10,000	10,000 to 25,000	25,000 to 50,000	50,000 to 100,000	100,000 to 250,000	250,000 to 500,000	500,000 to 2,500,000	2,500,000 and over
Number of Enterprises 1	12425	2402	9529	167	201	33	42	19	19	8	0	0	0
Revenues ($ in Thousands)													
Net Sales 2	27792218	322790	8353954	469619	1395483	519182	1716594	1246898	1837528	1177222	0	0	0
Interest 3	384629	818	517	495	1212	385	2744	3289	4838	1958	0	0	0
Rents 4	19630	937	46	0	271	2081	490	685	2981	839	0	0	0
Royalties 5	8816	0	0	0	0	0	0	306	2426	0	0	0	0
Other Portfolio Income 6	354207	8090	11208	0	451	434	6594	30535	18350	8060	0	0	0
Other Receipts 7	958098	77523	43174	1	18643	36907	57564	85152	60310	78574	0	0	0
Total Receipts 8	29517598	410158	8408899	470115	1416060	558989	1783986	1366865	1926433	1266653	0	0	0
Average Total Receipts 9	2376	171	882	2815	7045	16939	42476	71940	101391	158332	•	•	•
Operating Costs/Operating Income (%)													
Cost of Operations 10	56.0	61.3	69.8	53.8	60.8	74.2	68.0	48.8	45.8	51.0	•	•	•
Salaries and Wages 11	12.3	8.5	5.8	10.1	15.1	12.6	12.7	15.4	12.7	17.2	•	•	•
Taxes Paid 12	1.7	4.5	1.3	1.1	1.9	2.1	1.7	1.8	2.2	2.9	•	•	•
Interest Paid 13	1.0	0.2	0.2	0.3	0.1	0.1	0.3	0.3	0.9	0.5	•	•	•
Depreciation 14	1.2	1.8	0.8	2.2	0.6	1.0	0.8	1.3	1.7	1.5	•	•	•
Amortization and Depletion 15	0.3	0.3	0.0	0.0	0.1	0.1	0.1	0.1	0.8	1.3	•	•	•
Pensions and Other Deferred Comp. 16	0.4	•	0.3	0.0	0.3	0.2	0.4	0.4	1.0	0.3	•	•	•
Employee Benefits 17	1.0	1.0	0.3	1.3	0.5	0.9	1.0	1.3	2.2	1.3	•	•	•
Advertising 18	4.0	1.0	1.1	0.2	1.4	0.2	1.5	2.8	2.0	1.7	•	•	•
Other Expenses 19	20.2	21.7	14.5	25.0	13.1	8.5	10.6	30.4	28.8	22.6	•	•	•
Officers' Compensation 20	2.1	12.8	3.6	4.9	4.4	2.8	1.6	1.3	1.5	0.5	•	•	•
Operating Margin 21	•	•	2.4	1.1	1.5	•	1.1	•	0.4	•	•	•	•
Operating Margin Before Officers' Comp. 22	1.8	•	6.0	6.0	5.9	0.1	2.7	•	1.9	•	•	•	•

Selected Average Balance Sheet ($ in Thousands)

Net Receivables 23	336	0	8	103	614	1835	3340	3306	8865	22444
Inventories 24	5	0	2	0	10	15	51	552	294	169
Net Property, Plant and Equipment 25	114	0	16	112	201	1414	1552	3797	10688	11242
Total Assets 26	2955	0	99	767	2537	6686	16121	35967	70996	169069
Notes and Loans Payable 27	143	0	41	38	111	1033	1533	5089	9228	12646
All Other Liabilities 28	1338	0	33	349	1589	2625	9137	17983	35051	67498
Net Worth 29	1474	0	26	380	837	3028	5450	12896	26717	88924

Selected Financial Ratios (Times to 1)

Current Ratio 30	1.5	•	2.3	1.4	1.2	1.7	1.2	0.9	1.1	1.1
Quick Ratio 31	1.2	•	1.8	1.1	1.1	1.3	0.9	0.7	0.8	0.9
Net Sales to Working Capital 32	9.2	•	21.7	26.4	21.2	8.9	17.8	•	45.0	18.0
Coverage Ratio 33	7.2	84.7	20.2	5.1	27.2	55.4	20.2	22.4	6.9	12.9
Total Asset Turnover 34	0.8	•	8.8	3.7	2.7	2.4	2.5	1.8	1.4	0.9
Inventory Turnover 35	251.1	•	294.4	•	409.5	804.2	544.3	58.0	150.7	444.1
Receivables Turnover 36	10.2	•	96.2	54.7	14.7	•	11.9	13.8	16.1	6.5
Total Liabilities to Net Worth 37	1.0	•	2.9	1.0	2.0	1.2	2.0	1.8	1.7	0.9
Current Assets to Working Capital 38	2.9	•	1.8	3.4	5.9	2.4	5.0	•	15.8	8.1
Current Liabilities to Working Capital 39	1.9	•	0.8	2.4	4.9	1.4	4.0	•	14.8	7.1
Working Capital to Net Sales 40	0.1	•	0.0	0.0	0.0	0.1	0.1	•	0.0	0.1
Inventory to Working Capital 41	0.0	•	0.0	•	0.0	0.0	0.0	•	0.2	0.0
Total Receipts to Cash Flow 42	4.2	3.6	6.5	4.4	7.3	8.7	7.3	2.9	3.2	3.9
Cost of Goods to Cash Flow 43	2.4	2.2	4.6	2.3	4.4	6.4	4.9	1.4	1.5	2.0
Cash Flow to Total Debt 44	0.4	•	1.8	1.7	0.6	0.5	0.5	1.0	0.7	0.5

Selected Financial Factors (in Percentages)

Debt Ratio 45	50.1	•	74.1	50.4	67.0	54.7	66.2	64.1	62.4	47.4
Return on Total Assets 46	5.4	•	29.2	5.5	8.6	11.8	13.4	10.7	8.1	6.1
Return on Equity Before Income Taxes 47	9.3	•	107.2	9.0	25.0	25.5	37.6	28.5	18.5	10.7
Return on Equity After Income Taxes 48	7.7	•	106.0	8.7	22.2	22.6	32.8	23.6	13.2	8.7
Profit Margin (Before Income Tax) 49	6.1	13.9	3.1	1.2	3.0	4.9	5.0	5.6	5.1	6.4
Profit Margin (After Income Tax) 50	5.1	13.4	3.1	1.2	2.7	4.3	4.4	4.6	3.7	5.3

Table I

Corporations with and without Net Income

OTHER ADMINISTRATIVE AND SUPPORT SERVICES

MONEY AMOUNTS AND SIZE OF ASSETS IN THOUSANDS OF DOLLARS

Item Description for Accounting Period 7/04 Through 6/05	Total	Zero Assets	Under 500	500 to 1,000	1,000 to 5,000	5,000 to 10,000	10,000 to 25,000	25,000 to 50,000	50,000 to 100,000	100,000 to 250,000	250,000 to 500,000	500,000 to 2,500,000	2,500,000 and over
Number of Enterprises 1	187218	27142	147920	6356	4787	469	287	113	50	47	26	17	3

Revenues ($ in Thousands)

Item Description for Accounting Period 7/04 Through 6/05	Total	Zero Assets	Under 500	500 to 1,000	1,000 to 5,000	5,000 to 10,000	10,000 to 25,000	25,000 to 50,000	50,000 to 100,000	100,000 to 250,000	250,000 to 500,000	500,000 to 2,500,000	2,500,000 and over
Net Sales 2	180928003	3652059	53298793	14908344	25472046	8045834	8690338	7048744	4706617	8421818	8244296	18668861	19770253
Interest 3	1969698	5120	41993	5634	25853	6977	9225	12178	41379	58356	126336	264786	1371860
Rents 4	161448	0	5412	6969	5403	1789	3380	14617	14	8206	8824	9028	97804
Royalties 5	1355612	1999	0	8719	0	3885	1636	8006	14195	16172	1820	129281	1169899
Other Portfolio Income 6	1106733	64991	132769	29489	44592	11791	26195	5523	72112	22912	116317	104136	475909
Other Receipts 7	6954785	684182	1768778	55170	210385	164415	264613	257781	186497	571988	220216	796609	1774152
Total Receipts 8	192476279	4408351	55247745	15014325	25758279	8234691	8995387	7346849	5020814	9099452	8717809	19972701	24659977
Average Total Receipts 9	1028	162	373	2362	5381	17558	31343	65016	100416	193605	335300	1174865	8219959

Operating Costs/Operating Income (%)

Item Description for Accounting Period 7/04 Through 6/05	Total	Zero Assets	Under 500	500 to 1,000	1,000 to 5,000	5,000 to 10,000	10,000 to 25,000	25,000 to 50,000	50,000 to 100,000	100,000 to 250,000	250,000 to 500,000	500,000 to 2,500,000	2,500,000 and over
Cost of Operations 10	37.8	33.0	34.1	40.6	50.8	43.0	48.5	43.0	44.2	36.6	18.6	32.4	33.2
Salaries and Wages 11	21.4	29.0	20.4	22.4	17.4	20.4	20.0	20.7	20.7	28.6	34.9	25.5	16.1
Taxes Paid 12	3.6	4.5	3.9	4.0	3.7	3.3	3.6	2.9	2.7	3.9	4.1	4.7	1.8
Interest Paid 13	2.2	2.9	0.7	0.6	0.7	0.6	1.2	1.3	2.0	2.9	4.2	2.4	9.5
Depreciation 14	2.9	2.4	2.8	3.4	2.2	2.2	2.1	1.8	1.8	2.9	2.8	2.9	5.6
Amortization and Depletion 15	1.2	1.7	0.1	0.1	0.1	0.2	0.4	0.7	1.4	1.4	2.0	2.1	5.5
Pensions and Other Deferred Comp. 16	0.4	0.5	0.2	0.4	0.3	0.5	0.4	0.5	0.2	0.5	0.4	0.9	0.4
Employee Benefits 17	2.0	2.2	0.9	1.3	1.3	1.6	2.8	9.1	2.1	2.0	3.8	2.8	2.1
Advertising 18	1.3	1.2	1.5	0.7	0.5	0.7	1.0	1.7	0.6	1.6	1.1	0.3	3.2
Other Expenses 19	27.0	37.6	26.0	16.4	16.8	25.3	17.8	18.2	27.7	22.5	29.9	25.2	58.3
Officers' Compensation 20	4.0	6.8	7.6	7.2	3.6	2.4	2.2	1.5	1.7	1.2	1.1	0.6	0.1
Operating Margin 21	•	•	1.8	2.8	2.5	•	0.0	•	•	•	•	0.1	•
Operating Margin Before Officers' Comp. 22	0.3	•	9.4	10.0	6.1	2.2	2.2	0.0	•	•	•	0.8	•

Selected Average Balance Sheet ($ in Thousands)

Net Receivables 23	90	0	10	154	499	2189	4189	9715	17763	31088	45640	170877	756932
Inventories 24	12	0	2	33	78	46	510	1062	3302	3712	2765	9502	203043
Net Property, Plant and Equipment 25	99	0	23	214	409	1629	2442	4515	8696	19601	45327	184573	1391295
Total Assets 26	685	0	72	715	1838	7049	15547	35172	69703	161734	338913	1123663	17828335
Notes and Loans Payable 27	201	0	47	323	734	2204	5944	15289	23145	58703	125352	298412	2791521
All Other Liabilities 28	272	0	16	218	769	3133	6375	12185	23152	48922	121672	227969	9460031
Net Worth 29	211	0	9	174	335	1711	3228	7698	23405	54109	91889	597282	5576783

Selected Financial Ratios (Times to 1)

Current Ratio 30	1.2	•	1.4	1.3	1.2	1.2	1.3	1.4	1.1	1.6	1.0	1.5	0.7
Quick Ratio 31	0.9	•	1.1	1.0	0.9	1.1	1.0	1.1	0.8	1.2	0.7	1.1	0.5
Net Sales to Working Capital 32	32.3	•	40.5	27.6	23.6	19.4	14.0	12.1	22.6	6.8	75.1	9.8	•
Coverage Ratio 33	2.2	0.6	8.5	6.9	6.3	4.9	4.0	3.1	1.8	2.4	1.7	4.0	•
Total Asset Turnover 34	1.4	•	5.0	3.3	2.9	2.4	1.9	1.8	1.4	1.1	0.9	1.0	0.4
Inventory Turnover 35	29.3	•	64.6	28.9	34.5	159.3	28.8	25.2	12.6	17.7	21.3	37.5	10.8
Receivables Turnover 36	10.6	•	41.5	17.0	10.0	9.6	7.2	7.1	5.3	6.6	7.0	6.3	6.5
Total Liabilities to Net Worth 37	2.2	•	7.3	3.1	4.5	3.1	3.8	3.6	2.0	2.0	2.7	0.9	2.2
Current Assets to Working Capital 38	6.9	•	3.6	4.7	5.0	5.2	4.2	3.8	8.6	2.6	30.9	2.9	•
Current Liabilities to Working Capital 39	5.9	•	2.6	3.7	4.0	4.2	3.2	2.8	7.6	1.6	29.9	1.9	•
Working Capital to Net Sales 40	0.0	•	0.0	0.0	0.0	0.1	0.1	0.1	0.0	0.1	0.0	0.1	•
Inventory to Working Capital 41	0.4	•	0.3	0.4	0.3	0.1	0.2	0.2	1.0	0.1	0.6	0.1	•
Total Receipts to Cash Flow 42	4.1	3.3	3.8	6.0	6.0	4.2	5.5	5.6	4.1	4.5	3.6	3.6	2.9
Cost of Goods to Cash Flow 43	1.6	1.1	1.3	2.4	3.0	1.8	2.7	2.4	1.8	1.7	0.7	1.2	1.0
Cash Flow to Total Debt 44	0.5	•	1.5	0.7	0.6	0.8	0.4	0.4	0.5	0.4	0.4	0.6	0.2

Selected Financial Factors (in Percentages)

Debt Ratio 45	69.1	•	88.0	75.7	81.8	75.7	79.2	78.1	66.4	66.5	72.9	46.8	68.7
Return on Total Assets 46	6.9	•	30.9	13.6	12.5	6.7	9.3	7.3	4.8	7.6	6.7	9.4	•
Return on Equity Before Income Taxes 47	12.2	•	227.7	47.8	57.5	21.8	33.7	22.7	6.4	13.2	10.1	13.3	•
Return on Equity After Income Taxes 48	10.1	•	224.3	46.5	54.5	18.3	30.3	17.8	3.3	10.4	7.4	9.2	•
Profit Margin (Before Income Tax) 49	2.7	•	5.4	3.5	3.6	2.2	3.6	2.8	1.6	4.0	2.9	7.2	•
Profit Margin (After Income Tax) 50	2.2	•	5.4	3.4	3.4	1.8	3.2	2.2	0.8	3.1	2.1	5.0	•

Table II

Corporations with Net Income

OTHER ADMINISTRATIVE AND SUPPORT SERVICES

MONEY AMOUNTS AND SIZE OF ASSETS IN THOUSANDS OF DOLLARS

Item Description for Accounting Period 7/04 Through 6/05	Total	Zero Assets	Under 500	500 to 1,000	1,000 to 5,000	5,000 to 10,000	10,000 to 25,000	25,000 to 50,000	50,000 to 100,000	100,000 to 250,000	250,000 to 500,000	500,000 to 2,500,000	2,500,000 and over
Number of Enterprises 1	117391	13009	94951	5244	3532	311	180	73	29	27	0	0	0
Revenues ($ in Thousands)													
Net Sales 2	129118367	1792370	37863891	12210324	21873464	5222089	6390332	5283594	3082642	6366021	0	0	0
Interest 3	663119	2196	38509	4354	10756	4707	5278	7502	3924	28494	0	0	0
Rents 4	51909	0	3617	4365	3340	1042	1614	14177	14	4976	0	0	0
Royalties 5	180739	1999	0	8719	0	3885	1636	640	14111	16172	0	0	0
Other Portfolio Income 6	519425	22496	116870	13527	33464	6455	22064	3876	69275	12696	0	0	0
Other Receipts 7	4754325	666688	1662857	10998	211244	130587	204164	212845	73915	537491	0	0	0
Total Receipts 8	135287884	2485749	39685744	12142287	22132268	5368765	6625088	5522634	3243881	6965850	0	0	0
Average Total Receipts 9	1152	191	418	2315	6266	17263	36806	75653	111858	257994	.	.	.
Operating Costs/Operating Income (%)													
Cost of Operations 10	38.1	30.8	31.1	43.8	50.4	44.6	46.7	46.2	51.9	41.7	.	.	.
Salaries and Wages 11	21.6	39.8	21.5	16.2	17.9	22.8	20.6	21.2	16.9	26.3	.	.	.
Taxes Paid 12	3.7	5.3	3.6	3.7	3.6	3.5	3.7	3.0	3.1	3.5	.	.	.
Interest Paid 13	1.5	0.7	0.7	0.6	0.5	0.3	0.6	0.7	1.8	2.1	.	.	.
Depreciation 14	2.6	1.7	2.4	3.8	1.8	2.0	2.3	1.7	1.8	2.7	.	.	.
Amortization and Depletion 15	0.8	0.3	0.1	0.1	0.0	0.1	0.2	0.3	1.1	0.5	.	.	.
Pensions and Other Deferred Comp. 16	0.4	0.2	0.2	0.4	0.3	0.3	0.4	0.5	0.2	0.6	.	.	.
Employee Benefits 17	1.7	2.3	0.9	1.4	1.0	1.8	2.9	4.7	2.2	2.0	.	.	.
Advertising 18	1.0	1.6	1.4	0.8	0.5	0.8	0.5	1.3	0.9	2.0	.	.	.
Other Expenses 19	21.6	30.8	25.6	15.6	15.4	16.7	16.2	17.1	16.9	19.5	.	.	.
Officers' Compensation 20	3.9	6.9	6.8	7.6	3.6	2.8	2.1	1.5	1.8	1.3	.	.	.
Operating Margin 21	3.0	.	5.8	6.1	5.1	4.3	3.9	1.8	1.2	.	.	.	.
Operating Margin Before Officers' Comp. 22	6.9	.	12.6	13.7	8.7	7.1	6.0	3.3	3.0	.	.	.	.

Selected Average Balance Sheet ($ in Thousands)

Net Receivables 23	99	0	10	154	494	1855	4351	10672	19889	38612
Inventories 24	14	0	2	36	65	44	544	1202	5069	6170
Net Property, Plant and Equipment 25	112	0	21	221	353	1588	2749	4777	10181	21093
Total Assets 26	569	0	75	728	1802	6917	16013	34033	69995	166273
Notes and Loans Payable 27	177	0	36	305	487	1625	4024	9342	24637	38131
All Other Liabilities 28	165	0	13	237	709	2625	5795	12605	25283	56439
Net Worth 29	227	0	26	186	605	2666	6193	12087	20075	71703

Selected Financial Ratios (Times to 1)

Current Ratio 30	1.4	•	1.8	1.4	1.3	1.6	1.5	1.4	1.2	1.7
Quick Ratio 31	1.1	•	1.5	1.1	1.0	1.4	1.1	1.2	0.8	1.4
Net Sales to Working Capital 32	16.2	•	23.9	20.1	21.9	9.9	11.6	11.4	14.0	6.7
Coverage Ratio 33	6.1	28.7	16.4	12.3	14.2	23.8	13.1	9.4	4.6	4.5
Total Asset Turnover 34	1.9	•	5.3	3.2	3.4	2.4	2.2	2.1	1.5	1.4
Inventory Turnover 35	29.5	•	60.0	28.0	47.7	171.7	30.4	27.8	10.9	15.9
Receivables Turnover 36	10.3	•	42.3	17.8	12.5	9.1	8.4	7.5	5.7	8.4
Total Liabilities to Net Worth 37	1.5	•	1.9	2.9	2.0	1.6	1.6	1.8	2.5	1.3
Current Assets to Working Capital 38	3.4	•	2.2	3.7	4.0	2.7	3.1	3.3	5.4	2.4
Current Liabilities to Working Capital 39	2.4	•	1.2	2.7	3.0	1.7	2.1	2.3	4.4	1.4
Working Capital to Net Sales 40	0.1	•	0.0	0.0	0.0	0.1	0.1	0.1	0.1	0.1
Inventory to Working Capital 41	0.2	•	0.1	0.3	0.2	0.0	0.2	0.2	0.9	0.2
Total Receipts to Cash Flow 42	4.0	2.2	3.2	5.5	5.5	5.1	4.8	4.9	5.3	4.3
Cost of Goods to Cash Flow 43	1.5	0.7	1.0	2.4	2.7	2.3	2.3	2.3	2.8	1.8
Cash Flow to Total Debt 44	0.8	•	2.5	0.8	0.9	0.8	0.7	0.7	0.4	0.6

Selected Financial Factors (in Percentages)

Debt Ratio 45	60.1	•	65.8	74.4	66.4	61.5	61.3	64.5	71.3	56.9
Return on Total Assets 46	18.0	•	60.1	22.1	23.2	18.1	18.2	15.0	12.6	13.4
Return on Equity Before Income Taxes 47	37.7	•	164.8	79.4	64.1	44.9	43.6	37.7	34.2	24.2
Return on Equity After Income Taxes 48	34.7	•	163.1	77.9	62.0	41.6	40.7	33.0	28.1	20.5
Profit Margin (Before Income Tax) 49	7.8	18.3	10.6	6.4	6.3	7.1	7.6	6.3	6.5	7.4
Profit Margin (After Income Tax) 50	7.2	17.3	10.5	6.3	6.1	6.6	7.1	5.5	5.3	6.2

Table I

Corporations with and without Net Income

WASTE MANAGEMENT AND REMEDIATION SERVICES

MONEY AMOUNTS AND SIZE OF ASSETS IN THOUSANDS OF DOLLARS

Item Description for Accounting Period 7/04 Through 6/05	Total	Zero Assets	Under 500	500 to 1,000	1,000 to 5,000	5,000 to 10,000	10,000 to 25,000	25,000 to 50,000	50,000 to 100,000	100,000 to 250,000	250,000 to 500,000	500,000 to 2,500,000	2,500,000 and over
Number of Enterprises **1**	12132	1768	6875	1553	1459	254	126	45	20	14	7	7	5
Revenues ($ in Thousands)													
Net Sales **2**	52800619	399547	4106909	3346892	6217356	2935506	2998431	1301053	1701978	2440500	2006243	4750649	20607555
Interest **3**	657447	433	511	2626	808	967	4057	1551	4411	9595	4942	78817	548729
Rents **4**	59459	98	1397	271	997	1912	2969	283	1350	619	33	5735	43796
Royalties **5**	41601	0	0	321	6066	0	20	491	0	1182	0	13380	20142
Other Portfolio Income **6**	697350	62074	29479	38044	17495	1090	18855	3516	2858	2540	16477	6578	498343
Other Receipts **7**	1451716	5890	3158	5193	91274	23311	40825	15539	8477	39390	12695	217417	988545
Total Receipts **8**	55708192	468042	4141454	3393347	6333996	2962786	3053157	1322433	1719074	2493826	2040390	5072576	22707110
Average Total Receipts **9**	4592	265	602	2185	4341	11665	24231	29387	85954	178130	291484	724654	4541422
Operating Costs/Operating Income (%)													
Cost of Operations **10**	41.8	20.7	52.2	11.3	54.5	58.5	54.9	53.7	54.9	29.4	38.5	29.5	39.8
Salaries and Wages **11**	14.1	12.1	6.7	12.4	8.3	8.9	9.6	8.9	8.7	25.7	14.8	19.3	17.1
Taxes Paid **12**	4.1	13.6	2.1	2.4	3.3	4.3	2.7	3.0	2.3	3.4	3.8	3.4	5.5
Interest Paid **13**	4.9	0.9	0.7	1.1	1.8	1.0	1.3	2.5	1.5	2.6	4.5	6.3	8.8
Depreciation **14**	6.9	4.6	3.0	3.9	4.9	3.1	5.1	5.7	4.8	5.3	6.1	8.9	9.6
Amortization and Depletion **15**	1.7	0.6	0.1	0.3	0.1	0.4	0.5	1.1	0.8	1.5	2.0	4.3	2.6
Pensions and Other Deferred Comp. **16**	0.5	0.5	0.0	0.5	0.4	0.2	0.4	0.3	0.3	0.6	1.5	1.0	0.5
Employee Benefits **17**	2.1	2.1	0.5	1.2	1.2	1.2	2.1	2.2	2.1	4.1	3.8	3.0	2.3
Advertising **18**	0.3	1.3	0.8	0.4	0.3	0.4	0.3	0.3	0.4	0.2	0.1	0.3	0.3
Other Expenses **19**	24.4	27.1	25.6	60.4	17.2	20.2	19.8	18.0	20.6	28.1	24.8	30.2	20.7
Officers' Compensation **20**	1.5	9.4	4.6	3.8	3.1	1.6	1.9	1.9	1.2	1.0	0.6	0.4	0.0
Operating Margin **21**	•	7.1	3.6	2.4	4.8	0.4	0.8	2.3	2.4	3.8	3.0	•	•
Operating Margin Before Officers' Comp. **22**	•	16.5	8.2	6.1	8.0	1.9	3.3	4.3	3.6	•	0.1	•	•

Selected Average Balance Sheet ($ in Thousands)

Net Receivables 23	656	0	9	130	512	2040	3948	5388	12346	24704	49428	116697	788067
Inventories 24	57	0	3	12	102	134	299	737	356	380	1508	30333	33626
Net Property, Plant and Equipment 25	2149	0	48	211	828	2067	5568	9931	18858	47780	130764	439880	3496425
Total Assets 26	6042	0	99	708	2020	6140	15249	34873	70283	144808	371027	1143856	9896675
Notes and Loans Payable 27	2681	0	68	449	966	2624	6028	14667	32407	64833	150102	462253	4404463
All Other Liabilities 28	1954	0	19	90	539	2798	5178	10155	21682	38285	130077	453209	3155418
Net Worth 29	1406	0	11	169	515	718	4043	10051	16195	41690	90848	228395	2336794

Selected Financial Ratios (Times to 1)

Current Ratio 30	0.9	•	1.3	3.0	1.3	1.1	1.3	1.6	1.3	1.1	1.2	0.5	0.8
Quick Ratio 31	0.7	•	1.0	2.3	1.1	0.9	1.0	1.1	0.9	1.0	0.9	0.3	0.7
Net Sales to Working Capital 32	•	•	90.3	8.6	20.7	77.4	14.7	6.6	13.6	42.4	20.9	•	•
Coverage Ratio 33	1.7	28.6	7.1	4.4	4.7	2.2	3.4	2.5	3.3	1.1	1.3	1.0	1.3
Total Asset Turnover 34	0.7	•	6.1	3.0	2.1	1.9	1.6	0.8	1.2	1.2	0.8	0.6	0.4
Inventory Turnover 35	31.9	•	119.0	20.7	22.8	50.5	43.6	21.1	131.2	134.8	73.2	6.6	48.8
Receivables Turnover 36	7.4	•	73.4	16.6	7.6	7.6	6.5	5.1	7.1	8.6	7.7	5.8	6.2
Total Liabilities to Net Worth 37	3.3	•	7.6	3.2	2.9	7.5	2.8	2.5	3.3	2.5	3.1	4.0	3.2
Current Assets to Working Capital 38	•	•	4.5	1.5	4.1	20.5	4.4	2.7	4.6	8.4	7.0	•	•
Current Liabilities to Working Capital 39	•	•	3.5	0.5	3.1	19.5	3.4	1.7	3.6	7.4	6.0	•	•
Working Capital to Net Sales 40	•	•	0.0	0.1	0.0	0.0	0.1	0.2	0.1	0.0	0.0	•	•
Inventory to Working Capital 41	•	•	0.7	0.1	0.2	1.1	0.2	0.2	0.1	0.1	0.2	•	•
Total Receipts to Cash Flow 42	4.6	2.3	4.5	1.8	5.5	5.9	5.4	5.6	4.9	5.0	4.7	3.9	5.7
Cost of Goods to Cash Flow 43	1.9	0.5	2.3	0.2	3.0	3.5	2.9	3.0	2.7	1.5	1.8	1.2	2.3
Cash Flow to Total Debt 44	0.2	•	1.5	2.2	0.5	0.4	0.4	0.2	0.3	0.3	0.2	0.2	0.1

Selected Financial Factors (in Percentages)

Debt Ratio 45	76.7	•	88.4	76.1	74.5	88.3	73.5	71.2	77.0	71.2	75.5	80.0	76.4
Return on Total Assets 46	5.8	•	31.2	14.7	17.9	4.4	6.6	5.3	5.9	3.5	4.7	3.8	4.9
Return on Equity Before Income Taxes 47	10.0	•	231.1	47.5	55.4	20.6	17.4	11.2	17.7	1.5	4.9	0.5	5.1
Return on Equity After Income Taxes 48	8.0	•	230.3	44.3	53.4	18.2	13.3	8.7	17.3	•	2.7	•	3.4
Profit Margin (Before Income Tax) 49	3.2	24.3	4.4	3.7	6.7	1.3	3.0	3.9	3.4	0.4	1.5	0.2	2.9
Profit Margin (After Income Tax) 50	2.6	24.2	4.4	3.5	6.5	1.1	2.3	3.0	3.3	•	0.8	•	1.9

363

Table II

Corporations with Net Income

WASTE MANAGEMENT AND REMEDIATION SERVICES

MONEY AMOUNTS AND SIZE OF ASSETS IN THOUSANDS OF DOLLARS

Item Description for Accounting Period 7/04 Through 6/05	Total	Zero Assets	Under 500	500 to 1,000	1,000 to 5,000	5,000 to 10,000	10,000 to 25,000	25,000 to 50,000	50,000 to 100,000	100,000 to 250,000	250,000 to 500,000	500,000 to 2,500,000	2,500,000 and over
Number of Enterprises 1	7566	1097	4157	920	1122	132	82	24	11	9	0	4	0
Revenues ($ in Thousands)													
Net Sales 2	37905478	323458	3342822	2430771	5057328	1297469	2326321	876180	1126772	1437998	0	2044107	0
Interest 3	208120	0	245	2280	570	794	2231	1106	526	2394	0	13161	0
Rents 4	21839	9	1397	271	89	1912	2935	271	55	421	0	2140	0
Royalties 5	22641	0	0	321	0	0	20	0	0	1182	0	977	0
Other Portfolio Income 6	494727	60327	29419	31323	16709	149	15562	1526	1384	254	0	4187	0
Other Receipts 7	1074518	6026	2755	4610	83685	13976	33817	12360	3032	36791	0	145103	0
Total Receipts 8	39727323	389820	3376638	2469576	5158381	1314300	2380886	891443	1131769	1479040	0	2209675	0
Average Total Receipts 9	5251	355	812	2684	4597	9957	29035	37143	102888	164338	•	552419	•
Operating Costs/Operating Income (%)													
Cost of Operations 10	40.0	13.0	59.4	6.9	52.0	50.9	56.5	55.5	56.1	43.5	•	25.6	•
Salaries and Wages 11	14.5	13.7	5.2	9.6	8.3	12.3	8.4	6.8	9.2	12.9	•	21.7	•
Taxes Paid 12	4.6	16.0	1.9	1.9	3.1	3.1	2.5	2.8	1.7	2.4	•	3.5	•
Interest Paid 13	2.5	0.6	0.4	0.2	1.7	0.8	0.9	1.6	0.7	1.7	•	5.5	•
Depreciation 14	7.0	4.4	1.7	2.3	4.6	3.6	4.3	4.4	4.0	6.0	•	7.0	•
Amortization and Depletion 15	1.4	0.7	0.1	0.0	0.0	0.0	0.2	0.9	0.6	1.3	•	4.6	•
Pensions and Other Deferred Comp. 16	0.5	0.1	0.0	0.6	0.5	0.2	0.5	0.4	0.4	0.3	•	0.5	•
Employee Benefits 17	2.2	2.5	0.3	0.9	1.2	2.1	1.8	2.0	2.2	2.6	•	2.7	•
Advertising 18	0.4	0.8	0.8	0.4	0.4	0.7	0.2	0.2	0.4	0.2	•	0.3	•
Other Expenses 19	23.0	24.2	20.8	68.6	16.5	17.4	17.9	15.3	16.0	26.8	•	23.2	•
Officers' Compensation 20	1.4	11.2	3.1	2.5	3.3	1.5	2.3	2.0	1.2	1.3	•	0.5	•
Operating Margin 21	2.5	12.6	6.4	6.2	8.4	7.4	4.4	7.9	7.5	1.0	•	4.9	•
Operating Margin Before Officers' Comp. 22	3.9	23.8	9.5	8.6	11.7	8.9	6.7	10.0	8.7	2.4	•	5.4	•

Selected Average Balance Sheet ($ in Thousands)

Net Receivables 23	714	0	9	149	501	1237	4410	6516	15568	23067	100210
Inventories 24	54	0	2	20	122	187	367	847	421	468	10022
Net Property, Plant and Equipment 25	2368	0	47	153	841	2367	5444	9012	20069	50825	353923
Total Assets 26	6541	0	96	730	2101	5838	15339	35906	68307	138208	1021938
Notes and Loans Payable 27	2445	0	51	98	959	1406	5106	10551	19965	61122	404390
All Other Liabilities 28	1876	0	19	117	366	2105	4373	12143	21528	37488	277322
Net Worth 29	2220	0	25	515	776	2326	5861	13212	26815	39599	340226

Selected Financial Ratios (Times to 1)

Current Ratio 30	1.2	•	1.6	4.4	1.8	1.3	1.6	1.6	1.4	1.2	0.6
Quick Ratio 31	0.9	•	1.3	3.3	1.5	1.1	1.3	1.2	1.1	0.9	0.5
Net Sales to Working Capital 32	28.9	•	70.9	6.3	12.4	18.2	9.7	7.4	11.0	29.0	•
Coverage Ratio 33	4.0	53.6	21.0	41.9	7.1	11.9	8.5	7.1	11.9	3.3	3.4
Total Asset Turnover 34	0.8	•	8.4	3.6	2.1	1.7	1.8	1.0	1.5	1.2	0.5
Inventory Turnover 35	37.3	•	210.1	9.1	19.1	26.7	43.7	23.9	136.6	148.6	13.1
Receivables Turnover 36	8.6	•	82.4	19.8	7.8	10.1	7.3	5.9	6.9	8.2	2.1
Total Liabilities to Net Worth 37	1.9	•	2.8	0.4	1.7	1.5	1.6	1.7	1.5	2.5	2.0
Current Assets to Working Capital 38	7.3	•	2.7	1.3	2.3	4.5	2.6	2.7	3.5	6.2	•
Current Liabilities to Working Capital 39	6.3	•	1.7	0.3	1.3	3.5	1.6	1.7	2.5	5.2	•
Working Capital to Net Sales 40	0.0	•	0.0	0.2	0.1	0.1	0.1	0.1	0.1	0.0	•
Inventory to Working Capital 41	0.3	•	0.3	0.1	0.1	0.5	0.2	0.2	0.1	0.1	•
Total Receipts to Cash Flow 42	4.1	2.0	4.8	1.4	4.6	4.7	4.8	4.8	4.8	5.1	3.2
Cost of Goods to Cash Flow 43	1.6	0.3	2.8	0.1	2.4	2.4	2.7	2.7	2.7	2.2	0.8
Cash Flow to Total Debt 44	0.3	•	2.4	8.6	0.7	0.6	0.6	0.3	0.5	0.3	0.2

Selected Financial Factors (in Percentages)

Debt Ratio 45	66.1	•	73.5	29.4	63.1	60.2	61.8	63.2	60.7	71.3	66.7
Return on Total Assets 46	7.5	•	65.6	28.8	26.0	16.0	14.1	11.4	13.0	6.4	9.3
Return on Equity Before Income Taxes 47	16.5	•	235.6	39.8	60.4	36.8	32.5	26.6	30.3	15.6	19.6
Return on Equity After Income Taxes 48	14.5	•	235.0	38.0	58.7	35.4	28.2	23.0	29.9	11.7	16.6
Profit Margin (Before Income Tax) 49	7.3	33.1	7.4	7.8	10.4	8.7	6.7	9.6	7.9	3.9	13.0
Profit Margin (After Income Tax) 50	6.4	33.0	7.4	7.4	10.1	8.4	5.8	8.3	7.8	2.9	11.0

Table I

Corporations with and without Net Income

EDUCATIONAL SERVICES

MONEY AMOUNTS AND SIZE OF ASSETS IN THOUSANDS OF DOLLARS

Item Description for Accounting Period 7/04 Through 6/05	Total	Zero Assets	Under 500	500 to 1,000	1,000 to 5,000	5,000 to 10,000	10,000 to 25,000	25,000 to 50,000	50,000 to 100,000	100,000 to 250,000	250,000 to 500,000	500,000 to 2,500,000	2,500,000 and over
Number of Enterprises 1	43956	6153	35704	810	998	137	72	28	21	19	7	7	0
Revenues ($ in Thousands)													
Net Sales 2	32364218	446479	9442718	766753	4200217	1665013	1550391	1384299	1406918	3218605	2223232	6059592	0
Interest 3	85530	859	1472	4062	6287	1926	3106	1870	2986	12993	7684	42285	0
Rents 4	17757	0	450	0	1863	874	477	432	227	4600	906	7929	0
Royalties 5	186561	18808	2762	0	59109	0	152	976	563	0	26349	77841	0
Other Portfolio Income 6	150303	25224	22425	9319	1720	10862	2430	5225	5722	9408	8677	49293	0
Other Receipts 7	511330	10876	93060	5374	42314	17785	50814	18591	45855	20072	21537	185051	0
Total Receipts 8	33315699	502246	9562887	785508	4311510	1696460	1607370	1411393	1462271	3265678	2288385	6421991	0
Average Total Receipts 9	758	82	268	970	4320	12383	22325	50407	69632	171878	326912	917427	•
Operating Costs/Operating Income (%)													
Cost of Operations 10	14.1	12.0	7.8	30.0	7.6	33.8	18.0	22.1	17.4	35.9	22.7	2.6	•
Salaries and Wages 11	30.3	26.5	28.7	9.5	36.3	24.2	32.9	28.1	34.5	22.4	29.9	36.7	•
Taxes Paid 12	3.5	4.7	3.9	1.9	4.1	3.8	3.8	3.8	2.7	2.5	5.3	2.3	•
Interest Paid 13	1.0	1.5	0.5	1.7	0.9	0.7	1.6	0.9	1.1	1.6	2.6	0.9	•
Depreciation 14	3.0	2.2	1.6	1.6	2.7	4.3	3.1	3.0	3.8	3.2	3.9	4.6	•
Amortization and Depletion 15	0.7	2.1	0.3	0.2	0.1	0.4	0.5	1.3	0.7	1.2	1.4	0.9	•
Pensions and Other Deferred Comp. 16	0.7	0.4	1.1	0.7	1.1	0.7	0.5	0.3	0.4	0.3	1.3	0.1	•
Employee Benefits 17	2.4	4.1	2.7	0.2	1.2	1.9	2.2	2.4	1.5	1.9	2.3	3.6	•
Advertising 18	4.7	3.2	2.0	2.2	2.5	1.6	5.9	5.1	9.0	3.7	4.6	11.1	•
Other Expenses 19	30.0	44.2	37.1	37.6	31.3	19.6	28.1	27.6	25.8	21.1	22.2	28.2	•
Officers' Compensation 20	5.2	6.4	9.6	9.7	7.2	3.0	3.5	4.1	2.1	1.9	1.8	1.5	•
Operating Margin 21	4.4	•	4.7	4.7	4.9	6.0	•	1.4	1.0	4.3	1.9	7.5	•
Operating Margin Before Officers' Comp. 22	9.6	•	14.3	14.4	12.2	9.0	3.3	5.5	3.1	6.2	3.7	9.0	•

Selected Average Balance Sheet ($ in Thousands)

Net Receivables 23	90	0	10	32	450	1642	3261	5412	11587	32260	44754	189614	•
Inventories 24	6	0	2	8	26	362	216	1083	719	1374	1815	4418	•
Net Property, Plant and Equipment 25	115	0	19	447	605	1371	4421	7265	16840	28342	77350	181624	•
Total Assets 26	506	0	72	738	2033	6998	15790	34620	70169	152295	392908	977579	•
Notes and Loans Payable 27	144	0	50	595	685	2342	5024	9390	16335	30423	103163	112931	•
All Other Liabilities 28	167	0	22	119	1214	2867	5678	11393	24523	56281	127663	236005	•
Net Worth 29	194	0	0	24	134	1790	5089	13837	29310	65591	162083	628643	•

Selected Financial Ratios (Times to 1)

Current Ratio 30	1.3	•	1.4	1.6	0.9	1.1	1.3	1.4	1.5	1.2	1.3	1.4	•
Quick Ratio 31	1.1	•	1.2	1.4	0.9	0.9	1.0	1.0	1.2	1.0	0.8	1.2	•
Net Sales to Working Capital 32	15.1	•	25.2	11.9	•	33.6	12.7	11.9	6.0	13.5	12.4	7.2	•
Coverage Ratio 33	8.0	4.3	11.9	5.3	9.4	12.4	3.2	4.7	5.7	4.6	2.9	15.5	•
Total Asset Turnover 34	1.5	•	3.7	1.3	2.1	1.7	1.4	1.4	1.0	1.1	0.8	0.9	•
Inventory Turnover 35	16.2	•	10.7	35.4	12.4	11.3	17.9	10.1	16.2	44.3	39.7	5.1	•
Receivables Turnover 36	8.0	•	28.4	29.0	7.1	7.8	6.7	9.1	4.2	6.4	6.8	4.5	•
Total Liabilities to Net Worth 37	1.6	•	33541.6	30.1	14.2	2.9	2.1	1.5	1.4	1.3	1.4	0.6	•
Current Assets to Working Capital 38	4.6	•	3.4	2.7	•	10.4	4.6	3.8	3.0	5.2	4.8	3.6	•
Current Liabilities to Working Capital 39	3.6	•	2.4	1.7	•	9.4	3.6	2.8	2.0	4.2	3.8	2.6	•
Working Capital to Net Sales 40	0.1	•	0.0	0.1	•	0.0	0.1	0.1	0.2	0.1	0.1	0.1	•
Inventory to Working Capital 41	0.1	•	0.2	0.1	•	1.2	0.1	0.3	0.1	0.1	0.1	0.0	•
Total Receipts to Cash Flow 42	3.4	3.3	2.8	2.7	3.2	4.7	4.2	4.6	4.0	4.6	5.2	3.0	•
Cost of Goods to Cash Flow 43	0.5	0.4	0.2	0.8	0.2	1.6	0.7	1.0	0.7	1.6	1.2	0.1	•
Cash Flow to Total Debt 44	0.7	•	1.3	0.5	0.7	0.5	0.5	0.5	0.4	0.4	0.3	0.8	•

Selected Financial Factors (in Percentages)

Debt Ratio 45	61.6	•	100.0	96.8	93.4	74.4	67.8	60.0	58.2	56.9	58.7	35.7	•
Return on Total Assets 46	12.1	•	23.8	11.3	17.6	14.8	7.0	6.2	5.8	8.1	6.1	12.5	•
Return on Equity Before Income Taxes 47	27.5	•	729879.2	286.3	238.2	53.2	15.0	12.2	11.5	14.7	9.6	18.2	•
Return on Equity After Income Taxes 48	22.0	•	711561.0	285.1	229.8	47.0	12.7	8.1	9.4	9.2	6.7	11.7	•
Profit Margin (Before Income Tax) 49	7.3	5.1	6.0	7.2	7.6	7.8	3.5	3.4	5.0	5.7	4.9	13.2	•
Profit Margin (After Income Tax) 50	5.8	3.3	5.8	7.1	7.3	6.9	3.0	2.3	4.1	3.6	3.4	8.5	•

Table II
Corporations with Net Income

EDUCATIONAL SERVICES

MONEY AMOUNTS AND SIZE OF ASSETS IN THOUSANDS OF DOLLARS

Item Description for Accounting Period 7/04 Through 6/05	Total	Zero Assets	Under 500	500 to 1,000	1,000 to 5,000	5,000 to 10,000	10,000 to 25,000	25,000 to 50,000	50,000 to 100,000	100,000 to 250,000	250,000 to 500,000	500,000 to 2,500,000	2,500,000 and over
Number of Enterprises 1	24789	2806	20834	222	714	101	53	20	18	11	0	0	0
Revenues ($ in Thousands)													
Net Sales 2	25946063	233579	6722783	415958	3607584	1449565	1278821	1121394	1237567	2459428	0	0	0
Interest 3	60535	458	1328	823	3847	1405	2697	1560	2761	11475	0	0	0
Rents 4	13612	0	0	0	620	874	395	432	130	2327	0	0	0
Royalties 5	157169	0	2762	0	52558	0	152	976	563	0	0	0	0
Other Portfolio Income 6	123061	25067	21450	7342	1720	10708	1332	5225	5356	7795	0	0	0
Other Receipts 7	451146	11447	90409	192	32218	17170	46757	14162	32398	15528	0	0	0
Total Receipts 8	26751586	270551	6838732	424315	3698547	1479722	1330154	1143749	1278775	2496553	0	0	0
Average Total Receipts 9	1079	96	328	1911	5180	14651	25097	57187	71043	226959	·	·	·
Operating Costs/Operating Income (%)													
Cost of Operations 10	14.7	13.5	9.6	22.2	5.8	37.2	20.2	18.6	13.3	43.3	·	·	·
Salaries and Wages 11	29.5	10.9	27.8	8.7	35.8	21.7	30.2	28.8	36.1	18.5	·	·	·
Taxes Paid 12	3.3	4.6	3.6	2.0	4.1	3.3	3.5	3.6	2.9	2.4	·	·	·
Interest Paid 13	0.6	1.0	0.5	0.7	0.3	0.3	0.5	0.6	1.1	0.7	·	·	·
Depreciation 14	2.8	1.6	1.2	1.1	1.8	4.3	2.8	3.0	4.2	2.8	·	·	·
Amortization and Depletion 15	0.4	0.3	0.1	0.3	0.0	0.1	0.3	0.8	0.5	0.6	·	·	·
Pensions and Other Deferred Comp. 16	0.8	0.2	1.5	0.0	1.2	0.7	0.5	0.3	0.5	0.4	·	·	·
Employee Benefits 17	2.4	5.4	2.6	0.3	1.3	2.0	1.9	2.6	1.7	1.5	·	·	·
Advertising 18	4.8	0.8	1.4	3.0	2.5	1.2	6.2	5.0	5.1	4.0	·	·	·
Other Expenses 19	26.5	49.2	30.2	31.7	30.0	15.9	26.3	27.9	27.9	15.1	·	·	·
Officers' Compensation 20	5.2	8.3	11.3	8.1	7.2	2.8	3.6	1.8	2.2	1.8	·	·	·
Operating Margin 21	8.9	4.1	10.3	22.0	9.8	10.6	3.9	7.0	4.6	9.0	·	·	·
Operating Margin Before Officers' Comp. 22	14.1	12.4	21.5	30.1	17.1	13.4	7.5	8.8	6.8	10.8	·	·	·

Selected Average Balance Sheet ($ in Thousands)

Net Receivables 23	102	0	11	99	542	2016	3676	4392	13057	46189
Inventories 24	9	0	3	27	34	368	224	1448	485	2107
Net Property, Plant and Equipment 25	149	0	19	188	654	1408	4213	8566	18315	30561
Total Assets 26	622	0	81	721	2097	7085	15740	34251	70305	143731
Notes and Loans Payable 27	100	0	30	196	264	1829	3262	7087	15567	11890
All Other Liabilities 28	198	0	22	218	1333	2800	5865	9887	21348	66206
Net Worth 29	324	0	29	306	499	2455	6612	17276	33391	65635

Selected Financial Ratios (Times to 1)

Current Ratio 30	1.4	•	1.8	2.0	1.0	1.3	1.3	1.5	1.7	1.6
Quick Ratio 31	1.2	•	1.5	1.9	1.0	1.0	1.0	1.1	1.4	1.4
Net Sales to Working Capital 32	11.1	•	17.5	8.4	88.1	15.1	11.6	9.0	4.6	7.1
Coverage Ratio 33	19.9	20.4	23.9	35.0	40.5	49.5	15.6	15.3	8.2	15.5
Total Asset Turnover 34	1.7	•	4.0	2.6	2.4	2.0	1.5	1.6	1.0	1.6
Inventory Turnover 35	16.5	•	12.1	15.3	8.6	14.5	21.8	7.2	18.9	46.0
Receivables Turnover 36	10.3	•	44.5	28.8	8.2	8.7	7.2	12.0	4.6	•
Total Liabilities to Net Worth 37	0.9	•	1.8	1.4	3.2	1.9	1.4	1.0	1.1	1.2
Current Assets to Working Capital 38	3.2	•	2.3	2.0	23.4	4.6	4.0	2.8	2.4	2.7
Current Liabilities to Working Capital 39	2.2	•	1.3	1.0	22.4	3.6	3.0	1.8	1.4	1.7
Working Capital to Net Sales 40	0.1	•	0.1	0.1	0.0	0.1	0.1	0.1	0.2	0.1
Inventory to Working Capital 41	0.1	•	0.1	0.1	0.4	0.6	0.1	0.3	0.0	0.1
Total Receipts to Cash Flow 42	3.2	2.3	2.9	2.0	2.9	4.3	3.7	3.7	3.4	4.6
Cost of Goods to Cash Flow 43	0.5	0.3	0.3	0.5	0.2	1.6	0.7	0.7	0.4	2.0
Cash Flow to Total Debt 44	1.1	•	2.2	2.2	1.1	0.7	0.7	0.9	0.6	0.6

Selected Financial Factors (in Percentages)

Debt Ratio 45	47.9	•	64.3	57.5	76.2	65.3	58.0	49.6	52.5	54.3
Return on Total Assets 46	21.1	•	49.8	64.2	30.6	26.2	13.0	15.9	9.0	17.3
Return on Equity Before Income Taxes 47	38.4	•	133.9	146.8	125.3	74.0	28.9	29.5	16.6	35.4
Return on Equity After Income Taxes 48	32.6	•	131.6	146.4	122.2	67.8	26.5	25.0	14.4	25.9
Profit Margin (Before Income Tax) 49	11.9	19.9	12.0	24.0	12.4	12.7	7.9	9.1	8.1	10.4
Profit Margin (After Income Tax) 50	10.1	16.5	11.8	23.9	12.1	11.6	7.3	7.7	7.0	7.6

OFFICES OF PHYSICIANS

Table I

Corporations with and without Net Income

MONEY AMOUNTS AND SIZE OF ASSETS IN THOUSANDS OF DOLLARS

Item Description for Accounting Period 7/04 Through 6/05	Total	Zero Assets	Under 500	500 to 1,000	1,000 to 5,000	5,000 to 10,000	10,000 to 25,000	25,000 to 50,000	50,000 to 100,000	100,000 to 250,000	250,000 to 500,000	500,000 to 2,500,000	2,500,000 and over
Number of Enterprises **1**	142141	13906	121859	4152	1874	153	125	43	16	8	4	0	0
Revenues ($ in Thousands)													
Net Sales **2**	199672363	6104174	119203077	21324633	28679083	5653228	5875033	3986063	1845041	1092141	5909891	0	0
Interest **3**	98090	5408	29095	7602	13558	3447	8629	3156	3505	3130	20559	0	0
Rents **4**	108753	75	54463	3611	19274	874	8545	13371	6767	1032	741	0	0
Royalties **5**	12148	0	2820	0	0	0	483	0	0	8845	0	0	0
Other Portfolio Income **6**	250385	40347	63505	1787	105724	288	5278	2847	12836	812	16961	0	0
Other Receipts **7**	4480320	81958	3002158	251010	418369	82987	245060	73015	70140	16835	238787	0	0
Total Receipts **8**	204622059	6231962	122355118	21588643	29236008	5740824	6143028	4078452	1938289	1122795	6186939	0	0
Average Total Receipts **9**	1440	448	1004	5200	15601	37522	49144	94848	121143	140349	1546735	·	·
Operating Costs/Operating Income (%)													
Cost of Operations **10**	3.6	3.0	2.2	6.4	3.1	10.9	9.7	14.8	15.1	9.0	1.1	·	·
Salaries and Wages **11**	26.8	19.4	24.0	24.6	30.1	35.4	40.6	39.9	33.3	35.9	47.9	·	·
Taxes Paid **12**	3.0	3.1	3.1	3.4	2.5	2.1	2.8	2.5	2.5	3.2	4.1	·	·
Interest Paid **13**	0.3	0.2	0.2	0.4	0.2	0.5	0.5	0.5	0.6	1.3	0.3	·	·
Depreciation **14**	1.3	0.7	1.1	1.5	1.9	2.3	1.6	2.4	1.8	2.6	0.3	·	·
Amortization and Depletion **15**	0.1	0.1	0.0	0.1	0.1	0.1	0.2	0.2	0.2	1.5	0.4	·	·
Pensions and Other Deferred Comp. **16**	3.7	3.9	4.0	3.6	2.9	2.3	2.4	2.1	1.3	2.1	6.6	·	·
Employee Benefits **17**	2.0	1.1	1.8	2.1	1.8	1.2	3.4	3.1	4.0	2.6	5.3	·	·
Advertising **18**	0.6	0.1	0.7	0.3	0.6	0.4	0.3	0.2	0.2	2.3	0.1	·	·
Other Expenses **19**	31.9	33.3	30.8	23.0	38.2	34.7	39.4	32.5	45.2	38.8	36.9	·	·
Officers' Compensation **20**	25.1	35.9	29.5	31.6	17.6	11.1	2.8	2.1	0.6	1.2	0.5	·	·
Operating Margin **21**	1.6	·	2.4	3.1	1.0	·	·	·	·	·	·	·	·
Operating Margin Before Officers' Comp. **22**	26.7	35.1	32.0	34.7	18.6	10.2	1.7	·	·	·	·	·	·

Selected Average Balance Sheet ($ in Thousands)

Net Receivables 23	21	0	2	38	377	2008	3417	10113	12427	23423	76127
Inventories 24	1	0	0	1	10	44	189	304	462	623	1129
Net Property, Plant and Equipment 25	52	0	25	239	704	2751	3832	10906	23774	22820	13069
Total Assets 26	184	0	82	687	2192	6911	14920	33571	65396	121995	683958
Notes and Loans Payable 27	85	0	48	345	1069	4106	6422	9434	18885	21726	107914
All Other Liabilities 28	73	0	28	282	730	2227	7406	18738	31933	56985	351024
Net Worth 29	26	0	6	59	394	578	1092	5399	14578	43284	225020

Selected Financial Ratios (Times to 1)

Current Ratio 30	1.0	•	1.0	1.2	1.1	1.0	0.9	1.1	2.2	0.9	•
Quick Ratio 31	0.9	•	0.9	1.1	1.0	0.8	0.7	0.9	2.0	0.7	•
Net Sales to Working Capital 32	510.6	•	951.6	100.7	194.5	•	•	38.7	5.1	•	•
Coverage Ratio 33	16.0	7.0	24.1	13.9	2.2	2.5	4.7	1.4	2.9	4.3	•
Total Asset Turnover 34	7.6	•	11.9	7.5	5.3	3.2	2.8	1.8	1.1	2.2	•
Inventory Turnover 35	62.7	•	74.8	45.5	92.3	24.0	45.2	37.8	19.6	13.8	•
Receivables Turnover 36	57.7	•	450.3	124.7	13.9	14.0	10.4	11.0	6.2	•	•
Total Liabilities to Net Worth 37	6.1	•	11.8	10.6	11.0	12.7	5.2	3.5	1.8	•	•
Current Assets to Working Capital 38	30.5	•	37.4	7.4	16.9	•	•	8.4	1.8	•	•
Current Liabilities to Working Capital 39	29.5	•	36.4	6.4	15.9	•	•	7.4	0.8	•	•
Working Capital to Net Sales 40	0.0	•	0.0	0.0	0.0	•	•	0.0	0.2	•	•
Inventory to Working Capital 41	0.3	•	0.3	0.1	0.0	•	•	0.2	0.0	•	•
Total Receipts to Cash Flow 42	3.2	3.6	3.2	2.8	3.2	2.9	3.3	2.4	2.8	3.0	•
Cost of Goods to Cash Flow 43	0.1	0.1	0.1	0.3	0.4	0.3	0.5	0.4	0.3	0.0	•
Cash Flow to Total Debt 44	2.8	•	4.0	1.8	1.8	1.2	1.0	0.9	0.6	1.1	•

Selected Financial Factors (in Percentages)

Debt Ratio 45	85.8	•	92.2	91.4	82.0	91.6	92.7	83.9	77.7	64.5	67.1
Return on Total Assets 46	33.2	•	63.0	35.0	22.1	5.7	4.2	6.5	1.4	4.1	2.5
Return on Equity Before Income Taxes 47	219.5	•	776.1	371.0	114.4	37.8	34.7	31.6	1.7	7.6	5.9
Return on Equity After Income Taxes 48	214.6	•	767.0	365.3	112.8	31.5	27.2	20.4	1.7	6.2	2.7
Profit Margin (Before Income Tax) 49	4.1	1.2	5.1	4.3	2.9	0.6	0.8	1.8	0.2	2.4	0.9
Profit Margin (After Income Tax) 50	4.0	1.1	5.0	4.2	2.9	0.5	0.6	1.2	•	2.0	0.4

Table II

Corporations with Net Income

OFFICES OF PHYSICIANS

MONEY AMOUNTS AND SIZE OF ASSETS IN THOUSANDS OF DOLLARS

Item Description for Accounting Period 7/04 Through 6/05	Total	Zero Assets	Under 500	500 to 1,000	1,000 to 5,000	5,000 to 10,000	10,000 to 25,000	25,000 to 50,000	50,000 to 100,000	100,000 to 250,000	250,000 to 500,000	500,000 to 2,500,000	2,500,000 and over
Number of Enterprises **1**	85427	5800	74948	3255	1237	77	65	29	0	0	0	0	0
Revenues ($ in Thousands)													
Net Sales **2**	120348362	4833173	71099614	14346067	17699779	3733689	3405839	3021718	0	0	0	0	0
Interest **3**	59590	3998	19616	4966	6862	2802	5081	2911	0	0	0	0	0
Rents **4**	44944	75	9367	1209	18188	0	4504	8133	0	0	0	0	0
Royalties **5**	3303	0	2820	0	0	0	483	0	0	0	0	0	0
Other Portfolio Income **6**	194079	33881	37016	1370	105580	188	3746	519	0	0	0	0	0
Other Receipts **7**	2605476	6886	1577849	230981	265497	61953	176246	44726	0	0	0	0	0
Total Receipts **8**	123255754	4878013	72746282	14584593	18095906	3798632	3595899	3077007	0	0	0	0	0
Average Total Receipts **9**	1443	841	971	4481	14629	49333	55322	106138	•	•	•	•	•
Operating Costs/Operating Income (%)													
Cost of Operations **10**	3.6	3.3	1.6	9.2	2.7	0.6	12.6	17.7	•	•	•	•	•
Salaries and Wages **11**	23.1	21.1	21.1	21.9	22.3	38.9	38.6	35.6	•	•	•	•	•
Taxes Paid **12**	2.8	3.0	2.9	3.1	2.4	2.2	2.8	2.5	•	•	•	•	•
Interest Paid **13**	0.3	0.2	0.2	0.3	0.2	0.4	0.5	0.4	•	•	•	•	•
Depreciation **14**	1.2	0.7	1.0	1.4	1.8	1.6	1.6	1.7	•	•	•	•	•
Amortization and Depletion **15**	0.1	0.1	0.0	0.1	0.0	0.1	0.1	0.2	•	•	•	•	•
Pensions and Other Deferred Comp. **16**	3.3	4.4	3.5	3.4	2.6	2.3	1.8	2.3	•	•	•	•	•
Employee Benefits **17**	1.6	1.1	1.6	1.7	1.6	0.7	3.0	2.5	•	•	•	•	•
Advertising **18**	0.6	0.1	0.8	0.2	0.3	0.5	0.3	0.2	•	•	•	•	•
Other Expenses **19**	31.3	26.7	30.7	20.1	40.3	37.8	37.1	33.3	•	•	•	•	•
Officers' Compensation **20**	26.2	36.1	28.7	33.0	21.9	13.6	3.0	2.3	•	•	•	•	•
Operating Margin **21**	5.9	3.3	7.8	5.6	3.8	1.2	•	1.4	•	•	•	•	•
Operating Margin Before Officers' Comp. **22**	32.1	39.5	36.5	38.7	25.7	14.8	1.4	3.7	•	•	•	•	•

Selected Average Balance Sheet ($ in Thousands)

Net Receivables 23	17	0	3	29	267	420	2966	10286
Inventories 24	1	0	0	1	11	70	255	281
Net Property, Plant and Equipment 25	52	0	24	203	662	3306	4265	9051
Total Assets 26	191	0	91	690	2258	6836	14835	34134
Notes and Loans Payable 27	73	0	38	288	753	3710	5713	7440
All Other Liabilities 28	52	0	25	177	582	2018	5879	16745
Net Worth 29	66	0	28	225	924	1108	3243	9949

Selected Financial Ratios (Times to 1)

Current Ratio 30	1.3	•	1.3	1.5	1.6	0.8	1.0	1.1
Quick Ratio 31	1.2	•	1.2	1.4	1.5	0.7	0.8	0.9
Net Sales to Working Capital 32	64.0	•	84.6	39.0	32.7	•	491.1	45.3
Coverage Ratio 33	30.7	20.6	43.2	23.5	29.0	7.5	8.5	9.3
Total Asset Turnover 34	7.4	•	10.4	6.4	6.3	7.1	3.5	3.1
Inventory Turnover 35	57.8	•	49.9	391.3	36.2	4.4	25.9	65.5
Receivables Turnover 36	78.2	•	335.7	181.5	69.5	28.6	15.2	11.8
Total Liabilities to Net Worth 37	1.9	•	2.3	2.1	1.4	5.2	3.6	2.4
Current Assets to Working Capital 38	4.2	•	4.1	3.1	2.7	•	71.5	7.8
Current Liabilities to Working Capital 39	3.2	•	3.1	2.1	1.7	•	70.5	6.8
Working Capital to Net Sales 40	0.0	•	0.0	0.0	0.0	•	0.0	0.0
Inventory to Working Capital 41	0.0	•	0.0	0.0	0.0	•	2.7	0.2
Total Receipts to Cash Flow 42	2.9	3.9	2.8	4.3	2.4	2.6	2.8	3.0
Cost of Goods to Cash Flow 43	0.1	0.1	0.0	0.4	0.1	0.0	0.4	0.5
Cash Flow to Total Debt 44	3.9	•	5.3	2.2	4.4	3.2	1.6	1.5

Selected Financial Factors (in Percentages)

Debt Ratio 45	65.5	•	69.6	67.4	59.1	83.8	78.1	70.9
Return on Total Assets 46	63.3	•	107.2	48.6	39.8	23.7	15.9	11.2
Return on Equity Before Income Taxes 47	177.4	•	343.9	142.8	94.0	127.0	64.3	34.2
Return on Equity After Income Taxes 48	174.1	•	340.5	140.8	92.9	120.4	59.5	25.1
Profit Margin (Before Income Tax) 49	8.3	4.3	10.1	7.3	6.1	2.9	4.0	3.3
Profit Margin (After Income Tax) 50	8.1	4.2	10.0	7.2	6.0	2.8	3.7	2.4

Table I

Corporations with and without Net Income

OFFICES OF DENTISTS

MONEY AMOUNTS AND SIZE OF ASSETS IN THOUSANDS OF DOLLARS

Item Description for Accounting Period 7/04 Through 6/05	Total	Zero Assets	Under 500	500 to 1,000	1,000 to 5,000	5,000 to 10,000	10,000 to 25,000	25,000 to 50,000	50,000 to 100,000	100,000 to 250,000	250,000 to 500,000	500,000 to 2,500,000	2,500,000 and over
Number of Enterprises **1**	67724	5876	58458	3053	324	0	6	4	4	0	0	0	0
Revenues ($ in Thousands)													
Net Sales **2**	49835882	1122174	40329897	4932434	2275568	0	193125	100706	881978	0	0	0	0
Interest **3**	17860	9	16104	1266	151	0	94	223	14	0	0	0	0
Rents **4**	11789	0	11429	0	0	0	0	0	360	0	0	0	0
Royalties **5**	0	0	0	0	0	0	0	0	0	0	0	0	0
Other Portfolio Income **6**	93163	6389	79003	6314	28	0	244	1131	55	0	0	0	0
Other Receipts **7**	617859	35156	540822	25461	1818	0	3647	7049	3905	0	0	0	0
Total Receipts **8**	50576553	1163728	40977255	4965475	2277565	0	197110	109109	886312	0	0	0	0
Average Total Receipts **9**	747	198	701	1626	7030	•	32852	27277	221578	•	•	•	•
Operating Costs/Operating Income (%)													
Cost of Operations **10**	5.7	2.6	5.7	5.2	4.5	•	11.9	18.6	16.1	•	•	•	•
Salaries and Wages **11**	23.1	23.9	21.7	25.9	33.0	•	41.7	24.5	38.3	•	•	•	•
Taxes Paid **12**	3.7	3.9	3.7	3.8	3.4	•	4.2	3.8	3.4	•	•	•	•
Interest Paid **13**	0.9	0.5	0.8	1.9	0.4	•	0.7	7.3	1.1	•	•	•	•
Depreciation **14**	2.0	1.9	2.1	2.5	0.8	•	2.4	5.7	2.1	•	•	•	•
Amortization and Depletion **15**	0.4	0.5	0.3	0.8	0.1	•	0.5	3.1	1.9	•	•	•	•
Pensions and Other Deferred Comp. **16**	2.2	1.5	2.3	2.2	0.9	•	3.3	0.2	0.0	•	•	•	•
Employee Benefits **17**	1.1	0.1	1.2	0.7	1.0	•	2.9	1.3	1.8	•	•	•	•
Advertising **18**	1.3	0.9	1.3	1.3	2.2	•	1.2	2.1	1.9	•	•	•	•
Other Expenses **19**	33.5	50.5	34.0	25.1	36.3	•	22.3	40.4	30.6	•	•	•	•
Officers' Compensation **20**	20.0	13.5	21.3	20.7	8.7	•	1.8	2.1	0.1	•	•	•	•
Operating Margin **21**	6.0	0.3	5.7	10.0	8.8	•	7.2	•	2.9	•	•	•	•
Operating Margin Before Officers' Comp. **22**	26.0	13.8	27.0	30.7	17.5	•	9.0	•	3.0	•	•	•	•

Selected Average Balance Sheet ($ in Thousands)

Net Receivables 23	6	0	3	18	171	•	4231	6496	26896
Inventories 24	1	0	1	0	3	•	77	584	2030
Net Property, Plant and Equipment 25	60	0	52	248	538	•	2639	5754	21564
Total Assets 26	155	0	126	642	1500	•	15310	38471	112341
Notes and Loans Payable 27	103	0	87	477	459	•	2597	22949	41326
All Other Liabilities 28	25	0	21	50	389	•	4661	6363	29443
Net Worth 29	27	0	18	115	653	•	8052	9158	41572

Selected Financial Ratios (Times to 1)

Current Ratio 30	1.3	•	1.2	1.2	1.8	•	1.4	1.0	1.5
Quick Ratio 31	1.2	•	1.1	1.1	1.7	•	1.2	0.9	1.2
Net Sales to Working Capital 32	71.4	•	88.4	81.5	18.4	•	17.4	308.9	19.1
Coverage Ratio 33	9.3	9.8	10.0	6.5	24.7	•	14.7	0.9	4.2
Total Asset Turnover 34	4.7	•	5.5	2.5	4.7	•	2.1	0.7	2.0
Inventory Turnover 35	45.2	•	45.7	288.2	96.8	•	49.6	8.0	17.5
Receivables Turnover 36	123.5	•	246.5	124.3	64.8	•	6.3	1.8	•
Total Liabilities to Net Worth 37	4.7	•	6.1	4.6	1.3	•	0.9	3.2	1.7
Current Assets to Working Capital 38	4.5	•	5.0	6.4	2.2	•	3.7	101.4	3.0
Current Liabilities to Working Capital 39	3.5	•	4.0	5.4	1.2	•	2.7	100.4	2.0
Working Capital to Net Sales 40	0.0	•	0.0	0.0	0.1	•	0.1	0.0	0.1
Inventory to Working Capital 41	0.1	•	0.1	0.0	0.0	•	0.0	4.0	0.2
Total Receipts to Cash Flow 42	2.9	2.4	2.9	3.3	2.4	•	3.6	3.3	3.6
Cost of Goods to Cash Flow 43	0.2	0.1	0.2	0.2	0.1	•	0.4	0.6	0.6
Cash Flow to Total Debt 44	2.0	•	2.2	0.9	3.5	•	1.2	0.3	0.9

Selected Financial Factors (in Percentages)

Debt Ratio 45	82.4	•	85.9	82.1	56.5	•	47.4	76.2	63.0
Return on Total Assets 46	40.0	•	44.2	31.8	43.6	•	20.8	4.3	8.8
Return on Equity Before Income Taxes 47	202.4	•	281.5	150.5	96.1	•	36.9	•	18.1
Return on Equity After Income Taxes 48	201.0	•	279.5	150.5	95.9	•	35.5	•	17.3
Profit Margin (Before Income Tax) 49	7.5	4.0	7.3	10.7	8.9	•	9.2	•	3.4
Profit Margin (After Income Tax) 50	7.5	3.9	7.2	10.7	8.9	•	8.9	•	3.3

Table II

Corporations with Net Income

OFFICES OF DENTISTS

MONEY AMOUNTS AND SIZE OF ASSETS IN THOUSANDS OF DOLLARS

Item Description for Accounting Period 7/04 Through 6/05	Total	Zero Assets	Under 500	500 to 1,000	1,000 to 5,000	5,000 to 10,000	10,000 to 25,000	25,000 to 50,000	50,000 to 100,000	100,000 to 250,000	250,000 to 500,000	500,000 to 2,500,000	2,500,000 and over
Number of Enterprises **1**	47470	3680	40954	2532	294	0	6	0	4	0	0	0	0
Revenues ($ in Thousands)													
Net Sales **2**	35556613	990432	27499501	3830160	2154180	0	200362	0	881978	0	0	0	0
Interest **3**	14993	0	13346	1243	151	0	239	0	14	0	0	0	0
Rents **4**	1740	0	1380	0	0	0	0	0	360	0	0	0	0
Royalties **5**	0	0	0	0	0	0	0	0	0	0	0	0	0
Other Portfolio Income **6**	82464	0	74855	6310	28	0	1216	0	55	0	0	0	0
Other Receipts **7**	462065	28923	386583	25258	6738	0	10658	0	3905	0	0	0	0
Total Receipts **8**	36117875	1019355	27795665	3862971	2161097	0	212475	0	886312	0	0	0	0
Average Total Receipts **9**	761	277	683	1526	7351	.	35412	.	221578	.	.	.	.
Operating Costs/Operating Income (%)													
Cost of Operations **10**	5.3	2.9	5.0	6.6	1.7	.	20.8	.	16.1	.	.	.	.
Salaries and Wages **11**	23.3	21.3	21.5	26.2	34.0	.	37.5	.	38.3	.	.	.	.
Taxes Paid **12**	3.7	3.5	3.7	3.9	3.3	.	4.3	.	3.4	.	.	.	.
Interest Paid **13**	0.9	0.2	0.9	1.7	0.3	.	2.4	.	1.1	.	.	.	.
Depreciation **14**	1.7	0.7	1.8	1.7	0.8	.	2.9	.	2.1	.	.	.	.
Amortization and Depletion **15**	0.4	0.3	0.3	0.7	0.1	.	0.8	.	1.9	.	.	.	.
Pensions and Other Deferred Comp. **16**	1.8	1.7	1.9	1.9	0.9	.	2.9	.	0.0	.	.	.	.
Employee Benefits **17**	1.0	.	1.1	0.8	0.9	.	2.5	.	1.8	.	.	.	.
Advertising **18**	1.4	0.6	1.3	1.3	2.3	.	1.2	.	1.9	.	.	.	.
Other Expenses **19**	32.0	44.9	32.3	24.1	37.2	.	18.2	.	30.6	.	.	.	.
Officers' Compensation **20**	18.3	12.6	20.1	17.2	9.1	.	2.1	.	0.1	.	.	.	.
Operating Margin **21**	10.2	11.3	10.1	13.7	9.3	.	4.4	.	2.9	.	.	.	.
Operating Margin Before Officers' Comp. **22**	28.5	23.9	30.1	30.9	18.5	.	6.5	.	3.0	.	.	.	.

Selected Average Balance Sheet ($ in Thousands)

Net Receivables 23	8	0	15	188	•	4655	26896
Inventories 24	1	0	0	4	•	77	2030
Net Property, Plant and Equipment 25	60	0	224	545	•	2965	21564
Total Assets 26	168	131	630	1535	•	23809	112341
Notes and Loans Payable 27	97	79	416	387	•	8281	41326
All Other Liabilities 28	26	20	54	417	•	5320	29443
Net Worth 29	46	32	161	731	•	10209	41572

Selected Financial Ratios (Times to 1)

Current Ratio 30	1.4	1.4	1.1	2.2	•	1.1	1.5
Quick Ratio 31	1.3	1.3	1.1	2.0	•	0.9	1.2
Net Sales to Working Capital 32	45.7	50.7	93.0	14.9	•	54.1	19.1
Coverage Ratio 33	13.4	14.0	9.4	33.5	74.8	5.4	4.2
Total Asset Turnover 34	4.4	5.1	2.4	4.8	•	1.4	2.0
Inventory Turnover 35	41.2	37.0	286.1	34.0	•	90.0	17.5
Receivables Turnover 36	111.1	204.1	126.0	61.3	•	8.4	
Total Liabilities to Net Worth 37	2.7	3.1	2.9	1.1	•	1.3	1.7
Current Assets to Working Capital 38	3.4	3.4	8.5	1.8	•	11.7	3.0
Current Liabilities to Working Capital 39	2.4	2.4	7.5	0.8	•	10.7	2.0
Working Capital to Net Sales 40	0.0	0.0	0.0	0.1	•	0.0	0.1
Inventory to Working Capital 41	0.1	0.1	0.0	0.0	•	0.1	0.2
Total Receipts to Cash Flow 42	2.7	2.7	3.0	2.3	2.1	4.0	3.6
Cost of Goods to Cash Flow 43	0.1	0.1	0.2	0.0	0.1	0.8	0.6
Cash Flow to Total Debt 44	2.3	2.6	1.1	4.0	•	0.6	0.9

Selected Financial Factors (in Percentages)

Debt Ratio 45	73.0	75.5	74.5	52.4	•	57.1	63.0
Return on Total Assets 46	56.8	65.2	39.0	47.4	•	18.0	8.8
Return on Equity Before Income Taxes 47	194.3	247.3	136.6	96.6	•	34.1	18.1
Return on Equity After Income Taxes 48	193.1	245.7	136.6	96.4	•	31.5	17.3
Profit Margin (Before Income Tax) 49	11.8	11.8	14.5	9.6	14.2	10.4	3.4
Profit Margin (After Income Tax) 50	11.7	11.7	14.5	9.6	14.0	9.6	3.3

Table I

Corporations with and without Net Income

OFFICES OF OTHER HEALTH PRACTITIONERS

MONEY AMOUNTS AND SIZE OF ASSETS IN THOUSANDS OF DOLLARS

Item Description for Accounting Period 7/04 Through 6/05	Total	Zero Assets	Under 500	500 to 1,000	1,000 to 5,000	5,000 to 10,000	10,000 to 25,000	25,000 to 50,000	50,000 to 100,000	100,000 to 250,000	250,000 to 500,000	500,000 to 2,500,000	2,500,000 and over
Number of Enterprises 1	87323	10938	74732	794	689	83	44	19	11	11	0	0	0
Revenues ($ in Thousands)													
Net Sales 2	43384377	1764648	24921790	896919	4463689	3366871	1337028	1540368	725569	4847495	0	0	0
Interest 3	62648	124	3361	527	883	4313	2533	4417	6419	40071	0	0	0
Rents 4	15520	174	1991	106	1056	210	2695	1683	2108	5498	0	0	0
Royalties 5	42	42	0	0	0	0	0	0	0	0	0	0	0
Other Portfolio Income 6	46553	9177	3986	635	4618	2545	4747	12040	974	7831	0	0	0
Other Receipts 7	1015953	111462	165550	33351	29614	18200	137108	290159	92254	138255	0	0	0
Total Receipts 8	45005093	1885627	25096678	931538	4499860	3392139	1484111	1848867	827324	5039150	0	0	0
Average Total Receipts 9	515	172	336	1173	6531	40869	33730	97298	75211	458105	·	·	·
Operating Costs/Operating Income (%)													
Cost of Operations 10	14.0	11.1	10.8	8.9	6.2	66.9	17.0	7.9	9.4	5.0	·	·	·
Salaries and Wages 11	22.4	21.2	20.3	29.7	32.0	12.1	23.3	18.5	28.7	30.3	·	·	·
Taxes Paid 12	2.9	5.0	3.3	5.3	2.6	1.8	2.1	1.9	2.3	1.5	·	·	·
Interest Paid 13	0.7	1.7	0.4	1.8	0.6	0.1	0.6	1.5	1.2	1.9	·	·	·
Depreciation 14	1.5	1.9	1.5	2.8	2.3	0.7	1.3	1.1	3.3	1.0	·	·	·
Amortization and Depletion 15	0.2	0.2	0.1	0.8	0.1	0.0	0.2	0.3	1.0	0.7	·	·	·
Pensions and Other Deferred Comp. 16	1.1	1.5	1.4	0.5	1.1	0.2	1.1	0.8	0.1	0.1	·	·	·
Employee Benefits 17	2.2	2.1	1.0	0.9	2.1	0.8	16.8	7.1	3.9	3.5	·	·	·
Advertising 18	1.4	1.4	1.7	6.0	1.1	0.5	0.3	0.5	0.4	0.4	·	·	·
Other Expenses 19	39.6	39.2	35.0	35.2	48.3	13.1	44.8	80.3	56.4	57.7	·	·	·
Officers' Compensation 20	9.6	9.5	14.8	9.1	3.9	1.0	1.5	0.6	0.9	0.3	·	·	·
Operating Margin 21	4.4	5.2	9.5	·	·	2.7	·	·	·	·	·	·	·
Operating Margin Before Officers' Comp. 22	14.0	14.6	24.3	8.2	3.7	3.7	·	·	·	·	·	·	·

Selected Average Balance Sheet ($ in Thousands)

Line Item										
Net Receivables 23	19	0	4	202	300	1162	4207	7882	11662	38004
Inventories 24	2	0	2	28	1	27	212	566	576	830
Net Property, Plant and Equipment 25	29	0	18	84	519	1356	2439	6247	16603	25316
Total Assets 26	124	0	58	574	1593	6705	16375	39270	68679	196241
Notes and Loans Payable 27	49	0	26	376	869	515	3785	9503	17833	74403
All Other Liabilities 28	38	0	11	94	324	3616	5167	16102	21578	98693
Net Worth 29	38	0	21	104	400	2574	7423	13666	29268	23145

Selected Financial Ratios (Times to 1)

Line Item										
Current Ratio 30	1.5	•	1.9	2.9	1.6	1.4	1.1	1.2	1.4	1.2
Quick Ratio 31	1.2	•	1.8	2.3	1.2	0.7	0.9	0.9	1.2	0.9
Net Sales to Working Capital 32	23.0	•	24.2	4.7	22.3	28.2	27.3	22.5	8.8	28.3
Coverage Ratio 33	11.5	8.3	30.2	2.7	2.2	40.6	4.4	0.7	6.2	1.8
Total Asset Turnover 34	4.0	•	5.7	2.0	4.1	6.1	1.9	2.1	1.0	2.2
Inventory Turnover 35	34.9	•	23.3	3.5	350.8	992.8	24.5	11.3	10.7	26.4
Receivables Turnover 36	26.2	•	76.7	5.1	22.5	45.2	6.9	10.6	5.4	11.3
Total Liabilities to Net Worth 37	2.3	•	1.8	4.5	3.0	1.6	1.2	1.9	1.3	7.5
Current Assets to Working Capital 38	2.9	•	2.1	1.5	2.8	3.6	8.8	5.7	3.5	5.8
Current Liabilities to Working Capital 39	1.9	•	1.1	0.5	1.8	2.6	7.8	4.7	2.5	4.8
Working Capital to Net Sales 40	0.0	•	0.0	0.2	0.0	0.0	0.0	0.0	0.1	0.0
Inventory to Working Capital 41	0.1	•	0.1	0.1	0.0	0.0	0.2	0.1	0.1	0.1
Total Receipts to Cash Flow 42	2.5	2.4	2.7	3.4	2.3	7.1	2.3	1.3	1.7	1.7
Cost of Goods to Cash Flow 43	0.3	0.3	0.3	0.3	0.1	4.8	0.4	0.1	0.2	0.1
Cash Flow to Total Debt 44	2.3	•	3.3	0.7	2.4	1.4	1.5	2.5	1.0	1.5

Selected Financial Factors (in Percentages)

Line Item										
Debt Ratio 45	69.7	•	64.4	81.9	74.9	61.6	54.7	65.2	57.4	88.2
Return on Total Assets 46	31.0	•	60.6	9.4	4.9	21.7	4.5	2.1	7.2	7.6
Return on Equity Before Income Taxes 47	93.6	•	164.5	32.5	10.5	55.0	7.6	•	14.2	28.5
Return on Equity After Income Taxes 48	91.0	•	164.0	32.1	8.5	50.9	6.1	•	9.4	15.5
Profit Margin (Before Income Tax) 49	7.0	12.0	10.2	3.0	0.6	3.5	1.9	•	6.3	1.5
Profit Margin (After Income Tax) 50	6.8	12.0	10.2	3.0	0.5	3.2	1.5	•	4.2	0.8

Table II

Corporations with Net Income

OFFICES OF OTHER HEALTH PRACTITIONERS

MONEY AMOUNTS AND SIZE OF ASSETS IN THOUSANDS OF DOLLARS

Item Description for Accounting Period 7/04 Through 6/05	Total	Zero Assets	Under 500	500 to 1,000	1,000 to 5,000	5,000 to 10,000	10,000 to 25,000	25,000 to 50,000	50,000 to 100,000	100,000 to 250,000	250,000 to 500,000	500,000 to 2,500,000	2,500,000 and over
Number of Enterprises 1	60709	6659	53148	466	325	68	22	0	8	0	0	0	0
Revenues ($ in Thousands)													
Net Sales 2	31184653	1151036	19528641	745437	1330634	3090733	831465	0	604241	0	0	0	0
Interest 3	49299	8	2010	362	171	4119	1557	0	5891	0	0	0	0
Rents 4	4264	0	4	106	1056	104	1529	0	1465	0	0	0	0
Royalties 5	0	0	0	0	0	0	0	0	0	0	0	0	0
Other Portfolio Income 6	31466	3901	2064	635	64	2470	3501	0	974	0	0	0	0
Other Receipts 7	738870	67271	111250	23850	7106	13436	77416	0	25183	0	0	0	0
Total Receipts 8	32672552	1222216	19643969	770390	1339031	3110862	915468	0	637754	0	0	0	0
Average Total Receipts 9	538	184	370	1653	4120	45748	41612	•	79719	•	•	•	•
Operating Costs/Operating Income (%)													
Cost of Operations 10	15.5	16.5	8.9	10.7	17.9	72.9	21.8	•	10.8	•	•	•	•
Salaries and Wages 11	20.9	17.5	18.5	31.2	37.8	9.5	23.7	•	20.9	•	•	•	•
Taxes Paid 12	2.8	2.7	3.2	3.9	3.3	1.7	2.4	•	2.3	•	•	•	•
Interest Paid 13	0.6	1.3	0.3	1.1	0.4	0.1	0.5	•	1.1	•	•	•	•
Depreciation 14	1.4	1.7	1.4	2.1	3.3	0.6	1.2	•	3.5	•	•	•	•
Amortization and Depletion 15	0.2	0.1	0.1	0.2	0.1	0.0	0.1	•	1.0	•	•	•	•
Pensions and Other Deferred Comp. 16	1.1	0.7	1.4	0.5	3.3	0.2	1.3	•	0.1	•	•	•	•
Employee Benefits 17	2.0	1.5	1.1	0.9	0.7	0.5	14.0	•	3.2	•	•	•	•
Advertising 18	1.5	2.0	1.8	5.0	2.2	0.5	0.4	•	0.5	•	•	•	•
Other Expenses 19	34.7	26.1	34.5	23.9	17.3	9.4	35.6	•	53.5	•	•	•	•
Officers' Compensation 20	9.9	10.6	14.4	8.2	5.5	0.9	1.5	•	0.7	•	•	•	•
Operating Margin 21	9.3	19.3	14.2	12.4	8.2	3.7	•	•	2.3	•	•	•	•
Operating Margin Before Officers' Comp. 22	19.2	29.9	28.6	20.5	13.7	4.6	•	•	3.0	•	•	•	•

Selected Average Balance Sheet ($ in Thousands)

	1	2	3	4	5	6	7	8	9
Net Receivables 23	18	0	5	228	228	590	4292	•	10125
Inventories 24	2	0	2	26	1	24	198	•	655
Net Property, Plant and Equipment 25	30	0	20	123	465	1438	1753	•	20185
Total Assets 26	125	0	67	554	1472	6864	16112	•	70764
Notes and Loans Payable 27	42	0	24	304	490	450	3040	•	19128
All Other Liabilities 28	35	0	13	63	182	3458	1397	•	18016
Net Worth 29	48	0	30	187	800	2956	11675	•	33620

Selected Financial Ratios (Times to 1)

	1	2	3	4	5	6	7	8	9
Current Ratio 30	1.8	•	2.0	4.5	4.0	1.5	1.3	•	1.5
Quick Ratio 31	1.5	•	1.8	3.5	2.5	0.7	1.1	•	1.4
Net Sales to Working Capital 32	18.1	•	22.0	5.6	6.5	27.0	14.8	•	8.2
Coverage Ratio 33	19.5	20.8	44.4	15.4	23.2	56.2	16.9	•	8.0
Total Asset Turnover 34	4.2	•	5.5	2.9	2.8	6.6	2.3	•	1.1
Inventory Turnover 35	44.3	•	21.4	6.5	530.6	1402.4	41.5	•	12.4
Receivables Turnover 36	30.7	•	83.8	5.2	22.3	•	8.5	•	7.5
Total Liabilities to Net Worth 37	1.6	•	1.2	2.0	0.8	1.3	0.4	•	1.1
Current Assets to Working Capital 38	2.2	•	2.0	1.3	1.3	3.1	4.1	•	2.9
Current Liabilities to Working Capital 39	1.2	•	1.0	0.3	0.3	2.1	3.1	•	1.9
Working Capital to Net Sales 40	0.1	•	0.0	0.2	0.2	0.0	0.1	•	0.1
Inventory to Working Capital 41	0.1	•	0.1	0.2	•	0.0	0.1	•	0.1
Total Receipts to Cash Flow 42	2.5	2.3	2.5	3.0	4.3	8.9	2.4	•	1.7
Cost of Goods to Cash Flow 43	0.4	0.4	0.2	0.3	0.8	6.5	0.5	•	0.2
Cash Flow to Total Debt 44	2.7	•	4.1	1.5	1.4	1.3	3.5	•	1.2

Selected Financial Factors (in Percentages)

	1	2	3	4	5	6	7	8	9
Debt Ratio 45	61.5	•	54.6	66.3	45.7	56.9	27.5	•	52.5
Return on Total Assets 46	52.5	•	83.0	48.5	25.6	29.2	19.1	•	9.5
Return on Equity Before Income Taxes 47	129.3	•	178.9	134.4	45.1	66.5	24.7	•	17.5
Return on Equity After Income Taxes 48	126.5	•	178.3	134.0	43.0	62.2	22.9	•	11.8
Profit Margin (Before Income Tax) 49	11.9	25.5	14.8	15.7	8.8	4.3	7.6	•	7.8
Profit Margin (After Income Tax) 50	11.6	25.5	14.7	15.7	8.4	4.0	7.1	•	5.2

Table I

Corporations with and without Net Income

OUTPATIENT CARE CENTERS

MONEY AMOUNTS AND SIZE OF ASSETS IN THOUSANDS OF DOLLARS

Item Description for Accounting Period 7/04 Through 6/05	Total	Zero Assets	Under 500	500 to 1,000	1,000 to 5,000	5,000 to 10,000	10,000 to 25,000	25,000 to 50,000	50,000 to 100,000	100,000 to 250,000	250,000 to 500,000	500,000 to 2,500,000	2,500,000 and over
Number of Enterprises 1	4892	234	4020	334	184	42	36	12	9	4	7	6	3
Revenues ($ in Thousands)													
Net Sales 2	27812636	12461	2736176	413357	2883941	480705	1380364	1013703	1015352	1129679	2352440	5923347	8471112
Interest 3	114212	745	157	672	1453	2831	5585	1740	7118	521	16310	33290	43792
Rents 4	36643	0	0	0	88	91	952	731	165	0	555	6581	27480
Royalties 5	79604	0	0	0	0	0	0	0	0	0	0	73000	6604
Other Portfolio Income 6	137229	0	7108	8379	31	6986	1587	31	867	0	82217	22442	7580
Other Receipts 7	905830	3356	31416	-791	11770	4381	24024	19968	44767	6104	143691	380519	236624
Total Receipts 8	29086154	16562	2774857	421617	2897283	494994	1412512	1036173	1068269	1136304	2595213	6439179	8793192
Average Total Receipts 9	5946	71	690	1262	15746	11786	39236	86348	118697	284076	370745	1073196	2931064
Operating Costs/Operating Income (%)													
Cost of Operations 10	28.3	4.3	15.2	30.5	11.4	6.1	30.0	34.7	2.9	1.4	42.0	40.6	32.5
Salaries and Wages 11	21.5	3.6	13.7	29.7	43.0	7.0	12.8	19.1	11.7	16.6	28.7	21.3	18.7
Taxes Paid 12	3.1	3.5	2.5	4.0	2.9	1.0	1.5	1.9	1.5	1.3	2.7	4.2	3.7
Interest Paid 13	2.7	0.0	0.9	1.8	0.6	1.0	0.8	0.9	1.4	2.5	1.6	1.8	5.7
Depreciation 14	2.6	0.0	0.9	6.0	1.3	1.2	1.1	1.2	1.2	3.6	2.0	2.8	3.9
Amortization and Depletion 15	1.5	•	0.0	0.5	0.0	0.0	0.3	1.7	0.7	0.6	1.8	1.9	2.6
Pensions and Other Deferred Comp. 16	0.6	•	0.3	0.2	3.3	0.1	0.3	0.1	0.2	0.0	0.1	0.5	0.4
Employee Benefits 17	4.1	43.2	2.3	3.2	3.9	0.5	5.1	2.0	1.9	1.6	1.5	7.5	3.8
Advertising 18	0.4	•	1.0	0.3	0.2	0.2	0.3	0.7	0.9	0.5	1.0	0.1	0.1
Other Expenses 19	33.4	47.8	46.6	27.7	26.2	78.2	47.1	35.5	77.3	67.5	18.5	18.9	31.4
Officers' Compensation 20	1.7	•	7.2	2.5	5.5	0.9	1.0	1.1	1.0	0.3	1.3	0.4	0.3
Operating Margin 21	0.2	•	9.2	•	1.7	3.9	•	1.1	•	3.9	•	•	•
Operating Margin Before Officers' Comp. 22	1.9	•	16.4	•	7.2	4.8	0.6	2.3	0.4	4.2	0.3	•	0.3

Selected Average Balance Sheet ($ in Thousands)

Net Receivables 23	871	0	5	43	944	316	3024	6356	4680	13210	32754	228438	720057
Inventories 24	77	0	2	0	136	12	263	616	565	519	3129	25612	97555
Net Property, Plant and Equipment 25	1015	0	71	324	527	671	4453	5125	8201	52628	24470	115180	1026533
Total Assets 26	5338	0	120	704	2566	6685	16529	30793	65639	191060	284961	1082460	4611845
Notes and Loans Payable 27	918	0	131	289	1420	1850	6216	6667	18137	84922	39126	302547	212435
All Other Liabilities 28	2464	0	35	344	995	3241	5044	15189	20447	54661	69460	494380	2419619
Net Worth 29	1956	0	-46	71	151	1594	5269	9037	27055	51477	176375	285534	1979790

Selected Financial Ratios (Times to 1)

Current Ratio 30	1.5	·	0.3	0.9	1.0	1.0	1.2	1.4	1.0	1.6	2.1	1.5	1.8
Quick Ratio 31	1.2	·	0.3	0.5	0.8	0.7	1.0	1.2	0.6	1.3	1.4	1.3	1.5
Net Sales to Working Capital 32	9.6	·	·	·	438.2	·	28.6	16.7	·	10.1	6.8	6.6	5.1
Coverage Ratio 33	2.9	1906.5	12.4	·	4.5	7.9	3.4	4.9	4.4	2.8	6.5	6.3	1.2
Total Asset Turnover 34	1.1	·	5.7	1.8	6.1	1.7	2.3	2.7	1.7	1.5	1.2	0.9	0.6
Inventory Turnover 35	20.8	·	59.0	·	13.2	59.4	43.8	47.6	5.7	7.8	45.2	15.7	9.4
Receivables Turnover 36	7.6	·	159.4	58.1	12.5	15.7	12.7	12.3	19.6	10.6	10.5	3.4	·
Total Liabilities to Net Worth 37	1.7	·	·	8.9	16.0	3.2	2.1	2.4	1.4	2.7	0.6	2.8	1.3
Current Assets to Working Capital 38	3.1	·	·	·	52.2	·	6.0	3.8	·	2.7	1.9	3.1	2.3
Current Liabilities to Working Capital 39	2.1	·	·	·	51.2	·	5.0	2.8	1.7	0.9	2.1	1.3	·
Working Capital to Net Sales 40	0.1	·	·	·	0.0	·	0.0	0.1	·	0.1	0.1	0.2	0.2
Inventory to Working Capital 41	0.1	·	·	·	3.6	·	0.2	0.1	·	0.0	0.0	0.0	0.2
Total Receipts to Cash Flow 42	3.0	1.3	2.1	·	3.9	1.2	2.1	2.8	1.3	1.5	4.6	4.1	3.9
Cost of Goods to Cash Flow 43	0.9	0.1	0.3	2.4	0.4	0.1	0.6	1.0	0.0	0.0	1.9	1.7	1.3
Cash Flow to Total Debt 44	0.6	·	2.0	0.2	1.7	1.9	1.6	1.4	2.3	1.4	0.7	0.3	0.3

Selected Financial Factors (in Percentages)

Debt Ratio 45	63.4	·	138.2	89.9	94.1	76.2	68.1	70.7	58.8	73.1	38.1	73.6	57.1
Return on Total Assets 46	8.2	·	65.6	·	16.9	13.4	6.3	11.5	10.9	10.5	12.5	10.4	4.0
Return on Equity Before Income Taxes 47	14.5	·	·	·	222.8	49.1	13.9	31.2	20.5	24.9	17.1	33.2	1.2
Return on Equity After Income Taxes 48	10.4	·	·	·	212.5	43.8	9.8	29.0	13.5	24.7	12.6	22.4	·
Profit Margin (Before Income Tax) 49	5.0	30.6	10.6	·	2.1	6.8	1.9	3.3	4.9	4.5	9.0	9.6	0.9
Profit Margin (After Income Tax) 50	3.6	27.9	10.4	·	2.1	6.1	1.3	3.1	3.2	4.5	6.6	6.5	·

Table II

Corporations with Net Income

OUTPATIENT CARE CENTERS

MONEY AMOUNTS AND SIZE OF ASSETS IN THOUSANDS OF DOLLARS

Item Description for Accounting Period 7/04 Through 6/05	Total	Zero Assets	Under 500	500 to 1,000	1,000 to 5,000	5,000 to 10,000	10,000 to 25,000	25,000 to 50,000	50,000 to 100,000	100,000 to 250,000	250,000 to 500,000	500,000 to 2,500,000	2,500,000 and over
Number of Enterprises **1**	3187	3	2713	238	155	29	22	0	0	0	7	6	0
Revenues ($ in Thousands)													
Net Sales **2**	21003917	6709	2302095	219077	2428637	140798	1004888	0	0	0	2352440	10088996	0
Interest **3**	67907	745	156	6	1191	2628	4466	0	0	0	16310	34428	0
Rents **4**	8234	0	0	0	88	91	907	0	0	0	555	6483	0
Royalties **5**	73000	0	0	0	0	0	0	0	0	0	0	73000	0
Other Portfolio Income **6**	128782	0	7108	8379	31	6986	722	0	0	0	82217	22442	0
Other Receipts **7**	685376	3357	30939	326	13872	2911	16218	0	0	0	143691	418399	0
Total Receipts **8**	21967216	10811	2340298	227788	2443819	153414	1027201	0	0	0	2595213	10643748	0
Average Total Receipts **9**	6893	3604	863	957	15767	5290	46691	•	•	•	370745	1773958	•
Operating Costs/Operating Income (%)													
Cost of Operations **10**	33.4	•	13.3	26.2	13.6	20.8	38.9	•	•	•	42.0	46.7	•
Salaries and Wages **11**	18.2	•	9.7	16.0	41.3	22.9	11.3	•	•	•	28.7	14.0	•
Taxes Paid **12**	3.0	0.3	1.8	1.4	2.9	3.4	1.3	•	•	•	2.7	4.0	•
Interest Paid **13**	1.7	0.0	0.3	3.3	0.6	3.1	0.4	•	•	•	1.6	2.5	•
Depreciation **14**	2.2	0.0	0.5	8.0	1.1	3.5	0.8	•	•	•	2.0	3.2	•
Amortization and Depletion **15**	1.3	•	0.0	1.0	0.0	0.1	0.1	•	•	•	1.8	2.0	•
Pensions and Other Deferred Comp. **16**	0.7	•	0.1	0.0	3.9	0.2	0.4	•	•	•	0.1	0.5	•
Employee Benefits **17**	4.4	80.3	2.4	2.6	4.5	1.4	6.6	•	•	•	1.5	6.0	•
Advertising **18**	0.4	•	1.0	0.0	0.2	0.6	0.4	•	•	•	1.0	0.1	•
Other Expenses **19**	28.8	17.0	46.3	29.0	22.8	24.6	37.0	•	•	•	18.5	18.3	•
Officers' Compensation **20**	2.0	•	8.6	0.5	5.9	3.2	0.8	•	•	•	1.3	0.2	•
Operating Margin **21**	4.1	2.3	15.9	12.0	3.3	16.4	2.0	•	•	•	•	2.6	•
Operating Margin Before Officers' Comp. **22**	6.1	2.3	24.5	12.6	9.2	19.6	2.8	•	•	•	•	2.8	•

Selected Average Balance Sheet ($ in Thousands)

Net Receivables 23	832	0	0	736	457	2730	•	32754	354252
Inventories 24	92	0	2	162	0	129	•	1710	39787
Net Property, Plant and Equipment 25	606	0	51	520	704	3329	•	24470	215101
Total Assets 26	5513	0	96	2358	5794	15409	•	284961	2215068
Notes and Loans Payable 27	1002	0	36	1501	2299	5260	•	39126	347647
All Other Liabilities 28	1542	0	38	900	602	5553	•	69460	609145
Net Worth 29	2970	0	23	-43	2894	4596	•	176375	1258276

Selected Financial Ratios (Times to 1)

Current Ratio 30	1.4	•	0.4	0.8	1.0	2.6	1.4	•	2.1	1.4
Quick Ratio 31	1.1	•	0.3	0.3	0.7	1.7	1.2	•	1.4	1.1
Net Sales to Working Capital 32	13.5	•	•	•	•	1.8	17.8	•	6.8	10.2
Coverage Ratio 33	6.3	2129.5	56.9	5.9	7.5	9.2	11.2	•	6.5	4.4
Total Asset Turnover 34	1.2	•	8.8	1.4	6.6	0.8	3.0	•	1.2	0.8
Inventory Turnover 35	24.0	•	48.1	•	13.2	•	137.9	•	82.7	19.7
Receivables Turnover 36	7.8	•	2041.8	24341.9	13.3	•	19.6	•	14.4	4.8
Total Liabilities to Net Worth 37	0.9	•	3.1	4.3	1.0	2.4	•	•	0.6	0.8
Current Assets to Working Capital 38	3.6	•	•	•	1.6	3.5	•	•	1.9	3.8
Current Liabilities to Working Capital 39	2.6	•	•	•	0.6	2.5	•	•	0.9	2.8
Working Capital to Net Sales 40	0.1	•	•	•	0.6	0.1	•	•	0.1	0.1
Inventory to Working Capital 41	0.2	•	•	•	•	0.1	•	•	0.0	0.2
Total Receipts to Cash Flow 42	3.0	1.2	1.8	3.0	2.5	2.6	•	•	4.6	4.5
Cost of Goods to Cash Flow 43	1.0	•	0.2	0.8	0.5	1.0	•	•	1.9	2.1
Cash Flow to Total Debt 44	0.9	•	6.6	0.6	0.7	1.6	•	•	0.7	0.4

Selected Financial Factors (in Percentages)

Debt Ratio 45	46.1	•	75.8	81.2	101.8	50.1	70.2	•	38.1	43.2
Return on Total Assets 46	12.7	•	157.2	26.6	30.1	23.8	13.7	•	12.5	8.5
Return on Equity Before Income Taxes 47	19.8	•	637.7	117.0	•	42.5	41.9	•	17.1	11.6
Return on Equity After Income Taxes 48	15.7	•	627.5	116.8	•	38.3	34.3	•	12.6	7.7
Profit Margin (Before Income Tax) 49	8.9	63.5	17.5	16.0	3.9	25.3	4.2	•	9.0	8.7
Profit Margin (After Income Tax) 50	7.1	58.5	17.3	16.0	3.8	22.8	3.4	•	6.6	5.8

HEALTH CARE AND SOCIAL ASSISTANCE
621515

Table I

Corporations with and without Net Income

MISC. HEALTH CARE AND SOCIAL ASSISTANCE

MONEY AMOUNTS AND SIZE OF ASSETS IN THOUSANDS OF DOLLARS

Item Description for Accounting Period 7/04 Through 6/05	Total	Zero Assets	Under 500	500 to 1,000	1,000 to 5,000	5,000 to 10,000	10,000 to 25,000	25,000 to 50,000	50,000 to 100,000	100,000 to 250,000	250,000 to 500,000	500,000 to 2,500,000	2,500,000 and over
Number of Enterprises 1	49619	4908	39984	2202	2048	204	122	54	38	34	10	14	0
Revenues ($ in Thousands)													
Net Sales 2	71639366	871309	18869939	3945275	10567951	4379193	3578998	3063285	3665072	3842292	4084986	14771065	0
Interest 3	107445	751	2184	223	3639	3205	5849	9596	16893	31610	9600	23896	0
Rents 4	25009	926	6176	446	2681	3214	2041	1830	2777	3885	0	1033	0
Royalties 5	69300	10	974	0	0	39	294	2458	28138	194	36051	1142	0
Other Portfolio Income 6	531887	151883	10369	693	30752	9045	23624	7147	12176	140718	27471	118009	0
Other Receipts 7	1402593	27066	245585	726	179318	246611	76329	37091	72071	129506	19071	369219	0
Total Receipts 8	73775600	1051945	19135227	3947363	10784341	4641307	3687135	3121407	3797127	4148205	4177179	15284364	0
Average Total Receipts 9	1487	214	479	1793	5266	22752	30222	57804	99924	122006	417718	1091740	•
Operating Costs/Operating Income (%)													
Cost of Operations 10	22.6	33.5	13.9	14.7	34.3	44.0	28.0	32.3	18.0	21.5	19.2	19.4	•
Salaries and Wages 11	29.8	25.7	33.1	34.4	26.8	21.2	29.3	30.1	32.2	31.0	35.6	26.8	•
Taxes Paid 12	3.8	5.1	4.3	4.5	3.9	2.4	3.3	4.4	4.2	3.7	3.4	3.1	•
Interest Paid 13	1.8	4.3	0.6	1.1	1.1	1.2	1.2	1.4	2.1	3.7	1.9	3.7	•
Depreciation 14	2.9	0.6	1.5	2.5	1.6	1.4	3.0	2.8	2.9	5.2	1.9	6.0	•
Amortization and Depletion 15	0.9	0.7	0.1	2.0	0.3	0.1	0.4	0.6	1.3	2.0	1.9	2.0	•
Pensions and Other Deferred Comp. 16	0.5	0.1	1.0	0.2	0.4	0.1	0.4	0.9	0.7	0.7	0.5	0.1	•
Employee Benefits 17	2.7	4.6	1.4	1.8	1.9	1.2	3.9	3.1	2.2	2.8	3.2	5.1	•
Advertising 18	0.6	0.8	0.8	0.4	0.5	0.4	0.7	0.5	0.4	0.6	0.4	0.6	•
Other Expenses 19	29.1	42.4	29.9	30.0	23.6	31.4	28.0	26.1	37.3	41.5	33.1	24.8	•
Officers' Compensation 20	5.2	4.1	11.2	7.3	5.5	1.3	2.3	1.5	2.0	1.5	0.6	2.4	•
Operating Margin 21	0.2	•	2.2	1.1	0.2	•	•	•	•	•	•	6.0	•
Operating Margin Before Officers' Comp. 22	5.3	•	13.4	8.4	5.7	1.9	•	•	•	•	•	8.4	•

Selected Average Balance Sheet ($ in Thousands)

Net Receivables 23	138	0	6	96	533	2026	4932	7398	15246	20700	61241	142253	•
Inventories 24	15	0	3	11	45	118	376	586	2117	2162	6525	15286	•
Net Property, Plant and Equipment 25	184	0	32	306	566	1017	3487	7211	12582	29280	45853	217361	•
Total Assets 26	888	0	72	663	1945	6776	16100	34717	69993	166501	343160	1342871	•
Notes and Loans Payable 27	372	0	62	386	866	2440	5755	10346	25807	61008	116792	525312	•
All Other Liabilities 28	225	0	18	137	478	3360	5128	10390	18351	35984	80884	325563	•
Net Worth 29	292	0	-8	140	601	977	5217	13981	25836	69509	145484	491995	•

Selected Financial Ratios (Times to 1)

Current Ratio 30	1.5	•	1.1	1.3	1.7	1.2	1.5	1.4	1.4	2.1	1.7	1.4	•
Quick Ratio 31	1.1	•	0.9	1.1	1.4	1.0	1.3	1.0	1.0	1.5	1.4	0.8	•
Net Sales to Working Capital 32	13.6	•	231.1	45.4	11.2	28.6	9.5	14.2	10.2	3.4	8.1	10.5	•
Coverage Ratio 33	2.7	0.8	6.7	2.0	3.1	2.1	3.3	•	1.1	•	1.3	3.5	•
Total Asset Turnover 34	1.6	•	6.6	2.7	2.7	3.2	1.8	1.6	1.4	0.7	1.2	0.8	•
Inventory Turnover 35	21.5	•	25.8	23.4	39.3	80.2	21.8	31.3	8.2	11.3	12.0	13.4	•
Receivables Turnover 36	9.5	•	85.6	12.3	10.4	11.5	6.6	6.8	6.8	4.9	7.4	5.5	•
Total Liabilities to Net Worth 37	2.0	•	•	3.7	2.2	5.9	2.1	1.5	1.7	1.4	1.4	1.7	•
Current Assets to Working Capital 38	3.1	•	15.2	4.8	2.5	5.6	2.8	3.8	3.6	1.9	2.4	3.4	•
Current Liabilities to Working Capital 39	2.1	•	14.2	3.8	1.5	4.6	1.8	2.8	2.6	0.9	1.4	2.4	•
Working Capital to Net Sales 40	0.1	•	0.0	0.0	0.1	0.0	0.1	0.1	0.1	0.3	0.1	0.1	•
Inventory to Working Capital 41	0.1	•	1.1	0.1	0.1	0.2	0.1	0.1	0.3	0.1	0.1	0.1	•
Total Receipts to Cash Flow 42	3.8	5.4	3.9	3.8	4.6	3.4	3.9	5.0	3.3	3.9	3.3	3.4	•
Cost of Goods to Cash Flow 43	0.9	1.8	0.6	0.6	1.6	1.5	1.1	1.6	0.6	0.8	0.6	0.7	•
Cash Flow to Total Debt 44	0.6	•	1.5	0.9	0.8	1.1	0.7	0.6	0.7	0.3	0.6	0.4	•

Selected Financial Factors (in Percentages)

Debt Ratio 45	67.1	•	111.5	78.9	69.1	85.6	67.6	59.7	63.1	58.3	57.6	63.4	•
Return on Total Assets 46	7.9	•	27.8	6.2	8.9	7.6	7.1	•	3.2	•	3.0	10.1	•
Return on Equity Before Income Taxes 47	15.2	•	•	14.8	19.6	27.1	15.4	•	0.9	•	1.8	19.6	•
Return on Equity After Income Taxes 48	10.4	•	•	13.8	17.4	22.9	11.9	•	•	•	•	12.6	•
Profit Margin (Before Income Tax) 49	3.1	•	3.6	1.2	2.3	1.2	2.7	•	0.2	•	0.7	9.2	•
Profit Margin (After Income Tax) 50	2.1	•	3.5	1.1	2.0	1.0	2.1	•	•	•	•	5.9	•

Table II

Corporations with Net Income

MISC. HEALTH CARE AND SOCIAL ASSISTANCE

MONEY AMOUNTS AND SIZE OF ASSETS IN THOUSANDS OF DOLLARS

Item Description for Accounting Period 7/04 Through 6/05	Total	Zero Assets	Under 500	500 to 1,000	1,000 to 5,000	5,000 to 10,000	10,000 to 25,000	25,000 to 50,000	50,000 to 100,000	100,000 to 250,000	250,000 to 500,000	500,000 to 2,500,000	2,500,000 and over
Number of Enterprises 1	26275	2996	20654	1115	1241	107	83	31	19	14	7	7	0
Revenues ($ in Thousands)													
Net Sales 2	50331887	624683	13490624	2466013	7790306	1422176	2668063	2248359	1998754	2221243	3270674	12130993	0
Interest 3	40578	634	1708	17	1230	1141	3663	5982	5095	9378	4260	7470	0
Rents 4	22118	0	6176	266	2596	2891	1946	1830	2777	2747	0	890	0
Royalties 5	40050	10	974	0	0	39	225	1242	27772	0	9317	469	0
Other Portfolio Income 6	479642	149973	10353	20	30265	4693	21279	5873	7557	138210	1935	109484	0
Other Receipts 7	927879	24025	203159	-2167	174223	235873	61891	28113	48742	11728	1882	140409	0
Total Receipts 8	51842154	799325	13712994	2464149	7998620	1666813	2757067	2291399	2090697	2383306	3288068	12389715	0
Average Total Receipts 9	1973	267	664	2210	6445	15578	33218	73916	110037	170236	469724	1769959	•
Operating Costs/Operating Income (%)													
Cost of Operations 10	22.7	28.9	13.2	17.1	43.2	29.8	29.6	31.5	17.7	17.5	16.1	20.3	•
Salaries and Wages 11	27.8	25.6	31.3	26.0	19.5	34.0	27.7	29.7	35.0	29.7	35.6	25.2	•
Taxes Paid 12	3.6	5.1	4.1	3.8	3.4	3.7	3.4	4.1	5.2	3.6	3.5	2.8	•
Interest Paid 13	1.2	5.3	0.4	0.7	0.6	0.3	1.0	1.0	1.2	1.2	1.1	2.4	•
Depreciation 14	2.5	0.5	1.2	1.7	1.2	3.3	2.8	2.1	3.0	3.0	1.7	4.8	•
Amortization and Depletion 15	0.7	0.7	0.1	0.1	0.2	0.1	0.3	0.4	1.2	1.1	1.3	1.6	•
Pensions and Other Deferred Comp. 16	0.7	0.1	1.4	0.2	0.4	0.4	0.4	1.0	0.8	1.0	0.6	0.1	•
Employee Benefits 17	3.1	4.8	1.4	2.1	1.7	2.7	4.1	2.9	2.5	2.7	3.0	5.9	•
Advertising 18	0.6	0.6	0.8	0.2	0.5	0.6	0.4	0.4	0.5	0.4	0.2	0.6	•
Other Expenses 19	25.9	35.3	26.3	31.8	20.9	27.3	24.0	23.5	30.1	35.2	32.7	23.4	•
Officers' Compensation 20	5.3	3.2	12.4	8.6	3.6	3.0	2.1	1.1	1.3	0.9	0.8	2.4	•
Operating Margin 21	6.1	•	7.2	7.7	4.9	•	4.0	2.3	1.8	3.6	3.5	10.4	•
Operating Margin Before Officers' Comp. 22	11.4	•	19.7	16.3	8.4	•	6.1	3.4	3.1	4.5	4.2	12.8	•

Selected Average Balance Sheet ($ in Thousands)

Net Receivables 23	169	0	10	126	434	1734	4958	8597	17170	23702	63158	227390	•
Inventories 24	19	0	3	15	59	187	368	587	1571	2188	5116	25504	•
Net Property, Plant and Equipment 25	188	0	35	309	447	1399	3549	7273	16647	23768	48085	235605	•
Total Assets 26	1043	0	89	699	1827	6438	15652	34496	71390	161783	355061	1908982	•
Notes and Loans Payable 27	349	0	50	245	571	1032	5542	9233	16974	36466	113680	668104	•
All Other Liabilities 28	238	0	12	185	539	1902	4768	9476	18660	35671	70579	413742	•
Net Worth 29	456	0	28	269	717	3505	5342	15786	35756	89646	170802	827135	•

Selected Financial Ratios (Times to 1)

Current Ratio 30	1.6	•	1.7	1.6	1.8	2.0	1.5	1.5	1.3	1.8	2.1	1.3	•
Quick Ratio 31	1.2	•	1.6	1.4	1.4	1.7	1.3	1.2	1.0	1.5	1.8	0.8	•
Net Sales to Working Capital 32	13.6	•	33.6	21.7	11.5	6.7	11.2	14.0	12.8	5.6	6.9	14.1	•
Coverage Ratio 33	8.7	4.4	21.1	11.9	13.9	39.3	8.2	5.2	6.6	9.7	4.5	6.1	•
Total Asset Turnover 34	1.8	•	7.3	3.2	3.4	2.1	2.1	2.1	1.5	1.0	1.3	0.9	•
Inventory Turnover 35	22.7	•	25.5	26.0	46.4	21.2	25.9	38.9	11.8	12.7	14.7	13.8	•
Receivables Turnover 36	9.5	•	82.6	12.8	12.6	7.8	7.4	7.9	7.2	5.4	7.4	5.1	•
Total Liabilities to Net Worth 37	1.3	•	2.2	1.6	1.5	0.8	1.9	1.2	1.0	0.8	1.1	1.3	•
Current Assets to Working Capital 38	2.8	•	2.4	2.6	2.2	2.0	2.9	3.0	4.0	2.2	1.9	4.1	•
Current Liabilities to Working Capital 39	1.8	•	1.4	1.6	1.2	1.0	1.9	2.0	3.0	1.2	0.9	3.1	•
Working Capital to Net Sales 40	0.1	•	0.0	0.0	0.1	0.1	0.1	0.1	0.1	0.2	0.1	0.1	•
Inventory to Working Capital 41	0.1	•	0.1	0.0	0.1	0.1	0.1	0.1	0.3	0.1	0.0	0.2	•
Total Receipts to Cash Flow 42	3.4	3.8	3.5	2.8	4.1	2.9	3.8	4.2	3.5	2.7	2.9	3.2	•
Cost of Goods to Cash Flow 43	0.8	1.1	0.5	0.5	1.8	0.9	1.1	1.3	0.6	0.5	0.5	0.6	•
Cash Flow to Total Debt 44	1.0	•	3.1	1.8	1.4	1.5	0.8	0.9	0.9	0.8	0.9	0.5	•

Selected Financial Factors (in Percentages)

Debt Ratio 45	56.3	•	69.1	61.5	60.8	45.6	65.9	54.2	49.9	44.6	51.9	56.7	•
Return on Total Assets 46	18.6	•	68.2	26.2	27.9	25.7	17.2	10.9	11.1	11.8	6.7	13.2	•
Return on Equity Before Income Taxes 47	37.7	•	210.3	62.5	66.0	45.9	44.3	19.3	18.9	19.0	10.9	25.5	•
Return on Equity After Income Taxes 48	31.9	•	206.7	61.5	63.1	43.9	39.4	16.7	14.9	15.1	7.6	17.2	•
Profit Margin (Before Income Tax) 49	9.0	17.8	8.9	7.6	7.5	12.1	7.4	4.2	6.4	10.8	4.0	12.2	•
Profit Margin (After Income Tax) 50	7.6	16.4	8.7	7.5	7.2	11.6	6.6	3.6	5.1	8.6	2.8	8.2	•

Table I

Corporations with and without Net Income

HOSPITALS, NURSING, AND RESIDENTIAL CARE FACILITIES

MONEY AMOUNTS AND SIZE OF ASSETS IN THOUSANDS OF DOLLARS

Item Description for Accounting Period 7/04 Through 6/05	Total	Zero Assets	Under 500	500 to 1,000	1,000 to 5,000	5,000 to 10,000	10,000 to 25,000	25,000 to 50,000	50,000 to 100,000	100,000 to 250,000	250,000 to 500,000	500,000 to 2,500,000	2,500,000 and over
Number of Enterprises **1**	18885	2298	13069	749	1931	233	218	78	33	40	9	22	5
Revenues ($ in Thousands)													
Net Sales **2**	99031915	485851	6892785	1028665	9130550	1980083	4532336	3974802	3470725	7354857	2839991	25144378	32196893
Interest **3**	460264	5303	8	833	1032	475	5002	11452	4098	34272	9688	196567	191533
Rents **4**	374019	205	0	58	510	46	4269	6576	8081	54668	3633	59420	236552
Royalties **5**	27413	0	0	0	0	0	0	1432	0	0	0	25980	0
Other Portfolio Income **6**	645425	675	509	33828	981	5496	21198	19664	6698	86372	64198	149950	255855
Other Receipts **7**	2853453	25952	10761	1653	301252	33745	71280	79994	41200	236254	50917	753922	1246526
Total Receipts **8**	103392489	517986	6904063	1065037	9434325	2019845	4634085	4093920	3530802	7766423	2968427	26330217	34127359
Average Total Receipts **9**	5533	225	528	1422	4886	8669	21257	52486	106994	194161	329825	1196828	6825472
Operating Costs/Operating Income (%)													
Cost of Operations **10**	7.7	4.2	4.4	3.8	4.4	9.2	14.0	7.3	14.8	8.9	4.9	14.7	2.2
Salaries and Wages **11**	41.4	33.8	36.0	32.7	46.9	28.7	36.6	41.9	41.2	43.9	47.7	31.9	48.9
Taxes Paid **12**	5.5	6.7	5.4	4.4	7.1	5.7	6.1	5.7	5.1	5.5	6.7	4.8	5.6
Interest Paid **13**	3.1	3.3	1.7	2.5	1.6	3.8	2.8	2.1	2.4	3.0	3.2	2.8	4.2
Depreciation **14**	3.4	1.5	1.5	2.3	1.9	2.5	2.4	2.3	1.9	2.8	3.0	2.9	5.3
Amortization and Depletion **15**	0.7	1.8	0.2	0.2	0.1	0.3	0.4	0.2	0.3	0.8	1.2	1.0	0.7
Pensions and Other Deferred Comp. **16**	0.6	0.0	0.1	0.7	0.1	0.1	0.4	0.4	0.2	0.2	0.0	0.2	1.3
Employee Benefits **17**	4.4	1.6	1.7	1.6	3.0	2.4	4.7	3.4	4.4	4.9	5.5	3.9	5.8
Advertising **18**	0.4	0.4	0.5	0.3	0.4	0.3	0.4	0.3	0.2	0.3	0.3	0.4	0.4
Other Expenses **19**	34.4	59.7	41.5	44.4	35.7	48.9	30.9	36.9	28.6	31.0	31.7	38.6	29.4
Officers' Compensation **20**	1.2	9.4	5.9	10.2	0.9	1.2	1.0	0.7	0.8	0.4	0.5	1.0	0.2
Operating Margin **21**	•	1.2					0.2		0.1				
Operating Margin Before Officers' Comp. **22**	•	•	7.1	7.2			1.3		0.9			•	•

Selected Average Balance Sheet ($ in Thousands)

Net Receivables 23	649	0	10	241	465	1134	3261	6088	11003	25504	53155	127312	959274
Inventories 24	13	0	0	1	3	19	84	133	405	1005	799	3711	13283
Net Property, Plant and Equipment 25	1959	0	78	277	1050	4892	6018	15789	28073	70751	117291	423042	3108691
Total Assets 26	5464	0	122	679	2147	7405	15066	34407	65855	145870	320877	1165183	10325493
Notes and Loans Payable 27	2369	0	217	409	1524	6472	9383	18250	36596	82196	141220	447522	3520290
All Other Liabilities 28	1483	0	30	181	748	1521	4674	10619	22686	42397	136132	294871	2674612
Net Worth 29	1612	0	-125	89	-125	-587	1008	5538	6573	21277	43524	422789	4130591

Selected Financial Ratios (Times to 1)

Current Ratio 30	1.2	•	0.6	1.4	0.9	0.7	1.3	1.1	1.0	1.1	1.1	1.4	1.3
Quick Ratio 31	0.9	•	0.5	1.4	0.7	0.7	1.0	0.8	0.8	0.9	0.9	1.1	0.8
Net Sales to Working Capital 32	28.4	•	•	15.9	•	•	16.9	37.9	167.4	62.0	27.2	14.1	18.9
Coverage Ratio 33	1.6	•	1.8	1.2	1.7	0.7	1.9	2.0	1.8	2.2	0.9	1.9	1.4
Total Asset Turnover 34	1.0	•	4.3	2.0	2.2	1.1	1.4	1.5	1.6	1.3	1.0	1.0	0.6
Inventory Turnover 35	30.6	•	955.2	68.7	71.0	41.6	34.7	27.8	38.4	16.3	19.4	45.4	10.9
Receivables Turnover 36	8.2	•	38.5	6.0	11.6	7.1	6.8	9.2	8.2	7.9	7.3	8.9	6.4
Total Liabilities to Net Worth 37	2.4	•	•	6.7	•	•	13.9	5.2	9.0	5.9	6.4	1.8	1.5
Current Assets to Working Capital 38	6.7	•	•	3.5	•	•	4.8	9.7	38.3	16.4	8.5	3.7	4.8
Current Liabilities to Working Capital 39	5.7	•	•	2.5	•	•	3.8	8.7	37.3	15.4	7.5	2.7	3.8
Working Capital to Net Sales 40	0.0	•	•	0.1	•	•	0.1	0.0	0.0	0.0	0.0	0.1	0.1
Inventory to Working Capital 41	0.1	•	•	0.0	•	•	0.1	0.1	0.6	0.4	0.1	0.0	0.0
Total Receipts to Cash Flow 42	3.4	3.0	3.6	2.6	3.5	2.4	3.6	3.1	4.2	3.6	5.1	2.8	4.0
Cost of Goods to Cash Flow 43	0.3	0.1	0.2	0.1	0.2	0.2	0.5	0.2	0.6	0.3	0.3	0.4	0.1
Cash Flow to Total Debt 44	0.4	•	0.6	0.9	0.6	0.4	0.4	0.6	0.4	0.4	0.2	0.5	0.3

Selected Financial Factors (in Percentages)

Debt Ratio 45	70.5	•	203.0	86.9	105.8	107.9	93.3	83.9	90.0	85.4	86.4	63.7	60.0
Return on Total Assets 46	4.7	•	13.3	6.0	6.1	3.0	7.3	6.1	6.7	8.5	2.9	5.1	3.6
Return on Equity Before Income Taxes 47	5.7	•	•	7.7	•	17.1	50.5	18.8	29.5	31.7	•	6.6	2.3
Return on Equity After Income Taxes 48	1.8	•	•	•	•	20.0	45.1	15.1	17.6	25.1	•	3.8	•
Profit Margin (Before Income Tax) 49	1.7	•	1.3	0.5	1.2	2.4	2.0	1.8	3.7	2.4	•	1.5	•
Profit Margin (After Income Tax) 50	0.6	•	1.3	•	1.1	2.2	1.6	1.1	2.9	1.4	•	•	•

Table II

Corporations with Net Income

HOSPITALS, NURSING, AND RESIDENTIAL CARE FACILITIES

MONEY AMOUNTS AND SIZE OF ASSETS IN THOUSANDS OF DOLLARS

Item Description for Accounting Period 7/04 Through 6/05	Total	Zero Assets	Under 500	500 to 1,000	1,000 to 5,000	5,000 to 10,000	10,000 to 25,000	25,000 to 50,000	50,000 to 100,000	100,000 to 250,000	250,000 to 500,000	500,000 to 2,500,000	2,500,000 and over
Number of Enterprises 1	9431	847	6768	347	1103	100	145	48	19	28	0	15	0
Revenues ($ in Thousands)													
Net Sales 2	66863216	257178	3247966	460782	4655542	983147	3490063	3207991	2684589	5675985	0	17697679	0
Interest 3	343126	5	1	823	849	365	2297	6394	3864	18411	0	129274	0
Rents 4	250296	0	0	58	0	46	4023	1754	8081	39501	0	40581	0
Royalties 5	25980	0	0	0	0	0	0	0	0	0	0	25980	0
Other Portfolio Income 6	589831	675	497	33828	810	4809	17187	18570	5253	81524	0	111699	0
Other Receipts 7	2185757	7362	3573	1562	273276	18616	53394	62980	34336	162485	0	505885	0
Total Receipts 8	70258206	265220	3252037	497053	4930477	1006983	3566964	3297689	2736123	597906	0	18511098	0
Average Total Receipts 9	7450	313	481	1432	4470	10070	24600	68702	144006	213497	.	1234073	.
Operating Costs/Operating Income (%)													
Cost of Operations 10	8.9	0.7	5.4	8.5	3.9	7.7	14.9	7.5	17.6	10.7	.	16.1	.
Salaries and Wages 11	40.1	22.5	33.8	35.1	47.0	43.4	35.6	40.8	40.2	40.1	.	29.3	.
Taxes Paid 12	5.5	5.3	5.3	5.1	7.6	6.3	6.2	5.5	4.8	5.2	.	4.7	.
Interest Paid 13	3.1	1.9	1.3	2.2	1.7	3.4	2.0	1.6	1.1	2.2	.	3.0	.
Depreciation 14	3.7	2.4	1.8	2.5	2.1	2.2	2.1	2.0	1.6	2.9	.	3.1	.
Amortization and Depletion 15	0.7	0.6	0.0	0.0	0.1	0.1	0.2	0.1	0.2	0.6	.	1.3	.
Pensions and Other Deferred Comp. 16	0.6	0.1	0.2	0.3	0.1	0.3	0.3	0.3	0.2	0.2	.	0.2	.
Employee Benefits 17	4.5	1.7	1.0	1.7	2.8	4.2	4.3	3.2	4.5	4.6	.	4.2	.
Advertising 18	0.4	0.2	0.3	0.4	0.6	0.2	0.4	0.3	0.2	0.3	.	0.5	.
Other Expenses 19	29.3	44.7	33.4	34.8	32.8	26.4	29.6	36.6	26.8	31.7	.	36.6	.
Officers' Compensation 20	1.0	16.0	6.9	8.8	0.8	1.5	1.1	0.7	0.8	0.5	.	0.7	.
Operating Margin 21	2.2	4.0	10.6	0.4	0.6	4.4	3.3	1.3	2.0	1.1	.	0.5	.
Operating Margin Before Officers' Comp. 22	3.2	20.0	17.5	9.2	1.4	5.9	4.4	2.0	2.8	1.6	.	1.2	.

Selected Average Balance Sheet ($ in Thousands)

Net Receivables 23	882	0	4	214	366	1083	3662	7349	14067	26924	•	128296
Inventories 24	17	0	0	0	2	17	97	156	603	990	•	1847
Net Property, Plant and Equipment 25	2666	0	93	311	1066	4217	5832	13817	27389	71656	•	415595
Total Assets 26	8048	0	139	650	2122	6447	15169	35133	67275	150061	•	1182964
Notes and Loans Payable 27	3000	0	105	298	1255	4599	8092	17020	32085	77141	•	443868
All Other Liabilities 28	1729	0	13	139	360	1372	4793	10432	26423	37736	•	330824
Net Worth 29	3318	0	20	213	508	476	2284	7681	8767	35184	•	408273

Selected Financial Ratios (Times to 1)

Current Ratio 30	1.2	•	1.1	1.8	1.7	1.0	1.3	1.2	1.0	1.2	•	1.3
Quick Ratio 31	0.9	•	1.0	1.7	1.4	0.9	1.1	0.9	0.8	1.0	•	1.0
Net Sales to Working Capital 32	27.8	•	271.6	11.4	14.3	113.0	15.7	32.5	•	20.4	•	15.8
Coverage Ratio 33	3.3	4.7	9.3	4.8	4.9	3.0	3.8	3.6	4.6	3.9	•	2.7
Total Asset Turnover 34	0.9	•	3.5	2.0	2.0	1.5	1.6	1.9	2.1	1.4	•	1.0
Inventory Turnover 35	37.3	•	553.9	•	95.9	45.4	37.0	32.2	41.1	21.9	•	102.9
Receivables Turnover 36	7.9	•	117.1	6.4	15.8	8.8	7.9	11.2	9.1	9.5	•	9.8
Total Liabilities to Net Worth 37	1.4	•	5.9	2.0	3.2	12.5	5.6	3.6	6.7	3.3	•	1.9
Current Assets to Working Capital 38	6.1	•	14.3	2.3	2.5	21.3	4.1	7.2	•	5.3	•	4.0
Current Liabilities to Working Capital 39	5.1	•	13.3	1.3	1.5	20.3	3.1	6.2	•	4.3	•	3.0
Working Capital to Net Sales 40	0.0	•	0.0	0.1	0.1	0.0	0.1	0.0	•	0.0	•	0.1
Inventory to Working Capital 41	0.1	•	•	•	0.0	0.3	0.1	0.1	•	0.1	•	0.0
Total Receipts to Cash Flow 42	3.3	2.5	2.9	3.1	3.1	3.7	3.5	2.9	4.0	3.2	•	2.7
Cost of Goods to Cash Flow 43	0.3	0.0	0.2	0.3	0.1	0.3	0.5	0.2	0.7	0.3	•	0.4
Cash Flow to Total Debt 44	0.5	•	1.4	1.0	0.8	0.5	0.5	0.8	0.6	0.6	•	0.6

Selected Financial Factors (in Percentages)

Debt Ratio 45	58.8	•	85.5	67.2	76.1	92.6	84.9	78.1	87.0	76.6	•	65.5
Return on Total Assets 46	9.0	•	41.6	21.4	16.1	15.6	11.9	10.8	10.6	11.7	•	8.1
Return on Equity Before Income Taxes 47	15.3	•	256.2	51.7	53.7	141.5	58.2	35.5	63.7	37.0	•	14.8
Return on Equity After Income Taxes 48	11.6	•	254.7	37.6	52.8	133.1	54.6	31.1	48.3	31.3	•	10.6
Profit Margin (Before Income Tax) 49	7.2	7.1	10.7	8.3	6.5	6.9	5.5	4.1	4.0	6.4	•	5.1
Profit Margin (After Income Tax) 50	5.4	7.1	10.7	6.0	6.4	6.4	5.2	3.6	3.0	5.4	•	3.7

Table I

Corporations with and without Net Income

OTHER ARTS, ENTERTAINMENT, AND RECREATION

MONEY AMOUNTS AND SIZE OF ASSETS IN THOUSANDS OF DOLLARS

Item Description for Accounting Period 7/04 Through 6/05	Total	Zero Assets	Under 500	500 to 1,000	1,000 to 5,000	5,000 to 10,000	10,000 to 25,000	25,000 to 50,000	50,000 to 100,000	100,000 to 250,000	250,000 to 500,000	500,000 to 2,500,000	2,500,000 and over
Number of Enterprises **1**	62139	11710	48394	1103	631	108	92	39	17	28	8	7	0
Revenues ($ in Thousands)													
Net Sales **2**	32520419	1063410	14191693	2139564	2175224	668887	1584484	1124725	1272940	3683044	1571775	3044674	0
Interest **3**	127254	1122	3964	1557	1977	1743	2972	3253	1925	27560	9135	72047	0
Rents **4**	70590	0	1628	2457	809	1988	1899	1589	322	20879	11490	27528	0
Royalties **5**	88633	184	236	0	17	1	650	786	7320	45365	30323	3751	0
Other Portfolio Income **6**	194318	29516	11976	2405	11034	37258	26615	2471	155	53950	11092	7843	0
Other Receipts **7**	1807874	22221	363764	16562	125019	137811	107104	68702	164825	513708	282560	5598	0
Total Receipts **8**	34809088	1116453	14573261	2162545	2314080	847688	1723724	1201526	1447487	4334506	1916375	3161441	0
Average Total Receipts **9**	560	95	301	1961	3667	7849	18736	30808	85146	155161	239547	451634	•
Operating Costs/Operating Income (%)													
Cost of Operations **10**	15.1	7.2	8.1	30.3	21.5	8.7	25.7	21.4	18.7	15.7	49.6	8.8	•
Salaries and Wages **11**	17.0	5.7	11.7	9.2	15.9	24.3	14.8	33.2	38.2	34.8	22.2	11.8	•
Taxes Paid **12**	2.9	2.0	2.0	5.5	3.3	4.3	2.9	3.7	2.7	4.1	3.8	3.1	•
Interest Paid **13**	1.4	1.4	0.3	0.6	0.4	1.4	0.9	1.7	1.2	2.8	3.4	4.8	•
Depreciation **14**	3.1	4.7	1.5	2.3	2.0	3.5	3.3	4.6	2.5	3.7	5.6	8.5	•
Amortization and Depletion **15**	1.0	0.5	0.0	0.0	0.1	0.2	5.8	0.3	1.3	2.9	0.9	2.5	•
Pensions and Other Deferred Comp. **16**	1.8	1.7	2.1	3.2	2.0	0.5	0.4	0.5	0.6	2.0	1.6	1.0	•
Employee Benefits **17**	1.0	1.0	0.4	0.4	0.5	0.8	0.9	1.3	1.8	1.9	3.8	1.9	•
Advertising **18**	2.6	0.9	2.9	3.3	1.9	2.6	1.6	1.6	5.7	2.2	2.1	2.3	•
Other Expenses **19**	38.9	60.3	41.6	28.9	26.4	47.7	35.9	32.7	32.2	37.4	21.1	50.9	•
Officers' Compensation **20**	16.5	21.2	27.8	10.2	16.5	18.6	6.6	4.5	5.3	4.2	1.4	3.5	•
Operating Margin **21**	•	•	1.6	6.1	9.5	•	1.2	•	•	•	•	0.9	•
Operating Margin Before Officers' Comp. **22**	15.3	14.6	29.4	16.3	25.9	6.0	7.8	25.9	•	•	•	4.4	•

Selected Average Balance Sheet ($ in Thousands)

Net Receivables 23	33	0	2	33	187	171	3033	2778	8905	20844	35995	51272	•
Inventories 24	7	0	3	49	163	26	325	409	872	1330	1023	3904	•
Net Property, Plant and Equipment 25	109	0	8	162	340	1162	3706	9085	15055	41171	117994	396904	•
Total Assets 26	385	0	56	666	1914	7585	15780	33770	67642	160172	349174	1034578	•
Notes and Loans Payable 27	178	0	66	207	411	2497	6182	10534	38214	56173	137665	401270	•
All Other Liabilities 28	125	0	18	187	501	1421	4560	11689	31118	64138	83590	335137	•
Net Worth 29	82	0	-28	273	1003	3667	5039	-1690	11547	39861	127920	298170	•

Selected Financial Ratios (Times to 1)

Current Ratio 30	1.3	•	1.6	1.4	2.2	2.8	1.9	1.5	1.3	1.0	1.7	0.8	•
Quick Ratio 31	1.0	•	1.0	1.0	1.7	2.5	1.4	1.1	0.9	0.7	1.1	0.7	•
Net Sales to Working Capital 32	14.9	•	21.2	21.9	5.3	1.9	4.9	7.5	16.5	918.2	4.3	•	•
Coverage Ratio 33	5.2	•	13.6	12.9	36.5	10.8	11.6	1.7	4.1	3.2	2.8	2.0	•
Total Asset Turnover 34	1.4	•	5.2	2.9	1.8	0.8	1.1	0.9	1.1	0.8	0.6	0.4	•
Inventory Turnover 35	10.6	•	6.8	12.0	4.5	20.5	13.6	15.1	16.1	15.5	95.2	9.8	•
Receivables Turnover 36	16.7	•	146.5	40.4	15.3	9.0	5.5	10.2	7.8	7.1	7.0	11.0	•
Total Liabilities to Net Worth 37	3.7	•	•	1.4	0.9	1.1	2.1	1.9	•	3.0	1.7	2.5	•
Current Assets to Working Capital 38	4.2	•	2.7	3.3	1.8	1.6	2.1	3.1	4.8	415.0	2.5	•	•
Current Liabilities to Working Capital 39	3.2	•	1.7	2.3	0.8	0.6	1.1	2.1	3.8	414.0	1.5	•	•
Working Capital to Net Sales 40	0.1	•	0.0	0.0	0.2	0.5	0.2	0.1	0.1	0.0	0.2	•	•
Inventory to Working Capital 41	0.2	•	0.3	0.6	0.1	0.0	0.1	0.1	0.3	11.6	0.0	•	•
Total Receipts to Cash Flow 42	2.5	1.9	2.3	3.3	2.7	1.9	2.4	3.3	3.4	2.6	4.5	1.9	•
Cost of Goods to Cash Flow 43	0.4	0.1	0.2	1.0	0.6	0.2	0.6	0.7	0.6	0.4	2.2	0.2	•
Cash Flow to Total Debt 44	0.7	•	1.5	1.5	1.4	0.8	0.7	0.4	0.3	0.4	0.2	0.3	•

Selected Financial Factors (in Percentages)

Debt Ratio 45	78.8	•	150.3	59.1	47.6	51.7	68.1	65.8	102.5	75.1	63.4	71.2	•
Return on Total Assets 46	9.7	•	24.0	22.7	29.3	12.7	11.9	2.5	5.2	7.5	5.3	4.1	•
Return on Equity Before Income Taxes 47	36.9	•	•	51.2	54.4	23.9	34.0	3.0	•	20.8	9.3	7.2	•
Return on Equity After Income Taxes 48	32.4	•	•	50.6	53.1	21.5	28.7	•	•	18.2	5.3	4.0	•
Profit Margin (Before Income Tax) 49	5.8	•	4.3	7.2	15.8	14.1	9.9	1.2	3.5	6.3	6.1	4.9	•
Profit Margin (After Income Tax) 50	5.1	•	4.2	7.1	15.4	12.7	8.4	•	2.2	5.5	3.5	2.7	•

Table II

Corporations with Net Income

OTHER ARTS, ENTERTAINMENT, AND RECREATION

MONEY AMOUNTS AND SIZE OF ASSETS IN THOUSANDS OF DOLLARS

Item Description for Accounting Period 7/04 Through 6/05	Total	Zero Assets	Under 500	500 to 1,000	1,000 to 5,000	5,000 to 10,000	10,000 to 25,000	25,000 to 50,000	50,000 to 100,000	100,000 to 250,000	250,000 to 500,000	500,000 to 2,500,000	2,500,000 and over
Number of Enterprises **1**	30559	6572	22802	621	405	51	53	18	10	17	0	0	0
Revenues ($ in Thousands)													
Net Sales **2**	23546700	755120	10066419	1845792	1436686	420226	1132209	796154	1145797	2220692	0	0	0
Interest **3**	82729	264	1227	1553	674	1057	2855	1278	1488	21358	0	0	0
Rents **4**	65580	0	15	2457	0	1058	1899	1206	322	19847	0	0	0
Royalties **5**	87266	0	0	0	17	1	650	19	7320	45185	0	0	0
Other Portfolio Income **6**	171283	22231	11805	1703	8156	32699	24392	727	137	53420	0	0	0
Other Receipts **7**	1542634	62180	250805	17721	178976	146655	94334	54085	120805	332375	0	0	0
Total Receipts **8**	25496192	839795	10330271	1869226	1624509	601696	1256339	853469	1275869	2692877	0	0	0
Average Total Receipts **9**	834	128	453	3010	4011	11798	23705	47415	127587	158405	•	•	•
Operating Costs/Operating Income (%)													
Cost of Operations **10**	12.1	8.1	4.1	32.8	9.4	7.7	20.9	20.2	20.6	11.0	•	•	•
Salaries and Wages **11**	16.9	5.3	14.1	8.1	14.8	24.3	15.5	27.2	32.1	31.4	•	•	•
Taxes Paid **12**	2.8	1.9	1.8	5.7	2.2	4.4	2.8	3.1	2.6	3.5	•	•	•
Interest Paid **13**	1.0	0.3	0.1	0.2	0.3	0.3	0.6	1.3	0.9	2.7	•	•	•
Depreciation **14**	2.6	1.3	1.0	1.3	1.9	1.8	2.5	3.1	2.6	3.5	•	•	•
Amortization and Depletion **15**	1.1	0.0	0.0	0.0	0.0	0.0	8.1	0.0	1.1	2.9	•	•	•
Pensions and Other Deferred Comp. **16**	1.8	1.0	2.0	3.7	2.5	0.3	0.4	0.5	0.6	2.0	•	•	•
Employee Benefits **17**	0.8	0.6	0.3	0.4	0.2	0.2	0.8	1.2	1.5	1.8	•	•	•
Advertising **18**	2.7	1.1	3.3	3.0	1.5	2.7	2.0	1.1	6.2	1.6	•	•	•
Other Expenses **19**	37.6	49.7	41.1	26.6	23.5	47.6	27.4	24.9	27.8	41.7	•	•	•
Officers' Compensation **20**	14.3	16.8	23.3	10.2	21.3	14.7	7.9	5.1	5.7	3.7	•	•	•
Operating Margin **21**	6.2	14.0	8.9	7.9	22.4	•	11.0	12.2	•	•	•	•	•
Operating Margin Before Officers' Comp. **22**	20.5	30.7	32.3	18.1	43.7	10.6	19.0	17.2	3.9	•	•	•	•

Selected Average Balance Sheet ($ in Thousands)

Net Receivables 23	38	0	1	59	213	130	2745	2147	12695	16647
Inventories 24	4	0	0	38	9	31	132	607	1440	1153
Net Property, Plant and Equipment 25	153	0	9	73	257	864	3214	7198	20115	37944
Total Assets 26	471	0	65	710	1855	6527	16218	34602	67850	154378
Notes and Loans Payable 27	133	0	19	82	287	1845	4076	6579	36261	60655
All Other Liabilities 28	159	0	28	315	311	1314	4345	14468	24792	57072
Net Worth 29	179	0	18	313	1256	3368	7797	13554	6797	36650

Selected Financial Ratios (Times to 1)

Current Ratio 30	1.4	•	1.6	1.3	3.7	2.7	2.2	1.7	1.2	1.1
Quick Ratio 31	1.1	•	1.2	1.0	3.0	2.4	1.7	1.3	0.9	0.8
Net Sales to Working Capital 32	13.3	•	25.2	33.6	4.0	3.9	4.7	6.1	23.4	32.1
Coverage Ratio 33	15.5	96.3	121.0	58.3	139.4	127.7	36.5	15.4	11.6	6.7
Total Asset Turnover 34	1.6	•	6.8	4.2	1.9	1.3	1.3	1.3	1.7	0.8
Inventory Turnover 35	23.2	•	36.3	25.7	36.8	20.4	34.0	14.8	16.4	12.4
Receivables Turnover 36	21.8	•	270.9	88.4	13.4	15.3	9.2	15.8	8.2	10.3
Total Liabilities to Net Worth 37	1.6	•	2.7	1.3	0.5	0.9	1.1	1.6	9.0	3.2
Current Assets to Working Capital 38	3.4	•	2.7	4.9	1.4	1.6	1.8	2.4	5.6	14.5
Current Liabilities to Working Capital 39	2.4	•	1.7	3.9	0.4	0.6	0.8	1.4	4.6	13.5
Working Capital to Net Sales 40	0.1	•	0.0	0.0	0.2	0.3	0.2	0.2	0.0	0.0
Inventory to Working Capital 41	0.1	•	0.0	0.4	0.0	0.0	0.0	0.1	0.5	0.2
Total Receipts to Cash Flow 42	2.1	1.5	2.0	3.1	1.8	1.3	2.2	2.4	3.3	1.9
Cost of Goods to Cash Flow 43	0.2	0.1	0.1	1.0	0.2	0.1	0.5	0.5	0.7	0.2
Cash Flow to Total Debt 44	1.3	•	4.7	2.4	3.2	2.0	1.1	0.9	0.6	0.6

Selected Financial Factors (in Percentages)

Debt Ratio 45	62.0	•	72.6	56.0	32.3	48.4	51.9	60.8	90.0	76.3
Return on Total Assets 46	25.3	•	79.0	39.1	68.3	49.7	29.7	26.4	17.7	15.4
Return on Equity Before Income Taxes 47	62.3	•	286.5	87.3	100.1	95.6	60.1	63.0	161.5	55.4
Return on Equity After Income Taxes 48	58.3	•	284.9	86.4	98.5	90.0	54.1	59.8	136.7	50.6
Profit Margin (Before Income Tax) 49	14.5	25.2	11.5	9.2	35.5	39.1	21.9	19.3	9.6	15.5
Profit Margin (After Income Tax) 50	13.5	24.4	11.5	9.1	34.9	36.8	19.8	18.3	8.1	14.2

Table I

Corporations with and without Net Income

AMUSEMENT, GAMBLING, AND RECREATION INDUSTRIES

MONEY AMOUNTS AND SIZE OF ASSETS IN THOUSANDS OF DOLLARS

Item Description for Accounting Period 7/04 Through 6/05	Total	Zero Assets	Under 500	500 to 1,000	1,000 to 5,000	5,000 to 10,000	10,000 to 25,000	25,000 to 50,000	50,000 to 100,000	100,000 to 250,000	250,000 to 500,000	500,000 to 2,500,000	2,500,000 and over
Number of Enterprises 1	56716	9054	38921	3750	3828	675	309	104	32	24	8	8	3
Revenues ($ in Thousands)													
Net Sales 2	42288229	970657	8843947	3294903	7774984	4451214	2904067	1789623	1196582	1991964	1755833	4828283	3086173
Interest 3	570750	2227	11065	3956	8403	4044	6312	7366	5469	17226	18667	148387	337628
Rents 4	139643	3313	6364	9404	12678	21233	7829	10059	5589	6058	9798	26393	20923
Royalties 5	121730	29130	0	0	3868	0	20075	4	11	1717	597	4353	61975
Other Portfolio Income 6	636065	67375	138191	70415	167214	22953	20333	9071	10508	9719	59501	52006	8780
Other Receipts 7	3529840	5963	209664	620357	236135	194595	232525	159539	282050	118569	189899	1017430	263115
Total Receipts 8	47886257	1078665	9209231	3999035	8203282	4694039	3191141	1975662	1500209	2145253	2034295	6076852	3778594
Average Total Receipts 9	844	119	237	1066	2143	6954	10327	18997	46882	89386	254287	759606	1259531
Operating Costs/Operating Income (%)													
Cost of Operations 10	22.5	19.4	18.9	30.9	23.9	37.3	31.9	24.0	15.6	14.7	14.8	11.6	19.3
Salaries and Wages 11	22.3	20.3	17.0	17.4	22.5	20.1	23.1	25.4	34.3	21.9	30.9	33.7	16.8
Taxes Paid 12	7.3	7.2	5.1	5.3	6.3	5.2	7.0	7.0	14.2	9.6	7.1	11.4	11.1
Interest Paid 13	5.2	3.0	1.6	1.9	3.4	2.6	3.4	2.9	3.7	6.2	7.1	10.4	21.8
Depreciation 14	7.7	5.3	5.0	6.7	7.1	6.9	8.3	10.6	8.4	12.3	9.6	8.1	13.3
Amortization and Depletion 15	0.7	0.5	0.2	0.6	0.5	0.6	0.8	0.5	1.0	1.4	0.9	1.2	1.2
Pensions and Other Deferred Comp. 16	0.3	0.0	0.1	0.7	0.4	0.5	0.3	0.4	0.5	0.1	0.5	0.1	0.3
Employee Benefits 17	1.7	1.1	0.8	1.0	1.6	1.1	2.2	1.9	1.6	2.0	2.3	3.6	2.1
Advertising 18	2.9	3.9	2.2	2.5	2.2	3.6	2.2	2.3	6.2	3.3	2.9	3.4	4.3
Other Expenses 19	35.8	51.1	41.7	41.1	31.2	24.8	28.2	30.9	35.3	37.5	36.6	44.7	30.7
Officers' Compensation 20	3.2	1.9	8.2	3.1	3.2	1.7	1.7	1.8	1.2	1.3	1.8	0.6	0.5
Operating Margin 21	•	•	•	•	•	•	•	•	•	•	•	•	•
Operating Margin Before Officers' Comp. 22	•	7.4	•	0.9	•	•	•	•	•	•	•	•	•

Selected Average Balance Sheet ($ in Thousands)

Net Receivables 23	306472	131577	8728	7864	2163	1708	844	626	119	42	2	0	68
Inventories 24	16551	31923	3959	2168	414	666	399	247	59	24	5	0	22
Net Property, Plant and Equipment 25	1073717	485706	188628	78055	39823	22005	9228	4852	1406	495	49	0	517
Total Assets 26	3480092	1207836	340939	148885	65421	36033	15594	7820	2117	751	93	0	1003
Notes and Loans Payable 27	2210991	608172	187216	65804	24985	12146	6904	3739	1355	465	93	0	562
All Other Liabilities 28	262213	414709	94213	33905	13806	6994	2681	1731	328	66	20	0	196
Net Worth 29	1006887	184955	59511	49176	26630	16892	6010	2350	434	219	-20	0	246

Selected Financial Ratios (Times to 1)

Current Ratio 30	2.5	1.0	0.5	0.8	0.7	1.0	1.3	0.6	1.0	1.7	1.2	•	1.1
Quick Ratio 31	1.9	0.7	0.3	0.6	0.5	0.7	0.8	0.4	0.8	1.3	0.8	•	0.8
Net Sales to Working Capital 32	2.3	123.0	•	•	•	•	12.7	•	177.4	11.1	42.2	•	54.9
Coverage Ratio 33	1.0	0.7	1.2	0.6	1.9	1.9	1.2	1.5	1.9	6.5	3.1	0.2	1.4
Total Asset Turnover 34	0.3	0.5	0.6	0.6	0.6	0.5	0.6	0.8	1.0	1.2	2.4	•	0.8
Inventory Turnover 35	12.0	2.2	8.2	5.6	14.1	6.2	7.5	10.0	8.3	11.2	8.9	•	7.8
Receivables Turnover 36	•	2.6	36.9	10.7	18.8	10.2	11.7	12.2	17.1	26.4	154.9	•	10.7
Total Liabilities to Net Worth 37	2.5	5.5	4.7	2.0	1.5	1.1	1.6	2.3	3.9	2.4	•	•	3.1
Current Assets to Working Capital 38	1.7	56.5	•	•	•	•	4.7	•	33.8	2.4	5.8	•	15.5
Current Liabilities to Working Capital 39	0.7	55.5	•	•	•	•	3.7	•	32.8	1.4	4.8	•	14.5
Working Capital to Net Sales 40	0.4	0.0	•	•	•	•	0.1	•	0.0	0.1	0.0	•	0.0
Inventory to Working Capital 41	0.0	4.8	•	•	•	•	0.5	•	4.5	0.4	0.9	•	1.7
Total Receipts to Cash Flow 42	3.8	3.9	4.1	5.1	3.2	3.8	5.0	5.6	4.4	2.6	3.7	4.5	4.0
Cost of Goods to Cash Flow 43	0.7	0.5	0.6	0.8	0.5	0.9	1.6	2.1	1.0	0.8	0.7	0.9	0.9
Cash Flow to Total Debt 44	0.1	0.2	0.2	0.2	0.3	0.2	0.2	0.2	0.3	0.6	0.5	•	0.2

Selected Financial Factors (in Percentages)

Debt Ratio 45	71.1	84.7	82.5	67.0	59.3	53.1	61.5	70.0	79.5	70.8	121.1	•	75.5
Return on Total Assets 46	6.8	3.7	5.5	1.9	4.0	2.6	2.5	3.2	6.3	14.4	12.1	•	5.5
Return on Equity Before Income Taxes 47	1.1	•	5.5	•	4.7	2.6	1.1	3.3	14.8	41.9	•	•	6.4
Return on Equity After Income Taxes 48	•	•	1.8	•	3.8	1.9	0.4	2.7	14.2	41.7	•	•	5.0
Profit Margin (Before Income Tax) 49	1.1	•	1.5	0.5	3.4	2.5	0.7	1.2	3.2	10.4	3.4	•	2.1
Profit Margin (After Income Tax) 50	•	•	0.5	0.2	2.7	1.9	0.2	1.0	3.0	10.4	3.0	•	1.6

Table II

Corporations with Net Income

AMUSEMENT, GAMBLING, AND RECREATION INDUSTRIES

MONEY AMOUNTS AND SIZE OF ASSETS IN THOUSANDS OF DOLLARS

Item Description for Accounting Period 7/04 Through 6/05	Total	Zero Assets	Under 500	500 to 1,000	1,000 to 5,000	5,000 to 10,000	10,000 to 25,000	25,000 to 50,000	50,000 to 100,000	100,000 to 250,000	250,000 to 500,000	500,000 to 2,500,000	2,500,000 and over
Number of Enterprises 1	25761	2968	18359	2010	1989	245	120	39	11	10	0	0	0
Revenues ($ in Thousands)													
Net Sales 2	22506277	159703	4684926	2523606	4160319	2643503	1539995	1085113	596791	841263	0	0	0
Interest 3	230438	30	1334	3549	3801	1275	2743	3649	3204	1937	0	0	0
Rents 4	63325	0	551	4799	5425	5920	3781	5183	5097	5848	0	0	0
Royalties 5	115412	29130	0	0	3868	0	20072	4	11	337	0	0	0
Other Portfolio Income 6	511056	66630	133675	70311	136447	16159	12101	6754	9195	6721	0	0	0
Other Receipts 7	1966871	3268	170916	610669	67219	109350	134833	93292	262540	85300	0	0	0
Total Receipts 8	25393379	258761	4991402	3212934	4377079	2776207	1713525	1193995	876838	941406	0	0	0
Average Total Receipts 9	986	87	272	1598	2201	11331	14279	30615	79713	94141	•	•	•
Operating Costs/Operating Income (%)													
Cost of Operations 10	26.5	5.5	20.5	34.3	23.8	46.1	31.0	21.4	19.3	16.1	•	•	•
Salaries and Wages 11	18.6	26.4	12.4	17.1	20.8	17.5	22.0	25.5	38.1	22.8	•	•	•
Taxes Paid 12	6.9	7.7	3.8	5.0	5.3	3.7	7.5	6.9	16.3	5.0	•	•	•
Interest Paid 13	3.5	2.5	0.9	1.2	2.7	0.8	2.4	1.7	1.5	2.7	•	•	•
Depreciation 14	6.4	3.4	3.0	5.3	6.4	4.1	6.6	5.9	6.0	14.5	•	•	•
Amortization and Depletion 15	0.5	2.2	0.3	0.6	0.4	0.1	0.4	0.4	0.1	0.2	•	•	•
Pensions and Other Deferred Comp. 16	0.4	0.0	0.1	0.8	0.3	0.7	0.3	0.6	0.9	0.3	•	•	•
Employee Benefits 17	1.4	0.3	0.3	0.9	1.5	0.9	2.1	1.6	1.2	3.4	•	•	•
Advertising 18	2.4	2.7	1.9	2.7	1.7	3.3	2.2	2.3	8.8	2.0	•	•	•
Other Expenses 19	29.4	53.1	38.1	39.6	24.9	16.6	22.5	24.6	36.4	30.6	•	•	•
Officers' Compensation 20	3.2	3.8	7.5	2.8	3.7	1.1	1.8	1.8	1.7	2.3	•	•	•
Operating Margin 21	0.8	•	11.2	•	8.5	5.0	1.1	7.4	•	•	•	•	•
Operating Margin Before Officers' Comp. 22	4.0	•	18.7	•	12.2	6.1	2.9	9.2	•	2.2	•	•	•

Selected Average Balance Sheet ($ in Thousands)

Net Receivables 23	72	0	1	46	87	172	831	2858	3268	9461
Inventories 24	30	0	5	40	64	577	467	429	588	2913
Net Property, Plant and Equipment 25	443	0	32	452	1348	3835	8393	19476	36505	84363
Total Assets 26	1009	0	91	786	2044	7554	15894	35498	65741	137621
Notes and Loans Payable 27	453	0	46	270	1021	2207	5789	7921	14633	36913
All Other Liabilities 28	181	0	14	76	244	2155	3155	7737	11655	29740
Net Worth 29	374	0	32	441	779	3192	6950	19839	39454	70968

Selected Financial Ratios (Times to 1)

Current Ratio 30	1.2	•	2.0	2.2	1.2	0.6	1.5	1.3	1.1	1.2
Quick Ratio 31	0.9	•	1.3	1.7	1.0	0.3	0.9	1.1	0.9	0.9
Net Sales to Working Capital 32	18.0	•	12.9	7.8	27.1	•	9.6	14.4	55.8	17.7
Coverage Ratio 33	4.9	22.6	19.8	14.8	6.1	13.0	6.2	11.0	12.4	5.4
Total Asset Turnover 34	0.9	•	2.8	1.6	1.0	1.4	0.8	0.8	0.8	0.6
Inventory Turnover 35	7.7	•	10.1	10.8	7.7	8.6	8.5	13.9	17.8	4.6
Receivables Turnover 36	11.2	•	241.8	38.0	23.4	74.7	14.6	10.4	14.8	8.6
Total Liabilities to Net Worth 37	1.7	•	1.9	0.8	1.6	1.4	1.3	0.8	0.7	0.9
Current Assets to Working Capital 38	5.1	•	2.0	1.9	5.0	•	3.1	4.6	13.1	5.1
Current Liabilities to Working Capital 39	4.1	•	1.0	0.9	4.0	•	2.1	3.6	12.1	4.1
Working Capital to Net Sales 40	0.1	•	0.1	0.1	0.0	•	0.1	0.1	0.0	0.1
Inventory to Working Capital 41	0.7	•	0.2	0.3	0.5	•	0.4	0.2	0.5	0.6
Total Receipts to Cash Flow 42	3.0	1.1	2.6	2.3	3.5	4.6	3.6	2.8	2.1	2.7
Cost of Goods to Cash Flow 43	0.8	0.1	0.5	0.8	0.8	2.1	1.1	0.6	0.4	0.4
Cash Flow to Total Debt 44	0.5	•	1.6	1.6	0.5	0.5	0.4	0.6	1.0	0.5

Selected Financial Factors (in Percentages)

Debt Ratio 45	62.9	•	65.4	44.0	61.9	57.7	56.3	44.1	40.0	48.4
Return on Total Assets 46	14.8	•	52.2	29.1	16.8	15.5	11.9	15.0	15.0	8.9
Return on Equity Before Income Taxes 47	31.9	•	143.3	48.4	36.9	33.9	22.9	24.5	22.9	14.0
Return on Equity After Income Taxes 48	29.8	•	137.0	48.3	36.2	32.8	21.3	22.9	21.1	11.4
Profit Margin (Before Income Tax) 49	13.6	54.5	17.7	17.0	13.7	10.0	12.4	17.4	16.7	11.8
Profit Margin (After Income Tax) 50	12.8	49.4	16.9	17.0	13.5	9.7	11.5	16.4	15.3	9.6

Table I

Corporations with and without Net Income

ACCOMMODATION

Money Amounts and Size of Assets in Thousands of Dollars

Item Description for Accounting Period 7/04 Through 6/05	Total	Zero Assets	Under 500	500 to 1,000	1,000 to 5,000	5,000 to 10,000	10,000 to 25,000	25,000 to 50,000	50,000 to 100,000	100,000 to 250,000	250,000 to 500,000	500,000 to 2,500,000	2,500,000 and over
Number of Enterprises 1	36553	2564	19914	3565	9171	691	358	124	53	46	26	25	16

Revenues ($ in Thousands)

Item	Total	Zero Assets	Under 500	500 to 1,000	1,000 to 5,000	5,000 to 10,000	10,000 to 25,000	25,000 to 50,000	50,000 to 100,000	100,000 to 250,000	250,000 to 500,000	500,000 to 2,500,000	2,500,000 and over
Net Sales 2	87657067	1495668	3786604	1570878	9586250	2816041	3989308	2951508	2835030	8330222	4132574	13693121	32469864
Interest 3	2078895	6120	4580	5238	14781	5413	11970	22651	20285	26430	77845	285348	1598234
Rents 4	449841	6046	696	9386	7033	6858	13039	5342	10969	35284	15775	103981	235431
Royalties 5	1627969	2414	0	0	5174	0	365	1685	6	6114	161363	43822	1407026
Other Portfolio Income 6	2054429	51927	80192	99446	136340	30714	57998	52100	58586	262132	120199	493629	611168
Other Receipts 7	7691142	78467	131578	52392	317828	174608	166644	71550	95365	365092	131185	417817	5688614
Total Receipts 8	101559343	1640642	4003650	1737340	10067406	3033634	4239324	3104836	3020241	9025274	4638941	15037718	42010337
Average Total Receipts 9	2778	640	201	487	1098	4390	11842	25039	56986	196202	178421	601509	2625646

Operating Costs/Operating Income (%)

Item	Total	Zero Assets	Under 500	500 to 1,000	1,000 to 5,000	5,000 to 10,000	10,000 to 25,000	25,000 to 50,000	50,000 to 100,000	100,000 to 250,000	250,000 to 500,000	500,000 to 2,500,000	2,500,000 and over
Cost of Operations 10	23.3	8.3	13.1	4.6	16.1	29.8	23.5	21.9	27.3	43.3	22.5	45.4	13.1
Salaries and Wages 11	23.2	32.9	14.1	19.9	20.0	14.3	17.3	13.7	16.3	8.3	17.2	13.2	36.8
Taxes Paid 12	7.5	9.2	7.6	7.8	7.3	6.4	5.0	4.6	4.0	2.9	5.2	8.3	9.6
Interest Paid 13	7.1	7.2	2.0	4.6	8.4	6.8	3.9	4.9	3.2	2.2	5.3	5.8	10.4
Depreciation 14	6.5	7.4	4.7	6.3	9.0	6.0	6.1	6.3	5.3	4.0	7.4	5.4	7.1
Amortization and Depletion 15	0.7	0.5	0.2	0.5	0.6	0.5	0.5	0.5	0.4	0.7	0.7	0.8	0.8
Pensions and Other Deferred Comp. 16	0.5	0.6	0.4	0.0	0.1	0.0	0.1	0.8	0.2	0.2	0.6	0.6	0.8
Employee Benefits 17	2.6	3.8	0.4	1.0	1.0	1.1	1.9	1.7	1.4	1.0	1.9	2.8	4.2
Advertising 18	3.0	2.5	1.7	2.9	2.4	2.6	3.0	2.0	2.8	1.8	4.5	1.8	4.0
Other Expenses 19	36.4	49.6	51.4	54.1	34.9	35.9	51.0	48.4	46.5	42.1	42.2	23.4	33.3
Officers' Compensation 20	1.4	0.9	2.9	3.0	2.8	2.9	1.1	0.8	0.7	0.5	0.8	0.7	1.4
Operating Margin 21	•	•	1.6	•	•	•	•	•	•	•	•	•	•
Operating Margin Before Officers' Comp. 22	•	•	4.5	•	0.1	•	•	•	•	•	•	•	•

Selected Average Balance Sheet ($ in Thousands)

Net Receivables 23	232	0	3	21	39	309	843	1855	4260	9651	45905	48656	258692
Inventories 24	73	0	2	6	14	50	154	327	991	1579	7733	22084	91792
Net Property, Plant and Equipment 25	2375	0	88	480	1613	4535	8983	21613	36165	90213	184136	513502	2239299
Total Assets 26	5584	0	136	670	2151	6420	14932	34669	68993	170536	354863	1125298	7271478
Notes and Loans Payable 27	2720	0	88	619	1903	4513	9057	23496	32068	69877	172250	457977	2993286
All Other Liabilities 28	1033	0	15	54	171	711	2561	6569	16398	46683	56729	224003	1460426
Net Worth 29	1831	0	32	-4	77	1196	3313	4604	20527	53976	125883	443318	2817766

Selected Financial Ratios (Times to 1)

Current Ratio 30	1.2	•	1.3	2.0	1.4	1.5	1.3	1.0	1.1	1.1	1.5	1.4	1.0
Quick Ratio 31	0.8	•	1.0	1.4	0.8	1.0	0.9	0.6	0.7	0.6	1.2	0.7	0.8
Net Sales to Working Capital 32	18.8	•	22.3	6.8	13.0	10.7	16.9	•	30.5	33.2	5.4	10.3	52.9
Coverage Ratio 33	1.5	•	4.7	2.3	1.3	1.2	•	0.9	0.5	1.6	1.7	1.3	1.8
Total Asset Turnover 34	0.4	•	1.4	0.7	0.5	0.6	0.7	0.7	0.8	1.1	0.4	0.5	0.3
Inventory Turnover 35	7.7	•	13.7	3.4	12.4	24.3	17.0	15.9	14.7	49.6	4.6	11.3	2.9
Receivables Turnover 36	11.2	•	35.7	20.7	32.2	14.5	12.8	15.7	12.3	20.3	3.2	14.4	8.6
Total Liabilities to Net Worth 37	2.0	•	3.2	•	26.9	4.4	3.5	6.5	2.4	2.2	1.8	1.5	1.6
Current Assets to Working Capital 38	6.4	•	4.3	2.0	3.5	2.9	5.0	•	9.9	7.8	3.1	3.7	21.3
Current Liabilities to Working Capital 39	5.4	•	3.3	1.0	2.5	1.9	4.0	•	8.9	6.8	2.1	2.7	20.3
Working Capital to Net Sales 40	0.1	•	0.0	0.1	0.1	0.1	0.1	•	0.0	0.0	0.2	0.1	0.0
Inventory to Working Capital 41	0.6	•	0.2	0.1	0.2	0.2	0.2	•	0.6	0.3	0.2	0.4	2.4
Total Receipts to Cash Flow 42	3.6	4.7	2.7	2.6	3.5	4.3	3.9	3.9	4.2	4.7	3.5	6.4	2.9
Cost of Goods to Cash Flow 43	0.8	0.4	0.3	0.1	0.6	1.3	0.9	0.9	1.2	2.0	0.8	2.9	0.4
Cash Flow to Total Debt 44	0.2	•	0.7	0.2	0.1	0.2	0.2	0.2	0.3	0.3	0.2	0.1	0.2

Selected Financial Factors (in Percentages)

Debt Ratio 45	67.2	•	76.4	100.5	96.4	81.4	77.8	86.7	70.2	68.3	64.5	60.6	61.2
Return on Total Assets 46	4.6	•	13.0	6.9	5.2	5.3	•	2.9	1.3	3.8	4.1	3.6	5.1
Return on Equity Before Income Taxes 47	4.8	•	43.6	•	31.5	5.3	•	•	•	4.7	4.9	2.0	5.8
Return on Equity After Income Taxes 48	2.7	•	41.3	•	28.4	4.1	•	•	•	•	2.5	0.7	3.7
Profit Margin (Before Income Tax) 49	3.7	•	7.3	6.0	2.3	1.6	•	•	•	1.4	1.6	1.6	8.1
Profit Margin (After Income Tax) 50	2.1	•	6.9	5.4	2.1	1.2	•	•	•	1.4	2.0	0.6	5.1

383

Table II

Corporations with Net Income

ACCOMMODATION

MONEY AMOUNTS AND SIZE OF ASSETS IN THOUSANDS OF DOLLARS

Item Description for Accounting Period 7/04 Through 6/05	Total	Zero Assets	Under 500	500 to 1,000	1,000 to 5,000	5,000 to 10,000	10,000 to 25,000	25,000 to 50,000	50,000 to 100,000	100,000 to 250,000	250,000 to 500,000	500,000 to 2,500,000	2,500,000 and over
Number of Enterprises **1**	18382	934	9448	2431	4856	364	206	60	19	22	15	0	0
Revenues ($ in Thousands)													
Net Sales **2**	57337347	945041	2592980	1093082	5864526	1041535	2373153	1123544	684738	2537821	2015271	0	0
Interest **3**	1818723	1473	3011	3115	13170	5232	5771	13100	6401	11601	65408	0	0
Rents **4**	353275	3918	696	0	6534	1343	7266	3473	3285	32526	12882	0	0
Royalties **5**	1598979	0	0	0	5174	0	365	1	6	141	160910	0	0
Other Portfolio Income **6**	1874343	37302	75593	98929	123280	28624	33731	43226	48311	249220	118651	0	0
Other Receipts **7**	6713628	29572	121456	28947	264213	151887	86461	30161	21758	99106	87316	0	0
Total Receipts **8**	69732395	1017306	2793736	1224073	6276897	1228621	2506747	1213505	764499	2930415	2460438	0	0
Average Total Receipts **9**	3794	1089	296	504	1293	3375	12169	20225	40237	133201	164029		•
Operating Costs/Operating Income (%)													
Cost of Operations **10**	14.1	8.5	8.9	3.7	18.0	26.3	21.4	21.4	17.6	21.2	15.5	•	•
Salaries and Wages **11**	28.9	23.6	12.3	17.1	17.7	18.2	21.7	20.2	22.1	16.6	26.1	•	•
Taxes Paid **12**	9.1	7.6	6.4	7.4	7.0	7.3	5.7	5.9	5.7	5.5	5.6	•	•
Interest Paid **13**	8.0	3.9	1.5	5.2	6.3	5.9	4.0	6.5	4.5	3.0	6.9	•	•
Depreciation **14**	7.1	5.6	3.2	6.5	7.1	6.1	6.2	7.9	7.8	7.2	10.0	•	•
Amortization and Depletion **15**	0.6	0.6	0.2	0.7	0.5	0.2	0.2	0.4	0.6	0.7	0.8	•	•
Pensions and Other Deferred Comp. **16**	0.6	0.9	•	•	0.1	0.1	0.2	0.1	0.2	0.4	1.1	•	•
Employee Benefits **17**	3.1	3.6	0.6	0.3	1.2	0.4	2.5	2.2	2.5	2.7	2.4	•	•
Advertising **18**	3.5	2.8	1.7	3.0	1.8	2.3	3.0	2.4	3.2	3.3	4.0	•	•
Other Expenses **19**	33.4	38.4	48.4	51.5	29.7	30.4	31.7	27.8	34.9	37.8	31.2	•	•
Officers' Compensation **20**	1.7	0.3	3.3	1.4	3.7	3.9	1.3	1.3	0.5	0.9	1.1	•	•
Operating Margin **21**	•	4.2	13.7	3.1	6.9	•	2.2	3.7	0.4	0.8	•	•	•
Operating Margin Before Officers' Comp. **22**	•	4.5	16.9	4.5	10.6	2.7	3.6	5.1	0.9	1.7	•	•	•

Selected Average Balance Sheet ($ in Thousands)

Net Receivables 23	322	0	6	26	34	113	859	1873	2530	10834	48502
Inventories 24	110	0	1	8	14	53	112	253	346	1184	11812
Net Property, Plant and Equipment 25	3315	0	81	531	1501	4254	9167	22795	37235	83786	199305
Total Assets 26	8541	0	162	693	2135	6047	15313	34364	73789	176355	368738
Notes and Loans Payable 27	3742	0	73	675	1494	3192	8673	20522	31073	55699	205763
All Other Liabilities 28	1564	0	14	29	122	377	2099	4099	8340	48169	24290
Net Worth 29	3235	0	75	-11	519	2478	4541	9743	34376	72487	138685

Selected Financial Ratios (Times to 1)

Current Ratio 30	1.2	.	2.6	1.7	2.5	1.6	1.5	1.5	1.8	2.2	1.3
Quick Ratio 31	0.8	.	2.1	1.0	1.8	1.3	1.1	1.0	1.4	1.0	1.0
Net Sales to Working Capital 32	16.3	.	6.5	8.4	7.1	10.0	10.2	9.1	6.0	3.7	6.8
Coverage Ratio 33	2.5	4.1	15.7	3.9	3.2	3.8	3.0	2.8	3.6	6.4	3.5
Total Asset Turnover 34	0.4	.	1.7	0.6	0.6	0.5	0.8	0.5	0.5	0.7	0.4
Inventory Turnover 35	4.0	.	21.1	2.2	15.8	14.3	21.9	15.8	18.3	20.7	1.8
Receivables Turnover 36	11.2	.	50.6	16.3	40.4	34.3	14.9	14.9	10.3	14.6	2.6
Total Liabilities to Net Worth 37	1.6	.	1.2	.	3.1	1.4	2.4	2.5	1.1	1.4	1.7
Current Assets to Working Capital 38	6.1	.	1.6	2.4	1.7	2.6	2.9	3.2	2.2	1.9	4.8
Current Liabilities to Working Capital 39	5.1	.	0.6	1.4	0.7	1.6	1.9	2.2	1.2	0.9	3.8
Working Capital to Net Sales 40	0.1	.	0.2	0.1	0.1	0.1	0.1	0.1	0.2	0.3	0.1
Inventory to Working Capital 41	0.5	.	0.0	0.1	0.1	0.2	0.1	0.2	0.0	0.0	0.4
Total Receipts to Cash Flow 42	2.8	2.8	2.0	2.3	2.7	2.6	3.6	3.3	3.0	2.8	2.5
Cost of Goods to Cash Flow 43	0.4	0.2	0.2	0.1	0.5	0.7	0.8	0.7	0.5	0.6	0.4
Cash Flow to Total Debt 44	0.2	.	1.5	0.3	0.3	0.3	0.3	0.2	0.3	0.4	0.2

Selected Financial Factors (in Percentages)

Debt Ratio 45	62.1	.	53.8	101.5	75.7	59.0	70.3	71.6	53.4	58.9	62.4
Return on Total Assets 46	7.2	.	38.8	13.2	11.4	10.7	8.9	9.9	8.1	12.6	8.9
Return on Equity Before Income Taxes 47	11.2	.	78.7	.	32.4	19.3	19.8	22.6	12.6	25.8	16.9
Return on Equity After Income Taxes 48	8.8	.	76.6	.	31.5	18.2	18.3	20.3	11.5	18.3	13.2
Profit Margin (Before Income Tax) 49	11.6	11.8	21.4	15.1	13.9	16.7	7.8	11.7	12.0	16.2	17.5
Profit Margin (After Income Tax) 50	9.1	10.3	20.8	14.3	13.5	15.7	7.2	10.5	11.0	11.5	13.6

Table I

Corporations with and without Net Income

FOOD SERVICES AND DRINKING PLACES

ACCOMMODATION AND FOOD SERVICES
722115

MONEY AMOUNTS AND SIZE OF ASSETS IN THOUSANDS OF DOLLARS

Item Description for Accounting Period 7/04 Through 6/05	Total	Zero Assets	Under 500	500 to 1,000	1,000 to 5,000	5,000 to 10,000	10,000 to 25,000	25,000 to 50,000	50,000 to 100,000	100,000 to 250,000	250,000 to 500,000	500,000 to 2,500,000	2,500,000 and over
Number of Enterprises 1	243964	28486	193348	13285	7627	571	383	112	48	45	21	24	12
Revenues ($ in Thousands)													
Net Sales 2	288647602	3423759	94288297	25840396	33639889	8039383	10615246	7191251	6758616	10969137	9714583	25232766	52954279
Interest 3	1367695	5647	21090	8376	10148	5924	7869	4961	4079	21000	17541	302466	958594
Rents 4	644039	219	48630	11656	6710	10491	7995	15929	9398	33730	47672	248385	203224
Royalties 5	4195071	4224	1046	1692	361	779	43210	63437	40350	152489	567928	820604	2498949
Other Portfolio Income 6	1159067	145916	203040	76502	53495	20053	20130	12703	13283	82318	92089	62344	377191
Other Receipts 7	7367941	92814	519797	403134	359454	240479	195187	113456	66036	192984	450856	1256031	3477718
Total Receipts 8	303381415	3672579	95061900	26341756	34070057	8317109	10889637	7401737	6891762	11451658	10890669	27922596	60469955
Average Total Receipts 9	1244	129	492	1983	4467	14566	28432	66087	143578	254481	518603	1163442	5039163
Operating Costs/Operating Income (%)													
Cost of Operations 10	41.8	43.6	42.8	39.9	40.9	41.5	43.5	47.5	38.5	43.4	35.6	42.7	40.9
Salaries and Wages 11	19.8	15.3	17.0	19.6	19.1	20.2	19.3	16.7	19.7	19.3	27.2	22.2	23.5
Taxes Paid 12	4.1	5.6	4.4	4.2	3.8	4.2	3.7	3.5	3.6	4.1	4.5	4.0	3.7
Interest Paid 13	1.7	1.1	0.6	0.9	1.0	1.3	1.9	1.9	1.8	2.4	2.7	2.8	3.4
Depreciation 14	3.2	2.6	1.9	3.1	2.7	2.9	3.5	3.4	3.6	4.1	4.6	5.8	4.3
Amortization and Depletion 15	0.5	0.5	0.2	0.3	0.3	0.7	0.7	0.6	0.7	0.5	0.7	0.6	1.1
Pensions and Other Deferred Comp. 16	0.2	0.0	0.1	0.1	0.1	0.4	0.1	0.1	0.2	0.1	0.8	0.3	0.4
Employee Benefits 17	1.2	0.5	0.4	0.8	0.9	1.5	1.3	1.3	1.5	1.6	1.6	1.8	2.5
Advertising 18	2.5	2.7	1.6	3.4	3.2	3.2	3.5	2.4	2.2	3.1	3.1	3.2	2.3
Other Expenses 19	24.8	37.2	25.5	24.8	23.1	24.3	22.5	23.0	28.9	22.3	24.2	22.8	25.9
Officers' Compensation 20	2.3	3.5	4.3	2.7	2.2	1.5	1.4	1.2	1.0	0.7	1.0	0.6	0.6
Operating Margin 21	•	1.0	1.0	0.1	2.7	•	•	•	•	•	•	•	•
Operating Margin Before Officers' Comp. 22	0.2	5.3	2.9	4.9	4.9	•	0.2	•	•	•	•	•	•

Selected Average Balance Sheet ($ in Thousands)

Net Receivables 23	42	0	4	25	77	212	891	3122	4161	10275	19233	53312	452770
Inventories 24	20	0	7	29	63	462	399	1010	2035	4511	8881	20726	109515
Net Property, Plant and Equipment 25	287	0	51	374	971	3506	7957	17669	38427	82366	167001	471422	1688619
Total Assets 26	739	0	107	690	1871	6561	15401	34808	70229	158128	344425	910027	6932579
Notes and Loans Payable 27	289	0	87	437	1004	3664	8884	16615	33751	60975	147054	263940	1599329
All Other Liabilities 28	192	0	21	110	466	1301	3466	9462	21920	50835	99805	269536	1896672
Net Worth 29	258	0	-1	142	401	1596	3052	8732	14558	46318	97565	376551	3436577

Selected Financial Ratios (Times to 1)

Current Ratio 30	0.9	•	1.3	1.2	1.1	0.8	0.9	0.9	0.6	1.1	1.0	0.9	0.8
Quick Ratio 31	0.7	•	0.8	0.8	0.7	0.5	0.6	0.6	0.4	0.7	0.7	0.5	0.6
Net Sales to Working Capital 32	•	•	65.6	69.1	162.6	•	•	•	•	130.7	295.8	•	•
Coverage Ratio 33	2.9	•	4.2	3.3	4.9	2.4	1.7	1.8	1.2	2.1	3.3	2.3	2.8
Total Asset Turnover 34	1.6	•	4.6	2.8	2.4	2.1	1.8	1.8	2.0	1.5	1.3	1.2	0.6
Inventory Turnover 35	24.1	•	31.0	26.8	28.6	12.7	30.2	30.2	26.7	23.5	18.5	21.7	16.5
Receivables Turnover 36	29.8	•	113.2	86.3	52.0	50.9	33.3	26.3	33.4	27.7	26.5	22.1	10.5
Total Liabilities to Net Worth 37	1.9	•	•	3.8	3.7	3.1	4.0	3.0	3.8	2.4	2.5	1.4	1.0
Current Assets to Working Capital 38	•	•	4.4	5.8	18.3	•	•	•	•	19.1	46.0	•	•
Current Liabilities to Working Capital 39	•	•	3.4	4.8	17.3	•	•	•	•	18.1	45.0	•	•
Working Capital to Net Sales 40	•	•	0.0	0.0	0.0	•	•	•	•	0.0	0.0	•	•
Inventory to Working Capital 41	•	•	0.9	1.1	2.2	•	•	•	•	2.2	6.0	•	•
Total Receipts to Cash Flow 42	5.3	5.9	5.8	5.7	5.4	5.5	6.3	6.0	4.6	6.1	4.4	5.4	4.2
Cost of Goods to Cash Flow 43	2.2	2.6	2.5	2.3	2.2	2.3	2.7	2.8	1.8	2.6	1.6	2.3	1.7
Cash Flow to Total Debt 44	0.5	•	0.8	0.6	0.6	0.5	0.4	0.4	0.5	0.4	0.4	0.4	0.3

Selected Financial Factors (in Percentages)

Debt Ratio 45	65.1	•	100.9	79.4	78.6	75.7	80.2	74.9	79.3	70.7	71.7	58.6	50.4
Return on Total Assets 46	7.6	•	11.3	8.4	11.7	6.7	5.9	6.4	4.2	7.8	11.8	7.7	6.1
Return on Equity Before Income Taxes 47	14.3	•	•	28.3	43.4	16.2	12.7	11.4	3.0	13.9	28.8	10.6	8.0
Return on Equity After Income Taxes 48	11.0	•	•	27.3	41.8	15.4	11.0	8.8	0.7	10.2	21.5	6.6	4.8
Profit Margin (Before Income Tax) 49	3.1	•	1.9	2.1	4.0	1.8	1.4	1.6	0.3	2.6	6.1	3.8	6.2
Profit Margin (After Income Tax) 50	2.4	•	1.8	2.0	3.8	1.7	1.2	1.2	0.1	1.9	4.5	2.4	3.8

Table II

Corporations with Net Income

FOOD SERVICES AND DRINKING PLACES

MONEY AMOUNTS AND SIZE OF ASSETS IN THOUSANDS OF DOLLARS

Item Description for Accounting Period 7/04 Through 6/05	Total	Zero Assets	Under 500	500 to 1,000	1,000 to 5,000	5,000 to 10,000	10,000 to 25,000	25,000 to 50,000	50,000 to 100,000	100,000 to 250,000	250,000 to 500,000	500,000 to 2,500,000	2,500,000 and over
Number of Enterprises **1**	124365	8300	101697	7620	5882	444	245	67	34	31	18	0	0
Revenues ($ in Thousands)													
Net Sales **2**	219773848	1126279	62725839	18532017	27973198	676796	7089795	4260727	4662598	7869104	8926489	0	0
Interest **3**	1132249	3745	17448	7055	8937	5234	4643	3268	3584	13737	17505	0	0
Rents **4**	359415	0	22981	9115	5907	10113	4644	14379	8365	25383	47275	0	0
Royalties **5**	3265076	3053	0	392	56	779	31514	41076	29807	127182	562571	0	0
Other Portfolio Income **6**	981676	87396	179341	39433	45846	15208	17083	9104	3689	76829	92089	0	0
Other Receipts **7**	6253750	7248	373065	163747	351755	216884	140729	59438	51679	184243	432851	0	0
Total Receipts **8**	231766014	1298721	63318674	18751759	28385699	7015014	7288408	4387992	4759722	8296478	10078780	0	0
Average Total Receipts **9**	1864	156	623	2461	4826	15800	29749	65492	139992	267628	559932	•	•
Operating Costs/Operating Income (%)													
Cost of Operations **10**	41.4	42.2	42.4	40.8	41.8	39.5	42.9	48.0	36.1	43.1	34.0	•	•
Salaries and Wages **11**	19.6	8.9	16.6	17.8	17.7	21.3	19.8	16.1	18.8	19.3	28.4	•	•
Taxes Paid **12**	3.9	5.3	4.2	3.7	3.7	4.4	3.6	3.1	3.3	4.0	4.7	•	•
Interest Paid **13**	1.5	1.2	0.5	0.6	0.9	1.1	1.5	1.3	1.4	1.8	2.3	•	•
Depreciation **14**	2.9	2.3	1.4	1.5	2.3	2.3	3.1	2.6	3.5	3.9	4.6	•	•
Amortization and Depletion **15**	0.5	0.2	0.2	0.2	0.3	0.7	0.5	0.4	0.5	0.5	0.7	•	•
Pensions and Other Deferred Comp. **16**	0.2	0.0	0.0	0.1	0.1	0.5	0.1	0.1	0.2	0.2	0.9	•	•
Employee Benefits **17**	1.3	0.2	0.5	0.8	0.9	1.5	1.3	1.2	1.4	1.6	1.6	•	•
Advertising **18**	2.5	2.1	1.6	3.6	3.2	2.9	3.4	2.1	2.1	3.2	3.2	•	•
Other Expenses **19**	23.4	30.5	22.8	23.5	22.5	24.8	20.8	21.6	31.2	21.8	24.5	•	•
Officers' Compensation **20**	2.1	6.1	4.3	2.4	1.8	1.3	1.5	1.4	0.9	0.8	1.0	•	•
Operating Margin **21**	0.7	1.0	5.5	4.9	4.7	•	1.5	2.1	0.6	0.0	•	•	•
Operating Margin Before Officers' Comp. **22**	2.8	7.1	9.8	7.3	6.5	0.9	3.1	3.6	1.5	0.8	•	•	•

Selected Average Balance Sheet ($ in Thousands)

Net Receivables 23	63	0	5	30	82	240	929	3043	3418	8280	21263
Inventories 24	31	0	7	31	61	508	404	1098	1712	4734	9095
Net Property, Plant and Equipment 25	427	0	54	326	886	3064	7684	15319	37498	82012	172842
Total Assets 26	1146	0	124	697	1844	6496	15108	33598	70312	154748	344882
Notes and Loans Payable 27	365	0	68	317	868	3143	7675	12541	28117	48768	139581
All Other Liabilities 28	276	0	20	110	452	1398	3275	7506	19953	41926	108630
Net Worth 29	506	0	35	270	524	1955	4157	13551	22242	64054	96671

Selected Financial Ratios (Times to 1)

Current Ratio 30	1.0	•	1.8	1.8	1.2	0.9	1.0	1.1	0.7	1.2	1.0
Quick Ratio 31	0.7	•	1.3	1.2	0.8	0.5	0.7	0.8	0.5	0.8	0.7
Net Sales to Working Capital 32	487.4	•	31.4	24.9	70.0	•	841.9	63.2	•	52.4	240.2
Coverage Ratio 33	5.1	15.1	14.5	10.3	7.6	3.9	3.9	4.8	2.9	4.1	3.9
Total Asset Turnover 34	1.5	•	5.0	3.5	2.6	2.3	1.9	1.9	2.0	1.6	1.4
Inventory Turnover 35	23.7	•	34.9	32.0	32.3	11.8	30.8	27.8	28.9	23.1	18.5
Receivables Turnover 36	28.5	•	110.0	85.2	53.4	52.0	34.1	24.4	34.8	30.8	32.5
Total Liabilities to Net Worth 37	1.3	•	2.5	1.6	2.5	2.6	2.6	1.5	2.2	1.4	2.6
Current Assets to Working Capital 38	61.9	•	2.3	2.3	7.6	•	108.4	9.5	•	7.4	37.4
Current Liabilities to Working Capital 39	60.9	•	1.3	1.3	6.6	•	107.4	8.5	•	6.4	36.4
Working Capital to Net Sales 40	0.0	•	0.0	0.0	0.0	•	0.0	0.0	•	0.0	0.0
Inventory to Working Capital 41	8.9	•	0.4	0.4	1.0	•	12.3	1.2	•	0.9	4.8
Total Receipts to Cash Flow 42	4.7	3.0	4.9	4.8	5.0	5.1	5.6	5.2	3.8	5.2	4.2
Cost of Goods to Cash Flow 43	1.9	1.3	2.1	1.9	2.1	2.0	2.4	2.5	1.4	2.3	1.4
Cash Flow to Total Debt 44	0.6	•	1.4	1.2	0.7	•	0.5	0.6	0.8	0.5	0.5

Selected Financial Factors (in Percentages)

Debt Ratio 45	55.9	•	71.4	61.2	71.6	69.9	72.5	59.7	68.4	58.6	72.0
Return on Total Assets 46	12.1	•	34.5	23.4	18.3	10.2	11.1	12.2	7.9	11.8	13.1
Return on Equity Before Income Taxes 47	21.9	•	112.5	54.5	55.8	25.3	30.0	23.9	16.4	21.5	34.6
Return on Equity After Income Taxes 48	18.6	•	111.2	53.6	54.2	24.4	28.1	21.1	14.3	17.6	26.0
Profit Margin (Before Income Tax) 49	6.3	16.3	6.5	6.1	6.2	3.2	4.3	5.1	2.7	5.4	6.7
Profit Margin (After Income Tax) 50	5.3	15.9	6.4	6.0	6.0	3.1	4.0	4.5	2.3	4.4	5.1

Table I

Corporations with and without Net Income

AUTOMOTIVE REPAIR AND MAINTENANCE

MONEY AMOUNTS AND SIZE OF ASSETS IN THOUSANDS OF DOLLARS

Item Description for Accounting Period 7/04 Through 6/05	Total	Zero Assets	Under 500	500 to 1,000	1,000 to 5,000	5,000 to 10,000	10,000 to 25,000	25,000 to 50,000	50,000 to 100,000	100,000 to 250,000	250,000 to 500,000	500,000 to 2,500,000	2,500,000 and over
Number of Enterprises 1	106732	10787	88401	5288	2040	148	46	8	7	4	4	0	0
Revenues ($ in Thousands)													
Net Sales 2	61469613	1416817	38495836	8019328	7715664	1644622	1181702	539648	878429	237769	1339798	0	0
Interest 3	31245	7	5095	4884	6723	2296	558	840	159	9684	997	0	0
Rents 4	38873	0	23055	8987	3841	178	1785	333	0	165	530	0	0
Royalties 5	66923	0	0	0	0	0	9397	0	1450	54466	1610	0	0
Other Portfolio Income 6	140970	23683	34710	1149	34342	42306	3309	50	470	486	463	0	0
Other Receipts 7	257531	7643	88111	25016	33580	20871	17903	4747	2031	54863	2768	0	0
Total Receipts 8	62005155	1448150	38646807	8059364	7794150	1710273	1214654	545618	882539	357433	1346166	0	0
Average Total Receipts 9	581	134	437	1524	3821	11556	26406	68202	126077	89358	336542	.	.
Operating Costs/Operating Income (%)													
Cost of Operations 10	49.9	43.8	47.0	55.3	57.4	55.1	55.9	38.0	51.7	44.2	59.0	.	.
Salaries and Wages 11	12.8	10.9	13.2	9.4	14.6	11.6	12.2	19.6	18.5	22.7	5.9	.	.
Taxes Paid 12	3.6	4.6	3.8	3.6	3.4	3.6	3.1	2.9	3.6	4.4	1.7	.	.
Interest Paid 13	1.2	0.7	0.8	1.8	1.1	1.9	1.5	2.4	2.9	9.6	4.1	.	.
Depreciation 14	2.3	4.2	2.0	2.8	2.2	2.5	3.0	3.4	3.3	7.3	3.8	.	.
Amortization and Depletion 15	0.4	3.3	0.2	0.2	0.3	0.4	0.4	2.2	1.2	5.8	1.9	.	.
Pensions and Other Deferred Comp. 16	0.2	0.0	0.2	0.1	0.1	0.7	0.2	0.1	0.0	1.9	1.0	.	.
Employee Benefits 17	1.2	0.7	1.0	1.9	1.1	1.0	1.7	2.2	0.9	3.6	1.7	.	.
Advertising 18	1.7	1.9	1.5	2.1	1.6	2.4	2.1	4.1	0.4	1.3	3.2	.	.
Other Expenses 19	19.8	34.8	21.0	18.4	13.1	16.6	19.2	24.8	19.2	57.4	15.7	.	.
Officers' Compensation 20	6.4	7.0	8.1	4.0	4.0	3.1	1.8	0.9	0.8	2.9	0.5	.	.
Operating Margin 21	0.5	.	1.3	0.5	1.1	1.1	.	.	.	.	1.4	.	.
Operating Margin Before Officers' Comp. 22	6.9	.	9.4	4.4	5.1	4.2	0.7	0.3	.	.	1.9	.	.

Selected Average Balance Sheet ($ in Thousands)

Net Receivables 23	19	0	10	74	216	772	1998	4206	3428	10612	9842
Inventories 24	20	0	11	53	255	614	1615	2094	4656	5305	30757
Net Property, Plant and Equipment 25	85	0	44	371	788	3377	5764	9295	21380	55682	104944
Total Assets 26	194	0	101	700	1818	6693	15664	32936	67255	164228	307936
Notes and Loans Payable 27	118	0	68	489	924	2804	6018	26961	35964	82815	167545
All Other Liabilities 28	38	0	25	94	205	1256	4622	8982	19749	25406	59427
Net Worth 29	38	0	9	117	689	2633	5023	-3006	11543	56006	80965

Selected Financial Ratios (Times to 1)

Current Ratio 30	1.4	•	1.2	1.7	2.1	1.4	1.1	1.0	0.7	1.1	2.0
Quick Ratio 31	0.9	•	0.8	1.1	1.3	0.7	0.6	0.4	0.5	0.5	0.3
Net Sales to Working Capital 32	27.2	•	57.6	16.0	9.6	16.9	53.7	•	•	15.4	7.4
Coverage Ratio 33	2.2	•	3.0	1.5	2.9	3.7	2.1	1.2	0.3	•	1.5
Total Asset Turnover 34	3.0	•	4.3	2.2	2.1	1.7	1.6	2.0	1.9	0.4	1.1
Inventory Turnover 35	14.6	•	19.0	15.7	8.5	10.0	8.9	12.2	13.9	5.0	6.4
Receivables Turnover 36	31.0	•	45.3	20.1	19.3	13.0	14.3	17.6	26.0	•	34.1
Total Liabilities to Net Worth 37	4.1	•	10.2	5.0	1.6	1.5	2.1	•	4.8	1.9	2.8
Current Assets to Working Capital 38	3.4	•	5.3	2.5	1.9	3.3	12.4	•	•	12.1	2.0
Current Liabilities to Working Capital 39	2.4	•	4.3	1.5	0.9	2.3	11.4	•	•	11.1	1.0
Working Capital to Net Sales 40	0.0	•	0.0	0.1	0.1	0.1	0.0	•	•	0.1	0.1
Inventory to Working Capital 41	1.0	•	1.5	0.6	0.7	0.8	3.1	•	•	1.4	0.7
Total Receipts to Cash Flow 42	6.8	7.2	6.4	7.3	9.3	6.4	7.7	5.8	8.5	3.2	8.8
Cost of Goods to Cash Flow 43	3.4	3.2	3.0	4.0	5.3	3.5	4.3	2.2	4.4	1.4	5.2
Cash Flow to Total Debt 44	0.5	•	0.7	0.4	0.4	0.4	0.3	0.3	0.3	0.2	0.2

Selected Financial Factors (in Percentages)

Debt Ratio 45	80.4	•	91.1	83.2	62.1	60.7	67.9	109.1	82.8	65.9	73.7
Return on Total Assets 46	7.6	•	10.8	6.0	6.8	11.5	5.2	5.9	1.7	•	6.7
Return on Equity Before Income Taxes 47	20.8	•	80.7	12.5	11.8	21.5	8.4	•	•	•	8.5
Return on Equity After Income Taxes 48	19.3	•	78.2	11.8	10.5	20.8	7.8	•	•	•	5.1
Profit Margin (Before Income Tax) 49	1.4	•	1.7	1.0	2.2	5.1	1.6	0.5	•	•	2.1
Profit Margin (After Income Tax) 50	1.3	•	1.6	0.9	1.9	4.9	1.5	0.2	•	•	1.2

Table II

Corporations with Net Income

AUTOMOTIVE REPAIR AND MAINTENANCE

MONEY AMOUNTS AND SIZE OF ASSETS IN THOUSANDS OF DOLLARS

Item Description for Accounting Period 7/04 Through 6/05	Total	Zero Assets	Under 500	500 to 1,000	1,000 to 5,000	5,000 to 10,000	10,000 to 25,000	25,000 to 50,000	50,000 to 100,000	100,000 to 250,000	250,000 to 500,000	500,000 to 2,500,000	2,500,000 and over
Number of Enterprises **1**	57965	4858	48495	3359	1100	118	25	0	0	0	0	0	0
Revenues ($ in Thousands)													
Net Sales **2**	38671089	612372	24867948	5411104	4567085	1318287	796345	0	0	0	0	0	0
Interest **3**	11504	0	3302	2413	3259	1453	358	0	0	0	0	0	0
Rents **4**	14768	0	6410	3012	3318	100	1363	0	0	0	0	0	0
Royalties **5**	11007	0	0	0	0	0	9397	0	0	0	0	0	0
Other Portfolio Income **6**	109631	19551	20043	222	25709	40725	2747	0	0	0	0	0	0
Other Receipts **7**	140533	7013	58189	19821	11041	20262	8169	0	0	0	0	0	0
Total Receipts **8**	38958532	638936	24955892	5436572	4610412	1380827	818379	0	0	0	0	0	0
Average Total Receipts **9**	672	132	515	1619	4191	11702	32735	·	·	·	·	·	·
Operating Costs/Operating Income (%)													
Cost of Operations **10**	47.1	41.8	44.7	52.6	52.3	49.9	58.2	·	·	·	·	·	·
Salaries and Wages **11**	12.6	9.2	13.2	9.3	14.8	13.6	10.9	·	·	·	·	·	·
Taxes Paid **12**	3.5	2.9	3.6	3.3	3.9	3.4	3.0	·	·	·	·	·	·
Interest Paid **13**	0.9	0.3	0.6	1.6	1.1	2.0	1.0	·	·	·	·	·	·
Depreciation **14**	2.0	3.2	1.7	2.6	1.8	2.6	1.7	·	·	·	·	·	·
Amortization and Depletion **15**	0.2	·	0.1	0.1	0.2	0.5	0.2	·	·	·	·	·	·
Pensions and Other Deferred Comp. **16**	0.2	·	0.2	0.1	0.2	0.2	0.3	·	·	·	·	·	·
Employee Benefits **17**	1.1	0.0	1.0	1.6	1.0	1.0	1.2	·	·	·	·	·	·
Advertising **18**	1.9	2.4	1.6	2.4	2.3	2.7	1.9	·	·	·	·	·	·
Other Expenses **19**	18.9	29.1	19.9	18.6	13.2	17.5	17.2	·	·	·	·	·	·
Officers' Compensation **20**	6.8	4.4	8.3	4.8	4.8	3.8	1.8	·	·	·	·	·	·
Operating Margin **21**	4.7	6.6	5.2	3.0	4.4	2.5	2.5	·	·	·	·	·	·
Operating Margin Before Officers' Comp. **22**	11.5	11.1	13.5	7.8	9.3	6.4	4.3	·	·	·	·	·	·

Selected Average Balance Sheet ($ in Thousands)

Net Receivables 23	20	0	11	77	165	656	2774
Inventories 24	21	0	10	42	336	582	1825
Net Property, Plant and Equipment 25	87	0	39	358	806	3559	4657
Total Assets 26	209	0	107	704	1895	6813	15217
Notes and Loans Payable 27	104	0	55	415	799	2889	5076
All Other Liabilities 28	35	0	21	89	193	1184	4973
Net Worth 29	70	0	31	200	903	2739	5167

Selected Financial Ratios (Times to 1)

Current Ratio 30	1.7	•	1.6	1.7	2.6	1.5	1.3
Quick Ratio 31	1.1	•	1.2	1.2	1.6	0.8	0.8
Net Sales to Working Capital 32	18.7	•	29.4	15.6	7.8	17.8	18.6
Coverage Ratio 33	6.8	34.0	10.7	3.2	5.8	4.6	6.4
Total Asset Turnover 34	3.2	•	4.8	2.3	2.2	1.6	2.1
Inventory Turnover 35	15.1	•	22.8	20.0	6.5	9.6	10.2
Receivables Turnover 36	32.2	•	47.4	21.3	20.1	13.2	14.2
Total Liabilities to Net Worth 37	2.0	•	2.5	2.5	1.1	1.5	1.9
Current Assets to Working Capital 38	2.4	•	2.7	2.4	1.6	3.1	4.3
Current Liabilities to Working Capital 39	1.4	•	1.7	1.4	0.6	2.1	3.3
Working Capital to Net Sales 40	0.1	•	0.0	0.1	0.1	0.1	0.1
Inventory to Working Capital 41	0.6	•	0.6	0.5	0.6	0.5	1.2
Total Receipts to Cash Flow 42	5.5	3.6	5.3	6.1	7.1	5.6	6.6
Cost of Goods to Cash Flow 43	2.6	1.5	2.3	3.2	3.7	2.8	3.8
Cash Flow to Total Debt 44	0.9	•	1.3	0.5	0.6	0.5	0.5

Selected Financial Factors (in Percentages)

Debt Ratio 45	66.7	•	71.1	71.5	52.4	59.8	66.0
Return on Total Assets 46	20.4	•	29.3	11.6	14.2	15.2	13.2
Return on Equity Before Income Taxes 47	52.3	•	91.9	27.9	24.7	29.6	32.7
Return on Equity After Income Taxes 48	50.8	•	90.6	27.3	22.8	28.8	31.5
Profit Margin (Before Income Tax) 49	5.5	11.0	5.5	3.5	5.4	7.3	5.3
Profit Margin (After Income Tax) 50	5.3	10.9	5.5	3.4	5.0	7.1	5.1

Table I

Corporations with and without Net Income

OTHER REPAIR AND MAINTENANCE

MONEY AMOUNTS AND SIZE OF ASSETS IN THOUSANDS OF DOLLARS

Item Description for Accounting Period 7/04 Through 6/05	Total	Zero Assets	Under 500	500 to 1,000	1,000 to 5,000	5,000 to 10,000	10,000 to 25,000	25,000 to 50,000	50,000 to 100,000	100,000 to 250,000	250,000 to 500,000	500,000 to 2,500,000	2,500,000 and over
Number of Enterprises **1**	52949	7104	42468	1807	1372	104	70	13	5	6	0	0	0
Revenues ($ in Thousands)													
Net Sales **2**	28477651	779353	12277316	3678623	5256647	1644117	2236995	760828	407765	1436008	0	0	0
Interest **3**	14769	2280	1995	1951	3706	759	1775	369	329	1604	0	0	0
Rents **4**	5109	0	702	749	2272	404	541	440	0	1	0	0	0
Royalties **5**	5815	0	4443	0	0	0	36	0	359	977	0	0	0
Other Portfolio Income **6**	80838	23186	28375	2283	6445	10280	4680	2488	774	2329	0	0	0
Other Receipts **7**	209482	2309	56248	4779	48849	16472	49843	7183	4511	19285	0	0	0
Total Receipts **8**	28793664	807128	12369079	3688385	5317919	1672032	2293870	771308	413738	1460204	0	0	0
Average Total Receipts **9**	544	114	291	2041	3876	16077	32770	59331	82748	243367	•	•	•
Operating Costs/Operating Income (%)													
Cost of Operations **10**	49.9	51.8	41.0	34.0	60.5	58.4	69.2	62.6	76.1	73.6	•	•	•
Salaries and Wages **11**	14.3	5.8	15.8	26.4	8.9	15.0	8.3	11.3	6.7	6.8	•	•	•
Taxes Paid **12**	3.1	1.6	3.3	4.5	2.7	2.6	2.5	3.3	1.2	2.5	•	•	•
Interest Paid **13**	0.8	1.0	0.5	0.7	1.2	0.8	0.9	1.9	1.2	1.4	•	•	•
Depreciation **14**	2.1	3.0	2.3	1.2	1.8	3.1	2.6	2.0	2.3	1.3	•	•	•
Amortization and Depletion **15**	0.3	0.1	0.0	0.8	0.3	0.1	0.1	0.6	3.9	1.3	•	•	•
Pensions and Other Deferred Comp. **16**	0.3	0.1	0.2	0.3	0.3	0.8	0.9	0.3	0.5	0.1	•	•	•
Employee Benefits **17**	2.7	2.2	1.3	9.0	1.9	2.9	2.3	2.7	1.5	1.9	•	•	•
Advertising **18**	0.6	1.3	0.9	0.3	0.6	0.3	0.3	0.3	0.1	0.1	•	•	•
Other Expenses **19**	17.5	24.7	22.1	17.7	13.3	13.9	9.2	11.8	8.7	12.4	•	•	•
Officers' Compensation **20**	5.9	1.4	9.1	4.4	4.9	2.4	2.4	1.3	1.0	0.5	•	•	•
Operating Margin **21**	2.4	7.0	3.5	0.7	3.5	•	1.3	1.9	•	•	•	•	•
Operating Margin Before Officers' Comp. **22**	8.3	8.4	12.7	5.1	8.4	2.2	3.7	3.2	•	•	•	•	•

Selected Average Balance Sheet ($ in Thousands)

Net Receivables 23	51	0	11	207	516	2360	5176	10909	21780	50215
Inventories 24	38	0	13	85	492	1569	2934	9469	14203	14849
Net Property, Plant and Equipment 25	40	0	20	156	332	1118	3232	4519	9369	13496
Total Assets 26	193	0	65	740	1854	6409	15110	35522	68059	177128
Notes and Loans Payable 27	86	0	39	396	700	1726	5151	8368	26622	72356
All Other Liabilities 28	58	0	16	127	464	3002	4972	17576	21651	91125
Net Worth 29	49	0	10	217	691	1681	4987	9578	19786	13648

Selected Financial Ratios (Times to 1)

Current Ratio 30	1.6	•	1.8	2.2	1.8	1.4	1.6	1.9	2.3	0.9
Quick Ratio 31	1.0	•	1.2	1.6	1.0	1.0	1.0	1.0	1.3	0.5
Net Sales to Working Capital 32	11.1	•	17.4	8.4	6.9	10.5	8.0	4.6	3.3	•
Coverage Ratio 33	5.3	11.3	9.5	2.3	4.8	2.9	5.1	2.7	•	0.7
Total Asset Turnover 34	2.8	•	4.5	2.8	2.1	2.5	2.1	1.6	1.2	1.4
Inventory Turnover 35	7.1	•	9.5	8.2	4.7	5.9	7.5	3.9	4.4	11.9
Receivables Turnover 36	10.4	•	26.5	11.6	6.4	6.7	7.6	4.9	2.9	4.9
Total Liabilities to Net Worth 37	2.9	•	5.4	2.4	1.7	2.8	2.0	2.7	2.4	12.0
Current Assets to Working Capital 38	2.6	•	2.2	1.8	2.3	3.3	2.6	2.1	1.8	•
Current Liabilities to Working Capital 39	1.6	•	1.2	0.8	1.3	2.3	1.6	1.1	0.8	•
Working Capital to Net Sales 40	0.1	•	0.1	0.1	0.1	0.1	0.1	0.2	0.3	•
Inventory to Working Capital 41	0.8	•	0.7	0.4	0.9	0.9	0.8	0.7	0.6	•
Total Receipts to Cash Flow 42	5.9	3.6	4.6	6.6	6.7	9.0	10.0	8.4	18.7	10.8
Cost of Goods to Cash Flow 43	2.9	1.9	1.9	2.2	4.0	5.3	6.9	5.2	14.3	8.0
Cash Flow to Total Debt 44	0.6	•	1.1	0.6	0.5	0.4	0.3	0.3	0.1	0.1

Selected Financial Factors (in Percentages)

Debt Ratio 45	74.6	•	84.5	70.7	62.7	73.8	67.0	73.0	70.9	92.3
Return on Total Assets 46	12.2	•	21.4	4.5	12.2	5.6	10.1	8.5	•	1.4
Return on Equity Before Income Taxes 47	38.8	•	122.9	8.6	25.8	13.9	24.6	19.9	•	•
Return on Equity After Income Taxes 48	35.4	•	119.3	8.3	25.0	3.4	21.1	15.7	•	•
Profit Margin (Before Income Tax) 49	3.5	10.5	4.3	0.9	4.6	1.5	3.8	3.3	•	•
Profit Margin (After Income Tax) 50	3.2	8.0	4.1	0.9	4.5	0.4	3.3	2.6	•	•

Table II

Corporations with Net Income

OTHER REPAIR AND MAINTENANCE

MONEY AMOUNTS AND SIZE OF ASSETS IN THOUSANDS OF DOLLARS

Item Description for Accounting Period 7/04 Through 6/05	Total	Zero Assets	Under 500	500 to 1,000	1,000 to 5,000	5,000 to 10,000	10,000 to 25,000	25,000 to 50,000	50,000 to 100,000	100,000 to 250,000	250,000 to 500,000	500,000 to 2,500,000	2,500,000 and over
Number of Enterprises **1**	32333	3324	26878	980	984	96	57	0	0	0	0	0	0
Revenues ($ in Thousands)													
Net Sales **2**	21214821	635989	8823910	2869668	3976697	1391233	1904172	0	0	0	0	0	0
Interest **3**	9596	2239	848	839	1363	555	1657	0	0	0	0	0	0
Rents **4**	3345	0	702	749	1098	306	490	0	0	0	0	0	0
Royalties **5**	1372	0	0	0	0	0	36	0	0	0	0	0	0
Other Portfolio Income **6**	77039	23186	28248	1166	4385	10046	4603	0	0	0	0	0	0
Other Receipts **7**	133697	2302	39316	2737	29945	14687	20861	0	0	0	0	0	0
Total Receipts **8**	21439870	663716	8893024	2875159	4013488	1416827	1931819	0	0	0	0	0	0
Average Total Receipts **9**	663	200	331	2934	4079	14759	33892	·	·	·	·	·	·
Operating Costs/Operating Income (%)													
Cost of Operations **10**	49.2	58.8	38.6	32.4	61.0	57.0	69.0	·	·	·	·	·	·
Salaries and Wages **11**	14.6	6.3	16.6	29.3	7.2	14.2	7.9	·	·	·	·	·	·
Taxes Paid **12**	2.8	1.6	2.9	4.4	2.4	2.7	2.7	·	·	·	·	·	·
Interest Paid **13**	0.6	0.8	0.4	0.4	1.3	0.4	0.5	·	·	·	·	·	·
Depreciation **14**	1.8	2.1	2.1	1.0	1.6	2.6	2.1	·	·	·	·	·	·
Amortization and Depletion **15**	0.1	0.0	0.0	0.2	0.3	0.0	0.1	·	·	·	·	·	·
Pensions and Other Deferred Comp. **16**	0.3	0.1	0.2	0.2	0.3	0.9	0.9	·	·	·	·	·	·
Employee Benefits **17**	2.7	1.2	0.8	11.1	1.6	3.0	2.7	·	·	·	·	·	·
Advertising **18**	0.6	0.4	1.0	0.4	0.6	0.4	0.3	·	·	·	·	·	·
Other Expenses **19**	15.6	13.3	21.2	12.9	13.2	12.1	7.7	·	·	·	·	·	·
Officers' Compensation **20**	5.1	0.8	7.8	3.6	4.6	2.6	2.4	·	·	·	·	·	·
Operating Margin **21**	6.3	14.4	8.4	4.2	5.9	4.1	3.8	·	·	·	·	·	·
Operating Margin Before Officers' Comp. **22**	11.4	15.3	16.2	7.8	10.6	6.7	6.2	·	·	·	·	·	·

Selected Average Balance Sheet ($ in Thousands)

Net Receivables 23	64	0	13	262	569	2382	5538
Inventories 24	41	0	10	60	517	1373	3007
Net Property, Plant and Equipment 25	43	0	20	137	321	1070	2937
Total Assets 26	226	0	68	778	1948	6326	15441
Notes and Loans Payable 27	74	0	31	326	699	1458	3488
All Other Liabilities 28	69	0	17	141	509	1977	5053
Net Worth 29	84	0	20	312	740	2890	6900

Selected Financial Ratios (Times to 1)

Current Ratio 30	1.8	•	1.8	2.1	1.9	1.8	1.8
Quick Ratio 31	1.1	•	1.2	1.6	1.1	1.3	1.1
Net Sales to Working Capital 32	9.9	•	18.9	11.1	6.3	6.4	6.8
Coverage Ratio 33	12.7	24.5	21.8	12.6	6.4	14.5	11.6
Total Asset Turnover 34	2.9	•	4.8	3.8	2.1	2.3	2.2
Inventory Turnover 35	7.8	•	12.6	15.8	4.8	6.0	7.7
Receivables Turnover 36	11.1	•	29.0	12.4	6.9	7.2	7.8
Total Liabilities to Net Worth 37	1.7	•	2.4	1.5	1.6	1.2	1.2
Current Assets to Working Capital 38	2.3	•	2.2	1.9	2.1	2.2	2.3
Current Liabilities to Working Capital 39	1.3	•	1.2	0.9	1.1	1.2	1.3
Working Capital to Net Sales 40	0.1	•	0.1	0.1	0.2	0.2	0.1
Inventory to Working Capital 41	0.6	•	0.6	0.2	0.8	0.6	0.7
Total Receipts to Cash Flow 42	5.1	3.7	3.8	6.8	5.8	7.0	9.4
Cost of Goods to Cash Flow 43	2.5	2.2	1.5	2.2	3.5	4.0	6.5
Cash Flow to Total Debt 44	0.9	•	1.8	0.9	0.6	0.6	0.4

Selected Financial Factors (in Percentages)

Debt Ratio 45	62.9	•	71.0	59.9	62.0	54.3	55.3
Return on Total Assets 46	23.3	•	46.3	17.9	16.8	14.6	12.4
Return on Equity Before Income Taxes 47	57.8	•	152.4	41.1	37.4	29.7	25.4
Return on Equity After Income Taxes 48	54.6	•	149.6	40.7	36.4	23.2	22.3
Profit Margin (Before Income Tax) 49	7.4	18.8	9.1	4.4	6.8	5.9	5.2
Profit Margin (After Income Tax) 50	7.0	15.7	9.0	4.3	6.7	4.6	4.6

Table I

Corporations with and without Net Income

PERSONAL AND LAUNDRY SERVICES

MONEY AMOUNTS AND SIZE OF ASSETS IN THOUSANDS OF DOLLARS

Item Description for Accounting Period 7/04 Through 6/05	Total	Zero Assets	Under 500	500 to 1,000	1,000 to 5,000	5,000 to 10,000	10,000 to 25,000	25,000 to 50,000	50,000 to 100,000	100,000 to 250,000	250,000 to 500,000	500,000 to 2,500,000	2,500,000 and over
Number of Enterprises **1**	133600	25675	98515	4344	4465	378	124	41	21	17	5	14	0
Revenues ($ in Thousands)													
Net Sales **2**	68719870	1442645	26071924	4270585	11867838	3642690	2261969	1430498	1466057	2607411	1047881	12610371	0
Interest **3**	238616	2945	9850	6841	18855	4443	5724	7847	5249	8332	22211	146318	0
Rents **4**	59057	455	1903	2725	5493	546	3065	1929	1679	5848	1614	33799	0
Royalties **5**	102793	0	0	0	0	0	61	1	94	7338	5085	90214	0
Other Portfolio Income **6**	525331	44543	84502	6282	38695	29009	38042	6731	2904	86758	2335	185527	0
Other Receipts **7**	1050513	1904	201827	30102	201017	47193	43326	47386	112834	166674	-26817	225074	0
Total Receipts **8**	70696180	1492492	26370006	4316535	12133898	3723881	2352187	1494392	1588817	2882361	1052309	13291303	0
Average Total Receipts **9**	529	58	268	994	2717	9852	18969	36449	75658	169551	210462	949379	•
Operating Costs/Operating Income (%)													
Cost of Operations **10**	28.7	14.5	23.0	28.0	28.5	45.4	33.2	30.9	36.7	31.3	37.4	34.3	•
Salaries and Wages **11**	20.9	15.5	21.3	20.2	23.2	13.1	22.4	23.7	20.4	18.0	25.8	20.6	•
Taxes Paid **12**	4.2	4.0	4.0	4.3	4.9	4.2	4.3	3.8	3.3	2.4	3.7	4.4	•
Interest Paid **13**	2.1	1.9	0.9	1.3	2.3	1.4	1.9	2.8	2.3	4.0	2.9	4.3	•
Depreciation **14**	3.8	1.9	3.3	6.4	3.5	6.7	4.3	4.1	4.6	3.7	4.7	3.6	•
Amortization and Depletion **15**	1.2	0.8	0.6	0.6	0.4	0.4	0.7	0.6	0.7	2.3	1.1	3.4	•
Pensions and Other Deferred Comp. **16**	0.5	1.1	0.3	0.6	0.4	0.4	0.4	0.5	0.7	0.2	0.6	0.7	•
Employee Benefits **17**	1.6	0.6	0.6	1.7	2.0	1.3	3.1	2.6	7.8	1.4	4.1	2.1	•
Advertising **18**	2.1	1.5	2.5	1.8	1.2	2.2	1.1	4.4	1.4	3.8	1.3	2.0	•
Other Expenses **19**	31.0	53.6	34.0	26.4	31.7	20.5	27.9	27.4	28.2	45.1	24.1	24.8	•
Officers' Compensation **20**	5.1	8.5	7.9	10.7	4.6	2.9	2.3	3.0	1.4	1.1	1.1	0.5	•
Operating Margin **21**	•	•	1.7	•	•	1.5	•	•	•	•	•	•	•
Operating Margin Before Officers' Comp. **22**	4.1	4.6	9.6	8.7	1.9	4.4	0.6	•	•	•	•	•	•

Selected Average Balance Sheet ($ in Thousands)

Net Receivables 23	47	0	5	54	197	908	2388	3940	8265	14491	64497	224171	•
Inventories 24	17	0	3	21	55	250	742	1442	3860	7146	6528	59371	•
Net Property, Plant and Equipment 25	138	0	36	347	935	2513	4768	9850	27216	29153	56765	423454	•
Total Assets 26	403	0	86	707	1749	6719	15605	34195	68870	149264	352559	1628148	•
Notes and Loans Payable 27	170	0	65	280	1118	2588	5508	15229	26415	71099	64616	413313	•
All Other Liabilities 28	117	0	15	95	325	1848	5108	13791	16802	66625	160262	580312	•
Net Worth 29	115	0	6	331	305	2283	4988	5175	25654	11541	127682	634522	•

Selected Financial Ratios (Times to 1)

Current Ratio 30	1.6	•	1.5	1.7	1.5	1.6	1.5	1.4	1.5	0.7	1.2	2.2	•
Quick Ratio 31	1.1	•	1.1	1.2	1.0	1.2	1.0	0.9	0.9	0.4	1.0	1.3	•
Net Sales to Working Capital 32	11.7	•	29.2	13.3	17.2	10.1	8.2	9.8	10.2	•	11.1	3.9	•
Coverage Ratio 33	1.9	0.7	4.2	0.3	0.7	3.7	2.2	1.1	1.4	0.3	•	2.1	•
Total Asset Turnover 34	1.3	•	3.1	1.4	1.5	1.4	1.2	1.0	1.0	1.0	0.6	0.6	•
Inventory Turnover 35	8.5	•	18.2	12.8	13.9	17.5	8.2	7.5	6.6	6.7	12.0	5.2	•
Receivables Turnover 36	9.8	•	54.3	15.5	13.7	11.4	8.5	9.6	8.0	11.8	3.2	4.4	•
Total Liabilities to Net Worth 37	2.5	•	13.1	1.1	4.7	1.9	2.1	5.6	1.7	11.9	1.8	1.6	•
Current Assets to Working Capital 38	2.6	•	2.9	2.5	3.2	2.6	3.0	3.6	3.0	•	5.3	1.8	•
Current Liabilities to Working Capital 39	1.6	•	1.9	1.5	2.2	1.6	2.0	2.6	2.0	•	4.3	0.8	•
Working Capital to Net Sales 40	0.1	•	0.0	0.1	0.1	0.1	0.1	0.1	0.1	0.1	0.1	0.3	•
Inventory to Working Capital 41	0.4	•	0.4	0.3	0.3	0.3	0.4	0.4	0.6	•	0.2	0.4	•
Total Receipts to Cash Flow 42	4.6	3.2	4.2	5.9	5.5	5.7	4.5	5.6	4.6	3.5	7.3	4.8	•
Cost of Goods to Cash Flow 43	1.3	0.5	1.0	1.6	1.6	2.6	1.5	1.7	1.7	1.1	2.7	1.7	•
Cash Flow to Total Debt 44	0.4	•	0.8	0.4	0.3	0.4	0.4	0.2	0.3	0.3	0.1	0.2	•

Selected Financial Factors (in Percentages)

Debt Ratio 45	71.5	•	92.9	53.1	82.6	66.0	68.0	84.9	62.8	92.3	63.8	61.0	•
Return on Total Assets 46	5.1	•	11.4	0.5	2.5	7.4	4.9	3.3	3.2	1.3	•	5.1	•
Return on Equity Before Income Taxes 47	8.5	•	122.5	•	•	15.8	8.2	2.8	2.5	•	•	6.9	•
Return on Equity After Income Taxes 48	6.2	•	119.7	•	•	14.5	6.0	•	1.6	•	•	3.7	•
Profit Margin (Before Income Tax) 49	1.9	•	2.8	•	•	3.8	2.2	0.4	0.9	•	•	4.9	•
Profit Margin (After Income Tax) 50	1.4	•	2.8	•	•	3.4	1.6	•	0.6	•	•	2.6	•

Table II

Corporations with Net Income

PERSONAL AND LAUNDRY SERVICES

MONEY AMOUNTS AND SIZE OF ASSETS IN THOUSANDS OF DOLLARS

Item Description for Accounting Period 7/04 Through 6/05	Total	Zero Assets	Under 500	500 to 1,000	1,000 to 5,000	5,000 to 10,000	10,000 to 25,000	25,000 to 50,000	50,000 to 100,000	100,000 to 250,000	250,000 to 500,000	500,000 to 2,500,000	2,500,000 and over
Number of Enterprises **1**	70544	8643	56635	2669	2166	294	80	23	15	0	0	0	0
Revenues ($ in Thousands)													
Net Sales **2**	44922638	754790	17363231	2885014	6479997	2797185	1640438	889694	1035557	0	0	0	0
Interest **3**	103869	2584	5890	5462	18039	4097	3621	4040	3448	0	0	0	0
Rents **4**	39257	288	1888	2381	4312	512	3049	592	963	0	0	0	0
Royalties **5**	76622	0	0	0	0	0	1	1	0	0	0	0	0
Other Portfolio Income **6**	296703	43203	47166	5947	23654	26293	34342	2250	2614	0	0	0	0
Other Receipts **7**	551701	9405	82806	9696	61958	37712	29755	38379	100280	0	0	0	0
Total Receipts **8**	45990790	810270	17500981	2908500	6587960	2865799	1711206	934956	1142862	0	0	0	0
Average Total Receipts **9**	652	94	309	1090	3042	9748	21390	40650	76191	·	·	·	·
Operating Costs/Operating Income (%)													
Cost of Operations **10**	29.6	11.9	25.3	30.9	24.0	42.5	31.1	37.0	41.3	·	·	·	·
Salaries and Wages **11**	18.8	13.3	18.1	14.9	23.4	13.2	23.5	19.6	18.3	·	·	·	·
Taxes Paid **12**	4.1	4.1	3.6	4.2	5.5	4.2	4.1	3.3	3.1	·	·	·	·
Interest Paid **13**	1.1	1.4	0.6	1.0	1.4	1.1	1.2	2.0	1.1	·	·	·	·
Depreciation **14**	3.2	2.2	2.2	5.5	2.2	7.0	3.4	3.9	4.6	·	·	·	·
Amortization and Depletion **15**	1.0	0.1	0.5	0.3	0.3	0.3	0.3	0.4	0.4	·	·	·	·
Pensions and Other Deferred Comp. **16**	0.4	1.9	0.1	0.8	0.7	0.2	0.4	0.6	0.9	·	·	·	·
Employee Benefits **17**	1.7	0.7	0.6	1.7	2.5	0.8	3.2	1.8	8.0	·	·	·	·
Advertising **18**	1.7	0.6	2.0	1.8	1.2	1.4	0.8	6.2	1.5	·	·	·	·
Other Expenses **19**	27.5	39.1	29.6	26.1	30.9	21.9	27.7	19.7	24.4	·	·	·	·
Officers' Compensation **20**	5.2	7.4	8.1	9.4	5.7	2.6	2.4	3.6	1.6	·	·	·	·
Operating Margin **21**	5.6	17.9	9.3	3.5	2.0	4.8	1.8	1.9	·	·	·	·	·
Operating Margin Before Officers' Comp. **22**	10.8	25.3	17.4	12.9	7.7	7.4	4.2	5.5	·	·	·	·	·

Selected Average Balance Sheet ($ in Thousands)

Net Receivables 23	47	0	3	57	217	780	2831	2735	9410
Inventories 24	24	0	4	27	60	233	847	2039	4343
Net Property, Plant and Equipment 25	135	0	36	345	753	2533	4583	9501	25122
Total Assets 26	421	0	86	718	1669	6516	15990	32815	67828
Notes and Loans Payable 27	145	0	47	235	801	2063	4357	9530	21465
All Other Liabilities 28	94	0	10	78	247	1863	5391	13230	15489
Net Worth 29	182	0	28	405	621	2590	6241	10055	30874

Selected Financial Ratios (Times to 1)

Current Ratio 30	1.8	.	2.6	2.2	1.9	1.5	1.6	1.3	1.9
Quick Ratio 31	1.2	.	2.0	1.5	1.5	1.1	1.1	0.8	1.3
Net Sales to Working Capital 32	10.7	.	17.7	8.8	12.7	11.8	6.8	11.5	7.6
Coverage Ratio 33	8.2	18.5	19.1	5.2	3.4	7.8	5.8	4.4	5.6
Total Asset Turnover 34	1.5	.	3.6	1.5	1.8	1.5	1.3	1.2	1.0
Inventory Turnover 35	7.8	.	20.3	12.4	11.9	17.4	7.5	7.0	6.6
Receivables Turnover 36	10.2	.	71.1	17.7	14.0	13.7	8.3	13.2	.
Total Liabilities to Net Worth 37	1.3	.	2.1	0.8	1.7	1.5	1.6	2.3	1.2
Current Assets to Working Capital 38	2.2	.	1.6	1.9	2.1	2.9	2.6	3.9	2.1
Current Liabilities to Working Capital 39	1.2	.	0.6	0.9	1.1	1.9	1.6	2.9	1.1
Working Capital to Net Sales 40	0.1	.	0.1	0.1	0.1	0.1	0.1	0.1	0.1
Inventory to Working Capital 41	0.4	.	0.2	0.3	0.2	0.4	0.3	0.6	0.5
Total Receipts to Cash Flow 42	4.1	2.1	3.6	4.6	5.5	4.5	3.7	5.1	4.6
Cost of Goods to Cash Flow 43	1.2	0.3	0.9	1.4	1.3	1.9	1.1	1.9	1.9
Cash Flow to Total Debt 44	0.7	.	1.5	0.7	0.5	0.5	0.6	0.3	0.4

Selected Financial Factors (in Percentages)

Debt Ratio 45	56.9	.	67.4	43.6	62.8	60.2	61.0	69.4	54.5
Return on Total Assets 46	13.9	.	38.2	8.0	8.7	12.1	9.3	10.6	6.3
Return on Equity Before Income Taxes 47	28.2	.	111.1	11.4	16.7	26.6	19.8	26.7	11.4
Return on Equity After Income Taxes 48	25.4	.	110.0	11.0	16.1	25.1	17.0	23.7	10.4
Profit Margin (Before Income Tax) 49	8.0	25.2	10.1	4.3	3.5	7.2	6.0	6.9	5.1
Profit Margin (After Income Tax) 50	7.2	24.5	10.0	4.1	3.3	6.8	5.2	6.2	4.7

Table I

Corporations with and without Net Income

RELIGIOUS, GRANTMAKING, CIVIC AND PROFESSIONAL ORGANIZATIONS

MONEY AMOUNTS AND SIZE OF ASSETS IN THOUSANDS OF DOLLARS

Item Description for Accounting Period 7/04 Through 6/05	Total	Zero Assets	Under 500	500 to 1,000	1,000 to 5,000	5,000 to 10,000	10,000 to 25,000	25,000 to 50,000	50,000 to 100,000	100,000 to 250,000	250,000 to 500,000	500,000 to 2,500,000	2,500,000 and over
Number of Enterprises **1**	39382	3327	31500	2516	1831	117	66	10	7	6	0	0	0
Revenues ($ in Thousands)													
Net Sales **2**	9960406	176102	3429713	1127839	1993274	204691	831944	280339	999620	916883	0	0	0
Interest **3**	120850	27	25618	20040	38116	4911	3459	1303	821	26556	0	0	0
Rents **4**	34742	203	11106	3297	11626	1683	1346	11	0	5470	0	0	0
Royalties **5**	5953	0	0	0	19	0	5934	0	0	0	0	0	0
Other Portfolio Income **6**	61634	0	62	15509	16045	6868	756	9650	0	12741	0	0	0
Other Receipts **7**	2546200	-87	475734	189470	541545	149456	125230	12007	30563	1022283	0	0	0
Total Receipts **8**	12729785	176245	3942233	1356155	2600625	367609	968669	303310	1031004	1983933	0	0	0
Average Total Receipts **9**	323	53	125	539	1420	3142	14677	30331	147286	330656	·	·	·
Operating Costs/Operating Income (%)													
Cost of Operations **10**	34.5	23.7	27.0	8.3	27.3	9.6	56.1	36.2	89.9	37.3	·	·	·
Salaries and Wages **11**	13.8	1.8	8.2	10.7	22.0	35.9	13.4	14.0	3.3	29.5	·	·	·
Taxes Paid **12**	2.2	2.5	1.6	1.5	3.7	6.0	2.3	2.0	0.3	3.8	·	·	·
Interest Paid **13**	0.4	1.6	0.1	0.4	0.5	4.3	0.6	0.4	0.1	0.2	·	·	·
Depreciation **14**	2.1	1.3	1.0	1.3	2.7	14.6	3.5	3.2	1.5	2.8	·	·	·
Amortization and Depletion **15**	0.2	·	0.0	0.1	0.1	0.2	0.0	0.1	0.3	1.1	·	·	·
Pensions and Other Deferred Comp. **16**	0.3	·	0.2	0.1	0.2	0.4	0.3	1.1	0.2	1.1	·	·	·
Employee Benefits **17**	1.4	·	0.7	0.7	2.4	5.8	1.2	1.5	0.1	4.1	·	·	·
Advertising **18**	0.7	0.1	0.2	0.0	0.6	1.1	0.3	0.7	0.1	4.9	·	·	·
Other Expenses **19**	68.5	67.8	69.7	95.6	70.7	99.7	36.2	41.5	7.0	124.1	·	·	·
Officers' Compensation **20**	2.7	·	6.5	0.5	0.7	0.7	0.6	1.5	0.3	1.3	·	·	·
Operating Margin **21**	·	1.2	·	·	·	·	·	·	·	·	·	·	·
Operating Margin Before Officers' Comp. **22**	·	1.2	·	·	·	·	·	·	·	·	·	·	·

Selected Average Balance Sheet ($ in Thousands)

Net Receivables 23	23	0	4	39	112	189	1503	2000	12448	41215	•
Inventories 24	2	0	0	0	14	28	202	137	108	1914	•
Net Property, Plant and Equipment 25	81	0	7	62	589	4081	9394	14385	36369	37932	•
Total Assets 26	312	0	87	696	1977	7155	15266	34501	64846	256704	•
Notes and Loans Payable 27	26	0	7	113	92	1076	2259	2036	4817	4250	•
All Other Liabilities 28	84	0	16	180	386	1099	3342	9797	15480	180900	•
Net Worth 29	203	0	65	404	1499	4980	9666	22668	44549	71553	•

Selected Financial Ratios (Times to 1)

Current Ratio 30	2.7	•	5.6	2.4	4.2	2.5	1.5	2.0	1.3	1.0	•
Quick Ratio 31	2.4	•	5.2	2.2	3.8	2.3	1.2	1.4	1.2	0.7	•
Net Sales to Working Capital 32	2.1	•	1.7	1.4	1.3	1.1	8.9	4.7	26.8	•	•
Coverage Ratio 33	3.5	1.8	•	4.2	0.4	1.3	3.8	13.8	1.8	32.3	•
Total Asset Turnover 34	0.8	•	1.2	0.6	0.6	0.2	0.8	0.8	2.2	0.6	•
Inventory Turnover 35	57.5	•	414.9	77.8	20.8	6.0	35.0	74.3	1193.8	29.8	•
Receivables Turnover 36	11.2	•	33.3	13.4	9.1	12.9	8.4	14.5	17.8	3.2	•
Total Liabilities to Net Worth 37	0.5	•	0.4	0.7	0.3	0.4	0.6	0.5	0.5	2.6	•
Current Assets to Working Capital 38	1.6	•	1.2	1.7	1.3	1.6	3.1	2.0	3.9	•	•
Current Liabilities to Working Capital 39	0.6	•	0.2	0.7	0.3	0.6	2.1	1.0	2.9	•	•
Working Capital to Net Sales 40	0.5	•	0.6	0.7	0.8	0.9	0.1	0.2	0.0	•	•
Inventory to Working Capital 41	0.0	•	0.0	0.0	0.0	0.0	0.2	0.0	0.0	•	•
Total Receipts to Cash Flow 42	1.7	1.7	1.8	1.3	1.7	1.3	3.0	2.3	18.1	0.8	•
Cost of Goods to Cash Flow 43	0.6	0.4	0.5	0.1	0.5	0.1	1.7	0.8	16.3	0.3	•
Cash Flow to Total Debt 44	1.3	•	2.6	1.2	1.3	0.6	0.8	1.0	0.4	1.0	•

Selected Financial Factors (in Percentages)

Debt Ratio 45	35.1	•	26.0	42.1	24.2	30.4	36.7	34.3	31.3	72.1	•
Return on Total Assets 46	1.1	•	•	0.9	0.1	1.4	2.0	4.8	0.3	3.8	•
Return on Equity Before Income Taxes 47	1.2	•	•	1.2	•	0.5	2.3	6.8	0.2	13.2	•
Return on Equity After Income Taxes 48	0.5	•	•	0.8	•	0.2	1.6	4.4	•	9.3	•
Profit Margin (Before Income Tax) 49	0.9	1.3	•	1.1	•	1.4	1.7	5.5	0.1	6.2	•
Profit Margin (After Income Tax) 50	0.4	1.2	•	0.7	•	0.6	1.2	3.6	•	4.4	•

Table II

Corporations with Net Income

RELIGIOUS, GRANTMAKING, CIVIC AND PROFESSIONAL ORGANIZATIONS

MONEY AMOUNTS AND SIZE OF ASSETS IN THOUSANDS OF DOLLARS

Item Description for Accounting Period 7/04 Through 6/05	Total	Zero Assets	Under 500	500 to 1,000	1,000 to 5,000	5,000 to 10,000	10,000 to 25,000	25,000 to 50,000	50,000 to 100,000	100,000 to 250,000	250,000 to 500,000	500,000 to 2,500,000	2,500,000 and over
Number of Enterprises 1	19573	1618	14707	1897	1259	40	37	0	3	0	0	0	0
Revenues ($ in Thousands)													
Net Sales 2	6256032	110263	2400876	849782	1084191	119806	435118	0	78129	0	0	0	0
Interest 3	99466	1	18210	17489	31287	2248	2187	0	316	0	0	0	0
Rents 4	28009	0	8351	2452	11021	0	703	0	0	0	0	0	0
Royalties 5	5934	0	0	0	0	0	5934	0	0	0	0	0	0
Other Portfolio Income 6	58077	0	62	14984	13382	6772	484	0	0	0	0	0	0
Other Receipts 7	1013459	-1	188730	128244	223226	63538	68354	0	9766	0	0	0	0
Total Receipts 8	7460977	110263	2616229	1012951	1363107	192364	512780	0	88211	0	0	0	0
Average Total Receipts 9	381	68	178	534	1083	4809	13859	•	29404	•	•	•	•
Operating Costs/Operating Income (%)													
Cost of Operations 10	28.5	36.1	35.5	10.6	17.1	7.1	37.7	•	1.7	•	•	•	•
Salaries and Wages 11	15.4	2.8	9.4	8.7	21.2	34.5	13.9	•	34.5	•	•	•	•
Taxes Paid 12	2.6	3.9	1.5	1.3	4.9	5.0	2.8	•	3.3	•	•	•	•
Interest Paid 13	0.3	1.7	0.1	0.3	0.4	2.1	0.7	•	1.1	•	•	•	•
Depreciation 14	1.7	1.4	0.6	1.1	2.3	6.4	2.8	•	9.9	•	•	•	•
Amortization and Depletion 15	0.2	•	0.0	0.1	0.0	0.1	0.1	•	3.5	•	•	•	•
Pensions and Other Deferred Comp. 16	0.4	•	0.3	•	0.2	0.4	0.6	•	2.6	•	•	•	•
Employee Benefits 17	1.7	•	0.9	0.8	2.6	3.1	1.1	•	1.5	•	•	•	•
Advertising 18	1.1	0.2	0.2	0.0	0.8	1.4	0.5	•	1.2	•	•	•	•
Other Expenses 19	58.3	47.5	47.8	92.3	69.9	87.1	51.5	•	46.6	•	•	•	•
Officers' Compensation 20	4.1	•	9.0	0.7	0.7	1.2	1.2	•	4.0	•	•	•	•
Operating Margin 21	•	6.4	•	•	•	•	•	•	•	•	•	•	•
Operating Margin Before Officers' Comp. 22	•	6.4	3.6	•	•	•	•	•	•	•	•	•	•

Selected Average Balance Sheet ($ in Thousands)

Net Receivables 23	25	0	4	39	75	272	1902	3114
Inventories 24	2	0	0	17	48	297		219
Net Property, Plant and Equipment 25	70	0	8	34	374	2457	7740	31212
Total Assets 26	403	0	117	691	1876	7105	15336	57580
Notes and Loans Payable 27	19	0	9	8	42	848	2610	6549
All Other Liabilities 28	110	0	17	174	357	2150	4004	4454
Net Worth 29	274	0	91	509	1476	4108	8722	46577

Selected Financial Ratios (Times to 1)

Current Ratio 30	3.3	•	6.7	3.7	5.4	2.2	1.7	3.0
Quick Ratio 31	3.0	•	6.5	3.6	4.9	2.2	1.4	2.4
Net Sales to Working Capital 32	1.7	•	1.9	1.0	0.9	1.3	4.9	3.6
Coverage Ratio 33	16.6	4.7	38.6	13.2	16.6	6.8	8.9	3.6
Total Asset Turnover 34	0.8	•	1.4	0.6	0.5	0.4	0.8	0.5
Inventory Turnover 35	36.9	•	463.4	142.5	8.8	4.5	15.0	2.0
Receivables Turnover 36	11.9	•	44.9	15.1	9.8	13.5	6.3	•
Total Liabilities to Net Worth 37	0.5	•	0.3	0.4	0.3	0.7	0.8	0.2
Current Assets to Working Capital 38	1.4	•	1.2	1.4	1.2	1.8	2.4	1.5
Current Liabilities to Working Capital 39	0.4	•	0.2	0.4	0.2	0.8	1.4	0.5
Working Capital to Net Sales 40	0.6	•	0.5	1.0	1.1	0.8	0.2	0.3
Inventory to Working Capital 41	0.0	•	0.0	0.0	0.0	0.0	0.2	0.0
Total Receipts to Cash Flow 42	1.9	1.9	2.4	1.2	1.5	1.2	1.9	2.6
Cost of Goods to Cash Flow 43	0.5	0.7	0.8	0.1	0.3	0.1	0.7	0.0
Cash Flow to Total Debt 44	1.3	•	2.7	2.0	1.4	0.8	0.9	0.9

Selected Financial Factors (in Percentages)

Debt Ratio 45	32.0	•	21.8	26.4	21.3	42.2	43.1	19.1
Return on Total Assets 46	4.0	•	5.1	2.3	2.8	6.0	4.5	1.8
Return on Equity Before Income Taxes 47	5.6	•	6.4	2.9	3.4	8.8	7.1	1.6
Return on Equity After Income Taxes 48	4.5	•	5.8	2.5	2.6	7.8	5.7	1.1
Profit Margin (Before Income Tax) 49	4.8	6.4	3.6	3.3	5.8	12.1	5.3	2.9
Profit Margin (After Income Tax) 50	3.9	6.2	3.2	2.8	4.4	10.7	4.2	2.0

Index

Index